INTERNATIONAL

MARKETING

SECOND EDITION

INTERNATIONAL

MARKETING

MICHAEL R. CZINKOTA
Georgetown University

ILKKA A. RONKAINEN
Georgetown University

SECOND EDITION

THE DRYDEN PRESS
A HARCOURT BRACE JOVANOVICH COLLEGE PUBLISHER
Fort Worth   Philadelphia   San Diego   New York   Orlando   Austin   San Antonio
Toronto   Montreal   London   Sydney   Tokyo

Acquisitions Editor: Rob Zwettler
Developmental Editor: Judy Sarwark
Project Editor: Paula Dempsey
Design Supervisor: Rebecca Lemna
Production Manager: Bob Lange
Permissions Editor: Cindy Lombardo
Director of Editing, Design, and Production: Jane Perkins

Text and Cover Designer: Frances Hasegawa
Copy Editor: Jean Berry
Indexer: Joyce Goldenstern
Compositor: G&S Typesetters, Inc.
Text Type: 10/12 Melior

Library of Congress Cataloging-in-Publication Data

Czinkota, Michael R.
    International marketing / Michael R. Czinkota, Ilkka A. Ronkainen.
  —2nd ed.
    p. cm.
    Includes bibliographical references.
    ISBN 0-03-032239-1
    1. Export marketing. I. Ronkainen, Ilkka A. II. Title.
  HF1009.5.C95 1990
  658.8′48—dc20   89-23364

Printed in the United States of America
 12-032-9876543

Requests for permission to make copies of any part of the work should be mailed to: Permissions Department, Harcourt Brace Jovanovich Publishers, 8th Floor, Orlando, FL 32887.

Address orders:
The Dryden Press
Orlando, FL 32887

Address editorial correspondence:
The Dryden Press
301 Commerce Street, Suite 3700
Fort Worth, TX 76102

The Dryden Press
Harcourt Brace Jovanovich

Map Insert: Copyright John Bartholomew & Son Limited.

Cover photographs: Murray Alcosser/The Image Bank; Harold Sund/The Image Bank; Weinberg Clark/The Image Bank; Gerard Champlong/The Image Bank.

To Ilona ▪ *MRC*

_____

To Susan and Sanna ▪ *IAR*

The Dryden Press Series in Marketing

Preface

Being competitive means not resting on one's laurels but seeking further strategic advantage. This guideline for the international marketer applies in equal measure to this book. The resounding market acceptance experienced with the first edition of *International Marketing* gave us the impetus to work even harder to make this second edition an even better, more up-to-date, and user-friendly text.

The international dimension affects all companies and individuals making marketing decisions today. We all must focus on the international market in order to remain competitive. Even if not engaged in marketing goods or services abroad, we will be affected by the marketing activities of foreign entities. International marketing therefore is no longer in the domain of a few multinational corporations; increasingly, a broad spectrum of individuals, firms, and institutions are participants in the international marketplace.

Although most marketing practices are applicable to any type of company, regardless of the level of international expertise, the way in which marketing management is executed will vary. Multinational corporations typically have the ability to command financial, personnel, and information resources that smaller firms do not have. Furthermore, operating on a worldwide scale requires a different set of marketing coordination activities than when exports or imports are limited to one country.

Even though the activities of a few large companies account, in terms of dollar value, for the largest portion of international marketing activities in the United States, on a transaction basis most business is done by smaller firms with limited international exposure. In addition, the less experienced firms will have more questions and will need more help. As a result, employment opportunities are available both in multinational firms and in companies that are only now beginning to internationalize. Yet, the need for international marketing expertise and the ability on the part of the recent graduate to make a difference in international marketing are greatest within firms that have had only limited international exposure.

International marketing textbooks have traditionally concentrated on the more glamorous and extensive operations of the multinational corporation. This text differs from that approach and reflects the realities of educational needs by discussing the international marketing concerns of all types of companies. A full discussion of international start-up operations is presented, followed by a presentation of the international concerns of the beginning marketer, and finally the issues confronting giant global marketers. Therefore, the instructor and the student are able to explore the entire breadth of international marketing rather than only a specialized subsegment.

This text is designed primarily for the advanced undergraduate student. Because of the in-depth development of topical coverage, however, it also presents an excellent challenge for graduate instruction. Throughout the text, the material is presented with a focus on ease of communication and reader-friendliness, without compromising rigor.

ORGANIZATION

The text is divided into three parts. First the basic concepts of international marketing are outlined, and the environments that the international marketer has to consider are discussed. The second part focuses on the various activities necessary for international marketing planning and concentrates on the beginning of international marketing activities. Export and import operations are covered here, together with elements of the marketing mix that tend to be most important for firms at an initial level of international experience. The third part discusses marketing management and strategy issues most relevant for the multinational corporation.

Both the instructor and the student can work with this text in two ways. One alternative is to cover the material sequentially, progressing from the initial international effort to multinational activities. In this way, marketing dimensions such as distribution, promotion, and pricing are covered in the order in which they are most relevant for the particular level of expertise within the firm. Another approach is to use the text in a parallel manner, by pairing comparable chapters from Parts Two and Three. In this way, the primary emphasis can be placed on the functional approach to international marketing.

CHANGES IN THE SECOND EDITION

The basic structure of the text remains the same, but the highly dynamic nature of the international marketplace is reflected in the number of new features in this second edition. The objective of the revision was to enhance the text's up-to-date information, practical nature, and reader-friendliness with both the student and the instructor in mind. "The International Marketplace" boxes are virtually all based on the most recent market developments. Chapter content also reflects recent research as well as governmental and corporate practice. This has been achieved by having scores of academic reviewers and practitioners read sections of the text and comment on them. One-third of the cases are either new or revised.

The chapters in Part One have all been updated with the latest available trade and corporate information. The emphasis is on changing trade patterns and their effect on the international marketer. Special attention is given to discussion of economic integration. Entire new sections are devoted to the effects of foreign investment, the European 1992 phenomenon, political risk assessment, lobbying, cultural training, as well as to changes in public and private sources of international trade financing.

Part Two has been positioned to more clearly reflect the challenges of small and medium-sized businesses in the international marketing environment. New and substantially revised sections are devoted to the utility of various international trade data, international negotiations, and parallel importation.

The revision of Part Three focuses on new forms of advanced marketing activities. Strategic alliances, cooperative manufacturing, international marketing decision support systems, intellectual property protection, taxation changes affecting transfer pricing, as well as globalization in product, promotion, and organizational decisions have been highlighted in the second edition. The chapters on services marketing, marketing with governments, and countertrade have all undergone major revision and updating as a result of the changes that have occurred in the past three years. The final chapter now has a substantially strengthened discussion on career and educational opportunities in international marketing.

SPECIAL FEATURES

Contemporary Realism

Each chapter offers a variety of "The International Marketplace" boxes, which focus on real marketing situations and are intended to help students understand and absorb the presented materials. The instructor can highlight the boxes to exemplify theory or use them as mini-cases for class discussion.

Research Emphasis

A special effort has been made to provide current research information and data. Chapter notes are augmented by lists of relevant recommended readings incorporating the latest research findings. In addition, a wide variety of sources and organizations that provide international information are listed in the text. These materials enable the instructor and the student to go beyond the text whenever time permits.

Maps

In order to improve students' geographic literacy, several full-color maps are furnished in this text following page 66, covering the social, economic, and political features of the world. They provide the instructor with the means to visually demonstrate concepts such as political blocs and socioeconomic variables. A separate full-color world map is included free with the text.

Cases

Following each of the three parts of the text are a variety of cases, most written especially for this book, that present students with real business situations. In addition, a video case has been developed to accompany Part Two that further assists in enlivening classroom activity. Challenging questions accompany each case, permitting in-depth discussion of the materials covered in the chapters.

Instructor's Materials

The text is accompanied by an in-depth *Instructor's Manual*, devised to provide major assistance to the professor. The material in the manual includes the following:

Teaching Plans   Alternative teaching plans and syllabi are presented to accommodate the instructor's preferred course structure and varying time constraints. Time plans are developed for the course to be taught in a semester format, on a quarter basis, or as an executive seminar.

Discussion Guidelines   For each chapter, specific teaching objectives and guidelines are developed to help stimulate classroom discussion. In addition, teaching notes referencing the transparency masters are provided within appropriate chapters.

End-of-Chapter Questions   Each question is fully developed in the manual to accommodate different scenarios and experience horizons. Where appropriate, the relevant text section is referenced.

Cases   A detailed case-chapter matrix is supplied that delineates which cases are most appropriate for each area of the international marketing field. In addition, detailed case discussion alternatives are provided, outlining discussion strategies and solution alternatives.

Video and Film References   An extensive listing of video and film materials available from educational institutions, companies, and government agencies is provided. Materials are briefly discussed, possible usage patterns are outlined, and ordering/availability information is supplied. In addition, each adopter of this text will receive a free video on international marketing, which is tied to the Lakewood Forest Products case following Part Two (page 472).

Test Bank   The manual includes a greatly expanded test bank, consisting of more than 900 short essay questions, true/false questions, and multiple choice questions. This test bank is also computerized and available to adopters on IBM computer diskettes.

Transparency Masters   The manual contains a substantial number of transparency masters, including some materials from the text, but also drawing heavily on non-text materials such as advertisements, graphs, and figures, which can be used to further enliven classroom interaction and to develop particular topics in more depth.

ACKNOWLEDGMENTS

We are deeply grateful to the professors, students, and professionals using this book. Your interest demonstrates the need for more knowledge about international marketing. As our market, you are telling us that our product adds value to your lives. As a result, you add value to ours. Thank you!

We also thank the many reviewers for their constructive and imaginative comments and criticisms, which were instrumental in making this second edition even better. These are:

Van Wood
Texas Tech University

Denise Johnson
University of Louisville

Andrew Gross
Cleveland State University

John Ryans
Kent State University

Sudhir Kale
Arizona State University

Nittaya Wongtada
George Mason University

Fred Miller
Murray State University

Sanjeev Agarwal
Iowa State University

Alex Christofides
Ohio State University

Mushtaq Luqmani
Western Michigan University

We remain indebted to the reviewers of the first edition of this text:

Warren Bilkey
University of Wisconsin

Sudhir Kale
Arizona State University

S. Tamer Cavusgil
Michigan State University

Hertha Krotkoff
Towson State University

John Dyer
University of Miami

Bertil Liander
University of Massachusetts

Donna Goehle
Michigan State University

James Maskulka
Lehigh University

Paul Groke
Northern Illinois University

Henry Munn
California State University, Northridge

Andrew Gross
Cleveland State University

Jacob Naor
University of Maine, Orono

Basil Janavaras
Mankato State University

Marta Ortiz
Florida International University

Fernando Robles
George Washington University

Barry Rosen
Baruch College, CUNY

W. Daniel Rountree
Middle Tennessee State University

James H. Sood
American University

Brian Toyne
University of South Carolina

Theafanis Varvoglis
San Diego State University

Many thanks to the faculty and students at Georgetown University and other academic institutions who have helped us in sharpening our thinking by cheerfully providing challenging comments and questions. Thanks are also due to the many fine employees of the U.S. Department of Commerce and all our business associates who have assisted us greatly by letting us work with and learn from them. Without the direct link to business and policy you have all provided, this book would have lost much of its refreshing realism. In particular, we thank Lyn Amine, St. Louis University; Tamer Cavusgil, Michigan State University; Zuhair Al-Obaidi, Helsinki School of Economics; James Wills, University of Hawaii; William Casselman, Popham, Haik; Robert Conkling, Conkling Associates; Lew Cramer, U.S. West; Mark Dowd, IBM Corporation; H. P. Goldfield, Swidler and Berlin; Louis Guadagnoli, Camac Interests; Robert Kaiser, Export-Import Bank of the United States; Robert Keezer, Keezer and Company; William Morris, Global USA; Robert Schott, Sea Schott; and David Barton, Mike Hand, Allen Lenz, and Henry Misisco, U.S. Department of Commerce; and the Wakemans of Brookside. The assistance in manuscript preparation given by Dorothy Sykes, Jennifer Smith, Bao-Nga Tran, and Joseph Kuranda, all of Georgetown University, is also especially appreciated.

At The Dryden Press, Rob Zwettler and Judy Sarwark shepherded this project to conclusion with continued professionalism, enthusiasm, patience, and a lot of humorous cajoling. Major assistance was also provided by the expertise, help, and friendliness of Jean Berry, Paula Dempsey, Shelly Dettmer, Rebecca Lemna, and Bob Lange.

Last, but foremost, we are grateful to our families, who have truly participated in the writing of this book. Only the patience, understanding, and love of Ilona, Ursula, Michael, and Thomas Czinkota and Susan and Sanna Ronkainen enabled us to have the energy, stamina, and inspiration to write this book.

Michael R. Czinkota
Ilkka A. Ronkainen
Washington, D.C.
December 1989

About the Authors

MICHAEL R. CZINKOTA

Michael R. Czinkota is a member of the faculty of marketing and international business at the School of Business Administration of Georgetown University. From 1981 to 1986 he was the Chairman of the National Center for Export-Import Studies at the university.

During a leave of absence from 1986 to 1989, Dr. Czinkota served in the U.S. government as Deputy Assistant Secretary of Commerce. He was responsible for macro trade analysis, departmental support of international trade negotiations and retaliatory actions, and policy coordination for international finance, investment, and monetary affairs. He served as Head of the U.S. Delegation to the OECD Industry Committee in Paris and as Senior Trade Advisor for Export Administration and Controls.

Dr. Czinkota's background includes eight years of private-sector business experience as a partner in an export-import firm and in an advertising agency and ten years of research and teaching in the academic world. He has received research grants from various organizations, including the National Science Foundation, the General Electric Company, and the Organization of American States. He has written extensively for leading academic journals and the trade press and has published several books, including *International Business, Export Policy, Export Development Strategies,* and *Japan's Market: The Distribution System.*

Dr. Czinkota serves on the Board of Directors of the American Marketing Association, where he is also Vice President of the Global Division; the Board of Governors of the Academy of Marketing Science; and the editorial boards of the *Journal of Business Research, International Marketing Review,* the *Journal of International Consumer Marketing,* the *Journal of Teaching of International Business,* and the *Singapore Marketing Review.* In 1985, he was appointed a member of the District Export Council.

Dr. Czinkota has served as consultant to a wide range of individuals and institutions in the United States and abroad. He has worked with corporations such as AT&T, IBM, and Nestlé and has been instrumental in fostering interregional economic dialogue at the policy level through the sponsorship of international symposia on trade relations.

Dr. Czinkota studied law and business administration at the University of Erlangen-Nürnberg in Germany and was awarded a two-year Fulbright Scholarship. He holds an MBA in international business and a Ph.D. in marketing from The Ohio State University. He and his wife, Ilona, live in Luray, located in Virginia's Shenandoah Valley.

ILKKA A. RONKAINEN

Ilkka A. Ronkainen is a member of the faculty of marketing and international business at the School of Business Administration at Georgetown University. From 1981 to 1986 he served as Associate Director and from 1986 to 1987 as Chairman of the National Center for Export-Import Studies.

Dr. Ronkainen serves as docent of international marketing at the Helsinki School of Economics. He was visiting professor at HSE during the 1987–88 academic year and continues to teach in its Executive MBA and International MBA programs.

Dr. Ronkainen holds a Ph.D. and a master's degree from the University of South Carolina as well as an M.S. (Economics) degree from the Helsinki School of Economics.

Dr. Ronkainen has published extensively in academic journals and the trade press. He is a co-author of *International Business*. He serves on the review boards of the *Journal of Business Research, International Marketing Review,* and *Journal of Travel Research* and has reviewed for the *Journal of Advertising* and the *Journal of International Business Studies*. He serves as the North American coordinator for the European Marketing Academy. He was a member of the board of the Washington International Trade Association from 1981 to 1986 and started the association's newsletter, *Trade Trends*.

Dr. Ronkainen has served as a consultant to a wide range of U.S. and international institutions. He has worked with entities such as IBM, the Rank Organization, and the Organization of American States. He maintains close relations with a number of Finnish companies and their internationalization and educational efforts.

Brief Contents

Contents

P A R T   T W O   *Beginning International Marketing Activities*   *209*

C H A P T E R   **7**   **The Export Process**   **210**

MOTIVATIONS TO INTERNATIONALIZE   211
Proactive Motivations   212
Reactive Motivations   214

CHANGE AGENTS   217
Internal Change Agents   217
External Change Agents   219

INTERNATIONALIZATION STAGES   221
INTERNATIONALIZATION PROBLEMS   222

C H A P T E R   **8**   **Secondary International Marketing Research**   **232**

DEFINING THE ISSUE   233
LINKING RESEARCH TO THE DECISION-MAKING PROCESS   234
DIFFERENTIATING BETWEEN INTERNATIONAL AND
   DOMESTIC RESEARCH   235
New Parameters   235
New Environments   236

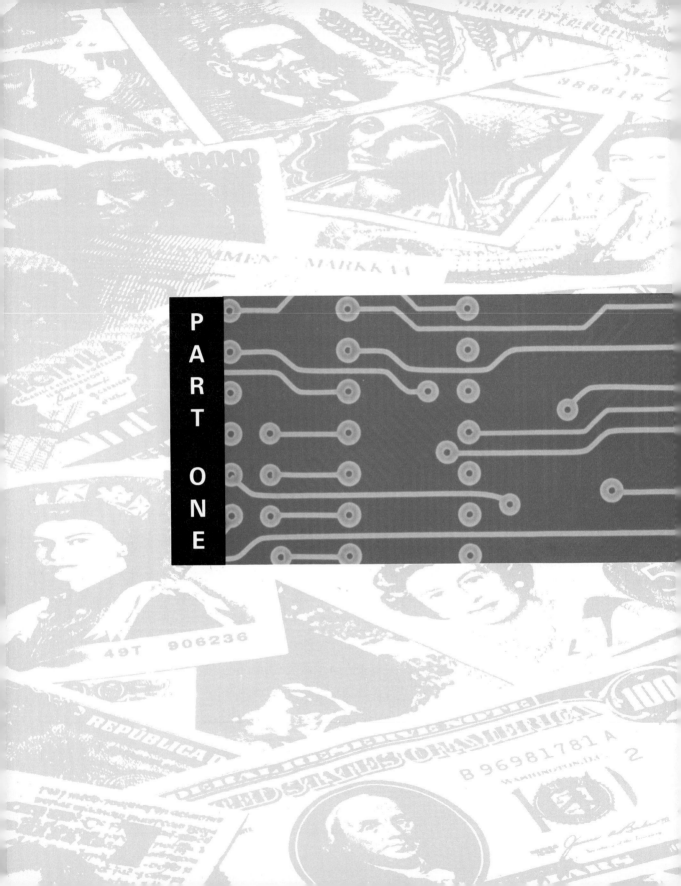

PART ONE

The International Environment

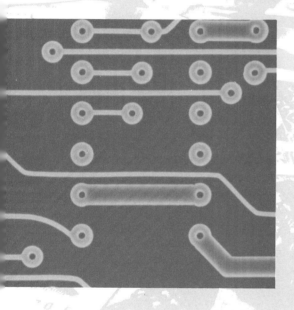

PART ONE introduces the international trade framework and environment. It highlights the need for international marketing activities and explains why the international market is an entirely new arena for a firm and its managers.

The chapters devoted to macroenvironmental factors explain the many forces to which the firm is exposed. The marketer will need to adapt to these foreign environments and adeptly resolve conflicts between political, cultural, and legal forces in order to be successful.

CHAPTER 1

The International Marketing Imperative

1.1 THE INTERNATIONAL MARKETPLACE

A New Age of Boundless Competition A one-world market exists for products ranging from cars to consumer electronics to carbonated drinks. Build a better microchip in Omaha, and buyers will be there from Osaka to Oslo. Even if you don't export, your competitors are likely to hail from all over. See how foreign manufacturers, including some from the so-called Third World, hasten the industrial sunset for USX, LTV, and America's other stay-at-home steel makers. Now squint into the sunrise and ask American Express about the high-quality, low-cost software programming it gets from Bombay-based TaTa Consultancy Services.

Instead of competing with you, your overseas rival may buy you. Firestone has agreed to sell most of its tire business to Japan's Bridgestone Corporation. In 1987 British Petroleum, Unilever, and Hoechst took three of the seven top spots on Fortune's ranking of U.S. deals of the year. Bruce Springstein and Michael Jackson toil for owners from abroad since Sony plunked down $2 billion for CBS records.

Even if you run a drugstore in Knoxville and all of the above seems irrelevant, you still need to cultivate a more planetary planning horizon. The cost of the merchandise you sell, the sales pitches that captivate new customers, even the price of your mortgage and the size of your tax bite, increasingly reflect the exotic influence of the decisions made on the Tokyo stock exchange, over lunch by London admen, or by monetary boffins in the bowels of West Germany's Bundesbank.

Source: Richard I. Kirkland, Jr., "Entering a New Age of Boundless Competition," Fortune, March 14, 1988, 40–41.

You are about to begin an exciting, important, and necessary task: the exploration of international marketing. International marketing is exciting because it combines the science and the art of business with many other disciplines. Economics, anthropology, cultural studies, geography, history, languages, jurisprudence, statistics, demographics, and many other fields combine to help you explore the global market. Environmental differences will stimulate your intellectual curiosity, which will enable you to absorb and understand new phenomena. International marketing has been compared by many who have been active in the field to the task of mountain climbing: challenging, arduous, and exhilarating.

International marketing is important because the world has become globalized. International marketing takes place all around us, every day, and has a major effect on our lives, as The International Marketplace 1.1 shows. After reading through this book, and observing international marketing phenomena, you will see what happens, understand what happens, and at some time in your future perhaps even make it happen. All of this is much better than to stand by and wonder what happened.

International marketing is necessary because, from a national standpoint, economic isolationism has become impossible. Failure to participate in the global marketplace assures a nation of declining economic influence and a decrease in the standard of living of its citizens. Successful international marketing, however, holds the promise of an improved quality of life, a better society, and, as some have stated, even a more peaceful world.

This chapter is designed to increase your awareness of what international marketing is all about. It describes the current levels of world trade activities, projects future developments, and discusses the resulting repercussion on countries, institutions, and individuals worldwide. Both the opportunities and the threats that emanate from the global marketplace are highlighted and the need for an international "marketing" approach on the part of individuals and institutions is emphasized.

This chapter text ends with an explanation of the major organizational thrust of this book, which is a differentiation between the beginning internationalist and the multinational corporation. This theme, which carries through the entire book, takes into account that the concerns, capabilities, and goals of firms will differ widely based on their level of international expertise, resources, and involvement. The stepwise approach to international marketing taken here will therefore permit you to understand the entire range of international activities and allow a useful and early transfer of the acquired knowledge into practice.

WHAT INTERNATIONAL MARKETING IS

In brief, **international marketing** is concerned with the planning and conducting of transactions across national borders to satisfy the objectives of individuals and organizations. In its many forms, it ranges from export–import trade to licensing, joint ventures, wholly owned subsidiaries, turnkey operations, and management contracts.

As this definition indicates, international marketing very much retains the basic marketing tenet of "satisfaction." International marketing is the tool used to obtain the goal of improvement of one's present position. The fact that a transaction takes place "across national borders" highlights the difference between domestic and international marketing. The international marketer is subject to a new set of macroenvironmental factors, to different constraints, and to quite frequent conflicts resulting from different laws, cultures, and societies. The basic principles of marketing still apply, but their applications, complexity, and intensity may vary substantially. Yet the capability to successfully master these challenges affords the international marketer the potential for more opportunities and higher rewards.

The definition also focuses on international transactions. The use of the term recognizes that marketing internationally is an activity, which needs to be pursued, often aggressively. Those who do not participate in the transactions are only exposed to international marketing and subject to its changing influences. The international marketer is part of the exchange, recognizes the changing nature of transactions, and adjusts to a constantly moving target subject to environmental shifts. This need for adjustment, for comprehending change and, in spite of it all, successfully carrying out transactions highlights the fact that international marketing is as much art as science.

To achieve success in the art of international marketing, it is necessary to be firmly grounded in the scientific aspects. Only then will individual consumers, policymakers, and business executives be able to incorporate international marketing considerations into their thinking and planning. Only then will they be able to consider international issues and repercussions and make decisions based on the answers to such questions as these:

- How will my idea, product, or service fit into the international market?
- What adjustments are or will be necessary?
- What threats from global competition should I expect?
- How can I work with these threats to turn them into opportunities?
- What are my strategic global alternatives?

If all of these issues are integrated into each decision made by individuals and by firms, international markets can become a source of growth, profit, and needs satisfaction that would not have existed had they limited themselves to domestic activities. To aid in this decision process is the purpose of this book.

THE IMPORTANCE OF WORLD TRADE

World trade has assumed a heretofore unknown importance to the global community. In past centuries trade was conducted internationally, but not at the level or with the impact on nations, firms, and individuals that it has recently achieved. In the past two decades world trade has expanded from

$200 billion to over $4 trillion. Countries that had never been considered major participants in world trade have suddenly emerged as major economic powers. Individuals and firms have come to recognize that they are competing not only domestically but in a global marketplace. World trade has given rise to global linkages of markets, technology, and living standards that were previously unknown and unanticipated. At the same time it has deeply affected domestic policy-making and has often resulted in the emergence of totally new opportunities and threats to firms and individuals.

Global Linkages

World trade has forged a network of **global linkages** that bind us all— countries, institutions, and individuals—much closer than ever before. These linkages were first widely reorganized during the worldwide oil shock of 1970. But they continue to increase. A drought in Brazil and its effects on coffee production are felt around the world. A cutoff of strategic materials produced in South Africa affects many other nations, firms, and individuals. The global crash of 1987 reverberated in financial quarters all around the globe.

World trade has also brought about a global reorientation in production strategies. As an example, only a few decades ago it would have been thought impossible to produce parts for a car in more than one country, assemble the car in yet another country, and sell it in still other nations. Yet such global investment strategies coupled with production and distribution sharing are occurring with increasing frequency.

The level of global investment is at an unprecedented high. The United States, after having been a net creditor to the world for many decades, has been a **world debtor** since 1985. This means that the United States owes more to foreign institutions and individuals than they owe to U.S. entities. The shifts in financial flows have had major effects. Currently well over 30 percent of the workers in the U.S. chemical industry toil for foreign owners. Many of the office buildings we work in are held by foreign landlords. The opening of plants abroad and in the United States increasingly takes the place of trade. All these developments make us more and more dependent on one another.

This interdependence, however, is not stable. On virtually a daily basis realignments take place on both micro and macro levels that make past orientations at least partially obsolete. For example, for the first two hundred years of its history, the United States looked to Europe for markets and sources of supply. However, despite the maintenance of this orientation by many individuals, firms, and policymakers, the reality of trade relationships is gradually changing. U.S. two-way trade across the Pacific totalled $290 billion in 1988, $96 billion more than our trade across the Atlantic. This gap will continue to grow, because the newly industrializing countries in Asia average a 7 percent annual growth, while the nations

FIGURE 1.1   ▪   **The Changing U.S. Share of World Trade**

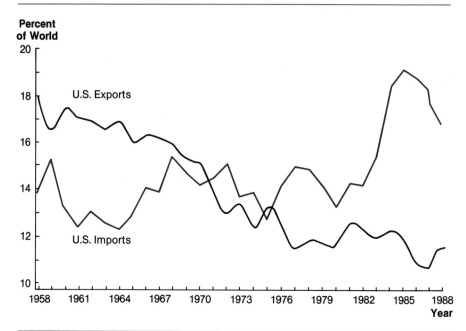

Source: International Monetary Fund (IMF), *International Financial Statistics,* March 1989.

of the European Community struggle for nominal increases in their domestic economic growth.[1]

Not only is the environment changing, but the pace of change grows faster. "A boy who saw the Wright brothers fly for a few seconds at Kitty Hawk in 1903 could have watched Apollo II land on the moon in 1969. The first electronic computer was built in 1946; today the world rushes from the mechanical into the electronic age. The double helix was first unveiled in 1953; today biotechnology threatens to remake mankind."[2]

These changes and the speed with which they come about significantly affect both corporations and individuals. During the past few decades the United States was widely seen as the hub of world trade. While this is still true in terms of the United States being the locomotive of market flows, its participation in world trade measured as a portion of world market share has declined drastically. In the early 1950s the United States accounted for nearly 25 percent of world trade flows; in 1988 this figure had declined

[1] U.S. Department of Commerce, *Survey of Current Business* (Washington, D.C.: Government Printing Office, March 1989), 41–42.

[2] Arthur M. Schlesinger, Jr., *The Cycles of American History* (Boston: Houghton Mifflin, 1986), *XI.*

to 14 percent. Figure 1.1 shows the striking changes that have taken place. As a result, it is fair to claim that "world trade is becoming more important to the United States, while at the same time the United States is becoming less important to world trade."[3]

Domestic Policy Repercussions

The effects of increasing global linkages on the economies of countries have been dramatic. Policymakers have increasingly come to recognize that it is very difficult to isolate domestic economic activity from international market events. Again and again, domestic policy measures are vetoed or counteracted by the activities of global market forces. Decisions that once were clearly in the domestic purview have now become subject to revision by influences from abroad.

Agricultural and farm policies, for example, which historically have been a major domestic issue, are suddenly thrust into the international realm. Any industrial policy consideration must now be seen in light of international repercussions. This results from our increased reliance on trade. The following examples highlight the penetration of our society by foreign trade and its influences:

- One out of every four U.S. farm acres is producing for export.
- One of every six U.S. manufacturing jobs produces for export.
- One of every seven dollars of U.S. sales is to someone abroad.
- One of every three cars, nine of every ten television sets, two out of every three suits, and every video recorder sold in the United States is imported.
- One of every four dollars of U.S. bonds and notes is issued to foreigners.[4]

To some extent the economic world as we knew it has been turned upside down. For example, trade flows used to determine currency flows and therefore the level of the exchange rate. In the more recent past **currency flows** took on a life of their own and have, independent of trade, set the value of exchange rates. These exchange rates in turn have now begun to determine the level of trade. Governments that wish to counteract these developments with monetary policies find that currency flows outnumber trade flows by ten to one. Also, private sector financial flows vastly outnumber the financial flows that can be marshaled by governments, even when acting in concert. Similarly, constant rapid technological change and

[3] Suresh Desai, "International Business and Management Education," *Issues in International Business* 2 (Summer–Fall 1985): 31–32.

[4] Raymond J. Waldmann, *Managed Trade: The Competition between Nations* (Cambridge, Mass.: Ballinger, 1986), 6; and *Ward's Automotive Report*, January 9, 1989.

1.2   THE INTERNATIONAL MARKETPLACE

Does International Marketing Create Peace?   One really big surprise of the postwar era has been that historic enemies, such as West Germany and France, or Japan and the United States, have not had the remotest threat of war since 1945. Why should they? Anything Japan has that we want we can buy, and on very easy credit terms, so why fight for it? Why should the Japanese fight the United States and lose all those profitable markets? France and West Germany, linked intimately through marketing and the European Community, are now each other's largest trading partners. Closed systems build huge armies and waste their substance on guns and troops; open countries spend their money on new machine tools to crank out Barbie dolls or some such trivia. Their bright young people figure out how to tool the machines, now how to fire the latest missile. For some reason they not only get rich fast, but also lose interest in military adventures. Japan, that peculiar superpower without superguns, confounds everyone, simply because no one has ever seen a major world power that got that way by selling you to death, not shooting you to death. In short, if you trade a lot with someone, why fight? The logical answer—you don't—is perhaps the best news mankind has had in millennia.

Source: Richard N. Farmer, "Would You Want Your Granddaughter to Marry a Taiwanese Marketing Man?" *Journal of Marketing* 51 (October 1987): 114–115.

vast advances in communication permit firms and countries to quickly emulate innovation and counteract carefully designed plans. As a result, governments are often powerless to implement effective policy measures, even when they know what to do.

Policymakers therefore find themselves with increasing responsibilities, yet with fewer and less effective tools to carry out these responsibilities. At the same time that more parts of a domestic economy are vulnerable to international shifts and changes, these parts are becoming less controllable. To regain some of their power to influence, nations have sought to restrict the influence of world trade by erecting barriers, charging tariffs, and implementing import regulations. However, these measures too have been restrained by the existence of international agreements that regulate trade restrictions. World trade has therefore changed many previously held notions about nation-state sovereignty and extraterritoriality. The same interdependence that has made us more affluent has also left us more vulnerable. Because this vulnerability is spread out over all major trading nations, however, some have credited international marketing with being a pillar of international peace, as The International Marketplace 1.2 shows.

THE INTERNATIONAL MARKETPLACE `1.3`

Domestic Market Saturation at POM   *POM is the Russellville,*
Arkansas, successor to Park-O-Meter, which developed the first of
the ubiquitous coin crunchers in 1935. POM is operating in a ma-
ture U.S. market because the average machine, once implanted in
the pavement, lasts 20 to 25 years.

In 1981, POM dropped its flag on the new industrialized coun-
tries, where prosperity is clogging urban streets with traffic and
straining parking resources. Since 1982, POM's exports have grown
20 percent a year.

Its meters sprout from sidewalks in such far-flung metropolises
as Malacca, Malaysia; Thunder Bay, Ontario; Santiago, Chile; and
Sittard, Holland. To keep its momentum going, the company has
introduced the first solar-powered parking meter. It features a pro-
grammable timer driven by a microprocessor. The first shipment
was to Shepparton, Australia, a city promoting the use of solar
power. POM is counting heavily on exports to help it double its
$10 million annual sales over the next four years.

Source: Christopher Knowlton, "The New Export Entrepreneurs," *Fortune*, June 6,
1988, 94–98.

OPPORTUNITIES AND CHALLENGES IN INTERNATIONAL MARKETING

In order to prosper in a world of abrupt changes and discontinuities, of
newly emerging forces and dangers, of unforeseen influences from abroad,
firms need to prepare themselves and develop active responses. New
strategies need to be envisioned, new plans need to be made, and our way
of doing business needs to change. The way to retain leadership, economically, politically, or morally, is—as the examples of Rome, Constantino-
ple, and London have amply demonstrated—not through passivity but
rather through innovation and a continuous, alert adaptation to the changing world environment. In order to stay on top, firms need to aggressively
participate in the changes that take place and respond with innovation
and creativity.

The growth of global business activities offers increased opportunities.
Firms that heavily depend on long production runs, for example, can expand their activities far beyond their domestic markets and benefit from
reaching many more customers. Market saturation can be avoided by
lengthening or rejuvenating product life cycles in other countries, as seen
in The International Marketplace 1.3. Production policies that once were
inflexible suddenly become variable when plants can be shifted from one
country to another, and suppliers can be found on every continent. Cooperative agreements can be formed that enable all parties to bring their

major strengths to the table and emerge with better products, services, and ideas than they could produce on their own. In addition, research has found that multinational corporations face a lower probability of insolvency and less average risk than do domestic companies.[5] At the same time, international marketing enables consumers all over the world to find greater varieties of products at lower prices and to improve their lifestyles and comfort.

Realization of Opportunities

All of these opportunities need careful exploration. What is needed is an awareness of global developments, an understanding of their meaning, and a development of capabilities to adjust to change. Furthermore, firms must adapt to the international market.

One key facet of the marketing concept is adaptation to the environment. The validity of this concept was recognized some time ago, and it has been implemented domestically to such an extent that the United States has been called a marketing society. The transference of the concept to the international realm, however, has not occurred with equal speed. International marketing is a field of underdeveloped knowledge, only now beginning to attract attention and to be considered worthwhile to teach and learn in an academic setting.

Academic concern with international marketing has been much greater abroad. For example, at the turn of this century Emperor Franz Joseph of Austria founded the Exportakademie in Vienna; it is now the Vienna University of Economic Sciences. In the United States it was not until the late 1970s that the American Assembly of Collegiate Schools of Business (AACSB) began to require the incorporation of international dimensions into the business school curriculum. International marketing has therefore only recently begun the tortuous process of becoming an academic discipline in the United States. Initial exploratory research is now used to gradually identify relevant building blocks for a general foundation of the field. As these building blocks are put into place, it becomes possible to carry out research with a general focus based on this foundation. Currently we are in the midst of building a framework of knowledge that can be called international marketing and of disseminating this knowledge toward the end of improving the way society functions.

This development is necessary and long overdue, because business firms have been aware for some time that many of the key difficulties encountered in doing business internationally are marketing problems. Judging by corporate needs, a background in international marketing for business students seeking emloyment is highly desirable,[6] not only for to-

[5] Israel Shaked, "Are Multinational Corporations Safer?" *Journal of International Business Studies* 17 (Spring 1986): 100.

[6] Theodor Kohers, "Corporate Employment Needs and Their Implications for an International Business Curriculum: A Survey of Firms Located in the Southeastern United States," *Issues in International Business* 2 (Summer–Fall 1985): 33–37.

THE INTERNATIONAL MARKETPLACE `1.4`

The Chief Executive in the Year 2000   *Since World War II, the typical corporate chief executive officer has looked something like this: He started out as a finance man with an undergraduate degree in accounting. He methodically worked his way up through the company from the comptroller's office in a division, to running that division, to the top job. His military background shows; he is used to giving orders—and to having them obeyed. As the head of the United Way drive, he is a big man in his community. However, the first time he traveled overseas on business was as a chief executive. Computers make him nervous.*

But peer into the executive suite of the year 2000 and see a completely different person. The undergraduate degree is in French literature, but he—or she—also has a joint MBA/engineering degree. He started in research and was quickly picked out as potential CEO. He zigzagged from research to marketing to finance. He proved himself in Brazil by turning around a failing joint venture. He speaks Portuguese and French and is on a first-name basis with commerce ministers in half a dozen countries. Unlike his predecessors, he is not a drill sergeant. He is first among equals in a five-person Office of the Chief Executive.

As the 40-year postwar epoch of growing markets and domestic-only competition fades, so too is vanishing the narrow one-company, one-industry chief executive. By the turn of the century, many experts predict, companies' choices of leaders will be governed by increasing international competition, the globalization of companies, the spread of technology, demographic shifts, and the speed of overall change.

Source: Amanda Bennett, "The Chief Executives in the Year 2000 Will Be Experienced Abroad," *The Wall Street Journal*, February 27, 1989, 1.

---

day but for long-term career plans, as The International Marketplace 1.4 shows.

Threats to Firms and Individuals

Most firms in the United States do not participate in the global market. In an era in which countries such as Japan and West Germany launched national export drives, the great majority of U.S. firms ignored international opportunities. Even though the growth in world trade is a continuing phenomenon, 92 percent of all U.S. firms still sell only in the United States.[7]

[7] U.S. Department of Commerce, Industry and Trade Administration, "Seven Surprising Facts about Exporting" (Washington, D.C.: Government Printing Office, not dated), 1.

TABLE 1.1 ∎ **The 50 Leading U.S. Exporters, 1988**

Rank	Company	Products	Export Sales[a]	Total Sales[a]	Exports as Percent of Sales
1	General Motors (Detroit)	Motor vehicles and parts	9,392.0	121,085.4	7.8
2	Ford Motor (Dearborn, Mich.)	Motor vehicles and parts	8,822.0	92,445.6	9.5
3	Boeing (Seattle)	Commercial and military aircraft	7,849.0	16,962.0	46.3
4	General Electric (Fairfield, Conn.)	Jet engines, generators, medical systems	5,744.0	49,414,0	11.6
5	Int'l Business Machines (Armonk, N.Y.)	Computers and related equipment	4,951.0	59,681.0	8.3
6	Chrysler (Highland Park, Mich.)	Motor vehicles and parts	4,343.9	35,472.7	12.2
7	E.I. Du Pont de Nemours (Wilmington, Del.)	Specialty chemicals; energy products	4,196.0	32,514.0	12.9
8	McDonnell Douglas (St. Louis)	Commercial and military aircraft	3,471.0	15,072.0	23.0
9	Caterpillar (Peoria, Ill.)	Heavy machinery, engines, turbines	2,930.0	10,435.0	28.1
10	United Technologies (Hartford)	Jet engines, helicopters, cooling equipment	2,848.1	18,087.8	15.8
11	Eastman Kodak (Rochester, N.Y.)	Imaging equipment and supplies	2,301.0	17,034.0	13.5
12	Digital Equipment (Maynard, Mass.)	Computers and related equipment	2,083.0	11,475.4	18.2
13	Hewlett-Packard (Palo Alto, Calif.)	Computers, electronics	2,064.0	9,831.0	21.0
14	Unisys (Blue Bell, Pa.)	Computers and related equipment	2,012.9	9,902.0	20.3
15	Philip Morris (New York)	Tobacco, beverages, food	1,863.0	25,860.0	7.2
16	Motorola (Schaumburg, Ill.)	Radio equipment, semiconductors	1,742.0	8,250.0	21.1
17	Occidental Petroleum (Los Angeles)	Agricultural products, coal	1,684.0	19,417.0	8.7
18	General Dynamics (St. Louis)	Tanks, aircraft, missiles, gun systems	1,597.1	9,551.0	16.7
19	Allied-Signal (Morristown, N.J.)	Aircraft and vehicle parts, chemicals	1,464.0	11,909.0	12.3
20	Weyerhaeuser (Tacoma)	Wood, pulp, paper, logs, lumber	1,398.0	10,004.2	14.0
21	Union Carbide (Danbury, Conn.)	Chemicals, plastics	1,388.0	8,324.0	16.7
22	Raytheon (Lexington, Mass.)	Electronic weaponry, aircraft	1,307.0	8,192.1	16.0
23	Textron (Providence)	Aerospace, consumer goods	1,127.0	7,111.2	15.8
24	Westinghouse Electric (Pittsburgh)	Air traffic and weapons electronics	1,115.0	12,499.5	8.9
25	Dow Chemical (Midland, Mich.)	Chemicals, plastics, polymer products	1,109.0	16,682.0	6.6
26	Archer Daniels Midland (Decatur, Ill.)	Protein meals, vegetable oils, flour	1,087.7	6,798.4	16.0

Rank	Company	Products	Export Sales[a]	Total Sales[a]	Exports as Percent of Sales
27	Monsanto (St. Louis)	Herbicides, chemicals, pharmaceuticals	1,083.0	8,293.0	13.1
28	International Paper (Purchase, N.Y.)	Pulp, paper, wood products	1,000.0	9,533.0	10.5
29	Hoechst Celanese (Somerville, N.J.)	Chemicals, plastics, fibers	967.0	5,679.0	17.0
30	Exxon (New York)	Petroleum, chemicals	937.0	79,557.0	1.2
31	Intel (Santa Clara, Calif.)	Microcomputer components	925.6	2,874.8	32.2
32	Minnesota Mining & Mfg. (St. Paul)	Industrial, electronic, and health goods	836.0	10,581.0	7.9
33	Bayer USA (Pittsburgh)	Health goods, chemicals, photographics	700.0	4,718.5	14.8
34	Lockheed (Calabasas, Calif.)	Aircraft, electronics, information systems	686.0	10,667.0	6.4
35	Phillips Petroleum (Bartlesville, Okla.)	Liquefied natural gas, chemicals, plastics	675.0	11,304.0	6.0
36	Warner Communications (New York)	Video production, videocasettes	673.5	4,206.1	16.0
37	FMC (Chicago)	Armored cars, electronics, chemicals	647.3	3,286.9	19.7
38	Deere (Moline, Ill.)	Farm and industrial equipment	622.0	5,364.8	11.6
39	Rockwell Int'l (El Segundo, Calif.)	Electronics, automotive parts	620.0	11,946.3	5.2
40	Merck (Rahway, N.J.)	Drugs, specialty chemicals	619.4	5,939.5	10.4
41	Compaq Computer (Houston)	Computers and related equipment	611.7	2,065.6	29.6
42	Honeywell (Minneapolis)	Control and flight systems	610.0	7,148.3	8.5
43	Aluminum Co. of America (Pittsburgh)	Aluminum products	590.6	9,795.3	6.0
44	North American Philips (New York)	Electronics, televisions, lighting	588.1	5,423.5	10.8
45	Dresser Industries (Dallas)	Oil, coal, and gas equipment	584.6	3,941.7	14.8
46	Amoco (Chicago)	Chemicals	578.0	21,150.0	2.7
47	Combustion Engineering (Stamford, Conn.)	Industrial control systems, generators	560.0	3,483.9	16.1
48	Abbott Laboratories (Abbott Park, Ill.)	Drugs, diagnostic equipment	547.0	4,937.0	11.1
49	Ethyl (Richmond)	Specialty and petroleum chemicals	542.7	2,718.0	20.0
50	Baxter International (Deerfield, Ill.)	Health goods	521.0	6,861.0	7.6
	Totals		96,615.3	885,485.4	

[a]In millions of dollars.

Source: Edward Prewitt, "America's 50 Biggest Exporters," *Fortune* 120, no. 2 (July 17, 1989), 50–51.

Even though the United States is a major participant in world trade, most of these activities are carried out by relatively few firms. For example, the 50 firms listed in Table 1.1 account for over 30 percent of U.S. exports.

This lack of international orientation by U.S. firms, which is surprising in view of American entrepreneurship, is explained in various ways. First, the United States has historically been a closed economy, relatively independent of foreign trade. Also, the vast size of the American economy offers substantial possibilities for corporate expansion and does not force firms to look abroad. Finally, the distance to foreign markets (except those of Canada and Mexico) has resulted in frequent unfamiliarity with trade activities.

Yet, individual firms and entire industries are coming to recognize that, in today's trade environment, isolation has become impossible. Willing or unwilling, U.S. firms are becoming participants in global business affairs. Even if not by choice, most firms are affected directly or indirectly by the economic and political developments that occur in the international marketplace. Those that refuse to participate are relegated to reacting to the global marketplace and therefore expose themselves to harsh competition from abroad because they are unprepared.

Some industries are now beginning to recognize the need for international adjustments. U.S. farmers, because of high costs, increased international competition, and unfair foreign trade practices, have increasingly lost world market share. Firms in technologically advanced industries, such as semiconductor producers, have seen the prices of their products drop precipitously and their sales volumes shrink by half.

Other industries were exposed earlier to adjustment needs and have partially adjusted, but with great pain. Examples abound in the steel, automotive, and textile sectors of the U.S. economy.

Still other U.S. industries never fully recognized what had happened and therefore, in spite of attempts to adjust, were not successful and have ceased to exist. VCRs are no longer produced domestically. The U.S. television industry is vanishing. Only a small percentage of motorcycles are produced in the United States. The shoe industry is in its death throes.

These developments demonstrate that it has become virtually impossible to disregard the powerful impact that world trade now has on all of us. Temporary isolation may be possible and delay tactics may work for a while, but the old adage applies: you can run, but you cannot hide. Participation in the world market has become truly imperative.

THE GOALS OF THIS BOOK

This book aims to make the reader a better, more successful participant in the international marketplace by providing information about what is going on in international markets, and helping to translate knowledge into successful business transactions. By learning about both theory and practice the reader can obtain a good conceptual understanding of the field of international marketing as well as become firmly grounded in the realities of the global marketplace. Therefore, this book approaches international marketing in the way the manager of a firm does, reflecting different levels of international involvement and the importance of business–government relations.

Firms differ widely in their international activities and needs, depending on their level of experience, resources, and capabilities. For the firm that is just beginning to enter the global market, the level of knowledge about international complexities is low, the demand on time is high, expectations about success are uncertain, and the international environment is often inflexible. Conversely, for a multinational firm that is globally oriented and employs thousands of people in each continent, much more leeway exists in terms of resource availability, experience, and information. In addition, the multinational firm has the option of responding creatively to the environment by shifting resources, or even shaping the environment itself. For example, the heads of large corporations have access to government ministers to plead their case for a change in policy, an alternative that is rarely afforded to smaller firms.

In order to become a large, international corporation, however, a firm usually has to start out small. Similarly, in order to direct far-flung global operations, managers first have to learn the basics. The structure of this text reflects this reality by presenting initially an environmental perspective, which covers national and global marketing and policy issues, and their economic, political, legal, cultural, and financial dimensions.

Subsequently, the book discusses in detail the beginning internationalization of the firm. The emphasis is on the needs of those who are starting out, with a very limited international awareness, and the operational questions that are crucial to success. Some quite basic, yet essential issues addressed are: What is the difference between domestic and international marketing? Does the applicability of marketing principles change when they are transferred to the global environment? How do marketers find out whether there is a market for a product abroad without spending a fortune in time and money on research? How can the firm promote its products in foreign markets? How do marketers find and evaluate a foreign distributor and how do they make sure that the firm gets paid? How can marketers minimize government red tape, yet take advantage of any governmental programs that are of use to them?

These questions are addressed both conceptually and empirically, with a strong focus on export and import operations. The reader will see how the international commitment is developed within the firm and is strengthened.

Once these important dimensions are covered, the transition is made to the multinational corporation. The focus is not on the transnational allocation of resources, the coordination of multinational marketing activities, and the attainment of global synergism. Finally, emerging issues of challenge to both policymakers and multinational firms, such as countertrade, marketing to governments, the international marketing of services, and the future outlook of the global market, are discussed.

All of the marketing issues are considered in relation to national policies so as to apprise the reader of the divergent forces at play in the global market. Increased awareness of and involvement with international marketing on the part of governments requires managers to be aware of the role of governments and also to be able to work with them in order to attain marketing goals. Therefore, the continued references in the text to business–government interaction represent a vital link in the development of international marketing strategy.

We expect that this gradual approach to international marketing will permit the reader not only to master another academic subject but also to become well versed in both the operational and the strategic aspects of the field. The result should be a better understanding of how the global market works and the capability to participate in the international marketing imperative.

SUMMARY

In the past two decades, world trade has expanded from $200 billion to over $4 trillion. As a result, nations are much more affected by international business than in the past. Global linkages have made possible investment strategies and marketing alternatives that offer tremendous opportunities. Yet these changes and the speed of change also can represent threats to nations and firms.

On the policy front, decision makers have come to realize that it is very difficult to isolate domestic economic activity from international market events. Factors such as currency exchange rates, financial flows, and foreign economic actions increasingly render the policymaker powerless to implement a domestic agenda. International interdependence that has contributed to greater affluence has also increased our vulnerability.

Both firms and individuals are also greatly affected by international trade. Whether willing or not, they are participating in global business affairs. Entire industries have been threatened in their survival as a result of international trade flows and have either adjusted to new market realities or left the market. Individuals have experienced the loss of their workplace and reduced salaries. At the same time, global business changes have increased the opportunities available. Firms can now reach many more customers, product life cycles are lengthened, sourcing policies have become variable, new jobs have been created, and consumers all over the world can find greater varieties of products at lower prices.

In order to benefit from the opportunities and deal with the adversities of international trade, business needs to adopt the international marketing concept. The new set of macroenvironmental factors has to be understood and responded to in order to let international markets become a source of growth, profit, and needs satisfaction.

Questions for Discussion

1. Will expansion of world trade in the future be similar to that in the past?

2. Discuss reasons for the decline in the U.S. share of the world market.

3. Does increased world trade mean increased risk?

4. Discuss specific effects of world trade on domestic economic policy making.

5. Is it beneficial for nations to become dependent on one another?

6. With foreign wages at one-tenth of U.S. wages, how can America compete?

7. Compare and contrast domestic and international marketing.

8. Why do more firms in other countries enter international markets than do U.S. firms?

9. Can you think of examples of international marketing contributing to world peace?

APPENDIX

BASICS OF MARKETING

This appendix provides a summary of the basic concepts in marketing for the reader who wishes to review them before applying them to international marketing.

A new definition of marketing that reflects the wide range of activities and entities covered by marketing was approved in 1985 by the American Marketing Association.[1] Marketing is defined as "the process of planning and executing the conception, pricing, promotion, and distribution of ideas, goods, and services to create exchanges that satisfy individual and organizational objectives." The concepts of satisfaction and exchange are at the core of marketing. For an exchange to take place, two or more parties must come together physically, through the mails, or through technology, and they must communicate and deliver things of perceived value. Potential customers should be perceived as information seekers who evaluate marketers' efforts in terms of their own drives and needs. When the offering is consistent with their needs, they tend to choose the product; if it is not, other alternatives are chosen. A key task of the marketer is to recognize the ever-changing nature of needs and wants. Increasingly, the task of marketing has been expanded from sensing, serving, and satisfying individual customers to taking into consideration the long-term interests of society.

Marketing is not limited to business entities but involves governmental and nonbusiness units as well. Marketing techniques are applied not only to goods but also to ideas (for example, the "Made in the U.S.A." campaign) and to services (for example, international advertising agencies). The term business marketing is used for activities directed at other businesses, governmental entities, and various types of institutions. Business marketing comprises well over 50 percent of all marketing activities.

STRATEGIC MARKETING

The marketing manager's task is to plan and execute programs that will ensure a long-term competitive advantage for the company. This task has two integral parts: (1) the determining of specific target markets and (2) marketing management, which consists of manipulating marketing mix elements to best satisfy the needs of individual target markets.

Target Market Selection

Characteristics of intended target markets are of critical importance to the marketer. These characteristics can be summarized by eight Os: occu-

---

[1] "AMA Board Approves New Marketing Definition," *Marketing News*, March 1, 1985, 1.

pants, objects, occasions, objectives, outlets, organization, operations, and opposition.[2]

Occupants are targets of the marketing effort. The marketer must determine which customers to approach and also define them along numerous dimensions, such as demographics (age, sex, and nationality, for example), geography (country or region), psychographics (attitudes, interests, and opinions), or product-related variables (usage rate and brand loyalty, for example). Included in this analysis must be the major influences on the occupants during their buying processes.

Objects are what is being bought at present to satisfy a particular need. Included in this concept are physical objects, services, ideas, organizations, places, and persons.

Occasions are when members of the target market buy the product or service. This characteristic is important to the marketer because a product's consumption may be tied to a particular time period—for example, imported beer and a festival.

Objectives are the motivations behind the purchase or adoption of the marketed concept. A computer manufacturer does not market hardware but, instead, solutions to problems. Additionally, many customers look for hidden value in the product they purchase, which may be expressed, for example, through national origin of the product or through brand name.

Outlets are where customers expect to be able to procure a product or to be exposed to messages about it. This includes not only the entities themselves but also location within a particular outlet. Although aseptic packaging made it possible to shelve milk outside the refrigerated area in supermarkets, customers' acceptance of the arrangement was not automatic: the product was not where it was supposed to be. In the area of services, outlet involves (1) making a particular service available and communicating its availability and (2) the particular types of facilitators (such as brokers) who bring the parties together.

Organization describes how the buying or acceptance of a (new) idea takes place. Organization expands the analysis beyond the individual consumer to the decision-making unit (DMU). The DMU varies in terms of its size and its nature from relatively small and informal groups to large groups (more than ten people) to quite formal buying committees. Compare, for example, the differences in the processes between a family buying a new home entertainment center and the governing board at a university deciding which architectural firm to use. In either case, it is in the marketer's best interest to know as much as possible about the decision-making processes and the roles various individuals take in order to develop proper products and services and also to manipulate the process.

Operations represents the behavior of the organization buying products and services. Increasingly, industrial organizations are concentrating their

---

[2]Philip Kotler presents eight Os in the sixth edition of *Marketing Management: Analysis, Planning, and Control* (Englewood Cliffs, N.J.: Prentice-Hall, 1988), 174–175.

purchases to fewer suppliers and making longer term commitments. Supermarkets may make available only the leading brands in a product category, thereby complicating the marketer's attempts to place new products in these outlets.

Opposition refers to the competition to be faced in the marketplace. The nature of competition will vary from direct product-type competition to products that satisfy the same need. For example, Prince tennis rackets face a threat not only from other racket manufacturers but from any company that provides a product or service for leisure-time use. Competitive situations will vary from one market and from one segment to the next. Gillette is number one in the U.S. market for disposable razors, with Bic a distant runner up; however, elsewhere, particularly in Europe, the roles are reversed. In the long term, threats may come from outside the industry in which the marketer operates. As an example, digital watches originated in the electronics industry rather than the watch industry.

Analyzing the eight Os, and keeping in mind other uncontrollable environments (cultural, political, legal, technological, societal, and economic), the marketer must select the markets to which efforts will be targeted. In the short term, the marketer has to adjust to these environmental forces; in the long term, they can be manipulated to some extent by judicious marketing activity. Consumerism, one of the major forces shaping marketing activities, is concerned with protecting the consumer whenever an exchange relationship exists with any type of organization. Manifestations of the impact of consumerism on marketing exist in labeling, product specifications, and the conduct of promotional campaigns.

Because every marketer operates in a corporate environment of scarcity and comparative strengths, the target market decision is a crucial one. In some cases, the marketer may select only one segment of the market (for example, motorcycles of +1,000 cc) or multiple segments (for example, all types of motorized, two-wheeled vehicles) or may opt for an undifferentiated product that is to be mass marketed (for example, unbranded commodities or products that satisfy the same need worldwide, such as Coca-Cola).

Marketing Management

The marketing manager, having analyzed the characteristics of the target market(s), is in a position to specify the mix of marketing variables that will best serve each target market. The elements the marketing manager controls are known as the elements of the marketing mix, or the four Ps[3]: product, price, place, and promotion. Each consists of a submix of variables, and policy decisions must be made on each.

Product policy is concerned with all of the elements that make up the product, service, or idea that is offered by the marketer. Included are all

---

[3]The four Ps were popularized by E. Jerome McCarthy. See E. Jerome McCarthy and William Perreault, *Basic Marketing: A Managerial Approach*, 9th ed. (Homewood, Ill.: Irwin, 1987).

possible tangible characteristics (such as the core product and packaging) and intangible characteristics (such as branding and warranties). Many products are a combination of a concrete product and the accompanying service; for example, in buying an Otis elevator, the purchaser buys not only the product but an extensive service contract as well.

Pricing policy determines the cost of the product to the customer—a point somewhere between the floor created by the costs to the firm and the ceiling created by the strength of demand. An important consideration of pricing policy is pricing within the channel of distribution; margins to be made by the middlemen who assist in the marketing effort must be taken into account. Discounts to middlemen include functional, quantity, seasonal, and cash discounts, as well as promotional allowances. An important point to remember is that price is the only revenue-generating element of the marketing mix.

Distribution policy covers the *place* variable of the marketing mix and has two components: channel management and logistics management. Channel management is concerned with the entire process of setting up and operating the contractual organization, consisting of various types of middlemen (such as wholesalers, agents, retailers, and facilitators). Logistics management is focused on providing product availability at appropriate times and places in the marketing channel.[4] Place is the most long term of all of the marketing mix elements, that is, the most difficult to change in the short term.

Communications policy uses *promotion* tools to interact with customers, middlemen, and the public at large. The communications element consists of these tools: advertising, sales promotion, personal selling, and publicity. Because the purpose of all communications is to persuade, this is the most visible and sensitive of the marketing mix elements.

Blending the various elements into a coherent program requires trade-offs based on the type of product or service being offered (for example, detergents versus fighter aircraft), the stage of the product's life cycle (a new product versus one that is being revived), and resources available for the marketing effort (money and manpower) as well as the type of customer to whom the marketing efforts are directed.

THE MARKETING PROCESS

The actual process of marketing consists of four stages: analysis, planning, implementation, and control.

Analysis begins with the collecting of data on the eight Os, using various quantitative and qualitative techniques of marketing research. Data sources will vary from secondary to primary, internal to external (to the company), and from informal to formal. The data are used to determine

[4]Bert Rosenbloom, *Marketing Channels: A Management View*, 3d ed. (Hinsdale, Ill.: Dryden, 1987), 8–9.

company opportunities by screening a plethora of environmental opportunities. The company opportunities must then be checked against the company's resources to judge their viability. The key criterion is competitive advantage.

Planning refers to the blueprint generated to react to and exploit the opportunities in the marketplace. The planning stage involves both long-term strategies and short-term tactics. A marketing plan developed for a particular market includes a situation analysis, objectives and goals to be met, strategies and tactics, and cost and profit estimates. Included in the activity is the formation of new organizational structure or adjustments in the existing one to prepare for the execution of the plan.

Implementation is the actual carrying out of the planned activity. If the plans drawn reflect market conditions and if they are based on realistic assessments of the company's fit into the market, the implementation process will be a success. Plans must take into account unforeseeable changes within the company and the environmental forces, and allow for corresponding changes to occur in implementing the plans.

For this reason, concurrently with implementation, control mechanisms must be put into effect. The marketplace is ever dynamic and requires the monitoring of environmental forces, competitors, channel participants, and customer receptiveness. Short-term control tools include annual plan control (such as comparing actual sales to quota), profitability control, and efficiency control. Long-term control is achieved through comprehensive or functional audits to make sure that marketing is not only doing things right but is doing the right things. The results of the control effort provide valuable input for subsequent planning efforts.

These marketing basics do not vary, regardless of the type of market one is planning to enter or to continue to operate. They have been called the technical universals of marketing.[5] The different environments in which the marketing manager must operate will give varying emphases to the variables and will cause the values of the variables to change more drastically.

---

[5] Robert Bartels, "Are Domestic and International Marketing Dissimilar?" *Journal of Marketing* 36 (July 1968): 56–61.

CHAPTER 2

International Trade and the United States

2.1 THE INTERNATIONAL MARKETPLACE

Toward a New Era of World Trade *The coincidence of widespread layoffs and slow income growth, coupled with record trade deficits and burgeoning foreign debt, has led many Americans to question whether the United States will enjoy a more prosperous future. Concerns are being expressed about the ability of the United States to control its own destiny. Some ask whether it is the beginning of the end of the American dream. Many Americans today worry that the increasing competition facing U.S. firms is hurting their standard of living. The nation's support for free trade is wavering, and foreign economic development is seen increasingly as a threat to U.S. welfare, rather than a help.*

The most important policy questions concern the adjustment process: Which countries will have reduced surpluses, and how will the surpluses be reduced? Will the internal adjustment process be smooth or fraught with political friction? A second important policy question concerns the governance at the end of the process: If the United States is no longer willing or able to continue to bear the burden of leadership, who will assume more of the burden?

Change is inevitable, and it is the key to growth and a better future. America must meet head-on the challenge of its changing global role by adapting to the increased competition in the global economy. America should welcome the competition. Competition is what prods us all to do better.

Source: C. Michael Aho, "Looking at the Options," *Journal of Japanese Trade and Industry* 4 (July/August, 1988):14.

We are at a crossroads, as The International Marketplace 2.1 shows. The global environment is changing rapidly, and many of these changes will have a profound impact on the United States and the world.

This chapter begins by highlighting the importance of trade to mankind. Selected historical developments that were mainly influenced by international trade are delineated. International trade developments since 1945 are then presented, together with the international institutions that have emerged to regulate and facilitate trade.

The chapter will analyze and discuss the position of the United States in the world trade environment and explain the impact of trade on the United States. Various efforts undertaken by governments to manage trade by restricting or promoting exports, imports, technology transfer, and investments will be described. Finally, the chapter will present a strategic outlook for future developments in trade.

THE HISTORICAL DIMENSION

One of the major world powers in ancient history was the Roman Empire, which covered most of the known world. Its impact on thought, knowledge, and development can still be felt today. Even while expanding their territories through armed conflicts, the Romans placed primary emphasis on encouraging international business activities. The principal devices used to implement this emphasis were the Pax Romana and the common coinage. The Pax Romana, or the Roman Peace, ensured that merchants were able to travel safely on roads that were built, maintained, and protected by the Roman legions and their affiliated troops. The common coinage in turn ensured that business transactions could be carried out easily throughout the empire. In addition, Rome developed a systematic law, central market locations through the founding of cities, and an excellent communication system resembling an early version of the Pony Express; all of these measures contributed to the functioning of the international marketplace and a reduction of business uncertainty. As a result, economic well-being within and outside the empire started to differ sharply.

Soon city-nations and tribes that were not part of the empire wanted to share in the benefits of belonging. They joined the empire as allies and agreed to pay tribute and taxes. Thus the immense growth of the Roman Empire did not occur mainly through the marching of its legions and war but rather through the linkages of business. Of course, the Romans had to engage in substantial effort to facilitate business in order to make it worthwhile for others to belong. For example, when pirates threatened the seaways, Rome under Pompeius sent out a large fleet to subdue them. The cost of international distribution, and therefore the cost of international marketing, was substantially reduced because fewer goods were lost to pirates. As a result, goods could be made available at lower prices, which in turn translated into larger demand.

The fact that international business was one of the primary factors holding the empire together can also be seen in its decay. When "barbaric" tribes overran the empire, it was not mainly through war and prolonged battles that Rome lost ground. The outside tribes were actually attacking an empire that was already substantially weakened because it could no longer offer the benefits of affiliation. Former allies no longer saw any advantage in being associated with the Romans and, rather than face prolonged battles, willingly cooperated with the invaders.

In a similar fashion, one could interpret the evolution of European feudalism to be a function of trade and marketing. Because farmers were frequently deprived of their harvests as a result of incursions by other (foreign) tribes, or even individuals, they decided to band together and provide for their own protection. By delivering a certain portion of their "earnings" to a protector, they could be assured of retaining most of their gains. While this system initially worked quite well in reducing the cost of production and the cost of marketing, it did ultimately result in the emergence of the feudal system which, perhaps, was not what the initiators had intended it to be.

Interesting in the context of the feudal system is the fact that it encouraged the development of a closed-state economy that was inwardly focused and ultimately conceived for self-sufficiency and security. This static system resulted in a dearth of local commerce.

However, medieval commerce still thrived by developing through export trade. In Italy, the Low Countries, and the German Hanse towns, the impetus for commerce was provided by East–West trade. Profits from the spice trade through the Middle East created the wealth of Venice and other Mediterranean ports. Europe also imported rice, oranges, dyes, cotton, and silk. Western European merchants in turn exported timber, arms, and woolen clothing in exchange for these luxury goods. A remaining legacy of this trade are the many English and French words of Arabic origin, such as divan, bazaar, artichoke, orange, jar, and tariff.[1]

Trade has not always persisted in all countries, however. For example, when in 1896 the Empress Dowager Tz'u-hsi, in order to finance the renovation of the summer palace, impounded government funds that had been designated for Chinese shipping and its navy, China's participation in world trade virtually ground to a halt. As a result, China operated in the subsequent decades in virtual total isolation, without any transfer of knowledge from the outside, without major inflow of goods, and without the innovation and productivity increases that result from exposure to international trade.

International business and international trade have long been seen as valuable tools for national policy purposes. The use of economic coercion—for example, by nations or groups of nations- –can be traced back as far as the time of the Greek city-states and the Peloponnesian War or, in more recent times, to the Napoleonic wars, during which the combatants used blockades to achieve their goal of "bringing about commercial ruin and shortage of food by dislocating trade."[2] Similarly, during the Civil War in the United States, the North consistently pursued a strategy of

---

[1] Henri Pirenne, *Economic and Social History of Medieval Europe* (New York: Harcourt, Brace, and World, 1933), 142–146.

[2] Margaret P. Doxey, *Economic Sanctions and International Enforcement* (New York: Oxford University Press, 1980), 10.

denying international trade opportunities to the South and thus deprived it of export revenue needed to import necessary products.

More recently, the importance of international trade was highlighted during the 1930s. The Smoot-Hawley Act raised duties to reduce the volume of imports into the United States, in the hopes that this measure would restore domestic employment. The result, however, was a raising of duties and other barriers to imports by most other trading nations as well. These measures were contributing factors in the subsequent worldwide depression and the collapse of the world financial system, and these in turn set the scene for World War II.

Global Developments after 1945

After 1945, the United States was the leading proponent of creating a "Pax Americana" for the Western World, driven by the belief that international trade was a key to worldwide prosperity. Many months of international negotiations in London, Geneva, and Lake Success (New York) culminated on March 24, 1948, in Havana, Cuba, with the signing of the charter for an International Trade Organization (ITO). This charter, a series of agreements between 53 countries, was designed to cover international commercial policies, restrictive business practices, commodity agreements, employment and reconstruction, economic development and international investment, and a constitution for a new United Nations agency to administer the whole.[3] In addition, a General Agreement on Tariffs and Trade was initiated, with the purpose of reducing tariffs among countries, and international institutions such as the World Bank and the International Monetary Fund were negotiated.

Even though the International Trade Organization incorporated many farsighted notions, most nations refused to ratify it, fearing its power, its bureaucratic size, and its threats to national sovereignty. As a result, the most forward-looking approach to international trade never came about. However, other organizations conceived at the time are still in existence and have made major contributions toward improving international trade.

Transnational Institutions Affecting World Trade

GATT The General Agreement on Tariffs and Trade (GATT) has been called "a remarkable success story of a postwar international organization that was never intended to become one."[4] It began in 1947 as a set of rules for nondiscrimination, transparent procedures, and settlement of disputes in international trade. Gradually it evolved into an institution that sponsored successive rounds of international trade negotiations.

Early in its existence the GATT achieved the liberalization of trade in 50,000 products, amounting to two-thirds of the value of the trade among

[3] Edwin L. Barber III, "The Investment–Trade Nexus," in U.S. International Economic Policy 1981, ed. Gary Clyde Hufbauer (Washington: The International Law Institute, 1982), 9-4.

[4] Thomas R. Graham, "Global Trade: War and Peace," Foreign Policy (Spring 1983): 124–137.

2.2 | THE INTERNATIONAL MARKETPLACE

***A GATT-Uruguay Round Glossary: What They Said and
What They Really Meant***

"An ambitious proposal"
(It is unlikely to get any support.)

"An innovative proposal"
(This one really is out of the trees.)

"The paper is unbalanced."
(It does not contain any of our views.)

"This proposal strikes a good balance."
(Our interests are completely safeguarded.)

"I should like to make some brief comments."
(You have time for a cup of coffee.)

"We will be making detailed comments at a later stage."
(Expect that your posting will be over before you hear from us.)

"This paper contains some interesting features."
*(I am going to give some face-saving reasons why it should be
withdrawn.)*

"The paper will provide useful background to our discussions."
(I haven't read it.)

"We need transparency in the process."
*(I am worried that I won't be included in the back-room
negotiations.)*

"English is not my mother tongue."
(I am about to give you a lecture on a fine point of syntax.)

"The delegate of . . . spoke eloquently on this subject."
(I haven't got the faintest idea what he means.)

"A comprehensive paper"
*(It's over two pages in length and seems to have an awful lot of
headings.)*

Source: Anonymous.

---

its participants.[5] In subsequent years, special GATT negotiations such as
the Kennedy Round and the Tokyo Round further reduced trade barriers
and developed improved dispute settlement mechanisms, better provisions dealing with subsidies, and a more explicit definition of rules for
import controls.

In spite of, or perhaps because of, these impressive gains, GATT has become less effective today. Duties have already been drastically reduced—
for example, the average U.S. tariff rate fell from 26 percent in 1946 to

[5] Barber, "The Investment–Trade Nexus," 9-5.

5 percent in 1987[6]—and further reductions are unlikely to have a major impact on world trade. Concurrently, many nations have developed new tools for managing and distorting trade flows that are not covered under GATT rules. Examples are "voluntary agreements" to restrain trade, bilateral or multilateral special trade agreements such as the multifiber accord that restricts trade in textiles and apparel, and nontariff barriers. Also, GATT does not cover certain types of trade, for example trade in services or trade in military goods. Because these types of trade comprise an increasing portion of world trade, the impact of GATT shrinks even more. Finally, GATT, which was founded by 24 like-minded governments, is designed to operate by consensus. With a current membership of 95, this consensus rule often leads to a stalemate of many GATT activities. As a result of all these constraints, the GATT is torn between protection and free trade and has lost much of its impact—yet there is no replacement for it in sight. The International Marketplace 2.2 gives some tongue-in-cheek examples of how difficult negotiations in the GATT are described.

IMF   The International Monetary Fund (IMF), conceived in 1944 at Bretton Woods in New Hampshire, was designed to provide stability for the international monetary framework. It obtained funding from its members, who subscribed to a quota based on expected trade patterns and paid in 25 percent of the quota in gold or dollars and the rest in their local currencies. These funds were to be used to provide countries with protection against temporary fluctuations in the value of their currency. Therefore, it was the original goal of the IMF to provide for fixed exchange rates between countries.

The perhaps not so unintended result of using the U.S. dollar as the main world currency resulted in a glut of dollar supplies in the 1960s. This forced the United States to abandon the gold standard and devalue the dollar, and resulted in flexible or floating exchange rates in 1971. However, even though this major change occurred, the IMF as an institution has clearly contributed toward providing international liquidity and to facilitating international trade.

Although the system has functioned well so far, it is currently under severe challenge due to substantial debts incurred by less-developed countries, which are the result of overextended development credits and changes in the cost of energy. The IMF has not been able to find means and ways to resolve this debt "crisis." It has nevertheless made a major contribution toward maintaining the world financial system and has provided time for the parties involved to find new avenues to resolve their problems.

World Bank   The World Bank, whose official name is the International Bank for Reconstruction and Development, has had similar success. It was initially formed in 1944 to aid countries suffering from the destruction of war. After completing this process most successfully it has since taken on the task of aiding world development. With more and more new nations

---

[6]Graham, "Global Trade," 127.

emerging from the colonial fold of the world powers of the early 20th century, the Bank has played a major role in assisting fledgling economies to participate in a modern economic trade framework. More recently, the bank has begun to participate actively with the IMF to resolve the debt problems of the developing world.

Regional Institutions   GATT, IMF, and the World Bank operate on a global level. Regional changes have also taken place, based on the notion that trade between countries needs to be encouraged. Of particular importance was the formation of **economic blocs** that integrated the economic and political activities of nations.

The concept of regional integration was used more than 100 years ago when Germany developed the Zollverein. Its modern-day development began in 1952 with the establishment of the European Coal and Steel Community, which was designed to create a common market among six countries in coal, steel, and iron. Gradually, these nations developed a Customs Union and created common external tariffs. The ultimate goal envisioned was the completely free movement of capital, services, and people across national borders and the joint development of common international policies. Over time, parts of the goal have been attained. The European Community (EC) now encompasses a 12-country group, which represents a formidable market size internally and market power externally. Even though not all restrictions have been dropped as envisioned, the well-being of all EC members has increased substantially since the bloc's formation. Successful implementation of the EC's 1992 plans should lead to even more economic and political integration.

Similar market agreements have been formed by other groups of nations. Examples are the European Free Trade Association (EFTA), the Council for Mutual Economic Assistance (COMECON), and the Gulf Cooperation Council (GCC). Each of these unions was formed for different reasons and operates with different degrees of cohesiveness as appropriate for the specific environment. They focus on issues such as forming a customs union, a common market, an economic union, or a political union. They demonstrate that the joining of forces internationally permits better, more successful international marketing activities, results in an improved standard of living, and provides an effective counterbalance to other large economic blocs. Just as in politics, trade has refuted the old postulate of "the strong is most powerful alone." Nations have come to recognize that trade activities are of substantial importance to their economic well-being. A nation or a group of nations has to generate sufficient outflow activities to compensate for the inflow activities taking place. In the medium and long run, the balance of payments has to be maintained. In the short run, "an external deficit can be financed by drawing down previously accumulated assets or by accumulating debts to other countries. In time, however, an adjustment process must set in to eliminate the deficit."[7]

[7]Mordechai E. Kreinin, *International Economics: A Policy Approach*, 5th ed. (New York: Harcourt Brace Jovanovich, 1987), 12.

The urgency of the adjustment will vary according to the country in question. Some countries find it very hard to obtain acceptance for an increasing number of IOUs. Others, like the United States, can run deficits of hundreds of billions of dollars and still be a preferred borrower because of political stability and perceived economic security. Yet, over the long term, it is the outward orientation of international business activities that is the key to the facilitation of inward flows.

As a result of this understanding, virtually all nations today wish to take part in international trade and make efforts to participate in as much of it as possible.

The Current U.S. International Trade Position

Over the years the U.S. international trade position has eroded substantially when measured in terms of world market share. In the 1950s U.S. exports comprised 25 percent of total world exports. This share has declined precipitously. It is not that U.S. exports have actually dropped during that time. The history of the U.S. decline in world market share began with the fact that the U.S. economy was not destroyed by the war. Because other countries had little to export and a great need for imports, the U.S. export position was powerful. Over time, however, as other trade partners entered the picture and aggressively obtained a larger world market share for themselves, U.S. export growth was not able to keep pace with total growth of world exports. Table 2.1 provides an overview of recent devel-

TABLE 2.1 ▪ Shares of Free-World Exports

Period	United States	France	West Germany	Italy	Netherlands	United Kingdom	Japan	Canada
1970	15.3	6.4	12.1	4.7	4.1	6.9	6.8	5.9
1977	11.9	6.3	11.4	4.4	4.2	5.4	7.8	4.2
1978	12.3	6.7	12.0	4.7	4.2	5.7	8.3	4.1
1979	12.4	6.7	11.4	4.8	4.2	5.7	6.8	3.9
1980	12.3	6.3	10.5	4.2	4.0	6.0	7.1	3.7
1981	13.2	5.9	9.7	4.3	3.8	5.6	8.4	4.0
1982	12.9	5.8	10.5	4.4	3.9	5.8	8.2	4.2
1983	12.6	5.8	10.4	4.5	4.0	5.6	9.0	4.7
1984	13.0	5.7	9.9	4.3	3.8	5.4	9.8	5.2
1985	12.6	5.8	10.5	4.4	3.9	5.8	10.2	5.2
1986	11.7	6.4	12.6	5.0	4.2	5.5	10.9	4.7
1987	11.1	6.5	12.8	5.1	4.0	5.7	10.1	4.3
1988[a]	12.2	6.4	12.1	4.7	3.8	5.7	9.9	4.4

[a] January–September.

Sources: U.S. Department of Commerce, *International Economic Indicators,* March 1985; Bureau of the Census, *FT 900;* and International Monetary Fund, *International Financial Statistics,* 1988 Yearbook and January 1989.

TABLE 2.2 ▪ **Merchandise Exports as a Percentage of Gross National Product**[a]

Period	United States	France	West Germany	Italy	Nether-lands	United Kingdom	Japan	Canada
1980	8.1	17.5	23.6	17.1	43.7	20.5	12.2	24.6
1981	7.7	18.2	25.7	18.4	48.5	19.8	13.0	23.5
1982	6.7	17.5	26.8	18.2	48.0	20.0	12.8	22.6
1983	5.9	18.0	25.7	17.5	48.3	19.9	12.4	22.3
1984	5.8	19.5	27.6	17.7	52.4	21.6	13.5	25.2
1985	5.3	19.3	29.1	18.4	53.7	22.0	13.2	24.9
1986	5.1	17.2	27.1	16.1	45.4	19.1	10.7	23.7
1987	5.4	16.8	26.1	14.7	43.4	19.3	9.5	22.6
1988[b]	6.3	NA	26.0	NA	NA	NA	9.2	NA

NA—Not available.

[a] Gross domestic product for France, Italy, and Canada.

[b] January–September.

Sources: U.S. Department of Commerce, *International Economic Indicators*, March 1985, 36; IMF, *International Financial Statistics*, January 1989; OECD, *Quarterly National Accounts*, No. 2, 1988; *Bank of Canada Review*, January 1988; *Japan Economic Statistics Monthly*, November 1988; Reihe 4, *Saisonbereinigte Wirtschaftszahlen*, December 1988 (Statistische Beihefte zu den Monatsberichten der Deutschen Bundesbank).

TABLE 2.3 ▪ **Exports and Imports per Capita for Selected Countries, 1987**

Country	Exports per Capita	Imports per Capita
United States	$1,041	$1,740
Canada	3,827	3,610
France	2,667	2,849
West Germany	4,807	3,731
Netherlands	6,298	6,224
United Kingdom	2,306	2,712
Japan	1,894	1,237

Source: U.S. Department of Commerce, *FT 900*; IMF, *International Financial Statistics*, January 1989; and OECD, *Main Economic Indicators*, December 1988.

opments in the free world export share distribution among major trading countries.

In spite of the decline in world market share, U.S. exports as a share of the GNP have grown substantially in recent years. However, this increase pales when compared to the international trade performance of other nations. West Germany, for example, has consistently maintained an export share of over 20 percent of GNP. Japan, in turn, which so often is maligned as the export problem child in the international trade arena, exports only about 10 percent of its GNP. Comparative developments of exports across countries in terms of percentage of GNP can be seen in Table 2.2.

The impact of international trade and marketing is even more visible when trade is scrutinized from a per-capita perspective. Table 2.3 presents this information on a comparative basis. Among the major industrialized nations the United States has the lowest exports per capita, amounting to less than one-fourth of Germany's figure, and less than one-sixth of the per-person exports of the Netherlands. Even though imports per capita are also relatively low, they far exceed the level of export activity, thus producing major trade deficits for the United States.

A Diagnosis of the U.S. Trade Position

The developments just enumerated foster the question, why did these shifts occur? We should not attribute the decrease in U.S. trade performance merely to temporary factors such as the high value of the dollar, the subsidization of exports from abroad, or the high price of oil. We need to search further to determine the root causes for the decline in U.S. international competitiveness.

Since World War II it had been ingrained in the minds of American policy makers that the United States is the leading country in world power and world trade. Together with this opinion came the feeling that the United States should assist other countries with their trade performance, because without American help they would never be able to play a meaningful role in the world economy. At the same time, there was admiration for "Yankee ingenuity"—for the idea that U.S. firms were the most entrepreneurial, the most innovative, and the most aggressive in the world. Therefore, the U.S. private sector appeared not to need any help in its international trade efforts.

The result of this overall philosophy was a continuing effort to aid countries abroad in their economic development. At the same time, no particular attention was paid to U.S. domestic firms. This policy was well conceived and well intentioned and resulted in spectacular successes. Books written in the late 1940s describe the overwhelming economic power of the United States and the apparently impossible task of resurrecting foreign economies. Comparing those texts with the economic performance of countries such as Japan and West Germany today demonstrates that the policies of helping to stimulate foreign economies were indeed crowned by success.

These policies were so successful that no one wished to tamper with them. The United States continued to encourage trade abroad and not to aid domestic firms throughout the 1960s and the 1970s. Although the policies were well conceived, the environment to which they were applied was changing. In the 1950s and early 1960s the United States successfully encouraged other nations again to become full partners in world trade.

However, U.S. firms were placed at a distinct disadvantage when these policies continued into the late 1970s.

U.S. firms were assured that, "because of its size and the diversity of its resources, the American economy can satisfy consumer wants and national needs with a minimum of reliance on foreign trade."[8] The availability of a large U.S. domestic market and the relative distance to foreign markets resulted in U.S. manufacturers simply not feeling a compelling need to seek business beyond national borders. Subsequently, the perception emerged within the private sector that exporting and international marketing is "too risky, complicated, and [therefore] not worth it."[9]

This perception also resulted in increasing gaps in international marketing knowledge between managers in the United States and those abroad. While business executives abroad were forced, by the small size of their markets, to look abroad very quickly and to learn about cultural sensitivity and market differences, most U.S. managers remained blissfully ignorant of foreign markets. Similarly, U.S. education, until recently, did not make knowledge about the global environment, foreign languages, and cultures an area of major priority.

Given such lack of global interest, inadequacy of information, ignorance of where and how to market internationally, unfamiliarity with foreign market conditions, and complicated trade regulations, the private sector became fearful of conducting international business activities.

THE IMPACT OF TRADE AND INVESTMENT ON THE UNITED STATES

If complacency with the status quo and fear of change exist with regard to foreign market activities, why should we not simply let U.S. business managers worry about the domestic market and get on with it? Why should we be bothered that the largest portion of U.S. exports are carried out by only 2,500 companies? Why should we be concerned that the Department of Commerce estimates that thousands of U.S. firms are believed to be capable of exporting but do not do so?

The Effect of Trade

Exports are important in a macroeconomic sense, in terms of balancing the trade account. The steady erosion of the American share of total world exports that took place in the 1960s and 1970s has had more than purely optical repercussions. It has also resulted in a merchandise **trade deficit,** which since 1975 has been ever growing. In 1983, imports of products into

---

[8]Kreinin, *International Economics*, 6.

[9]House Subcommittee of the Committee on Government Operations, *Commerce and State Department's Export Promotion Programs*, 95th Cong., 1st sess., 1977, 66.

the United States exceeded exports by over $70 billion. This deficit rose in 1984 to $118 billion; in 1985 to $142 billion; in 1986 to $159 billion; in 1987 to 171 billion; and declined to $138 billion in 1988.

Such trade deficits have a major impact on the United States and its citizens. One billion dollars worth of exports creates, on average, 22,800 jobs.[10] In 1988, over 10 million U.S. jobs depended on trade. It has been estimated that, in addition, $2 billion of GNP are generated per billion of exports, together with $400 million in state and federal tax revenue.[11]

Increases in exports can become a major contributor to economic growth. This fact became particularly evident during the first quarter of 1988, when rapid export growth accounted for almost three-quarters of the entire domestic economic growth rate, and produced most new employment.[12]

More importantly, by marketing internationally, firms can achieve **economies of scale** that may not be obtainable through domestic marketing alone. As a result of increased production a firm may lengthen production runs more quickly and therefore make goods available more cheaply in the United States. Most importantly, international trade permits firms to hone their competitive skills abroad by meeting the challenge of foreign products. By going abroad, U.S. firms can learn from their foreign competitors, challenge them on their ground, and translate the absorbed knowledge into product and marketing improvements at home.

The Effect of International Investment

International marketing activities consist not only of trade, but of a spectrum of involvement, much of which results in international direct investment activities. For decades the United States was the leading foreign direct investor in the world. U.S. multinationals and subsidiaries sprouted everywhere. Of late, however, because of the low value of the dollar, which has made acquisitions in the United States cheap, and because of fears of being excluded from trade by means of governmental action, foreign firms increasingly invest in the United States, as The International Marketplace 2.3 shows.

The extent of **foreign direct investment** in different U.S. manufacturing industries is shown in Table 2.4 on page 37. Foreign affiliates account for about one-eighth of total U.S. manufacturing assets. However, the foreign ownership is not equally distributed across all manufacturing sectors. For example, in the chemical industry, U.S. affiliates of foreign corporations own roughly one-third of all assets.

---

[10] Lester A. Davis, *Contribution of Exports to U.S. Employment: 1980–87* (Washington, D.C.: Government Printing Office, 1989).

[11] Robert G. Shaw in House Subcommittee of the House Committee on Operations, 95th Congress, *Commerce and State Department's Export Promotion Programs* (1977), 94.

[12] Gary R. Teske and Lester A. Davis, "The U.S. Export Boom and Economic Growth," in *U.S. Industrial Outlook* (Washington, D.C.: U.S. Government Printing Office, 1989), 12–15.

2.3 THE INTERNATIONAL MARKETPLACE

Foreign Investment Surrounds Us   You don't need to be an international economist to understand how foreign money is transforming the United States. Take a typical day. You awaken and wash up with a bar of Dove soap. You dress in a Brooks Brothers suit or an outfit purchased at Bloomingdale's and hop into your car, which sports Michelin tires and parts supplied by Marada Inc. At your office in the U.S. News and World Report Building in Washington, you cozy up to a Fujitsu computer and use a Northern Telecom phone system. At lunchtime you pick up a business associate who is staying at the Embassy Suites Hotel. After work you shop at a Benetton Store or maybe Laura Ashley, paying for your purchases with money from a First American Bank cash machine. For a late snack, you eat Keebler cookies.

In each instance, foreign-owned companies with operations a few miles from the White House produced or marketed what you are eating, wearing, driving, and working on. Other foreign investors own your office building, the hotel, the stores, and the bank.

Most consumers know that Sony ships VCRs here from Japan and Hyundai brings over cars from South Korea. But less obvious is that a bar of Dove soap comes from a Baltimore factory owned by the giant Dutch marketer Unilever, whereas Brooks Brothers is owned by a British concern, Marks & Spencer PLC. And while General Motors makes its own cars in Baltimore, parts are produced by Marada, a Canadian-owned company.

Source: Paul Farahi, "How Foreign Money Is Changing Washington," *The Washington Post*, June 20, 1988, 1, 33.

Many of these investments are carried out by the largest trading partners of the United States. Although the United Kingdom still leads all foreign countries in terms of the value of direct investment, Japan is rapidly catching up. As Figure 2.1 on page 38 shows, Japanese corporations alone operated over 640 plants in the United States in 1988.

To some extent these foreign direct investments substitute for trade activities. As a result, firms operating only in the domestic market may be surprised by the onslaught of foreign competition and, by being unprepared to respond quickly, lose their domestic market share. However, the substitution for trade is far from complete. For example, U.S. affiliates of foreign corporations accounted for over 34 percent of U.S. merchandise imports and more than 23 percent of U.S. merchandise exports. They also provided for almost 8 percent of U.S. employment in manufacturing industries and had a highly concentrated employment effect in many states.[13]

[13] U.S. Department of Commerce, Bureau of Economic Analysis, unpublished data, May 1988.

Even though the United States has an open investment policy that welcomes foreign corporations to U.S. shores, some degree of unease exists about the rapid growth of such investment. Increasingly, major foreign investments are reviewed by a specially created U.S. government interagency committee called the Committee for Foreign Investments in the United States (CFIUS). This committee primarily scrutinizes foreign investment activities from the standpoint of their impact on U.S. national security.

A general restriction of foreign investments aimed to help U.S. firms might well be contrary to the general good of U.S. citizens. Industries may be preserved, but only at great peril to the free flow of capital and at substantial cost to consumers. A restriction of investments may permit more domestic control over industries, yet it also denies access to foreign capital, and often innovation. This in turn can result in a tightening up of credit markets, higher interest rates, and a decrease in willingness to adapt to changing world market conditions.

In order to avoid these negative repercussions, the United States as a nation and its citizens must encourage more involvement in the international market by U.S. firms. Greater participation in international trade

TABLE 2.4 ■ **Total Assets of U.S. Affiliates of Foreign Corporations and of All U.S. Businesses in Manufacturing, 1986**

Products	Affiliates (in millions of dollars)	All Businesses (in millions of dollars)	Affiliates as a Percentage of All Businesses
Chemicals and Allied Products	70,497	217,166	32.5%
Stone, Clay, and Glass Products	10,660	46,784	22.8
Primary Metal Industries	15,138	73,942	20.5
Petroleum and Coal Products	50,049	334,952	14.9
Printing and Publishing	11,064	94,154	11.8
Electric and Electronic Equipment	19,662	173,262	11.3
Food and Kindred Products	20,988	219,791	9.5
Paper and Allied Products	5,568	69,082	8.1
Fabricated Metal Products	6,456	84,491	7.6
Instruments and Related Products	4,008	62,943	6.4
Machinery, except Electrical	11,636	211,901	5.5
Textile Products	1,182	26,729	4.4
Rubber and Plastics Products	1,660	41,329	4.0
Transportation Equipment	7,172	251,406	2.9
Other	4,784	86,187	5.6
Total	240,524	1,994,119	12.1

Source: U.S. Bureau of the Census, U.S. Department of Commerce, unpublished data, 1988.

FIGURE 2.1   ▪   **U.S. Plants Operated by Japanese Corporations**

❷ Japanese corporations were operating 640 plants in the US as of May 1987.

Distribution of Japanese Manufacturer's Factory Sites in US (As of May 1987)

Source: JETRO

❸ Japanese corporations made the most number of investments of any country in the US in 1986. In manufacturing, many Japanese corporations built new plants or expanded existing ones in the automotive, electrical machine and other fields.

Number of Investments in US by Major Countries (1986)

Japan	**351**
United Kingdom	178
Canada	114
West Germany	60
France	45

Source: Foreign Direct Investment in the United States, US Department of Commerce

Source: *Handy Facts on U.S.–Japan Economic Relations* (Tokyo: Japan External Trade Organization, 1988), 10–11.

can be achieved by exporting more, by investing, licensing, or franchising abroad, or alternatively by participating in joint ventures domestically. For all these activities, however, the key issue will be the maintenance of high levels of U.S. international competitiveness in order to retain and regain domestic and international market share.

U.S. AND FOREIGN POLICY RESPONSES TO TRADE PROBLEMS

The word policy implies that there is a coordinated set of continuous activities in the legislative and executive branches of government that attempts to deal with U.S. international trade. Unfortunately, such concerted efforts only rarely come about. Policy responses have consisted mainly of political ad-hoc reactions, which over the years have changed from deploration to protectionism. Whereas in the mid-1970s most lawmakers and administration officials simply regretted the lack of U.S. performance in international markets, more recently industry pressures have forced increasing action.

Restrictions of Imports

The U.S. Congress in the past ten years has increasingly been ready to provide the President with more powers to restrict trade. Many resolutions have also been passed and legislation enacted admonishing the President to pay closer attention to trade. However, most of these admonitions only provided for an increasing threat against foreign importers, not for better conditions for U.S. exporters. The power of the executive to improve international trade opportunities for U.S. firms through international negotiations and a relaxation of rules, regulations, and laws has become increasingly restricted over time.

A tendency has also existed to disregard the achievements of past international negotiations. For example, in the 98th Congress an amendment was attached to protectionistic legislation, stipulating that U.S. international trade legislation should not take effect if it is not in conformity with internationally negotiated rules. The amendment was voted down by an overwhelming majority, demonstrating a legislative lack of concern for such international trade agreements.

Worldwide there is a desire to maintain, on the surface at least, agreement with international principles. Yet many countries resort to new trade barriers, examples of which are listed in Table 2.5. One typical method consists of "voluntary" import restraints that are applied selectively against trading partners. Because they are "voluntary," they do not fall under the purview of previously negotiated international agreements. Such measures have been used mainly in areas such as textiles, automobiles, and steel. Such voluntary restrictions, which are of course implemented with the assistance of severe threats against trading partners, are intended to aid domestic industries to reorganize, restructure, and recapture their trade prominence of years past. They fail to take into account that foreign importers may not have caused the economic decline of the domestic industry.

The steel industry provides a good example. World steel production capacity and supply clearly exceed world demand. This is the result both of overly ambitious industrial development projects motivated by nationalistic aspirations and of technological innovation. However, a closer look at the steel industries of developed nations shows that demand for steel has been reduced. In the automobile industry, for example, fewer automobiles are being produced, and they are being produced differently from ten years ago. Automobiles are more compact, lighter, and much more fuel efficient as a result of different consumer tastes and higher oil prices. The average automobile in the 1980s weighed 700 pounds less than in the 1970s. Accordingly, less steel is needed for its production. In addition, many components formerly made of steel are now being replaced by components made from other products such as plastic. Even if imports of steel were to be excluded totally from the markets of industrialized nations, the steel industries could not regain the sales lost from a substantial change in the automotive industry.

TABLE 2.5 ▪ **Types of Trade Barriers**

- Tariff and other import charges (for example, high tariffs, surtaxes, and other import duties)
- Quantitative restrictions (for example, quotas or embargoes on imports)
- Import licensing (for example, restrictive licensing practices)
- Customs barriers (for example, uplift of invoice value for duty assessment purposes and certain practices related to rules of origin)
- Standards, testing, labeling, and certification (for example, use of regional rather than international product standards, unnecessarily restrictive application of phytosanitary standards, and refusal to accept importing manufacturers' self-certification of conformance to foreign product standards)
- Government procurement (for example, "buy national" policies and closed bidding)
- Export subsidies (for example, export financing on preferential terms and agricultural export subsidies that displace exports in third country markets)
- Lack of intellectual property protection (for example, piracy of copyrighted works, inadequate patent protection, and counterfeiting of trademarks)
- Countertrade and offsets (for example, foreign-government-mandated barter agreements that displace exports in third country markets and government requirements for company exports as a condition for allowing imports)
- Services barriers (for example, prohibitions on imports, screen time quotas for foreign films, and requirements that imports be carried by national flag vessels)
- Investment barriers (for example, limitations on foreign equity participation, local content and export performance requirements, and restrictions on transferring earnings and capital)

Source: Office of the United States Trade Representative, *Foreign Trade Barriers* (Washington, D.C.: U.S. Government Printing Office, 1988), 2.

If countries do not resort to the subtle mechanism of voluntary agreements, they often resort to old-fashioned quotas and tariffs. For example, Japanese heavy motorcycles imported into the United States were assessed a duty of 49.4 percent. This regulation kept the last U.S. producer of motorcycles, the Harley-Davidson Company, in business, at a very high cost to the consumer. Similarly, quotas have been proposed on imports of tuna fish packed in water. U.S. producers have complained that Japanese processors are taking away their market share in this field. However, from a historical perspective, it was U.S. processors who encouraged Japanese concentration in water-packed tuna by preventing them in the early 1970s from entering the U.S. market with tuna fish packed in oil. At that time the vast majority of canned tuna sold in the United States was packed in oil; only 7 percent was packed in water. Today the situation has reversed itself; most canned tuna purchased is now packed in water. The Japanese, having had to concentrate since the 1970s on this small market niche, have grown quite successful in penetrating it and have become even more successful since it became a larger market niche. The market share situation changed not because of Japanese ingenuity but because of changing consumer tastes, to which the Japanese were ready to respond while many U.S. manufacturers were not.

A third major method by which trade has been restricted is through **nontariff barriers.** These barriers consist of "buy domestic" campaigns, of providing preferential treatment to domestic bidders as compared to foreign bidders, of using national standards that are not comparable to international standards, of placing emphasis on design rather than performance, and of providing for general difficulties in the market entry of foreign products. Most famous in this regard are probably the measures implemented by France. In order to stop or at least to reduce the importation of foreign video recorders, France ruled in 1983 that all of them had to be sent through the customs station at Poitiers. This customs house is located in the middle of the country, was woefully understaffed, and was open only a few days each week. In addition, the few customs agents at Poitiers insisted on opening each package separately in order to inspect the merchandise. Within a few weeks, imports of video recorders in France came to a halt. The French government, however, was able to point to international agreements and to the fact that officially all measures were in full conformance with the law.

The primary result of all of these trade restrictions is that many actions are taken that are contrary to what we know is good for the world and its citizens. Industries are preserved, but only at great peril to the continued existence of the world trade framework and at a substantial cost to consumers. The direct costs of these actions are hidden and do not evoke much public complaint because they are spread out over a multitude of individuals. Yet, as Table 2.6 shows, these costs are real and burdensome and directly affect the standard of living of individuals. It has been esti-

TABLE 2.6 ▪ **1986 Back-to-School Bill**

Item	Free Market Price[a]	1986 Price with Current Trade Restraints
1 boy's sweater	$20	$25
1 pair cotton blue jeans	$14.50	$18
1 book bag knapsack	$12	$16
1 vinyl handbag	$10	$12
1 leather handbag	$40	$44
1 clock radio	$30	$32
1 Walkman-style radio	$18.70	$20
1 tuna sandwich	$1.80	$2
1 peanut butter sandwich	$1	$1.50
1 candy bar	$0.15	$0.30

[a] Prices calculated based on G. Hufbauer, Diane T. Berliner, and Kimberly Ann Elliott, *Trade Protection in the United States* (Washington: Institute for International Economics, 1986), and 1986 tariff rates quoted by the U.S. International Trade Commission and the U.S. Commerce Department.

mated that in 1988 the total cost to U.S. consumers due to import restraints amounted to $81 billion.[14]

Restrictions of Exports

In addition to imposing restraints on imports, nations also control their
exports. The United States, for example, places a major emphasis on export controls because it regards trade as a privilege rather than a right or a
necessity. U.S. export-controls legislation focuses on national security
controls—that is, the controls of exports that might adversely affect the
safety of the nation in areas such as weapons exports or high-technology
exports. In addition, exports are controlled for the purposes of foreign policy and short supply. These controls restrict the international marketing
activities of firms if an administration feels that such a restriction would
or could send a necessary foreign policy message to another country. This is
done regardless of whether the message will have any impact or whether
similar products can easily be obtained from companies in other nations.
Although perhaps valuable as a tool of international relations, such policies give U.S. firms the reputation of being unreliable suppliers and may
divert sales orders to firms in other countries.

Countries also often establish and implement domestic regulations
without regard for their international trade effects. In the United States,
for example, the breakup of AT&T and the subsequent changes in the purchasing practices of this organization were never considered in light of the
potential impact they might have on foreign sourcing. The same holds true
for the deregulation of the airline industry in the United States. All over
the world, countries pass legislation that has a profound impact on the
ability of firms to compete abroad. The "side effects" of such laws on
the international marketplace are often ignored because countries view
the setting of domestic policies as their sovereign right. Yet, given the linkages among economies, this view is unwarranted and often very dangerous. It places firms at a competitive disadvantage in the international
marketplace and makes easier the competition of foreign firms in the domestic market.

Export Promotion Efforts in the United States

U.S. policymakers have taken several steps to improve the international
trade performance of U.S. firms. The Department of Commerce has added
new information services that provide data on foreign trade and marketing
developments to U.S. companies. Also, the Foreign Commercial Service,
which formerly was part of the Department of State, has been reformed

---

[14]Private communication with Gary Hufbauer, Georgetown University, July 1989.

FIGURE 2.2 ▪ **U.S. Rank for Selected Export Promotion Indicators**

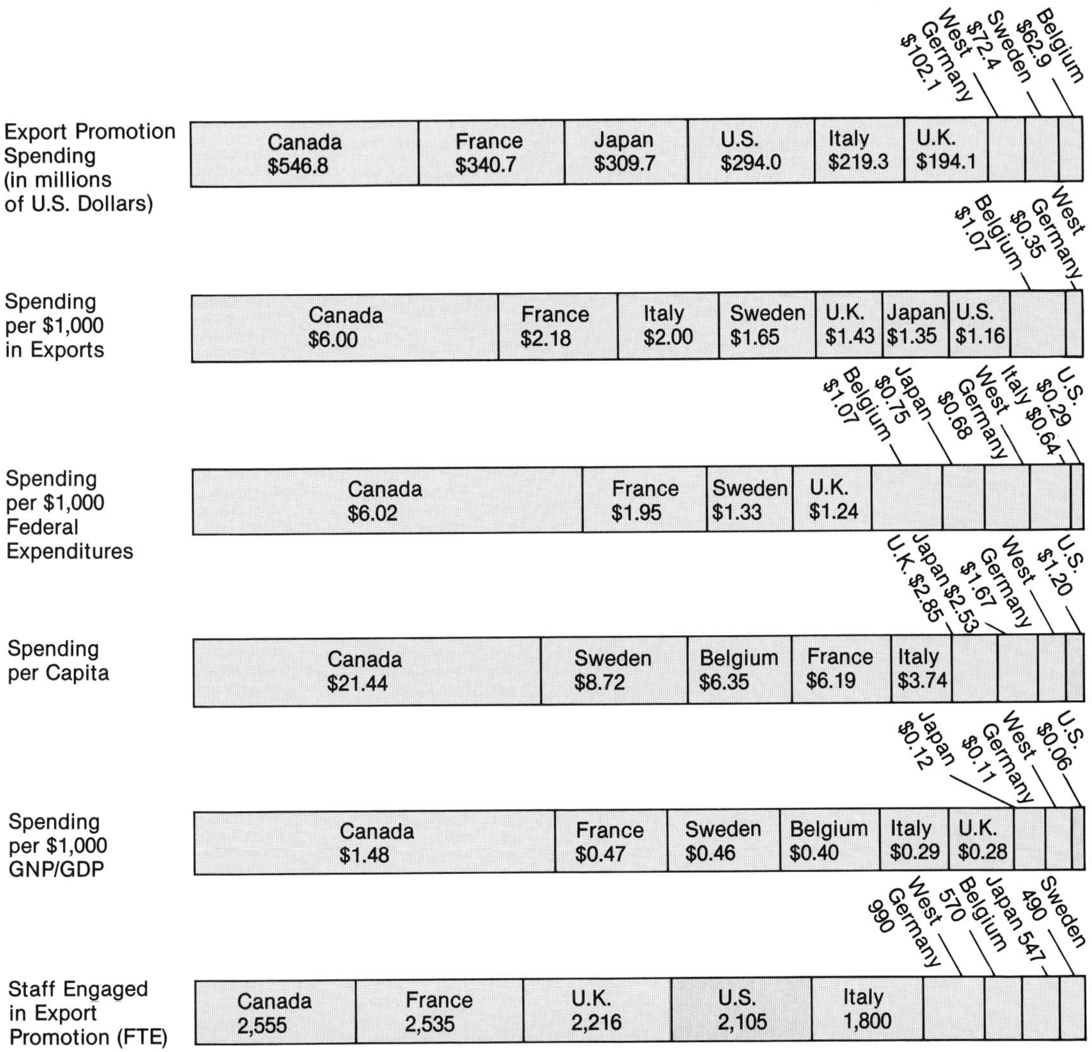

							West Germany $102.1	Sweden $72.4	Belgium $62.9
Export Promotion Spending (in millions of U.S. Dollars)	Canada $546.8	France $340.7	Japan $309.7	U.S. $294.0	Italy $219.3	U.K. $194.1			

						Belgium $1.07	West Germany $0.35	
Spending per $1,000 in Exports	Canada $6.00	France $2.18	Italy $2.00	Sweden $1.65	U.K. $1.43	Japan $1.35	U.S. $1.16	

				Belgium $1.07	Japan $0.75	West Germany $0.68	Italy $0.64	U.S. $0.29
Spending per $1,000 Federal Expenditures	Canada $6.02	France $1.95	Sweden $1.33	U.K. $1.24				

				U.K. $2.85	Japan $2.53	West Germany $1.67	U.S. $1.20
Spending per Capita	Canada $21.44	Sweden $8.72	Belgium $6.35	France $6.19	Italy $3.74		

					Japan $0.12	West Germany $0.11	U.S. $0.06
Spending per $1,000 GNP/GDP	Canada $1.48	France $0.47	Sweden $0.46	Belgium $0.40	Italy $0.29	U.K. $0.28	

				West Germany 990	West Germany 570	Belgium 547	Japan 490	Sweden
Staff Engaged in Export Promotion (FTE)	Canada 2,555	France 2,535	U.K. 2,216	U.S. 2,105	Italy 1,800			

Source: U.S. Department of Commerce, U.S. and Foreign Commercial Service, (Washington, D.C., 1988).

and now falls under the aegis of the U.S. Department of Commerce. Many new professionals were hired to provide an inward and outward link for U.S. business in terms of information flow and market assistance.

In terms of comparative efforts, however, U.S. export promotion activities still lag far behind the support provided by other major industrial nations. The United States ranks rather low in both financial expenditures and manpower, as Figure 2.2 shows. Moreover, the numbers reflect only official—that is, public sector—export promotion support. Many of the countries also provide substantial levels of private sector support, which exists to a much lesser degree in the United States.

A new focus has come about in the area of export financing. Although many efforts were made in the past to reduce the activities of the Export–Import Bank of the United States, policymakers have increasingly recognized that U.S. business may be placed at a disadvantage if it cannot meet the subsidized financing rates of foreign suppliers. The bank, charged with the new mission of aggressively meeting foreign export financing conditions, has in recent years even resorted to offering mixed aid credits. These take the form of loans composed partially of commercial interest rates and partially of highly subsidized developmental aid interest rates.

Tax legislation that inhibited the employment of Americans by U.S. firms abroad has also been altered to be more favorable to U.S. firms. In the past, U.S. nationals living abroad were, with some minor exclusion, fully subject to federal taxation. Because the cost of living abroad can often be quite high—rent for a small apartment can approach the range of $2,000-plus per month—this tax structure often imposed a significant burden on U.S. firms and citizens abroad. Therefore, companies frequently were not able to send U.S. employees abroad. However, as the result of a revision of the tax code that allows a substantial amount of income (up to $70,000) to remain tax free, more Americans can now be posted abroad. In their work they may specify the use of American products and thus enhance the competitive opportunities of U.S. firms.

A major export promotion development in the recent past was the passage of the Export Trading Company Act of 1982. Intended to be the American response to Japanese sogoshoshas, this legislation permits firms to work together to form **export consortia.** The basic idea was to provide a one-stop shopping center for the foreign buyer in which a group of U.S. firms could offer a variety of complementary and competitive products. By exempting U.S. firms from current antitrust statutes, and by permitting banks to cooperate in the formation of these ventures through direct capital participation and the financing of trading activities, it was hoped that more firms could participate in the international marketplace. Although this legislation was originally hailed as a masterstroke and a key measure in turning around the decline in U.S. competitiveness abroad, so far it has not attracted a large number of successful firms. However, too little time may have passed to measure its full impact.

A STRATEGIC OUTLOOK

Even though the United States currently may not appear to have an international trade policy, men and women in responsible positions are increasingly recognizing the crucial importance of international trade to the national well-being. The U.S. national economy has simply become too intertwined with world trade to be considered independent from it.

Critical in the years to come will be the development of a trade policy in a positive fashion rather than in a reactive way that aims only at reducing imports. Protectionistic legislation can be helpful if it is not enacted. Proposals in Congress can be quite useful as bargaining chips in international negotiations. However, if passed, signed into law, and implemented, protectionistic legislation can result in the destruction of the international trade framework.

Most important is the consideration of the **locus of control of trade policy.** Given current proposals, a variety of regulatory agencies could become involved in administering U.S. trade policy. Although such agencies would be useful from the standpoint of addressing narrowly defined grievances, they carry the danger that commercial policy will be determined by a new chorus of discordant voices. This seems even more threatening when one considers that many regulatory agencies see themselves mainly responsible to Congress or to specific constituencies rather than to the administration. By shifting the power of setting trade policy from the administration to agencies or even to states, the term "new federalism" could be given a quite unexpected meaning and might cause progress at the international negotiation level to grind to a halt. No U.S. negotiator can expect to retain the goodwill of his foreign counterparts if he or she cannot place issues on the table that can be negotiated without constantly having to check back with different authorities.

Trade policy can also take either a multilateral or a bilateral approach. In a **bilateral approach,** negotiations are carried out mainly between two nations, while in a **multilateral approach,** negotiations are carried out between a wide variety of nations. The approach can also be broad in terms of covering a wide variety of products and services, or it can be narrow in that it focuses on specific sectoral problems.

As a quick and temporary measure, bilateral approaches and a **sectoral focus** seem quite appealing. Very specific problems can be discussed and can be resolved expediently. Yet, even though negotiators may be well intentioned, **sectoral negotiation** outcomes may, on occasion, produce some quite unexpected results. An example of such a situation is provided in The International Marketplace 2.4.

Bilateral approaches in turn may seem quite appealing, particularly in an era in which there appears to be an emergence of new trading blocs in both Europe and the Western Hemisphere. However, every time bilateral negotiations take place, their very nature excludes a multitude of other interested parties. In order to be successful, negotiations need to produce winners. If a constant set of winners and losers is produced, then negotiations have no chance for long-term success, because no one wants to take the position of the loser. This points in the direction of multilateral negotiation approaches on a broad scale. Here concessions can be traded off, thus making it possible for all nations to emerge and declare themselves as winners. The difficulty lies in devising enough incentives to bring the appropriate and desirable partners to the bargaining table.

2.4 THE INTERNATIONAL MARKETPLACE

U.S.–Japan Accord Benefits Brazil   In June 1988, Washington and Tokyo announced an accord to gradually reduce Japanese barriers to U.S. citrus fruits and juice imports. Japan had agreed to increase citrus imports over the next three years and to eliminate import quotas within four years.

Even though the negotiations were driven by the desire of the United States to open up access to the Japanese market for U.S. firms, the primary beneficiaries of the accord appeared to be Brazilian firms. Because Brazil is the dominant factor in international trade in processed oranges, and the reduction of barriers in Japan is nondiscriminatory, the accord offered much greater market access to Brazil. In addition, Florida suppliers frequently use Brazilian orange juice in the blends they export. Therefore, the increased access would also assist Brazilian orange juice producers indirectly. Finally, most Brazilian orange-growing operations are owned by Japanese. Therefore, established business ties and linkages are likely to lead to increased Brazilian sales in Japan.

Source: James Bruce, "Brazil Expects to Benefit from U.S.–Japan Accord," *The Journal of Commerce,* July 29, 1988, 4A.

SUMMARY

International trade has often played a major role in world history. The rise and fall of the Roman Empire and the emergence of feudalism can be attributed to trade. Since 1945, the Western nations have made concerted efforts to improve the trade environment and expand trade activities. In order for them to do so, various multinational organizations, such as the GATT, the IMF, and the World Bank were founded. In addition, several economic blocs like the EC, the GCC, and EFTA were formed. Many of these organizations have been very successful in their mission, yet new realities of the trade environment demand new types of action.

Over the years, the U.S. international trade position has eroded substantially, and the U.S. share of world exports has declined precipitously from 25 percent in the 1950s. This has occurred mainly because other countries have expanded their trade activities. U.S. firms have been too complacent and disinterested in foreign markets to keep up the pace. As a result, the great majority of U.S. exports are carried out by only 2,500 companies.

Successful foreign competitiveness in international trade has resulted in major trade deficits for the United States. Since each billion dollars worth of exports creates, directly and indirectly, almost 23,000 jobs, it is important for U.S. firms to begin to concentrate on the opportunities the international market has to offer.

Some policymakers have responded to the poor U.S. trade performance by threatening the world with increasing protectionism. The danger of such a policy lies in the fact that world trade would shrink, and standards of living would decline. Protectionism cannot, in the long run, prevent adjustment or increase productivity and competitiveness. It is therefore important to improve the capability of firms to compete internationally and to provide an international trade framework that facilitates international marketing activities.

Questions for Discussion

1. Why is international trade important to a nation?
2. Give examples of the effects of the "Pax Americana."
3. Discuss the role of "voluntary" import restraints in international marketing.
4. What is meant by multilateral negotiations?
5. How have consumer demands changed international trade?
6. Discuss the impact of import restrictions on consumers.
7. Discuss the effect of foreign direct investment on trade.

Recommended Readings

Cohen, Stephen D. *The Making of United States International Economic Policy.* 3d ed. New York: Praeger, 1988.

Conybeare, John A. C. *Trade Wars.* New York: Columbia University Press, 1987.

Czinkota, Michael R., ed. *Improving U.S. Competitiveness.* Washington, D.C.: Government Printing Office, 1988.

Czinkota, Michael R., and George Tesar, eds. *Export Policy: A Global Assessment.* New York: Praeger, 1982.

Diebold, William, Jr., ed. *Bilateralism, Multilateralism and Canada in U.S. Trade Policy.* Cambridge, Mass.: Ballinger, 1988.

Guide to the Evaluation of Trade Promotion Programmes. Geneva: International Trade Centre, UNCTAD/GATT, 1987.

Spiegelman, James M. *Trade and Politics.* Washington, D.C.: Center for International Business and Trade, Georgetown University, 1987.

U.S. Department of Commerce. International Trade Administration. *United States Trade Performance Report.* Washington, D.C.: Government Printing Office, 1988.

Waldman, Raymond J. *Managed Trade.* Cambridge, Mass.: Ballinger, 1986.

CHAPTER 3

The International Economic Environment

THE INTERNATIONAL MARKETPLACE

The Coming Boom in Europe *The Pacific Rim will not have a monopoly on fast growth in the 1990s. Managers are beginning to realize that Western Europe may well be the fastest growing market for a host of businesses. The economic picture had not been good in the late 1970s and 1980s, but the European Community's drive to create a single market of 320 million consumers by the end of 1992 has become a potent engine of change.*

Governments are determined to make Europe's comeback more than a cyclical happening. They are sticking tenaciously to free-market programs that sparked the revival. Probusiness policies have turned out to be good politics. "Eurosclerosis" is turning into "Europhoria."

Underlying all of it is Europe's sturdy economic outlook. The EC's gross national product rose 3.7 percent in 1988, a 13-year high. The EC foresees growth at 3 percent to 3.5 percent annually in the 1990s, almost twice the pace in the 1980s. Strong growth has also had an impact on a perennial problem: joblessness. Europe is creating 1.5 million jobs a year, the most since the 1960s. In the United Kingdom, 1.2 million unemployed went to work in 1988 and early 1989, cutting the rate from 12 percent to 7.2 percent. Overall European unemployment, which was about 10 percent in early 1989, should continue to fall.

Inflation is being kept at bay. During 1987 and 1988, prices increased only about 3 percent. Furthermore, Europe is determined to tame inflation by sticking to tight monetary and fiscal policies. Investment is soaring. Wages rose 3.8 percent in 1988, about half the increase five years earlier, which helped boost profits. Cash-rich companies in France, West Germany, Italy, and Britain spent a record $52 billion on equipment, an increase of 14 percent over the previous year.

As incomes rise and tastes may become more uniform, Europe will turn into a booming market for consumer goods from appliances to soft drinks. Deregulation will trigger growth. Businesses that have been held down by regulation and government monopolies, such as advertising and telecommunications, will grow far faster in Europe than in the United States. Foreign companies will be able to break into protected national markets for the first time.

Source: Shawn Tully, "The Coming Boom in Europe," *Fortune*, April 10, 1989, 108–114.

The assessment of a foreign market environment should start with the evaluation of economic variables relating to the size and nature of the markets. Because of the large number of worthwhile alternatives, initial screening of markets should be done efficiently yet effectively enough, with a wide array of economic criteria, to establish a preliminary estimate of market potential. One of the most basic characterizations of the world economy is provided in Figure 3.1, which incorporates many of the economic variables pertinent to marketers.

The **Group of Five**—listed in Figure 3.1 as the United States, Britain, France, West Germany, and Japan—consists of the major industrialized countries of the world. This group is sometimes expanded to the **Group of Seven** (by adding Italy and Canada) and to the **Group of Ten** (by adding Sweden, the Netherlands, and Belgium). It may also be expanded to encompass the members of the Organization for Economic Cooperation and Development, OECD (which consists of 24 countries: Western Europe, the United States, Canada, Japan, Australia, and New Zealand).

An important group in the middle-income developing countries are the newly industrialized countries (NICs), which include Singapore, Taiwan, Korea, Hong Kong, Brazil, and Mexico (some propose adding Malaysia and the Philippines to the list as well). Some of these NICs will earn a new acronym, RIC (rapidly industrializing countries); for example, by the end of the 1990s South Korea expects to claim 7 percent of the global electronics market.[1]

The major oil-exporting countries, in particular members of the Organization of Petroleum Exporting Countries (OPEC) and countries such as Nigeria, Venezuela, and Indonesia, are dependent on the price of oil for their world market participation. Few analysts expect the price per barrel to climb much higher than the mid-20s by 1995, which will not work in these countries' favor.

Many of the less-developed countries will depend on the success of their industrialization efforts in the years to come, even in the case of resource-rich countries that may find commodity prices being driven down by man-made substitutes. China, one of the major less-developed countries, became the second-largest exporter of textiles to the United States after it began increasing production in the 1980s. Despite an image of hopeless poverty, India has over 75 million middle-class consumers, more than West Germany. A special group in this category are the countries

---

[1] Richard I. Kirkland, "We're All in This Together," *Fortune*, February 2, 1987, 26–29.

FIGURE 3.1 ▪ **The Global Economy**

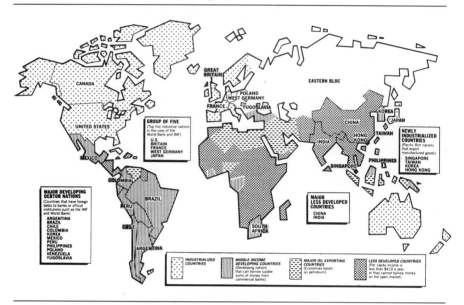

Source: "The Global Economy," *The Washington Post,* January 19, 1986, H1. Reprinted with permission.

saddled with a major debt burden, such as Peru and Yugoslavia. The degree and form of their participation in the world market will largely depend on how the debt issue is solved with the governments of the major industrialized countries and the multilateral and commercial banks.

The centrally planned economies, mainly members of the Council of Mutual Economic Assistance (COMECON), are undergoing major economic experimentation in varying degrees and as a result are allowing market forces to work. Trade ties with the West, for example between the EC and COMECON, will expand possibilities to market in countries like Hungary and the Soviet Union.

Classifications of markets will vary by originator and intended use. Marketers will combine economic variables to fit their planning purposes by using those that relate directly to the product and/or service the company markets, such as the market's ability to buy. For example, Table 3.1 provides a summary of an economic classification system used by the General Electric Company. This approach has countries divided into four basic categories, with the centrally planned economies given separate consideration because of their unique characteristics of strict governmental control and centralized procurement. This format takes into account both general country considerations—such as population, GNP, geography, manufacturing as a percentage of national product, infrastructure and per-capita income—and narrower industry-specific considerations of interest

TABLE 3.1 ▪ **Economic Development Variable in Countries' Use of Electricity and Electrical Goods**

Less developed: These countries have primarily agrarian and/or extractive economies. High birthrates, along with limited infrastructures, account for the low per-capita income and usage of electricity. Electrification is limited to the main population centers. Generally, basic electrical equipment is imported.

Early developing: These countries have begun initial development of an infrastructure and have infant industries, especially mining and selected cottage manufactures. Target economic sectors may enjoy high growth rates even though per-capita income and electricity consumption are still modest. Progressively more sophisticated electrical equipment is imported, frequently to achieve forward integration of extractive industries.

Semideveloped: These countries have started an accelerated expansion of infrastructure and wide industrial diversification. Thus, per-capita income and electricity consumption are growing rapidly. Increased discretionary income and electrification allow greater ownership of autos and electrical appliances among the expanding middle class. Larger quantities of high-technology equipment are imported.

Developed: These countries enjoy well-developed infrastructures, high per-capita income and electricity consumption, and large-scale industrial diversification. They are also characterized by low rates of population and economic growth, as well as shifts in emphasis from manufacturing to service industries—notably transportation, communication, and information systems.

Communist: The separate listing for these countries does not imply that they represent either a higher or a lower stage of economic development. They could have been distributed among each of the above four categories.

Source: V. Yorio, *Adapting Products for Export* (New York: Conference Board, 1983), 11.

to the company and its marketing efforts, such as extent of use of the product, total imports, and U.S. share of these imports.

The discussion that follows is designed to summarize a set of criteria that help identify foreign markets and screen the most opportune ones for future entry or change of entry mode. Discussed are variables on which information is readily available from secondary sources such as international organizations, individual governments, and private organizations or associations.

The Statistical Yearbook of the United Nations, World Bank publications, and individual countries' *Statistical Abstracts* provide the starting point for market investigations. The more developed the market, the more abundantly data are available. Data are available on past developments as well as on projections of broader categories such as population and income. *Business International,* for example, annually compiles market-size indicators for 117 countries that account for over 90 percent of the world's output in goods and services. The most recent summary, provided in the Appendix to Chapter 3, will be used throughout the discussion.

MARKET CHARACTERISTICS

The main dimensions of a market can be captured by considering variables such as those relating to the population and its various characteristics, infrastructure, geographical features of the environment, and foreign involvement in the economy.

Population

The total world population is expected to exceed five billion people by 1990. The number of people in a particular market provides one of the most basic indicators of market size and is, in itself, indicative of the potential demand for certain staple items that have universal appeal and are generally affordable. As indicated by the data in Table 3.2, population is not evenly divided among the major regions of the world; Asia holds over half of the world's population.

These population figures can be analyzed in terms of marketing implications by noting that countries belonging to the European Community (EC) constitute 65 percent of the Western European population, and the two largest entities in Asia, China and India, constitute nearly 70 percent of Asia's. The greatest population densities are also to be found in Europe, providing the international marketer with a strategically located center of operation and ready access to the major markets of the world. (Western Europe as a fast-growing market in the 1990s is discussed in The International Marketplace 3.1.)

Population figures themselves must be broken down into meaningful categories in order for the marketer to take better advantage of them. Because market entry decisions may lie in the future, it is worthwhile to analyze population projections in the areas of interest and focus on their possible implications. Table 3.3 includes projections provided by the United Nations that point to a population explosion, but mainly in the developing countries. Northern Europe will show nearly zero population growth for the next 30 years, whereas the population of Africa will triple. Even in the low- or zero-growth markets the news is not necessarily bad for the international marketer. The 25 to 45 age group, whose numbers will be increasing between now and 1995, are among the most affluent consumers of all, having formed family units and started to consume household goods in

TABLE 3.2 ▪ **World Population Distribution, 1986 (in millions)**

Western Europe	426.7	Middle East	157.4
Eastern Europe	391.5	Latin America	356.0
North America	265.8	Caribbean	34.9
Asia	2,718.9	Africa	432.8
Oceania	19.2		

Source: "Indicators of Market Size," *Business International*, 1988.

TABLE 3.3 ∎ Population Projections by Region and Countries, 1990 to 2025

Region and Country	1990	1995	2000	2025	Region and Country	1990	1995	2000	2025
World, total	5,248.5	5,679.3	6,127.1	8,177.1	Temperate South America[b]	49.1	52.3	55.5	70.1
More developed[a]	1,208.8	1,242.8	1,275.7	1,396.7	Argentina	32.9	35.1	37.2	47.4
Less developed[a]	4,039.7	4,436.4	4,851.5	6,780.4	Chile	13.1	14.0	14.9	18.8
Africa	645.3	753.2	877.4	1,642.9	Uruguay	3.1	3.2	3.4	3.9
Eastern Africa[b]	189.7	224.7	266.2	531.4	Tropical South America[b]	249.8	276.9	304.1	436.3
Burundi	5.3	6.1	7.0	11.0	Bolivia	7.3	8.4	9.7	18.3
Ethiopia	42.7	50.1	58.4	112.0	Brazil	150.4	165.1	179.5	245.8
Kenya	25.4	31.4	38.5	82.9	Colombia	31.8	34.9	38.0	51.7
Madagascar	11.6	13.4	15.6	29.7	Equador	10.9	12.7	14.6	25.7
Malawi	8.3	9.8	11.7	23.2	Paraguay	4.2	4.8	5.4	8.6
Mozambique	16.2	18.8	21.8	39.7	Peru	22.3	25.1	28.0	41.0
Rwanda	7.3	8.8	10.6	22.2	Venezuela	21.3	24.2	27.2	42.8
Somalia	5.9	6.2	7.1	13.2	Northern America[b]	275.2	286.8	297.7	347.3
Tanzania	27.0	32.5	39.1	83.8	Canada	27.1	28.3	29.4	34.4
Uganda	18.8	22.5	26.8	52.3	United States	248.0	258.3	268.1	312.7
Zambia	7.9	9.4	11.2	23.8	East Asia[b]	1,317.2	1,390.4	1,470.0	1,696.1
Zimbabwe	10.5	12.6	16.1	32.7	China: Mainland	1,119.6	1,184.2	1,255.7	1,460.1
Middle Africa[b]	71.9	83.0	96.1	183.5	Hong Kong	6.1	6.6	6.9	7.9
Angola	10.0	11.5	13.2	24.5	Japan	122.7	125.1	127.7	127.6
Cameroon	11.1	12.6	14.4	25.2	North Korea	22.4	24.9	27.3	37.6
Cen. African Rep.	2.9	3.3	3.7	6.7	South Korea	43.8	46.8	49.5	58.6
Chad	5.7	6.4	7.3	13.1	South Asia	1,740.2	1,909.4	2,073.7	2,770.6
Zaire	38.4	44.8	52.4	104.4	Eastern South Asia[b]	440.4	480.8	519.7	684.7
Northern Africa[b]	143.8	164.3	185.7	295.0	Burma	44.5	49.8	55.2	82.2
Algeria	26.0	30.5	35.2	57.3	Indonesia	178.4	191.9	204.5	255.3
Egypt	52.7	58.9	65.2	97.4	Kampuchea	8.4	9.2	9.9	12.5
Libya	4.3	5.2	6.1	11.1	Laos	5.0	5.6	6.2	9.2
Morocco	27.6	31.9	36.3	59.9	Malaysia	17.3	19.1	20.6	26.9
Sudan	24.9	28.7	32.9	55.4	Philippines	61.4	68.3	74.8	102.3
Tunisia	8.1	8.9	9.7	13.6	Singapore	2.7	2.9	3.0	3.2
Southern Africa[b]	42.3	48.1	54.5	90.7	Thailand	56.2	61.1	66.1	88.3
South Africa	36.8	41.6	46.9	76.3	Vietnam	55.4	71.7	78.1	105.1
Western Africa[b]	197.6	233.1	275.0	542.4	Middle South Asia[b]	1,189.9	1,279.9	1,386.7	1,815.9
Benin	4.7	5.4	6.4	12.2	Afghanistan	19.3	21.7	24.2	35.9
Burkina Faso[c]	8.0	9.1	10.5	19.5	Bangladesh	115.2	130.3	145.8	219.4
Ghana	15.9	18.7	21.9	37.7	India	831.9	899.1	961.5	1,188.5
Guinea	6.1	7.0	7.9	13.9	Iran	51.8	58.7	65.5	96.2
Ivory Coast	11.5	13.4	15.6	28.1	Nepal	18.5	20.7	23.0	33.9
Mali	9.3	10.7	12.4	21.4	Pakistan	113.3	128.0	142.6	212.8
Niger	7.1	8.3	9.8	18.9	Sri Lanka	18.0	19.5	20.8	26.2
Nigeria	113.3	135.5	161.9	338.1	Western South Asia[b]	129.9	148.7	168.3	270.0
Senegal	7.5	8.7	10.0	18.9	Iraq	18.5	21.6	24.9	42.7
Togo	3.4	3.9	4.6	9.0	Israel	4.7	5.0	5.4	7.0
Latin America	453.2	501.3	550.0	786.6	Jordan	4.3	5.2	6.4	13.4
Caribbean[b]	34.6	37.7	40.8	57.7	Lebanon	3.0	3.3	3.6	5.2
Cuba	10.5	11.2	11.7	13.6	Saudi Arabia	13.5	16.1	18.9	33.5
Dominican Republic	7.0	7.7	8.4	12.2	Syria	12.8	15.3	18.1	32.3
Haiti	7.5	8.6	9.9	18.3	Turkey	56.0	62.4	68.5	99.3
Middle America[b]	119.7	134.4	149.6	222.6	Yemen Arab Rep.	7.5	8.6	9.9	16.5
El Salvador	6.5	7.5	8.7	15.0					
Guatemala	9.7	11.1	12.7	21.7					
Honduras	5.1	6.0	7.0	13.3					
Mexico	89.0	99.2	109.2	154.1					
Nicaragua	3.9	4.5	5.3	9.2					

(Continued)

TABLE 3.3 ▪ Continued

Region and Country	1990	1995	2000	2025	Region and Country	1990	1995	2000	2025
Europe (excluding					Southern Europe[b]	146.4	150.0	153.1	162.8
Soviet Union)	499.5	506.5	513.1	526.9	Albania	3.4	3.8	4.1	5.8
Eastern Europe	115.7	118.2	121.0	131.2	Greece	10.2	10.5	10.7	11.8
Bulgaria	9.4	9.6	9.7	10.2	Italy	57.4	57.9	58.2	56.9
Czechoslovakia	16.0	16.3	16.8	18.8	Portugal	10.4	10.7	11.0	11.9
East Germany	16.6	16.5	16.6	16.1	Spain	40.5	42.0	43.4	49.2
Hungary	10.8	10.8	10.9	10.9	Yugoslavia	23.9	24.6	25.2	26.6
Poland	39.0	40.2	41.4	45.9	Western Europe[b]	154.8	155.3	155.6	149.3
Romania	23.9	24.8	25.6	29.2	Austria	7.5	7.5	7.5	7.3
Northern Europe[b]	82.6	83.0	83.4	83.6	Belgium	9.9	9.9	9.9	9.8
Denmark	5.2	5.1	5.1	4.8	France	55.4	56.3	57.1	58.5
Finland	4.9	5.0	5.0	4.8	Netherlands	14.7	14.9	15.0	14.6
Ireland	3.8	4.0	4.2	5.2	Switzerland	6.2	6.0	5.9	4.9
Norway	4.2	4.2	4.2	4.3	West Germany	60.7	60.3	59.8	53.8
Sweden	8.2	8.2	8.1	7.5	Soviet Union	291.3	303.1	314.8	367.1
United Kingdom	55.8	56.0	56.2	56.4	Oceania[b]	26.7	28.5	30.4	39.5
					Australia	16.7	17.7	18.7	23.5
					New Zealand	3.4	3.6	3.7	4.2
					Papua New Guinea	4.2	4.8	5.3	8.2

[a] Regions.

[b] Includes countries not shown separately.

[c] Formerly Upper Volta.

Source: Bureau of the Census, *Statistical Abstract of the United States, 1989* (Washington, D.C.: Government Printing Office, 1989), 816–818.

large quantities as they reach the peak of their personal earnings potential. By the year 2000, they are expected to start spending more on leisure goods and health care and related services.[2]

In order to influence population growth patterns, governments will have to undertake, with the help of private enterprise, quite different social marketing tasks. These will range from promoting and providing incentives for larger families (in Scandinavia, for example) to increased family planning efforts (in Thailand, for example). Regardless of the outcome of such government programs, current trends will further accelerate the division of world markets into the "haves" and the "have-nots." More adjustment capability will be required on the part of companies that want to market in the developing countries because of lower purchasing power of individuals and increasing government participation in the marketing of basic products.

Depending on the marketer's interest, population figures can be classified to show specific characteristics of their respective markets. Age distribution and life expectancy correlate heavily with the level of development of the market. Industrialized countries, with their increasing median age and a larger share of the population above 65, will open unique opportuni-

[2] *Consumer Europe* (London: Euromonitor 1988), 24.

ties for international marketers with new products and services. A number of companies in the United States, for example, are marketing an adult diaper.

As the life expectancy in a market extends and new target markets become available, international marketers may be able to extend their products' life cycles by marketing them abroad. Interpretation of demographics will require some degree of experiential knowledge. As an example, which age categories of females should be included in an estimate of market potential for a new contraceptive? This would vary from the very early teens in the developing countries to higher age categories in Northern countries, where the maturing process is later.

An important variable for the international marketer is the size of the household. A **household** describes all the persons, both related and unrelated, who occupy a housing unit.[3] Among the EC, the average household size has shrunk from 2.9 to 2.7 persons since 1977, and is expected to decline further.[4] One factor behind the overall growth in households, and subsequent decline in the average size, has been the increase in the numbers of divorced and sole-survivor households. One-person households are most common in Norway and West Germany. This compares strikingly to countries such as Turkey, where the average household size is 5. With economic development usually bringing about more, but smaller sized, households, international marketers of food products, appliances, and household goods have to adjust to patterns of demand; for example, they may offer single-serving portions of frozen foods and smaller appliances.

The increased urbanization of many markets has distinctly changed consumption patterns. Urban populations as a percentage of the total will vary from a low of 4 percent in Nepal to a high of 86 percent in Australia.[5] The degree of urbanization often dictates the nature of the marketing task the company faces, not only in terms of distribution but also in market potential and buying habits. Urban areas provide larger groups of consumers who may be more receptive to marketing efforts because of their exposure to other consumers (the demonstration effect) and to communication media. In markets where urbanization is recent and taking place rapidly, the marketer faces additional responsibility as a change agent, especially when incomes may be low and the conditions for the proper use of the products may not be adequate. This is especially true in countries where rapid industrialization is taking place, such as Greece, Spain, and Portugal.

When using international data sources, the international marketer must recognize that definitions of a construct may vary among the many secondary sources. The concept of **urbanization,** for example, has different

---

[3] James F. Engel, Roger D. Blackwell, and Paul W. Miniard, *Consumer Behavior* (Hinsdale, Ill.: Dryden), 270.

[4] *European Marketing Data and Statistics* (London: Euromonitor 1988/89), 26–27.

[5] U.S. Bureau of the Census, *World Population Profile* (Washington, D.C.: U.S. Government Printing Office, 1985), 21–24.

TABLE 3.4 ▪ Gross National Product by Country

Country	Current Dollars (billions)						Constant (1984) Dollars (billions)			Per Capita (dollars)		
	1975	1980	1982	1983	1984	1985	1975	1980	1985	1975	1980	1985
United States	1,598.0	2,732.0	3,166.0	3,406.0	3,772.0	4,010.0	2,903.0	3,434.0	3,887.0	13,440	15,080	16,240
Afghanistan	2.1	3.3	3.8[a]	3.8[a]	3.7[a]	3.5[a]	3.8	4.2	3.4[a]	268	278	248
Algeria	16.7	33.4	42.5	46.8	51.3	54.9	30.3	41.9	53.2	1,875	2,225	2,413
Argentina	40.6	64.7	64.2	68.0	72.4	71.6	73.7	81.4	69.4	2,830	2,882	2,287
Austria	27.6	48.1	56.9	61.1	63.8	67.7	50.2	60.5	65.6	6,642	8,015	8,674
Bangladesh	5.2	9.6	12.0	12.9	14.0	15.0	9.4	12.1	14.5	123	137	143
Belgium	36.7	60.6	70.4	73.1	77.0	80.6	66.6	76.1	78.1	6,797	7,731	7,923
Brazil	81.1	160.9	182.8	182.4	197.5	220.6	147.3	202.3	213.8	1,355	1,642	1,527
Bulgaria	28.1	42.8	52.8	53.9	57.8	57.8	51.0	53.8	56.0	5,850	6,079	6,259
Burma	2.1	4.0	5.3	5.7	6.3	6.9	3.8	5.1	6.7	124	152	179
Canada	142.5	240.0	276.1	296.1	322.5	346.1	258.9	301.6	335.4	11,390	12,530	13,220
Chile	7.4	15.3	15.4	16.0	17.2	18.6	13.4	19.3	18.0	1,309	1,738	1,490
China:												
Mainland[a]	94.7	179.0	236.5	270.0	319.6	368.9	172.1	225.0	357.5	187	229	342
Taiwan	14.7	35.2	44.9	50.3	57.9	62.2[a]	26.8	44.3	60.3[a]	1,661	2,489	3,127
Colombia	14.6	27.8	33.0	34.7	36.7	38.7	26.5	34.9	37.5	1,100	1,316	1,274
Czechoslovakia	61.7	99.5	117.6	124.0	131.9	136.8	112.0	125.0	132.6	7,584	8,197	8,556
East Germany	77.1	125.3	148.4	157.3	167.9	177.4	140.0	157.5	171.9	8,309	9,412	10,330
Egypt	12.3	27.8	36.0	39.3	41.6	44.4	22.3	34.9	43.0	602	827	875
Ethiopia	2.1	3.5	4.3	4.6	4.7	4.5	3.8	4.4	4.4	106	115	101
France	220.4	375.4	446.7	465.3	487.9	508.5	400.3	471.9	492.8	7,588	8,759	8,932
Ghana	4.3	6.4	6.7	6.7	7.6	8.1	7.7	8.1	7.9	771	745	604
Greece	14.8	26.6	30.6	31.6	33.5	35.0	26.8	33.4	33.9	2,965	3,461	3,411
Hungary	37.4	59.9	72.9	74.9	79.9	80.6	68.0	75.3	78.1	6,454	7,031	7,331
India	67.8	117.1	148.9	166.6	179.1	196.5	123.1	147.1	190.5	198	214	248
Indonesia	25.5	52.9	69.2	73.9	81.3	86.2	46.3	66.5	83.5	336	429	483
Iran[a]	76.4	116.2	143.7	161.7	163.4	164.2	138.8	146.0	159.1	4,160	3,729	3,385
Iraq[a]	18.9	54.1	34.4	34.2	37.5	37.9	34.3	67.9	36.8	3,085	5,147	2,326
Italy	155.3	272.5	313.9	325.6	347.2	366.4	282.0	342.4	355.1	5,075	6,066	6,216
Japan	458.5	850.5	1,067.0	1,145.0	1,256.0	1,361.0	832.8	1,069.0	1,319.0	7,464	9,151	10,920
Kenya	2.2	4.1	5.1	5.5	5.7	6.2	4.0	5.2	6.0	294	311	291
Madagascar	1.4	2.1	2.2	2.2	2.2	2.3	2.5	2.7	2.3	330	309	225
Malaysia	9.4	20.3	26.6	28.7	31.7	32.4	17.0	25.6	31.4	1,385	1,857	2,038
Mexico	64.0	125.3	150.0	148.5	161.3	173.4	116.2	157.4	168.1	1,890	2,245	2,139
Morocco	4.4	8.3	10.1	10.7	11.3	12.0	8.0	10.4	11.6	442	507	501

meanings depending on where one operates. In the United States an urban area is defined as a place of 2,500 or more inhabitants; in Sweden, it is a built-up area with at least 200 inhabitants with no more than 200 meters between houses; in Mauritius, it is a town with proclaimed legal limits. Comparability, therefore, is concerned with the ends and not the means (or the definition).

Income Markets require not only people but also purchasing power, which is a function of income, prices, savings, and credit availability.

Apart from basic staple items, for which population figures provide an estimate, income is most indicative of the market potential for most con-

Country	Current Dollars (billions)						Constant (1984) Dollars (billions)			Per Capita (dollars)		
	1975	1980	1982	1983	1984	1985	1975	1980	1985	1975	1980	1985
Mozambique	2.0[a]	3.0	3.3	2.9	2.5	2.2	3.7[a]	3.7	2.1	356	308	156
Nepal	1.0	1.7	2.2	2.3	2.5	2.7	1.9	2.1	2.6	143	143	152
Netherlands	58.9	97.1	110.9	117.1	124.1	130.7	107.0	122.0	126.7	7,837	8,625	8,741
Nigeria	43.6	75.6	79.8	78.7	77.8	79.4	79.2	95.0	77.0	1,027	1,055	749
North Korea[a]	9.0	15.5	20.5	21.6	23.0	24.3	16.4	19.5	23.6	1,031	1,089	1,155
Pakistan	10.7	21.3	27.8	31.1	33.7	37.4	19.5	26.8	36.3	261	315	367
Peru	10.2	16.3	19.9	17.8	19.2	20.1	18.5	20.5	19.5	1,223	1,164	989
Philippines	12.9	25.3	31.0	32.6	31.5	31.3	23.5	31.8	30.3	528	624	520
Poland	122.1	183.3	200.3	218.4	235.0	245.6	221.8	230.4	238.0	6,529	6,476	6,398
Portugal	8.1	14.7	17.3	18.1	18.1	19.4	14.7	18.5	18.8	1,562	1,892	1,853
Romania	50.6	88.9	106.0	110.3	121.3	126.6	91.9	111.8	122.7	4,325	5,034	5,399
South Africa	31.5	52.2	63.5	64.5	70.4	71.6	57.2	65.6	69.3	2,247	2,251	2,115
South Korea	23.4	48.1	63.0	73.3	82.4	89.4	42.4	60.4	86.6	1,157	1,585	2,110
Soviet Union	937.0	1,541.0	1,868.0	1,991.0	2,091.0	2,197.0	1,702.0	1,937.0	2,129.0	6,689	7,270	7,635
Spain	73.6	116.5	137.0	145.1	153.8	162.9	133.6	146.5	157.8	3,758	3,907	4,089
Sri Lanka	2.1	3.9	4.9	5.4	5.9	6.3	3.8	4.9	6.1	276	327	380
Sudan	3.7	6.4	8.0	8.6	8.3	7.3	6.6	8.1	7.1	414	427	317
Sweden	46.2	70.4	81.4	86.4	93.0	98.0	83.9	88.5	95.0	10,240	10,640	11,380
Switzerland	45.9	72.8	85.7	89.9	96.2	103.2	83.4	91.5	100.0	13,020	14,330	15,320
Syria	7.4	14.0	18.0	19.1	19.1	19.8	13.4	17.6	19.2	1,820	2,020	1,854
Tanzania	2.6	4.3	5.0	5.2	5.4	5.7	4.8	5.5	5.5	302	290	250
Thailand	13.1	26.5	33.6	37.1	40.3	43.0	23.8	33.3	41.7	564	710	805
Turkey	19.7	32.2	40.8	44.0	48.2	52.5	35.8	40.4	50.9	883	896	1,004
Uganda	2.8	3.1	4.2	4.6	5.0	NA	5.1	3.9	NA	456	309	NA
United Kingdom	206.7	321.1	373.8	404.2	428.8	460.4	375.4	403.6	446.2	6,679	7,167	7,882
Venezuela	24.8	42.3	47.9	46.3	48.1	48.9	45.1	53.2	47.4	3,562	3,542	2,733
West Germany	276.2	477.0	549.1	577.9	616.0	649.9	501.8	599.5	629.9	8,115	9,738	10,320
Yugoslavia	18.2	34.9	40.9	42.0	44.3	45.9	33.1	43.9	44.5	1,552	1,966	1,924
Zaire	2.7	3.7	4.3	4.4	4.4	4.7	4.8	4.6	4.6	208	174	150

NA = Not available.

[a] Estimated.

Source: Bureau of the Census, *Statistical Abstract of the United States, 1989* (Washington, D.C.: Government Printing Office, 1989), 822.

sumer and industrial products and services. For the marketer to make use of information on gross national products of various nations, such as that summarized in Table 3.4, further knowledge is needed on distribution of income. Per-capita GNP is often used as a primary indicator for evaluating purchasing power. This figure shows great variation between countries as indicated by Switzerland's $15,320 and Bangladesh's $143. The wide use of GNP figures can be explained by their easy availability but they should, nevertheless, be used with caution. In industrialized countries, the richest 5 percent of the population receives 14 percent of the income, while the respective figure for the developing countries is 25 percent of the income.[6]

[6] United Nations, *Demographic Yearbook 1982* (New York: United Nations, 1983), 8.

In some markets, income distribution produces wide gaps between population groups. The more developed the economy, the more income distribution tends to converge toward the middle class.

The international marketer can use the following classification as a planning guide:

1. Very low family incomes. Subsistence economies tend to be characterized by rural populations in which consumption relies on personal output or barter. Some urban centers may provide markets. Example: Cameroon.
2. Mostly low family incomes. Economies that are industrializing along Marxist lines sacrifice personal income to allow as much industrial capital formation as possible. Most goods are produced domestically by state-owned enterprises or enter into the market as a result of bilateral trade agreements. Example: Romania.
3. Very low, very high family incomes. Some countries exhibit strongly bimodal income distributions. The majority of the population may live barely above the subsistence level, while there is a strong market for imported (luxury) items. The affluent are truly affluent and will consume accordingly. Examples: India, Mexico.
4. Low, medium, high family incomes. Industrialization produces an emerging middle class with increasing disposable income. The very low and very high income classes tend to remain for traditional reasons of social class barriers. Example: Portugal.
5. Mostly medium family incomes. The advanced industrial nations tend to develop institutions and policies that reduce extremes in income distribution, resulting in a large and comfortable middle class able to purchase a wide array of both domestic and imported products and services. Example: Denmark.[7]

Although the national income figures provide a general indication of a market's potential, they suffer from various distortions. Figures available from secondary sources are often in U.S. dollars. The per-capita income figures may not be a true reflection of purchasing power if the currencies involved are distorted in some way. For example, fluctuations in the value of the U.S. dollar may distort real-income and standard-of-living figures. The goods and services in different countries have to be valued consistently if the differences are to reflect real differences in the volumes of goods produced. The use of **purchasing power parities (PPP)** instead of exchange rates is intended to achieve this objective. PPPs show how many units of currency are needed in one country to buy the amount of goods and services that one unit of currency will buy in another country. Table 3.5 provides an example of such data.

Secondly, using a monetary measure may not be a proper and all-

[7] Philip Kotler, *Marketing Management* (Englewood Cliffs, N.J.: Prentice-Hall, 1988), 383.

TABLE 3.5 ∎ **Gross Domestic Product/Purchasing Power Parities**

| Country | Gross Domestic Product (billions of dollars) | | | | | | Gross Domestic Product per Capita (dollars) | | | | | |
	1970	1975	1980	1984	1985	1986	1970	1975	1980	1984	1985	1986
United States	1,009.2	1,583.9	2,688.5	3,722.3	3,959.6	4,185.5	4,922	7,334	11,804	15,705	16,548	17,324
OECD Europe[a]	1,056.2	1,727.6	2,880.5	3,741.6	3,966.9	4,188.2	2,864	4,511	7,320	9,330	9,847	10,347
Belgium	28.9	48.0	80.4	101.2	105.9	111.2	2,989	4,899	8,166	10,272	10,741	11,276
Denmark	17.4	26.9	43.9	58.4	62.8	66.7	3,523	5,308	8,563	11,431	12,282	13,030
France	163.2	278.6	472.7	615.6	645.5	676.6	3,215	5,287	8,773	11,203	11,701	12,218
Greece	13.7	24.7	44.1	56.2	59.7	62.1	1,562	2,726	4,572	5,674	6,006	6,224
Ireland	5.5	9.6	17.2	23.0	23.9	24.5	1,852	3,007	5,066	6,509	6,765	6,903
Italy	163.4	258.3	450.3	583.9	618.9	652.7	3,045	4,660	7,982	10,247	10,833	11,406
Luxembourg	1.3	2.1	3.3	4.6	4.9	5.2	3,714	5,733	9,184	12,482	13,361	14,070
Netherlands	45.6	75.0	123.2	155.1	163.7	172.0	3,500	5,487	8,704	10,752	11,296	11,809
Portugal	12.3	21.3	40.0	50.0	53.3	57.0	1,454	2,441	4,303	5,218	5,524	5,868
Spain	73.8	135.5	215.6	277.5	292.1	310.8	2,179	3,816	5,760	7,262	7,613	8,065
United Kingdom	182.1	284.1	445.1	577.5	617.9	652.7	3,273	5,053	7,905	10,224	10,913	11,498
West Germany	207.0	321.8	547.4	698.5	739.2	777.8	3,413	5,204	8,891	11,418	12,114	12,741
Austria	20.6	35.0	59.8	76.9	81.6	85.1	2,757	4,622	7,925	10,183	10,793	11,254
Finland	13.4	22.9	38.4	52.9	56.4	59.3	2,902	4,865	8,032	10,827	11,509	12,059
Iceland	.6	1.2	2.3	3.0	3.2	3.5	2,980	5,316	10,018	12,392	13,163	14,299
Norway	12.1	21.3	38.9	53.5	58.2	62.3	3,113	5,306	9,510	12,923	14,008	14,956
Sweden	31.0	49.4	76.2	100.3	105.7	109.7	3,855	6,035	9,173	12,031	12,655	13,111
Switzerland	30.3	44.3	69.5	87.9	94.3	99.4	4,840	6,919	10,891	13,506	14,439	15,153
Turkey	34.1	67.7	112.2	165.7	179.7	199.7	958	1,679	2,508	3,395	3,606	3,927
Australia	44.4	75.9	124.7	170.8	185.3	193.0	3,465	5,462	8,486	10,979	11,765	12,084
Canada	84.6	153.1	267.9	362.8	390.0	413.5	3,969	6,737	11,131	14,427	15,366	16,105
Japan	291.5	505.2	929.1	1,321.6	1,424.6	1,497.9	2,811	4,531	7,954	11,012	11,798	12,339
New Zealand	9.4	16.1	22.9	31.9	33.1	33.8	3,331	5,231	7,281	9,793	10,106	10,311

[a]European Community.

Source: Bureau of the Census, *Statistical Abstract of the United States, 1989* (Washington, D.C.: Government Printing Office, 1989), 823.

inclusive measure of income. For example, in developing economies where most of the consumption is either self-produced or bartered, reliance on financial data alone would seriously understate the standard of living. Further, several of the service-related items (for example, protective services and travel), characteristic of the industrialized countries' national income figures, do not exist for markets at lower levels of development. Moreover, the cost of products and services must be considered, because they vary dramatically between nations. As an example, despite the country's wealth, the Japanese do not enjoy the same type of lifestyle that average families in other industrialized democracies appear able to afford. By the Japanese Construction Ministry's own standards, 11.4 percent of Japanese families live in substandard housing (less than a 50-square-meter house or apartment with a kitchen and three rooms for a family of four or a 29-square-meter dwelling for a couple). In many respects, Japanese living standards have been subjugated to the goals of an export-led economy.

TABLE 3.6 ▪ **Housing Costs versus Average Income**

	Average Price of New House (A)	Average Family Income (B)	Ratio (A/B)
United States	$ 69,300	$23,400	3.0
United Kingdom	38,800[a]	10,800[a]	3.6
West Germany	80,500[a]	15,300[a]	5.3
France	21,500[a]	7,900[a]	2.7
Japan	143,900[a]	21,100[a]	6.5

[a]Conversion at the 1985 exchange rate.

Source: "The Rabbit-Hutch Image—Embarrassing, But True," *Far Eastern Economic Review,* June 13, 1985, 91–92.

Table 3.6 provides a comparison of housing costs versus average income in the Group of Five countries.

In general, income figures are useful in the initial screening of markets. However, in product-specific cases, income may not play a major role and startling scenarios may emerge. Some products, such as bicycles and television sets in China, are in demand regardless of their high price in relation to wages because of their high prestige value. Some products are in demand because of their foreign origin. As an example, European luxury cars have lucrative markets in countries where per-capita income figures may be low but there are wealthy consumers who are able and willing to buy them. Further, the lack of income in a market may preclude the marketing of a standardized product but, at the same time, provide an opportunity for an adjusted product. A packaged goods company, confronted with considerable disparity in income levels within the same country, adapted a deodorant product to fit two separate target income groups—the regular product version in an aerosol can and the less expensive one in a plastic squeeze bottle. By substituting cheaper parts and materials, successful international marketers can make both consumer and industrial products more affordable in less affluent markets and therefore reach a wider target audience.[8]

Consumption Patterns Depending on the sophistication of a country's data collection systems, economic data on consumption patterns can be obtained and analyzed. The share of income spent on necessities will provide an indication of the market's development level as well as an approximation of how much money the consumer has left for other purchases. Engel's laws provide some generalizations about consumers' spending patterns, which are useful generalizations when precise data are not available. They state that as a family's income increases, the percentage spent on food will decrease, the percentage spent on housing and household

[8]V. Yorio, *Adapting Products for Export* (New York: Conference Board, 1983), 29–39.

TABLE 3.7 ▪ **Consumer Spending by Category, as Percent of Total, 1986**

	Food, Beverages, Tobacco	Clothing, Footwear, Textiles	House- hold Fuels	House- hold Goods	Housing	Health	Leisure and Education	Transport and Com- munica- tions	Other
Argentina	34.0	5.3	6.0	6.4	28.0	5.1	5.2	6.2	3.8
Australia	20.8	6.1	2.4	6.8	22.3	6.4	7.8	13.6	13.8
Brazil	27.3	5.0	6.1	5.0	31.0	5.2	5.2	9.1	6.1
Canada	15.7	6.1	3.2	8.0	17.7	3.9	7.1	15.0	23.2
China	52.4	14.1	2.6	11.1	0.9	2.0	7.7	1.1	7.9
Colombia	49.2	4.9	1.7	4.0	9.2	4.6	4.3	9.6	12.4
India	54.4	10.1	4.4	4.5	2.7	2.0	3.8	12.0	6.1
Indonesia	56.8	4.8	NA	8.8	17.4	NA	2.3	3.8	6.1
Israel	29.4	5.5	2.2	10.2	17.5	6.4	8.9	12.0	7.9
Japan	22.6	6.2	5.1	3.6	4.3	2.1	12.7	8.7	34.6
Mexico	37.8	10.1	NA	12.0	8.4	5.0	4.9	12.2	9.5
Singapore	24.6	9.7	NA	12.5	12.5	4.5	15.1	14.2	6.8
South Korea	43.5	6.7	NA	5.0	11.1	4.5	10.0	9.7	9.6
Thailand	41.8	12.0	3.3	6.7	3.7	5.5	4.4	14.0	8.6
United Kingdom	24.1	7.0	4.3	6.0	10.6	1.2	14.9	12.2	19.2
United States	17.8	6.0	3.7	11.4	15.6	11.4	6.7	13.0	14.4
USSR	43.7	19.2	3.8	8.0	3.6	2.6	2.9	8.3	8.0
West Germany	23.0	8.4	6.3	9.8	13.5	4.5	13.4	9.0	11.9
Zimbabwe	15.7	12.2	10.7	7.4	7.3	3.6	4.6	4.5	33.9

NA—Not available.

Source: *International Marketing Data and Statistics 1988/89* (London: Euromonitor, 1989), 385; and *European Marketing Data and Statistics 1988/89* (London: Euromonitor, 1989), 238–239.

operations will be roughly constant, and the amount saved or spent on other purchases will increase. Private expenditure comparisons reveal that the percentage spent on food in 1986 varied from 18 percent in the United States to 57 percent in Indonesia (see Table 3.7).

In Western Europe, expenditures on clothing typically account for 5 to 7 percent of all spending, but in poorer countries the proportion may be lower. In some low-wage areas, a significant proportion of clothing is homemade or locally made at low cost, making comparisons not entirely accurate. Eastern European households spend an inordinate proportion of their incomes on foodstuffs, but quite a low proportion on housing. The remaining, less absolutely central areas of consumption (household goods, leisure, and transportation) are most vulnerable to short-term cancellation or postponement and thus serve as indicators for the strength of confidence in the market in general.

Data on product saturation or diffusion—information on the percentage of households in a market that own a particular product—allow a further evaluation of market potential. Table 3.8 presents the percentage of households that own certain appliances and indicates that saturation levels in the markets for which the data exist are quite high. This does not necessarily indicate lack of market potential; replacement markets or the demand

TABLE 3.8 ▪ **Percentage of Households Owning Selected Appliances, 1984**

Appliance	United States[a]	France	Italy	Nether-lands	Poland	Soviet Union	Spain	Sweden	United King-dom	West Ger-many	Yugo-slavia
Clothes Washer	73	83	92	90	NA	55	93	67	83	91	NA
Dishwasher	38	22	19	12	1	NA	9	26	6	21	NA
Freezer (separate)	37	33	39	47	NA	NA	13	68	80	53	47
Range:											
Electric	54	12	5	10	53	NA ⎱	92	⎰ 93	40	73 ⎱	88
Gas	45	NA	NA	NA	NA	NA ⎰		⎱ NA	NA	NA ⎰	
Refrigerator	100	97	86	98	NA	65	94	96	58	82	82
Television Set:											
Black and White	43	61	75	33	NA ⎱	38	⎰ 84	NA	14	56 ⎱	61
Color	88	56	45	84	NA ⎰		⎱ 47	86	88	69 ⎰	

NA—Not available.

[a]Represents appliances possessed and generally used by households.

Source: Bureau of the Census, *Statistical Abstract of the United States, 1989* (Washington, D.C.: Government Printing Office, 1989), 812.

for auxiliary products may offer attractive opportunities to the international marketer. Low rates of diffusion should be approached cautiously, because they can signal a market opportunity or lack thereof resulting from low income levels, use of a substitute product, or lack of acceptance. As an example of lack of acceptance, the timesaving feature of microwave ovens may not be as attractive in more tradition-bound societies as in the United States.

General consumption figures are valuable, but they must be viewed with caution because they may conceal critical product-form differences; for example, refrigerators in European households are far smaller than their U.S. counterparts. Information about existing product usage can nevertheless provide indirect help to international marketers. As an example, a large number of telephones, and their even distribution among the population or a target group, may make market research via telephone interviewing a possibility.

A problem for marketers in general is **inflation;** varying inflation rates complicate this problem in international markets. Many of the industrialized countries have recently been able to keep inflation rates at single-digit levels (the U.S. rate for 1988 was 4.5 percent while Japan's was 1.1 percent). At the same time countries such as Bolivia, Argentina, and Israel have suffered from chronic inflation (see Table 3.9). Inflation affects the ability of both industrial customers and consumers to buy and also introduces uncertainty into both the marketer's planning process and consumers' buying habits, as can be seen in The International Marketplace 3.2. In high-inflation markets, the marketer may have to make changes in the product (more economical without compromising quality), promotion (more rational), and distribution (more customer involvement) to meet customer needs and maintain demand. In response to rapidly escalating

TABLE 3.9 ▪ **Consumer Price Index**

Country	1981–1982	1982–1983	1983–1984	1984–1985	1985–1986	Country	1981–1982	1982–1983	1983–1984	1984–1985	1985–1986
United States	6.2	3.2	4.3	3.6	1.9	Kenya	20.4	11.5	10.2	13.0	4.0
						Malasia	5.8	3.7	3.9	.3	.7
Argentina	164.8	343.8	626.7	672.1	90.1	Mexico	58.9	101.8	65.5	57.7	86.2
Australia	11.1	10.1	4.0	6.7	9.1	Netherlands	5.9	2.8	3.3	2.2	.2
Austria	5.4	3.3	5.7	3.2	1.7	Nigeria	7.7	23.2	39.6	5.5	1.1
Bangladesh	12.5	9.4	10.5	10.7	11.0	Norway	11.4	8.4	6.3	5.7	7.2
Belgium	8.7	7.7	6.3	4.9	1.3	Pakistan	5.9	6.2	6.6	5.8	3.7
Bolivia	133	269	1,281	11,750	NA	Peru	64.4	111.2	110.2	163.4	77.9
Brazil	98.0	142.1	197.0	226.9	145.2	Philippines	10.2	10.0	50.3	23.1	.8
Canada	10.8	5.8	4.3	4.0	4.2	Portugal	22.7	25.1	28.9	19.6	11.8
Chile	9.9	27.3	19.9	30.7	19.5	Romania	16.9	5.2	1.1	−.4	−.1
Colombia	24.5	19.8	16.1	24.0	18.9	South Africa	14.7	12.3	11.7	16.2	18.6
Ecuador	16.3	48.4	31.2	28.0	23.0	South Korea	7.3	3.4	2.3	2.5	2.3
Egypt	14.8	16.1	17.1	13.3	22.6	Spain	14.4	12.2	11.3	8.8	8.8
France	11.8	9.6	7.4	5.8	2.5	Sri Lanka	10.8	14.0	16.6	1.5	8.0
Ghana	22.3	122.9	39.7	10.3	24.6	Sweden	8.6	8.9	8.0	7.4	4.2
Greece	21.0	20.2	18.4	19.3	23.0	Switzerland	5.7	3.0	2.9	3.4	.8
Guatemala	.3	4.5	3.4	18.7	36.9	Thailand	5.3	3.7	.9	2.4	1.8
India	7.9	11.9	8.3	5.6	8.7	Turkey	30.8	32.9	48.4	45.0	34.6
Indonesia	9.5	11.8	10.5	4.7	5.8	United Kingdom	8.6	4.6	5.0	6.1	3.5
Iran	18.7	19.7	12.5	4.4	NA	Venezuela	9.6	6.3	12.2	11.4	11.5
Israel	120.4	145.6	373.8	304.6	48.1	West Germany	5.3	3.3	2.4	2.2	−.2
Italy	16.5	14.6	10.8	9.2	5.9	Yugoslavia	32.9	40.2	54.7	72.3	70.3
Japan	2.6	1.9	2.3	2.0	.6	Zaire	36.2	77.1	52.2	23.8	46.7

NA—Not available.

Source: *International Statistics* (Washington, D.C.: International Monetary Fund, 1988), monthly.

prices, a government will often invoke price controls. The setting of maximum prices for products may cause the international marketer to face unacceptable profit situations, future investments will not be made, and production may even have to be stopped.[9]

Another challenge for international marketers is the **debt problem.** Many of the developing countries are saddled with a collective debt of $1.2 trillion (see Figure 3.2). Latin America calls the 1980s "the lost decade," but other countries have suffered indirectly. In 1980 the United States sold $6 billion more in goods and services to Latin America than it imported. The debt crisis crushed the region's purchasing power and forced up exports to meet interest payments. By 1987 the United States was running a $15 billion trade deficit with Latin America; the $21 billion swing accounted for nearly 10 percent of the record trade gap that year.[10] To continue growing, many companies are looking at developing nations because of the potential they see 10 to 15 years ahead. U.S. companies

[9]Victor H. Frank, Jr., "Living with Price Control Abroad," *Harvard Business Review* 62 (March–April 1984): 137–142.

[10]"Fitting into a Global Economy," *U.S. News and World Report,* January 2, 1989, 80–82.

3.2   THE INTERNATIONAL MARKETPLACE

Inflation Jeopardizing Brazil's Export Efforts   *Of the $93 billion in exports generated by all of Latin America in 1987, Brazil originated one-third. These sales generated a solid enough trade surplus for Brazil to resume interest payments on its $120.1 billion foreign debt. And Brazil, more than any of the other countries of the region, has diversified its exports substantially. Its exports range from shoes to military hardware, with 500 products in between. This has spilled into other areas as well. With a 130 percent jump in foreign orders for steel in 1988, layoffs have been averted in that industry. Orders for Cummins Engine Company diesel truck engines made in Brazil grew 33 percent, keeping employees working overtime.*

But trouble is predicted. Hyperinflation, nearing 1,000 percent annually, is beginning to erode the low cost structure that made Brazil export in the first place. Price hikes on such products as chemicals, pulp and paper, coffee, and soybeans accounted for much of the $6 billion gain in 1988 over 1987. The crippling inflation rate "is yielding hidden costs that are hurting the export sector," said Cummins Brasil president Jack Edwards. The vast network of state companies that control the supply of energy, fuel, and raw materials has been raising prices above inflation levels to offset their massive operating losses. Higher costs are causing some companies to reconsider Brazil as an export base. Already, auto producers Volkswagen and Ford are reducing the number of cars and trucks from Brazil to compensate for rising costs.

President Jose Sarney says that the worst enemy of democracy in Latin America is inflation. A tough anti-inflation plan could mean political havoc, thereby reducing Brazil's attractiveness further.

Source: "Brazil's Export Engine Is Starting to Sputter," *Business Week,* November 14, 1988, 84.

---

typically face competition in these regions from Japanese companies, which are often aided by their government's aid grants, as well as by Europeans, who do business with the help of government export credits that have interest rates lower than those provided by U.S. entities. Access to these markets can be achieved by helping political leaders provide jobs and by increasing exports. Heinz, for example, operates in many developing countries through joint ventures in which Heinz holds 51 percent. To sell copiers and printers in Brazil, Xerox exports Brazilian steel to Europe and Brazilian venetian blinds to the United States, among other products worth $100 million annually.[11] Many industrialized countries, such as

[11]Louis Kraar, "How to Sell to Cashless Buyers," *Fortune,* November 7, 1988, 147–154.

FIGURE 3.2 ▪ **Nations in Debt: 1988 Debt Outstanding (in billions of dollars)**

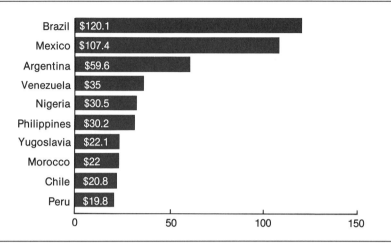

Source: "Nations in Debt," *The Washington Post*, March 14, 1989, D1. © The Washington Post, reprinted with permission.

Japan, France, and the United States are seeking ways to ease the burden facing debtor nations.[12]

Infrastructure

The availability and quality of an infrastructure is of critical importance in evaluating marketing operations abroad. Every international marketer will depend heavily on services provided by the local market for transportation, communication, and energy as well as on organizations participating in the facilitating functions of marketing: marketing communications, distributing, information, and financing. Indicators such as steel consumption, cement production, and electricity production relate to the overall industrialization of the market and can be used effectively by suppliers of industrial products and services. As an example, energy consumption per capita may serve as an indicator of market potential for electrical markets, provided evenness of distribution exists over the market. Yet the marketer must make sure that the energy is affordable and compatible (in terms of current and voltage) with the products to be marketed.

The existence and expansion of basic infrastructure has contributed significantly to increased agricultural output in Asia and Latin America. The Philippines has allocated 5 percent of agricultural development funds to rural electrification programs. On a similar level, basic roads are essential to moving agricultural products. In many parts of Africa, farmers are more than a day's walk from the nearest road. As a result, measures to improve production without commensurate improvements in transportation and

[12]"Washington's New, Softer Line on Latin Debt," *Business Week*, March 20, 1989, 58.

communications are of little use because the crops cannot reach the market. In addition, the lack of infrastructure cuts the farmers off from new technology, inputs, and ideas.

Transportation networks by land, rail, waterway, or air are essential for physical distribution. The major world land and ocean transportation flows are summarized in the following color map insert. An analysis of rail traffic by freight tons per kilometer offers a possible way to begin an investigation of transportation capabilities; however, these figures may not always indicate the true state of the system. For example, in China, rail freight, which accounted for half of the total freight volume, logged 742.7 billion ton-kilometers in 1984. By comparison, India's well-utilized 61,230-kilometer rail network handled 164.3 billion ton-kilometers. China's 52,000 kilometers of railway carried five times as much freight for each kilometer of track; this is an amazing feat in light of the fact that only 9,000 kilometers of the network are double tracked, and shared use of tracks by passenger and freight trains requires frequent diversions of the slower freights to sidings. Passenger loading has nearly doubled since 1978, with the average overloading factor being 30 to 50 percent.[13] In spite of the greater use of rail in China, the international marketer would, therefore, be ill-advised to rely on distribution via trains. With the same type of caution, the number of passenger cars as well as buses and trucks can be used to analyze the state of road transportation and transportation networks.

Communication is as important as transportation. The ability of a firm to communicate with entities both outside and within the market can be estimated by using indicators of the communications infrastructure: telephones, broadcast media, and print media in use. Again, the figures do not reveal the quality of the services provided and their possible reach. For example, the telephone system in Egypt, especially in Cairo, is notorious for its frequent breakdowns and lack of capacity.

Data on the availability of commercial (marketing-related) infrastructure are often not readily available. Data on which to base an assessment may be provided by government sources, such as Overseas Business Reports; trade associations, such as the Business Equipment Manufacturers' Association; and trade publications, such as *Advertising Age*. The more extensive the firm's international involvement, the more it can rely on its already existing support network of banks, advertising agencies, and distributors to assess new markets.

Geography

The physical characteristics of individual markets in terms of distance, topography, climate, and natural resources will have an impact on the international marketer's decision to enter a market and the possible adjustments needed in the marketing mix.

---

[13]"I Think I Can, I Think . . . ," *Far Eastern Economic Review*, June 13, 1985, 120.

World Maps

Trade and Travel Networks

Gross National Product and
Working Populations

Economic Groups

Trade and Travel Networks

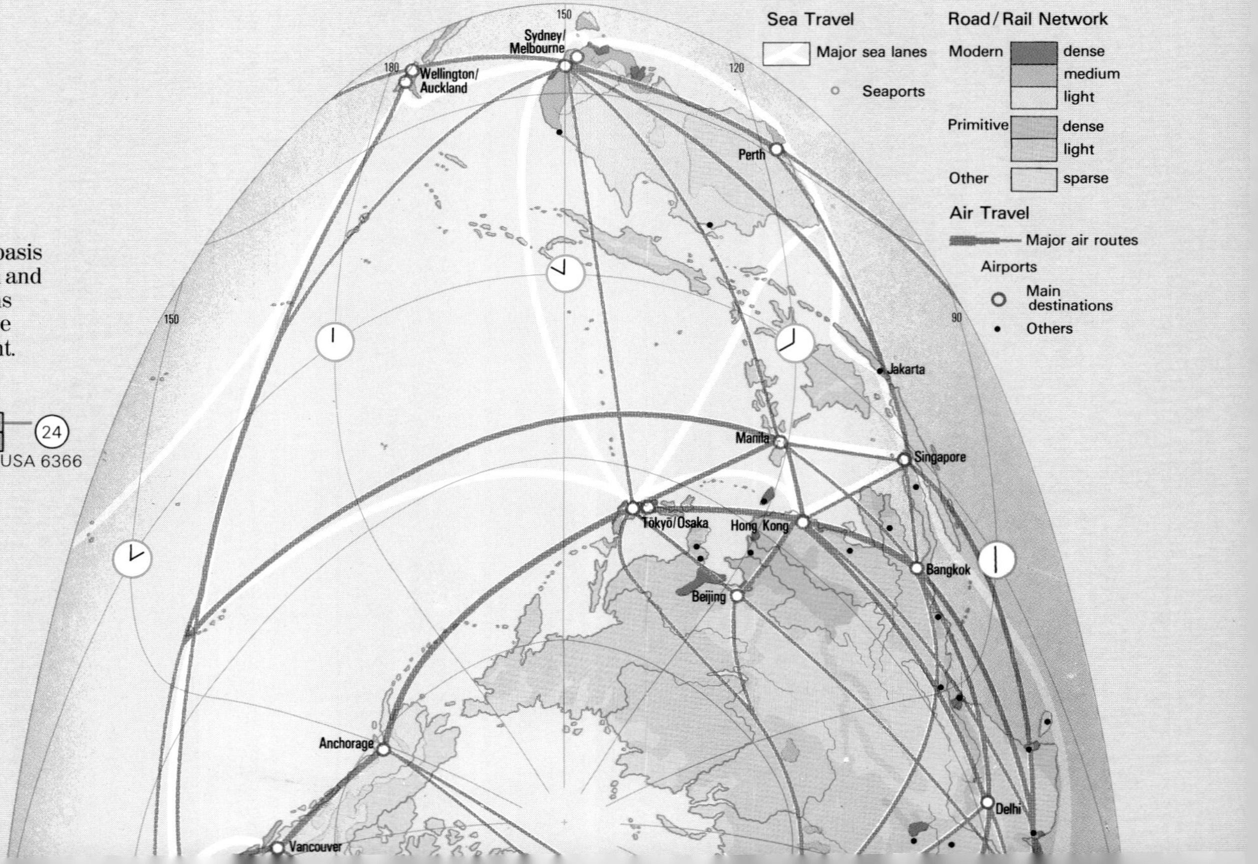
Sea Travel
Major sea lanes
Seaports
Road/Rail Network
Modern
dense
medium
light
Primitive
dense
light
Other
sparse
Air Travel
Major air routes
Airports
Main destinations
Others
Sydney/Melbourne
Wellington/Auckland
Perth
Jakarta
Manila
Singapore
Tokyō/Osaka
Hong Kong
Bangkok
Beijing
Anchorage
Delhi
Vancouver
150
180
120
90

Road and Rail

Integrated road and rail networks are the basis of industrialised society. Containerisation and the extension of modern highway systems have increased flexibility and reduced the emphasis on railways transporting freight.

Roads – comparative lengths (Log scale)

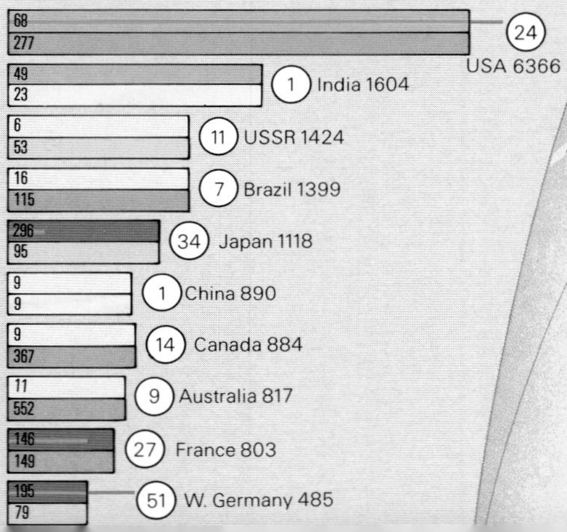
68
277
24
USA 6366
49
23
1
India 1604
6
53
11
USSR 1424
16
115
7
Brazil 1399
296
95
34
Japan 1118
9
9
1
China 890
9
367
14
Canada 884
11
552
9
Australia 817
146
149
27
France 803
195
79
(51)
W. Germany 485

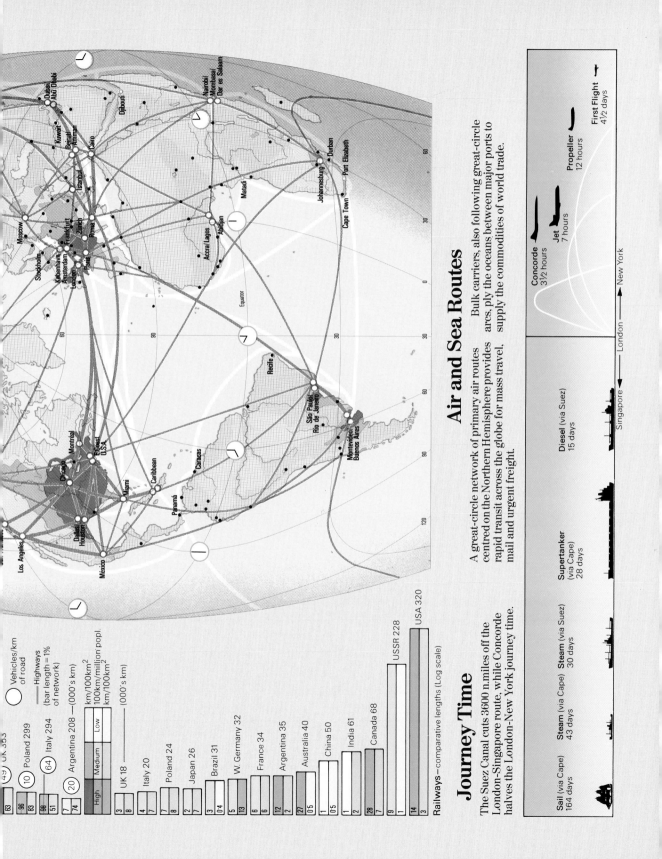

Air and Sea Routes

A great-circle network of primary air routes centred on the Northern Hemisphere provides rapid transit across the globe for mass travel, mail and urgent freight.

Bulk carriers, also following great-circle arcs, ply the oceans between major ports to supply the commodities of world trade.

Journey Time

The Suez Canal cuts 3600 n.miles off the London-Singapore route, while Concorde halves the London-New York journey time.

First Flight 4½ days

Propeller 12 hours

Jet 7 hours

Concorde 3½ hours

London — New York

Singapore — London — New York

Sail (via Cape) 164 days

Steam (via Cape) 43 days

Steam (via Suez) 30 days

Supertanker (via Cape) 28 days

Diesel (via Suez) 15 days

Map labels

Los Angeles, Dallas Houston, Chicago, Montreal, E.Coast U.S.A., México, Miami, Caribbean, Panamá, Caracas, Recife, São Paulo, Rio de Janeiro, Montevideo, Buenos Aires, Cape Town, Port Elizabeth, Durban, Johannesburg, Matadi, Abidjan, Accra/Lagos, Nairobi, Mombasa, Dar es Salaam, Djibouti, Cairo, Amman, Beirut, Kuwait, Dubai, Abu Dhabi, Istanbul, Roma, Zürich, Frankfurt, Paris, London, Amsterdam, København, Stockholm, Moscow

Equator

Railways – comparative lengths (Log scale)

Country	(000's km)
UK 18	3 / 8
Italy 20	4 / 7
Poland 24	7 / 8
Japan 26	2 / 7
Brazil 31	3 / 04
W. Germany 32	5 / 13
France 34	6 / 6
Argentina 35	12 / 2
Australia 40	27 / 05
China 50	1 / 05
India 61	1 / 2
Canada 68	28 / 7
USSR 228	9 / 1
USA 320	14 / 3

(key)

○ Vehicles/km of road

— Highways (bar length = 1% of network)

Argentina 208 — (000's km)

	km/100km² High	Medium	Low 100km/million popl. km/100km²

(49) UK 353	63
⑩ Poland 299	96 / 83
Italy 294	98 / 51
㉖ 64	7 / 74
⑳ 20	

Gross National Product and Working Populations

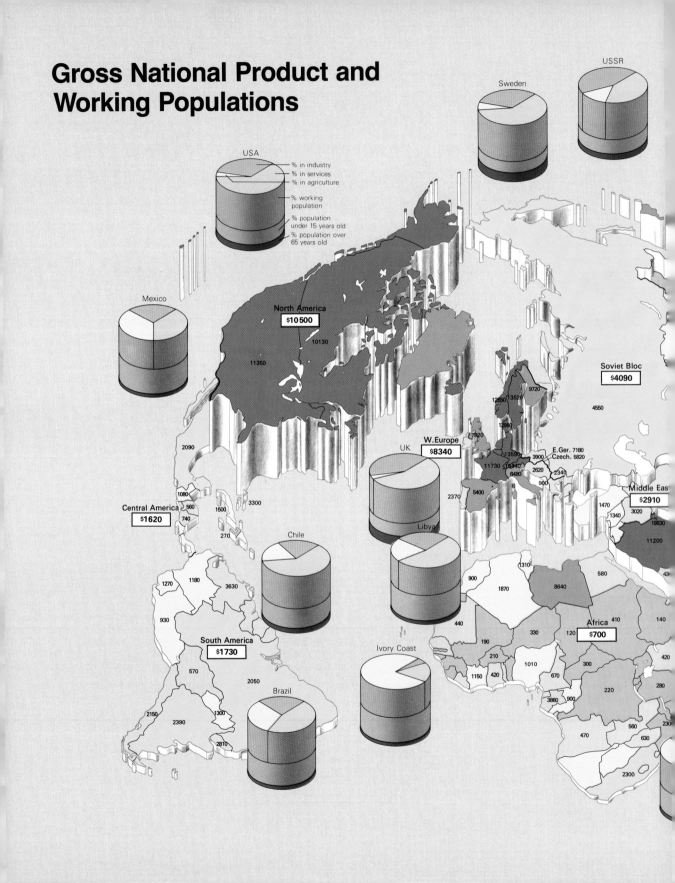

USSR

Sweden

USA
- % in industry
- % in services
- % in agriculture
- % working population
- % population under 15 years old
- % population over 65 years old

Mexico

North America
$10500

10130

11360

Soviet Bloc
$4090

9720
12650 13520
4550
12960
W.Europe
UK $8340
7920

E.Ger. 7180
13590 Czech. 5820
3900
11730 13410
6480 2620 2340
900

2090

Middle East
$2910

1470
1340 3020
19830
11200

Central America
$1620

1080
560
740
1500
3300
270

2370 5400

Chile

Libya

900 1310
1870 8640

580

43

1270 1180
3630

930

South America
$1730

570

2050

Brazil

1300

2150
2390

2810

Ivory Coast

440

190
210 1010
1150 420
3860 900

330

Africa 410
$700

120
300
670
220

140

420

280

560
470 630

230

2300

China

Japan
$8730

Japan

290

S. & E. Asia
$310

690

130   170   670

300   300   240

850

270

Israel   India

780

11890

1620

Indonesia

Oceania
$7000

9820

7090

Australia

350

S. Africa

Economic Groups

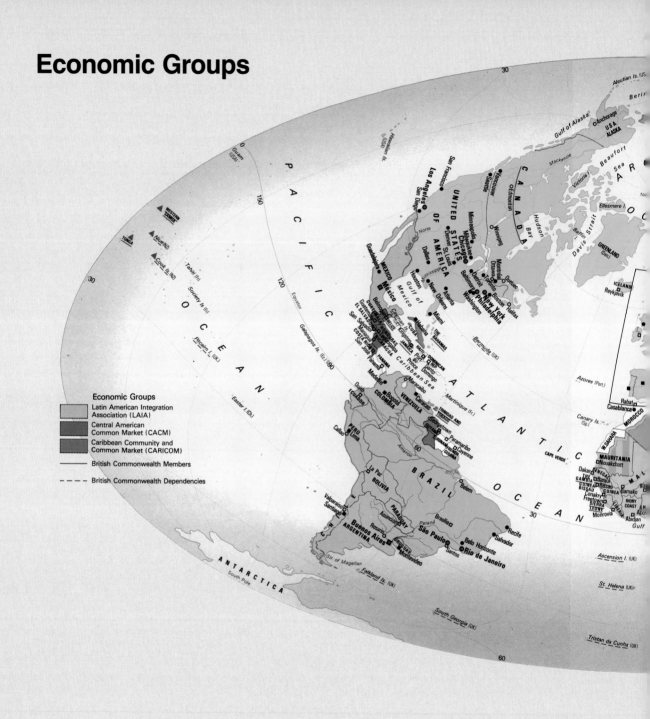

Economic Groups

Latin American Integration
Association (LAIA)

Central American
Common Market (CACM)

Caribbean Community and
Common Market (CARICOM)

——— British Commonwealth Members

- - - British Commonwealth Dependencies

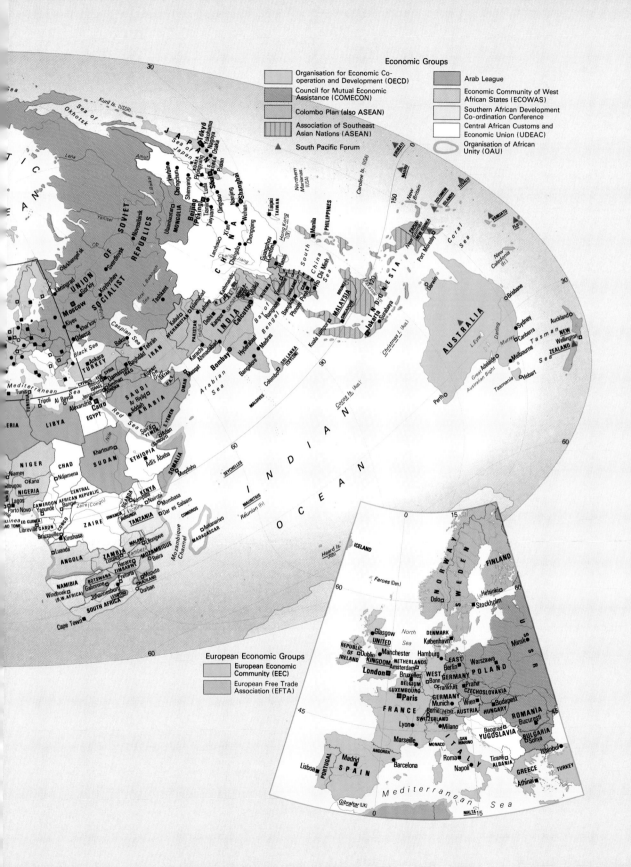

Economic Groups

- Organisation for Economic Co-operation and Development (OECD)
- Council for Mutual Economic Assistance (COMECON)
- Colombo Plan (also ASEAN)
- Association of Southeast Asian Nations (ASEAN)
- ▲ South Pacific Forum
- Arab League
- Economic Community of West African States (ECOWAS)
- Southern African Development Co-ordination Conference
- Central African Customs and Economic Union (UDEAC)
- Organisation of African Unity (OAU)

European Economic Groups

- European Economic Community (EEC)
- European Free Trade Association (EFTA)

In this context **distance** relates to the physical separation of the marketer from potential customers. In many cases physical distance is accompanied by psychological distance, which manifests itself in cultural differences. Physical distances between locations are often quite extensive and can affect marketers in many ways, not the least of which is pricing. The landed cost of Indonesian textiles on the West Coast of the United States can easily be two-and-a-half times their cost in Bali. Long distances may require the use of more expensive modes of transportation to secure availability and proper quality of the product. Air transportation, for example, must be used when marketing fresh flowers from Europe or the Caribbean in the United States.

For marketers, **topography** can mean complicating factors such as barriers formed by land and water. These barriers can signify separate target groups within a target market because of cultural differences. For example, people living in the highlands of a country may display behavioral characteristics very different from those in the valleys.

Certain markets that have few access points may be vulnerable to international incidents. For example, Iraq's oil flow to the West was severely hindered because the Syrians did not allow use of a pipeline that runs through their territory during the Iran–Iraq conflict. Finally, for some marketers, topography may be a major determinant in their product offering—the Club Med in its site location to attract tourists, for example.

Which products a company can market and how they may have to be adjusted for logistics or marketing purposes may be affected by **climate.** The market's climatic conditions, and the degree of their variation during the year, can have a direct effect on the consumption pattern of any market. The major caveat is stereotyping or making hasty decisions. As an example, windsurfing or sailing equipment may not, offhand, seem to have major markets in Northern Europe because of the shortness of the summer season. However, windsurfers have extended their season by using wetsuits. As a result of the five-month sailing season and the expense involved, sailing has a well-defined, quite affluent target market.

Products must be modified to withstand extremes in temperature, humidity, or altitude. Among the products that are usually modified are engines for altitude or to meet emissions-control requirements, electric devices for humidity, oil-refining controls for insulation against Arctic cold and desert heat, and measuring and precision instruments with tolerance levels changed in order to maintain their accuracy under extreme temperatures. For example, Soviet-made Belarus tractors, when first marketed in the United States, had cabs fitted with heating devices designed for Russian winters, which naturally made them too warm for American conditions.

Climate may have an impact on distribution as well. Products must be protected (by extra coats of preservatives, for example) for long periods in transit as well as the possibility of longer-than-normal shelf life in a foreign market.

TABLE 3.10 ▪ **Strategic Mineral Reserves**

Mineral	Reserve Base (million tonnes)	Years' Supply at 1981 Consumption	Major Location of Reserves
Antimony	4.5	70	Bolivia, South Africa, Mexico
Bauxite	20,300	260	Guinea, Australia, Brazil, Jamaica
Beryllium	NA	NA	Brazil
Bismuth	0.1	30	Australia, Bolivia, Canada
Cadmium	0.7	39	Canada, U.S., Australia
Chromium	3,350	374	South Africa, Zimbabwe, Finland
Cobalt	3.1	116	Zaire, Zambia, Morocco
Columbium	3,450 (tonnes)	206	Brazil, Canada, Nigeria
Copper	505	65	Chile, U.S., Zambia, Canada, U.S.S.R.
Diamond	620 (m. carats)	20	Zaire, Botswana, Australia
Gallium	1	50	Contained in bauxite (see above)
Germanium	very large	very large	Zaire, U.S.
Gold	37,000 (tonnes)	30	South Africa, U.S.S.R., U.S.
Hafnium	0.5	NA	Contained in zirconia (see below)
Ilmenite	660	138	Norway, South Africa, Canada, Finland
Indium	1,500 (tonnes)	36	Canada, U.S., Peru, U.S.S.R.
Iron Ore	108,000	410	U.S.S.R., Brazil, Australia, India
Lead	165	48	U.S., Australia, Canada
Lithium	2.22	large	Chile, U.S., Zaire, Canada
Manganese	5,000	186	U.S.S.R., South Africa, Australia
Mercury	1.5	23	Spain, U.S.S.R., Algeria
Molybdenum	9.8	97	U.S., Chile, Canada
Nickel	54	76	New Caledonia, Canada, Cuba
Platinum Group	37,000 (tonnes)	176	South Africa, U.S.S.R., Zimbabwe
Rare Earths	NA	large	U.S., India, Australia
Rhenium	3.175 (tonnes)	254	U.S., Chile, U.S.S.R., Peru
Rutile	131	337	Brazil, Australia, India
Selenium	0.1	84	U.S., Canada, Chile, Peru
Silver	262,000 (tonnes)	24	U.S., Canada, Mexico
Tantalum	22,000 (tonnes)	49	Thailand, Australia, Canada, Zaire
Tellurium	32,000 (tonnes)	156	U.S., Canada, Peru
Tin	10	40	Malaysia, Indonesia, Thailand, China
Tungsten	2.9	56	China, Canada, U.S., Korea
Vanadium	19	520	South Africa, U.S.S.R., China
Yttrium	44,000 (tonnes)	large	India, Australia, U.S.
Zinc	240	41	Canada, U.S., Australia
Zirconium	43	83	Australia, U.S., South Africa

NA—Not available.

Source: *World Index of Strategic Minerals* by S. Hargreaves and S. Fromson. © 1983. Reprinted with permission of Facts on File, Inc., New York.

Charting the **natural resources** of markets will provide the international marketer with an assessment of both marketing and procurement potential. The endowment of natural resources alone does not determine the level of economic development of a particular region, because resources are required for their exploitation. If they are not on hand, they must be imported and access to supplies guaranteed. Some countries without natural resources (such as Japan) have obtained resources through the exchange processes and achieved success, whereas some countries with rich endowments (such as Angola) have not developed because internal strife has kept interested parties out. Increasingly, the issue of resources has focused on fossil fuels and strategic minerals. The capital-surplus oil-exporting countries—Kuwait, Libya, Oman, Qatar, Saudi Arabia, and United Arab Emirates—have been able to fuel their economic development through their resource base. Similarly, South Africa has done well with its minerals.

The possibility of exhausting these resource bases is of concern to industrialized countries, which remain the main users, with dwindling supplies of their own. Furthermore, the industrial marketer's decisions are affected by risks associated with production (capacity, labor disputes, and violent conflicts), transportation (disruptions in the flow of materials and derived products), and trade (collusive price agreements and embargoes).[14] A joint venture in an extractive industry, for example, may not be attractive in its own right, but as a means of securing long-term supply it may be invaluable. The main strategic mineral reserves are summarized in Table 3.10. The data indicate that, in the case of some minerals such as platinum and vanadium, U.S. supplies might be cut off in the event of adverse political developments—with major repercussions for manufacturers that need these materials. U.S. action against the South African government on apartheid resulted in threats by the Pretoria government to cut off exports of strategic minerals to the United States.

The international marketer has to make contingency plans for the eventuality of **shortages.** In cases of temporary shortages (lack of cocoa for chocolate or coffee affected by adverse weather, for example), companies prepare by stockpiling adequate reserves. For longer term shortages, the company may reassess the use of certain raw materials and search for substitutes. Shortages and the price increases that usually result are problems for some companies, opportunities for others. For example, the Bandeirante, a 12- to 18-passenger turboprop plane designed for markets in the developing countries by Embraer (a Brazilian mixed state-private enterprise), found a niche in industrialized countries for feeder routes as fuel prices rose.

Foreign Involvement in the Economy

For the international marketer interested in entering a foreign market, it is important to know the extent to which such entry is accepted by a country. An economy's overall acceptance of foreign involvement can be estimated by analyzing the degree of foreign direct investment by country and by industry in a given market as well as by the rules governing such investment.

A summary of the conditions for foreign direct investment in selected countries is provided in Figure 3.3. Restrictions exist mainly by industry

[14]D. Hargreaves and S. Fromson, *World Index of Strategic Minerals* (New York: Facts on File, 1983), 15–34.

FIGURE 3.3 ▪ **Regulations Governing Foreign Direct Investment**

Who Helps —and Hampers— Foreign Investors

CANADA
Canada took down its KEEP OUT sign with the Investment Canada Act of 1985. But the government is still reluctant to approve deals in film, publishing, and other areas that could compromise Canada's "cultural heritage or national identity."

UNITED STATES
Come one, come all, unless you come from Cambodia, Cuba, Libya, Nicaragua, North Korea, or Vietnam. Buy anything, anywhere, but not more than 25% of a freshwater or coastal shipping enterprise, airline, or broadcast station. Expect heat from the government if you're eyeing a company that affects national security.

MEXICO
The Law to Promote Mexican Investment and Regulate Foreign Investment is a bureaucratic migraine. Don't expect government clearance mañana. And save your breath if your business is oil, nuclear power, mining, electricity, railroads, or communications.

BRAZIL
Best bet: Buy some of Brazil's foreign debt and swap it for an equity stake in a local business. Like the rest of Latin America, Brazil is desperate to cut its debt burden.

BRITAIN
Official stance: total congeniality. But the government can influence who buys what by exerting behind-the-scenes pressure. Scandinavian Airways found that out recently and dropped plans to bid for British Caledonian.

SAUDI ARABIA
Wanted: foreign investors willing to take in Saudi partners and teach them technical, managerial, and marketing skills. Not wanted: investments in legal services, cleaning, and businesses considered sensitive. A word to the wise businesswoman: Go elsewhere.

FRANCE, GERMANY, & SWITZERLAND
France has loosened up considerably since 1984, and Germany is a breeze. Switzerland has no laws against foreign investment, but as in many European countries, tacit prohibitions abound. Smaller countries don't want their tiny industrial bases swallowed by foreign buyers.

HONG KONG
A foreign investor's dream: Disclosure laws are nil and restrictions virtually nonexistent. But beware of 1997, when the island reverts to Chinese control.

JAPAN
The world's most frenetic shoppers don't want a reciprocal onslaught. Vague prohibitions against acquisitions that would harm national security or disturb the public order give the government ample room to trip up deals. That's one reason foreigners have only $8 billion invested in Japanese hard assets—3% of what foreigners own in the U.S.

SOUTH KOREA
Look elsewhere if you want to invest in publishing, flowers, electric power plants, bars, savings banks, transportation, communications, or gambling. What's left? High-tech industries. Approval is a snap and comes with a tax holiday.

TAIWAN
The Statute for Investment by Foreign Nationals and Overseas Chinese is essentially a toothless tiger. Capital-intensive and high-tech ventures get swift approval; textiles and other light manufacturing businesses do not.

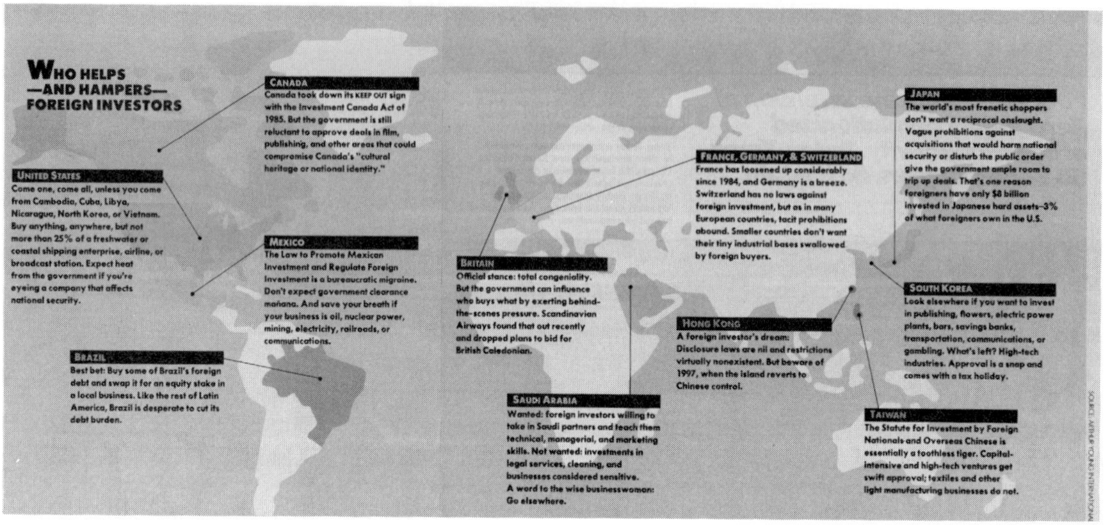

Source: Jaclyn Fierman, "The Selling of America," *Fortune*, May 23, 1988, 56–57. © 1988 Time Inc. All rights reserved.

type, but also by origin of investor. Many nations have established investment screening agencies to assess foreign direct investment proposals. For example, in the United States, major foreign direct investments must be reviewed by the Committee for Foreign Investments in the United States (CFIUS). Concerns have been raised mainly in terms of national security and origin of investors: in the 1970s, Arabs, and in the late 1980s, the Japanese.

Over 3,200 U.S. corporations had over 21,000 subsidiaries in 121 foreign countries in 1984, ranging from companies like Bata Shoe with operations in Panama to Hewlett-Packard, which has operations in 70 different countries.[15] On the other hand, 4,270 U.S.-based companies were wholly or in part owned by 2,700 foreign companies, ranging from Siemens (Federal Republic of Germany) to Kawasaki Jukogyo K.K. (Japan). In a survey, foreign firms reported investing in the United States for the same reason that prompts U.S. companies to invest overseas: to participate directly in the growing international market that cannot be adequately reached by exports and imports alone.[16] For example, in 1987, U.S. companies spent $2.4 billion in acquiring European companies, mostly to prepare themselves for the 1992 phenomenon.[17]

[15] *Directory of American Firms Operating in Foreign Countries* (New York: Uniworld Business Publications, 1984), 15.

[16] Juvenal L. Angel, *Directory of Foreign Firms Operating in the U.S.* (New York: World Trade Academy Press, 1978), 3.

[17] "Will the New Europe Cut U.S. Giants Down to Size?" *Business Week*, December 12, 1988, 54–58.

FIGURE 3.4 ▪ **Japanese Foreign Direct Investment by Region, 1987**

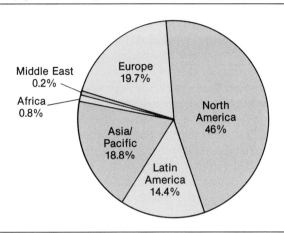

Source: "Foreign Investment Outlook: What the Japanese Are Doing Around the World," *Business International*, August 8, 1988, 248–249.

The favored investment regions of U.S. companies are Europe and Canada; for Japanese companies, North America and Asia; and for companies based in West Germany, Europe and North America. In general, direct investments are growing in the Far East (for example, Singapore and Malaysia), while certain regions are witnessing decline (for example, South Africa for political reasons).

The foreign investment activities of Japan are quite interesting. With its $33.4 billion in foreign direct investment, Japan is competing with West Germany to be the third largest foreign direct investor in the world after the United States and Great Britain. In 1987, U.S. total foreign direct investment amounted to nearly $300 billion.[18] However, the rapid rise of Japan's foreign stakes in recent years, and the assured prospect of further high growth, are certain to result in increasing dominance of both Japanese products and financial influence. The areas in which Japanese investment has concentrated are provided in Figure 3.4. This development has been boosted both by countries competing for Japanese investment with incentives and by the Japanese Ministry of Finance through loan programs. The United States remains a favorite destination with 44 percent of regional foreign direct investment. In the late 1980s, the low value of the dollar made U.S. assets particularly attractive for foreign buyers. European companies were active as well: they spent $37.1 billion in the United States in 1987. The Japanese are concentrating their efforts to North America and Europe because of their market size and advanced technology, while investment in Asia is driven by the desire to have a base for exports to third countries, re-exports to Japan, and production for foreign firms.

[18] U.S. Department of Commerce, *United States Trade Performance in 1987* (Washington, D.C.: U.S. Government Printing Office, 1988), 58–59.

Foreign direct investment in Japan, however, is relatively modest. Foreign-affiliated companies accounted for only 1.5 percent of total sales and 2.8 percent in the manufacturing sector. (In the United States the figure for the manufacturing sector is 15 percent; however, some sectors are higher, chemicals are 32 percent owned by foreigners.[19]) Japan ranks low among the investment priorities of U.S. and European companies. Reasons cited are active discouragement by Japan through rigorous case-by-case reviews of applications, favoritism toward licensing rather than joint manufacturing ventures between Japanese and foreign companies, high start-up costs (although eventual rewards may be considerable), difficulty in hiring, and the companies' own negative feelings toward joint ventures rather than wholly owned or controlled subsidiaries.

IMPACT OF THE ECONOMIC ENVIRONMENT ON SOCIAL DEVELOPMENT

Many of the characteristics discussed are important beyond the numbers. Because of the close relationship between economic and social development, many of the figures can be used as social indicators as well. Consider the following factors and their significance: share of urban population, life expectancy, number of physicians per capita, literacy rate, percentage of income received by the richest 5 percent of the population, and percentage of the population with access to electricity. In addition to these factors, several other variables can be used as cultural indicators: number of public libraries, registered borrowings, book titles published, and number of daily newspapers. The **Physical Quality of Life Index (PQLI)** is a composite measure of the level of welfare in a country. It has three components: life expectancy, infant mortality, and adult literacy rates.[20] The three components of the PQLI are among the few social indicators available to provide a comparison of progress through time in all of the countries of the world.

Differences in the degree of urbanization of target markets in lesser developed countries influence international marketers' product strategies. If products are targeted only to urban areas, products need minimal adjustments mainly to qualify them for market entry. However, when targeting national markets, adaptations may need to be extensive to match more closely the expectations and the more narrow consumption experiences of the rural population.[21]

In terms of infrastructure, improved access brings with it in rural areas an expansion of nonfarm enterprises such as shops, repair services, and

[19] John J. Curran, "What Foreigners Will Buy Next," *Fortune*, February 13, 1989, 94–98.

[20] Ben Crow and Alan Thomas, *Third World Atlas* (Milton Keynes, England: Open University Press, 1984), 85.

[21] John S. Hill and Richard R. Still, "Effects of Urbanization on Multinational Product Planning: Markets in Lesser-Developed Countries," *Columbia Journal of World Business* 19 (Summer 1984): 62–67.

grain mills. It also changes customs, attitudes, and values. As an example, a World Bank study on the impact of rural roads of Yucatan in Mexico found that roads offered an opportunity for enlarging women's role by introducing new ideas, education, medical care, and economic alternatives to maize cultivation.[22] In particular, women married later, had fewer children, and pursued more nondomestic activities. The same impact has been observed with increased access to radio and television. These changes can, if properly understood and utilized, offer major new opportunities to the international marketer.

The presence of multinational corporations, which by their very nature are change agents, will accelerate social change. If government control is weak, the multinational corporation bears the social responsibility for its actions. In some cases, governments restrict the freedom of multinational corporations if their actions may affect the environment. As an example, the Indonesian government places construction restrictions (such as building height) on hotels in Bali to avoid the overcrowding and ecological problems incurred in Hawaii when that state developed its tourism sector vigorously in the 1960s and 1970s.

REGIONAL ECONOMIC INTEGRATION

Economic integration has been one of the main economic developments affecting world markets since World War II. Countries have wanted to engage in economic cooperation to use their respective resources more effectively and to provide larger markets for member-country producers. Some integration efforts have had quite ambitious goals, such as political integration; some have failed as the result of perceptions of unequal benefits from the arrangement or parting of ways politically. A summary of the major forms of economic cooperation in regional markets in Figure 3.5 shows the varying degrees of formality with which integration can take place. Three major trading blocs that emerged during the late 1980s are described in The International Marketplace 3.3.

The Free Trade Area

The **free trade area** is the least restrictive and loosest form of economic integration among nations. In a free trade area, all barriers to trade among member countries are removed. Goods and services are freely traded among member countries. Each member country maintains its own trade barriers vis-à-vis nonmembers.

The most well-known of the free trade areas is the European Free Trade Area (EFTA). Formed in 1960 by eight European countries, it has since lost three members (Denmark, Portugal, and the United Kingdom) to the

[22] The World Bank, *World Development Report 1982* (New York: Oxford University Press, 1982), 63.

FIGURE 3.5 ■ **Forms of Economic Integration in Regional Markets**

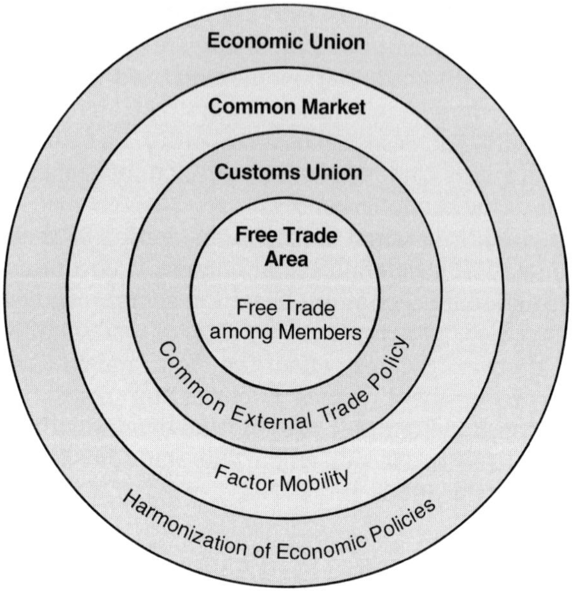

European Community (EC). All of the EFTA countries have bilateral free trade arrangements with the EC. EFTA countries are harmonizing their trade rules and regulations with those of the EC to effectively form a larger entity called the European Economic Space (EES).

After three failed tries during this century, the United States and Canada signed a free trade agreement that went into effect January 1, 1989. The agreement created a single, $5 trillion continental economy—10 percent bigger than the United States on its own and 15 percent larger than the EC.[23] The two countries had already had sectoral free trade arrangements; for example, one for automotive products had existed for 23 years. The new agreement eliminates duties in three stages: (1) immediately, (2) five equal cuts of 20 percent beginning January 1, 1989, and (3) ten equal cuts of 10 percent beginning January 1, 1989.[24] For example, the first round eliminated a 3.9 percent tariff on U.S. computers shipped to Canada as well as 4.9 percent to 22 percent duties on trade in whiskey, skates, furs, and unprocessed fish. The sensitive sectors, such as textiles, steel, and agricultural products, will not be liberalized until the latter part of the ten-year transitionary period. Both countries see the free trade agreement as an important path to world competitiveness. Although there will be

[23] "Getting Ready for the Great American Shakeout," *Business Week*, April 4, 1988, 44–46.
[24] "Summary of the U.S.–Canada Free Trade Agreement," *Export Today* 4 (November–December 1988): 57–61.

THE INTERNATIONAL MARKETPLACE 3.3

Building Blocs During the late 1980s, three major trading blocs have emerged: North American, Western European, and Asian. Statistics show that trade inside these blocs has grown at a rapid pace, while trade among these blocs or with outsiders is either declining or growing far more moderately.

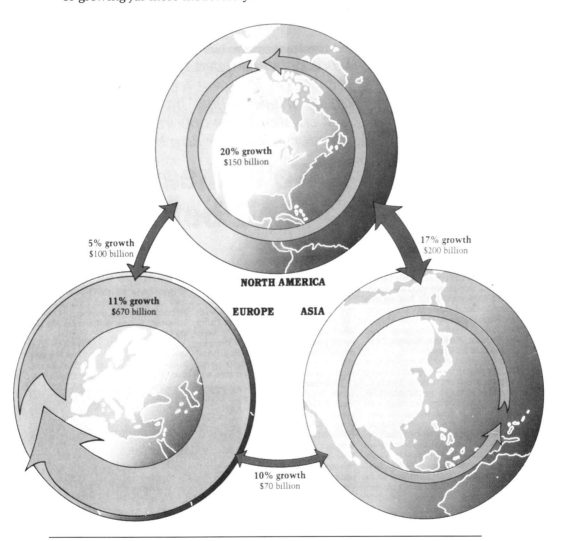

NORTH AMERICA

EUROPE **ASIA**

Source: Andrew Christie, "Building Blocs?" *Forbes*, February 6, 1989, p. 39. Reprinted by permission of Forbes Magazine. © Forbes Inc., 1989.

The trend has been most pronounced in Western Europe, where regional integration is most advanced. Inside the European Com-

munity, trade increased nearly 15 percent from 1986 through 1988, while EC trade with nonmembers actually fell by 10 percent. Considering that trade with European Free Trade Association members is still rigorous, trade with countries outside Western Europe declined substantially.

In 1988, trade among the United States, Canada, and Mexico grew by almost 20 percent, compared with a 5 percent increase in trade with Western Europe (see the chart for growth rates in 1988). These trade patterns are expected to intensify as the Canada–U.S. Free Trade Agreement and the European Community's 1992 unification plans take full effect.

Japan, on its part, has led the integration of Asia. Overall trade within the Asian region (consisting of Japan, South Korea, Taiwan, Hong Kong, Singapore, Indonesia, Malaysia, Thailand, and the Philippines) grew at a 32 percent pace in 1988. The group's trade grew significantly with North America and Western Europe, but not nearly as quickly.

Source: Edwin A. Finn, "Sons of Smoot-Hawley," *Forbes*, February 6, 1989, 38–40.

some dislocations due to consolidation of production, for example, the pact is expected to create 750,000 jobs in the United States and 150,000 in Canada. It is also expected to add as much as 1 percent in growth to both countries' economies as it takes effect in various stages.

The Customs Union

The **customs union** is one step further along the spectrum of economic integration. As in the free trade area, members of the customs union dismantle barriers to trade in goods and services among members. In addition, however, the customs union establishes a common trade policy with respect to nonmembers. Typically, this takes the form of a common external tariff, whereby imports from nonmembers are subject to the same tariff when sold to any member country. The Benelux countries formed a customs union in 1921 that was later integrated into the EC framework.

The Common Market

The **common market** amounts to a customs union covering the exchange of goods and services, the prohibition of duties in exports and imports between members, and the adoption of a common external tariff in respect to nonmembers. In addition, factors of production (labor, capital, and technology) are mobile among members. Restrictions on immigration and cross-border investment are abolished. The importance of **factor mobility** for economic growth cannot be overstated. When factors of production are mobile, then capital, labor, and technology may be employed in their most productive uses.

Despite the obvious benefits, members of a common market must be prepared to cooperate closely in monetary, fiscal, and employment policies. Furthermore, while a common market will enhance the productivity of members in the aggregate, it is by no means clear that individual member countries will always benefit. Because of these difficulties, the goals of common markets have proved to be elusive in many areas of the world, notably Central and South America and Asia. Although certainly not perfect, the EC may be cited as an example of the success of common market policies.

The Economic Union

The creation of a true **economic union** requires integration of economic policies in addition to the free movement of goods, services, and factors of production across borders. Under an economic union, members will harmonize monetary policies, taxation, and government spending. In addition, a common currency is to be used by members. This could be accomplished, de facto, by a system of fixed exchange rates. Clearly, the formation of an economic union requires members to surrender a large measure of their national sovereignty to supranational authorities in community-wide institutions such as the European Parliament. The final step would be a **political union** calling for political unification. At present, the EC is moving toward an economic union as witnessed by the so-called 1992 phenomenon.

Discussion has repeatedly emerged on the linking of the United States, Canada, and Mexico together in a North American Common Market.[25] The strongest supporters see it as a means of increasing the flow of oil and gas from Canada and Mexico. Apart from certain economic advantages, major problems exist. The NACM would never be a confederation of economic equals like the EC. Furthermore, it took more than three years of tough bargaining to reach an agreement between the United States and Canada— two countries whose economic, industrial, and social systems parallel each other.[26]

The main economic integration arrangements are summarized in Table 3.11. The Council of Mutual Economic Assistance (COMECON or CMEA) is an integration effort more politically than economically motivated. Led largely by the Soviet Union, the organization has mainly favored intrabloc trade. With recent changes in the economies of some of the member coun-

---

[25] Herbert E. Meyer, "Why a North American Common Market Won't Work—Yet," *Fortune*, September 10, 1979, 118–124.

[26] "A Giant Step Closer to North America Inc.," *Business Week*, December 5, 1988, 44–45.

TABLE 3.11 ▪ **Major Regional Trade Associations**

ANCOM	Andean Common Market
	Bolivia, Colombia, Ecuador, Peru, Venezuela
ASEAN	Association of Southeast Asian Nations
	Indonesia, Malaysia, Philippines, Singapore, Thailand
BENELUX	Belgium-Netherlands-Luxembourg
	Belgium, Netherlands, Luxembourg
CACM	Central American Common Market
	Costa Rica, El Salvador, Guatemala, Honduras, Nicaragua
CARICOM	Caribbean Community
	Antigua, Bahamas, Barbados, Belize, Dominica, Grenada, Guayana, Jamaica, Montserrat, St. Kitts-Nevis-Anguilla, St. Lucia, St. Vincent and the Grenadines, Trinidad-Tobago
CMEA	Council of Mutual Economic Assistance (COMECON)
	Bulgaria, Czechoslovakia, East Germany, Hungary, Mongolia, Poland, Romania, U.S.S.R., Cuba, Vietnam
ECOWAS	Economic Community of West African States
	Benin, Burkina Faso, Cape Verde, Gambia, Ghana, Guinea, Guinea-Bissau, Ivory Coast, Liberia, Mali, Mauritania, Niger, Nigeria, Senegal, Sierra Leone, Togo
EC	European Community (Common Market)
	Belgium, Denmark, France, Greece, Ireland, Italy, Luxembourg, Netherlands, Portugal, Spain, United Kingdom, West Germany
EFTA	European Free Trade Association
	Austria, Finland, Iceland, Norway, Sweden, Switzerland
LAIA	Latin American Integration Association
	Argentina, Bolivia, Brazil, Chile, Colombia, Ecuador, Mexico, Paraguay, Peru, Uruguay, Venezuela

tries (especially the Soviet Union), CMEA has started formal contacts with the EC. ASEAN, on the other hand, is a cooperative effort by its members to maintain and expand access to industrialized countries' markets. In mid-1987, ASEAN members agreed on a package of proposals to institute more prefential treatment among members and to promote more private sector cooperation, especially in the form of joint ventures.[27]

1992

The European Community has embarked on an ambitious effort to remove the barriers between the 12 member countries to free the movement of goods, services, capital, and people. The process is spelled out in the White Paper, Completing the Internal Market, published in 1985 and ratified by the passing of the **Single European Act** in July 1987. The act commits the member states to the target date of December 31, 1992, to complete the internal market. Approximately 300 measures or areas requiring action will need to be addressed.

[27] "ASEAN Ministers Propose Improved Trade Links," *Far Eastern Economic Review*, July 23, 1987, 79.

   The barriers targeted for action are in eight general categories:[28] The EC has estimated that marketers could save more than $200 billion over the years through the removal of the various barriers.[29]

1. Border controls: Dismantling border controls will make it much easier to deliver goods. With the "single administrative document," drivers hauling cargo will be able to clear border crossings with one piece of paper rather than two pounds of documents needed earlier. The benefit is in increased efficiency, making the EC more competitive. Furthermore, the entire European transportation landscape can be expected to change.

2. Freedom of movement of people: Although nonprofessionals have enjoyed the ability to move to other EC countries to work, the acceptance of academic and professional qualifications acquired in different member states is only now possible. This will result in the widening of labor markets in the professional sectors and will help the international marketer in recruiting efforts.

3. Different indirect taxation regimes: The EC sets a high priority for the harmonization of the main national systems of indirect taxes, value-added taxes (VAT), and excise taxes. A smoothing of widely varying VAT rates into a range of 4 to 19 percent, from the current range of 0 to 38 percent, is proposed to coincide with the dismantling of border stations. Because these taxes tend to hit luxury goods the hardest in southern Europe, a $17,500 BMW in Frankfurt costs $50,000 in Athens. VCRs in France are taxed at 28 percent, while the rate in West Germany is 14 percent.[30] Without trade barriers, parallel imports will flourish.

4. Lack of a common legal framework: There is considerable need to establish community-wide laws and regulations to govern in areas such as intellectual property and the treatment accorded firms in the member states. The European Community has already begun to articulate the principle of reciprocity; that is, the EC will give access to foreign firms on the same terms that the foreign country gives access to EC companies in the same industry.

5. Controls on movement of capital: The EC seeks to increase the effectiveness of the financial markets by liberalizing capital markets. Labor unions fear that this will mean lost jobs to countries like Spain where both wages and costs are lower.

6. Regulation of services: Much of the attention is focused on financial services, especially on the right and conditions for banks and insurance companies to be established. Allowing for freer access, competition in the service sector will increase tremendously.

---

[28] Michael Calingaert, *The 1992 Challenge from Europe: Development of the EC's Internal Market* (Washington, D.C.: The National Planning Association 1988), Chapter 3.

[29] "1992: Europe Becomes One," *Advertising Age*, July 11, 1988, 46.

[30] "Reshaping Europe: 1992 and Beyond," *Business Week*, December 12, 1988, 48–51.

7. Harmonization of technical standards: In addition to major cost savings (estimated at $1 billion for foodstuffs), the development cycle of a product from invention to commercialization can be shortened and the product made available to larger markets at once.

8. Public procurement policies: Discriminatory procurement policies favoring national companies have created fragmented markets; for example, in boilers, locomotives, turbine generators, and telephones there is virtually no trade within the EC. An open procurement system would bring about estimated cost savings of $21 billion but also result in a dramatic reduction in the number of firms; for example, turbine manufacturers from ten to two and electric locomotive producers from sixteen to three.[31]

Most of these measures are expected to take effect by the set deadline. Some others, such as an agreement on a common currency, are unlikely to occur in this century. However, enough momentum has developed to bring the members of the EC closer in the years before 1992 than anything since the founding of the entity in 1957.

A number of challenges need to be met by the international marketing manager. First, most industries within the EC have to reduce overcapacity. For example, the U.S. market, which is comparable to that of the EC in many respects, only supports two turbine manufacturers and two locomotive producers. Secondly, companies operating in the market will have to build scale. This can be accomplished through acquisitions, mergers, or the formation of strategic alliances. Finally, the international marketer needs to work on homogenizing local tastes. Finding and shaping common denominators will enable the adoption of pan-European or global strategies to benefit the marketing effort.[32]

For firms from nonmember countries, 1992 presents various possibilities depending on the firm's position within the EC.[33] Table 3.12 provides four different scenarios with proposed courses of action. Well-established U.S.-based multinational marketers such as H.J. Heinz and Colgate-Palmolive will be able to take advantage of the new economies of scale. For example, 3M plants earlier turned out different versions of the company's products for various markets. Now, the 3M plant in Wales, for example, makes videotapes and videocassettes for all of Europe.[34] Colgate-Palmolive has to watch out for competitors like West Germany's Henkel in the brutally competitive detergent market. At the same time, large-scale retailers, such as France's Carrefour and West Germany's Aldi group, are undertaking their own efforts to exploit the situation with hypermarkets supplied by

---

[31] "Painful Challenges, Important Gains," *Financial Times*, November 17, 1988, VIII.

[32] Eric G. Friberg, "1992: Moves Europeans Are Making," *Harvard Business Review* 67 (May–June 1989): 85–89.

[33] John F. Magee, "1992: Moves Americans Must Make," *Harvard Business Review* 67 (May–June 1989): 78–84.

[34] Richard I. Kirkland, "Outsider's Guide to Europe in 1992," *Fortune*, October 24, 1988, 121–127.

TABLE 3.12 ▪ **Proposed Company Responses to 1992**

Company Status	Challenges	Response
Established Multinational Marketer/Multiple Markets	Exploit opportunities from improved productivity	
	Meet challenge of competitors	Pan-European strategy
	Cater to customers/ intermediaries doing same	
Marketer with One European Subsidiary	Competition Loss of niche	Expansion Strategic alliances Rationalization Divestment
Exporter to Europe	Competition Access	European branch Selective acquisition Strategic alliance
No Interest	Competition at home Lost opportunity	Entry

Source: John F. Magee, "1992: Moves Americans Must Make," *Harvard Business Review* 67 (May–June 1989): 78–84.

central warehouses with computerized inventories. Their procurement policies have to be met by companies like Heinz. Many multinationals are developing pan-European strategies to exploit the emerging situation; that is, they are standardizing their products and processes to the greatest extent possible without compromising local input and implementation.

A company with a foothold in only one European market is faced with the danger of competitors who can use the strength of multiple markets. Furthermore, the elimination of barriers may do away with the company's competitive advantage. For example, over half of the 45 major European food companies are in just one or two of the individual European markets and seriously lag behind broader-based U.S. and Swiss firms. Similarly, automakers Peugeot and Fiat are nowhere close to the cross-manufacturing presence of Ford and GM. The courses of action include expansion through acquisitions or mergers, formation of strategic alliances (for example, AT&T's joint venture with Spain's Telefonica to produce state-of-the-art microchips), rationalization by concentrating only on business segments in which the company can be a pan-European leader, and, finally, divestment.

Exporters will need to worry about maintaining their competitive position and continued access to the market. Companies with a physical presence may be in a better position to assess and to take advantage of the developments. In some cases, fears of 1992 amounting to "Fortress Europe" may be valid, especially in industries in which national champions are preferred (such as telecommunications, autos, and computers). This may very well be the case with Japanese exports into the EC from production points in the United States. The EC is trying to negotiate a Europe-wide auto quota that would limit Japan's market share to 11 percent. One way the Japanese may try to get around this could be reexporting from the United States.[35] Some firms, like Filament Fiber Technology Inc. of New Jersey, establish production units in Europe. Digital Microwave Corporation of California decided to defend its market share in Europe by joining two British communications companies and setting up a digital microwave radio and optical-fiber plant in Scotland.[36] In some industries, marketers do not see a reason either to be in Europe at all or to change from exporting to more involved modes of entry. Machinery and machine tools, for example, are in great demand in Europe, and marketers in these companies say they have little reason to manufacture there. Whatever the approach, U.S. exporters will have to make critical decisions on Europe 1992 soon. Although the phenomenon is a journey and not a destination, the markets will start taking new shape in the early 1990s.

Early efforts in the United Kingdom to prepare for 1992 are described in The International Marketplace 3.4. Various entities, both from the public and private sectors, are gearing up their efforts to promote and facilitate firms' adjustment to 1992. An example of such an event is provided in Figure 3.6 covering one of the markets that has heretofore been protected but to which 1992 will provide access, telecommunications.

Arguments Surrounding Economic Integration

Regional economic integration creates opportunities and potential problems for the international marketer. It may have an impact on a company's entry mode by favoring direct investment, because one of the basic rationales of integration is to generate favorable conditions for local production and intraregional trade. By design, larger markets are created with potentially more opportunity. Because of harmonization efforts, regulations may be standardized, thus positively affecting the international marketer.

The individual member states benefit also from the creation of larger markets that will tend to increase the number of competing firms, resulting in greater efficiency and lower prices for consumers. Moreover, less productive entities may be spurred into action by competition from the more energetic bloc members.

Although some believe that it is no longer possible to remain local and survive, many are concerned about the loss of their sovereignty and cultural heritage with increasing economic integration. This was one of the main arguments voiced by Canadians who opposed the U.S.–Canadian free trade agreement.

[35] "Is Japan Using the U.S. as a Back Door to Europe?" *Business Week*, November 14, 1988, 57.
[36] "Should Small U.S. Exporters Take the Plunge?" *Business Week*, November 14, 1988, 64–68.

THE INTERNATIONAL MARKETPLACE 3.4

Preparation for 1992   As 1992 approaches, British marketers are the subject of an effort to prepare them for the event. The Confederation of British Industry (CBI) has prepared a series of ten seminars on special topics related to 1992, each to be held in 13 regions of the United Kingdom.

In April 1988, Prime Minister Margaret Thatcher launched a lavish 1992 information campaign at a cost of more than $17 million. The Department of Trade and Industry (DTI) produced 32 fact sheets that include information on items such as technical standards in the EC, language skills, and a checklist designed to make companies think about whether they are doing enough.

Not much practical action had been triggered by the end of 1988. A telephone survey of 200 manufacturing and service companies revealed that even among companies expecting to be affected by 1992, 5 percent had reorganized their company in response, 6 percent had looked at acquisitions/joint ventures, 3 percent had opened sales offices, while 31 percent had done nothing at all. The responses to the survey were as follows:

What, if anything, has your company done to prepare for 1992?

Reorganized own company	9	(5%)
Appointed an executive responsible for 1992	13	(7%)
Carried out a strategy review	39	(20%)
Introduced an in-house training scheme	7	(4%)
Attended seminars/courses	24	(12%)
Introduced language training	13	(7%)
Undertaken market research	20	(10%)
Looked at acquisitions/joint ventures	12	(6%)
Opened manufacturing operations	1	(1%)
Opened sales office/offices	5	(3%)
Appointed sales agent/agents	7	(4%)
Nothing	61	(31%)
Specified other	50	(25%)

The DTI will provide increasingly specific material as time goes on. For many businesses this free information is likely to be enough. The CBI scheme, which has a hefty (though subsidized) price tag, is expected to score with companies that want much more detailed information and the chance to follow up on their own particular questions.

Source: "Preparing Britain for 1992," *Financial Times*, November 1, 1988, 8.

FIGURE 3.6 ▪ **Seminar on 1992**

Source: Reprinted with permission of the publisher, BCR Enterprises, Inc.

SUMMARY

Economic variables relating to the various markets' characteristics—population, income, consumption patterns, infrastructure, geography, and attitudes toward foreign involvement in the economy—form a starting point for assessment of market potential for the international marketer. These data are readily available but should be used in conjunction with other, more interpretive data, because the marketer's plans often require a long-term approach. Data on the economic environment produce a snapshot of the past; in some cases old data are used to make decisions affecting operations two years in the future. Even if the data are recent, they cannot themselves indicate the growth and the intensity of development. Some economies remain stagnant, plagued by natural calamities, internal problems, and lack of export markets, while some witness booming economic development.

Economic data provide a baseline from which other more market/product-specific and even experiential data can be collected. Understanding the composition and interrelationships between economic indicators is essential for the assessment of the other environments and their joint impact on market potential. The international marketer needs to understand the impact of the economic environment on social development.

The emergence of economic integration in the world economy poses unique opportunities and challenges to the international marketer. Eliminating barriers between member markets and erecting new ones vis-à-vis nonmembers will call for adjustments in past strategies to fully exploit the new situations. In the late 1980s, economic integration increased substantially. The signing of the U.S.–Canadian free trade agreement produced the largest trading bloc in the world, whereas the "1992 phenomenon" in Europe is an ambitious attempt to remove physical, fiscal, and technical barriers separating the 12 member countries of the EC.

Questions for Discussion

1. Place these markets in the framework provided below:

a. Indonesia	g. Turkey	m. Peru
b. Mozambique	h. Spain	n. Jamaica
c. India	i. Singapore	o. Poland
d. Bangladesh	j. Nigeria	p. United Kingdom
e. Niger	k. Algeria	q. Iraq
f. Brazil	l. Zambia	r. Saudi Arabia

   Income Level

   Low Income   Middle Income   High Income

   Trade Structure
   Industrial
   Developing
   •Semi-Industrial
   •Oil-Exporting
   •Primary Producing
   •Populous South Asia
   •Least Developed

2. Comment on this statement: "A North American Common Market, if established, would be more of a mirror image of COMECON than the EC."

3. Using the data in the Appendix to Chapter 3, assess the market potential for (a) power generators and (b) consumer appliances in (1) the Philippines, (2) Jordan, and (3) Portugal.

4. From the international marketer's point of view, what are the opportunities and problems caused by increased urbanization in developing countries?

5. Comment on this statement: "A low per-capita income will render the market useless."

6. Comment on the statement that "the economic straits of developing countries have cost the United States more than $60 billion in exports and 1.7 million jobs in the past five years."

7. Discuss the impact of distance on the marketing mix of an exporter.

8. What is the function of economic data for the international marketer? Are not the categories too broad and too open to variations, deviations, and exceptions for them to be of real use?

Recommended Readings

Current issues of *Business International, Business Europe, Business East Europe, Business Asia, Business Latin America, Business China.*

Farmer, Richard N., and Barry M. Richman. *Comparative Management and Economic Progress.* Homewood, Ill.: Irwin, 1965.

Yearbook of International Trade Statistics. New York: United Nations, 1988.

U.S. Department of Commerce. "Annual Survey of Foreign Direct Investment Activity." Washington, D.C.: U.S. Government Printing Office, 1984.

Vernon, Raymond, and Louis T. Wells. *Manager in the International Economy.* Englewood Cliffs, N.J.: Prentice-Hall, 1981.

The World in Figures. London: The Economist Publications, 1988.

Rostow, Walt W. *The Stages of Economic Growth.* London: Cambridge University Press, 1960.

International Marketing Data and Statistics 1988/89. London: Euromonitor, 1989.

Europe 1992: The Single Market. Brussels: Ernst & Whinney, 1988.

INDICATORS OF MARKET SIZE FOR 117 COUNTRIES

APPENDIX

Some terms require a word of explanation in order to make country-by-country comparisons more meaningful.

Population figures are midyear UN estimates. Working age is defined as ages 16 to 64 inclusive.

Gross Domestic Product (GDP) is the total value at current market prices of all goods and services produced by residents of a country before deduction of depreciation charges on fixed capital. It is equal to the sum of (1) personal consumption expenditures; (2) gross domestic capital formation (investments), including inventory changes; (3) the net of exports minus imports of goods and services; and (4) government consumption expenditures. GDP differs from GNP by excluding net factor incomes received from abroad (an amount usually about 1 percent of GDP). GDP and GNP reports tend to run later and are subject to constant revision (the United States normally makes about a half dozen changes after its first estimate). Thus, the 1984 figures are often provisional or are estimates made by Business International analysts.

National Income is the sum of the incomes of nationals of a country, whether resident or not, before deduction of direct taxes. The main components are wages and salaries, employees' benefits, corporate earnings accruing to residents, income from business operations, net interest, and royalties. Source: *International Financial Statistics* (IMF).

Average Wages in Manufacturing are subject to inconsistencies in reporting and definitions of manufacturing, as well as differences in the workweek and treatment of overtime, benefits, payments in kind, etc. Wages at current prices have been adjusted for inflation using the private consumption deflator to obtain real growth in manufacturing wages. Source: *Yearbook of Labor Statistics* (International Labor Organization).

Total Exports are presented f.o.b. (approximately the seller's price before transportation). Often in trade statistics, this is compared to imports f.o.b. to obtain the country's balance of trade. However, BI believes imports c.i.f. (which include transportation and insurance costs) gives a better picture of the significance of imports to a nation's economy. Sources: *Direction of Trade Statistics* (IMF), central banks', and government publications.

Source: "Indicators of Market Size for 117 Countries," *Business International*, June 1988.

Sources used by BI editors include: *Monthly Bulletin of Statistics* (UN); *OECD Economic Surveys: Direction of Trade Statistics* (IMF); *International Financial Statistics* (IMF); U.S. Department of Commerce; Agency for International Development; *World Automotive Market* (Johnston International Publishing Corp.); *The World's Telephones* (American Telephone and Telegraph); *World Radio-TV Handbook* (AT&T Communications); *Statistical Yearbook* (UN); *Yearbook of Labor Statistics* (ILO); *Yearbook of National Accounts Statistics* (UN); *Yearbook of Energy Statistics* (UN); *International Iron and Steel Institute; Key Indicators of Developing Member Countries of ADB* (Asian Development Bank); *Selected World Demographic Indicators by Countries, 1950–2000* (UN); central banks', and government publications.

Private Consumption Expenditure is the value of final expenditure by households and private nonprofit institutions on current goods and services, less sales of similar goods. Sources: BI area forecasting studies, *Monthly Bulletin of Statistics* (UN), *International Financial Statistics* (IMF), *Yearbook of National Accounts Statistics* (UN).

Passenger Cars in Use denotes motor vehicles seating fewer than eight persons, including taxis, jeeps, and station wagons. Source: *World Automotive Report* (Johnston International Publishing Company).

Trucks and Buses in Use includes vans, lorries, buses, and tractor and semitrailer combinations (except trailers and farm tractors). Source: *World Automotive Report* (Johnston International Publishing Company).

Telephone Access Lines includes both public and private telephones installed that can be connected to a central exchange. Source: *The World's Telephones* (AT&T).

Television Sets in Use is a total number of receiving sets in each country. Source: *World Radio and TV Handbook.*

Computers refers to the total number of installed large-scale systems. Large-scale systems are either general-purpose computers or high-speed scientific computers with a typical system price of over $1 million. Generically referred to as mainframes, these systems typically support more than 128 users in a normal commercial environment. Source: International Data Corporation.

Steel Consumption is apparent consumption of crude steel (that is, production plus imports minus exports) disregarding inventory changes. Source: International Iron and Steel Institute.

Cement Production includes all types. Sources: *Monthly Bulletin of Statistics* (UN), *European Annual Review* (Cembureau).

Electricity Production combines generation of electricity by utility firms for public use and production by companies for their own use. If grand totals for electricity production in 1984 were not available, estimates made on available monthly data were used. Source: *Monthly Bulletin of Statistics* (UN).

Energy Consumption is denominated in per-capita oil equivalent. Coal equivalent can be calculated by dividing the oil equivalent figure by 0.687623. Source: *Yearbook of Energy Statistics* (UN).

In addition to the caveats accompanying the definition of terms, the following should also be kept in mind.

Currency conversion. For the presentation of GDP and private consumption expenditure on a comparative basis, BI has converted data in local currencies to U.S. dollars, using average exchange rates for the year from the *Monthly Bulletin of Statistics* (U.S.). In cases in which multiple exchange rates are used, a choice was made based on BI's best judgment.

Although conversion to a common currency is often essential for comparisons between countries, it should be recognized that a degree of distortion is inevitably involved. An important contribution to this distortion is the fact that exchange rates apply only to goods in world trade. Countries vary in their degree of involvement in international trade, which results in differences in the volumes and prices of nontraded goods among economies.

Another source of distortion is the tendency of floating currencies to overshoot in the process of adjusting to market forces. In some countries, inflation and managed currency rates are not necessarily in step. In both cases, data converted to dollars may appear relatively high or low compared with those of other countries in a given year or with data for the same country in previous years.

Variation in national accounting. East European countries and the Soviet Union use Net Material Product instead of Gross Domestic Product as a measure of economic activity for the nation as a whole. This concept deliberately excludes certain services, including government services, and is thus 20 to 30 percent lower than GDP would be if these services were counted.

In general, data reported in national accounts must be regarded with special care because they are subject to frequent revision and sometimes underestimate the contribution of inflation in early estimates.

Market Size shows the relative dimensions of each national or regional market as a percentage of the total world market. The percentages for each market are derived by averaging the corresponding data on total population (doubled weighted), urban population, private consumption expenditure, steel consumption, cement and electricity production, and ownership of telephones, passenger cars, and televisions.

Market Intensity measures the richness of the market, or the degree of concentrated purchasing power it represents. BI's measure of world-economy intensity is designated as 1.00, and the intensity of each market is calculated in proportion to it. The intensity figure is arrived at by averaging per-capita energy consumption, telephone access lines, and passenger cars. Double weight is given to private consumption expenditure. The proportion of urban population is also taken into account (and double weighted), since in many developing countries much of the rural population does not actively participate in the money economy.

Market Growth is an average of the growth rates of several indicators over the past five years: population; steel consumption; electricity production; and ownership of passenger cars, trucks, and buses; televisions, private consumption expenditure; and real GNP.

Adjustments have been made for missing or misleading data in computing the three composite indices. The estimates that have been made for LDCs with scant data are likely to be on the low side.

The table demonstrates how some key markets have changed over the past decade. For the sake of historical comparability, China has been omitted. However, because it is emerging as one of the world's more interesting markets, we have recalculated the 1986 intensities to include it in the chart.

	Population				GDP[1]		National Income[10]		Average Hourly Wage[11]	
	Total 1986 (million)	Past 5-year constant compound % increase	Working age 1986 (million)	Past 5-year constant compound % increase	Total 1986 ($ billion)	Past 5-year constant compound % increase	Total 1985 ($ billion)	Per capita 1986 ($)	1985 ($)	Past 5-year constant compound % increase
WESTERN EUROPE										
EC										
Belgium	9.9	0.1	6.7	—	109.6	1.2	86.2	8,707	5.84	−5.5
Denmark	5.1	0.0	3.4	0.0	82.4	3.2	58.7	11,510	8.51	1.0
France	54.8	0.3	36.3	0.9	723.8	1.5	537.0	9,835	4.97	−0.7
Germany	60.7	−0.2	42.7	0.9	1,001.6	1.7	643.0	10,558	6.48	0.3
Greece	9.9	0.5	6.5	2.1	40.1	1.6	34.2[6]	3,455	2.13	−1.2
Ireland	3.7	1.2	2.2	3.2	13.7	0.9	16.9	4,694	5.19	2.4
Italy	57.3	0.1	38.8	0.8	408.0[5]	1.9	363.3[6]	6,340	4.41[4]	−5.5
Luxembourg	0.4	0.0	0.3	—	4.6[5]	1.3	5.0	9,974	6.44	—
Netherlands	14.5	0.5	10.0	1.0	171.2	1.2	132.4	9,131	5.33[4]	−6.2
Portugal	10.3	0.7	6.7	1.4	29.3	1.8	18.8[4]	1,861	1.09[4]	−7.3
Spain	38.8	0.6	25.1	0.8	229.1	2.1	142.4[4]	3,680	3.66	−2.9
United Kingdom	56.2	0.1	36.7	0.1	548.9	2.5	330.5	5,891	5.29	−1.0
TOTAL EC[1]	321.57		215.3		3,362.3		2,368.4			
EFTA										
Austria	7.5	0.0	5.1	1.0	94.4	2.0	76.8[6]	10,240	5.51	4.0
Finland	4.9	0.5	3.4	0.5	70.6	3.1	51.7	10,551	5.94	1.7
Iceland	0.2	1.2	0.2	2.1	3.7	1.6	2.2	10,476	—	—
Norway	4.2	0.3	2.7	0.9	69.7	4.0	58.4[6]	13,661	8,09	0.5
Sweden	8.3	0.1	5.4	0.0	132.3	2.1	97.5	11,747	7.71	−6.2
Switzerland	6.4	0.2	4.4	0.5	135.5	1.7	103.9	16,492	9.07	6.9
TOTAL EFTA	31.51		21.1		506.2		390.5			
Turkey	50.3	2.1	29.9	2.4	58.1	5.4	38.9[4]	780	0.26[4]	—
Yugoslavia	23.3	0.8	15.8	—	41.6[5]	1.0	28.8[4]	1,252	0.69	—
TOTAL WESTERN EUROPE[1]	426.72		282.1		3,968.2		2,826.6			
EASTERN EUROPE										
Bulgaria	9.1	0.5	6.0	—	25.1[5][9]	·3.8	—	—	1.58	9.7
Czechoslovakia	15.6	0.4	10.1	—	79.3[5][9]	2.4	—	—	1.36	−11.2
East Germany	16.8	0.0	11.3	—	93.9[5][9]	4.4	—	—	2.68	—
Hungary	10.7	0.0	7.0	—	19.2[9]	1.0	19.4	1,813	0.78	7.6
Poland	37.5	0.9	24.5	—	54.1[9]	2.9	—	—	0.86	−6.8
Romania	23.2	0.7	11.4	—	47.8[9]	5.4	46.5[6]	2,004	1.28	—
USSR	278.6	1.0	185.2	—	836.0[9]	3.3	—	—	1.49[4]	5.4
TOTAL EASTERN EUROPE[1]	391.47		255.6		1,155.4[9]		65.9			
MIDDLE EAST										
Bahrain	0.5	4.4	0.3	—	4.0	0.0	—	—	—	—
Egypt	48.0	2.4	27.1	1.8	45.5	4.8	40.9[4]	887	—	—
Iran	45.9	2.9	24.7	4.9	165.0	3.8	94.3[4]	2,188	—	—
Iraq	16.5	3.6	8.3	4.0	63.5	—	23.9[4]	1,593	—	—
Israel	4.3	1.8	2.6	0.9	27.5	1.9	14.5	3,452	2.58	−0.4
Jordan	3.7	3.7	1.8	4.0	4.8	3.0	5.0[6]	1,351	—	—
Kuwait	1.9	5.5	1.1	12.7	18.3	−4.7	25.7[4]	16,063	—	—
Libya	3.7	3.9	1.9	4.3	19.9	—	—	—	—	—
Oman	1.3	4.7	0.7	—	9.0[5]	5.3	7.6[4]	6,333	—	—
Qatar	0.3	6.8	0.2	—	6.4[5]	4.2	—	—	—	—
Saudi Arabia	12.0	4.2	6.4	6.1	77.4	−8.9	111.3[4]	10,702	—	—
Syria	10.9	3.5	5.3	2.2	23.1[5]	−0.2	—	—	—	—
United Arab Emirates	1.4	6.0	0.9	—	25.6[5]	−3.2	22.9[4]	1,877	—	—
North Yemen	7.0	2.7	3.5	3.2	2.6	6.8	3.6[2]	571	—	—
TOTAL MIDDLE EAST[1]	157.41		84.8		492.6		349.7			

Total Exports		Total Imports		Imports from U.S.		Imports from Japan		Imports from EEC	
1986 f.o.b. ($ million)	Average annual % increase (past 5 years)	1986 c.i.f. ($ million)	Average annual % increase (past 5 years)	1986 c.i.f. ($ million)	Average annual % increase (past 5 years)	1986 c.i.f. ($ million)	Average annual % increase (past 5 years)	1986 c.i.f. ($ million)	Average annual % increase (past 5 years)
68,819[8]	6.2	68,624[8]	3.7	3,463[8]	−3.6	1,896[8]	15.8	49,678[8]	8.5
21,158	8.8	22,844	8.4	1,207	2.1	1,293	28.2	11,892	10.6
124,946	7.1	129,399	3.4	9,676	2.1	4,666	13.6	76,927	9.5
243,515	9.2	191,068	5.7	12,351	1.7	11,112	22.2	99,784	7.9
5,652	7.7	11,358	3.4	342	−4.8	688	−3.4	6.667	10.6
12,571	11.9	11,612	4.9	1,840	10.6	442	11.6	7,819	3.7
97,827	7.8	99,925	4.0	5,669	−0.2	2,099	18.5	55,540	12.1
—	—	—	—	—	—	—	—	—	—
80,550	5.2	75,738	4.5	5,950	1.0	2,490	20.8	48,344	9.0
7,345	15.5	9,766	1.8	687	−7.7	322	4.5	5,797	15.7
27,206	7.7	35,056	3.1	3,445	−5.2	1,729	18.1	17,665	18.1
107,088	2.6	126,326	6.3	12,549	1.9	7,243	12.5	65,410	10.6
796,677		781,716		57,179		33,980		445,523	
22,473	10.1	26,823	9.3	865	4.6	1,168	23.8	18,016	11.9
16,356	6.2	15,335	3.8	735	−2.0	992	16.5	6,612	10.9
1,098	13.2	1,119	18.6	78	0.9	21	−14.1	592	9.2
18,261	1.1	20,289	8.1	1,400	0.3	1,500	16.9	10,171	11.1
37,315	8.9	32,228	4.2	2,492	1.6	1,747	15.0	18,351	7.3
37,456	10.5	41,409	10.4	2,214	3.1	1,909	17.7	29,996	13.0
132,959		137,203		7,784		7,337		83,738	
7,205	6.5	11,917	7.8	1,275	15.7	752	26.6	5,120	21.2
10,298	0.1	11,756	189.8	673	−1.2	148	12.8	3,860	−3.0
947,139		942,592		66,911		42,217		538,241	
2,033	1.0	3,731	7.7	106	20.3	178	32.7	1,608	15.0
5,821	2.6	6,013	8.7	101	8.2	68	0.1	2,129	13.2
5,296	2.1	5,168	−0.2	53	−29.9	132	−1.7	1,159	12.3
9,158	0.9	9,596	2.3	184	9.8	141	12.0	2,159	4.7
11,950	1.1	12,029	4.5	151	2.0	147	39.0	2,384	4.8
10,705	−9.9	9,315	−9.2	251	3.4	112	7.1	961	−0.7
33,696	−1.3	42,807	4.0	1,372	−8.5	3,496	−0.8	10,654	7.2
78,659		88,659		2,218		4,274		21,054	
2,501	−15.4	2,390	−9.6	214	12.9	134	−11.3	560	0.2
3,761	5.0	12,132	11.3	2,180	21.8	624	27.7	4,959	10.5
9,005	−13.1	9,775	−0.9	38	−16.6	1,270	31.4	4,013	5.9
7,634	−6.2	8,847	−16.9	580	−5.5	1,346	1.8	3,012	−22.0
7,130	8.3	10,491	2.2	1,789	3.8	307	19.7	4,950	13.9
804	3.4	3,694	4.7	343	−12.2	200	−6.1	952	−11.1
7,707	−7.3	5,634	−9.1	723	−7.4	1,354	−8.1	2,063	−7.9
6,412	−16.1	4,553	−12.8	51	−15.4	216	−5.1	2,803	−14.2
2,687	−8.0	2,741	4.0	175	−2.6	320	−8.8	1,184	7.2
2,106	−9.0	1,095	−1.3	68	−19.2	164	−20.8	500	−10.4
24,776	−23.1	22,114	−13.9	3,794	−19.4	3,065	−19.7	8,888	−10.5
1,136	−3.5	2,616	−10.0	44	−24.4	76	−8.7	734	−9.6
11,397	−5.8	6,750	−8.3	543	−19.1	1,147	−9.5	2,713	−5.8
50	25.3	1,412	−2.1	87	30.7	137	−9.5	119	−16.7
87,106		94,244		10,629		10,360		37,450	

	Population				GDP[1]		National Income[10]		Average Hourly Wage[11]	
	Total 1986 (million)	Past 5-year constant compound % increase	Working age 1986 (million)	Past 5-year constant compound % increase	Total 1986 ($ billion)	Past 5-year constant compound % increase	Total 1985 ($ billion)	Per capita 1986 ($)	1985 ($)	Past 5-year constant compound % increase
AFRICA										
Algeria	22.4	3.0	11.4	3.3	51.4	2.5	—	—	—	—
Angola	9.0	2.5	4.7	5.9	—	—	—	—	—	—
Burkina Faso	7.1	2.4	3.8	−0.9	0.9[4]	—	0.8[3]	107	—	—
Cameroon	10.2	2.7	5.4	3.1	13.2	7.0	6.2[4]	667	—	—
Congo	1.8	2.6	0.9	1.7	2.2	2.4	1.5[3]	882	—	—
Ethiopia	44.7	2.5	23.5	11.0	5.5	1.7	4.9[4]	141	—	—
Gabon	1.1	1.6	0.7	5.3	3.7	2.2	—	—	—	—
Ghana	14.0	3.2	7.1	3.0	6.4[5]	2.5	5.9[3]	457	—	—
Ivory Coast	10.2	3.7	5.2	3.7	—	1.2	—	—	—	—
Kenya	21.5	4.1	9.8	5.1	5.8[5]	3.2	5.7[4]	292	0.79	—
Madagascar	10.3	2.8	5.4	2.7	2.7	0.5	—	—	—	—
Malawi	7.2	3.1	3.7	2.9	1.2	3.1	0.9[3]	132	0.27[4]	—
Mauritius	1.1	1.9	0.7	—	1.4	—	1.0	1,000	0.27	—
Morocco	22.5	2.5	12.4	2.5	15.1	4.2	11.4[4]	498	—	—
Mozambique	14.3	2.8	7.7	9.3	3.4[5][9]	−8.0	—	—	—	—
Nigeria	98.5	3.3	48.6	4.8	67.1	−4.0	62.3[3]	731	—	—
Senegal	6.6	2.6	3.5	3.0	—	4.8	—	—	—	—
Sierra Leone	3.7	1.8	2.0	0.7	3.8	1.8	—	—	—	—
South Africa	33.2	2.5	18.2	2.0	64.4	0.4	51.5[6][7]	1,551	1.45	—
Tanzania	23.3	3.5	11.4	4.7	—	2.2	—	—	—	—
Tunisia	7.2	2.0	4.1	2.5	8.9	2.8	8.4[6]	1,167	—	—
Uganda	16.0	3.3	7.9	1.8	—	2.8	—	—	—	—
Zaire	30.9	2.9	16.1	3.1	2.6[5]	2.3	2.5	143	—	—
Zambia	6.9	3.3	3.4	2.6	2.9[5]	−0.2	2.2[4]	333	0.59[4]	—
Zimbabwe	9.1	3.5	4.5	3.3	—	1.9	—	—	—	—
TOTAL AFRICA[1]	432.82		222.2		262.7		165.2			
NORTH AMERICA										
Canada	25.7	1.1	17.5	0.2	366.0	2.8	291.4	11,472	8.28	3.2
United States	240.1	0.9	159.4	0.9	4,168.9	2.8	3,750.6[8]	15,621	9.53	4.5
TOTAL NORTH AMERICA	265.8		176.9		4,534.9		4,042.0			
LATIN AMERICA										
LAIA										
Argentina	31.0	1.6	18.8	2.0	76.1[4]	0.4	76.0	2,676	1.17	—
*Bolivia	6.5	2.7	3.5	2.8	1.4	−3.0	3.2	516	0.23[4]	—
Brazil	141.5	2.2	82.0	2.9	270.9	3.7	242.8[6]	1,716	—	—
Chile	12.2	1.6	7.8	2.4	15.9	−0.1	9.7	815	0.87	−13.8
*Colombia	29.3	2.2	17.4	2.9	26.4	2.7	32.5	1,157	—	—
*Ecuador	9.6	2.9	5.3	4.8	9.3	1.6	10.0[6]	1,042	—	—
Mexico	81.0	2.6	43.9	3.1	127.5	−0.6	131.8[3]	1,734	0.90	−25.4
Paraguay	3.8	3.0	2.1	3.0	7.6	0.7	6.8[6]	1,789	—	—
*Peru	20.2	2.6	11.3	2.5	21.2	0.8	10.4	528	0.24[4]	−9.7
Uruguay	3.0	0.7	1.9	1.7	6.2	−5.8	4.9	1,633	0.85	—
*Venezuela	17.8	2.8	10.1	1.7	49.6[5]	−0.1	43.7	2,526	—	—
*Ancom Subtotal[1]	83.5		47.5		107.9		99.8			
TOTAL LAIA[1]	356.0		203.9		612.1		571.8			
CACM										
Costa Rica	2.7	2.6	1.6	4.4	4.3	1.6	4.5[6]	1,667	0.91	−5.3
El Salvador	5.7	2.9	3.0	3.4	4.0	0.1	3.7[6]	649	1.42	8.0
Guatemala	8.2	2.8	4.2	3.4	11.1[5]	−1.6	10.8[6]	1,317	—	—
Honduras	4.5	3.4	2.3	4.7	3.7	1.3	3.4[6]	756	0.28	39.8
Nicaragua	3.4	3.3	1.7	4.7	—	2.2	—	—	—	—
TOTAL CACM[1]	24.5		12.8		23.1[5]		22.4			

Total Exports		Total Imports		Imports from U.S.		Imports from Japan		Imports from EEC	
1986 f.o.b. ($ million)	Average annual % increase (past 5 years)	1986 c.i.f. ($ million)	Average annual % increase (past 5 years)	1986 c.i.f. ($ million)	Average annual % increase (past 5 years)	1986 c.i.f. ($ million)	Average annual % increase (past 5 years)	1986 c.i.f. ($ million)	Average annual % increase (past 5 years)
7,953	−8.9	8,251	−4.4	498	−14.8	262	−21.4	5,645	−0.3
1,787	1.9	1,080	5.4	91	−9.0	20	−2.8	603	19.3
88	11.3	397	13.2	11	11.3	16	25.0	221	16.1
1,790	21.8	1,809	11.3	52	−9.4	114	12.0	1,277	9.3
795	−1.5	527	−13.3	10	−23.7	20	−3.7	423	−8.1
496	6.6	1,257	13.3	114	68.6	73	5.1	563	18.2
1,211	−9.2	878	2.8	28	0.8	45	−1.7	87	−14.9
876	7.2	875	7.6	92	3.6	37	18.2	427	13.8
3,348	10.7	1,917	−2.1	65	−3.0	107	16.6	1,164	5.0
1,339	7.7	1,831	2.1	76	−5.0	190	12.2	898	14.3
351	1.5	442	−3.6	28	12.5	25	28.1	203	0.3
282	3.8	287	−8.3	3	−5.4	13	−1.1	97	6.9
662	18.0	676	10.7	12	−11.2	47	27.8	241	17.2
2,312	3.0	3,962	−1.5	511	31.4	67	4.7	2,237	6.7
166	−13.3	485	−11.2	26	19.0	20	10.2	177	0.8
8,823	−11.9	5,650	−17.1	450	−22.2	217	−35.0	3,155	−17.2
589	13.0	1,087	6.0	55	30.4	21	9.2	617	0.6
176	−13.4	180	−6.5	25	72.7	10	−9.7	93	2.6
19,713	3.2	12,781	−6.9	1,229	−13.6	1,338	−1.0	4,657	−6.5
379	−1.0	1,003	3.6	42	5.9	110	3.5	354	−1.8
1,730	−3.1	2,853	−4.3	189	−4.4	46	9.6	1,951	−2.2
453	5.7	332	−1.5	5	−7.6	17	28.0	129	−1.4
1,532	33.1	1,548	38.7	115	4.6	53	0.0	848	11.0
688	−9.9	591	−10.6	35	9.9	40	4.9	226	−1.5
1,001	−5.2	1,160	−3.6	68	−11.8	43	−9.3	338	−4.3
58,540		51,859		3,830		2,951		26,631	
89,706	6.2	85,686	10.2	56,094	10.1	5,496	18.1	9,104	18.9
217,291	0.7	387,075	11.3	—	—	85,457	21.4	79,520	16.1
306,997		472,761		56,094		90,953		88,624	
7,477	−0.2	5,067	0.8	935	−3.2	376	0.7	1,561	7.8
657	−5.2	685	9.8	123	3.3	32	18.6	88	9.5
24,551	5.6	16,390	−5.3	4,029	8.4	1,063	9.0	3,648	13.7
4,226	−2.7	3,132	−1.5	641	−7.9	296	20.6	674	4.9
5,174	15.1	4,077	−7.1	1,450	−8.5	428	9.6	933	6.3
2,940	11.0	2,074	3.5	661	−6.2	301	21.4	486	7.9
16,579	−5.2	12,899	2.2	8,272	6.7	771	14.4	1,766	2.7
234	−4.2	579	−0.4	70	25.7	29	7.5	93	−0.1
2,505	−5.7	2,089	−8.9	473	−16.1	165	−12.7	368	−11.6
1,355	10.4	1,066	6.3	110	11.4	34	14.8	236	21.0
8,412	−14.5	8,475	−6.4	3,503	−5.5	529	−6.0	2,053	2.1
19,688		17,400		6,210		1,455		3,928	
74,110		56,533		20,267		4,024		11,906	
1,213	9.0	1,137	7.2	485	11.1	117	34.2	167	18.2
789	4.2	1,186	8.5	570	21.1	37	11.9	106	8.7
1,471	7.4	1,106	−5.0	440	1.7	50	1.2	160	5.8
925	6.0	890	5.9	400	7.6	78	20.9	104	17.3
315	−5.9	544	−7.6	3	−39.9	10	17.4	166	20.7
4,713		4,863		1,898		292		703	

	Population				GDP[1]		National Income[10]		Average Hourly Wage[11]	
	Total 1986 (million)	Past 5-year constant compound % increase	Working age 1986 (million)	Past 5-year constant compound % increase	Total 1986 ($ billion)	Past 5-year constant compound % increase	Total 1985 ($ billion)	Per capita 1986 ($)	1985 ($)	Past 5-year constant compound % increase
CARIBBEAN AND OTHERS										
Barbados	0.3	0.3	0.2	0.0	1.2	1.0	—	—	—	—
Cuba	10.1	0.6	6.8	2.8	15.3[5]	—	—	—	1.16	—
Dominican Republic	6.4	2.3	3.6	0.9	5.1	1.0	9.8[4]	1,485	—	—
Guyana	1.0	2.0	0.6	4.9	0.5	−4.8	0.4	444	—	—
Haiti	6.8	2.5	3.6	2.8	0.5	0.7	2.2[6]	150	—	—
Jamaica	2.4	1.5	1.4	1.5	2.1[5]	0.0	1.8	783	—	—
Netherlands Antilles	0.3	—	—	—	—	—	—	—	6.87	—
Panama	2.2	2.2	1.3	2.7	4.8	2.5	4.4	2,095	—	—
Puerto Rico	4.3	1.5	2.2	2.8	15.8	2.6	13.8[6]	3,209	5.18	4.2
Trinidad and Tobago	1.2	1.6	0.7	1.5	4.8	−4.9	4.5	4,091	—	—
TOTAL CARIBBEAN AND OTHERS[1]	34.9		20.3		50.1		36.9			
TOTAL LATIN AMERICA	415.5		237.0		685.3		631.1			
ASIA										
Afghanistan	17.2	0.6	9.3	0.6	—	—	—	—	—	—
Bangladesh	103.9	2.7	53.1	2.2	15.5	3.3	—	—	0.13[4]	—
Burma	37.9	1.9	22.0	1.8	8.0	4.7	7.5[6]	198	—	—
China	1,072.2	1.2	696.5	2.4	263.4	8.2	241.9[6]	226	0.15	—
Hong Kong	5.6	1.9	3.9	1.6	37.4	5.7	34.1	6,200	1.41	11.0
India	772.7	1.9	454.5	2.7	185.9	5.2	158.8[4]	215	—	—
Indonesia	169.5	2.0	97.7	2.2	73.3	2.9	77.9	460	—	—
Japan	121.4	0.7	82.3	0.5	1,576.6	3.7	1,357.6	11,248	7.52	3.7
Dem. Kampuchea	7.5	2.6	4.8	2.5	—	—	—	—	—	—
Korea, North	20.9	2.5	12.0	3.2	—	—	—	—	—	—
Korea, South	42.6	1.9	27.2	2.0	77.7	8.4	73.7[4]	1,793	1.31	1.7
Laos	4.2	2.2	2.3	1.4	0.5	—	—	—	—	—
Malaysia	15.9	2.5	9.3	2.7	28.1	4.0	25.6[6]	1,610	—	—
Nepal	16.9	2.3	9.1	2.7	2.3	3.5	1.8	109	—	—
Pakistan	102.9	3.1	55.0	3.4	33.4	6.5	33.4[6]	325	—	—
Philippines	55.8	2.4	31.3	1.6	30.4	−1.5	26.4[6]	473	0.47	—
Singapore	2.6	1.2	1.7	0.0	17.3	4.5	—	—	1.65	9.1
Sri Lanka	16.5	1.8	10.0	1.4	6.4	4.7	5.8[4]	360	0.19	4.9
Taiwan	19.6	1.4	—	—	70.5	6.8	53.1[4]	2,780	2.18	6.5
Thailand	52.3	2.0	31.4	2.9	42.4	4.7	263.8[6]	5,044	—	—
Vietnam	60.9	2.0	34.5	3.0	—	5.4	—	—	—	—
TOTAL ASIA[1]	2,718.9		1,648.0		2,469.1		2,361.4			
OCEANIA										
Australia	15.9	1.3	10.5	2.1	162.0	3.1	140.7	9,019	6.69	−2.9
New Zealand	3.3	0.9	2.2	0.0	22.1[5]	1.9	19.5	5,909	4.27	−5.2
TOTAL OCEANIA	19.2		12.7		184.1		160.2			

*Member of Andean Common Market (Ancom).

Footnotes: (1) Total of available data; (2) 1982; (3) 1983; (4) 1984; (5) 1985; (6) 1986; (7) including Namibia; (8) includes Luxembourg; (9) Net Material Product; (10) Business International estimate; (11) See text on currency conversion.

Total Exports		Total Imports		Imports from U.S.		Imports from Japan		Imports from EEC	
1986 f.o.b. ($ million)	Average annual % increase (past 5 years)	1986 c.i.f. ($ million)	Average annual % increase (past 5 years)	1986 c.i.f. ($ million)	Average annual % increase (past 5 years)	1986 c.i.f. ($ million)	Average annual % increase (past 5 years)	1986 c.i.f. ($ million)	Average annual % increase (past 5 years)
280	3.7	572	1.3	235	7.4	33	18.2	120	11.0
875	−8.7	2,543	17.6	1	0.0	326	35.4	741	17.8
212	−18.4	861	−10.5	12	−24.6	128	22.1	154	19.4
242	6.5	231	−4.2	52	1.7	19	67.7	47	2.3
163	0.0	654	29.9	426	7.4	30	2.3	76	9.8
583	−4.1	969	−7.5	491	−0.6	36	2.6	119	−3.7
1,434	−17.8	1,732	−25.9	437	−10.0	53	−7.2	308	−7.7
576	16.4	4,685	66.0	783	10.8	546	61.0	665	105.6
11,202	8.6	10,182	7.5	6,172	3.8	—	—	—	—
1,372	−16.9	1,332	−22.2	571	−14.5	142	−12.9	280	−15.2
16,939		23,761		9,180		1,313		2,510	
95,762		85,157		31,345		5,629		15,119	
636	−2.7	1,026	16.8	8	9.5	130	6.5	73	0.1
889	4.7	2,502	6.4	212	6.5	348	7.7	412	4.4
506	14.1	304	4.8	17	−8.7	234	−1.0	112	−13.2
31,366	9.5	43,503	25.1	4,718	7.6	12,463	39.9	7,757	44.4
35,420	17.6	35,360	14.0	2,980	4.6	7,228	9.0	4,059	9.8
10,317	8.1	18,830	12.7	1,690	−0.4	2,331	13.3	6,251	11.0
14,824	−1.6	10,724	−9.9	1,482	−5.8	3,128	−7.4	1,838	−10.3
210,804	11.3	127,660	−0.6	29,410	5.2	—	—	14,173	18.6
—	—	—	—	—	—	—	—	—	—
684	3.3	820	−5.6	0	—	204	−11.3	81	−4.1
35,624	13.3	33,335	8.3	6,735	3.1	10,999	20.7	3,584	20.5
14	−6.9	70	−2.4	0	—	14	30.5	6	1.5
18,382	11.7	10,819	−2.9	2,034	—	2,221	−6.2	1,585	1.7
144	19.4	316	−10.9	8	20.8	73	9.0	43	11.3
3,383	11.3	5,367	0.1	705	9.2	874	5.5	1,450	9.0
4,787	−0.6	5,213	−10.6	1,293	−8.4	887	−12.2	571	−6.9
22,490	2.2	25,506	−2.4	3,819	1.6	5,078	0.7	2,971	0.6
1,163	4.8	1,829	−2.0	118	4.0	319	4.9	284	−0.4
39,785	17.3	24,175	7.4	5,415	4.8	8,244	15.6	—	—
8,776	6.9	9,303	2.7	1,278	7.1	2,440	4.7	1,479	12.5
320	14.6	629	2.0	33	2.9	209	20.6	63	−5.3
440,314		357,291		61,955		57,424		46,792	
22,541	0.9	26,211	1.3	5,235	0.8	5,348	3.5	5,850	4.9
5,930	1.7	5,997	1.3	1,050	4.3	1,264	5.2	1,355	6.8
28,471		32,208		6,285		6,612		7,205	

	Private Consumption Expenditure					Passenger Cars		Trucks and Buses		Telephone Access Lines
	1985 total ($ billions)	Average annual % real increase (past 5 years)	1985 % for food	1985 % for clothing	1985 % for house-hold	1986 (thousands)	Cumula-tive % increase (past 5 years)	1986 (thousands)	Cumula-tive % increase (past 5 years)	1984 (thousands)
WESTERN EUROPE										
EC										
Belgium	60.7	0.5	21.6	7.4	10.1	3,494	3.0	366	3.1	2,818
Denmark	37.5	2.9	23.9	5.9	7.0	1,501	9.4	267	9.4	2,458
France	392.6	1.8	20.8	6.3	8.3	20,940	3.2	3,426	27.4	31,483
Germany	423.3	0.9	22.6	8.6	8.9	26,099	5.1	1,723	4.6	23,630
Greece	20.3	2.3	42.2	9.0	8.1	1,264	26.5	621	17.8	2,714
Ireland	12.2	−2.1	45.0[4]	6.2[4]	6.0[4]	710	0.1	102	36.0	613
Italy	253.6	1.0	29.2	6.6	—	21,500	13.1	1,824	12.9	15,601
Luxembourg	2.4	1.1	24.7	7.0	9.8	—	—	—	—	142
Netherlands	88.3	0.2	19.1	6.7	7.2	4,901	5.9	428	10.3	5,462
Portugal	15.2	—	—	—	—	1,185	4.7	356	−7.0	1,248
Spain	116.7	0.5	29.4	7.6	7.4	9,274	11.0	1,610	6.9	8,457
United Kingdom	305.9	2.6	18.9	7.0	6.6	19,349	20.4	2,753	52.4	20,200
TOTAL EC[1]	1,728.7					110,217		13,476		114,826
EFTA										
Austria	44.8	2.1	23.5	11.0	7.2	2,531	4.4	258	17.8	7,548
Finland	33.2	3.2	25.3	5.0	6.5	1,546	14.3	200	10.5	4,870
Iceland	1.6	—	19.4	19.5	13.3	103	19.8	13	30.0	99
Norway	31.9	3.6	24.6	7.3	7.6	1,514	13.2	250	38.1	1,554
Sweden	58.1	0.9	23.8	7.3	6.3	3,151	7.3	231	11.6	5,017
Switzerland	67.9	1.2	27.5	4.5	5.1	2,617	4.0	211	14.7	3,095
TOTAL EFTA	237.5					11,462		1,163		22,183
Turkey	—	—	—	—	—	984	20.1	553	13.1	1,673
Yugoslavia	19.0	—	—	—	—	2,849	—	299	—	2,091
TOTAL WESTERN EUROPE[1]	1,985.2					125,512		15,491		140,773
EASTERN EUROPE										
Bulgaria	—	—	—	—	—	1,030	88.3	150	12.8	—
Czechoslovakia	—	—	—	—	—	2,695	9.6	425	8.7	1,772
East Germany	—	—	—	—	—	3,306	19.6	417	−25.4	16,701
Hungary	—	—	—	—	—	1,436	25.0	223	43.1	658
Poland	—	—	—	—	—	3,671	37.4	863	15.9	2,217
Romania	—	—	—	—	—	250	0.0	150	12.8	—
USSR	—	—	—	—	—	11,000	11.9	9,000	7.0	—
TOTAL EASTERN EUROPE[1]						23,388		11,228		21,348
MIDDLE EAST										
Bahrain	1.5[3]	—	—	—	—	70	—	26	30.0	56
Egypt	—	—	—	—	—	426	−1.8	244	37.1	—
Iran	96.5[4]	6.1	43.8[4]	9.7[4]	6.4[4]	1,589	43.3	539	18.2	1,202
Iraq	—	—	—	—	—	258	0.8	273	−1.4	323
Israel	11.0	1.8	28.9	4.1	2.6	636	23.5	128	13.3	1,103
Jordan	3.9	—	—	—	—	136	34.7	64	18.5	—
Kuwait	9.1	—	—	—	—	555	18.3	204	2.5	232
Libya	—	—	—	—	—	415	0.0	320	−4.2	—
Oman	3.4	—	—	—	—	109	—	166	159.4	—
Qatar	—	—	—	—	—	78	—	65	—	67
Saudi Arabia	40.4[2]	—	—	—	—	1,300	21.7	1,450	8.3	891
Syria	12.5	−3.4	—	—	—	95	25.0	190	150.0	81
United Arab Emirates	6.9	3.6	—	—	—	240	—	143	57.1	181
North Yemen	3.1	—	—	—	—	20	11.1	61	19.6	—
TOTAL MIDDLE EAST[1]	188.3					5,927		3,873		4,136

Televisions 1987 (thousands)	Televisions Cumulative % increase (past 5 years)	Computers 1986 (thousands)	Steel 1986 (K MT)	Steel Average annual % increase (past 5 years)	Cement 1986 (K MT)	Cement Cumulative % increase (past 5 years)	Electricity 1985 (M KWH)	Electricity Cumulative % increase (past 5 years)	Energy kg per capita 1984 oil equivalent
3,040	1.7	213	3,568	−7.3	5,760	−9.3	56.36	11.3	3,499
1,952	3.4	118	1,796	1.5	2.028	15.0	29.06	59.7	3,734
17,950	4.8	1,046	14,541	−4.0	22,584	−13.6	326.40	25.2	2,809
22,908	4.4	1,527	30,508	2.4	26,460	−11.8	406.71	10.3	4,024
1,725	1.1	—	1,721	1.0	12,828	−2.9	27.74	29.6	1,632
918	34.2	—	365	−5.6	1,248	−23.0	11.74	7.6	2,159
14,521	6.2	708	22,508	1.9	37,152 [5]	−11.7	182.24	5.2	2,303
91	0.0	—	—	—	—	—	0.50	−58.5	8,072
4,633	5.0	256	4,019	3.9	3,096	−0.4	62.94	−1.8	4,027
1,530	0.6	—	1,227	−4.9	5,412	−8.0	19.01	18.6	911
9,920	0.1	222	8,925	2.0	21,924	−25.9	125.56	13.4	1,528
18,716	−1.0	1,402	14,350	−0.7	13,416	3.5	294.77	6.1	3,439
97,904		5,492	103,528		151,908		1,543.03		
2,600	−17.9	119	2,523	1.2	4,548	−9.3	43.92	2.4	2,768
1,792	3.9	90	1,844	−2.7	1,260	−30.0	47.10	20.0	3,664
64	2.0	—	—	—	—	—	4.04	25.2	3,539
1,369	4.1	98	1,562	0.0	1,752	2.8	103.19	10.3	4,555
3,266	1.2	211	3,537	0.4	2,388 [4]	−5.2	136.54	36.6	3,472
2,216	5.7	216	2,431	5.3	4,368	0.5	53.87	12.3	2,664
11,307		734	11,897		14,316		388.67		
5,010	2.2	—	5,366	7.7	20,016	27.3	33.31	33.5	646
4,000	−17.5	—	5,565	1.7	9,120	−6.1	73.94	23.1	1,764
118,221		6,226	126,356		195,360		2,038.95		
2,100	6.3	—	2,950	−1.6	5,724	1.9	41.63	12.6	4,004
4,366	0.5	—	11,157	−0.1	10,296	−0.2	80.63	8.9	4,362
5,985	0.3	—	8,932	−2.4	11,988	2.3	113.83	15.2	5,454
3,500	28.8	—	3,499	−1.3	3,864	−11.5	26.78	−1.5	2,724
9,467	13.5	—	15,997	2.7	15,828	−1.3	137.71	19.7	3,245
3,910	0.3	—	11,471	−0.6	11,196 [5]	−24.1	75.27	9.6	3,345
90,000	15.6	—	165,122	2.4	135,108	9.0	1,544.0	16.5	4,292
119,328			219,128		194,004		2,019.85		
135	13.3	—	59	−10.5	—	—	2.13	—	8,956
2,010	−59.9	—	2,452	0.1	5,364 [5]	56.3	23.23	21.2	463
2,100	0.0	—	3,817	−3.9	—	—	37.30	97.9	876
605	−5.9	—	605	−12.0	—	—	18.76	112.1	454
620	3.1	—	804	11.4	1,884 [4]	−9.8	15.70	13.5	1,704
240	−17.9	—	194	−15.4	1,800	127.3	2.47	109.3	660
450	−28.0	—	328	−14.6	—	—	15.69	57.7	4,993
235	46.8	—	506	11.9	—	—	8.17	136.3	2,475
400	962.0	—	208	−2.5	—	—	2.85	—	5,807
150	43.9	—	132	39.2	—	—	3.52	—	14,600
3,700	60.0	—	2,830	−16.7	—	—	32.41	216.8	2,524
400	−25.0	—	241	−4.5	4,356	62.8	7.32	54.3	860
145	39.8	—	—	—	—	—	6.69	—	5,092
44	660.7	—	—	—	—	—	0.30	15.0	131
11,234			12,176		13,404		176.52		

	Private Consumption Expenditure					Passenger Cars		Trucks and Buses		Telephone Access Lines
	1985 total ($ billions)	Average annual % real increase (past 5 years)	1985 % for food	1985 % for clothing	1985 % for household	1986 (thousands)	Cumulative % increase (past 5 years)	1986 (thousands)	Cumulative % increase (past 5 years)	1984 (thousands)
AFRICA										
Algeria	—	—	—	—	—	589	2.6	377	46.7	444
Angola	—	—	—	—	—	126	−10.0	42	−4.5	—
Burkina Faso	0.7[4]	—	—	—	—	11	−15.4	13	0.0	—
Cameroon	5.3[3]	—	—	—	—	85	21.4	74	39.6	—
Congo	0.8[4]	—	—	—	—	26	18.2	20	25.0	—
Ethiopia	—	—	—	—	—	41	0.0	19	58.3	—
Gabon	—	—	—	—	—	—	—	—	—	2
Ghana	3.5	0.9	—	—	—	59	−9.2	46	−8.0	38
Ivory Coast	4.7	—	—	—	—	161	20.1	89	11.3	—
Kenya	0.2	3.4	—	—	—	126	−3.1	133	13.7	96
Madagascar	1.9	1.5	—	—	—	49	−9.3	44	−8.3	—
Malawi	0.7[4]	—	—	—	—	15	7.1	15	7.1	—
Mauritius	0.8	3.7	—	—	—	31	24.0	12	−20.0	38
Morocco	8.8	—	—	—	—	446	5.2	199	10.6	201
Mozambique	—	—	—	—	—	87	−10.3	24	0.0	—
Nigeria	41.8[3]	—	—	—	—	786	23.6	619	8.0	—
Senegal	2.4	2.3	—	—	—	62	5.1	37	8.8	—
Sierra Leone	0.9[9]	—	—	—	—	19	−20.8	10	−9.1	—
South Africa	25.4	0.8	33.6	7.7	9.7	2,912	18.9	1,216	18.2	2,120
Tanzania	—	—	—	—	—	42	—	51	0.0	—
Tunisia	5.8	4.2	—	—	—	175	32.6	179	35.6	152
Uganda	—	—	—	—	—	32	0.0	13	0.0	—
Zaire	—	—	—	—	—	94	0.0	86	0.0	—
Zambia	0.7	3.1	—	—	—	98	−3.9	68	3.0	43
Zimbabwe	2.9	−4.2	35.1	12.1	7.3	176	−0.6	80	8.1	104
TOTAL AFRICA[1]	107.3					6,248		3,466		3,238
NORTH AMERICA										
Canada	194.0	2.5	17.8	6.3	8.7	11,118	5.2	3,149	−4.4	10,468
United States	2,584.3	3.6	14.7	11.7	6.1	132,108	5.8	39,583	11.0	106,239
TOTAL NORTH AMERICA	2,778.3					143,226		42,732		116,707
LATIN AMERICA										
LAIA										
Argentina	19.1[3]	—	—	—	—	3,832	11.7	1,427	8.1	2,523
*Bolivia	3.0	−1.8	—	—	—	33	−2.9	47	−2.1	158
Brazil	90.1	—	—	—	—	10,027	18.0	2,214	7.7	6,325
Chile	—	—	—	—	—	496	−1.2	241	3.4	484
*Colombia	15.7[4]	1.6	36.8[3]	6.0[3]	5.3[3]	591	−27.4	599	201.0	1,384
*Ecuador	7.7	1.0	38.6	11.4	7	77	0.0	178	2.3	296
Mexico	90.7[4]	−0.5	—	—	—	5,157	12.3	2,254	18.8	3,223
Paraguay	4.4	2.4	—	—	—	61	69.4	30	7.1	84
*Peru	11.0[4]	−2.8	—	—	—	385	4.1	209	7.2	361
Uruguay	3.0	−6.1	—	—	—	166	−4.6	83	−5.7	244
*Venezuela	31.0	—	52.4	4.6	6.2	1,564	6.6	916	8.8	1,514
*Ancom Subtotal[1]	68.4					2,650		1,949		3,713
TOTAL LAIA[1]	275.7					22,389		8,198		16,596
CACM										
Costa Rica	2.2	1.9	—	—	—	79	−2.5	66	8.2	—
El Salvador	2.3	−0.3	—	—	—	53	0.0	65	0.0	75
Guatemala	9.3	−1.0	—	—	—	97	2.1	94	0.0	106
Honduras	2.5	1.1	—	—	—	27	0.0	50	2.0	34
Nicaragua	—	—	—	—	—	32	−8.6	28	−6.7	—
TOTAL CACM	16.3					288		303		215

Televisions		Computers	Steel		Cement		Electricity		Energy
1987 (thousands)	Cumulative % increase (past 5 years)	1986 (thousands)	1986 (K MT)	Average annual % increase (past 5 years)	1986 (K MT)	Cumulative % increase (past 5 years)	1985 (M KWH)	Cumulative % increase (past 5 years)	kg per capita 1984 oil equivalent
1,540	8.7	—	1,969	−6.5	4,500 [4]	—	12.27	81.6	537
32	48.9	—	—	—	—	—	1,79	16.1	85
41	131.3	—	—	—	—	—	0.12	—	20
2	—	—	—	—	—	—	2.24	55.8	313
5	0.0	—	—	—	—	—	0.24	81.3	67
40	−13.9	—	—	—	—	—	0.83	20.0	12
37	95.2	—	—	—	—	—	0.54	20.0	814
140	157.3	—	—	—	—	—	3.04	−30.3	63
550	77.2	—	—	—	—	—	1.79	−0.7	—
192	190.8	—	223	3.3	1,116 [5]	−22.8	2.49	56.7	58
96	675.0	—	—	—	36	0.0	0.45	5.8	28
—	—	—	—	—	70	16.7	0.51	35.3	26
110	31.3	—	—	—	—	—	0.10	−71.4	202
1,099	8.0	—	527	−6.3	3,636 [5]	−1.9	6.95	48.2	229
20	375.0	—	—	—	—	—	1.95	−71.8	63
500	10.9	—	1,932	−6.7	3,600 [4]	—	9.00	66.7	159
55	9.8	—	—	—	408 [5]	8.1	0.70	3.2	117
25	17.0	—	—	—	—	—	0.28	13.2	51
2,500	23.8	—	5,302	−3.1	6,252	−24.8	122.29	7.1	2,147
8	−25.0	—	49	−10.4	372 [5]	−6.0	0.88	—	—
400	0.0	—	445	−5.8	2,964	61.4	4.02	50.0	532
90	23.0	—	—	—	—	—	0.65	—	18
15	19.2	—	22	12.0	—	—	4.62	—	45
66	−90.6	—	28	34.4	204 [5]	41.7	10.09	—	226
112	16.4	—	415	27.6	612 [5]	4.1	4.34	−3.7	307
7,675			10,912		23,770		192.16		
15,300	12.0	1,045	12,539	7.9	10,272	26.4	460.41	21.6	6,937
145,037	2.5	12,350	94,872	3.8	71,112	22.6	2,525.19	6.6	6,694
101,220		13,395	107,411		81,384		2,985.60		
5,925	0.2	—	2,517	−0.5	4,692 [5]	−32.1	45.27	28.3	1,192
300	−28.1	—	41	−0.5	—	—	1.73	11.9	214
36,000	70.7	—	14,477	9.6	20,616 [5]	−17.1	192.95	33.7	484
2,000	−30.5	—	632	19.0	1,440	27.7	13.89	16.9	623
3,800	138.7	—	1,330	5.7	5,736	25.5	26.80	24.9	588
600	41.7	—	369	14.0	—	—	4.49	35.4	447
9,490	32.1	—	6,694	−3.7	19,500	0.4	93.41	27.8	1,174
231	227.1	—	—	—	—	—	1.54	74.6	178
1,701	118.0	—	550	7.6	—	—	12.12	19.6	414
500	17.0	—	—	—	—	—	6.60	81.9	424
2,750	46.7	—	2,746	3.6	—	—	45.40	16.7	2,205
9,151			5,036		5,736		90.53		3,868
63,297			29,356		51,984		444,18		7,943
470	5.6	—	163	30.3	—	—	2.83	22.3	340
400	41.7	—	70	9.4	—	—	1.70	5.5	121
300	57.9	—	130	0.6	—	—	1.76	−9.1	139
90	−42.3	—	84	32.5	—	—	1.07	27.6	154
171	27.7	—	—	—	—	—	1.06	5.8	7,553
1,431			447		—		8.40		

	Private Consumption Expenditure					Passenger Cars		Trucks and Buses		Telephone Access Lines
	1985 total ($ billions)	Average annual % real increase (past 5 years)	1985 % for food	1985 % for clothing	1985 % for household	1986 (thousands)	Cumulative % increase (past 5 years)	1986 (thousands)	Cumulative % increase (past 5 years)	1984 (thousands)
CARIBBEAN AND OTHERS										
Barbados	0.7	—	—	—	—	35	29.6	7	16.7	51
Cuba	—	—	—	—	—	—	—	—	—	265
Dominican Republic	7.8⁴	0.6	—	—	—	106	3.9	6.5	1.6	136
Guyana	—	—	—	—	—	29	−6.5	12	0.0	—
Haiti	—	—	—	—	—	31	14.8	17	41.7	—
Jamaica	1.4	3.4	50.7	4.3	6.9	107	0.0	30	3.4	—
Netherlands Antilles	—	—	—	—	—	66	13.8	14	27.3	45
Panama	3.1	7.5	—	—	—	144	26.3	65	41.3	156
Puerto Rico	15.5	3.8	28.3	8.3	6.2	1,102	12.9	192	2.1	493
Trinidad & Tobago	2.6⁴	−4.9	—	—	—	242	46.7	79	51.9	66
TOTAL CARIBBEAN¹	31.1					1,862		481		1,212
TOTAL LATIN AMERICA¹	323.1					24,539		8,982		18,023
ASIA										
Afghanistan	—	—	—	—	—	32	−3.0	25	−7.4	—
Bangladesh	13.6	2.8	—	—	—	47	0.0	34	6.3	—
Burma	—	—	—	—	—	28	−6.7	43	−2.3	—
China	—	—	—	—	—	182	160.0	1,830	103.3	—
Hong Kong	22.2	6.4	19.5	19.0	12.0	186	−20.2	87	−2.2	1,554
India	133.9	4.1	57.0	10.1	4.2	1,128	24.4	1,189	32.0	2,667
Indonesia	48.5	5.1	—	—	—	956	30.8	1,040	27.8	503
Japan	919.8	3.2	22.1	6.3	5.5	27,845	9.0	18,313	15.9	44,967
Dem. Kampuchea	—	—	—	—	—	—	—	—	—	—
Korea, North	—	—	—	—	—	—	—	—	—	—
Korea, South	89.2	5.7	44.2	6.7	4.6	557	82.0	557	63.3	4,810
Laos	—	—	—	—	—	—	—	—	—	—
Malaysia	16.6	3.4	—	—	—	1,124	30.4	324	62.8	700
Nepal	1.6	—	—	—	—	—	—	—	—	—
Pakistan	26.4	5.7	—	—	—	392	11.0	270	35.0	409
Philippines	25.5	0.1	56.0	65.0	13.9	360	4.3	521	−0.6	379
Singapore	8.3	3.9	29.2	9.0	11.5	240	23.7	140	29.6	680
Sri Lanka	4.3	—	54.4	6.8	4.5	149	10.4	132	20.0	80
Taiwan	—	—	—	—	—	916	54.7	429	28.4	3,577
Thailand	25.7	4.7	45.4	11.8	6.6	485	12.3	702	34.0	479
Vietnam	—	—	—	—	—	—	—	—	—	—
TOTAL ASIA¹	1,335.6					34,627		25,636		60,805
OCEANIA										
Australia	96.2	2.5	22.6	6.2	6.7	6,842	8.7	2,137	28.7	6,187
New Zealand	13.1	—	—	—	—	1,500	9.0	302	7.9	1,189
TOTAL OCEANIA¹	109.3					8,342		2,439		7,376

*Member of Andean Common Market (Ancom).

Footnotes: (1) Total of available data; (2) 1982; (3) 1983; (4) 1984; (5) 1985; (6) 1986; (7) including Namibia; (8) includes Luxembourg; (9) Net Material Product; (10) Business International estimate; (11) See text on currency conversion.

Televisions		Computers	Steel		Cement		Electricity		Energy
1987 (thousands)	Cumulative % increase (past 5 years)	1986 (thousands)	1986 (K MT)	Average annual % increase (past 5 years)	1986 (K MT)	Cumulative % increase (past 5 years)	1985 (M KWH)	Cumulative % increase (past 5 years)	kg per capita 1984 oil equivalent
60	11.4	—	—	—	—	—	0.36	13.7	968
1,525	2.1	—	1,183	8.2	3,312	4.5	12.20	18.1	1,000
500	35.3	—	123	2.9	—	—	4.02	14.6	333
—	—	—	—	—	—	—	0.39	−14.2	487
25	−76.9	—	—	—	—	—	0.38	4.2	36
350	92.7	—	—	—	240 [5]	55.6	2.40	2.5	822
60	6.6	—	—	—	—	—	2.40	31.9	7,553
300	31.3	—	—	—	—	—	2.57	35.3	463
820	0.8	—	—	—	1,028	12.5	12.32	−8.3	1,722
345	47.5	—	110	13.8	324 [5]	122.0	3.04	54.1	3,535
3,985		—	1,416		4,904		40.07		
68,713			31,219		56,888		492.64		
20	67.3	—	—	—	—	—	1.06	7.7	72
302	23.0	—	439	21.4	288	4.3	4.87	73.4	40
64	125.0	—	—	—	432 [5]	−36.3	1.76	19.0	62
9,950	0.6	—	75,716	16.8	161,364	78.1	410.70	34.0	485
1,312	3.3	34	2,388	4.4	2,232	55.0	19.24	63.0	1,169
5,000	172.6	450	14,784	1.4	25,896 [5]	24.7	188.48	55.5	178
4,900	78.8	—	2,838	3.1	10,104 [5]	80.3	12.90	80.7	179
30,250	0.2	5,750	69,941	0.4	71,265	−10.0	673.41	29.0	2,600
7	−107.8	—	—	—	—	—	0.08	−41.7	2
175	—	—	—	—	—	—	48.00	31.0	1,877
10,100	40.0	258	11,600	11.1	23,400	30.8	62.72	55.8	1,130
31	4.2	—	—	—	—	—	1.35	31.5	26
1,505	55.5	—	2,146	−2.2	3,216	11.3	14.92	56.3	1,103
18	—	—	—	—	—	—	0.41	85.5	12
1,850	105.1	—	1,064	−10.3	4,980	34.7	25.73	50.0	175
3,997	374.6	—	1,237	0.0	3,075 [5]	−30.5	21.02	31.8	203
485	3.4	—	1,937	−6.1	—	—	9.88	32.7	5,385
350	732.8	—	—	—	556	2.4	2.46	31.8	77
6,085	20.3	18	7,840	11.7	—	—	—	—	—
3,300	12.5	—	2,135	−0.9	7,920 [5]	−44.8	24.18	61.4	292
5,000	152.8	—	—	—	—	—	5.00	—	82
84,701		6,573	194,065		314,728		1,528.15		
6,000	2.0	725	5,925	1.5	6,012	4.4	118.97	15.3	4,591
931	−1.7	—	607	−6.2	900	15.4	26.76	17.9	2,402
6,931		725	6,532		6,912		145.73		

The International Political and Legal Environment

THE INTERNATIONAL MARKETPLACE

Software Piracy in China   *U.S. business executives consider China to be the "worst violator of intellectual property rights" in the world. Piracy of America's computer software, they say, has cost them between $100 million and $400 million per year in lost revenue.*

Piracy apparently became rampant in China beginning in 1988. U.S. Commerce Department officials charged that China was engaged in a sophisticated type of software copying that required concerted efforts by Chinese engineers, who had to break complex codes designed to protect the software. The officials said that the copying, therefore, must have required decisions at a high level in the Chinese ministries, research institutes, and state-run corporations that use U.S. software. Some of the pirated software is even being offered through catalogs prepared by Chinese corporations.

U.S. Ambassador Winston Lord said that the unauthorized copying of American software by Chinese engineers was an acute issue in U.S. relations with China. "It has come to the top of our agenda among economic questions." The piracy of what is called intellectual property—not just software but also other patented and trademarked items—was important enough for President Bush to raise it when he met with Chinese Premier Li Peng in early 1989.

Source: Daniel Southerland, "U.S. Businesses Urge Trade Sanctions to Stop Piracy of Software in China," *The Washington Post*, April 11, 1989, E7.

Much as most managers would like to ignore them, political and legal factors often play a critical role in international marketing activities. Even the best business plans can go awry as a result of unexpected political or legal influences, and the failure to anticipate these factors can be the undoing of an otherwise successful business venture.

Of course, a single international political and legal environment does not exist. The business executive must be aware of political and legal factors on a variety of planes. For example, while it is useful to understand the complexities of the host-country legal system, such knowledge does not protect against a home-country-imposed export embargo.

The study of the international political and legal environment must therefore be broken down into several subsegments. Many researchers do this by separating the legal from the political. This separation—although perhaps analytically useful—is somewhat artificial, because laws generally are the result of political decisions. Here no attempt will be made to separate legal and political factors, except when such a separation is essential.

Instead, this chapter will examine the political-legal environment from the manager's point of view. In making decisions about his or her firm's international marketing activities, the manager will need to concentrate on three areas: the political and legal circumstances of the home country; those of the host country; and the bilateral and multilateral agreements, treaties, and laws governing the relations between host and home countries.

HOME COUNTRY POLITICAL AND LEGAL ENVIRONMENT

No manager can afford to ignore the policies and regulations of the country from which he conducts international marketing transactions. Wherever a firm is located, it will be affected by government policies and the legal system.

Many of these laws and regulations may not be designed specifically to address international marketing issues, yet they can have a major impact on a firm's opportunities abroad. Minimum wage legislation, for example, affects the international competitiveness of a firm using production processes that are highly labor intensive. The cost of domestic safety regulations may significantly affect the pricing policies of firms in their international marketing efforts. For example, U.S. legislation that created the **Environmental Superfund** requires payment by chemical firms based on their production volume, regardless of whether the production is sold domestically or exported. As a result, these firms are at a disadvantage internationally when exporting their commodity-type products, because they must compete against foreign firms that are not required to make such a payment in their home countries and therefore have a cost advantage.

Other legal and regulatory measures, however, are clearly aimed at international marketing activities. Some may be designed to help firms in their international efforts. The lack of enforcement of others may hurt the international marketer. For example, as The International Marketplace 4.1 shows, the U.S. government is quite concerned about lacking safeguards of intellectual property rights in China. Not only may counterfeiting result in inferior products and damage to the reputation of a company, but it also reduces the chances of an innovative firm to recoup its investment in research and development and spawn new products.

Violations of intellectual property rights can occur anywhere, however. As an example, in 1988 Anheuser-Busch agreed with Czechoslovak authorities to settle a trademark dispute with Budjovicki Budvar over the use of the name Budweiser. Anheuser-Busch agreed to give the Czech brewery a $15 million package, $10.3 million in brewing equipment, and $4.7 million in cash in return for which the two firms agreed to a division of the world into specified exclusive and shared markets. Chapter 16 will provide further in-depth discussions of intellectual property right problems and ways to protect a firm from infringements.

Another area in which governments may attempt to aid and protect the international marketing efforts of companies is that of **gray market** activities. Gray market goods are products that enter markets in ways not desired by their manufacturer. Companies may be hurt by their own products if they reach the consumer via uncontrolled distribution channels. Chapter 12 provides more details on gray market activities.

Apart from specific areas that result in government involvement, the political environment in most countries tends to provide general support for the international marketing efforts of the country's firms. For example, a government may work to reduce trade barriers or to increase trade opportunities through bilateral and multilateral negotiations. Such actions will affect individual firms to the extent that they affect the international climate for free trade.

Often, however, governments also have specific rules and regulations restricting international marketing. Such regulations are frequently political in nature and are based on the fact that governments believe commerce to be only one objective among others, such as foreign policy and national security. Four main areas of governmental activities are of major concern to the international marketer here. These are: embargoes or trade sanctions, export controls, import controls, and the regulation of international business behavior.

Embargoes and Sanctions

The terms **trade sanctions** and **embargoes** as used here refer to governmental actions that distort the free flow of trade in goods, services, or ideas for decidedly adversarial and political, rather than economic, purposes. To understand them better, it is useful to examine the auspices and legal justifications under which they are imposed.

Trade sanctions have been used quite frequently and successfully in times of war or to address specific grievances. For example, in 1284, the Hansa, an association of north German merchants, felt that its members were suffering from several injustices by Norway. On learning that one of its ships had been attacked and pillaged by the Norwegians, the Hansa called an assembly of its members and resolved an economic blockade of Norway. The export of grain, flour, vegetables, and beer was prohibited on pain of fines and confiscation of the goods. The blockade was a complete success. Deprived of grain from Germany, the Norwegians were unable to obtain it from England or elsewhere. As a contemporary chronicler reports: "Then there broke out a famine so great that they were forced to make atonement." Norway was forced to pay indemnities for the financial losses that had been caused and to grant the Hansa extensive trade privileges.[1]

The League of Nations set a precedent for the international legal justification of economic sanctions by subscribing to a covenant that provided for penalties or sanctions for breaching its provisions. The members of the League of Nations did not intend to use military or economic measures separately, but the success of the blockades of World War I fostered the opinion that "the economic weapon, conceived not as an instrument of war but as a means of peaceful pressure, is the greatest discovery and most precious possession of the League."[2] The basic idea was that economic sanctions could force countries to behave peacefully in the international community.

The idea of the multilateral use of economic sanctions was again incorporated into international law under the charter of the United Nations, but greater emphasis was placed on the enforcement process. Once decided upon, sanctions are mandatory, even though each permanent member of the Security Council can veto efforts to impose sanctions. The charter also allows for sanctions as enforcement action by regional agencies such as the Organization of American States, the Arab League, and the Organization of African Unity, but only with the Security Council's authorization.

The apparent strength of the United Nations' enforcement system was soon revealed to be flawed. Stalemates in the Security Council and vetoes by permanent members often led to a shift of emphasis to the General Assembly, where sanctions are not enforceable. Further, concepts such as "peace" and "breach of peace" are seldom perceived in the same way by all members, and thus no systematic sanctioning policy has developed in the United Nations.[3]

Over the years, economic sanctions and embargoes have become a major tool of foreign policy for many countries. Often they are imposed unilaterally in the hope of changing a country's government or at least changing its policies. Between 1914 and 1983, 99 incidents occurred in which sanctions were used to pursue political goals, 46 of them since 1970.[4] Reasons for the impositions have varied, ranging from human rights to nuclear nonproliferation to antiterrorism.

The problem with sanctions is that frequently their unilateral imposition has not produced the desired result. Sanctions may make the obtaining of goods more difficult or expensive for the sanctioned country, yet achievement of the purported objective almost never occurs. In order to

---

[1]Philippe Dollinger, *The German Hansa* (Stanford, Calif.: Stanford University Press, 1970), 49.

[2]Robin Renwick, *Economic Sanctions* (Cambridge, Mass.: Harvard University Press, 1981), 11.

[3]Margaret P. Doxey, *Economic Sanctions and International Enforcement* (New York: Oxford University Press, 1980), 10.

[4]Gary Clyde Hufbauer and Jeffrey J. Schott, "Economic Sanctions: An Often Used and Occasionally Effective Tool of Foreign Policy" in *Export Controls*, ed. Michael R. Czinkota (New York: Praeger Publishers, 1984), 18–33.

work, sanctions need to be imposed multilaterally, a goal that is clear, yet difficult to implement. Quite often individual countries have different relationships with the country subject to the sanctions, and for one reason or another they cannot or do not wish to terminate trade relations.

In addition, sanctions imposed by governments always raise the issue of compensation for the domestic firms that are affected. Obviously, a cutoff of trade with certain regions may result in significant losses of business, forcing selected firms to bear the brunt of governmental policy. Trying to impose sanctions slowly, in order to ease the burden on these firms, undercuts their ultimate chance for success. The international marketer often finds himself caught in this political web and loses business as a result. Frequently a firm can anticipate sanctions based on its evaluations of the international political climate. Nevertheless, even if substantial precautions are taken, firms may still suffer substantial losses.

One case in which sanctions had a major impact on a wide variety of firms involved the efforts by the U.S. government to block the construction of the Yamal pipeline, which was supposed to carry natural gas from the Soviet Union to Western Europe. The Reagan administration opposed the project on the grounds that it would make Europeans too dependent on Soviet gas and would provide the Soviets with large amounts of hard currency. Despite this U.S. opposition, several U.S. and European firms bid successfully for contracts to work on the pipeline. Following the imposition of martial law in Poland in December 1981, however, the United States imposed an embargo on the export of all U.S.-origin oil and gas transmission equipment, services, and technology to the Soviet Union.

John Brown Engineering, a British firm involved in providing gas turbines for the pipeline, was one of the firms affected by the embargo because it relied on General Electric, a U.S. company, for parts and technology. John Brown had already signed a contract with the Soviet Union to deliver turbines for the pipeline, but the U.S. actions prevented the company from effectively fulfilling its contract. In this case, a firm's international marketing effort was damaged by a deterioration in the international political relationship between two countries, even though the firm was operating in a third country. The details of this incident are given in two cases at the end of Part I.

Export Controls

Many nations have export control systems designed to deny the acquisition of strategically important goods to adversaries or at least to delay their acquisition. In the United States the export control system is based on the Export Administration Act and the Munitions Control Act. These laws control all exports of goods, services, and ideas from the United States. The reasons for these controls are concerns about national security, foreign policy, short supply, or nuclear proliferation. In order for any export from the United States to take place, the exporter must obtain an export

FIGURE 4.1   ■   **U.S. Export Control System**

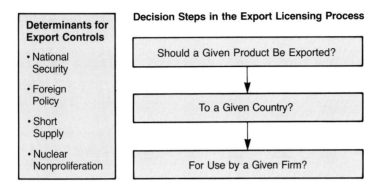

Determinants for Export Controls

• National Security

• Foreign Policy

• Short Supply

• Nuclear Nonproliferation

Decision Steps in the Export Licensing Process

Should a Given Product Be Exported?

To a Given Country?

For Use by a Given Firm?

license from the Department of Commerce, which administers the Export Administration Act.[5] In consultation with other government agencies—particularly the Departments of State, Defense, and Energy—the Department of Commerce has drawn up a list of commodities whose export is considered particularly sensitive. In addition, a list of countries differentiates nations according to their political relationship with the United States. Finally, a list of individual firms that are considered to be unreliable trading partners because of past trade diversion activities exists for each country.

For any export license application, specialists in the Department of Commerce match the commodity to be exported with a file containing information about products that are either particularly sensitive to national security (the **Critical Commodities List**) or controlled for other purposes. A match of these products is then made with the country of destination and the recipient company. If no concerns regarding any of them exist, a validated export license is issued. Control determinants and the steps in the decision process are summarized in Figure 4.1.

This process may sound overly cumbersome, but it does not apply in equal measure to all exports. Many international marketing activities can be carried out with a general license. Under such a license, which is not even in writing, the export can be freely shipped to most trading partners if neither the product nor the country is considered to be sensitive. The process becomes more complicated and cumbersome, however, when it involves products incorporating high-level technologies and countries not friendly to the United States. Corporations then need to apply for a validated export license, which consists of written authorization to send a product abroad. In 1988, more than 96,000 validated license applications

[5] Robert M. Springer, Jr., "New Export Law and Aid to International Marketers," *Marketing News*, January 3, 1986, 10, 67.

were received by the U.S. Department of Commerce, of which over 90,000 were approved.

Given this volume of requests, time delays are inevitable and make the process burdensome. They complicate the international marketing effort because firms trying to close a sale often do not know whether they will be permitted to ship the product abroad. This is particularly the case if a license application must be referred to another U.S. government agency or, more troublesome yet, to **COCOM,** an international coordinating committee for export controls.

The international marketing repercussions of export controls have become increasingly important. To design a control system that is effective and, in consideration of important national concerns, restricts some international business activities is one thing. It is quite another when controls lose their effectiveness and when, because of a control system, firms are placed at a competitive disadvantage with firms in other countries whose control system is less severe or nonexistent.

Export controls are increasingly difficult to implement and enforce for several reasons. First, the number of countries that are able to manufacture products of strategic importance has increased. Industrializing nations, which only a decade ago were seen as poor imitators at best, are now at the forefront of cutting-edge technology. Their products can have a decidedly significant impact on the balance of power in the world. Second, products that are in need of control are developed and disseminated very quickly. Product life cycles have been shortened to such an extent that even temporary delays in distribution may result in a significant setback for a firm. Third, products that are in need of control are shrinking in size because of advancements in miniaturization. The smuggling and diversion of such products has become much easier because they are easier to conceal. Finally, quite apart from products, the transfer of technology and know-how has increasingly taken on major strategic significance. Yet such services are often invisible, are performed by individuals, and are highly personalized. They are easy to transship and therefore difficult to trace and control.

In order for the control process to work to any meaningful extent, alliances must therefore be forged between nations that possess strategic goods and can export them. The United States has done this by harmonizing export control systems in the Western world through the COCOM mechanism. COCOM, an acronym for the coordinating committee for export controls headquartered in Paris, attempts on behalf of most NATO countries and Japan continuously to determine which items need to be controlled, which ones need to be decontrolled, and how national policies can be structured to result in a unified international export control system. In addition, the United States has tried over the years to bring neutral countries into the fold by asking them to join in the overall export control aims of COCOM. In order to encourage these countries to participate, U.S. technology flow to them is offered freely if their control system works. If they are unwilling to forge effective export controls, however, the flow of

THE INTERNATIONAL MARKETPLACE ▊4.2

An Electronic Export License   *For years, the U.S. Commerce Department had been accused by business groups of costing them
high-tech sales because of the time it took to get export licenses. In
response, the department expended major efforts to upgrade the
licensing procedure, while tightening the net to ensure that overseas sales that could harm national security do not slip through.*

*A new system allows applicants for export licenses to noncom-
munist countries, which comprise 80 percent of all requests, to file
their applications electronically. The application is screened by a
computer to check whether the product is eligible for a license
and whether the buyer or seller has a record of diverting high-
technology products to Soviet bloc nations. A licensing agency
employee double-checks the computer, and the license is approved
or denied within three days. Before the electronic system went into
effect, it took 13 days to win license approval; in 1984 the approval
time was as long as 54 days.*

Source: Stuart Auerbach, "Export Licenses Can Be Issued Electronically," The
Washington Post, January 22, 1988, F2.

U.S. products and technology is necessarily reduced because of the risk of
diversion.

In spite of all these harmonization efforts, export controls are a major
obstacle to international marketing activities. The staff and time required
to comply with them can represent a major burden, particularly for the
small or medium-sized firm. Even multinational corporations find it difficult to deal with complex control laws. For example, at Siemens A.G. of
West Germany, 93 people are needed in the high-tech division simply to
assure that the company complies with export control regulations.

Given increasing advances in technology, substantial efforts are under-
way to streamline the licensing system, to control only those commodities
that are truly in need of control, and to ease the licensing burden through
automation. A new electronic system for issuing licenses is described in
The International Marketplace 4.2. Making export controls less onerous is
crucial in order to avoid a strangulation of international marketing efforts
with bureaucratic red tape.

Import Controls

Many nations exert substantial restraints on international marketers through
import controls. This is particularly true of countries that suffer from
major balance-of-trade deficits or major infrastructural problems. In these
countries, either all imports or the imports of particular products are controlled through mechanisms such as tariffs, voluntary restraint agree-

ments, or **quota systems.** On occasion, countries cut off imports of certain products entirely in order to stimulate the development of a domestic industry.

For the international marketer, such restrictions may mean that the most efficient sources of supply are not available, because government regulations restrict importation from those sources. The result is either second-best products or higher costs for restricted supplies. This in turn means that the customer is served less well and often has to pay significantly higher prices.

Policymakers are faced with several problems when trying to administer import controls. First, most of the time such controls exact a huge price from domestic consumers. Even though the wide distribution of the burden among many consumers may result in a less obvious burden, the social cost of these controls may be damaging to the economy and subject to severe attack by individuals. However, these attacks are counteracted by pressures from protected groups that benefit from import restrictions. For example, while citizens of the European Community may be forced—because of import controls—to pay an elevated price for all agricultural products they consume, agricultural producers in the region benefit from higher levels of income. Achieving a proper trade-off is often difficult if not impossible for the policymaker.

A second major problem resulting from import controls is the downstream change in import composition that results from these controls. For example, if the import of copper ore is restricted, either through voluntary restraints or through quotas, producing countries may opt to shift their production systems and produce copper wire instead, which they then export. As a result, initially narrowly defined protectionist measures may have to snowball in order to protect one downstream industry after another.

A final major problem that confronts the policymaker is that of efficiency. Import controls that are frequently designed to provide breathing room to a domestic industry either to grow or to recapture its competitive position often turn out not to work. Rather than improve the productivity of an industry, such controls provide it with a level of safety and a cushion of increased income, yet let overall technological advancement fall behind. Alternatively, supply may respond to artificial stimulation and grow totally out of proportion.

Regulation of International Business Behavior

Home countries may implement special laws and regulations in order to ensure that the international business behavior of their firms is conducted within the legal, moral, and ethical boundaries considered appropriate. The definition of appropriateness may vary from country to country and from government to government. Therefore such regulations, their enforcement, and their impact on firms may differ substantially among nations.

The three major areas in which the United States attempts to govern the international marketing activities of its firms are **boycotts,** antitrust measures, and corruption.

Arab nations, for example, have developed a blacklist of companies that deal with Israel. In addition, Arab customers frequently demand from their suppliers assurances that the source of the products purchased is not Israel, and that the company does not do any business with Israel. The goal of these actions clearly is to impose a boycott on business with Israel. Because of U.S. political ties to Israel, the U.S. government in response to these Arab actions has adopted a variety of laws to prevent U.S. firms from complying with this boycott. These laws include a provision to deny foreign income tax benefits to companies that comply with the boycott and also to require notification of the U.S. government in case any boycott requests are received. U.S. firms that comply with the boycott are subject to heavy fines and denial of export privileges.

These boycott measures put U.S. firms in a difficult position. Caught in a web of governmental activity, they may be forced either to lose business or to pay fines. This is particularly the case if a firm's products are competitive yet not unique, so that the supplier can opt to purchase them elsewhere. Heightening of such conflict can sometimes force companies to withdraw operations from a country entirely.

The second area of regulatory activity affecting international marketing efforts of U.S. firms is U.S. **antitrust laws.** These apply to the international operations of firms as well as to domestic business. The Justice Department watches closely when any U.S. firm buys an overseas company, engages in a joint venture with a foreign firm, or makes an agreement abroad with a competing firm.

Given increasing worldwide cooperation among companies, however, substantial rethinking is going on regarding the validity of extending U.S. antitrust legislation to cover international activities. Some limitations to tough antitrust provisions were implemented decades ago. For example, the Webb-Pomerene Act of 1918 excludes from antitrust prosecution firms that are cooperating to develop foreign markets. This act was passed as part of an effort to aid U.S. export efforts in the face of strong foreign competition by oligopolies and monopolies. The exclusion of international marketing activity from antitrust regulation was further enhanced by the Export Trading Company Act of 1982, which does not expose cooperating firms to the threat of treble damages. It was designed specifically to assist small and medium-sized firms in their export efforts by permitting them to join forces in their international market development activities. Because of increased competition by state-supported enterprises and megacorporations from abroad, however, further steps to loosen U.S. antitrust laws in their application to international marketing activities are under consideration.

Third, U.S. firms operating overseas are affected by U.S. laws against bribery and **corruption.** In many countries, payments or favors are a way of life, and "a greasing of the wheels" is expected in return for government

4.3   THE INTERNATIONAL MARKETPLACE

Paying Bribes Is Expensive   *Napco International Inc. and its parent company, Venturian Corporation of Hopkins, Minnesota, pleaded guilty to paying more than $130,000 in bribes to officials in the Republic of Niger. The purpose of the bribes was to obtain and keep an aircraft service contract funded by the U.S. government's foreign military sales program. The companies plead guilty to conspiracy, to tax violations, and to violating the 1977 Foreign Corrupt Practices Act, which prohibits U.S. companies from paying bribes to foreign officials.*

The company paid the bribes to Tahirou Barke Doka, then the First Counselor at Niger's embassy in Washington, D.C., and Captain Ali Tiemogo, then the Chief of Maintenance of the nation's air force, to use their influence to make certain that Napco obtained and retained the contracts to provide spare parts and maintenance service for C-130 cargo aircraft. The contract was worth more than $3 million.

From 1983 to 1987 the company engaged in an elaborate effort to set up and conceal the bribery scheme. The firm opened a Minnesota bank account in the name of a fictitious commission agent named "E. Dave" and listed two relatives of Tiemogo as Napco's agents in Niger, when in fact they served as intermediaries for the bribe payments. The fraud was uncovered when the name of one of the agents was checked by U.S. officials with the government of Niger.

Under the terms of the plea agreement, the company will pay $685,000 for violating the Foreign Corrupt Practices Act, $100,000 for filing a false tax return, and $75,000 to the Internal Revenue Service to settle its civil tax liabilities. It also will pay $140,000 in civil penalties to be credited to the Republic of Niger's Foreign Military Sales Account. Napco, which sells spare parts, components, and service for American-made military equipment to about 60 countries, could also be barred by the Defense Department from receiving new U.S. government business and could lose its export privileges.

Source: Ruth Marcus, "Minnesota Defense Contractor Fined for Bribing Two Niger Officials," *The Washington Post,* May 3, 1989, F1.

---

services. In the past many U.S. companies doing business internationally routinely paid bribes or did favors for foreign officials in order to gain contracts. In the 1970s major national debate erupted over these business practices, led by arguments that U.S. firms should provide ethical and moral leadership and that contracts won through bribes do not reflect competitive market activity. As a result, the Foreign Corrupt Practices Act

was passed in 1977, making it a crime for U.S. firms to bribe a foreign official for business purposes.

A number of U.S. firms have complained about the act, arguing that it
hinders their efforts to compete internationally against companies from
countries that have no such antibribery laws. The problem is one of ethics
versus practical needs and also, to some extent, of the amounts involved.
For example, it may be difficult to draw the line between providing a generous tip and paying a bribe in order to speed up a business transaction.
Many business managers argue that the United States should not apply its
moral principles to other societies and cultures in which bribery and corruption are endemic. If they are to compete internationally, these managers argue, they must be free to use the most common methods of competition in the host country.

On the other hand, applying different standards to management and
firms, depending on whether they do business abroad or domestically, is
difficult to envision. Also, bribes may open the way for shoddy performance and loose moral standards among managers and employees, and
may result in a spreading of general unethical business practices. Unrestricted bribery could result in concentration on how to bribe best rather
than on how best to produce and market products.

The international manager must carefully distinguish between reasonable ways of doing business internationally—including compliance with
foreign expectations—and outright bribery and corruption. In order to assist the manager in this task, revisions were made in the 1988 Trade Act to
clarify the applicability of the Foreign Corrupt Practices legislation. These
revisions clarify when a manager is expected to know about violation of
the act, and a distinction is drawn between the facilitation of routine governmental actions and governmental policy decisions. Routine actions
concern issues such as the obtaining of permits, licenses, processing of
governmental papers such as visas and work orders, the providing of mail
and phone service, and the loading and unloading of cargo. Policy decisions refer mainly to situations in which the obtaining or retaining of contracts is at stake. While the facilitation of routine actions is not prohibited,
the illegal influencing of policy decisions can result in the imposition of
severe fines and penalties, as The International Marketplace 4.3 shows.

All of these issues of governmental regulation pose difficult and complex problems, for they place managers in the position of having to choose
between home country regulations and foreign business practices. This
choice is made even more difficult because of diverging standards of behavior applied to businesses in different countries.

HOST COUNTRY POLITICAL AND LEGAL ENVIRONMENT

The host country environment, both political and legal, affects the international marketing operations of firms in a variety of ways. The good manager will understand the country in which the firm operates so that he or

she is able to work within the existing parameters and can anticipate and plan for changes that may occur.

Political Action and Risk

Firms usually prefer to conduct business in a country with a stable and friendly government, but such governments are not always easy to find. Therefore international managers need to analyze the host country's government, its policies, and its stability to determine the potential for political change that could adversely affect corporate operations.

Political risk occurs in every nation, but the range of risks varies widely from country to country. In general, political risk is lowest in countries with a history of stability and consistency. Conversely, political risk is highest in nations lacking this kind of history. Nevertheless, in a substantial number of countries consistency and stability were apparent on the surface, yet were quickly swept away by major popular movements that benefited from pent-up frustrations of the population.

A manager will want to think twice before conducting business in a country in which the likelihood of conflict and violent change is high. If conflict breaks out, the firm and its employees will possibly face violence in the form of guerrilla warfare, civil disturbances, or terrorism. Such violence often has an anti-industry element, making companies and their employees potential targets. U.S. corporations or firms linked to the United States are often subject to major threats, even in countries that boast of great political stability. In 1986, for example, Dr. Karl-Heinz Beckhurst, director of research for the German multinational company Siemens, was assassinated by the Red Army Faction because of his alleged involvement with the U.S.-sponsored Strategic Defense Initiative (SDI).

International terrorists have frequently targeted U.S. corporate facilities, operations, and personnel abroad for attack in order to strike a blow against the United States and capitalism. U.S. firms are prominent symbols of the U.S. presence abroad, and by their nature they cannot have the elaborate security and restricted access of U.S. diplomatic offices and military bases. The methods used by terrorists against business facilities include bombing, arson, hijacking, and sabotage. To obtain funds the terrorists resort to kidnapping of executives, armed robbery, and extortion.[6] How such incidents against businesses are distributed around the world is shown in Figure 4.2.

In many countries, particularly in the developing world, coups d'etat can result in drastic changes in government. The new government may attack foreign multinational corporations as remnants of the Western-dominated colonial past, as has happened in Cuba, Nicaragua, and Iran. Even if such changes do not represent an immediate physical threat to firms and their employees, they can have drastic effects. The past few de-

---

[6]Harvey J. Iglarsh, "Terrorism and Corporate Costs," *Terrorism*, vol. 10, no. 3, 1987, 227–230.

FIGURE 4.2   ▪   **Location of Incidents against Business**

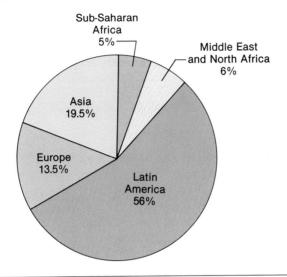

Note: U.S. and Canada had no incidents.

Source: Business Risks International, Nashville, Tennessee, as printed in *The Journal of Commerce*, August 4, 1988, p. 1. Reprinted by permission of The Journal of Commerce.

cades have seen such coups in the countries of Ghana, Ethiopia, and Iraq, to name a few, that have seriously impeded the conduct of international marketing.

Less dramatic but still worrisome are changes in government policies that are caused, not by changes in the government itself, but as a result of pressure from nationalist or religious factions or widespread anti-Western feeling. The aware manager will work to anticipate these changes and plan ways to cope with them.

What sort of changes in policy result from the various events described? The range of possible actions is broad. All of them can affect international marketing operations, but not all are equal in weight. Except for extreme cases, companies do not usually have to fear violence against employees, although violence against company property is quite common. Common also are changes in policy that take a strong nationalist and antiforeign investment stance. The most drastic steps resulting from such policy changes are usually confiscation and expropriation.

An important governmental action is **expropriation.** According to the World Bank, in the 1960s and 70s, a total of 1,535 firms from 22 different countries have been expropriated in 511 separate actions by 76 nations.[7] Expropriation was an appealing action to many countries because it demonstrated nationalism and transfered a certain amount of wealth and re-

[7]Joseph V. Miscallef, "Political Risk Assessment," *Columbia Journal of World Business,* January 1981, 47.

sources from foreign companies to the host country immediately. It did have costs to the host country, however, to the extent that it made other firms more hesitant to invest in the country. Expropriation does not relieve the host government of providing compensation to the former owners. However, these compensation negotiations are often protracted and result in settlements that are frequently unsatisfactory to the owners. For example, governments may offer compensation in the form of local, nontransferable currency or may base the compensation on the book value of the firm. Even though firms that are expropriated may deplore the low levels of payment obtained, they frequently accept them in the absence of better alternatives.

The use of expropriation as a policy tool has sharply decreased over time. In the mid-1970s, more than 83 expropriations took place in a single year. By the 1980s the annual average had declined to fewer than three. Apparently, governments have come to recognize that the damage inflicted on themselves through expropriation exceeds the benefits.[8]

In that it results in a transfer of ownership from the foreign firm to the host country, **confiscation** is similar to expropriation. It differs, however, in that it does not involve compensation for the firm. Some industries are more vulnerable than others to confiscation and expropriation because of their importance to the host country economy and their lack of ability to shift operations. For this reason, sectors such as mining, energy, public utilities, and banking have been targets of such government actions.

Confiscation and expropriation constitute major political risks for foreign investors. Other government actions, however, are nearly as damaging. Many countries are turning from confiscation and expropriation to more subtle forms of control, such as **domestication.** The goal of domestication is the same, to gain control over foreign investment, but the method is different. Through domestication, the government demands partial transfer of ownership and management responsibility, and imposes regulations to ensure that a large share of the product is locally produced and a larger share of the profit is retained in the country.

Domestication can have profound effects on the international marketer for a number of reasons. First, if a firm is forced to hire nationals as managers, poor cooperation and communication can result. If the domestication is imposed within a very short time span, corporate operations overseas may have to be headed by poorly trained and inexperienced local managers. Further, domestic content requirements may force a firm to purchase supplies and parts locally, which can result in increased costs, inefficiency, and lower quality products, thus further damaging a firm's interest. Export requirements imposed on companies may also create havoc for the international distribution plan of a corporation and force it to change or even shut down operations in third countries. Finally, domes-

[8]Michael Minor, "LDCs, TNCs, and Expropriation in the 1980s," *The CTC Reporter*, Spring 1988, 53.

tication usually will shield the industry within one country from foreign competition. As a result, inefficiencies will be allowed to grow due to a lack of market discipline. In the long run this will affect the international competitiveness of an operation abroad and may become a major problem when, years later, the removal of domestication is considered by the government.

Most businesses operating abroad face a number of other risks that are less dangerous, but probably more common, than the drastic ones already described. Host governments that face a shortage of foreign currency sometimes will impose controls on the movement of capital in and out of the country. Such controls may make it difficult for a firm to remove its profits or investments from the host country. Sometimes **exchange controls** are also levied selectively against certain products or companies in an effort to reduce the importation of goods that are considered to be a luxury or unnecessary. Such regulations are often difficult to deal with because they may affect the importation of parts, components, or supplies that are vital for production operations. Restrictions on such imports may force a firm either to alter its production program or, worse yet, to shut down its entire plant. Prolonged negotiations with government officials may be necessary in order to reach a compromise agreement on what constitutes a "valid" expenditure of foreign currency resources. Because the goals of government officials and corporate managers may often be quite different, such compromises, even when they can be reached, may result in substantial damage to the international marketing operations of a firm.

Countries may also raise the tax rates applied to foreign investors in an effort to control the firms and their capital. Such tax increases may result in much needed revenue for the coffers of the host country, but they can severely damage the operations of the foreign investors. This damage, in turn, will frequently result in decreased income for the host country in the long run.

The international marketing manager must also worry about **price controls.** In many countries, domestic political pressures can force governments to control the prices of imported products or services, particularly in sectors that are considered to be highly sensitive from a political perspective, such as food or health care. If a foreign firm is involved in these areas, it is a vulnerable target of price controls because the government can play upon its people's nationalistic tendencies to enforce the price controls. Particularly in countries that suffer from high inflation and frequent devaluations, the international marketer may be forced to choose between shutting down the operation or continuing production at a loss in the hope of recouping that loss once the government chooses to loosen or remove its price restrictions. How a firm can adjust to price controls is discussed in greater detail in Chapter 17.

Managers face political and economic risk whenever they conduct business overseas, but there may be ways to lessen the risk. Obviously, if a new government comes into power that is dedicated to the removal of all for-

FIGURE 4.3 ▪ **Assistance for Risk Management**

Source: Courtesy Palisade Corporation, Newfield, NY.

eign influences, a firm can do little. In less extreme cases, however, managers can take actions to reduce the risk if they understand the root causes of the host country policies.

Adverse governmental actions are usually the result of a host country's nationalism, desire for independence, and opposition to colonial remnants. If a country's citizens feel exploited by foreign firms, government officials are more likely to take antiforeign action. In order to reduce the risk of government intervention, a firm needs to demonstrate that it is concerned with the host country's society and that it considers itself an integral part of the host country rather than simply an exploitative foreign corporation. Ways to do this include intensive local hiring and training practices, good pay, more charity, and more societally useful investment.

In addition, a company can form joint ventures with local partners in order to demonstrate a willingness to share its benefits with nationals. Although such actions will not guarantee freedom from risk, they will certainly lessen the exposure.

Other actions that can be taken by corporations to protect against political risk consist of the close monitoring of political developments. Increasingly, private sector firms offer assistance in such monitoring activities, permitting the overseas corporation to discover potential trouble spots as early as possible and react quickly to prevent major losses. Figure 4.3 provides an example of such a service. Firms can also take out insurance to cover losses due to political risk. In the United States, for example, the Overseas Private Investment Corporation (OPIC) offers such insurance. Rates vary by country and type of activity, but for $100 of coverage per year they average $0.30 to protect against inconvertibility, $0.60 to protect against expropriation, and $1.05 to compensate for damage to business income and assets from political violence.[9]

Clearly, the international marketer must consider the likelihood of negative political factors in making decisions on conducting business overseas. On the other hand, host-country political and legal systems can have a positive impact on the conduct of international business. Many governments, for example, encourage foreign investments, especially if they believe that the investment will produce economic and political benefits domestically. Some governments have opened up their economy to foreign investors, placing only minimal constraints on them, in the hope that such policies will lead to rapid economic development. Others have provided for substantial subsidization of new investment activities in the hope that investments will generate additional employment. The international marketer, in his investment decision, can and should therefore also pay close attention to the extent and forms of incentives available from foreign governments. Although international marketing decisions should be driven by market forces, the basic economies of these decisions may change depending on incentives offered.

In this discussion of the political environment, laws have been mentioned only to the extent that they appear to be the direct result of political changes. However, each nation has laws regarding marketing, and the international manager must understand their effects on the firm's efforts.

Legal Differences and Restraints

Countries differ in their laws as well as in their use of these laws. For example, the United States has developed into an increasingly litigious society, in which institutions and individuals are quick to take a case to

[9]Overseas Private Investment Corporation, Washington, D.C., 1989.

4.4   THE INTERNATIONAL MARKETPLACE

Two Air Disasters, Two Cultures, Two Remedies   When two
jumbo jets crashed ten days apart in Dallas and in the mountains
near Tokyo, Americans and Japanese shared a common bond of
shock and grief. Soon, however, all parties in Japan—from the airline to the employers of victims—moved to put the tragedy behind
them. In the United States legal tremors will be felt for years.

Lawyers hustled to the scene of the Delta Air Lines accident
at the Dallas–Fort Worth airport and set up shop at an airport
hotel. Proclaimed San Francisco attorney Melvin Belli: "I'm not an
ambulance chaser—I get there before the ambulance." "We always
file the first suit," bragged Richard Brown, a Melvin Belli associate who flew to Dallas "to get to the bottom of this and to make
ourselves available." He added, "We never solicited anyone directly. We were called to Texas by California residents who lost
their loved ones." Within 72 hours, the first suit against Delta was
filed. Insurance adjusters working for Delta went quickly to work
as well.

Seven thousand miles away, Japan Air Lines President Yasumoto
Takagi humbly bowed to families of the 520 victims and apolo-
gized "from the bottom of our hearts." He vowed to resign once the
investigation was complete. Next of kin soon received "condolence
payments" and negotiated settlements with the airline. Traditionally few if any lawsuits are filed following such accidents.

Behind these differences lie standards of behavior and corporate
responsibility that are worlds apart. "There is a general Japanese
inclination to try to settle any disputes through negotiations between the parties before going to court," said Koichiro Fujikura, a
Tokyo University law professor. Added Carl Green, a Washington,
D.C., attorney and specialist on Japanese law, "There is an assumption of responsibility. In our adversarial society, we don't admit responsibility. It would be admitting liability."

After a JAL jet crashed into Tokyo Bay in 1982, killing 24, JAL
President Takagi visited victims' families, offered gifts, and knelt
before funeral altars. JAL offered families about $2,000 each in
condolence payments, then negotiated settlements reported to be
worth between $166,000 and $450,000, depending on the age and
earning power of each victim. Only one family sued.

Japanese legal experts expect settlements to be as high as 500
million yen—about $2.1 million—apiece. Negotiations may be
prolonged. But if families believe that JAL is sincerely sorry, "I
think their feelings will be soothed," predicted attorney Takeshi
Odagi.

Japan's legal system encourages these traditions. "Lawyers don't
descend in droves on accident scenes because they barely have

enough time to handle the suits they have," said John Haley, a law professor at the University of Washington who has studied and worked in Japan. "There are fewer judges per capita than there were in 1890," Haley added. Only 500 lawyers are admitted to the bar each year.

Source: Clemens P. Work, Sarah Peterson, and Hidehiro Tanakadate, "Two Air Disasters, Two Cultures, Two Remedies," *U.S. News and World Report*, August 26, 1985, 25–26.

---

court. As a result, court battles are often protracted and costly, and the threat itself of a court case can reduce marketing opportunities. In contrast, Japan, for example, still has only approximately 12,500 fully licensed lawyers, compared to some 650,000 in the United States. Whether cause or effect, the result is that the Japanese tend not to litigate.[10] The International Marketplace 4.4 relects some of the subsequent differences in litigation.

Apart from understanding the use of the law, the international marketer must understand the type of legal system in a host country. Two major legal systems exist worldwide: common law and code law. **Common law** is based on tradition and depends less on written statutes and codes than on precedent and custom. Common law originated in England and is the system of law found today in the United States.

On the other hand, **code law** is based on a comprehensive set of written statutes. Countries with code law try to spell out all possible legal rules explicitly. Code law is based on Roman law and is found in the majority of the nations of the world.

In general, countries with the code law system have much more rigid laws than those with the common law system. In the latter, courts adopt precedents and customs to fit the cases, allowing the marketer a better idea of the basic judgment likely to be rendered in new situations.

The differences between code law and common law, and their impact on the international marketer, although wide in theory, are not always as broad in practice. For example, many common law countries, including the United States, have adopted commercial codes to govern the conduct of business.

Host countries may adopt a number of laws that affect a company's ability to market. To begin with, there can be laws affecting the entry of goods, such as tariffs and quotas. Also in this category are **antidumping laws,** which prohibit below-cost sales of products, and laws that require export and import licensing. In addition, many countries have health and safety standards that may, by design or by accident, restrict the entry of foreign

[10] "Japan Still Has Only 12,500 Lawyers," *The Exporter*, September 1986, 18.

goods. The United States, for example, has often complained about Japan's strict standards for imports. U.S. business executives and policymakers argue that such standards are designed specifically as barriers to trade, because they focus primarily on the design or content of products rather than on their performance.

Other laws may serve to restrict entrepreneurial activities. For example, in Argentina, a law requires that pharmacies be owned by the pharmacist. This legislation prevents a sharp businessman from hiring a couple of druggists and starting a pharmacy chain. Similarly, a marketer is prevented from adding a drug counter to an existing business, such as a supermarket, to broaden the product offering to consumers.[11]

Very specific legislation may also exist to regulate, for example, where a firm can advertise or what constitutes deceptive advertising. Many countries prohibit specific claims by marketers comparing their products to that of the competition and restrict the use of promotional devices. Even when no laws exist, the marketer may be hampered by regulations. For example, in many countries, governments require a firm to join the local chamber of commerce or become a member of the national trade association. These institutions in turn may have internal regulations that set standards for the conduct of business and may be seen as quite confining to the international marketer.

Finally, seemingly innocuous local regulations that may be overlooked by the international marketer can have a major impact on a firm's success. For example, the Japanese government's desire to protect smaller merchants has led to an intricate process regulating the building of a new department store or supermarket. Consequently, the opening of large stores has come to a virtual standstill. Because large stores serve as the major conduit for the sale of imported consumer products, the opportunities for market penetration of imported merchandise have been severely affected.[12]

The Influencing of Politics and Laws

To succeed in a market, the international marketer needs much more than business know-how. He or she must also deal with the intricacies of national politics and laws. Although to fully understand another country's legal and political system will rarely be possible, the good manager will be aware of its importance and will work with people who do understand how to operate within the system.

Many areas of politics and law are not immutable. Viewpoints can be modified or even reversed, and new laws can supersede old ones. There-

---

[11] James L. Rowe, Jr., "Inflation Slowed, Argentina's Alfonsin Now Tackling Economic Stagnation," *The Washington Post*, July 13, 1986, G1, G8.

[12] Michael R. Czinkota and Jon Woronoff, *Japan's Market: The Distribution System* (New York: Praeger Publishers, 1986), 111–113.

fore, existing political and legal restraints do not always need to be accepted. In order to achieve change, however, there must be some impetus for it, such as the clamors of a constituency. Otherwise systemic inertia is likely to allow the status quo to prevail.

The international marketer has various options. One sometimes used is simply to ignore prevailing rules and expect to get away with it. Pursuing this option is a high-risk strategy, because the possibility of objection and even prosecution exists. A second, traditional option is to provide input to trade negotiators and expect any problem areas to be resolved in multilateral negotiations. The drawback to this option is of course the quite time-consuming process involved.

A third option involves the development of coalitions or constituencies that can motivate legislators and politicians to consider and ultimately implement change. This option can be pursued in various ways. First of all, direct linkages and their cost and benefit can be highlighted to legislators and politicians. For example, the manager can explain the employment and economic effects of certain laws and regulations and demonstrate the benefits of change. The picture can be enlarged by including indirect linkages. For example, suppliers, customers, and distributors can be asked to participate in delineating to decision makers the benefit of change.

Developing such coalitions is not an easy task. Companies often seek assistance in effectively influencing the government decision-making process. Such assistance usually is particularly beneficial when narrow economic objectives or single-issue campaigns are needed. Typical providers of this assistance are lobbyists. Usually, these are well-connected individuals and firms that can provide access to policymakers and legislators.

Foreign countries and companies have been particularly effective in their lobbying in the United States. For example, in 1975, only 35 U.S. firms had filed with the U.S. Department of Justice that they were lobbyists for foreign interests. By 1985, this number had grown to 105 U.S. firms retained under contract to represent foreign economic interests in the United States, beyond traditional diplomatic representation. As an example, Brazil has held on average nearly a dozen contracts per year with U.S. firms covering trade issues. Brazilian citrus exporters and computer manufacturers have hired U.S. legal and public relations firms to provide them with information on relevant U.S. legislative activity. The Banco do Brasil lobbied for the restructuring of Brazilian debt and favorable banking regulations. Examples of how foreign lobbying activity in the United States has grown are given in Table 4.1.

U.S. firms also have representation in Washington, D.C., as well as state capitals. Often, however, they are less adept at ensuring proper representation abroad. For example, a survey of U.S. international marketing executives found that knowledge and information about foreign trade and government officials was ranked lowest among critical international business information needs. This low ranking appears to reflect the fact that many U.S. firms are far less successful in their interaction with govern-

TABLE 4.1 ▪ **Changes in U.S.-Directed Lobbying Activities**

	1975		
	Contracts with U.S. Firms	*Number Directed at U.S. Legislation*	*Total Real Lobbying Expenditures*
BRAZIL Trade	6	2	NA

BRAZIL Trade: Two contracts with U.S. firms involved lobbying on potential U.S. trade legislation by presenting the views of the Brazilian sugar, alcohol, and coffee institutes. Three covered publicity campaigns to promote Brazilian coffee and industrial product exports, and one provided legal representation for the Banco do Brasil and Banco do Estado de Sao Paulo.

Finance

HONG KONG Trade	2	0	NA

HONG KONG Trade: The Hong Kong Trade Development Council held a contract with a U.S. firm to design and place advertising to promote export trade to the United States. One contract provided legal advice and representation for a Hong Kong trading house in pending litigation.

Finance: The Hong Kong Trade Development Council also disseminated a monthly investment newsletter promoting the nation as a profitable manufacturing location.

SOUTH KOREA Trade	6	0	NA

SOUTH KOREA Trade: Two commercial contracts—on behalf of the Korea Steel Corporation and Korean Traders Association—provided public relations advice and consultations aimed at expanding Korean share of the U.S. import market. Three contracts arranged for legal representation of several Korean industrial groups.

Finance: The Korean Trade Promotion Corporation hired a U.S. public relations and advertising agency to design campaigns to promote U.S. private investment in Korea.

Source: U.S. Department of Justice Records.

1980		
Contracts with U.S. Firms	Number Directed at U.S. Legislation	Total Real Lobbying Expenditures
9	6	$617,332

Six contracts targeted at U.S. legislation put special emphasis on U.S. countervailing duties, the Generalized System of Preferences, and trade legislation that could affect Brazilian coffee, sugar, and alcohol exports. Tactics included monitoring Congressional trade proposals and reporting on market developments. Two contracts provided legal services in connection with Brazilian banking.

One contract between a U.S. firm and the Banco do Brasil provided advice on U.S. tax law as a potential guide for Brazilian tax law revision. A separate contract directed a U.S. firm to protect the commercial interests of the Brazilian aviation industry by contacting U.S. executive and legislative officials on tax matters.

3	1	$83,117

One contract directed at U.S. economic legislation consisted of contacting members of Congress and their aides to give them alternative views on U.S. legislation that would place a moratorium on acquisitions of domestic banks by foreign banks. Two other contracts covered legal services for the government of Hong Kong on bilateral trade disputes with the United States.

The Hong Kong Trade Development Council promoted U.S. investment by furnishing U.S. firms with information on manufacturing resources in Hong Kong.

21	14	$605,699

Fourteen contracts monitored and furnished advice regarding potential U.S. legislation on U.S. fisheries policy, footwear and leather imports, and the bilateral textiles agreement. Four contracts promoted South Korean commercial interests by publicizing two-way trade opportunities through trade missions and orientation trips for U.S. businessmen. Three contracts arranged for legal representation on behalf of Korean electronics, leather, and footwear exporters before U.S. government agencies.

1985		
Contracts with U.S. Firms	Number Directed at U.S. Legislation	Total Real Lobbying Expenditures
26	20	$1,497,465

Two-thirds (20) of Brazilian lobbying contracts were set up to monitor or attempt to influence pending U.S. legislation on steel imports, tax regulations, sugar and alcohol import quotas, textile trade, and footwear imports. Three were for legal representation in U.S. trade complaints under Section 301 of the Trade Act, and general legal services for the Banco do Brasil. Three covered trade promotion for Brazilian products.

One contract between Banco do Brasil and a U.S. firm included research and advice on U.S. government attitudes toward the Bretton Woods Agreement Act and assistance in securing the restructuring of Brazilian external debt.

8	5	$790,281

The five contracts directed against U.S. legislation sought favorable treatment for Hong Kong textile exports under the new U.S. tariff schedule and included testimony before the International Trade Commission to promote favorable country-of-origin legislation. Of the three remaining, one covered legal advice on trade matters and two represented Hong Kong commercial interests by publicizing the region's stability and prosperity.

One contract primarily for promotion of U.S.–Hong Kong trade included publicity for U.S. foreign investment opportunities. Tactics included dissemination of news features, audiotapes, and videotapes to promote the view that Hong Kong's stability and prosperity will continue and that the territory is a receptive area for U.S. investment of money and technology.

27	10	$3,293,520

Ten contracts attempted to influence U.S. policy on fishery quotas, textiles, countervailing duty investigations on carbon steel products, landing rights for Korea Air Lines, and electronic imports. Tactics included meetings with members of the executive and legislative branches and U.S. private industry and labor representatives. Nine contracts kept Korean firms informed of the status of trade deliberations in the United States; six trade-related lobbying contracts represented Korean legal interests in color-television-dumping complaints as well as other trade issues.

One contract coordinated joint ventures between U.S. and Korean firms and arranged visits of U.S. technical experts to Korea to solve manufacturing problems that could hinder foreign investment. Korean banks hired a U.S. firm to help lobby for favorable treatment under U.S. tax laws.

4.5   THE INTERNATIONAL MARKETPLACE

Does Japan Shape U.S. Trade Policy?   *A new wave of Japanese wealth is washing over America, and it has little to do with government bonds or corporate securities. The new currency is influence. As Japan increases its investment in the west, it is also becoming a full-fledged member of the American political, cultural, and intellectual debate in a way—and on a scale—that no other nation has ever achieved.*

Japanese companies are spending heavily to shape the way Americans view them. They are pouring tens of millions of dollars into U.S. education, from Ivy League colleges to elementary schools in Kentucky. Museums, universities, public television stations, and think tanks are competing for—and getting—Japanese money. The Japanese are also wielding political power from the grass roots to the top echelons of Washington. The same words that describe Japan's economic strategy applied to what the Japanese called their "soft side" activities: systematic, coordinated, long term.

There is nothing improper about it. America and most larger nations attempt to spread their ideas around the world. For Japan, though, the motive is primarily economic. As Japan's investments overflow from financial assets into real property such as plants and skyscrapers, the Japanese want more than just an open U.S. market for their exports; they want to protect their broad stake here. That means becoming sophisticated in pulling America's political strings.

Japanese companies spend an estimated $45 million a year on public relations—much of it for image building. For lawyers, public relations advisors, academics, economists, journalists, and political consultants, Japan's spending is a major growth industry. In addition, Japan is able to gain, in many cases, leverage from its business relationships with American companies. Major Wall Street firms have important Japanese shareholders. And it is only prudent for them to consider the impact of public pronouncements on their Japanese partners. Likewise, a host of U.S. manufacturers enjoy joint ventures or marketing agreements with the Japanese. If the domestic political environment becomes threatening, they often go to bat to defend their partners.

Although many argue that funding by, or association with, Japan has no impact on their views, critics argue that basic ethical questions are involved. They say that Japan's wealth tempts some of America's elite to accept Japanese funds at the expense of broader U.S. interest.

Source: William J. Holstein, "Japan's Clout in the U.S.," *Business Week*, July 7, 1988, 64–66.

ments abroad and far less intensive in their lobbying attempts than are foreign entities in the United States.[13]

Although representation of the firm's interests to government decision makers and legislators is entirely appropriate, the international marketer must consider also any potential side effects. Major questions can be raised if such representation becomes very strong, as The International Marketplace 4.5 shows. In such instances, short-term gains may be far outweighed by long-term negative repercussions if the international marketer is perceived as exerting too much political influence.

THE INTERNATIONAL ENVIRONMENT

In addition to the politics and laws of both the home and the host countries, the international marketer must consider the overall international political and legal environment. Relations between countries can have a profound impact on firms trying to do business internationally.

International Politics

The effect of politics on international marketing is determined by both the bilateral political relations between home and host countries and by multilateral agreements governing the relations among groups of countries.

The government-to-government relationship can have a profound effect, particularly if it becomes hostile. Numerous examples exist of the linkage between international politics and international marketing. The premier example is perhaps U.S.-Iranian relations following the 1979 Iranian revolution. Although the internal political and legal changes in the aftermath of that revolution would certainly have affected international marketing in Iran, the deterioration in U.S.-Iranian political relations that resulted from the revolution had a significant impact. U.S. firms were injured not only by physical damage caused by the violence but also by the anti-American feelings of the Iranian people and their government. The clashes between the two governments completely destroyed any business relationships, regardless of corporate feelings or agreements on either side.

International political relations do not always have harmful effects on international marketers. If bilateral political relations between countries improve, business can benefit. An example is provided by U.S.-Chinese relations for about a decade. Political warming between the two countries opened the potentially lucrative Chinese market to U.S. businesses. The Coca-Cola Company gained access to the Chinese market on the coattails

---

[13] Michael R. Czinkota, "Governmental Trade Data: Utility and Usage," paper presented at the 1989 Annual Meeting of the Academy of International Business, Singapore, 1989.

of the Carter administration's political efforts. Subsequently many high-technology firms benefited from this rapprochement by exporting technologies to China that previously had been considered much too sensitive for distribution to that country. However, these benefits derived by business turned into drawbacks once internal civil unrest in China resulted in a cooling off of relations. Sanctions imposed by the United States jeopardized existing business contracts, and investments that had appeared sound were now viewed in a different light.

The good international marketer will be aware of political currents worldwide and will attempt to anticipate changes in the international political environment, good or bad, so that his or her firm can plan for them.

International Law

International law plays an important role in the conduct of international business. Although no enforceable body of international law exists, certain treaties and agreements respected by a number of countries profoundly influence international business operations. As an example, the General Agreement on Tariffs and Trade (GATT) defines internationally acceptable economic practices for its member nations. Although it does not directly affect individual firms, it does affect them indirectly by providing a more stable and predictable international market environment.

A number of efforts have been made to simplify business procedures. For example, firms wanting to patent their products in the past had to register them separately in each country in order to have protection. In response to the chaos and expense of such procedures, several multilateral simplification efforts have been undertaken. European countries have been at the forefront of such efforts, having developed the European Patent Convention and the Community Patent Convention.

Similar efforts have been undertaken with regard to trademarks so that firms can benefit from various multilateral agreements. The two major international conventions on trademarks are the International Convention for the Protection of Industrial Property and the Madrid Arrangement for International Registration of Trademarks. Several regional conventions include the Inter-American Convention for Trademark Protection and a similar agreement in French West Africa.

In addition to multilateral agreements, firms are affected by bilateral treaties and conventions. The United States, for example, has signed bilateral treaties of friendship, commerce, and navigation (FCN) with a wide variety of countries. These agreements generally define the rights of U.S. firms doing business in the host country. They normally guarantee that the U.S. firms will be treated by the host country in the same manner in which domestic firms are treated. Although these treaties provide for some stability, they can be canceled, as the withdrawal of the United States from its FCN agreement with Nicaragua shows.

The international legal environment also affects the marketer to the extent that firms must concern themselves with jurisdictional disputes. Because no single body of international law exists, firms usually are restricted by both home and host country laws. If a conflict occurs between contracting parties in two different countries, a question arises concerning which country's laws will be followed. Sometimes the contract will contain a jurisdictional clause, which settles the matter. If not, the parties to the dispute can follow either the laws of the country in which the agreement was made or those of the country in which the contract will have to be fulfilled. Deciding on the laws to be followed and the location to settle the dispute are two different decisions. As a result, a dispute between a U.S. exporter and a French importer could be resolved in Paris with the resolution based on New York State law.

If no satisfactory arrangement can be agreed upon, the parties can choose either arbitration or litigation. Litigation is usually avoided for several reasons. It often involves extensive delays and is very costly. In addition, firms may fear discrimination in foreign countries. Companies therefore tend to prefer conciliation and arbitration, because these processes result in much quicker decisions. Arbitration procedures are often spelled out in the original contract and usually provide for an intermediary who is judged to be impartial by both parties. Frequently intermediaries will be representatives of chambers of commerce, trade associations, or from third country institutions.

SUMMARY

The political and legal environment in the home country, the environment in the host country, and the laws and agreements governing relationships between nations are all important to the international marketer. Compliance with them is mandatory in order to do business successfully abroad. To avoid the problems that can result from changes in the political and legal environment, the international marketer must anticipate changes and develop strategies for coping with them. Whenever possible, the manager must avoid being taken by surprise and thus not let events control business decisions.

On occasion, the international marketer may be caught between clashing home and host country laws. In such instances, the firm needs to conduct a dialogue with the governments in order to seek a compromise solution. Alternatively, managers can encourage their government to engage in government-to-government negotiations in order to settle the dispute. By demonstrating the business volume at stake and the employment that may be lost through such governmental disputes, government negotiators can often be motivated to press hard for a settlement of such intergovernmental difficulties. Finally, the firm can seek redress in international court. Such international legal action, however, may be quite slow, and, even if resulting in a favorable judgment for the firm, may not be adhered to by the government against which the judgment is rendered.

In the final analysis, a firm conducting business internationally is subject to the vagaries of political and legal changes and may lose business as a result. The best the manager can do is to be aware of political influences and laws and strive to adopt them as far as possible.

Questions for Discussion

1. Discuss this statement: "High political risk requires companies to seek a quick payback on their investments. Striving for such a quick payback, however, exposes firms to charges of exploitation and results in increased political risk."

2. How appropriate is it for governments to help drum up business for their companies abroad? Should commerce not be completely separate from politics?

3. Discuss this statement: "The national security that our export control laws seek to protect may be threatened by the resulting lack of international competitiveness of U.S. firms."

4. U.S. antiboycott statutes prohibit the participation of a U.S. firm in a foreign boycott. Should that regulation be applied equally to the boycott of South Africa?

5. After you hand your passport to the immigration officer in country X, he misplaces it. A small "donation" would certainly help him find it again. Should you give him money? Is this a business expense to be charged to your company? Should it be tax deductible?

6. Discuss the advantages and disadvantages for the international marketer of common versus code law.

7. Research examples of multinational corporations that have remained untouched by waves of expropriation. What was the secret of their success?

8. The United States has been described as a "litigious" society. How does frequent litigation affect the international marketer, particularly in comparison to the situation in other countries?

9. What are your views on lobbying efforts by foreign firms?

Recommended Readings

Carter, Barry E. *International Economic Sanctions.* Cambridge: Cambridge University Press, 1988.

Czinkota, Michael R., ed. *Export Controls.* New York: Praeger Publishers, 1984.

Hufbauer, Gary Clyde, Diane T. Berlinger, and Kimberly Ann Elliot. *Trade Protection in the United States.* Washington, D.C.: Institute for International Economics, 1986.

Hufbauer, Gary Clyde, and Jeffrey J. Schott. *Economic Sanctions in Support of Foreign Policy Goals*. Washington, D.C.: Institute for International Economics, 1984.

Jeffries, Francis M. *American Business and International Political Risk: Past, Present, and Future*. Poolesville, Md.: Jeffries and Associates, 1985.

Sagafi-nejad, Tagi, Richard W. Moxon, and Howard V. Perlmutter. *Controlling International Technology Transfer*. New York: Pergamon Press, 1981.

CHAPTER **5**

The International Cultural Environment

THE INTERNATIONAL MARKETPLACE

Meeting the Cultural Challenge at United   On February 11, 1986, United Airlines acquired the entire Pacific division of Pan American Airways. Virtually overnight, United began serving 13 cities in 10 Pacific Rim countries, the fastest growing and probably one of the most competitive regions in the world. The speed and magnitude of the airline's entry into such a market had few, if any, precedents. Consequently, it also brought up new challenges:

■ The map United inserted into its sales promotion brochure left out one of Japan's main islands.

■ United's magazine ad campaign, "We Know the Orient," listed the names of Far Eastern countries below pictures of local coins. Unfortunately, the coins did not match up with the countries.

■ Most Chinese business travelers were shocked during the inauguration of United's concierge services for first-class passengers. To mark the occasion, each concierge was proudly wearing a white carnation—a well-known oriental symbol of death.

■ Perhaps the most embarrassing mistake was United's inflight magazine cover that showed Australian actor Paul Hogan wandering through the Outback. The caption read, "Paul Hogan Camps It Up." Hogan's lawyer alerted the airline that "camps it up" is Australian slang for "flaunts his homosexuality."

■ United's international ticket specialists were well trained in rate and fare calculation, technical documentation, passport regulations, and various currencies—the technical part of their task. However, once on the job, these employees still felt they were unprepared. One of the concerns expressed was that United did not take the time to teach them how to pronounce the names of destination cities correctly. They knew, quite *correctly, that they would never get away with mispronouncing someone's hometown.*

Source: John R. Zeeman, "Service—the Cutting Edge of Global Competition," speech given at the annual meeting of the Academy of International Business, November 14, 1987, Chicago, Illinois.

Although the world has become smaller as a result of improvements in transportation and information systems, the behavioral patterns, values, and attitudes that govern human interaction remain relatively unchanged. Technological innovation is bringing about the internationalization of business, and employees at all levels are becoming involved in cross-cultural interaction. Firms expanding internationally acquire foreign clients as well as foreign personnel with whom regular communication is necessary, with the result that day-to-day operations require significant cross-cultural competence. As the distinction between domestic and international activities diminishes cultural sensitivity in varying degrees is required from every employee, as The International Marketplace 5.1 illustrates.

In the past, marketing managers who did not want to worry about the cultural challenge could simply decide not to do so and concentrate on domestic markets. In today's business environment, a company has no choice but to face international competition. In this new environment, believing that concern about culture and its elements is a waste of time often proves to be disastrous.

Cultural differences often are the subject of anecdotes, and business blunders may provide a good laugh. Cultural incompetence, however, can easily jeopardize millions of dollars in wasted negotiations, potential purchases, sales and contracts, and customer relations. Furthermore, the internal efficiency of a firm may be weakened if managers, employees, and intermediaries are not "on the same wavelength."

The intent of this chapter is first to analyze the concept of culture and its various elements and then to provide suggestions for meeting the cultural challenge. Culture does, after all, affect each and every aspect of business.

CULTURE DEFINED

Culture gives an individual an anchoring point—an identity—as well as codes of conduct. Of the more than 160 definitions of culture analyzed by Kroeber and Kluckhohn, some conceive of culture as separating humans from nonhumans, some define it as communicable knowledge, and some as the sum of historical achievements produced by man's social life.[1] All of

[1] Alfred Kroeber and Clyde Kluckhohn, *Culture: A Critical Review of Concepts and Definitions* (New York: Random House, 1985), 11.

the definitions have common elements: Culture is learned, shared, and transmitted from one generation to the next. Culture is primarily passed on from parents to their children but also by social organizations, special interest groups, the government, the schools, and the church. Common ways of thinking and behaving that are developed are then reinforced through social pressure. Hofstede calls this the "collective programming of the mind."[2] Culture is also multidimensional, consisting of a number of common elements that are interdependent. Changes occurring in one of the dimensions will affect the others as well.

For the purposes of this text, culture is defined as an integrated system of learned behavior patterns that are distinguishing characteristics of the members of any given society. It includes everything that a group thinks, says, does, and makes—its customs, language, material artifacts, and shared systems of attitudes and feelings.[3] The definition therefore encompasses a wide variety of elements from the materialistic to the spiritual. Culture is inherently conservative, resisting change and fostering continuity. Every person is encultured into a particular culture, learning the "right way" of doing things. Problems may arise when a person encultured in one culture has to adjust to another one. The process of **acculturation**—adjusting and adapting to a specific culture other than one's own—is one of the keys to success in international operations.

Edward T. Hall, who has made some of the most valuable studies on the effects of culture on business, makes a distinction between high and low context cultures.[4] In **high context cultures,** such as Japan and Saudi Arabia, context is at least as important as what is actually said. The speaker and the listener rely on a common understanding of the context. In **low context cultures,** however, most of the information is contained explicitly in the words. North American cultures engage in low-context communications. Unless one is aware of this basic difference, messages and intentions can easily be misunderstood. If performance appraisals of marketing personnel are to be centrally guided or conducted in a multinational corporation, those involved must be acutely aware of cultural nuances. One of the interesting differences is that the U.S. system emphasizes the individual's development, whereas the Japanese system focuses on the group within which the individual works. In the United States, criticism is more direct and recorded formally, whereas in Japan it is more subtle and verbal. What is not being said can carry more meaning than what is said.

Few cultures today are as homogeneous as those of Japan and Saudi Arabia. Elsewhere intracultural differences based on nationality, religion, race, or geographic areas have resulted in the emergence of distinct subcultures. The international manager's task is to distinguish relevant cross-cultural and intracultural differences and then to isolate potential oppor-

---

[2]Hofstede, Geert, "National Cultures Revisited," *Asia–Pacific Journal of Management* 1 (September 1984): 22–24.

[3]Robert L. Kohls, *Survival Kit for Overseas Living* (Chicago: Intercultural Press, 1979), 3.

[4]Edward T. Hall, *Beyond Culture* (Garden City, N.Y.: Anchor Press, 1976), 15.

tunities and problems. Good examples are the Hispanic subculture in the United States and the Flemish and the Walloons in Belgium. On the other hand, borrowing and interaction between national cultures may lead to narrowing gaps between cultures. Here the international business entity will act as a change agent by introducing new products or ideas and practices. Although this may consist of no more than shifting consumption from one product brand to another, it may lead to massive social change in the manner of consumption, the type of products consumed, and social organization. Consider, for example, that in a ten-year period the international portion of McDonald's annual sales grew from 13 percent to 23 percent. In markets such as Taiwan, the entry of McDonald's and other fast-food entities dramatically changed eating habits, especially of the younger generation.

THE ELEMENTS OF CULTURE

The study of culture has led to generalizations that may apply to all cultures. Such characteristics are called **cultural universals,** which are manifestations of the total way of life of any group of people. These include such elements as bodily adornments, courtship, etiquette, family, gestures, joking, mealtimes, music, personal names, status differentiation, and trade.[5] These activities occur across cultures, but their manifestation may be unique in a particular society, bringing about **cultural diversity.** Common denominators can indeed be found, but how they are actually accomplished may vary dramatically.[6] Observation of the major ones summarized in Table 5.1 suggests that the elements are both material (such as tools) and abstract (such as attitudes). The sensitivity and adaptation to these elements by an international firm depends on the firm's level of involvement in the market—for example, licensing versus direct investment—and the product or service marketed. Naturally, some products and services or management practices require very little adjustment, whereas others have to be adapted dramatically.

Language

Language has been described as the mirror of culture. Language itself is multidimensional by nature. This is true not only of the spoken word but also of what can be called the nonverbal language of international business. Messages are conveyed by the words used, by how the words are spoken (for example, tone of voice), and through nonverbal means such as gestures, body position, and eye contact.

[5] George P. Mundak, "The Common Denominator of Cultures," in *The Science of Man in the World,* ed. Ralph Linton (New York: Columbia University Press, 1945), 123–142.

[6] Philip R. Harris and Robert T. Moran, *Managing Cultural Differences* (Houston, Tex.: Gulf, 1987), 201.

TABLE 5.1 ▪ **Elements of Culture**

> Language
>   • Verbal
>   • Nonverbal
> Religion
> Values and Attitudes
> Manners and Customs
> Material Elements
> Aesthetics
> Education
> Social Institutions

Very often mastery of the language is required before a person is accultured to a culture other than his or her own. Language mastery must go beyond technical competency because every language has words and phrases that can be readily understood only in context. Such phrases are carriers of culture; they represent special ways a culture has developed to view some aspect of human existence.

Language capability serves four distinct roles in international marketing.[7] Language is important in information gathering and evaluation efforts. Rather than rely completely on the opinions of others, the manager is able to see and hear personally what is going on. People are far more comfortable speaking their own language, and this should be treated as an advantage. The best intelligence is gathered on a market by becoming part of the market rather than observing it from the outside. For example, local managers of a multinational corporation should be the firm's primary source of political information to assess potential risk. Second, language provides access to local society. Although English may be widely spoken, and may even be the official company language, speaking the local language may make a dramatic difference. Third, language capability is increasingly important in company communications, whether within the corporate family or with channel members. Imagine the difficulties encountered by a country manager who must communicate with employees through an interpreter. Finally, language provides more than the ability to communicate. It extends beyond mechanics to the interpretation of contexts.

The manager's command of the national language(s) in a market must be greater than simple word recognition. Consider, for example, how dramatically different English terms can be when used in Australia, the United Kingdom, or the United States. In negotiations, U.S. delegates "tabling a proposal" mean that they want to delay a decision, while their British counterparts understand the expression to mean that immediate action is to be taken. If the British promise something "by the end of the day," this does not mean within 24 hours, but rather when they have completed the job. Additionally, they may say that negotiations "bombed," meaning

---

[7]David A. Ricks, *Big Business Blunders* (Homewood, Ill.: Irwin, 1983), 4.

FIGURE 5.1 ▪ **Example of an Ad That Will Transfer Badly**

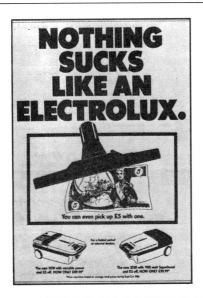

Source: "Viewpoint: Letters," *Advertising Age*, June 29, 1987, 20.

that they were a success, which to an American could convey exactly the opposite message.

An example of this separation of Americans and British by the same language is provided in Figure 5.1. Electrolux's theme in marketing its vacuum cleaners is interpreted in the United Kingdom without connotations, while in the United States the slang implications would earn the campaign blunder honors. Similar problems occur with other languages and markets. Swedish is spoken as a mother tongue by 8 percent of the population in Finland, where it has idioms that are not well understood by Swedes.

Difficulties with language usually arise through carelessness, which is manifested in a number of translation blunders. The old saying, "If you want to kill a message, translate it," is true. A classic example involves GM and its "Body by Fisher" theme; when translated into Flemish, this became "Corpse by Fisher."[8] A similar incident for Braniff is reported in The International Marketplace 5.2. There is also the danger of sound-alikes. For example, Chanel No. 5 would have fared poorly in Japan had it been called Chanel No. 4, because the Japanese word for four (shih) also sounds like the word for death. This is the reason that IBM's series 44 computers had a different number classification in Japan than in any other market in which they were introduced. The danger of using a translingual

[8]Ibid., 24–28.

5.2 THE INTERNATIONAL MARKETPLACE

> ***Braniff's Bare Bones Advertising Campaign*** Braniff Inc. got *some extra miles out of its advertising campaign designed to attract Spanish-speaking passengers. The advertisement invited customers to try the airline's leather seats. But that was not apparently all. "Sentado en cuero," or "to be seated in leather," sounds and looks too much like "sentado en cueros," or "to be seated naked."*
>
> *The company's marketing vice president, Diego Garrido, did not mind all the publicity that ensued. Having a little fun with the situation, he put out a news release that said "en cuero—leather—should not be confused with en cueros—naked—although we do not want to limit your imagination."*
>
> *Garrido said that, when the ads were designed, Braniff knew the slogan could be taken the wrong way. However, the only other Spanish word for leather is "piel," which can also mean animal hide and human skin.*
>
> Source: "Braniff Inc.'s Spanish Ad Bears Cause for Laughter," *The Wall Street Journal*, February 9, 1987, 5.

homonym also exists; that is, an innocent English word may have strong aural resemblance to a word not used in polite company in another country. Examples in French-speaking areas include Pet milk products and a toothpaste called Cue. A French firm trying to sell pâté to a Baltimore importer experienced a problem with the brand name Tartex, which sounded like shoe polish. Kellogg renamed Bran Buds in Sweden, where the brand name translated roughly to "burned farmer."

Another consideration is the capability of language to convey different shades of meaning. As an example, a one-word equivalent to "aftertaste" does not exist in many languages and in others is far-fetched at best. To communicate the idea may require a lengthy translation of "the taste that remains in your mouth after you have finished eating or drinking."

The role of language extends beyond that of a communications medium. Linguistic diversity often is an indicator of other types of diversity. In Quebec, the French language has always been a major consideration of most francophone governments, because it is one of the clear manifestations of the identity of the province vis-à-vis the English-speaking provinces. The Charter of the French Language states that the rights of the francophone collectivity are (1) the right of every person to have the civil administration, semipublic agencies, and business firms communicate with him or her in French; (2) the right of workers to carry on their activities in French; and (3) the right of consumers to be informed and served in French. The Bay, a major Quebec retailer, spends $8 million annually on its translation operations. It even changed its name to La Baie in appropriate areas.

If a brand name or an advertising theme is to be extended, care has to be taken to make sure of a comfortable fit. Kellogg's Rice Krispies snap, crackle, and pop in most markets; the Japanese, who have trouble pronouncing these words, watch the caricatures "patchy, pitchy, putchy" in their commercials.

Dealing with the language problem invariably requires the use of local assistance. A good local advertising agency and a good local market research firm can prevent many problems. When translation is required, as when communicating with suppliers or customers, care should be taken in selecting the translator. One of the simplest methods of control is **back-translation**—the translating of a foreign-language version back to the original language by a different person than the one who made the first translation.

Nonverbal Language

Managers must analyze and become familiar with the hidden language of foreign cultures.[9] Five key topics—time, space, material possessions, friendship patterns, and business agreements—offer a starting point from which managers can begin to acquire the understanding necessary to do business in foreign countries. In many parts of the world, time is flexible and not seen as a limited commodity; people come late to appointments or may not come at all. In Hong Kong, for example, it is futile to set exact meeting times, because getting from one place to another may take minutes or hours depending on the traffic situation. Showing indignation or impatience at such behavior would astonish an Arab, Latin American, or Asian.

In some countries, extended social acquaintance and the establishment of appropriate personal rapport are essential to conducting business. The feeling is that one should know one's business partner on a personal level before transactions can occur. Therefore rushing straight to business will not be rewarded, because deals are made not only on the basis of the best product or price but also the entity or person deemed most trustworthy. Contracts may be bound on handshakes, not lengthy and complex agreements—a fact that makes some, especially Western, business people uneasy.

Individuals vary in the amount of space they want separating them from others. Arabs and Latin Americans like to stand close to people they are talking with. If an American, who may not be comfortable at such close range, backs away from an Arab, this might incorrectly be taken as a negative reaction. Also, Westerners are often taken aback by the more physical nature of affection between Slavs—for example, being kissed squarely on the lips by a business partner, regardless of sex.

[9]Edward T. Hall, "The Silent Language of Overseas Business," *Harvard Business Review* 38 (May–June 1960): 87–96.

International body language must be included in the nonverbal language of international business. For example, an American manager may, after successful completion of negotiations, impulsively give a finger-and-thumb OK sign. In Southern France, the manager will have indicated that the sale is worthless, and in Japan that a little bribe has been asked for; the gesture is grossly insulting to Brazilians. An interesting exercise is to compare and contrast the conversation styles of different nationalities. Northern Europeans are quite reserved in using their hands and maintain a good amount of personal space, whereas Southern Europeans involve their bodies to a far greater degree in making a point.

Religion

Most cultures find in religion a reason for being. Religion can provide the basis for transcultural similarities under shared beliefs in Islam, Buddhism, or Christianity, for example.

An obvious example of the effect of religious beliefs on international marketing is the prohibition of pork products and alcoholic beverages in the Middle East. When beef or poultry is exported to a Muslim country, the animal must be killed in the "halal" method. Currently 12 Islamic centers slaughter and certify meat for export. Recognition of religious restrictions can reveal opportunities as well as liabilities, as evidenced by the successful launch of several nonalcoholic beverages in some Middle Eastern countries. The impact of religion may vary from one country to another. For example, Islam requires extensive fasting during the holy month of Ramadan, the start and duration of which varies because the lunar year is 11 to 12 days shorter than that based on the Gregorian calendar. Tunisia, however, has discouraged its people from too diligent observance of Ramadan to avoid marked drops in productivity. In Saudi Arabia the pilgrimage to Mecca has forced the government to improve its transportation system. The primary responsibility for building a traffic system to Mecca was assumed by a Swedish firm, which found that non-Muslims are not allowed access to the sacred place. The solution was to use closed-circuit television to supervise the work.

Major holidays are often tied to religion. These holidays will be observed differently from one culture to the next, to the extent that the same holiday may have different connotations. Most Western cultures, because they are predominantly Christian, observe Christmas and exchange gifts either December 24 or December 25. However, the Dutch exchange gifts on St. Nicholas Day (December 6) and the Russians on Frost Man's Day (January 1). Tandy Corporation, in its first year in Holland, targeted its major advertising campaign for the third week of December with disastrous results. The international manager must see to it that local holidays are taken into account in the scheduling of events, ranging from fact-finding missions to marketing programs, and in preparing local work schedules.

The role of women in business is tied to religion, especially in the Middle East, where they are not able to function as they would in the

West. This affects management in two ways: the firm may not be able to use women managers or personnel in certain countries, and women's role as consumers and influencers in the consumption process may be altogether different. Access to women in Islamic countries, for example, may be available only by using female sales personnel, direct marketing, and women's specialty shops.[10]

International marketing managers must be aware of religious divisions in the countries of operation. The impact of these divisions may range from hostilities, as in Sri Lanka, to below-the-surface suspicion—for example, in many European markets where Protestant and Catholic are the main religious divisions.

Values and Attitudes

Values are shared beliefs or group norms that have been internalized by individuals.[11] Attitudes are evaluations of alternatives based on these values. The Japanese culture raises an almost invisible—yet often unscalable—wall against all *gaijin*, foreigners. Many middle-aged bureaucrats and company officials, for example, feel that buying foreign products is unpatriotic. The resistance therefore is not so much against foreign products as those who produce and market them. Similarly, foreign-based corporations have had difficulty in hiring university graduates or mid-career personnel because of bias against foreign employers.

Even under these adverse conditions the race can be run and won through tenacity, patience, and drive. As an example, Procter & Gamble has made impressive inroads with its products by adopting a long-term, Japanese-style view of profits. Since the mid-1970s, the company has gained some 20 percent of the detergent market and made Pampers a household word among Japanese mothers. The struggle toward such rewards can require foreign companies to take big losses for five years or more.

The more rooted values and attitudes are in central beliefs (such as religion), the more cautiously the international marketing manager has to move. Attitude toward change is basically positive in industrialized countries, whereas in more tradition-bound societies change is viewed with great suspicion, especially when it comes from a foreign entity. These situations call for thorough research, most likely a localized approach, and a major commitment at the top level for a considerable period of time. For example, before launching Colac laxative in Japan, Richardson-Vicks studied the psychological dimensions of constipation. The reticent Japanese are willing to discuss such delicate subjects once they realize they are members of a group with a common problem, but not with Westerners

---

[10]Mushtaq Luqmami, Zahir A. Quraeshi, and Linda Delene, "Marketing in Islamic Countries: A Viewpoint," *MSU Business Topics* 23 (Summer 1980): 17–24.

[11]James F. Engel, Roger D. Blackwell, and Paul W. Miniard, *Consumer Behavior* (Hinsdale, Ill.: Dryden, 1986), 223.

present at the meetings. Research showed that Japanese were dissatisfied with slow-acting herbal medicines but wary that a Western laxative might be too strong. Thus Colac is presented as two little pink pills with natural qualities: "Three things to consider for stubborn constipation—salad, beauty exercise, and Colac before bedtime."

Cultural differences in themselves can be a selling point suggesting luxury, prestige, or status. Sometimes U.S. companies use domestic marketing approaches when selling abroad because they believe the American look will sell the product. In Japan, Borden sells Lady Borden ice cream and Borden cheese deliberately packaged and labeled in English, exactly as they are in the United States. Similarly, in France, General Foods sells a chewing gum called Hollywood with an accompanying Pepsi-generation type of ad campaign that pictures teenagers riding bicycles on the beach.

Occasionally, U.S. firms successfully use American themes abroad that would not succeed at home. In Japan, Levi Strauss promoted its popular jeans with a television campaign featuring James Dean and Marilyn Monroe, who represent the epitome of Japanese youth's fantasy of freedom from a staid, traditional society. The commercials helped to establish Levi's as *the* prestige jeans, and status-seeking Japanese youth willingly pay 40 percent more for them than for local brands. Their authentic Levi's, however, are designed and mostly made in Japan, where buyers like a tighter fit than do Americans.[12] At the same time, in the U.S. market many companies have been quite successful in emphasizing a foreign, imported image.

Manners and Customs

Changes occurring in manners and customs must be carefully monitored, especially in cases that seem to indicate narrowing of cultural differences between peoples. Phenomena such as McDonald's and Coke have met with success around the world, but this does not mean that the world is becoming Westernized. Modernization and Westernization are not at all the same, as can be seen in Saudi Arabia, for example.

Understanding manners and customs is especially important in negotiations, because interpretations based on one's own frame of reference may lead to a totally incorrect conclusion. To negotiate effectively abroad, all types of communication should be read correctly. Americans often interpret inaction and silence as a negative sign, with the result that Japanese executives tend to expect by saying little to get Americans to lower prices or sweeten the deal. Even a simple agreement may take days to negotiate in the Middle East because the Arab party may want to talk about unrelated issues or do something else for a while. The abrasive style of Soviet negotiators, and their usual last-minute change requests, may cause astonishment and concern on the part of ill-prepared negotiators. And consider the reaction of an American business person if a Finnish counterpart were to

[12]"Learning How to Please the Baffling Japanese," *Fortune*, October 5, 1981, 122.

THE INTERNATIONAL MARKETPLACE   5.3

Coordinating European Schedules   *Can Europe have a single market before it has a single lunchtime? Europeans' determination to have lunch at three o'clock (Spain) or 12 o'clock (Federal Republic of Germany) or one o'clock (United Kingdom) means that catching a European business contact may be challenging. In Greece, no one makes telephone calls between two and five in the afternoon. Greeks doing business with Germans have to get to their West German counterparts in the morning hours because the Germans start going home at four.*

The British tend to arrive at their desks at 9:30, but do not like to be rung on the telephone at that hour. They do paperwork and drink their morning beverage while collecting themselves. They can rarely be reached after 5:30 even if they are at their desks: switchboards have closed down by then. The French, like the West Germans, tend to start earlier, occasionally attending working breakfasts. Civil servants in Italy work from eight to two and then go home (although they do work a six-day week).

Stereotyping about national hours and national character are risky. The levantine Turkish business community keeps hours rather like the British. The Irish (who used to say that when God created time he made plenty of it) have produced a new breed of business person who prides himself or herself on taking phone calls from Hong Kong at four o'clock in the morning.

The challenges are as great in European countries outside the EC. Norwegians get to the office at eight, leave for lunch at eleven, and may have dinner as early as five. Visitors are often mystified at finding restaurants getting ready to close at nine. Zurich bankers have been known to make appointments for seven in the morning, with visitors expected to arrive five minutes early.

Source: "Europe Sans Horaires," *The Economist,* May 21, 1988, 60.

---

propose the continuing of negotiations in the sauna. Many business customs may seem trivial, or even humorous, until the international manager must cope with them, as illustrated in The International Marketplace 5.3.

In many cultures, certain basic customs must be observed by the foreign business person. One of them concerns use of the right and left hands. In so-called right-hand societies, the left hand is the "toilet hand" and using it to eat, for example, is considered impolite.

Managers must be concerned with differences in the ways products are used. For example, General Food's Tang is positioned as a breakfast drink in the United States; in France, where orange juice usually is not consumed at breakfast, Tang is positioned as a refreshment. The questions that the international manager must ask are: "What are we selling?" and "What are the use benefits we should be providing?"

Usage differences have to be translated into product form and promotional decisions. Maxwell House coffee is a worldwide brand name. It is used to sell coffee in both ground and instant form in the United States. In the United Kingdom, Maxwell House is available only in instant form. In France and Germany, it is sold in freeze-dried form only, while in the Scandinavian countries Maxwell House is positioned as the top-of-the-line entry. As a matter of fact, Maxwell House is called simply Maxwell in France and Japan, because "House" is confusing to consumers in those countries. In one South American market, a shampoo maker was concerned about poor sales of the entire product class. Research uncovered the fact that many women wash their hair with bars of soap and use shampoo only as a brief rinse or topper.

Many Western companies have stumbled in Japan because they did not learn enough about the distinctive habits of Japanese consumers. Purveyors of soup should know that the Japanese drink it mainly for breakfast. Johnson & Johnson had relatively little success selling baby powder in Japan until research was conducted on use conditions. In their small homes, mothers fear that powder will fly around and get into their spotlessly clean kitchens. The company now sells baby powder in flat boxes with powder puffs so that mothers can apply it sparingly. Adults will not use it at all. They wash and rinse themselves before soaking in hot baths; powder would make them feel dirty again. Another classic case involves General Mills' Betty Crocker cake mix. The company designed a mix to be prepared in electric rice cookers. After the product's costly flop, the company found that the Japanese take pride in the purity of their rice, which they thought would be contaminated by cake flavors. General Mills' mistake was comparable to asking an English housewife to make coffee in her teapot.

Package sizes and labels must be adapted in many countries to suit the needs of the particular culture. In Mexico, for example, Campbell's sells soup in cans large enough to serve four or five, because families are generally large. In Britain, where consumers are more accustomed to ready-to-serve soups, Campbell's prints "one can makes two" on its condensed soup labels to ensure that shoppers understand how to use it.

In the United States, men buy diamond engagement rings for their fiancées. This custom is not global, however. In Germany, for example, young women tend to buy diamond rings for themselves. This precludes the use of global advertising campaigns by a company like De Beers.

Managers must be careful of myths and legends. One candy company was ready to launch a new peanut-packed chocolate bar in Japan, aimed at giving teenagers quick energy while they crammed for exams. The company then learned about a Japanese folk legend that eating chocolate with peanuts can cause nosebleed. The launch never took place.

Meticulous research plays a major role in avoiding these types of problems. Concept tests determine the potential acceptance and proper understanding of a proposed new product. **Focus groups,** each consisting of 8 to 12 consumers representative of the proposed target audience, can be interviewed and their responses used as disaster checks and to fine-tune research findings. The most sensitive types of products, such as consumer packaged goods, require consumer usage and attitude studies as well as retail distribution studies and audits to analyze the movement of the product to retailers and eventually to households.

Material Elements

Material culture results from technology and is directly related to how a society organizes its economic activity. It is manifested in the availability and adequacy of the basic economic, social, financial, and marketing **infrastructures.** The basic economic infrastructure consists of transportation, energy, and communications systems. Social infrastructure refers to housing, health, and educational systems. Financial and marketing infrastructures provide the facilitating agencies for the international firm's operation in a given market in terms of, for example, banks and research firms. In some parts of the world, the international firm may have to be an integral partner in developing the various infrastructures before it can operate, whereas in others it may greatly benefit from their high level of sophistication.

The level of material culture can serve in segmentation efforts if the degree of industrialization is used as a basis. For companies selling industrial goods, such as General Electric, this can provide a convenient starting point. In developing countries, demand may be highest for basic energy-generating products. In fully developed markets time-saving home appliances may be more in demand.

Technological advances have probably been the major cause of cultural change in many countries. For example, the increase in leisure time so characteristic in Western cultures has been a direct result of technological development. Workers in West Germany are now pushing for a 35-hour work week. With technological advancement also comes **cultural convergence.** Black-and-white television sets extensively penetrated the U.S. market more than a decade before they reached similar levels in Europe and Japan. With color television, the lag was reduced to five years. With videocassette recorders, the difference was only three years, but this time the Europeans and the Japanese led the way while Americans concentrated on cable systems. With the compact disk, penetration rates were even after only one year. Today, with MTV available by satellite across Europe, no lag exists at all.[13]

Material culture—mainly the degree to which it exists and how it is esteemed—will have an impact on marketing decisions. Many exporters do not understand the degree to which Americans are package-conscious; for

[13]Kenichi Ohmae, "Managing in a Borderless World," *Harvard Business Review* 67 (May–June 1989): 152–161.

example, cans must be shiny and beautiful. On the other hand, packaging problems may arise in other countries due to lack of certain materials, different specifications when the material is available, different line-fill machinery, and immense differences in quality and consistency of printing ink, especially in South America and the Third World. Even the ability of media to reach target audiences will be affected by ownership of television sets and radios.

Aesthetics

Each culture makes a clear statement concerning good taste, as expressed in the arts and in the particular symbolism of colors, form, and music. What is and what is not acceptable may vary dramatically even in otherwise highly similar markets. Sex in advertising is an example. In an apparent attempt to preserve the purity of Japanese womanhood, Japanese advertisers frequently turn to blonde, blue-eyed foreign models to make the point. In the same vein, Commodore International, the U.S.-based personal computer manufacturer, showed a totally naked young man in ads that ran in the German version of *Cosmopolitan*. Approaches of this kind would not be possible in the United States because of regulations and opposition from consumer groups.

Color is often used as a mechanism for brand identification, feature reinforcement, and differentiation. In international markets, colors have more symbolic value than in domestic markets. Black, for instance, is considered the color of mourning in the United States and Europe, whereas white has the same symbolic value in Japan and most of the Far East. A British bank interested in expanding its operations to Singapore wanted to use blue and green as its identification colors. A consulting firm was quick to tell the client that green is associated with death there. Although the bank insisted on its original choice of colors, the green was changed to an acceptable shade.[14] Similarly, music used in broadcast advertisements is often adjusted to reflect regional differences.

International firms, such as McDonald's, have to take into consideration local tastes and concerns in designing their facilities. They may have a general policy of uniformity in building, or office space design, but local tastes may often warrant modifications.

Education

Education, either formal or informal, plays a major role in the passing on and sharing of culture. Educational levels of a culture can be assessed using literacy rates, enrollment in secondary education, or enrollment in higher education available from secondary data sources. International firms also need to know about the qualitative aspects of education, namely

[14]Joe Agnew, "Cultural Differences Probed to Create Product Identity," *Marketing News*, October 24, 1986, 22.

varying emphases on particular skills, and the overall level of the education provided. Japan and the Republic of Korea, for example, emphasize
the sciences, especially engineering, to a greater degree than do Western
countries.

Educational levels will have an impact on various business functions.
Training programs for a production facility will have to take the educational backgrounds of trainees into account. For example, a high level of
illiteracy will suggest the use of visual aids rather than printed manuals.
Local recruiting for sales jobs will be affected by the availability of suit-
ably trained personnel. In some cases, international firms routinely send
locally recruited personnel to headquarters for training.

The international marketing manager may also have to be prepared to
fight obstacles in recruiting a suitable sales force or support personnel. For
example, the Japanese culture places a premium on loyalty, and employees
consider themselves to be members of the corporate family. If a foreign firm
decides to leave Japan, employees may find themselves stranded in mid-
career, unable to find a place in the Japanese business system. University
graduates are therefore reluctant to join all but the largest and most well
known of foreign firms.[15]

If technology is marketed, the level of sophistication of the product will
depend on the educational level of future users. Product-adaptation decisions are often influenced by the extent to which targeted customers are
able to use the product or service properly.

Social Institutions

Social institutions affect the ways in which people relate to each other.
The family unit, which in Western industrialized countries consists of
parents and children, in a number of cultures is extended to include
grandparents and other relatives. This will have an impact on consumption patterns and must be taken into account, for example, when conducting market research.

The concept of kinship, or blood relations between individuals, is defined in a very broad way in societies such as those in sub-Saharan Africa.
Family relations and a strong obligation to family are important factors to
be considered in human resource management in those regions. Understanding tribal politics in countries such as Nigeria may help the manager
avoid unnecessary complications in executing business transactions.

The division of a particular population into classes is termed **social
stratification.** Stratification ranges from the situation in Northern Europe,
where most people are members of the middle class, to highly stratified
societies in which the higher strata control most of the buying power and
decision-making positions.

[15] Joseph A. McKinney, "Joint Ventures of United States Firms in Japan: A Survey," *Venture
Japan* 1 (No. 2, 1988): 14–19.

An important part of the socialization process of consumers worldwide is **reference groups.**[16] These groups provide the values and attitudes that become influential in shaping behavior. Primary reference groups include the family, coworkers, and other intimate groupings, whereas secondary groups are social organizations in which less continuous interaction takes place, such as professional associations and trade organizations. Besides socialization, reference groups develop an individual's concept of self, which manifests itself, for example, through the use of products. Reference groups also provide a baseline for compliance with group norms through either conforming to or avoiding certain behaviors.

Social organization also determines the roles of managers and subordinates and how they relate to one another. In some cultures, managers and subordinates are separated explicitly and implicitly by various boundaries ranging from social class differences to separate office facilities. In others, cooperation is elicited through equality. For example, Nissan USA has no privileged parking spaces and no private dining rooms, everyone wears the same type of white coveralls, and the president sits in the same room with a hundred other white-collar workers.[17] The fitting of an organizational culture for internal marketing purposes to the larger context of a national culture has to be executed with care. Changes that are too dramatic may cause disruption of productivity or, at the minimum, suspicion.

SOURCES OF CULTURAL KNOWLEDGE

The concept of cultural knowledge is broad and multifaceted. Cultural knowledge can be defined by the way it is acquired. Objective or factual information is obtained from others through communication, research, and education. **Experiential knowledge,** on the other hand, can be acquired only by being involved in a culture other than one's own.[18] A summary of the types of knowledge needed by the international manager is provided in Table 5.2. Both factual and experiential information can be general or country specific. In fact, the more a manager becomes involved in the international arena, the more he or she is able to develop a meta-knowledge; that is, ground rules that apply to a great extent whether in Kuala Lumpur, Malaysia, or Asunción, Paraguay. Market-specific knowledge does not necessarily travel well; the general variables on which the information is based does.

In a survey of managers on how to acquire international expertise, they ranked eight factors in terms of their importance, as shown in Table 5.3. These managers emphasized the experiential acquisition of knowledge. Written materials were indicated to play an important but supplementary

---

[16]Engel, Blackwell, and Miniard, *Consumer Behavior,* 318–324.

[17]"The Difference That Japanese Management Makes," *Business Week,* July 14, 1986, 47–50.

[18]James H. Sood and Patrick Adams, "Model of Management Learning Styles as a Predictor of Export Behavior and Performance," *Journal of Business Research* 12 (June 1984): 169–182.

TABLE 5.2 ▪ **Types of International Information**

| | Type of Information | |
Source of Information	General	Country-Specific
Objective	Examples: • Impact of GNP • Regional integration	Examples: • Tariff barriers • Government regulations
Experiential	Example: • Corporate adjustment to internationalization	Examples: • Product acceptance • Program appropriateness

TABLE 5.3 ▪ **Managers' Ranking of Factors Involved in Acquiring International Expertise**

	Factor	Considered Critical	Considered Important
1.	Business Travel	60.8%	92.0%
2.	Assignments Overseas	48.8	71.2
3.	Reading/Television	16.0	63.2
4.	Training Programs	6.4	28.8
5.	Precareer Activities	4.0	16.0
6.	Graduate Course	2.4	15.2
7.	Nonbusiness Travel	0.8	12.8
8.	Undergraduate Courses	0.8	12.0

Source: Stephen J. Kobrin, *International Expertise in American Business* (New York: Institute of International Education, 1984), 38.

role, very often providing general or country-specific information before operational decisions must be made. Interestingly, many of today's international managers have precareer experience in government, the Peace Corps, the armed forces, or missionary service. Although the survey emphasized travel, a one-time trip to London with a stay at a large hotel and scheduled sightseeing tours does not contribute to cultural knowledge in a significant way. Travel that involves meetings with company personnel, intermediaries, facilitating agents, customers, and government officials, on the other hand, does contribute.[19]

A variety of sources and methods are available to the manager for extending his or her knowledge of specific cultures. Most of these sources deal with factual information that provides a necessary basis for market studies. Beyond the normal business literature and its anecdotal information, specific country studies are published by the U.S. government, private companies, and universities. *Country Studies* are available for 108

[19] Stephen J. Kobrin, *International Expertise in American Business* (New York: Institute of International Education, 1984), 36.

countries from the U.S. Government Printing Office, while *Country Up-dates,* produced by Overseas Briefing Associates, feature 22 countries. *In-formation Guide for Doing Business in X* is the basic title for a series of publications produced by Price Waterhouse; so far, 48 countries are in-cluded. *Brief Culturegrams* for 63 countries and the more extensive *Build-ing Bridges for Understanding with the People of X* are published by the Language and Intercultural Research Center of Brigham Young Univer-sity.[20] Many facilitating agencies—such as banks, advertising agencies, and transportation companies—provide background information on the markets they serve for their clients. One of the more attractive sources is provided by the Hong Kong and Shanghai Banking Corporation, which has a *Business Profile Series* that is especially good for the Middle East.

Blunders in foreign markets that could have been avoided with factual information are generally inexcusable. A manager who travels to Taipei without first obtaining a visa, and is therefore turned back, has no one else to blame. Other oversights may lead to more costly mistakes. For example, Brazilians are several inches shorter than the average American, but this was not taken into account when Sears erected American-height shelves that block Brazilian shoppers' view of the rest of the store.

International business success requires not only comprehensive fact finding and preparation but also an ability to understand and appreciate fully the nuances of different cultural traits and patterns. Gaining this **in-terpretive knowledge** requires "getting one's feet wet" over a sufficient length of time.

CULTURAL ANALYSIS

To try to understand and explain differences among cultures and subse-quently in cross-cultural behavior, checklists and models showing perti-nent variables and their interaction can be developed. An example of such a model is provided in Figure 5.2. This model is based on the premise that all international business activity should be viewed as innovation and as producing change processes.[21] After all, exporters and multinational cor-porations introduce marketing practices as well as products and services from one country to other cultures, where they are perceived to be new and different. Although many question the usefulness of such models, they do bring together, into one presentation, all or most of the relevant variables that have an impact on how consumers in different cultures may perceive, evaluate, and adopt new behaviors. However, any manager using such a tool should periodically cross-check its results with reality and experience.

[20] Lennie Copeland, "Training Americans to Do Business Overseas," *Training,* July 1984, 22–23.

[21] Jagdish N. Sheth and S. Prakash Sethi, "A Theory of Cross-Cultural Buying Behavior," in *Consumer and Industrial Buying Behavior,* eds. Arch G. Woodside, Jagdish N. Sheth, and Peter D. Bennett (New York: Elsevier North-Holland, 1977), 369–386.

FIGURE 5.2 ▪ **A Model of Cross-Cultural Behavior**

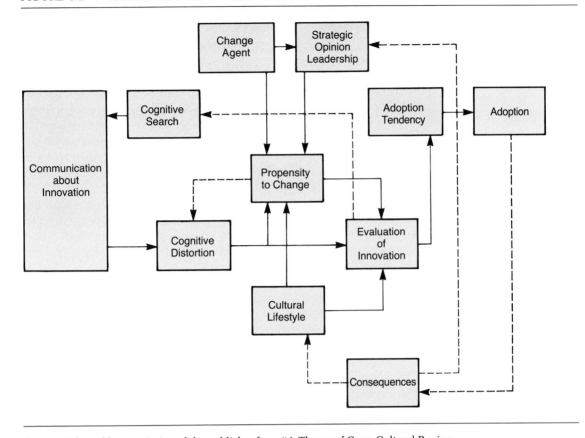

Source: Adapted by permission of the publisher from "A Theory of Cross-Cultural Buying Behavior," by Jagdish N. Sheth and S. Prakash Sethi, in *Consumer and Industrial Buyer Behavior,* eds. Arch G. Woodside, Jagdish N. Sheth, and Peter D. Bennett, 1977, 373. Copyright 1977 by Elsevier Science Publishing Co., Inc.

The key variable of the model is propensity to change, which is a function of three constructs: (1) cultural lifestyle of individuals in terms of how deeply held their traditional beliefs and attitudes are, and also which elements of culture are dominant; (2) change agents (such as multinational corporations and their practices) and strategic opinion leaders (for example, social elites); and (3) communication about the innovation from commercial sources, neutral sources (such as government), and social sources, such as friends and relatives.

Communication about the innovation takes place through the physical product itself (samples) or experiencing a new policy in the company. If a new practice, such as quality circles or pan-regional planning, is in question, results may be communicated in reports or through word-of-mouth by the participating employees. Communication content depends on the following factors: the product's or policy's relative advantage over existing alternatives; compatibility with established behavioral patterns; complexity, or the degree to which the product or process is perceived as difficult to understand and use; trialability, or the degree to which it may be experimented with and not incur major risk; and observability, which is the extent to which the consequences of the innovation are visible.

Before the product or policy is evaluated, information about it will be compared with existing beliefs about the circumstances surrounding the situation. Distortion will occur as a result of selective attention, exposure, and retention. As examples, anything foreign may be seen in a negative light, another multinational company's efforts may have failed, or the government may implicitly discourage the proposed activity. Additional information may then be sought from any of the input sources or from opinion leaders in the market.

Adoption tendency refers to the likelihood that the product or process will be accepted. Examples of this are advertising in the People's Republic of China and equity joint ventures with Western participants in the Soviet Union, both of them unheard of a few years ago. If an innovation clears the hurdles, it may be adopted and slowly diffused into the entire market. An international manager has two basic choices: to adapt company offerings and methods to those in the market or try to change market conditions to fit company programs. In Japan, a number of Western companies have run into obstructions in the Japanese distribution system, where great value is placed on established relationships; everything is done on the basis of favoring the familiar and fearing the unfamiliar. In most cases, this problem is solved by joint venturing with a major Japanese entity that has established contacts. On occasion, when the company's approach is compatible with the central beliefs of a culture, the company may be able to change existing customs rather than adjust to them. Initially, Procter & Gamble's traditional hard-selling style in television commercials jolted most Japanese viewers accustomed to more subtle approaches. Now the ads are being imitated by Japanese competitors.

Although models like the one in Figure 5.2 may aid in strategy planning by making sure that all variables and their linkages are considered, any analysis is incomplete without the basic recognition of cultural differences. Adjusting to differences requires putting one's own cultural values aside. James E. Lee proposes that the natural **self-reference criterion**—the unconscious reference to one's own cultural values—is the root of most international business problems.[22] However, recognizing and admitting this are often quite difficult. The following analytical approach is recommended to reduce the influence of one's own cultural values:

1. Define the problem or goal in terms of domestic cultural traits, habits, or norms.

---

[22] James A. Lee, "Cultural Analysis in Overseas Operations," *Harvard Business Review* 44 (March–April 1966): 106–114.

2. Define the problem or goal in terms of foreign cultural traits, habits, or norms. Make no value judgments.

3. Isolate the self-reference criterion influence in the problem and examine it carefully to see how it complicates the problem.

4. Redefine the problem without the self-reference criterion influence and solve for the optimum goal situation.

This approach can be applied to product introduction. If Kellogg's wants to introduce breakfast cereals into markets where breakfast is traditionally not eaten or where consumers drink very little milk, managers must consider very carefully how to instill this new habit. The traits, habits, and norms in terms of the importance of breakfast are quite different in the United States, France, and Brazil, and they have to be outlined before the product can be introduced. In France, Kellogg's commercials are aimed as much at providing nutrition lessons as they are at promoting the product. In Brazil, the company advertised on a soap opera to gain entry into the market, because Brazilians often emulate the characters of these television shows.

Analytical procedures require constant monitoring of changes caused by outside events as well as the changes caused by the business entity itself. Controlling **ethnocentricism**—regarding one's own culture superior to others—can be achieved only by acknowledging it and properly adjusting to its possible effects in managerial decision making. The international manager needs to be prepared and able to put that preparedness to effective use.[23]

THE TRAINING CHALLENGE

International managers face a dilemma in terms of international and intercultural competence. The lack of adequate foreign language and international business skills has cost U.S. firms lost contracts, weak negotiations, and ineffectual management. A UNESCO study of 10- and 14-year-old students in nine countries placed Americans next to last in their comprehension of foreign cultures. A sad 61 percent of U.S. business schools offer few or no courses in international business.[24] Although the types of jobs for which cross-cultural training has been deemed most important—mainly expatriate positions—are on the decline, the increase in overall international activity of firms has increased the need for cultural sensitivity training at all levels of the organization. Further, today's training must take into consideration not only outsiders to the firm but interaction within the corporate family as well. However inconsequential the degree of interaction may seem, it can still cause problems if proper understand-

[23] Peter D. Fitzpatrick and Alan S. Zimmerman, *Essentials of Export Marketing* (New York: American Management Organization, 1985), 16.

[24] Copeland, "Training Americans to Do Business Overseas."

ing is lacking. Consider, for example, the date 11/12/90 on a telex; a European will interpret this as the eleventh of December, an American as the twelfth of November.

Some companies try to avoid the training problem by hiring only nationals or well-traveled Americans for their international operations. This makes sense for the management of overseas operations but will not solve the training need, especially if transfers are likely to a culture unfamiliar to the manager. International experience may not necessarily transfer from one market to another.

To foster cultural sensitivity and acceptance of new ways of doing things within the organization, management must institute internal education programs. These may include written communication (for example, newsletters), interaction between management and employees, and formal training programs for those who will have front-line duty in this respect. The objective of formal training programs is to foster the four critical characteristics of preparedness, sensitivity, patience, and flexibility in managers and other personnel. These programs vary dramatically in terms of their rigor, involvement, and, of course, cost.[25] One such program is described in The International Marketplace 5.4.

Environmental briefings and cultural orientation programs are types of **area studies** programs. These programs provide factual preparation for a manager to operate in, or work with people from, a particular country. Area studies should be a basic prerequisite for other types of training programs. Alone, area studies serve little practical purpose because they do not really get the manager's feet wet. Other, more involved, programs contribute the context in which to put facts so that they can be properly understood.

The **cultural assimilator** is a program in which trainees must respond to scenarios of specific situations in a particular country. These programs have been developed for the Arab countries, Iran, Thailand, Central America, and Greece.[26] The results of the trainees' assimilator experience are evaluated by a panel of judges. This type of program has been used in particular in cases of transfers abroad on short notice.

When more time is available, managers can be trained extensively in language. This may be required if an exotic language is involved. **Sensitivity training** focuses on enhancing a manager's flexibility in situations that are quite different from those at home. The approach is based on the assumption that understanding and accepting oneself is critical to understanding a person from another culture. Finally, training may involve field experience, which exposes a manager to a different cultural environment for a limited amount of time. Although the expense of placing and maintaining an expatriate is high (and, therefore, the cost of failure is high), field experience is rarely used in training.

---

[25] Rosalie Tung, "Selection and Training of Personnel for Overseas Assignments," *Columbia Journal of World Business* 16 (Spring 1981): 68–78.

[26] Harris and Moran, *Managing Cultural Differences*, 267–295.

THE INTERNATIONAL MARKETPLACE 5.4

Raising Cross-Cultural Awareness at Honeywell Honeywell, the large Minnesota-based high-technology firm, receives more than one-third of its $5 billion sales revenue from foreign operations. As a result, the firm needed to develop intercultural training for managers who live and travel abroad. The president of Honeywell Control Systems, Jim Renier, working with the corporate human resource development staff, initiated a program in 1981 to advance both international managerial skills and intercultural awareness.

A need analysis was developed that surveyed most of the employees who traveled extensively, lived abroad, or interacted regularly with those from abroad. This survey was designed to determine cultural barriers as well as strengths and weaknesses of management practices in worldwide operations, in order to design an effective program that could assist employees in preparing to live abroad and to reenter the home country when their assignments were completed. The results of the survey were analyzed by using standard statistical procedures and by collecting anecdotal data that respondents provided. Evidently, the top executives needed to be kept informed of the changing economic and market conditions, exchange rates, and ethical practices found in the countries in which Honeywell operates.

A seminar was developed for top executives and management to discuss issues such as international marketing and cultural values. The survey also indicated the need to address cross-cultural problems that Honeywell American employees experienced overseas. To raise cross-cultural awareness, a training program was designed to focus on three specific areas.

1. Culture-specific information: *data covering other countries and particularly a country one would be entering*
2. Cultural general information: *values, practices, and assumptions of countries other than the United States*
3. Self-specific information: *identifying one's own cultural paradigm including values, assumptions, and perceptions about others*

In addition to seminars and training programs, videopacks on "how to enter another culture" and "cultural grams" about specific countries and cultures are provided for self-study to those going overseas. This cross-cultural program has lessened the cultural gap between expatriate and native personnel, and it has increased employees' efficiency and productivity on a worldwide basis.

Source: W. Chan Kim and R. A. Mauborgne, "Cross-Cultural Strategies," *The Journal of Business Strategy* 7 (Spring 1987): 33.

Regardless of the degree of training, preparation, and positive personal characteristics, a manager will always remain foreign. A manager should never rely on his or her own judgment when local managers can be consulted. In many instances, a manager should have an interpreter present at negotiations, especially if the manager is not completely bilingual. Overconfidence in one's language capabilities can create problems.

SUMMARY

Culture is one of the most challenging elements of the international marketplace. This system of learned behavior patterns characteristic of the members of a given society is constantly shaped by a set of dynamic variables: language, religion, values and attitudes, manners and customs, aesthetics, technology, education, and social institutions. An international manager, to cope with this system, needs both factual and interpretive knowledge of culture. To some extent, the factual can be learned; the interpretation comes only through experience.

The most complicated problems in dealing with the cultural environment stem from the fact that one cannot learn culture—one has to live it. Two schools of thought exist in the business world on how to deal with cultural diversity. One is that business is business the world around, following the model of Pepsi and McDonald's. In some cases, globalization is a fact of life; however, cultural differences are still far from converging.

The other school proposes that companies must tailor business approaches to individual cultures. Setting up policies and procedures in each country has been compared to an organ transplant; the critical question centers around acceptance or rejection. The major challenge to the international manager is to make sure that rejection is not a result of cultural myopia or even blindness.

Fortune examined the international performance of a dozen large companies that earn 20 percent or more of their revenue overseas.[27] The internationally successful companies all share an important quality: patience. They have not rushed into situations but rather built their operations carefully by following the most basic business principles. These principles are to know your adversary, know your audience, and know your customer.

Questions for Discussion

1. Comment on the assumption, "If people are serious about doing business with you, they will speak English."

2. You are on your first business visit to the Federal Republic of Germany. You feel confident about your ability to speak the language (you studied German in school and have taken a refresher course),

[27] Kenneth Labich, "America's International Winners," *Fortune*, April 14, 1986, 34–46.

and you decide to use it. During introductions, you want to break the ice by asking "Wie geht's?" and insisting that everyone call you by your first name. Speculate as to the reaction.

3. What can a company do to culture sensitize its staff?

4. What can be learned about a culture from reading and attending to factual materials?

5. Given the tremendous increase in international marketing activities, where will companies in a relatively early stage of the internationalization process find the personnel to handle the new challenges?

6. Management at an American company trying to market tomato paste in the Middle East did not know that, translated into Arabic, tomato paste is "tomato glue." How could they have known in time to avoid problems?

7. Give examples of how the self-reference criterion might be manifested.

8. Is any international business entity not a cultural imperialist? How else could one explain the phenomenon of multinational corporations?

Recommended Readings

Bhagat, Ravi S., and Harry V. Triandis. *Management across Cultures.* Glenview, Ill.: Scott Foresman, 1984.

Bristin, R. W., W. J. Lonner, and R. M. Thorndike. *Cross-Cultural Research Methods.* New York: Wiley, 1973.

Copeland, Lennie, and L. Griggs. *Going International: How to Make Friends and Deal Effectively in the Global Marketplace.* New York: Random House, 1985.

Graham, John L., and S. Yoshihiro. *Smart Bargaining: Doing Business with the Japanese.* Cambridge, Mass.: Ballinger, 1984.

Hofstede, Geert. *Culture's Consequences.* London: Sage Publications, 1981.

Mathews, E. *Culture Clash.* Warmouth, Maine: Intercultural Press, 1982.

Segall, Marshall. *Cross-Cultural Psychology: Human Behavior in a Global Perspective.* Monterey, Calif.: Brooks/Cole, 1979.

Terpstra, Vern, and K. David. *The Cultural Environment of International Business.* Cincinnati, Ohio: Southwestern, 1985.

Ward, T. *Living Abroad: The Book of Preparations.* New York: The Free Press, 1984.

CHAPTER 6

The International Financial Environment

6.1 THE INTERNATIONAL MARKETPLACE

Credit as a Marketing Tool *Sales are often won or lost on the availability of favorable credit terms to the buyer. With large numbers of competent firms active in international markets, financing packages—often put together with the help of governments—have become more important. This is especially true in the area of engineering and construction where superior technical capability and attractive cost may not be enough to secure a contract today.*

Today, many buyers ask foreign contractors to submit financing proposals along with their bids; Bechtel Financial Services, for example, has been involved in many such projects. In cash-poor countries, outside financing may be necessary to create a market. Because the major U.S. construction and engineering firms are among the largest and financially strongest in the world, they have in some cases gone so far as to take equity positions in new projects. In 1986, Bechtel Power Corporation signed a protocol with the Turkish Electric Authority to build a $1 billion coal-fired power plant. Under this protocol, Bechtel and its partners are not only to design, build, and finance the project, but also enter a 15-year joint venture with the Turkish government; some of their revenues will come through the sale of power.

Of course, only a few firms are capable of participating in such arrangements, which not only demand an unusual commitment of capital, but may force a contractor into an unfamiliar and uncomfortable role. Managers of U.S. firms also face another challenge: the roles taken by other industrialized nations in project financing. For example, in France, Italy, and Japan, government agencies have stepped in, both with development aid and with export credits at below-market interest rates. A Japanese-led consortium won a major contract from the Turkish government to build a bridge over the Bosporus with a package including a $205 million Japanese loan at 5 percent, at least $130 million in Italian export credits at 2.5 to 7.75 percent, and commercial loans totaling $230 million.

Sources: Kenan B. Jarboe, Robert R. Miller, and John A. Alic, "Project Financing: The Case of the International Construction Industry," in *Trade Finance: Current Issues and Developments,* ed. Michael R. Czinkota (Washington, D.C.: Government

Printing Office, 1988), 86–92; D. Barchard, "Ozal Model Sets Pattern for the Future," *Financial Times*, December 18, 1986, 6; and L. Ingrassia, "How Japan Sealed Deal to Build Bridge Spanning the Bosporus," *The Wall Street Journal*, May 29, 1985, 1.

In the extremely competitive international environment, a marketing entity cannot always expect to sell for its own currency with cash in advance, especially when large or long-term contracts are sought. Most companies will be required to go beyond their own working capital and banking lines of credit and expose themselves to new types of risk. The marketer can be sure that if he or she does not finance customers' international trade, the company's competitors probably will.

This chapter will include a discussion of the financial concerns of the international marketer: Am I going to be paid? What are the payment risks in executing the transaction? Who can I count on for support both in getting paid and avoiding financial risk?

MACRO-DEVELOPMENTS

The financial environment is uncontrollable to the international marketer and thus needs to be analyzed carefully and understood in terms of the company's ability to operate within its restrictions. Export industries in the United States during the high value of the dollar and in Japan during the high value of the yen provide examples of corporate reaction and adjustment.

Major adjustments are called for when factors in the financial environment create long-term barriers to a firm's international competitiveness. From 1981 to the end of 1985, the value of the dollar made U.S. exports too expensive for many foreigners to buy, while competitors abroad were able to flood their home markets with less expensive goods. Over that period, the dollar rose by more than 60 percent against the average of other major currencies. A Frenchman had to put up more than twice as many francs to acquire dollars in order to buy American products. Americans received three-quarters again as many German marks for their dollars and so bought German products rather than U.S.[1] U.S. exporters of telecommunication, heating, and air-conditioning equipment claim that they lost as much as $2 billion in contracts during 1982 and 1983 because of the low value of the Japanese yen against the dollar. Some companies had to change their procurement policies. For example, machine toolmaker Cross & Trecker used Japanese parts in some of its products. Many U.S. manufacturers added less expensive imported products to their lines. After a decline of $100 million in exports of U.S. products, Dow Chemical began serving overseas markets from its facilities in other countries, such as Brazil.[2]

[1] "Our Trading Balance: A Growing Crisis," *New York Times*, December 7, 1984, A31.

[2] "For Business, a Painful Adjustment to High Dollar," *U.S. News & World Report*, December 4, 1984, 57–59.

Since 1986, Japanese exporters have been faced with the dilemma created by a high currency value. For example, Japanese companies exporting to the United States have had to choose between two general alternatives. If dollar prices were kept at similar levels with domestic companies, revenue would decline. If dollar prices were raised to offset the rising yen, however, sales would be lost to competition. Since the dollar peaked and started its decline in February 1985, foreign currencies have climbed nearly 70 percent in value—the yen well over 100 percent—against the dollar, but import prices in the United States have risen only 30 percent. This means that less than half of the currency change has been passed through to prices. During a similar situation of a high yen in the period 1967 to 1978, Japanese exporters quickly translated the entire exchange rate change into higher U.S. prices. This time, however, the Japanese decided to protect their hard-earned share of the U.S. market and let profit margins sink.[3]

In some cases, however, currency swings have been too dramatic for lower profit margins to completely solve pricing problems. For example, Caterpillar's prices rose just 5 percent a year from 1986 to 1989, while Komatsu, Caterpillar's Japanese competitor, was forced to tack on seven price increases in the three years. As a result, Caterpillar's market share in North America rose to 32 percent while Komatsu dropped to 9 percent from its all-time high of 12 percent.[4]

Beyond **price manipulation,** other adjustment mechanisms exist. Table 6.1 summarizes the results of a survey of Japanese firms concerning their responses to the strength of the yen. Matsushita Electric, Japan's largest consumer electronics manufacturer, adopted two strategies to combat the effect of the yen. First, it accelerated a shift in production from Japan to the ASEAN nations, and secondly, it began to focus on products that are less sensitive to exchange rate changes.[5] Komatsu launched a $1 billion joint venture with Texas-based Dresser Industries to build equipment in the United States.

In some cases, even adverse developments in the currency market have not had an effect on some international markets or marketers. In the Far East, U.S. oil toolmakers and oil-field service companies were never hurt by the high value of the dollar because their expertise was in demand. Similarly, many U.S. firms, such as IBM, did not suffer because their exported products are both built and sold in other countries. In some cases, imported goods may be in demand because no domestic production exists, which is the case in the United States with consumer goods such as electronics and cameras.

Despite the conditions, responsive action will enable companies to stay competitive in the long term. Effective financial arrangements significantly support the marketing program if it is carefully formulated in coop-

[3] "Will We Ever Close the Trade Gap?" *Business Week*, February 27, 1989, 86—92.

[4] Ronald Henkoff, "This Cat Is Acting like a Tiger," *Fortune*, December 19, 1988, 69—76.

[5] "Burden of the Yen," *Far Eastern Economic Review*, December 25, 1986, 61—67.

TABLE 6.1 ▪ **Survey Results: What Will Japanese Firms Do If the Yen Stays High?**

	All Industries	Manufac- turing	Nonmanu- facturing
Increase direct investment	30.9%	28.8%	34.1%
Change export destinations	1.1	1.9	—
Link with firms in same industry	3.4	4.3	2.2
Link with firms in other industries	5.1	3.4	8.0
Emphasize domestic market	50.4	52.9	45.6
Other	9.1	8.7	10.1
Total	100%	100%	100%

Source: "The Yen Strikes Home," *Far Eastern Economic Review*, December 25, 1986, 61.

eration between the finance and marketing areas of the firm. Customers abroad may be prepared to accept higher prices if they can obtain attractive credit terms.[6]

CREDIT POLICY

The seller's primary concern is to be paid for the goods shipped. Before a particular order is received, the marketer has already formulated a policy on the acceptable degree of risk and preferable terms of international transactions. The extent of credit offered is determined by (1) firm-specific factors such as size, experience in international trade, and capacity for financing transactions; (2) market characteristics such as degree of economic development and availability of means of payment; and (3) factors relating to a particular transaction such as the amount of payment and the need for protection, terms offered by competitors, the relative strength and attractiveness of the trading partner, and the type of goods involved (for example, perishables or custom-made items). In some cases the marketing and financial departments of the firm are at odds. Marketing wants to expand sales and move into new markets, whereas finance wants to minimize risks and, as a result, market selectively. Before finalizing any contract, the marketer must analyze the risks involved and decide how to manage them.[7]

The development of a credit policy requires teamwork between the company's marketing and finance departments and its commercial banks.[8] To

[6] Llewellyn Clague and Rena Grossfield, "Export Pricing in a Floating Rate World," *Columbia Journal of World Business* 9 (Winter 1974): 17–22.

[7] U.S. Department of Commerce, *A Basic Guide to Exporting* (Washington, D.C.: Government Printing Office, 1981), 57.

[8] Christine Topoulos, "The Link between Export Sales and Financing," *Export Today* 4 (November–December 1988): 37–40.

FIGURE 6.1   ▪   **Financing Services of a Bank**

Source: Citicorp.

get the best assistance, most companies need to access both regional banks, with which exporters maintain day-to-day relationships, and money-center banks, which typically provide more sophisticated services than regional banks can (for an example see Figure 6.1). The larger banks provide a full range of finance, insurance, and advisory services. These are at the disposal of the exporter through the correspondent relationship that regional banks have with the large banks, although many large companies have direct relationships with money-center banks.

Both marketers and finance people need to properly understand the role of financing as a marketing tool. Export finance managers may not have time to listen to marketers and understand the kind of financing terms that are needed to make sales or to work on the more complicated financing solutions needed. This can be overcome by helping marketing personnel better understand financing options and by allowing marketers to communicate their needs directly to the banks. Action to accomplish this may include regular roundtable discussions between marketers and bankers and trips abroad by teams of marketers and finance people working together to understand the sale and financing package from start to finish. The goal is to seek and provide the kind of financing that wins business.

The credit policy, once developed, should (1) help the exporter determine the extent of risk he or she is willing to absorb, (2) allow the exporter to explore new ways of financing exports, and (3) prepare the exporter for a changing environment. Each of these elements will be discussed.

TYPES OF FINANCIAL RISK

Overseas political and commercial developments can overnight destroy even the most careful of credit judgments. In addition to macro-developments causing nonpayment, the buying entity may go out of business before paying the seller. The major types of financial risk are commercial risk, political risk, foreign exchange risk, and other risks such as those related to inflation.

The term **commercial risk** refers primarily to the insolvency of or protracted payment default by an overseas buyer. Commercial defaults, in turn, usually result from deterioration of conditions in the buyer's market, fluctuations in demand, unanticipated competition either domestically or internationally, or technological changes. The range of specific reasons may include:

1. Internal changes, such as the death or retirement of a key person. This is a likelihood because many importing entities are dependent on the owner–operator.
2. The buyer losing a key customer. This can occur when an importer buys raw materials or components to be used in production.
3. Unexpected difficulty experienced by the buyer in meeting operating expenses. As an example, the importer's final product may fall under price controls while inputs may not be controlled, especially if this takes place in a high-inflation market.
4. Natural disasters, such as floods and industrial accidents. These can affect the ability of a buyer to operate in a market.
5. Slow payment by government buyers.

All of these risks can emerge in the domestic environment as well, but the geographic and psychological distances to international markets make the risks more severe and more difficult to anticipate.

Noncommercial or **political risk** is completely beyond the control of either the buyer or the seller. For example, the foreign buyer may be willing to pay, but the government may use every trick in the book to delay payment as far into the future as possible. In addition to exchange transfer delay, which has the most direct impact on a transaction, other political risks include war, revolution, or similar hostilities; unforeseen withdrawal or nonrenewal of a license to export or import; requisition, expropriation, confiscation, or intervention in the buyer's business by a government authority; transport or insurance charges caused by interruption or diversion of shipments; and certain other government acts that may prevent or unduly delay payment beyond the control of either the buyer or the seller.

The term **foreign exchange risk** refers to the effects of fluctuating exchange rates. The currency of quotation depends largely on the bargaining positions of the buyer and the seller as well as on accepted business practices in the industry. However, if the price quotation is not in the seller's currency, the seller firm must be prepared to protect itself against losses resulting from changes in the value of the currency transaction.

SOURCES OF FINANCING

Except in the case of larger companies that may have their own financing entities (such as Bechtel's, which is described in The International Marketplace 6.1), most international marketers assist their customers abroad in securing appropriate financing. Export financing terms can significantly affect the final price paid by buyers. Consider, for example, two competitors for a $1 million sale. Exporter A offers an 8 percent interest rate over a ten-year payment period, while B offers 9 percent for the same term. Over the ten years, the difference in interest is $55,000. In some cases, buyers will award a contract to the provider of cheaper credit and overlook differences in quality and price.

Financing assistance is available from both the private and the public sectors. The international marketer should assess not only domestic programs but also those in other countries. For example, Japan, Taiwan, and Korea have import financing programs that provide U.S. exporters added potential in penetrating these significant markets.

Commercial Banks

Commercial banks the world over provide trade financing depending on their relationship with the exporter, the nature of the transaction, the country of the borrower, and the availability of export insurance. This usually means that financing assistance is provided only to first-rate credit risks, leaving many U.S. exporters to report major problems in enlisting assistance from U.S. commercial banks. This is best indicated by a 1988 survey of exporters in which 65 percent of respondents reported that competitive financing is generally not available from commercial lenders for exports even to markets where sales opportunities are promising and repayment would be likely.[9] The problem is most serious when developing-country markets are involved.

This pullback has been strongly driven by debt problems of less-developed countries and by major changes in the U.S. banking system, notably the erosion of "relationship" banking.[10] Many banks see profits from international trade transactions as too small, too risky, and too time consuming. In addition, investor pressures have led banks to minimize foreign credit risks. Earlier, banks—in return for interest-free corporate deposits—provided companies with loans on preferential terms and low-cost access to bank services, such as trade finance. With changes in the U.S. financial services industry, such financial ties have broken. The result is that exporters have to look abroad for such financing and that some sales are lost to other countries because of the lack of financing.

Forfaiting and Factoring

A trade financing technique that was developed in Europe has only in the past decade become widely known in the United States. **Forfaiting** was first used by European commercial banks in financing trade to the Eastern European countries and has since spread to banks throughout the world. Forfaiting provides the exporter with cash at the time of the shipment. In a typical forfait deal, the importer pays the exporter with bills of exchange or promissory notes guaranteed by a leading bank in the importer's country. The exporter can sell them to a third party (for example, Citicorp) at a discount from their face value for immediate cash. The sale is without recourse to the exporter and the buyer of the notes assumes all of the risks. The discount rate takes into account the buyer's creditworthiness and country, the quality of the guaranteeing bank, and the interest cost over the term of the credit.[11]

The benefits to the exporter are the reduction of risk, simplicity of documentation (because the documents used are well-known in the market), and 100 percent coverage, which official sources such as export-import banks do not provide. In addition, forfaiting does not involve either content or country restrictions. In contrast, Eximbank in the United States, for example, does not cover financing of military goods, and its charter pre-

[9] Rosemary Mazon, "Where Have All the Banks Gone?" *Export Today* 4 (September–October 1988): 71–73.

[10] William F. Kolarik, "Financing American Exports: The Diminishing Role of U.S. Commercial Banks," in *Trade Finance*, ed. Michael R. Czinkota (Washington, D.C.: Government Printing Office, 1981), 76–85.

[11] Louis G. Guadagnoli, *Practical Guide to Export Financing and Risk Management* (Arlington, Va.: Government Information Services, 1989), III-33.

vents it from participating in deals with the Soviet Union.[12] The major complaints about forfaiting center around availability and cost. Forfaiting is not available where exporters need it most; that is, the high-risk countries. Furthermore, it is usually a little more expensive than using public sources of trade insurance.

Certain companies, known as **factoring** houses, may purchase an exporter's receivables for a discounted price (2 to 4 percent less than face value). Factors enable the exporter to receive payment for goods and provide relief of the administrative burden of collection. Arrangements are typically with recourse, leaving the exporter ultimately liable for repaying the factor in case of a default. Some factors accept export receivables without recourse but require a large discount.

Official Trade Finance[*]

Official financing can take the form of either a loan or a guarantee, including credit insurance. In a loan, the government provides funds to finance the sale and charges interest on those funds at a stated rate. The government lender accepts the risk of a possible default. In a guarantee, a private sector lender provides the funds and sets the interest rate, with the government assuring that it will reimburse the lender if the loan is unpaid. The government is not providing funds but rather risk protection.[13] The programs provide assurance the governmental agency will pay for a major portion of the loss should the foreign buyer default on payment. The advantages are significant: (1) protection in the riskiest part of an exporter's business (foreign sales receivables), (2) protection against political and commercial risks over which the exporter does not have control, (3) encouragement to exporters to make competitive offers by extending terms of payment, (4) broadening of potential markets by minimizing exporter risks, and (5) the possibility of leveraging exporter accounts receivable.[14]

Because credit has emerged as an increasingly important component in export selling, governments of most industrialized countries have established entities that insure credit risks for exports. The international union of export credit and investment insurers, or the "Berne Union," was established in 1934 by the leading trading nations for the purpose of establishing a voluntary international understanding on export insurance terms by recommending the length of periods for which credit can be extended. Recommended periods range from five years for heavy capital goods to 18 months for consumer durable goods. In 1981, an international agreement

[*] The authors acknowledge the assistance of Robert J. Kaiser of the Export-Import Bank of the United States and Louis G. Guadagnoli in the preparation of this section.

[12] "How U.S. Exporters Can Benefit from Forfait Financing," *Business International Money Report*, December 21, 1987, 418–420.

[13] Office of Trade Finance, "Survey of Finance Topics of Current Interest," in *Trade Finance*, ed. Michael R. Czinkota (Washington, D.C.: Government Printing Office, 1988), 34–43.

[14] "EXIM-Bank Program Summary," in *Export-Import Bank of the United States* (Washington, D.C.: EXIM Bank, 1985), 1.

TABLE 6.2 ∎ **International Agreement on Financing**

	Repayment Terms[a]	
Borrower	2 to 5 years	Over 5 years
Relatively Rich (e.g., Finland)	10.15%	10.40%
Intermediate (e.g., Jordan)	9.15	9.66
Relatively Poor (e.g., Ethiopia)	8.30	8.30

[a] The minimum rates are reviewed each January and July.

was reached on the standardization of international financing, which is summarized in Table 6.2. Increasingly, however, countries tend to circumvent this agreement by providing mixed credits—that is, a combination of commercial export financing funds with "soft" development aid funds.

The Export-Import Bank of the United States (Eximbank) was created in 1934 and established as an independent U.S. government agency in 1945. The purpose of the bank is "to aid in financing and facilitating exports." Since its inception, Eximbank has supported more than $193 billion in U.S. export sales, such as those described in The International Marketplace 6.2. Eximbank's support for short-term export sales (up to 180 days) rests exclusively with the export credit insurance program that is administered by the Foreign Credit Insurance Association, which is Eximbank's agent.

The Foreign Credit Insurance Association (FCIA) was created in 1961 to give U.S. exporters the means to become internationally competitive. The FCIA is an association of the nation's leading insurance companies (such as American International Group, American Foreign Insurance Association, and Chubb). They underwrite the commercial credit risks, while Eximbank covers the political risks and reinsures certain excess commercial risks. More than 70 percent of FCIA's insureds are small businesses and FCIA accounts for the majority of Eximbank's activity.

The data in Table 6.3 matches products and services with the customary financing term and the appropriate Eximbank and Foreign Credit Insurance Association programs, although the applicability of a particular program depends on the details of the specific transaction.

FCIA Policies Any entity including the U.S. exporter, a U.S. or foreign bank, or the foreign buyer may apply to FCIA for a premium quote, at no cost, to determine the availability and cost of FCIA's export credit insurance.[15] FCIA offers ten standard policies that fall into two basic categories:

[15] John A. Hanson, "The Government Can Help," Export Today 4 (July–August 1988): 62–63.

6.2   THE INTERNATIONAL MARKETPLACE

Inside the Export-Import Bank   *A working capital guarantee helped Mertz Inc. of Ponca City, Oklahoma, to fulfill a $9.2 million export order from the People's Republic of China for seismic testing equipment. Mertz will supply 31 seismic vibrator trucks to be used for oil exploration in China. The customers are state-owned China National Technical Import Corporation and China National Technical Import and Export Corporation. Eximbank's working capital guarantee covers 90 percent of a $5.3 million loan extended by Bank of Oklahoma to finance costs related to manufacturing the vibrators. Mertz has been making seismic vibrators, used to determine the potential for resources under the earth's surface, since the 1960s. Mertz has produced the majority of seismic vibrators used in the world today and has sold about 280 of them to China since 1974.*

Satellite Earth Station. Scientific Atlanta of Atlanta, Georgia, supplied a $7.1 million satellite earth station to the Office of Post and Telecommunications of Gabon with the help of a $6 million loan to finance the deal. Scientific Atlanta will provide management services in addition to the equipment for the project. The new station provides international links in conjunction with the INTELSAT satellite system to Gabon's existing network. Eximbank financing covers 85 percent of the export value of the equipment and services through a loan at 9.35 percent interest. Repayment is scheduled in 20 semiannual installments beginning in January 1990.

Gas Turbines. Phimar International Inc. in Rockville, Maryland, won a $2.5 million contract from Energie Electrique de la Cote d'Ivoire (EECI), the national utility company of the Ivory Coast. Phimar will be the prime contractor for the inspection and refurbishment of both conventional steam turbine-generators and combustion turbine-generators in Abidjan. Phimar will provide engineering services and will purchase necessary equipment from a variety of U.S. manufacturers such as General Electric. In the past, Phimar has won a number of smaller contracts from EECI, but has lost larger orders to the French company Alsthom. Eximbank financing enabled Phimar to win the current order over competition from Alsthom. The transaction represented Eximbank's first loan to the Ivory Coast in many years, and the first use of Eximbank's programs by Phimar. EECI will make cash payments of $370,779 and will borrow $2.1 million from Eximbank at an annual interest rate of 8.25 percent. Repayment will be in 10 semiannual installments beginning six months from completion of services.

Hydropower. C.V.G. Electrificacion del Caroni C.A. (EDELCA) was guaranteed a loan of $103.7 million by Eximbank to assist in financing U.S. exports of construction and project management services, construction equipment, mechanical and electrical equipment, and *consumables for the Macaqua II Hydropower Project on the Caroni River in southeastern Venezuela. EDELCA selected a consortium that includes the U.S. company Guy F. Atkinson Construction Company of California to undertake the major civil works portion of the project. Atkinson will be responsible for construction management services and procurement of U.S. equipment. PEFCO extended a loan, guaranteed by Eximbank, to cover 85 percent of the $122.0 million eligible project costs: $107.9 million in U.S. costs and $14.1 million in eligible foreign components. Repayment will be in 17 semiannual installments beginning in June 1995.*

Source: *Exim News* of April 22, 1988, July 12, 1988, July 20, 1988, and April 18, 1989, published by Eximbank, Washington, D.C.

TABLE 6.3 ∎ **Selection Chart for Eximbank and Foreign Credit Insurance Association Programs**

Exports	*Appropriate Programs*
Pre-Export Any product or service when working capital is needed to fill an export order	Working Capital Loan Guarantee
Short Term (up to 180 days) Consumables Small Manufactured Items Spare Parts Raw Materials Services Less Than 1 Year	Export Credit Insurance
Short Term (up to 360 days) Consumer Durables Bulk Agricultural Commodities	Export Credit Insurance
Medium Term (181 days to 5 years) Capital Equipment Mining and Refining Equipment Construction Equipment Agricultural Equipment General Aviation Aircraft Planning/Feasibility Studies Breeding Livestock	Export Credit Insurance Intermediary Credit Financial Guarantees
Long Term (5 years and longer) Power Plants LNG and Gas Processing Plants Other Major Projects	Direct Loans Financial Guarantees PEFCO

multibuyer and single-buyer types. These policies accommodate the special needs of various types of exporters and financing institutions, either of which can be an insured party. The insurance premiums charged are based on the buyer, the length of the repayment term, the country of importation, the experience of the insured, and the volume of business. The coverage offered under the policies may be comprehensive, meaning that both commercial and political risks of default are covered, or political only. A comprehensive policy is advisable because of the difficulty in predicting events. Also, devaluation is not covered as a political risk but, if it causes default, may be covered as a commercial risk. FCIA does not offer commercial risk cover alone. The policies have U.S. content requirements in order to fulfill the basic mission of supporting U.S. jobs. Products sold with short-term repayment periods must be at least 50 percent U.S. content, exclusive of markup. Products sold with medium-term repayment periods must be 100 percent U.S. content. No value may be added after shipment from the United States.

Multibuyer policies may cover short- or medium-term sales or a combination of both. They require that the insured pay premium on all, or a reasonable spread, of export credit sales. This requirement exists to prevent the insured from making an adverse selection of sales to be insured and increasing FCIA's risk. Typically it is used by an exporter for comprehensive coverage on worldwide short-term sales. The FCIA assigns an aggregate policy limit, which is the maximum dollar amount in claims that will be paid in a policy year. However, the insured must submit credit information to FCIA and receive approval for each buyer whose receivables are to be insured. A discretionary credit limit may be granted to experienced insureds to relieve them from obtaining preapproval for sales under a certain dollar amount, provided they maintain a credit file on the buyer. A first-loss deductible for commercial risk claims is typical. The minimum premium is usually $500 per year paid up front and the insured pays premiums monthly, based on shipments.

Single-buyer policies may also cover short- or medium-term sales or a combination of both. This type of policy allows exporters to select the sales they desire to insure. There is no first-loss deductible. It may cover single or repetitive sales to one buyer. An example of an FCIA medium-term single-buyer policy is provided in Table 6.4.

The many standard FCIA policies include several designed specifically for financing institutions such as banks. These include the Bank Letter of Credit Policy, which covers the obligation of a foreign bank to remit funds to a bank that has confirmed a letter of credit opened by that foreign bank for the purchase of U.S. goods. Also, the Financial Institution Buyer Credit Policy covers the short-term credit obligations of a foreign buyer of U.S. goods to its funding bank and the Bank Supplier Credit Policy covers the short-term financing provided to a U.S. exporter by its bank related to export credit sales. Other policies, such as the Trade-Association Policy and Umbrella Policy, allow organizations experienced in export trade and financing to act as intermediaries between FCIA and potential insureds. The administrators of these policies are not insured, but assist the exporter in obtaining insurance, maintaining documentation, and filing claims. FCIA offers insurance for leases as well as sales. The Operating Lease Policy covers a specific number of lease payments plus the depreciated value of

TABLE 6.4 ▪ **Example of Foreign Credit Insurance Association Coverage for a Medium-Term Repayment**

(1)	Contract value	$100,000
(2)	Cash payment (15%)	15,000
(3)	Financed portion (85%)	85,000
(4)	Exporter commercial retention (10% of line 3)	8,500
(5)	Eximbank commercial risks coverage (90% of line 3)	76,500
(6)	Eximbank political risks (100% of line 3)	85,000

Source: Louis G. Guadagnoli.

the equipment if expropriation occurs. No down payment is required for this medium-term cover. The Financing Lease Policy covers the total of the lease payments but a 15 percent cash payment is required.

A combination of short- and medium-term insurance is available, used mainly to protect U.S. exporters who offer floor plans to overseas dealers and distributors. This option offers protection on parts and accessories sales on terms up to 180 days and capital equipment inventory financing for up to 270 days that can be converted to a medium-term receivable of up to three years.

To insure against risks from the date of signing the sales contract instead of from the date of shipment, comprehensive preshipment coverage is available. This coverage is necessary when goods are specially manufactured or require a long factory lead time. Nonacceptance cover against the arbitrary refusal of the buyer to accept products that conform to the contract of sale may be offered at no extra cost in addition to the normal cover except when greater than normal risk exists, such as with perishable items. In addition, the FCIA will insure political risks for goods on consignment where payment is made to the exporter only after the goods have been sold. Should an exporter consummate a sale requiring payment in foreign currency rather than U.S. dollars, FCIA will cover such transactions under all policies; however, cover is limited to "freely transferable" currencies and no exchange or transfer risk is insurable under this endorsement.

To encourage U.S. firms to expand their foreign business during a period when there is a strong overseas demand for services, services coverage was developed. Industries benefiting from this include management consultants, engineering service firms, transportation companies, and other firms offering the services of U.S.-based personnel to foreign buyers with repayment being made in U.S. dollars in the United States. The New-to-Export Policy is for companies without exporting experience or those that have had limited export sales in the past. The policy gives added commercial risk protection of 95 percent in order to further cushion any potential losses. These criteria have to be met by the applying company: average annual export credit sales of less than $750,000 per year during the preceding two years, and prior direct coverage under any FCIA insurance program.

FCIA does not finance export sales, but the exporter who insures accounts receivable is often able to obtain financing from banks and other lending institutions with this coverage. As a result, the exporter can extend credit on more favorable terms to overseas customers without tying up resources required for internal operations.

Claims may be submitted immediately upon default or there may be a waiting period of up to eight months, depending on the provisions of the policy and the cause of the default. At the time of the claim, the exporter must submit certain documents, such as copies of bills of lading, the debt instrument, evidence of attempts to collect, and evidence of compliance with any special conditions imposed by FCIA. The exporter must therefore retain all documents until the claim has been paid.

Eximbank Programs   During the fall of 1986 and extending into the spring of 1987, Eximbank undertook a major revision of all its programs. Many of the programs, especially those that supported small business, were inconsistent from one program to another or were not responsive to the specific needs of the smaller exporter.

One of the greatest impediments small businesses experience in attempting to fulfill export orders is a lack of adequate working capital to build the necessary inventory for the export order. In response to this need, Eximbank created a Working Capital Guarantee Program (WCG). It is the only preexport program offered by Eximbank. All other Eximbank or FCIA programs finance exports after shipment or performance.

Under this program, Eximbank guarantees the lender against default by the exporter. The guarantee is for 90 percent of the loan and interest up to 1 percent over the Treasury borrowing rate. The lender must retain 10 percent of the risk. Should the exporter default, only the commercial bank is covered. For example, if the foreign buyer of the U.S. goods defaults, only the exporter's outstanding loan to the commercial bank is covered under the Working Capital Guarantee. For this reason, many secure FCIA insurance to protect themselves against failure of the foreign buyer to pay the obligation for either commercial or political reasons. In some cases, Eximbank, as a condition of approving a Working Capital Guarantee application, may require that an FCIA policy be secured by the exporter.

The Working Capital Guarantee may be used for single sales or as a revolving facility. It may also be used for marketing and promotion purposes. However, most of the WCGs approved by Eximbank are for single-sale transactions. The exporter must put up collateral equal to 110 percent of the value of the loan. Eximbank takes a broad interpretation of acceptable collateral and will accept raw materials, fixed assets in certain cases, foreign receivables or collateral. Frequently, the personal guarantee of the exporting company's officers is also required. The exporter may approach Eximbank directly for a WCG, or through its bank.

Medium-Term Guarantees are available for export transactions up to $10 million, with a maximum repayment term not to exceed seven years. Most typically, they are used by commercial banks that do not want exposure in a certain country or that have reached their internal "exposure limit" in a given country. The Eximbank guarantee overcomes these limitations. The medium-term guarantee provides the lender 100 percent political and commercial risk protection. However, the exporter in the transaction must provide a 2 percent counterguarantee for the commercial risk. Under this guarantee, the foreign buyer is required to make a 15 percent cash down payment, so the guarantee covers the "financed portion" of 85 percent.

Eximbank's fee schedule is determined by country risk and the repayment terms of the transaction. Rates vary from the highest rated "A" country to the lowest rated "E" country. By having a rate schedule based on perceived risk assumption, Eximbank is able to remain open for business longer in more countries because it is compensated for the risk it is being asked to take.

Long-Term Guarantees are used for transactions in excess of $10 million and repayment periods of eight or more years. The commercial and political risk cover is 100 percent, and there is no requirement for an exporter 2 percent commercial risk counterguarantee. The same fee structure detailed under "medium-term guarantees" applies. One major difference in the long-term guarantee is that loans made under the long-term guarantee may be denominated in foreign currencies acceptable to Eximbank. This enables foreign buyers with access to foreign currency earnings to use this currency to repay loans. A good example of this would be a foreign airline with earnings, through its flight routes, in Japanese yen. The airline wishes to buy U.S.-made airplanes, but wants to borrow in yen and use its yen earnings to service the debt. An Eximbank long-term guarantee could be utilized for such a transaction.

Eximbank, by statute, does not compete with commercial banks. It complements and supplements commercial bank support for exports by assuming risks unacceptable to the banks. As is well known, commercial banks will only rarely provide fixed interest rate loans for any type of commercial transaction. Yet today, in the highly competitive international marketplace, many foreign buyers can demand financial support as a precondition to their purchase of goods from abroad. These foreign buyers often require fixed rate financing as a condition of their purchase.

Eximbank offers medium-term loans to commercial banks at a discount from the official Organization for Economic Cooperation and Development (OECD) rates for the country of the purchaser. The commercial bank then on-lends to the foreign buyer at the full OECD rate. The discount the commercial bank receives varies from 50 to 150 basis points based on the dollar amount of the medium-term credit. The maximum amount that a bank can borrow from Eximbank under this facility and still receive the discount is $10 million. Amounts in excess of $10 million do not receive a discount. The discount is available only to commercial banks. All other intermediary lenders, including the exporters themselves, may borrow from Eximbank at the official OECD rate and on-lend at the same OECD rate to the foreign buyer.

For fixed rate loans in excess of $10 million and repayment periods of eight years or longer, Eximbank acts as a lender directly to the foreign buyer. This is because most commercial banks simply do not extend loans beyond seven-year repayment terms. Often, too, these transactions are large ones, in excess of $100 million, and commercial banks do not want such large exposure for long periods of time in one country. Such major projects, or large product purchases, are often let through international bids and competition is keen to secure these major orders. Without Eximbank participation, American exporters would be unable to successfully compete. Under OECD regulations, a 15 percent cash down payment by the foreign buyer is required. Thus the "financed portion" is 85 percent of the export value. Eximbank has eased its U.S. content requirements somewhat and is now prepared to finance up to a maximum of 15 percent foreign content in the export order. The rest of the export must be U.S.-produced goods and services. If the foreign content exceeds 15 percent of the shipment, then that foreign content will be excluded entirely from Eximbank support. Payment terms are normally determined by studying cash flow projections from the proposed project or the useful life of the product. In any case, repayment rarely exceeds a ten-year term. Normally, if a project is involved, repayment begins six months after the project commences commercial operations. For a product, such as a commercial jet aircraft, repayment begins six months after the plane goes into service.

An example of typical financing for a turnkey project is provided in Table 6.5. Eximbank funds or guarantees 85 percent of U.S. costs at a fixed rate, with the rate varying by country classification. The bank financing for infrastructure is a separate transaction. For security, Eximbank requires the government as borrower or as guarantor. To be involved, Eximbank and commercial banks must be satisfied that the project is technically and financially feasible. For this they require extensive information, including a feasibility study. The balance of the financing requirements usually comes out of the project owner's resources.

Under its charter, Eximbank must have "reasonable assurance of repayment." Therefore, a careful analysis of the foreign buyer's creditworthiness and the project's viability is conducted. If necessary, government guarantees of the loan repayment, representing the full faith and credit of the host country of the foreign buyer, may be required. In other cases, guarantees of a commercial bank in the host country may also be satisfactory and necessary.

The export-import banks of other countries should also be monitored to assess the structures, terms, and rates of import financing programs for U.S. goods and services. Included could be such entities as the Export-Import Bank of Japan or the Export Development Corporation of Canada.[16]

---

[16] Martin R. Brill, "The East Asian Edge," *Export Today* 4 (July–August 1988): 50–53.

TABLE 6.5 ▪ **Typical Financing Plan for a Turnkey Project**

Costs (in millions)		Financing Plan (in millions)	
Hardware	$10.0	Eximbank Credit/Guarantee	$ 8.5
Infrastructure	5.0	U.S. Banks—U.S. Costs	1.5
Interest during		U.S. Banks—Infrastructure	5.0
Construction	2.0	Sponsor's Equity	4.0
Working Capital		Total	$19.0
Requirements	2.0		
Total	$19.0		

Source: Louis G. Guadagnoli.

Other Public-Sector Financing Sources The Overseas Private Investment Corporation (OPIC) is a federal agency that offers investment guarantees comparable to those offered by the FCIA and Eximbank to U.S. manufacturers who wish to establish plants in less-developed countries, either by themselves or as a joint venture with local capital. OPIC finances and/ or insures only foreign direct investment through (1) direct loans from $100,000 to $6 million per project with terms of 7 to 12 years, (2) loan guarantees to U.S. institutional lenders of up to $50 million per project, and (3) political risk insurance against currency inconvertibility, expropriation, or takeover, and physical damage resulting from political strife.[17] The importance of this activity is increasing rapidly because foreign direct investment enables firms to remain competitive in the world marketplace. It is difficult to maintain viable market share without presence as a producer, making trade more dependent on investment with time.[18]

The Agency for International Development (AID) administers most of the foreign economic assistance programs for the U.S. government. Because many AID agreements require that commodities be purchased from the United States, exporters should use this support mechanism. AID estimates that 70 percent of all U.S. aid comes back in purchases of goods and services from U.S. companies. In the long term, the agency's objective is to increase potential for increased exports by follow-up sales and by creating potential in the market for other purchases.[19] As a sister agency to AID, the U.S. Trade Development Program (TDP) uses foreign assistance funds to increase U.S. exports by financing the planning of projects and dispersing grants for feasibility studies of development projects.

In addition to these U.S. entities, the international marketer will find it worthwhile to monitor the activities of development banks such as the World Bank, regional development banks (such as the Inter-American De-

[17] Craig A. Nalen, "Direct Investment: An Entree to Exporting," *Export Today* 4 (March–April 1988): 10–13.

[18] Peter Drucker, "From World Trade to World Investment," *The Wall Street Journal*, May 26, 1987, 33.

[19] "Foreign Assistance Funds: Marketing U.S. Exports through Economic Development," *Export Today* 4 (March–April 1988): 6–9.

velopment Bank), and many national development banks. These banks specialize in financing investment activities and can provide valuable leads for future business activity.

The World Bank Group has, since its inception, provided over $200 billion in financing for over 5,000 projects. In 1988, loans totaled $19.2 billion for 217 new operations. Projects cover a wide spectrum, including agriculture, industry, transportation, telecommunications, and population planning. Loans are at variable rates, based on the cost of borrowing, and for 15 to 20-year terms. All loans must be guaranteed by the government of the borrowing country.[20] In order to get business from World Bank projects, international marketers have to closely monitor the entire process—from the identification of the project to the approval of the loan.

In April 1988, an affiliate of the World Bank began operation. The Multilateral Investment Guaranty Agency (MIGA) will encourage the flow of financial resources to its developing member countries. To accomplish this, MIGA is authorized to issue guarantees against noncommercial risks in host countries, so that investors may assess the benefits of projects on economic and financial grounds rather than political risk.

Private Sector Export-Credit Insurance

The Private Export Funding Corporation (PEFCO) is a private corporation founded in 1970 for the purpose of making fixed rate U.S. dollar loans to foreign importers to finance purchases of goods and services of U.S. manufacture or origin. PEFCO's stockholders consist of 54 commercial banks, including most of the major U.S. banks involved in export financing, one investment banking firm, and seven manufacturing firms (Boeing, Cessna, Combustion Engineering, General American Transportation, General Electric, McDonnell Douglas Finance, and United Technologies). The Eximbank and PEFCO maintain an agreement whereby Eximbank guarantees the principal and interest on debt obligations that are issued by foreign purchasers of U.S. products and services by PEFCO. PEFCO thereby acquires a portfolio of Eximbank-guaranteed paper that can be used as the basis for raising funds in the private market. Because all of its loans are guaranteed, PEFCO itself does not evaluate credit risks, appraise economic conditions in foreign countries, or review other factors that might affect the collectibility of its loans.

The role of private export credit insurers has increased in the past few years.[21] For example, American International Underwriters, a division of American International Group, offers coverage of commercial credit and political risks similar to that offered by FCIA. Other firms that offer limited forms of commercial and political risks are entities such as Citicorp

[20]Carol Stitt, "The World Bank and Project Finance," *Export Today* 5 (February 1989): 50–54.

[21]H. Allan Legge, Jr., "Private-Sector Export Insurance: Taking Care of Business," *Export Today* 4 (September–October 1988): 74–75.

International Trade and American Credit Indemnity. Private underwriters offer political risk coverage for investments covering confiscation, expropriation, and nationalization risks that is similar to that provided by OPIC.

Proponents of the private insurers cite their faster processing time, lower rates because of selectivity, absence of U.S.-origin requirement, and ability to do business in countries embargoed by the U.S. government. The drawbacks, however, are that they require a minimum but substantial amount of business to be covered, they cater mainly to the large multinational corporations and are not as interested in smaller firms, and, the most important caveat, their insurance may not be as acceptable to commercial banks that will be providing the financing.

FINANCIAL RISK MANAGEMENT

After financial risks have been assessed, the international marketer needs to decide whether to do business in the particular environment. If the decision is to do so, risk needs to be minimized through actions by either the company itself or support systems. The decision must be an informed one, based on detailed and up-to-date information in international credit and country conditions. In many respects, the assessment of a buyer's creditworthiness requires the same attention to credit checking and financial analysis as that for domestic buyers; however, the assessment of a foreign private buyer is complicated by some of the following factors:

1. Credit reports may not be reliable.
2. Audited reports may not be available.
3. Financial reports may have been prepared according to a different format.
4. Many governments require annual upward revaluation of assets that can distort results.
5. Statements are in local currency.
6. The buyer may have the financial resources in local currency but may be precluded from converting to dollars because of exchange controls and other government actions.

More than one credit report should be obtained, and it should be determined how each credit agency obtains its reports. They may use the same correspondent agency. It does the exporter no good to obtain the same information from two sources and to pay for it twice. Table 6.6 provides a summary of the major sources of credit information. At least one of the credit reports solicited by the exporter should be the World Traders Data Report compiled by the U.S. Department of Commerce.

In many cases, financing requirements may go beyond export credits, and financial risk management gains added dimensions. In a hotly contested bid for its first two communications satellites, Brazil managed to bargain the price down to $150 million. In addition, it pressured the two consortia competing for the business, one French and one Canadian, to

TABLE 6.6 ▪ **Sources of International Credit Information**

Source	Response Time	Cost	Comments
1. Dun & Bradstreet	2 to 4 weeks, depending on location	$60 to $240	Standard in the industry. Data are often sketchy as subjects are reticent to respond to a credit inquiry.
2. World Traders Data Report	Variable; if known name, quick; otherwise, lengthy delays	$100	If prominent name, comprehensive. Tendency to be out of date
3. Local Credit Agency Report	Long, start from scratch	$100 to $200	Quality varies. International market perspective lacking
4. Bank Reports	Slow	None	Limited in scope
5. Federal Credit Interchange Bureau	5 to 6 weeks	Part of membership fee ($500)	Narrow in scope

Source: Richard Loth, American Export Group International Services.

promise to buy shoes, coffee, and iron ore as partial payment. **Countertrade** provisions are making their way into many financing arrangements, especially when developing countries or centrally planned economies are concerned. Because of the prominent position of countertrade in international trade (approximately 25 percent of the total), many firms not only have had to accept it but also have made major adjustments financially and organizationally to cope with it. Some U.S. construction companies are hoping to open up new construction projects by devising ways to help debt-strapped developing countries with their financing problems. In Latin America, U.S. contractors, led by McDermott International, are experimenting with countertrade. McDermott is already grossing $700 million a year in countertrade in such commodities as steel, fertilizer, and chemicals. It also bought the international trading arm of West Germany's Coutinho, Caro & Co. to help dispose of the items it takes in compensation for work performed abroad.[22]

A development related to the debt crisis is the emergence of debt/equity and debt/product swaps. Under a **debt/equity swap,** a firm wishing to invest in a country with debt problems arranges to swap the country's debt for an equity investment. For example, Chrysler purchased $110 million in Mexican debt for about 55 cents on the dollar. The debt was then converted into about $100 million in pesos and invested in the Mexican sub-

[22]"The Shrinking World of Engineering Contractors," *Business Week*, September 24, 1984, 84–90.

TABLE 6.7   ▪   **Example of Foreign Exchange Impact**

Monthly contract, £1,000
Cost of goods to marketer, $1,650

Date	Exchange Rate	Revenue	Cost	Net Income
1/1	1£ = $1.70	$1,700	$1,650	$50
2/1	1£ = 1.65	1,650	1,650	0
3/1	1£ = 1.60	1,600	1,650	(50)

sidiary.[23] As suitable investments may not be available, **debt/product swaps** may be used as another vehicle for marketing debt. Peru has negotiated deals in which creditors have committed themselves to buying $3 worth of Peruvian products for every $1 of products paid by Peru against debt.[24]

Foreign Exchange Risk

Any time the international marketer is to receive payment in a currency other than that of his or her country, the risk exists of a decline (devaluation) in the foreign currency during the time between the signing of the contract and the receipt of the foreign currency. If the marketer takes no action to manage an exchange rate fluctuation, losses will be incurred. This is illustrated in Table 6.7, in which the British pound depreciates against the U.S. dollar. Protection against foreign exchange risk cannot be secured from the same sources as for commercial and political risk. It must emerge from sound management practices.

The Foreign Exchange Market

The foreign exchange market is the mechanism by which purchasing power between countries is transferred, credit is provided for international transactions, and exposure to the risks of exchange rate fluctuations can be minimized.[25] The participants in this market include banks, governments, and speculators as well as individuals and firms conducting transactions.

The price of one currency in terms of another is called the **exchange rate.** Sources for daily exchange rates such as those shown in Figure 6.2 are available from newspapers such as *The Wall Street Journal* and *The Financial Times.* The marketer, however, has to contact a particular bank's

[23]"Debt-Business Boom in Latin America," *Euromoney*, September 1987, 81.

[24]"Drexel's Milken Is Trying to Find a Lode in Latin Debt," *The Wall Street Journal*, September 14, 1987, 6.

[25]David K. Eiteman and Arthur I. Stonehill, *International Business Finance* (Reading, Mass.: Addison-Wesley, 1986), 88.

FIGURE 6.2 ▪ **Foreign Exchange Rates**

EXCHANGE RATES
Friday, April 28, 1989

The New York foreign exchange selling rates below apply to trading among banks in amounts of $1 million and more as quoted at 3 p.m. Eastern time by Bankers Trust Co. Retail transactions provide fewer units of foreign currency per dollar.

Country	U.S. $ equiv. Fri.	U.S. $ equiv. Thurs.	Currency per U.S. $ Fri.	Currency per U.S. $ Thurs.
Argentina (Austral)	.014092	.014092	70.96	70.96
Australia (Dollar)	.7940	.7947	1.2594	1.2583
Austria (Schilling)	.07557	.07577	13.23	13.19
Bahrain (Dinar)	2.6518	2.6518	.37710	.37710
Belgium (Franc)				
Commercial rate	.02542	.02547	39.33	39.26
Financial rate	.02532	.02536	39.48	39.42
Brazil (Cruzado)	.980392	.980392	1.0200	1.0200
Britain (Pound)	1.6900	1.6910	.5917	.5913
30-Day Forward	1.6858	1.6870	.5931	.5927
90-Day Forward	1.6776	1.6788	.5961	.5956
180-Day Forward	1.6665	1.6676	.6000	.5996
Canada (Dollar)	.8435	.8389	1.1855	1.1920
30-Day Forward	.8416	.8370	1.1881	1.1947
90-Day Forward	.8384	.8338	1.1927	1.1993
180-Day Forward	.8343	.8298	1.1985	1.2051
Chile (Official rate)	.0039671	.0039671	252.07	252.07
China (Yuan)	.268672	.268672	3.7220	3.7220
Colombia (Peso)	.002747	.002747	364.00	364.00
Denmark (Krone)	.1368	.1370	7.3070	7.2970
Ecuador (Sucre)				
Floating rate	.001988	.001988	503.00	503.00
Finland (Markka)	.2383	.2389	4.1950	4.1845
France (Franc)	.1574	.1575	6.3525	6.3465
30-Day Forward	.1576	.1577	6.3450	6.3403
90-Day Forward	.1578	.1579	6.3335	6.3305
180-Day Forward	.1583	.1584	6.3165	6.3130
Greece (Drachma)	.006250	.006250	160.00	160.00
Hong Kong (Dollar)	.128509	.128518	7.7815	7.7810
*ia (Rupee)	.0634920	.0634920	15.75	15.75
nesia (Rupiah)	.0005740	.0005740	1742.00	1742.00
Ireland (Punt)	1.4357	1.4357	.6965	.6965
Israel (Shekel)	.5503	.5503	1.8170	1.8170
Italy (Lira)	.0007267	.0007278	1376.00	1374.00
Japan (Yen)	.007530	.007570	132.80	132.10
30-Day Forward	.007564	.007605	132.19	131.49
90-Day Forward	.007663	.007667	130.49	130.42
180-Day Forward	.007716	.007757	129.60	128.90
Jordan (Dinar)	1.8968	1.8968	.5272	.5272
Kuwait (Dinar)	3.4482	3.4482	.2900	.2900
Lebanon (Pound)	.001851	.001851	540.00	540.00
Malaysia (Ringgit)	.37174	.37174	2.6900	2.6900
Malta (Lira)	2.9282	2.9282	.3415	.3415
Mexico (Peso)				
Floating rate	.0004123	.0004123	2425.00	2425.00
Malta (L.ra)	2.9282	2.9282	.3415	.3415
Mexico (Peso)				
Floating rate	.0004123	.0004123	2425.00	2425.00
Netherland (Guilder)	.4715	.4727	2.1205	2.1155
New Zealand (Dollar)	.6165	.6140	1.6220	1.6286
Norway (Krone)	.1465	.1468	6.8225	6.8075
Pakistan (Rupee)	.05012	.05012	19.95	19.95
Peru (Inti)	.0006191	.0006191	1615.00	1615.00
Philippines (Peso)	.048076	.048076	20.80	20.80
Portugal (Escudo)	.006508	.006508	153.65	153.65
Saudi Arabia (Riyal)	.2666	.2666	3.7505	3.7505
Singapore (Dollar)	.5138	.5136	1.9460	1.9468
South Africa (Rand)				
Commercial rate	.3901	.3916	2.5633	2.5538
Financial rate	.2392	.2430	4.1800	4.1150
South Korea (Won)	.0015015	.0015015	666.00	666.00
Spain (Peseta)	.008580	.008591	116.55	116.40
Sweden (Krona)	.1567	.1571	6.3800	6.3625
Switzerland (Franc)	.5977	.6033	1.6730	1.6575
30-Day Forward	.5994	.6050	1.6682	1.6528
90-Day Forward	.6024	.6083	1.6598	1.6437
180-Day Forward	.6073	.6136	1.6464	1.6297
Taiwan (Dollar)	.03716	.03716	26.91	26.91
Thailand (Baht)	.039292	.039292	25.45	25.45
Turkey (Lira)	.0004899	.0004899	2041.00	2041.00
United Arab (Dirham)	.2722	.2722	3.6725	3.6725
Uruguay (New Peso)				
Financial	.001901	.001901	526.00	526.00
Venezuela (Bolivar)				
Floating rate	.02684	.02684	37.25	37.25
W. Germany (Mark)	.5319	.5330	1.8800	1.8760
30-Day Forward	.5335	.5346	1.8742	1.8703
90-Day Forward	.5339	.5376	1.8728	1.8600
180-Day Forward	.5403	.5417	1.8505	1.8460
SDR	1.29566	1.29710	0.771807	0.770949
ECU	1.10719	1.10878		

Special Drawing Rights (SDR) are based on exchange rates for the U.S., West German, British, French and Japanese currencies. Source: International Monetary Fund.

European Currency Unit (ECU) is based on a basket of community currencies. Source: European Community Commission.

Source: "Foreign Exchange," *The Wall Street Journal*, May 2, 1989, C13.

foreign exchange trader for a firm quote. Both spot and forward transactions are made in the market. The market for buying and selling on the current day is the **spot market.** The market for closing contracts on subsequent periods of 30, 60, or 90 days is called the **forward market.** For example, for the rates quoted for April 28, 1989, the forward quote for Britain is less than spot (the pound is selling at a discount), whereas the forward quotes for Japan are higher, and the yen is said to be selling at a premium. Forward contracts for lesser known currencies are not readily available, and for unstable currencies they are quite expensive.

Forward contracts provide a form of protection, or **hedge,** against exchange risks. When a forward exchange contract is signed, the forward quote (such as the 90-day quote for West Germany) is the rate that applies although no payment is generally made until the settlement date of the contract. The user pays the price of forgoing possible gains in order to ensure protection against possible losses.

Foreign exchange quotations are given either directly or indirectly. The quote, $.1574/FF, is a direct quote for the French franc because it is the home currency price of one unit of a foreign currency. The indirect quote, the amount of foreign currency for one unit of the domestic currency, in this case is FF6.3525/$.

The rate of exchange between two countries is the result of supply and demand as well as possible governmental policy. Changes in the supply and demand conditions will have an impact on the currency's value. For example, an increase in a country's exports or its interest rates would increase demand for its currency and thus lead to an increase in its currency value. In some cases, governments will establish an exchange rate for their currency and absorb and counter market pressures (and thus accept foreign currency losses) up to a point before allowing the exchange rate to change. Occasionally, governments will coordinate their actions to rectify an imbalance in demand and supply conditions. In September 1985, for example, the United States, together with Great Britain, West Germany, Japan, and France, decided on a coordinated effort to bring the dollar down. Because market participants then expected the dollar to fall, they sold dollars, sparking a sharp decline in the value of the currency. The spot market exchange rate therefore reflects international trade flows, international capital flows, and governmental policy.

Forward markets exist for only a relatively small number of major currencies used in international transactions. The principal determinant for forward rates is the spot rate. Anything having an impact on the spot rate, such as balance-of-payments problems, will have the same impact on forward rates.

The Management of Foreign Exchange Risk

When an international marketer conducts transactions in foreign currencies, he or she runs the risk of suffering financial losses resulting from the change in the value of the currency used. Naturally, changes can also affect the marketer favorably. A firm is exposed to foreign exchange in three ways. **Transaction exposure** refers to the effect of outstanding contracts (for example, payables and receivables). Table 6.7 is an example of a loss to the U.S. exporter if he or she has chosen not to make any changes in his policies or decided not to protect himself against such changes. If the contract had called for payment in U.S. dollars, however, the loss would have been that of the British buyer.

If the financial statements of the marketer are affected as a result of having to report consolidated worldwide results in home-country currency, the firm has **translation exposure.** If the exporter in the example maintained a British bank account with a balance of £100,000, it would initially be worth $170,000 (1/1). Two months later, the exporter would report in its own books the British bank balance to be worth $160,000. Translation exposure for a U.S. firm is a function of the rules issued by the Financial Accounting Standards Board (FASB), in particular FASB 52

FIGURE 6.3 ▪ An Example of a Currency Options and Futures Provider

Risk control for businesses that bruise easily.

When you ship $1.2 billion worth of bananas worldwide, a small flip in currency exchange rates could make a big difference in profits.

Chiquita, like many smart international companies, gets a good grip on those risks with currency options at the Chicago Mercantile Exchange. Hedging Deutschemarks, Pound Sterling and Yen, Chiquita has successfully guarded against financial bruising for years. And because 80% of all the exchange traded currency worldwide was traded on the CME's International Monetary Market, they've found it easy to slip in and out of currency options quickly.

"The IMM is where all information that impacts foreign exchange prices comes together," says David Groelinger, Chiquita VP and Treasurer. "That's where the most efficient pricing takes place."

Now, it will become even more efficient with the launch of GLOBEX—the computer network that expands futures and options trading around the world, around the clock.

If you're like the top bananas at Chiquita, and don't want your international earnings frittered away, the CME's currency futures and options should hold great appeal for you.

CHICAGO MERCANTILE EXCHANGE
The Exchange of Ideas

1-800-331-3332 (US) 01-920-0722 (Europe) 03-595-2251 (Pacific)

Source: Reprinted by permission of the Chicago Mercantile Exchange.

("Foreign Currency Translation"), issued in 1981.[26] If the long-term health of a business entity is affected by foreign exchange beyond transaction and translation exposure, the entity has **economic exposure.** Response to economic exposure involves the application of long-term strategy by all of the functional units of the firm. Marketers can avoid unnecessary economic exposure by careful selection of target markets and prudent pricing and credit policies. Any firm with ongoing international marketing activities will have economic exposure.

Three types of devices to protect against currency-related risk have been proposed: (1) risk modifying, such as increasing prices and incurring local debt; (2) self-insuring, such as manipulating the leads and lags in terms of export and import payments in anticipation of either currency revaluations or devaluations; and (3) risk shifting, such as purchasing of options or futures.[27]

Options and futures are a relatively new development in the foreign exchange markets. An **option** gives the holder the right to buy or sell foreign currency at a prespecified price on or up to a prespecified date. The difference between the currency options market and the forward market is that the transaction in the options market gives the participant the *right* to buy or sell whereas a transaction in the forward market entails a contractual obligation to buy or sell. The currency **futures** market is conceptually similar to the forward market; that is, to buy futures on the pound implies an obligation to buy in the future at a prespecified price. However, the minimum transaction sizes are considerably smaller on the futures market. Forward quotes apply to transactions of $1 million or more, while on the futures market transactions will typically be well below $100,000. This market, therefore, allows relatively small firms engaged in international trade to lock in exchange rates and lower their risk. An example of an entity providing both such services for the international marketer is in Figure 6.3.

SUMMARY

The financing terms of a transaction are an important marketing tool. The basics of an international marketer's credit policy involve two major concerns: (1) getting paid and (2) avoiding unnecessary risk in the process. This requires a good understanding not only of the mechanisms of the foreign exchange market but also of the various types of financial assistance available to the international marketer.

To help the international marketer deal with financial risk, various programs have been put in place by both the government and the private sec-

---

[26] "Foreign Currency Translation," *FASB Statement No. 52* (December 1981), par. 15.

[27] Richard D. Robinson, *Internationalization of Business: An Introduction* (Hinsdale, Ill.: Dryden Press, 1984), 200–207.

tor. Support systems exist as well to get information on international credit and country conditions.

Foreign exchange risk is present any time the international marketer is to receive payment in a currency different from his or her own. The marketer can be protected through the purchase of forward contracts, for example.

Use of the resources described in this chapter will allow the exporter to (1) offer competitive terms of payment to the buyer, (2) prudently penetrate foreign markets of higher risk, and (3) have greater financial liquidity and flexibility in administering the foreign receivables portfolio.

Questions for Discussion

1. Discuss the various types of financial risk in terms of their impact on an international marketing entity and their degree of difficulty.

2. FCIA does not finance export sales, yet it indirectly is quite involved. How?

3. At times, subsidized export credit rates have been as low as half the rates at which national treasuries were borrowing. What is the rationale for this?

4. Compare and contrast FCIA and PEFCO.

5. Suggest possible reasons why Eximbank does not cover 100 percent of commercial risk.

6. What accounts for the fact that export finance managers and export marketing managers have traditionally not worked as closely together as possible?

7. Comment on this statement: "Many commercial banks today have only two objections to financing international trade: one, it is international; two, it involves trade."

8. Suggest benefits and drawbacks of debt/product swaps.

Recommended Readings

Exporter's Encyclopedia. 1988/89. New York: Dun & Bradstreet, 1988.

Chamber of Commerce of the United States. *Foreign Commerce Handbook.* Washington, D.C.: Chamber of Commerce, 1986.

Czinkota, Michael R., ed. *Trade Finance: Current Issues and Developments.* Washington, D.C.: Government Printing Office, 1988.

Foreign Credit Insurance Association. *Your Competitive Edge in Selling Overseas.* New York: FCIA, 1988.

Guadagnoli, Louis G. *A Practical Guide to Export Financing and Risk Management.* Arlington, Va.: Government Information Services, 1989.

Lanze, L. B. *Import/Export Can Make You Rich.* Englewood Cliffs, N.J.: Prentice-Hall, 1988.

Shapiro, Alan C. *Multinational Financial Management.* Boston, Mass.: Allyn and Bacon, 1989.

Wamsley, Julian. *The Foreign Exchange Handbook.* New York: Wiley, 1983.

One Afternoon at the United States International Trade Commission

Chairwoman Stern: We turn now to investigation TA-201-55 regarding nonrubber footwear. Staff has assembled. Are there any questions? Vice Chairman Liebeler has a question. Please proceed.

Vice Chairman Liebeler: My questions are for the Office of Economics, Mr. Benedick. Do foreign countries have a comparative advantage in producing footwear?

Mr. Benedick: Yes, foreign producers generally have a comparative advantage vis-à-vis the domestic producers in producing footwear. Footwear production generally involves labor intensive processes which favor the low wage countries such as Taiwan, Korea, and Brazil, which are the three largest foreign suppliers by volume. For instance, the hourly rate for foreign footwear workers in these countries range from about one-twelfth to one-fourth of the rate for U.S. footwear workers.

Vice Chairman Liebeler: Is it likely that this comparative advantage will shift in favor of the domestic industries over the next several years?

Mr. Benedick: It is not very likely. There seems to be little evidence that supports this. The domestic industry's generally poor productivity performance over the last several years, which includes the period 1977 to 1981, roughly corresponding to the period of OMAs (Orderly Marketing Arrangements Agreements) for Taiwan and Korea, suggest that U.S. producers must significantly increase their modernization efforts to reduce the competitive advantage of the imported footwear.

Vice Chairman Liebeler: Have you calculated the benefits and costs of import relief using various assumptions about the responsiveness of supply and demand to changes in price?

Mr. Benedick: Yes. On the benefit side, we estimated benefits of import restrictions to U.S. producers, which included both increased domestic production and higher domestic prices. We also estimated the terms of trade benefits resulting from import restrictions. These latter benefits result from an appreciation of the U.S. dollar as a result of the import restrictions.

On the cost side, we estimated cost to consumers of the increase in average prices on total footwear purchases under the import restrictions and the consumer costs associated with the drop in total consumption due to the higher prices.

Vice Chairman Liebeler: In your work, did you take into account any retaliation by our trading partners?

Mr. Benedick: No.

Vice Chairman Liebeler: What was the 1984 level of imports?

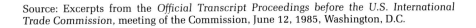

Source: Excerpts from the *Official Transcript Proceedings before the U.S. International Trade Commission,* meeting of the Commission, June 12, 1985, Washington, D.C.

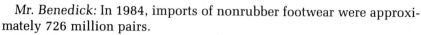

Mr. Benedick: In 1984, imports of nonrubber footwear were approximately 726 million pairs.

Vice Chairman Liebeler: If a six hundred million pair quota were imposed, what would the effect on price of domestic and foreign shoes be, and what would the market share of imports be?

Mr. Benedick: At your request, the Office of Economics estimated the effects of the six hundred million pair quota. We estimate that prices of domestic footwear would increase by about 11 percent, and prices of imported footwear would increase by about 19 percent.

The import share, however, would drop to about 59 percent of the market in the first year of the quota.

Vice Chairman Liebeler: What would aggregate cost to consumers be of that kind of quota?

Mr. Benedick: Total consumer cost would approach 1.3 billion dollars in each year of such a quota.

Vice Chairman Liebeler: What would be the benefit to the domestic industry of this quota?

Mr. Benedick: Domestic footwear production would increase from about 299 million pairs for 1984, to about 367 million pairs, or by about 23 percent. Domestic sales would increase from about $3.8 billion to about $5.2 billion, an increase of about 37 percent.

Vice Chairman Liebeler: How many jobs would be saved?

Mr. Benedick: As a result of this quota, domestic employment would rise by about 26,000 workers over the 1984 level.

Vice Chairman Liebeler: What is the average paid to those workers?

Mr. Benedick: Based on questionnaire responses, each worker would earn approximately $11,900 per year in wages and another $2,100 in fringe benefits, for a total of about $14,000 per year.

Vice Chairman Liebeler: So what then would be the cost to consumers of each of these $14,000 a year jobs?

Mr. Benedick: It would cost consumers approximately $49,800 annually for each of these jobs.

Vice Chairman Liebeler: Thank you very much, Mr. Benedick.

Commissioner Eckes: I have a question for the General Counsel's Representative. I heard an interesting phrase a few moments ago, "comparative advantage." I don't recall seeing that phrase in Section 201. Could you tell me whether it is there and whether it is defined?

Ms. Jacobs: It is not.

Chairwoman Stern: I would like to ask about cost/benefit analysis. Perhaps the General Counsel's Office again might be the best place to direct this question. It is my understanding that the purpose of Section 201 is to determine whether a domestic industry is being injured, the requisite level for requisite reasons, imports being at least as important a cause of the serious injury as any other cause, and then to recommend a remedy which we are given kind of a short menu to select from to remedy the industry's serious injury.

Are we to take into account the impact on the consumer?

Are we to do a cost/benefit analysis when coming up with the remedy which best relieves the domestic industry's serious injury?

Ms. Jacobs: As the law currently stands, it is the responsibility of the Commission to determine that relief which is a duty or import restriction which is necessary to prevent or remedy the injury that the Commission has determined to exist. The President is to weigh such considerations as consumer impact, etc. The Commission is not necessarily responsible for doing that. Of course, the Commission may want to realize that, knowing the President is going to consider those factors, they might want to also consider them, but in fact, that is not the responsibility of the Commission. It is the responsibility of the Commission only to determine that relief which is necessary to remedy the injury they have found.

Chairwoman Stern: I can understand our reporting to the President other material which aren't part of our consideration, but nevertheless necessary for the President in his consideration, but having that information and providing it to the President is different from its being part of the Commission's consideration in its recommendations.

Ms. Jacobs: That's right. Your roles are quite different in that respect.

Vice Chairman Liebeler: Nations will and should specialize in production of those commodities in which they have a comparative advantage. Fortunately, our country has a large capital stock which tends to provide labor with many productive employments. Our comparative advantage is in the production of goods that use a high ratio of capital to labor. Shoes, however, are produced with a low ratio of capital to labor.

Therefore, American footwear cannot be produced as cheaply as foreign footwear. The availability of inexpensive imports permits consumers to purchase less expensive shoes and it allows the valuable capital and labor used in this footwear industry to shift to more productive pursuits.

This situation is not unique to the footwear industry. The classic example is agriculture, where the share of the labor force engaged in farming declined from 50 percent to 3 percent over the last 100 years. This shift did not produce a 47 percent unemployment rate. It freed that labor to produce cars, housing, and computers.

The decline of the American footwear industry is part of this dynamic process. This process is sometimes very painful. Congress, by only providing for temporary relief, has recognized that our continued prosperity depends on our willingness to accept such adjustments.

The industry has sought this so-called "temporary import relief" before. The ITC has conducted approximately 170 investigations relating to this industry. This is the fourth footwear case under Section 201, and so far the industry has gotten relief twice. The 1975 petition resulted in adjustment assistance. The 1976 case resulted in orderly marketing agreements with Taiwan and Korea.

In spite of the efforts of the domestic industry to suppress imports, the industry has been shrinking. Between 1981 and 1984, 207 plants closed;

94 of these closings occurred just last year. The closing of unprofitable plants is a necessary adjustment. Import relief at this stage will retard this process and encourage entry into a dying industry.

Because there is no temporary trade restriction that would facilitate the industry's adjustment to foreign competition, I cannot recommend any import barrier.

Chairwoman Stern: The intent of the General Import Relief law is to allow a seriously injured industry to adjust to global competition. The Commission must devise a remedy which corresponds to the industry and the market forces it must face.

No other manufacturing sector of our economy faces stiffer competition from abroad than the U.S. shoe industry. Imports have captured three-fourths of our market. No relief program can change the basic conditions of competition that this industry must ultimately face on its own. The best that we as a Commission can do—and under Section 201 that the President can do—is to give the industry a short, predictable period of relief to allow both large and small firms to adjust, coexist, and hopefully prosper.

I am proposing to the President an overall quota on imports of 474 million pairs of shoes in the first year. Shoes with a customs value below $2.50 would not be subject to this quota. The relief would extend for a full five years.

Commissioner Lodwick: Section 201 is designed to afford the domestic industry a temporary respite in order to assist it making an orderly adjustment to import competition. The fact that the law limits import relief to an initial period of up to five years, to be phased down after three years to the extent feasible, indicates that Congress did not intend domestic producers to find permanent shelter from import competition under the statute.

Accordingly, I intend to recommend to the President a five-year quota plan which affords the domestic nonrubber footwear industry ample opportunity to implement feasible adjustment plans which will facilitate, as the case may be, either the orderly transfer of resources to alternative uses or adjustments to new conditions of competition.

Commissioner Rohr: In making my recommendation, I emphasize the two responsibilities which are placed on the Commission by statute. First, it must provide a remedy which it believes will effectively remedy the injury which is found to exist.

Secondly, Congress has stated that we, as Commissioners, should attempt, to the extent possible, to develop a remedy that can be recommended to the President by a majority of the Commission. I have taken seriously my obligation to attempt to fashion a remedy with which at least a majority of my colleagues can agree. Such remedy is a compromise.

I am concurring in the remedy proposal which is being presented today by a majority of the Commission. This majority recommendation provides for an overall limit on imports of 474 million pairs; an exclusion from such limitation of shoes entering the United States with a value of less than $2.50 per pair; a growth in such limitation over a five-year period of zero percent, three percent, and nine percent; and the sale of import licenses through an auctioning system.

Commissioner Eckes: It is my understanding that a majority of the Commission has agreed on these points. I subscribe to that and will provide a complete description of my views in my report to the President.

Questions for Discussion

1. What are your views of the ITC recommendation?
2. Should the principle of comparative advantage always dictate trade flows?
3. Why are the consumer costs of quotas so often neglected?
4. Discuss alternative solutions to the job displacement problem.
5. How would you structure a "temporary relief program"?

John Brown (A)

John Brown Public Limited Company (PLC) is an internationally oriented holding company in the United Kingdom. Under its roof are a wide variety of firms, operating mainly in the industrial field. In 1982, sixty percent of group sales were outside the United Kingdom, 24 percent of all sales were exports by John Brown PLC's British companies, and 36 percent were sales by its foreign subsidiaries. The Americas are John Brown's largest international market, mostly through the sales of its 12 U.S. companies and one Canadian corporation. The U.S. companies construct oil and petrochemical plants, make machinery for the plastics and textile industries, and manufacture machine tools. In 1982, total group sales were 681 million pounds and profits were 14.2 million pounds.

One of the firms under the John Brown PLC holding umbrella is John Brown Engineering Limited (JBE). Since 1899, JBE had been a shipbuilder and supplier of engineered marine equipment. In the mid-1960s, the firm was beginning to make and sell small gas turbines. In the early 1970s, JBE became a manufacturing associate of General Electric of the United States. The thrust of the GE-JBE agreement was that GE would supply the technology and the rotor component of gas turbines, while JBE manufactured and sold the turbines. JBE was not restricted in its marketing domain and is not a license company.

By the mid-1970s, JBE had one product: an industrial gas turbine that it made in five different sizes, all at its single location in Clydebank, Scotland, near Glasgow. The gas turbine is used either for power generation or in mechanical drive applications such as the pumping of fluids. Since JBE began building such turbines in 1965, it has delivered a total of 385 of them to its customers. In the five years from 1979 to 1983, it shipped 18 to 41 turbines annually. In 1982, JBE's contribution to the total sales of the holding company was 94 million pounds, with profits of 1.8 million pounds.

DOING BUSINESS WITH THE SOVIET UNION

The Soviet Union is an important business partner to the John Brown group. Soviet business for the group dates from the 1860s, when Mr. John Brown first sold steel for railways to Russia. Since 1960 the U.S.S.R. has represented a significant market for the John Brown group.

JBE's business is mostly export business. Ninety-two percent of its turbines are sold to foreign customers in 45 countries around the world, with the Middle East accounting for the largest share. The company is no stranger to political risk, having done business in Iraq, Syria, Libya,

Source: Stanley D. Nollen, "Commercial Ties with Political Adversaries: The Case of John Brown Engineering and the Soviet Gas Pipeline," Staff Paper 12 (Washington, D.C.: National Center for Export-Import Studies, 1984).

Algeria, and Argentina, as well as in the Soviet Union. Among these countries the Soviet Union has been the largest single purchaser of gas turbines in the world in the last several years and has also been JBE's best customer. Since JBE's first sale to the Soviet Union in 1975, the company has sold 67 turbines for Soviet natural gas transmission pipelines, which accounted for about 30 percent of its business.

As a result, JBE had become an old hand at dealing with the Soviet Union. Over the years, JBE had systematically nurtured the expertise required to do business with the Soviets: adaptation to bureaucratic methods, submission of several modified sales quotations, long negotiations, arrangement of credit facilities, and meticulous preparation and fulfillment of contracts. JBE management had also found that while the Soviets were hard-nosed negotiators, once they agreed to a contract, they always followed it strictly and paid on time.

THE JBE PIPELINE DEAL

On October 6, 1981, JBE announced that it had signed a contract for 61 million pounds to supply 21 gas turbines for the Soviet natural gas pipeline in Western Europe. JBE was one of six European companies to win major contracts for the pipeline from V/O MachinoImport, the Soviet foreign trade organization. Delivery was to commence in the late summer of 1982. Subsequently, JBE announced on October 13 that it had obtained further orders for spare parts and service for the pipeline worth 43 million pounds. Total contract value to JBE was therefore 195 million dollars, the largest contract in the company's history. By itself, the contract accounted for about two-thirds of the company's entire order book. Coming off a loss the year before, John Brown needed the new business badly. Given the high unemployment levels in Scotland, a widespread sigh of relief was heard in Britain, as threatened layoffs did not have to occur at JBE.

Because there had been occasional controversy between Europe and the United States over the building of the pipeline, JBE knew that the turbine contract was politically sensitive. As a result, prior to signing, the firm's management discussed the business with the British government, which agreed to help work out the commercial details of export credits necessary for the deal. The firm also touched base with the U.S. government before the contract was signed, to inquire whether its existing general import license would apply to these turbines. Informal conversations indicated that this was to be the case and that JBE could therefore count on no interference from the U.S. government with its supplies from GE.

THE U.S. EMBARGO

On December 29, 1981, President Reagan, using the authority granted him in the Export Administration Act, placed an embargo on the export of all U.S. oil- and gas-refining equipment, services, and technology to

the Soviet Union. The embargo included the transmission of data and also applied to the re-export of U.S. goods from foreign locations.

The statement from the White House read: "Effective December 30, 1981, the processing of all applications for validated licenses, re-export authorizations for shipment of any commodities, or transfer of any technical data to the U.S.S.R. has been suspended. Furthermore, outstanding validated licenses and authorizations to export may be reviewed to determine whether suspension or revocation is necessary."

The object of the embargo, which followed closely the imposition of martial law in Poland, was to further U.S. foreign policy objectives in light of the Soviet Union's heavy and direct responsibility for the repression in Poland.

The President's announcement meant that, from then on, a validated license would be required in order for JBE to obtain rotors or technical data from GE. Any application for such a license, however, would not be acted upon. The embargo thus prevented GE from shipping any rotors to JBE for use in turbines destined for the Soviet pipeline and from communicating data about the turbines. The embargo also prevented JBE from shipping any turbines already in Scotland that contained GE parts.

Questions for Discussion

1. Could JBE have anticipated the U.S. embargo?
2. How could JBE have changed its international marketing strategy?
3. How can the U.S. government and GE differentiate between rotors for Iraq and rotors for the Soviet Union?
4. Discuss the rationale for economic sanctions.

John Brown (B)

On December 29, 1981, the United States imposed an embargo against shipment of pipeline-related equipment to the Soviet Union. At that time, John Brown Engineering (JBE) already had six rotors from GE in stock. The remaining 15 turbines were to be delivered in the spring of 1983, 15 months away. However, because of the embargo, GE would not be able to make such a shipment.

JBE'S ACTIONS IN THE UNITED STATES

Only days after the U.S. embargo was officially recorded in the Federal Register of January 5, 1982, a delegation of JBE executives visited Washington. Their mission was threefold:

1. To clarify the U.S. action with the officials at the Departments of Commerce and State. The British Embassy in Washington assisted by identifying the appropriate officials and arranging meetings. Clarification meant establishing that only JBE was affected, not the entire John Brown group, or any other John Brown operating company. Clarification also meant establishing that only JBE's Soviet oil and gas industry was affected, not the turbines for power generation for other countries.
2. To explain how the U.S. action affected JBE and sketch the implications of special interest to the United States. For example, JBE had large contracts with Abu Dhabi and Oman for power generation turbines.
3. To get advice from legal experts on how to proceed further in response to the embargo.

In these meetings, John Brown Engineering's principal argument was that the U.S. embargo was retroactive. The JBE contract had been made three months before the embargo, after a check with the United States about the question of export licenses. While an embargo on further JBE business with the Soviet Union would have been opposed by JBE, it would have been understood and accepted.

A second point made by JBE was that it had a legally binding contract freely entered into, and that no government, least of all the United States, should erode this essential foundation of free enterprise. The argument was both one of principle—the inviolability of private contracts—and one of practice—the likelihood of extreme economic damage to the company if it had to default on its contract.

Source: Stanley D. Nollen, "Commercial Ties with Political Adversaries: The Case of John Brown Engineering and the Soviet Gas Pipeline," Staff Paper 12 (Washington, D.C.: National Center for Export-Import Studies, 1984).

Throughout the meetings, company officials stressed that they were not taking issue with Washington's foreign policy views about martial law in Poland. The executives received a very sympathetic hearing in Washington, yet it was pointed out to them that the rules of the embargo were inflexible.

INVESTIGATION OF ALTERNATIVES

A common response to trade controls is to avoid the controls by either making the product oneself or by substituting another country's or company's product. Such a substitution will never match the original (or it would have been chosen in the first place) but it could be a plausible short-term solution.

JBE had the technological ability to make the 15 rotors, but they would first have to be reverse engineered, because JBE did not prosess the specifications. The plant would then have to be tooled up. The total investment in time and money would have been quite substantial. In addition, deliveries of turbines to the Soviet Union would be late, the U.S. embargo would be violated unless the already shipped GE rotors were not used, and JBE's manufacturing associate agreement with GE would be jeopardized, with unknown adverse legal and financial consequences.

Another crucial consideration in this do-it-yourself option were the long-term implications. What would happen after the Soviet contract was completed? The Soviet-bound turbine was one of five sizes and types. The overall world demand for turbines is limited, which would make it very difficult to achieve economies of scale.

A second major alternative was to source rotors from Alsthom Atlantique, a French firm, which was equipped to make the GE rotor. Alsthom Atlantique executives indicated that they could complete the first rotor in late 1983. They also made it clear that they were under substantial pressure from the French government not to give the appearance of contravening the U.S. embargo. In any event, a large new investment would be necessary to meet an expanded and accelerated production schedule.

If JBE used this alternative, its deliveries to the Soviet Union would likely be late, in spite of using the six GE rotors on hand. As per contract, a late delivery would trigger a five percent penalty of total contract value. JBE would also have to cancel its order for 15 more GE rotors with unknown consequences for that essential business relationship.

Because other European contractors of the Soviet pipeline were also affected, a third alternative was for all the European contractors to agree jointly on a revised method of pumping the natural gas through the pipeline, using the rotors on hand in all the companies (they had 23 out of the required 125) to make gas-fired turbines, and then driving steam turbines via heat recovery from the gas turbines. This, plus the use of some Soviet-made turbines, might get the job done. A meeting of all European contractors was held in Köln, Germany. However, at this meeting many problems surfaced, some of which were similar to the problems of other options, such as late delivery, violation of the U.S. embargo, and cancellation of the GE order. The principal uncertainty, however, was the willingness of the Soviet Union to cooperate in such a "half loaf" contract.

A final alternative was to simply scrap the Soviet contract. However, the cost of such an action would be substantial. It would mean the loss of 104 million pounds in contract revenues; probable penalty levies of five percent of the contract and severe consequential damages; possible loss of future Soviet business; loss of an unquantified number of jobs in an already depressed area; disfavor of the British government; and perhaps future problems with GE.

In return for suffering these costs, JBE would get two benefits. It would be in compliance with the U.S. embargo and could possibly get partial reimbursement for losses from the British Export Guaranty Department (ECGD). Such coverage is limited to 85 percent of the contract value and to actual costs and expenditures of the contractor. It does not include damage suits or loss of profit. Yet, whether coverage would actually be extended was doubtful. Customarily, export credit guarantees are triggered by customers' nonpayment, whereas in this case the problem was the sellers. Because there was no precedent for such a case, there was no way of putting odds on receiving coverage.

Questions for Discussion

1. Evaluate the alternatives available to JBE.
2. What is your view of JBE's Washington argument of retroactivity?
3. How do export controls mesh with the freedom of entrepreneurship?
4. In your view, should JBE be eligible for insurance coverage by ECGD?

Food for Thought

The following story line has been slightly modified in order to protect the identities of the companies involved. However, the facts presented are essentially accurate.

Mrs. McIntosh's Applesauce Company (MMAC) cannot meet the growing consumer demand for its applesauce. It has a manufacturing facility in San Diego that dates to the early 1940s. The company is unable to hire the labor necessary to man the production line at the rates it pays. This may be due to the immigration bill passed by Congress that places a burden on U.S. companies to hire only legal U.S. residents. In addition, MMAC's facility is outmoded and should be updated to keep up with current demand.

MMAC, after considering the alternatives, has decided to relocate its plant to Vancouver, Canada. The Canadian government has agreed to a five-year tax haven and a low-cost loan to purchase the building. All planned production will be consumed in the U.S. marketplace. MMAC has sent out a bid package for a turnkey plant to make its applesauce. The request-for-price package was sent to the ten largest food processing plant manufacturers, only one of which is located in the United States. Part of the bid package advises the bidders that financing is to be included as part of the proposal. MMAC is willing to put down 30 percent of the total factory price, with the successful bidder responsible for finding financing for the other 70 percent.

The only U.S. company capable of bidding on the factory is Food Processors Inc. (FPI), an Oregon corporation. Because of its proximity to the Canadian site and because it has already built a nearly identical facility for orange juice, FPI expects to be the lowest price bidder on the program. The sole question is financing.

The other major bidders are from France, England, and Germany. The German government does not provide financing for such programs. On the other hand, the French and British governments are able and willing, through their export promotion programs, to provide very attractive ten-year financing. The rates that they offer are definitely below market rates.

FPI, the U.S. company, submits a request for financing to the Export-Import Bank of the United States (EXIM). EXIM turns down the request without stating a reason. The president of FPI calls a high U.S. government official, who sets up a meeting among all concerned parties. FPI's president explains that the project is of vital importance to the company. Failure to obtain financing may cause FPI to lose the project. If it does, several hundred workers will have to be laid off. All FPI asks is that EXIM match the rate to be used by financing agencies of the other countries.

The EXIM official refuses, explaining that EXIM will not use its funds

Source: This case was prepared by David W. Danjczek of Litton Industries. Reprinted with permission.

for any project that results in economic dislocation to the United States. If it provides financing in this case, the funds will be used to relocate a plant now in the United States to a foreign country, thereby causing economic dislocation.

FPI's president explains that the decision by MMAC has already been finalized to relocate to Canada. The dislocation will occur regardless of EXIM's position, and the only result of such an obstinate position by EXIM will be the layoff of several hundred workers in Oregon. EXIM's position does not change. FPI loses the job to a French company. The workers in Oregon are laid off.

Questions for Discussion

1. Is EXIM's position logical? Should EXIM have lent the money, provided it was certain that MMAC was going to relocate?

2. Could FPI have handled its case better? Should it have obtained assistance from government officials prior to making its initial request to EXIM?

3. Does FPI have any other means open to it? (Remember that there is a General Agreement on Tariffs and Trade [GATT] that covers both tariff and nontariff barriers to trade.) Do the Canadian government's favorable terms for the facility represent government subsidies?

4. When the finished product—the applesauce—enters the United States from Canada, will its price be considered to be subsidized by the Canadian government?

5. Should MMAC move to Canada at all? Is the move fair to its California employees?

Retaliation against Brazil

In October 1986, President Reagan determined that certain Brazilian policies were unreasonable and a burden and restriction on U.S. commerce. In particular he was concerned about administrative burdens on imports, prohibitions on foreign investment, and the lack of copyright protection for computer software.

After more than a year of negotiations, Brazil still had not rectified its unfair trade practices. As a result, President Reagan decided to impose sanctions on selected Brazilian exports to the United States. A notice was placed in the Federal Register listing products upon which sanctions might be imposed in the form of increased tariffs. As required by statute, the Commerce Department scheduled public hearings in order to take U.S. industry concerns into consideration before finalizing the sanctions. During these hearings various industry positions emerged.

The position of the American Electronics Association was that the electronics industry already suffered from Brazil's informatics policies; therefore any sanctions the administration finally decided on should not further hurt that industry. The acting president of the Computer and Business Equipment Manufacturer's Association testified that products manufactured by overseas subsidiaries and affiliates of U.S. firms should not be subject to sanctions because of U.S. investment in Brazil. His reasons were that the sanctions would add to the burden already exerted on these firms by Brazil's policies and that high-technology companies were already hurt by trade sanctions.

The Computer Software and Services Industry Association supported the sanctions. An association representative said the message "must be sent" that other countries cannot build their export industries at the expense of U.S. firms.

The Footwear Group of the American Association of Exporters and Importers objected to sanctions on leather footwear for men and boys. Sanctions would hurt lower income U.S. consumers by raising prices of Brazilian shoes since no competing products were available from domestic firms. The International Footwear Association also opposed sanctions in the belief that they would hurt its members—importers, wholesalers, and domestic manufacturers. The Footwear Industries of America Inc. favored sanctions on nonrubber footwear, however, believing that they would restrain Brazilian trade and encourage a change in its trade restraining policies. In addition, sanctions would help the U.S. footwear industry.

Source: This case, written by Michael R. Czinkota, draws on public secondary source materials: "Tariff on Brazilian Exports," White House Fact Sheet, November 13, 1987; "Industry Testifies on Brazil Retaliation As Administration Moves toward Sanctions," *International Trade Reporter*, December 23, 1987, 1590–1591; and various newspaper articles and press releases.

The president of the Ferroalloy Association said that inclusion of ferrosilicon and silicon metal on the sanctions list would be appropriate because they are important exports from Brazil. Moreover, Brazil's "very lax" pollution and safety regulations give that country an unfair advantage over U.S. industry. He added that U.S. imports have cost jobs and that Brazil accounts for more than 25 percent of the imports. However, the American Iron and Steel Institute disagreed, citing negative consequences for U.S. specialty steel producers.

According to the American Restaurant China Council Inc., restrictions on all Brazilian commercial chinaware would be an effective and appropriate response to Brazil's trade practices. The council was in favor of including imports of all Brazilian chinaware on the list of sanctioned products.

Following the hearings, administration officials met to determine the most appropriate products for sanctioning. Shortly before sanctions were announced, Brazilian officials suggested that the view being taken in the trade dispute was far too narrow, because Brazilian exports were directly linked to Brazil's ability to service and repay its international debt. Should exports be curtailed, payments would probably be affected. In addition, the Brazilian government was working hard at resolving the issue but simply needed more time. The U.S. Department of the Treasury promised to raise that concern on the interagency level.

As a result of the subsequent interagency consultations, the Office of the United States Trade Representative announced on February 29, 1988, that the imposition of sanctions against Brazil would be postponed.

Questions for Discussion

1. How would you characterize the positions taken by the various industries?

2. How should policymakers resolve such conflicting advice?

3. Should overseas subsidiaries of U.S. firms be exempt from trade policy actions by the U.S. government?

4. If debt repayment is the reason for not imposing sanctions, does that not give preferential treatment to banks over service providers and manufacturers?

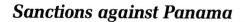

Sanctions against Panama

For many years the United States has maintained a close relationship with the country and government of Panama. On an international level, U.S.–Panamanian relations reached a historic high when President Carter signed the Panama Canal treaties, which began to transfer control of the Panama Canal from the United States to the Panamanian people. Relationships were also closely intertwined militarily because of the location of the U.S. military's Southern Command, which is headquartered in Panama. Economically, the close linkage between Panama and the United States could be seen by the fact that Panama uses U.S. dollar bills as its national currency.

These relations took a sharp turn for the worse when General Manuel Antonio Noriega, commander of Panama's national defense forces, was indicted at the beginning of 1988 by a U.S. grand jury in Miami, Florida, for drug smuggling. On February 25, 1988, President Eric Arturo Delvalle of Panama dismissed General Noriega from his position, only to be ousted himself by the Panamanian legislature. On March 11, 1988, President Reagan, in an effort to "rapidly restore democracy" in Panama, announced several policy steps that were to lead to the resignation or ouster of General Noriega. The steps announced by the President consisted of the following:

- A suspension of the trade preferences available to Panama under the Generalized System of Preferences (GSP) and the Caribbean Basin Initiative
- Suspension of Panama's sugar export quotas to the United States for 1988
- Instructions to U.S. businesses and individuals not to make tax and other trade-related payments to the Panamanian government
- The placement of all funds due or payable to the Republic of Panama from the U.S. government in an escrow account for the Delvalle government
- The placement of all payments due to Panama from the Panama Canal Commission into an escrow account
- Cessation of all payments of assistance by the U.S. government; these included any credits for arms sales, donations of food and nonfood commodities, and financing by the Export-Import Bank
- Instruction of the U.S. representatives to the World Bank, the International Finance Corporation, and the Inter-American Development Bank to vote against any loans to Panama

Source: This case, written by Michael R. Czinkota, draws on public secondary source materials such as: "Statement by the President," March 11, 1988, The White House, Office of the Press Secretary, Washington, D.C.; "Press Release by Secretary of State George Schultz," The White House, Office of the Press Secretary, March 11, 1988, Washington, D.C.; Statement by Eric Arturo Delvalle, Embassy of Panama, March 1, 1988, Washington, D.C.; William Branigin, "U.S. Campaign to Oust Noriega Appears Nearing a Dead End," *The Washington Post*, Thursday, February 9, 1989, A30.

In addition, based on a coordinated statement with President Delvalle, all payments of debts, taxes, fees, or other obligations due to the Republic of Panama were to be made into an escrow account.

Clearly, the goal of these policy actions was to economically starve Panama under General Noriega. It was expected that, with an imminent acute cash crisis, the government would not be able to meet its obligations and that the Noriega regime would collapse shortly. In interviews given by Washington policymakers, the end of the Noriega regime was predicted to be only a matter of days or weeks at most.

All the policy measures had an almost immediate economic effect on the Republic of Panama. With $50 million worth of assets frozen in New York, the Bank of Panama had to close. Deprived of $145 million worth of canal toll revenues, the cash shortage became very acute. A general bank closure took place from March to May of 1988. The Panamanian government defaulted on all of its foreign commercial bank loans. In a matter of months, gross domestic product dropped by 10 percent, government revenues by 30 percent, and unemployment rose from 11.6 percent to 23 percent. Many of the offshore deposits that had accumulated in the international banking haven of Panama were withdrawn. From 1987 to 1988, the level of deposits dropped from $20.6 billion to $7.5 billion.

But General Noriega hung in there. In spite of the cash shortage, and the closure of all banks, he managed to make at least partial payments on national payroll requirements. Checks were monetized and made negotiable for limited purposes. The government began issuing payroll and pension checks in several denominations and began distributing multiple checks to employees and pensioners. These checks were then accepted in the Panamanian economy for commercial transactions including payment of rent, grocery purchases, and payment of debt to the government, such as taxes and utility bills.

The government also issued new financial instruments, called *Cedis*, backed by time deposits. These certificates were circulated for commercial transactions. In addition, the government cashed some checks in dollars, even though on occasion cash was delivered in the form of coins. Over time, the population of Panama began to get used to the acute cash shortage. Banks began to reopen and permit the withdrawal of funds on a very limited basis.

As Panama began to adjust to a new economic situation, the same could not be said about the U.S. holders of $4 billion worth of investment in Panama, their employees and managers, and the U.S. embassy staff. Their problems continued to mount. For example, the more than 160 Americans assigned to the U.S. Embassy in Panama soon were unable to use their cars because of the U.S. refusal to deal with the new Panamanian government. This refusal resulted in their inability to get new license plates. Many U.S. businesses in Panama, according to the American Chamber of Commerce in Panama, were being forced to close their doors. Because they were unable under the sanctions to pay import duties to the Panamanian government, they were not permitted to import goods vital to their survival. Within five months of the announcement of the sanctions, U.S. firms in Panama were operating at 40 to 70 percent of capacity.

The U.S. government tried to remedy this problem by having the Treasury Department quietly publish regulations that permitted payments to the Noriega regime of import duties, other import-related expenses, and port fees. Even though these measures helped, they were of little use for thousands of Panamanian employees of U.S. agencies and companies in Panama who, because taxes were no longer deducted and paid by their employers, were unable to sell property or conduct other business and occasionally had their property confiscated in lieu of withheld taxes.

U.S. executives were severely hampered in their mobility. They could not obtain visas to travel to Panama because the U.S. government recognized only the Delvalle government, and documentation issued by the Delvalle Embassy in Washington was not accepted in Panama. Similarly, U.S. executives working in Panama had major problems leaving the country. In order to leave, they had to produce a "Paz y Salvo" document at immigration. However, these documents are issued only if the applicant is current on all tax payments. Because it was illegal to pay these taxes, many U.S. executives were unable to leave Panama.

By the Spring of 1989, a new administration had come to Washington, D.C. In Panama, however, General Noriega was still in firm command. U.S. firms were still suffering major hardships in Panama, and it became an issue of major debate whether the provision in the Panama Canal treaties, which called for a Panamanian to be appointed administrator of the canal in 1990, should be adhered to. Nonadherence would be clearly regarded by many in Latin America as a U.S. abrogation of the treaties and would heighten the danger of anti-American sentiments inside Panama.

Questions for Discussion

1. What is your view of economic sanctions to enforce foreign policy?
2. What went wrong in applying economic sanctions to Panama?
3. How can sanctions be devised that do not affect U.S. businesses operating in the sanctioned country?
4. If U.S. businesses are hurt due to sanctions, should they be compensated, and by whom? How about compensation for affected foreign firms and individuals?
5. Which laws and regulations should subsidiaries of U.S. multinationals adhere to? Those of the home country or those of the host country?
6. Should the United States honor treaties if they benefit inconvenient foreign leaders?

IKEA in the USA

IKEA, the world's largest home furnishings retail chain, was founded in Sweden in 1943 as a mail-order company and opened its first showroom ten years later. From its headquarters in Almhult, IKEA has since expanded to worldwide sales of $2.6 billion from 83 outlets in 20 countries (see Table 1). In fact, the second store that IKEA built was in Oslo, Norway. Today, IKEA operates large warehouse showrooms in Sweden, Norway, Denmark, Holland, France, Belgium, West Germany, Switzerland, Austria, Canada, the United States, Saudi Arabia, and the United Kingdom. It has smaller stores in Kuwait, Australia, Hong Kong, Singapore, the Canary Islands, and Iceland. A store near Budapest was expected to open by 1990, with others to follow in Poland and Yugoslavia. Even the Soviet Union is not considered out of bounds.

The international expansion of IKEA has progressed in three phases, all of them continuing at the present time: Scandinavian expansion, begun in 1963; West European expansion, begun in 1973; and North American expansion, begun in 1974. Of the individual markets, West Germany is the largest, accounting for 30 percent of company sales. The phases of expansion are detectable in the worldwide sales shares depicted in Figure 1. "We want to bring the IKEA concept to as many people as possible," IKEA officials have said.

THE IKEA CONCEPT

Ingvar Kamprad, the founder, formulated as IKEA's mission to "offer a wide variety of home furnishings of good design and function at prices so low that the majority of people can afford to buy them." The principal target market of IKEA, which is similar across countries and regions in which IKEA has a presence, is composed of people who are young, highly educated, liberal in their cultural values, white-collar workers, and not especially concerned with status symbols.

IKEA follows a standardized product strategy with an identical assortment around the world. Today, IKEA carries an assortment of 12,000 different home furnishings that range from plants to pots, sofas to soup spoons, and wine glasses to wallpaper. The smaller items are carried to

Source: This case, prepared by Ilkka A. Ronkainen, is based on: Rita Martenson, "Is Standardization of Marketing Feasible in Culture-Bound Industries? A European Case Study," *International Marketing Review* 4 (Autumn 1987): 7–17; Eleanor Johnson Tracy, "Shopping Swedish Style Comes to the U.S.," *Fortune*, January 27, 1986, 63–67; Mary Krienke, "IKEA— Simple Good Taste," *Stores*, April 1986, 58; Jennifer Lin, "IKEA's U.S. Translation," *Stores*, April 1986, 63; "Furniture Chain Has a Global View," *Advertising Age*, October 26, 1987, 58; and Bill Kelley, "The New Wave from Europe," *Sales and Marketing Management*, November 1987, 46–48. Special thanks are due Dan Tavares for information on IKEA.

TABLE 1 ▪ **IKEA's International Expansion**

Year	Outlets	Countries	Coworkers	Catalog Circulation	Turnover in Swedish Crowns
1954	1	1	15	285,000	3,000,000
1964	2	2	250	1,200,000	79,000,000
1974	10	5	1,500	13,000,000	616,000,000
1984	66	17	8,300	45,000,000	6,770,000,000
1988	75(83[a])	19(20[a])	13,400[b]	50,535,000[c]	14,500,000,000[d]

[a]Stores/countries being opened by the end of 1990.

[b]13,400 coworkers are equivalent to 10,700 full-time workers.

[c]14 languages, 27 editions.

[d]Corresponding to net sales of the IKEA group of companies.

Source: *IKEA Facts, 88/89.*

FIGURE 1 ▪ **IKEA Worldwide Sales Expressed as Percentages of Turnover**

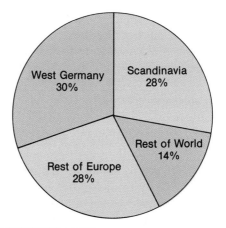

complement the bigger ones. IKEA does not have its own manufacturing facilities but designs all of its furniture. The network of subcontracted manufacturers numbers nearly 1,500 in 50 different countries. IKEA shoppers have to become "prosumers"—half producers, half consumers—because most products must be assembled.

Manufacturers are responsible for shipping the components to large warehouses, for example, to the central one in Almhult. These warehouses then supply the various stores, which are in effect miniwarehouses. The final distribution is the customer's responsibility. IKEA does cooperate with car-rental companies to offer vans and small trucks at reasonable rates for customers needing delivery service.

TABLE 2 ▪ **The IKEA Concept**

Target market:	"Young people of all ages"
Product:	IKEA offers the same products worldwide. The countries of origin of these products are: Scandinavia (52 percent), Western Europe (21 percent), Eastern Europe (20 percent), and others (7 percent). Most items have to be assembled by the customer. The furniture design is modern and light. Textiles and pastels.
Distribution:	IKEA has built its own distribution network. Outlets are outside the city limits of major metropolitan areas. Products are not delivered but IKEA cooperates with car rental companies that offer small trucks. IKEA offers mail order in Europe and Canada.
Pricing:	The IKEA concept is based on low price. The firm tries to keep its price image constant.
Promotion:	IKEA's promotional efforts are mainly through its catalogs. IKEA has developed a prototype communications model that must be followed by all stores. Its advertising is attention getting and provocative. Media choices vary by market.

Although IKEA has concentrated on company-owned, larger scale outlets, franchising has been used in areas in which the market is relatively small or where uncertainty may exist as to the response to the IKEA concept. IKEA uses mail order in Europe and Canada but has resisted expansion into it in the United States, mainly because of capacity constraints.

IKEA offers prices that are 30 to 50 percent lower than fully assembled competing products. This is a result of large-quantity purchasing, low-cost logistics, store location in suburban areas, and the do-it-yourself approach to marketing. IKEA's prices do vary from market to market, largely because of fluctuations in exchange rates and differences in taxation regimes, but price positioning is kept as standardized as possible.

IKEA's promotion is centered on the catalog. The IKEA catalog is printed in 14 languages and has a worldwide circulation of over 50 million copies (see Table 1). The catalogs are uniform in layout except for minor regional differences. The company's advertising goal is to generate word-of-mouth publicity through innovative approaches. Local store managers have substantial leeway in promotional decision making (for example, in choosing an advertising agency) but have to adhere to certain guidelines to ensure a universal image.

The IKEA concept is summarized in Table 2.

IKEA IN THE COMPETITIVE ENVIRONMENT

IKEA's strategic positioning is unique. As Figure 2 illustrates, few furniture retailers anywhere have engaged in long-term planning or achieved scale economies in production. European furniture retailers, especially those in Sweden, Switzerland, West Germany, and Austria, are much

FIGURE 2 ▪ **Competition in Furniture Retailing**

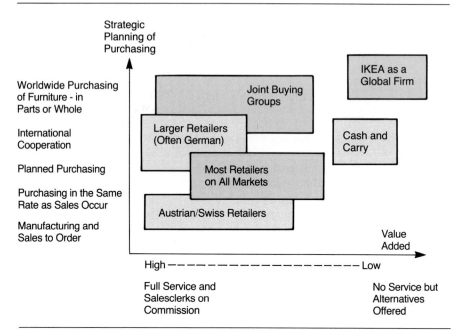

Source: Rita Martenson, "Is Standardization of Marketing Feasible in Culture-Bound Industries? A European Case Study," *International Marketing Review* 4 (Autumn 1987): 14.

smaller than IKEA. Even when companies have joined forces as buying groups, their heterogeneous operations have made it difficult for them to achieve the same degree of coordination and concentration as IKEA. Because customers are usually content to wait for the delivery of furniture, retailers have not been forced to take purchasing risks.

The value-added dimension differentiates IKEA from its competition. IKEA offers no customer assistance but creates opportunities for consumers to choose, transport, and assemble units of furniture. The best summary of the competitive situation was provided by a manager at another firm: "We can't do what IKEA does, and IKEA doesn't want to do what we do."

IKEA IN THE UNITED STATES

After careful study and assessment of its Canadian experience, IKEA decided to enter the U.S. market in 1985 by establishing outlets on the East Coast. IKEA's three stores (Philadelphia, Woodbridge near Washington, D.C., and Baltimore) generated $93 million in 1988. The overwhelming level of success in 1987 led the company to invest in a warehousing facility near Philadelphia that receives goods from Sweden. Plans call for

60 additional stores over the next 25 years with only gradual expansion to the West Coast.

Questions for Discussion

1. What accounts for IKEA's success with a standardized product and marketing strategy in a business that is usually described as having some of the strongest cultural influences? Consider, for example, that an American buying IKEA beds will also have to buy IKEA sheets, because the beds are in European sizes.

2. Which features of the "young people of all ages" are universal and can be exploited by a global/regional marketing strategy?

3. Is IKEA destined to succeed everywhere it cares to establish itself?

PART TWO

Beginning International Marketing Activities

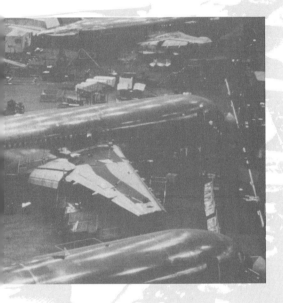

IN PART TWO the major focus is on the company that is considering whether to fill an unsolicited export order, the manager who wants to find out how the current product line can be marketed abroad, or the firm searching for ways to expand its currently limited international activities.

It concentrates on low-cost, low-risk international expansion, which permits a firm to enter the global market without an extraordinary commitment of human or financial resources. The reader will share the concerns of small and medium-sized firms—those that need international marketing assistance most and that supply the largest employment opportunities—before progressing to the advanced international marketing activities described in Part Three.

CHAPTER 7

The Export Process

7.1 THE INTERNATIONAL MARKETPLACE

The Wrong Price List   Michael Hand is the sales representative of a Wisconsin manufacturer. His firm purchases sheepskins, tans them, and produces a variety of merchandise, such as sheepskin rugs, pillows, and stuffed animals. The company has also developed a series of products targeted exclusively to the automotive aftermarket in the Great Lakes area. Steering-wheel covers and seat covers from sheepskin account for 20 percent of total sales.

During a vacation in the United Kingdom, Michael took along some samples to show to a friend he was visiting, simply to explain how he was earning a living back home. Ever the salesman, he then could not resist visiting some car dealers in London to gauge their interest level. The response was enthusiastic, and dealers wanted to order. Michael showed them his price list and was about to explain that the prices would be lower when adjusted to reflect the exchange rate for the pound and the dollar, when he was told that the prices were "indeed" very reasonable.

Four years after that trip Michael's division accounted for over 40 percent of the firm's total sales. Michael had been promoted to the position of Vice President of International Marketing.

Participation in the international marketplace is a potentially very profitable activity, although firms cannot simply jump into international marketing and expect to be successful. They must adjust to the needs and opportunities of international markets in order to become long-term participants. Because of the gradual globalization of the marketplace,[1] however, firms have less and less time to adjust to new market realities. In addition, many firms are so exposed to international competition that they must participate, whether they want to or not.

Because most firms start their international involvement with exporting, this chapter will discuss the export process by addressing the activities that take place within the firm preparing to enter the international marketplace.

[1] Theodore Levitt, "The Globalization of Markets," *Harvard Business Review* 61 (May–June 1983): 92–102.

It will focus on the basic stimuli for exporting and will discuss the change agents, both internal and external, that activate these stimuli. In addition, the concerns and preoccupations of firms as they begin their international marketing operations will be discussed. Finally, a model of the export development process within the firm will be presented.

Managers must understand what "sells" to owners and decision makers in the firm so that they can aid in the move toward internationalization. Current and prospective employees must be able to assess the strategic direction of the firm. An awareness of the inherent attributes that make firms international can aid students in selecting the best environment in which to become active in international marketing.

MOTIVATIONS TO INTERNATIONALIZE

Many researchers have worked on determining the reasons why firms go international. A key factor is apparently the type and quality of management. Some researchers have shown that dynamic management is important when firms take their first international steps.[2] Also, managers of exporting firms typically show a higher level of formal education and foreign language fluency than do managers of nonexporting firms.[3] Other researchers have differentiated between active and passive firms and shown linkages with internationalization efforts.[4] Similarly, firms have been segmented into aggressive and nonaggressive.[5] All of the differentiations point toward a conclusion that the international marketing behavior of firms is related to managerial aspirations and the level of commitment that management is willing to give to the international marketing effort. To a large extent, this conclusion has been formulated by reverse deduction: the managers of firms that are unsuccessful or inactive in the international marketplace usually exhibit a lack of determination or devotion to international marketing. Because international markets cannot be penetrated overnight—but rather require a vast amount of market development activity, market research, and sensitivity to foreign market factors—the issue of managerial commitment is a crucial one.

In most business activities, one factor alone rarely accounts for any given action. Usually a mixture of factors result in firms taking steps in a

[2] Warren J. Bilkey and George Tesar, "The Export Behavior of Smaller Sized Wisconsin Manufacturing Firms," *Journal of International Business Studies* 8 (Spring/Summer 1977): 93–98.

[3] F. N. Burton and B. B. Schlegelmilch, "Profile Analyses of Non-Exporters versus Exporters Grouped by Export Involvement," *Management International Review* 27 (First Quarter, 1987): 38–49.

[4] Finn Wiedersheim-Paul, H. C. Olson, and L. S. Welch, "Pre-Export Activity: The First Step in Internationalization," *Journal of International Business Studies* 9 (Spring/Summer 1978): 47–58.

[5] George Tesar and Jesse S. Tarleton, "Comparison of Wisconsin and Virginia Small and Medium-Sized Exporters: Aggressive and Passive Exporters" in *Export Management*, eds. Michael R. Czinkota and George Tesar (New York: Praeger Publishers, 1982), 85–112.

TABLE 7.1 ▪ **Major Motivations to Internationalize Small and Medium-Sized Firms**

Proactive
- Profit Advantage
- Unique Products
- Technological Advantage
- Exclusive Information
- Managerial Urge
- Tax Benefit
- Economies of Scale

Reactive
- Competitive Pressures
- Overproduction
- Declining Domestic Sales
- Excess Capacity
- Saturated Domestic Markets
- Proximity to Customers and Ports

Source: Michael R. Czinkota, *Export Development Strategies* (New York: Praeger Publishers, 1982), 53.

given direction. This is true of internationalization; motivation consists of a variety of factors both pushing and pulling firms along the international path.[6] Table 7.1 provides an overview of the major motivations to internationalize. They are differentiated into proactive and reactive motivations. Proactive motivations represent stimuli to attempt strategic change. Reactive motivations influence firms that are responsive to environmental changes and adjust to them by changing their activities over time.

Proactive Motivations

The most stimulating proactive motivation to become involved in international marketing is the profit advantage. Management may perceive international sales as a potential source of higher profit margins or of more added-on profits. Of course, the perceived profitability, when planning to enter into international markets, is often quite different from profitability actually attained. The gap between perception and reality may be particularly large when the firm has not previously engaged in international market activities. Despite thorough planning, imponderable influences often shift the profit picture substantially. For example, a sudden shift in exchange rates may drastically alter profit forecasts even though they were based on careful market evaluation.

A second major stimulus emanates either from unique products or from a technological advantage. A firm may produce goods or services that are not widely available from international competitors or may have made

[6]Tamer S. Cavusgil, "Global Dimensions of Marketing," in *Marketing*, eds. Patrick E. Murphy and Ben M. Enis (Glenview, Ill.: Scott, Foresman, 1985), 577–599.

technological advances in a specialized field. Again, real and perceived advantages should be differentiated. Many firms believe that theirs are unique products or services, even though this may not be the case in the international market. If products are unique, however, they certainly can provide a competitive edge. One issue to consider is how long such a technological or product advantage will continue. Historically, a firm with a competitive edge could count on being the sole supplier to foreign markets for years to come. This type of advantage, however, has shrunk dramatically because of competing technologies and a frequent lack of international patent protection.

Exclusive market information is another proactive stimulus. This includes knowledge about foreign customers, marketplaces, or market situations that is not widely shared by other firms. Such special knowledge may result from particular insights by a firm based on international research, special contacts a firm may have, or simply being in the right place at the right time (for example, recognizing a good business situation during a vacation trip). Although exclusivity can serve well as an initial stimulus for international marketing activities, it will rarely provide prolonged motivation because competitors—at least in the medium run—can be expected to catch up with the information advantage of the firm.

Managerial urge is a motivation that reflects the desire, drive, and enthusiasm of management toward international marketing activities. This enthusiasm can exist simply because managers like to be part of a firm that operates internationally. (It sounds impressive.) Further, it can often provide a good reason for international travel—for example, to call on a major customer in the Bahamas during a cold winter month. Such travel can be deducted as a business rather than a personal expense. Often, however, the managerial urge to internationalize is simply the reflection of general entrepreneurial motivation—of a desire for continuous growth. The International Marketplace 7.1 provides an example of general entrepreneurial motivation.

Tax benefits can also play a major motivating role. Historically, such benefits were obtainable to U.S. firms through the formation of a Domestic International Sales Corporation (DISC). However, because of discrepancies between DISC legislation and international trade agreements in the GATT, this method of providing tax benefits to firms that engage in international marketing efforts ended on December 31, 1984. Since then, a new tax mechanism called a Foreign Sales Corporation (FSC) has been instituted. It is in conformity with the international agreements and provides firms with certain tax deferrals, thus making international marketing activities potentially more profitable. Whether FSC tax benefits exceed the costs firms incur by having to comply with the regulations depends on the extent of international marketing activities. Among other things, the regulations require the formation of a foreign subsidiary and the holding of directors' meetings abroad. If realized, FSC tax benefits allow the firm either to offer its products at a lower cost in foreign markets or to accumulate a higher profit. This may therefore tie in closely with the profit motivation.

A final major proactive motivation is that of economies of scale. Becoming a participant in international marketing activities may enable the firm to increase its output and therefore climb more rapidly on the learning curve. Ever since the Boston Consulting Group showed that a doubling of output can reduce production costs up to 30 percent, this effect has been very much sought. Increased production for the international market can therefore also help in reducing the cost of production for domestic sales and make the firm more competitive domestically as well.[7] This effect often results in the seeking of market share as a primary objective of firms. At an initial internationalization stage, this may mean an increased search for export markets; at a later stage, it can result in the opening of foreign subsidiaries and foreign production facilities. The latter effects, however, are primarily applicable to multinational firms and are therefore discussed in Part Three.

Reactive Motivations

A second set of motivations, primarily characterized as reactive, influences firms to respond to environmental changes and pressures rather than attempt to blaze trails.

A prime form of reactive motivation is that of competitive pressures. A firm may fear losing domestic market share to competing firms that have benefited from the effect of the economies of scale gained by international marketing activities. Further, it may fear losing foreign markets permanently to domestic competitors that decide to focus on these markets. Observing that domestic competitors are beginning to internationalize, and knowing that market share is most easily retained by the firm that obtains it initially, firms frequently enter the international market head over heels. Quick entry may result in similarly quick withdrawal once the firm recognizes that its preparation has been insufficient.

Similarly, overproduction can serve as a major reactive motivation. Historically, during downturns in the domestic business cycle, foreign markets were initially unaffected because of lag time. They provided an ideal outlet for inventories that were significantly above desired levels. Frequently, however, international market expansion motivated by overproduction did not represent full commitment by management, but rather **safety-valve activity.** As soon as domestic market demand returned to previous levels, international marketing activities were curtailed or even terminated. Firms that have used such a strategy may encounter difficulties when trying to employ it again because many foreign customers are not interested in temporary or sporadic business relationships. The impact of this motivation is therefore decreasing, particularly because the last long business cycle recession taught firms to be careful in building up excess inventory.

[7]Michael R. Czinkota and Michael L. Ursic, "An Experience Curve Explanation of Export Expansion," *Journal of Business Research* 12 (Spring 1984): 159–168.

Declining domestic sales, whether measured in sales volume or market share, have a similar motivating effect. Products marketed by the firm domestically may be at the declining stage of the product life cycle. Instead of attempting a push-back of the life cycle process domestically, or in addition to such an effort, firms may opt to prolong the product life cycle by expanding the market. In the past such efforts often met with success because customers in many countries outside the United States only gradually reached a level of need and sophistication already attained by U.S. customers. Increasingly, however, if lag times exist at all in foreign markets, particularly in the industrialized nations, they are quite short. Nevertheless, this motivation is still a valid one in the context of developing nations, which often still have very good use for U.S. products for which the U.S. demand is already on the decline. The International Marketplace 7.2 provides an example.

Excess capacity can also be a powerful motivation. If equipment for production is not fully utilized, firms may see expansion into the international market as an ideal possibility for achieving broader distribution of fixed costs. Alternately, if all fixed costs are assigned to domestic production, the firm can penetrate international markets with a pricing scheme that focuses mainly on variable costs. Although such a strategy may be useful in the short term, it may result in the offering of products abroad at a cost lower than at home, which in turn may trigger dumping charges. In the long run fixed costs have to be recovered in order to assure replacement of production equipment that growing international marketing activities may overtax. Market penetration strategy based on variable cost alone is therefore not feasible over the long term.

The reactive motivation of a saturated domestic market is similar in results to that of declining domestic sales. Again, firms in this situation can use the international market to prolong the life cycle of their product and of their organization.

A final major reactive motivation is that of proximity to customers and ports. Physical and psychological closeness to the international market can often play a major role in the export activities of a firm. For example, U.S. firms established near the Canadian border may not even perceive of their market activities in Canada as international marketing. Rather, they are simply an extension of domestic activities without any particular attention being paid to the fact that some of the products go abroad. Except for some firms close to the Canadian or Mexican border, however, this factor is much less prevalent in the United States than in many other countries. Unlike European firms, most American firms are situated far away from foreign countries. Considering the radius of activity of many U.S. firms, which may be 200 miles, and applying such a radius to a European scenario, most European firms automatically become international marketers simply because their neighbors are so close. As an example, a European company operating in Belgium need go only 50 miles to be in multiple foreign markets.

THE INTERNATIONAL MARKETPLACE

Reviving a Product through Export Sales   Facing a shrinking U.S. market for its mobile telephone systems, Freeman Engineering & Associates, Inc., in Metairie, Louisiana, decided to look for overseas customers. Harrell Freeman, president of the 12-person firm, reassessed his marketing strategy after observing a shift in the United States away from his product toward cellular telephones. He discovered that in countries with a developing communication industry there continues to be a need for more basic telephone systems that are less expensive, easy to maintain, and do not require sophisticated technical skills to operate.

Freeman has described his thoughts at that point: "How does a small company like ours get started in selling overseas? We were apprehensive. We didn't know which way to turn." He went to the New Orleans Commerce Department district office for advice. Trade specialists gave Freeman some names to contact, and he sent a representative to China and New Guinea to talk to prospective customers.

The firm made its first overseas sale to China, where the car telephone is used for road maintenance work and the fixed radio for rural telephone systems, thus avoiding the costly construction of lines. China sent a delegation to the United States to inspect Freeman's equipment and to learn how to install and repair it. Next, Freeman outbid several international firms to win an order in New Guinea. He is sending an employee to the country to train nationals to use the equipment. Car telephones there are popular with business people, as they are in the United States. Freeman also sees a potential large market for his other equipment in 700 New Guinea villages that suffer from telephone shortages. Now Freeman is exploring market opportunities in the Middle East.

Source: "Exporting Pays Off," *Business America*, August 3, 1987, 20.

In this context, the concept of psychic or **psychological distance** needs to be understood.[8] Geographic closeness to foreign markets may not necessarily translate into real or perceived closeness to the foreign customer. Sometimes cultural variables, legal factors, and other societal norms make a foreign market that is geographically close seem psychologically distant. For example, research has shown that U.S. firms perceive Canada to be much closer psychologically than Mexico. Even England, mainly because of the similarity in language, is perceived by many U.S. firms to be much closer than Mexico or other Latin American countries, despite the geographic distances.

[8] Wiedersheim-Paul, "Pre-Export Activity," 47–58.

An overall contemplation of these motivations should also consider the following factors. First, firms that are most successful in exporting are motivated by proactive—that is, firm-internal—factors. Second, the motivations of firms do not seem to shift dramatically over time, but are rather stable. For the student who seeks involvement in international markets and searches for firms that provide the most adequate environment, an important strategic consideration is whether a firm is proactive or reactive.

The proactive firm is also more likely to be service oriented than reactive firms. Further, it is frequently more marketing and strategy oriented than reactive firms, which have as their major concern operational issues. The clearest differentiation between the two types of firms can probably be made *ex post facto* by determining how they initially entered international markets. Proactive firms are more likely to solicit their first international marketing order, whereas reactive firms frequently begin international marketing activities after receiving an unsolicited order from abroad.

All of these considerations lead to the question of how the activities of firms can be changed and, ideally, of how the student and future employee can be part of this change.

CHANGE AGENTS

In order for change to take place, someone or something within the firm must initiate it and shepherd it through to implementation. This intervening individual or variable is here called a **change agent.** Change agents in the internationalization process are shown in Table 7.2.

Internal Change Agents

A primary internal change agent is enlightened management. The current management of a firm discovers and understands the value of international markets and decides to pursue international marketing opportunities. Trigger factors frequently are foreign travel, during which new busi-

TABLE 7.2 ▪ **Change Agents in the Internationalization Process**

Firm Internal
- Enlightened Management
- New Management
- Significant Internal Event

Firm External
- Demand
- Other Firms
- Distributors
- Banks
- Chambers of Commerce
- Export Agents
- Governmental Activities

TABLE 7.3 ▪ **Export Decision Makers in Small and Medium-Sized Firms: Percentages of Influence**

| | Type of Decision | | | | | | | |
| Decision Makers | Deciding to Export | | Initiating Export Activities | | Implementing Export Activities | | Evaluating Export Activities | |
	Small	Medium	Small	Medium	Small	Medium	Small	Medium
Chairman	10%	12%	6%	6%	4%	3%	6%	7%
President	56	48	43	27	38	20	47	30
VP—Finance	4	3	4	4	5	6	9	10
VP—Marketing	20	22	30	40	29	42	24	31
VP—Production	2	4	3	2	4	3	1	3
Executive VP	2	2	2	2	1	2	1	3
International Manager	3	3	6	10	12	12	7	8
Other	3	6	6	9	7	12	5	8

Source: Michael R. Czinkota, *Export Development Strategies: U.S. Promotion Policy* (New York: Praeger Publishers, 1982), 112–118.

ness opportunities are discovered, or the receipt of information that leads management to believe that such opportunities exist. Managers who have lived abroad, have learned foreign languages, or are particularly interested in foreign cultures are likely to sooner rather than later investigate whether international marketing opportunities would be appropriate for their firm.

A second set of major internal change agents consists of new management or new employees. Often managers enter a firm having already had some international marketing experience in previous positions and try to use this experience to further the business activities of their new firm. Also, in developing their goals in the new job, managers frequently consider an entirely new set of options, one of which may be international marketing activities.

A significant internal event can be another major change agent. A new employee who firmly believes that the firm should undertake international marketing may find ways to motivate management. Overproduction or a reduction in domestic market size can serve as such an event, as can the receipt of new information about current product uses. As an example, a manufacturer of hospital beds learned that beds it was selling domestically were being resold in a foreign country. Further, the beds it sold for $600 each were resold overseas for approximately $1,300. This new piece of information served to trigger a strong interest on the part of the company's management in entering international markets.

Research has shown that in small and medium-sized firms, meaning firms with fewer than 250 employees, the initial decision to export usually is made by the president, with substantial input provided by the marketing department (see Table 7.3). The carrying out of the decision—that is, the initiation of actual international marketing activities and the implementation of these activities—is then primarily the responsibility of marketing personnel. Only in the final decision stage of evaluating international marketing activities does the major emphasis rest again with the president of the firm. In order to influence a firm internally, it therefore appears that the major emphasis should be placed first on convincing the president to enter the international marketplace and then on convincing the marketing department that international marketing is an important activity. Conversely, the marketing department is a good place to be if one wants to become active in international business.

External Change Agents

The primary outside influence on a firm's decision to become international is foreign demand. Expressions of such demand through, for example, inquiries from abroad have a powerful effect on initial interest in entering the international marketplace. Unsolicited orders from abroad are the one major factor that encourages firms to begin exporting—even though over the past decade U.S. firms increasingly have come to recognize that they must take the initiative in getting started in exporting.[9]

Another major outside influence is the statements and actions of other firms in the same industry. Information that an executive in a competing firm considers international markets to be valuable and worthwhile to develop easily captures the attention of management. Such statements not only have source credibility but are viewed with a certain amount of fear, because a too-successful competitor may eventually infringe on the firm's business. Formal and informal meetings among managers from different firms at trade association meetings, conventions, or business roundtables therefore often serve as a major change agent.

A third, quite influential change agent is comprised of distributors. Often distributors of firms are engaged, through some of their other business activities, in international marketing, and in order to increase their international distribution volume encourage purely domestic firms also to participate in the international market. This is true not only for exports but also for imports. For example, a major customer of a manufacturing firm may find that materials available from abroad, if used in the domestic production process, would make the product available to him or her at lower cost. In such instances, the customer may approach the supplier and strongly encourage foreign sourcing. Many firms, although they may not like the suggestion, are flexible when they face the loss or potential loss of a major account.

Banks and other service firms, such as accountants, can serve as major change agents by alerting domestic clients to international opportunities.

[9] Anthony C. Koh and Robert A. Robicheaux, "Variation in Export Performance Due to Differences in Export Marketing Strategy: Implications for Industrial Marketers," *Journal of Business Research* 17 (November 1988): 249–258.

While these service providers historically follow their major multinational clients abroad, increasingly they are establishing a foreign presence. They frequently work with domestic clients on expanding their market reach in the hope that their services will be used for any international transactions that result.

Chambers of commerce and other business associations that interact with firms locally can frequently heighten their international marketing interests. In most instances these organizations only function as secondary intermediaries, because true change is brought about by the presence and encouragement of other managers.

Export agents are experienced in bringing about an international marketing orientation through two major kinds of activities. Some agents actively seek new international business activities. They visit firms and encourage them to penetrate international markets. In the past, firms often paid a basic fee to such agents and, subsequent to any sales, a commission on these sales. The incidence of such business transactions, however, is decreasing because fewer and fewer firms are willing to pay up-front fees. Increasingly, firms themselves seek out agents to market their products.[10]

In either case, several issues need to be considered. First, agents have limited expertise and usually are knowledgeable only in some markets or some product lines. Second, agents take on a product to generate a profit for themselves. Either they are quite selective in choosing customers and new products or they are not able to provide a substantial enough international marketing effort to be successful. In addition, agents charge directly or indirectly for all of the marketing functions they perform, which often may make international marketing efforts less profitable than originally expected.

Governmental efforts can also serve as a major change agent. In the United States, the Department of Commerce is particularly involved in encouraging exports. Its district offices are charged with increasing the international marketing activities of U.S. firms. Frequently district officers, with the help of voluntary groups such as district export councils, visit firms and attempt to analyze their international marketing opportunities. Such activities raise questions about market and product specialization. Only rarely will Department of Commerce employees have expertise in all areas. However, they can draw on the vast resources of the department in order to provide more information to an interested firm. For a firm new to exporting, Department of Commerce activities can be quite useful. As firms acquire more expertise in international marketing, the assistance may decline in value (see Figure 7.1).

Increasingly, other governmental entities are also actively encouraging firms to participate in the international market. This takes place primarily on the state and local level. Many states have formed agencies for eco-

---

[10]John J. Brasch, "Using Export Specialists to Develop Overseas Sales," *Harvard Business Review* 59 (May–June 1981): 6–8.

FIGURE 7.1 ▪ **Belief in the Helpfulness of the U.S. Department of Commerce (by Stage of Internationalization)**

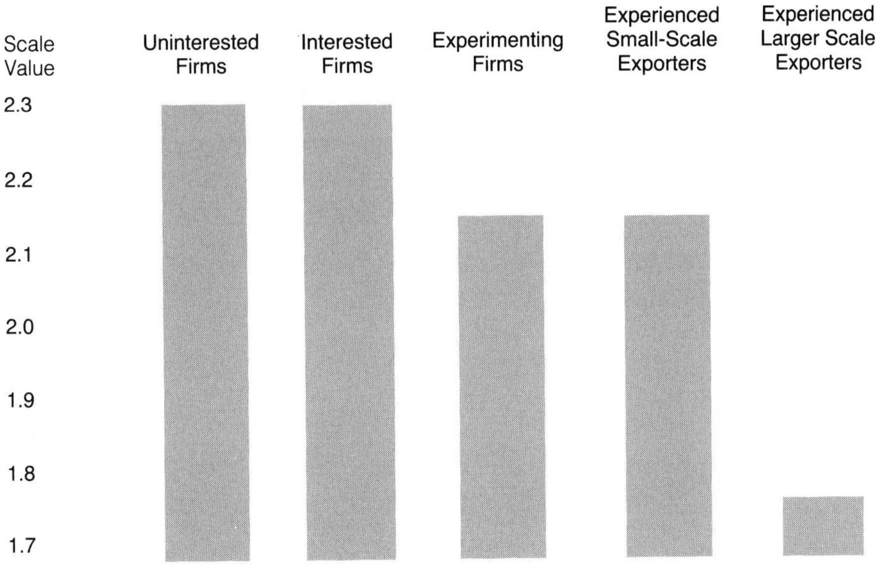

Source: Michael R. Czinkota, *Export Development Strategies: U.S. Promotion Policy* (New York: Praeger Publishers, 1982), 104.

nomic development that assist companies through the providing of information, the display of products abroad, and sometimes even through financing. Trade missions and similar activities are also being carried out by some of the larger cities. Although it is difficult to measure the effects of these efforts,[11] it appears that due to their closeness to firms, such state and local government authorities can become a major factor in influencing firms to become international.

INTERNATIONALIZATION STAGES

Normally internationalization is a gradual process. Only rarely is a firm formed expressly to engage in international marketing activities. Usually firms begin their operations in the domestic market, and over time some of them become interested in the international market.

The vast majority of firms are not at all interested in the international marketplace. Frequently management will not even fill an unsolicited ex-

[11] F. H. Rolf Seringhaus, "The Impact of Government Export Marketing Assistance," *International Marketing Review* 3 (Summer 1986): 55–66.

port order if one is received. Should unsolicited orders or other international market stimuli continue over time, however, a firm may gradually become a potentially interested exporter. Management will then fill unsolicited export orders. Gradually the firm begins to explore international markets, and management is willing to consider the feasibility of exporting. After this exploratory stage, the firm becomes an **experimental exporter,** usually to psychologically close countries. However, management is still far from being committed to international marketing activities.

At the next stage, the firm evaluates the impact of exporting on its general activities. Here, of course, the possibility exists that a firm is disappointed with its international market performance and withdraws from these activities. On the other hand, frequently, it will continue to exist as an experienced small exporter. The final stage of this process is that of **export adaptation.** Here a firm is an experienced exporter to a particular country and adjusts exports to changing exchange rates, tariffs, and other variables. Management is ready to explore the feasibility of exporting to additional countries that psychologically are farther away. Frequently this level of adaptation is reached once export transactions comprise 15 percent of sales volume. Just as parking ticket income, originally seen as surprise revenue, gradually became incorporated into city budgets, the income from export marketing may become incorporated in the budget and in strategic plans of the firm. In these instances, the firm can be considered a full participant in the international market.

INTERNATIONALIZATION PROBLEMS

As can be expected, firms that enter the international marketplace are faced with a host of new problems. Table 7.4 lists main problem areas at the different internationalization stages. Uninterested firms are not included because the international marketplace appears too problematic and unrewarding to them to become active.

Firms at an export awareness stage—partially interested in the international market—are primarily concerned with operational matters such as information flow and the mechanics of carrying out international business transactions. They understand that a totally new body of knowledge and expertise is needed and try to acquire it. Companies that already have had some exposure to international markets begin to think about tactical marketing issues such as communication and sales effort. Finally, firms that have reached the export adaptation phase are mainly strategy and service oriented, which is to say that they worry about longer range issues such as service delivery and regulatory changes. Utilizing the traditional marketing concept, one can therefore recognize that increased sophistication in international markets translates into increased application of marketing knowledge on the part of firms. The more they become active in international markets, the more firms recognize that a marketing orientation internationally is just as essential as it is in the domestic market.

TABLE 7.4 ▪ **Main Problem Areas in Each of the Internationalization Stages**[a]

Rank	2 Partially Interested Firm	3 Exploring Firm	4 Experimental Exporter	5 Experienced Small Exporter	6 Experienced Large Exporter
1	Financing	Communication	Sales effort	Communication	Communication
2	Information on business practices	Sales effort	Obtaining financial information	Sales effort	Sales effort
3	Communication	Marketing information gathering	Physical product	Marketing information gathering	Marketing information gathering
4	Providing technical advice	Information on business practices	Marketing information gathering	Obtaining financial information	Providing repair service
5	Sales effort	Obtaining financial information	Information on business practices	Handling documentation	Information on business practices

[a]Firms in Stage 1 are uninterested in international activities.

Source: Michael R. Czinkota, *Export Development Strategies: U.S. Promotion Policy* (New York: Praeger Publishers, 1982), 101.

All of these developments take place within both small and medium-sized firms. Crucial here is the establishment of a specific export structure in which someone has responsibility for exporting. Without some specified responsibility center, the focus on and interest in exporting that is necessary for planning activity is highly unlikely.[12] Just one person assigned part-time to international marketing activities can begin exploring and entering international markets. More important than an international marketing department staffed with experts is the commitment of management to international market investigation, exploration, and penetration. This commitment must be able to endure stagnation and sometimes even setbacks and failure. The International Marketplace 7.3 highlights the importance of management commitment.

A model of the internationalization process of the small and medium-sized firm, with particular focus on exporting, is presented in Figure 7.2. It shows how the decision components discussed so far combine into the export development process and how the gradual internationalization of the firm takes place. Alternative strategies such as licensing and franchising will be discussed in Chapter 13.

Both management and the prospective employee must determine the firm's stage in the export development process and the changes needed to attain continued progress. The Appendix to Chapter 7 provides a profile of firms at each stage and detailed information on assistance requirements and implementation strategies.

[12]Peter G. Walters, "A Study of Planning for Export Operations," *International Marketing Review* (Autumn 1985): 74–81.

7.3   THE INTERNATIONAL MARKETPLACE

Management Commitment Crucial to Export Success   An export-oriented person at the top is essential to success in foreign marketing, according to Richard Lee, president of Econocorp, manufacturer of packaging machinery. "A company must have an export mentality, and it must start with the person at the top," Lee has said. "The company has to be committed to exporting to make it really go, and the commitment must go right down to the employees in shipping and receiving."

Econocorp's commitment to exporting is evident: It seeks a 50–50 split between domestic and foreign markets. Lee said the "outrageous dollar exchange rate" in the mid-1980s caused the company's export ratio to drop to 20 percent. With the lower dollar, the ratio has been increasing. It was 42 percent during the fiscal year that ended June 30, 1988, and Lee was confident it would be back at 50 percent for 1989.

Lee sees exporting as a stabilizer for his company. When the U.S. economy slows down, he likes to have the assurance of overseas business, and vice versa. Econocorp's domestic and foreign sales plan evens out the peaks and valleys in both the U.S. economy and the international economies. Econocorp sells in 68 countries and is trying to set up sales operations in additional foreign markets.

Source: "50 Firms Share Export Techniques," *Business America*, September 12, 1988, 24.

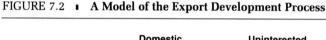 FIGURE 7.2   ▪   **A Model of the Export Development Process**

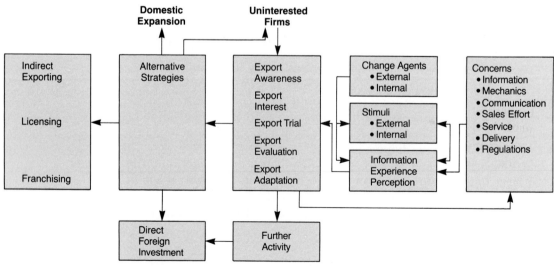

SUMMARY

Firms do not become experienced exporters overnight, but rather progress gradually through an export development process. This process is the result of different motivations to internationalize.

These motivations can be either proactive or reactive. Proactive motivations are initiated by the firm's management and can consist of a perceived profit advantage, technological advantage, product advantage, exclusive market information, or managerial urge. Reactive motivations are the responses of management to environmental changes and pressures. Typical are competitive pressures, overproduction, declining domestic sales, or excess capacity. Firms that are primarily stimulated by proactive motivations are more likely to enter international markets aggressively and successfully.

An international orientation can also be brought about by change agents both external and internal to the firm. Typically these are individuals and institutions that, due to their activities or goals, highlight the benefits of international activities. They can be managers who travel abroad or have carried out successful international marketing ventures, foreign distributors who inquire about the possibility of representing a firm, or organizations such as banks, government agencies, or trading consortia.

Over time, firms will progress through stages of international expertise and activity. In each one of these stages, firms are likely to have a distinct level of interest in the international market and require different types of information and help. Their outlook toward international markets is likely to progress gradually from purely operational concerns to a strategic international orientation. Only at that level will the firm have become a truly international marketer.

Questions for Discussion

1. Discuss the difference between a proactive and a reactive firm, focusing your discussion on the international market.

2. How have the benefits that accrue to firms from unique products or technological advantages changed over time?

3. Explain the benefits that international sales can have for domestic market activities.

4. Discuss the benefits and the drawbacks of treating international market activities as a safety-valve mechanism.

5. What is meant by the concept of "psychological or psychic distance"?

6. Give some of the reasons why distributors would want to help a firm gain a greater foothold in the international market.

7. To what well-known marketing concept does the export development process of the small and medium-sized firm relate?

8. How do the concerns of firms change as they progress in their internationalization effort?

Recommended Readings

Cavusgil, Tamer S., and Michael R. Czinkota, eds. *Trade Promotion and Assistance: International Perspectives.* Westport, Conn.: Quorum Books, 1990.

Czinkota, Michael R., and George Tesar, eds. *Export Management: An International Context.* New York: Praeger Publishers, 1982.

Czinkota, Michael R., and George Tesar. *Export Policy: A Global Assessment.* New York: Praeger Publishers, 1982.

Joyner, Nelson, and Richard G. Lurie. *How to Build an Export Business.* Washington: U.S. Department of Commerce, Office of Minority Business Enterprise, n.d.

Root, Franklin R. *Entry Strategies for International Markets.* Lexington, Mass.: Lexington Books, 1987.

Rosson, Philip J., and Stanley D. Reid. *Managing Export Entry and Expansion.* New York: Praeger Publishers, 1987.

Sheth, Jagdish N., and Hanns-Martin Schoenfeld, eds. *Export Marketing: Lessons from Europe.* Urbana, Ill.: Bureau of Economic and Business Research, University of Illinois, 1980.

U.S. Department of Commerce. *A Basic Guide to Exporting.* Washington, D.C.: Government Printing Office, 1986.

FIRM PROFILES

This appendix provides general profiles of U.S. firms in each stage of export development and describes their main assistance requirements.

Stage 1: The Completely Uninterested Firm

Profile   Most firms at this stage have an annual sales volume of less than $5 million and fewer than 100 employees. The main decision maker is the president. The firm does not export and does not plan to do so in the future. Management is not exploring the possibility of exporting nor will unsolicited export orders be filled. Management tends to believe that exports will not contribute to the firm's profits or growth.

Assistance Requirements   Raise awareness level of exporting.

Implementation Strategies   Increase communication that expounds the value of exporting on an unsolicited basis. Communicate the tangible benefits of exporting to such firms through trade associations and mini-conferences. Use successful small exporters from a peer or reference group as role models, asking them to provide testimonials and case studies to firms not interested in exporting. Increase information dissemination showing the size and profitability of foreign markets. Increase international education in schools to foster awareness of the international marketplace. Regularly publish export activity figures by industry, export profitability statistics, and data about the impact of specific export activities on the balance of trade.

Stage 2: The Partially Interested Firm

Profile   Most firms have an annual sales volume below $5 million and fewer than 100 employees. The current average annual export volume is below $200,000, which is sold to fewer than ten customers. One-quarter of the firms have actively sought their first export order. Almost half of the firms started exporting to Canada, to which they currently ship half of their exports. The president of the firm has the most input in the export decision; the marketing manager is a close second. Management knows that the firm has exportable products and tries to fill export orders. Management tends to believe that exporting may be a desirable activity and undertakes some exploration of export possibilities. Management is uncertain whether the firm will export more in the future and whether exports will contribute to the firm's growth and profits. The main reasons that motivate exporting are a unique product and profit advantage.

Areas that the firm tends to see as being to some degree a problem in the export effort are financing, information on business practices, communi-

Source: Michael R. Czinkota, *Export Development Strategies: U.S. Promotion Policy* (New York: Praeger Publishers, 1982), 107.

cations, the providing of technical advice, and sales effort. Firms believe that the Department of Commerce can be of substantial help to their export effort by assisting with obtaining financial information, financing, handling documentation, communication, and funds transfer.

Assistance Requirements   Raise awareness levels of export benefits; assist with information about the mechanics of exporting.

Implementation Strategies   Use case studies to demonstrate the benefits that can be derived from exporting. Increase communications to make firms more aware of existing services. Provide these services in an accurate and timely fashion. Respond to export financing requests from such firms through more active small-volume export financing by Eximbank or by establishing a facility that provides occasional exporters with small-sized credits (below $100,000) in a rapid fashion; an alternative could be a government guarantee of small export loans to banks similar to current student loan programs. Train Department of Commerce field officers to handle routine documentation problems and to have a general knowledge of the mechanics of the international transfer of funds. Hire more multilingual field officers so that they can assist with communication problems. Institute a centralized task force within the Department of Commerce to provide rapid access for field officers with nonroutine problems. Encourage universities to include commercial aspects in their foreign language courses. Create student language banks at universities that, for a small fee, aid firms in translating foreign documents.

Stage 3: The Exploring Firm

Profile   Most firms have an annual sales volume below $10 million and fewer than 100 employees. These firms export about $500,000 worth of merchandise to fewer than 20 customers. More than one-third of the firms have actively sought the first export order, which mainly originated from Canada. Currently, about one-third of their exports go to Canada.

In management, the president is the major export decision maker. The desirability of exporting is well known, as is the fact that the firm has exportable products. The firm is planning on exporting and is actively exploring export possibilities. The potential contribution of exporting to the firm's growth and profits is acknowledged, but past export profits have not met expectations. Having a unique product and obtaining a profit advantage are principal motivating factors for exporting. Important problems are encountered in the areas of communication, sales effort, marketing information gathering, information on business practices, and obtaining financial information.

Assistance by the Department of Commerce is seen as valuable in the areas of obtaining financial information, information on business practices, marketing information gathering, handling documentation, and communication.

Assistance Requirements   Make exporting more profitable. Provide general information and practical assistance.

Implementation Strategies   To increase the profitability of exports, the use of a Foreign Sales Corporation (FSC) by such firms could be increased, resulting in a tax deferral. Tax legislation reducing the corporate tax rate on the first $200,000 of exports may also be a significant incentive. An increase in deductions for export losses may also help increase the profitability of exploring firms. The possibility of entering into risk- and profit-sharing agreements for a specified amount of initial exports with a government agency could also be considered. Publication of books and brochures containing current general market data and a wide distribution of these publications would help satisfy the general information needs. Department of Commerce field officers should be trained in handling documentation problems of these firms. The use of multilingual officers and cooperation with universities as mentioned for Stage 2 would also help.

Stage 4: The Experimental Exporter

Profile   Most firms have an annual sales volume of less than $5 million and have fewer than 100 employees. Average exports are about $750,000 and are shipped to about ten customers. One-third of the firms actively sought their first export order, which came mostly from Canada. Currently, one-third of the exports go to Canada.

The president is the major decision maker. Exporting is seen favorably but little active exploration of export possibilities takes place. Principal motivating factors for exporting are a unique product, technological advantage, and profit advantage.

Important exporting problems are seen in the areas of sales effort, obtaining financial information, physical product adaptation, marketing information gathering, and information on business practices.

Assistance by the Department of Commerce is seen as somewhat helpful in the areas of marketing information gathering, information on business practices, handling documentation, obtaining financial information, and communication.

Assistance Requirements   Encourage the active exploration of exporting. Provide general assistance and help with product adaptation.

Implementation Strategies   Provide management with foreign purchasing requests for products manufactured by these firms. Increase participation of these firms in foreign exhibitions. Search for contacts for these firms and carry out initial contacts for them. By functioning as an intermediary placing export orders with firms, an institution could clearly demonstrate the benefits of exporting without forcing firms to partake in the initial risk. Apart from the general assistance, increased information on foreign product standards should be communicated to these firms. Tax legislation that would permit increased deductions for costs incurred in product adaptations would help reduce the strength of this problem.

Stage 5: The Experienced Small Exporter

Profile   Average annual sales volume is below $10 million. Most firms employ fewer than 100 people. The export volume is slightly below $1.5 million and is shipped to an average of 40 customers. Four out of ten firms actively sought their first export order. One-third of the firms started their exporting to Canada, to which they currently ship one-fourth of their exports.

The president is the major decision maker with strong input from the vice president for marketing. Exporting is seen in a very favorable light. Only the past profitability of export activities is called into question. Profit advantage, a unique product, managerial urge, and a technological advantage are the main factors motivating exporting. Problems encountered in exporting are important in the areas of communication, sales effort, marketing information gathering, obtaining financial information, and handling documentation. Assistance by the Department of Commerce is seen as somewhat helpful in the areas of gathering information on business practices, marketing information gathering, obtaining financial information, communication, and financing.

Assistance Requirements   Make exporting more profitable, provide general assistance, and help with financing.

Implementation Strategies   Encourage the use of FSC (Foreign Sales Corporation) for these groups and implement legislation reducing the taxation of initial export profits. Financial assistance is now needed in greater size and for longer time periods than for firms in lower stages. Rapid responses to financing requests are not that important here. An increase in the cooperation with Eximbank will help satisfy this need. Training seminars on export financing would be of value to firms in this stage. Requests for financial information need to be responded to rapidly and accurately. Improvements in the training of commercial officers stationed abroad will help achieve that goal. By introducing a specific lead time of one week, and assuming limited liability for incorrect information, such service would be more highly regarded, used more, and would strongly help firms in this international stage with their exporting effort.

Stage 6: The Experienced Large Exporter

Profile   Most firms have an average annual sales volume below $50 million and employ between 100 and 250 persons. Average annual export volume is about $6 million, shipped to about 140 customers. About one-half of the firms actively sought their first export order. One-fifth of the firms began their export activities with Canada, to which they now ship one-eighth of their exports.

The president and the marketing manager are the main export decision makers in the firm. Exporting is seen in a very favorable light with the firm planning to be continuously active in the future. Main motivating factors for exporting are profit advantage, technological advantage, competitive pressures, FSC legislation, a unique product, and managerial urge. Important problems are encountered in the areas of communication, sales effort, marketing information gathering, the providing of repair service, and information on business practices. Assistance by the Department of Commerce is seen as possibly helpful in the areas of marketing information gathering, information on business practices, obtaining financial information, financing, and funds transfer.

Assistance Requirements Facilitate customer service and provide general assistance.

Implementation Strategies To facilitate customer service abroad, companies should be encouraged to train foreign personnel, enabling them to provide such services abroad. Such training costs, jointly with the indirect cost of customer service, such as the translation of repair manuals, could receive preferential tax treatment through multiple deductions in order to allow firms export expansion without strong hindrance by customer service cost consideration. The further granting of tax incentives to such firms should be reconsidered because they are currently satisfied with the profitability of the exporting efforts and sufficiently committed to the continuation of their international activities even without tax benefits.

CHAPTER 8

Secondary International Marketing Research

THE INTERNATIONAL MARKETPLACE

A Corporation Describes Its International Market Research
"When we go into a foreign market on an agent basis, we do not engage in any in-depth analysis since our investment is small. It may be a blind decision. If the agent sends someone here for training, we know he is committed and serious.

"Identifying potential in a new foreign market is a real problem for us. Well over half of our information comes from the U.S. Department of Commerce. [Their materials] are comprehensive, basic, and make you aware of the trends. Of course, like information from other sources, it has to be filtered and used cautiously; one must develop some history with it.

"In developing countries, statistics are not available or reliable; so we tend to depend on the Department of Commerce more. In many cases, there will be a significant divergence in the potential implied by the U.S. Department of Commerce figures versus competitive activity information. Information from competitors is more credible but at the same time more difficult to come by. We try to gather and use both types of information."

Source: S. Tamer Cavusgil, "International Marketing Research: Insights into Company Practices," in *Research in Marketing*, vol. 7, ed. J. N. Sheth (Greenwich, Conn.: JAI Press, 1984), 261–268.

Even though most managers recognize the need for domestic marketing research, the single most important cause for failure in the international marketplace is insufficient preparation and information. When analyzing an international marketing failure, one often finds that errors could have been avoided if only the firm and its managers had an adequate understanding of the business environment.[1] This hindsight, however, does not lead to an automatic increase in international marketing research. Instead, failures continue to occur because firms either do not believe that international market research is worthwhile or face manpower and resource bottlenecks that impede research.

[1]David A. Ricks, *Big Business Blunders: Mistakes in Multinational Marketing* (Homewood, Ill.: Dow Jones–Irwin, 1983).

This chapter will introduce ways of obtaining necessary information quickly, ensuring that the information is reasonably accurate, and doing so with a limited commitment of corporate resources. For smaller firms and those beginning international operations, market research must be quick and relatively inexpensive in order to be feasible. Therefore, it is often not possible to go out in the field and collect original data. Rather, the firm may have to resort to the use of data that have already been collected; in short, to secondary data. This emphasis should not detract from the value of primary research activities in the international market or the need for firms with extensive international experience also to make use of secondary data.

More sophisticated forms of international market research such as primary data collection and the development of management information systems will be covered in Chapter 15.

DEFINING THE ISSUE

In order to discuss international marketing research, we first need to clearly understand the meaning of marketing research. The definitions committee of the American Marketing Association (AMA) defines **marketing research** as "the systematic gathering, recording, and analyzing of data about problems relating to the marketing of goods and services."[2] This statement highlights several important aspects of marketing research. It emphasizes the need for systematic work, indicating that research should be the result of planned and organized activity, rather than of coincidence. Second, it highlights the need to work with data rather than with judgment alone, therefore making information accumulation a necessary prerequisite for marketing research. Finally, it addresses the need for the data-gathering process to relate to specific problems. Marketing research cannot take place in a void; rather, it must take place on a prescribed course.

A more recent and even more appropriate definition states that marketing research is "a systematic and objective approach to the development and provision of information for the marketing management decision-making process."[3] This statement enriches the AMA's definition. It includes the term "objective," which indicates that marketing research should strive to be unbiased and unemotional. In other words, research must apply the scientific method to marketing and be based on a common standard. The statement also uses the word "information" instead of "data," highlighting management's need for meaningful data. Finally, it appropriately emphasizes the relationship between marketing research and the decision-making process. In order for marketing research carried out by

[2] Report of the Definitions Committee of the American Marketing Association (Chicago: American Marketing Association, 1961).

[3] Thomas C. Kinnear and James R. Taylor, *Marketing Research: An Applied Approach*, 3d ed. (New York: McGraw-Hill, 1987), 18.

the corporate world to be useful, it must obtain information that can be acted upon and that improves management's ability to guide the firm.

LINKING RESEARCH TO THE DECISION-MAKING PROCESS

International marketing research should be linked to the decision-making process within the firm. The recognition that a situation exists that requires action is the factor that initiates the decision-making process. The problem must then be defined. Often symptoms are mistaken for causes, with the result that action determined by symptoms is oriented in the wrong direction. The research process begins here, because information must often be obtained to determine the precise nature of the problem.

FIGURE 8.1 ▪ **Steps in the Secondary Data Research Process**

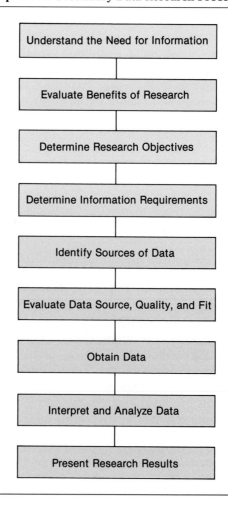

The next step in the decision-making process is to identify alternative courses of action. More data and information are frequently necessary in order to understand the alternatives that exist. This also holds true for the next step, which consists of an evaluation of possible courses of action. As much information as possible is needed so that an intelligent comparison and rank ordering of alternatives can take place.

The role of research ends here. Management selects from among the alternatives the one course of action that harmonizes most closely with the corporate mission and management goals. In the implementation and modification stage, the role of research is not a major one. Obviously, research can be used to continuously collect information on the implementation of a given course of action. However, the implementation itself is beyond the reach of market research.

Figure 8.1 provides an overview of the steps in the secondary data research process. It begins with the recognition of the need for information. The value of research is then determined and research objectives are defined. Although this process appears simplistic, various groups within a firm often have different research objectives. These must be fully understood and integrated into one common research plan. The next steps in the research process are to determine information requirements and to identify possible sources of data. Time and financial constraints require the researcher to evaluate the quality of the data available and to assess how well the data fit with research objectives and information requirements. Next the data are obtained and then interpreted and analyzed. Finally, the researcher presents the results to management, which can take appropriate action based on the research report.

DIFFERENTIATING BETWEEN INTERNATIONAL AND DOMESTIC RESEARCH

The tools and techniques of international marketing research are said by some to be exactly the same as those of domestic marketing research, and only the environment differs. However, the environment is precisely what determines how well the tools, techniques, and concepts apply to the international market. Although the objectives of marketing research may be the same, the execution of research may differ substantially in international research as compared to domestic research. The four primary reasons for this difference are new parameters, new environments, an increase in the number of factors involved, and the broader definition of competition.

New Parameters

In crossing national borders, a firm encounters parameters not found in domestic marketing. Examples include duties, foreign currencies and changes in their value, different modes of transportation, international documentation, and port facilities. A firm that has done business only do-

FIGURE 8.2 ▪ **New Environments Confronting the International Firm**

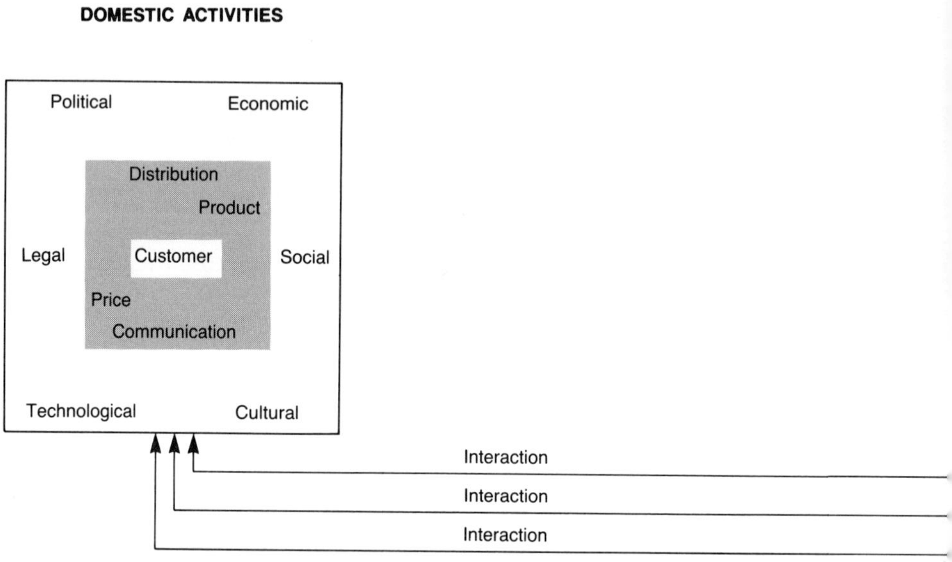

DOMESTIC ACTIVITIES

mestically will have had little or no prior experience with these requirements and conditions. Information on each of them must be obtained in order for management to make appropriate business decisions. New parameters also emerge because of differing modes of operating internationally. For example, a firm can export, it can license its products, it can engage in a joint venture, or it can carry out foreign direct investment.

New Environments

When it decides to **go international** in its marketing activities, a firm exposes itself to an unfamiliar environment. Many of the assumptions on which the firm was founded and its domestic activities were based may not hold true internationally. Firms need to learn about the culture of the host country, understand its political systems and determine its stability, and understand the differences in societal structures and language. In addition, they must fully comprehend pertinent legal issues in the host country in order to avoid operating contrary to local legislation. They should also incorporate the technological level of the society in the marketing plan and understand the economic environment. In short, all the assumptions formulated over the years in the domestic market must be reevaluated. This crucial point has often been neglected because most managers are born into the environment of their domestic operations and only subconsciously learn to understand the constraints and opportunities of

INTERNATIONAL ACTIVITIES

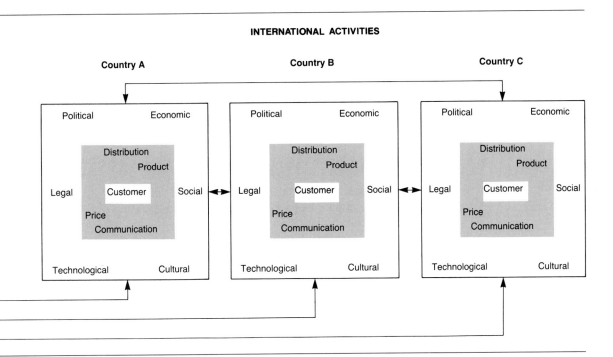

their business activities. The process is analogous to learning one's native language. Speakers with little knowledge of rules of grammar may nevertheless use the language correctly. Only in attempting to learn a foreign language will they begin to appreciate the complex structure of languages and the need for rules. Figure 8.2 illustrates the multiplicity of new environments and their interactions that firms must consider when they begin international activities.

The Number of Factors Involved

Going international often means entering into more than one market. As a result, the number of changing dimensions increases geometrically. Even if every dimension is understood, management must also understand the interaction between them. Because of their sheer number, coordination of this interaction becomes increasingly difficult. The international marketing research process can help management with this undertaking.

Broader Definition of Competition

By entering the international market, the firm also exposes itself to a much greater variety of competition than existed in the domestic market. For example, fishery products compete not only with other fishery products, but competition may be found in meat or even vegetarian substitutes. Similarly, firms that offer labor-saving devices in the domestic marketplace may suddenly face competition from cheap manual labor. As a result, the firm must determine the breadth of the competition, track the competitive activities, and finally evaluate their actual and potential impact on its own operations.

RECOGNIZING THE NEED FOR RESEARCH

Even though most firms recognize the need for domestic marketing research, this need is not fully understood for international marketing activities. Most small or medium-sized firms conduct no international market research before they enter a foreign market. Often decisions concerning entry and expansion in overseas markets and the selecting and appointing of distributors are made after a cursory subjective assessment of the situation. The research done is less rigorous, less formal, and less quantitative than for domestic marketing activities. Further, once a small or medium-sized firm has entered a foreign market, it is likely to discontinue the research of that market.[4,5] Many business executives therefore appear to view foreign market research as relatively unimportant.

A major reason why firms are reluctant to engage in international marketing activities is the lack of sensitivity to differences in consumer tastes and preferences. Often managers tend to assume that their methods are both best and acceptable to all others. This is fortunately not true. What a boring place the world would be if it were!

A second reason is a limited appreciation for the different marketing environments abroad. Often firms are not prepared to accept that distribution systems, the availability of media, or advertising regulations may be entirely different from the home market. Barely aware of the differences, they are unwilling to spend money to find out about them.

A third reason is the lack of familiarity with national and international data sources, and the inability to use them if obtained. As a result, the cost of conducting international marketing research is seen as prohibitively high, and therefore not a worthwhile investment relative to the benefits to be gained.[6] Finally, firms often build up their international marketing activities gradually, often on the basis of unsolicited orders. Over time, actual business experience in a country or with a specific firm may then be used as a substitute for organized research.[7]

Despite their reservations about international marketing research, firms must learn what customers want, why they want it, and how they go about filling their needs in order to serve them efficiently. They must understand

[4] Vinay Kothari, "Researching for Export Marketing" in *Export Promotion: The Public and Private Sector Interaction*, ed. M. Czinkota (New York: Praeger Publishers, 1983), 155.

[5] S. Tamer Cavusgil, "International Marketing Research: Insights into Company Practices," in *Research in Marketing*, vol. 7, ed. J. N. Sheth (Greenwich, Conn.: JAI Press, 1984), 261–288.

[6] Susan P. Douglas and C. Samuel Craig, *International Marketing Research* (Englewood Cliffs, N.J.: Prentice Hall, 1983), 2.

[7] Cavusgil, "International Market Research," 261–288.

that entering foreign markets without marketing research places them, their assets, and their entire international operation at risk.

International marketing research permits management to identify and develop strategies for internationalization. This task includes the identification, evaluation, and comparison of potential foreign market opportunities and subsequent market selection. Second, research is necessary for the development of a marketing plan. In the initial internationalization process, the factors necessary for market entry and initial market penetration need to be determined. Subsequently, the research should define the appropriate marketing mix for each international market and should maintain a continuous feedback in order to fine-tune the various marketing elements. Finally, research can provide management with foreign market intelligence in order to help it anticipate events, take appropriate action, and adequately prepare for global changes.

EVALUATING BENEFITS OF RESEARCH

A primary constraint for international marketing research is that of resource allocation. In order to carry out international research, firms require resources in terms of both time and money. For the typical smaller firm, those two types of resources are its most precious and scarce commodities. In order to make a justifiable case for allocating resources to international marketing research, management must understand what the value of research will be. This is even more important for international market research than domestic market research because the cost tends to be higher. The research efforts of one firm are described in The International Marketplace 8.1.

The value of research can be assessed from two perspectives. One approach analyzes the benefits accruing to the firm based on research. The other identifies the downside risk that the firm incurs if it does not carry out research.

The Benefits of Research

The value of research in making a particular decision may be determined by applying the following equation:

$$V(dr) - V(d) > C(r)$$

where:
   $V(dr)$ is the value of the decision with the benefit of research;
   $V(d)$ is the value of the decision without the benefit of research; and
   $C(r)$ is the cost of research.

Obviously, the value of the decision with the benefit of research should be greater than the value of the decision without research by an amount exceeding the cost of the research. Otherwise, carrying out international marketing research would be a waste of resources. It is frequently difficult to quantify the individual values because often the risks and benefits are not easy to ascertain. Yet the use of decision theory permits a comparison of alternative research strategies.[8] Using such a justification for research, however, may place the researcher at risk because, once the research is carried out, the actual benefits are measurable and can be compared to the anticipated ones. If all the benefits do not materialize, the researcher may be charged with having inappropriately inflated his or her benefit expectation.

The Risks of Inadequate Research

The researcher can point out in a "what if" fashion the risks that the company may incur by operating internationally without sufficient information. Such risks might include a loss of market penetration effectiveness, development of ill will abroad that precludes any further internationalization, and expropriation. In the long run, this justification is easier for the researcher to use than the benefit formula because he or she can point out that some of the worst-case scenarios have not materialized.

In any event, the researcher must demonstrate to management the need for information and therefore justify the allocation of scarce resources. This requirement suggests that international market research should aim at managerial rather than statistical significance. It should clearly aid management in improving its decision-making process in international marketing. At the same time international market research should be recognized as a tool and not a substitute for judgment. Enough of the "right" information is never obtained within the time constraints to dictate the action or course to follow. However, research will aid in avoiding gross errors.

DETERMINING RESEARCH OBJECTIVES

The researcher should take great care in determining research objectives. These objectives will vary from firm to firm because of the views of management, the corporate mission, and the marketing situation. In addition, as discussed in Chapter 7, the information needs of firms are closely linked with the level of already existing international expertise.

Going International: Exporting

The most frequent objective of international market research is that of **foreign market opportunity analysis.** When a firm launches its international activities, information can be accumulated to provide basic guidelines. The aim is not to conduct a painstaking and detailed analysis of the world on a market-by-market basis, but instead to utilize a broadbrush approach. Accomplished quickly at low cost, this can narrow down the possibilities for international marketing activities.

[8] For an excellent exposition on measuring the value of research, see Gilbert A. Churchill, *Marketing Research,* 4th ed. (Hinsdale, Ill.: Dryden Press, 1987), 43–60.

Such an approach should begin with a cursory analysis of general market variables. These consist of proxy factors such as total and per-capita GNP, mortality rates, and population figures. Although these factors in themselves will not provide detailed market information, they will enable the researcher and management to determine whether the corporation's objectives might be met in those markets. For example, highly priced consumer products are not likely to be successful in the People's Republic of China, because their price may comprise a significant proportion of the annual salary of a worker, and the benefit to the worker may only be minimal. Such cursory evaluation will help reduce the number of markets to be considered to a more manageable number—for example, from 147 to 25.

Next the researcher will require information on each individual market for a preliminary evaluation. This information typically locates the fastest growing markets, the largest markets for a particular product, market trends, and market restrictions. Although precise and detailed information for each product probably cannot be obtained, it is available for general product categories.

Both foreign markets and domestic restrictions relating to them must be considered. As an example, one can determine that the Soviet Union represents a fast-growing market for computer hardware and software. However, an inspection of U.S. export licensing regulations will reveal that computer trade with the Soviet Union is quite restricted. Again, this overview will be cursory, but will serve to quickly evaluate markets and narrow down their number for closer investigation.

At this stage, the researcher must select appropriate markets. The emphasis will shift to focus on market opportunities for a specific product or brand, including existing, latent, and incipient markets. Even though the aggregate industry data have already been obtained, general information is insufficient to make company-specific decisions. For example, the market demand for medical equipment should not be confused with the potential demand for a specific brand.[9] In addition, the research should identify demand and supply patterns and evaluate any regulations and standards. Finally, a competitive assessment needs to be made that matches markets with corporate strengths and provides an analysis of the best market potential for specific products. Figure 8.3 offers a summary of the various stages in the determination of market potential.

Going International: Importing

When importing, the major focus shifts from supplying to sourcing. Management must identify markets that produce supplies or materials desired or that have the potential to do so. Foreign firms must be evaluated in terms of their capabilities and competitive standing.

Just as management would wish to have some details on a domestic supplier, the importer needs to know, for example, about the reliability of a

[9] S. Tamer Cavusgil, "Guidelines for Export Market Research," *Business Horizons* 28 (November–December 1985): 27–33.

FIGURE 8.3 ▪ **A Sequential Process of Researching Foreign Market Potentials**

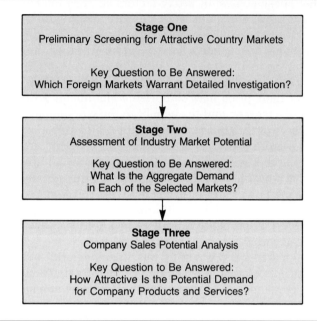

Source: S. Tamer Cavusgil, "Guidelines for Export Market Research," *Business Horizons* 28 (November–December 1985): 29. Copyright by the Foundation for the School of Business at Indiana University. Reprinted by permission.

foreign supplier, the consistency of his product or service quality, and the length of delivery time. Information obtained through the subsidiary office of a bank or one's embassy can be very helpful.

In addition, foreign rules must be scrutinized as to whether exportation is possible. For example, India may set limits on the cobra handbags it allows to be exported and laws protecting the cultural heritage may prevent the exportation of pre-Columbian artifacts from Latin American countries.

The international manager must also analyze domestic restrictions and legislation that may prohibit the importation of certain goods into the home country. Even though a market may exist in the United States for foreign umbrella handles, for example, quotas may restrict their importation in order to protect domestic industries. Similarly, even though domestic demand may exist for ivory, its importation may be illegal because of legislation enacted to protect wildlife worldwide.

Market Expansion

Research objectives may include the obtaining of detailed information for market penetration, for the design and fine-tuning of the marketing mix, or the monitoring of the political climate of a country so that the firm can expand its operation successfully. The better defined the research objective is, the better the researcher will be able to determine the information requirements and thus conserve time and financial resources to the firm.

DETERMINING INFORMATION REQUIREMENTS

Using the research objective as a guide, the researcher will be able to pinpoint the type of information needed. For example, if only general initial market information is required, perhaps macro data such as world population statistics will be sufficient. If research is to identify market restraints, then perhaps information is required about international accords, negotiations in the GATT, and any "voluntary" agreements. Alternatively, broad product category and production and trade figures may be desired in order to pinpoint general market activities. For the fine-tuning of a marketing mix, very specific detailed product data may be necessary in order to conduct a relevant analysis. Table 8.1 lists the types of international trade data considered most critical by business executives.

In determining information requirements, the researcher should formulate appropriate research questions that he or she intends to answer. Table 8.2 provides samples of possible research questions on broad stategic issues, foreign market assessment and selection, and marketing mix determination.

IDENTIFYING SOURCES OF DATA

Secondary data for international marketing research purposes are available from a wide variety of sources. The major ones are briefly reviewed here. In addition, Appendix A to Chapter 8 lists over 100 publications and organizations that monitor international issues.

TABLE 8.1 ▪ **Most Critical International Trade Data**

Type of Data	Importance Rating[a]
Nontariff Measures	1.18
U.S. Export-Import Data	1.22
Foreign Export-Import Data	1.26
Tariff Data	1.27
Local Laws and Regulations	1.33
Size of Market	1.44
Competition in Market	1.44
Local Standards and Specifications	1.48
Government Trade Policy	1.49

[a] Rated on a three-point scale with 1 = critical, 2 = useful, 3 = of little value.

Source: Michael R. Czinkota, "Governmental Trade Data: Utility and Usage," presented at the annual meeting of the Academy of International Business, Singapore, 1989.

TABLE 8.2 ■ **International Marketing Questions Determining Information Requirements**

Broad Strategic Issues
What objectives should be pursued in the foreign market?
Which foreign market segments should the firm strive to satisfy?
Which are the best product, place/distribution, pricing, and promotion strategies for the foreign market?
What should be the product-market-company mix to take advantage of the available foreign marketing opportunities?

Foreign Market Assessment/Selection
Do opportunities exist in a foreign market for the firm's products and services?
What is the market potential abroad?
Are there foreign markets that the firm can serve?
What new markets are likely to open up abroad?

What are the major economic, political, legal, social, technological, and other environmental facts and trends in a foreign country?
What impact do these environmental dimensions have on the specific foreign market for the firm's products and services?

Who are the firm's present and potential customers abroad?
What are their needs and desires?
What are their demographic and psychographic characteristics—disposable income, occupation, age, sex, opinions, interests, activities, tastes, values, etc.?
What is their lifestyle?
Who makes the purchase decisions?
Who influences the purchase decisions?
How are the purchase decisions made?
Where are the products purchased?
How are the products used?
What are the purchase and consumption patterns and behaviors?

What is the nature of competition in the foreign market?
Who are major direct and indirect competitors?
What are the major characteristics of the competitors?
What are the firm's competitive strengths and weaknesses in reference to such factors as product quality, product lines, warranties, services, brands, packaging, distribution, sales force, advertising, prices, experience, technology, capital and human resources, and market share?

What attitudes do different governments (domestic and foreign) have toward foreign trade?
Are there any foreign trade incentives and barriers?
Is there any prejudice against imports or exports?
What are different governments doing specifically to encourage or discourage international trade?
What specific requirements—for example, import or export licenses—have to be met to conduct international trade?
How difficult are certain government regulations for the firm?

How well developed are the foreign mass communication media? Are the print and electronics media abroad efficient and effective?
Are there adequate transportation and storage/warehouse facilities in the foreign market?
Does the foreign market offer efficient channels of distribution for the firm's products?

TABLE 8.2   ■   **Continued**

What are the characteristics of the existing domestic and foreign distributors?
  How effectively can the distributors perform specific marketing functions?
What is the state of the retailing institutions?

Marketing Mix Assessment and Selection
Product
Which product should the firm offer abroad?
What specific features—design, color, size, packaging, brand, warranty, etc.—
  should the product have?
What foreign needs does the product satisfy?
Should the firm adapt/modify its domestic market product and sell it abroad?
  Should it develop a new product for the foreign market?
Should the firm make or buy the product for the foreign market?
How competitive is or will be the product abroad?
Is there a need to withdraw the product from the foreign market?
At which stage in its life cycle is the product in the foreign market?
What specific services are necessary abroad at the presale and postsale stages?
Are the firm's service/repair facilities adequate?
What is the firm's product and service image abroad?
What patents or trademarks does the firm have that can benefit it abroad? How
  much legal protection does the firm have concerning patents, trademarks, etc.?
What should be the firm's product mission philosophy in the foreign market?
Are the firm's products socially responsible? Do the products create a good
  corporate image?

Price
At what price should the firm sell its product in the foreign market?
Does the foreign price reflect the product quality?
Is the price competitive?
Should the firm pursue market penetration or market-skimming pricing objec-
  tives abroad?
What type of discounts (trade, cash, quantity) and allowances (advertising, trade-
  off) should the firm offer its foreign customers?
Should prices differ with market segment?
What should the firm do about product line pricing?
What pricing options are available if costs increase or decrease? Is the demand in
  the foreign market elastic or inelastic?
How are prices going to be viewed by the foreign government—reasonable,
  exploitative?

Place/Distribution
Which channels of distribution should the firm use to market its products
  abroad?
Where should the firm produce its products and how should it distribute them in
  the foreign market?
What types of agents, brokers, wholesalers, dealers, distributors, retailers, etc.,
  should the firm use?
What are the characteristics and capabilities of the available intermediaries?
Should the assistance of EMCs (export management companies) be acquired?
What forms of transportation should the firm use?
Where should the product be stored?
What is the cost of distribution by channel?
What are the costs of physical distribution?
What type of incentives and assistance should the firm provide its intermediaries
  to achieve its foreign distribution objectives?

(continued)

TABLE 8.2 ▪ **Continued**

Which channels of distribution are used by the firm's competitors and how effective are these channels?

Promotion—Nonpersonal (Advertising and Sales Promotion)
How should the firm promote its products in the foreign market? Should it advertise? Should it participate in international trade fairs and exhibits?
What are the communication needs of the foreign market?
What communication or promotion objectives should the firm pursue abroad?
What should be the total foreign promotion budget?
What advertising media are available to promote in the foreign market? What are their strengths and limitations? How effective are different domestic and foreign advertising media?
Should the firm use an advertising agency? How should it be selected?
How effective and competitive are the firm's existing advertising and promotion programs concerning the foreign market?
What are the legal requirements?
Are there foreign laws against competitive advertising?

Promotion—Personal Selling
Is there a need for personal selling to promote the product abroad?
What assistance or services do foreign customers need from the sales force?
What should be the nature of personal selling abroad?
How many salespeople should the firm have?
How should the sales personnel be trained, motivated, compensated, assigned sales goals and quotas, and assigned foreign territories?
What should the nature of foreign sales effort be?
How does the firm's sales force compare with its competitors?
What criteria should the firm use to evaluate sales performance?
How should the firm perform sales analysis?

Source: Vinay Kothari, "Researching for Export Marketing." From *Export Promotion: The Public and Private Sector Interaction,* edited by Michael R. Czinkota, pp. 169–172, 1983.

U.S. Government

Of all the sources, the U.S. government has the greatest variety of data available. Most of them are collected by the Department of Commerce, the Department of Agriculture, the Department of State, the Department of the Treasury, and by U.S. embassies abroad.

Typically, the information provided by the U.S. government addresses either macro or micro issues, or it offers specific data services. Macro information includes population trends, general trade flows between countries, and world agricultural production. Micro information includes materials on specific industries in a country, their growth prospects, and their foreign trade activities. Specific data services might provide custom-tailored information responding to the detailed needs of a firm. More information on selected U.S. government publications and research services is presented in Appendix B to Chapter 8. The International Marketplace 8.2 provides an example of how the U.S. government is attempting to assist U.S. firms abroad with information and research services.

THE INTERNATIONAL MARKETPLACE   8.2

The U.S. and Foreign Commercial Service   The Department of
Commerce introduces its exporting experts:

Our more than 1,100 trade professionals around the world are
dedicated to your export success. We're available to help you export your goods or services in virtually all major world markets,
and offer highly effective services to help you every step of the way.

We can analyze foreign markets, conduct customized in-country
studies of your product's competition, help you find buyers and
representatives overseas—even take your product on tour abroad
via catalog or video shows. Our programs are strategically structured to meet your international marketing needs and to make your
exporting ventures as profitable and painless as possible.

Established in 1982 to help American exporters compete more
effectively in the world marketplace, the U.S. and Foreign Commercial Service (US&FCS) is the U.S. Government's only international
trade agency with a worldwide delivery system.

Our experienced international trade specialists are based in 66
major U.S. cities and 126 locations abroad. We are there for you,
whether you're in Cleveland or Calcutta, San Francisco or
Singapore.

U.S.-based trade specialists reach out to businesses with export
potential, conducting more than 100,000 one-on-one counseling
sessions with U.S. companies every year. Most business clients
work with one trade specialist in their local office throughout their
exporting experience. This close working relationship enables your
trade specialist to develop an in-depth understanding of your export needs.

Drawing from a large commercial database fed by our commercial officers overseas, your trade specialist can develop marketing
packages for your company, individually tailored to your specific
products or services and oriented to your marketing goals.

Your trade specialist keeps you posted on upcoming export
workshops, conferences and seminars in your area, as well as domestic and overseas trade events that offer good potential for promoting your products or services.

Trade specialists overseas do on-the-spot market research, including customized individual studies; search for sales leads,
qualified agents and distributors; make appointments with key
buyers and government officials; and counsel firms frustrated by
trade barriers. They speak the host-country language, understand
local customs, traditions and trade regulations, and can be a particularly valuable resource when you're visiting overseas markets
in person.

With this global network of trade specialists and commercial officers, supported by overseas market research and a Washington,

D.C., staff, the U.S. and Foreign Commercial Service is in a unique position to serve you. We can support your export efforts with sophisticated marketing information and the most direct product promotion assistance available anywhere.

Source: U.S. Department of Commerce, *Export Now: It Makes Good Business Sense* (Washington, D.C.: Government Printing Office, 1988).

Other Governments

Even though many other governments do not collect as extensive data as does the United States, many countries have a wide array of national and international trade data available. Unfortunately, the data are often published only in their home countries and in their native languages. However, these information sources are often available at embassies and consulates, whose mission includes the enhancement of trade activities. The commercial counselor or commercial attaché can provide the information available from these sources.

International Organizations

Some international organizations provide useful data for the researcher. The *Statistical Yearbook* produced by the United Nations contains international trade data on products and provides information on exports and imports by country. The *World Atlas* published by the World Bank provides useful general data on population, growth trends, and GNP figures. The Organization for Economic Cooperation and Development (OECD) also publishes quarterly and annual trade data on its member countries. Finally, organizations such as the International Monetary Fund (IMF) and the World Bank publish occasional staff papers that evaluate region- or country-specific issues in depth.

Service Organizations

A wide variety of service organizations that may provide information include banks, accounting firms, freight forwarders, airlines, and **international trade consultants.** Frequently they are able to provide data on business practices, legislative or regulatory requirements, and political stability as well as basic trade data. However, although this information is available without charge, its basic intent is to serve as an "appetizer." Much of the initial information is quite general in nature; more detailed answers require an appropriate fee.

Trade Associations

Associations such as world trade clubs and domestic and international chambers of commerce (for example, the American Chamber of Commerce abroad) can provide good information on local markets. Often files are maintained on international trade flows and trends affecting international marketers. Valuable information can also be obtained from industry associations. These groups, formed to represent entire industry segments, often collect from their members a wide variety of data that are then published in an aggregate form. Because most of these associations represent the viewpoints of their member firms to the federal government, they usually have one or more publicly listed representatives in Washington. The information provided is often quite general in nature because of the wide variety of clientele served. However, it can provide valuable initial insights into international markets.

Directories, Newsletters, and Databases

A large number of industry directories are available on local, national, and international levels. These directories primarily serve to identify firms and to provide very general background information such as the name of the chief executive officer, the location, the address and telephone number, and some information on a firm's products. In the past few years, newsletters have sprung up devoted to specific international issues such as international trade finance, bartering, countertrade, international payment flows, and customs news. Often they are published by banks or accounting firms in order to keep their clientele current on international developments. Usually newsletters cater to narrow audiences but can provide important information to the firm interested in a specific area.

Increasingly, on-line electronic **databases** also provide international marketing information, ranging from the latest developments in financial markets to new writings in the academic and trade press and late-breaking political developments. Currently, over 3,700 databases are available worldwide. With approximately 900 database producers and 300 database distributors, the United States is the largest provider of database services.[10]

These information services are available for a subscription fee and often require payment on an as-used basis. In spite of their cost, data services are often well worth their price because of the rapid updates received, the convenience of access, and their frequently extensive search capabilities. With continuing improvements and progress in the area of telecommunications and computerization, the use of such databases can be expected to increase in the future and eventually become a key information source.

Other Firms

Often firms can provide useful information for international marketing purposes. Firms appear to be more open about their international than about their domestic marketing activities. On some occasions, valuable information can also be obtained from foreign firms and distributors.

---

[10] Mary C. Inoussa, "Electronic Database Services," *U.S. Industrial Outlook* (Washington, D.C.: U.S. Department of Commerce, 1989), 45–54.

EVALUATING DATA SOURCE AND QUALITY

Before too much time and energy are spent obtaining the data, evaluations should be made of the quality of the data source, the quality of the actual data, and the compatibility of the data with information requirements.

Source Quality

In evaluating the quality of the data source, the researcher should determine who collected the data, the purpose of the original data collection, and how the data were collected. Ideally, the researcher would obtain the initial research specifications that were drawn up for the data collection. If these are not readily available, the organization that collected the data is occasionally willing to supply the specifications. In reviewing the specifications, the researcher can clearly determine the purpose and the method of the original data collection and therefore evaluate the data quality and fit.

Checking the quality of the source is important because there may be ulterior motives behind a specific form of data presentation, particularly for international statistics. As an example, some countries may wish to demonstrate that their economy is improving in order to attract foreign direct investment. As a result, some factors may be overstated. Other countries may wish to indicate a need for increased foreign aid and may therefore understate some statistics. Many nations simply do not have sophisticated data collection systems in place and therefore tend to supply data estimates that reflect wishes or goals rather than reality. Because the international organizations publishing these data serve only as information disseminators, all footnotes and introductory remarks that may clarify unusual methods of data collection should be carefully scrutinized.

Data Quality

The relevance of data to the researcher's information requirements plays a major role in assessing the quality of the data. The first test therefore is to determine whether the data provide responses to the firm's particular questions.

The compatibility and comparability of data need to be considered. Often in international marketing research, the researcher compares different sets of data from different countries. Great care must therefore be taken to ensure that identical or at least similar units of measurement and definitional units are used. The International Marketplace 8.3 provides an example of how different countries use different definitions of the term "urban" in their data collection processes.

The accuracy and reliability of the data must be determined. Often, international data are approximated. Geographic or manpower limitations may render some countries unable, even if they are not unwilling, to be precise in their data collection. Exploring the accuracy of the data, to the

THE INTERNATIONAL MARKETPLACE   8.3

An Example of Data Equivalence Problems   *The definition of "urban" used by the United Nations in its Demographic Yearbook to establish the proportion of urban population varies substantially from country to country, depending largely on population density. In Japan, for example, urban population is defined as shi (city) with 50,000 inhabitants or more, or shis (population usually 30,000 inhabitants) with urban facilities. In India, the definition includes all places with 5,000 inhabitants or more. In Nigeria it includes the 40 largest towns; in Kenya and in Zaire, agglomerations with at least 2,000 inhabitants are classified as urban. Similarly, in France and West Germany, communities with 2,000 or more inhabitants are included, while in Norway and Sweden the population requirement decreases to include localities or built-up areas with as few as 200 inhabitants.*

Source: Susan P. Douglas and C. Samuel Craig, *International Marketing Research* (Englewood Cliffs, N.J.: Prentice-Hall, 1983), 80.

---

extent possible, can be carried out by investigating three dimensions. First, the researcher should determine the primacy of the data source. A primary source is the source that originated the data, whereas a secondary source has secured the data from an original source. The researcher should always attempt to obtain information from the primary source, because this permits an evaluation of source credibility. Further, the primary source usually provides the most detail about data collection methods. Second, the collection methods should be examined to determine whether proper research procedures were followed and whether definitions used are acceptable. Third, the researcher should investigate the purpose of data publication. If the data have been published by a partisan organization or serve to advance a cause, proper caution is appropriate.[11]

The recency of data can also be important. Few countries conduct data collection as often as does the United States, and even in the United States international data are often found to be insufficient or outdated.[12] In many nations, the most recent data available may be three to five years old. The effect of economic changes during these years on a firm's international business operations may be quite significant. Obtaining misleading information may lead to inappropriate decisions, a result that is contrary to the intent of marketing research.

---

[11] Gilbert A. Churchill, Jr., *Basic Marketing Research* (Hinsdale, Ill.: Dryden Press, 1988), 148–149.

[12] Frank G. Vukmanic, Michael R. Czinkota, and David A. Ricks, "National and International Data Problems and Solutions in the Empirical Analysis of Intra-Industry Direct Foreign Investment" in *Multinationals as Mutual Invaders*, ed. Asím Erdilek (London: Croon Helm, 1985), 160–184.

Finally, although data have been collected, some countries do not make them available. The Soviet Union, for example, engages in massive data collection efforts. Most of the data on economic issues, however, are closely held and are not readily available to an outsider, even though an increasing openness can be anticipated.

Before a commitment is made to acquire data, both data sources and data quality must be carefully evaluated in terms of coverage, availability, accuracy, and timeliness.[13] This step is necessary not only to screen out data that may be expensive to obtain but also to minimize unnecessary cluttering of information. Even if data are free, working through them requires corporate resources that are usually scarce. The researcher therefore must ensure not only that data are acquired, but that the right ones are obtained, using paucity as key criterion. Otherwise, large data acquisitions are likely to lead to information overload within the firm, with the result that either the data are not used at all or their use becomes so time consuming that the research becomes inefficient.

OBTAINING THE DATA

The existence and the availability of international marketing data do not necessarily indicate that the data can be obtained. Obviously, in order to be useful for the corporation and the researcher, data need to be obtained in a timely manner and with relative ease. Furthermore, cost is a factor to consider.

The Department of Commerce will make U.S. government data available upon request, charging only a modest user fee. However, several weeks may elapse before the data are finally received. This of course applies only to readily packaged information that has already been published and not to individual data runs, which may take even longer. Rather than wait for mail from Washington, researchers often can seek recourse from a local Department of Commerce district office that maintains substantial library holdings of department materials.

Many universities are designated as **official depositories** of U.S. government documents. Data can be rapidly reviewed in these libraries. Many public libraries maintain a holding of data from international organizations. If they are not available there, data can be ordered from the organizations directly.

As a word of caution, the researcher must carefully scrutinize the data in advance in order to minimize the risk of having to discard data once the information is obtained. This is best done by precisely determining the information requirements, carefully matching the sources of data with these requirements, and selecting the data with the best fit.

Secondary data have been collected by other parties for their own purposes. As a result, data will not always be available for the precise require-

---

[13]Gillian Rice and Essam Mahmoud, "Forecasting and Data Bases in International Business," *Management International Review* 24 (Fourth Quarter 1984): 59–70.

ments of a firm. As an example, at this time the major emphasis of the U.S. government is on exporting. As a result, obtaining detailed import data is very difficult. Although some private organizations are beginning to make such data available, obtaining them is expensive and time consuming.

INTERPRETING AND ANALYZING THE DATA

A critical task for the researcher begins after the data have been collected. At this stage, the individual must use his or her research creativity to make good use of the data.

Secondary data, having originally been collected to serve other purposes, must be combined in a useful manner. This often requires the combination and crosstabulation of various sets of data or the use of proxy information in order to arrive at conclusions that address the research objectives. For example, the market penetration of television sets may be used as a **proxy variable** for the potential market demand for video recorders. Similarly, in an industrial setting, information about plans for new port facilities may be useful to determine future containerization requirements. Also, the beginning computerization of a society may highlight the need for software.

The researcher must go beyond the scope of the data and use creative inferences to arrive at knowledge useful to the firm. However, such creativity brings risks. Once the interpretation and analysis have taken place, a consistency check must be conducted. The researcher should always cross-check the results with other possible sources of information or with experts.

In addition, the researcher should take another look at the research methods employed, and, based on their usefulness, determine any necessary modifications for future projects. This will make possible the continuous improvement of international market research activities and enables the corporation to learn from experience.

PRESENTING RESEARCH RESULTS

Communicating the results to management is a crucial step to the success of the research. Care taken in preparing the research reports will reflect the desire of the researcher to communicate important knowledge to management.

Managers may not be aware of the many intricacies and subtleties of research, nor do they necessarily need to know about them. Management requires a palatable and useful demonstration of the information. Although the temptation may be great to cart reams of computer printout into a meeting to demonstrate the vast data resources the researcher has used, such actions are inappropriate. Rather, the researcher's task is to distill the data into core components that will enable management to understand the course of action that is necessary.

The report to management therefore needs to be concise. Restricting the length of memos to one page, for example, is not an unreasonable measure. Rather, it acknowledges the value and scarcity of managerial time and the need to conserve it. Reports should be preceded by short and incisive abstracts. The researcher should then clearly define the major issues, highlight research information that will give management confidence in the results presented, and clearly demonstrate the conclusions. Detailed information that may or may not be necessary should be placed in appendixes. The data are then preserved but do not clutter the report.

The purpose of the presentation is effective communication—and a demonstration of both the utility of the results and the need for implementation. Because the report shapes the perception of the entire research, it is a crucial component in the research process. No matter how valuable the research, any report not understood or utilized by management results in a waste of resources.

SUMMARY

Constraints of time, resources, and expertise are the major inhibitors to international marketing research. Nevertheless, firms need to carry out planned and organized research in order to explore foreign market alternatives successfully. Such research needs to be linked closely to the decision-making process.

International market research differs from domestic research in that the environment, which determines how well tools, techniques, and concepts apply, is different abroad. In addition, the manager needs to deal with new parameters, such as duties, exchange rates, and international documentation; a greater number of interacting factors; and a much broader definition of the concept of competition.

The research process starts by recognizing the need for research, which is often not well understood. When the firm is uninformed about international differences in consumer tastes and preferences and about the foreign market environments, the need for international research is high. Yet an appropriate trade-off needs to be made between the costs and the benefits of research in order to spend resources wisely. The research objectives need to be determined, based on the corporate mission, the level of international expertise, and the marketing intent. These objectives will enable the researcher to identify the information requirements.

Given the scarcity of resources, companies beginning their international effort often need to seek recourse to data that have already been collected, that is, secondary data. Such data are available from sources such as governments, international organizations, directories, or trade associations. Before using these data, however, the researcher needs to recognize that the quality, reliability, and usefulness of these data may be limited.

It is important to evaluate the quality of the data. This means exploring the purpose of the original data collection, the method underlying the data collection, the compatibility and comparability of the data, and their usefulness for the research task at hand.

Once the data are obtained, the researcher must analyze them with creativity, resorting often to proxy variables in order to draw inferences useful to management. A presentation of research results in a concise and clear fashion will then result in a contribution to the decision-making process that can lead to the implementation of activities.

Questions for Discussion

1. What is the difference between domestic and international marketing research?

2. How does "going international" affect the environmental perspective of a firm?

3. What does international marketing research aim to achieve?

4. How would you justify the need for international marketing research?

5. You are employed by National Engineering Corporation, a U.S. firm that designs subways. Knowing that you had a course in international marketing, your boss asks you to explore international market entry possibilities and report within a week. How will you go about this task?

6. Discuss the possible shortcomings of secondary data.

7. Why would a firm use secondary data in spite of their shortcomings?

Recommended Readings

Churchill, Gilbert A. *Marketing Research: Methodological Foundations*, 4th ed. Hinsdale, Ill.: Dryden Press, 1987.

Delphos, William A. *Inside Washington: The International Business Executive's Guide to Government Resources*. Lanham, Md.: Madison Books, 1988.

Department of Commerce, International Trade Administration, *Partners in Export Trade*. Washington, D.C.: Government Printing Office, 1987.

Directory of Online Databases. Santa Monica, Calif.: Cuadra Associates, published annually.

Douglas, Susan P., and C. Samuel Craig. *International Marketing Research*. Englewood Cliffs, N.J.: Prentice-Hall, 1983.

Interagency Task Force on Trade, *Exporter's Guide to Federal Resources for Small Business*. Washington, D.C.: Government Printing Office, 1988.

Predicasts Services. Cleveland, Ohio, published monthly.

Sheth, Jagdish N., ed. *Research in Marketing*, vol. 10. Greenwich, Conn.: JAI Press, 1988.

Sheth, Jagdish N., and Abdolreza Eshghi. *Global Marketing Perspectives*. Cincinnati, Ohio: South-Western, 1989.

MONITORS OF INTERNATIONAL ISSUES

Selected Organizations

American Bankers Association
1111 14th Street N.W. Suite 300
Washington, D.C. 20005

American Bar Association
750 N. Lake Shore Drive
Chicago, Ill. 60611
and
1800 M Street N.W.
Washington, D.C. 20036

American Management
  Association
440 First Street N.W.
Washington, D.C. 20001

American Marketing Association
250 S. Wacker Drive Suite 200
Chicago, Ill. 60606
and
1518 K Street N.W.
Washington, D.C. 20005

American Petroleum Institute
1220 L Street N.W.
Washington, D.C. 20005

Asian Development Bank
2330 Roxas Boulevard
Pasay City, Philippines

Chamber of Commerce of the
  United States
1615 H Street N.W.
Washington, D.C. 20062

Commission of the European
  Communities to the
  United States
2100 M Street N.W. Suite 707
Washington, D.C. 20037

Conference Board
845 Third Avenue
New York, N.Y. 10022

and
1755 Massachusetts Avenue N.W.
Suite 312
Washington, D.C. 20036

Center for International Business
  and Trade
School of Business Administration
Georgetown University
1242 35th Street N.W. Suite 501
Washington, D.C. 20057

Electronic Industries Association
2001 I Street N.W.
Washington, D.C. 20006

European Community Information
  Service
200 Rue de la Loi
1049 Brussels, Belgium
and
2100 M Street N.W. 7th Floor
Washington, D.C. 20037

Export-Import Bank of the
  United States
811 Vermont Avenue N.W.
Washington, D.C. 20571

Federal Reserve Bank of New York
33 Liberty Street
New York, N.Y. 10045

Inter-American Development Bank
1300 New York Avenue N.W.
Washington, D.C. 20577

International Bank for
  Reconstruction and
  Development (World Bank)
1818 H Street N.W.
Washington, D.C. 20433

International Monetary Fund
700 19th Street N.W.
Washington, D.C. 20431

Marketing Research Society
111 E. Wacker Drive Suite 600
Chicago, Ill. 60601

National Association of
Manufacturers
1331 Pennsylvania Avenue
Suite 1500
Washington, D.C. 20004

National Federation of
Independent Business
600 Maryland Avenue S.W.
Suite 700
Washington, D.C. 20024

Organization for Economic
Cooperation and Development
2 rue Andre Pascal
75775 Paris Cedex Ko, France

and
2001 L Street N.W.
Suite 700
Washington, D.C. 20036

Organization of American States
17th and Constitution
Avenue N.W.
Washington, D.C. 20006

Society for International
Development
1401 New York Avenue N.W.
Suite 1100
Washington, D.C. 20005

United Nations

Conference of Trade and
Development
Palais des Nations
1211 Geneva 10
Switzerland

Department of Economic and
Social Affairs
1 United Nations Plaza
New York, N.Y. 10017

Industrial Development
Organization
1660 L Street N.W.
Washington, D.C. 20036

and
Post Office Box 300
Vienna International Center
A-1400 Vienna, Austria

Publications
Room 1194
1 United Nations Plaza
New York, N.Y. 10017

Statistical Yearbook
1 United Nations Plaza
New York, N.Y. 10017

U.S. Government

Agency for International
Development
Office of Business Relations
Washington, D.C. 20523

Customs Service
1301 Constitution Avenue N.W.
Washington, D.C. 20229

Department of Agriculture
12th Street and Jefferson Drive S.W.
Washington, D.C. 20250

Department of Commerce
Herbert C. Hoover Building
14th Street and Constitution
Avenue N.W.
Washington, D.C. 20230

Department of State
2201 C Street N.W.
Washington, D.C. 20520

Department of the Treasury
15th Street and Pennsylvania
    Avenue N.W.
Washington, D.C. 20220

Federal Trade Commission
6th Street and Pennsylvania
    Avenue N.W.
Washington, D.C. 20580

International Trade Commission
701 E Street N.W.
Washington, D.C. 20436

Small Business Administration
Imperial Building
1441 L Street N.W.
Washington, D.C. 20416

Trade Development Program
1621 North Kent Street
Rosslyn, Va. 22209

World Trade Centers Association
1 World Trade Center Suite 7701
New York, N.Y. 10048

Indexes to Literature

Business Periodical Index
H.W. Wilson Co.
950 University Avenue
Bronx, N.Y. 10452

New York Times Index
University Microfilms International
300 N. Zeeb Road
Ann Arbor, Mich. 48106

Public Affairs Information Service
    Bulletin
11 W. 40th Street
New York, N.Y. 10018

Readers' Guide to Periodical
    Literature
H.W. Wilson Co.
950 University Avenue
Bronx, N.Y. 10452

Wall Street Journal Index
Dow Jones & Company
200 Liberty Street
New York, N.Y. 10281

Periodic Reports, Newspapers, Magazines

Advertising Age
Crain Communications Inc.
740 N. Rush Street
Chicago, Ill. 60611

Advertising World
Directories International Inc.
150 Fifth Avenue Suite 610
New York, N.Y. 10011

Arab Report and Record
84 Chancery Lane
London WC2A 1DL, England

Barron's
University Microfilms International
300 N. Zeeb Road
Ann Arbor, Mich. 48106

Business America
U.S. Department of Commerce
14th Street and Constitution
    Avenue N.W.
Washington, D.C. 20230

Business International
Business International Corp.
One Dag Hammarskjold Plaza
New York, N.Y. 10017

Business Week
McGraw-Hill Publications Co.
1221 Avenue of the Americas
New York, N.Y. 10020

Commodity Trade Statistics
United Nations Publications
1 United Nations Plaza
Room DC2-853
New York, N.Y. 10017

Conference Board Record
Conference Board Inc.
845 Third Avenue
New York, N.Y. 10022

Customs Bulletin
U.S. Customs Service
1301 Constitution Avenue N.W.
Washington, D.C. 20229

Dun's Business Month
Goldhirsh Group
38 Commercial Wharf
Boston, Mass. 02109

The Economist
Economist Newspaper Ltd.
25 St. James Street
London SW1A 1HG, England

Europe Magazine
2100 M Street N.W. Suite 707
Washington, D.C. 20037

The Financial Times
Bracken House
10 Cannon Street
London EC4P 4BY, England

Forbes
Forbes, Inc.
60 Fifth Avenue
New York, N.Y. 10011

Fortune
Time, Inc.
Time & Life Building
1271 Avenue of the Americas
New York, N.Y. 10020

Global Trade
North American Publishing Co.
401 N. Broad Street
Philadelphia, Pa. 19108

Industrial Marketing
Crain Communications, Inc.
740 N. Rush Street
Chicago, Ill. 60611

International Financial Statistics
International Monetary Fund
Publications Unit
700 19th Street N.W.
Washington, D.C. 20431

Investor's Daily
Box 25970
Los Angeles, Calif. 90025

Journal of Commerce
110 Wall Street
New York, N.Y. 10005

Sales and Marketing Management
Bill Communications Inc.
633 Third Avenue
New York, N.Y. 10017

Wall Street Journal
Dow Jones & Company
200 Liberty Street
New York, N.Y. 10007

World Agriculture Situation
U.S. Department of Agriculture
Economics Management Staff
Information Division
1301 New York Avenue N.W.
Washington, D.C. 20005

World Development
Pergamon Press Inc.
Journals Division
Maxwell House
Fairview Park
Elmsford, N.Y. 10523

World Trade Center Association
   (WTCA) Directory
World Trade Centers Association
1 World Trade Center
New York, N.Y. 10048

Directories

American Register of Exporters
   and Importers
38 Park Row
New York, N.Y. 10038

Arabian Year Book
Dar Al-Seuassam Est.
Box 42480
Shuwakh, Kuwait

Directories of American Firms
   Operating in Foreign Countries
World Trade Academy Press
Uniworld Business
   Publications Inc.
50 E. 42nd Street
New York, N.Y. 10017

Encyclopedia of Associations
Gale Research Company
Book Tower
Detroit, Mich. 48226

Polk's World Bank Directory
R.C. Polk & Co.
2001 Elm Hill Pike
P.O. Box 1340
Nashville, Tenn. 37202

Verified Directory of
   Manufacturers' Representatives
MacRae's Blue Book Inc.
817 Broadway
New York, N.Y. 10003

World Guide to Trade
   Associations
K.G. Saur & Company
175 Fifth Avenue
New York, N.Y. 10010

Encyclopedias, Handbooks, and Miscellaneous

A Basic Guide to Exporting
U.S. Government Printing Office
Superintendent of Documents
Washington, D.C. 20402

Doing Business in . . . Series
Price Waterhouse
1251 Avenue of the Americas
New York, N.Y. 10020

Economic Survey of Europe
The United Nations
United Nations Publication
   Division
1 United Nations Plaza
Room DC2-0853
New York, N.Y. 10017

Export-Import Bank of the United
   States Annual Report
U.S. Government Printing Office
Superintendent of Documents
Washington, D.C. 20402

Exporting for the Small Business
U.S. Government Printing Office
Superintendent of Documents
Washington, D.C. 20402

Exporting to the United States
U.S. Government Printing Office
Superintendent of Documents
Washington, D.C. 20402

Export Shipping Manual
U.S. Government Printing Office
Superintendent of Documents
Washington, D.C. 20402

Foreign Business Practices:
    Materials on Practical Aspects
    of Exporting, International
    Licensing, and Investing
U.S. Government Printing Office
Superintendent of Documents
Washington, D.C. 20402

A Guide to Financing Exports
U.S. Government Printing Office
Superintendent of Documents
Washington, D.C. 20402

Handbook of Marketing Research
McGraw-Hill Book Company
1221 Avenue of the Americas
New York, N.Y. 10020

Economic Survey of Latin America
United Nations
United Nations Publishing
    Division
1 United Nations Plaza
Room DC2-0853
New York, N.Y. 10017

Encyclopedia Americana,
    International Edition
Grolier Inc.
Danbury, Conn. 06816

Encyclopedia of Business
    Information Sources
Gale Research Company
Book Tower
Detroit, Mich. 48226

Europa Year Book
Europa Publications Ltd.
18 Bedford Square
London WC1B 3JN, England

Export Administration Regulations
U.S. Government Printing Office
Superintendent of Documents
Washington, D.C. 20402

Exporters' Encyclopedia—World
    Marketing Guide
Dun's Marketing Services
49 Old Bloomfield Rd.
Mountain Lake, N.J. 07046

International Encyclopedia of the
    Social Sciences
MacMillan and the Free Press
866 Third Avenue
New York, N.Y. 10022

Marketing and Communications
    Media Dictionary
Media Horizons Inc.
50 W. 25th Street
New York, N.Y. 10010

Market Share Reports
U.S. Government Printing Office
Superintendent of Documents
Washington, D.C. 20402

Media Guide International:
    Business/Professional
    Publications
Directories International Inc.
150 Fifth Avenue
Suite 610
New York, N.Y. 10011

Overseas Business Reports
U.S. Government Printing Office
Superintendent of Documents
Washington, D.C. 20402

Trade Finance
U.S. Department of Commerce
International Trade Administration
Washington, D.C. 20230

World Economic Conditions in
   Relation to Agricultural Trade
U.S. Government Printing Office
Superintendent of Documents
Washington, D.C. 20402

Yearbook of International Trade
   Statistics
United Nations
United Nations Publishing
   Division
1 United Nations Plaza
Room DC2-0853
New York, N.Y. 10017

DESCRIPTION OF SELECTED U.S. GOVERNMENT PUBLICATIONS AND SERVICES

Macrodata

World Population is issued by the U.S. Bureau of the Census, which collects and analyzes worldwide demographic data. Information is provided about total population, fertility, mortality, urban population, growth rate, and life expectancy. Also published are detailed demographic profiles, including an analysis of the labor force structure of individual countries.

Foreign Trade Highlights are annual reports published by the Department of Commerce. They provide basic data on U.S. merchandise trade with major trading partners and regions. They also contain brief analyses of recent U.S. trade developments.

United States Trade Performance and Outlook is published by the Department of Commerce and provides an overview of trade flows among nations. In addition, a special topics section addresses major changes in trade regulation and trade policy that have taken place during the year.

Foreign Trade Report FT410 provides a monthly statistical record of shipments of all merchandise from the United States to foreign countries, including both the quantity and dollar value of exports to each country. It also contains cumulative export statistics from the first of the calendar year.

World Agriculture, a publication of the U.S. Department of Agriculture, provides production information, data, and analyses by country along with a review of recent economic conditions and changes in agricultural and trade policies. Frequent supplements provide an outlook of anticipated developments for the coming year.

Country Information

Country Market Profiles (CMP) are multicountry, multi-industry reports that include trade contacts, specific trade leads, and statistical analyses.

International Market Research (IMR) reports provide in-depth analyses of one industry in one country. Each report typically includes information such as behavioral characteristics, trade barriers, market share figures, and trade contacts.

Overseas Business Reports (OBR) present economic and commercial profiles on specific countries and provide background statistics. Selected information on the direction and the volume and nature of U.S. foreign trade is also provided.

Background Notes, prepared by the Department of State, present a survey of a country's people, geography, economy; government, and foreign policy. The reports also include important national economic and trade information.

Foreign Economic Trends presents recent business and economic developments and the latest economic indicators of more than 100 countries.

Product Information

Export Statistics Profiles analyzes exports for a single industry, product by product, country by country, over a five-year period. Data are rank-ordered by dollar value for quick identification of the leading products and industries. Tables show the sales of each product in an industry to each country as well as competitive information, growth, and future trends. Each profile also contains a narrative analysis that highlights the industry's prospects, performance, and leading products.

Custom Statistical Service offers data on products not covered in one of the standard export statistics profiles. It allows firms access to data tailored specifically to their needs. Data are available in formats such as quantity, unit quantity, unit value, and percentages as well as on imports.

Annual Worldwide Industry Review publications provide a combination of country by country market assessments, export trends, and five-year statistical tables of U.S. exports for a single industry integrated into one report. They show the industry's performance for recent years in many countries.

U.S. Industrial Outlook, an annual publication of the U.S. Department of Commerce, provides an overview of the domestic and international performance of all major U.S. industries, complete with employment and shipment information and a forecast of future developments.

Market Share Reports provide basic data to evaluate overall trends in the size of markets for exporters. They also measure changes in the import demand for specific products and compare the competitive position of U.S. and foreign exporters.

Country Trade Statistics provides details of all U.S. exports to a single country over a five-year period. It shows leading U.S. exports by industry and country. Each country report contains four key statistical tables showing the top U.S. exports of about 150 product categories and other indicators of which U.S. products are in demand.

Export Information System Data Reports, available from the U.S. Small Business Administration, provide small businesses with a list of the 25 largest importing markets for their products and the 10 best markets for U.S. exporters of the products. Trends within those markets and the major sources of foreign competition are also discussed.

Services

Agent Distributor Service (ADS): The Foreign Commercial Service (FCS) provides a customized search for interested and qualified foreign representatives for a firm's product.

Catalog Exhibitions: The Department of Commerce organizes displays of product literature and videotape presentations overseas.

Comparison Shopping Service: The FCS provides a custom foreign market survey on a product's overall marketability, names of competitors, comparative prices, and customary business practices.

Economic Bulletin Board: The Department of Commerce provides access to the latest economic data releases, including trade opportunities, for on-line users.

Foreign Buyer Program: The FCS brings foreign buyers to U.S. trade shows for industries with high export potential.

Matchmaker Events: The Department of Commerce introduces U.S. companies to new markets through short visits abroad to match the U.S. firm with a representative or prospective partner.

Seminar Missions: The Department of Commerce sponsors technical seminars abroad designed to promote sales of sophisticated products and technology.

Trade Missions: Groups of U.S. business executives, led by Commerce Department staff, are brought in direct contact with potential foreign buyers, agents, and distributors.

Trade Opportunity Program: The FCS daily collection of trade opportunities worldwide is published and electronically distributed to subscribers.

World Traders Data Reports: The FCS publishes background research conducted by FCS officers abroad on potential trading partners, such as agents, distributors, and licensees.

CHAPTER 9

International Product Adaptation

9.1 THE INTERNATIONAL MARKETPLACE

EC Court Throws Out Purity Laws   As part of the 1992 integration effort, the European Court of Justice has struck down a number of laws that have been de facto barriers to the importation of a number of products. Two examples are beer in West Germany and pasta in Italy, both of which until recently have been protected by "purity laws," thereby effectively keeping most foreign-produced versions out.

In March 1987 the court took exception with the West German "beer purity mandate," which dates back to 1516 and forbids the drinking of beer containing anything but water, hops, malt, and yeast. Most non-German brewers use rice or corn in their beers. The German Brewers League argued that additives in foreign beers, although not specifically prohibited by law, are a threat to public health, and beer not brewed according to the mandate might contain chemical additives such as preservatives and sulphur dioxide. The issue is of special significance because German per-capita consumption averages 38.3 gallons per year.

In a similar ruling, the court in July 1988 threw out Italy's "pasta purity" law, arguing that Italy cannot ban imports under a 1967 law requiring that all pasta be made with durum wheat. Such pasta is firmer but more expensive. The case was brought up by the West German pasta producer Drei Glocken, which was blocked in 1985 from importing pasta made with mixed wheat into Italy. Under the ruling, Italy can still require its own pasta makers to use only durum wheat, but it cannot use the law to block imports from other EC countries. The Italian reaction was one of distaste. "That flavorful and firm macaroni, the product of our able pasta makers, will be challenged, and maybe even replaced, by the gluey and insipid pasta from West Germany or Holland."

In both cases, the European Court ruled that the restrictions go far beyond what is necessary to protect consumers and represent unjustifiable trade barriers. The decision is based on the provision in the Treaty of Rome, the EC's founding charter, that forbids member states to place limits on trade in goods.

Source: "German Brewers and EEC Will Meet in Court," *Advertising Age*, July 23, 1984, 57; "EC Claims Victory as Court Overturns Age-Old Ban on Beer Imports," *The Wall Street Journal*, March 13, 1987, 29; and "Italy Finds Pasta Ruling Distasteful," *The Washington Post*, July 15, 1988, D1.

This chapter is concerned with how the international marketer should adjust the firm's product offering to the international marketplace. An array of both external and internal variables influence the degree to which the firm will cater to the unique needs of each of the markets it will enter. The decision is critical to all marketers, small and large, in their attempt to serve customers better, regardless of their geographic location, while maintaining overall profitability.

PRODUCT VARIABLES

The core of a firm's international operations is a product or service. This can be defined as the complex of tangible and intangible elements that distinguishes it from the other entities in the marketplace. The firm's success depends on how good its product or service is and on how well the firm is able to differentiate it from the offerings of competitors. Theodore Levitt has stated that there is no such thing as a commodity; all goods and services are differentiable.[1] Products can be differentiated by their composition, by their country of origin, by their tangible features such as packaging or quality, or by their augmented features such as warranty. Further, the positioning of the product in consumers' minds (for example, 7UP, the Uncola) will add to its perceived value. The elements of the total product are summarized in Figure 9.1. The **core product**—for example, the bios-ROM component of a personal computer or the recipe for a soup—may indeed be the same or highly similar to those of competitors, leaving the marketer with the other tangible and **augmented features** of the product to achieve differentiation. Very often, the accompanying service may be a good share of what the company is marketing; for example, Otis Elevator Company generates half of its worldwide revenues from the service contracts on its elevators.

To the potential buyer, a product is a complete cluster of value satisfactions. A customer attaches value to a product in proportion to its perceived ability to help solve problems or meet needs. Therefore, IBM does not sell personal computers but rather help for problem solutions its customers are seeking. Charles Revson of Revlon summed it up best by stating that he manufactured cosmetics but sold hope. Within international markets these psychological expectations may vary dramatically from one

[1]Theodore Levitt, "Marketing Success Through Differentiation—of Anything," *Harvard Business Review* 58 (January–February 1980): 83–91.

FIGURE 9.1   ▪   **Elements of a Product**

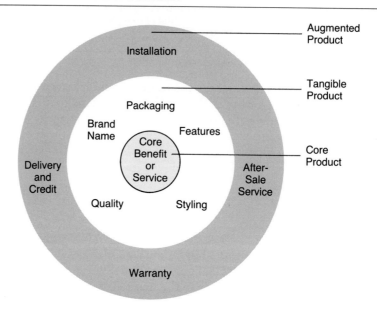

Source: Philip Kotler, *Principles of Marketing*, 3/e, © 1986, 297. Reprinted by permission of Prentice-Hall, Inc., Englewood Cliffs, New Jersey.

market to another without having a dramatic effect on the core product, yet warranting a careful assessment of choices to be made.

Standardization versus Adaptation

The first question after the internationalization decision has been made concerns the product modifications that are needed or warranted. A firm has four basic alternatives in approaching international markets: (1) selling the product as is in the international marketplace, (2) modifying products for different countries and/or regions, (3) designing new products for foreign markets, and (4) incorporating all the differences into one product design and introducing a global product. Firms may identify potential target markets and then choose products that can easily be marketed there with little or no modification.

The question of whether to standardize or to custom-tailor marketing programs in each country has continued to trouble practitioners and academics alike and has produced many and varied opinions. In the early 1960s Robert Buzzell stated that it depends on the strengths of the barriers to standardization, such as national differences in consumer preferences and legal restrictions, and on the potential payoffs of standardizing marketing strategy.[2] Studies of how firms view standardization have found

[2] Robert Buzzell, "Can You Standardize Multinational Marketing?" *Harvard Business Review* 46 (November–December 1968): 98–104.

TABLE 9.1 ▪ **Standardization versus Adaptation**

> Factors encouraging standardization
> - Economies of scale in production
> - Economies in product R&D
> - Economies in marketing
> - "Shrinking" of the world marketplace/integration
> - Global competition
>
> Factors encouraging adaptation
> - Differing use conditions
> - Government and regulatory influences
> - Differing consumer behavior patterns
> - Local competition
> - True to the marketing concept

that arguments in favor of standardizing whenever possible fall into two categories: better marketing performance and lower marketing cost.[3] The general benefits and disadvantages of standardization versus adaptation are summarized in Table 9.1.

The benefits of standardization—that is, selling the same product worldwide—are cost savings in production and marketing. In addition to the economies of scale, many point to economic integration as a driving force to make markets more unified. As a response to 1992, many international marketers are indeed standardizing many of their marketing approaches, such as branding and packaging, across markets.[4] Similarly, having to face the same competitors in the major markets of the world will add to the pressure of a worldwide approach to international marketing. However, in most cases, demand and usage conditions vary sufficiently to require some changes in the product or service itself.

Coca-Cola, Levi's jeans, and Colgate toothpaste have been cited as evidence that universal product and marketing strategy can work.[5] Yet the argument that the world is becoming more homogenized may actually be true only for a limited number of products that have universal brand recognition and minimal product knowledge requirements for use.[6] Although product standardization is generally increasing, there are still substantial differences in company practices depending on the products they market and where they are marketed.[7] As shown in Figure 9.2, industrial prod-

[3] Ralph Z. Sorenson and Ulrich E. Wiechmann, "How Multinationals View Marketing Standardization," *Harvard Business Review* 53 (May–June 1975): 38–56.

[4] Theodore Levitt, "The Globalization of Markets," *Harvard Business Review* 61 (May–June 1983): 92–101.

[5] W. Chan Kim and R. A. Mauborgne, "Cross-Cultural Strategies," *The Journal of Business Strategy* 7 (Spring 1987): 28–36.

[6] "Marketers Turn Sour on Global Sales Pitch Harvard Guru Makes," *The Wall Street Journal*, May 12, 1988, 1, 13.

[7] J. J. Boddewyn, Robin Soehl, and Jacques Picard, "Standardization In International Marketing: Is Ted Levitt in Fact Right?" *Business Horizons* 29 (November–December 1986): 69–75.

FIGURE 9.2 ▪ **Strategic Adaptation to Foreign Markets**

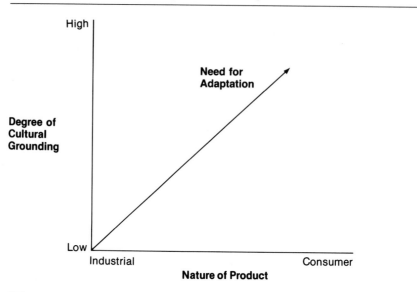

Source: W. Chan Kim and R. A. Mauborgne, "Cross-Cultural Strategies," *The Journal of Business Strategy* 7 (Spring 1987): 31; and John A. Quelch and Edward J. Hoff, "Customizing Global Marketing," *Harvard Business Review* 64 (May–June 1986): 92–101.

ucts, such as steel, chemicals, and agricultural equipment, tend to be less culturally grounded and warrant less adjustment than consumer goods.

Adaptation needs in the industrial sector may exist even though the need may not be overt. As an example, capacity–performance is seen from different perspectives in different countries. Typically, the performance specifications of a German product are quite precise; for example, if a German product is said to have a lifting capacity of 1,000 kg, it will perform precisely up to that level. The U.S. counterpart, however, is likely to maintain a safety factor of 1.5 or even 2.0, resulting in a substantially higher payload capacity. Buyers of Japanese machine tools have also found that they will perform at the specified level, not beyond them, as would their U.S.-made counterparts.

Consumer goods generally require product adaptation because of their higher degree of cultural grounding. The degree of change introduced in consumer goods depends not only on cultural differences but also on economic conditions in the target market. Low incomes may cause pressure to simplify the product to make it affordable in the market.

Beyond the dichotomy of standardization and adaptation exist other approaches. The international marketer may design and introduce new products for foreign markets in addition to the firm's relatively standardized "flagship" products and brands. Some of these products developed specifically for foreign clients may later be introduced elsewhere, including the domestic market.

Even companies that are noted for following the same methods world-wide have made numerous changes in their product offering. Some, like Coca-Cola Company's Hi-C Soy Milk in Hong Kong, may be restricted to markets for which they were specifically developed. Although Colgate toothpaste is available worldwide, the company also markets some products locally, such as a spicy toothpaste formulated especially for the Middle East.[8] McDonald's serves abroad the same menu of hamburgers, soft drinks, and other foods that it does in the United States, and the restaurants look the same. But McDonald's has also tried to tailor its product to local styles; for example, in Japan the chain's trademark character, known as Ronald McDonald in the United States, is called Donald McDonald because it is easier to pronounce that way.[9] Menu adjustments include beer in Germany and wine in France. Of course, marketers may have similar adaptation needs in their domestic operations; for example, menus of fast food restaurants in the South carry iced tea, while those in the Northeast do not.

Increasingly, companies are attempting to develop global products by incorporating differences regionally or worldwide into one basic design. This is not pure standardization, however. To develop a standard in the United States, for example, and use it as a model for other markets is dramatically different from obtaining inputs from the intended markets and using the data to create a standard. What is important is that adaptability is built into the product. For example, IBM makes more than 20 different keyboards for its relatively standardized personal computers to adjust to language differences in Europe alone. The international marketer attempts to exploit the common denominators, but local needs are considered from product development to the eventual marketing of the product. Car manufacturers like Ford and Nissan may develop basic models for regional, or even global, use, but they allow for substantial discretion in adjusting the models to local preferences. Such an approach encourages "thinking globally, acting locally." Often this is best done in collaboration with a local joint venture partner or, in the case of large companies, in collaboration with the subsidiary.

Factors Affecting Adaptation

In deciding the form in which the product is to be marketed abroad, the firm should consider three sets of factors: (1) the market(s) that have been targeted, (2) the product and its characteristics, and (3) company characteristics, in terms of factors such as resources and policy. In a survey of firms with products or services in the international marketplace, 40 percent said that the adaptation issue comes up frequently, while another

[8]"Marketers Turn Sour on Global Sales Pitch Harvard Guru Makes," *The Wall Street Journal,* May 12, 1988, 1, 13.

[9]"Why Some U.S. Companies Crack Japan's Market," *Business Week,* August 29, 1983, 33–34.

FIGURE 9.3 ▪ **Factors Affecting Product-Adaptation Decisions**

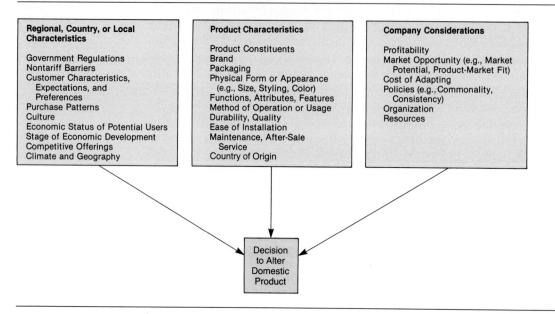

Source: V. Yorio, *Adapting Products for Export* (New York: The Conference Board, 1983), 7. Reprinted with permission.

40 percent reported that the issue arises sometimes.[10] For most firms the key question linked to adaptation is whether the effort is worth the cost involved—in adjusting production runs, stock control, or servicing, for example—and the investigative research involved in determining, for example, features that would be most appealing. For six out of ten firms surveyed, the expense of modifying products was moderate. This may mean, however, that the expense is moderate when modifications are considered and acted upon, whereas modifications are considered but rejected when the projected cost is substantial.

A detailed examination of 174 consumer-packaged goods destined for the developing countries has shown that, on the average, 4.1 changes per product were made in terms of brand name, packaging, measurement units, labeling, constituents, product features, and usage instructions.[11] Only one out of ten products was transferred without modification.

There is no panacea for resolving questions of adaptation. Many firms are formulating decision-support systems to aid in situations concerning product adaptation, while some consider every situation independently. The factors presented in Figure 9.3 provide a summary of the factors that

[10] V. Yorio, *Adapting Products for Export* (New York: The Conference Board, 1983), 1.

[11] John S. Hill and Richard R. Still, "Adapting Products to LDC Tastes," *Harvard Business Review* 62 (March–April 1984): 92–101.

determine the need for either **mandatory** or **discretionary product adaptation.** All products have to conform to the prevailing environmental conditions, over which the marketer has no control. These relate to legal, economic and climatic conditions in the market. Further adaptation decisions are made to enhance the exporter's competitiveness in the marketplace. This is achieved by matching competitive offers, catering to customer preferences, and meeting demands of local distribution systems.

THE MARKET ENVIRONMENT

Government Regulations

Government regulations often present the most stringent of requirements to the firm. Some of the requirements may serve no purpose other than political (such as protection of domestic industry or response to political pressures). Because of the sovereignty of nations, individual firms need to comply but can influence the situation by lobbying directly or through their industry associations for the issue to be raised during trade negotiations. Government regulations may be spelled out, but firms need to be ever vigilant in terms of changes and exceptions. As an example, the metric standard applies to all commercial importation of distilled spirits to the United States. Bottle sizes must be 1.75 liters, 1.00 liters, and so on. Shipments that do not conform to these metric standards are denied entry by customs, except upon written authorization by the Bureau of Alcohol, Tobacco, and Firearms, which is part of the U.S. Treasury Department. In order to claim exemption from these requirements, the importer must produce a statement from an authorized official in the country of origin to the effect that the spirits were bottled or packed prior to January 1, 1980, the date on which the regulation became effective.

Sweden was the first country in the world to enact legislation against most aerosol sprays on the grounds that they may harm the atmosphere. The ban, which went into effect January 1, 1979, covers thousands of hair sprays, deodorants, air fresheners, insecticides, paints, waxes, and assorted sprays that use Freon gases as propellants. It does not apply to certain medical sprays, especially those used by people who suffer from asthma. The Swedish government, which has one of the world's most active environmental protection departments, is taking seriously warnings by some scientists that continued release of these chemicals could eventually degrade the earth's ozone layer. Germany has exceptionally stringent food laws, in part because the Germans are health conscious. An outsider has difficulty entering the health-food market.

Although economic integration usually reduces discriminatory governmental regulation (as seen in The International Marketplace 9.1), some national environmental restrictions may stay in place. For example, a 1989 ruling by the European Court of Justice let stand Danish laws that require returnable containers for all beer and soft drinks. These laws seriously restrict foreign brewers, whose businesses are not on a scale large enough to justify the logistics system necessary to handle returnables.[12]

On occasion, it may be in the marketer's best interest to gain governmental approval for a product even though it may not be required. Testing by a governmental agency or an independent testing laboratory (equivalent to Underwriters Laboratory) may add to the product's acceptability in the foreign marketplace.

Government regulations are probably the single most important factor contributing to product adaptation and, because of bureaucratic red tape, often one of the most cumbersome and frustrating to deal with. In some cases government regulations have been passed to serve as nontariff barriers to trade. To ease the situation, some industries are following agreed-upon international standards.

Nontariff Barriers

Nontariff barriers include product standards, testing or approval procedures, subsidies for local products, and bureaucratic red tape. The nontariff barriers affecting product adjustments usually concern elements outside the core product. For example, France requires the use of the French language in any offer, presentation, or advertisement whether written or spoken, in instructions for use, and in specification or guarantee terms for goods or services, as well as for invoices and receipts.

Because nontariff barriers are usually in place to keep foreign products out and/or to protect domestic producers, getting around them may be the toughest single problem for the international marketer. The expense of compliance with government regulations is high. As an example, Mack International has to pay $10,000 to $25,000 for a typical European engine certification. Brake system changes to conform with other countries' regulations run from $1,500 to $2,500 per vehicle. Wheel equipment changes will cost up to $1,000 per vehicle. Even with these outlays and the subsequent higher price, the company is still able to compete successfully in the international marketplace.

Small companies with limited resources may simply give up in the face of seemingly arbitrary harassment. For example, product testing and certification requirements have made the entry of many foreign companies into Japanese markets quite difficult, if not impossible.[13] Japan requires testing of all pharmaceutical products in Japanese laboratories, maintaining that these tests are needed because the Japanese may be physiologically different from Americans or Swiss. Similarly, foreign ski products were kept out because Japanese snow was somehow unique. Many exporters, rather than try to move mountains of red tape, have found ways to accommodate Japanese regulations. Famous Amos, for example, creates sep-

[12] Eric C. Friberg, "1992: Moves Europeans Are Making," *Harvard Business Review* 67 (May–June 1989): 85–89.

[13] Vernon R. Alden, "Who Says You Can't Crack Japanese Markets?" *Harvard Business Review* 64 (January–February 1986): 52–56.

arate product batches to meet Japanese requirements and avoid problems with the Japanese Health and Welfare Agency.[14]

With a substantial decrease in tariff barriers, nontariff forms of protectionism have increased. On volume alone, agriculture dominates the list. Many barriers have been in existence for decades, because agriculture is exempted from the GATT framework, but new ones emerge as needed. In 1989, for example, the United States and the EC fought over beef produced with the aid of hormones. The hormones the Europeans banned in beef imports to the EC are almost undetectable and were declared safe by the U.N. health authorities in 1987.[15]

One way to keep a particular product out of a market is to make it hard to sell by insisting on certain standards. In preparation for 1992, the EC's postal and telecommunications administrations are developing harmonized standards for equipment. Many U.S. manufacturers are worried that many of the new standards will reduce the U.S. market share in the $12 billion annual market. Similar policies already exclude most imported equipment from the growing Korean market.

Customer Characteristics, Expectations, and Preferences

The characteristics and behavior of intended customer groups are as important as governmental influences on the product adaptation decision. Even when the benefits sought are quite similar, the physical characteristics of customers may dictate product adaptation. For example, U.S.-based Erno Laszlo tried to market the same skin-care product to "fair-skinned Australians, swarthy Italians, and delicate Asian women" and failed in its effort.[16] The company also found that in Asia skin-care customs vary widely from region to region. GE Medical Systems has designed a product specifically for Japan in addition to computerized tomography scanners produced for the U.S. market. The unit is smaller because Japanese hospitals are smaller than most U.S. facilities, but also because of the smaller size of Japanese patients.[17]

Product decisions of consumer-product marketers are especially affected by local behavior, tastes, attitudes, and traditions—all reflecting the marketer's need to gain customers' approval. This group of variables is critical in that it is the most difficult to quantify, but is nevertheless essential in making a go/no-go decision. The reason most Europeans who wear Western boots buy those made in Spain may be that American footwear manufacturers are unaware of style-conscious Europeans' preference for pointed toes and narrow heels. They view American-made boots as "practical but uninteresting," as described in The International Marketplace 9.2.

[14] "Going Through Customs," *Inc.*, December 1984, 180–184.

[15] Rahul Jacob, "Export Barriers the U.S. Hates Most," *Fortune*, February 27, 1989, 88–89.

[16] "Marketers Turn Sour on Global Sales Pitch Harvard Guru Makes," *The Wall Street Journal*, May 12, 1988, 1, 13.

[17] Kate Bertrand, "Marketing to the Land of the Rising Yen," *Business Marketing* 12 (October 1986): 77–86.

9.2 THE INTERNATIONAL MARKETPLACE

Do Round-Toed Boots Contribute to the Trade Gap? *The sales of Western footwear, especially cowboy boots, have been boosted dramatically in Europe since the mid-1980s by a fashion theme emphasizing the West and the outdoors. Estimates indicate that Germans, for example, buy up to 500,000 pairs of cowboy boots annually with sales growing at an 8 percent rate. U.S. companies, however, are not part of the evolving market. The boots may be as American as John Wayne, but most of those sold are European brands made in Spain. The main reason cited: the toes of U.S. boots are not pointy enough.*

"American brands are not very popular because they are of a different style," says the owner of Dynamo, one of the largest shops specializing in boots in Germany. The U.S. style has a round toe, whereas Europeans prefer a pointed tip. An added problem is that American heels are perceived to be too wide as well. "They are practical, but not interesting."

Certainly, U.S. shoemakers have the technology to make pointy toes and narrow heels, which raises the question of why they do not do so. German buyers respond with two often-heard criticisms of U.S. manufacturers. First, U.S. companies do not export seriously, and, second, they are unaware of foreign needs and tastes or are unwilling to adapt their products to foreign markets. The latter comment is highlighted by the market trend of another product born in the American West: jeans. Denim is popular in Europe, and traditional American brands are worn widely. But European brands have captured a large part of the market with vanguard designs.

Frank Scivetti, vice president for sales and marketing at Justin Boot Company in Fort Worth, Texas, said the higher prices of U.S. footwear, as well as import duties and other costs, give Spanish manufacturers an edge. "Germans are willing to settle for lower priced products, while the French will pay higher prices for authentic boots made in the United States." German retailers agree that price is a consideration but the difference of style is the main factor hurting the popularity of "authentic" Western footwear.

Source: "Do Round-Toed Boots Contribute to Trade Gap?" *The Journal of Commerce,* April 5, 1989, 1A, 12A.

Three groups of factors determine cultural and psychological specificity in relation to products and services: consumption patterns, psychosocial characteristics, and general cultural criteria.[18] The types of questions asked in Table 9.2 should be answered and systematically recorded for every

[18] Steuart Henderson Britt, "Standardizing Marketing for the International Market," *Columbia Journal of World Business* 9 (Winter 1974): 32–40.

TABLE 9.2   ■   **Cultural and Psychological Factors Affecting Product Adaptation**

I.   Consumption Patterns
   A.   Pattern of Purchase
      1.   Is the product or service purchased by relatively the same consumer income group from one country to another?
      2.   Do the same family members motivate the purchase in all target countries?
      3.   Do the same family members dictate brand choice in all target countries?
      4.   Do most consumers expect a product to have the same appearance?
      5.   Is the purchase rate the same regardless of the country?
      6.   Are most of the purchases made at the same kind of retail outlet?
      7.   Do most consumers spend the same amount of time making the purchase?
   B.   Pattern of Usage
      1.   Do most consumers use the product or service for the same purpose or purposes?
      2.   Is the product or service used in different amounts from one target area or country to another?
      3.   Is the method of preparation the same in all target countries?
      4.   Is the product or service used along with other products or services?

II.   Psychosocial Characteristics
   A.   Attitudes toward the Product or Service
      1.   Are the basic psychological, social, and economic factors motivating the purchase and use of the product the same for all target countries?
      2.   Are the advantages and disadvantages of the product or service in the minds of consumers basically the same from one country to another?
      3.   Does the symbolic content of the product or service differ from one country to another?
      4.   Is the psychic cost of purchasing or using the product or service the same, whatever the country?
      5.   Does the appeal of the product or service for a cosmopolitan market differ from one market to another?
   B.   Attitudes toward the Brand
      1.   Is the brand name equally known and accepted in all target countries?
      2.   Are customer attitudes toward the package basically the same?
      3.   Are customer attitudes toward pricing basically the same?
      4.   Is brand loyalty the same throughout target countries for the product or service under consideration?

III.   Cultural Criteria
      1.   Does society restrict the purchase and/or use of the product or service to a particular group?
      2.   Is there a stigma attached to the product or service?
      3.   Does the usage of the product or service interfere with tradition in one or more of the targeted markets?

Source: Steuart Henderson Britt, "Standardizing Marketing for the International Market," *Columbia Journal of World Business* 9 (Winter 1974): 32−40.

product under consideration. Use of the list of questions will guide the international marketer through the analysis, ensuring that all of the necessary points are dealt with before a decision is made.

Because Brazilians are rarely breakfast eaters, Dunkin' Donuts is marketing doughnuts in Brazil as snacks, desserts, and for parties. To further appeal to Brazilians, doughnuts are made with local fruit fillings like papaya and guava. Campbell Soup Company failed in Brazil with its offerings of vegetable and beef combinations mainly because Brazilian housewives prefer the dehydrated products of competitors such as Knorr and Maggi, which they could use as soup starter but still add their own flair and ingredients. The only way of solving this problem is through proper customer testing, which can be formidably expensive for a company interested only in exports.

Often no concrete product changes are needed, only a change in the product's **positioning.** Positioning refers to consumers' perception of brand as compared to those of competitors' brands; that is, the mental image a brand, or the company as a whole, evokes. For example, Gillette has a consistent image worldwide as a masculine, hardware, sports-oriented company. A brand's positioning, however, may have to change to reflect the differing lifestyles of the targeted market. Coca-Cola Company took a risk in marketing Diet Coke in Japan, because trying to sell a diet drink is difficult in a nation where "diet" is a dirty word and the population is not overweight by Western standards. The problem was addressed by changing the name of the drink to Coke Light and subtly shifting the promotional theme from "weight loss" to "figure maintenance." Japanese women do not like to admit that they are dieting by drinking something clearly labeled diet (see Figure 9.4).

Health and beauty care products often rely on careful positioning to attain a competitive advantage. Timotei shampoo, which is Unilever's brand leader in that category, has a natural-looking image with a focus on mildness and purity. Because people around the world have different hair, Timotei's formula varies, but it always has the same image. The selling of "lifestyle" brands is common in consumer goods for which differentiation may be more difficult. Lifestyles may be more difficult for competitors to copy but they are also more susceptible to changes in fashion.[19]

Culture

Variables discussed in Chapter 5 affect product decisions. Culture reflects the social, political, and religious heritage of the country, often presenting the hardest variable for any company to try to change. U.S. and European marketers have been accused of equating Japan's modernization with Westernization. More and more universal values certainly are seen, but these are interpreted differently in each country. A good example is symbols.

[19] "Better to Be on the Inside Looking Out," *The Economist,* December 24, 1988, 96–98.

FIGURE 9.4   ▪   **Diet Coke Marketed as Coke Light in Japan**

Had the woman in Unilever's Surf detergent commercial in India not worn a "mangalsutra" necklace many would have taken her white sari as a sign that she was a widow. Because "yellow" in Thai means "pus," Coca-Cola shortened the product name from Mello Yellow to simply Mello when it was introduced in Thailand in 1983. The international slogan, "world's fastest soft drink," was replaced by "smooth through the throat and refreshing."[20] A correct interpretation of a culture in terms of language, religion, aesthetics, values and attitudes, and education require help from people experienced in the particular market area.

The influence of culture is especially of concern where society may restrict the purchase of the product or when the product or one of its features may be subject to a stigma. Uncle Ben's, Australia's foremost producer of pet foods, produces pork-free pet products for Muslim markets. A symbol in packaging may seem fully appropriate in one culture, yet be an insult elsewhere. Dogs, for example, were alleged to have eaten one of Mohammed's regiments and therefore are considered signs of bad luck and uncleanliness in parts of North Africa. An American cologne manufacturer discovered this after launching a product featuring a man and his dog in a rural setting.

Another primary cultural consideration is the perception of numbers. In the West, 7 is considered lucky, while 13 is regarded as the opposite. In Japan, however, the ideogram for the number 4 can also be read as "death." Therefore, consumer goods shipped to Japan in packages of four have experienced limited sales. On the other hand, 3 and 5 are considered luckier numbers.[21]

Economic Development

Management must take into account the present stage of economic development of the overseas market. As a country's economy advances, buyers are in a better position to buy and to demand more sophisticated products and product versions. With broad country considerations in mind, the firm can determine potentials for selling certain kinds of products and services. In some cases, the situation in a developing market may require **backward innovation;** that is, the market may require a drastically simplified version of the firm's product due to lack of purchasing power or usage conditions.

Economic conditions will affect packaging in terms of size and units sold in a package. In developing markets products such as cigarettes and razor blades are often sold by the piece rather than packaged so that consumers with limited incomes can afford them. Soft-drink companies have introduced four-can packs in Europe, where cans are sold singly, even in large stores. On the other hand, products oriented to families, such as food

---

[20]"One Mello, Please," *Advertising Age*, August 1, 1983, 26.

[21]Nancy Hollander, "Judging a Book by Its Cover," *Export Today* 4 (July–August 1988): 47–49.

products, appear in larger sizes in developing markets. Pillsbury packages its products in six- and eight-serving sizes for developing country markets whereas the most popular size in the North American market is for two.[22]

Competitive Offerings

The monitoring of competitors' product features, as well as determining what has to be done to meet and beat them, is critical. Competitive offerings may provide a baseline against which the firm's resources can be measured—for example, what it takes to reach a critical market share in a given competitive situation. An analysis of competitors' offerings may reveal holes in the market or suggest staying away from certain market segments, as illustrated in The International Marketplace 9.3. American Hospital Supply, a Chicago-based producer of medical equipment, adjusts its product in a preemptive way by making products that are hard to duplicate. As a result, the firm achieved increases of about 40 percent per year in sales and earnings in Japan over a ten-year period.[23] The products are so specialized that it would be hard for Japanese firms to duplicate them on a mass-production basis.

In many markets, the international marketer is competing with local manufacturers and must overcome traditional purchasing relationships and the certainty they provide. Companies like BBN, a marketer of highly interactive data processing equipment and support services, is facing with its $30 million in export sales giants such as Siemens and Philips. BBN must prove not only that its products are competitive in price and quality but also that the company will honor its commitments and provide any necessary after-sales service. However, by concentrating on one area alone, and targeting carefully, BBN can invest far more resources and stay ahead of its competition.[24]

Climate and Geography

Climate and geography will usually have an effect on the total product offering: the core product, tangible elements, mainly packaging, and the augmented features. The international marketer must consider two sometimes contradictory aspects of packaging for the international market. On the one hand, the product itself has to be protected against longer transit times and possibly for longer shelf life; on the other hand, care has to be taken that no nonallowed preservatives are used. One firm experienced this problem when it tried to sell Colombian guava paste in the United States. Because the packaging could not withstand the longer distribution

[22] John S. Hill and Richard R. Still, "Adapting Products to LDC Tastes," *Harvard Business Review* 62 (March–April 1984): 92–101.

[23] "Why Some U.S. Companies Crack Japan's Market," *Business Week*, August 29, 1983, 33–34.

[24] "Divide and Conquer," *Export Today* 5 (February 1989): 10.

9.3 THE INTERNATIONAL MARKETPLACE

How Foreign Markets Saved the 737 *The Boeing 737 was introduced in the late 1960s to compete with McDonnell Douglas's
DC-9. Sales did not meet expectations and Boeing was on the verge
of killing the program. The DC-9 was in some respects a superior
plane—a little faster, for one thing—and it had been introduced
three years before the 737.*

*Giving it one last chance, the company engineers and marketers
looked at underdeveloped parts of the world—mainly the Middle
East, Africa, and South America, where they figured competitive
clashes between airframe manufacturers to occur. It was not to be
an immediate sales bonanza, but rather an effort to build a customer base for the long term.*

*Boeing needed to adapt the plane to the idiosyncracies of Third
World aviation. First of all, the runways in developing countries
were too short to accommodate the jet, and too soft, made of as-
phalt rather than concrete. Boeing's engineers redesigned the wings
to allow for shorter landings and added thrust to the engines for
quicker takeoffs. In studying the pilots, Boeing found that "they
tended to come in hard when they landed, and when the plane
bounces up in the air, the brakes cannot work. So they run out of
runway." Boeing redesigned the landing gear and installed low-
pressure tires so the plane would stick to the ground when it
touched down. "You can crash a 737, but you cannot bounce it,"
say Boeing representatives with pride.*

*Boeing's gamble worked. In addition to selling enough 737s
throughout the developing world to keep production rates at reasonable levels, the plane built its reputation around the world.
Many of the adaptations made for particular regions of the world
met with approval elsewhere as well. Recently, the 737 became the
best-selling commercial jet in history.*

Source: Andrew Kupfer, "How to Be a Global Manager," *Fortune*, March 14, 1988,
24–27.

channels and the longer time required for distribution, the product arrived in stores in poor condition and was promptly taken off the shelves.

PRODUCT CHARACTERISTICS

Product characteristics are the inherent features of the product offering,
whether actual or perceived. The inherent characteristics of products, and
the benefits they provide to consumers in the various markets in which
they are marketed, make certain products good candidates for standardization, others not. Figure 9.5 summarizes product characteristics most often

FIGURE 9.5 ▪ **Product Characteristics Affecting the Adaptation Decision**

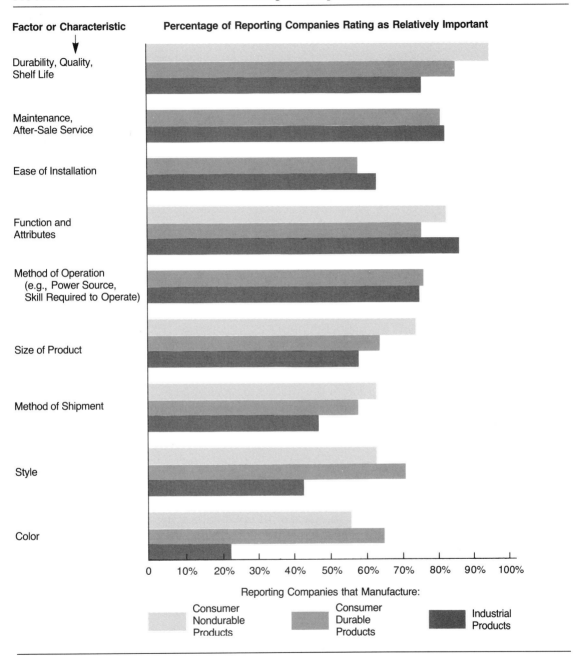

Source: V. Yorio, *Adapting Products for Export* (New York: The Conference Board, 1983), 13.
Reprinted with permission.

reported to be potentially important in management's evaluation of export adaptation requirements. Consumer nondurables, such as food products, show generally the highest amount of sensitivity given differences in national tastes and habits. Consumer durables, such as cameras and home electronics, are subject to far more homogeneous demand and more predictable adjustment (for example, adjustment to a different technical system in television sets and videotape recorders). Industrial products tend to be more shielded from cultural influences. However, substantial modifications may sometimes be required—in the telecommunications industry, for example—as a result of government regulations and restraints.

The influence of the various market factors on product features varies dramatically by type and by impact.

Product Constituents

The international marketer must make sure products do not contain ingredients that might be in violation of legal requirements or religious or social customs. As an example, DEP Corporation, a Los Angeles manufacturer with $19 million annual sales of hair and skin products, takes particular pains to make sure that no Japan-bound products contain formaldehyde—an ingredient commonly used in the United States but illegal in Japan. To ensure the purity of the Japanese batches, the chemical vats are repeatedly cleaned and sterilized, all ingredients checked for traces of formaldehyde, and the finished product checked before shipment.[25] When religion or custom determines consumption, ingredients may have to be replaced in order for the product to be acceptable. In Islamic countries, for example, animal fats have to be replaced by ingredients such as vegetable shortening.

Branding

Brand names convey the image of the product or service. The term brand refers to a name, term, symbol, sign, or design used by a firm to differentiate its offerings from those of its competitors. Brands are one of the most standardizable items in the product offering; they may allow further standardization of other marketing elements such as promotional items. Figure 9.6 presents a collection of some of the best-known brand names. The brand name is the vocalizable part of the brand, brand mark the nonvocalizable part (for example, Camel's "camel"). The brand mark may become invaluable when the product itself cannot be promoted but the symbol can be used. As an example, Marlboro cannot be advertised in most European countries because of legal restrictions on cigarette advertising; however, Philip Morris features advertisements showing only the Marlboro cowboy, who is known throughout the world. Unfortunately, most

[25] Joel Kotkin, "Going Through Customs," *Inc.*, December 1984, 180–184.

FIGURE 9.6   ▪   **Examples of World Brand and Trade Names**

Source: "If You're an Advertiser Who's Decided to Take on the World," *Advertising Age*, June 25, 1984, 51–54.

brands do not have such recognition. The term trademark refers to the legally protected part of the brand, indicated by the symbol ®. Increasingly, international marketers have found their trademarks violated by counterfeiters who are illegally using or abusing the brand name of the marketer.

The international marketer has a number of options in choosing a branding strategy. The marketer may choose to be a contract manufacturer to a distributor (the generics approach) or to establish national, regional, or worldwide brands. The international diffusion of U.S. brands, for example, is quite limited. Except for certain **global brands,** the majority of U.S. brands achieve roughly four-fifths of their sales in the domestic market.[26] The use of standardization in branding is strongest in culturally similar markets; for example, for U.S. marketers, Canada and the United Kingdom. Standardization of product and brand do not necessarily move

[26]Barry N. Rosen, J. J. Boddewyn, and Ernst A. Louis, "U.S. Brands Abroad: An Empirical Study of Global Branding," *International Marketing Review* 6 (Spring 1989): 7–19.

hand in hand; a regional brand may well have local features or a highly standardized product may have local brand names.[27]

The establishment of worldwide brands is difficult; how can a consumer marketer establish world brands when it sells 800 products in more than 200 countries, and most of them under different names? This is Gillette's situation. A typical example is Silkience hair conditioner, which is sold as Soyance in France, Sientel in Italy, and Silkience in Germany. Gillette has announced, however, a massive standardization program of brand names, packaging, and advertising.[28] Many consumer-product companies are engaging in similar moves in preparation for 1992. For example, Johnson & Johnson's rollout of Silhouette feminine hygiene products in 1989 was the first time the company had approached Europe as a single market, rather than as a collection of distinct countries.[29] Standardizing names to reap promotional benefits is difficult because names are established in each market and the action raises objections from local managers.

The psychological power of brands is enormous. Surveys of American consumer goods have shown the number-one brand in a product category to be earning a 20 percent return, the number-two brand around 5 percent, and the rest are losing money.[30] Brand loyalty translates into profits despite the fact that favored brands may not be superior by any tangible measure. New brands may be very difficult and expensive to build, and as a result the company may seek a tie-in with something that the customer feels positively toward. For instance, a small Hong Kong-based company markets a product line called American No. 1. This is because the market prefers U.S. products.

Brand names often do not travel well. Semantic variations can hinder a firm's product overseas. Even the company name or the trade name should be checked out. For instance, when Pet Inc. tried to expand into French Canadian markets, the name had to be changed because the word "pet" in French is a vulgarism. Parker Bros. is known as Parker outside the United States because of translation problems with "Bros." Most problems associated with brands are not as severe, but require attention nevertheless. To avoid problems with brand names in foreign markets, NameLab, a California-based name development and testing laboratory, suggests these approaches:

1. Translation. Little Pen Inc. would become La Petite Plume, S.A., for example.
2. Transliteration. This requires the testing of an existing brand name for connotative meaning in the language of the intended market. Flic

[27] J. J. Boddewyn, Robin Soehl, and Jacques Picard, "Standardization in International Marketing: Is Ted Levitt in Fact Right?" *Business Horizons* 29 (November–December 1986): 69–75.

[28] Dean M. Peebles, "Don't Write Off Global Advertising: A Commentary," *International Marketing Review* 6 (Spring 1989): 73–78.

[29] "1992: Europe Becomes One," *Advertising Age*, July 11, 1988, 46.

[30] "The Year of the Brand," *The Economist*, December 24, 1988, 95–96.

Pen Corporation, for example, would be perceived in France as a manufacturer of writing instruments for the police, because the slang term "flic" connotes something between "cop" and "pig."

3. Transparency. This can be used to develop a new, essentially meaningless brand name to minimize trademark complexities, transliteration problems, and translation complexities. (Sony is an example.)

4. Transculture. This would mean using a foreign language name for a brand.[31] Vodkas, regardless of where they originate, should have Russian-sounding names or at least Russian lettering, whereas perfumes should sound French.

Brands are powerful marketing tools; for example, the chemicals and natural ingredients in one popular perfume now retailing for $140 an ounce may be worth less than $3.[32]

Firms must also be aware of trademark registration requirements in foreign countries. Under U.S. law, based on English common law, rights to a trademark are created and maintained through use; registration of the trademark is an added protection. In some other countries, such as in Europe, the law is based on the Roman civil code and trademarks are generally awarded to the first one that registers. The trademark must be protected by registering it in any market where there is even a remote chance of using it. This calls for constant vigilance, which McDonald's found out in Latin America. McDonald's trademark was registered at the Venezuelan development ministry. The registration expired, and before anything could be done a Mr. McDonald locked up the name in Valencia and Maracaibo, two of the country's largest cities, for his fast food outlets featuring a plastic cup with drinking straws arched like the U.S. logo and an ad slogan that reads "Millions and millions will be served."[33]

In some markets brand name changes are required by the government. In Korea, unnecessary foreign words are barred from use; for example, "Sprite" has been renamed as "Kin." The same situation has emerged in Mexico, where the reasoning for local branding is primarily to control foreign companies in terms of the marketing leverage they would have with a universal brand.

Packaging

Packaging serves three major functions: protection, promotion, and user convenience. The major consideration for the international marketer is making sure the product reaches the ultimate user in the form intended. Packaging will vary as a function of transportation mode, transit condi-

---

[31]"How Names Work," *NameLab* (San Francisco: NameLab, 1981), 3–4.

[32]"What Lies Behind the Sweet Smell of Success," *Business Week*, February 27, 1984, 139–140.

[33]"Will the Real Big Mac Please Stand Up?" *Advertising Age*, August 22, 1983, 34.

tions, and length of time in transit. Because of the longer time that products spend in channels of distribution, firms in the international marketplace, especially those exporting food products, have had to use more expensive packaging materials and/or more expensive transportation modes. The solution of food processors has been to utilize airtight, reclosable containers that reject moisture and other contaminants.

Pilferage is a problem in a number of markets and has forced companies to use only shipping codes in outside packaging. With larger shipments, containerization has helped alleviate the theft problem. An exporter should anticipate inadequate, careless, or primitive loading methods. The labels and loading instructions should be not only in English but also in the market's language as well as in symbols.

The promotional aspect of packaging relates mostly to labeling. The major adjustments concern legally required bilinguality, as in the case of Canada (French and English), Belgium (French and Flemish), and Finland (Finnish and Swedish). Other governmental requirements include more informative labeling on products, as described in The International Marketplace 9.4. Inadequate identification, failure to use the needed languages, or inadequate or incorrect descriptions printed on the labels may cause problems. If in doubt, a company should study foreign competitors' labels.

Incorrect labeling can be serious, as Coca-Cola found in 1977 when trying to extend the U.S. product to the Italian market. Its whole operation was brought to a standstill by a judicial order. *The New York Times* reported: "A judge in Genoa ordered the nationwide seizure of all bottled Coca-Cola on the ground that its ingredients were not properly labeled. The Magistrate, Mario Sossi, also banned any further distribution or production of bottled Coca-Cola, a $120 million-a-year business in Italy."[34] The ruling did not apply to canned Coca-Cola, which does list the ingredients. The company claimed the ingredients for the bottled product were listed on the bottle cap; the judge felt the description did not meet Italy's label laws.

Package aesthetics must be a consideration in terms of the promotional role of packaging. This mainly involves the prudent choice of colors and package shapes. African nations, for example, often prefer bold colors, but flag colors may be alternately preferred or disallowed. Red is often associated with death or witchcraft. Color in packaging may be faddish. White is losing popularity in industrialized countries because name brands do not want to be confused with generic products. Black, on the other hand, is increasingly popular, and is now used to suggest quality, excellence, and "class." Package shapes can be selected for promotional as well as handling and storage reasons, but marketers should also recognize reuse and waste as considerations.

Package size varies according to purchasing patterns and market conditions. For instance, a six-pack format for soft drinks may not be fea-

---

[34]"Coca-Cola Brought to a Standstill in Italy," *New York Times*, November 16, 1977, 32.

THE INTERNATIONAL MARKETPLACE 9.4

Tobacco Companies Face Special International Packaging Obstacles *R.J. Reynolds Tobacco Company of Winston-Salem, North Carolina, exports 16 billion cigarettes to 160 countries and territories each year. In addition to packaging variations caused by different brand styles, requirements of foreign governments force the company to produce more than 250 different packages for Winston cigarettes, its biggest selling brand worldwide. Only about 15 Winston package variations were in use in the mid-1960s and 50 variations in the mid-1970s. One reason for the increase is that the company has grown and exports to more countries, but most of the complexity has come about because of the large increase in governmental health warnings and local duty and excise tax regulations. For instance, when the Ethiopian Tobacco Monopoly places an order for 7,500 cases of Winstons, the company has to imprint the name Ethiopia on the paper used for those cigarettes. A special closure seal also must be applied to every pack. The closure indicates the retail price in Ethiopian currency.*

Almost all export packaging is printed in Winston-Salem. To prevent typesetting errors when working with Greek, Arabic, Japanese, and other languages, someone in the foreign country prepares a precise, handmade replica of the new or revised package. Altogether the company has more than 1,400 different product codes in order to cover all brands in all of the markets.

Source: "Tobacco Companies Face Special International Packaging Obstacles," *Marketing News*, February 24, 1984, 20.

sible in certain markets because of the lack of refrigeration capacity in households. Quite often, consumers overseas with modest or low discretionary purchasing power buy smaller sizes or even single units (such as cigarettes) in order to stretch a limited budget. As a result, the smaller size or unit may sell for more per gram or ounce than the respective U.S. economy size, which has caused concern among supranational organizations and consumer groups monitoring the marketing activities of foreign firms.

Marketers are wise to monitor packaging technology developments in the world marketplace. One of the major innovations of the 1980s was in aseptic containers for fruit drinks and milk. Tetra Pak International, the $1.5 billion Swedish company, converted 40 percent of milk sales in Western Europe to its aseptic packaging system, which keeps perishables fresh for five months without refrigeration. The company claimed 5 percent of the fruit juice packaging market and 20 percent of the fruit drink market in the United States.

Appearance

Adaptations in product styling, color, size, and other appearance features are more common in consumer marketing than in industrial marketing. Color plays an important role in how consumers perceive a product, and marketers must be aware of the signal being sent by the product's color. Color can be used for brand identification—for example, the yellow of Hertz, red of Avis, and green of National. It can be used for feature reinforcement; for example, Honda adopted the color black to give its motorcycles a Darth Vader look, whereas Rolls Royce uses a dazzling silver paint that spells luxury. Colors communicate in a subtle way in developed societies; they have direct meaning in more traditional societies. For instance, in the late 1950s, when Pepsi Cola changed the color of its coolers and vending machines from deep regal blue to light ice blue, the result was catastrophic in Southeast Asia. Pepsi had a dominant market share, which it lost to Coca-Cola, because light blue is associated with death and mourning in that part of the world. The only way companies can protect themselves against incidents of this kind is through thorough on-site testing.

Product Uses

The international marketer should be open to ideas for new uses for the product being offered. New uses may substantially expand the market potential of the product. For example, Turbo Tek Inc., which produces a hose attachment for washing cars, has found that foreign customers have expanded the product's functions. In Japan, TurboWash is used for cleaning bamboo, while the Dutch use it to wash windows, plants, and the sidings of their houses.[35]

Method of Operation

The product as it is offered in the domestic market may not be operable in the foreign market. One of the major differences faced by appliance manufacturers is electrical power systems. In some cases, variations may exist within a country, such as Brazil. An exporter can learn about these differences through local government representatives or various trade publications such as the U.S. Department of Commerce publication, *Electric Current Abroad.* However, exporters should determine for themselves the adjustments that are required by observing competitive products or having their product tested by a local entity.

Many complicating factors may be eliminated in the future through standardization efforts by international organizations and by the conversion of most countries to the metric system. Some companies have ad-

---

[35] "Awash in Export Sales," *Export Today* 5 (February 1989): 11.

justed their products to operate in different systems; for example, Japanese VCR equipment will record and play back on different color systems.

The most blatant blunders in international marketing are usually the result of exporters' failure to adjust their products to local systems. But different operating systems and environments can also provide opportunities. When Canada adopted the metric system in 1977 to 1978, many U.S. companies were affected. Perfect Measuring Tape Company in Toledo, for example, had to convert to metric if it wanted to continue selling disposable paper measuring tape to textile firms in Canada. Once the conversion had been made, the company found an entire world of untapped markets. It was soon shipping nearly 30 percent of its tape to overseas markets as disparate as Australia and Zimbabwe.[36]

Quality

Many Western exporters must emphasize quality in their strategies, because they cannot compete on price alone. Many new exporters compete on value in the particular segments in which they have chosen to compete. In some cases, producers of cheaper Asian products have forced international marketers to reexamine their strategies, allowing them to win contracts on the basis of technical advantage. To maintain a position of product superiority, exporting firms must invest in research and development for new products as well as manufacturing methods. For example, Sargent and Burton, a small Australian producer of high-technology racing boats with only 18 employees, invested in CAD/CAM technology to develop state-of-the-art racing boats that have proven successful in international competition against sophisticated overseas entries.[37]

An important aspect of improving quality is an emphasis on design. Some countries, such as Singapore and Taiwan, provide financial assistance to help companies improve product design. Some of the programs are directed toward companies in the form of cash grants to help defer design costs, while some are publicity oriented to increase overall design consciousness.[38]

Some products have fared well in the international marketplace because of their durability, this despite negative features, such as **country-of-origin effects.** For example, Russian-made Belarus tractors have fared well in the West not only because of their reasonable price tag but also because of their ruggedness. Similarly, the Russian-made automatic rifle, AK-47, is the most used weapon in the world partly because of its reliability.

---

[36] "Made in the U.S.A.," *Business Week*, February 29, 1988, 60–66.

[37] Ian Wilkinson and Nigel Barrett, "In Search of Excellence in Exports: An Analysis of the 1986 Australian Export Award Winners," paper given at the Australian Export Award presentations, Sydney, November 28, 1986.

[38] John S. Blyth, "Other Countries Lead U.S. in Supporting Design Efforts," *Marketing News*, February 13, 1989, 14–15.

Service

When a product sold overseas requires repairs, parts, or service, the problem of obtaining, training, and holding a sophisticated engineering or repair staff is not easy. If the product breaks down, and the repair arrangements are not up to standard, the image of the product will suffer. In some cases, products abroad may not even be used for their intended purpose, and may thus require not only modifications in product configuration but also in service frequency. For instance, snow plows exported from the United States are used to remove sand from driveways in Saudi Arabia. Closely related to servicing is the issue of product warranties. Warranties are not only instructions to customers about what to do if the product fails within a specified period of time but also effective promotional tools.

Country-of-Origin Effects

The country of origin of a product, typically communicated by the phrase "made in (country)," has a considerable influence on the quality perceptions of a product. The manufacture of products in certain countries is affected by a built-in positive or negative stereotype on the perception of product quality. One study of machine-tool buyers found that the United States and West Germany were rated higher than Japan, with Brazil being rated below all three.[39] These types of findings indicate that steps must be taken by the international marketer to overcome or at least neutralize biases. This issue may be especially important to developing countries, which need to increase exports, and for importers who source products from countries different from where they are sold.[40]

Country-of-origin effects have been characterized as minor as customers become more informed. Also, as more countries develop the necessary bases to manufacture products, the origin of the products becomes less important. This can already be seen with so-called hybrid products (for example, a U.S. multinational manufacturing the product in Malaysia). The argument has been made that with the advent of more economic integration, national borders become less important.[41]

COMPANY CONSIDERATIONS

Before launching a product in the international marketplace, the marketer needs to consider organizational capabilities in addition to the nature of the product and the level of adaptation needed to acommodate various market-related differences between domestic and international markets.

[39]Phillip D. White and Edward W. Cundiff, "Assessing the Quality of Industrial Products," *Journal of Marketing* 42 (January 1978): 80–86.

[40]Warren J. Bilkey and Erik Nes, "Country-of-Origin Effects on Product Evaluations," *Journal of International Business Studies* 13 (Spring–Summer 1982): 89–99.

[41]Johny K. Johansson, "Determinants and Effects of the Use of 'Made in' Labels," *International Marketing Review* 6 (1989): 47–58.

THE INTERNATIONAL MARKETPLACE ▐9.5▌

The Sound of Success   *Infinity Inc. is a manufacturer of high-end audio component loudspeakers employing 120 people. Infinity has taken a global approach to its export operations and has made it the top priority for the company. Exports account for 25 percent of the company's present sales, having grown at a 50 percent rate in the late 1980s.*

Infinity's strategy is to design products that will have global appeal and then cultivate a niche in every market possible, incorporating state-of-the-art technology in all products, and then move from upscale, higher priced markets to more mass appeal, lower priced markets. "We try to take the technology that was developed for the most expensive speakers and then put it into our lowest priced product. Generally it takes a couple of years."

This approach requires that the company make few modifications from one market to another—a big cost savings on product development as the company expands its global sales base. Although it may save the company costs in launching into new markets, the money is spent elsewhere in overall product development, however. "We use the cutting edge of technology in all of our products. The first thing the buyer has to know is that we stand for quality in every sense of the word."

The company's goal is to reach a 50–50 split between domestic and international sales. And although the best markets are West Germany and Southeast Asia, the company is doing well in its toughest market—Japan. Lately the company's American image is beginning to pay off. "In the last two years 'Made in the USA' has become magic again."

It would certainly be unfair to attribute too much of Infinity's success to its American image. In Japan, where competition for audio products is intense, there are no mercy buys—quality and performance are the real measuring sticks.

Source: "America: The Export Edge," *Export Today*, February 1989, 13.

The question of product adaptation most often climaxes in the question, "Is it worth it?" The answer depends on the firm's ability to control costs, correctly estimate market potential and, finally, secure profitability. However, the question that used to be posed as "Can we afford to do it?" should now be "Can we afford not to do it?"

The decision to adapt should be preceded by a thorough analysis of the market. Formal market research with primary data collection and/or testing is warranted. From the financial standpoint, some firms have specific return-on-investment levels to be satisfied before adaptation (for instance, 25 percent), while some let the requirement vary as a function of the market considered and also the time in the market—that is, profitability may be initially compromised for proper market entry.

Most companies aim for consistency in their marketing efforts. This translates into the requirement that all products fit in terms of quality, price, and user perceptions. An example of where consistency may be difficult to exercise is in the area of warranties. Warranties can be uniform only if the use conditions do not vary drastically and if the company is able to deliver equally on its promise anywhere it has a presence.

A critical element of the adaptation decision has to be human resources, that is, individuals to make the appropriate decisions. Individuals are needed who are willing to make risky decisions and who know about existing market conditions. The strategy of one medium-sized company with a goal of achieving a 50–50 split between domestic and international sales is described in The International Marketplace 9.5. A characteristic of the American export boom in the late 1980s was that foreigners and recent immigrants were often the first to see overseas opportunities. Foreign-born managers may look for goods that many native Americans overlook or consider too difficult for the international marketplace.[42]

SUMMARY

The international marketer must pay careful attention to variables that may call for an adaptation in the product offering. The target market will influence the adaptation decision through factors such as government regulation and customer preferences and expectations. The product itself may not be in a form ready for international market entry in terms of its brand name, its packaging, or its appearance. Some marketers make a conscious decision to offer only standardized products; some adjust their offerings by market.

Like the soft-drink and cigarette marketers that have led the way, the newest marketers of world brands are not producing necessarily identical products, but recognizable products. As an example, the success of McDonald's in the world marketplace has been based on variation, not offering the same product worldwide.[43] Had it not been for the variations, its only customers overseas would have been American tourists.

Firms entering or participating in the international marketplace will certainly find it difficult to cope with the conflicting needs of the domestic and international markets. They will be certain to ask whether adjustments in their product offerings, if the marketplace requires them, are worthwhile. There are, unfortunately, no magic formulas for addressing the problem of product adaptation. The answer seems to lie in adopting formal procedures to assess products in terms of the markets' and the company's own needs.

---

[42] "The Little Guys Are Making It Big Overseas," *Business Week*, February 27, 1989, 94–96.
[43] "Colleague [Philip Kotler] Says Levitt Wrong," *Advertising Age*, June 25, 1984, 50.

Questions for Discussion

1. Comment on the statement, "It is our policy not to adapt products for export."

2. What are the major problems facing companies, especially smaller ones, in resolving product-adaptation issues?

3. How do governments affect product-design decisions of firms?

4. Is the metric standard required by the U.S. government for imported distilled spirits actually a nontariff barrier?

5. Is any product ever the same everywhere it is sold?

6. Which of these groups of factors—product, market, or company—is the most important influence on product adaptation decisions?

7. Can a company make its products so tough from the beginning that they meet all of the regulations and other key requirements of any market, thus avoiding the discussion on adaptation altogether?

8. Choose three of the questions asked in Table 9.2 and relate them to a particular market. For example, a French shopper will buy meat at a butcher (specialized outlet), an American at a supermarket (broad mixed-merchandise outlet).

Recommended Readings

Johansson, Johny K., and Hans B. Thorelli. "International Product Positioning." *Journal of International Business Studies* 16 (Fall 1985): 57–75.

Kaynak, Erdener. *International Marketing Management.* New York: Praeger Publishers, 1984.

Keegan, Warren J., and Charles S. Mayer. *Multinational Product Management.* Chicago: American Marketing Association, 1977.

Levitt, Theodore. *The Marketing Imagination.* New York: The Free Press, 1986.

Ohmae, Kenishi. *Triad Power: The Coming Shapes of Global Competition.* New York: The Free Press, 1985.

Ries, Al, and Jack Trout. *Positioning: A Battle for Your Mind.* New York: McGraw-Hill, 1981.

Urban, Glen L., and John Hauser. *Design and Marketing of New Products.* Englewood Cliffs, N.J.: Prentice-Hall, 1980.

CHAPTER 10

Export Pricing Strategies

10.1 THE INTERNATIONAL MARKETPLACE

The Squeeze Is On *From champagne, cookies, and cheeses to sports cars and jetliners, exporters to the United States are responding to the lower value of the dollar by sacrificing profits to hold onto their market share. Since the dollar peaked in February 1985, foreign currencies have climbed nearly 70 percent in value. Although the least painful approach in the short term would be to pass through the currency swing to prices, foreign manufacturers decided to protect their hard-won market share in the U.S. and let profit margins sink.*

British construction equipment maker J. C. Bamford Excavators Ltd., which sells 20 percent of its output to the United States, has kept American price hikes to a minimum despite the pound's 40 percent rise since 1985. "Our competitors all produce locally," said Chief Executive Gilbert Johnston, "we cannot increase our prices." Some companies have been able to do this because of the "beachhead effect." These companies spent heavily to establish sales and distribution networks in the United States between 1980 and 1985, and all those early investments have enabled them to take slimmer profits now.

Not all are in a similar position. Arms and aerospace manufacturers, for example, are in a nosedive. French fighter manufacturer Avions Marcel Dassault-Breguet saw profits plunge more than 90 percent in 1987 as overseas orders nearly dried up. And British Aerospace PLC, running up mounting deficits on sales of commercial jet aircraft and wings for the European-built Airbus, set aside $350 million to cover anticipated foreign-exchange losses. An official said, "We simply cannot go to the customer every time the dollar moves down and say we are going to put our prices up by 20 percent."

Those who raise prices know that all too well. Since the dollar peaked in early 1985, Sweden's Saab-Scania group has boosted the American price of the Saab 9000 Turbo sedan by 31 percent. With prices up, Saab's U.S. car sales slipped 6.3 percent in 1987. As wineries from California, Chile, and Australia battle French producers, sales to the U.S. are collapsing, according to Parisian wine brokers. In Italy, some 150 shoe manufacturers have already been forced out of business after a drop of more than 40 percent in U.S. sales since 1985.

Some companies are looking for sales in other markets. German automakers Daimler-Benz and BMW are expecting sharp rises in sales to Japan. The West German mark's value has changed little against the yen since 1985, and the market has become more attractive with increased affluence and fewer trade barriers.

Source: "The Dollar Is Casting a Widening Pall over Europe," *Business Week*, February 8, 1988, 42–43; "Made in the U.S.A.," *Business Week*, February 29, 1988, 60–62; and "Will We Ever Close the Trade Gap?" *Business Week*, February 27, 1989, 86–92.

This chapter will focus on the pricing decision from the exporter's point of view: the setting of export price, terms of sale, and terms of payment. The setting of price is complicated by such factors as duties and intermediary margins. Two special considerations in export pricing—leasing and dumping—are discussed at the end of this chapter. Chapter 17 will cover foreign-market pricing (by subsidiaries) and intracompany transfer pricing; that is, pricing for transactions between corporate entities.

PRICE DYNAMICS

Price is the only element of the marketing mix that is revenue generating; all of the others are costs. It should therefore be used as an active instrument of strategy in the major areas of marketing decision making. Price serves as a means of communication with the buyer by providing a basis for judging the attractiveness of the offer. Price is a major competitive tool in meeting and beating close rivals and substitutes. Competition will often force prices down, whereas intracompany financial considerations have an opposite effect. Prices, along with costs, will determine the long-term viability of the enterprise.

Price should not be determined in isolation from the other marketing mix elements. Price may be used effectively in positioning of the product in the marketplace—for example, Perrier as a premium entry in the United States. It may be a major determinant in how the product is to be distributed. The feasibility range for price setting established by demand, competition, costs, and legal considerations may be narrow or wide in a given situation (for example, the pricing of a commodity versus an innovation). Regardless of how narrow the gap allowed by these factors, however, pricing should never be considered a static element.

A summary of international pricing situations is provided as a matrix in Figure 10.1. Pricing problems—such as pricing for a new market entry, changing price either as an attack strategy or in response to competitive

FIGURE 10.1 ▪ **International Pricing Situations**

Pricing Situation	International Involvement		
	Exporting	Foreign-Market Pricing	Intracompany Pricing
First-Time Pricing			
Changing Pricing			
Multiple-Product Pricing			

Source: Adapted from Helmut Becker, "Pricing: An International Marketing Challenge," in *International Marketing Strategy*, eds. Hans Thorelli and Helmut Becker (New York: Pergamon Press, 1980), 207. Adapted with permission.

changes, and multiple-product coordination in cases of related demand—are technically the same as problems encountered in domestic markets. The scope of these pricing situations will vary according to the degree of foreign involvement and the type of market encountered.

In first-time pricing, the general alternatives are (1) skimming, (2) following the market price, and (3) penetration pricing. The objective of **skimming** is to achieve the highest possible contribution in a short time period. For an exporter to use this approach, the product has to be unique and some segments of the market must be willing to pay the high price. As more segments are targeted and more of the product is made available, the price is gradually lowered. The success of skimming depends on the ability and speed of competitive reaction.

If similar products already exist in the target market, **market pricing** can be used. The final customer price is determined based on competitive prices, and then both production and marketing must be adjusted to the price. This approach requires the exporter to have a thorough knowledge of product costs and confidence that the product life cycle is long enough to warrant entry into the market. It is a reactive approach and may lead to problems if sales volumes never rise to sufficient levels to produce a satisfactory return. Although firms typically use pricing as a differentiation tool, the international marketing manager may have no choice but to accept the prevailing world-market price.

When **penetration pricing** is used, the product is offered at a low price intended to generate volume sales and achieve high market share, which would compensate for a lower per-unit return. This approach requires mass markets, price-sensitive customers, and decreasing production and marketing costs as sales volumes increase. The basic assumption of penetration pricing is that the lower price will increase sales, which may not always be the case.

Price changes are called for when a new product is launched, when a change occurs in overall market conditions (such as a change in the value of the billing currency), or when there is a change in the exporter's internal situation, such as costs of production. As seen in The International Marketplace 10.1, an exporter may elect not to change price even though the result may be lower profitability. However, if a decision is made to change prices, related changes must also be considered. For example, if an increase in price is required, it may at least initially be accompanied by increased promotional efforts. Price changes usually follow changes in the product's stage in the life cycle. As the product matures, more pressure will be put on the price to keep the product competitive despite increased competition and less possibility of differentiation.

With multiple-product pricing, the various items in the line may be differentiated by pricing them appropriately to indicate, for example, an economy version, a standard version, and the top-of-the-line version. One of the products in the line may be priced to protect against competitors or to gain market share from existing competitors. The other items in the line are then expected to make up for the lost contribution of such a "fighting brand."

Although foreign-market pricing and intracompany pricing are discussed later in conjunction with multinational pricing challenges, they do have an impact on the exporter as well. For example, distributors in a particular market may want to keep their profit margins up. This means that the exporter will have to lower prices to the distributor and take less profit to ensure sales and to remain competitive.[1] Similarly, the exporter, in providing products to its own sales offices abroad, may have to adjust its transfer prices according to foreign-exchange fluctuations.

THE SETTING OF EXPORT PRICE

The setting of prices in general is summarized in Figure 10.2. As in all marketing decisions, the intended target market will establish the basic premise for pricing. Factors to be considered include the importance of price in customer decision making, the strength of the perceived price-quality relationship, and potential reactions to price manipulations by marketers. Customers' demands will also have to be considered in terms of support required by the intermediary. The marketing mix must be planned to match the characteristics of the target market. Pricing will be a major factor in determining the desired brand image as well as the distribution channels to be used and the level of promotional support required.

Pricing policies follow from the overall objectives of the firm for a particular target market and involve general principles or rules that a firm follows in making pricing decisions. Policies include profit maximization, market share, survival, achieving a certain percentage return on invest-

[1] "Sizing Up the Customers' Needs," Export Today 5 (February 1989): 32–35.

FIGURE 10.2　▪　**Stages in Setting of Prices**

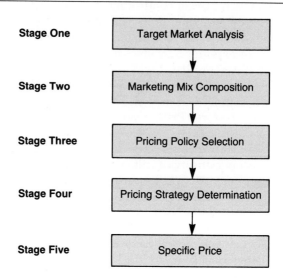

Stage One	Target Market Analysis
Stage Two	Marketing Mix Composition
Stage Three	Pricing Policy Selection
Stage Four	Pricing Strategy Determination
Stage Five	Specific Price

Source: Alfred R. Oxenfeldt, "Multistage Approach to Pricing," *Harvard Business Review* 38 (July–August 1960): 125–133.

ment, and various competitive policies such as copying competitors' prices, following a particular competitor's prices, or pricing in such a way as to discourage competitors from entering the market.[2] For example, an exporter entering a new market may allow wholesalers and retailers above-normal profit margins to encourage maximum sales volume, geographic distribution, and loyalty.

Three Strategies

Three general price-setting strategies in international marketing are a standard worldwide price; dual pricing, which differentiates between domestic and export prices; and market-differentiated pricing.[3] The first two are cost-oriented pricing methods that are relatively simple to establish, easy to understand, and cover all of the necessary costs. The **standard worldwide price** is based on average unit costs of fixed, variable, and export-related costs.

In **dual pricing,** the export price is often based on marginal cost pricing, resulting in a lower export price than domestic price. This method, based

[2]Donald V. Harper and Jack L. Caldwell, "Pricing," in *Marketing Manager's Handbook,* ed. Steuart Henderson Britt and Norman Guess (Chicago: Dartnell, 1983), 723–736.

[3]Richard D. Robinson, *Internationalization of Business: An Introduction* (Hinsdale, Ill.: The Dryden Press, 1984), 49–54.

on incremental costs, considers the direct costs of producing and selling products for export as the floor beneath which prices cannot be set, while other fixed costs (such as basic R&D) are considered to have been recaptured by domestic operations. This may open the firm to dumping charges, because determination of dumping has generally been based on average total costs, which can be considerably higher. Lower export prices are common, especially among Western European companies, which have a heavier tax burden on their domestically sold products than on exported products. The reason is that the value-added tax is refunded for the exported products. Cost-oriented pricing creates some major problems because it (1) is based on arbitrary cost allocations, (2) does not take into consideration highly differing market conditions, and (3) is subject to differing internal conditions with respect to the various markets, such as entry mode and stage of the product's life cycle in the respective markets.

On the other hand, **market-differentiated pricing** is based on a demand-oriented strategy and is thus more consistent with the marketing concept. This method also allows the exporter to consider competitive forces in setting of the export price. The major problem is the exporter's perennial dilemma: lack of information. Therefore, in most cases, marginal costs provide a basis for competitive comparisons, on which the export price is set.

Export-Related Costs

In preparing a quotation, the exporter must be careful to take into account and, if possible, include unique export-related costs. These are in addition to the normal costs shared with the domestic side. They include:

1. The cost of modifying the product for foreign markets (see Chapter 9).
2. Operational costs of the export operation. Examples are personnel, market research, additional shipping and insurance costs, communications costs with foreign customers, and overseas promotional costs.
3. Costs incurred in entering the foreign markets. These include tariffs and taxes; risks associated with a buyer in a different market (mainly commercial credit risks and political risks); and dealing in other than the exporter's domestic currency—that is, foreign exchange risk.

The combined effect of both clear-cut and hidden costs results in export prices far in excess of domestic prices. The cause is termed **price escalation.**

Four different export scenarios are compared with a typical domestic situation in Table 10.1. The first case is relatively simple, adding only the C.I.F. (cost, insurance, freight) and tariff charges. The second adds a foreign importer and thus lengthens the foreign part of the distribution channel. In the third, a **value-added tax (VAT)** is included in the calculations. This is imposed on the full export selling price, which represents the

TABLE 10.1 ▪ **Export-Price Escalation**

International Marketing Channel Elements and Cost Factors	Domestic Wholesale–Retail Channel	Export Market Cases			
		Case 1 Same as Domestic with Direct Wholesale Import C.I.F./Tariff	Case 2 Same as 1 with Foreign Importer Added to Channel	Case 3 Same as 2 with VAT Added	Case 4 Same as 3 with Local Foreign Jobber Added to Channel
Manufacturer's Net Price	6.00	6.00	6.00	6.00	6.00
+ Insurance and Shipping Cost (C.I.F.)	—	2.50	2.50	2.50	2.50
= Landed Cost (C.I.F. value)	—	8.50	8.50	8.50	8.50
+ Tariff (20% on C.I.F. value)	—	1.70	1.70	1.70	1.70
= Importer's Cost (C.I.F. value + tariff)	—	10.20	10.20	10.20	10.20
+ Importer's Margin (25% on cost)	—	—	2.55	2.55	2.55
+ VAT (16% on full cost plus margin)	—	—	—	2.04	2.04
= Wholesaler's Cost (= Importer's Price)	6.00	10.20	12.75	14.79	14.79
+ Wholesaler's Margin (33⅓% on cost)	2.00	3.40	4.25	4.93	4.93
+ VAT (16% on margin)	—	—	—	.79	.79
= Local Foreign Jobber's Cost (= Wholesale Price)	—	—	—	—	20.51
+ Jobber's Margin (33⅓% on cost)	—	—	—	—	6.84
+ VAT (16% on margin)	—	—	—	—	1.09
= Retailer's Cost (= Wholesale or Jobber Price)	8.00	13.60	17.00	20.51	28.44
+ Retailer's Margin (50% on cost)	4.00	6.80	8.50	10.26	14.22
+ VAT (16% on margin)	—	—	—	1.64	2.28
= Retail Price (what consumer pays)	12.00	20.40	25.50	32.41	44.94
Percentage Price Escalation over Domestic		70%	113%	170%	275%
Percentage Price Escalation over Case 1			25%	59%	120%
Percentage Price Escalation over Case 2				27%	76%
Percentage Price Escalation over Case 3					39%

Source: Helmut Becker, "Pricing: An International Marketing Challenge," in *International Marketing Strategy*, eds. Hans Thorelli and Helmut Becker (New York: Pergamon Press, 1980), 215. Reprinted with permission.

"value added" to or introduced into the country from abroad. In Italy, for example, where most food items are taxed at 2 percent, processed meat is taxed at 18 percent because the government wants to use the VAT to help reduce its trade deficit. The fourth case simulates a situation typically found in less-developed countries where distribution channels are longer. Lengthy channels can easily double the landed (C.I.F.) price.

FIGURE 10.3 ▪ **Distribution Adjustment to Decrease Price Escalation**

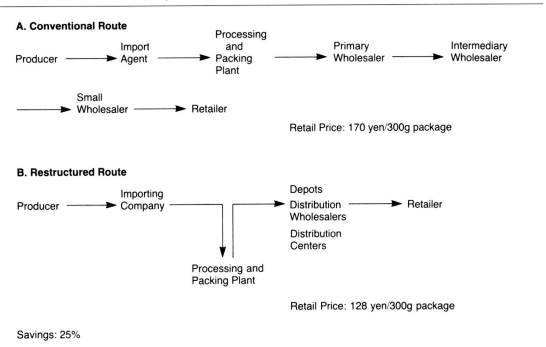

A. Conventional Route

Producer ⟶ Import Agent ⟶ Processing and Packing Plant ⟶ Primary Wholesaler ⟶ Intermediary Wholesaler

⟶ Small Wholesaler ⟶ Retailer

Retail Price: 170 yen/300g package

B. Restructured Route

Producer ⟶ Importing Company ⟶ Depots / Distribution Wholesalers / Distribution Centers ⟶ Retailer

Processing and Packing Plant

Retail Price: 128 yen/300g package

Savings: 25%

Source: Michael R. Czinkota, "Distribution of Consumer Products in Japan: An Overview," *International Marketing Review* 2 (Autumn 1985): 39–51.

Price escalation can be combated through creative strategies such as re-organizing the channel of distribution. The example in Figure 10.3, based on import channels for spaghetti and macaroni in Japan, shows how the flow of merchandise through the various wholesaling levels has been reduced to comprise only a company internal wholesaler distribution center, resulting in savings of 25 percent and increasing the overall potential for imports. Careful planning may also help avoid later surprises in the form of hidden costs. For example, Korelska GmbH of Vienna, a manufacturer of office supplies, found that in selling to the Soviet Union, the company's travel and accommodations costs were three times the costs incurred under similar circumstances in the West.[4] The U.S. Department of Commerce suggests that price quotations should be as complete as possible in describing the product, the price at a specified delivery point, and the terms of payment.[5]

[4]"Developments in Countertrade. VIII. Soviet Union," *Business Eastern Europe*, October 17, 1980, 322–323.

[5]United States Department of Commerce, *A Basic Guide to Exporting* (Washington: International Trade Administration, 1986), 41–44.

FIGURE 10.4 ▪ **Selected Trade Terms**

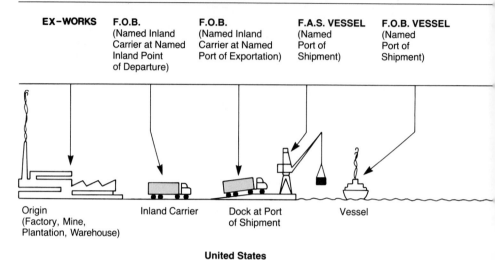

| EX-WORKS | F.O.B. (Named Inland Carrier at Named Inland Point of Departure) | F.O.B. (Named Inland Carrier at Named Port of Exportation) | F.A.S. VESSEL (Named Port of Shipment) | F.O.B. VESSEL (Named Port of Shipment) |

Origin (Factory, Mine, Plantation, Warehouse)   Inland Carrier   Dock at Port of Shipment   Vessel

United States

TERMS OF SALE

The responsibilities of the buyer and the seller should be spelled out as they relate to what is and what is not included in the price quotation. Although the same terms may be used in domestic transactions, they gain new meaning in the international arena. In the U.S. domestic market, it is customary to use F.O.B. (free on board) with a specified place and with payment usually C.O.D. (cash on delivery). However, exporters should use the **C.I.F. (cost, insurance, freight)** quotation, because it gives the would-be importer a clear understanding of costs involved. The most common terms used in international marketing are summarized in Figure 10.4.

Prices quoted **ex-works** (factory, mine, plantation, or warehouse) apply only at the point of origin and the seller agrees to place the goods at the disposal of the buyer at the specified place on the date or within the fixed period. All other charges are for the account of the buyer.

Free alongside ship (F.A.S.) at a named U.S. port of export means that the exporter quotes a price for the goods, including charges for delivery of the goods alongside a vessel at the port. The seller handles the cost of unloading and wharfage; loading, ocean transportation, and insurance are left to the buyer.

Under the term **free on board (F.O.B.)**, the seller quotes a price for the goods, including the cost of loading them into transport vessels at a named point. There are a number of variations of this term, including:

▪ F.O.B. (named inland point). The price quoted applies only at a designated inland shipping point. The seller is responsible for loading goods into the transport vessel; the buyer, for all subsequent expenses.

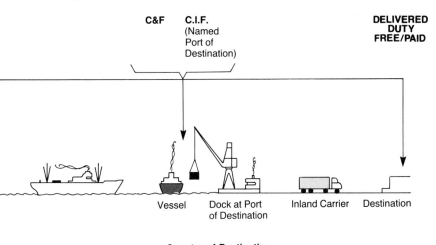

- F.O.B. (named port of exportation) includes the cost of transporting the goods to the named port.
- F.O.B. vessel (named port of shipment). The seller quotes a price covering all expenses up to, and including, delivery of goods upon an overseas vessel provided by or for the buyer.

Under **cost and freight (C&F)** to a named overseas port of import the seller quotes a price for the goods, including the cost of transportation to the named port of debarkation. The cost of insurance and choice of insurer is left to the buyer.

With cost, insurance, and freight (C.I.F.) to a named overseas port of import, the seller quotes a price including insurance, all transportation, and miscellaneous charges to the point of debarkation from vessel or aircraft. Items that may enter into the calculation of the C.I.F. cost are (1) port charges: unloading, wharfage (terminal use) handling, storage, cartage, heavy lift, and demurrage; (2) documentation charges: certification of invoice, certificate of origin, weight certificate, and consular forms; and (3) other charges, such as fees of the freight forwarder, and freight (inland and ocean) insurance premiums (marine, war, credit).

With **delivery duty free/paid,** the seller delivers the goods, import duties paid, including inland transportation from import point to the buyer's premises. Ex-works signifies the maximum obligation for the buyer; delivered duty free/paid puts the maximum burden on the seller.

The careful determination and clear understanding of terms used and their acceptance by the parties involved are vital if subsequent misunderstandings and disputes are to be avoided. The widely accepted trade terms, **INCOTERMS, 1980,** are sponsored by these organizations: American Importers Association, National Association of Councils on International Banking, Chamber of Commerce of the United States, National Committee on International Trade Documentation, National Foreign Trade Council, and U.S. Council of the International Chamber of Commerce. Copies are available from the U.S. Council of the International Chamber of Commerce.[6]

These terms are also powerful competitive tools. The exporter should therefore learn what importers usually prefer in the particular market and what the specific transaction may require. An exporter should quote C.I.F. whenever possible, because it clearly shows the buyer the cost to get the product to a port in or near a desired country.

An inexperienced importer might be discouraged from further action by a quote such as ex-plant Jessup, Maryland, whereas C.I.F. Kotka will enable the Finnish importer to handle the remaining costs because they are incurred at home. The responsibility for keeping track of the shipment until it reaches the destination remains with the exporter. Despite its customer orientation, C.I.F. has its risks in that many of the costs may change, sometimes dramatically, between the quote and the actual time of shipment. Freight forwarders are useful in determining costs and preparing quotations and making sure that unexpected changes do not end up losing money for the exporter. Most exporters do not want to go beyond the C.I.F. quotation because of uncontrollables and unknowns in the destination country.

Freight forwarders are useful to the exporter not only as facilitators and advisors but also in keeping down some of the export-related costs. Rates for freight and insurance provided to freight forwarders may be far more economical than to an individual exporter because of large-volume purchases, especially if export sales are infrequent.

TERMS OF PAYMENT

Export credit and terms add another dimension to the profitability of an export transaction. The exporter has in all likelihood already formulated a credit policy that determines the degree of risk the firm is willing to assume and the preferred selling terms. The main objective is to meet the importer's requirements without jeopardizing the firm's financial goals. The exporter will be concerned over being paid for the goods shipped and will therefore consider the following factors in negotiating terms of payment: (1) the amount of payment and the need for protection, (2) terms offered by competitors, (3) practices in the industry, (4) capacity for financing international transactions, and (5) relative strength of the parties in-

---

[6]Ann Dwyer Maffry, *Foreign Commerce Handbook* (Washington, D.C.: Chamber of Commerce of the United States, 1981), 128–129.

FIGURE 10.5 ▪ **Risk Triangle**

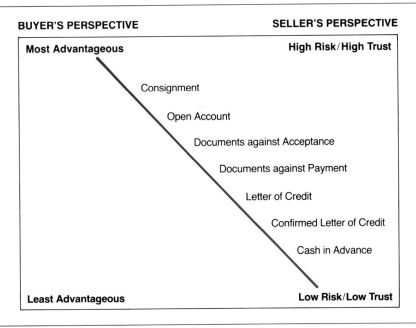

BUYER'S PERSPECTIVE   SELLER'S PERSPECTIVE

Most Advantageous   High Risk/High Trust

Consignment

Open Account

Documents against Acceptance

Documents against Payment

Letter of Credit

Confirmed Letter of Credit

Cash in Advance

Least Advantageous   Low Risk/Low Trust

Source: Chase Manhattan Bank, *Dynamics of Trade Finance* (New York: Chase Manhattan Bank, 1984), 5.

volved.[7] If the exporter is well established in the market with a unique product and accompanying service, price and terms of trade can be set to fit the exporter's desires. If, on the other hand, the exporter is breaking into a new market or if competitive pressures call for action, pricing and selling terms should be used as major competitive tools.

The basic methods of payment for exports vary in terms of their attractiveness to the buyer and the seller, from cash in advance to open account or consignment selling. Neither of the extremes will be feasible for longer term relationships, but they do have their use in certain situations. These methods are depicted in the risk triangle presented in Figure 10.5.

The most favorable term to the exporter is cash in advance, because it relieves the exporter of all risk and allows for immediate use of the money. It is not widely used, however, except for smaller, first-time transactions or situations in which the exporter has reason to doubt the importer's ability to pay. Cash-in-advance terms are also found when orders are for custom-made products, because the risk to the exporter is beyond that of a normal transaction. In some instances, the importer may not be able to buy on a cash-in-advance basis because of insufficient funds or government restrictions.

[7]Chase Manhattan Bank, *Dynamics of Trade Finance* (New York: Chase Manhattan Bank, 1984), 10–11.

FIGURE 10.6 ▪ **Parties to a Letter of Credit**

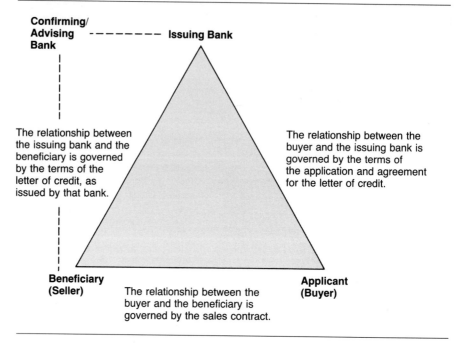

Source: First National Bank of Chicago, *Financing of U.S. Export* (Chicago: First National Bank of Chicago, 1975), 21.

A **letter of credit** is an instrument issued by a bank, at the request of a buyer, in which the bank promises to pay a specified amount of money upon presentation of documents stipulated in the letter of credit, usually the bill of lading, consular invoice, and a description of the goods.[8] Letters of credit are one of the most-used methods of payment in international transactions. Figure 10.6 summarizes the relationships between the partners to the letter of credit. The issuing bank is typically the buyer's bank, while the confirming/advising bank is the exporter's bank. Letters of credit can be classified along three dimensions:

1. Irrevocable versus revocable. An irrevocable letter of credit can be neither canceled nor modified without the consent of the beneficiary (exporter), thus guaranteeing payment.
2. Confirmed versus unconfirmed. In the case of a U.S. exporter, a U.S. bank might confirm the letter of credit and thus assume the risk, including the transaction (exchange) risk. The single best method of

[8]David K. Eiteman and Arthur I. Stonehill, *Multinational Business Finance* (Reading, Mass.: Addison-Wesley, 1986), 503–525.

payment for the exporter in most cases is a confirmed, irrevocable letter of credit. Banks may also assume an advisory role but not assume the risk; the underlying assumption is that the bank and its correspondent(s) are better able to judge the credibility of the bank issuing the letter of credit than is the exporter.

3. Revolving versus nonrevolving. Most letters of credit are nonrevolving; that is, valid for the one transaction only. In case of established relationships a revolving letter of credit may be issued.

Figure 10.7 provides an example of a letter of credit.

The letter of credit provides advantages to both the exporter and the importer, which explains its wide use. The approach substitutes the credit of the bank for the credit of the buyer, and is as good as the issuing bank's access to dollars. In custom-made orders, an irrevocable letter of credit may help the exporter secure pre-export financing. The importer will not need to pay until the documents have arrived and been accepted by the bank, thus giving an additional float. The major caveat is that the exporter has to comply with all of the terms of the letter of credit. For example, if the documents state that shipment is made in crates measuring $4 \times 4 \times 4$, and the goods are shipped in crates measuring $4 \times 3 \times 4$, the bank will not honor the letter of credit. If there are changes, the letter of credit can be amended to ensure payment. In some cases, the exporter must watch out for fraudulent letters of credit, especially in the case of less-developed countries.

The letter of credit is a promise to pay but not a means of payment. Actual payment is accomplished by means of a **draft**, which is similar to a personal check. Like a check, it is an order by one party to pay another. Most drafts are documentary, which means that the buyer must obtain possession of various shipping documents before obtaining possession of the goods involved in the transaction. Clean drafts—orders to pay without any other documents—are mainly used by multinational corporations in their dealings with their own subsidiaries and in well-established business relationships.

In **documentary collection** situations, the seller ships the goods, and the shipping documents and the draft demanding payment are presented to the importer through banks acting as the seller's agent. The draft, also known as the bill of exchange, may be either a sight draft or a time draft (see Figure 10.8). A sight draft documents against payment and is payable upon presentation to the drawee, that is, the party to whom the draft is addressed. A time draft documents against acceptance and allows for a delay of 30, 60, or 90 days. When a time draft is drawn on and accepted by a bank, it becomes a banker's acceptance, which is sold in the short-term money market. Time drafts drawn on and accepted by a business firm become trader's acceptances, which are normally not marketable. A draft is presented to the drawee, who accepts it by writing or stamping a notice of acceptance on it. With both sight and time drafts the buyer can effectively

FIGURE 10.7 ■ **Letter of Credit**

1st AMERICAN
FIRST AMERICAN BANK, N.A.

INTERNATIONAL DEPARTMENT
740 15TH. STREET, N.W.
WASHINGTON, D.C. 20005

CABLE: FSTAMERICA
TELEX: 89-2354 FSTAMERICA
248427 FSTAM UR
197638 1STAM UT

DATE ▶ February 10, 19___

DOCUMENTARY CREDIT · IRREVOCABLE

CREDIT NUMBER

of issuing bank   of advising bank

ADVISING BANK

Japanese Bank, Ltd.
P.O. Box 567
Tokyo, Japan

ID-0000C

APPLICANT

XYZ Importers, Inc.
1234 Main Street
Anywhere, U.S.A. 54321

BENEFICIARY

ABC Exporters, Ltd.
9876 First Street
Anywhere, Japan

AMOUNT

Five Hundred Thousand and 00/100 United
States Dollars
(US$500,000.00)

EXPIRY

November 10, 19___

Dear Sir(s):
We hereby issue this letter of credit in your favor available by your draft drawn on us at   sight

bearing the clause "Drawn under First American Bank, N.A. Letter of Credit No.   ID-0000C
accompanied by the following documents:

1. Commercial Invoice in Triplicate

2. Certificate of Origin

3. Insurance Policy or Certificate

4. Packing List in Duplicate

5. Full Set Clean On Board Ocean Bills of Lading Issued To Order of First American
   Bank, N.A. marked Notify XYZ Importers, Inc. Also to be marked Freight Prepaid.

covering Merchandise per P.O. Number 10203

Shipment from Any Japanese Port
to CIF USA Port
Special conditions

Partial Shipments
Permitted

Transhipments
Prohibited

THIS CREDIT IS SUBJECT TO THE UNIFORM CUSTOMS AND PRACTICES FOR DOCUMENTARY CREDITS (1983 REVISION) INTERNATIONAL CHAMBER OF COMMERCE PUBLICATION NO 400.

We hereby engage with drawers and/or bonafide holders that drafts
drawn and negotiated in conformity with the terms of this credit will
be duly honored on presentation and that drafts accepted within the
terms of this credit will be duly honored at maturity.
The amount of each draft must be endorsed on the reverse of this
credit by the negotiating bank.

☐ This refers to our cable of today through the advising bank
☒ This credit is forwarded to the advising bank by airmail
Advising bank's notification

Yours very truly,
First American Bank, N.A.

SAMPLE

Issuing Bank (authorized signature)

Place, date, name and signature of advising bank

FORM NO 1045 REV 3-80

ORIGINAL

Source: First American Bank, Washington, D.C.

FIGURE 10.8 ▪ **Drafts**

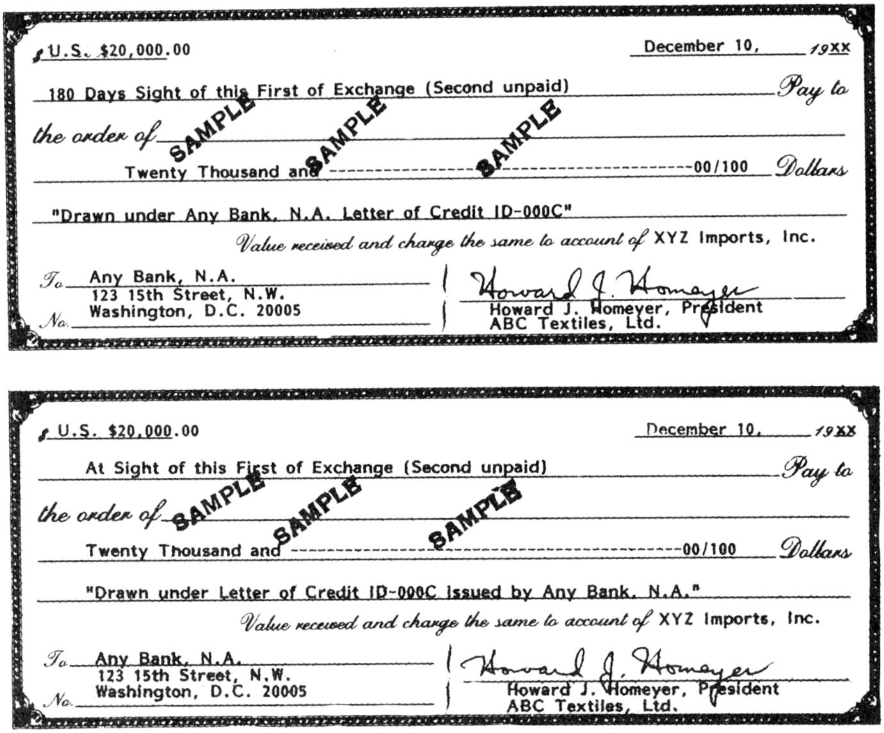

U.S. $20,000.00   December 10,   19XX

180 Days Sight of this First of Exchange (Second unpaid)   Pay to

the order of _____ SAMPLE _____ SAMPLE _____ SAMPLE _____

_____ Twenty Thousand and --00/100   Dollars

"Drawn under Any Bank, N.A. Letter of Credit ID-000C"

Value received and charge the same to account of XYZ Imports, Inc.

To   Any Bank, N.A.
     123 15th Street, N.W.
No. Washington, D.C. 20005   Howard J. Homeyer
                                               Howard J. Homeyer, President
                                               ABC Textiles, Ltd.

U.S. $20,000.00   December 10,   19XX

At Sight of this First of Exchange (Second unpaid)   Pay to

the order of SAMPLE _____ SAMPLE _____ SAMPLE _____

Twenty Thousand and --00/100   Dollars

"Drawn under Letter of Credit ID-000C issued by Any Bank, N.A."

Value received and charge the same to account of XYZ Imports, Inc.

To   Any Bank, N.A.
     123 15th Street, N.W.
No. Washington, D.C. 20005   Howard J. Homeyer
                                               Howard J. Homeyer, President
                                               ABC Textiles, Ltd.

Source: First American Bank, Washington, D.C.

extend the period of credit by avoiding receipt of the goods. A date draft requires payment on a specified date, regardless of the date on which the goods and the draft are accepted by the buyer.

To illustrate, an exporter may have a time draft accepted by Citibank for $1 million to be paid in 90 days. Like many exporters who extend credit for competitive reasons, the firm may have immediate need for the funds. It could contact an acceptance dealer and sell the acceptance at a discount, with the rate depending on the market rate of interest. If the annual interest rate were 12 percent, for example, the acceptance could be sold for $970,873 ($1 million divided by 1.03). Interest rates for banker's acceptances of various maturities are listed daily in *The Wall Street Journal*.

Even if the draft is not sold in the secondary market, the exporter may convert it into cash by **discounting.** To discount the draft simply means that the draft is sold to a bank at a discount from face value. If the discounting is with recourse, the exporter is liable for the payment to the bank if the importer defaults. If it is without recourse, the exporter will not be liable even in the event that the importer does not pay the bank. Discounting without recourse is known as factoring or, in the case of higher credit risk and longer term receivables, forfaiting (see Chapter 6).

The normal manner of doing business in the domestic market is **open account** (open terms). The exporter selling on open account removes both real and psychological barriers to importing. However, no written evidence of the debt exists, and the exporter has to put full faith in the references contacted. Worst of all, there is no guarantee of payment. If the debt turns bad, the problems of overseas litigation are considerable. Bad debts are normally easier to avoid than to rectify. The open-account arrangement is common in trade between European countries, and a European company asking for a letter of credit would not be popular.[9] Trade practice does allow for letters of credit in certain industries or when goods are imported from countries more geographically removed such as the United States, Japan, and Australia. In less-developed countries, importers will usually need proof of debt in the application to the central bank for hard currency, which will not allow them to deal on an open-account basis. Again, open account is used by multinationals in their internal transactions and when there is implicit trust among the partners.

The most favorable term to the importer is **consignment selling,** which allows the importer to defer payment until the goods are actually sold. This approach places all of the burden on the exporter and its use should be carefully weighed against the objectives of the transaction. If the exporter wants entry into a specific market through specific intermediaries, consignment selling may be the only method of gaining acceptance by the middlemen. The arrangement will require clear understanding as to the parties' responsibilities—for example, which party is responsible for insurance until the goods have actually been sold.

Adjusting to Foreign Currency Fluctuations

Another important matter to be resolved over payment for exports is the currency in which to invoice. Unless currencies are closely linked, as for example between West Germany and Austria, exchange rate movements may harm one or the other of the parties. If the price is quoted in the exporter's currency, the exporter will get exactly the price he wants, but may lose the sale as a result. The currency chosen will depend on the parties themselves and the particular transaction. If the exporter needs the sale, the invoice may be in the importer's currency and the exchange risk the burden of the exporter. These exchange risks may be a result of an appreciating or depreciating currency. Exchange risks may also result from a revaluation or devaluation of a currency by a central bank,

---

[9] Paul Jermer, *Europe: An Exporter's Handbook* (New York: Facts on File, 1981), 145–147.

resulting in a higher or lower export bill. Assume that a U.S. importer bought $250,000 or DM525,000 worth of goods from a German company, which agreed to accept U.S. dollars for payment within 90 days. At the time of the quotation the exchange rate for $1 was DM2.10, whereas the time of payment the rate for $1 was DM2.00. This means that the German exporter, instead of eventually receiving DM525,000, received only DM500,000.

When invoicing in foreign currencies, an exporter cannot insulate himself from the problems of currency movements but he can at least know how much he will eventually receive by using the mechanism of the **forward exchange market.** In essence, the exporter gets a bank to agree to a rate at which it will buy the foreign currency the exporter will receive when the importer makes payment. The rate is expressed as either a premium or a discount on the current spot rate. The risk still remains if the exchange rate does not move as anticipated and the exporter may be worse off than if he had not bought forward. See also Chapter 6 for a discussion on exchange-rate determinations.

The steep decline in the value of the dollar has substantially altered the competitive environment in various industries. Many non-U.S. companies are facing a serious pricing versus margin dilemma. Some of them have already left the international arena, unable to compete without major changes in their international marketing strategies. For U.S. companies the decision has been how to adjust their pricing to international customers in view of the more favorable dollar exchange rate.

For U.S. exporters three alternatives are available. First, making no change in the dollar price could result in a more favorable price in foreign currencies and likely higher sales. Second, the export price could be increased in conjunction with decreases in the value of the dollar to maintain stable export prices in foreign currencies. This would result in improved margins if sales volume remained steady. The third alternative is to pass only a share of the savings to the customers with the hope of increasing sales with improved margins.

The data in Table 10.2 show that on the average foreign manufacturers absorbed about half of the decline in the trading value of the dollar between March 1985 and September 1987. If prices of nonfuel imports to the United States had fully reflected the dollars, they would have risen 34 percent on average; instead they rose only about 19 percent.

Meanwhile, U.S. exporters have in general lowered their foreign-currency denominated prices to improve their competitive positions. The dollar price index for exports was up only 2.8 percent and the foreign currency index was down 21.5 percent.[10] Some industries in the United States, such as the automobile industry, have been criticized for raising their domestic prices as the prices of Japanese imports have been forced

---

[10]"How Dollar Weakness Affects Pricing Policies of U.S. and Non-U.S. Firms," *Business International*, December 7, 1987, 387.

TABLE 10.2 ▪ **Effect of Dollar Fall on Trade Pricing**

Product Category	Imports to United States: Percent of Pass-Through	Exports to United States: Percent of Pass-Through
BEVERAGES AND TOBACCO	23.5	89.9
Beverages	27.1	98.6
Tobacco	NA	89.1
CHEMICALS AND RELATED PRODUCTS	8.7	78.7
Pharmaceuticals	54.2	54.3
Essential Oils and Perfumes	46.1	66.8
Manufactured Fertilizers	38.1	130.2
Artificial Resins and Plastics	20.4	42.1
Organic Chemicals	NA	54.3
Miscellaneous Chemical Materials	21.3	106.8
INTERMEDIATE MANUFACTURES	39.9	63.7
Paper and Paperboard	69.9	29.4
Textiles	24.8	NA
Nonmetallic Minerals	57.1	29.4
Iron and Steel	17.2	58.5
MACHINERY	46.5	92.8
Specialized	59.0	95.9
Metalworking	75.6	65.7
General Industrial	71.2	82.6
Office and Data Processing	37.1	113.0
Telecommunications and Sound	11.4	78.1
Electric	38.8	92.4
Motor Vehicles and Parts	55.3	50.0
Power Generating	NA	81.9
MISCELLANEOUS FINISHED MANUFACTURES	72.8	77.2
Plumbing, Heating, Light	44.8	NA
Furniture and Parts	58.9	37.4
Apparel	89.7	NA
Footwear	43.8	NA
Scientific Instruments	76.7	78.6
Photographic, Watches, etc.	48.7	96.9

Note: The numbers indicate the percentage of foreign exchange loss U.S. exporters passed through to their overseas customers in the form of stable dollar prices, and the percentage of exchange gain non-U.S. exporters passed through to U.S. customers in the form of higher dollar prices, between March 1985 and September 1987.

Source: "How Dollar Weakness Affects Pricing Policies of U.S. and Non-U.S. Firms," *Business International*, December 7, 1988, 387. Reprinted with permission.

up by the higher value of the yen. Rather than try to capture market share, the automakers went for extra profits.[11]

[11]"Did U.S. Car Makers Err by Raising Prices When the Yen Rose?" *The Wall Street Journal*, April 18, 1988, 1, 14.

LEASING

Organizational customers frequently prefer to lease major equipment. About 30 percent of all capital goods are leased in the United States, with eight out of ten companies involved in leasing.[12] Although a major force in the United States, leasing has grown significantly elsewhere as well; for example, one of the major international trade activities of the Soviet Union, in addition to shipping and oil, is equipment leasing. The Russians view leasing not only as a potential source of hard currency but also as a way of attracting customers who would be reluctant to buy an unfamiliar product.[13]

For the industrial marketing manager selling products such as printing presses, forklift trucks, and machine tools, leasing may allow penetration of markets that might otherwise not exist for the firm's products if it had to sell them outright. Balance of payment problems have forced some countries to prohibit the purchase and importation of equipment into their markets; an exception has been made if the import is to be leased.[14] In less-developed countries, the fact that leased products are serviced by the lessor may be a major benefit because of the shortage of trained personnel and availability of spare parts. The main benefit for the lessor is that total net income, after charging off pertinent repair and maintenance expenses, is often higher than it would be if the unit were sold.

In today's competitive business climate, traditional financial considerations are often only part of the asset-financing formula. Many leasing companies have become more than a source of capital, developing new value-added services that have taken them from asset financiers to asset managers, or forming relationships with others that can provide these services. In some cases, lessors have even evolved into partners in business activities. Xerox Credit, for example, finances assets worth about $2 billion every year—$1 billion under captive leasing services from its parent, Xerox Corporation, and $1 billion as an equipment lessor competing in the open market. It has some copy equipment leases in which it provides both machinery and the personnel to operate it.

DUMPING

Inexpensive imports often trigger accusations of dumping—that is, selling goods overseas for less than in the exporter's home market or at a price below the cost of production, or both. Dumping cases that have been re-

---

[12] "Leasing: A New Role," *Business Week*, May 15, 1989, 141–152.

[13] Herbert E. Meyer, "The Communist Internationale Has a Capitalist Accent," *Fortune*, February 1977, 134–142.

[14] David A. Ricks and Saeed Samiee, "Leasing: It May Be Right Abroad Even When It Is Not at Home," *Journal of International Business Studies* 5 (Fall 1974): 87–90.

ported range from Florida tomato growers charging that Mexican vegetables were being dumped across the border to the Canadian Anti-Dumping Tribunal ruling that U.S. firms were dumping radioactive diagnostic reagents in Canada.[15] Such disputes have become quite common, especially in highly competitive industries such as computer chips, ball bearings, and steel. In 1989, for example, AT&T, asserting that it had experienced "heavy and growing injury," asked the U.S. government to investigate its complaint that companies in Japan, Korea, and Taiwan were selling telephone equipment in the United States at unfair prices.[16] Similarly, in Europe, the European Community's Executive Commission investigated the imports of audiocassette tapes from Asia that were allegedly being sold at below-market prices in the 12-nation trading bloc.[17]

Dumping ranges from predatory dumping to unintentional dumping. **Predatory dumping** refers to a tactic whereby a foreign firm intentionally sells at a loss in another country in order to increase its market share at the expense of domestic producers, which amounts to an international price war. **Unintentional dumping** is the result of time lags between the dates of sales transaction, shipment, and arrival. Prices, including exchange rates, can change in such a way that the final sales price turns out to be below the cost of production or below the price prevailing in the exporter's home market.

In the United States, domestic producers may petition the government to impose antidumping duties on imports alleged to be dumped (see The International Marketplace 10.2). The duty is imposed if the Department of Commerce determines that sales have occurred at less than fair market value, and if the U.S. International Trade Commission finds that domestic industry is being, or threatened with being, materially injured by the imports. The remedy is an **antidumping duty** equal to the dumping margin. International agreements and U.S. law provide for **countervailing duties,** which may be imposed on imports that are found to be subsidized by foreign governments and which are designed to offset the advantages imports would otherwise receive from the subsidy. In one of these cases, the United States ruled that Israel was subsidizing exports of freshly cut flowers and ordered a countervailing duty of 1.55 percent on the imports, far below the 27 percent the industry requested.[18] Governmental action against dumping and subsidized exports violating GATT may result in hurting the very industries seeking relief. Action against European steel, for example, could result in retaliatory measures against U.S. steelmakers who themselves export billions of dollars worth of steel products. Euro-

[15] Steven Plaut, "Why Dumping Is Good for Us," *Fortune*, May 5, 1980, 11–22.

[16] "AT&T Files a Complaint on 'Dumping,'" *The New York Times*, December 29, 1988, D1, D18.

[17] "Europe Inquiry on Asian Tapes," *The New York Times*, January 16, 1989, D11.

[18] "How Four Industries Are Hurt by Dumping," *U.S. News & World Report*, July 5, 1982, 45–46.

THE INTERNATIONAL MARKETPLACE 10.2

United States to Take a New Look at Dumping Laws U.S. law prohibits dumping but the federal government has been cautious in enforcing the law, especially in the case of allies. In the 1970s, Timken had to sue the U.S. government to force it to carry out its own dumping order against Japanese tapered roller bearings. Zenith labored for a decade to get U.S. dumping duties assessed against Japanese TV manufacturers, and then the governments of the two countries negotiated the penalty down to 10 cents on the dollar. Three times Hitachi was charged with dumping different types of semiconductors. But by the time the cases were resolved, Hitachi was dumping a whole new generation of chips. Between 1985 and 1988, the Japanese doubled their U.S. market share from 12 percent to 24 percent.

Timken, Smith Corona, Zenith, and the semiconductor industry claim that the way the United States calculates dumping margins—the difference between the home market price and the import price as a percentage of import price—makes it harder to prove dumping in the United States than in Europe. This is especially true when transactions include so-called related parties such as manufacturers and their in-house distributors. In such cases, the United States, unlike most of its competitors, includes profits in its import price estimate (making the price higher) and excludes indirect selling costs in its calculation of the home market price (making that price lower). As a result dumping margins can be lower in the United States than in Europe.

Importers counter that these companies are trying to use the dumping laws as protection. As a result of this debate, the U.S. Department of Commerce has agreed to take a new look at how dumping laws are enforced and the way dumping margins are calculated.

Source: Ann Reilly Dowd, "What to Do About Trade Policy," *Fortune*, May 8, 1989, 106–112.

---

pean governments have also threatened to retaliate against U.S. exports of other products.

In some cases, dumping suits have strong competitive motivations; for example, to discourage an aggressive competitor by accusing it of selling at unfair prices. Antidumping and unfair-subsidy suits have led in some cases to formal agreements on voluntary restraints, whereby foreign producers agree that they will supply only a certain percentage of the U.S. market. One such arrangement is the semiconductor trade agreement between the United States and Japan signed in 1986 that required the Japanese to stop selling computer chips at below their cost. The agreement also called for the Japanese to make efforts to increase sales of foreign-made computer chips in Japan.[19]

SUMMARY

The status of price has changed to that of a dynamic marketing mix element. This has resulted from both internal and external pressures on business firms. Management must analyze the interactive effect pricing has on the other elements of the mix, and how pricing can assist in meeting the overall goals of the marketing strategy.

Setting of export price must start with the determination of an appropriate cost baseline and include variables such as export-related costs in order to avoid compromising the desired profit margin. The quotation needs to spell out the respective responsibilities of the buyer and the seller in getting the goods to their intended destination. The terms of sale are used to indicate this but may also be used as a competitive tool. The terms of payment have to be clarified to ensure that the exporter will indeed get paid for the products and services rendered. Facilitating agents such as freight forwarders and banks are often used to absorb some of the risk and uncertainty in preparing price quotations and establishing terms of payment.

Exporters need also to be ready to defend their pricing practices. Competitors may petition their own government to investigate the exporter's pricing to determine the degree to which it reflects costs and prices prevailing in the exporter's domestic market.

Questions for Discussion

1. What are the implications of price escalation?
2. Discuss the use of the currency of quotation as a competitive tool.
3. Who is harmed and who is helped by dumping?
4. Why is there a tendency to underestimate the importance of price in developing a marketing mix?
5. Propose scenarios in which export prices are higher/lower than domestic prices.
6. Based on the data in Table 10.2, which industries show the most tight competitive situations?
7. What are the benefits of leasing to the lessor? To the lessee? Why would a U.S. company lease rather than sell equipment outright?
8. What are the possible exporter reactions to extreme foreign-exchange fluctuations?

[19]"Chip Pact Falls Short of Goals," *The New York Times*, August 2, 1988, D1.

Recommended Readings

Chase Manhattan Bank. *Dynamics of Trade Finance*. New York: Chase Manhattan Bank, 1984.

Monroe, Kent B., and Albert DellaBitta. "Models for Pricing Decisions." *Journal of Marketing Research* 15 (August 1978): 413–428.

Oxenfeldt, Alfred R. "Multistage Approach to Pricing." *Harvard Business Review* 38 (July–August 1960): 125–133.

U.S. Department of Commerce. *Basic Guide to Exporting*. Washington, D.C.: Government Printing Office, 1986.

CHAPTER 11

International Communications

11.1 THE INTERNATIONAL MARKETPLACE

Interpreter Can Be an Asset Abroad *An international marketing executive on a business trip abroad faces a risk seldom encountered at home: losing something in the translation—literally. Whether to take along an interpreter or have company materials translated into a foreign language is an early, key decision. To assume that English will be understood when speaking before a group of businessmen overseas, and then to discover that it is not, provides a rude shock.*

Sarah Pilgrim, president of OmniLingua, Inc., has suggested: "You need to do some research and think about what you are doing. Are you going to sell your product? Or going for social reasons to develop contacts? Do the people you are meeting speak English—and with what level of competency? If you are making initial contacts, trying to find out about the market potential, you may not want to spend the money for an interpreter or translation of your literature. But if you are trying to sell something in a foreign country, it is important to have literature in the language of the target country. Although an interpreter costs $150 to $300 a day, it is wise to take one to important negotiations. If you bring your own interpreter, you can be sure that person is on your side. The interpreter should be well briefed ahead of time so he or she is familiar with the product and can act as a company representative."

Some of the drawbacks of interpreters are that (1) interpreters can slow down negotiations or inject their own point of view into the discussion, (2) they may diminish the spontaneity and negotiating strength of the presentation, (3) using an interpreter may offend a foreign business executive who thinks his or her English is good, and (4) interpreters are a risk in communicating confidential information.

Translating brochures and information usually is seen as a sign that a company is serious about doing business in the country. It also allows technical products to be explained more precisely to a foreign business executive whose command of English may not be good enough to understand a product's finer points. An entire bro-

chure can be printed in a foreign language or an inset may be placed inside the company's English-language brochure. The costs vary widely depending on the language, technical level of the information, and graphic treatment desired. Translating business cards is even more important than brochures, especially for use in the Orient and Middle East. Business cards in many countries are considered the equivalent of a handshake. Because a marketing executive's reception abroad often depends on his or her hierarchical level, careful translation of business titles is important.

In the United States there are about 20 translation companies, in addition to private translators and interpreters. Increasingly, hotels have begun to provide translation services to foreign business people.

Source: Barbara Zigli, "Interpreter Can Be an Asset Abroad," *USA Today*, April 15, 1985, 15E.

Effective communication is particularly important in international marketing because of the geographic and psychological distances that separate a firm from its intermediaries and customers. By definition, communication is a process of establishing a "commonness" of thought between a sender and a receiver.[1] This process extends beyond the conveying of ideas to include persuasion, and thus enables the marketing process to function more effectively and efficiently. Ideally marketing communication is a dialogue that allows organizations and consumers to achieve mutually satisfying exchange agreements.[2] This definition emphasizes the two-way nature of the process, with listening and responsiveness as integral parts. The majority of communication is verbal, but nonverbal communication and the concept of silent languages must also be considered because they often create problems for international marketers.

This chapter will include an overview of the principles of marketing communications in international markets. Because face-to-face, buyer–seller negotiations are possibly the most fundamental marketing process,[3] guidelines for international business negotiations are first discussed. Second, the chapter will focus on the management of the international communications mix from the exporter's point of view. Because the exporter's alternatives may be limited by the entry mode and by resources available,

[1] Wilbur Schramm and Donald F. Roberts, *The Process and Effects of Mass Communications* (Urbana, Ill.: University of Illinois Press, 1971), 12–17.

[2] William G. Nickels, *Marketing Communication and Promotion* (Columbus, Ohio: Grid Publishing, 1980), 10.

[3] John L. Graham, Dong Ki Kim, Chi-Yuan Lin, and Michael Robinson, "Buyer-Seller Negotiations around the Pacific Rim: Differences in Fundamental Exchange Processes," *Journal of Consumer Research* 15 (June 1988): 48–54.

the tools and the challenges are quite different from those of the multinational entity. The promotional approaches used by multinational marketers are discussed in Chapter 19.

THE MARKETING COMMUNICATIONS PROCESS

As shown in the communications model presented in Figure 11.1, effective communication requires three elements—the sender, the message, and the receiver—to be connected by a message channel. The process may begin with an unsolicited inquiry from a potential customer or as a planned effort by the marketer. Whatever the reason for the communications process, the sender needs to study receiver characteristics before encoding the message to be sent in order to achieve maximum impact. **Encoding** the message simply means converting the message into symbolic form that is properly understood by the receiver. This is not a simple task, however. For example, a U.S. firm quoting an export price F.O.B. may inadvertently convey to overseas clients that it is not overly interested in obtaining orders, because the more inclusive C.I.F. is typically preferred by most importers. On occasion, the message in itself may be silence, allowing the receiver an opportunity to change an earlier position.

The message channel is the path through which the message moves from sender (source) to receiver. This link that ties the receiver to the sender ranges from sound waves conveying the human voice in personal selling to transceivers or intermediaries such as print and broadcast media. Although technological advances (for example, telex, telefax, and video-conferencing) may have made buyer–seller negotiations more efficient, the fundamental process and its purpose have remained unchanged. Complications in international marketing may arise if a particular medium is not available at all for commercial purposes, such as radio in the Northern European countries. Other examples of complications are the banning of advertising for certain product categories, such as cigarette advertising in the EC countries, and the fact that some marketing practices may not be allowed, such as door-to-door selling in France.

Once a sender has placed a message into a channel or a set of channels and directed them to the intended destination, the completion of the process is dependent on the receiver's **decoding**—that is, transforming the message symbols back into thought. If there is an adequate amount of overlap between sender characteristics and needs reflected in the encoded message and receiver characteristics and needs reflected in the decoded message, the communications process has worked.

A message moving through a channel is subject to the influence of extraneous and distracting stimuli, which interfere with the intended accurate reception of the message. This interference is referred to as **noise.** In the international marketing context noise might be a bad telephone connection, failure to express a quotation in the inquirer's system of currency and

FIGURE 11.1 ▪ **The Marketing Communications Process**

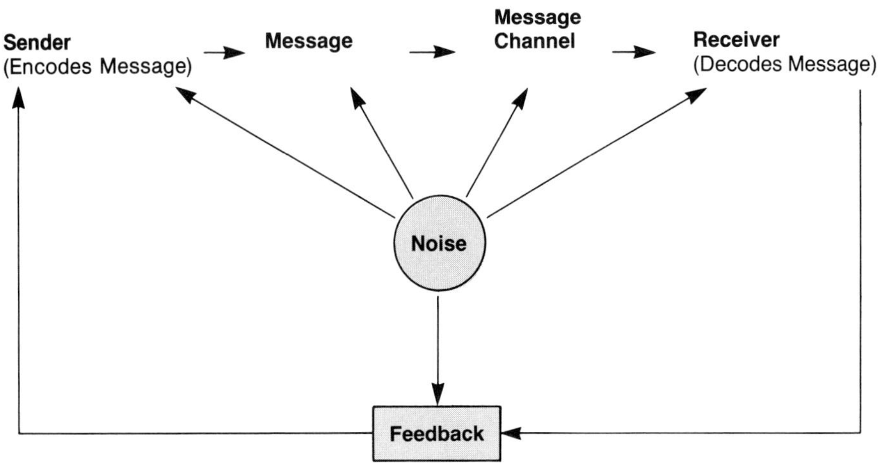

Source: Terence A. Shimp and M. Wayne DeLozier, *Promotion Management and Marketing Communications* (Hinsdale, Ill.: Dryden Press, 1986), 27.

measurement, or a highly cluttered medium such as Italian television, where all advertisements are aired in one half-hour period each night. A valid inquiry from overseas may not be considered seriously by a U.S. marketer because of noise consisting of low-quality paper, grammatical errors, or a general appearance unlike domestic correspondence.

The international marketer should be most alert to cultural noise. The lack of language skills may hinder successful negotiations while translation errors may render an advertising campaign or brochure useless. Similarly, nonverbal language and its improper interpretation may cause problems. For example, in the United States lack of eye contact is a signal that something is wrong. This is not necessarily so in Japan, where the cultural style of communication involves markedly less eye contact.[4]

Regardless of whether the situation calls for interpersonal or mass communications, the collection and observation of feedback is necessary to analyze the success of the communications effort. The initial sender–receiver relationship is transposed, and interpretative skills similar to those needed in developing messages are needed. To make effective and efficient use of the communications requires considerable strategic planning. Examples of concrete ways in which feedback can be collected are inquiry cards or toll-free numbers distributed at trade shows to gather additional information.

[4]John L. Graham, "A Hidden Cause of America's Trade Deficit with Japan," *Columbia Journal of World Business* 16 (Fall 1981): 5–15.

INTERNATIONAL NEGOTIATIONS

When international marketing managers travel abroad to do business, they are frequently shocked to discover the extent to which the many variables of foreign behavior and custom complicate their efforts.[5] One of these differences is negotiation. The process of negotiation differs in most countries from that typical in the United States. This means that international marketing managers have to adjust their approaches to establishing rapport, information exchange, persuasion, and concession making if they are to be successful in dealing with their clients and partners, such as intermediaries.[6] The negotiation process can be a short one with the stages collapsing into one session or a prolonged endeavor taking weeks.

Stages of the Negotiation Process

The process of international business negotiations can be divided into five stages: the offer, informal meetings, strategy formulation, negotiations, and implementation.[7]

The offer stage allows the two parties to assess each other's needs and degree of commitment. The initiation of the process and its progress are determined to a great extent by background factors of the parties (such as objectives) and the overall atmosphere (for example, a spirit of cooperativeness). As an example, many European buyers may be skittish about dealing with an American exporter, given the number of U.S. companies that "fold their tents and go away when an initial sale blitz fizzles" or when environmental factors turn sour.[8]

After the buyer has received the offer, the parties meet to discuss the terms and get acquainted. In many parts of the world (Asia, the Middle East, and Latin America) informal meetings may often make or break the deal. Foreign buyers may want to ascertain that they are doing business with someone who is sympathetic and whom they can trust. In some cases, it may be necessary to utilize facilitators (such as consultants or agents) to establish the contact. For example, in the Soviet Union, well-established foreign business people who know their way around the Soviet business bureaucracy may act as a go-between for newcomers seeking to do business.[9]

Both parties have to formulate strategies for formal negotiations. This means not only careful review and assessment of all of the factors affecting

[5]Edward T. Hall, "The Silent Language of Overseas Business," *Harvard Business Review* 38 (May–June 1960): 87–96.

[6]John L. Graham, "Across the Negotiating Table from the Japanese," *International Marketing Review* 4 (Autumn 1986): 58–71.

[7]Pervez N. Ghauri, "Guidelines for International Business Negotiations," *International Marketing Review* 4 (Autumn 1986): 72–82.

[8]"Made in the U.S.A.," *Business Week*, February 29, 1988, 60–66.

[9]Phyllis Berman, "The Five-Percenters, Moscow's Pet Capitalists," *Forbes*, February 6, 1989, 93–97.

the deal to be negotiated but also preparation for the actual give-and-take of the negotiations. For example, research studies have found that U.S. and Canadian anglophone bargainers can be taken advantage of by competitive bargainers,[10] and that they are more trusting than other cultural groups.[11] Thus, these managers should consciously and carefully consider competitive behaviors of clients and partners. Especially in the case of governmental buyers, it is imperative to realize that public-sector needs may not necessarily fit into a mold that the marketer would consider rational.

The actual face-to-face negotiations and the approach used in them will depend on the cultural background and business traditions prevailing in different countries.

How to Negotiate in Other Countries[12]

A combination of attitudes, expectations, and habitual behavior influences negotiation style. Although some of the following recommendations may go against the approach used at home, they may allow the negotiator to adjust to the style of the host country negotiators.

1. *Team assistance.* Using specialists will strengthen the team substantially and allow for all points of view to be given proper attention. Further, observation of negotiations can be valuable training experience for less-experienced participants.

2. *Traditions and customs.* For newcomers, status relations and business procedures must be carefully considered with the help of consultants or local representatives. For example, in highly structured societies, such as Korea, great respect is paid to age and position.[13]

3. *Language capability.* Ideally the international marketing manager should be able to speak the customer's language, but that is not always possible. The use of interpreters allows for longer response time and a more careful articulation of arguments (see The International Marketplace 11.1).

4. *Determination of authority limits.* The disadvantages of having full authority must be weighed against the expenses of communication with the home office. Announcing that the negotiators do not have the final authority to conclude the contract may be perceived negatively; however, if it is used as a tactic to probe the moves of the buyer, it can be quite effective.

5. *Patience.* In many countries, such as the Soviet Union and the People's Republic of China, business negotiations may take three times the

[10] Nancy J. Adler, John L. Graham, and Theodore Schwarz Gehrke, "Business Negotiations in Canada, Mexico, and the United States," *Journal of Business Research* 15 (1987): 411–429.

[11] D. L. Harnett and L. L. Cummings, *Bargaining Behavior: An International Study* (Houston, Tex.: Dame Publications, 1980), 231.

[12] John L. Graham and Roy A. Herberger, Jr., "Negotiators Abroad—Don't Shoot from the Hip," *Harvard Business Review* 61 (July–August 1983): 160–168.

[13] Lennie Copeland and L. Griggs, *Going International: How to Make Friends and Deal Effectively in the Global Marketplace* (New York: Ballinger, 1985), 113.

amount of time that they do in Western Europe. Showing impatience in countries such as Brazil or Thailand may prolong negotiations rather than speed them up. Also, Americans tend to start relatively close to what they consider a fair price in their negotiations, whereas Chinese negotiators may start with "unreasonable" demands.

6. *Negotiation ethics.* Attitudes and values of foreign negotiators may be quite different from those that a U.S. marketing executive is accustomed to. Being tricky can be valued in some parts of the world whereas it is frowned upon elsewhere. For example, Western negotiators may be taken aback by last minute changes or concession requests by Soviet negotiators.[14]

7. *Silence.* To negotiate effectively abroad, all types of communication should be read correctly. Americans often interpret inaction and silence as a negative sign. As a result, Japanese executives tend to expect that they can get Americans to lower prices or sweeten the deal.[15]

8. *Persistence.* Insisting on answers and an outcome may be seen as a threat by negotiating partners abroad. In some markets, negotiations are seen as a means of establishing long-term commercial relations, not as an event with winners and losers. Confrontations are to be avoided because minds cannot be changed at the negotiation table; this has to be done informally.

9. *Holistic view.* Concessions should be avoided until all issues have been discussed so as to preclude the possibility of granting unnecessary benefits to the negotiation partners. Furthermore, in the Far East and elsewhere concessions traditionally come at the end of bargaining.

10. *The meaning of agreements.* What constitutes an agreement will vary from one market to another. In many parts of the world, legal contracts are still not needed; as a matter of fact, reference to legal counsel may indicate that the relationship is in trouble.

When a verbal agreement is reached, it is critical that both parties leave with a clear understanding of what they have agreed to. This may entail only the relatively straightforward act of signing a distributor agreement but, in the case of large-scale projects, details must be explored and spelled out. For example, in contracts that call for cooperative efforts, the responsibilities of each partner must be clearly specified. Otherwise, obligations that were anticipated to be the duty of one contracting party may result in costs to another. Rosenlew Oy, a major Finnish industrial corporation, had to pay a $600,000 fine to Hungary's Chemokomplex for delays in the completion of a plant. Parts provided by Hungarian suppliers seldom arrived on time, and Rosenlew, as the major contractor, was held responsible.[16]

[14] Ilkka A. Ronkainen, "Project Exports and the CMEA," in *International Marketing Management*, ed. Erdener Kaynak (New York: Praeger, 1984), 305–317.

[15] "Crossing Cultural Divides: Conducting Business Internationally," *T&E*, October 1985, 1.

[16] "Negotiating in Eastern Europe," *Business Eastern Europe*, October 17, 1980, 320–330.

MARKETING COMMUNICATIONS STRATEGY

The international marketing manager has the responsibility of formulating a communications strategy for the promotion of the company and its products and services. The basic steps of such a strategy are outlined in Figure 11.2.

Few if any firms can afford expenditures for promotion in international markets that is done as "art for art's sake" or only because major competitors do it. The first step in developing communications strategy is therefore assessing what company or product characteristics and benefits should be communicated to the export market. This requires constant monitoring of the various environments and target audience characteristics. For example, Volvo has used safety and quality as its primary themes in its worldwide promotional campaigns since the 1950s. This approach has provided continuity, repetition, and uniformity in positioning Volvo with respect to its primary competitors: Mercedes Benz (prestige) and BMW (sportiness).

Absolut, which is owned by the Swedish government, in 1979 started exporting its vodka into the United States with 45,000 cases and an introductory promotion effort. In 1988 sales reached two million cases as a result of changing American drinking habits. Vodkas are now the largest category in the distilled-spirits business, with Absolut ruling the high-

FIGURE 11.2 ▪ **Steps in Formulating Marketing Communications Strategy**

Step One	Assess Marketing Communications Opportunities
Step Two	Analyze Marketing Communications Resources
Step Three	Set Marketing Communications Objectives
Step Four	Develop/Evaluate Alternative Strategies
Step Five	Assign Specific Marketing Communications Tasks

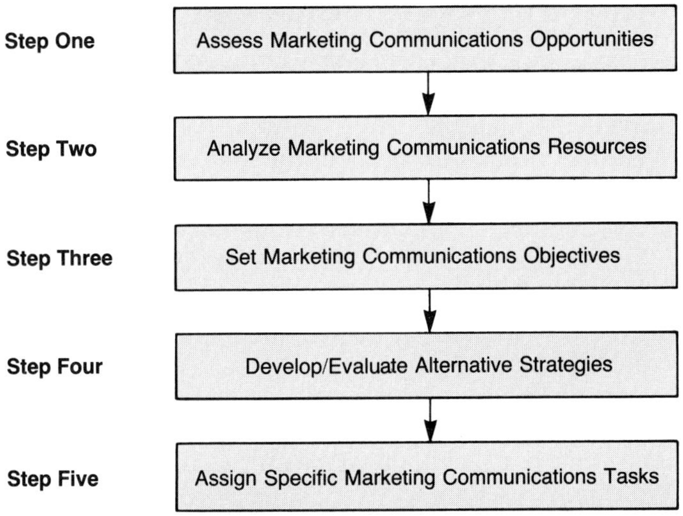

Source: Wayne DeLozier, *The Marketing Communication Process* (New York: McGraw-Hill, 1976), 272.

class vodka crowd.[17] Certain rules of thumb can be followed in evaluating resources to be allocated for export communications efforts. A sufficient commitment is necessary, which means a relatively high absolute amount of money. The exporter has to operate in foreign markets according to the rules of the marketplace, which in the United States, for example, means high promotional costs—perhaps 30 percent of exports or even more during the early stage of entry. For example, Absolut's promotional budget for 1988 was $22.5 million, a significant amount when compared to retail sales of $260 million.

Because of monetary constraints that most exporters face, promotional efforts should be concentrated on key markets. For example, European liquor marketers traditionally concentrate their promotional efforts on the United States, where volume consumption is the greatest, and Great Britain, which is considered the world capital of the liquor trade. A specific objective might be to spend more than the closest competitors do in the U.S. market. In some cases, an exporter will have to limit this to one country, even one area, at a time to achieve set goals with the available budget. International campaigns require patient investment; the market has to progress through awareness, knowledge, liking, preference, and favorable purchase intentions before payback begins. Payback periods of one or two years cannot be realistically expected. For many exporters a critical factor is the support of the intermediary. Whether a distributor is willing to contribute a $3 million media budget or a few thousand dollars makes a big difference. In some cases, intermediaries take a leading role in the promotion of the product in a market. In the case of Absolut, for example, Carillon Importers has been credited with the creative advertising widely acknowledged as a primary reason for the brand's success. In most cases, however, the exporter should retain control of the campaign rather than allow a free hand in the various markets operated. Although markets may be dissimilar, common themes and common objectives need to be incorporated into the individual campaigns.

Alternative strategies are needed to spell out how the firm's resources can be combined and adapted to market opportunities. The tools that the international marketer has available to form a total communications program for use in the targeted markets are referred to as the **promotional mix.** They consist of the following:

1. Advertising: any form of nonpersonal presentation of ideas, goods, or services by an identified sponsor, with predominant use made of the media of mass communication
2. Personal selling: the process of assisting and persuading a prospect to buy a good or service or to act upon an idea through use of person-to-person communication
3. Publicity: any form of nonpaid commercially significant news or editorial comment about ideas, products, or institutions

[17] "Neat Shot," *Marketing & Media Decisions* 24 (March 1989): 73–78.

4. Sales promotion: direct inducements that provide extra product value or incentive to the sales force, distributors, or the ultimate consumers [18]

In some cases, packaging serves a promotional role—for example, when it is distinctive and unique in its color or shape. The use of tools will vary by company and by situation as seen in The International Marketplace 11.2.

[18]Irving Shapiro, *Dictionary of Marketing Terms* (Totowa, N.J.: Rowmen and Littlefield, 1981), 203.

THE INTERNATIONAL MARKETPLACE 11.2

Stepping Out *John Stollenwerk bought Allen Edmonds, the Milwaukee maker of classic American shoes, in 1980 and learned that although the company purchased the leather for uppers in Europe, it did not sell any finished shoes there. In fact, the company had no sales at all outside the United States. By 1989 Allen Edmonds was earning more than 10 percent of its $33 million total sales abroad.*

Breaking into foreign markets was not easy. Starting in 1980, Stollenwerk took Edmonds' wares to trade shows in Italy, Germany, and France—where he was ignored. He traveled continually, displaying his shoes for several years until finally a distributor approached him, impressed with his perseverance. Thanks to that distributor, Allen Edmonds broke into Europe.

Next, Stollenwerk turned to Japan. But to sell in Japan he needed to get his foot in the door of the Tokyo Trade Fair, something that no other American shoemaker had ever been able to do. At first, he was no different. He applied and was politely rejected on the pretense that the fair was closed to foreigners. Then Stollenwerk found out that certain European manufacturers had been expressly invited to attend. "That really ticked us off."

With classic American flair, Stollenwerk packed his bags, booked a flight to Tokyo, and called a press conference. The story was quickly picked up by the international press and almost overnight Tokyo was welcoming him with open arms. In 1988, Allen Edmonds sold more than 3,000 pairs of shoes to the Japanese—at $500 a pair.

Allen Edmonds tries to find the right fit for each market, modifying shoe styles to account for differing tastes and needs. Edmonds also alters its advertising styles market by market. The company advertises in 15 languages and maintains in-house communication capabilities in four.

Source: "America: The Export Edge," *Export Today* 5 (February 1989): 5–19.

The choice of tools leads to either a push or a pull emphasis in marketing communications. **Push strategies** focus on the use of personal selling. Despite its higher cost per contact, personal selling is appropriate for the international marketing of industrial goods, which have shorter channels of distribution and smaller target populations than do consumer goods. Governmental clients are typically serviced through personal selling efforts. Some industries, such as pharmaceuticals, traditionally rely on personal selling to service the clientele.

On the other hand, **pull strategies** depend on mass communications tools, mainly advertising. Advertising is appropriate for consumer-oriented products with large target audiences and long channels of distribution. Of its promotional budget, Absolut spends 85 percent in print media in the United States, with the balance picked up by outdoor advertising, mainly billboards. The base of the advertising effort is formed by magazines such as *Sports Illustrated, Vanity Fair, Business Week, Rolling Stone, Esquire, Time,* and *Newsweek.*

No promotional tool should be used in isolation or without regard to the others. Their use should be coordinated according to target market and product characteristics, the size of the promotional budget, the type and length of international involvement, and control considerations. As an example, industrial purchasing decisions typically involve 8 to 11 people. Because a salesperson may not reach all of them, the use of advertising may be necessary to influence the participants in the decision-making process.

Some exporters maintain an overall umbrella campaign to support the product-specific campaigns of their product divisions and individual distributors. An example of such a campaign is presented in Table 11.1. The company engaged in an umbrella campaign not only because of its diverse operations but also to take advantage of the economic integration in Europe.

Finally, specific marketing communications tasks must be assigned, which may involve deciding on a division of labor with foreign intermediaries or with other exporters for cooperative communications efforts.[19] For example, Koss, a Milwaukee-based company that is one of the most recognized names in stereophones, concentrates on in-store display through a cooperative program with its distributors.[20] More money is thus available for promotion, and its execution is carried out locally with central control from Koss.

COMMUNICATIONS TOOLS

The main communications tools used by exporters to communicate with the foreign marketplace from their domestic base are business and trade journals, direct mail, trade fairs and missions, and personal selling. If the

[19] M. Wayne DeLozier, *The Marketing Communications Process* (New York: McGraw-Hill, 1976), 163–173.

[20] "The Sound of America," *Export Today* 5 (February 1989): 33–34.

TABLE 11.1 ▪ **Key Ingredients of Kemira's International Corporate Image Campaign**

- Short-term goals: to increase awareness of the company and to support sales and advertising efforts in export markets
- Long-term goals: to assist in competing against larger competitors and to position the company above weaker competitors
- Corporate image goal: to convey that Kemira is a creative company, its personnel are highly motivated and can cope with its clients' toughest problems, and Kemira is an internationally significant company in its specialty areas
- Duration: August 1982 through Spring 1983
- Budget: two million Fmks (approximately $400,000)
- Targets: public administrators, financing organizations, and higher management levels of present and potential clients in Europe, Africa, the Far East, and Latin America
- Creative requirement: five black-and-white full-page advertisements, each featuring a description of one of the company's divisions—fertilizers, industrial chemicals, titanium oxide, viscosity fibers, and protective devices
- Media vehicles: *Economist, Business Week, International Management, Scientific American, Far Eastern Economic Review, Capital, L'Expansion,* and *Africa*
- Sales promotion: campaign brochure provided to 200 sales agents as well as a general corporate brochure in English, French, and Spanish
- Results: more than 350 letters from 60 different countries, 70 percent from upper management, as well as a prize in *International Management* magazine's corporate-image advertising competition

Source: Timo Holtari, "Rahaa ja Strategiaa," *Fakta* (February 1983): 35–37.

exporter's strategy calls for a major promotional effort in a market, it is advisable either to use a U.S.-based agency with extensive operations in the intended market or to use a local agency and work closely with the company's local representatives in media and message choices.

The challenges to be faced within individual markets in terms of advertising, sales promotion, and personal selling and their multinational coordination are discussed in Chapter 19. The focus of this section is on international promotional activities rather than local activities; for example, selling directly to clients abroad across multiple markets rather than local selling.

Business and Trade Journals

A wide range of business and trade publications is available to the exporter, as Figure 11.3 indicates. Many business publications, such as *Business Week, Fortune, The Economist, The Wall Street Journal,* and *Financial Times,* are standard information sources worldwide. An extension of these are their regional editions; for example, *Asian Wall Street Journal* or

FIGURE 11.3 ▪ **Examples of International Business Publications**

Source: Standard Rate & Data Service.

Business Week–Europe. Trade publications can be classified as (1) horizontal, which cater to a particular job function cutting across industry lines, such as *Purchasing World*, and (2) vertical, which deal with a specific industry, such as *Chemical Engineering.* These journals are either global, regional, or country-specific in their approaches. Many U.S.-based publications are available in national language editions, with some offering regional buys for specific export markets—for example, the Spanish edition of *Reader's Digest,* titled *Selecciones.*

The two main concerns when selecting media are those of effectiveness in reaching the appropriate target audience(s) and efficiency in minimizing the cost of doing so, measured in terms of cost per thousand. If the exporter is in a position to clearly define the target audience (for example, in terms of demographics or product-related variables), the choice of media will be easier. The advertisement shown in Figure 11.4 is directed to an audience with a particular income level and product interest.

In deciding which publications to use, the exporter must apply the general principles of marketing communications strategy. Coverage and circulation information is available from **Standard Rate & Data.** SRDS provides a complete list of international publications in the International Section of *The Business Publication,* and audit information similar to that on the U.S. market is provided for the United Kingdom, Italy, France, Austria, Switzerland, West Germany, Mexico, and Canada. Outside of these areas, the exporter has to rely on the assistance of publishers or local representatives. Actual choices are usually complicated by lack of sufficient funds and concern over the information gap. The simplest approach may be to use U.S. publishers, in which the exporter may have more confidence in terms of rates and circulation data. If a more localized approach is needed, a regional edition or national publications can be considered. Before advertising is placed in an unfamiliar journal, its content and overall quality of presentation should be analyzed.

Direct Mail

Direct mail can be a highly personalized tool of communication if the target audience can be identified and defined narrowly. Ranging from notices to actual samples, it allows for flexibility in the amount of information conveyed and in its format. Direct mail is directly related in its effectiveness to the quality of the mailing lists, which generally are not as readily available or as up-to-date as they are in the United States. Many mailing lists do not specify an individual as recipient, which means that the materials sent will probably be discarded before they reach the decision maker. In the People's Republic of China, for example, lists are available to send literature directly to factories, ministries, professional societies, research institutes, and universities. However, such mailings can be extremely costly and produce few results. An effective and efficient direct mail campaign requires extensive market-by-market planning of materials, format, and mode of mailing.

FIGURE 11.4 ▪ **A Targeted Advertisement**

WHEN DR. DINGER PROMISES YOU 965 HORSEPOWER, HE DOESN'T MEAN 964.

If you'd like your new diesel yacht to speed up to 60 miles per hour with a whopping 6,000 hours minimum between overhauls, the best friend you could have is Dr. Hans Dinger of MTU. Why?

Thirty years ago his discoveries in hydrodynamic behavior made design predictions of power more accurate than ever before. Today he heads hundreds of heirs by the engineering genius of MTU's founders ... Gottlieb Daimler, Karl Benz, Wilhelm Maybach and Rudolf Diesel.

And every one of his high-speed marine diesels from Friedrichshafen, West Germany, can deliver all the power you paid for without compromising the durability you deserve.

Which is why most of the big, fast yachts on the Mediterranean rely on MTUs. And over 70 navies throughout the world. And more and more American builders like Denison and Palmer Johnson and Hatteras.

Engines that keep their promise

MTU won't ship an engine until tests prove it delivers all the horsepower promised. Whether that is 665 horses or ten thousand. And every single engine has to pass the test.

But anyone can soup up an engine for awhile, right? (And some do.) So the key is whether that power keeps pumping out next month and next year.

A stunning truth revealed

How long can you expect MTU's power to last between recommended overhauls? A stunning fact is revealed by comparing other engines' owner manuals. MTU's suggests 6,000 hours as the minimum for even our highest RPM engines, not a measly two or three thousand. That's twelve years for most yacht owners, not just five or six.

And even after an MTU overhaul, you can expect another 6,000 hours of specified power before the second one. Ask any other engine to do that!

Why less means more

While other engine companies crank out tens of thousands of marine diesels a year, MTU crafts a few hundred. So it's much easier for MTU to incorporate new power technology. Example, our 94 series 396s have nearly 35% more power than our 93 series with only 10% more weight.

There are scores more reasons why MTUs deliver the power you pay for. Including a predictable German pride in craftsmanship.

Here to stay

When MTU announced its U.S. invasion last year, a few

skeptics wondered where we'd be this year. We'll tell you.

We're twice as far ahead in sales as we ever hoped. We're keeping a staff naval architect busy all day every day custom tailoring and supervising every installation. We opened our U.S. parts and service center ahead of schedule. And have already successfully introduced the only jet propulsion system for large yachts available in the U.S. Not bad, eh?

Your first phone call to MTU is the start of a one-on-one partnership between you

and MTU's factory representative. For the life of your yacht. And our service here in the U.S. can even include direct maintenance performed by factory-trained personnel.

For more information

Write MTU of North America, Inc., Dept. B, 10450 Corporate Drive, Houston, TX 77478. Or call us at 713-240-4100. Or telex 203137 MTU UR. Find out how MTU delivers Dr. Dinger's promise of more dependable, longer lasting high-speed marine power.

OF NORTH AMERICA

Source: Courtesy MTU of North America, Inc.

Catalogs are typically distributed to overseas customers through direct mail. Their function is to make the exporter's name known, generate requests for further information, stimulate orders, and to serve as a reminder between transactions. Catalogs are particularly useful if a firm's products are in a highly specialized field of technology and if only the most highly qualified specialists are to be contacted.

The Soviet market features a unique catalog distribution system. Western firms can conveniently and inexpensively acquaint Soviet scientific, technical, and production end-users with their products by distributing catalogs through the U.S.S.R. State Public Scientific-Technical Library System. The system distributes catalogs through more than 85 industrial information agencies, 15 republic divisions, and 10,000 scientific–technical bureaus that reach end-user organizations and personnel.[21] Because a great unsatisfied demand exists for these catalogs, a very small investment can reach many potential end-users.

Trade Fairs and Missions

Marketing goods and services through trade fairs is a European tradition that dates back over 1,200 years. After salesforce costs, trade shows are one of the most significant cost items in marketing budgets. Although trade fairs are usually associated with industrial firms, some consumer-products firms are represented as well. Typically, a trade show is an event at which manufacturers, distributors, and other vendors display their products or describe their services to current and prospective customers, suppliers, other business associates, and the press. The International Automotive Services Industries Show or the International Coal Show, for example, run eight hours for three days, plus one or two preview days, and register 25,000 attendees. Trade fairs in the Soviet Union are described in The International Marketplace 11.3. In the consumer-goods area, expositions are the most common type of show. Tickets are usually sold; typical expositions include home–garden, boat, auto, hi-fi, and antiques. Although a typical trade show or typical participant does not exist, an estimated $73,000 is allocated for each show, and the median manufacturer or distributor attends nine or ten shows annually.[22]

Whether an exporter should participate in a trade fair depends largely on the type of business relationship it wants to develop with a particular country. A company looking only for one-time or short-term sales might find the expense prohibitive, but a firm looking for long-term involvement may find the investment worthwhile. Arguments in favor of participation include the following:

1. Some products, by their very nature, are difficult to market without providing the potential customer a chance to examine them or see

[21] "Tactics for the Russian Front," *Business Marketing* 74 (January 1989): 42–49.

[22] Thomas V. Bonoma, "Get More Out of Your Trade Shows," *Harvard Business Review* 61 (January–February 1983): 137–145.

11.3   THE INTERNATIONAL MARKETPLACE

At a Soviet Trade Fair   *Exhibitions in the Soviet Union are not much different from those in the United States or Western Europe. Usually planned well in advance and well promoted, the major ones are held in Moscow, usually at Sokolinika Fairgrounds or at the World Trade Center. Because exhibitions seldom if ever compete, exhibitors can count on the major buying influences to show up.*

The U.S.S.R. Chamber of Commerce and Industry generally sponsors the trade fairs (such as the Equipment and Materials for Toy Manufacturing Exhibition held in February 1989), and the U.S. Department of Commerce, Trade Promotion Division, frequently sponsors U.S. participation at major international exhibitions.

Exhibitions are an excellent window on the Soviet marketplace. They provide an opportunity to examine products offered by Soviets to buyers domestically and within the East Bloc, and those offered to the Soviets by competitors worldwide. And exhibitions are an economical way to meet potential business partners.

The language barrier is significant on the exhibit floor. An interpreter should be brought along or arranged for. A good approach is to talk with an agent or consultant with offices in the Soviet Union and arrange for one of its staffers to serve as a guide. Service may be rendered willingly and without charge if it leads to potential future business.

Source: "Tactics for the Soviet Front," *Business Marketing*, 74 (January 1989): 42–49.

---

them in action. Trade fairs provide an excellent opportunity to introduce, promote, and demonstrate new products.

2. An appearance produces goodwill and allows for periodic cultivation of contacts. Beyond the impact of displaying specific products, many firms place strong emphasis on "waving the company flag" against competition.[23] This facet also includes morale boosting of the firm's sales personnel and distributors.

3. Attendance is one of the best ways to contact government officials and decision makers, especially in Eastern European countries and the People's Republic of China. For example, participation in the Leipzig Fair in East Germany is "expected" by the host government.

4. Trade fairs provide an excellent chance for market research and collecting competitive intelligence. The exporter is able to view most rivals at the same time and to test comparative buyer reactions. Trade fairs provide one of the most inexpensive ways of

---

[23]Richard Barovick, "Exporters Fit Trade Fairs into Larger Marketing Strategy," *Business America*, December 10, 1984, 3–5.

obtaining evaluative data on the effectiveness of a promotional campaign.

5. Exporters are able to reach a sizable number of sales prospects in a brief time period at a reasonable cost per contact. More than 86 percent of all attendees represent buying influences (managers with direct responsibility for purchasing products and services). Of equal significance is the fact that trade show visitors are there because they have a specific interest in the exhibits.[24]

On the other hand, these are among the reasons cited for nonparticipation in trade fairs:

1. High costs. These can be avoided by participating in events sponsored by the U.S. Department of Commerce or exhibiting at U.S. trade centers or export development offices. An exporter can also lower costs by sharing expenses with distributors or representatives. Further, costs of closing a sale through trade shows are estimated to be much lower than for those closed through personal sales.

2. Difficulty in choosing the appropriate trade fairs for participation. This is a critical decision. Because of scarce resources, many firms rely on suggestions from their foreign distributors on which fairs to attend and what specifically to exhibit. Caterpillar, for example, usually allows its foreign dealers to make the selections for themselves. In markets where conditions are more restricted for exporters, such as the People's Republic of China, Caterpillar in effect serves as the dealer and thus participates itself.

3. For larger exporters with multiple divisions, coordination becomes an additional concern. Several divisions may be required to participate in the same fair under the company banner. Similarly, coordination is required with distributors and agents if joint participation is desired, which requires joint planning.

Trade show participation is too expensive to be limited to the exhibit alone. A clear set of promotional objectives would include targeting accounts and attracting them to the show with preshow promotion. Major customers and attractive prospects often attend and they should be acknowledged, for example, by arranging for a hospitality suite.[25] Finally, a system is needed to evaluate postshow performance and to track qualified leads.

Exporters may participate in general or specialized trade fairs. Examples of general trade fairs are the ones held in Hanover in West Germany and Milan in Italy. An example of a highly specialized one is the fire prevention equipment fair in Ostrava, Czechoslovakia.

---

[24] "Taking Advantage of Trade Fairs for Maximum Sales Impact," *Business International*, October 12, 1987, 321–323.

[25] "Don't Just Exhibit—Do Something," *Business Marketing* 74 (May 1989): 78.

Other promotional events that the exporter can use are trade missions, seminar missions, solo exhibitions, and video/catalog exhibitions. **Trade missions** can be either U.S. specialized trade missions or industry-organized, government-approved (IOGA) trade missions, both of which aim at expanding the sales of U.S. goods and services and the establishment of agencies and representation abroad. The U.S. Department of Commerce is actively involved in assistance of both types. **Seminar missions** are events in which eight to ten firms are invited to participate in a one- to four-day forum, during which the team members conduct generic discussions on technological issues—that is, follow a soft-selling approach. This is followed up by individual meetings with end-users, government agencies, research institutions, and other potentially useful contacts. Individual firms may introduce themselves to certain markets by proposing a technical seminar there. Synopses of several alternative proposed lectures together with company details and the qualifications of the speakers must be forwarded to the proper body, which will circulate the proposals to likely interested bodies and coordinate all the arrangements. The major drawback is the time required to arrange for such a seminar, which may be as much as a year. **Solo exhibitions** are generally limited to one or, at the most, a few product themes and are held only when market conditions warrant them. **Video/catalog exhibitions** allow exporters to publicize their products at low cost. These programs are organized by the Department of Commerce and related industry associations and consist of 20 to 35 product presentations on videotapes, each lasting five to ten minutes. They provide the advantage of actually showing the product in use to potential customers. All of the approaches require follow-up. An exporter may decide to follow up by letter, personal calls, by calling on embassies or foreign trade organizations (especially when centrally planned economies are concerned), or by combining any of these methods.

Personal Selling

Personal selling is the most effective of the promotional tools available to the marketer; however, its costs per contact are high. The average cost of sales calls may vary from $200 to $1,100, depending on the industry and the product or service. Given the high cost, personnel choices become very important as discussed in The International Marketplace 11.4.

Personal selling may take place through intermediaries or as a direct effort. Intermediaries include manufacturers' representatives, selling agents, or distributors. Communication with intermediaries must ensure both that they are satisfied with the arrangement and that they are equipped to market and promote the exporter's product appropriately. Whatever the distribution arrangement, the exporter must provide basic selling aid communications, such as product specification and data literature, catalogs, the results of product testing, and demonstrated performance information—everything needed to present products to potential customers. In some cases, the exporter has to provide the intermediaries with incentives to en-

THE INTERNATIONAL MARKETPLACE | 11.4

Finding an International Sales Manager   For companies with a long-established history of international marketing or for smaller firms just beginning to test the overseas market, there is no more important position to fill than that of the international sales manager.

Spalding, which does about $500 million in business annually, including $200 million overseas, has offered the following basic guidelines for selecting a good international sales manager:

- Look for someone with experience inside the company, or provide a thorough training program.
- Choose someone in a senior position, or provide a high-level contact in upper management.
- Pick a person with a flexible personality.
- Look for someone with extensive international knowledge or someone willing to gain it.

The first choice is an inside person who knows the company. If this is not possible, an outsider should be given thorough training. In any case, the international sales manager should report to someone at a high level in the company. Otherwise, the need to obtain approval from several people on the color of a package, for example, will cause the international sales effort to suffer.

For someone from outside the company, knowledge of the industry is important. However, someone who is very familiar with the trade channels in a country is as useful as a person with thorough knowledge of the industry, especially for a consumer product.

Where the international sales manager should be based depends on the size of the international operation and the distribution network. The location will also depend on the relationship with an overseas distributor. If the relationship is good, it is not necessary to have someone overseas until the company is doing enough business to warrant a presence abroad.

Source: Stephen J. Simurda, "Finding an International Sales Manager," *Northeast International Business* 1 (September 1988): 15–16.

---

gage in local advertising efforts. They may include special discounts, push money, or cooperative advertising. Cooperative advertising will give the exporter's product local flavor and increase the overall promotional budget for the product. However, the exporter needs to be concerned about its quality and that the funds are spent as agreed.

A number of exporters employ sales representatives whose main function is to represent the firm abroad to existing and potential customers and to seek new leads. This type of presence is essential at some stage of the firm's international involvement. Other promotional tools can facilitate foreign market entry but eventually some personal selling must take place.

The role of personal selling is greatest when the exporter sells directly to the end-user or to governmental agencies, such as foreign trade organizations. Firms selling products with high price tags (such as Boeing commercial aircraft) or companies selling to monopsonies (such as Seagrams liquor to certain Scandinavian countries where all liquor sales are through state-controlled outlets) must rely heavily on person-to-person communication, oral presentations, and direct marketing efforts. Many of these firms can expand their business only if their markets are knowledgeable about what they do. This may require corporate advertising and publicity generation through extensive public relations efforts.

Whatever the sales task, effectiveness is determined by a number of interrelated factors that are summarized in Figure 11.5.[26] One of the keys to personal selling is the salesperson's ability to adapt to the customer and the selling situation.[27] This aspect of selling requires cultural knowledge and empathy; for example, in the Middle East, sales presentations may be broken up by long discussions of topics that have little or nothing to do with the transaction at hand. The characteristics of the buying task, whether routine or unique, have a bearing on the sales presentation. The exporter may be faced by a situation in which the idea of buying from a foreign entity is the biggest obstacle in terms of the risks perceived. If the exporter's product does not provide a clear-cut relative advantage over that of competitors, the analytical, interpersonal skills of the salesperson are needed to assist in the differentiation. A salesperson, regardless of the market, must have a thorough knowledge of the product or service. The more the salesperson is able to apply that knowledge to the particular situation, the more likely that he or she will obtain a positive result. The salesperson usually has front-line responsibility for the firm's customer relations, having to handle conflict situations such as the parent firm's bias for domestic markets and thus the possibility that shipments of goods to foreign clients receive low priority.

In the past, U.S. marketers thought that offices were almost essential to bring their companies closer to overseas customers. Now international **telemarketing** is being promoted by Service 800 SA in Europe and AT&T in the United States. The main uses of the service are data transmission, service calls, customer inquiries, and even office-to-office communication. The quasi-toll-free service allows customers and prospects from 40 countries to contact a firm for little more than the cost of a local call. The service can handle both inbound and outbound calls. Many companies see this as a preliminary step to entering a foreign market with a branch office.

---

[26] Barton A. Weitz, "Effectiveness in Sales Interactions: A Contingency Framework," *Journal of Marketing* 45 (Winter 1981): 85–103.

[27] Alf H. Walle, "Conceptualizing Personal Selling for International Business: A Continuum of Exchange Perspective," *Journal of Personal Selling and Sales Management* 6 (November 1986): 9–17.

FIGURE 11.5 ▪ **Determinants of Effectiveness in Personal Selling**

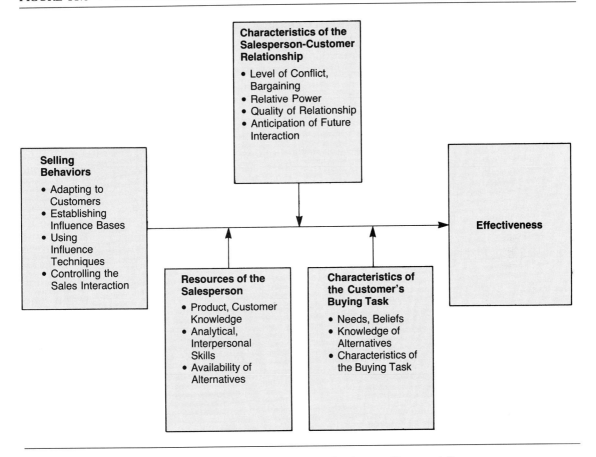

Source: Barton A. Weitz, "Effectiveness in Sales Interactions: A Contingency Framework," *Journal of Marketing* 45 (Winter 1981): 85–103.

In Europe companies using the service publicize their assigned local phone numbers on television and print ads, direct mailings, and catalogs, and calls are routed to Switzerland. The name of the country in which the call originates is displayed above the switchboard so it can be taken by an operator who speaks the language native to that country.[28]

SUMMARY

Effective communication is essential in negotiating agreements. To maximize the outcome of negotiations with clients and partners from other cultural backgrounds, international marketers must show adjustment capability to different standards and behaviors. Success depends on being

[28] Kevin T. Higgins, "Toll-Free Calling Offered to Global Marketers," *Marketing News*, November 22, 1985, 29, 34.

prepared and remaining flexible, whatever the negotiation style in the host country.

Effective and efficient communication is needed for the dual purpose of (1) informing prospective customers about the availability of products or services and (2) persuading customers to opt for the marketer's offering over those of competitors. Within the framework of the company's opportunities, resources, and objectives, decisions must be made about whether to direct communications to present customers, potential customers, the general public, or intermediaries. Decisions must be made on how to reach each of the intended target audiences without wasting valuable resources. A decision also has to be made about who will control the communications effort: the exporter, an agency, or local representatives. The U.S. Department of Commerce is the single best source of export promotion support, which is essential to alleviating the environmental threats perceived by many exporters.

The exporting international marketer must also choose tools to use in the communications effort. Usually two basic tools are used: (1) mass selling through business and trade journals, direct mail, trade fairs, and missions and (2) personal selling, which brings the international marketer face to face with the targeted customer.

Questions for Discussion

1. What is potentially harmful in going out of one's way to make clients feel comfortable by playing down status distinctions such as titles?

2. Discuss this statement: "Lack of foreign-language skills puts American negotiators at a disadvantage."

3. Compare and contrast the usefulness to a novice exporter of elements of the promotional mix.

4. Why do exporters usually choose U.S.-based publishers' services when placing advertisements to boost export sales specifically?

5. Some exporters report that they value above all the broad exposure afforded through exhibiting at a trade fair, regardless of whether they are able to sell directly at the event. Comment on this philosophy.

6. Discuss the benefits of horizontal versus vertical trade journals.

7. What specific advice would you give to an exporter who has used domestic direct mail extensively and wishes to continue the practice abroad?

8. Can an exporter be successful and yet not use local (national) media?

Recommended Readings

Contractor, Farok J., and Peter Lorange. *Cooperative Strategies in International Business.* Lexington, Mass.: Lexington Books, 1988.

Dunn, S. Watson, Arnold M. Barban, Dean M. Krugman, and Leonard N. Reid. *Advertising: Its Role in Modern Marketing,* 7th ed. Hinsdale, Ill.: Dryden Press, 1990.

Graham, John L., and Y. Sano. *Smart Bargaining, Doing Business with the Japanese.* Cambridge, Mass.: Ballinger, 1984.

Hendon, Donald, and Rebecca A. Hendon. "International Body Language and Effective Marketing." *Journal of International Consumer Marketing* 1 (Spring 1988): 51–74.

Jain, Subhash, and Lewis R. Tucker. *International Marketing: Managerial Perspectives.* Boston: CBI Publishing, 1979.

Manville, Richard. "Caveats for the Overseas Marketer." *Marketing News,* March 10, 1978, 8–9.

Shimp, Terence A. *Promotion Management and Marketing Communications.* Hinsdale, Ill.: Dryden Press, 1990.

Young, James R., and R. Wayne Mondy. *Personal Selling: Function, Theory, and Practice.* Hinsdale, Ill.: Dryden Press, 1982.

CHAPTER 12

International Channels of Distribution

12.1 THE INTERNATIONAL MARKETPLACE

Putting the Best Foot Forward In the early 1980s, when most American exporters were getting out of foreign markets, Timberland Shoes decided to find a new market for its line of rugged, outdoor footgear. Initially, the firm had no idea it could be successful in international sales. "A tremendous amount of our decision was really luck. We were discovered by people in Europe who saw an opportunity for us to export at a time we did not believe we could. The goods news is that once we realized there was an opportunity, we went after it," said the company's president.

Timberland's first choice—Italy—surprised many in the industry. Home to many of the world's best-known and high-priced brands of leather footwear, Italy had earned the reputation as the most sophisticated market in Europe. Today, Italy is the most profitable of Timberland's five export markets. The success gave Timberland the confidence to make exporting a major profit center for the company: 1987 exports accounted for 28 percent of net sales, with export sales growth at 50 percent.

To find new markets, Timberland takes a somewhat unconventional approach. Instead of scouting for markets where management thinks it could get a foothold, the company responds only to those distributors who approach it. "We have talented distributors who understand the market better than we ever could." Timberland looks at the line of footwear the distributor carries and how it is marketed. If the line is high quality and the distributor has a good success rate, then Timberland will go into the market.

Timberland also maintains close relationships with each distributor. Every year the company conducts two sales meetings in the United States for its foreign distributors. And despite a preference for coordinating international sales efforts from the United States, Timberland sends top officers from the company on periodic visits to each local market.

Source: "Sizing up the Customers' Needs," Export Today 5 (February 1989): 32–33.

Channels of distribution provide the essential linkages that connect producers and customers. The links are intracompany and extracompany entities that perform a number of functions. This chapter will focus on the ways an exporter can form an optimal distribution system in terms of design and choice of the individual **intermediaries.** More than a simple sequence of marketing institutions between producers and consumers, a channel of distribution should be a team working toward a common goal. The effort must be seen as a joint one by all of the participants in order to be successful in the long run.

The channel decision is the most long-term of the marketing mix decisions in that it cannot be readily changed. This makes the choice of channel structure crucial. Firm and market factors influence export task performance in various ways, as shown in The International Marketplace 12.1. An experienced exporter may decide that control is of utmost importance and choose to perform tasks itself and incur the information collection and adaptation costs. An infrequent exporter, on the other hand, may be quite dependent on experienced intermediaries to get its product to markets. Whether export tasks are self-performed or assigned to export intermediaries, the distribution function should be planned in such a way that the channel will function as one rather than a collection of different or independent units. The decisions involved in the structuring and management of the export channel of distribution are discussed first. The chapter will end with a discussion of the steps needed in the preparation of an international shipment. Logistics issues will be discussed in detail in Chapter 18.

CHANNEL STRUCTURE

A generalization of channel configurations for consumer and industrial products as well as services is provided in Figure 12.1. Channels can vary from direct, producer-to-consumer ones, to elaborate, multilevel channels employing many types of intermediaries, each serving a particular purpose. For example, Amstrad, a British computer manufacturer, sells its products in Spain in more than 4,200 retail outlets. To have this reach it sells through four types of channels: (1) large accounts, such as the country's largest department stores, (2) buyer groups consisting of national and regional associations of consumer electronics retailers, (3) independent appliance retailers and informatics stores, and (4) wholesalers who reach accounts that the other channel types cannot reach.[1] Channel configurations will vary within industries, even within the same firm for the same product because national markets quite often have their unique features. This may mean dramatic departures from accepted policy for a company. For example, IBM signed a deal in Britain to let Ferranti PLC sell PS/2s

---

[1] *Business International/Ideas in Action,* "How Amstrad Successfully Set Up a Distribution Channel in Spain," March 14, 1988, 4–6.

FIGURE 12.1 ▪ **Channel Configurations**

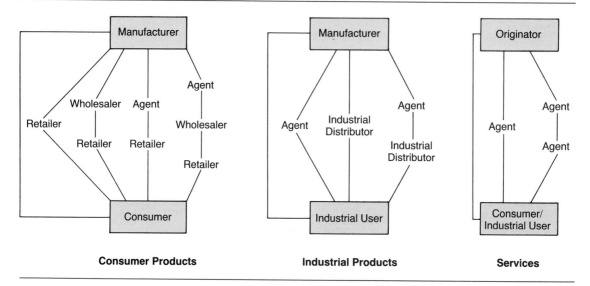

Consumer Products   **Industrial Products**   **Services**

under its name to niche markets that are not often reached by IBM—a first time for IBM to use such an approach.[2]

The type and number of channel members can differ to accommodate customer characteristics and other environmental variables, as can be seen from the two examples in Figure 12.2. Whereas PepsiCo has millions of customers and needs saturation coverage to reach them, Boeing has relatively few, easily targetable customers and thus has a direct channel between the manufacturer and the user. When a government-owned airline in a Third World country is the customer, Boeing often leases the plane.

The connections made by marketing institutions are not solely for the physical movement of goods. They also serve as transactional title flows and informational communications flows. Rather than unidirectional, downward from the producer, the flows are usually multidirectional, both vertical and horizontal. As an example, the manufacturer relies heavily on the retailer population for data on possible changes in demand. Communications from retailers may be needed to coordinate a cooperative advertising campaign instituted by a manufacturer. The three flows—physical, transactional, and informational—do not necessarily take place simultaneously or occur at every level of the channel. Agent intermediaries, for example, act only to facilitate the information flow. They do not take title and often do not physically handle the goods.

Because only a few products are sold directly to ultimate users, an international marketer has to decide on alternative ways to move products to chosen markets. The basic marketing functions of exchange, physical

[2] *Business Week,* "Mike Armstrong Is Improving IBM's Game in Europe," June 20, 1988, 96–101.

FIGURE 12.2 ▪ **Channels of Distribution for PepsiCo and Boeing**

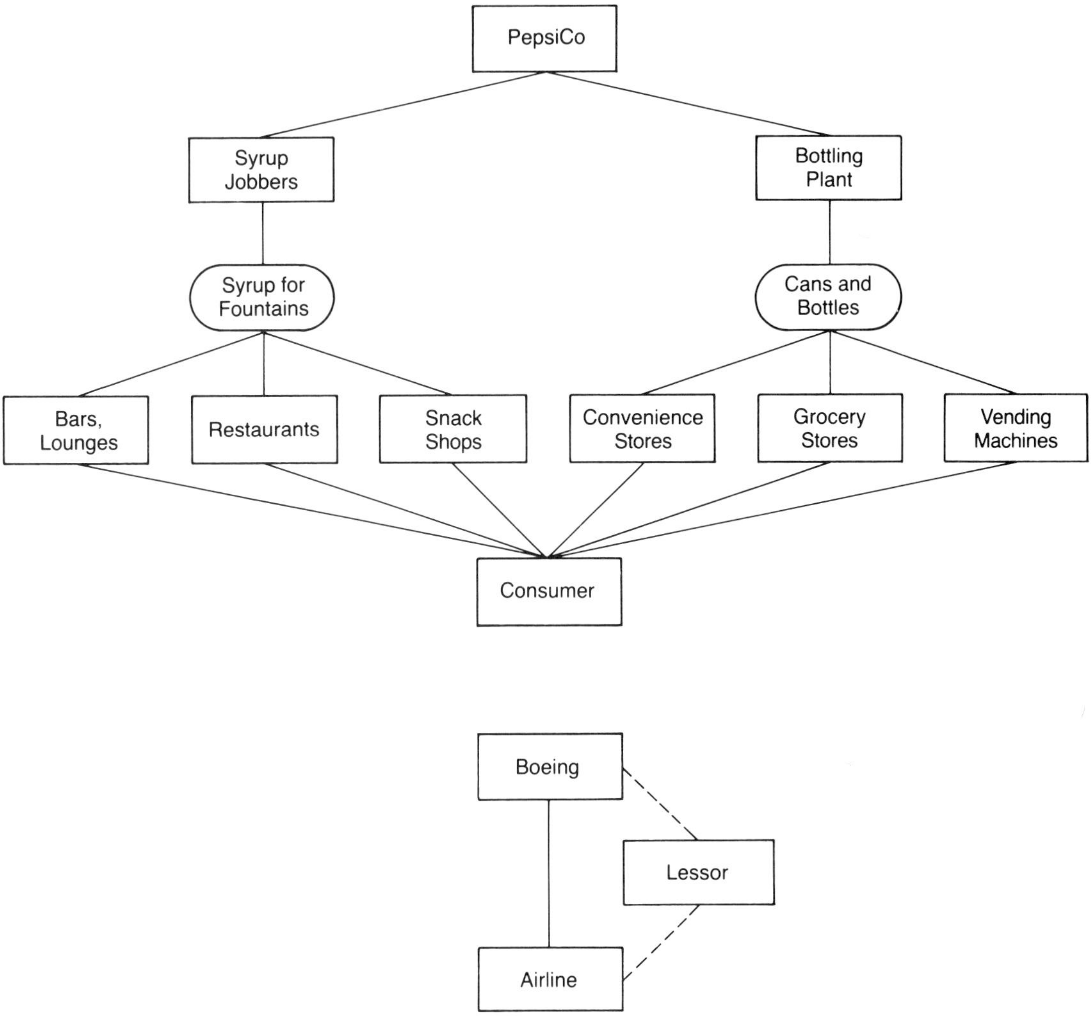

movement, and various facilitating activities must be performed but the marketer may not be equipped to handle them. Intermediaries can therefore be used to gain quick, easy, and relatively low-cost entry to a targeted market.

CHANNEL DESIGN

The term channel design refers to the length and the width of the channel employed. Length is determined by the number of levels, or different types, of intermediaries. The most traditional is the producer-wholesaler-

TABLE 12.1 ▪ **Determinants of Channel Structure**

Customer Characteristics
Culture
Competition
Company Objectives
Character
Capital
Cost
Coverage
Control
Continuity
Communication

retailer-customer configuration. Channel width is determined by the number of institutions of each type in the channel. An industrial-goods marketer may grant exclusive distribution rights to a foreign entity, whereas a consumer-goods marketer may want to use as many intermediaries as possible to ensure intensive distribution.

Channel design is determined by factors that can be summarized as the 11 Cs, as listed in Table 12.1. These factors are integral to both the development of new marketing channels and the modification of existing ones. Their individual influences will vary from one market to another and seldom, if ever, can one factor be considered without the interactive effects of the others. The marketer should use the 11 Cs checklist to determine the proper approach to reach intended target audiences before selecting channel members to fill the roles. The first three factors are givens in that the firm must adjust to the existing structures. The other eight are controllable to a certain extent by the international marketer.

Customer Characteristics

The demographic and psychographic characteristics of targeted customers will form the basis for channel design decisions. Answers to questions such as what customers need as well as why, when, and how they buy are used to determine ways in which the products should be made available in order to generate a competitive advantage. As an example, Anheuser-Busch's success in Japan began when Suntory, one of the country's largest liquor distillers, acquired the importing rights. Suntory's marketing plan stressed distribution of Budweiser in discos, pubs, and other night spots where Japan's affluent, well-traveled youth gather. Young people in Japan are influenced by American culture and adapt themselves more readily to new products than do older Japanese. Taking advantage of this fact, Suntory concentrated its efforts on one generation, and on-premise sales led to major off-premise (retail outlet) sales as well.

In the early stages of product introduction, the international marketer may concentrate efforts on only the most attractive markets and later, having attained a foothold, expand distribution. When Kronenbourg, the best-selling beer in Europe, entered the U.S. market, distribution was initiated in New York City and then extended to the metropolitan area. The reason was the area's prominence in both domestic and imported beer consumption. The national rollout took place five years later. In the industrial sector, certain industries cluster geographically, allowing the international marketer to take a more direct approach.

Customer characteristics may cause the same product to be distributed through two different types of channels. All sales of Caterpillar's earth-moving equipment are handled by 247 independent dealers, except that sales are direct to the U.S. government, the Soviet Union, and the People's Republic of China. Furthermore, primary target audiences may change from one market to another. For example, in Japan McDonald's did not follow the U.S. pattern of locating restaurants in the suburbs. The masses of young pedestrians that flood Japanese cities were more promising than affluent but tradition-minded car owners in the suburbs.[3]

Culture

In planning a distribution system, the marketer must analyze existing channel structures, or what might be called **distribution culture.** As an example, the manner in which Japanese channels of distribution are structured and managed presents one of the major reasons for the apparent failure of foreign firms to establish major market penetration in Japan.[4] The new firm must therefore be prepared to spend more time developing a working knowledge of the market for its products than is usually the case in other countries. The Japanese argue that channel patterns develop over time for a particular reason to "provide the most economical and efficient means of serving the market environment."[5] In any case, and in every country, international marketers must study distribution systems in general and the types of linkages between channel members for their specific type of product. Usually the international marketer has to adjust to existing structures to gain distribution. For example, in Finland 92 percent of all distribution of nondurable consumer goods is through four wholesale chains. Without their support, no significant penetration of the market is possible.

In addition to structure, functions performed by the various types of intermediaries have to be outlined. Retailers in Japan demand more from manufacturers and wholesalers than do American retailers; for example, they expect returns of merchandise to be fully accepted even if there is no reason other than lack of sales. Retailers also expect significant amounts

[3] Frederick H. Katayama, *Fortune*, "Japan's Big Mac," September 15, 1986, 114–120.

[4] Randolph Ross, "Understanding the Japanese Distribution System: An Explanatory Framework," *European Journal of Marketing* 17 (Winter 1983): 5–15.

[5] Yoshi Tsurumi, "Managing Consumer and Industrial Systems in Japan," *Sloan Management Review*, Fall 1982, 36–45.

TABLE 12.2 ▪ **Examples of Function Performance in the Channel System for the Japanese Cosmetics Industry**

Channel Member		
Manufacturer	*Intermediary*	*Retail*
Production	Order Taking	Selling
Advertising	Inventory Maintenance	Organizing Consumers
National Sales Promotion	Space Control at the	In-Store Promotion
Dealer Aids	Retail Level	
Education of Dealers	Product Assortment	
Financing	Dispatching of Sales	
	Support Personnel	
	Area Marketing	
	Financing	

Source: Michael R. Czinkota, "Distribution of Consumer Products in Japan," *International Marketing Review* 2 (Autumn 1985): 39–51.

of financing and frequent delivery of products. Retailers, on their part, offer substantial services to their clientele and take great pains to build close relationships with their customers. As can be seen in Table 12.2, which lists channel members in the Japanese cosmetics industry, functions are—and should be—clearly delineated. Manufacturers concentrate mainly on production and promotional activities; intermediaries work on logistics activities, financing, and communication with manufacturers and retailers; retailers focus on sales and promotional activities.

Trying to change existing distribution systems may be quite difficult. Porsche tried to change the way it sold automobiles in the United States from traditional independent franchised dealers to a "dealerless system." Whereas dealers buy cars for resale, Porsche would have instituted agents who would order cars as they sold them and work on an 8 percent commission rather than the normal 16 to 18 percent margin. After an uproar, Porsche abandoned the plan.[6]

Additionally, an analysis is needed of the relationships between channel members—for example, the extent of vertical integration. The linkage can be based on ownership, contract, or the use of expert or referent power by one of the channel members. The Japanese distribution system often financially links producers, importers, distributors, and retailers, either directly or through a bank or a trading company. Interdependence in a number of southern European markets is forged through family relationships or is understood as an obligation.

Foreign legislation affecting distributors and agents is an essential part of the distribution culture of a market. For example, legislation may re-

[6]David B. Tinnin, "Porsche's Civil War with Its Dealers," *Fortune*, April 16, 1984, 63–68.

quire that foreign firms be represented only by firms that are 100 percent locally owned. Some nations have totally prohibited the use of dealers in order to protect consumers from abuses attributed to intermediaries.

Competition

Channels used by competitors may be the only distribution system for a particular product that is accepted by both the trade and consumers. In this case, the international marketer's task is to use the structure effectively and efficiently. One challenge, even for a sizable entity such as IBM, may be to create a distribution system as extensive as an established competitor. IBM can send a sales team out of its Tokyo office or one of its 50 branch offices to sell a system to a large buyer, such as a bank or industrial company. Hitachi, on the other hand, has 10,000 exclusive retail dealers and a salesforce already selling motors and other machinery to hundreds of commercial customers. To emulate the distribution approach of this major competitor, IBM enlisted the help of more than 60 outside dealers, such as Nissan Motor outlets, to sell small computers to their customers.

The alternative is to use a totally different distribution approach from that of the competition and hope to develop a competitive advantage. A new approach will have to be carefully analyzed and tested against the cultural, political, and legal environments in which it is to be introduced. For example, Black Box, a Pittsburgh-based manufacturer of computer-communications equipment, found that its independent foreign distributors often pushed only the most profitable lines regardless of who made them. Black Box's solution was to form jointly owned sales companies.[7] In some cases, the international marketer cannot manipulate the distribution variable. For example, in Sweden and Finland all alcoholic beverages must be distributed through state monopoly-owned outlets. In Japan, the Japan Tobacco & Salt Public Corporation is a state monopoly that controls all tobacco imports and charges a 20 percent fee for distribution.

In some cases, all feasible channels may be blocked by domestic competitors either through contractual agreements or through other means. U.S. suppliers of soda ash, which is used in glass, steel, and chemical products, have not been able to penetrate the Japanese market even though they offer a price advantage. The reason is the cartel-like condition developed by the Japan Soda Industry Association, which allegedly sets import levels, specifies which local trading company is to deal with each U.S. supplier, and buys the imports at lower U.S. prices for resale by its members at higher Japanese prices. Efforts by U.S. producers to distribute directly or through smaller, unaffiliated traders have faced strong resistance. The end-users and traders fear alienating the domestic producers, on whom their business depends.

---

[7] *Business Week,* "Made in the U.S.A.," February 29, 1988, 60–66.

Company Objectives

A set of management considerations will have an effect on channel de-sign.[8] No channel of distribution can be properly selected unless it meets the requirements set by overall company objectives for market share and profitability. Sometimes management may simply want to use a particular channel of distribution, and there may be no sound business basis for the decision.

Channels of distribution will have to change as the operations of the company expand. For example, Xerox set a goal of having noncopier sales account for 50 percent of the company's worldwide business by 1990. Be-fore this decision, copiers, accounting for 95 percent of sales, were sold mainly through the company's own direct salesforce. In France, Xerox changed its distribution dramatically by setting up a chain of retail sales outlets, wholly owned and run by the company. To improve its coverage of rural areas and small towns, Xerox withdrew its direct salesforce and re-placed it with independent distributors, called **concessionaires,** who work on an exclusive basis.[9]

Often some management goals may have conflicting results. When in-vestment in the restaurant business in Japan was liberalized, a number of U.S. fast food chains rushed to capitalize on the development. Because they were unfamiliar with the features of the Japanese distribution system, most formed joint ventures with Japanese partners, partially adapting sales methods and American-type products to fit the market. The com-panies attempted to establish mass sales as soon as possible by opening numerous restaurants in the busiest sections of several Japanese cities. Unfortunately, control proved to be quite difficult because of the sheer number of openings over a relatively short period of time. The individual stores changed the product as they grew, ruining the major asset—stan-dardization—that the U.S. companies offered.[10]

Character

The nature of the product, its character, will have an impact on the design of the channel. Generally, the more specialized, expensive, bulky, or per-ishable the product and the more after-sale service it may require, the more likely the channel is to be relatively short. Staple items, such as soap, tend to have longer channels.

The type of channel chosen must match the overall positioning of the product in the market. Changes in overall market conditions, such as cur-

[8]C. Glenn Walters and Blaise J. Bergiel, *Marketing Channels* (Glenview, Ill.: Scott, Foresman, 1982), 142–162.

[9]*Business International/Ideas in Action,* "Rank Xerox Reorganizes Distribution to Succeed in Europe," February 15, 1988, 2–5.

[10]Robert H. Luke, "Successful Marketing in Japan: Guidelines and Recommendations" in *Contemporary Perspectives in International Business,* eds. Harold W. Berkman and Ivan R. Vernon (Chicago: Rand McNally, 1979), 307–315.

FIGURE 12.3 ▪ **Variety of Distribution Alternatives: The Channels for Soap in Japan**

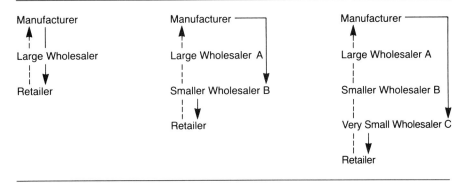

Source: Michael R. Czinkota, "Distribution of Consumer Products in Japan," *International Marketing Review* 2 (Autumn 1985): 39–51.

rency fluctuations, may require changes in distribution as well. An increase in the value of the dollar may cause a repositioning of the marketed product as a luxury item, necessitating an appropriate channel (such as an upper-grade department store) for its distribution.

Rules of thumb aside, particular products may be distributed in a number of ways even to the same target audience. Figure 12.3 shows the variety of distribution alternatives for soap in Japan. Case 1 presents the most frequently used channel. Product deliveries are made from the manufacturer to a wholesaler who in turn delivers to a retailer. Payment flows go from the retailer to the wholesaler who in turn pays the manufacturer. In case 2, the larger wholesaler acts as an agent, receiving a 5 percent commission on the sale from the manufacturer. Case 3 is an example of channel structures necessary to ensure the most intensive type of distribution.

Capital

The term capital is used to describe the financial requirements in setting up a channel system. The international marketer's financial strength will determine the type of channel and the basis on which channel relationships will be built. The stronger the marketer's finances, the more able the firm is to establish channels it either owns or controls. Intermediaries' requirements for beginning inventories, selling on a consignment basis, preferential loans, and need for training all will have an impact on the type of approach chosen by the international marketer. For example, an industrial goods manufacturer may find that potential distributors in a particular country all lack the capability of servicing the product. The marketer then has two options: (1) set up an elaborate training program at headquarters or regionally or (2) institute company-owned service centers to help distributors. Either approach will require a significant investment.

Cost

Closely related to the capital dimension is cost—that is, the expenditure incurred in maintaining a channel once it is established. Costs will naturally vary over the life cycle of a relationship with a particular channel member as well as over the life cycle of the products marketed. An example of the costs involved is promotional monies spent by a distributor for the marketer's product. In 1982, a total of $1.4 million was spent to promote Budweiser in Japan, with Anheuser-Busch and its Japanese distributor, Suntory, splitting the cost evenly.

Costs will vary in terms of the relative power of the manufacturer vis-à-vis its intermediaries. In the United Kingdom, for example, retail power is in the hands of giant multiple stores, such as Tesco, Sainsbury, and Asda. The centralized distribution systems being developed by these giants are eroding the marketing strength of manufacturers, which lay in their networks of distribution depots that delivered direct to stores. Now, retailers want delivery to their central distribution centers. In addition, they are pushing stockholding costs to manufacturers by demanding more frequent deliveries, in smaller, mixed loads, with shorter delivery time.[11]

Costs may also be incurred in protecting the company's distributors against adverse market conditions. A number of U.S. manufacturers helped their distributors maintain competitive prices through subsidies when the exchange rate for the U.S. dollar caused pricing problems. Extra financing aid has been extended to distributors that have been hit with competitive adversity. Such support, although often high in monetary cost, will pay back manyfold through a faultless manufacturer-distributor relationship.

Coverage

The term coverage is used to describe both the number of areas in which the marketer's products are represented and the quality of that representation. Coverage is therefore two dimensional in that horizontal and vertical coverage need to be considered in channel design. The number of areas to be covered depends on the dispersion of demand in the market and also the time elapsed since the product's introduction to the market. Three different approaches are available:

1. Intensive coverage, which calls for distributing the product through the largest number of different types of intermediaries and the largest possible number of individual intermediaries of each type
2. Selective coverage, which entails choosing a number of intermediaries for each area to be penetrated
3. Exclusive coverage, which involves only one entity in a market for its distributive effort

---

[11] *Business International/Ideas in Action,* "How Dairy Crest Transformed Customer Service by Better Physical Distribution," April 11, 1988, 8–11.

TABLE 12.3 ▪ **Advantages of a Single Distributor**

1. One corporate presence eliminates confusion among buyers and local officials.
2. The volume of business that results when exports are consolidated will attract a larger distributor. The larger distributor will have greater influence in its local business community.
3. Communication is less plagued by noise. This will have a positive effect in many areas, from daily information flows to supervising and training.
4. More effective coordination of the sales and promotional effort can be achieved.
5. Logistics flows are more economical.
6. A stronger presence can be maintained in smaller markets or markets in which resources may dictate a holding mode, until more effective penetration can be undertaken.
7. Distributor morale and overall principal–intermediary relationship are better.

Source: Business International Corporation, *201 Checklists: Decision Making in International Operations* (New York: Business International Corporation, 1980), 26–27.

Generally, intensive and selective coverage call for longer channels using different types of intermediaries, usually wholesalers and agents. Exclusive distribution is conducive to more direct sales. For some products, such as ethnic products, markets are concentrated geographically and allow for more intensive distribution with a more direct channel. A company typically enters a market with one local distributor, but as volume expands the distribution base often has to be adjusted. The advantages of a single distributor are listed in Table 12.3.

Expanding distribution too quickly may cause problems. Benetton, one of Italy's major exporters of clothing, had planned to have 1,000 stores in the United States by 1990. The plan was abandoned because of concerns about oversaturation of certain urban areas and overprojection of retail sales. Rather, more emphasis is being put on consumer service.[12]

Control

The use of intermediaries will automatically lead to loss of some control over the marketing of the firm's products. The looser the relationship is between the marketer and intermediaries, the less control the marketer can exert. The longer the channel, the more difficult it becomes for the marketer to have a final say over pricing, promotion, and the types of outlets in which the product will be made available.

Foreign-market entry requires a major trade-off for an exporter between the desire to control export efforts and the desire to minimize resource commitment costs.[13] In the initial stages, the use of intermediaries is typi-

[12] Curtis Pepper, "Fast Forward," *Business Month*, February 1989, 25–30.

[13] Erin Anderson and Hubert Gatignon, "Modes of Foreign Entry: A Transaction Cost Analysis and Propositions," *Journal of International Business Studies* 17 (Fall 1986): 1–26.

cal, but as the exporter becomes more familiar with export tasks, they are performed increasingly in-house.

The issue of control correlates heavily with the type of product or service being marketed. In the case of industrial and high-technology products, control will be easier to institute because intermediaries are dependent on the marketer for new products and service. The marketer's ability and willingness to exercise any type of power—whether reward, coercive, legitimate, referent, or expert—determines the extent of control. The exercise of control causes more incidents of conflict in channels of distribution than any other activity in the relationship. This points to the need for careful communication with foreign intermediaries about the marketer's intentions and also the need for certain control measures. These might include the marketer's need to be the sole source of advertising copy or in charge of all product modification activities. Generally, the more control the marketer wishes to have, the more cost is involved in securing that control.

Continuity

Channel design decisions are the most long term of the marketing-mix decisions. Utmost care must therefore be taken in choosing the right type of channel, given the types of intermediaries available and any environmental threats that may affect the channel design. Occasionally, however, unpredictable events may occur. As an example, Cockspur, the largest distiller of rum in Barbados, negotiated an arrangement with one of the largest distributors in the United States. Almost immediately the distributor was acquired by Nabisco, which did not perceive liquor distribution as fitting its mission and eliminated the products and reassigned the salespeople. Years later, Cockspur was still without substantial distribution in the United States.[14]

Nurturing continuity rests heavily on the marketer because foreign distributors may have a more short-term view of the relationship. For example, Japanese wholesalers believe that it is important for manufacturers to follow up initial success with continuous improvement of the product. If such improvements are not forthcoming, competitors are likely to enter the market with similar, but lower priced, products and the wholesalers of the imported product will turn to the Japanese suppliers.

The U.S. manufacturers of Odoreaters experienced such a development. After three years of costly market development efforts together with a Japanese wholesaler, the firm had reached a sales level of 3.8 million pairs. However, six months after product introduction, 12 comparable Japanese products had already been introduced. Because Odoreaters was not able to improve its product substantially over time, its wholesaler made an exclusive agreement with a competing firm—Scholl Inc.—and terminated

---

[14] We are indebted to Dr. James H. Sood of the American University for this example.

the relationship with Odoreaters. Even though Odoreaters managed to find a new distributor, its sales dropped significantly.[15]

Continuity is also expressed through visible market commitment. Industries abroad may be quite conservative and distributors will not generally support an outsider until they are sure it is in the market to stay. Such commitments have included Kraft's listing on the Tokyo exchange[16] and some exporters' setting up wholly owned sales subsidiaries from the start in Europe—and staffing them with locals to help communicate that the company is there for the long term.[17]

Communication

Communication provides the exchange of information that is essential to the functioning of the channel. Communication is an important consideration in channel design, and it gains more emphasis in international distribution because of various types of distances that may cause problems. In analyzing buyer-seller relationships in industrial markets, the distance that is perceived to exist between a buyer and a seller has five aspects:[18]

1. Social distance: the extent to which each of the two entities in a relationship is familiar with the other's ways of operating
2. Cultural distance: the degree to which the norms, values, or working methods between the two entities differ because of their separate national characteristics
3. Technological distance: the differences between the product or process technologies of the two entities
4. Time distance: the time that must elapse between establishing contact or placing an order and the actual transfer of the product or service involved
5. Geographical distance: the physical distance between the locations of the two entities.

All of these dimensions must be considered when determining whether to use intermediaries and, if they are to be used, what types to use.

Communication, if properly utilized, will assist the international marketer in conveying the firm's goals to the distributors, in solving conflict situations, and in the overall marketing of the product. Communication is a two-way process that does not permit the marketer to dictate to intermediaries. Cases are well known in which the marketer is not able to make the firm's marketing program functional. Prices may not be competitive;

[15] Michael R. Czinkota, "Distribution of Consumer Products in Japan," *International Marketing Review* 2 (Autumn 1985): 39—51.

[16] *Business International*, "Opening of Japan's Food Market Spells Opportunity for Foreign Corporations," November 21, 1988, 366.

[17] *Business Week*, "Made in the U.S.A.," February 29, 1988, 60—66.

[18] David Ford, "Buyer/Seller Relationships in International Industrial Markets," *Industrial Marketing Management* 13 (May 1984): 101—112.

promotional materials may be obsolete or inaccurate and not well received overall.[19] Solving these problems is important to the welfare of both parties. However, the marketer's attempts to solve them may have met with resentment because of the way the distributor was approached.

Channels of distribution, because of their sequential positioning of the entities involved, are not conducive to noiseless communication. The marketer must design a channel and choose intermediaries that guarantee good information flow. Proper communication involves not only the passage of information between channel members but also a better understanding of what each party's needs and goals are. This can be achieved through personal visits, exchange of personnel, or establishing distribution advisory councils. Consisting of members from all channel participants, advisory councils meet regularly to discuss opportunities and problems that may have arisen.

SELECTION OF INTERMEDIARIES

Once the basic design of the channel has been determined, the international marketer must begin a search to fill the roles defined with the best available candidates and secure their cooperation.

Types of Intermediaries

Two basic decisions are involved in choosing the type of intermediaries to serve a particular market. First, the marketer must determine the type of relationship to have with intermediaries. The alternatives are distributorship and agency relationship. A **distributor** will purchase the product and will therefore exercise more independence than do agencies. Distributors are typically organized along product lines and provide the international marketer with complete marketing services. **Agents** have less freedom of movement than distributors because they operate on a commission basis and do not usually physically handle the goods. In addition to the business implications, the choice of type will have legal implications in terms of what the intermediary can commit its principal to and the ease of termination of the agreement.

Second, the marketer must decide whether to utilize a direct or an indirect distribution approach. In **direct marketing,** the U.S. firm markets through its own organization, either through its salesforce (where, for example, a salesforce has global product responsibility), an export department (which can vary from a one-person office to a sizable corporate unit), or a foreign sales corporation. **Indirect marketing** requires dealing with another U.S.-based firm that acts as a sales intermediary for the marketer,

[19]Philip J. Rosson, "Success Factors in Manufacturer-Overseas Distributor Relationships in International Marketing" in *International Marketing Management*, ed. Erdener Kaynak (New York: Praeger Publishing, 1984), 91–107.

TABLE 12.4 ▪ **International Channel Intermediaries**

Agents	
Foreign (Direct)	Domestic (Indirect)
Brokers	Brokers
Manufacturer's Representatives	Export Agents
Factors	EMCs
Managing Agents	

Distributors	
Distributors/Dealers	Domestic Wholesalers
Import Jobbers	EMCs
Wholesalers/Retailers	ETCs
	Complementary Marketing

Source: Peter B. Fitzpatrick and Alan S. Zimmermann, *Essentials of Export Marketing* (New York: American Management Association, 1985), 20.

often taking over the international side of the marketer's operations. Indirect exporting can provide the marketer additional volume without requiring major adjustment and risk, and will get the marketer's "feet wet." Direct marketing, on the other hand, will help retain more control over the marketing of the firm's product.

The major types of intermediaries are summarized in Table 12.4. Care should be taken to understand conceptual differences that might exist from one market to another. For example, a **commissionario** may sell in his own name (as a distributor would) but for an undisclosed principal (an agency concept). Similarly, a **del credere agent** guarantees the solvency of the customer and may therefore be responsible to the supplier for payment by the customer.[20]

The respective strengths and weaknesses of various intermediary types are discussed in Chapter 13.

The Sources for Finding Intermediaries

Firms that have successful international distribution attest to the importance of finding top representatives. This undertaking should be held in the same regard as recruiting and hiring within the company because "an ineffective foreign distributor can set you back years; it is almost better to have no distributor than a bad one in a major market."[21]

---

[20] Peter B. Fitzpatrick and Alan S. Zimmerman, *Essentials of Export Marketing* (New York: American Management Association, 1985), 43.

[21] "How to Evaluate Foreign Distributors: A BI Checklist," *Business International*, May 10, 1985, 145–149.

The approach can be either passive or active. Foreign operations for a number of smaller firms start through an unsolicited order; the same can happen with foreign distribution. Distributors, wherever they are, are always on the lookout for product representation that can be profitable and status enhancing. The initial contact may result from an advertisement or from a trade show the marketer has participated in.

The marketer's best interest lies in taking an active role. The marketer should not simply use the first intermediary to show an interest in the firm. The choice should be a result of a careful planning process. The exporter should start from understanding market conditions in order to define what is expected of an intermediary and what the exporter can offer in the relationship. At the same time, procedures need to be set for intermediary identification and evaluation.[22] The exporter does not have to do all of this independently; both governmental and private agencies can assist the marketer in locating intermediary candidates.

Governmental Agencies   The U.S. Department of Commerce has various services that can assist firms in identifying suitable representatives abroad. Some have been designed specifically for that purpose. The New Product Information Service (NPIS) provides worldwide publicity for new U.S. products available for export. This exposure enables foreign firms to identify and contact U.S. firms, thereby giving the U.S. company a direct indication of market interest. A firm can subscribe to the Department's Trade Opportunities Program (TOP), which matches product interests of foreign buyers with those indicated by the U.S. subscribers. The Commerce Department also collects data on foreign firms for the Foreign Traders Index (FTI). Covering 143 countries, the file contains information on more than 140,000 importing firms, agents, representatives, distributors, manufacturers, service organizations, retailers, and potential end-users.

Two services are specifically designed for locating foreign representatives. The Agent/Distributor Service (A/DS) locates foreign firms that are interested in export proposals submitted by U.S. firms and determines their willingness to correspond with the U.S. firm. Both U.S. and foreign commercial service posts abroad supply information on up to six representatives who meet these requirements. The World Traders Data Report (WTDR) is a valuable service, especially when the screening of potential candidates takes place. WTDRs provide a trade profile of specific foreign firms. They also provide a general narrative report by the Commercial Officer conducting the investigation on the reliability of the foreign firm. All of the services are available for relatively small fees; for example, the cost for an A/DS application is $90.[23] An example of a WTDR is provided in Figure 12.4. For the centrally planned economies, State-Controlled Trading Companies lists are available.

[22] *Business International,* "Finding a Distributor Takes Planning and Skill," March 8, 1985, 74–75.

[23] U.S. Department of Commerce, *Commerce Export Assistance Programs* (Washington, D.C.: Department of Commerce, 1983).

FIGURE 12.4   ▪   Sample Report from the World Traders Data Report

```
World                          This report, submitted to the U S
Traders                        Department of Commerce by the U S
                               Foreign Service—Department of State, is
Data                           transmitted in confidence  No
                               responsibility can be assumed by the
Report                         Government or its officers for any
                               transactions had with any persons or
                               firms herein mentioned The report is not
                               for publication  All correspondence
                               relating to information in this report
                               should be addressed to the Export
                               Information Division, Bureau of
                               International Commerce, DIBA, U S
                               Department of Commerce, Washington,
                               D C 20230

                               SECONDARY DISTRIBUTION PROHIBITED
```

```
R 100820Z APRIL 75
FM  AMCONSUL MUNICH
TO  USDOC WASHDC
UNCLASS MUNICH 0128
SUBJECT:  WTDR/FTI KINGFISHER SUESSWAREN GMBH              SAMPLE

REFERENCE:  USDOC 18345

1.  GERMANY   2.  CNTRY CODE: 428   3.  SER NO: 0709400

4.  KINGFISHER SUESSWAREN GMBH.

4A.  CODE:  K  4B.  CODE:  G  4C.  CODE:  X
5.  POSTFACH 1272; GERNESTR. 252
6.  8000 MUENCHEN 15, GERMANY

7.  ESTABL: 1952  8.  EMPL: 300  9.  SIZE: (19-X) LARGE
10.  REPUTATION:  (22-X) EXCELLENT

11.  SELLS ITS PRODUCTS IN THE FOLLOWING FOREIGN AREAS LISTED IN
ORDER OF IMPORTANCE:  UNITED KINGDOM, FRANCE, SPAIN, NORTH
AFRICA, MIDDLE EAST, JAPAN, REP. OF S. AFRICA, UNITED STATES AND
SOUTH AMERICA.

12.  RPT. DATE: 04/75

13A.  20650/0345  MFR. DIST. EXP. IMP. OF CONFECTIONERY AND
13B.  20660/0345    CHOCOLATE AND COCOA PRODUCTS
13C.  20670/532  AGT. IMP. DIST. OF CHEWING GUM
13D.  20520/04   MFR. DIST & EXP. OF COOKIES
13E.  20231/5G   IMP. OF DRY MILK PRODUCTS: INTEREST IN
                   LICENSE TO MANUF.
13F.  35891/5F   IMP. BAKING & RELATED EQUIP; INTEREST   IN
                   NEW LINES & DEVELOPMENTS
13G.  35512/F    INTEREST IN ANY NEW FOOD PACK. & BOXING
                   MACHINERY
```

```
14.  CONTACT:  KARL JOSEF NEFFE      TITLE:  MANAGER
15.  CABLE:  NEMET      16.  TELEX:  2258051
17.  TEL:  012/2437511 AND 2437586
18.  FINANCIAL REFS:  DEUTSCHE BANK AG, MUENCHNER LANDSTR. 17,
AUGSBURG:  COMMERZBANK AG, OPERNRING 2, MUNICH.
19.  TRADE REFS:  JOHNSON MACHINERY, INC., 862 S. LOS ANGELES
ST., LOS ANGELES, CA 96102: AND TEDENSON CO., INC., 125 SOUTH
ST., BOSTON, MA 02111.
20.  FOREIGN FIRMS REPRESENTED:  AGENT OF NORTH-AM CHICLE CO.,
P.O.B. 245, WASHINGTON, D.C. 20001, FOR CHEWING GUM, ACQUIRED
1954; LICENSEE OF ENGLISH TREACLE, LTD., NORTHGATE, LONDON E.C.
4, FOR HARD & SOFT CANDIES, ACQ. 1965; LICENSEE OF SCHWEIZERISCHE
SUESSWAREN, ZURICH, ACQ. 1965.

21.  THIS FIRM IS ONE OF GERMANY'S LEADING MANUFACTURERS OF
ALL TYPES OF CONFECTIONARY.  FIXED ASSETS LATEST REPORTED AT
DM 1.5 MILLION AND CAPITALIZATION AT DM 3 MILLION.  ANNUAL
SALES DM 6.5 MILLION.  MANUFACTURING FACILITIES AND HEAD OFFICES
LOCATED IN MUNICH.  FIRM RECENTLY MODERNIZED COOKIE PRODUCTION
FACILITY WITH INSTALLATION OF TWO HIGH VOLUME CONVEYOR-OVEN
UNITS FROM HAALFORS OF SWEDEN.  DISTRIBUTION WAREHOUSE IN MANN-
HEIM FOR SOME EUROPEAN SALES AND IN BREMEN FOR EXPORT SALES.
FIRM SELLS ITS PRODUCTS FINISHED AND PACKAGED TO FOOD BROKERS
AND LARGE FOOD CHAINS AS EXCLUSIVE AGENTS IN ALL MARKETS EXCEPT
U.S. WHERE TENDENSON COMPANY IMPORTS IN BULK AND PACKAGES WITH
AMERICAN LABELS.  THE MAJORITY STOCKHOLDER IS HEIDE DERRIG AG,
A HOLDING COMPANY LOCATED IN MUNICH.  BANKING SOURCES REPORT
FINANCES ARE SOUND, OBLIGATIONS MET PROMPTLY.  MANAGEMENT CON-
SIDERED HIGHLY REPUTABLE AND EXPERIENCED BY LOCAL BUSINESS SOURCES,
ESPECIALLY FOREIGN SALES MANAGER HELMUT SCHOLZE, FORMERLY WITH
NESTLE.  CONSULATE RECOMMENDS SUBJECT AS AN EXCELLENT TRADE
CONTACT FOR U.S. FIRMS.

                                                    SAMPLE
```

Source: U.S. Department of Commerce, *A Basic Guide to Exporting* (Washington, D.C.: Government Printing Office, 1981), 65–66.

Private Sources   The easiest approach for the firm seeking intermediaries is to consult trade directories. Country and regional business directories such as Kompass (Europe), Bottin International (worldwide), Nordisk Handelskalendar (Scandinavia), and the Japan Trade Directory are good places to start. Company lists by country and line of business can be ordered from Dun & Bradstreet, Reuben H. Donnelly, Kelly's Directory, and Johnston Publishing. Telephone directories, especially the yellow-page sections or editions, can provide distributor lists. The Jaeger and Waldmann International Telex Directory can also be consulted. Although not detailed, these listings will give addresses and an indication of the products sold.

The firm can solicit the support of some of its facilitating agencies, such as banks, advertising agencies, shipping lines, and airlines. All of them have substantial international information networks and can put them to work for their clients. The services available will vary by agency, depending on the size of its foreign operations. Some of the major U.S. flagship carriers—for example, Pan American and Northwest airlines—have spe-

FIGURE 12.5 ▪ **Advertisement for an Intermediary**

REAR BUSINESS OPPORTUNITY

Agent is wanted in Finland for a well known European Mail Order company.

The agent who will become a part of a newly established Scandinavia group of franchise agents, will be supported with marketing material, cataloques and computer system from our office in Copenhagen.

This is an ideal opportunity for someone looking for easy expansion into new business.

Please write to:

GRATTAN MAILORDER SCANDINAVIA APS

Solbrinken 44, 2750 Ballerup, Denmark.

All applications will be handled confidentally, and all will receive a reply.

(Ilmoitus)

Source: *Kauppalehti.*

cial staffs for this purpose within their cargo operations. Banks usually have the most extensive networks through their affiliates and correspondent banks.

The marketer can take an even more direct approach by buying space to solicit representation. Advertisements typically indicate the type of support the marketer will be able to give to its distributor. An example of this type of advertisement is provided in Figure 12.5 (which also points up the importance of language in foreign communications). Trade fairs are an important forum to meet potential distributors and to get data on intermediaries in the industry. The marketer may also deal directly with contacts from previous applications, launch new mail solicitations, use its own sales organization for the search, or communicate with existing customers to find prospective distributors. The latter may happen after a number of initial (unsolicited) sales to a market, causing the firm to want to enter the market on a more formal basis. If resources permit, the international marketer can use outside service agencies or consultants to generate a list of prospective representatives.

TABLE 12.5 ▪ **Data Sources for Locating Foreign Intermediaries**

1. Distributor inquiries
2. U.S. Department of Commerce
   − New Product Information Service
   − Trade Opportunities Program
   − Foreign Traders Index
   − Agent/Distributor Service
   − World Traders Data Report
3. Trade sources
   − Magazines, journals
   − Directories
   − Associations
   − Banks, advertising agencies, carriers
4. Field sales organizations
5. Customers
6. Direct mail solicitation/contact of previous applicants
7. Independent consultants

The purpose of using the sources summarized in Table 12.5 is to generate as many prospective representatives as possible for the next step, screening.

The Screening of Intermediaries

In most firms the evaluation of candidates involves both what to look for and where to go for the information. At this stage, the international marketer knows the type of distributor that is needed. The potential candidates must now be compared and contrasted against determining criteria. Although the criteria to be used vary by industry and by product, a good summary list is provided in Table 12.6.[24] Especially when various criteria are being weighed, these lists must be updated to reflect changes in the environment and the marketer's own situation. Some criteria can be characterized as determinant, in that they form the core dimensions along which candidates must perform well, whereas some criteria, although important, may be used only in preliminary screening. This list should correspond closely to the exporter's own determinants of success—all the things that have to be done better to beat out competition.

Before signing a contract with a particular agent or a distributor, international marketers should satisfy themselves on certain key criteria. A number of these key criteria can be easily quantified, thereby providing a solid base for comparisons between candidates, whereas others are qualitative and require careful interpretation and confidence in the data sources providing the information.

[24] Franklin R. Root, *Foreign Market Entry Strategies* (New York: American Management Association, 1983), 74–75.

TABLE 12.6 ▪ **Selection Criteria for Choosing an International Distributor**

Characteristics	Weight	Rating
Goals and Strategies		
Size of the Firm		
Financial Strength		
Reputation		
Trading Areas Covered		
Compatibility		
Experience		
Sales Organization		
Physical Facilities		
Willingness to Carry Inventories		
After-sales Service Capability		
Use of Promotion		
Sales Performance		
Relations with Local Government		
Communications		
Overall Attitude		

Source: Franklin R. Root, *Foreign Market Entry Strategies* (New York: American Management Association, 1983), 74–75.

Performance   The financial standing of the candidate is one of the most important criteria, as well as a good starting point. This figure will show whether the distributor is making money and is able to perform some of the necessary marketing functions such as extension of credit to customers and risk absorption. Financial reports are not always complete or reliable, or they may lend themselves to interpretation differences, pointing to a need for third party opinion.

Sales are another excellent indicator. What the distributor is presently doing gives an indication of how he or she could perform if chosen to handle the international marketer's product. The distributor's sales strength can be determined by analyzing management ability and the adequacy and quality of the sales team.

The distributor's existing product lines should be analyzed along four dimensions: competitiveness, compatibility, complementary nature, and quality. Quite often, international marketers find that the most desirable distributors in a given market are already handling competitive products and are therefore unavailable. In that case, the marketer can look for an equally qualified distributor handling related products. The complementary nature of products may be of interest to both parties, especially in industrial markets, where ultimate customers may be in the market for complete systems or one-stop shopping. The quality match for products is important for product-positioning reasons; a high-quality product may suffer unduly from a questionable distributor reputation. The number of product lines handled gives the marketer an indication of the level of effort to expect from the distributor. Some distributors are interested in carrying as many products and product lines as possible to enhance their own standing, but they have time and the willingness to actively sell only those that bring the best compensation. At this time, it is also important to check the candidate's physical facilities for handling the product. This is essential particularly for products that may be subject to quality changes, such as food products.

The distributor's market coverage must be determined. The analysis of coverage will include not only how much territory, or how many segments of the market, are covered but how well the markets are served. Again, the characteristics of the salesforce and the number of sales offices are good quantitative indicators. To study the quality of the distributor's market coverage, the marketer can check whether the salesforce visits executives, engineers, and operating people or concentrates mainly on purchasing agents. In some areas of the world, the marketer has to make sure that two distributors will not end up having territorial overlaps, which can lead to unnecessary conflict.

Professionalism The distributor's reputation must be checked. This rather abstract measure takes its value from a number of variables that all should help the marketer forecast effectiveness. The distributor's customers, suppliers, facilitating agencies, competitors, and other members of the local business community should be contacted for information on the business conduct of the distributor in such areas as buyer–seller relations and ethical behavior. This effort will shed light on variables that may be important only in certain parts of the world, such as political clout, which is essential in certain developing countries.

The marketer must acknowledge the distributor as an independent entity with its own goals. The distributor's business strategy must therefore be determined, particularly what the distributor expects to get from the relationship and where the international marketer fits into those plans. Because a channel relationship is long term, the distributor's views on future expansion of the product line or its distribution should be clarified. This phase will also require a determination of the degree of help the distributor would need in terms of price, credit, delivery, sales training, communication, personal visits, product modification, warranty, advertising, warehousing, technical support, and after-sales service.[25] Leaving uncertainties in these areas will cause major problems later.

Finally, the marketer should determine the distributor's overall attitude in terms of cooperation and commitment to the marketer. An effective way of testing this, and weeding out the less interested candidates, is to ask the distributor to assist in developing a local marketing plan or to develop one. This endeavor will bring out potential problem areas and will spell out which party is to perform the various marketing functions.

---

[25] "How to Evaluate Foreign Distributors: A BI Checklist," *Business International*, May 10, 1985, 145–149.

A criteria list is valuable only when good data are available on each and every criterion. Although the initial screening can take place at the firm's offices, the three to five finalists should be visited. No better method of assessing distributors exists than visiting them, inspecting their facilities, and interviewing their various constituents in the market. A number of other critical data sources exist that have importance for firms without the resources for on-site inspection. The distributor's suppliers or firms not in direct competition can provide in-depth information. A bona fide candidate will also provide information through a local bank. Credit reports are available through the Foreign Credit Interchange Bureau (FCIB) in New York, Dun & Bradstreet, and local credit reporting agencies. A list of the foreign sources of credit information is published by Trade Data Reports Inc.[26]

The Distributor Agreement

When the international marketer has found a suitable intermediary, a foreign sales agreement is drawn up. The agreement can be relatively simple but, given the numerous differences in the market environments, certain elements are essential. The checklist prepared by *Business International* (see Table 12.7) is the most comprehensive in stipulating the nature of the contract and the respective rights and responsibilities of the marketer and the distributor.

Contract duration is important, especially when an agreement is signed with a new distributor. In general, distribution agreements should be for a specified, relatively short period (one or two years). The initial contract with a new distributor should stipulate a trial period of either three or six months, possibly with minimum purchase requirements. Duration should be determined with an eye on the local laws and their stipulations on distributor agreements. These will be discussed later in conjunction with distributor termination.

Geographic boundaries for the distributor should be determined with care, especially by smaller firms. Future expansion of the product market might be complicated by a distributor claiming rights to certain territories. The marketer should retain the right to distribute products independently, reserving the right to certain customers. For example, Parker Pen maintains a dual distribution system, dealing directly with certain large accounts. This type of arrangement should be explicitly stated in the agreement.

The payment section of the contract should stipulate the methods of payment as well as how the distributor or agent is to draw compensation. Distributors derive compensation from various discounts, such as the functional discount, whereas agents earn a specific commission percentage of net sales (such as 15 percent). Given the volatility of currency markets, the agreement should also state the currency to be used. The inter-

---

[26] "How to Check Credit Overseas," *Business International*, May 10, 1985, 149.

TABLE 12.7 ▪ **Elements of a Distributor Agreement**

A. *BASIC COMPONENTS*
1. Parties to the agreement
2. Statement that the contract supersedes all previous agreements
3. Duration of the agreement (perhaps a three- or six-month trial period)
4. Territory:
   a. Exclusive, nonexclusive, sole
   b. Manufacturer's right to sell direct at reduced or no commission to local government and old customers
5. Products covered
6. Expression of intent to comply with government regulations
7. Clauses limiting sales forbidden by U.S. Export Controls or practices forbidden by the Foreign Corrupt Practices Act

B. *MANUFACTURER'S RIGHTS*
1. Arbitration:
   a. If possible, in the manufacturer's country
   b. If not, before International Chambers of Commerce or American Arbitration Association, or using the London Court of Arbitration rules
   c. Definition of rules to be applied (e.g., in selecting the arbitration panel)
   d. Assurance that award will be binding in the distributor's country
2. Jurisdiction that of the manufacturer's country (the signing completed at home); if not possible, a neutral site such as Sweden or Switzerland
3. Termination conditions (e.g., no indemnification if due notice given)
4. Clarification of tax liabilities
5. Payment and discount terms
6. Conditions for delivery of goods
7. Nonliability for late delivery beyond manufacturer's reasonable control
8. Limitation on manufacturer's responsibility to provide information
9. Waiver of manufacturer's responsibility to keep lines manufactured outside the United States (e.g., licensees) outside of covered territory
10. Right to change prices, terms, and conditions at any time
11. Right of manufacturer or agent to visit territory and inspect books
12. Right to repurchase stock
13. Option to refuse or alter distributor's orders
14. Training of distributor personnel in the United States subject to:
    a. Practicality
    b. Costs to be paid by the distributor
    c. Waiver of manufacturer's responsibility for U.S. immigration approval

C. *DISTRIBUTOR'S LIMITATIONS AND DUTIES*
1. No disclosure of confidential information
2. Limitation of distributor's right to assign contract
3. Limitation of distributor's position as legal agent of manufacturer
4. Penalty clause for late payment
5. Limitation of right to handle competing lines
6. Placement of responsibility for obtaining customs clearance
7. Distributor to publicize designation as authorized representative in defined area
8. Requirement to move all signs or evidence identifying distributor with manufacturer if relationship ends
9. Acknowledgment by distributor of manufacturer's ownership of trademark, trade names, patents

(Continued)

TABLE 12.7 ■ **Continued**

C. *DISTRIBUTOR'S LIMITATIONS AND DUTIES*
  10. Information to be supplied by the distributor:
    a. Sales reports
    b. Names of active prospects
    c. Government regulations dealing with imports
    d. Competitive products and competitor's activities
    e. Price at which goods are sold
    f. Complete data on other lines carried (on request)
  11. Information to be supplied by distributor on purchasers
  12. Accounting methods to be used by distributor
  13. Requirement to display products appropriately
  14. Duties concerning promotional efforts
  15. Limitation of distributor's right to grant unapproved warranties, make excessive claims
  16. Clarification of responsibility arising from claims and warranties
  17. Responsibility of distributor to provide repair and other services
  18. Responsibility to maintain suitable place of business
  19. Responsibility to supply all prospective customers
  20. Understanding that certain sales approaches and sales literature must be approved by manufacturer
  21. Prohibition of manufacture or alteration of products
  22. Requirement to maintain adequate stock, spare parts
  23. Requirement that inventory be surrendered in event of a dispute that is pending in court
  24. Prohibition of transshipments

Source: *"Elements of a Distributor Agreement,"* Business International, March 29, 1963, 23–24. Reprinted with permission from Business International. Some of the sections have been changed to reflect the present situation.

national marketer also needs to make sure that none of the compensation forwarded to the distributor is in violation of the Foreign Corrupt Practices Act. A violation occurs if a payment is made to influence a foreign official in exchange for business favors, depending on the nature of the action sought. So-called grease or **facilitating payments,** such as paying a small fee to expedite paperwork through customs, are not considered violations.[27]

Product and conditions of sale need to be agreed on. The products or product lines included should be stipulated as well as the functions and responsibilities of the intermediary in terms of carrying the goods in inventory, providing service in conjunction with them, and promoting them. Conditions of sale determine which party is to be responsible for some of the expenses involved, which will in turn have an effect on the price to the distributor. These conditions include credit and shipment terms.

[27] Michael G. Harvey and Ilkka A. Ronkainen, "The Three Faces of the Foreign Corrupt Practices Act: Retain, Reform, or Repeal" in *1984 AMA Educators' Proceedings* (Chicago: American Marketing Association, 1984), 290–294.

Effective means of communication between the parties must be provided for in the agreement if a marketer-distributor relationship is to succeed. The marketer should have access to all information concerning the marketing of his products in the distributor's territory, including past records, present situation assessments, and marketing research concerning the future. Communication channels should be formal for the distributor to voice formal grievances. The contract should state the confidentiality of the information provided by either party and protect the intellectual property rights (such as patents) involved.

CHANNEL MANAGEMENT

A channel relationship can be likened to a marriage in that it brings together two independent entities that have shared goals. For the relationship to work, each party must be open about its expectations and openly communicate changes perceived in the other's behavior that might be contrary to the agreement. The closer the relationship is to a distribution partnership, the more likely marketing success will materialize. Conflict will arise, ranging from small grievances (such as billing errors) to major ones (rivalry over channel duties), but it can be managed to enhance the overall channel relationship. In some cases, conflict may be caused by an outside entity, such as gray markets, in which unauthorized intermediaries compete for market share with legitimate importers and exclusive distributors. Nevertheless, the international marketer must solve the problem.

The relationship has to be managed for the long term. An exporter may in some countries have a seller's market situation that allows it to exert pressure on its intermediaries for concessions, for example. However, if environmental conditions change, the exporter may find that the channel support it needs to succeed is not there because of the manner in which it managed channel relationships in the past.[28]

Factors in Channel Management

An excellent framework for managing channel relationships is shown in Figure 12.6.[29] The complicating factors that separate the two parties fall into three categories: ownership, geographic and cultural distance, and different rules of law. Rather than lament over their existence, both parties need to take strong action to remedy them. Often the major step is acknowledgment that differences do indeed exist.

[28] Gary L. Frazier, James D. Gill, and Sudhir H. Kale, "Dealer Dependence Levels and Reciprocal Actions in a Channel of Distribution in a Developing Country," *Journal of Marketing* 53 (January 1989): 50–69.

[29] Philip J. Rosson, "Success Factors in Manufacturer-Overseas Distributor Relationships in International Marketing," in *International Marketing Management*, ed. Erdener Kaynak (New York: Praeger Publishing, 1984), 91–107.

FIGURE 12.6 ■ **Performance Problems and Remedies
When Using Overseas Distributors**

High Export Performance Inhibitors ⟶ Bring		Remedy Lies In
Separate Ownership	• Divided Loyalties • Seller-Buyer Atmosphere • Unclear Future Intentions	Offering good incentives, helpful support schemes, discussing plans frankly, and interacting in a mutually beneficial way
Geographic and Cultural Separation	• Communication Blocks • Negative Attitudes toward Foreigners • Physical Distribution Strains	Making judicious use of two-way visits establishing a well-managed communication program
Different Rules of Law	• Vertical Trading Restrictions • Dismissal Difficulties	Full compliance with the law, drafting a strong distributor agreement

Source: Philip J. Rosson, "Source Factors in Manufacturer-Overseas Distributor Relationships in International Marketing." From *International Marketing Management*, edited by Erdener Kaynak, 1984.

In international marketing, manufacturers and distributors are usually independent entities. Distributors typically carry the products of more than one manufacturer and judge products by their ability to generate revenue without added expense. The international marketer, in order to receive disproportionate attention for his concerns, may offer both monetary and psychological rewards.

Distance, whether it is geographic, psychological, or a combination of both, can be bridged through effective two-way communication. This should go beyond normal routine business communication to include innovative ways of sharing pertinent information. The international marketer may place one person in charge of distributor-related communications or put into effect an interpenetration strategy—that is, an exchange of personnel so that both organizations gain further insight into the workings of the other.[30]

Laws and regulations in many markets may restrict the manufacturer in terms of control. For example, in the European Community the international marketer cannot prevent a distributor from reexporting products to customers in another member country, even though the marketer has another distributor in that market. The only remedy is to include the necessary stipulations in the distributor agreement; for example, a clause prohibiting transshipments.

[30] Bert Rosenbloom, *Marketing Channels: A Management View*, 3d ed. (Hinsdale, Ill.: Dryden Press, 1987), 429–449.

Most of the criteria used in selecting intermediaries can be used to evaluate existing intermediaries as well. If not conducted properly and fairly, however, evaluation can be a source of conflict. In addition to being given the evaluation results in order to take appropriate action, the distributor should be informed of the evaluative criteria and should be a part of the overall assessment process. Again, the approach should be one of partnership, not a buyer-seller one.

A part of the management process is channel adjustment. This can take the form of channel shift (eliminating a particular type of channel), channel modification (changing individual members while leaving channel structure intact), or role or relationship modification (changing functions performed or the reward structure) as a result of channel evaluation.[31] The need for channel change should be well established and not executed hastily, because it will cause a major distraction in the operations of the firm. Some companies have instituted procedures that require executives to carefully consider all of the aspects and potential results of change before execution.

A Special Problem: Gray Markets

Gray markets, or **parallel importation,** refer to authentic and legitimately manufactured trademark items that are produced and purchased abroad but imported or diverted to the United States by bypassing designated channels.[32] The value of gray markets in the United States has been estimated at $6 to $10 billion at retail. The products may be as expensive to the consumer as automobiles or as inexpensive as chewing gum (see The International Marketplace 12.2 on Chiclets). The phenomenon is not restricted to the United States; Japan, for example, is witnessing gray markets because of the high value of the yen and the subsidization of cheaper exports through high taxes. Japanese marketers often find it cheaper to go to Los Angeles to buy export versions of Japanese-made products.[33]

An example of the phenomenon is provided in Figure 12.7, which shows the flow of Seiko watches through authorized and unauthorized channels. Seiko is a good example of a typical gray market product in that it carries a well-known trademark. Unauthorized importers, such as Progress Trading Company in New York, and retailers, such as Montgomery Ward, buy Seiko watches around the world at advantageous prices and then sell them to consumers at substantial discounts over authorized Seiko dealers. Seiko has fought back, for example, by advertising warnings to consumers against buying gray market watches on the grounds that

---

[31] J. Taylor Sims, J. Robert Foster, and Arch G. Woodside, *Marketing Channels: Systems and Strategies*, 3d ed. (New York: Harper & Row, 1977).

[32] Ilkka A. Ronkainen and Linda van de Gucht, "Making a Case for Gray Markets," *The Journal of Commerce*, January 6, 1987, 13A.

[33] Dan Koeppel, *Adweek's Marketing Week*, "'Gyakuyunyu' Takes Hold in Japan," March 20, 1989, 22.

12.2 THE INTERNATIONAL MARKETPLACE

Peppermint Chiclets from Zouk-Mikhail   *The distance between an upscale grocery on New York's Park Avenue and Zouk-Mikhail, a shattered suburb located seven miles north of Beirut, can be measured in miles—or in money.*

The money comes from peppermint Chiclets. Many of New York's Korean greengrocers have begun to use alternative sources to supply packaged goods. One of the most unusual gray goods they are currently stocking is Chiclets, manufactured not by Warner-Lambert Inc. in Morris Plains, New Jersey, but at a company-owned plant in Zouk-Mikhail in Lebanon. The 20-year-old plant has continued to operate even as Beirut has been transformed from "the Paris of the Mideast" to a battle zone.

Warner-Lambert is pleased that the facility has miraculously remained intact, but it is not happy that the plant's product has made its way to U.S. stores. The company has brought several lawsuits against importers of the Chiclets, and continues to try to stop the goods from coming into the country. But, as company officials say, despite slight flavor differences in the foreign and U.S. gums, consumers do not really notice where the particular packages come from. Those who do notice usually call to express disbelief that Warner-Lambert has a plant in Beirut.

The gray-market Chiclets trade is part of the thriving underground marketplace that has come to dominate Lebanon. Products ranging from television sets to truffles are often smuggled in and out of the country by taxicab owners who have seen their tourist trade dry up. Many are loaded onto boats from Cairo or Greek ports and sent to Paris, London, or New York. No American Warner-Lambert executive has visited Zouk-Mikhail since the U.S. government banned travel to Lebanon in 1987, but the company still believes that doing business in Lebanon is a good idea. "The company predates the conflict; we hope it outlasts the problem too."

Source: Dan Koeppel, "From War-Torn Beirut, Peppermint Chiclets," *Adweek's Marketing Week* 30 (1989): 24.

these products may be obsolete or worn-out models and that consumers might have problems with their warranties. Many gray marketers, however, provide their own warranty-related service and guarantee watches sold through them.

Various conditions allow unauthorized resellers to exist. The most important are price segmentation and exchange-rate fluctuations. Competitive conditions may require the international marketer to sell essentially the same product at different prices in different markets or to different cus-

FIGURE 12.7 ▪ **Seiko's Authorized and Unauthorized Channels of Distribution**

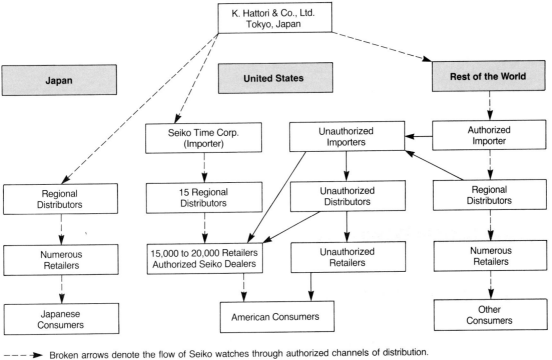

- - - ▶ Broken arrows denote the flow of Seiko watches through authorized channels of distribution.

───▶ Solid arrows denote the flow of Seiko watches through unauthorized channels of distribution.

Source: Jack Kaikati, "Parallel Importation: A Growing Conflict in International Channels of Distribution," Symposium on Export–Import Interrelationships, Georgetown University, November 14–15, 1985.

tomers. Because many products are priced higher in, for example, the United States, a gray marketer can purchase them in Europe or the Far East and offer discounts between 10 and 40 percent below list price when re-selling them in the U.S. market. Exchange-rate fluctuations can cause price differentials and thus opportunities for gray marketers. For example, during the high value of the dollar in 1984 and 1985, gray marketers im-ported Caterpillar excavators and loaders built in Scotland, Belgium, and Japan into the United States at prices 15 percent lower than those for the same equipment built in Caterpillar's domestic plants.[34] In some cases, gray markets emerge as a result of product shortages. For example, in 1988, many U.S. computer manufacturers had to turn to gray marketers to secure their supply of DRAMs or watch their production lines grind to a

[34] Frank V. Cespedes, E. Raymond Corey, and V. Kasturi Rangan, "Gray Markets: Causes and Cures," *Harvard Business Review* 66 (July–August 1988): 75–82.

halt.[35] However, in these cases, the gray market goods typically cost more than those usually available through authorized suppliers.

Opponents and supporters of the practice disagree on whether the central issue is price or trade rights. Detractors typically cite the following arguments: (1) the gray market unduly hurts the legitimate owners of trademarks; (2) without protection, trademark owners will have little incentive to invest in product development; (3) gray marketers will "free ride," or take unfair advantage of the trademark owners' marketing and promotional activities; and (4) parallel imports can deceive consumers by not meeting U.S. product standards or their normal expectations of after-sale service. Gray market goods can severely undercut local marketing plans, erode long-term brand images, and eat up costly promotion dollars. For example, Lever Brothers had to face the parallel importation of British-made Shield deodorant soap. The product was formulated for the hard water in the United Kingdom and dissolved quickly in American showers. The company estimates it lost $5 million in sales to the invading British Shield.

Proponents of parallel importation approach the issue from an altogether different point of view. They argue for their right to "free trade" by pointing to manufacturers who are both overproducing and overpricing in some markets. The main beneficiaries are consumers, who benefit from lower prices, and discount distributors with whom some of the manufacturers do not want to deal and who have now, because of gray markets, found a profitable market niche.

In response to the challenge, manufacturers have chosen various approaches. Despite the Supreme Court ruling in May 1988 to legitimize gray markets in the United States,[36] foreign manufacturers, U.S. companies manufacturing abroad, and authorized retailers have continued fighting the practice. The solution for the most part lies with the contractual relationships that tie businesses together. In almost all of the cases of gray marketing, someone in the authorized channel commits a diversion, thus violating the agreements signed. One of the standard responses is therefore disenfranchisement of such violators. This approach is a clear response to complaints from the authorized dealers who are being hurt by transshipments. Tracking down offenders is quite expensive and time consuming, however. Some of the gray marketers can be added to the authorized dealer network if mutually acceptable terms can be reached, thereby increasing control of the channel of distribution.

A one-price policy can eliminate one of the main reasons for gray markets. This means choosing the most efficient of the distribution channels through which to market the product but it may also mean selling at the lowest price to all customers regardless of location and size. A meaningful

---

[35] *Electronic Business,* "How the Gray Marketeers Are Cashing In on DRAM Shortages," June 1, 1988, 18–19.

[36] *Business Week,* "A Red-Letter Day for Gray Marketeers," June 13, 1988, 30.

one-price strategy must also include a way to reward the providers of other services, such as warranty repair, in the channel.

Other strategies have included producing different versions of products for different markets. For example, Minolta Camera Company markets an identical camera in the United States and Japan but gives it different names and warranties.[37] Some have introduced price incentives to consumers. Hasselblad, the Swedish camera manufacturer, offers rebates to purchasers of legally imported, serial-numbered camera bodies, lenses, and roll-fill magazines.[38]

Termination of the Channel Relationship

Termination conditions are one of the most important considerations in the distributor agreement, because the just causes for termination vary and the penalties for the international marketer may be substantial. Just causes include fraud or deceit, damage to the other party's interest, or failure to comply with contract obligations concerning minimum inventory requirements or minimum sales levels. These must be spelled out carefully because local courts are often favorably disposed toward local businesses. In some countries, termination may not even be possible.[39] In the EC and Latin America, terminating an ineffective intermediary is time consuming and expensive. One year's average commissions are typical for termination without justification. A notice of termination has to be given three to six months in advance. In Austria termination without just cause and/or failure to give notice of termination may result in damages amounting to average commissions for between 1 and 15 years.[40]

The time to think about such issues is before the overseas distribution agreement is signed. It is especially prudent to find out what local laws say about termination and to check what type of experience other firms have had in the particular country. Careful preparation can allow the exporter to negotiate a termination without litigation.[41] If the distributor's performance is unsatisfactory, careful documentation and clearly defined performance measures may help show that the distributor has more to gain going quietly than by fighting. If the company has to change for other reasons, the situation is more delicate but can be handled if dealt with fairly. This requires an understanding of the effect of termination on the distributor and open communication to implement a smooth transition.

[37] *Business Week*, "Now, Japan Is Feeling the Heat from the Gray Market," March 14, 1988, 50–51.

[38] Gay Jervey, "Gray Markets Hit Camera, Watch Sales," *Advertising Age*, August 15, 1983, 3, 62.

[39] Jack Kaikati, "The Marketing Environment in Saudi Arabia," *Akron Business and Economic Review* 7 (Summer 1976): 5–13.

[40] Ovidio M. Giberga, "Laws Restrain Agency Agreement Termination," in *Foreign Business Practices* (Washington: Department of Commerce, 1981), 86–95.

[41] *Business International*, "Foreign Distributors: How MNCs Can Avoid the Termination Minefield," July 12, 1985, 217–218.

THE INTERNATIONAL SHIPMENT

With a channel system in place, the next concern of the international marketer is getting the product to the distributor. In domestic operations this typically involves only (1) the shipper, a carrier, and the receiver and (2) relatively simple paperwork. International shipments are more complicated on both dimensions.

International shipments usually involve not just one carrier but multiple types of carriers. The shipment must be routed to the port of export, where it is transferred to another mode of transportation—for example, from truck or rail to vessel. Documentation for international shipments is universally perceived as so complicated, especially by smaller firms, that it becomes a trade barrier. A Canadian study found that 46 person-hours were needed for the processing of one export shipment;[42] the U.S. Department of Transportation pegged it at 36 hours.[43] As the result of recent efforts toward standardization, most of the documents needed are now aligned through a system called the U.S. Standard Master for International Trade. Certain standard entries, such as export carrier and document number, are in the same position in all of the forms. As part of the 1992 program, the EC is simplifying its required documentation for shipments. Whereas drivers earlier needed two pounds of documents on a route, for example, from Amsterdam to Lisbon, they now only need a single piece of paper. The savings on the elimination of this red tape is significant.[44] Increasingly, electronic data transfer will be replacing paperwork.

Few international marketers, especially small or medium-sized firms and those new to exporting, are familiar with the many and varied details involved in transportation. These may include arranging for shipment from the factory, transfer from train to vessel, securing of rates and space on vessels, clearing U.S. Customs, stowing, delivery at the port of destination to docks, clearance through local customs, and finally delivery to the buyer. Larger exporters have a separate department or staff to secure transportation services and proper documentation, whereas smaller firms rely on support agencies for this work.

Documentation

In the most simple form of exporting, the only documents needed are a bill of lading and an export declaration. Most exports fit under a general license, which is a generalized authorization consisting simply of a number

---

[42] Wayne D. Mays, "Documentary Problems of International Transportation," *Journal of World Trade Law* 12 (November–December 1978): 506–518.

[43] Ray J. Sampson, Martin Farris, and David L. Shrock, *Domestic Transportation: Practice, Theory, and Policy* (Boston: Houghton Mifflin, 1985), 106.

[44] *Business Week*, "Reshaping Europe: 1992 and Beyond," December 12, 1988, 48–51.

TABLE 12.8 ▪ **Documentation for an International Shipment**

> A. Documents required by the U.S. government
>   1. Shipper's export declaration
>   2. Export license
> B. Commercial documents
>   1. Commercial invoice
>   2. Packing list
>   3. Inland bill of lading
>   4. Dock receipt
>   5. Bill of lading or airway bill
>   6. Insurance policies or certificates
>   7. Shipper's declaration for dangerous goods
> C. Import documents
>   1. Import license
>   2. Foreign exchange license
>   3. Certificate of origin
>   4. Consular invoice
>   5. Customs invoice

Source: Dun & Bradstreet, *Exporter's Encyclopedia* (New York: Dun & Bradstreet, 1985), and Marta Ortiz-Buonafina, *Profitable Export Marketing* (Englewood Cliffs, N.J.: Prentice-Hall, 1984), 218–246.

to be shown on the documents. Certain goods and data require a special validated license for export, as discussed in Chapter 4. For importation the basic documents are a bill of lading and an invoice. Table 12.8 provides a summary of the main documents used in international shipments.

The **bill of lading** (see Figure 12.8) is the most important document to the shipper, the carrier, and the buyer. It acknowledges receipt of the goods, represents the basic contract between the shipper and the carrier, and serves as evidence of title to the goods for collection by the purchaser. Various types of bills of lading exist. The inland bill of lading is a contract between the inland carrier and the shipper. Bills of lading may be negotiable instruments in that they may be endorsed to other parties (order bill) or may be non-negotiable (straight). The shipper's **export declaration** (see Figure 12.9) states proper authorization for export and serves as a means for governmental data collection efforts.

The packing list, if used, lists in some detail the contents, the gross and net weights, and dimensions of each package. Some shipments, such as corrosives, flammables, and poisons, require a **shipper's declaration for dangerous goods.** When the international marketer is responsible for moving the goods to the U.S. port of export, a dock receipt (for ocean freight) or a warehouse receipt (if the goods are stored) is issued prior to the issuance of the bill of lading. Collection documents must be also produced, which always include a commercial invoice (a detailed description of the transaction), often a **consular invoice** (required by certain countries for data-

FIGURE 12.8 ▪ **Bill of Lading**

ACL

BILL OF LADING

ACL

SHIPPER/EXPORTER	DOCUMENT NO. BOOKING NO.
	EXPORT REFERENCES
	FORWARDER REF. NO.
	SHIPPER'S REF. NO.
CONSIGNEE	FORWARDING AGENT. F.M.C. NO.
	POINT AND COUNTRY OF ORIGIN PLACE OF RECEIPT *
NOTIFY PARTY	DOMESTIC ROUTING/EXPORT INSTRUCTIONS
PIER	
EXPORTING CARRIER PORT OF LOADING	PLACE OF DELIVERY *
PORT OF DISCHARGE FOR TRANSSHIPMENT TO	

PARTICULARS FURNISHED BY SHIPPER

MARKS AND NUMBERS	NO. OF PKGS.	DESCRIPTION OF PACKAGES AND GOODS	GROSS WEIGHT	MEASUREMENT

*APPLICABLE ONLY WHEN USED AS THROUGH BILL OF LADING
AS PER CLAUSE 3 (III) ON REVERSE HEREOF.

| PREPAID | COLLECT | FREIGHT AND CHARGES PAYABLE AT_____ | ALL CHARGES EX SHIPS
TACKLE FOR ACCOUNT OF CARGO |
|---|---|---|---|

ACL
an affiliate of:
Cie Generale Maritime
The Cunard Steam-Ship Company Ltd.
Intercontinental Transport (ICT) BV
Swedish American Line
Swedish Transatlantic Line
Wallenius Line

RECEIVED by ACL for shipment by ocean vessel, between port of loading and port of discharge, and for arrangement or procurement of precarriage from place of receipt and on-carriage to place of delivery where stated above, the goods as specified above in apparent good order and condition unless otherwise stated. The goods to be delivered at the above mentioned port of discharge or place of delivery, whichever applicable. Subject always to the exceptions, limitations, conditions and liberties set out on the reverse side hereof, to which the Merchant agrees by accepting this B/L.

In Witness whereof three (3) original Bs/L have been signed, if not otherwise stated above, one of which being accomplished the other(s) to be void.

For **ACL**

B/L NUMBER	DATE

Source: Seaschott.

FIGURE 12.9 ▪ **Shipper's Export Declaration**

U.S. DEPARTMENT OF COMMERCE — BUREAU OF THE CENSUS — INTERNATIONAL TRADE ADMINISTRATION	
FORM **7525-V** (1-1-88) **SHIPPER'S EXPORT DECLARATION**	OMB No. 0607-0018

1a. EXPORTER *(Name and address including ZIP code)*

ZIP CODE

2. DATE OF EXPORTATION

3. BILL OF LADING/AIR WAYBILL NO.

b. EXPORTER'S EIN (IRS) NO.

c. PARTIES TO TRANSACTION
☐ Related ☐ Non-related

4a. ULTIMATE CONSIGNEE

b. INTERMEDIATE CONSIGNEE

5. FORWARDING AGENT

6. POINT (STATE) OF ORIGIN OR FTZ NO. **7.** COUNTRY OF ULTIMATE DESTINATION

8. LOADING PIER *(Vessel only)*

9. MODE OF TRANSPORT *(Specify)*

10. EXPORTING CARRIER

11. PORT OF EXPORT

12. PORT OF UNLOADING *(Vessel and air only)*

13. CONTAINERIZED *(Vessel only)*
☐ Yes ☐ No

14. SCHEDULE B DESCRIPTION OF COMMODITIES.
15. MARKS, NOS., AND KINDS OF PACKAGES *(Use columns 17 – 19)*

VALUE (U.S. dollars, omit cents)
(Selling price or cost if not sold)
(20)

D/F (16)	SCHEDULE B NUMBER (17)	CHECK DIGIT	QUANTITY – SCHEDULE B UNIT(S) (18)	SHIPPING WEIGHT *(Kilos)* (19)

21. VALIDATED LICENSE NO./GENERAL LICENSE SYMBOL **22.** ECCN *(When required)*

23. Duly authorized officer or employee │ The exporter authorizes the forwarder named above to act as forwarding agent for export control and customs purposes.

24. I certify that all statements made and all information contained herein are true and correct and that I have read and understand the instructions for preparation of this document, set forth in the "**Correct Way to Fill Out the Shipper's Export Declaration.**" I understand that civil and criminal penalties, including forfeiture and sale, may be imposed for making false or fraudulent statements herein, failing to provide the requested information or for violation of U.S. laws on exportation (13 U.S.C. Sec. 305; 22 U.S.C. Sec. 401; 18 U.S.C. Sec. 1001; 50 U.S.C. App. 2410).

Signature

Title

Date

Confidential – For use solely for official purposes authorized by the Secretary of Commerce (13 U.S.C. 301 (g)).

Export shipments are subject to inspection by U.S. Customs Service and/or Office of Export Enforcement.

25. AUTHENTICATION *(When required)*

This form may be printed by private parties provided it conforms to the official form. For sale by the Superintendent of Documents, Government Printing Office, Washington, D.C. 20402, and local Customs District Directors. The "**Correct Way to Fill Out the "Shipper's Export Declaration**" is available from the Bureau of the Census, Washington, D.C. 20233.

Source: Seaschott.

collection purposes), and a **certificate of origin** (required by certain countries to ensure correct tariffs). Insurance documents are produced when stipulated by the transaction. In certain countries, especially in Latin America, two additional documents are needed. An **import license** may be required for certain types or amounts of particular goods, while a **foreign exchange license** allows the importer to secure the needed hard currency to pay for the shipment. The exporter has to provide the importer with the data needed to obtain these licenses from governmental authorities and should make sure, before the actual shipment, that the importer has indeed secured the documents. All commercial shipments to West Germany, irrespective of value or mode of transport, require a commercial invoice, bill of lading (or airway bill), certificate of origin, and any special documents required due to the type of goods being forwarded.

Whatever the required documents, their proper preparation is of utmost importance. Improper or missing documents can easily lead to difficulties that will delay payment or even prevent it. Furthermore, improper documentation may cause problems with customs, as shown in The International Marketplace 12.3. If a customs service seizes the merchandise, delays can be measured in weeks and may end up in total financial loss for the particular shipment. However, with adherence to release procedures, a seizure case can usually be guided through without major loss to the international marketer.[45]

Support Agencies for International Shipments

Several types of support agencies provide services in the physical movement of the goods. An **international freight forwarder** acts as an agent for the international marketer in moving cargo to the overseas destination. Independent freight forwarders are regulated and should be certified by the Federal Maritime Commission. The forwarder advises the marketer on shipping documentation and packing costs and will prepare and review the documents to ensure that they are in order. Forwarders will also book the necessary space aboard a carrier. They will make necessary arrangements to clear outbound goods with customs, and after clearance forward the documents to either the customer or to the paying bank. A **customs broker** serves as an agent for an importer with authority to clear inbound goods through customs and ship them on to their destination. These functions are performed for a fee. Customs brokers are regulated by the U.S. Customs Service. Nonvessel-operating **common carriers** consolidate freight into containers and thus provide attractive rates to international marketers whose shipments are less than full containerloads.

---

[45] David Serko and Barry Kaplan, "What to Do When Customs Seizes Your Merchandise," *Global Trade* 3 (October 1988): 15–16.

THE INTERNATIONAL MARKETPLACE **12.3**

Dealing with Customs   The United States Customs Service is responsible for enforcing the rules and regulations of more than 40 government agencies. In its effort to fulfill its expanding tasks in an era of tightening budgets, the agency has centralized inspections, reassessed personnel needs, and deployed the Automated Commercial Service, a computer network for the management and processing of trade information.

The extent of its task and the volume of trade make the agency a target of criticism. It processes over seven million merchandise entries a year, and for the majority of importers the main complaint is the delay in clearing their shipments. "You can get a shipment from the Orient in a matter of hours—and have it sit for 12 days in some cases," said Gordon Freund, chairman of the Textile and Apparel Group of the American Association of Exporters and Importers. Some shipments may be tied up longer if improprieties are alleged.

Customs officials reject the majority of such criticism. A rising percentage of goods—about 80 percent in large ports like New York—is cleared without requiring any inspection beyond simple document checks. The most expensive checks for importers, such as those involving the emptying of entire shipping containers, rarely occur unless customs agents find discrepancies in documents or discover violations during cursory dockside inspections.

Customs violations run the gamut from innocent mistakes and simple negligence, such as improper labeling, to outright fraud by importers seeking to bring in counterfeit goods, dodge quotas, or avoid duties. Penalties for criminal fraud can be as severe as two years' imprisonment and a $5,000 fine for each violation. False labeling that results in underpayment of duty can lead to a penalty of eight times the amount of underpayment in the case of fraud, or two times the value in the case of simple negligence.

Customs has the authority to seize goods, order them returned to their country of origin, damage them if necessary in its investigation, and order their return for further inspection if examination of samples raises questions. Disputes may last years if appealed to the federal courts.

Source: "Importers' 'Horror Stories,'" *The New York Times*, April 21, 1987, D1.

SUMMARY

Channels of distribution consist of the marketing intermediaries that facilitate the movement of goods and services. Decisions that must be made to establish an international channel of distribution focus on channel design and the selection of intermediaries for the roles that the international marketer will not perform. The channel must be designed to meet the requirements of the intended customer base, coverage, long-term continuity of the channel once it is established, and the quality of coverage to be achieved. Having determined the basic design of the channel, the international marketer will then decide on the number of different types of intermediaries to use and how many of each type. The process is important because the majority of international sales involve distributors, and channel decisions are the most long-term of all marketing decisions. Once the channel is in place, shipping goods may require the help of additional support agencies. The more the channel operation resembles a team, rather than a collection of independent businesses, the more effective the overall marketing effort will be.

Questions for Discussion

1. Relate these two statements: A channel of distribution can be compared to a marriage. The number one reason given for divorce is lack of communication.

2. Channels of distribution tend to vary according to the level of economic development of a market. The more developed the economy, the shorter the channels tend to be. Why?

3. If a small exporter lacks the resources for an on-site inspection, what measures would you propose for screening potential distributors?

4. The international marketer and the distributor will have different expectations concerning the relationship. Why should these expectations be spelled out and clarified in the contract?

5. What courses of action are open to an international marketer who finds all attractive intermediaries already under contract to competitors?

6. One method of screening candidates is to ask distributors for a simple marketing plan. What items would you want included in this plan?

7. What are the functions performed by an international freight forwarder?

8. Using the *Exporter's Encyclopedia* published by Dun & Bradstreet, outline the documentation needed for shipments to (a) France, (b) Senegal, (c) Argentina, (d) Papua New Guinea, (e) People's Republic of China, and (f) Canada.

Recommended Readings

Czinkota, Michael R., and Jon Woronoff. *Japan's Market: The Distribution System*. New York: Praeger Publishing, 1986.

Michman, Ronald D., and Stanley D. Sibley. *Marketing Channels and Strategies*. Columbus, Ohio: Grid Publishing, 1980.

Schary, Philip B. *Logistics Decisions: Text and Cases*. Hinsdale, Ill.: Dryden Press, 1984.

Stern, Louis W., and Adel I. El-Ansary. *Marketing Channels*. Englewood Cliffs, N.J.: Prentice-Hall, 1988.

CHAPTER 13

Licensing, Franchising, and Export Intermediaries

13.1 THE INTERNATIONAL MARKETPLACE

Land of the Licensing Sun *Most entrepreneurs would sooner sell their mothers than their technology. Not so Sun Microsystems. Through much cash, sweat, and tears, California's Sun has struggled to create desktop computers embodying some of the fastest microprocessors, flashiest graphics, and most convenient communications software on the market. But instead of guarding its innovations, Sun will license vital computer technologies to anybody who wants them—friend or foe.*

Sun is actively trying to get others to copy several of its key technologies. The company has licensed the microprocessor that powers most of its computers to five other firms, including Fujitsu and LSI Logic as well as Toshiba. And it has licensed its version of the Unix operating system to perhaps 20 or 30 others. In fact, Sun does not track exactly how many firms have licensed its software because it has granted some firms the power to relicense the technology to others without telling Sun—thus reassuring potential users that Sun cannot cut them off.

Doomsayers predict that Sun will grow its own rivals, which eventually will drive it out of business. So far, however, Sun's open-door policy has made it one of America's fastest growing computer companies, expanding to annual sales of $2 billion in seven years. Sun reckons that the benefits of sharing its technology far outweigh the problems of extra competition. Specifically, it reckons the advantages of sharing include:

- *Familiarity: Proprietary technologies make customers nervous. Such technologies are often unfamiliar and hard to modify to meet a customer's specific needs. And they tie a customer to a specific supplier who may in the future fall behind the pace of technological change.*
- *Innovation: By sharing its technology with others, Sun can take advantage of their improvements to it.*
- *Management Focus: Proprietary technology tempts companies to relax. Knowing that competitors will share basic technologies makes employees concentrate on staying ahead in other ways—by innovating faster, by quality, by service.*

- Market Size: *Computer markets often grow in a sort of virtuous circle; good hardware attracts good software, which attracts more and better hardware. The more machines that can share software with Sun computers, the more software will be written for them—and thus the bigger Sun's potential market.*
- Cash Flow: *Though licensing revenues account for well under a tenth of Sun's sales, profit margins are immense and help finance other initiatives.*

Source: "Land of the Licensing Sun," *The Economist*, June 3, 1989, 68–69.

Quite frequently firms recognize the value of marketing internationally but either lack sufficient capital or human resources for direct exporting or foreign direct investment, or they consider these strategies to be inappropriate. This chapter suggests alternative strategies for participation in the international marketplace. For the moving of services and expertise abroad, the chapter focuses primarily on licensing and franchising. It describes how they function, the opportunities they provide, and their drawbacks. For the marketing of products, the use of market intermediaries is explained. These include primarily export management companies, Webb-Pomerene associations, and export trading companies.

If international marketing functions are left entirely to others, the firm will not gain the international marketing expertise necessary to ready itself for subsequent world market penetration. As a way to initiate market entry, however, these alternatives are viable and useful if used properly by the firm.

Clearly, going international through licensing, franchising, and export intermediaries are alternatives open to and used by all types of firms, large and small. In addition, these options present only some of the international avenues beyond exporting—others are foreign direct investment, joint ventures, or management contracts. Yet, because they represent very viable entry alternatives for the small and medium-sized firm, licensing, franchising, and the use of export intermediaries are dealt with in this concluding chapter of Part Two. The more resource intensive ways of going international will then be addressed in Part Three.

LICENSING

Under a licensing agreement, one firm, the licensor, permits another to use its intellectual property in exchange for compensation designated as a royalty. The recipient firm is the licensee. The property might include patents, trademarks, copyrights, technology, technical know-how, or specific marketing skills. For example, a firm that has developed a new packaging proven for liquids can permit other firms abroad to use the same process. Licensing therefore amounts to exporting intangibles.

Assessment of Licensing

Licensing has intuitive appeal to many would-be international marketers. As an entry strategy, it requires neither capital investment nor knowledge and marketing strength in foreign markets. By earning royalty income, it provides an opportunity to exploit research and development already committed to. After initial costs, the licensor can reap benefits until the end of the contract period. Licensing reduces risk of exposure to government intervention in that the licensee is typically a local company that can provide leverage against government action. Licensing will help to avoid host country regulations that are more prevalent in equity ventures. Licensing may also serve as a stage in the internationalization of the firm by providing a means by which foreign markets can be tested without major involvement of capital or management time. Similarly, licensing can be used as a strategy to preempt a market before the entry of competition, especially if the licensor's resources permit full-scale involvement only in selected markets.

Licensing has nevertheless come under criticism from many supranational organizations, such as the United Nations Conference on Trade and Development (UNCTAD). They have alleged that licensing provides a mechanism by which older technology is capitalized on by industrialized country multinational corporations (MNCs). Licensees may often want labor-intensive techniques or machinery, however. Guinness Brewery, for example, in order to produce Guinness Stout in Nigeria, imported licensed equipment that had been used in Ireland at the turn of the century. Even though this equipment was obsolete by Western standards, it had additional economic life in Nigeria because it presented a good fit with Nigeria's productive needs.

In addition, licensing offers a foreign entity the opportunity for immediate market entry with a proven concept. It therefore eliminates the risk of R&D failures, the cost of designing around the licensor's patents, or the fear of patent infringement litigation. Furthermore, most licensing agreements provide for ongoing cooperation and support, thus enabling the licensee to benefit from new developments.

With increasing host country regulation, licensing may enable the international marketer to enter a foreign market that is closed to either imports or direct foreign investments. In addition, licensing arrangements may enable the licensor to negotiate parallel contracts that are not related directly to the agreement, and to provide for foreign purchases of materials and components. The licensor can thereby expand participation in the particular market.

Licensing is not without disadvantages. The most limited form of foreign-market participation, it does not in any way guarantee a basis for future expansion in market entry. As a matter of fact, quite the opposite may take place. In exchange for the royalty, the licensor may create its own competitor not only in the markets for which the agreement was made but also for third markets as well. As a result, some companies are hesitant to enter licensing agreements. As an example, Japanese firms are delighted to sell goods to China but are unwilling to license the Chinese to produce the goods themselves. They fear that, because of the low wage structure in China, such licenses could create a powerful future competitor in markets presently held by Japan. In contrast, Sun Microsystems became one of America's fastest growing companies through licensing of vital computer technologies, as described in The International Marketplace 13.1.

Licensing agreements typically have time limits. Although terms may be extended once after the start-up period, additional extensions are not readily permitted by a number of foreign governments. If the licensee ties in with the licensor's global marketing network, quality control in terms of both production and marketing effort becomes a concern.

U.S. Regulation of Licensing

The U.S. Department of Justice has nine specific patent license provisions (the nine no-nos of patent licensing) that it considers unlawful under the antitrust laws.[1] These provisions prohibit the licensor from controlling the licensee's distribution of a patented product. For example, it is illegal for the licensor to restrict a licensee's ability to resell a patented product, to restrict the licensee's ability to sell products that compete with the patented product (tie-out), or to require the licensee to adhere to a minimum price in the sale of the product. Other restrictions pertain to payments. It is illegal to require the licensee to purchase from the licensor products used with or in the patented product (tie-in), to offer to license only a group of patents rather than individual patents, or to base royalties on a measure other than one that corresponds to sales of products covered by the patent.

U.S. national security considerations must be kept in mind in terms of Export Administration regulations and U.S. jurisdiction over technology based on technical data originating in the United States. These regulations have to be considered especially in light of their match between national and regional policies, such as those of the EC.

The international marketer must also research national regulations concerning foreign involvement and foreign exchange restrictions that may have an impact on the payment of royalties by the licensee. An overview of typical licensing regulations is provided in Table 13.1.

Principal Issues in Negotiating Licensing Agreements

The key issues in negotiating licensing agreements include the scope of the rights conveyed, compensation, licensee compliance, dispute resolution, and the term and termination of the agreement.[2] The more clearly

[1] Roger B. Andewelt, "The Antitrust Division's Perspective on Intellectual Property Protection and Licensing—The Past, the Present, and the Future," paper presented at the annual meeting of the American Bar Association, London, England, 1985.

[2] Martin F. Connor, "International Technology Licensing," Seminars in International Trade, National Center for Export-Import Studies, Washington, D.C.

TABLE 13.1 ▪ Licensing Regulations in 18 Nations

	Registration Requirements	Royalty and Fee Patterns	Applicable Tax and Restrictions	Comments
Canada	Registration with government not compulsory. Exclusive license, patent assignments must be registered, but no penalty for failure to register.	Freely negotiated. A maximum royalty of 4 percent for pharmaceuticals.	Tax officials may be strict about "reasonable" royalty payments if they suspect tax avoidance.	Government agencies can be helpful in finding licensees.
United States	No government approval needed for foreign licensing of technology in U.S., but export controls on certain sensitive technologies apply for U.S. firms.	Freely negotiated. Rates vary, but generally range from 2.5 to 5 percent of net sales.	No controls or limitations on remittances.	Rapid obsolescence of technology has decreased average life of agreements and amount of royalties.
Belgium	No government approval required, but should be registered. Assignment of patents, trademarks, or design must be recorded at Patents Department or Benelux Bureau.	No special patterns, though officials question fees over 7.5 percent of sale price of licensed goods.	Freely remitted. No significant restrictions.	Investment by foreign companies more prevalent than straight licensing agreements.
France	French party to agreement must notify Service de la Propriete Industrielle within one month of signing.	Rates vary with industry. Declining rates often used to guarantee minimum income at beginning of contract. Rates fall as production increases.	Freely remitted, but French licensees may be denied tax deductions for payments in excess of 5 to 6 percent.	Licensing used extensively as substitute for or prelude to direct investment.
Germany	No government approval necessary for terms of licensing agreements or royalty payments to foreigners.	Royalties often based on per-unit basis of sales. Many agreements fix annual royalties, payable regardless of sales.	Royalties freely remitted. Disclosure fees sometimes charged.	Agreement can outlast patent right for which it was granted.
Italy	No government approval necessary, but royalty payments scrutinized by government.	Determined by commercial considerations and rarely publicized. Finance Ministry specifies level of royalties "acceptable" for tax and exchange purposes.	Royalty remittances subject to exchange control strictures.	Protection of industrial property is weak.
Netherlands	While there is no registration requirement for licensing agreements, it is advisable.	Terms concern only signing parties. No set rule bases royalties on gross or net sales; large concerns often agree on lump-sum payments.	Royalties freely remitted. No restrictions.	Well developed and often-used licensing system.

TABLE 13.1 ▪ **Continued**

	Registration Requirements	Royalty and Fee Patterns	Applicable Tax and Restrictions	Comments
Spain	Companies must file contract with DGTE, which sends it to Office of Technological Innovation and to competition authorities. If not rejected after 30 days, contract takes effect.	Royalties vary by industry. Percentage allowed depends on importance of products to national economy. Standard rate is 0.5 percent of sales for 5 years.	Government still monitors technology inflows, but has reduced restrictions under EC rules.	New system introduced January 1988 a major improvement over old, but still restrictive.
Sweden	Licensing agreements entirely free of official governmental regulation.	Entirely a matter of commercial negotiation.	No taxes or restrictions, but funds must go through authorized banks.	Tie-in clauses and other practices restricting free competition permitted if not to have "harmful effects" to industry.
United Kingdom	No registration necessary.	Determined solely by commercial considerations. Royalty range for most agreements is 5 to 10 percent of net sales.	Excessive royalty payments may be ruled dividend distribution, thus disallowed as corporate expenses for tax purposes.	Licensing agreements are popular and laws are pro-licensor.
Australia	Agreements require exchange control approval from Reserve Bank.	Royalties under 10 percent allowed. Specific terms vary.	Exchange control approval required for royalty payments.	Procedures for exchange control approval simple and usually granted readily.
India	Extensive requirements for government approval. Relevant ministries decide on arrangements that entail "useful or new" technology and no foreign-equity investment.	Government keeps royalties low. Maximum is 4 percent of sales computed by a complex formula. Guaranteed minimum, unrelated to sales, prohibited.	Stringent foreign exchange controls and applicable investment rules pose limitations to agreements.	Sound legal counsel, honest partners, and patience necessary for long negotiations. Intellectual property protection poor.
Japan	Proposal must be submitted to Ministry of Finance, and Ministry of Industry involved. Agreements not concluded until 30 days after submission.	No legal maximum rates, but MITI considers 5 percent "ideal maximum." Provisions for minimum royalties often included.	Disclosure fees common, but no tax or other limits. Complex approval requirements.	Number of gratis licenses up as a result of cross-licensing deals.
Korea	New law requires only technology imports be reported to Ministry of Finance. Approval automatic after 20 days if no modifications ordered.	Licensees must justify fees above 2 to 3 percent of net sales unless know-how highly advanced. Royalties tax exempt for 5 years.	Government may reject technology imports if deemed low quality, outmoded, or restrict conditions on exports.	New tax rules may discourage local licensees from taking on agreements greater than 3 percent of sales.

(continued)

TABLE 13.1 ▪ **Continued**

	Registration Requirements	Royalty and Fee Patterns	Applicable Tax and Restrictions	Comments
Taiwan	Agreements involving FX payments must be approved and are reviewed case-by-case. Details on products, services, etc., should be included. Usually takes one month if agreement is uncomplicated.	Royalties computed on net sales, but sometimes related to output. Most agreements fall below 5 percent and run 5 years.	MOEA won't review licenses for light or labor-intensive industries nor companies aiming at lower labor costs.	Government has tightened terms except in high tech, which it promotes. Intellectual property protection improved, but still weak.
Argentina	National Institute of Industrial Technology must approve when licensor owns 49 percent or more of sub. For others, contract need only be registered.	Unlimited by law, but must be in line with market rates. Royalties don't exceed 5 percent of net sales. Cash remittances permitted at FX rate.	Royalty tax of 45 percent applied on following percentages of: technical assistance (60%); patents (80%); and services (100%) not covered in transfer of technology law.	Licensee may not deduct royalty payments as operating expenses. Patents, trademarks should be registered.
Brazil	Must be approved and registered with National Institute of Industrial Property. Agreements between related companies illegal.	Royalties restricted to 1 to 5 percent of net sales. Companies may capitalize technology payments. Trademark royalties maximum 1 percent of net sales.	Severe limitations on remittances. Royalty tax is 25 percent (reduced by some tax treaties). Payments deductible with 1 to 5 percent of gross sales.	Patent piracy, copyright infringement growing problem. Technology transfer a limited profit-making operation.
Mexico	Must be registered with National Registry of Technology Transfer.	3 percent of net sales the norm, though special cases go up to 10 percent. Typical contract length is 10 years. Remittances at controlled exchange rate.	Royalty tax is 21 percent on payments for know-how, technical assistance and 42 percent on straight patents and trademarks.	Stronger intellectual property laws but enforcement still lax.

Source: "Licensing Regulations in 18 Nations," *Business International*, March 7, 1988, 68–69. Reprinted with permission.

these are spelled out, the more trouble-free the association between the two parties can be.

The rights conveyed are product and/or patent rights. Defining their scope involves specifying the technology, know-how, or show-how to be included; the format; and guarantees. An example of format specification is an agreement on whether manuals will be translated into the licensee's language.

Compensation issues may be heavily disputed and argued. The costs the licensor wants to cover are (1) **transfer costs,** which are all variable costs incurred in transferring technology to a licensee and all ongoing costs of maintaining the agreement, (2) R&D costs incurred in developing the licensed technology, and (3) **opportunity costs** incurred in the foreclosure of other sources of profit, such as exports or direct investment. In return, the licensor wants a share of the profits generated from the use of the license. Licensees usually do not want to include allowances for opportunity costs, and they often argue that R&D costs have already been covered by the licensor. In theory, royalties can be seen as profit sharing; in practice, royalties are a function of both the licensor's minimum necessary return and the cost of the licensee's next best alternative. In the past U.S. marketers have been able to obtain licensing returns above their transfer costs as a result of the unique features of their technology and intellectual property, but changes in the marketplace suggest a drastically different future.[3] These changes include maturing technologies, intensifying competition among suppliers, growing sophistication among licensees, and greater involvement by governments in arranging for the licensing agreements.

The methods of compensating the licensor can take the form of running royalties, such as 5 percent of the licensee sales, and/or up-front payments, service fees, and disclosure fees (for proprietary data). Sometimes government regulations pose an obstacle to the collection of royalties or know-how payments. In such instances, the know-how transferred can be capitalized as part of a cooperative venture, where a specific value is attributed to the information. Payments are then received as profits or dividends.[4]

Licensee compliance on a number of dimensions must be stipulated in the agreement: (1) U.S. export administration regulations, especially concerning sales to the Council of Mutual Economic Assistance; (2) confidentiality of the intellectual property and technology provided; and (3) record keeping and provisions for licensor audits, which are done periodically, usually a minimum of once a year.

Dispute resolution discussions center on the choice of law for contract interpretation and the choice of forum. Typically, the parties involved choose a third country's law to govern the agreement. Great care should be taken to determine the laws of the particular third country with respect to licensing. Swedish law, which is often used, stipulates on certain issues that the law of the licensee's country govern. When the parties cannot agree on an applicable legal system, an arbitration clause is warranted. This should be spelled out by using, for example, the International Chamber of Commerce model clause: "All disputes arising in connection with the present contract shall be finally settled under the Rules of Conciliation

[3] Franklin R. Root and Farok J. Contractor, "Negotiating Compensation in International Licensing Agreements," *Sloan Management Review* 22 (Summer 1981): 23–32.

[4] "International Licensing and Technology, Brazil," *Business International*, December 1987, 12.

and Arbitration of the International Chamber of Commerce by one or more arbitrators appointed in accordance with the said rules." Also needed is a statement regarding the arbitrators' authority.[5]

Finally, the term, termination, and survival of rights must be specified. Government regulations in the licensee's market will have to be studied, and if the conditions are not favorable (for example, in terms of the maximum allowable duration), a waiver should be applied for.

New Developments in Licensing

For companies that can trade on their names and characters, **trademark licensing** has become a substantial source of worldwide revenue. The total volume of trademark licensing was expected to reach $75 billion by 1990. The names or logos of designers, literary characters, sports teams, and movie stars appear on clothing, games, foods and beverages, gifts and novelties, toys, and home furnishings. British designer Laura Ashley started the first major furniture program, licensing her name to Henredon Furniture Industries. Coca-Cola licensed its name to Murjani to be used on blue jeans, sweatshirts, and windbreakers. The licensors are likely to make millions of dollars with little effort, while the licensees can produce a branded product that consumers will recognize immediately. Licensing costs in such instances are typically an average fee of five percent of the wholesale price.[6]

Both licensor and licensee may run into difficulty if the trademark is used for a product too far removed from the original success. In licensing a trademark, consumer perceptions have to be researched to make sure the brand's positioning will not change. As an example, when Löwenbräu was exported to the United States, it was the number one imported beer sold in the market. However, when the product name was licensed to Miller Brewing Company for domestic production, the beer's positioning (and subsequently its target audience) changed drastically in the minds of the consumers, resulting in a major decline in sales.

FRANCHISING

Franchising is a form of licensing in which a parent company (the franchisor) grants another, independent entity (the franchisee) the right to do business in a prescribed manner. This right can take the form of selling the franchisor's products, using its name, production and marketing tech-

---

[5] William W. Park, "Arbitration of International Contract Disputes," *The Business Lawyer* 39 (August 1984): 83–99.

[6] "What's in a Name? Millions If It's Licensed," *Business Week,* April 8, 1985, 97–98; and "Licensing Sales—The Name of the Game," *USA Today,* March 11, 1985, 7B.

niques, or general business approach.[7] Usually franchising involves a combination of many of these elements. The major forms of franchising are manufacturer–retailer systems (such as car dealerships), manufacturer–wholesaler systems (such as soft drink companies), and service firm–retailer systems (such as lodging services and fast food outlets). The International Marketplace 13.2 gives an example of an expanding international franchise operation.

Although franchising is not a U.S. innovation (its origins are in Bavaria), it has been adopted by various types of businesses, mainly in the United States. After impressive market penetration in the United States, where franchising sales for goods and services in more than 509,000 outlets accounted for almost $640 billion in 1988, international franchising activities have achieved major gains in the past decade. For example, in 1986, U.S. franchisors operated 31,626 outlets abroad, more than nine times the 1971 total, with Canada, Japan, and Australia as the leading markets.[8] Foreign franchisors are penetrating international markets as well. Examples include Holiday Rent-a-Car of Canada, and Descamps, a French firm selling linens and tablecloths. The principal types of U.S. international franchises and their locations around the world are listed in Table 13.2.

The typical reasons for the international expansion of franchise systems are market potential, financial gain, and saturated domestic markets. U.S. franchisors expanded dramatically in Europe in 1984, taking advantage of the strong U.S. dollar. The initial impetus for ComputerLand's expansion into the Asia/Pacific region was "Asian entrepreneurs coming knocking on our door asking for franchises."[9] In some cases, international expansion is a reaction to competitors' entry into foreign markets. In the mid-1980s, McDonald Corporation's biggest push was into France, because France was the only major European country where McDonald's lagged behind Burger King.[10]

From a franchisee perspective, the franchise is beneficial because it reduces risk by implementing a proven concept. In the United States, for example, between one-quarter and one-third of small businesses fail in their first year of operation. In contrast, only about 2.5 percent of franchise-owned outlets discontinue operations per year.[11]

Franchising by its very nature calls for a great degree of standardization. In most cases, this does not mean 100 percent uniformity but, instead, international recognizability. Fast-food franchisors, for example, will vary

[7] Donald W. Hackett, "The International Expansion of U.S. Franchise Systems," in *Multinational Product Management*, eds. Warren J. Keegan and Charles S. Mayer (Chicago: American Marketing Association, 1979), 61–81.

[8] Andrew Kostecka, *Franchising in the Economy 1986–1988* (Washington, D.C.: Government Printing Office, 1988), 1, 46.

[9] "ComputerLand Debugs Its Franchising Program for Asia/Pacific Region," *Business International*, September 13, 1985, 294–295.

[10] "U.S. Fast-Food Giants Moving in on France," *Advertising Age*, October 22, 1984, 54.

[11] "Franchising Is Management for Success," *Small Business Reporter* 7 (1986).

13.2 ## THE INTERNATIONAL MARKETPLACE

Domino's Driving Hard for International Success   Depending on
the product, international franchising can be an extremely effective
market entry method. The phenomenal international expansion of
some well-known food chains illustrates the potential of franchising as a method of expanding into new markets while retaining the
very elements of one's success: consistent products and services.
Following this recipe, Domino's Pizza, the $2 billion U.S. pizza de-
livery king, has already made impressive strides exporting its marketing concept to the rest of the world. It has 235 stores in 10
countries outside the United States and is aggressively aiming at
further international expansion. Underlying this growth is Domino's unique commitment to developing its own managerial talent.

Domino's approach to international expansion mirrors its expansion policy in the United States. The company is privately held,
and only qualified individuals who are already working for the
company are granted franchises. Thus, initial entry into a foreign
market is based not only on a country's market potential but also
on the existence of eligible individuals for the promising area.

To qualify for a domestic or an international franchise, the employee must be in an existing store as a manager or supervisor. In
order to attain this level, the individual must have completed six
months as a manager in training (MIT) and six classes—management basics, cost management, people management, dough management, sales building, and on-the-job training. After MIT, the
person must successfully manage an existing unit for no less than
one year. Once these requirements have been met, individuals are
eligible to apply for a single franchise. Subsequent store applications are granted based on the first unit's performance. Before a
foreign franchise is awarded, the potential franchisee must answer
an extensive market research questionnaire, which ensures that the
candidate has done the necessary homework. Besides the obvious
operating and marketing questions (for example, How many pizza
establishments exist? Do they deliver? Do people accept home delivery?), the survey also asks: Does the country promote entrepreneurs? Will the concept of "hustle" translate?

Source: Chris Matthews, "Domino's Driving Hard for International Success," *Business International*, September 19, 1988, 285–286. Reprinted with permission.

---

the products and product lines offered depending on local market conditions and tastes.

The problems encountered in using franchising as an entry mode are
summarized in Table 13.3 on page 396. Foreign government intervention
represents the major problem for franchise systems in their international

TABLE 13.2 ▪ **International Locations of U.S. Franchising Establishments**

| | | | | | Location | | | | |
| | | | | Europe | | | Asia | | |
Kinds of Franchised Business[a]	Total	Canada	Mexico	Carib-bean	United Kingdom	Other	Aus-tralia	Japan	Other	Other[b]
Total—All Franchising	31,626	9,031	559	792	2,415	4,844	2,816	7,366	2,042	1,761
Business Aids and Services	3,930	1,447	4	16	469	603	589	635	56	111
Construction, Home Improvement, Maintenance, and Cleaning Services	1,737	646	1	23	210	230	61	480	29	57
Restaurants (All Types)	6,769	1,869	121	280	608	642	691	1,548	552	458
Hotels, Motels, and Campgrounds	577	314	32	22	31	68	16	9	45	40
Recreation, Entertainment, and Travel	194	65	0	5	17	26	31	37	3	10
Rental Services (Auto–Truck)	5,928	721	232	293	365	1,832	635	512	435	903
Laundry and Drycleaning Services	67	61	0	0	1	0	0	0	5	0
Automotive Products and Services	2,274	1,084	27	38	106	563	168	123	57	108
Retailing (Nonfood)	3,619	1,580	68	51	489	616	463	180	118	54
Educational Products and Services, Rental Services (Equipment), Convenience Stores, and Miscellaneous	4,572	527	67	11	78	213	144	3,014	510	8
Retailing (Food Other Than Convenience Stores)	1,959	717	7	53	41	51	18	828	232	12

[a]Does not include automobile and truck dealers, gasoline service stations, and soft drink bottlers, for which data were not collected.

[b]Includes South America (521), Africa (641), New Zealand (420), and Central America (179).

Source: Andrew Kostecka, *Franchising in the Economy 1986–1988* (Washington, D.C.: Government Printing Office, 1988), 46.

expansion. In the Philippines, government restrictions on franchising and royalties hindered ComputerLand's Manila store from offering a fuller range of services, leading to a separation between the company and its franchisee. Selection and training of franchisees present another potential problem area. McDonald's lag behind Burger King in France was a result of the company's suing to revoke the license of its largest franchise for failure to operate 14 stores according to McDonald's standards. Many franchise systems have run into difficulty by expanding too quickly and granting franchises to unqualified entities. Although the local franchisee knows the market best, the franchisor still needs to understand the market for product adaptation purposes and operational details. The franchisor should be the conductor of a coordinated effort by the individual franchisees—for example, in terms of sharing ideas and engaging in joint marketing efforts, such as cooperative advertising.

In order to encourage better organized and more successful growth, companies increasingly turn to the **master franchising system,** wherein large foreign partners are selected and awarded the rights to a large ter-

TABLE 13.3   ▪   **Rank Order of Problems Encountered in International Markets by U.S. Franchise Systems**

1. Host government regulations and red tape
2. High import duties and taxes in foreign environment
3. Monetary uncertainties and royalty retribution to franchisor
4. Logistical problems in operation of international franchise system
5. Control of franchisees
6. Location problems and real estate costs
7. Patent, trademark, and copyright protection
8. Recruitment of franchisees
9. Training of foreign franchisee personnel
10. Language and cultural barriers
11. Availability of raw materials for company product
12. Foreign ownership limitations
13. Competition in foreign market areas
14. Adaptation of franchise package to local markets

Source: Donald W. Hackett, "The International Expansion of U.S. Franchise Systems," in *Multinational Product Management*, eds. Warren Keegan and Charles Mayer (Chicago: American Marketing Association, 1979), 78.

ritory in which they in turn can subfranchise. As a result, the franchisor gains market expertise and an effective screening mechanism for new franchises, without incurring costly mistakes.[12]

Franchising is often thought of as a strategy to be used for foreign market entry only by large firms. Yet franchising may be a viable alternative for small firms, if limited to undeveloped markets where the firm can establish its reputation relatively unopposed.[13] Automation Papers Company, a New Jersey-based supplier of high-technology paper products, opted for franchising to gain exclusive representation by a highly motivated sales force in its target markets. The franchisees receive rights to the Automation Papers trademarks; intensive training for local staff members; and the benefit of the franchisor's experience, credit lines, and advertising budget.

FACILITATING INTERMEDIARIES

Firms with products or devices that do not lend themselves to licensing or franchising can make use of the existing infrastructure of facilitating international market intermediaries. One obvious possibility is the selling of merchandise to a domestic firm that in turn sells it abroad. For example, many products are sold to multinational corporations that use them as input for their foreign sales. Similarly, products sold to the U.S. Department

[12] Agnes P. Olszewski, "International Marketing Strategies of U.S. Fast Food Franchises," in *Developments in Marketing Science*, eds. J. Hawes and J. Thanopoulos (Chicago: Academy of Marketing Science, 1989), 123–127.

[13] "One Company's Experience Shows How Franchising Can Help Overseas Sales," *Business International*, July 1, 1983, 201–203.

TABLE 13.4 ▪ **Exporting In Your Own Backyard: A Dozen Segments of the United States for Export Markets**

1. Large U.S. companies purchasing U.S. goods for their own foreign affiliates
2. Large design and construction firms purchasing U.S. goods for foreign projects awarded to them
3. U.S. branches of gigantic foreign trading companies purchasing U.S. goods for their affiliates
4. Export merchants buying for their own account
5. Large foreign companies purchasing U.S. goods through their U.S. buying office or agents
6. U.S. military purchasing for use abroad
7. U.S. exporters seeking U.S. goods to round out their own lines
8. United Nations members purchasing for development projects
9. Foreign governments purchasing U.S. goods
10. Foreign department stores purchasing U.S. goods through U.S. buying offices
11. Foreign buyers on purchasing trips
12. AID-financed transactions requiring U.S. goods

Source: Nelson Joyner, Georgetown University, teaching notes, 1989.

of Defense may ultimately be shipped to military outposts abroad. An exporter may buy products domestically to round out an international product line. Table 13.4 provides more examples of "exporting in your own backyard."

This section will consider three facilitating market intermediaries: export management companies (EMCs), Webb-Pomerene associations, and export trading companies (ETCs).

Export Management Companies

Export Management Companies (EMCs) are domestic firms that specialize in performing international marketing services as commission representatives or as distributors for several other firms. Although few directories listing such firms are available, more than 1,000 of these firms are estimated to be actively operating in the United States. A study conducted by the National Federation of Independent Businesses found that over 20 percent of all manufacturing exporters in the United States used EMCs.[14] Most EMCs are quite small. They were frequently formed by one or two major principals with experience in international marketing or in a particular geographic area. Their expertise enables them to offer specialized services to domestic corporations.

EMCs have two primary forms of operation. They either take title to goods and operate internationally on their own account, or they perform services as agents. In the first instance, the EMC offers a conventional ex-

[14]Economic Consulting Services, "A Study of the Feasibility of Using Export Associations to Promote Increased Exports by Small Businesses" (Washington, D.C.: Economic Consulting Services, 1982), 29.

port channel, in that it does not have any form of geographic exclusivity, and tends to negotiate price with suppliers on every transaction. As an agent, an EMC is likely to have either an informal or a formal contractual relationship, which results in exclusivity agreements and, often, sales quotas. However, price arrangements and promotional support payments are agreed upon, which simplifies ongoing transactions.[15] Because EMCs often serve a variety of clients, their mode of operation may vary from client to client and from transaction to transaction—that is, an EMC may act as an agent for one client whereas for another client, or even for the same one on a different occasion, it may operate as a distributor.

The EMC as an Agent   When serving as an agent, the EMC is primarily in charge of developing foreign marketing and sales strategies and establishing contact abroad. Because the EMC does not share in the profits from a sale, it depends heavily on a high sales volume, on which it charges commission. It may therefore be tempted to take on as many products and as many clients as possible, in order to obtain a high sales volume. The risk in this is that the EMC will spread itself too thin and cannot adequately represent all the clients and products it carries. This risk is particularly great for small EMCs.

In addition to its international activities, this type of EMC must concentrate a substantial amount of effort on the development of domestic clients. These clients often are exactly the firms that are unwilling to commit major resources to international marketing efforts. They must be convinced that it is worthwhile to consider international marketing. While developing or expanding its clientele, the EMC diverts some of its limited resources to the task.

EMCs that have specific expertise in selecting markets because of language capabilities, previous exposure, or specialized contacts appear to be the ones most successful and useful in aiding client firms in their export marketing efforts. For example, they can cooperate with firms that are already successful in international marketing but have been unable to penetrate a specific region. By sticking to their expertise and representing only a limited number of clients, such agent services can be quite valuable.

The EMC as a Distributor   When operating as a distributor, the EMC purchases products from the domestic firm, takes the title, and assumes the trading risk. Selling in its own name offers the opportunity to reap greater profits than does acting as an agent. The potential for greater profitability is appropriate, because the EMC has drastically reduced the risk for the domestic firm while increasing its own risk. The burden of the merchandise acquired provides a major motivation to complete an international sale successfully. The domestic firm selling to the EMC is in the comfort-

---

[15] Daniel C. Bello and Nicholas C. Williamson, "Contractual Arrangement and Marketing Practices in the Indirect Export Channel," *Journal of International Business Studies* 16 (Summer 1985): 65–82.

able position of having sold its merchandise and received its money without having to deal with the complexities of the international market. On the other hand, it is unlikely to gather much international marketing expertise and therefore relegates itself to some extent to remaining a purely domestic firm.

Compensation of EMCs The mechanism of an EMC may be very useful to the domestic firm if such activities produce additional sales abroad that otherwise would not have occurred. However, certain services must be performed that demand resources for which someone must pay. As an example, in order to develop foreign markets, market development expenses must be incurred. At the very least, products must be shown abroad, visits must be arranged, or contacts must be established in order to penetrate the market. Even though it may often not be discussed, the funding for these activities must be found.

One possibility is a fee charged to the manufacturer by the EMC for market development, sometimes in the form of a retainer and often on an annual basis. These retainers vary and are dependent on the number of products represented and the difficulty of foreign market penetration. Frequently, manufacturers are also expected to pay all or part of the direct expenses associated with foreign market penetration. Some of these expenses may involve the production and translation of promotional product brochures. Others may concern the rental for booth space at foreign trade shows, the provision of product samples, or trade advertising.[16] Often a firm will be asked to invest monies in these developmental efforts.

Alternatively, the EMC may set the price for the product. Because it will take on many of the marketing activities for the manufacturer, the EMC wants the price discounted for these activities. Therefore, sales to EMCs may occur only at a reduced price.

In one way or another, the firm that uses an EMC must pay the EMC for the international marketing effort. This compensation can be in the form of fees and/or cost-sharing or in terms of lower prices and resulting higher profits for the EMC. Otherwise, despite promises, the EMC may simply add the firm and product in name only to its product offering and do nothing to achieve international market penetration. Manufacturers need to be aware of this cost and the fact that EMCs do not offer a free ride. Depending on the complexity of a product and the necessity to carry out developmental research, promotion, and service, manufacturers must be prepared to part with some portion of the potential international profitability to compensate the EMC for its efforts.

Power Conflicts between EMCs and Clients The EMC in turn faces the continuous problem of retaining a client once foreign market penetration is achieved. Many firms use an EMC's services mainly to test international

---

[16]John J. Brasch, "Export Management Companies," *Journal of International Business Studies* 9 (Spring–Summer 1978): 69.

markets, with the clear desire to become a direct exporter once successful operations have been established. Of course this is particularly true if foreign demand turns out to be strong and profit levels are high. The conflict between the EMC and its clients, with one side wanting to retain market power by not sharing too much international market information, and the other side wanting to obtain that power, often results in short-term relationships and a lack of cooperation. Because international market development is based on long-term efforts, however, this conflict frequently precipitates unsuccessful international marketing efforts.

For the concept of an export management company to work, both parties must fully recognize the delegation of responsibilities; the costs associated with these activities; and the need for information sharing, cooperation, and mutual reliance. Use of an EMC should be viewed as a domestic channel commitment. This requires a thorough investigation of the intermediary and the advisability of relying on its efforts, a willingness to cooperate on a prolonged basis, and a willingness to reward it properly for these efforts.

Webb-Pomerene Associations

Legislation enacted in 1918 that led to **Webb-Pomerene associations** permits firms to cooperate in terms of sales allocation, financing, and pricing information. The associations must take care not to engage in activities that would reduce competition within the United States. To more successfully penetrate international markets, however, they can use mechanisms such as market allocation, quota fixing, and selection of exclusive distributors or brokers.

In spite of this early effort to encourage joint activities by firms in the international market, the effectiveness of Webb-Pomerene associations has not been substantial. At their peak from 1930 to 1934, fifty Webb-Pomerene associations accounted for about 12 percent of U.S. exports. By 1978, only 27 associations were active and accounted for less than 2 percent of U.S. exports.[17] In addition, it appears that most of the users of this particular form of export intermediary are not the small and medium-sized firms the act was initially intended to assist, but rather the dominant firms in their respective industries.

The lack of success of this particular intermediary has mainly been ascribed to the fact that the antitrust exemption granted was not sufficiently iron-clad. Further, specialized export firms are thought to have more to offer to a domestic firm than does an association, which may be particularly true if an association is dominated by one or two major competitors in an industry. This makes joining the association undesirable for smaller firms in that industry.

---

[17] Federal Trade Commission, *Webb-Pomerene Associations: Ten Years Later* (Washington, D.C.: Government Printing Office, 1978).

Trading Companies

A third major facilitating intermediary is the trading company. The concept was originated by the European trading houses such as the Fuggers and was soon formalized by the monarchs. Hoping to expand their imperial powers and wealth, kings chartered traders to form corporate bodies that enjoyed exclusive trading rights in certain areas of the world and protection by the naval forces in exchange for tax payments. Examples of such early trading companies are the East India Company of the Netherlands (Oost-Indische Compagnie), formed in 1602, followed shortly by the British East India Company and the French East India Company (La Compagnie des Indes).[18] Today, the most famous trading companies are the **sogoshosha** of Japan. Names like Mitsubishi, Mitsui, and C. Itoh have become household words around the world. The nine trading company giants of Japan in 1980 accounted, in their annual domestic sales, for about 30 percent of Japan's GNP.[19] These general trading companies play a unique role in world commerce by importing, exporting, countertrading, investing, and manufacturing. Because of their vast size, they can benefit from economies of scale and perform their operations at highly beneficial rates of return. Their profit margins, for example, are generally in the range of 2 percent.[20]

Four major reasons have been given for the success of the Japanese sogoshosha. First, by concentrating on obtaining and disseminating information about market opportunities and by investing huge funds in the development of information systems, these firms now have the mechanisms and organizations in place to gather, evaluate, and translate market information into business opportunities. Second, economies of scale permit them to take advantage of their vast transaction volume to obtain preferential treatment by, for example, negotiating transportation rates or even opening up new transportation routes. Third, these firms serve large internal markets, not only in Japan but also around the world, and can benefit from opportunities for barter trade. Finally, sogoshosha have access to vast quantities of capital, both within Japan and in the international capital markets. They can therefore carry out many transactions that are larger and more risky than is palatable or feasible for other firms.[21]

For many decades the emergence of trading companies was commonly believed to be a Japan-specific phenomenon. Particularly, Japanese cul-

[18] Dong-Sung Cho, *The General Trading Company: Concept and Strategy* (Lexington, Mass.: Lexington Books, 1987), 2.

[19] Thomas Capiello, "The Changing Role of Japan's General Traders," *Journal of Japanese Trade and Industry* 4 (Winter 1982): 19.

[20] Kiyoshi Kojima and Ozawa Terutomo, *Japan's General Trading Companies: Merchants of Economic Development* (Paris: Organization for Economic Cooperation and Development, 1984), 88.

[21] Yoshi Tsurumi, *Sogoshosha: Engines of Export Based Growth* (Montreal, Quebec: The Institute for Research on Public Policy, 1980).

tural factors were cited as the reason that such intermediaries could operate successfully only from that country. In 1975, however, trading companies were established by government declaration in Korea. The intent was to continue Korea's export-led growth in a more efficient fashion. With the new legislation, the Korean government tied access to financing and government contracts to the formation of trading companies. By 1981, the major trading companies of Korea (such as Hyundai, Samsung, and Daewoo) were handling 43 percent of Korea's total exports.[22] They were therefore considered to be a major success. Similarly, the Brazilian government stimulated the creation of trading companies by offering preferential financing arrangements. Within a short time, these Brazilian firms increased their activities dramatically and, by 1981, accounted for almost 20 percent of total Brazilian exports.[23]

Export trading company (ETC) legislation designed to improve the export performance of small and medium-sized firms has also been implemented in the United States. In order to improve export performance, bank participation in trading companies was permitted and the antitrust threat to joint export efforts was reduced through precertification of planned activities by the U.S. Department of Commerce. Businesses were encouraged to join together to export or offer export services by passage in 1982 of the Export Trading Company Act.

Permitting banks to participate in ETCs was intended to allow ETCs better access to capital and therefore to more trading transactions and easier receipt of title to goods. The relaxation of antitrust provisions in turn was to enable firms to form joint ventures more easily. The cost of developing and penetrating international markets would then be shared, with the proportional share being, for many small and medium-sized firms, much easier to bear. As an example, in case a warehouse is needed in order to secure foreign market penetration, one firm alone does not have to bear all the costs. A consortium of firms can jointly rent a foreign warehouse. Similarly, each firm need not station a service technician abroad at substantial cost. Joint funding of a service center by several firms makes the cost less prohibitive for each one. The trading company concept also offers a one-stop shopping center for both the firm and its foreign customers. The firm can be assured that all international functions will be performed efficiently by the trading company, and at the same time the foreign customer will have to deal with fewer individual firms.

The legislation permits a wide variety of possible structures for an ETC. General trading companies handle many commodities, perform import and export services, countertrade, and work closely with foreign distributors. Regional trading companies handle commodities produced in only one re-

---

[22]Chang-Kyun Shin, "Korean General Trading Companies: A Study of Their Development and Strategies," doctoral dissertation, George Washington University, Washington, D.C., 1984, 236.

[23]Umberto Costa Pinto, "Trading Companies: The Brazilian Experience," in *U.S. Latin American Trade Relations*, ed. M. Czinkota (New York: Praeger Publishers, 1983), 251.

gion, specializing in products in which this region possesses a comparative advantage. Product-oriented trading companies concentrate on a limited number of products and offer their market penetration services only for these products. Trading companies may also be geographically oriented, targeting on one particular foreign region, or can be focused on certain types of projects such as turnkey operations and joint ventures with foreign investors. Finally, trading companies may develop an industry-oriented focus, handling only goods of specific industry groups, such as metals, chemicals, or pharmaceuticals.[24]

Independent of its form of operation, an ETC can deliver a wide variety of services. Table 13.5 lists some of the services that an ETC formed by a trade association planned to offer. The services listed indicate that this particular ETC wishes to be active chiefly as an agent. Alternatively, the ETC can purchase products and act as a distributor abroad. It can provide information on distribution costs and even handle domestic and international distribution and transportation. This can range from identifying distribution costs to booking space on ocean or air carriers and handling shipping contracts.

Although ETCs seem to offer major benefits to many U.S. firms wishing to penetrate international markets, they have not been used very extensively. By 1989, only 108 individual ETCs had been certified by the U.S. Department of Commerce. Yet these certificates covered 4,360 firms, mainly because various trade associations had applied for certification for all of their members.[25] Perhaps the greatest potential of ETCs lies with trade associations. However, it may also be a worthwhile concept to consider by firms and banks.

Banks need to evaluate whether the mentalities of bankers and traders can be made compatible. Traders, for example, are known for seizing the opportune moment, whereas bankers often appear to move more slowly. A key challenge will be to find ways to successfully blend business entrepreneurship with banking regulations.

Banks also need to understand the benefits they can derive from working with small or medium-sized exporters. The first impression may be that an ETC offers only added risk and cost. Yet involvement with an ETC may provide the bank with a broader client base, profitable use of its extensive international information system and network of corresponding institutions, and a steppingstone toward the internationalization of its own banking services. Because of the current international debt situation, many banks are hesitant to increase the volume of their international activities. In the long run, however, an improved understanding of the type and profitability of transactions and increasing pressures of a highly com-

[24] *The Export Trading Company Act of 1982* (Washington, D.C.: Chamber of Commerce of the United States, 1983), 4.

[25] George Muller, Deputy Director, Office of Export Trading Companies, U.S. Department of Commerce, June 6, 1989.

National Machine Tool Builders' Association ("NMTBA"), a District of Columbia corporation, has applied to the Department of Commerce for a certificate of review under Title III of Pub. L. No. 97-290 (96 Stat. 1240–45), codified at 15 U.S.C. 4011-21 ("the Act"), and its implementing regulations, codified at 15 CFR pt. 325 (1986) ("the Regulations").

The application was deemed submitted on February 18, 1987, and a summary of the application was published in the Federal Register on March 5, 1987 (52 Fed. Reg. 6834).

The Department of Commerce and the Department of Justice have reviewed the application and other information in their possession.

Based on analysis of this information, the Department of Commerce has determined, and the Department of Justice concurs, that the Export Trade, Export Trade Activities, and Methods of Operation set forth below meet the four standards set forth in section 303(a) of the Act.

Accordingly, under the authority of the Act and the Regulations, NMTBA and its Members are certified to engage in the Export Trade Activities and Methods of Operation described below in the following Export Trade and Export Markets.

EXPORT TRADE

1. *Products*

   Machine tools, including metal cutting machine tools (SIC code 3541), metal forming machine tools (SIC code 3542), woodworking machinery (SIC code 3553), and special industry machinery (SIC code 3559); tooling, dies, jigs, and fixtures for machine tools (SIC code 3544); machine tool accessories (SIC code 3545); assembly, measuring, and inspection machines; computer controls for machine tools (including computer programs); robotics; industrial laser equipment; materials handling equipment; welding apparatus (SIC code 3623); wire-guided vehicles; and other machine tool related equipment.

2. *Services*

   Engineering and architectural services related to Products and to turnkey contracts that substantially incorporate Products; servicing of Products; training with respect to the use of Products.

3. *Export Trade Facilitation Services (as they relate to the export of Products and Services)*

   Consulting; international market research; marketing and trade promotion; trade show participation; insurance; legal assistance; transportation; trade documentation and freight forwarding; communication and processing of export orders; warehousing; foreign exchange; financing; and taking title to goods.

4. *Technology Rights*

   Patents, trademarks, service marks, copyrights, trade secrets, know-how, and semiconductor mask works.

EXPORT MARKETS

The Export Markets include all parts of the world except (a) the United States (the fifty states of the United States, the District of Columbia, the Commonwealth of Puerto Rico, the Virgin Islands, American Samoa, Guam, the Commonwealth of the Northern Mariana Islands, and the Trust Territory of the Pacific Islands) and (b) Canada.

Export Trade Activities and Methods of Operation

1. NMTBA and/or more of its members may:

   a. engage in joint bidding or other joint selling arrangements for Products and Services in Export Markets and allocate sales resulting from such arrangements;

   b. establish export prices for sales of Products and Services by the Members in Export Markets, with each Member being free to deviate from such prices by whatever amount it sees fit;

   c. discuss and reach agreements relating to the interface specifications and engineering requirements demanded by specific potential customers for Products for Export Markets;

   d. with respect to Products and Services, refuse to quote prices for, or to market or sell in, Export Markets;

   e. solicit non-member Suppliers to sell their Products and/or Services or offer their Export Trade Facilitation Services through the certified activities of NMTBA and/or its Members;

   f. coordinate with respect to the installation and servicing of Products in Export Markets, including the establishment of joint warranty, service, and training centers in such markets; .

TABLE 13.5 ▪ **Continued**

    g. license associated Technology Rights in conjunction with the sale of Products, but in all instances the terms of such licenses shall be determined solely by negotiations between the licensor Member and the export customer without coordination with NMTBA or any other Member;

    h. engage in joint promotional activities, such as advertising and trade shows, aimed at developing existing or new Export Markets; and

    i. bring together from time to time groups of Members to plan and discuss how to fulfill the technical Product and Services requirements of specific export customers or particular Export Markets.

2. NMTBA and/or its Members may enter into agreements wherein NMTBA and/or one or more Members agree to act in certain countries or markets as the Members' exclusive or non-exclusive Export Intermediary for Products and/or Services in that country or market. In such agreements, (i) NMTBA or the Member(s) acting as an exclusive Export Intermediary may agree not to represent any other Supplier for sale in the relevant country or market, and (ii) Members may agree that they will export for sale in the relevant country or market only through NMTBA or the Member(s) acting as exclusive Export Intermediary, and that they will not export independently to the relevant country or market, either directly or through any other Export Intermediary. When acting as an Export Intermediary, NMTBA shall make its services available to any Member on non-discriminatory terms.

3. NMTBA and/or its Members may exchange and discuss the following types of information solely about Export Markets:

    a. information (other than information about the costs, output, capacity, inventories, domestic prices, domestic sales, domestic orders, terms of domestic marketing or sale, or United States business plans, strategies or methods) that is already generally available to the trade or public;

    b. information about sales and marketing efforts for Export Markets; activities and opportunities for sales of Products and Services in Export Markets; selling strategies for Export Markets; pricing in Export Markets; projected demands in Export Markets; customary terms of sale in Export Markets; the types of Products available from competitors for sale in particular Export Markets, and the prices for such Products; and customer specifications for Products in Export Markets;

    c. information about the export prices, quality, quantity, source, and delivery dates of Products available from Members for export, provided however that exchanges of information and discussions as to Product quantity, source, and delivery dates must be on a transaction-by-transaction basis only;

    d. information about terms and conditions of contracts for sales in Export Markets to be considered and/or bid on by NMTBA and its members;

    e. information about joint bidding, selling, or servicing arrangements for Export Markets and allocation of sales resulting from such arrangements among the Members;

    f. information about expenses specific to exporting to and within Export Markets, including without limitation transportation, intermodal shipments, insurance, inland freight to port, port storage, commissions, export sales, documentation, financing, customs, duties, and taxes;

    g. information about U.S. and foreign legislation and regulations affecting sales in Export Markets; and

    h. information about NMTBA's or its Members' export operations, including without limitation sales and distribution networks established by NMTBA or its Members in Export Markets, and prior export sales by Members (including export price information).

4. NMTBA may provide its Members or other Suppliers the benefit of any Export Trade Facilitation Services to facilitate the export of Products to Export Markets. This may be accomplished by NMTBA itself, or by agreement with Members or other parties.

5. NMTBA and/or its Members may meet to engage in the activities described in paragraphs one through four above.

6. NMTBA and/or its Members may forward to the appropriate individual Member requests for information received from a foreign government or its agent (including private pre-shipment inspection firms) concerning that Member's domestic or export activities (including prices and/or costs), and if such individual Member elects to respond, it shall respond directly to the requesting foreign government of its agent with respect to such information.

Source: *NMTBA's Export Trade Certificate*, International Trade Department. NMTBA—
The Association for Manufacturing Technology, McLean, Virginia, 1987, 13–16. Reprinted
with permission.

FIGURE 13.1   ▪   **Service Requirements for American Export Trading Companies**

Suppliers Represented	Products Exported	
	Undifferentiated	Differentiated
Low Export Volume	Requires a Less Than Average Capability in Promotion, Market Contact, and Consolidation	Requires an Above Average Capability in Promotion, but an Average Capability in Market Contact and Consolidation
High Export Volume	Requires a Less Than Average Capability in Promotion, but an Average Capability in Market Contact and Consolidation	Requires an Above Average Capability in Promotion, Market Contact, and Consolidation

Source: Reprinted from Daniel C. Bello and Nicholas C. Williamson, "The American Export Trading Company: Designing a New International Marketing Institution," *Journal of Marketing* 49 (Fall 1985): 67, published by the American Marketing Association.

petitive deregulated home market will lead to more international involvement by U.S. banks.

Firms participating in trading companies by joining or forming them should be aware of the difference between product- and market-driven ETCs. Firms may have a strong tendency to use their trading company primarily to dispose of their merchandise. Successful foreign sales, however, depend primarily on the foreign demand and the foreign market. A blend of demand-driven activities and existing product lines needs to be achieved in order for a trading company to be successful.

The trading company itself must solicit continuous feedback on foreign market demands and changes in these demands so that its members will be able to maintain a winning international product mix. Substantial attention must be paid to gathering information on the needs and wants of foreign customers and disseminating this information to the participating U.S. producers. Otherwise, lack of responsiveness to foreign market demands will result in a decline of the ETC's effectiveness.[26] The ETC also should determine the activities on which to concentrate, basing this determination on the types of suppliers represented and the types of products exported. Figure 13.1 provides one possible differentiation for such service requirements.

Depending on whether products are differentiated or undifferentiated, the ETC should place varying degrees of emphasis on developing its capa-

[26]Michael R. Czinkota, "The Business Response to the Export Trading Company Act of 1982," *The Columbia Journal of World Business* 19 (Fall 1984): 111.

THE INTERNATIONAL MARKETPLACE   **13.3**

An Export Trading Company in a Business School   The
*Georgetown University School of Business Administration has
made the international component of business education a primary
focus in its educational activities. The goal is to have international
business issues permeate the entire graduate and undergraduate
business curriculum.*

*One approach used to achieve this goal was the formation of an
export trading company. With the help of a grant by the U.S. Department of Education, Georgetown Export Trading Company Inc.
(GETI) was formed by the school's affiliated National Center for
Export-Import Studies. The firm was allocated office space and
began to offer export trading services as an agent (to minimize financial risks) and consultant.*

*Students join the firm on a for-credit basis, devoting 15 hours
each week to learning about export trading. Some students concentrate on one specific function of exporting such as export licensing,
packaging, or pricing, and accumulate substantial expertise
through reading, interviewing, and carrying out transactions. Other
students concentrate on a geographic area—Japan, Germany, Austria, or England—and use old contacts in the area or establish new
ones. Still others develop product-specific knowledge.*

*Within a year after its formation GETI was certified as an export
trading company by the U.S. Department of Commerce. It offers a
wide variety of trading and consulting services. Most importantly,
the participating students, having learned about actual trading
activities, are able to knowledgeably enter firms seeking international business expertise.*

---

bility for international promotion. At the same time, undifferentiated
products require greater price competitiveness, which may be precisely
the chief advantage offered by an ETC as a result of economies of scale. For
differentiated products, an ETC may be able to place emphasis on promotion and have greater flexibility in price determination.

The future success of U.S. export trading companies is still uncertain.
Some believe that sufficient time has passed for the legislation to work,
and that businesses simply are not interested in joining forces to penetrate
international markets.[27] On the other hand, the concepts of synergism and
cooperation certainly make sense in terms of enhancing the international
competitiveness of U.S. firms. Yet the focus of ETCs should perhaps not be

---

[27] Donald G. Howard and James M. Maskulka, "Will American Export Trading Companies
Replace Traditional Export Management Companies?" *International Marketing Review* 5
(Winter 1988): 41–50.

pure exporting. Importing and countertrading may also generate substantial activity and profit. By carrying out a wide variety of export transactions, international market knowledge is obtained. This management and consulting expertise may in itself be a salable service. The International Marketplace 13.3 gives an example of how such service activities can be turned into salable products.

SUMMARY

In addition to direct exporting, other possibilities for international market entry are licensing, franchising, and the use of export intermediaries. The basic advantage of licensing is that it does not require capital investment or knowledge of foreign markets. The major disadvantage is that licensing agreements typically have time limits, often prescribed by foreign governments, and may even result in creating a competitor. The principal issues in negotiating licensing agreements are the scope of the rights conveyed, compensation, license compliance, dispute resolution, and the term and termination of the agreement. Franchising is a form of licensing. Since 1970 the expansion of U.S. franchisors into foreign markets has been dramatic. The reasons for this international expansion are typically market potential, financial gain, and saturated domestic markets. Franchisors must strike a balance between the need to adapt to local environments and to standardize to the degree necessary to maintain international recognizability.

Firms with products that do not lend themselves to licensing or franchising may use intermediaries in the existing infrastructure: EMCs, Webb-Pomerene associations, and trading companies. For international market entry mechanisms to be successful, a variety of international marketing functions need to be performed. Export intermediaries can take on these functions. In order for them to do so viably, however, a proper form of compensation must exist. The major disadvantage to using such intermediaries is that they may take on more clients or more diverse functions than they are staffed to perform. Although the potential of the newly created ETC mechanism is far from being fully utilized at this time, ETCs may yet become a useful and viable intermediary in the future.

Questions for Discussion

1. Comment on this statement: Licensing is really not a form of international involvement because it requires no substantial additional effort on the part of the licensor.

2. Assume that the government of Thailand wants to start producing F-20 Tigershark fighter aircraft under license from Northrop. What types of concerns will enter into the negotiations?

3. Suggest reasons for the explosive international expansion of U.S.-based franchise systems.

4. What is the purpose of export intermediaries?

5. How can an export intermediary avoid circumvention by a client or customer?

6. What makes an export agent different from any other channel member?

7. Is there a need for export trading companies?

8. What makes a U.S. export trading company different from Japanese trading companies?

9. Why is it useful to have antitrust exemption for an export trading company?

10. Give examples of product-based and geographic ETCs.

11. How can the discrepancy between product-driven and market-driven orientations within export trading companies be resolved?

12. Why would a trade association want to form an ETC?

Recommended Readings

Cho, Dong-Sung. *The General Trading Company: Concept and Strategy.* Lexington, Mass.: Lexington Books, 1987.

Contractor, Farok J. *Licensing in International Strategy: A Guide for Planning and Negotiations.* Westport, Conn.: Quorum Books, 1985.

Justis, Robert, and Richard Judd. *Franchising.* Cincinnati, Ohio: South-Western, 1989.

Kostecka, Andrew. *Franchising in the Economy 1986–1988.* Washington, D.C.: Government Printing Office, 1988.

Shanklin, William, and John K. Ryans. *Marketing High Technology.* Lexington, Mass.: Lexington Books, 1984.

Welt, Leo G. B., ed. *ETCs: New Method for Exporting.* New York: American Management Association, Membership Publications Division, 1984.

Yoshihara, Kunio. *Sogoshosha, the Vanguard of the Japanese Economy.* Tokyo: Oxford University Press, 1982.

Ski-Rumelt Ltd.

Ski-Rumelt Ltd. is a French corporation which manufactures skis, boots, and other ski equipment. It is the exclusive worldwide distributor of Ski-Rumelt products and is the owner of the rights to the Ski-Rumelt trademark in France. The U.S. Ski-Rumelt Corporation, a Delaware corporation, is a wholly owned subsidiary of Ski-Rumelt. U.S. Ski-Rumelt is the registered owner of the U.S. trademark rights for the Ski-Rumelt marks and is the exclusive distributor of Ski-Rumelt products in the United States. As the exclusive distributor of Ski-Rumelt products, U.S. Ski-Rumelt provides warranties and various servicing arrangements to the purchasers of Ski-Rumelt products. Because of the various market conditions, Ski-Rumelt products cost approximately 25 percent more in the United States than they do in France.

Mountain Discount, a Colorado corporation, is a regional retailer whose marketing strategy is to sell a wide variety of ski products to consumers at the lowest possible discount prices. For the past six months, Mountain Discount has been purchasing Ski-Rumelt products in France and has been selling them in the United States, without the written consent of U.S. Ski-Rumelt, at prices that are 15 percent below the regular price. Because Mountain Discount sells Ski-Rumelt products outside Ski-Rumelt's intended chain of distribution, it cannot provide the same warranties, servicing arrangements, or packaging as U.S. Ski-Rumelt.

Last week, U.S. Ski-Rumelt filed an action with the United States Court of International Trade seeking declaratory and injunctive relief against Mountain Discount, alleging that paragraph 526(a) of the Tariff Act of 1930 prohibits the importation of foreign manufactured goods bearing a registered trademark into the United States without the trademark owner's consent.

Mountain Discount argues that it is allowed to import Ski-Rumelt products because the U.S. Customs Service's regulation (19 C.F.R. paragraph 133.2) denies trademark owners the right to require exclusion of trademarked goods manufactured abroad where the U.S. and foreign trademarks are owned by the same entity or related entities, or where the trademark owner has authorized the foreign manufacturer to apply its trademark to the goods.

Questions for Discussion

1. Given the apparent inconsistency between the Tariff Act of 1930 and customs regulations, what will the U.S. Court of International Trade do?

Source: This case was prepared by Joseph Tasker, Jr., of Bishop, Cook, Purcell and Reynolds, for discussion purposes. The author acknowledges the support of Cathy L. Burgess in the preparation of the case. Reprinted with permission.

2. Assume that U.S. Ski-Rumelt is the parent corporation and Ski-Rumelt Ltd. is the wholly owned subsidiary. Would this change in facts affect the court's decision?

3. What legal and public policy factors would persuade the court to grant U.S. Ski-Rumelt an injunction which would prevent Mountain Discount from selling Ski-Rumelt products in the United States?

4. Would the result be different if Mountain Discount sold counterfeit goods instead of genuine Ski-Rumelt products?

5. Assume that Ski-Rumelt is an American firm, manufacturing in the United States and selling only to "authorized" dealers in the United States. Those dealers, in turn, are contractually required to sell only to customers who will use the products, not to other dealers. Nevertheless, Mountain Discount, which is not an "authorized" dealer, obtains some product and offers it for sale. Is there a federal remedy for the American Ski-Rumelt equivalent to the remedy offered by section 526(a) of the Tariff Act of 1930 for the French Ski-Rumelt?

Kenfair Manufacturing Company

Kenfair Manufacturing Company is a family owned and managed custom shade and awning corporation based in Alexandria, Virginia. Established in 1945, the firm was initially an industrial retail store. Later the erratic nature of activity in the construction industry and the spotty payment record of builders, on which Kenfair sales depended, led to a shift in the firm's focus from retailing to manufacturing and wholesaling. Kenfair became a supplier to Sears, Roebuck and Company in Washington, D.C., and by 1970 was supplying custom shades and window accessories nationwide to Montgomery Ward, J. C. Penney, and Sears, while continuing to maintain a small local distribution network.

Established to provide a stable income for the family owners, the company was run as a partnership from 1945 until January 1, 1961, when it was incorporated under the laws of the state of Virginia. In May 1981 the corporation formed a wholly owned subsidiary that operates as a domestic international sales corporation.

Kenfair's family origins are evident in its management structure. The founder, currently serving as chairman of the board, has responsibility for research and development. His son, who holds a baccalaureate in economics, is the company's president and handles production, billing, and financing. A daughter has a degree in fashion merchandising and serves as marketing and sales executive. The firm has a head office and plant in Alexandria, Virginia, and a plant in Orange, Virginia. Of the 105 employees, 5 are plant supervisors and 3 are in charge of computer operations, accounting, and customer service, respectively. All others are factory workers.

Kenfair's product range extends from assorted window shades (balloon shades, slat Roman shades, pleated shades) to blinds, tiebacks, and top treatments such as flat valances, box-pleat valances, swags, and cascades. Shades and blinds each account for 20 percent of sales volume and accessories represent 60 percent. Profits from sales are distributed approximately as follows: blinds, 12 percent; shades, 28 percent; and accessories, 60 percent. Table 1 provides selected data from Kenfair's financial statements.

In comparison with Burlington and J. P. Stevens, larger firms that are interested in producing high-volume items, Kenfair has made an asset of its small size and greater flexibility. It has carved out a niche for itself in smaller volume items such as valances, which are less economical for the larger firms to produce. To achieve the combined goals of increasing sales and expanding through new-product introduction, management uses the firm's established reputation for high product quality and punctual delivery.

Source: This case was prepared by Michael R. Czinkota.

TABLE 1 ▪ Selected Financial Data

	1965	1975	1977	1982	1983
Net Sales	$1,053,859	$1,134,217	$2,035,471	$5,296,300	$5,164,686
Cost of Goods Sold	580,449	872,606	1,575,512	3,744,542	3,295,220
Gross Profits	473,410	261,611	459,959	1,551,758	1,869,466
Operating Profits	(53,454)	22,723	122,932	206,818	429,900
Net Income	(51,529)	15,366	68,497	95,988	244,643

Although Kenfair's products are not inexpensive, they are price competitive in the upper levels of the market. The firm suffers from a number of weaknesses, however. Until recently external financing was difficult to obtain, but this problem has been overcome. Management is also dissatisfied with the firm's high inventory costs, which are the result of two- to three-month lead times of suppliers. However, additional computer resources are to be allocated to the inventory control system in the hope that the problem can be eased.

KENFAIR'S INTERNATIONAL DEVELOPMENT

Kenfair's interest in importing began in the early 1970s as a result of difficulties in obtaining 66-inch wide burlap domestically. At that time, the firm was manufacturing burlap-backed window shades of varying widths. Although domestic importers were capable of supplying 48- to 50-inch-wide rolled goods, burlap of greater width was unobtainable. As a result, narrow-width burlap had to be pieced together to produce shades for wider windows. These shades were not only costlier to manufacture but also less attractive to consumers than seamless shades. Repeated requests by Kenfair to domestic suppliers to increase the width of burlap were scoffed at. Allegedly it was too difficult and costly to develop machinery for such new production.

In 1972, the firm was sufficiently strong financially to consider importing as a solution to its problem; it was for the first time able to secure letters of credit of up to $40,000. Knowing of the existence of burlap factories in India, Kenfair's founder obtained a list of such firms from the Indian embassy and U.S. trade associations and initiated contact through the mail. After a year Kenfair located a factory in Calcutta that produced 60-inch burlap. After receiving a satisfactory sample, Kenfair placed a $15,000 "blind" order, because the price of the burlap was very attractive.

Although management was satisfied with the quality of the first shipment, several changes were desired. Kenfair's chairman therefore made

a trip to India to specify and verify quality and design standards for a second order ($30,000), which was to be filled within 90 days. Nevertheless, the following shipment was plagued with difficulties. As a result of the combined effects of a production strike, transport strike, and barge strike, 16 months elapsed before delivery was made. When it finally arrived, the product proved to be of inferior quality. Kenfair's president hypothesizes that the shipment may have suffered damage as a result of the delays. Kenfair was unable to obtain compensation for these damages from the Indian exporter who, management suspects, did not really need their business after the strikes caused a world shortage of burlap. Having prepaid by means of a letter of credit, Kenfair had no effective recourse.

As a result of the problems with the second order, Kenfair ceased dealing with the Indian firm. Price considerations made the relationship highly attractive, but quality was a negative factor. Importing proved to be less cost effective than expected because of higher working loss from inferior quality goods. Further, Kenfair's domestic burlap suppliers, reacting to the loss of business, had begun a search for extra-wide burlap of acceptable quality. A firm offering 66-inch burlap of better quality than that from India was located in Korea. Importing this burlap, Kenfair's former domestic suppliers were able to meet Kenfair's demand.

Since its initial dealings with the Indians, Kenfair has established a number of additional importing relationships. Although numerous unsolicited letters arrived from abroad offering a wide variety of goods for sale, Kenfair generally ignored these offerings. Instead management initiated relationships either to obtain a product not available domestically or, later, to take advantage of the significant price differential resulting from the strong U.S. dollar.

Although management is unable to point to any significant operational changes that have resulted from Kenfair's importing activities, attitudinal changes are in evidence. The president claims that experience has made them wiser and more skeptical. "We're not afraid to go out and contract for foreign products. We know the ins and outs of it now," he maintains. He believes that inspecting a product before buying it is important. Yet, in the long run, "it's like going to Vegas and throwing the dice. You take your chances."

On the whole, the president feels that Kenfair's importing activities have become more profitable over time. Top quality window-shade rollers are imported from Canada, and as long as the U.S. dollar remains strong vis-à-vis the Canadian dollar, Kenfair will not source domestically.

The strong dollar and increased confidence in its knowledge of importing have led Kenfair's management to consider Europe as a source of shade and vertical-blind fabrics. Current plans call for the marketing director to attend a trade show in Stuttgart to search for a fabric with "a different look."

SUPPLIER RELATIONS

In 1980, Kenfair initiated contact with Chii Hong Machine Industry Ltd., a Taiwanese firm that manufactures window shades. For some time, Kenfair had been having difficulty with the shade rollers obtained from domestic suppliers; the springs were not strong enough to support the heavy fabrics used. Product modification requests were shrugged off. An earlier attempt to solve this problem by importing $10,000 worth of rollers from Denmark had met with little success; the entire shipment was of inferior quality, and Kenfair sold the whole lot at a discount to a firm in Baltimore.

Initial contact between Kenfair and the Taiwanese firm was brought about through the efforts of the buyer for a large national consumer chain store with whom Kenfair did business. The buyer was going to Taiwan, and, knowing of Kenfair's problems with rollers, offered to obtain names of companies that might be able to supply them. The buyer expected that if Kenfair lowered production cost by buying Taiwanese rollers, this would reduce the price to his company for the finished shades.

Kenfair got in touch with the Taiwanese companies, and, on the basis of samples and price information sent, decided to buy two container loads of rollers from Chii Hong. The buyer making the connection took no commission for his services, benefiting instead from the fact that Kenfair's estimated cost savings of $18,000 to $23,000 per container permitted a 50-cent cut in the wholesale price of each shade. This allowed a price cut of $1.00 on regular shades and $3.00 on large shades at the retail level.

The Taiwanese rollers were purchased with a letter of credit, F.O.B. Keelung. The Taiwanese put the rollers on board and obtained insurance which, together with the ocean freight, brokerage fees, and freight to Alexandria, was paid for by Kenfair. These imports initially accounted for 50 percent of Kenfair's roller requirements. The remainder was supplied by three U.S. firms: Joanna Western Mills, Brenneman, and Graber Industries.

In its initial dealings with the Taiwanese firm, Kenfair imported standard one-inch diameter rollers that Chii Hong used in the manufacture of its own shades and modified them as needed. Some of the fabrics Kenfair used to make shades were too heavy to be suitable for rollers of this diameter. The Taiwanese were asked to supply 1⅛-inch diameter rollers as well. In time, the Taiwanese made modifications in their product to meet Kenfair's needs and offered 1⅛-inch rounds in shorter lengths to be used in the manufacture of narrower shades.

As a result of importing the 1⅛-inch diameter rollers from Taiwan, Kenfair made a few operational changes. Adjustments were made in the inventory system to account for the diversity of roller diameters, and care was taken to ensure that the new window-shade fabrics were matched with the correct rollers. To pay for the imports from Taiwan,

Kenfair employed letters of credit rather than the open invoices it used in its dealings with domestic suppliers.

During the five years that Kenfair maintained relations with Chii Hong, interaction was cordial but distant. Kenfair supplied some market information, product use, and technical data to the Taiwanese but was careful to limit its disclosure in order to minimize the possibility that Chii Hong might seek to enter the U.S. market and sell directly to Kenfair's customers. Chii Hong, for its part, supplied Kenfair with samples and descriptions of new products in the development stage.

On the whole, contact between the two firms was minimal. Kenfair's marketing vice president made one trip to Taiwan to review roller quality problems. The Taiwanese visited Alexandria twice, once when one of Chii Hong's owners was in the United States on personal business, and once when the manager of the window-shade division arrived to promote sales. Phone contact was limited to two or three calls made during the five years by Kenfair's purchasing agent and president, who generally was frustrated by these attempts to communicate because of the language barrier and the well-known East Asian disinclination to say no when negation is called for. Kenfair's purchasing agent or marketing vice president sent letters two or three times a year to request quotations or to make inquiries regarding orders. Chii Hong's president wrote about once a month asking when the next order would be placed. Telexes were exchanged once or twice a year, when the time factor was important.

During the five years, Kenfair imported window-shade rollers from Chii Hong in these dollar volumes:

1980	$ 56,000
1981	76,000
1982	200,000
1983	55,000
1984	29,000

Kenfair then ceased importing rollers from Chii Hong and has no plans to do so in the future. Because of exchange rate and quality considerations the firm has begun importing Canadian one-inch rollers, which are sufficiently sturdy to support its heavier window-shade fabrics.

From the outset, Kenfair's relationship with the Taiwanese was marked by a number of problems. Frequently the delivery time was slow and unpredictable, forcing Kenfair to place last-minute orders with U.S. suppliers. In addition, according to the firm's president, there was a major defect in every order. Sometimes the rollers were poorly spliced because insufficient glue had been applied. At other times the springs were rusted and unsightly. The locking mechanisms malfunctioned in one shipment. The Taiwanese were always informed of the defect, and in the subsequent shipment it was corrected, only to be replaced by another defect.

Kenfair operates in a market characterized by keen competition based on price and quality considerations. Initially, importing rollers from Taiwan had appeared profitable despite wastage and sorting costs. Narrow shades using Taiwanese rollers cost 15 percent to 20 percent less to produce, despite the cost of importation and a 10 percent trash factor. However, these savings were found to be illusory in the long term because roller defects were often not recognizable during shade production. Defects were often first detected by ultimate consumers, whose shades would roll up suddenly, unpredictably, and noisily. Kenfair's president, Nick Fairbanks, refers to this particular product failure as "the Holiday Inn surprise." Complaints became frequent and were transmitted to Kenfair by its major client retailers. Importing from Chii Hong proved prohibitively costly in terms of damage to Kenfair's reputation for product quality.

In 1987 Kenfair's import volume totaled $90,000; it forecast overall sales volume of approximately $6,000,000. Despite the difficulties encountered in importing, management continues to regard the experience favorably. Kenfair is currently importing from Canada, has made repeated attempts to purchase pleated shades from Taiwan, and is considering importing vinyl from Taiwan as well. In addition, Europe is regarded as a potential source of fabric for shades.

Questions for Discussion

1. Does a smaller firm have any international sourcing advantages over a larger company?
2. Should Kenfair import burlap from Korea?
3. Suggest steps for Kenfair's management to take to ensure import quality.
4. Discuss the difference in customer service responsiveness between domestic and foreign suppliers of Kenfair.
5. Why does Kenfair import only components rather than finished products?

Safco Inc.

Safco is a souvenir and promotional novelty business based in Washington, D.C. It was established as a "mom and pop" retail store in 1925 with the overriding goal of providing a stable and permanent source of income. Safco is wholly owned by the president, whose two sons are employed by the firm as vice presidents. Of the 17 other employees, 10 handle such tasks as bookkeeping, shipping, and packing; 5 work in sales; and 2 are in import management.

The president considers the firm's main strength to be the ability to handle an extremely wide range of advertising and promotional products in addition to souvenirs. Approximately 60 percent of the total sales volume comes from souvenirs for Washington and for tourist areas such as Disneyland and South of the Border. These items are primarily sold at souvenir shops and hotel gift shops. The remaining 40 percent of sales volume is from specialty items and accessories requested by companies for specific promotional purposes. Examples of the latter include ashtrays, lighters, and porcelain ware bearing a company logo.

THE DECISION TO GO INTERNATIONAL

Although Safco's growth has been characterized by the desire for stability and limitation of risk, the firm has proven itself capable of entrepreneurial risk taking. In 1955, for example, activities in the Washington area were expanded from retail to wholesale. This decision, made when the founder's son took over the business, laid the essential groundwork for the 1963 decision to reduce costs by bypassing the company's New York suppliers and importing souvenirs and novelties directly from the Far East.

At that time, the president made a number of informational visits to various Far Eastern embassies in Washington to talk with the commercial attachés; his primary aim was to obtain the names of exporters supplying products of interest to Safco. In addition, he advertised in a number of international trade magazines. As a result, the firm was bombarded by letters from exporters in the Far East desirous of establishing a working relationship.

Having made the decision to import, the president was nonetheless aware of some potential hazards involved. His main concern was that he might be "ripped off." Despite his attempts to find reputable exporters, he personally knew none of them. Going to the international court in the event of breach of contract, which he believed to be his only recourse, would be prohibitively expensive. Blacklisting fraudulent suppliers with the local Chamber of Commerce would not recoup losses. Therefore, he

Source: This case was prepared by Michael R. Czinkota and Laura M. Gould.

decided that the most important part of developing import activities was the forming of personal relationships. Armed with a list of potential exporters, the president made appointments to see a number of them during a trip to the Orient in order to get to know them better.

IMPORT ACTIVITIES

Safco's first imports were a result of the president's trip to Taiwan and Japan. At that time, financed by letters of credit, he placed orders for porcelain ware and stuffed toys with two agents, who in turn sourced products from a number of suppliers. The selection of suppliers and products was based on price and salability considerations. In effect, the items purchased were one-third the price of domestic items of similar quality.

During the next few years, Safco increased its importing activity. In addition to purchasing from agents in Japan and Taiwan, the firm began to import from Hong Kong and Korea. Korea was found to be the most suitable source for volume purchases because the factories are geared for economies of scale. This capability, however, made larger minimum orders necessary. In all cases, contacts with agents were made during annual trips to the Orient, and purchases were financed by letters of credit. Because the initial import activities had been successful, Safco had been able to obtain a substantial line of credit from its bank, which made such financing much easier.

Safco ceased dealing with domestic suppliers and focused exclusively on importing from the Far East. Sales in the United States grew because Safco was able to offer its products at very competitive prices as a result of the decreased costs of sourcing.

During the early stages of import development, the firm bought both products of its own design and items designed by the foreign sellers. At no time did the foreign sellers participate in any decisions regarding Safco's market development, pricing decisions to final customers, inventory policies, or physical distribution. All transactions were carried out using agents as intermediaries because Safco believed that dealing with one person was easier than dealing with 25 to 30 suppliers.

IMPORT PROBLEMS

During the early stages, there were isolated quality control problems—for example, words imprinted on products were misspelled. To a certain extent, this problem was mitigated by writing into the letter of credit a stipulation that a letter of approval of a sample must be submitted with the other documents before a bank could negotiate the letter of credit. If a quality problem was not too egregious, Safco was sometimes able to sell the item at a slight discount. If it was severe, only a very deep discount enabled Safco to sell the product.

On several occasions, nonetheless, Safco has had to return products to the Orient because of inferior quality. In such instances, even though payment is withheld, Safco still incurs losses due to the freight costs and the interest on the letter of credit. On occasion, the losses have been partially absorbed by the suppliers after extensive negotiations with the agent. At other times, Safco has had to absorb the entire loss.

There also were isolated instances of Safco's being "ripped off." For example, on one occasion rocks wrapped in newspaper were received and payment was made before the fraud was discovered. However, Safco found importing to be a highly profitable venture. The only major import failure Safco experienced was, in fact, a marketing mistake. Having invested $10,000 to import Rubik cubes from the Orient, management found that it had jumped on the bandwagon too late, and could hardly give them away. Over time, the firm was able to dispose of them at a deep discount, but only after incurring long-term warehousing costs. From this experience, Safco learned that once a fad has hit the market, it is too late to take advantage of it, particularly if one counts the 25 to 30 days lag for delivery from the time the order is filled.

OTHER IMPORT CONSIDERATIONS

A number of external factors affected the firm's importing activity. Management paid particular attention to changes in import duties, making a special effort to take advantage of the generalized system of preferences (GSP) by which certain products from developing countries could be imported duty free. All risk resulting from exchange rate fluctuations was borne by the exporter. Contracts were denominated in the currency of the exporting country with a clause stipulating that, if there was a currency appreciation relative to the dollar, the foreign currency price was adjusted downward so as to remain constant in dollars. However, if the currency depreciated relative to the dollar, prices were not revised upward.

As a result of importing, Safco has refocused its activities. Whereas initially the firm was engaged almost totally in importing souvenirs, it has recently begun to redirect its efforts toward becoming an advertising and promotional specialist, and a person was hired to cover the marketing of specialty items. This person is specifically targeting Washington area companies. Attempts are also being made to contact associations scheduled to hold conventions in the area.

An additional outcome of expanded import activity has been increased knowledge of international business. For example, management has become more sophisticated with respect to exchange rate risk. In addition, it has become better at international financing. Whereas Safco initially purchased a multitude of letters of credit for a large number of suppliers, it now consolidates international payments to the extent feasible so as to reduce financing charges. Stipulations included in letters of credit afford more protection in the firm's international transactions. Help is sought more often from the government, including U.S. embassy personnel. Import legislation and marketing are better understood. As a result, the company's import activities have become more profitable over time.

At present, Safco is the largest souvenir importer in Washington. The firm deals with two to three agents in Hong Kong, two in Taiwan, one in Korea, and one in Japan. Safco's orders represent about 90 percent of the business of each of its agents in the first three countries and 20 percent of the business of the Japanese agent. In general, Safco's orders also represent a large percentage of the various manufacturers' business. As of 1984, imports from the Far East totalled $1.5 million annually. To this, Safco applies a 20 percent to 25 percent markup.

RELATIONS WITH HONG KONG

Safco's principal business partner in Hong Kong is Friendship Trading Company. Safco first made contact with this firm in the mid-1960s during the third trip of the president to the Orient. The decision to import novelties from Hong Kong had been based on availability, price, and preferential duties. At the time of the president's visit, Friendship Trading Company was exhibiting souvenirs such as ashtrays, keychains, change purses, toys, and novelties at a trade show. While Safco was sourcing similar products at that time from suppliers in New York, the decision was made to cut out the intermediaries and reduce costs by importing.

Friendship was only one of the agents with whom the president chose to do business while on the trip. The firm was selected largely because the products were of good quality and the price was acceptable. Over time, Safco gave progressively more business to Friendship Trading Company because the firm proved to be "fast, reliable, and trust has developed." Initial purchases were made C.I.F. Later, when it had gained more knowledge about international shipping, Safco began to make purchases F.O.B.

The original products Friendship supplied were from the trade show or a catalog; the only changes Safco made were requests for specific lettering. On occasion, however, Safco also suggested modifications in Friendship's products, such as changes in the size of ashtrays and cups. Friendship was in no way involved in any of Safco's activities related to advertising, final pricing decisions, inventory, or physical distribution. For quality control, Safco mainly relied on Friendship.

Safco and Friendship maintain frequent contact. In addition to annual visits by Safco's president to Hong Kong to see new products, correspondence is exchanged between Friendship Trading Company and Safco's import manager on almost a daily basis. Telexes are used for urgent messages—for example, if the price or design is not approved—but routine business is conducted by mail. Generally, a purchase order is mailed to

the agent. About two weeks later, the import manager receives either a letter of confirmation with prices or a letter stating that the order cannot be filled. If the order is accepted, the import manager generally writes to request a sample for approval before purchasing the requisite letter of credit. In spite of this frequent interaction, no important exchange of market information or product use data has occurred.

Over time, Safco has steadily increased its business with Friendship. Since 1980, Safco has concentrated more and more on this supplier, which has been able to deliver faster than others, is extremely reliable, and is capable of supplying a broader line of products. Although some of Safco's competitors can offer certain products at a lower price, Friendship Trading Company's main advantage is that it can offer a broader, steadier, more complete line of products. Safco feels that "Friendship Trading Company can get us anything." At present, Safco believes that the volume of business supplied by Friendship is as large as it can get.

During the course of the relationship, a number of problems have arisen, but nothing that could be considered a crisis. When a design error or a mistake in spelling has been made, for example, Safco and Friendship have usually been able to negotiate a solution. Problems like breakage are normally covered by insurance. As a general rule, Safco feels that it has always been able to negotiate problems: "We do business with them. We want to keep good relations."

Over time, Safco's dealings with Friendship have increased to the point that 15 percent of Safco's total 1984 imports of $1.5 million are handled by Friendship. This represents 40 percent of Safco's imports in unit volume for the categories of plastics, toys, and novelties.

In the future, Safco plans to maintain its relations with Friendship. "You always take your chances, that's the problem for all imports. When you lose, you lose; but when you win, you make more money."

In general, Safco regards Friendship Trading Company as experienced, aggressive, very efficient, and trustworthy. "We know they are not out to rip us off."

Friendship Trading Company has also proven to be very reliable in dealing with the quota system. Even though some of its products, such as baseball caps, are strictly controlled, there has never been a quota problem. Friendship has always been able to obtain its quota allocation in sufficient size.

The loyalty it has been shown by Friendship is also very important to Safco. On the few occasions when one of its U.S. customers has tried to circumvent Safco and deal directly with the Hong Kong supplier, Friendship has always notified Safco immediately and has never responded to the inquiry. Safco's president stated, "That's important if you want to stay in the business. We value that."

The main lesson that Safco has learned in its dealings with Friendship Trading Company is that an importing relationship characterized by trust is possible. This trust has been particularly important in relation to prices. Safco feels that if someone else quotes a price, comparing it to what Friendship offers will indicate if the price is out of line. In addition to Friendship, Safco has 20 steady and 15 changing suppliers abroad. At present, relationships are maintained with two other agents in Hong Kong. These receive a smaller volume of Safco's business and work in product areas in which they have greater proficiency because of personal relationships with manufacturers. Despite Safco's trust in Friendship, management is reluctant to deal with only one agent, believing it is preferable to have some other agents upon whom they can rely "just in case."

Questions for Discussion

1. How can a supplier prevent the "circumvention" problem?
2. How will a decline in the value of the dollar affect Safco's international activities?
3. How can the U.S. government help Safco's import efforts?
4. Is such help appropriate in light of the large U.S. trade deficit?
5. Discuss the dangers of overdependence on one supplier.
6. Why can foreign suppliers offer their products at prices so much lower than U.S. suppliers?

American Box Company (ABCo)

Sam Smith, founder and president of American Box Company (ABCo), sat at his desk thinking of the decision he and the board had to make about ABCo's entry into the Icelandic market with fluid-box products. In addition to deciding whether or not to enter the market, ABCo's executives had to decide how to enter the market if they made a "go" decision. There were three possible ways: (1) simply export fluid boxes to Iceland, (2) make a direct investment in production facilities in Iceland, or (3) set up a licensing agreement with an Icelandic firm.

BACKGROUND

In the autumn of 1945, S. S. Smith bought a small corrugated box business in Columbus, Ohio. At that time, the company had only 25 employees and sold only $250,000 worth of boxes annually. Almost immediately, the company acquired a new building with a 50,000-square-foot production facility and a 20,000-square-foot warehouse. Six years later, the square footage had increased to 78,000 square feet.

In 1953, a Huntington, West Virginia, facility was opened in order to manufacture boxes from the corrugated sheets made in Columbus. The Columbus plant was expanded to 118,000 square feet in 1956, and increased to 165,000 square feet by 1962. The importance of the Columbus plant to the community was recognized when the city renamed the street passing the plant Corrugated Way.

ABCo now has the following divisions, in addition to the original corrugated operation: Fluid-Box Corporation and FilmCo.

FLUID-BOX CORPORATION

During 1961, the company began pilot production of plastic bags inside boxes. Used mainly by the dairy industry, the bag-in-a-box quickly supplanted the traditional five-gallon milk can. Fluid-Box Corporation, a subsidiary, was set up to manufacture and sell the new product. By 1962, Fluid-Box introduced a disposable ten-quart bag-in-a-box with its own dispensing valve. Designed for home delivery routes, the milk dispenser grew in popularity. Its acceptance led the company into manufacturing additional products. By 1963, the Fluid-Box subsidiary had 20,000 square feet of production facility in Columbus, and an additional 20,000 square feet leased in Dallas, Texas. A 10,000-square-foot addition in

Source: This case by Michael R. Czinkota and Wesley J. Johnston is reprinted from Roger D. Blackwell, Wesley J. Johnston, and W. Wayne Talarzyk, eds., *Cases in Marketing Management and Strategy* (Hinsdale, Ill.: Dryden Press, 1985), 151–164.

FIGURE 1 ∎ **ABCo Facilities**

∎ Corrugated Box Plants:
  Delaware, Ohio
  Huntington, West Virginia
  Muncie, Indiana
  Bowling Green, Kentucky
  Grand Rapids, Michigan

● Plastic Bottle Plants:
  Worthington, Ohio
  Auburn, Massachusetts
  Camden, New Jersey
  Waukegan, Illinois
  Houston, Texas
  Baltimore, Maryland
  Kansas City, Missouri
  La Mirada, California
  San Leandro, California

▲ Film Products Plants:
  Ashland, Ohio
  Jacksonville, Florida

◆ Paperboard Mill:
  Hawesville, Kentucky

1964 was devoted to corporate and Fluid-Box offices, and the other half was devoted to advanced research and development laboratories.

In 1967, to assure itself a regular supply of container board, the company built a paper mill in Hawesville, Kentucky. The ownership of the plant and its 300-ton daily output were shared by ABCo and another company. Later in the same year, the Fluid-Box division began blow-molding a polyethylene ten-quart dispenser to replace the bag-in-a-box version. Called Handi-tap, the new product was an instant success in test marketing. Blow-molding facilities were opened in Worthington, Ohio; Springfield, Massachusetts; Waukegan, Illinois; Los Angeles, California; Houston, Texas; and Orlando, Florida. Because the company was growing in the variety of its products as well as in size, it adopted the more generalized name ABCo Inc. in 1968. (Figure 1 shows the location and type of facilities ABCo owns.)

In 1969, at its Worthington plant, Fluid-Box began blow-molding one-gallon bottles in addition to the handy-tap dispenser. In the meantime, the company opened more blow-molding facilities for the gallon bottles at Baltimore, Maryland; Kansas City, Missouri; and Camden, New Jersey.

Early in 1970, ABCo opened its fifth corrugated box plant in Grand Rapids, Michigan. The company continued its expansion by moving the Columbus and Dallas operations of Fluid-Box to a new facility in Ashland, Ohio. A few months later, the bag-in-a-box operation of Weyerhaeuser was acquired. This purchase allowed ABCo to enlarge bag-in-a-box applications to include containers for battery acid and edible oils, thus broadening the product line even more.

Bag-in-a-Box Uses

The uses of a bag-in-a-box were almost unlimited. Some of the first uses were for milk and ice-cream mix. Then the firm began packaging items like food flavoring, condiments, citrus concentrates, hot foods, and recently wine. The plastic film that goes into the bag is also used for such items as disposable bags for kidney dialysis, inflatable bags for dunnage, and trashcan liners. One of the common problems in the industry was leakage. ABCo was able to solve the problem by introducing a double-lined bag, which was actually a bag inside a bag. According to ABCo, the biggest advantage of their bag is the seal for the filler tab. Many of ABCo's competitors are unable to manufacture and design a seal able to withstand heavy use. It is common for their seals to tear out of the bag when they are being filled.

The bag in the box is composed of three parts: the bag itself, the box that goes around the bag, and the seal and tube that are attached to the bag.

Equipment for Bag-in-a-Box

ABCo makes the machines to perform the packaging of the bag-in-a-box. The first machine is the sealer, which seals the plastic bags and installs the tap. ABCo also offers a model 620 bulk filler, which fills the bags with the desired liquid and seals a box around the bag. To companies that prefer to use their own machines to seal the boxes, ABCo offers two different models of fillers—C2B and C2T bulk fillers. The capacity of each machine is shown in Table 1.

The major problem ABCo has experienced with the machines is that they frequently need tuning. When ABCo sells machines to overseas affiliates, it usually trains their engineers for four weeks on the machines' uses and capabilities. ABCo will also send its engineers to a foreign facility to solve any mechanical problems their customers' engineers cannot.

FILMCO

The company's capacity for extruding plastic film opened the way for a new division—FilmCo—in 1973. This division makes and sells a variety of film items, including custom sheets and tubes, bags for packaging

TABLE 1 ▪ ABCo Bulk Fillers

	Output per Hour	
	---	---
Machine	For 2½-Gallon Container	For 5-Gallon Container
Sealer	840 bags	840 bags
Filler and Boxer		
(620 bulk filler)	300 boxes	300 boxes
C2B	500 bags	300 bags
C2T	1,000 bags	600 bags

bottles, shrink bundling, and trash-can liners. In mid-1974, ABCo transferred its Columbus corrugated container facility to Delaware, Ohio. The new plant's capacity exceeded the capacity of the old one by 50 percent. In the same year, the company also opened its second film plant, in Jacksonville, Florida.

As a result of this expansion, the company that S. S. Smith started grew to 17 plants, more than 700 employees, and sales of over $42 million.

FINANCIAL PERFORMANCE

ABCo's sales increased almost $20 million from 1977 to 1980, and its net income rose $1.2 million. Earnings per share increased by $1.30 during this time, and ABCo's cash dividends doubled (see Table 2). During this time, ABCo's assets grew by about $2.5 million, and its ratio of total debt to equity was about 1:2 (Table 3).

INTERNATIONAL PLANNING

The company has long considered entering foreign markets. The main reasons are the fear of a gradual saturation of the American market and management's desire for new ventures.

Since ABCo concentrates its products mostly in the dairy sector and most of the products are new even to the American market (most of ABCo's current products have been developed since 1976), it planned to look for new markets mostly in countries that had arrived at as sophisticated a dairy industry as the United States. It was feared that allocations of money for improvement in less-developed countries had to go to sectors of the economy that needed improvement more urgently; furthermore, the advantages of ABCo's products (short-time, large-scale filling and emptying, and safe transportation) could not be used to their full extent by such countries. Therefore, in search of foreign operations, ABCo considered only countries with considerable similarities to the

TABLE 2 ▪ ABCo Financial Data, 1977–1980

Operations (in thousands, except per share data)	1980	1979	1978	1977
Net sales	$48,617	$42,031	$33,679	$29,109
Costs and expenses:				
Selling, administrative, and general	5,175	4,487	3,643	3,501
Depreciation	1,664	1,469	1,457	1,217
Interest expense	748	496	546	559
LIFO adjustment	1,808			
Other cost of sales	34,923	32,175	25,469	22,169
	$44,318	$38,627	$31,115	$27,446
Income before income taxes	$ 4,299	$ 3,404	$ 2,564	$ 1,663
Income taxes	1,985	1,717	1,168	570
Net income per share of common stock:	$ 2,314	$ 1,687	$ 1,396	$ 1,093
Net income	$ 2.37	$ 1.73	$ 1.40	$ 1.07
Cash dividends	$ 0.70	$ 0.45	$ 0.36	$ 0.35
Other Financial Information (in thousands, except per share data)				
Cash flow	$ 4,462	$ 3,466	$ 2,982	$ 2,648
Working capital	6,931	4,534	3,143	2,411
Current ratio	2.8	2.2	2.2	1.8
Long-term debt	$10,275	$10,946	$ 6,735	$ 7,315
Shareholders' equity	$13,262	$11,641	$10,404	$ 9,920
Return on shareholders' equity	18.6%	15.3%	13.7%	11.4%
Market price of stock (approximate bid range)	$ 11–16	$ 12–16	$ 13–16	$ 10–16
Cash dividends payout percentage	29%	26%	26%	33%

TABLE 3 ▪ Consolidated Balance Sheet for ABCo and Subsidiaries

**ABCo Inc. and Subsidiaries
Consolidated Balance Sheet
December 28, 1980, and December 29, 1979**

Assets	Dec. 28, 1980	Dec. 29, 1979
Current assets:		
Cash	$ 133,000	$ 428,000
Short-term investments at cost (which approximates market)	1,500,000	700,000
Accounts receivable		
Trade	4,441,000	3,946,000
Other	117,000	162,000
Less allowance for doubtful accounts	(36,000)	(22,000)
Inventories	4,244,000	2,544,000
Current portion of advances to 50%-owned affiliate	400,000	400,000
Other current assets	64,000	32,000
Total current assets	$10,863,000	$ 8,190,000

TABLE 3 ▪ **Continued**

Investment in and advances to 50%-owned affiliate	$ 3,356,000	$ 3,627,000
Cash surrender value of life insurance, net loans of $426,000 and $411,000	$ 57,000	$ 46,000
Property, plant, and equipment, at cost		
Buildings and leasehold improvements	$ 5,021,000	$ 3,074,000
Equipment and vehicles	16,410,000	14,082,000
Less accumulated depreciation	(8,430,000)	(7,401,000)
Construction in process	290,000	678,000
Land	636,000	443,000
Funds held by trustee for construction of new plant	470,000	4,212,000
	$14,397,000	$15,088,000
Deferred charges and other assets	323,000	373,000
	$28,996,000	$27,324,000

Liabilities and Stockholders' Equity	*Dec. 28, 1980*	*Dec. 29, 1979*
Current liabilities:		
9% Note payable, bank	—	$ 300,000
Accounts payable, trade	$ 1,954,000	1,285,000
Dividends payable	137,000	124,000
Accrued expenses:		
Salaries and wages	548,000	454,000
Taxes, other than income taxes	230,000	308,000
Interest	127,000	121,000
Accrued income taxes	266,000	484,000
Current installments on term debt and lease obligations	670,000	580,000
Total current liabilities	$ 3,932,000	$ 3,656,000
Long-term obligations (net of current maturities):		
Term debt	$ 3,000,000	$ 3,500,000
Long-term lease obligations	7,275,000	7,446,000
Allowance for future costs	500,000	150,000
Deferred income taxes	641,000	754,000
Deferred investment tax credit	386,000	177,000
	$11,802,000	$12,027,000
Stockholders' equity:		
Common stock and additional capital, $2 stated value:		
Authorized: 2,000,000 shares		
Issued: 1,042,283 shares	$ 7,983,000	$ 6,653,000
Retained earnings	6,108,000	5,805,000
Less treasury stock: 65,274 shares and 65,660 shares at cost	(829,000)	(817,000)
Total stockholders' equity	$13,262,000	$11,641,000
	$28,996,000	$27,324,000

United States. Management had set forth some criteria that it thought countries should meet in order to be considered for ABCo's international activities. These criteria were:

1. A strong dairy sector
2. A high level of technology
3. A high percentage of disposable income
4. Much use of plastic

Having had business contacts through exports with a Canadian company for several years, ABCo decided to go into partnership with this company in 1974, thus establishing its first foreign affiliate. This venture works profitably, and close contact is maintained by monthly visits from ABCo officials. In considering other foreign operations, ABCo decided not to make use of government agencies, consulates, or banks. All contracts were to be joint ventures. Intending mostly to check markets first in order to see their possibilities, ABCo did not want to incur a high monetary risk. The company's policy was chiefly to offer technological assistance to firms abroad through licensing and royalty agreements. One licensee per country seemed ideal to ABCo's executives.

ABCo's Canadian affiliate provided the addresses of interested firms it worked with in English-speaking countries. ABCo, in turn, placed a salesman in charge of developing relations with such firms. For two years, this salesman and his two successors, appointed from within and outside the company, had no success. At the end of 1976, another salesman from within, this time with international experience (he had previously worked for Icelandic Oil), was promoted to the new rank of manager of international sales. This promotion from salesman to sales manager included a salary raise to the managerial level, permission to make international telephone calls, and the opportunity to make two trips to Europe.

LICENSING OPPORTUNITY IN ICELAND

Within six months, the sales manager had identified a licensing opportunity with a company in Iceland. The proposed agreement would give the Icelandic firm perpetual rights to market ABCo's bag-in-a-box in Iceland and Scandinavia (Denmark, Norway, and Sweden). ABCo was to supply the production machinery, the technological knowhow, and continuous updates on technological progress made in the bag-in-a-box manufacturing process. The Icelandic company was to buy the plastic film from ABCo in Norfolk, Virginia, at the going U.S. market price. ABCo had three choices: to commit itself to the licensing agreement and allow the Icelandic firm to retain the rights to the Scandinavian market, to ship fluid boxes to the Scandinavian market on its own, or to make a direct investment and produce the product in Scandinavia.

Pappirsvorur Proposal

Pappirsvorur Ltd., located in Reykjavik, Iceland, was the firm being considered for licensing by ABCo. Since the population of Iceland is only 200,000, the firm could effect a sizable operation only by exporting its products from Iceland. Exporting would be facilitated by Iceland's membership in the EFTA (Europe Free Trade Association), of which Austria, Denmark, Great Britain, Norway, Portugal, and Switzerland are also members. EFTA is also affiliated with the European Common Market. This affiliation entitles firms in the members' countries to favorable tariff and trade regulations.

Gilvi Henrickson, owner of Pappirsvorur, has large interests in Icelandic Oil, Icelandic Airlines, and Icelandic Steamship Corporation. He also has very good connections with Scandinavian business executives and politicians. He was able to persuade the Swedish legislature to pass a school-milk law requiring all school milk to be served in the bag-in-a-box.

Pappirsvorur proposed to share the Scandinavian market with two competitors. The firm's expected sales from approximately 14.1 million units of fluid boxes would be roughly $6 million annually. Of this income, ABCo would receive a 5 percent royalty plus its markup on the plastic film exported to Pappirsvorur.

Revenues from the Icelandic Market

The sale price of each unit is $377.81 per thousand fluid boxes of 2½ gallons, and $492.61 per thousand of 5-gallon fluid boxes. It is likely that ABCo would be able to absorb 50 percent of the market that Pappirsvorur intends to develop. Their competitors would probably absorb the rest. Roughly half of the mix would be 2½ gallon boxes; the other half, 5-gallon boxes. Pappirsvorur would also buy half of its plastic film from ABCo. The other half would be supplied by Pappirsvorur itself (see Tables 4 and 5).

There are many problems for ABCo to consider if it goes into the Icelandic market. ABCo has only a short time in which to decide. Pappirsvorur is already moving into the market, and two competitors are there. The market will soon be divided up.

ABCo might find a partner for a joint venture instead of licensing Pappirsvorur. This would be rather difficult in the time available, because checking out a partner, obtaining information, making an agreement, and starting operations take time. Or, ABCo might set up operations by itself. It still would have to move quickly, which could lead to costly errors in the long run. For example, it might choose the wrong location, or lose bargaining power. Also, few managers are available for a Scandinavian operation and none of ABCo's officers seems willing to head operations there.

TABLE 4 ▪ Financial Analysis of Pappirsvorur's Proposal to ABCo

Item	Cost of Manufacture* (per 1,000 units)	Sales Price in United States (per 1,000 units)	Sales Price in Iceland (per 1,000 units)
Tube	$ 35.40	$ 43.50	$ 47.01
2½-gallon bag	103.77	138.00	151.80
5-gallon bag	133.75	175.50	193.00
2½-gallon box	112.50	148.00	179.00
5-gallon box	169.25	224.75	251.60

Import and tariff from the United States to Sweden:
2½-gallon unit $57.54
5-gallon unit $70.20

* The cost of manufacture includes only variable overhead, labor, and material.

Cost breakdown based on the U.S. sales price:

Variable costs			Fixed costs		
	Revenue	$1.00		Auto-sealer (to put seals on the bag)	$ 42,000
	Labor	0.143		Box filler and sealer	59,000
	Materials	0.573		Filler only	38,500 (C2B)
	Overhead	0.036			63,000 (C2T)
	Transportation and duties	0.164		Building for Icelandic venture	110,000– 140,000

Note: One 2½-gallon bag contains approximately 1 square meter of plastic film. A 5-gallon bag contains approximately 1.4 square meters of plastic film.

TABLE 5 ▪ ABCo's Options

1. ABCo allows Pappirsvorur to develop the market:

Revenue

7 million, 2½ gal. @ .37781 per unit	=	$2,644,670
7.1 million, 5 gal. @ .4926 per unit	=	$3,497,531
Total		$6,142,201
5 percent royalty		$ 307,110

Plastic needed

7 million bags @ 1 square meter per bag	=	7,000,000 square meters
7.1 million bags @ 1.4 square meters per bag	=	9,940,000 square meters

ABCo will supply half of this material.

Sales price (1 square meter)	.09550
Transportation	(.00438)
Costs	(.07004)
	$.02108 per meter
	(8.5 million square meters)

Total costs	=	$179,180
Profit		$485,290
Less 1 − tax rate		.52
Net Profit		$252,350

2. ABCo decides to manufacture the product in the United States and ship it to Scandinavia. The net cash flows would be as follows:

Revenue: Figured at half of what Pappirsvorur could sell, because the competition would probably do better against ABCo since it does not have Pappirsvorur's political and economic connections.

Sales	=	$3,071,110

Costs:

2½-gallon units, 3.5 million @ .25167 per unit	=	$ 880,845
5-gallon units, 3.5 million @ .3384 per unit	=	$1,184,400
Duties (.147 of Scandinavian price)	=	$ 447,825
Manager of foreign operations	=	$ 80,000
Total cost		$2,593,070
Profit before taxes		478,040
Taxes (.48)		.52
Net Income		$ 245,600

Fixed Costs:

Machine capacity of sealer (250 days per year @ 7.5 hours per day)
= 840 units per hour
= 1,575,000 units

7.1 million units at 1,575,000 units per machine = 5 machines

It will be assumed that the distributors will fill their own boxes, because prices do not include this service.

5 machines @ $42,000	=	$210,000
Building (allocated space)	=	100,000
Initial investment		$310,000
Payback period $310,000/$245,600	=	1.26 years

(Continued)

TABLE 5 ▪ **Continued**

3. ABCo builds a factory in Scandinavia:

Costs:

All costs would be the same as 2, except that there would be no import duty.

Profit before taxes, from second choice	$478,040
Plus tariff and transportation costs	
to Sweden	30,660
	447,825
	$956,525
Minus Scandinavian tax rate = 0.53	.47
Net Income	$449,600
Payback period $310,000/$449,600	= 8 months

Even if all the planning were done carefully, ABCo might enter the market too late and have to fight for a market share from established competitors. Neither their strength nor the strength of Gilvi Henrickson is known, but a man who can induce a foreign legislature to pass a law must have strong ties with the country and could prove to be a strong competitor to ABCo.

ABCo is an aggressive company that in past years has steadily expanded. Building a plant in Scandinavia could be a financial success. But given the constraints of time, it would probably be better to continue to work with the Icelanders. ABCo could instead keep in mind the possibility of expanding abroad at a later time and start to train its management for foreign operations.

As Smith left for the board meeting, he felt confident that ABCo's executives would make a decision about the Icelandic market that would be compatible with the company's policy of international development.

Questions for Discussion

1. Discuss ABCo's progress in the internationalization process.
2. How could this progress have been improved?
3. Evaluate the foreign market criteria developed by ABCo.
4. Discuss ABCo's licensing opportunity with Pappirsvorur.
5. What decision do you recommend to ABCo's management?

Water from Iceland

Stan Otis was in a contemplative mood. He had just hung up the phone after talking with Roger Morey, vice president of Citicorp. Morey had made him a job offer in the investment banking sector of the firm. The interviews had gone well and Citicorp management was impressed with Stan's credentials from a major northeastern private university. "I think you can do well here, Stan. Let us know within a week whether you accept the job," Morey had said.

The three-month search had paid off well, Stan thought. However, an alternative plan complicated the decision to accept the position.

Stan had returned several months before from an extended trip throughout Europe, a delayed graduation present from his parents. Among other places, he had visited Reykjavik, Iceland. Even though he could not communicate well, he found the island enchanting. What particularly fascinated him was the lack of industry and the purity of the natural landscape. In particular, he felt the water tasted extremely good. Returning home, he began to consider making this water available in the United States.

THE WATER MARKET IN THE UNITED STATES

In order to consider the possibilities of importing Icelandic water, Stan knew that he first had to learn more about the general water market in the United States. Fortunately, some former college friends were working in a market research firm. Owing Stan some favors, these friends furnished him with a consulting report on the water market.

The Consulting Report

Primary types of water available for human consumption in the United States are treated or processed water, mineral water, sparkling or effervescent water, spring-well water, club soda, and tonic water.

Treated or processed water comes from a well stream or central reservoir supply. This water usually flows as tap water and has been purified and fluoridated.

Mineral water is spring water that contains a substantial amount of minerals, which may be injected or occur naturally. Natural mineral water is obtained from underground water strata or a natural spring. The composition of the water at its source is constant, and the source discharge and temperature remain stable. The natural content of the water at the source is not modified by an artificial process.

Source: This case was prepared by Michael R. Czinkota.

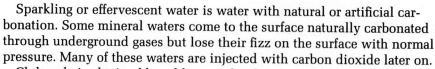

Sparkling or effervescent water is water with natural or artificial carbonation. Some mineral waters come to the surface naturally carbonated through underground gases but lose their fizz on the surface with normal pressure. Many of these waters are injected with carbon dioxide later on.

Club soda is obtained by adding artificial carbonation to distilled or regular tap water. Mineral content in this water depends upon the water supply used and the purification process the water has undergone. Tonic water is derived from the same process as club soda, but has bitters added to it.

Minerals are important to the taste and quality of water. The type and variety of minerals present in the water can make it a very healthy and enjoyable drink. The combination of minerals present in the water determines its relative degree of acidity. The level of acidity is measured by the pH factor. A pH 7 rating indicates a neutral water. A higher rating indicates that the water contains more solids, such as manganese calcium, and is said to be "hard." Conversely, water with a lower rating is classified as "soft." Most tap water is soft, whereas the majority of commercially sold waters tend to be hard.

Water Consumption in the United States

Tap water has generally been inexpensive, relatively pure, and plentiful in the United States. Traditionally, bottled water has been consumed in the United States by the very wealthy. In the past several years, however, bottled water has begun to appeal to a wider market. The four reasons for this change are:

1. An increasing awareness among consumers of the impurity of city water supplies
2. Increasing dissatisfaction with the taste and odor of city tap water
3. Rising affluence in society
4. An increasing desire to avoid excess consumption of caffeine, sugar, and other substances present in coffee and soft drinks

Bottled water consumers are found chiefly in the states of California, Florida, Texas, New York, and Illinois. Combined, these states represent 88 percent of nationwide bottled water sales. California alone represents one-half of industry sales. Nationwide, bottled water is drunk by one out of every two thousand persons. In California, however, one out of every six drinks bottled water.

Consumers differ in their reasons for drinking bottled water. In the Southwest, bottled water is regularly consumed in the home, the office, and restaurants. Consumers in this region are not as interested in the chic image of bottled water as they are its taste. In urban areas such as Chicago and New York City, bottled water is consumed as an alternative to alcoholic beverages, soft drinks, and coffee. Eighty-five percent of the consumers are women.

Prior to 1976, bottled water was considered primarily a gourmet specialty, an exotic demand of the rich. Since the entry of Perrier, an imported French water, however, U.S. bottled water consumption has shown exceptional growth. Bottled water sales rose from a level of 235 million gallons in 1971 to over 500 million gallons in 1983. Industry sales are expected to grow at a rate of 10 to 12 percent domestically. Imported water held a 5 percent share of the domestic market in terms of volume, but was expected to reach a 26 percent share of total market in 1983 in terms of sales dollars.

The bottled water market in the United States was estimated to be approximately $480 million in terms of producers' prices. Domestically purified and processed water was thought to hold a 45 percent market share, with domestic mineral water holding 29 percent and imported mineral water holding 26 percent of market share. The leading exporting country is France, with a 91.7 percent share of imports in the United States. Other countries are Italy with 2.6 percent, Canada with 4 percent, and West Germany with 1.7 percent of import share.

Among brands, Perrier is clearly the leader. Perrier is estimated to hold 5 percent of total unit volume of the bottled water market and 20 percent of the total dollar volume. Industry observers believe that the primary causes for Perrier's success are its heavy media budget, its national distribution network, and its focus on the soft drink market in general, rather than on the bottled water market. As a result, Perrier is able to charge a premium price, with most of its product selling in supermarkets at an average price of four cents per ounce, compared to an average price of two cents per ounce for the rest of the industry.

Overall, a cursory analysis indicates good potential for success for a new importer of bottled water in the United States. This is especially true if the water is exceptionally pure and can be classified as mineral water.

ADDITIONAL RESEARCH

Further exploring his import idea, Stan Otis gathered information on various other marketing facets. One of his main concerns was government regulations.

Bottled Water Regulations in the United States

The bottled water industry in the United States is regulated and controlled at two levels—by the federal government and various state governments. The federal government code defines bottled water as "water that is treated and bottled or out of containers and intended for human consumption." Bottled water does not include mineral water or any food defined in other sections. Any bottled water that is moved in interstate commerce is subject to Food and Drug Administration regulations. While the federal government has set quality and safety standards for bottled water that is consumed as a substitute for tap water, it has not defined and set such standards for mineral water. In cooperation with industry, and based mainly on the definition of mineral water in Europe, however, the federal government customarily sees mineral water as water that contains at least 500 parts per million of total dissolved solids (TDS) and that has not been artificially processed. If the water contains less than 500 parts TDS per million, it can still be labeled mineral water, but the TDS content must be shown on the label.

Some state regulatory officials hold that, to be labeled as mineral water, water must contain a minimum amount of dissolved solids. California Code regulations require bottled water to contain at least 500 parts TDS per million to qualify as a mineral water. Michigan is considering legislation that will require mineral water to contain at least one thousand parts TDS per million. In addition to state and federal regulation, the production and sale of bottled water can also be regulated by city and county agencies and public health authorities.

The Icelandic Scenario

Iceland is highly import dependent. In terms of products exported, it has little diversity and is dangerously dependent upon its fish crop and world fish prices. The government, troubled by high inflation rates and low financial reserves, is very interested in diversifying its export base. An Icelandic Export Board has been created and charged with developing new products for export and promoting them aggressively abroad.

The Ministry of Commerce, after consulting the Central Bank, has the ultimate responsibility in matters concerning import and export licensing. The Central Bank is responsible for the regulation of foreign exchange transactions and exchange controls, including capital controls. It is also responsible for ensuring that all foreign exchange due to residents is surrendered to authorized banks. All commercial exports require licenses. The shipping documents must be lodged with an authorized bank. Receipts exchanged for exports must be surrendered to the Central Bank.

All investments by nonresidents in Iceland are subject to individual approval. The participation of nonresidents in Icelandic joint venture companies may not exceed 49 percent. Nonresident-owned foreign capital entering in the form of foreign exchange must be surrendered.

Iceland is a member of the United Nations, the European Free Trade Association, and the General Agreement on Tariffs and Trade. Iceland enjoys "most favored nation" status with the United States. Under this designation, Iceland is subject to a tariff of 1.5 cents per gallon on imported water.

Questions for Discussion

1. Should water be bottled in Iceland for export or shipped in bulk and bottled in the United States?

2. Should the water from Iceland be marketed as natural, mineral, or sparkling water?

3. Which market segments would you recommend for an initial market introduction effort?

4. Develop a marketing mix for Otis. Be sure to focus on distribution, pricing, and promotion.

5. Should Otis become an investment banker or implement his vision?

Head Sports Wear Inc.

Head Sports Wear Inc., a wholly owned division of Leslie Fay Inc., is a sportswear company based in Columbia, Maryland. The firm has its roots in the Head Ski Company, a company founded in the mid-1960s to commercially exploit the new ski manufacturing techniques devised by Howard Head. Shortly after its inception, the ski company expanded its operations to include skiwear. Soon thereafter a separate sportswear division was formed. In the late 1960s this division was spun off from the ski company and became a separate firm. In 1969, both firms were bought out by AMF. In 1981, AMF sold the sportswear division to Leslie Fay Inc. A licensing agreement enables Leslie Fay to continue use of the Head name in its sportswear division.

Head Sports Wear is oriented primarily toward the merchandising and marketing of high-quality sportswear. Engaged in no actual production itself, the firm contracts work out to unaffiliated plants. These sub-contractors are located in various U.S. states—among them, Illinois, Virginia, Maryland, Pennsylvania, and New Jersey—as well as abroad. At present, foreign imports account for about two-thirds of the firm's annual income. With a staff of about 80 people, the firm maintains a relatively loose organizational structure. Approximately 15 percent of its personnel are engaged in merchandising tasks such as designing and setting up the product lines; an additional 15 percent work in the model room. Sales and marketing are handled by another 10 percent of the staff, while 10 percent deal with production concerns. The remaining 50 percent are divided between warehousing, inspection, and receiving, on the one hand, and data processing and accounting on the other.

The company views its ability to market high-quality, fashionable ski and tennis wear as its main strength, giving Head a niche in the highly competitive U.S. sportswear market. Competition is based largely on price, design, and perceived quality. Head's main skiwear competitors are C. B. Bogner and Rossignol. In tennis wear, the competition is so intense between the many firms involved that the main competitors "seem to change from day to day."

Not a mass merchandiser, Head would have difficulty selling large quantities of inexpensive garments. Head Sports Wear items are sold in department stores, ski-area ski shops, and specialty shops. At present, skiwear represents 55 percent of the firm's sales volume; tennis wear, 40 percent; and running wear, 5 percent. Head's current U.S. market share for skiwear is estimated to be 10 percent to 15 percent, and for tennis wear, about 18 percent. The market share of running wear is minuscule. Annual sportswear sales averaged between 25 and 30 million dollars during the past five years.

Source: This case was prepared by Michael R. Czinkota and Laura M. Gould.

INTERNATIONAL ACTIVITIES

Head Sports Wear first became involved in foreign contracting in the early 1970s. Management was dissatisfied with the product quality offered by domestic manufacturers and made the decision to go abroad in its search for high-quality ski sweaters, tennis skirts, and shorts.

At that time, contact was made with a small-scale agent in Hong Kong who was an acquaintance of one of Head's employees. Financed by a letter of credit backed by the parent company, AMF, a small order was placed with the agent for ski sweaters, tennis shorts, and skirts. It was decided that, if sales went well, Head would increase its purchases abroad in the future.

The initial purchase went well. Although the absence of a quality domestic source was the initial impetus for the decision to import, price subsequently became a supporting factor. As time went on and the business grew, Head increased its import activity proportionally. The company president, a German, had contacts in Germany, and as a result Head imported from Germany for one or two seasons until it became too expensive to do so. Ski boots were imported from Italy, zippers from Switzerland. While Japan was considered, it was deemed too expensive; imports from Hong Kong were increased. The firm also imported from Taiwan and Korea, but reduced its dealings with Korea after having a "disastrous" experience: the quality was extremely poor and delivery was late. In addition, management looked at manufacturers in the Philippines and Singapore but decided against them because of the poor workmanship at the plants there.

With the exception of such small items as zippers, Head has always designed its own products prior to marketing them in the United States with a Head label. Foreign manufacturers have in no way been involved in U.S. market development, pricing decisions, inventory policies, market research, or physical distribution. They received precise manufacturing instructions and carried them out.

The advent of importing activities initially caused no changes in the organizational structure of Head. As the volume of imports increased, however, one person was designated to monitor overseas purchases. Otherwise, employees' jobs in the various functional areas have expanded as necessary to accommodate the foreign activity. Despite the large proportion of import-related income, no department is expressly devoted to this area. The person in charge of imports has been working with the firm for eight years. Initially hired as manager of adjustments and in charge of returns from retailers, he was promoted after two years to the position of foreign purchasing coordinator. Although his educational background in the liberal arts offered no particular advantage for the position, he had lived and worked for two years in Taiwan and is fluent in Chinese, Russian, and German, making him the most eligible inside person for the job. His current position mainly involves coordinating the foreign purchasing process within the firm. He rarely travels

abroad, because specialized personnel is available for that task, and courtesy travel is carried out by senior management.

IMPORT PROBLEMS

When Head began importing, management expected quality, freight, and customs problems. In the course of the firm's importing activities, they have encountered all three. Quality problems have been the biggest concern because of the firm's dependence on its reputation for high-quality garments. Quality problems have included poor safety locking on seams and the substitution of inferior quality down in down garments. Head has often found a way to compromise with the supplier to obtain some compensation for quality problems. This is sometimes accomplished by negotiating a 10 percent discount off F.O.B. or by extracting an agreement from the exporter not to increase prices the following year. However, if the problem was egregious, this solution was of little worth and Head discontinued the relationship. On the whole, Head has found it more advantageous to send its employees abroad to catch quality problems before they happen than to haggle for a discount later on.

Freight problems have also arisen on occasion. Imported garments have arrived late as a result of poor routing, strikes, or shipping backlogs. Because of the extreme time sensitivity of the textile retail industry, these delays have occasionally led to lost sales. At such times, Head usually has to absorb the losses in terms of lost profits and increased inventory carrying costs. In an attempt to minimize its losses, the firm has tried to get the foreign firm either to pay part of the freight or to agree to a 25 percent to 50 percent discount. Even when successful, however, the savings on a $25 garment amount to no more than $2 to $4 because the cost of such a garment to Head is approximately $12, of which $8 is the F.O.B. cost.

The customs problems that Head encountered when it first began importing generally had to do with the definition of what would be considered an "assist." Having already paid duties on the zippers it imported from Switzerland, Head found that it was being charged duties a second time when these same zippers reentered the United States in finished garments manufactured in Hong Kong. As a result, the cost of the garments increased. Head ceased importing zippers from Switzerland and required Hong Kong to obtain the zippers directly. The firm did consider making use of foreign trade zones on a number of occasions but decided that the percentage saving would be small. Staffing another warehouse or paying someone else to do so would increase overhead, and this was deemed an unnecessary expense given the small volume of business involved.

An additional problem arose in conjunction with quota restrictions, which often caused uncertainty about the firm's ability to import the garments until well after production had been contracted. In general, U.S.

quota rights granted to a given country are distributed by that country's government on the basis of firms' exporting activity for the previous year. Obtaining such an allocation is, however, no easy task. Different textiles fall under different types of quota restrictions. The Hong Kong government will allocate a quota to a firm only after U.S. customs has ruled on the quota category into which a product will fall. U.S. customs in turn wants to see the shipment before making a binding determination regarding quota categories. A manufacturer in possession of quota rights in excess of foreign demand must either sell them to another firm or receive reduced quota rights the following year. Quota rights are therefore also held and sold for speculative purposes.

Head tries to divorce itself completely from the problem. Its contracts to import garments from abroad make the subcontractors responsible for having or acquiring sufficient quota rights; by accepting the order, the manufacturer is committed to having the quota. Thus, a shipment to Head has never actually been denied entry. However, contractors have occasionally had to scramble around at the last minute and pay a considerable amount for the requisite quota rights. Quota rights have sometimes worked to Head's advantage: a firm in fear of losing its allocation the following year because of decreased current exports would request Head to help out by increasing its order. At such times, Head obtained very good prices on a last-minute order for inventory.

Quota problems do not exist for the initial inspection of merchandise. Small shipments are sent in as a salesman's sample from abroad. As long as the total shipment value is under $250, no formal entry of the merchandise needs to be declared.

IMPORTS FROM HONG KONG

Products from Hong Kong constitute a major portion of Head's import activities. Except for a moderate amount of business placed through Leslie Fay's Hong Kong office, Head Sports Wear activity in Hong Kong is almost entirely conducted through an agent with whom contact was first established in the early 1970s. For the most part, Leslie Fay's Hong Kong office deals with tennis wear, while the agent is more involved with skiwear. This division of focus arose more or less by chance and has been maintained by inertia. Approximately 30 percent of the agent's time is devoted to Head. Of the various manufacturing firms to whom work is contracted, several devote as much as 50 percent of their capacity to Head Sports Wear during a particular season; for most, however, the figure is 1 percent to 10 percent.

The agent locates contractors in Hong Kong, but Head employees see to the actual design and quality control. To improve quality, the contractors in Hong Kong have often had to hire quality control people and purchase new equipment. If the equipment can be used for a variety of purposes, the manufacturer pays for it as a cost of doing business. If the

machine is peculiar to Head's needs, however, Head will either provide outright financial assistance or guarantee that a sufficiently large order will be placed to enable the manufacturer to amortize the machine's cost by adding approximately two cents to the cost of each garment. On occasion, manufacturers have set aside a separate work area and paid higher wages to those working on Head garments to foster higher quality workmanship.

Although contact between the agent and Head is frequent, little if any information is exchanged about product uses and market conditions. Between merchandising and production personnel, approximately 25 visits a year are made to Hong Kong in order to settle on contracts, clarify designs, determine pricing, and examine quality control. Telexes are often exchanged daily to clarify specific designs and specific orders. The agent generally travels to the United States once or twice a year, but contractors seldom come. When they do, it is usually as a treat rather than for any express business purpose. After a particularly good season, manufacturers will occasionally reward workers with a trip to the United States.

For the most part, the agent is considered to be experienced, astute, knowledgeable, businesslike, and a "little conniving." Head's volume of business with the agent has steadily increased and is expected to continue to do so in the future even though the quality of the goods has been uneven. At present, $3 million a year F.O.B., or approximately 50 percent of their imports, are acquired through this agent. The remainder comes from Leslie Fay's Hong Kong office and Taiwan.

Despite the fact that "something's always gonna go wrong," the benefits of importing from Hong Kong through this agent are perceived to outweigh the problems.

AN OVERALL ASSESSMENT OF INTERNATIONAL ACTIVITIES

On the whole, Head has found its import business profitable, although the level of profits is subject to change from year to year. Despite some internal debate about the need for an agent, Head's management decided not to eliminate the agent. From a purely financial standpoint it might be more profitable to work directly with manufacturers, as Head has done in Europe. This course of action was considered impractical in Hong Kong, where the intermediation of agents is standard business practice.

If dropped without cause, the agent might resort to any of the following actions: tell manufacturers not to deal with the firm; make sure that Head's garments are shipped last; see to it that the freight forwarders charge Head a higher rate; in general, bad-mouth Head with other agents in Hong Kong. Dealing through an agent is common throughout the Far East. The agent, who generally receives a commission of five percent or less, researches the market, monitors production, deals with the paperwork, and facilitates the resolution of quota problems.

Exchange rate changes are of no concern to Head. Contracts with suppliers are issued at the beginning of each season. Contract prices are denominated in U.S. dollars, and the firm does not undertake any hedging activities in the currency market. The risks and benefits of exchange rate fluctuations rest completely with the foreign supplier.

As a result of its importing activities, Head has become more sophisticated in its international business dealings and has increased its exporting activities as well. Head's exporting activity remains, nonetheless, a small part of its overall business. Although the firm does export some of its domestic garments to U.S. military outlets in Europe and to South America and the Middle East, it generally lets its licensees handle most exporting activity.

Questions for Discussion

1. How can Head overcome quality problems with imported skiwear?
2. How would the use of a foreign trade zone help Head?
3. Discuss the benefits and drawbacks of quotas.
4. Why should Head continue to use an agent in Hong Kong?
5. How can Head's suppliers protect themselves against currency fluctuations?

Intercoffee Incorporated

Intercoffee Incorporated, a coffee and cocoa importer located in New York City's financial district, was founded in 1932 by a wealthy New Yorker of Hispanic descent. His motives in entering the coffee and cocoa import business have been obscured by the passage of time. His successors speculate that this business was probably compatible with the freewheeling international lifestyle pursued by the founder, whose background included personal and family ties to a variety of Caribbean islands.

He appears to have capitalized on personal connections among growers in the Dominican Republic, from where he first imported coffee and cocoa beans in 1932. He acted chiefly as a middleman between these growers and U.S. processors.

In the ensuing years, Intercoffee expanded its import activities. Suppliers are presently located in Africa, Indonesia, and a variety of countries in Latin America, most notably, since 1979, Brazil. Although the number and location of suppliers has grown, Intercoffee's activities have remained restricted almost exclusively to the importation of coffee and cocoa. Only on rare occasions were forays into beeswax and wine made.

Intercoffee imports cocoa and all four kinds of coffee beans as well as spray-dried and freeze-dried instant coffee. The two major types of coffee are Robusta and Arabica. Robusta beans are considered to be of low grade, cheap, and easy to grow. They are found mainly in Africa and Indonesia. Arabica beans are of higher quality and are customarily subdivided into three groups: (1) Brazil beans, which are also known as unwashed or natural beans and are considered great blenders; (2) washed milds, originating mainly from Central America and Mexico, of somewhat higher quality; and (3) Colombia washed beans, which are generally considered to be of the highest quality.

Forty percent of the firm's revenues and profits derive from cocoa and 60 percent from coffee. Forty percent of the firm's coffee profits—and thus, 24 percent of the firm's total profits—derive from imports from Brazil, including Brazil beans, as well as both kinds of soluble (instant) coffee.

Over the years, both management and ownership of the firm have passed out of the hands of the founder's family. The firm is presently organized as a Subchapter S corporation, with its equity held entirely by management. Intercoffee currently has 15 employees. The executive committee, comprised of the president and three executive vice presidents, is responsible for trading activities and the day-to-day decision making. The firm's organizational structure is designed largely along product lines (see Figure 1). In addition, the firm employs two accoun-

Source: This case was prepared by Michael R. Czinkota and Laura M. Gould.

FIGURE 1 ▪ **Organization Chart**

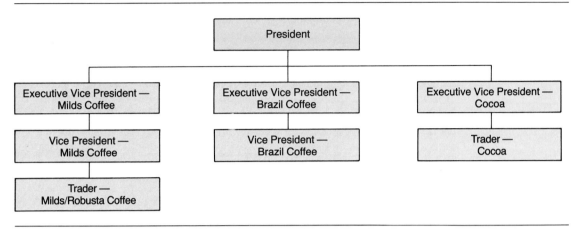

tants, two secretary–telex operators, and four persons whose primary concern is distribution, including the handling of documentation, flow of goods, customs, shipping and transportation, and billing.

The company's primary aim is to provide income to its share-holders–managers through the importation and resale of commodities, primarily cocoa and coffee. Its chief assets are its sales and trading skills and, in particular, its personal contacts with suppliers. Management believes that Intercoffee's main competitive disadvantage is the fact that it is subject to financial constraints on its ability to hedge its business risk in commodity futures markets and is therefore limited in its abilities to act as a principal. In most of the import transactions in which Intercoffee is involved, it acts only as an agent for the supplier in exchange for a commission on sales.

During recent years, Intercoffee's sales have totaled approximately $100 million a year. The firm's profits, like those of its industry in general, have been quite volatile. Net profits as a percentage of gross sales have ranged from 0.1 percent in bad years to 3.0 percent in good years.

At present, the firm ranks, by volume, in the top 20 percent of about 60 U.S. coffee and cocoa importers. In 1984 Intercoffee imported 200,000 bags of coffee and 100,000 bags of cocoa. (One bag weighs 60 kilograms.)

THE INTERNATIONAL COFFEE MARKET

Coffee and cocoa cannot be commercially grown in the United States except for a small amount in Hawaii because the climate is not suitable for their cultivation. As a result, virtually all of the coffee and cocoa sold in the United States is imported, making the United States the largest coffee buyer in the world. In 1984, 18 million bags of coffee were imported. Twenty-two percent of all U.S. coffee imports come from Brazil.

In its early days, coffee trade was regularly exposed to a boom and bust cycle. Stories still abound about the burning of coffee and the unloading of coffee into the ocean during times of oversupply. This situation was changed by the coordinated activities of the major coffee-producing nations.

The modern structure of the international coffee trade was created by the International Coffee Agreement (ICA) that originated in the early 1960s. Following the 1975 Brazilian coffee frost, the agreement gained additional members and became an effective instrument. It established dollar-denominated target floor and ceiling prices in the world market and allocated specified shares of world export production to each major coffee-producing nation. This management reduced uncertainty and competitive pressures on all participants in the industry.

INTERCOFFEE'S BUSINESS IN BRAZIL

Intercoffee is the exclusive U.S. agent for Cafe Soluvel Brasilia S.A. (CSB), one of the seven largest producers of instant coffee in Brazil. These producers were assisted substantially by the Brazilian government, which saw them as an effective means to expand employment and increase the value-added component of exported goods. Due in part to low-cost Brazilian instant coffee, a dramatic shift in U.S. domestic instant coffee production had already occurred. A large share of the instant coffee consumed in the United States is actually produced in Brazil and imported in bulk.

Intercoffee's relations with CSB date from 1979. Initial contact between the firms was established by Jack Smith, Intercoffee's current executive vice president in charge of Brazil operations. Prior to joining Intercoffee in 1979, Smith had enjoyed a successful career with Anderson Clayton, rising to the position of president of the Anderson Clayton Coffee Division in 1974. In 1972, a mutual friend introduced Smith to the president of Cafe Soluvel Brasilia, who was looking for a firm to represent CSB worldwide and to provide a preestablished distribution network. At that time, an agreement was reached between CSB and Anderson Clayton.

When Smith retired from Anderson Clayton and subsequently joined Intercoffee in 1979, CSB transferred its U.S. agency with him. This transfer was due to the strength of the personal relationship that had been developed, a relationship emphasized by the fact that CSB and Anderson Clayton never had a written contract.

Prior to establishing relations with CSB, Intercoffee had never imported instant coffee, although it had been available.

In its relationship with CSB, Intercoffee provides major input on required product quality based on information obtained from its clients, who are national brand packers and marketers, private label packers, and supermarket chains. The buyers also provide Intercoffee with a sample of the desired product and specifications for moisture, density, acidity, granulation, solubility, sediments, and taste. These specifications and samples are transmitted by Intercoffee to CSB, which supplies a product to match the buyers' needs.

Spray-dried instant coffee, which Intercoffee imports in 90-pound cartons, is subsequently run through an agglomerization process by the packer. Spray-dried coffee represents 90 percent of U.S. instant coffee imports and is shipped as finely granulated powder. Because of U.S. consumer preferences, this powder is agglomerated in a process that adds water and oils, resulting in chunky-style coffee rather than a powder mixture. Currently, 75 percent of spray-dried coffee is sold in agglomerated form. The 25 percent of nonagglomerated coffee is mostly sold as generic or off-brand product. The agglomerization process costs the buyer (or packer) about 20 cents per pound.

Freeze-dried instant coffee is already crystallized and requires no agglomerization. Produced from higher quality ingredients, it has already undergone a more costly process. It generally costs about $2.00 per pound F.O.B. more than spray-dried coffee.

Intercoffee imports instant coffee only from CSB. Approximately 99.8 percent of its imported coffee is presold. This is not necessarily the case, however, with its imported raw beans. Altogether, about 80 percent of Intercoffee's coffee bean imports are presold; for the remaining 20 percent, the firm acts a principal rather than an agent and consequently bears the market risk.

Intercoffee handles all distribution tasks for CSB in the United States. Pricing decisions are a function of the overall coffee market. Typically, supply exceeds demand, creating a buyer's market.

Intercoffee maintains no instant coffee inventory in the United States. All instant coffee remains in Brazil until it is needed. Market research and physical distribution are the responsibility of Intercoffee. The firm has not invested in CSB, which retains primary responsibility for manufacturing and quality control.

The nature of the market requires only minimal adaptation of the product by the supplier. From time to time, Intercoffee transmits information to CSB concerning changes in market trends and market specifications. In order to handle increased volume from CSB, Intercoffee has added additional traffic personnel and has modified its accounting procedures. Payment procedures have remained unchanged.

To meet Intercoffee's requirements, CSB has increased its productive capacity and has modified its equipment, such as extractors and aromatizing agents, to enhance the product and make it more marketable in the United States. Furthermore, CSB's export department was made more efficient through the addition of personnel and streamlining of operations.

CSB and Intercoffee enjoy a mutually beneficial exchange of information in a variety of areas. Intercoffee provides CSB with estimated sales figures and information about clients' requirements, quality standards,

competition, and pricing. On one occasion, after CSB had made initial contact with an instant coffee plant in Canada, Intercoffee assisted the Brazilians in purchasing the plant and having it shipped to Brazil by providing traffic expertise.

CSB for its part informs Intercoffee about technical improvements it is able to make, such as developing aromatizing capacity. Intercoffee, in turn, passes this information on to actual and prospective U.S. buyers. In addition, CSB keeps Intercoffee informed about changes in the European markets.

CSB and Intercoffee maintain frequent contact. Smith or his son, the vice president for Brazilian operations, maintains daily phone or telex contact with CSB's sales manager in order to discuss shipment posting, sales, and pricing. CSB's sales manager, an American who was formerly employed by Anderson Clayton, gives this information to the CSB vice president. Smith or his son visits CSB at least twice a year for face-to-face discussions of market strategies, performance, and means by which Intercoffee can better serve CSB. These strategy meetings are generally combined with trips to the six green coffee suppliers in Brazil with whom Intercoffee has business dealings. CSB people generally travel to New York at least once a year to visit the final customers.

Intercoffee has a high regard for CSB. It considers the Brazilian firm to be an efficient, technically expert company whose management is hard working and financially conservative. CSB's inexperience in the U.S. market renders it dependent on Intercoffee for agency services.

Intercoffee's business dealings with CSB have been characterized by a fairly steady upward growth of two to five percent a year. The U.S. firm imports about five million pounds of freeze-dried and spray-dried instant coffee a year, which it then distributes not only throughout the United States but also to Australia and Canada.

The relationship between CSB and Intercoffee has been characterized by an absence of problems, crises, and discontinuities, although price haggling is of course routine. The coffee and cocoa importing business is highly price competitive and characterized by low profit margins. Intercoffee believes that CSB's main advantage relative to its competitors is product quality. Because of higher quality, however, CSB is less price competitive.

Intercoffee expects to continue its mutually profitable business and close relationship with CSB. While problems are not expected, Intercoffee recognizes that long-run threats to its relationship with CSB might arise from a variety of sources. First, if the Brazilian government were to decide to increase its taxation of coffee exports, a larger share of the U.S. market would probably be seized by other countries from which Intercoffee is currently not sourcing instant coffee, such as Colombia or Ecuador. Second, amendments to the International Coffee Agreement might restrict Brazil's quota and thereby reduce Intercoffee's revenues. Third, a change of personnel at CSB or at Intercoffee would destroy the personal relationship on which Intercoffee's business critically depends.

Finally, an additional pressure on the relationship may occur in consequence of a recent decrease in the number of buyers, meaning more industry concentration, which may result in downward pressure on prices.

Because CSB was the first instant coffee supplier with whom Intercoffee has dealt, and is still the only one, the firm has learned a number of lessons from the relationship. Intercoffee has had to evaluate retailing and packaging considerations, and also has learned to deal with a supplier of a semifinished product rather than a supplier of raw materials (raw coffee beans). This in turn involved accommodating a more complex supplier perspective than had previously been necessary. Dealing with CSB, however, has also enabled Intercoffee to increase its penetration of the U.S. market and has opened up new channels of sales beyond the traditional green coffee sales to roasters.

Questions for Discussion

1. Discuss the value and effectiveness of the International Coffee Agreement.
2. How can the International Coffee Agreement affect Intercoffee Incorporated?
3. Evaluate the organizational structure of Intercoffee Incorporated.
4. Evaluate the relationships between Intercoffee and CSB. Would you recommend any changes?
5. Should CSB conduct its own market research in the United States?

Damar International

Damar International, a fledgling firm importing handicrafts of chiefly
Indonesian origin, was established in January 1984 in Burke, Virginia, a
suburb of Washington, D.C. Organized as a general partnership, the firm
is owned entirely by Dewi Soemantoro, its president, and Ronald I.
Asche, its vice president. Their part-time unsalaried efforts, and those of
Soemantoro's relatives in Indonesia, constitute the entire labor base of
the firm. Outside financing has been limited to borrowing from friends
and relatives of the partners in Indonesia and the United States.

Damar International imported its first shipment of handicrafts in April
1984 and estimates that its current annual sales revenues are between
$20,000 and $30,000. Although the firm has yet to reach the break-even
point, its sales revenues and customer base have expanded more rapidly
than anticipated in Damar's original business plan. The partners are generally satisfied with results to date and plan to continue to broaden their
operations.

Damar International was established in order to capitalize on Soemantoro's international experience and contacts. The daughter of an Indonesian Foreign Service officer, Soemantoro spent most of her youth and
early adulthood in Western Europe and has for the past 18 years resided
in the United States. Her immediate family, including her mother, now
resides in Indonesia. In addition to English and Malay, Soemantoro
speaks French, German, and Italian. Although she has spent the past four
years working in information management in the Washington area, first
for MCI and currently for Records Management, Inc., her interest in
importing derives from about six years she previously spent as a management consultant. In this capacity, she was frequently called on to advise
clients about importing clothing, furniture, and decorative items from
Indonesia. At the urging of family and friends, she decided to start her
own business. While Soemantoro handles the purchasing and administrative aspects of the business, Asche is responsible for marketing and
sales.

Damar International currently imports clothing, high-quality brassware, batik accessories, woodcarvings, and furnishings from Indonesia.
All of these items are handcrafted by village artisans working on a cottage industry basis. Damar International estimates that 30 percent of its
revenues from the sale of Indonesian imports are derived from clothing,
30 percent from batik accessories, 30 percent from woodcarvings, with
the remainder divided equally between brassware and furnishings. In addition, Damar markets in the eastern United States comparable Thai and
Philippine handcrafted items imported by a small California firm. This
firm in turn markets some of Damar's Indonesian imports on the West
Coast.

Source: This case was prepared by Michael R. Czinkota and Laura M. Gould.

Most of Damar's buyers are small shops and boutiques. Damar does not supply large department stores or retail chain outlets. By participating in gift shows, trade fairs, and handicraft exhibitions, the firm has expanded its customer base from the Washington area to many locations in the eastern United States.

In supplying small retail outlets with handcrafted Indonesian artifacts, Damar is pursuing a niche strategy. Although numerous importers market similar mass-produced manufactured Indonesian items chiefly to department stores and chain retailers, Damar knows of no competitors who supply handcrafted artifacts to boutiques. Small retailers find it difficult to purchase in sufficient volume to order directly from large-scale importers of mass-produced items. More important, it is difficult to organize Indonesian artisans to produce handcrafted goods in sufficient quantity to supply the needs of large retailers.

Damar's policy is to carry little if any inventory. Orders from buyers are transmitted by Soemantoro to her family in Indonesia, who contract production to artisans in the rural villages of Java and Bali. Within broad parameters, buyers can specify modifications of traditional Indonesian wares. Frequently, Soemantoro cooperates with her mother in creating designs that adapt traditional products to American tastes and to the specifications of U.S. buyers. Soemantoro is in contact with her family in Indonesia at least once a week by telex or phone in order to report new orders and check on the progress of previous orders. In addition, Soemantoro makes an annual visit to Indonesia to coordinate policy with her family and maintain contacts with artisans.

Damar also fills orders placed by Soemantoro's family in Indonesia. The firm therefore in essence acts as both an importer and an exporter despite its extremely limited personnel base. In this, as well as in its source of financing, Damar is highly atypical. The firm's great strength, which allows it to fill a virtually vacant market niche with extremely limited capital and labor resources, is clearly the Soemantoro family's nexus of personal connections. Without the use of intermediaries, this single bicultural family is capable of linking U.S. retailers and Indonesian village artisans and supplying products which, while unique and nonstandardized, are specifically oriented to the U.S. market.

Damar's principal weakness is its financing structure. There are obvious limits to the amount of money that can be borrowed from family and friends for such an enterprise. Working capital is necessary because the Indonesian artisans must be paid before full payment is received from U.S. buyers. Although a 10 percent deposit is required from buyers when an order is placed, the remaining 90 percent is not due until 30 days from the date of shipment F.O.B. Washington, D.C. However, the simplicity of Damar's financing structure has advantages: to date, it has been able to operate without letters of credit and their concomitant paperwork burdens.

One major importing problem to date has been the paperwork and red tape involved in U.S. customs and quota regulations. Satisfying these

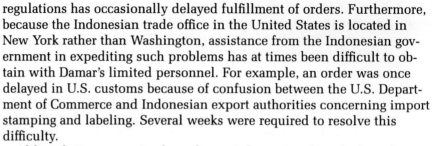

regulations has occasionally delayed fulfillment of orders. Furthermore, because the Indonesian trade office in the United States is located in New York rather than Washington, assistance from the Indonesian government in expediting such problems has at times been difficult to obtain with Damar's limited personnel. For example, an order was once delayed in U.S. customs because of confusion between the U.S. Department of Commerce and Indonesian export authorities concerning import stamping and labeling. Several weeks were required to resolve this difficulty.

Although Damar received regulatory information directly from the U.S. Department of Commerce when it began importing, its routine contact with the government is minimal because regulatory paperwork is contracted to customs brokers.

One of the most important lessons that the firm has learned is the critical role of participating in gift shows, trade fairs, and craft exhibitions. Soemantoro believes that the firm's greatest mistake to date was not attending a trade show in New York. In connecting with potential buyers, both through trade shows and "walk-in scouting" of boutiques, Damar has benefited greatly from helpful references from existing customers. Buyers have been particularly helpful in identifying trade fairs that would be useful for Damar to attend. Here too, the importance of Damar's cultivation of personal contacts is apparent.

Similarly, personal contacts offer Damar the possibility of diversifying into new import lines. Through a contact established by a friend in France, Soemantoro is currently planning to import handmade French porcelain and silk blouses.

Damar is worried about sustained expansion of its Indonesian handicraft import business because the firm does not currently have the resources to organize large-scale cottage industry production in Indonesia. Other major concerns are potential shipping delays and exchange rate fluctuations.

Questions for Discussion

1. Evaluate alternative expansion strategies for Damar International in the United States.
2. Discuss Damar's expansion alternatives in Indonesia and France and their implications for the U.S. market.
3. How can Damar protect itself against exchange rate fluctuations?
4. What are the likely effects of shipment delays on Damar? How can these effects be overcome?

Textilia

Textilia is a textile company based in Niteroi, state of Rio de Janeiro, Brazil. It is a closely held, family operated corporation. Founded in 1891, it is a traditional member of the Brazilian textile industry, producing raw cotton cloth for the domestic market. Raw and dyed fabrics are the principal products.

COMPANY BACKGROUND

The family's control of the company's stock has conservatively influenced the company's operations. Historically, the objective of the company has been to provide a stable and permanent source of income for the owners. As a result, corporate development has been affected by the immediate needs of the family versus entrepreneurship and risk taking. The company limited itself to manufacturing until recently, when important steps were taken toward implementing strategies to enter new markets.

The most significant decisions made in the history of the company were for the purchase and installation of new equipment for stamping fabric, which enabled the company to enter a new market selling printed fabrics. There were also improvements made in spinning and weaving production.

In spite of these advances, the firm still appears to be a technological throwback compared with other international firms, which affects its ability to compete in the world market. A labor-intensive operation, Textilia employs approximately 1,000 persons, most of whom are unskilled. About 15 employees have a middle-level technical background, and 6 are highly skilled technicians. In spite of the large number of workers, the firm's size compared with others in the sector would be considered medium, with less than one percent of the domestic market share.

The concern for a steady source of income resulted in a constant search for permanency and profits in the domestic marketplace. This approach did not change until the end of the 1970s, when significant strategy modifications were made. Until then, almost all of the production was absorbed by the domestic market, which had demonstrated rapid growth since the end of the 1960s. Export sales during this period were sporadic.

The change in the company's outlook was brought about by a series of factors affecting both domestic and international markets. On one hand,

Source: This case was prepared by Juan Luis Colaiácovo, Mario Eiris, and Antonio Assefh, staff members of the Centro Interamericano de Comercialización (CICOM), which is sponsored by the Organization of American States and the Fundação Getulio Vargas (Brasil). Reprinted with permission.

The names of the corporations in this text are intended to be fictitious even though the cases reflect situations that do occur in the world of business. Any similarity to any existing corporation is purely coincidental.

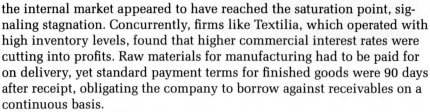

the internal market appeared to have reached the saturation point, signaling stagnation. Concurrently, firms like Textilia, which operated with high inventory levels, found that higher commercial interest rates were cutting into profits. Raw materials for manufacturing had to be paid for on delivery, yet standard payment terms for finished goods were 90 days after receipt, obligating the company to borrow against receivables on a continuous basis.

In response, the firm began a modernization program and hired managers and executive personnel charged with carrying it forward. The new phase was characterized by greater interest in rapid growth and a larger domestic market share.

In 1982 the company acquired control of Cia. Fábrica de Tecidos Doña Isabel, previously a state-owned enterprise, under a program of reintegration of public companies into the private sector. With this addition, the company further enhanced its product line. Textilia concentrated on producing printed fabric, whereas Cia. Doña Isabel produced solid, striped, and checked fabric.

Financial statement figures for 1981 and 1982, in cruzeiros, were as follows:

	1981	1982
Gross Sales	1,033,766,111.39	2,912,468,336.61
Net Sales	909,601,353.57	2,579,337,109.96
Cost of Goods Sold	563,126,485.45	1,886,489,336.61
Gross Profits	346,474,868.12	692,849,773.35
Operating Profits	81,175,222.11	343,740,918.84
Net Income	1,666,470.43	350,706,031.36

Output increased 29 percent in 1982, reaching a total production level of 8,345,088 meters. Then, in 1983, as a result of a domestic recession, production fell to 6,040,591 meters, or by 27.7 percent of the previous year's production. It should be noted that exports for the period increased.

The following is a breakdown of production:

Raw and Dyed Fabric	98.7%
Sheets	1.0
Bedspreads	0.3

The firm entered the international market with ready-made apparel, using its own fabric and a pool of subcontractor firms to produce the finished goods. In 1983 sales of these goods represented 30 percent of total corporate activity. Export sales were becoming more important to the company.

FIGURE 1 ▪ **Organization Chart**

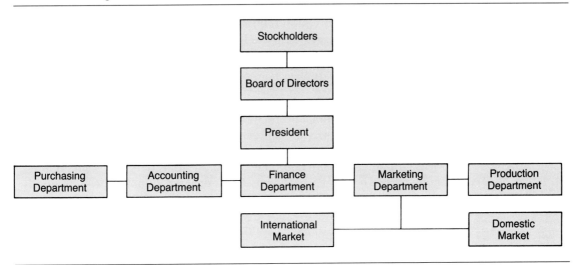

Sales for 1983 were as follows:

Raw Textiles	59%
Dyed Fabric	10
Sheets	0.8
Bedspreads	0.2
Ready-Made Apparel	30

Though raw textiles represented the bulk of sales, as they traditionally had, sales of dyed and finished goods increased. The company intends to support this trend, because profits on those sales are higher than on the sale of raw goods. To accomplish this, the company is trying to market directly to clothing manufacturers. Strides have been made in meeting the quality standards demanded by the market.

The administrative arm of the company is composed of a four-member board of directors. Three of the directors are family members representing 99 percent of corporate shares. The other director is the firm's legal counsel. The marketing department is the single most active department at present because of increased export sales. Nevertheless, the company does not have a modern infrastructure or its own international network. The organization chart is shown in Figure 1.

DEVELOPMENT OF THE EXPORT MARKET

Interest in exports began in the late 1960s, and by 1971 the company had begun delivering raw material to West Germany. Stimulus to enter the export market was provided by the government, which had embarked on

an export promotion program. Prior to that time, domestic demand had been strong. Further, domestic demand brought higher prices than the international market, which required competitive pricing, not to mention higher quality standards than the Brazilian marketplace. The company's management was largely unfamiliar with the export market, its characteristics, and requirements.

All of these factors had a negative effect on the development of export activity. Isolated export sales were realized mainly as a result of the efforts of the importers, and the company had no marketing strategy prepared for the international market. Nevertheless, as a consequence of the few export sales it made, the company gained some expertise in the area. For example, at first the company relied on intermediaries to handle the paperwork to export the goods. Later, it brought some of these functions in-house.

A noticeable change in company policy concerning exports took place after 1979. Three main factors influenced the change:

1. A foreseeable reduction in sales to the domestic market occurred because of a deep recession, leading to idle capacity and a corresponding increase in fixed costs.
2. Exports provided the company with improved cash flow, as payment terms were the standard letter of credit at sight. Traditional domestic market terms required financing on the company's part.
3. Government incentives were designed to help exporters improve the profitability of their export activities.

The need for new markets and financial liquidity together with the new policy favorable to exporters induced the company's management to consider international business as a viable, long-term activity. In an effort to enhance exports even further, the company adopted new initiatives oriented toward:

- Diversification of markets, with emphasis placed on countries without fixed import quotas (countries not traditional trading partners of Brazil)
- Advancement of products into markets where Brazilian producers were unable to fill export quotas
- Marketing directly to end-users, avoiding intermediaries and agents
- Increasing exports of finished goods, which proved more profitable than sales of raw materials
- Taking full advantage of government incentives for exporters

The United States is the company's biggest market. An intense, personalized marketing campaign was mounted to establish the company with U.S. importers. The resulting orders were of greater volume than Textilia could absorb alone. The company organized a group of subcontractor firms to produce the goods, using fabrics supplied by Textilia. In this way it was able to supply the volume required and increase its business in the United States.

The average export price is $0.82 per meter. As a wholesaler, the company is not concerned with pricing policy, inventory, marketing, or advertising. It will continue to respond to the importers' requirements as long as production capacity allows, negotiating price and delivery with payment by letter of credit at sight.

The principal concern of the company at present is rising production costs fueled by increased domestic cotton prices. World market textile prices have fallen as well (to 40 percent less than domestic prices) because of economic recession and increased competition, especially from Asiatic countries.

If these trends persist, only continued government incentives will permit the company to pursue its export markets. The firm has responded to the situation by implementing a policy to control costs. Studies are being made to further reduce costs and improve efficiency.

Questions for Discussion

1. How can export intermediaries remain indispensable?
2. Textilia liked the export market because of the resulting improved cash flow. Is that always the case for exporters?
3. Textilia entered the international market mainly because of governmental incentives. What is your view of such "market distortions"?
4. Should the government of Brazil increase its subsidies to Textilia in light of the greater competition from Asian countries?
5. In light of rising world protectionism in the textile field, what would you recommend to Textilia management? To the Brazilian government?

Pleamar S.A.

Pleamar S.A. is an Argentine corporation, located in Buenos Aires, dedicated to fishing and trading in seafood. Its processing plant and cold storage installations are in Necochea, a coastal town in the Buenos Aires province.

The firm was established in 1973 with capital contributions by a limited number of partners and financial support provided by banking institutions. The loans were part of government subsidies to the fishing industry and were administered by the national banking system. Pleamar S.A. was created with the objective of supplying overseas markets. Although the company began operations with a relatively small organization in terms of personnel and capital, it had reasonable access to credit. As a result, Pleamar could operate with a comfortable financial cushion, which made it easier to conclude initial international transactions.

The company began its operations by purchasing two fishing boats in Spain and registering the Pleamar trademark. First contacts with potential foreign buyers were initiated through a Spanish firm from which Pleamar had purchased the two fishing boats, the Pleamar S.A. trademark, and assignation of all business contacts. The first shipment, destined for Spain, took place in 1973. Whole fish was supplied and the operation was covered by a letter of credit. Pleamar contracted a third party to carry out all services connected with the export operation.

Consistent with the objectives of growth through exports, Pleamar initiated contacts with importers in other countries by sending sales personnel to potential buyers. Soon contracts were secured from Italy, Japan, Nigeria, and Brazil. As new contracts were being closed, the company realized the difficulties arising from the lack of a cold storage facility. The unavailability of such a plant proved to be a major hindrance to the logistics operation and increased the processing costs. Despite these difficulties, exports proved to be considerably more profitable than sales to the domestic market. Pleamar continued to improve its international competitiveness by focusing on three dimensions:

1. Quality. Strict quality control of the product was maintained, because even minor negligence could be highly detrimental to the company's growth.
2. Sales effort. An aggressive sales strategy was adopted that called for frequent personal visits to foreign clients.

Source: This case was written by Juan Luis Colaiácovo, Mario Eiris, and Antonio Assefh, staff members of the Centro Interamericano de Comercialización (CICOM), which is sponsored by the Organization of American States and the Fundação Getulio Vargas (Brasil). Reprinted with permission.

The names of the corporations in this text are intended to be fictitious even though the cases reflect situations that do occur in the world of business. Any similarity to any existing corporation is purely coincidental.

3. Financial support. The company concentrated on obtaining sufficient
    financing to expand its production and exports.

Pleamar's initial strategy, which remains unchanged, was primarily to
supply foreign markets. Only surplus quantities unfit for export were to
be sold locally. The main reasons for this strategy were the higher profits
and the greater business volume available in international markets.

With a desire for rapid growth, the company developed an aggressive
policy of penetrating international markets. Pleamar's expansion began
in 1977 with increased investments and improvements in its fishing
fleet. Pleamar acquired cold storage facilities in the port of Quequen of
Necochea with a capacity of 3,000 tons of warehousing space. The firm
currently owns six boats, one of them a highly sophisticated mothership.

A heavy flood in 1978 completely destroyed the floor of the warehouse
and the entire inventory was lost. Moreover, one of Pleamar's boats
equipped with processing equipment was sunk and all of the products
on the boat were lost. Because insurance covered only part of these
losses, this was a rather difficult time for the firm.

In 1979, Pleamar decided to forge closer contacts with importers in an
effort to improve business in nontraditional markets. This policy brought
good results in Nigeria, where the volume of business was substantially
increased and a long-term contract was signed. In Brazil, the company
became part of the bilateral trade agreement with Argentina. Major promotional efforts were also launched. These consisted of direct calls on
importers as well as frequent correspondence and telephone calls. In
addition, most international food fairs were visited. In 1982, Pleamar
participated for the first time with an exhibit in an international fair held
in the Canary Islands. Literature describing the company was printed
and distributed, and advertisements were inserted in trade publications.

In 1980, Pleamar purchased an idle cold storage plant in Necochea and
installed modern equipment. By 1981 that plant was used to prepare fish
for export. Until that time the company had used the boats to store and
process the fish. In 1983, the company added a new plant for filleted
fish. By then, the total investment in capital goods (plants, equipment,
machinery, boats, etc.) was in excess of U.S. $10,000,000, and Pleamar
had become the largest exporter of fish from Argentina.

Management of Pleamar is centralized. Decisions are made by the
board of directors, who are the main shareholders. Although some delegation of authority takes place in the production area, this is not the case
with marketing. The president has absolute control and is in charge of
contact with the clients. He conducts the negotiations for all international sales, which requires him to travel extensively (200 days each
year).

The organizational structure of the company has not kept pace with
the company's rapid growth. (See Figure 1 for an overview of the organizational structure.) As a result, to introduce a modern system of admin-

FIGURE 1 ▪ **Organizational Structure**

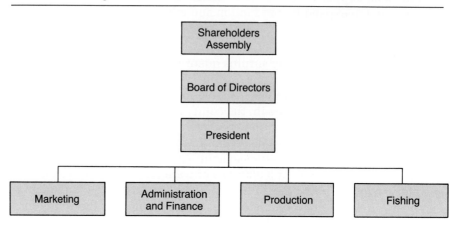

istration would be very difficult. Yet decisions are made quickly because of the standards of productivity imposed by the president.

Because local market operations have little significance, there is no structure to cover the domestic market. Even though, as a result of an agreement with the mayor of Buenos Aires, the company has been supplying retailers in the Buenos Aires fish market since 1985, the volume of domestic business is insignificant.

Pleamar employs about 450 persons. Forty hold administrative positions, and 50 are technicians, which indicates the high degree of technology used by Pleamar. Of the balance, 240 employees work on the boats, and 120 work in production on land. Pleamar uses two boats equipped with an installed freezing capacity of 1,000 tons and crews of 50 persons, and four vessels equipped with cooling capacity of 500 tons with crews of 35.

The most outstanding skill is the company's experience in foreign markets. Over the years, management has learned to deal with international operations and has developed an effective international sales organization. The requirements of the international market and the use of high-tech fishing methods have contributed to improved product quality. Although technological advances implemented thus far have not reached the highest levels available internationally, Pleamar can boast of substantial international competitiveness. In order to maintain its rapid growth, the company frequently innovates the processing of seafood intended for the overseas markets. Creative changes in the packing and freezing of fish and shellfish on board have made it possible to increase sales in foreign markets.

Seventy percent of the company's present production is accounted for by fish. The remaining 30 percent is shellfish. The main products are codfish, porgies, catfish, lobster, shrimp, and squid. Most of Pleamar's

TABLE 1 ▪ **Pleamar's Exports, 1973–1983**

Year	Volume Exported (in tons)
1973	13,000
1974	16,000
1975	16,000
1976	16,000
1977	22,000
1978	22,000
1979	22,000
1980	29,000
1981	39,893
1982	33,030
1983	36,281

TABLE 2 ▪ **Exports by Country of Destination: Values in U.S. Dollars**

Country	1981 Tons	1981 Value (in thousands)	1982 Tons	1982 Value (in thousands)	1983 Tons	1983 Value (in thousands)
Cameroon	722	$ 375	650	$ 330	600	$ 305
Republic of Congo	605	311	590	300	605	306
Nigeria	27,800	14,840	20,000	10,500	20,000	10,500
South Africa	67	66	48	47	50	49
Bolivia	2	4	—	—	—	—
Brazil	170	106	300	185	600	374
United States	30	43	—	—	—	—
Saudi Arabia	185	240	180	245	180	250
Cyprus	89	111	20	22	—	—
Taiwan	15	21	—	—	30	42
Israel	29	15	28	15	28	15
Japan	7,315	9,900	9,000	12,000	12,000	16,000
Jordan	219	198	200	180	210	190
Kuwait	16	20	6	8	—	—
Lebanon	10	12	—	—	—	—
West Germany	60	87	60	88	60	89
Denmark	20	24	—	—	—	—
Spain	26	15	28	17	30	18
France	12	15	15	20	18	25
Greece	392	901	400	940	420	960
Italy	1,472	1,606	1,480	1,650	1,450	1,600
The Netherlands	39	46	10	12	—	—
Portugal	46	74	15	25	—	—
United Kingdom	552	683	—	—	—	—
Total	39,893	$29,713	33,030	$26,584	36,281	$30,723

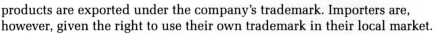

products are exported under the company's trademark. Importers are, however, given the right to use their own trademark in their local market.

Its continuous presence in international markets has enabled Pleamar to experiment with products and production, resulting in an improved production process and better quality. The company has acquired a good knowledge of markets and marketing channels. Market surveys are carried out from time to time and all markets are visited two or three times a year. The firm's pace is active, fast, and professional.

Currently, 24 countries are being supplied, with Nigeria, Japan, and Italy the most important ones. The best results of the firm's penetration policy were achieved in Africa, where Pleamar is now the largest Argentine fish and shellfish importer. Tables 1 and 2 provide an overview of the international operations.

The company's international strategy for the next few years has two major objectives: (1) to obtain deeper market penetration in developing countries (especially in the Middle East and Africa) where buyers' requirements are less strict and (2) to increase exports of products with higher aggregate value.

Questions for Discussion

1. Evaluate Pleamar's dependence on exports.
2. What changes in international marketing strategy would you recommend to Pleamar's management?
3. Discuss the effect of exchange rate changes and local inflation on Pleamar.
4. Design an organizational structure for Pleamar.

Joemarin Oy

Finland's first customers in the sailboat business are generally believed to have been the Vikings. More recently ships and boats were exported as part payment for World War II reparations. This long tradition in building sailboats is due, no doubt, to Finland's proximity to the sea, long coastline, and 60,000 lakes. Among luxury sailing yachts, the Swan boats of Nautor Oy and the Finnsailers of Fiskars Oy are internationally known and admired. There are, however, over one hundred other boat builders in Finland that turn out 10,000 sailing yachts yearly.

Although most of the Finnish sailboat companies are situated on the coast, for obvious reasons, Joemarin Oy is located in the town of Joensuu, roughly 450 kilometers northeast of Helsinki. Joemarin was founded in the town that lends part of its name to the company because of the efforts of Kehitysaluerahasto, which is the Development Area Foundation of the Finnish government. Kehitysaluerahasto provided a loan of four million Finnish marks to Joemarin, a privately owned company, to start its operations in the Joensuu area because of the town's high rate of unemployment.

The present product line consists of three types of fiberglass sailboats. The Joemarin 17 is a coastal sailing yacht with a new design approach. (See Figure 1.) This approach is to provide a craft that enables a family to make weekend and holiday cruises in coastal waters and also offers exciting sailing. The sailboat is very fast. The Finnish Yacht Racing Association stated in its test in which the Joemarin 17 was judged to be the best in her class: "She is delicate, lively, spacious, and easy to steer. She is well balanced and has a high-quality interior. She is especially fast on the beat and lively to handle in a free wind."

The Joemarin 17, a small day cruiser with berths for two adults and two children, has a sail area of 130 square feet, weighs one-half ton, and has an overall length of a little over 17 feet. The hull is made of glass-reinforced plastic (GRP), and the mast and boom are made of aluminum. The boat has a drop keel that is useful when negotiating shallow anchorages or when lifting the boat on a trailer for transportation. The layout of the boat is shown in Figure 2.

The Joemarin 34 is a relatively large motor sailer that sleeps seven people in three separate compartments. The main saloon contains an adjustable dining table, a complete galley, and a navigator's compartment. The main saloon is separated from the fore cabin by a folding door. The aft cabin, which is entered by a separate companionway, contains a double berth, wardrobe, wash basin, and lockers. The toilet and shower are situated between the fore cabin and the main saloon. The boat has a sail area of 530 square feet, weighs about five tons, and has an overall

Source: This case was prepared by James H. Sood of the American University. Reprinted with permission.

FIGURE 1 ▪ **Joemarin 17: Ideal for Family Cruising as Well as Exciting Racing**

length of 33 feet 9 inches. A significant feature of the craft is that she is equipped with a 47-horsepower diesel engine.

The Joemarin 34 has the same design approach as the 17. She is well appointed, with sufficient space for seven people to live comfortably. An important feature is that the three separate living compartments allow for considerable privacy. In addition, however, the modern hull is quite sleek, making her an excellent sailing yacht.

The Joemarin 36 was designed for a different purpose. While the 17 and 34 are oriented toward a family approach to sailing—combining the features of safety and comfortable accommodations with good sailing ability—the 36 is first and foremost a sailing craft. It does have two berths, a small galley, and toilet facilities, but the emphasis is on sailing and racing rather than comfort. The boat has a sail area of 420 square feet, weighs a little less than four tons, and has an overall length of 35 feet 10 inches. The boat is also equipped with a small (7 horsepower) diesel engine for emergency power situations. The Joemarin 36 is a traditional Swedish design and, therefore, is directed almost solely to the Swedish market.

The company was established in order to manufacture sailboats for export. The Finnish sailboat market is small because of the short sailing season. Nevertheless, the company has been successful in marketing the 17 in Finland, although this was difficult in the beginning because of the lack of boat dealers. To circumvent this problem, Joemarin persuaded a

FIGURE 2 ▪ **The Layout of the Joemarin 17**

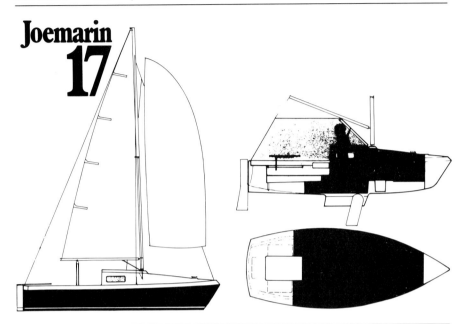

number of new car dealers throughout the country to handle the Joemarin 17 on an agency basis. This involved the company's providing one boat to each car dealer, who placed it in the showroom. The dealer then marketed the sailboats for a 15 percent sales commission.

While many people scoffed at this idea, the system produced reasonable sales and also made the company known throughout Finland. This contributed to an arrangement with one of the largest cooperative wholesale–retail operations in Finland. Like most cooperatives, this organization began with agricultural products; however, the product range of the company now includes virtually every conceivable consumer product. The present contract states that the cooperative will purchase 80 Joemarin 17 boats per year for the next three years.

The Swedish market is served by a selling agent, although this representative has not been particularly effective. Because Sweden is also the home of many sailboat builders, the company has tried to market only the 36 in that country. In Denmark, France, Holland, West Germany, and the United Kingdom, Joemarin has marketed the 34 through importers. These importers operate marinas in addition to new sailboat dealerships. They purchase the boats from Joemarin for their own accounts and mark up the price by about 20 percent. In return for exclusive marketing rights in their respective countries, they agree to purchase a minimum number (usually three or four) of the 34 design per year. None of these importers is interested in marketing the 17 or the 36; the shipping cost for the 17 is

too high compared to the value of the boat, and there is little customer interest in the 36.

Joemarin is planning to introduce a new sailboat. Whereas the present products were designed by people in the company who were relatively unknown (to the customers), the hull of the new sailboat has been designed by an internationally known boat designer. The cost of these design services was a $10,000 initial fee plus a $1,200 royalty fee to be paid for each boat produced. The new sailboat, the Joemarin 29, has an interior quite similar to that of the Joemarin 34. This is not unexpected because the same Joemarin people designed the interiors and decks of both sailboats.

The new boat is a motor sailer that sleeps six people in three separate compartments, is 28 feet 9 inches long, weighs four tons, has a joined cabin space and a separate aft cabin, small galley, toilet and shower facilities, and a 12-horsepower diesel engine. Because of a new construction technique that greatly reduces the amount of fiberglass required, the variable costs to construct the boat are only 60 percent of the costs for the 34. With a preliminary selling price of 195,000 Finnish marks, the Joemarin 29 is receiving favorable attention and the company is concerned that sales may have an adverse effect on sales of the 34.

The company categorizes the marketing expenses as fixed costs because allocating these expenses to specific products is difficult. The major element of the program is participation in international boat shows in London, Paris, Hamburg, Amsterdam, Copenhagen, and Helsinki. The initial purpose of participating in these shows was to locate suitable importers in the target markets; however, this effort is maintained in order to support the marketing programs of the importers. The importers are also supported by advertising in the leading yachting magazines in the national markets. Joemarin's personal selling effort consists primarily of servicing the importers and agents and staffing the exhibitions at the boat shows. Most of the sales promotion costs are the result of the elaborate sales brochures that the company has developed for each boat. These brochures are printed in four colors on three folded pages of high-quality paper. The costs are greatly increased, however, by having to print a relatively small number of each brochure in Finnish, French, English, German, and Swedish. The brochures are provided to the agents and importers and are used at the boat shows.

The company is in the process of preparing its production and marketing plan for the coming year in order to arrange financing. The president is strongly committed to the continued growth of the company, and the market indications suggest that there is a reasonably strong demand for the 17 in Finland and for the 34 in most of the other national markets. The sales results of the previous and present years are shown in Table 1; the profit statement for the present year is shown in Table 2.

The main problem in developing the plan for next year is determining the price for each sailboat in each market. In previous years Joemarin had established its prices in Finnish marks, on an ex-factory basis. Man-

TABLE 1 ▪ **Joemarin Sales**

		Last Year			Present Year	
	No.	Average Price[a]	Revenue	No.	Average Price[a]	Revenue
J/M-17	200	27,000	5,400,000	240	29,700	7,128,000
J/M-29	—	—	—	—	—	—
J/M-34	30	324,000	9,720,000	36	356,000	12,830,400
J/M-36	4	189,000	756,000	5	207,900	1,039,500
			15,876,000			20,997,900

[a] All prices are manufacturer's prices; prices and revenues are in Finnish marks; 1.00 Finnmark = U.S. $0.185.

TABLE 2 ▪ **Joemarin Profit Statement for Present Year**

	In Finnmarks	As a Percentage of Sales
Sales Revenue	20,790,000[a]	
Variable Costs (direct labor and materials)	13,510,000	65.0%
Fixed Costs:		
Production (building expense, production management salaries)	945,000	4.5
Product Design Costs (salaries, prototypes, testing, consultants)	1,323,000	6.4
Administration Costs (salaries, insurance, office expenses)	648,000	3.1
Marketing Costs (salaries, advertising, boat shows, sales promotion, travel expenses)	2,284,000	11.0
Total Fixed Costs	5,200,000	25.0
Profit before Taxes	2,080,000	10.0

[a] All prices are manufacturer's prices; prices and revenues are in Finnish marks; 1.00 Finnmark = U.S. $0.185.

agement has become convinced, however, that it must change the terms of its prices in order to meet competition in the foreign markets. Thus, the company has decided to offer C.I.F. prices to its foreign customers in the currency of the foreign country. The use of truck ferries between Finland and Sweden, Denmark, and Germany is expected to make this pricing approach more competitive.

Joemarin would also like to assure its agents and importers that the prices will remain in effect for the entire year, but the financial manager is concerned about the possible volatility of exchange rates because of the varying rates of inflation in the market countries. The present exchange rates, the expected inflation rates in the market countries, and the

TABLE 3 ▪ **Shipping Costs for Joemarin 36 to Sweden and Joemarin 29 and 34 to Other Countries**

Country	Present Exchange Rates in Finnish Marks	Expected Inflation Rates	Estimated Freight and Insurance Costs Per Boat
Denmark	Danish Kroner = 0.628	12%	13,500 Fmks.
France	French Franc = 0.778	10	19,000 Fmks.
Holland	Dutch Guilder = 2.015	9	17,000 Fmks.
Sweden	Swedish Kroner = 0.725	12	10,000 Fmks.
United Kingdom	English Pound = 8.308	14	22,000 Fmks.
West Germany	German Mark = 2.204	7	17,000 Fmks.
Finland	—	12	—

estimated costs to ship the Joemarin 36 to Stockholm and the Joemarin 29 and 34 to the other foreign marinas are shown in Table 3.

A second difficulty in pricing the product line of Joemarin is to establish a price for the 29 that will reflect the value of the boat, but will not reduce the sales of the 34. There are three schools of thought concerning the pricing of motor sailers. The predominant theory is that price is a function of the overall length of the sailboat. A number of people, however, believe that the overall weight of the craft is a more accurate basis. The third opinion argues that price is a function of the special features and equipment. Figure 3, which was prepared by a Swiss market research firm, shows the relationship between present retail prices and the length of new motor sailers in the West European market.

Questions for Discussion

1. Determine the optimum manufacturer's selling prices in the Finnish market for the four Joemarin sailboats for the coming year.

2. Determine the C.I.F. prices for the Joemarin 36 to the final customer in Sweden for the coming year. The agent's commission is 15 percent of the final selling price, and the final selling price should be in Swedish kroner.

3. Recommend a course of action for the company to take in regard to the Joemarin 36.

4. Determine the C.I.F. prices, in the foreign currencies, for the Joemarin 29 and 34 to the importers in Denmark, France, Holland, the United Kingdom, and West Germany for the coming year.

5. Develop a production and marketing plan for Joemarin for the coming year. What steps can the company take to ensure that the plan is in line with the demand for its products in its foreign markets?

FIGURE 3 ▪ **Retail Price in the European Market of Sailing Yachts as a Function of Overall Length**

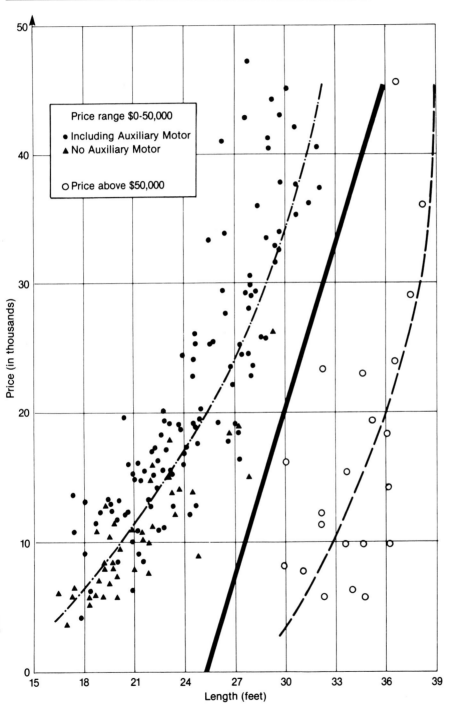

Note: All yachts to the right of the bold dividing line are priced above $50,000.

Lakewood Forest Products

Since the 1970s the United States has had a merchandise trade deficit with the rest of the world. Up to 1982, this deficit mattered little because it was relatively small. As of 1983, however, the trade deficit increased rapidly and became, due to its size and future implications, an issue of major national concern. Suddenly, trade moved to the forefront of national debate. Concurrently, a debate ensued on the issue of the international competitiveness of U.S. firms. The onerous question here was whether U.S. firms could and would achieve sufficient improvements in areas such as productivity, quality, and price to remain long-term successful international marketing players.

The U.S.–Japanese trade relation took on particular significance, because it was between those two countries that the largest bilateral trade deficit existed. In spite of trade negotiations, market-opening measures, trade legislation, and other governmental efforts, it was clear that the impetus for a reversal of the deficit through more U.S. exports to Japan had to come from the private sector. Therefore, the activities of any U.S. firm that appeared successful in penetrating the Japanese market were widely hailed. One company whose effort to market in Japan aroused particular interest was Lakewood Forest Products, in Hibbing, Minnesota.

COMPANY BACKGROUND

In 1983, Ian J. Ward was an export merchant in difficulty. Throughout the 1970s his company, Ward, Bedas Canadian Ltd., had successfully sold Canadian lumber and salmon to countries in the Persian Gulf. Over time, the company had opened four offices worldwide. However, when the Iran–Iraq war erupted, most of Ward's long-term trading relationships disappeared within a matter of months. In addition, the international lumber market began to collapse. As a result, Ward, Bedas Canadian Ltd. went into a survivalist mode and sent employees all over the world to look for new markets and business opportunities. Late that year, the company received an interesting order. A firm in Korea urgently needed to purchase lumber for the production of chopsticks.

Source: This case was written by Michael R. Czinkota based on the following sources: Mark Clayton, "Minnesota Chopstick Maker Finds Japanese Eager to Import His Quality Wari-bashi," *The Christian Science Monitor*, October 16, 1987, 11; Roger Worthington, "Improbable Chopstick Capital of the World," *Chicago Tribune*, June 5, 1988, 39; Mark Gill, "The Great American Chopstick Master," *American Way*, August 1, 1987, 34, 78–79; and personal interview with Ian J. Ward, president, Lakewood Forest Products.

Learning about the Chopstick Market

In discussing the wood deal with the Koreans, Ward learned that in order to produce good chopsticks more than 60 percent of the wood fiber would be wasted. Given the high transportation cost involved, the large degree of wasted materials, and his need for new business, Ward decided to explore the Korean and Japanese chopstick industry in more detail.

He quickly determined that chopstick making in the Far East is a fragmented industry, working with old technology and suffering from a lack of natural resources. In Asia, chopsticks are produced in very small quantities, often by family organizations. Even the largest of the 450 chopstick factories in Japan turns out only 5,000,000 chopsticks a month. This compares to an overall market size of 130 million pairs of disposable chopsticks a day. In addition, chopsticks represent a growing market. With increased wealth in Asia, people eat out more often and therefore have a greater demand for disposable chopsticks. The fear of communicable diseases has greatly reduced the utilization of reusable chopsticks. Renewable plastic chopsticks have been attacked by many groups as too new fangled and as causing future ecological problems.

From his research, Ward concluded that a competitive niche existed in the world chopstick market. He believed that, if he could use low-cost raw materials and assure that the labor cost component would remain small, he could successfully compete in the world market.

The Founding of Lakewood Forest Products

In exploring opportunities afforded by the newly identified international marketing niche for chopsticks, Ward set four criteria for plant location:

1. Access to suitable raw materials
2. Proximity of other wood product users who could make use of the 60 percent waste for their production purposes
3. Proximity to a port that would facilitate shipment to the Far East
4. Availability of labor

In addition, Ward was aware of the importance of product quality. Because people use chopsticks on a daily basis and are accustomed to products that are visually inspected one by one, he would have to live up to high quality expectations in order to compete successfully. Chopsticks could not be bowed or misshapen, have blemishes in the wood, or splinter.

In order to implement his plan, Ward needed financing. Private lenders were skeptical and slow to provide funds. This skepticism resulted from the unusual direction of Ward's proposal. Far Eastern companies have generally held the cost advantage in a variety of industries, especially those as labor-intensive as chopstick manufacturing. U.S. companies rarely have an advantage in producing low-cost items. Further, only a very small domestic market exists for chopsticks.

However, Ward found that the state of Minnesota was willing to participate in his new venture. Since the decline of the mining industry, regional unemployment had been rising rapidly in the state. In 1983, unemployment in Minnesota's Iron Range peaked at 22 percent. Therefore, state and local officials were anxious to attract new industries that would be independent of mining activities. They were excited about Ward's plans, which called for the creation of over 100 new jobs within a year.

Hibbing, Minnesota, turned out to be an ideal location for Ward's project. The area had an abundance of supply of aspen wood, which, because it grows in clay soil, tends to be unmarred. In addition, Hibbing boasted an excellent labor pool, and both the city and the state were willing to make loans totaling $500,000. Further, the Iron Range Resources Rehabilitation Board was willing to sell $3.4 million in industrial revenue bonds for the project. Together with jobs and training wage subsidies, enterprise zone credits, and tax increment financing benefits, the initial public support of the project added up to about 30 percent of its start-up costs. The potential benefit of the new venture to the region was quite clear. When Lakewood Forest Products advertised its first 30 jobs, more than 3,000 people showed up to apply.

THE PRODUCTION AND SALE OF CHOPSTICKS

Ward insisted that in order to truly penetrate the international market, he would need to keep his labor cost low. As a result, he decided to automate as much of the production as possible. However, no equipment was readily available to produce chopsticks, because no one had automated the process before.

After much searching, Ward identified a European equipment manufacturer who produced machinery for making popsicle sticks. He purchased equipment from this Danish firm in order to better carry out the sorting and finishing processes. However, because aspen wood was quite different from the wood the machine was designed for, as was the final product, substantial design adjustments had to be made. Sophisticated equipment was also purchased to strip the bark from the wood and peel it into long thin sheets. Finally, a computer vision system was acquired to detect defects in the chopsticks. This system rejected over 20 percent of the production, and yet some of the chopsticks that passed inspection were splintering. However, Ward firmly believed that further fine-tuning of the equipment and training of the new work force would gradually take care of the problem.

Given this fully automated process, Lakewood Forest Products was able to develop capacity for up to 7,000,000 chopsticks a day. With a unit manufacturing cost of $0.03 and an anticipated unit selling price of $0.057, Ward expected to earn a pretax profit of $4.7 million in 1988.

Due to intense marketing efforts in Japan and the fact that Japanese customers were struggling to obtain sufficient supplies of disposable chopsticks, Ward was able to presell the first five years of production quite quickly. By late 1987, Lakewood Forest Products was ready to enter the international market. With an ample supply of raw materials and an almost totally automated plant, Lakewood was positioned as the world's largest and least labor-intensive manufacturer of chopsticks. The first shipment of six containers with a load of 12,000,000 pairs of chopsticks to Japan was made in October 1987.

Questions for Discussion

1. What are the future implications of continuing large U.S. trade deficits?

2. What are the important variables for the international marketing success of chopsticks?

3. Rank in order the variables in question 2 according to the priority you believe they have for the foreign customers.

4. Why haven't Japanese firms thought of automating the chopstick production process?

5. How long will Lakewood Forest Products be able to maintain its competitive advantage?

PART THREE

Advanced International Marketing Activities

THE CORE marketing concerns of the beginning internationalist and the multinational corporation are the same. Yet multinational firms face challenges and opportunities that are different from those encountered by smaller firms. These firms are able to expend more resources on international marketing efforts, in terms of both financial and personnel considerations, than are small and medium-sized firms. In addition, their perspective can be more globally oriented. Multinational corporations also have more impact on individuals, economies, and governments, and therefore are much more subject to public scrutiny and need to be more concerned about the repercussions of their activities. Yet their very size often enables them to be more influential in setting international marketing rules.

CHAPTER 14

Foreign Direct Investment and Management Contracts

THE INTERNATIONAL MARKETPLACE

__The Transnational Corporation__   The traditional multinational corporation, invented in the middle years of the 19th century by U.S. and German industrialists, consists of a parent company with foreign "daughters." The parent company designs and manufactures for its domestic market. The daughters do not design at all. They produce locally whatever products the parent company designs and sell them in their own markets.

The distinction between parent and daughter is increasingly blurring. In the transnational company, design can be done anywhere within the system. Major pharmaceutical companies now have research laboratories in five or six countries: they do their research wherever there are research scientists. They produce wherever the economies of manufacturing dictate. IBM produces personal computers for all of Europe in two locations and disc drives in one. A major pharmaceutical manufacturer makes and sells prescription drugs in 164 countries, but all of its fermentation work is done in one plant in Ireland.

The treasurer of the transnational company manages money for all members of the group centrally, rather than having the British company manage money in London, the U.S. company manage money in New York, and so on. Each unit, including the parent company, has its own local management. Top management is transnational and so are the company's business plans, strategies, and decisions.

Source: Peter F. Drucker, "The New World according to Drucker," *Business Month,* May 1989, 48–59.

Global market expansion alternatives available primarily to the multinational firm are described in this chapter. The section on foreign direct investment strategies focuses on the rationale for such investment and on investment alternatives such as full ownership, joint ventures, and strategic alliances. The section on management contract activities focuses on the benefits and drawbacks of such arrangements.

FOREIGN DIRECT INVESTMENT

Foreign direct investment represents one component of the international investment flow. The other component is **portfolio investment,** which is the purchase of stocks and bonds internationally. Portfolio investment is a primary concern to the international financial community. The international marketer, on the other hand, makes foreign **direct investments** to create or expand a permanent interest in an enterprise. They imply a degree of control over the enterprise.[1]

This type of investment, although extremely important, has only recently received significant government attention. In 1974, for example, no comprehensive list was available of foreign firms investing in the United States, no one knew which firms were foreign owned, and major shortcomings existed in the foreign direct investment data that was available.[2] Because the U.S. data gathering system is one of the more sophisticated ones internationally, very likely even less information about foreign direct investment is available in other countries.

Concerted but old data gathering and estimation efforts by organizations such as the OECD and the International Monetary Fund (IMF) indicate that foreign direct investments have grown tremendously. The total global value of such investment, which in 1967 was estimated to be $105 billion, had climbed to an estimated $596 billion by the end of 1984.[3] Among foreign investors U.S. firms are major players due to major investments in the developed world and in some developing countries. In 1988, foreign direct investment by U.S. firms amounted to $327 billion. However, major foreign direct investment activity has also been carried out by firms from other countries, many of which decided to invest in the United States. In 1988, direct investment by foreign firms in the United States totaled approximately $329 billion, up from a level of $6.9 billion in 1960.[4] Foreign direct investment has clearly become a major avenue for foreign market entry and expansion.

Reasons for Foreign Direct Investment

Firms expand internationally for a wide variety of reasons. Table 14.1 provides an overview of the major determinants of foreign direct investment.

[1] Frank G. Vukmanic, Michael R. Czinkota, and David A. Ricks, "National and International Data Problems and Solutions in the Empirical Analysis of Intraindustry Direct Foreign Investment," in *Multinationals as Mutual Invaders: Intraindustry Direct Foreign Investment,* ed. A. Erdilek (Beckenham, Kent, England: Croom Helm Ltd., 1985), 160–184.

[2] Jeffrey Arpan and David A. Ricks, "Foreign Direct Investments in the U.S. and Some Attendant Research Problems," *Journal of International Business Studies* 5 (Spring 1974): 1–7.

[3] Harvey A. Poniachek, *Direct Foreign Investment in the United States* (Lexington, Mass.: D.C. Heath, 1986), 2.

[4] U.S. Department of Commerce, Bureau of Economic Analysis, *Survey of Current Business,* June 1989.

TABLE 14.1 ▪ **Major Determinants of Direct Foreign Investment**

MARKETING FACTORS

1. Size of market
2. Market growth
3. Desire to maintain share of market
4. Desire to advance exports of parent company
5. Need to maintain close customer contact
6. Dissatisfaction with existing market arrangements
7. Export base

TRADE RESTRICTIONS

1. Barriers to trade
2. Preference of local customers for local products

COST FACTORS

1. Desire to be near source of supply
2. Availability of labor
3. Availability of raw materials
4. Availability of capital/technology
5. Lower labor costs
6. Lower production costs other than labor
7. Lower transport costs
8. Financial (and other) inducements by government
9. More favorable cost levels

INVESTMENT CLIMATE

1. General attitude toward foreign investment
2. Political stability
3. Limitation on ownership
4. Currency exchange regulations
5. Stability of foreign exchange
6. Tax structure
7. Familiarity with country

GENERAL

1. Expected higher profits
2. Other

Source: *International Investment and Multinational Enterprises* (Paris: Organization for Economic Cooperation and Development, 1983), 41.

The Desire for Growth and Control Marketing factors and the corporate desire for growth and control are a major cause for the increase in foreign direct investment. This is understandable in view of John Kenneth Galbraith's postulation that "growth means greater responsibilities and more pay for those who contribute to it."[5] Even the huge U.S. market presents limitations to growth. Some have argued that future competitiveness demands require firms to operate simultaneously in the "triad" of the United States, Western Europe, and Japan.[6] Corporations therefore need to seek

[5] John Kenneth Galbraith, *A Life in Our Times* (Boston: Houghton, Mifflin, 1981), 518.

[6] Kenichi I. Ohmae, *Triad Power: The Coming Shape of Global Competition* (New York: The Free Press, 1985).

wider market access in order to maintain and increase their sales. This objective can be achieved most quickly through the acquisition of foreign firms. Through such expansion, the corporation also gains ownership advantages consisting of political know-how and expertise. Examples are better intelligence about political actors and opportunities, readier access to political opinion makers and decision makers, and superior skills for influencing the latter.[7]

Another incentive is that foreign direct investment permits corporations to circumvent current barriers to trade and operate abroad as a domestic firm, unaffected by duties, tariffs, or other import restrictions. The current enormous amount of U.S. investment in Canada would not have been attracted, had it not been for the barriers to trade created by the Canadian government to support domestic industry.

In addition to government-erected barriers, restrictions may be imposed by customers through their insistence on domestic goods and services, either as a result of nationalistic tendencies or as a function of cultural differences. Further, local buyers may wish to buy from sources that they perceive to be reliable in their supply, which means buying from local producers. For some products, country-of-origin effects may force a firm to establish a plant in a country that has a built-in positive stereotype for production location and product quality.[8]

Still another incentive is the cost factor, with corporations attempting to obtain low-cost resources and ensure their sources of supply. Finally, once the decision is made to invest internationally, the investment climate plays a major role. Corporations will seek to invest in those geographic areas where their investment is most protected and has the best chance to flourish.

These determinants will have varying impacts on the foreign direct investment decision, depending on the characteristics of the firm and its management, on its objectives, and on external conditions. Firms have been categorized as resource seekers, market seekers, and efficiency seekers.[9] **Resource seekers** search for either natural resources or human resources. Natural resources typically are based on mineral, agricultural, or oceanographic advantages and result in firms locating in areas where these resources are available. Firms are therefore tied in their availability of choices to the availability of the natural resources sought. Companies seeking human resources are likely to base their location decision on the availability of low-cost labor that matches their needs in terms of output quality. Alternatively, companies may select an area because of the availability of highly skilled labor. If natural resources are not involved, the location decision

[7]Jean J. Boddewyn, "Political Aspects of MNE Theory," *Journal of International Business Studies* 19 (Fall 1988): 341–363.

[8]Philip D. White and Edward W. Cundiff, "Assessing the Quality of Industrial Products," *Journal of Marketing* 42 (January 1978): 80–86.

[9]Jack N. Behrman, "Transnational Corporations in the New International Economic Order," *Journal of International Business Studies* 12 (Spring–Summer 1981): 29–42.

can be altered over time if the labor advantage changes. When the differential between labor costs in different locales becomes substantial, a corporation, in continuing to seek to improve its human resource access, may relocate to take advantage of the "better" resources.

Corporations primarily in search of better opportunities to enter and expand within markets are **market seekers.** Particularly when markets are closed or access is restricted, corporations have a major incentive to locate in them. **Efficiency seekers** attempt to obtain the most economic sources of production. They frequently have affiliates in various markets that are highly specialized in product lines or components and who exchange their production in order to maximize the benefits to the corporation.

Derived Demand   A second major cause for the increase in foreign direct investment is the result of **derived demand.** Often, as large multinational firms move abroad, they are quite interested in maintaining their established business relationships with other firms. Therefore, they frequently encourage their suppliers to follow them and continue to supply them from a foreign location. For example, many Japanese automakers have urged their suppliers in Japan to begin production in the United States in order for their new U.S. plants to have access to quality products. The same phenomenon holds true for service firms. For example, advertising agencies often move abroad in order to service foreign affiliates of their domestic clients. Similarly, engineering firms, insurance companies, and law firms often are invited to provide their services abroad. Yet not all of these developments are the result of co-optation by client firms. Often suppliers invest abroad out of fear that their clients might find good sources abroad and therefore begin to import the products or services they currently supply. Many firms therefore invest abroad in order to forestall such a potentially dangerous development.

Government Incentives   A third major cause for the increase in foreign direct investment, even though much more limited in its impact, is government incentives. Governments increasingly are under pressure to provide jobs for their citizens. Over time, many have come to recognize that foreign direct investment can serve as a major means to increase employment and income. Some countries such as Ireland have been promoting government incentive schemes for foreign direct investment for decades. Increasingly state and local governments are also participating in investment promotion activities. Some states, for example, are sending out investment missions on a regular basis, and others have opened offices abroad in order to inform local businesses about the beneficial investment climate at home. Figure 14.1 provides an example of such state investment promotion.

Government incentives are mainly of three types: fiscal, financial, and nonfinancial. **Fiscal incentives** are specific tax measures designed to serve as an attraction to the foreign investor. They typically consist of special depreciation allowances, tax credits or rebates, special deductions for capital expenditures, tax holidays, and the reduction of tax burdens on the

FIGURE 14.1 ▪ **An Advertisement for Foreign Direct Investment**

Source: Courtesy State of Rhode Island Department of Economic Development.

investor. **Financial incentives** offer special funding for the investor by providing, for example, land or buildings, loans, and loan guarantees. Finally, **nonfinancial incentives** can consist of guaranteed government purchases; special protection from competition through tariffs, import quotas, and local content requirements; and investments in infrastructure facilities.

All of these incentives are designed primarily to attract more industry and therefore create more jobs. They may slightly alter the advantage of a region and therefore make it more palatable for the investor to choose to invest in that region. By themselves, they are unlikely to spur an investment decision if proper market conditions do not exist. Consequently, when individual states within the United States offer special incentives to foreign direct investors, they may be competing against each other for a limited pie rather than increasing the size of the pie. Further, a question exists about the extent to which new jobs are actually created by foreign direct investment. Because many foreign investors import equipment, parts, and even personnel, the expected benefits in terms of job creation may often be either less than initially envisioned or only temporary. In spite of these concerns, any investment incentives that are offered will be seriously considered by the international marketer who seeks to choose the most appropriate location for foreign direct investment.

Types of Ownership

In carrying out its foreign direct investment, a multinational corporation has a wide variety of ownership choices, ranging from 100 percent ownership to a minority interest. Of course, the degree of control it can exercise over international marketing activities is of primary concern, and each level of ownership may indicate varying degrees of control. Full ownership assures control of business plans and strategies, as discussed in The International Marketplace 14.1.

Full Ownership   For many firms, the foreign direct investment decision is, initially at least, considered in the context of 100 percent ownership. Sometimes, this is the result of ethnocentric considerations, based on the belief that no outside entity should have an impact on corporation management. At other times, the issue is one of principle. For example, the management of IBM believes that by relinquishing portions of its ownership abroad, it would be setting a precedent for shared control with local partners that would cost more than could possibly be gained.[10]

In order to make a rational decision about the extent of ownership, management must evaluate the extent to which total control is important for the success of its international marketing activities. Often full ownership may be a desirable, but not a necessary, prerequisite for international success. At other times it may be necessary, particularly when strong linkages exist within the corporation. Interdependencies between and among local operations and headquarters may be so strong that anything short of total coordination will result in a benefit to the firm as a whole that is less than acceptable. This may be the case if central product design, pricing, or advertising is needed, as the following example illustrates:

> The Crane Company manufactures plumbing fixtures, pumps and valves, and similar equipment which is used in oil refineries, paper mills, and many other types of installations. The firm sells to design engineers throughout the world; these engineers may not be actual buyers, but they design equipment into the plants they build, and so they at least recommend the equipment to be used. In advertising to this important segment of the international market, Crane recognizes that the design engineer in São Paolo reads engineering journals published in the United States, Great Britain, and perhaps Germany or France, as well as Latin America. So Crane wants its advertising in these journals to be consistent. Therefore it does not let its foreign subsidiaries conduct their own advertising without advice and clearance from the New York headquarters. If Crane were to use joint ventures abroad, the partner would have to yield advertising authority to New York. This could conceiv-

[10]Dennis J. Encarnation and Sushil Vachani, "Foreign Ownership: When Hosts Change the Rules," *Harvard Business Review* 63 (September–October 1985): 152–160.

ably lead to discontent on the part of the local partner. To avoid arguments on advertising policies, Crane insists on full ownership.[11]

As this example shows, corporations sometimes insist on full ownership for major strategic reasons. Even in such instances, however, it is important to determine whether these reasons are important enough to warrant such a policy, or whether the needs of the firm can be accommodated in other ownership arrangements. Increasingly, the international environment is growing hostile to full ownership by multinational firms.

Many governments exert political pressure in order to obtain national control of foreign operations. Commercial activities under the control of foreigners are frequently believed to reflect the wishes, desires, and needs of headquarters abroad much more than those of the domestic economy. Governments fear that domestic economic policies may be counteracted by such firms, and employees are afraid that little local responsibility and empathy exist at headquarters. A major concern is the "fairness" of **profit repatriation,** or transfer of profits, and the extent to which firms operating abroad need to reinvest in their foreign operations. Governments often believe that transfer pricing mechanisms are used to amass profits in a place most advantageous for the firm and that, as a consequence, local operations often show very low levels of performance. By reducing the foreign control of firms they hope to put an end to such practices.

Ownership options are increasingly limited either through outright legal restrictions or through measures designed to make foreign ownership less attractive—such as profit repatriation limitations. The international marketer is therefore frequently faced with the choice either of abiding by existing restraints and accepting a reduction in control or of losing the opportunity to operate in the country.

In addition to the pressure from host governments, general market instability can also serve as a major deterrent to full ownership of foreign direct investment. Instability may result from political upheavals or changes in regimes. More often it results from threats of political action, complex and drawn-out bureaucratic procedures, and the prospect of arbitrary and unpredictable alterations in regulations after the investment decision has been made.[12]

Joint Ventures   Joint ventures are a collaboration of two or more organizations for more than a transitory period.[13] In this collaboration, the participating partners share assets, risks, and profits. Equality of partners is not necessary. In some joint ventures each partner holds an equal share; in

[11] Richard H. Holton, "Making International Joint Ventures Work," presented at the seminar on the Management of Headquarters/Subsidiary Relationships in Transnational Corporations, Stockholm School of Economics, June 2–4, 1980, 4.

[12] Isaiah Frank, *Foreign Enterprise in Developing Countries* (Baltimore: Johns Hopkins University, 1980).

[13] W. G. Friedman and G. Kalmanoff, *Joint International Business Ventures* (New York: Columbia University Press, 1961).

14.2 THE INTERNATIONAL MARKETPLACE

Joint Ventures in Developing Countries: The Heinz Philosophy
Having determined to expand our business through new geography, we developed what we think are sensible and realistic guidelines for undertaking this expansion. The key to our strategy has been to use the joint venture as our entrée to a region. A joint venture offers the twin advantages of familiarity and facilities.

Obviously, an established business has greater familiarity with the political, economic, and social environment of its home market. The pioneering spirit can take an investment only so far. Rather than plant our flag and hope for the best, we believe it far more prudent to seek an experienced and knowledgeable partner in each region we enter. That partner may be a successful private business or it may be the host government.

The facilities of an existing enterprise offer us an important financial advantage in the early stage of an overseas venture. Because so many developing countries find their foreign currency in short supply, they may have difficulty importing material and equipment to build a plant. That bottleneck may be avoided by finding a factory with equipment and infrastructure in place.

Before we begin our courtship of a prospective partner, we ask ourselves how well it reflects the criteria we have devised to assess a project's desirability. Such criteria include:

- *A company whose field is, or is closely related to, the food business.*
- *A company staffed by nationals and not reliant on expatriates.*
- *A company of sufficient size to serve as a continental base for expansion within the country and the region.*
- *A company not heavily dependent on imported raw materials.*
- *A company not dependent on exports and with ready markets for its products within its own country.*
- *A company with good profit potential to justify the greater risk of investment in the Third World.*

Source: Anthony J. F. O'Reilly, "Establishing Successful Joint Ventures in Developing Nations: A CEO's Perspective," *The Columbia Journal of World Business* 23 (Spring 1988): 66. Reprinted with permission.

others, one partner has the majority of shares. The partners' contributions to the joint venture can also vary widely. Contributions may consist of funds, technology, know-how, sales organizations, or plant and equipment. The International Marketplace 14.2 gives an example of one corporation's philosophy toward joint ventures.

Advantages of Joint Ventures   The two major reasons for carrying out foreign direct investments in the form of joint ventures are environmental and commercial. Environmental reasons consist mainly of government pressures on firms either to form or accept joint ventures or to forego participation in the local market. For example, India's Foreign Exchange Regulation Act (FERA) of 1973 restricts equity participation in local operations by foreigners to 40 percent.[14] This percentage is designed to reduce the extent of control that foreign firms can exercise over local operations. As a basis for defining control, most countries have employed percentage levels of ownership. Over time, countries have shown an increasing tendency to adopt lower thresholds of ownership as a basis for defining control. This tendency developed as it became apparent that even small, organized groups of stockholders may influence control of an enterprise, particularly if ownership is widely distributed.[15]

Another environmental reason, found mostly in socialist countries, may be the economic orientation of governments and a resulting requirement for joint venture collaboration. Joint ventures can help overcome traditional restrictions and open up or maintain market opportunities that otherwise would not be available.

Equally important to the formation of joint ventures are commercial considerations. If a corporation can identify a partner with a common goal, and if the international activities are sufficiently independent from each other not to infringe on the autonomy of the individual partner, joint ventures may represent the most viable vehicle for international expansion. The following is an example of a nearly ideal joint venture:

> The Trailmobile Company of Cincinnati, Ohio, produces truck trailers. It now participates in 27 joint ventures abroad. Truck trailers do not move in international markets in significant numbers because transportation costs are high and, more importantly, because tariffs typically serve to insulate the markets from each other. Therefore, pricing can be decided at the level of the joint venture, because one joint venture cannot invade the market of another. Each joint venture serves its own local market, and these differ from each other in significant ways; hence the marketing policy decisions are made at the local level. Only a modest part of the total cost of manufacturing the trailer is represented by components bought from Trailmobile. Thus the interdependencies are limited, decision making can be delegated to the level of the joint venture, and conflicts can be minimized.[16]

Joint ventures are valuable when the pooling of resources results in a better outcome for each partner than if each were to attempt to carry out its activities individually. This is particularly the case when each partner has a specialized advantage in areas that benefit the joint venture. For example, a firm may have new technology available, yet lack sufficient capital to carry out foreign direct investment on its own. By joining forces, the technology can be used more quickly and market penetration is easier. Similarly, one of the partners may have a distribution system already es-

[14] Encarnation and Vachani, "Foreign Ownership," 152–160.

[15] U.S. Department of Commerce, *Foreign Direct Investment in the United States*, vol. 1, April 1976, 5–6.

[16] Holton, "Making International Joint Ventures Work," 5.

tablished or have better access to local suppliers, either of which permits a greater volume of sales in a shorter period of time.

A good example is AT&T's joint venture with Brock Control Systems. Brock has 40 employees, while AT&T has 6,000 salespeople alone. The key is the synergism between Brock's automated telemarketing software system and the hardware and information-management-systems capabilities of AT&T. The combining of the products of the two companies provides proven solutions to business. As a result, AT&T sells more computer and network systems, and Brock sells more software packages.[17]

Joint ventures also permit better relationships with local organizations—government, local authorities, or labor unions. Particularly if the local partner can bring political influence to the undertaking, the new venture may be eligible for tax incentives, grants, and government support and be less vulnerable to political risk. Negotiations for certifications or licenses may be easier because authorities may not perceive themselves as dealing with a foreign firm. Relationships between the local partner and the local financial establishment may enable the joint venture to tap local capital markets. The greater experience—and therefore greater familiarity—with the local culture and environment of the local partner may enable the joint venture to be more aware of cultural sensitivities and benefit from greater insights into changing market conditions and needs.

A final major commercial reason to participate in joint ventures is the desire to minimize the risk of exposing long-term investment capital, while at the same time maximizing the leverage on the capital that is invested.[18] Economic and political conditions in many countries are increasingly volatile. At the same time, corporations tend to shorten their investment planning time span more and more. This financial rationale therefore takes on increasing importance.

Disadvantages of Joint Ventures   Problem areas in joint ventures, as in all partnerships, involve implementing the concept and maintaining the relationship.

Many of the governments that require a joint venture formation are inexperienced in foreign direct investment. Therefore, joint venture legislation and the ensuing regulations are often subject to substantial interpretation and arbitrariness. Frequently, for example, different levels of control are permitted depending on the type of product and the shipment destination. In some instances, only portions of joint venture legislation are made public. Other internal regulations are communicated only when necessary.[19] Such situations create uncertainty, which increases the risk for the joint venture participants.

---

[17] Stanley J. Modic, "Strategic Alliances," *Industry Week*, October 3, 1988, 46–52.

[18] Charles Oman, *New Forms of International Investment in Developing Countries* (Paris: Organization for Economic Cooperation and Development, 1984), 79.

[19] P. T. Bangsberg, "U.S. Lawyer Advises Companies on China," *The Journal of Commerce*, August 22, 1985, 5A.

Major problems can also arise in assuring the maintenance of the joint venture relationship. Seven out of ten joint ventures have been found to fall short of expectations and/or are disbanded.[20] The reasons typically relate to conflicts of interest, problems with disclosure of sensitive information, and disagreement over how profits are to be shared; in general, lack of communication before, during, and after the formation of the venture. In some cases, managers are interested in the launching of the venture but are too little concerned about the actual running of the enterprise. Many of the problems stem from a lack of careful consideration in advance of how to manage the new endeavor. A partnership works on the basis of trust and commitment, or not at all.

Areas of possible disagreement include the whole range of business decisions covering strategy, management style, accounting and control, marketing policies and practices, production, research and development, and personnel.[21] The joint venture may, for example, identify a particular market as a profitable target, yet the headquarters of one of the partners may already have plans for serving this market that would require competing against its own joint venture.

Similarly, the issue of profit accumulation and distribution may cause discontent. If one partner supplies the joint venture with a product, that partner will prefer that any profits accumulate at headquarters and accrue 100 percent to one firm rather than at the joint venture, where profits are partitioned according to equity participation. Such a decision may not be greeted with enthusiasm by the other partner. Further, once profits are accumulated, their distribution may lead to dispute. For example, one partner may insist on a high payout of dividends because of financial needs, whereas the other may prefer the reinvestment of profits into a growing operation.

Recommendations   The first requirement when forming a joint venture is to find the right partner. Partners should have a commonality of orientation and goals and should bring complementary and relevant benefits to the joint venture. The venture makes little sense if the expertise of both partners is in the same area—for example, if both have production experience but neither has distribution know-how. Similarly, bringing a good distribution system to the joint venture may be of little use if the established system is in the field of consumer products, and the joint venture will produce industrial products.

Second, great care needs to be taken in negotiating the joint venture agreement. In these negotiations, extensive provisions must be made for contingencies. Questions such as profit accumulation and distribution and market orientation must be addressed in the initial agreement; otherwise, they may surface as points of contention over time. A joint venture

---

[20] Yankelovich, Skelly and White, Inc., *Collaborative Ventures: A Pragmatic Approach to Business Expansion in the Eighties* (New York: Coopers and Lybrand, 1984), 10.

[21] Holton, "Making International Joint Ventures Work," 7.

14.3 THE INTERNATIONAL MARKETPLACE

Manufacturing Cooperation as Viewed by the Aerospace Industry   Internationalization describes a growing trend—business relationships that cross national borders. It has to do with issues of global trade, expanded international competition, and, in some instances, U.S. market share. Most significant, it involves cooperation and how the joint development and production of new technologies and products influence U.S. national security and economic prosperity.

Emerging from the dialogue, studies, and economic data is the realization that all sectors must work in concert to develop cohesive strategies and policies to keep the United States a key player in the new market environment. We have entered an era that involves cooperation with foreign manufacturers in order to meet the competitive challenges that could erode the U.S. market share. Capital and technology costs are major factors in internationalization, and the benefits—such as market access, reduced research and development cost, the elimination of duplication of effort, and technology flow back to the United States—need to be fully recognized and understood.

The U.S. aerospace industry is going through a major period of change, adjusting to the new global market environment, and, at the same time, adjusting to the new budget-driven defense environment. U.S. civil aerospace firms must be able to share the cost and risks of research and development at a time when the total investment in a new engine or aircraft program can exceed the net worth of the company. It is often found easier to partner with foreign companies and, as a result, we are seeing not only coproduction and licensing agreements, but, more recently, joint ventures and collaborative arrangements in the design, production, and marketing of aerospace products and systems.

The reality of internationalization has fostered trade-offs in both the civil and the military sectors of aerospace that did not exist for U.S. manufacturers in the past. It has become a buyer's market in which purchasers can demand concessions, such as domestic content requirement, from sellers in both military and commercial aerospace. With two-thirds of the market for commercial transport outside the United States and a substantial non-U.S. market for military products flourishing, foreign customers are frequently in a good position to call the shots. This is particularly true as collaboration increases among foreign firms in the defense sector and the United States faces a hard sell to market off-the-shelf defense products.

For the United States, though, the stakes can be high—market access in exchange for the development work and, often, technology. U.S. aerospace companies are challenged, therefore, to cooper-

ate with foreign firms without tipping their hand and losing the important assets that made them attractive partners in the first place. The key is to retain sufficient technological advantage, particularly in critical areas, so that a firm can incorporate still newer technology into its products and processes by the time the technology is transferred.

Source: "Internationalization: What Is It? Why Is It? Will It Go Away?" *Aerospace Industries Association Newsletter,* July 1988, 1–2.

---

agreement, although comparable to a marriage contract, should contain the elements of a divorce contract. In case the joint venture cannot be maintained to the satisfaction of the partners, plans must exist for the dissolution of the agreement and for the allocation of profits and cost.

Finally, joint ventures operate in dynamic business environments and therefore must be able to adjust to changing market conditions. The agreement therefore should provide for changes in the original concept so that the venture can grow and flourish.

Strategic Alliances One special form of joint ventures that is increasingly emerging is **strategic alliances,** or **partnerships.** The International Marketplace 14.3 provides an example.

Such ventures are central to the participant's future direction and means of achieving competitive advantages. The goals are to leverage critical capabilities, increase the flow of innovation, and improve flexibility in responding to market and technological changes.[22] A few years ago, it could be stated with impunity that "what the parent may get from a joint venture is money, but unlikely any substantial amount of new knowledge in technology, management, or the like."[23] However, given the growth of global competition, the large investment required for technological progress, and the resulting high risk of failure, corporations increasingly seek to join forces to spread the risk and share capabilities.

Strategic alliances can take place at either the industry or the corporate level. At the industry level, they are often an indication of government fiat and support for new technological developments that are believed to be critical in terms of competitiveness, but too expensive and risky for one firm alone. Examples of such alliances are EUREKA and JESSI in Europe, and SEMATECH in the United States. Common to all these programs is the collaboration of firms in the high-technology area with the benefit of governmental assistance and the goal of developing global leadership through the sharing of progress in research. Of course, companies must carefully evaluate the effects of entering such a coalition. Depending on the objec-

---

[22] Modic, "Strategic Alliances."

[23] Lars Otterbeck, "Management of Joint Ventures," presented at the seminar on the Management of Headquarters/Subsidiary Relationships in Transnational Corporations, Stockholm School of Economics, June 2–4, 1980, 27.

tives of the other partners, companies may wind up having their strategy partially driven by their competitors. Competitors may also gain strength through coalitions, unplanned transfers of technology might take place, and unexpected competitors might appear as a result.[24]

On the corporate level, such long-term partnerings are designed to open up major new strategic options to the participants. For example, the joining of forces between General Motors and Toyota in the New United Motor Manufacturing Inc. (NUMMI) venture was designed to enable GM to learn production and management techniques from a company renowned for them, while Toyota could gain low-cost entry to the U.S. auto industry with the assistance of the industry leader.[25] Given continued increases in the complexity of competitiveness and the cost of technology, strategic alliances are likely to continue to grow in importance.

MANAGEMENT CONTRACTS

As governments continue to insist on complete or majority ownership of firms, multinational corporations have turned to management contracts to expand their overseas operations. In a **management contract** the supplier brings together a package of skills that will provide an integrated service to the client without incurring the risk and benefit of ownership. It can be used by the international marketer in various ways. When equity participation, in the form of either full ownership or a joint venture, is not possible or must be relinquished, a management contract can serve to maintain participation in a venture. Depending on the extensiveness of the contract, it may even permit some measure of control. As an example, the manufacturing process might have to be relinquished to foreign firms, yet international distribution is needed for the product. A management contract could serve to maintain a strong hold on the operation by ensuring that all the distribution channels remain firmly controlled.

Yet management contracts should not be seen as a last line of defense. Whenever lack of expertise exists in a particular venture, management contracts can be a most useful tool to help overcome barriers to international marketing activities. This is particularly useful if an outside party has specialized knowledge that is crucial to international marketing success, whether in the area of distribution technology, marketing know-how, or worldwide contacts. Some companies in the service sector have independent entities that specialize in delivering management services. For example, the French airline UTA manages the operations of Air Zaire by handling the accounting system, setting salary and customer service levels, and providing training programs.[26]

[24] Pedro Nueno and Jan Oosterveld, "Managing Technology Alliances," *Long Range Planning* (June 1988): 11–17.

[25] Stephen E. Weiss, "Creating the GM–Toyota Joint Venture: A Case in Complex Negotiation," *Columbia Journal of World Business* 22 (Summer 1987): 22–37.

[26] "Air Zaire Improving with Help from UTA," *Air Transport World* (June 1987): 170–173.

Often a management contract is the critical element in the success of a project. For example, a financial institution may gain confidence in a project because of the existence of a management contract and sometimes may even make it a condition to the providing of funding.[27]

One specialized form of management contract is that of a **turnkey operation.** Here, the arrangement permits a client to acquire a complete operational system, together with the skills investment sufficient to allow unassisted maintenance and operation of the system following its completion.[28] The client need not search for individual contractors and subcontractors or deal with scheduling conflicts and difficulties in assigning responsibilities and blame. Instead, a package arrangement permits the accumulation of responsibility in one hand, and greatly eases the negotiation and supervision requirements and subsequent accountability issues for the client.

Management contracts have clear benefits for the client. They can provide organizational skills not available locally, expertise that is immediately available rather than built up, and management assistance in the form of support services that would be difficult and costly to replicate locally. In addition, the outside involvement is clearly limited. When a turnkey project is on line, for example, the system will be totally owned, controlled, and operated by the customer.

Similar advantages exist for the supplier. The risk of participating in an international venture is substantially lowered, because no equity capital is at stake. At the same time, a significant amount of operational control can be exercised. Existing know-how that has been built up with significant investment can be commercialized, and frequently the impact of fluctuations in business volume can be reduced by making use of experienced personnel who otherwise would have to be laid off. In industrialized countries like the United States, with economies that are increasingly service based, accumulated service knowledge and comparative advantage should be used internationally. Management contracts permit a firm to do so.

From the client's perspective, the main drawbacks to consider are the risks of overdependence and loss of control. For example, if the management contractor maintains all international relationships, little if any expertise may be passed on to the local operation. Instead of a gradual transfer of skills leading to increasing independence, the client may have to rely more and more on the performance of the contractor.

On the contractor's side, the major risks to consider are (1) the effects of the loss or termination of a contract and the resulting personnel problems, and (2) a bid made without fully detailed insight into actual expenses. The

---

[27]Michael Z. Brooke, *Selling Management Services Contracts in International Business* (London: Holt, Rinehart & Winston, 1985), 7.

[28]Richard W. Wright and Colin Russel, "Joint Ventures in Developing Countries: Realities and Responses," *Columbia Journal of World Business* 10 (Spring 1975): 74–80.

winning of a management contract could result in Pyrrhic victories, with the income not worth the expense.

SUMMARY

Foreign direct investment represents a major market expansion alternative to larger sized firms and multinational corporations. Market factors, the desire for control, barriers to trade, cost factors, and investment climate are the major causes of foreign direct investment, with market factors usually playing the major role.

Different ownership levels of foreign investments are possible, ranging from wholly owned subsidiaries to joint ventures. Although many firms prefer full ownership in order to retain full control, such a posture is often not possible because of governmental regulations. It may not even be desirable. Depending on the global organization of the firm, joint ventures with only partial ownership may be a profitable alternative.

In a joint venture, the partners can complement each other by contributing the strengths and resources that each is best equipped to supply. Joint ventures offer significant benefits in terms of closeness to markets, better acceptance by the foreign environment, and a lessening of the risks involved, but they also pose new problems due to potential clashes of corporate cultures, business orientations, and marketing policies. It is therefore important to select the appropriate joint venture partner and to design an agreement that ensures the long-term approval of all participants.

Strategic alliances, or partnerings, are a special form of joint venture in which the participants, at either the industry or the corporate level, join forces in order to make major strategic progress toward technology development and competitiveness. Given the complexities and cost of technological progress, the number of these alliances is rapidly growing.

As the United States is increasingly becoming a service-based economy, the usefulness of management contracts is increasing. Such contracts can maintain the involvement of the international marketer in a project when equity participation is not possible or desirable. They also permit a client to acquire operational skills and turnkey systems without relinquishing ownership of a project. Because management assistance, service delivery, and project planning are increasingly important, international marketers can use management contracting to carve out a profitable market niche.

Questions for Discussion

1. How is an increase in protectionism likely to affect foreign direct investment activities?

2. As a government official, would you prefer the foreign direct investment of a resource seeker, efficiency seeker, or market seeker?

3. Give some reasons why a multinational corporation might insist on 100 percent ownership abroad.

4. Discuss possible reasons why IBM withdrew from India's computer market rather than share ownership, yet Burroughs and International Computer entered the market at the same time as minority owners.

5. At what level of ownership would you consider a firm to be foreign controlled?

6. Do investment promotion programs of state governments make sense from a national perspective?

7. Suggest a way of reducing the transfer pricing problem in joint ventures.

8. How can a management contractor have more control than the client? What can the client do under such circumstances?

9. The joining of forces in strategic industry alliances may enhance technological progress, yet antitrust laws have prohibited such coalitions. Why? And why are they now possible?

10. Discuss the benefits and drawbacks of strategic partnerings at the corporate level.

Recommended Readings

Brooke, Michael Z. *Selling Management Services Contracts in International Business.* London: Holt, Rinehart & Winston, 1985.

Frank, Isaiah. *Foreign Investment in Developing Countries.* Baltimore: Johns Hopkins Press, 1981.

Franko, Lawrence G. "Use of Minority and 50-50 Joint Ventures by United States Multinationals during the 1970's: The Interaction of Host Country Policies and Corporate Strategies." *Journal of International Business Studies* 20 (Spring 1989): 19–40.

Harrigan, K. R. *Strategies for Joint Ventures.* Lexington, Mass.: Lexington Books, 1985.

Moran, Theodore H. (ed.). *Multinational Corporations: The Political Economy of Foreign Direct Investment.* Lexington, Mass.: Lexington Books, 1985.

Porter, Michael (ed.). *Competition in Global Industries.* Boston: Harvard Business School Press, 1986.

Sharma, D. B. *Swedish Firms and Management Contracts.* Uppsala, Sweden: Uppsala University, 1983.

U.S. Department of Commerce, International Trade Administration. *International Direct Investment.* 1988 Edition. Washington, D.C.: Government Printing Office, 1988.

Weiss, Stephen E. "Creating the GM–Toyota Joint Venture: A Case in Complex Negotiation." *Columbia Journal of World Business* 22 (Summer 1987): 23–37.

CHAPTER 15

Primary International Marketing Research and the Marketing Decision Support System

15.1 THE INTERNATIONAL MARKETPLACE

Selling Paint Mixers in Japan *Most paint stores in the United States do not stock all colors and shades of paint that may be wanted by a customer. In keeping with the "principle of postponement," customization of the product is undertaken at the latest possible moment. Only after a customer has chosen a color is base paint mixed with powder of the color desired. This process results in large savings in inventory costs and storage space.*

Anoli Inc., is a major producer of the paint mixers used in this process. H. Giv, president of Anoli, upon learning of the small size of Japanese retail stores, decided that perhaps Anoli's products would be useful for Japanese paint stores. In order to explore the idea further, she needed the answer to one major question: do Japanese retailers store different colors of paints or do they mix them on demand? Mrs. Giv contacted various sources of information— the Japanese Embassy, the Japanese Consulate, the Japan External Trade Organization (JETRO), and the Desk Officer for Japan in the U.S. Department of Commerce. Everyone sent voluminous information on the Japanese paint market, some even giving data on the sales volume. None, however, could answer Mrs. Giv's question. After three months, she finally recognized that the only way to get the desired information was to go to Japan and visit some paint stores.

The research section of this chapter focuses on the conduct of research abroad, the collection of primary data, and the minimization of research cost. The primary research process is explained by addressing the need for primary international research and the steps necessary for conducting it. Other issues are research administration, research technique, and research instruments.

In addition to specific international research projects, multinational corporations quite frequently desire to maintain continuous updates of changing market environments abroad and to obtain glimpses into the future in order to plan corporate strategy. The marketing decision support system necessary to achieve these goals is the topic of the second section of the chapter. Primary emphasis is on environmental scanning, the use of the Delphi research technique, and scenario building.

THE PRIMARY RESEARCH PROCESS

Primary research is conducted to fill specific information needs. The research may not actually be conducted by the firm with the need, but the work must be carried out for a specific research purpose. Primary research therefore goes beyond the activities of secondary data collection, which often cannot supply answers to the specific questions posed. The orientation may be limited and/or different or, in some instances, secondary research may not address issues that are of particular concern. The International Marketplace 15.1 provides an example of such a situation.

The use of primary research internationally is much less widespread than it should be. Frequently, corporations are reluctant to engage in international research because of its cost. A basic cost–benefit evaluation would, for example, suggest that "management should simply fill a $10,000 order to an otherwise trustworthy distributor operating under a teetering Latin American junta rather than spend several thousand dollars on further research as well as divert managerial resources from elsewhere." [1] Also, doubts about the competence and reliability of foreign research companies and of international research agencies are often cause for hesitation. [2]

In spite of these major barriers, corporations are increasingly recognizing the need for primary international research because of the large volume of their international business transactions and the growth in international risk. As the extent of a firm's international involvement increases, so does the importance and complexity of its international marketing research. Large companies are likely to engage in foreign marketing research more frequently and to use more rigorous techniques than are small or medium-sized firms. This difference results from the diversity of managerial talents and other resources in a larger firm and the increased dependence on profits from abroad. [3] Because the cost of research is often evaluated as a percentage of total business activity resulting from the research, the larger the intended or projected sales, the easier it becomes to justify primary research expenditures. The marketing research practices of one company with overseas sales exceeding $150 million are described in The International Marketplace 15.2.

[1] S. Tamer Cavusgil, "International Marketing Research: Insights into Company Practices," in *Research in Marketing*, vol. 7, ed. J. N. Sheth (Greenwich, Conn.: JAI Press, 1984), 261–288.
[2] Susan P. Douglas and C. Samuel Craig, *International Marketing Research* (Englewood Cliffs, N.J.: Prentice Hall, 1983), 2.
[3] Cavusgil, "International Marketing Research," 261–288.

15.2 THE INTERNATIONAL MARKETPLACE

Investigating and Tracking Market Potential   The company is a product division of a very large multinational firm. The division produces industrial motor controls, aircraft relays, circuit breakers, and related equipment. Overseas sales for the division exceed $150 million a year. Insights into the international marketing research practices of the company are offered in the following report.

"Indonesia is a market we are watching very closely now; sometime in the future Indonesia is going to demand a lot more attention than we are giving it. We watch it continuously and evaluate political and economic trends because any country with that many people and that much mineral wealth ultimately is going to be an important market. And we try and evaluate markets long term in this way. What is its natural resource capability and what is its human resource capability?

"In identifying new potential markets, we proceed in the following fashion. We have a market research department here at headquarters, and we will send people overseas and do market studies. We will use personnel at the local level as well. We have on occasion used outside consultants. . . . To the extent we are able to, we gather government statistics and analyze those ahead of time. As is well known, in some markets most government statistics are just a great amount of fiction. They're not very good to use. Even with our own government statistics—FT410 for instance—I find a lot of the categories so broad that you can't possibly identify a market for a specific product.

"We do market surveys for specific products all the time. They are very specific and very narrow. First, is the product being used or might it be used? Are there opportunities for the product to be sold; do they exist? Second, if there is a market, what is the competition; what is the current competitive price level; how is the product distributed; is it sold directly to the user; is it sold through OEMs; is it sold through distributors; is there any local fabrication or manufacturer? Is it a product that requires extended credit terms to obtain business? Is it a product that you would have substantial inventories in the country, or is it the kind of product where you can have relatively long lead times and still satisfy the customer requirements and therefore use inventories from the United States or some other central location? . . .

"As a rule of thumb for most products, if the potential sales is less than $250,000 a year, we are not going to spend much time. Of course, $250,000 on a product that produces a 50 percent margin might be more attractive to you than $500,000 on a product that generates only a 25 percent margin. With the former, you probably have a high turnover rate, so your ROI is good. While if you have a *low-margin product, the chances are that the turnover is not so good even though the market might be bigger. In sum, you have to look at many factors: the gross margins that are achievable; the amount of investment needed to sustain a position in the market; and the return you expect to get on the investment."*

Source: Quoted from S. Tamer Cavusgil, "International Marketing Research: Insights into Company Practices," in *Research in Marketing*, vol. 7, ed. J. N. Sheth (Greenwich, Conn.: JAI Press, 1984), 283–285. Used with permission.

Understanding the Need for Primary Research

An overview of the steps necessary to conduct primary research internationally is provided in Figure 15.1. As it does for secondary research, the first step consists of understanding the need for carrying out the research. Quite frequently, in a misguided effort to conserve funds, corporation management may insist on carrying out all research with secondary data. However, particularly for large-scale operations and pioneering activities, sooner or later issue-specific questions must be answered. Secondary data only rarely provide sufficient information for issue-specific inquiries. Management must therefore clearly recognize when the benefits and usefulness of secondary data are exhausted and make the decision to conduct primary research. This decision is complicated by the relative ease of identifying additional sources of secondary data, acquiring them, and anticipating an eventual answer. However, the process of gathering secondary data costs money and will waste time if the answer is not found. The experienced international researcher can soon determine the likelihood that the information sought will be found through secondary data. Even though these judgments may sometimes be inaccurate, in most instances this experience should be drawn on to decide on the need to conduct primary research.

Determining Research Objectives

One of three possible research objectives must be selected: exploratory, descriptive, or causal. This differentiation is necessary because the objectives require varying commitments of time and funding. Further, the answers supplied will have varying utility to the corporation, ranging from purely tactical to strategic and long term. Figure 15.2 depicts the changes in corporate usefulness of the three types of research. Each objective has merit, depending on corporate needs.

Exploratory Research Exploratory research is most appropriate when the primary objective is to identify problems, to define problems more precisely, or to investigate the possibility of new alternative courses of action. Exploratory research can also aid in formulating hypotheses regard-

FIGURE 15.1   ▪   **Steps in Primary International Research**

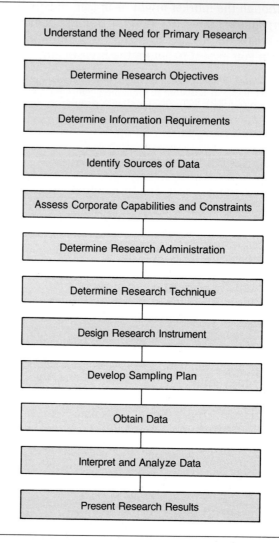

FIGURE 15.2   ▪   **Corporate Usefulness of Different Types of Research**

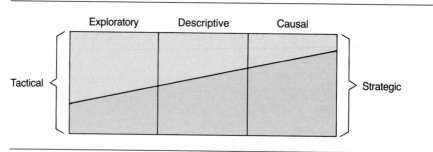

ing potential problems or opportunities present in the decision situation.[4] Frequently, exploratory research is only the first step in further research activity. To some extent, it can be compared to a fishing expedition or to a charting of the waters for the uninitiated.

As a result, exploratory research is often characterized by the need for great flexibility and versatility. Because the researcher is not knowledgeable about the phenomenon under investigation, he or she needs to be able to quickly adapt to newly emerging situations in order to make the research worthwhile. The emphasis is on qualitative rather than quantitative data collection, and quick rather than slow answers are sought. This of course means that exploratory research is less subject to the rigors of more precise research, and therefore is less reliable.

Exploratory research can be most useful in answering the basic question for the researcher: "What is the problem?" The defining and formulation of the problem is often far more essential than its solution, which may be merely a matter of mathematical or experimental skill. If the basic research objective is to define a problem or to gain "a feel" for a situation or to provide an overview, exploratory research may be the most appropriate activity from the standpoint of both time and money.

Descriptive Research   The aim of descriptive research is to provide a description of existing market phenomena. For example, market characteristics such as the socioeconomic position of customers or their purchasing intent may be analyzed. Such research is often used to determine the frequency of occurrence of marketing events, such as the frequency of customers visiting a store, of machines needing to be replaced, or of lawyers being consulted. Descriptive research can also be used to determine, in a noncausal fashion, the degree to which marketing variables are associated with one another. Based on this determination, predictions can then be made regarding future occurrences in the market. In the international setting, the researcher typically uses descriptive work to look for similarities and differences between markets and consumer groups. Similarities can then be exploited through standardization, while differences can assist in formulating an adaptive business strategy.

Although several interviews may be sufficient for exploratory research, descriptive studies often require larger quantities of data because the requirements for accurately portraying the population under study are much more stringent. In order to carry out descriptive work, the researcher needs a substantial amount of information about the phenomenon under study. Hypotheses are customarily preformulated and subsequently tested with the accumulated data. The research design needs to be carefully planned and structured. The intent of descriptive research is to maximize accuracy and to minimize systematic error. The researcher aims to increase reliability by keeping the measurement process as free from random error as possible.

[4] Thomas C. Kinnear and James R. Taylor, *Marketing Research: An Applied Approach*, 3d ed. (New York: McGraw-Hill, 1987), 125.

Descriptive research does not provide any information about causal interrelationships, but this does not necessarily detract from its value. Quite often firms have little interest in the underlying causes for interaction and are satisfied if linkages can be described. As an example, a firm may benefit from knowing that in January soft drink sales will drop by 30 percent from December's levels. Whether this development results from lower temperatures or from decreased humidity may be much less useful information.

Causal Research   The aim of causal research is to identify precise cause and effect relationships present in the market. The level of precision is higher than that for other types of research, because reasonably unambiguous conclusions regarding causality must be presented. Therefore causal research is often the most demanding type in terms of time and financial resources. It intends to present answers as to why things happen and to highlight details of the relationships among variables. In order to extract the causality from a variety of unrelated factors, investigations often need to resort to longitudinal and experimental measures. Longitudinal measures are required because after-the-fact measurement alone cannot fully explain the effect of causality. Similarly, experimentation is often necessary in order to introduce systematic variation of factors and then measure the effect of these variations. Obviously, causal research is useful only if the research objective is to identify these interrelationships, and if this knowledge makes a contribution to the corporate decision process that justifies the investment.

Descriptive studies comprise the vast majority of international marketing research. Many times, exploratory research is seen as an insufficient basis for major corporate decisions, and causal research is seen as too time consuming, too expensive, and not providing sufficient benefit to be justified. Corporations are mostly satisfied when management believes that a thorough understanding of a market situation has been obtained, and reasonable predictability is possible. Unlike academic research, corporate research is usually measured by its bottom-line effect, and descriptive studies often appear to contribute most to a desirable bottom line.

Determining Information Requirements

Specific research questions must be formulated in order to determine precisely the information that is required. For primary research purposes, most of the time, corporations pose clear-cut marketing questions:

- What is our market potential in market X?
- How much does the typical consumer spend on our type of product?
- What will happen to demand if we raise the price by 10 percent?
- What effect will a new type of packaging have on our sales?

Only when information requirements are determined as precisely as possible will the researcher be able to develop a research program that will deliver a useful product.

Identifying Data Sources

Location of Data Sources   The focus of study for the international market researcher will customarily be a foreign market. However, primary data do not always have to be collected abroad. On some occasions such data may be collected domestically. Interviews about foreign buyer behavior can, for example, be conducted with embassy personnel, foreign students, or domestic experts on the foreign market. Yet, in spite of the ease of access, the researcher needs to be cautious in using these sources. Often they are not representative of typical consumers but rather reflect the thinking and behavior of a country's elite class. The likelihood of obtaining biased information from these data sources is extremely high. The researcher therefore frequently needs to extend his or her efforts abroad. The specific country or region to be investigated must first be determined. Research in an entire country may not be necessary if, for example, only urban centers are to be penetrated. At other times, multiple regions of a country must be investigated if there is a lack of homogeneity between these regions as a result of different economic, geographic, or behavioral factors. The researcher must of course have a clear concept of what the population under study should be and where it is located before deciding on the country or region to be investigated.

Industrial Versus Consumer Sources of Data   Whether to conduct research with consumers or with industrial users must then be decided. This will in part determine the size of the universe and respondent accessibility. For example, consumers usually are a very large group and can be reached through interviews at home or intercept techniques. On the other hand, the total population of industrial users may be smaller and more difficult to reach. Further, cooperation by respondents may be quite different, ranging from very helpful to very limited. In the industrial setting, differentiating between users and decision makers may be much more important because their personality, their outlook, and their evaluative criteria may differ widely.

Assessing Corporate Capabilities and Constraints

The researcher must obtain input on what a corporation can and cannot do. Frequently over-optimism may result in wrong decisions that come back to haunt the researcher and the firm.

Corporations often tend to estimate their own strengths as greater than they are. As an example, a sales manager who is a native of Spain may not be the best person to entrust with research in that country. The individual may have outdated knowledge about the market, or the terminology used in Spain may differ substantially from what has been picked up in the United States. Friends who offer help may often not be qualified to provide such help professionally. Cost figures obtained may be totally out of date. Research skills that may have proven highly effective domestically may be inappropriate internationally. The research department possessing these domestic skills may therefore not be qualified to conduct international research.

Corporation management should not reject out of hand the possibility of using its own staff to conduct international marketing research. However, a precise assessment is needed of corporate capabilities and strengths as well as possible weaknesses in an international marketing research effort. Estimates made of cost and time requirements should be increased generously in order to accurately reflect reality.

Determining Research Administration

The major issues in determining who will do the research are whether to use a centralized, coordinated, or decentralized approach and whether to engage an outside research service.

Degree of Research Centralization   The level of control that corporation headquarters exercises over international marketing research activities is a function of the overall organizational structure of the firm and the nature and importance of the decision to be made. The three major approaches to international research organization are the centralized, coordinated, and decentralized approaches.[5] An overview of these approaches is provided in Figure 15.3.

The centralized approach clearly affords most control to headquarters. All **research specifications** such as focus, thrust, and design are directed by the home office and are forwarded to the local country operations for implementation. The subsequent analysis of gathered information again takes place at headquarters. Such an approach can be quite valuable when international marketing research is intended to influence corporate policies and strategy. It also ensures that all international market studies remain comparable to one another. On the other hand, downside risks exist. For example, headquarters management may be insufficiently familiar with the local market situation to be able to adapt the research appropriately. Also, headquarter cultural bias may influence the research activities. Finally, headquarters staff may be too small or insufficiently prepared to provide proper guidance for multiple international marketing research studies.

A coordinated research approach uses an intermediary to bring headquarters and country operations together. The intermediary can be the corporation's regional headquarters or an outside research agency. This approach provides for more interaction and review of the international marketing research plan by both headquarters and the local operations, and ensures more responsiveness to both strategic and local concerns. If

[5]John W. Ewen, "Industrial Research in International Markets," presented at the American Marketing Association/Market Research Society Conference, New York, October 20, 1981.

FIGURE 15.3 ▪ **Alternative Modes of Organizing and Coordinating Multicountry Research**

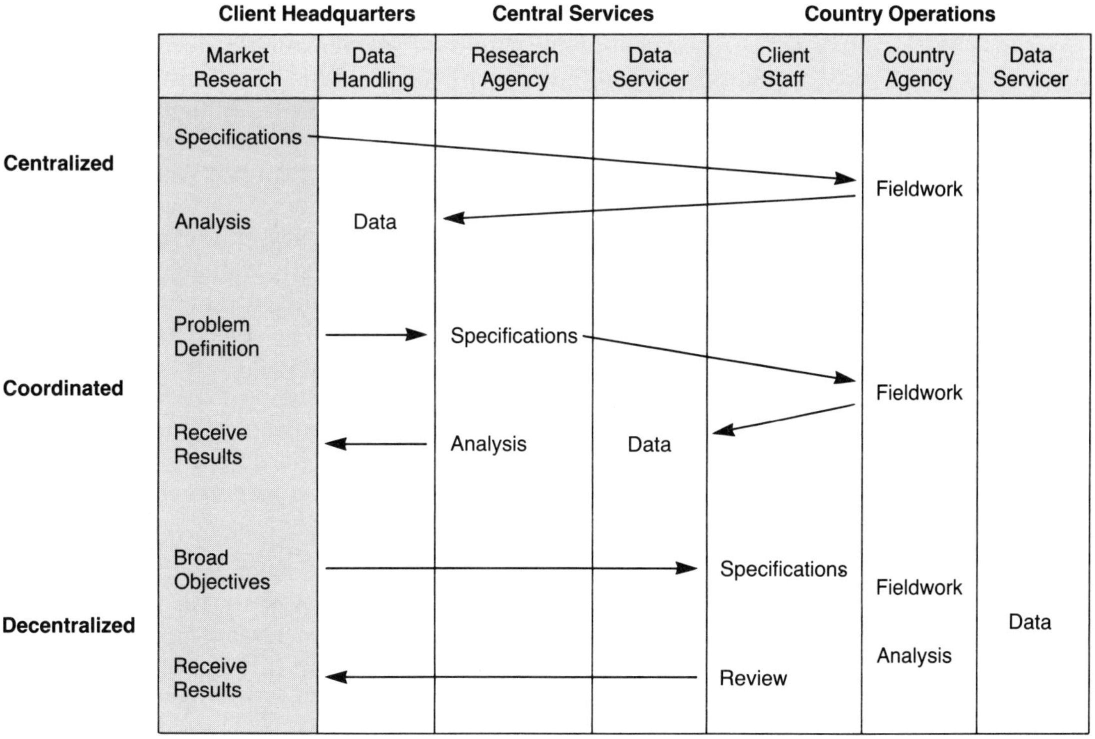

	Client Headquarters		Central Services		Country Operations		
	Market Research	Data Handling	Research Agency	Data Servicer	Client Staff	Country Agency	Data Servicer
Centralized	Specifications					Fieldwork	
	Analysis	Data					
Coordinated	Problem Definition		Specifications			Fieldwork	
	Receive Results		Analysis	Data			
Decentralized	Broad Objectives				Specifications	Fieldwork	Data
	Receive Results				Review	Analysis	

Source: Susan P. Douglas and C. Samuel Craig, *International Marketing Research* (Englewood Cliffs, N.J.: Prentice-Hall, 1983), 43.

the intermediary used is of high quality, the research capabilities of a corporation can be greatly enhanced through a coordinated approach.

The decentralized approach requires corporate headquarters to establish the broad thrust of research activities and then to delegate the further design and implementation to the local countries. The entire research is then carried out locally under the supervision of the local country operation, and only a final report is provided to headquarters. This approach has particular value if international markets differ significantly, because it permits detailed adaptation to local circumstances. However, implementing research activities on a country-by-country basis may cause unnecessary duplication, lack of knowledge transference, and lack of comparability of results.

Local country operations may not be aware of research carried out by corporate units in other countries and may reinvent the wheel. This problem can be avoided if a proper intracorporate flow of information exists so that local units can check whether similar information has already been collected elsewhere within the firm. Corporate units that operate in markets similar to one another can then benefit from the exchange of research findings.

Local units may also develop their own research thrusts, tools, and analyses. A researcher in one country may, for example, develop a creative way of dealing with a nonresponse problem. This new technique could be valuable to company researchers who face similar difficulties in other countries. However, for the technique to become widely known, systems must be in place to circulate information to the firm as a whole.

Finally, if left to their own devices, researchers will develop different ways of collecting and tabulating data. As a result, findings in different markets may not be comparable, and potentially valuable information about major changes and trends may be lost to the corporation.

International marketing research activities will always be carried out subject to the organizational structure of a firm. Ideally, a middle ground between centralization and decentralization will be found that permits local flexibility together with an ongoing exchange of information within the corporation. The exchange of information is particularly important because global rather than local optimization is the major goal of the multinational corporation.

The Use of Outside Research Services One major factor in deciding whether or not to use outside research services is, of course, the size of the international operations of a firm. No matter how large a firm is, however, it is unlikely to possess specialized expertise in international marketing research for every single market it currently serves or is planning to serve. Rather than overstretch the capabilities of its staff, or assert a degree of expertise that does not exist, a corporation may wish to delegate the research task to outside groups. This is particularly the case when corporate headquarters has little or no familiarity with the local research environment. The use of outside research agencies may be especially appropriate for large-scale international marketing research or if highly specialized research skills are required.[6] Many organizations stand ready to provide such outside assistance. Figure 15.4 provides an example. The selection process for outside research agencies should emphasize the quality of information rather than the cost. An agency that offers a low price may turn out to be expensive if it cannot furnish pertinent and accurate data.[7] Before a decision is made, the capabilities of an outside organization should be carefully evaluated and compared with the capabilities available in-house and from competing firms.

Although general technical capabilities are important, the prime selection criterion should be previous research experience in a particular country and a particular industry. Some experience is transferable from one industry or country to another; however, the better the corporation's re-

---

[6] Douglas and Craig, *International Marketing Research*, 49.

[7] Vinay Kothari, "Researching for Export Marketing," in *Export Promotion: The Public and Private Sector Interaction*, ed. M. Czinkota (New York: Praeger Publishers, 1983), 165.

FIGURE 15.4 ▪ **Ad for Burke International Research of New York**

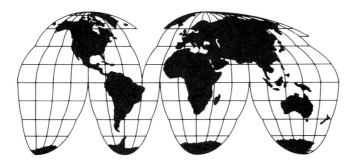
search needs overlap an agency's past research accomplishment, the more likely the research task will be carried out satisfactorily. Although the research may be more difficult to administer, multinational corporations should consider subcontracting each major international marketing research task to specialists, even if research within one country is carried out by various international marketing research agencies as a result. To have experts working on a problem is usually more efficient than to conserve corporate resources by centralizing all research activities with one

15.3 THE INTERNATIONAL MARKETPLACE

Primary Research in China   *China's Statistical Information and Consultancy Service Center will conduct a sample survey of households on what they think of Japanese goods such as televisions, refrigerators, and videoplayers. Zhou Zhilin, Deputy Manager of the center's information department said that the survey will be conducted in Beijing, Tianjin, Shanghai, Harbin, and Nanjing. Three thousand households will be asked more than 20 questions.*

In 1987, the center conducted a survey on the consumption habits of Beijing residents. Another survey provided information on 10,000 small Chinese factories and regularly provides basic data on 2,200 large and medium-sized Chinese enterprises. The center, founded in May 1985, has conducted nearly 600 surveys for foreign and Chinese firms and public institutions.

Zhou said that the center is under direct administration of the State Statistical Bureau, but the functions and aims of the two are quite different. The bureau serves only government bodies and Party organizations, whereas the center provides services for the public.

Source: Wang Xingcun, "Center Sells Foreigners Information," *China Daily Business Weekly*, April 10, 1988, 4.

---

service provider, who may only be marginally familiar with certain aspects of the research.

Occasionally, of course, the rules and regulations of a country will permit research to be carried out only by a government agency. The International Marketplace 15.3 provides an example. In such an instance, the choices for a firm are narrowed down very quickly, and the decision reverts to whether or not to do research.

Determining the Research Technique

Selection of the research technique depends on a variety of factors. First, the objectivity of the data sought must be determined. Standardized techniques are more useful in the collection of objective data than of subjective data. Also, the degree of structure sought in the data collection needs to be determined. Unstructured data will require more open-ended questions and more time than structured data. Whether the data are to be collected in the real world or in a controlled environment must be decided. Finally, a decision needs to be made as to whether the research technique is to collect historical facts or gather information about future developments. This is particularly important for consumer research, because firms frequently desire to determine the future intention of consumers to purchase a certain product.

Cultural and individual preferences play a major role in determining research techniques. U.S. managers frequently prefer to gather large quantities of data through surveys, which provide numbers that can be manipulated statistically, but managers in other countries appear to prefer the "soft" approach. For example, much of Japanese-style market research relies heavily on two kinds of information: **soft data** obtained from visits to dealers and other channel members and **hard data** about shipments, inventory levels, and retail sales. As the head of Matsushita's videocasette recorder division is reported to have said, "Why do Americans do so much marketing research? You can find out what you need by traveling around and visiting the retailers who carry your product."[8]

Once the structure of the type of data sought is determined, a choice must be made among the types of research instruments available. Each provides a different depth of information and has its unique strengths and weaknesses.

Interviews   Often interviews with knowledgeable persons can be of great value to the corporation desiring international marketing information. Because bias from the individual may be part of the findings, the intent should be to obtain in-depth information rather than a wide variety of data. Particularly when specific answers are sought to very narrow questions, interviews can be most useful.

One government program that attempts to be responsive to such a need has been implemented by the U.S. Foreign and Commercial Service of the Department of Commerce. On a pilot basis, the service offers, for a set fee, the answers to ten company-specific questions. The questions are forwarded to the service in Washington, which in turn relays them to its foreign commercial outpost in the country under study. A Foreign Commercial Officer will then gather facts to provide the response.

Focus Groups   Focus groups are a useful research tool resulting in interactive interviews. A group of knowledgeable persons is gathered for a limited period of time (two to four hours). Usually, seven to ten participants are the ideal size for a focus group. A specific topic is introduced and thoroughly discussed by all group members. Because of the interaction, hidden issues are sometimes raised that would not have been in an individual interview. The skill of the group leader in stimulating discussion is crucial to the success of a focus group. Discussions are often recorded on tape and subsequently analyzed in detail. Focus groups, like in-depth interviews, do not provide statistically significant information; however, they can be helpful in providing information about perceptions, emotions, and other nonovert factors. In addition, once individuals are gathered, focus groups are highly efficient in terms of rapidly accumulating a substantial amount of information.

---

[8]Johny K. Johansson and Ikujiro Nonaka, "Market Research the Japanese Way," *Harvard Business Review* 65 (May–June 1987): 16–22.

When conducting international research via focus groups, the researcher must be aware of the importance of culture in the discussion process. Not all societies encourage frank and open exchange and disagreement among individuals. Status consciousness may result in situations in which the opinion of one is reflected by all other participants. Disagreement may be seen as impolite, or certain topics may be taboo.

Observation   Observation techniques require the researcher to play the role of a nonparticipating observer of activity and behavior. Observation can be personal or impersonal—for example, mechanical. Observation can be obtrusive or inobtrusive, depending on whether the subject is aware or unaware of being observed. In international marketing research, observation can be extremely useful in shedding light on practices not previously encountered or understood. This aspect is particularly valuable for the researcher who is totally unfamiliar with a market or market situation. It can help in the understanding of phenomena that would have been difficult to assess with other techniques.

All of the research instruments discussed so far—interviews, focus groups, and observation—are useful primarily for the gathering of qualitative information. The intent is not to amass data, or to search for statistical significance, but rather to obtain a better understanding of given situations, behavioral patterns, or underlying dimensions. The researcher using these instruments must be cautioned that even frequent repetition of the measurements will not lead to a statistically valid result. However, statistical validity often is not the major focus of corporate international marketing research. Rather, it is the better understanding, description, and prediction of events that have an impact on marketing decision making. When quantitative data may also be desired, particularly when the research objectives are not exploratory but descriptive or causal, surveys and experimentation are the most appropriate types of research instruments.

Surveys   Survey research is useful in providing the opportunity to quantify concepts. In the social sciences, it is generally accepted that "the cross-cultural survey is scientifically the most powerful method of hypothesis testing."[9] Surveys are usually conducted via questionnaires that are administered personally, by mail, or by telephone. Use of the survey technique presupposes that the population under study is able to comprehend and respond to the questions posed. Also, particularly in the case of mail and telephone surveys, a major precondition is the feasibility of using the postal system or the widespread availability of telephones. Obviously, this is not a given in all countries. In many countries only limited records are available about dwellings, their location, and their occupants. In Venezuela, for example, most houses are not numbered, but rather are given individual names like "Casa Rosa" or "El Retiro." In some countries,

---

[9]Lothar G. Winter and Charles R. Prohaska, "Methodological Problems in the Comparative Analysis of International Marketing Systems," *Journal of the Academy of Marketing Science* 11 (Fall 1983): 421.

street maps are not even available. As a result, it becomes virtually impossible to reach respondents by mail.

In other countries, obtaining a correct address may be easy but the postal system may not function well. The Italian postal service, for example, repeatedly has suffered from scandals that exposed such practices as selling undelivered mail to paper mills for recycling. In Hong Kong, one researcher mailed out surveys with a dollar bill as a cash incentive. Based on a zero percent response rate, he concluded that he had either run into a fascinating cultural aversion to incentives or that—however unlikely— post office personnel had pocketed the money.[10]

Telephone surveys may also be inappropriate if telephone ownership is rare. In such instances, any information obtained would be highly biased even if the researcher randomizes the calls. In some instances, telephone networks and systems may also prevent the researcher from conducting surveys. Frequent line congestion or a lack of telephone directories are examples.

Surveys can be hampered by social and cultural constraints. Recipients of letters may be illiterate or may be reluctant to respond in writing.[11] In some nations entire population segments—for example, women—may be totally inaccessible to interviewers.

In spite of all these difficulties, however, the survey technique remains a useful one because it allows the researcher to rapidly accumulate a large quantity of data amenable to statistical analysis. Even though quite difficult, **international comparative research** has been carried out very successfully between nations, particularly if the environments studied are sufficiently similar so that uncontrollable macro-variables are limited in their impact.[12] With constantly expanding technological capabilities, international marketers will be able to use this technique more frequently in the future.

Experimentation   Experimental techniques are most useful in carrying out causal research. By determining the effect of an intervening variable, precise cause and effect relationships can be established. However, experimental techniques are difficult to implement in international marketing research. The researcher faces the task of designing an experiment in which most variables are held constant or are comparable across cultures. For example, an experiment that intends to determine a causal effect within the distribution system of one country may be difficult to transfer to another country, where the distribution system is different. As a result,

---

[10]Charles F. Keown, "Foreign Mail Surveys: Response Rates Using Monetary Incentives," *Journal of International Business Studies* 16 (Fall 1985): 151–153.

[11]Erdener Kaynak, "The Use of Marketing Research to Facilitate Marketing within Developing Countries," in *International Marketing Management*, ed. E. Kaynak (New York: Praeger Publishers, 1984), 155–171.

[12]Peter Banting, David Ford, Andrew Gross, and George Holmes, "Similarities in Industrial Procurement Across Four Countries," *Industrial Marketing Management* 14 (1985): 133–144.

experimental techniques are only rarely used, even though their potential value to the international market researcher is recognized.

Designing the Research Instrument

The research instrument most appropriate to international marketing surveys is the questionnaire. It should contain questions that are clear and easy to comprehend by the respondents as well as easy for the data collector to administer. Major attention must therefore be paid to question format, content, and wording.

Question Format   Questions can be structured or unstructured. Unstructured or open-ended questions permit the capture of more in-depth information, but they also increase the potential for interviewer bias. Even at the cost of potential bias, however, "the use of open-ended questions appears quite useful in cross-cultural surveys, because they may help identify the frame of reference of the respondents, or may even be designed to permit the respondent to set his own frame of reference." [13]

Another question format decision is the choice between direct and indirect questions. Societies have different degrees of sensitivity to certain questions. For example, questions related to the income or age of a respondent may be accepted differently in different countries. Also, the social desirability of answers may vary. As a result, the researcher must be sure that the questions are culturally acceptable. This may mean that questions that can be asked directly in some cultures because of their low sensitivity will have to be asked indirectly in others.

The question format should also ensure data equivalence in international marketing research. This requires categories used in questionnaires to be comparatively structured. In a developed country, for example, a white-collar worker may be part of the middle class, while in a less developed country the same person would be part of the upper class. Before using categories in a questionnaire, the researcher must therefore determine their appropriateness in different environments. This is particularly important for questions that attempt to collect attitudinal, psychographic, or lifestyle data, because cultural variations are most pronounced in these areas.

Question Content   When question content is planned, major consideration must be given to the ability and willingness of respondents to supply the answers. The knowledge and information available to respondents may vary substantially because of different educational levels, and may affect their ability to answer questions. Further, societal demands and restrictions may influence the willingness of respondents to answer certain questions. For various reasons, respondents may also be motivated to sup-

---

[13] Sydney Verba, "Cross-National Survey Research: The Problem of Credibility," in *Comparative Methods in Sociology: Essays on Trends and Applications*, ed. I. Vallier (Berkeley: University of California Press, 1971), 322–323.

ply incorrect answers. For example, in countries where the tax collection system is consistently eluded by taxpayers, questions regarding the level of income may deliberately be answered inaccurately. Distrust in the researcher, and the fear that research results may be passed on to the government, may also lead individuals to consistently understate their assets. Because of government restrictions in Brazil, for example, individuals will rarely admit to owning an imported car. Nevertheless, when the streets of Rio de Janeiro are observed, a substantial number of foreign cars are seen. The international market researcher is unlikely to change the societal context of a country. The objective of the content planning process should therefore be to adapt the questions to societal constraints.

Question Wording   The impact of language and culture are of particular importance when wording questions. The goal for the international marketing researcher should be to ensure that the potential for misunderstandings and misinterpretations of spoken or written words is minimized. Both language and cultural differences make this issue an extremely sensitive one in the international marketing research process. As a result, attention must be paid to the translation equivalence of verbal and nonverbal questions that can change in the course of translation. In one frequently cited example, a translation from the Bible of "the spirit is willing but the flesh is weak" was retranslated into English as "the bourbon is good but the steak leaves a lot to be desired."

The key is to keep questions clear by using simple rather than complex words, by avoiding ambiguous words and questions, by omitting leading questions, and by asking questions in specific terms, thus avoiding generalizations and estimates.[14] To reduce problems of question wording, it is helpful to use a **translation–retranslation approach.** The researcher formulates the questions, has them translated into the language of the country under investigation, and subsequently has a second translator return the foreign text to the researcher's native language. The researcher can hope to detect possible blunders through use of this method. An additional safeguard is the use of alternative question wording. Here the researcher uses questions that address the same issue but are worded differently and that resurface at various points in the questionnaire in order to check for consistency in question interpretation by the respondents.

In spite of superb research planning, a poorly designed instrument will yield poor results. No matter how comfortable and experienced the researcher is in international research activities, an instrument should always be pretested. Ideally such a pretest is carried out with a subset of the population under study. At least a pretest with knowledgeable experts and individuals should be conducted. Even though a pretest may mean delays in terms of time and additional cost, the downward risks of poor research are simply too great for this process to be omitted.

---

[14]Gilbert A. Churchill, Jr., *Marketing Research: Methodological Foundations*, 4th ed. (Hinsdale, Ill.: Dryden, 1987), 292–296.

Developing the Sampling Plan

In order to obtain representative results, the researcher must reach representative members of the population under study. Many methods that have been developed in industrialized countries for this purpose are useless abroad. For example, address directories may simply not be available. Multiple families may live in one dwelling. Differences between population groups living, for example, in highlands and lowlands may make it imperative to differentiate these segments. Lack of basic demographic information may make it impossible to design a sampling frame.

The international marketing researcher must keep in mind the complexities of the market under study and prepare his or her sampling plan accordingly. Often samples need to be stratified in order to reflect different population groups, and innovative sampling methods need to be devised in order to assure representative responses.

Obtaining the Data

When obtaining data, the international marketing researcher must check the quality of the data collection process. In some foreign cultures, questionnaire administration is seen as useless by the local population. Instruments are administered primarily to humor the researcher. In such cases, interviewer cheating may be quite frequent. Spot checks on the administration procedures are vital in order to ensure reasonable data quality. A **realism check** of data should be also used. For example, if marketing research in Italy reports that very little spaghetti is consumed, the researcher should perhaps consider whether individuals responded to their use of purchased spaghetti rather than homemade spaghetti. The collected data should therefore be compared to secondary information and to analogous information from a similar market in order to obtain a preliminary understanding of data quality.

Interpreting and Analyzing Data

Interpretation and analysis of accumulated information are required to answer the research questions that were posed initially. Analytical tools used in international marketing research are often quite shallow, and the sketchy evidence available suggests that analytical techniques, particularly quantitative ones, are not widely used by international marketing managers.[15] The researcher should of course use the best tools available and appropriate for analysis. The fact that a market may be in a less developed country does not preclude the subjecting of good data to good analysis. On the other hand, international researchers should be cautioned

---

[15] Essam Mahmoud and Gillian Rice, "Use of Analytical Techniques in International Marketing," *International Marketing Review* 5 (Autumn 1988): 7–13.

against using overly sophisticated tools for unsophisticated data. Even the best of tools will not improve data quality. The quality of data must be matched with the quality of the research tools to achieve appropriately sophisticated analysis and yet not overstate the value of the data.

Presenting Research Results

The primary focus in the presentation of research results must be communication. In multinational marketing research, communication must take place not only with management at headquarters but also with managers in the local operations. Otherwise, little or no transference of research results will occur, and the synergistic benefits of a multinational operation are lost. In order to minimize time devoted to the reading of reports, research results must be presented clearly and concisely. In the worldwide operations of a firm, particularly in the communication efforts, lengthy data and analytical demonstrations should be avoided. The availability of data and the techniques used should be mentioned, however, so that subsidiary operations can receive the information upon request.

The researcher should also demonstrate in the presentation how research results relate to the original research objective and fit in with overall corporate strategy. At least schematically, possibilities for analogous application should be highlighted. These possibilities should then also be communicated to local subsidiaries, perhaps through a short monthly newsletter. A newsletter format can be used regardless of whether the research process is centralized, coordinated, or decentralized. The only difference will be the person or group providing the input for the newsletter.

THE MARKETING DECISION SUPPORT SYSTEM

Many organizations have data needs going beyond specific international marketing research projects. Most of the time, daily decisions must be made for which there is neither time nor money for special research. An information system already in place is needed to provide the decision maker with basic data for most ongoing decisions. Information and data management for the international market are more complex than for the domestic market because of separation in time and space as well as wide differences in cultural and technological environments.[16] Yet these same factors highlight the increased need for an information system that assists in the decision-making process. Corporations have responded by developing marketing decision support systems such as the one described in Table 15.1. Defined as "an integrated system of data, statistical analysis, modeling, and display formats using computer hardware and software technol-

---

[16] Sayeste Daser, "International Marketing Information Systems: A Neglected Prerequisite for Foreign Market Planning," in *International Marketing Management,* ed. E. Kaynak (New York: Praeger Publishers, 1984), 139–154.

TABLE 15.1 ▪ **An Example of an International Decision Support System (IDSS)**

RJR Tobacco International, Inc.

This multinational cigarette manufacturer utilizes various methods of operation—exporting, licensing, wholly owned subsidiary—in major geographic markets around the world. Examples of subsystems of its IDSS might be:

a. Central databank on customers from different regions regarding demographic, psychological, sociological, and behavioral characteristics and sales data on each region. Tools from the statistical bank, like experimental design, can be used to measure the impact of competitive actions on company's sales.

b. Shipment reports data system to provide information regarding export shipments. Control data would be provided to management to measure program results against forecasted goals.

c. Subsidiary operations subsystem to provide financial and accounting information flows.

d. Econometric modeling procedures to be applied to forecasting economic and other trends affecting the cigarette industry around the world.

Source: Sayeste Daser, "International Marketing Information Systems: A Neglected Prerequisite for Foreign Market Planning." From *International Marketing Management*, edited by Erdener Kaynak, 1984.

ogy," such a system serves as a mechanism to coordinate the flow of information to corporate managers for decision-making purposes.[17]

In order to be useful to the decision maker, the system needs to benefit from various attributes. First, the information must be *relevant*. The data gathered must have meaning for the manager's decision-making process. Only rarely can corporations afford to spend large amounts of money on information that is simply "nice to know." Second, the information must be *timely*. It is of little benefit to the manager if decision information help that is needed today does not become available until a month from now. Third, information must be *flexible*—that is, it must be available in the forms needed by management. A marketing decision support system must therefore permit manipulation of the format and combining of the data. Fourth, information contained in the system must be *accurate*. This attribute is particularly relevant in the international field because information quickly becomes outdated as a result of major changes. Obviously, a system is of little value if it provides incorrect information that leads to poor decisions. Fifth, the system's information bank must be reasonably *exhaustive*. Because of the interrelationship between variables, factors that may influence a particular decision must be appropriately represented in the information system. This means that the marketing decision support system must be based on a broad variety of factors. Finally, in order to be useful to managers, the system must be *convenient*, both in use

[17] Kinnear and Taylor, *Marketing Research*, 146.

TABLE 15.2 ▪ **Factors Contributing to the Success of Marketing Decision Support Systems**

DATA AVAILABILITY

More internal data captured
More external data available on a commercial basis
Data now captured of unique value for marketing analysis
Data available on an instantaneous basis

INFORMATION TECHNOLOGY

Automated data capture at point of creation
Point-of-sale systems
Telecommunications
Videotex
Integrated and flexible software and hardware
Increased computer accessibility

REFINED DECISION MODELING APPROACHES

Manual decomposition techniques
Automated system-marketer decision analysis

PROFESSIONAL SOPHISTICATION

Familiarity with computer technology
Greater emphasis on decision methodology
Higher levels of education and training
Recognition of marketing function as necessary to success of the firm

MARKET CONDITIONS

Increased corporate competition
Smaller margin for error
Faster decision feedback
Rapidly evolving marketplace
Increasingly volatile distribution channels and consumer demand

Source: Stephen W. Brown and Martin D. Goslar, "New Information Systems for Marketing Decision Making," *Business* 38 (July-August-September 1988): 23.

and accessibility. Systems that are cumbersome and time consuming to reach and to use will not be used enough to justify corporate expenditures to build and maintain them.

There are various reasons why international marketing decision support systems are being developed successfully. As Table 15.2 shows, these are based on computer technology in both hardware and software, environmental changes such as increased familiarity with technology, and the necessity to deal with increasing shifts in market conditions. In addition, the advances made in utilizing vast quantities of information—through progress in research on artificial intelligence and the development of expert systems—make it important for a firm from a competitive viewpoint to explore the use of decision support systems.[18]

[18] Rowland T. Moriarty and Gordon S. Swartz, "Automation to Boost Sales and Marketing," *Harvard Business Review* 67 (January–February 1989): 100–108.

To build a market decision support system, corporations use the internal data that are available from divisions such as accounting and finance and also from various subsidiaries. In addition, many organizations put mechanisms in place to enrich the basic data flow. Three such mechanisms are environmental scanning, Delphi studies, and scenario building.

Environmental Scanning

Any changes in the environment, whether domestic or foreign, may have serious repercussions on the marketing activities of the firm. Corporations therefore understand the necessity for tracking developments in the environment. The remoteness from international markets requires continuous informational updates on developments in these environments. In order to carry out this task, some large multinational organizations have formed environmental scanning groups. Examples of such scanning activities and their rationale are provided in Table 15.3 on pages 520–521.

Environmental scanning activities are useful to continuously receive information on political, social, and economic affairs internationally; on changes of attitudes held by public institutions and private citizens; and to provide hints as to possible upcoming alterations in international markets. Environmental scanning models are used for a variety of purposes. Some of these are:

1. The provision of a mind-stretching or educational experience for management
2. The development of broad strategies and long-term policies
3. The development of action plans and operating programs
4. The development of a frame of reference for the annual budget [19]

Obviously, the precision required for environmental scanning varies with its purpose. Whether the information is to be used for mind stretching or for budgeting, for example, must be taken into account when constructing the framework and variables that will enter the scanning process. The more immediate and precise the exercise is to be in its application within the corporation, the greater the need for detailed information. At the same time, such heightened precision may lessen the utility of environmental scanning for the strategic corporate purpose, which is more long term in its orientation.

Environmental scanning can be performed in various ways. One component consists of obtaining factual input regarding many variables. For example, the International Data Base (IDB) of the U.S. Census Bureau collects, evaluates, and adjusts a wide variety of demographic, social, and economic characteristics of foreign countries. Estimates are being provided for all countries of the world, particularly on economic variables such as labor-force statistics, GNP, and income statistics. Health and nutri-

---

[19] Robert N. Anthony, John Dearden, and Richard F. Vancil, *Management Control Systems,* rev. ed. (Homewood, Ill.: Irwin, 1972), 471–472.

tional variables are also covered.[20] Similar factual information can be obtained from international organizations such as the World Bank or the United Nations.

Frequently, corporations believe that such factual data alone are insufficient for their information needs. Particularly for forecasting future developments, other methods are used to capture underlying dimensions of social change. One significant method is that of **content analysis.** This technique investigates the content of communication in a society, and entails literally counting the number of times preselected words, themes, symbols, or pictures appear in a given medium. It can be used productively in international marketing to monitor the social, economic, cultural, and technological environment in which the marketing organization is operating. The use of content analysis is facilitated by the emergence of new tools such as optical scanners and new software packages. For example, the Apple MacIntosh PC can accommodate texts in Chinese, Japanese, Hebrew, Korean, and Arabic.[21]

Corporations can use content analysis to pinpoint upcoming changes in their line of business and new opportunities, by attempting to identify trendsetting events. For example, the Alaska oil spill by the tanker *Valdez* is likely to set an entirely new trend in national concern about environmental protection and safety, reaching far beyond the incident itself.

Environmental scanning is conducted by a variety of groups within and outside the corporation. Quite frequently, small corporate staffs are created at headquarters to coordinate the information flow. In addition, subsidiary staff can be used to provide occasional intelligence reports. Groups of volunteers are also formed that gather and analyze information worldwide and feed their individual analyses back to corporate headquarters, where they can be used to form the "big picture." Increasingly, large corporations also offer services in environmental scanning to outsiders. In this way profits can be made from an in-house activity that has to be conducted anyway. Figure 15.5 on page 522 gives an example of such a service.

Typically, environmental scanning is designed primarily to aid the strategic planning process rather than the tactical activities of the corporation. A survey of corporate environmental scanning activities found that "the futurity of the scanning exercise ranges from the medium term (say about 5 years) to the truly long term (around 20 years) with the mode being about 10 years."[22] Environmental scanning, therefore, addresses itself mostly to the future in order to complement the continuous flow of factual data to the corporation.

Although environmental scanning is perceived by many corporations as quite valuable for the corporate planning process, there are dissenting

---

[20] "IDB Provides Demographics of Foreign Markets," *Marketing News*, May 24, 1985, 14.

[21] David R. Wheeler, "Content Analysis: An Analytical Technique for International Marketing Research," *International Marketing Review* (Winter 1988): 34–40.

[22] Phillip S. Thomas, "Environmental Scanning—The State of the Art," *Long Range Planning* 13 (February 1980): 24.

TABLE 15.3 ▪ **The Practice of Scanning for Planning**

Organization	Rationale for Scanning	Scope
American Council of Life Insurance	The primary goal of such a (trend analysis) program must be to change the process of thinking and decision making on the part of company management, not to directly shape decisions or corporate policy. If it succeeds in the former, however, it will certainly affect the latter.	Science and technology, social sciences, business and economics and politics, and government
Ciba-Geigy	The purpose of the information base on which all planning depends is to provide a sound perspective for identifying major opportunities and then as a basis for setting meaningful objectives.	Political affairs, economic conditions
Citicorp	We need more sophisticated global intelligence systems to provide early warning of possible emergencies. New intelligence systems must account for discrepancies between the political and economic realities.	Social, economic, political conditions and constraints
General Motors	Our ultimate goal is to make the social policy input commensurate with the quantification of financial and technological inputs.	General economic outlook plus government policies Public attitudes on major social issues
IBM	Management recognizes to a much greater extent that the success of a company increasingly depends on knowledge of the economic environment, because there is a parallel recognition that the overall external environment affects corporations much more than it used to.	Mainly economic conditions; also other environmental factors, e.g., consumerism, privacy and data security, international political and economic relationships
Royal Dutch Shell	Our forecasting cannot function without having a quality of management which we look for in Shell called the helicopter quality. That means having a person who is able to take off a little bit and overview the total scenario so that he can get things in perspective and yet remain in contact with the ground.	Economic, political, and social developments

Source: Reprinted with permission from *Long Range Planning*, 13, Phillip S. Thomas, "Environmental Scanning–The State of the Art," February 1980, pp. 26–28. Copyright 1980 Pergamon Press PLC.

Range	Futurity	Organizational Level
Nationwide	TAP does not make predictions; rather it describes the environment and shows what some possible futures might be	Centralized Abstracts Analysis Committee: 100 part-time volunteer staff in member companies who monitor 60 key publications
Each national market plus "world portraits"	Not disclosed	Headquarters and field units
Each national market	Current plus forecasts	Field units plus special officers at HO
Nationwide	Short term plus long term	Headquarters staff: Economics Department Societal Research Group
Nationwide and global	Not discussed	Two organizational mechanisms—one the operating units affected and the second the corporate staff
Country level plus global level	Alternative scenarios for up to 20 years	Headquarters plus field units

FIGURE 15.5 ▪ **Ad Offering Environmental Scanning as a Service**

World Information Services delivers:

▪ Data and guidance to enable you to operate more securely and efficiently in foreign markets

▪ A point of reference for management in dealing with financial and international business questions

▪ A tool to guide funding and financial management decisions

▪ A reliable database of quantitative information

▪ Authoritative global economic and strategic projections

▪ Access to a global intelligence network that is essential to informed policy debate and recommendations

▪ Practical working knowledge of the global economic and business environment

Country Outlooks	**$495 a year**
Country Data Forecasts	**$495 a year**
Country Risk Monitor	**$495 a year**
ALL THREE SERVICES	**$1290 a year**

Bank of America
World Information Services
Department 3015   **1-800-645-6667**
555 California Street   **In California 1-800-645-4004**
San Francisco, California 94104   **From Outside the U.S. (415) 622-1446**

BANK OF AMERICA NT&SA MEMBER FDIC   © 1989 Bank of America

Source: © 1989 Bank of America World Information Services. Reprinted with permission.

voices. For example, it has been noted by researchers "that in those constructs and frameworks where the environment has been given primary consideration, there has been a tendency for the approach to become so global that studies tend to become shallow and diffuse, or impractical if pursued in sufficient depth."[23] Obviously, this presents one of the major

[23] Winter and Prohaska, "Methodological Problems," 429.

continuous challenges corporations face in their international environmental scanning. The trade-off still exists between the breadth and depth of information. However, the continuous evolution of manipulative power through the ever-increasing capabilities of data processing may reduce at least the scope of the manipulative problem. However, the cost of data acquisition and the issue of actual data use will continue to form major restraints on the development of environmental scanning systems.

Delphi Studies

In order to enrich the information obtained from factual data, corporations frequently resort to the use of creative and highly qualitative data-gathering methods. One way of doing so is through Delphi studies. These studies are particularly useful in the international marketing environment, because they are "a means for aggregating the judgments of a number of . . . experts . . . who cannot come together physically."[24] This type of research approach clearly aims at qualitative rather than quantitative measures by aggregating the information of a group of experts. It seeks to obtain answers from those who know instead of seeking the average responses of many with only limited knowledge.

Typically, Delphi studies are carried out with groups of about 30 well-chosen participants who possess particular in-depth expertise in an area of concern, such as future developments in the international trade environment. These participants are asked, most frequently via mail, to identify the major issues in the area of concern. They are also requested to rank order their statements according to importance and explain the rationale behind the order. Next the aggregated information is returned to all participants, who are encouraged to clearly state their agreements or disagreements with the various rank orders and comments. Statements can be challenged and, in another round, the challenges can be responded to. After several rounds of challenge and response, a reasonably coherent consensus can be developed.

The Delphi technique is particularly valuable because it uses the mail communication method to bridge large distances, and therefore makes individuals quite accessible. It does not suffer from the drawback of ordinary mail investigations, which is the lack of interaction among the participants. One drawback of the technique is that it requires several steps and therefore months may elapse before the information is obtained. Also, substantial effort must be expended in selecting the appropriate participants and in motivating them to participate in this exercise with enthusiasm and continuity. When obtained on a regular basis, Delphi information can provide crucial augmentation to the factual data available for the marketing information system.

---

[24] Andrel Delbecq, Andrew H. Van de Ven, and David H. Gustafson, *Group Techniques for Program Planning* (Glenview, Ill.: Scott, Foresman, 1975), 83.

Scenario Building

For information enrichment purposes, some companies use **scenario analysis.** The principal method here is to look at different configurations of key variables in the international market. For example, economic growth rates, import penetration, population growth, and political stability can be varied. By projecting such variations for medium- to long-term periods, completely new environmental conditions can emerge. These conditions are then analyzed for their potential domestic and international impact on corporate strategy.

Of major importance in scenario building is the identification of crucial trend variables and the degree of their variation. Frequently key experts are used in order to gain information about potential variations and the viability of certain scenarios. The International Marketplace 15.4 provides an example of input from such experts.

A wide variety of scenarios must be built in order to expose corporate executives to multiple potential occurrences. Ideally, even far-fetched variables deserve some consideration, if only to build worst-case scenarios. A scenario for Union Carbide Corporation, for example, could have included the possibility of a disaster such as occurred in Bhopal.

Scenario builders also need to recognize the nonlinearity of factors. To simply extrapolate from currently existing situations is insufficient. Frequently extraneous factors may enter the picture with a significant impact. Finally, in scenario building the possibility of joint occurrences must be recognized, because changes may not come about in an isolated fashion but may be spread over wide regions. An example of a joint occurrence is the indebtedness of Latin American nations. Although the inability of any one country to pay its debts would not have presented a major problem for the international banking community, large and simultaneous indebtedness posed a problem of major severity. Similarly, given large technological advances, the possibility of "wholesale" obsolescence of current technology must also be considered. For example, quantum leaps in computer development and new generations of computers may render obsolete the technological investment of a corporation or even a country.

In order for scenarios to be useful, management must analyze and respond to them by formulating contingency plans. Such planning will broaden horizons and may prepare management for unexpected situations. Familiarization in turn can result in shorter response times to actual occurrences by honing response capability.

The development of a marketing decision support system is of major importance to the multinational corporation. It aids the ongoing decision process and becomes a vital corporate tool in carrying out the strategic planning task. Only by observing global trends and changes will the firm be able to maintain and increase its international competitive position. Much of the data available is quantitative in nature, but attention must also be paid to qualitative dimensions. Quantitative analysis will continue to improve, as the ability to collect, store, analyze, and retrieve data in-

THE INTERNATIONAL MARKETPLACE   15.4

Advice from Kissinger Associates   *Kissinger Associates is a New York-based consulting firm established in 1982 by former Secretary of State Henry Kissinger, former Undersecretary of State Lawrence S. Eagleburger, and former National Security Advisor Brent Scowcroft. For its corporate clients, the firm offers broadbrush pictures of political and economic conditions in particular countries or regions along with analyses of political and economic trends. Because none of the founders is particularly known for his business or economic expertise, an investment banker and an economist were brought on board.*

Some have argued that the pointing out of political trends is an insufficient base from which to make a living. Kissinger himself stated that to provide only abstract information on the political condition in a foreign country is not fair to the client. The firm sees its primary strength to be its sensitivity to the international political situation and its continued closeness to information sources. Although Kissinger Associates offers no voluminous country reports, the principals believe that by correctly assessing, for example, the political outlook in Greece for the next five years, they can help a client decide whether to make new investments there or preparations to leave in anticipation of a hostile socialist government. Similarly, the firm might help a U.S. oil company with limited Middle East experience in its first attempts to negotiate and work with a government in the region. Although this type of work does not involve Kissinger Associates deeply in specific business decisions, it does require a good understanding of clients' businesses and goals.

One practical reason for using high-powered consulting input was explained by a former member of Kissinger Associates: "These days, in case an investment goes sour, it is useful for (management) to be able to say, 'We got this expert advice and acted on that basis.' They have to show due diligence in exercising their fiduciary duties."

Even though client identities and fees are well-guarded secrets, congressional confirmation hearings for former employees of Kissinger Associates revealed that clients such as Union Carbide, Coca-Cola, Volvo, Fiat, and Daewoo pay between $150,000 and $400,000 per year for the firm's services.

Source: Christopher Madison, "Kissinger Firm Hopes to Make Its Mark as Risk Advisors to Corporate Chiefs," *National Journal,* June 22, 1985, 1452–1456; and "The Out-of-Office Reign of Henry I," *U.S. News and World Report,* March 27, 1989, 10.

creases through the use of computer equipment. Nevertheless, qualitative analysis will remain a major component for corporate research and planning activities.

SUMMARY

In order to respond to specific information requirements, frequently primary research is needed. Depending on the research objective at hand and on the existing level of expertise within the firm, exploratory, descriptive, or causal research needs to be carried out.

In developing a research program, care must be taken to properly determine the information requirements of the firm. Subsequently, the data sources available and the type of data needed have to be investigated. The researcher then must critically assess corporate capabilities and constraints in order to determine where the research is to be carried out, and whether the research program is to be centralized or decentralized. Although the latter decision may vary depending on the corporate orientation, research activities should always be coordinated across corporate functions in order to minimize overlap and to benefit from synergism.

The researcher then needs to select an appropriate research technique to collect the information needed. Particular sensitivity to different international environments and cultures will guide the researcher in the decision whether to use interviews, focus groups, observation, surveys, or experimentation as data collection techniques. The same sensitivity applies to the design of the research instrument, where issues such as question format, content, and wording are decided. Also, the sampling plan needs to be appropriate for the local environment in order to ensure representative and useful responses.

Once the data are collected, care must be taken to use analytical tools appropriate for the quality of data collected so that management is not misled about the sophistication of the research. Finally, the research results must be presented in a concise and useful form so that management can benefit in its decision making.

In order to provide ongoing information to management, a marketing decision support system is useful. Such a system will provide for the systematic and continuous gathering, analysis, and reporting of data for decision-making purposes. It uses firm internal information and gathers data via environmental scanning, Delphi studies, or scenario building, thus enabling management to prepare for the future and hone its decision-making skills.

Questions for Discussion

1. Why should a firm collect primary data in its international marketing research?

2. Should corporations conduct more causal international marketing research?

3. Discuss the trade-offs between centralized and decentralized international marketing research.

4. How is international market research affected by differences in language?

5. Compare the use of telephone surveys in the United States and in Egypt.

6. What are your thoughts on the characterization of international marketing research as unsophisticated and shallow?

7. Is highly priced personalized advice from an individual really worth the money?

8. What use do you see for an international marketing decision support system?

9. Does it make sense to spend money on 20-year forecasts?

10. What are some of the crucial variables you would track in a decision support system?

Recommended Readings

Barnard, Philip. "Conducting and Co-ordinating Multicountry Quantitative Studies across Europe." In *Global Marketing Perspectives*, edited by Jagdish Sheth and Abdolreza Eshghi, 56–73. Cincinnati, Ohio: South-Western, 1989.

Bartos, Rena. *Marketing to Women around the World*. Cambridge, Mass.: Harvard Business School Press, 1989.

Churchill, Gilbert A., Jr. *Marketing Research: Methodological Foundations*. 4th ed. Hinsdale, Ill.: Dryden, 1987.

Davidson, James Dale, and Sir William Rees-Mogg. *Blood in the Streets*. New York: Summit Books, 1987.

Douglas, Susan P., and C. Samuel Craig. *International Marketing Research*. Englewood Cliffs, N.J.: Prentice-Hall, 1983.

Malhotra, Naresh K. "A Methodology for Measuring Consumer Preferences in Developing Countries," *International Marketing Review*, Autumn 1988, 52–66.

Naisbitt, John. *Megatrends: Ten New Directions Transforming Our Lives*. New York: Warner Books, 1982.

Zikmund, William G. *Exploring Marketing Research*. 3d ed. Hinsdale, Ill.: Dryden, 1989.

CHAPTER 16

Product Management for Multinational Corporations

THE INTERNATIONAL MARKETPLACE

Different Strokes for Different Markets   *Procter & Gamble's sales volume was up only 4 percent for 1988 in the United States, whereas international shipments were growing at 8 to 10 percent. Thirty percent of the company's worldwide profit came from abroad. The improved performance in overseas markets was led by strong performances in disposable diapers, liquid detergents, and Richardson-Vicks over-the-counter drugs. The company's overall international effort involved 165 brands in 11 categories.*

P&G had become, according to industry experts, more aggressive in its marketing. Although the company was still only number two or number three in certain categories, boosting market share had become its top priority.

In Japan, where P&G trailed well-established Kao Corporation in share for diapers and detergents, new-product sales grew enough to push the subsidiary into the black. P&G had had to work quite hard in the market because it is not a category innovator there. Although Kao's Merries commanded about 40 percent of the disposable-diaper market with three brands, Pampers' sales grew to 23 percent of the market. This growth was primarily due to the introduction of a redesigned, superabsorbent, and smaller, thinner diaper.

In Europe, P&G faced its toughest competition from Unilever, which had made inroads into the company's detergent and fabric softener market shares. Liquid detergents commanded 30 percent of the $600 million U.K. detergent category, and P&G rushed two new items into the market in 1988 without test marketing; this was a rarity for the company, but necessitated by competitive pressures. By mid-1989 P&G's Ariel held 12 percent of the category, Unilever's Wisk only 8 percent. P&G's success in the liquid-detergent category was attributed to building brand leverage by simply extending the name of its Ariel powder entry, the leading detergent in the market. Unilever used different names for its liquid and powder brands.

In West Germany, P&G's acquisition of Blendax put the company into new personal-care categories, including toothpaste, where it had never competed. The company planned to use Richardson-

Vicks' distribution channels to expand Blendax brands into other parts of Europe.

Source: "P&G on a Roll Overseas," *Advertising Age*, June 27, 1988, 30; and "Kao Ready to Move with Jergens Line," *Advertising Age*, June 27, 1988, 30.

Developing and managing a product portfolio for international markets is a complex process as shown in The International Marketplace 16.1, which describes the various environmental challenges faced by Procter & Gamble. The basic issue discussed in Chapter 9 was the adaptation of products; this chapter will focus on the adaptation of product portfolios to markets in varying stages of development. The degree to which "thinking globally but acting locally" allows marketers to reap the benefits of economies of scale in offering standard product portfolios is discussed, as opposed to catering to needs of local segments with additional entries.

The development of product portfolios depends on an appropriate multinational product development effort that takes into consideration the needs of major markets without forgetting the needs of smaller national markets. The management of such portfolios will have to consider the competitiveness of the company's product lines globally, regionally, and locally in terms of risks and returns.

The chapter closes with a discussion of two intellectual-property issues. The first one is a major challenge facing international marketers worldwide: product counterfeiting. For products based on patents and trademarks, for example, violations can be harmful. Through foreign direct investment, international marketers transfer technology to target markets. The transfer process will be analyzed from the marketing point of view.

INTERNATIONAL PRODUCT PLANNING AND DEVELOPMENT

Product development is at the heart of the marketing process. New products should be developed, or old ones modified, to cater to new or changing customer needs. At the same time, corporate objectives of technical feasibility and financial profitability must be satisfied.

To illustrate, Black & Decker, manufacturer of power tools for do-it-yourself household repairs, has done some remodeling of its own. With total sales of $1.17 billion, the company in the early 1980s was the consummate customizer: the Italian subsidiary made tools for Italians, the British subsidiary for the British. At the same time Japanese power-tool makers such as Makita Electric Works Ltd. saw the world differently. Makita was Black & Decker's first competitor with a global strategy. Makita management did not care that Germans prefer high-powered, heavy-duty drills and that the Americans want everything lighter. They reasoned that a good drill at a low price will sell from Baden-Baden to Brooklyn. Using this strategy, Makita effectively cut into Black & Decker's market share. In 1984 Black & Decker unveiled 50 new models—each standardized for world production.[1]

With increasing competition able to react quickly when new products are introduced, worldwide planning at the product level provides a number of tangible benefits. A firm that adopts a worldwide product management approach is better able to develop products with specifications compatible on a worldwide scale. A firm that leaves product development to independent units will incur greater difficulties in transfering its experience and technology.

In many multinational corporations, each product is developed for potential worldwide usage, and unique multinational market requirements are incorporated whenever technically feasible. Some design their products to meet the regulations and other key requirements in their major markets and then, if necessary, smaller markets' requirements are met on a country-by-country basis. For example, Nissan develops lead-country models that can, with minor changes, be made suitable for local sales in the majority of markets. For the remaining situations, the company also provides a range of additional models that can be adapted to the needs of local segments. Using this approach, Nissan has been able to reduce the number of basic models from 48 to 18.[2] This approach also means that the new product can be introduced concurrently into all of the firm's markets. Companies like 3M and Xerox consider the introduction concurrent if initial shipments into all of their markets occur within a six-month period.

The main goal of the product development process, therefore, is not the development of a standard product or product line, but to build adaptability into products that are being developed to achieve worldwide appeal.

The Multinational Product Development Process

The product development process begins with idea generation. Ideas may come from within the company—from the research and development staff, sales personnel, or almost anyone who becomes involved in the company's efforts. Intermediaries may suggest ideas because they are closer to the changing, and often different, needs of international customers. Competitors are a major outside source of ideas. A competitive idea from abroad may be modified and improved to suit another market's characteristics. As an example, when the president of d-Con returned from a trip to Europe, he brought with him what would seem in the United States to be

[1]"Black & Decker's Gamble on 'Globalization,'" *Fortune*, May 14, 1984, 40–48.

[2]Kenichi Ohmae, "Managing in a Borderless World," *Harvard Business Review* 67 (May–June 1989): 152–161.

an unusual idea for packaging insecticides. In a market dominated by aerosols, the new idea called for offering consumers insect repellent in a "felt-tip pen." d-Con obtained U.S. rights for the product, which in Europe is marketed by Tamana, a subsidiary of Shell Oil.[3]

For a number of companies, especially those producing industrial goods, customers provide the best source of ideas for new products.[4] This situation is quite advantageous because the developing company is not obligated to limit marketing to the company that provided the idea. For some companies, procurement requisitions from governments and supranational organizations (for example, the United Nations) are a good source of new product ideas.

Most companies develop hundreds of ideas every year; for example, 3M may have 1,000 new product ideas competing for scarce development funds annually. Product ideas are screened on market, technical, and financial criteria: is the market substantial and penetrable, can the product be mass produced, and, if the answer to both of these questions is affirmative, can the company produce and market it profitably? For example, cereal producers may refrain from introducing their products to a market like Brazil, where breakfast is not normally eaten, because an expensive education process would be necessary.

A product idea that at some stage fails to earn a go-ahead is not necessarily scrapped. Most progressive companies maintain databanks of "miscellaneous opportunities." Often, data from these banks are used in the development of other products. One of the most famous examples concerns 3M. After developing a new woven fabric some 50 years ago, 3M's Commercial Office Supply Company did not know what to do with the technology. Among the applications rejected were seamless brassiere cups (too expensive) and disposable diapers. The fabric was finally used to make surgical and industrial masks.[5]

When a new product idea earns a go-ahead, the first pilot models are built. This means a major commitment of funds, especially if the product requires separate facilities and special personnel. In the scaleup phase, which precedes full-scale commercialization, preliminary production units are tested on-site or in limited minilaunches.

All of the development phases—idea generation, screening, product and process development, scaleup, and commercialization—should be multinational in nature with inputs into the process from all affected markets. If this is possible, original product designs can be adapted easily and inexpensively later on. The process has been greatly facilitated through the use of **computer-aided design (CAD)**. Some companies are able to de-

---

[3] "D-Con Finds New Product Idea in Europe," *Advertising Age*, July 9, 1984, 58.

[4] Eric von Hippel, "Successful Industrial Products from Customer Ideas," *Journal of Marketing* 42 (January 1978): 39–49.

[5] "Herzog: New Products Mean New Opportunities," *International Ambassador*, March 23, 1979, 3.

sign their products so that they meet most standards and requirements around the world with minor modifications on a country-by-country basis. The product development process can be initiated by any unit of the organization, in the parent country or abroad. If the initiating entity is a subsidiary that lacks technical and financial resources for implementation, another entity of the firm is assigned the responsibility. Most often this is the parent and its central R&D department. Larger multinational corporations naturally have development laboratories in multiple locations that can assume the task. Gillette, for example, maintains two toiletries laboratories, one in the United States and the other in the United Kingdom.[6] In these cases coordination and information flow between the units is especially critical.

In some cases, the assignment of product development responsibility may be based on a combination of special market and technical knowledge. When a major U.S. copier manufacturer was facing erosion of market share in the smaller copier segment in Europe because of Japanese incursions, its Japanese subsidiary was charged with developing an addition to the company's product line. This product, developed and produced outside the United States, has subsequently been marketed in the United States.

Even though the product development activity may take place in the parent country, all of the affected units actively participate in development and market planning for a new product. For example, a subsidiary would communicate directly with the product division at the headquarters level and also with the international staff, who could support the subsidiary on the scene of the actual development activity. This often also involves the transfer of people from one location to another for such projects.

The activities of a typical multinational program are summarized in Figure 16.1. The managing unit has prime responsibility for accomplishing: (1) single-point worldwide technical development and design of a new product that conforms to the multinational design standard and multinational manufacturing and procurement standards as well as transmittal of the completed design to each affected unit; (2) all other activities necessary to plan, develop, manufacture, introduce, and support the product in the managing unit as well as direction and support to affected units to ensure that concurrent introductions are achieved; and (3) integration and coordination of all multinational program activities.

The affected units, on the other hand, have prime responsibility for achieving: (1) identification of unique requirements to be incorporated in the product goals and specifications as well as in the managing unit's technical effort; (2) all other activities necessary to plan, manufacture, introduce, and support products in affected units; and (3) identification of any nonconcurrence with the managing unit's plans and activities.

---

[6]"How Gillette Keeps Research and Development Close to Local Markets," *Business International*, February 1, 1985, 33–34.

FIGURE 16.1   ▪   **Multinational Program Management**

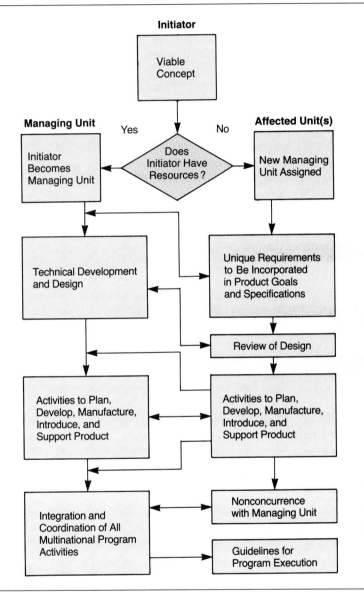

Source: Ilkka A. Ronkainen, "Product Development in the Multinational Firm," *International Marketing Review* 1 (Winter 1983): 24–30.

During the early stages of the product development process, the multinational emphasis is on identifying and evaluating the requirements of both the managing unit and the affected units and incorporating them into the plan. During the later stages, the emphasis is on the efficient development and design of a multinational product with a minimum of configuration differences and on the development of supporting systems capabilities in each of the participating units. The result of the interaction and communication is product development activity on a global basis as well as products developed primarily to serve world markets.

This approach cuts effectively through the standardized-versus-localized debate and offers a clear-cut way of determining and implementing effective programs in several markets simultaneously. It offers headquarters the opportunity to standardize certain aspects of the product while permitting maximum flexibility, whenever technically feasible, to differing market conditions. For instance, in terms of technical development, members of subsidiaries' staffs take an active part in the development processes to make sure that multinational specifications are built into the initial design of the product.[7]

The process has to be streamlined, however. In industries characterized by technological change, coming to market 9 to 12 months late can cost a new product half its potential revenues.[8] To cut down on development time, companies like NEC and Canon use multidisciplinary teams that stay with the project from start to finish, using a parallel approach toward product launch. Designers start to work before feasibility testing is over; manufacturing and marketing begin gearing up well before the design is finished. Such teams depend on computer systems for designing, simulating, and analyzing products. Toyota Motor Company estimates that it can in the future develop a new automobile in one year whereas most of its competitors now take up to five years.[9] However, with new uncertain technologies for which market response is not clear, longer development cycles are still common and advisable.[10]

Firms using worldwide product management are better able to develop products that can be quickly introduced into any market.[11] Foreign market introduction can take the form of either production or marketing abroad. The average time lags between initial production or marketing and introduction in other markets are summarized in Table 16.1 for firms in several industries.

These lags will grow shorter, according to *Business Week*, because "computers and telecommunications will speed up the spread of innovations. You do not have to go to the patent office anymore; once the idea is in the public domain, you can call it up on your desk computer through an information service firm."[12] In general, the length of the lag will depend

[7]Ilkka A. Ronkainen, "Product Development in the Multinational Firm," *International Marketing Review* 1 (Winter 1983): 24–30.

[8]Bro Uttal, "Speeding New Ideas to Market," *Fortune*, March 2, 1987, 62–66.

[9]"Advantage for Toyota," *The Wall Street Journal*, August 5, 1988, 35.

[10]Edward G. Krubasik, "Customize Your Product Development," *Harvard Business Review* 66 (November–December 1988): 46–52.

[11]Georges LeRoy, *Multinational Product Strategies: A Typology for Analysis of Worldwide Product Innovation Diffusion* (New York: Praeger, 1976), 1–3.

[12]"The Breakdown of U.S. Innovation," *Business Week*, February 16, 1976, 56–68.

TABLE 16.1 ▪ **Average Time Lags (in Months) between Initial Production or Marketing of New Products and Their Introduction into Other Markets**[a]

	Electronics Firms	Agricultural Machinery Firm	Aluminum Manufacturer	Visual Communication Equipment Manufacturer	Toiletries and Personal Care Manufacturer
Market	4.7	21.7	55.8	5.0	30.1
Production	36.0	64.0	62.0	6.0	50.0

[a]The average lag is for all the products selected in the firm and all the countries they were diffused to.

Source: Georges P. LeRoy, "An Innovation Diffusion Perspective," in *Multinational Product Management*, eds. Warren Keegan and Charles S. Mayer, 1977, p. 37. Reprinted from *Multinational Product Management*, published by the American Marketing Association.

on (1) the product involved, with industrial products having shorter lags because of their more standardized general nature; (2) degree of newness; (3) customer characteristics—both demographics and psychographics; (4) geographic proximity; (5) firm-related variables—the number and type of foreign affiliations as well as overall experience in international marketing; and (6) degree of commitments of resources.

The Location of Foreign R&D Activities

The past tendency of most multinational corporations has been to locate most of their product development operations within the parent corporation. Recently, however, a number of experts have called for companies to start using foreign-based resources to improve their ability to compete internationally. The experts' proposals are based on acquiring international contacts and having R&D investments abroad as ways to add new items to the company's existing product line. For example, in 1988, W. R. Grace opened an $8 million R&D center in Japan. Although the costs are high and recruitment difficult, benefits are numerous as well. Japan provides the company heightened awareness of and access to technological developments that can be used to be more responsive not only to local markets but to global markets as well. The R&D center is part of Grace's **triad** approach involving the three leading areas for diffusion of technology: the United States, Europe, and Japan.[13] A dozen other companies, including DuPont, Upjohn, and Eastman Kodak have launched similar centers.

[13] "W. R. Grace Extends Global R&D to Japan," *Business International*, December 5, 1988, 377, 382.

THE INTERNATIONAL MARKETPLACE

The Car of the Future Is Designed in California   Toyota was first, but now most of the major automakers have design studios in Los Angeles, Orange, or San Diego counties in California. The location of these design centers for cars two or three generations away allows for the monitoring of technical, social, and aesthetic values of the area. Californians spend more time in their cars than most Americans—and more energy caring both for and about their cars. The state is also the fifth largest auto market in the world in its own right. Half of all new cars sold in the state are imports, compared to approximately 30 percent for all of the United States. The many technological innovations and design trends that have originated there give it a trend-setting image. For many car manufacturers, California represents the world.

The responsibilities of the design studios of foreign-based manufacturers vary from fully developing specific models to collaborating with designers at home-market centers. Toyota's Japanese designers, for example, are concerned with the next generation of cars, whereas Calty, the company's studio in El Segundo, California, focuses on longer term designs. Isuzu's center in Cerritos, California, will either design or heavily influence more than 90 percent of Isuzu's products in the future.

In addition to their Michigan design studios, Chrysler, Ford, and General Motors have established their own facilities in Southern California. This is "not as a response to the Japanese, but more as a response to the area itself. California is right in the middle of the action, and you literally have to be there," according to an executive at GM.

Source: K. M. Chrysler, "For Car of Future, Go West, Young Man," *U.S. News & World Report*, September 10, 1984, 50; and Janice Steinberg, "Design Studios Go California Dreamin'," *Advertising Age*, July 25, 1988, S-18.

Investments for R&D abroad are made for four general reasons: (1) to aid technology transfer from parent to subsidiary, (2) to develop new and improved products expressly for foreign markets, (3) to develop new products and processes for simultaneous application in world markets of the firm, and (4) to generate new technology of a long-term exploratory nature. The commitment of the firm to international operations increases from the first type of investment to the third and the fourth, in which there is no or little bias toward headquarters performing the job.[14]

---

[14] Robert Ronstadt, "International R&D: The Establishment and Evolution of Research and Development Abroad by U.S. Multinationals," *Journal of International Business Studies* 9 (Spring–Summer 1978): 7–24.

TABLE 16.2   ▪   **Most Popular Sites for Foreign R&D Activities**

American Firms	*European Firms*
United Kingdom (11)	United States (14)
Australia (8)	France (10)
Canada (8)	Germany (9)
Japan (8)	India (6)
France (7)	Brazil (5)
Germany (6)	United Kingdom (5)
Mexico (6)	
Brazil (5)	

Note: Numbers in parentheses refer to the number of corporations reporting an R&D presence in a particular country.

Source: Jack N. Behrman and William A. Fischer, "Transnational Corporations and R&D Abroad," in *The Multinational Enterprise in Transition,* eds. Philip D. Grub et al. (Princeton, N.J.: Darwin Press, 1984), 383.

A sample of 35 U.S.-based and 18 Europe-based multinational corporations was used in an attempt to determine the type of R&D being performed abroad, how the sites were selected, how they are managed, and relations with local entities as well as collaborative efforts.[15] In many cases companies must be close to their markets to satisfy local styles and needs. This strategy or requirement is not limited to consumer-goods companies. Regulations in the pharmaceutical industry often require U.S. companies to have European formulation laboratories. In truly multinational companies, the location of R&D is determined by the existence of specific skills. For instance, all R&D concerning photography at 3M takes place in Italy at the Ferrania division, which was acquired by the company in the 1960s. Placing R&D operations abroad may also ensure access to foreign scientific and technical personnel and information, either in industry or at leading universities. The local decision may also be driven by the unique features of the market, as shown in The International Marketplace 16.2.

The most popular sites for foreign R&D activities are listed in Table 16.2. Most R&D activities are based in developed countries. Many companies regionalize their R&D efforts; for example, U.S.-based multinational corporations often base their European R&D facilities in Belgium because of its central location and desirable market characteristics, which include serving as headquarters for the European Community and providing well-trained personnel. Developing countries are increasingly demanding R&D facilities as a condition of investment or continued operation, to the extent that some companies have left countries where they saw no

[15] Jack N. Behrman and William A. Fischer, "Transnational Corporations: Market Orientations and R&D Abroad," in *The Multinational Enterprise in Transition,* eds. Philip D. Grub et al. (Princeton, N.J.: Darwin Press, 1984), 378–389.

need for the added expense. Countries that have been known to have attempted to influence multinational corporations are Japan, India, Brazil, and France.

Some governments, such as Canada, have offered financial rewards to multinational corporations to start or expand R&D efforts in the host markets. In addition to compliance with governmental regulation, local R&D efforts can provide positive publicity for the company involved. Internally, having local R&D may boost morale and elevate a subsidiary above the status of merely a manufacturing operation.[16]

Having R&D units abroad allows for division of labor, which may mean faster and more effective results. Marching orders still come from headquarters, but a regional or local laboratory may be the best choice for the actual development work.

In many multinational corporations, product development efforts amount to product modification—for example, making sure that a product satisfies local regulations. Local content requirements may necessitate major development input from the affected markets. In these cases, local technical people identify alternate, domestically available ingredients and prepare initial tests. More involved testing usually takes place at a regional laboratory or at headquarters.

The Organization of Multinational Product Development

The composition of a typical product development team is presented in Figure 16.2. Representatives of all of the affected functional areas are on each team to ensure the integrity of the project. A marketing team member is needed to assess the customer base for the new product, engineering to make sure that the product can be produced in the intended format, and finance to keep costs in control. An international team member should be assigned a permanent role in the product development process and not simply called in when a need arises. In addition to international representation on each product development team, some multinational corporations hold periodic meetings of purely international teams. A typical international team may consist of five members, each of whom also has a product responsibility (such as cable accessories) as well as a geographical responsibility (such as the Far East). Others may be from central R&D and domestic marketing planning. The function of international teams is to provide both support to subsidiaries and international input to overall planning efforts. A key input of international team members is the potential for universal features that can be used worldwide as well as unique features that may be required for individual markets.

---

[16] S. Tamer Cavusgil, "Multinational Corporations and the Management of Technology Transfers," in *Technology Transfer*, ed. A. Coskun Samli (Westport, Conn.: Quorum Books, 1985), 217–229.

FIGURE 16.2 ▪ **The Project-Team Approach to Product Development for International Markets**

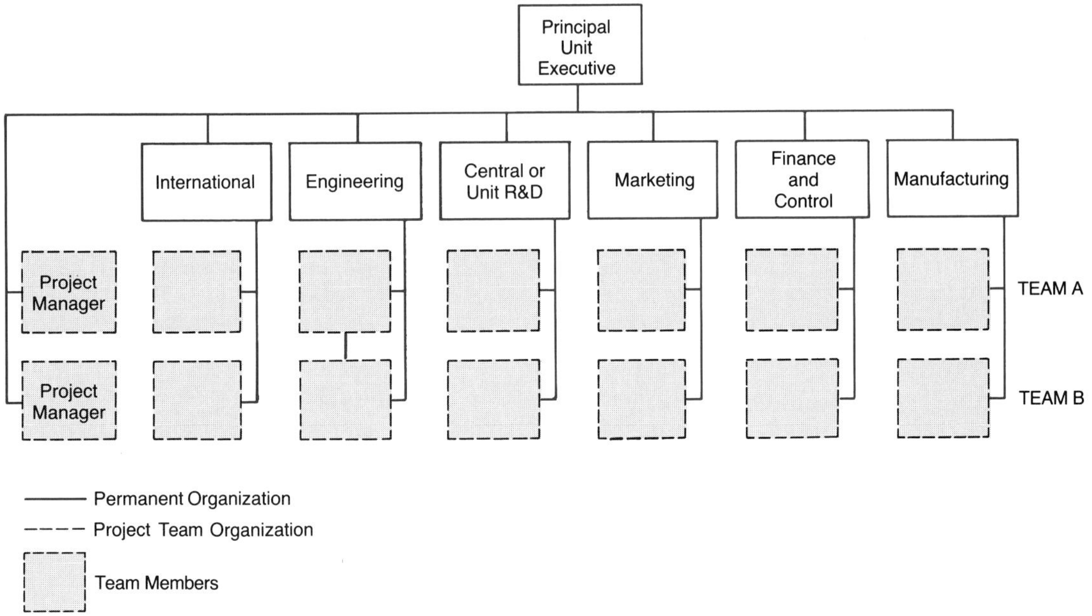

Source: Field research and interviews. A theoretical discussion on this approach can be found in Edgar A. Pessemier, *Product Management: Strategy and Organization* (New York: Wiley, 1977), 420; and in R. M. Hill and J. D. Hlavacek, "The Venture Team: A New Concept in Marketing Organization," *Journal of Marketing* 36 (July 1972): 48.

Such multidisciplinary teams maximize the payoff from R&D by streamlining decision making; that is, they reduce the need for elaborate reporting mechanisms and layers of committee approvals.[17] With the need to slash development time, these teams can be useful. For example, in response to competition, Honeywell set up a multidisciplinary "tiger team" to build a thermostat in 12 months rather than the usual four years.[18]

With the costs of basic research rising and product life cycles shortening, many companies have joined forces in R&D. The U.S. government and many U.S.-based multinational corporations have seen this approach as necessary to restore technological competitiveness. In 1984, the United States passed the National Cooperative Research Act, which allows companies to collaborate without the threat of antitrust suits in long-term R&D projects. Since then, more than 70 **R&D consortia** have been established to develop technologies ranging from artificial intelligence to those needed

[17] "Companies Try New Approaches to Maximize Payoff from R&D," *Business International,* January 25, 1988, 17–21.

[18] "Manufacturers Strive to Slice Time Needed to Develop Products," *The Wall Street Journal,* February 23, 1988, 1, 24.

to overtake the Japanese lead in semiconductor manufacturing.[19] The major consortia in those fields are Microelectronics and Computer Technology Corporation and Sematech, both founded to match similar Japanese alliances. The consortium approach is also proposed if U.S. firms are to compete in high definition television (HDTV).[20] Consortia exist in Europe as well, for example, the Joint European Submicron Silicon, which plans to spend $1 billion a year on research.

These consortia can provide the benefits and face the challenges of any strategic alliance (as discussed in Chapter 14). Countering the benefits of sharing costs and risks are management woes from mixing corporate cultures as well as varying levels of enthusiasm by the participants.[21]

The Testing of New Product Concepts

The final stages of the product development process will involve testing the product in terms of both its performance and its projected market acceptance. Depending on the product, testing procedures range from reliability tests in the pilot plant to minilaunches, from which the product's performance in world markets will be estimated. Any testing will prolong full-scale commercialization and increase the possibility of competitive reaction. Further, the cost of test marketing is substantial—on the average, $1 to $1.5 million per market.

Because of the high rate of new-product failure, estimated by the Conference Board at 67 percent in the United States,[22] most companies want to be assured that their product will gain customer acceptance. They therefore engage in a limited launch of the product. This may involve introducing the product in one country—for instance, Belgium—and basing the go-ahead decision for the rest of Europe on the performance of the product in that test market.

In many cases, companies rely too much on instinct and hunch in their marketing abroad, although in domestic markets they make extensive use of testing and research. Lack of testing has led to a number of major product disasters over the years.[23] The most serious blunder is to assume that other markets have the same priorities and lifestyles as the domestic market. The failure of Coca-Cola, when first introduced in Germany in the 1920s, was attributed to German dislike of both the taste and the bottle design. Refrigeration was not commonly available, and this affected the taste. The end result was the failure of a half-million-dollar ad campaign by J. Walter Thompson's Berlin branch. Campbell Soup Company repeated

[19] "Why High-Tech Teams Just Aren't Enough," *Business Week*, January 30, 1989, 63.

[20] Norm Alster, "TV's High-Stakes, High-Tech Battle," *Fortune*, October 24, 1988, 161–170.

[21] Lee Smith, "Can Consortiums Defeat Japan?" *Fortune*, June 5, 1989, 245–254.

[22] David S. Hopkins, "Survey Finds 67% of New Products Succeed," *Marketing News*, February 8, 1986, 1.

[23] David A. Ricks, *Big Business Blunders* (Homewood, Ill.: Dow Jones–Irwin, 1983), 23–35.

the failure experienced when it introduced canned soups in Italy in the 1960s by introducing them in Brazil in 1979. Research conducted in Brazil after the failure revealed that women fulfil their roles as homemakers in part by such tasks as making soups from scratch. A similar finding had emerged in Italy more than 20 years earlier.[24]

Other reasons for product failure are a lack of product distinctiveness, unexpected technical problems, and mismatches between functions.[25] Mismatches between functions may occur not only between, for example, engineering and marketing, but within the marketing function as well. Engineering may design features in the product that established distribution channels or selling approaches cannot exploit. Advertising may promise the customer something that the other functions within marketing cannot deliver.

The trend is toward a complete testing of the marketing mix. All the components of the brand are tested, including formulation, packaging, advertising, and pricing. Test marketing is indispensable because prelaunch testing is an artificial situation; it tells the researcher what people say they will do, not what they actually do. Test marketing carries major financial risks, which can be limited only if the testing can be conducted in a limited area. Ideally this would utilize localized advertising media—that is, broadcast and print media to which only a limited region would be exposed. However, localized media are lacking even in developed markets such as Western Europe.

Because test marketing in Europe and elsewhere is risky or even impossible, researchers have developed three research methods to cope with the difficulty.[26] **Laboratory test markets** are the least realistic in terms of consumer behavior over time, but they will allow introduction of television exposure, which is impossible otherwise. **Microtest marketing** involves a continuous panel of consumers serviced by a retail grocery operated by the research agency. New products enter the market with high-quality, color-print ads, coupons, and free samples. Initial penetration and repeat buying are monitored. **Forced distribution tests** are based on a continuously reporting panel of housewives, but they encounter new products in normal retail outlets. This is realistic, but competitors are immediately aware of the new product. An important criterion for successful testing is to gain the cooperation of key retailing organizations in the market. In Europe, retail trade is concentrated in a few companies; for example, in Finland by wholesaler cooperatives and in England by retail multiples. Mars Confectionery, which was testing a new chocolate malted-milk drink in England, could not get distribution in major supermarkets for test prod-

---

[24] "Campbell Soup Fails to Make It to the Table," *Business Week*, October 12, 1981, 66.

[25] Steven C. Wheelwright and W. Earl Sasser, Jr., "The New Product Development Map," *Harvard Business Review* 67 (May–June 1989): 112–125.

[26] B. C. Pymont, "Differences Make Europe Difficult Test Area," *Marketing News*, May 4, 1979, 12.

ucts. As a result, Mars changed its approach and focused its marketing on the home-delivery market.[27]

INTERNATIONAL MANAGEMENT OF THE PRODUCT PORTFOLIO

As a result of development efforts, most multinational marketers may have a considerable number of individual items in their product portfolios, consisting of different product lines—that is, groupings of products managed and marketed as a unit. For example, Richardson-Vicks' health-care division markets various cold medicines, the toiletries division markets personal care products, and the home products division caters to home-improvement needs. Each line will vary in the number of individual items as a function of market and marketer characteristics. For example, Mars has stayed out of the U.S. chocolate milk market, despite a product–company fit, because the market is dominated by Hershey and Nestlé. However, it has entered these particular markets elsewhere, such as in Europe.

Despite the challenge of the task, the multinational marketer needs to have a balanced product portfolio—a proper mix of new, growing, and mature products to provide a sustainable long-term competitive advantage for the firm.[28] Optimally, the portfolio will contain **cash cows,** which require little financing but generate cash flow, and **stars,** which are market leaders in growth markets.

Analyzing the International Product Portfolio

Using the product portfolio approach to analyze international markets requires the inclusion of additional dimensions to the exercise.[29] These dimensions would include countries, modes of operation, product markets, target segments, and marketing strategies. The specific approach and variables used will vary by company according to corporate objectives and characteristics as well as the nature of the product market.

Various portfolio models have been developed as tools for the analysis. They typically involve two measures—internal strength and external attractiveness—and the international extension includes the development of either (a) a worldwide matrix in which the units classified are products by countries (for example, personal computers or mainframes in the

[27] Laurel Wentz, "Mars Widens Its Line in U.K.," *Advertising Age,* May 16, 1988, 37.

[28] George S. Day, "Diagnosing the Product Portfolio," *Journal of Marketing* 41 (April 1977): 8–19.

[29] Yoram Wind and Susan P. Douglas, "International Portfolio Analysis and Strategy: Challenge of the 80s," *Journal of International Business Studies* 12 (Fall 1981): 69–82.

FIGURE 16.3 ▪ **Example of the International Product–Market Portfolio**

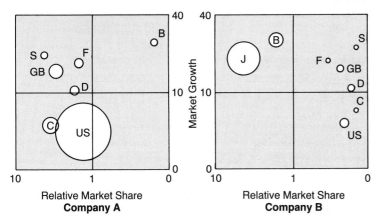

(B-Brazil, C-Canada, D-Germany, F-France, GB-Great Britain, J-Japan,
S-Spain, US-United States)

Source: Jean-Claude Larréché, "The International Product–Market Portfolio," in *1978
AMA Educators' Proceedings* (Chicago, Ill.: American Marketing Association, 1978), 276.

United Kingdom, France, and so on) or (b) a separate classification matrix
for each country.[30]

A product portfolio approach based on growth rates and market-share
positions allows the analysis of business entities, product lines, or individual products. Figure 16.3 represents the product–market portfolio of
Company A, which markets the same product line in several countries.
The company is a leader in most of the markets in which it has operations,
as indicated by its relative market shares. It has two cash cows (United
States and Canada), four stars (Germany, Great Britain, France, and Spain),
and one "problem child" (Brazil). In the mature U.S. market, Company A
has its largest volune, but only a small market share advantage compared
to competition. Company A's dominance is more pronounced in Canada
and in the EC countries.

At the same time Company B, its main competitor, although not a threat
in Company A's major markets, does have a commanding lead in two fast-
growing markets: Japan and Brazil. As this illustration indicates, an analysis should be conducted not only of the firm's own portfolio, but also of
competitors' portfolios, along with a projection of the firm's and the competitors' future international product–market portfolios.[31] Building future

[30] The models referred to are GE/McKinsey, Shell International, and A.D. Little product portfolio models.

[31] Jean-Claude Larréché, "The International Product-Market Portfolio" in *1978 AMA Educators' Proceedings* (Chicago, Ill.: American Marketing Association, 1978), 276–281.

16.3   THE INTERNATIONAL MARKETPLACE

Appliance Makers on a Global Quest   The $11 billion home-appliance market is undergoing major consolidation and globalization. Many U.S.-based manufacturers are faced in their home markets with increased competition from foreign companies, such as the world's largest appliance maker, Electrolux. In addition, industry fundamentals in the United States are rather gloomy: stagnating sales, rising raw material prices, and price wars. On the other hand, the European market, for example, is growing quite fast, and the breakdown of trade barriers within the EC by 1992 makes establishing business there even more attractive.

As a move toward globalization Maytag acquired Chicago Pacific Corporation, best known for the Hoover vacuum cleaners it markets in the United States and Europe. Chicago Pacific also makes washers, dryers, and other appliances carrying the Hoover name—and sells them exclusively in Europe and Australia. However, Hoover's position in Europe is tiny. It boasts a strong presence in the United Kingdom and Australia but is not a big player on the Continent. Thus Maytag will essentially be introducing new products into new markets. Because Hoover appliances do have strong name recognition in the United Kingdom, Maytag will be able to exploit some synergies there. Similarly, in Australia, where Hoover has a notable presence, the product line can be expanded to include Maytag's washers and dryers. In that market Maytag could be introduced as a premier line.

Other appliance manufacturers have formed strategic alliances. General Electric entered into a joint venture with Britain's General Electric PLC, and Whirlpool took a 53 percent stake in the appliance business of Dutch giant N. V. Philips. Whirlpool's move gave it 10 plants on the European continent and some popular appliance lines, which is a major asset in a region characterized by fierce loyalty to domestic brands. Product differences abound as well. The British favor front-loading washing machines, while the French swear by top-loaders. The French prefer to cook their food at high temperatures causing grease to splatter onto oven walls, which calls for self-cleaning ovens. This feature is in less demand in West Germany, where lower temperatures are used. Manufacturers are hoping that 1992 will bring about cost savings and product standardization. The danger to be avoided is the development of compromise products that in the end appeal to almost no one.

While opportunities do exist, competition is keen. Margins have suffered as manufacturers (over 300 in Europe alone) scrap for business. The major players have decided to compete in all the major markets of the world. "Becoming a global appliance player *is clearly the best use of our management expertise and well-established brand line-up," Whirlpool executives have said.*

Source: "Whirlpool Plots the Invasion of Europe," *Business Week*, September 5, 1988, 70−72; and "Can Maytag Clean Up around the World?" *Business Week*, January 30, 1989, 86−87.

---

scenarios based on industry estimates will allow Company A to take remedial long-term action to counter Company B's advances. In this case, Company A should direct resources to build market share in fast-growing markets such as Japan and Brazil.

In expanding markets, any company not growing rapidly risks falling behind for good. Growth may mean bringing out new items or lines or having to adjust existing products. Take, for example, the fastest growing market in 1988 and 1989 for PCs: Europe.[32] Tandon of Moorpark, California, started selling PCs in Europe before entering the U.S. market. Olivetti lost market share when it took 18 months longer than Compaq to incorporate new technology into its PCs. For some, market share can be gained only through acquisitions, as with Nokia's purchase of L. M. Ericsson's office automation division. Similar adjustments are described in The International Marketplace 16.3.

Advantages of the Product Portfolio Approach   The major advantages provided by the product portfolio approach are as follows:

1. A global view of the international competitive structure, especially when longer term considerations are included
2. A guide for the formulation of a global international marketing strategy based on the suggested allocation of scarce resources between product lines
3. A guide for the formulation of marketing objectives for specific international markets, based on an outline of the role of each product line in each of the markets served—for example, to generate cash or to block the expansion of competition
4. A convenient visual communication goal, achieved by integrating a substantial amount of information in an appealingly simple format.

Before making strategic choices based on such a portfolio, the international marketer should consider the risks related to variables such as entry mode and exchange rates; management preferences for idiosyncratic objectives, such as concentrating on countries with similar market characteristics; and marketing costs. For example, the cost of entry into one market may be less because the company already has a presence and the possi-

---

[32]Richard I. Kirkland, Jr., "Europe Goes Wild for Yankee PCs," *Fortune*, June 5, 1989, 257−260.

bility exists that distribution networks may be shared.[33] Hoover Company, the U.S. industry leader for vacuum cleaners with approximately one-third of the market, long relied on the good performance of its European subsidiaries, mainly because of the stagnant market at home. In the early 1980s, after the European operations began running into problems, Hoover decided to diversify on a worldwide basis. Its three-pronged strategy for European operations included (1) cutting high British manufacturing costs and shifting some production to France, (2) launching new lines of vacuum cleaners on the Continent, a market Hoover had neglected, and (3) concentrating on Britain's washing-machine market, at the same time conceding much of the Continent to lower cost washing machines from Italian competitors. Meanwhile, Hoover Ltd., the company's British subsidiary, diversified on its own to home security products, such as smoke detectors, fire extinguishers, and burglar alarms. This market in Europe is still in its infancy, while the vacuum cleaner markets in France, West Germany, and Britain have shown no growth in unit volume. Also, competition (AEG, Electrolux, Bosch-Siemens, and Vorwerk) have better name recognition on the Continent than does Hoover.[34] However, the Britons do not vacuum their homes, they "hoover" them.

Disadvantages of the Product Portfolio Approach   The application of the product portfolio approach has a number of limitations. International competitive behavior does not always follow the same rules as in the firm's domestic market; for example, a major local competitor may be a government-owned firm whose main objective is to maintain employment. The relationship between market share and profitability may be blurred by a number of factors in an international environment. Government regulations in every market will have an impact on the products a company can market. For instance, major U.S. tobacco manufacturers estimate they could capture 30 percent of Japan's cigarette market of $10 billion a year if it were not for restrictions that apply only to non-Japanese producers.

Product lines offered will also be affected by various local content laws—those stipulating that a prescribed percentage of the value of the final product must be manufactured locally. Market tastes have an important impact on product lines. These may not only alter the content of a product but may also require an addition in a given market that is not available elsewhere. The Coca-Cola Company has market leadership in a product category unique to Japan: coffee-flavored soft drinks. The market came into existence some 20 years ago and grew rapidly, accounting for 10 percent of soft drink sales in 1983. The beverage is packaged like any other soft drink and is available through vending machines, which dispense hot cans in the winter and cold servings during warm weather. Although Coca-Cola executives have considered introducing "Georgia" in the United

[33] Yoram Wind and Susan P. Douglas, "International Portfolio Analysis and Strategy: The Challenge of the 80s," *Journal of International Business Studies* 12 (Fall 1981): 69–82.

[34] "Hoover: Revamping in Europe to Stem an Earnings Drain at Home," *Business Week*, February 15, 1982, 144–146.

States, they are skeptical about whether the product would succeed, mainly because of declining coffee consumption and the lack of a vending machine network. Also, adoption by Americans of the concept is doubtful.[35] Sunbeam, which generates 30 percent of its sales overseas, was the first to develop the ladies' electric shaver. "Success was substantial," said the Sunbeam chairman, "but when we introduced it in Italy, it failed." His explanation: Italian men like their women with hair on their legs.[36]

The fact that multinational firms produce the same products in different locations may have an impact on consumer perceptions of product risk and quality. If the product is produced in a developing country, for example, the international marketer has to determine whether a well-known brand name can compensate for the concern a customer might feel. The situation may be more complicated for retailers importing from independent producers in developing nations under the retailers' private labels. In general, country-of-origin effects on product perceptions are more difficult to determine since the introduction of hybrid products.

Decisions in Product Portfolio Management

The multinational marketer will have to make specific product line decisions in terms of country markets, optimal combinations of product lines and items, and market segments targeted.[37]

In choosing country markets, decisions must be made beyond those relating to market attractiveness and company position. A market expansion policy will determine the allocation of resources among various markets. The basic alternatives are **concentration** on a small number of markets and **diversification,** which is characterized by growth in a relatively large number of markets. Expansion strategy is determined by market-, mix-, and company-related factors listed in Table 16.3.[38] Market-related factors determine the attractiveness of the market in the first place. With high and stable growth rates only in certain markets, the firm will likely opt for a concentration strategy, which is often the case for innovative products early in their life cycle. If demand is strong worldwide, as the case may be for consumer goods, diversification may be attractive. If markets respond to marketing efforts at increasing rates, concentration will occur; however, when the cost of market-share points becomes too high, marketers tend to begin looking for diversification opportunities. The uniqueness of the product offering with respect to competition is also a factor in expansion strategy. If lead time over competition is considerable, the decision to diversify may not seem urgent. Very few products, however, afford such a

[35] "Coke in Japan Riding High with Georgia Coffee," *Advertising Age*, March 19, 1984, 48–52.

[36] Anne Helming, "Culture Shock," *Advertising Age*, May 17, 1982, M-8, M-9.

[37] Susan P. Douglas and C. Samuel Craig, *International Marketing Research* (Englewood Cliffs, N.J.: Prentice-Hall, 1983), 298–303.

[38] Igal Ayal and Jehiel Zif, "Market Expansion Strategies in Multinational Marketing," *Journal of Marketing* 43 (Spring 1979): 84–94.

TABLE 16.3 ▪ **Factors Affecting the Choice between Concentration and Diversification Strategies**

Factor	Diversification	Concentration
Market Growth Rate	Low	High
Sales Stability	Low	High
Sales Response Function	Decreasing	Increasing
Competitive Lead Time	Short	Long
Spillover Effects	High	Low
Need for Product Adaptation	Low	High
Need for Communication Adaptation	Low	High
Economies of Scale in Distribution	Low	High
Extent of Constraints	Low	High
Program Control Requirements	Low	High

Source: Igal Ayal and Jehiel Zif, "Marketing Expansion Strategies in Multinational Marketing," *Journal of Marketing* 43 (Spring 1979): 89. Reprinted from *Journal of Marketing*, published by the American Marketing Association.

luxury. In many product categories marketers will be affected by spillover effects. Consider, for example, the impact of satellite channels on advertising in Europe, where ads for a product now reach most of the West European market. The greater the degree to which marketing mix elements can be standardized, the more diversification is probable. Overall savings through economies of scale can then be utilized in marketing efforts. Finally, the objectives and policies of the company itself will guide the decision making on expansion. If extensive interaction is called for with intermediaries and clients, efforts are most likely to be concentrated because of resource constraints.

In determining the optimal combination of products and product lines to be marketed, consideration will be given to choices for individual markets as well as transfer of products and brands from one region or market to another. This will often result in a particular country organization marketing product lines and products that are a combination of global, regional, and national brands.

Decisions on specific targeting may result in the choice of a narrowly defined segment in the countries chosen. This is a likely strategy for marketers of specialized products to clearly definable markets; for example, ocean-capable sailing boats. Catering to multiple segments in various markets is typical of consumer-oriented companies that have sufficient resources for broad coverage.

PRODUCT COUNTERFEITING

Counterfeit goods are any good bearing an unauthorized representation of a trademark, patented invention, or copyrighted work that is legally protected in the country where it is marketed. The International Trade Commission estimated that U.S. companies lost a total of $61 billion because of product counterfeiting and other infringement of intellectual property in 1986 alone.[39]

The practice of product counterfeiting has spread to high technology and services from the traditionally counterfeited products: high-visibility, strong-brand-name consumer goods. In addition, a dimension has emerged to further complicate the situation. Previously, the only concern was whether a company's product was being counterfeited; now companies have to worry about whether the raw materials and components purchased for production are themselves real.[40] The European Community estimates that trade in counterfeit goods now accounts for 2 percent of total world trade. The International Chamber of Commerce estimates the figure at close to 5 percent.[41]

Counterfeiting problems occur in three ways and, depending on the origin of the products and where they are marketed, require different courses of action. Approximately 75 percent of counterfeit goods are estimated to be manufactured outside the United States, and 25 percent are either made in this country or imported and then labeled here. Problems originating in the United States can be resolved through infringement actions brought up in federal courts. Counterfeit products originating overseas that are marketed in the United States should be stopped by the customs barrier. Enforcement has been problematic because of the lack of adequate personnel and the increasingly high-tech character of the products. When an infringement occurs overseas, action can be brought under the laws of the country in which it occurs. The sources of the most counterfeit goods are Brazil, Taiwan, Korea, and India. They are a problem to the legitimate owners of intellectual property on two accounts: the size of these countries' own markets and their capability to export. Countries in Central America and the Middle East are not sources but major markets for counterfeit goods.

Four types of action against counterfeiting are legislative action, bilateral and multilateral negotiations, joint private sector action, and measures taken by individual companies.

In the legislative arena, the Omnibus Tariff and Trade Act of 1984 amended Section 301 of the Trade Act of 1974 to clarify that the violation of intellectual property rights is an unreasonable practice within the statute. The act also introduced a major carrot-and-stick policy: the adequacy of protection of intellectual property rights of U.S. manufacturers is a factor that will be considered in the designation of **Generalized System of Preferences (GSP)** benefits to countries. In 1988, the U.S. denied Thailand

[39]"The Battle Raging over 'Intellectual Property,'" *Business Week*, May 22, 1989, 78–90.

[40]Ilkka A. Ronkainen, "Imitation as the Worst Kind of Flattery: Product Counterfeiting," *Trade Analyst* 2 (July–August 1986): 2.

[41]"MNCs Get New Ally in Their War against Counterfeiters," *Business International*, January 11, 1985, 11.

duty-free treatment on $165 million worth of goods because of lax enforcement of intellectual property laws.

The Trademark Counterfeiting Act of 1984 made trading in goods and services using a counterfeit trademark a criminal rather than a civil offense, establishing stiff penalties for the practice. The Semiconductor Chip Protection Act of 1984 clarified the status and protection afforded to semiconductor masks, which determine the capabilities of the chip. Protection will be available to foreign-designed masks in the United States only if the home country of the manufacturer also maintains a viable system of mask protection. The Intellectual Property Rights Improvement Act requires the U.S. Trade Representative to set country-specific negotiating objectives for reciprocity and consideration of retaliatory options to assure intellectual property protection. The U.S. imposed punitive tariffs on $39 million of Brazilian imports to retaliate against Brazil's refusal to protect American pharmaceutical patents.

The U.S. government is seeking to limit counterfeiting practices through bilateral and multilateral negotiations as well as education. A joint International Trade Administration and Patent and Trademark Office action seeks to assess the adequacy of foreign countries' intellectual property laws and practices, to offer educational programs and technical assistance to countries wishing to establish adequate systems of intellectual property protection, to offer educational services to the industry, and to review the adequacy of U.S. legislation in the area. Major legislative changes have occurred in the past few years in, for example, Taiwan and Singapore, where penalties for violations have been toughened. Since 1979, the United States and the EC have been urging the nations of GATT to adopt a counterfeiting code; however, it has been stalled by developing countries that believe that it would hinder their domestic industries.

A number of private sector joint efforts have emerged in the battle against counterfeit goods. In 1978, the International Anticounterfeiting Coalition was founded to lobby for stronger legal sanctions worldwide. The coalition consists of 375 members. The International Chamber of Commerce is establishing a Counterfeit Intelligence and Investigating Bureau in London that will act as a clearinghouse capable of synthesizing global data on counterfeiting.

In today's environment, companies are taking more aggressive steps to protect themselves, as can be seen in The International Marketplace 16.4. The victimized companies are not only losing sales. They are also losing goodwill in the longer term if customers believe they have the real product rather than a copy of inferior quality. In addition to the normal measures of registering trademarks and copyrights, companies are taking steps in product development to prevent knockoffs of trademarked goods. For example, new authentication materials in labeling are virtually impossible to duplicate.

Many companies maintain close contact with the government and the various agencies charged with helping them. Apple Computer, for example, loans testing equipment to customs officers at all major U.S. ports,

Which Is the Real Mickey?
The Mickey Mouse doll on the left is counterfeit; the authentic Mickey
is on the right.

© 1984 Walt Disney Productions.

Source: Eileen Hill, "Intellectual Property Rights," *Business America*, March 18,
1985, 3−9, a publication of the U.S. Department of Commerce.

THE INTERNATIONAL MARKETPLACE 16.4

Fighting Back against Counterfeiters   The American entertainment industry is enjoying a boom in Asia, but it has also suffered
losses between $10 and $20 million each year in royalties because
of counterfeiting. Walt Disney Productions has seen virtually all
lines of the company's merchandise faked: fluffy Mickey Mouse
dolls, videotapes of cartoon classics, children's clothing, books,
pens, stationery, figurines, and watches. The extent of the problem
reflects Disney's massive appeal among Asians. The retail value of
Disney's consumer products, excluding videotapes, in Asia is estimated at more than $1 billion and further growth is projected.

Although many foreign companies were reluctant to become involved in legal action, Disney decided to take action in mid-1989
after sales surged and local licensees began to complain about
rip-offs.

Thailand was chosen as the first target. The country affords
copyright protection by law but has become a haven for counterfeiters because of lax enforcement, low penalties, cheap labor, and
vigorous entrepreneurial spirit. It was also a big exporter of Disney

fakes to the Middle East. Perhaps more important, it was seen as a major future market for and a legitimate manufacturer of the company's consumer line. With the help of the police, Disney officials confiscated $30,000 worth of merchandise, which was burned at a city dump. The hope was that the bonfires would deter the fakers.

Similar campaigns were planned for Taiwan, South Korea, and Malaysia, and later action for the Philippines and Indonesia. China, despite its avalanche of counterfeits in recent years, was not an immediate priority due to the political turmoil of early 1989.

Disney wants to develop local business in Asia, and by mid-1989 had already licensed six companies in Thailand. These local companies were expected to be part of the fight against counterfeiters, because their profits would be most affected by the fakes.

Source: "Disney Attacks Asia Counterfeiters," *Honolulu Star-Bulletin*, June 26, 1989, C2, C4.

and company attorneys regularly conduct seminars in how to detect pirated software and hardware.[42] Others retain outside investigators to monitor the market and stage raids with the help of law-enforcement officers. A series of raids in California by GM resulted in the confiscation of $360,000 worth of bogus parts.[43]

The issue of intellectual property protection will become more important for the United States and the EC in future years. Counterfeiting is changing its nature from a decade ago when the principal victims were manufacturers of designer items. Today, the protection of intellectual property in high technology is crucial because it is one of the strongest areas of U.S. competitiveness in the world marketplace. The ease with which technology can be transferred and the lack of adequate protection of the developers' rights in certain markets make this a serious problem.[44]

INTERNATIONAL TRANSFER OF TECHNOLOGY

Technology transfer is the transfer of systematic knowledge for the manufacture of a product, for the application of a process, or for the rendering of a service. It does not extend to the mere sale or lease of goods.[45] Multina-

[42] "What Apple Does to Catch and Convict High Tech Pirates," *Business International*, January 18, 1985, 17–18.

[43] "Companies Are Knocking Off the Knockoff Outfits," *Business Week*, September 26, 1988, 86–88.

[44] Michael G. Harvey and Ilkka A. Ronkainen, "International Counterfeiters: Marketing Success without the Cost and the Risk," *Columbia Journal of World Business* 20 (Fall 1985): 37–45.

[45] United Nations, *Draft International Code of Conduct on the Transfer of Technology* (New York: United States, 1981), 3.

TABLE 16.4 ■ **Elements of Technology Transfer**

Human Ware	Software	Hardware
Product Know-How	Manuals	Building
Manufacturing Know-How	Procedures	Assembly Lines
Equipment Know-How	Documentation	Equipment
Training	Information	Tools
		Components
		Raw Materials

Source: J. C. Ramaer and P. H. Pijs, "Adapting Technology," undated working paper, Utrecht, The Netherlands: Philips.

tional corporations are one of the major vehicles for channeling technology to different countries to meet varying requirements.

The essential requirements for the transfer of technology are: (1) the availability of suitable technology, (2) social and economic conditions favoring transfer, and (3) the willingness and ability of the receiving party to use and adapt the technology. In industrialized countries sophisticated processes can be applied economically and specialists are available to solve problems and develop techniques. The problems arise with smaller developing countries with little industrial experience. Production facilities must be scaled down for small runs, and machinery and procedures must be simplified to offset the lack of skill and training. And yet, in most cases, the quality has to meet worldwide standards. To meet such challenges, a special pilot plant was built by Philips, the Dutch electronics firm. The plant develops ways to adapt to local circumstances the many elements constituting an industrial activity. The necessary know-how is then transferred to developing countries.

The elements of the transfer are summarized in Table 16.4. Human ware, software, and hardware are combined—through people and capital—to make possible the transfer of appropriate technology for manufacturing. The transfer cannot be accomplished by sending machinery and accompanying manuals; it is achieved by people who show the recipients what and how things should be done.

Technology transfer can occur both formally and informally, as summarized in Table 16.5. Most has traditionally taken place between developed countries. A significant proportion of the trade has also been effected through traditional equity interactions (subsidiaries or joint ventures), and nonequity interactions, such as licensing agreements between non-affiliated entities.[46] The basics of these modes were discussed in Chapter 14. The informal channels' share of the market is difficult to determine, but it is of concern to both the governments and the entities generating the

---

[46] Asim Erdilek, "International Technology Transfer in the Middle East," in *International Business with the Middle East*, ed. Erdener Kaynak (New York: Praeger, 1984), 85–99.

TABLE 16.5 ▪ **Principal Channels of International Technology Transfer**

A. Formal
  1. Licensing
  2. Direct foreign investment
  3. Sale of turnkey plants
  4. Joint ventures, cooperative research arrangements, and coproduction arrangements
  5. Export of high technology and capital goods
B. Informal
  1. Reverse engineering
  2. Exchange of scientific and technical personnel
  3. Science and technology conferences, trade shows, and exhibits
  4. Education and training of foreigners
  5. Commercial visits
  6. Open literature (journals, magazines, technical books, and articles)
  7. Industrial espionage
  8. End-user or third-country diversions
  9. Government assistance programs

Source: Asim Erdilek, "International Technology Transfer in the Middle East," in *International Business in the Middle East*, ed. Erdener Kaynak (New York: Praeger, 1984), 90.

technology, especially if informal channels result in intellectual property violation. Technology that is not protected by patent, copyright, or license has to be protected by an ongoing stream of innovation.

Technology transfer is likely to increase considerably with increased industrialization, which will generate not only new technological needs but also more sophisticated processes and technologies in existing sectors. Many countries are no longer satisfied to receive maximum know-how as quickly as possible; they want to possess technology themselves and to generate technology indigenously.

Internationally transferred technology usually must be adapted. For example, three standards for color television are used in the world: NTSC in the Americas (except for Brazil) and Japan; PAL in Europe, the British Commonwealth, and the Middle East; and SECAM in France, former French colonies, and the Eastern bloc countries. These standards differ from each other in terms of the amounts of fields and lines in the picture.

Technology must be adapted to factors that are quite often contradictory.[47] Customer requirements usually dictate that the output must be of the same caliber as that of the originator's. In some cases, performance requirements may even be more extensive; for example, machinery may have to be operated in a facility where it is not completely protected from the elements. If the multinational corporation's product has multiple production bases, technology has to be adjusted to technical specifications associated with quality requirements that may be based on one worldwide standard. The quantities to be produced have an impact on the technology

[47] J. C. Ramaer and P. H. Pijs, "Adapting Technology," undated working paper, Utrecht, the Netherlands: Philips.

THE INTERNATIONAL MARKETPLACE 16.5

A Technology Transfer Prognosis for the 1990s   *The changes and challenges of the 1990s in international technology transfer are, according to one expert, the following:*

1. The United States will maintain its lead in technologies closely related to military activities. This poses some problems in international technology transfer West/West or West/East in such areas as aircraft, space, nuclear materials, and electronics.

2. No new countries will join the select club at the world technological frontier. The newly industrializing countries continue to assimilate foreign technology through machinery imports, production know-how, licenses, and local contract agreements in supplier-dominated and scale-intensive sectors. Their indigenous capacity in production engineering and related production machinery will develop, but their industrial R&D will remain negligible.

3. Japan, West Germany, and some of the other European countries will maintain their technological dynamism and increase their innovative capacity in general and in particular sectors of comparative advantage, namely, chemicals (West Germany and Switzerland), automobiles (West Germany, Sweden, and Japan), electronics (Japan), and production machinery (West Germany, Japan, Sweden, and Switzerland).

Source: Keith Pavitt, "Technology Transfer among the Industrially Advanced Countries: An Overview," in *International Technology Transfer: Concepts, Measures, and Comparisons*, eds. Nathan Rosenberg and Claudio Frischtak (New York: Praeger, 1985), 3–23.

transferred. There is considerable difference between producing 700,000 television sets in Holland and 7,000 sets in Thailand.

The people involved in the production—their strengths and weaknesses in areas of practical knowledge, experience, abilities, and attitudes—are of critical concern in preparing the transfer. Machinery may have to be simplified and on-site maintenance made possible. Technology from a country like the United States or Japan may not be appropriate if the recipient's needs are for labor-intensive technology in order to create employment and income-earning opportunities. In these cases, adjustment may call for **backward invention.** Imported management and staff must also be adapted to the conditions awaiting them in the area where the technology is to be transferred.

Costs of the various input elements for the production process—such as labor, energy, materials, and components—will vary from market to market and thus require differing specifications in the technology transferred. The quality of the infrastructure may dictate special provisions; for example, if frequent power outages are characteristic of the area in which machinery is to be used, features are needed in the technology to avoid variations in output quality. An industry like home electronics may spend as much as 50 percent of each dollar earned on purchasing. In smaller developing countries supply industries may be insufficient and the existing suppliers may need extensive technical assistance to be in a position to produce desired goods.

In addition to providing technical assistance to the local supply industry, the designs for components must be simplified to allow for local production. This assistance is often critical because of governmental rules and regulations governing component imports. Other government policies that must be considered concern payment for technology, types of technology that can be transferred, and foreign involvement in the process; for example, foreigners may need work permits.

The majority of international technology transfer takes place between the more industrialized countries, and from them to the less-developed nations. Although the flows have started to change, with flows originating also in the less-developed nations, any major changes may take a substantial amount of time, as indicated in the forecast provided in The International Marketplace 16.5.

SUMMARY

The worldwide product planning of multinational corporations must address two critical questions: (1) how and where the company's products should be developed and (2) how and where present and future products should be marketed. The technical processes are similar to those performed in the domestic market; however, their execution must take into consideration the unique characteristics of the world marketplace.

In product development, multinational corporations are increasingly striving toward finding common denominators to rationalize worldwide production. This is achieved through careful coordination of the product development process by worldwide or regional development teams. No longer is the parent company the only source of new products. New product ideas emerge throughout the system and are developed by the entity most qualified to do so.

The multinational marketer's product line is not the same worldwide. The standard line items are augmented by local items or localized variations of products to better cater to the unique needs of individual markets. External variables such as competition and regulations often determine the final composition of the line and how broadly it is marketed.

Product counterfeiting is a threat to sales and also to the long-term image of the company producing the genuine product. Pirating of products will continue, especially in the developing countries, where consumers often cannot afford the real thing. However, the international marketer's worldwide image is in jeopardy and action should be taken.

As an indication of expanding selection of products and services, the multinational marketer is transferring not only products but the know-how for their manufacture. In technology transfer, the need for adaptation applies to hardware and also to the personnel affecting the transfer and the manuals and training involved. The issue has significance well beyond that of marketing of products and services as a controversial item in the dialogue concerning the industrialization of developing countries.

Questions for Discussion

1. If successful globalization calls for improved global planning, will this mean that only multinational corporations can reasonably be expected to succeed in the international marketplace?

2. Will an internationally involved company have an advantage over a domestic company in the generation of new product ideas?

3. Should the same criteria be used to screen new product ideas regardless of where the product is to be marketed?

4. What factors should be considered when deciding on the location of research and development facilities?

5. Comment on the maxim that product development should be centralized, product planning decentralized.

6. What are the major determinants influencing the composition of a company's product line in a given market?

7. Assess the pros and cons of using the product portfolio approach in making a product line decision.

8. What factors make product testing more complicated in the international marketplace?

9. The Middle East is an attractive market for technology transfer. How would Saudi Arabia, Egypt, and Iran differ in the types of technologies they seek?

10. Technology transfer plays a significant role in a developing country's industrialization efforts. What often-conflicting decisions do policymakers have to make in choosing the particular technology?

Recommended Readings

Davidson, William H. *Global Strategic Management.* New York: Wiley, 1982.

Diamond, Sidney A. *Trademark Problems and How to Avoid Them.* Lincolnwood, Ill.: NTC Business Books, 1988.

Foster, Richard. *Innovation: The Attacker's Advantage.* New York: Summit Books, 1986.

Marton, Katherin. *Multinationals, Technology, and Industrialization.* Lexington, Mass.: Lexington Books, 1986.

Robinson, Richard D. *The International Transfer of Technology.* Cambridge, Mass.: Ballinger, 1988.

Samli, A. Coskun, ed. *Technology Transfer: Geographic, Economic, Cultural, and Technical Dimensions.* Westport, Conn.: Quorum Books, 1985.

Still, Richard R., and John S. Hill. "Multinational Product Planning: A Meta-Market Analysis." *International Marketing Review* 2 (Spring 1985): 54–64.

CHAPTER 17

Multinational Pricing Strategies

17.1 THE INTERNATIONAL MARKETPLACE

Tax Authorities to Have More Say over Transfer Pricing *The U.S. Internal Revenue Service has begun to look more closely at transfer pricing on sales of goods and services among subsidiaries or between subsidiaries and the parent company. It has filed claims against hundreds of companies in recent years, claiming that multinational companies too often manipulate intracompany pricing to minimize their worldwide tax bills. Other countries have also strengthened their review systems. Japan has created specific transfer pricing legislation that penalizes marketers for not providing information in time to meet deadlines set by the government. West German tax authorities are carefully checking intracompany charges to deem their appropriateness.*

Increasing communication among tax authorities is having a dramatic effect and will continue to accelerate, especially with the trend toward shifting profits. Historically, transfer pricing from the point of view of a U.S. company meant the shifting of income out of the United States, but with the corporate tax rate at 34 percent, many U.S. companies are now trying to use transfer pricing to shift profits into the country. Thus U.S. multinationals must be prepared to justify transfer pricing policies on two or more fronts.

The entire tax equation has become more complicated because of changes in customs duties. In many countries, revenues from customs and indirect taxes are greater than revenue from corporate taxes. Authorities will jealously guard the income stream from customs taxes, and marketers could find gains on income taxes erased by losses on customs taxes.

Most multinationals are moving cautiously. Glen White, director of taxes at Dow Chemical, stresses this point. "I don't think anybody can afford to have a transfer-pricing system that cannot be revealed to all the relevant governments. If we were explaining to the Canadian tax auditor why we use our pricing system and our French tax inspector walked into the room, we would want to be able to invite him to sit down and then continue with the explanation."

Source: "Worldwide Tax Authorities Promise Increased Scrutiny of Transfer Pricing," *Business International Money Report*, February 22, 1988, 72; and "Smaller Bill Seen in Texaco Dispute," *The New York Times*, January 19, 1988, D2.

Successful pricing is a key element in the marketing mix. A study of 202 U.S. and non-U.S. multinational corporations found pricing to rank second only to the product variable in importance among the concerns of marketing managers.[1] Whereas the discussion in Chapter 10 was limited to export prices, this chapter will focus on price setting by multinational corporations that have direct inventories in other countries. This involves the pricing of sales to members of the corporate family as well as pricing within the individual markets in which the company operates. With increased economic integration and globalization of markets, the coordination of pricing strategies between markets becomes more important.

TRANSFER PRICING

Transfer pricing, or intracorporate pricing, is the pricing of sales to members of the corporate family. It has to be managed in a world characterized by different tax rates, different foreign exchange rates, varying governmental regulations, and other economic and social challenges. Allocation of resources among the various units of the multinational corporation requires the central management of the corporation to establish the appropriate transfer price to achieve these objectives:

1. Competitiveness in the international marketplace
2. Reduction of taxes and tariffs
3. Management of cash flows
4. Minimization of foreign exchange risks
5. Avoidance of conflicts with home and host governments
6. Internal concerns such as goal congruence and motivation of subsidiary managers.[2]

Intracorporate sales can so easily change the consolidated global results that they comprise one of the most important ongoing decision areas in the company. Transfer prices are usually set by the major financial officer—normally the financial vice president or comptroller—and parent company executives are uniformly unwilling to allow much participation by other department or subsidiary executives.[3,4]

[1] Saeed Samiee, "Elements of Marketing Strategy: A Comparative Study of U.S. and Non-U.S. Based Companies," *International Marketing Review* 1 (Summer 1982): 119–126.

[2] Wagdy M. Abdallah, "How to Motivate and Evaluate Managers with International Transfer Pricing Systems," *Management International Review* 29 (1989): 65–71.

[3] J. Fremgen, "Measuring Profit of Part of a Firm," *Management Accounting* 47 (January 1966): 7–18.

[4] Jeffrey Arpan, "Multinational Firm Pricing in International Markets," *Sloan Management Review* 15 (Winter 1973): 1–9.

TABLE 17.1 ▪ **Influences on Transfer Pricing Decisions**

1. Market conditions in the foreign country
2. Competition in the foreign country
3. Reasonable profit for the foreign affiliate
4. U.S. federal income taxes
5. Economic conditions in the foreign country
6. Import restrictions
7. Customs duties
8. Price controls
9. Taxation in the foreign country
10. Exchange controls

Source: Jane O. Burns, "Transfer Pricing Decisions in U.S. Multinational Corporations," *Journal of International Business Studies* 11 (Fall 1980): 23–39.

Transfer prices can be based on costs or on market prices. The cost approach uses an internally calculated cost with a percentage markup added. The market price approach is based on an established market selling price, and the products are usually sold at that price minus a discount to allow some margin of profit for the buying division. In general, cost-based prices are easier to manipulate,[5] because the cost base itself may be any one of these three: full cost, variable cost, or marginal cost.

Factors that have a major influence on intracompany prices are listed in Table 17.1. Market conditions in general, and those relating to the competitive situation in particular, were mentioned as key variables by 210 senior financial officers of multinational corporations.[6] In some markets, especially in the Far East, competition may prevent the international marketer from pricing at will. Prices may have to be adjusted to meet local competition with lower labor costs. This practice may provide entry to the market and a reasonable profit to the affiliate. However, in the long term it may also become a subsidy to an inefficient business. Further, tax and customs authorities may object, because underpricing means that the seller is earning less income than it would otherwise receive in the country of origin and is paying duties on a lower base price upon entry to the destination country.

Economic conditions in a market, especially the imposition of controls on movements of funds, may require the use of transfer pricing to allow the company to repatriate revenues. As an example, a U.S.-based multinational corporation with central procurement facilities required its subsidiaries to buy all raw materials from the parent; it began charging a standard 7 percent

[5] Paul Cook, "New Techniques for Intracompany Pricing," *Harvard Business Review* 35 (July–August 1957): 37–44.

[6] Jane O. Burns, "Transfer Pricing Decisions in U.S. Multinational Corporations," *Journal of International Business Studies* 11 (Fall 1980): 23–39.

for its services, which include guaranteeing on-time delivery and appropriate quality. The company estimates that its revenue remittances from a single Latin American country, which had placed restrictions on remittances from subsidiaries to parent companies, increased by $900,000 after the surcharge was put into effect.[7]

International transfer pricing objectives may lead to conflicting objectives, especially if the influencing factors vary dramatically from one market to another. For example, it may be quite difficult to perfectly match subsidiary goals with the global goals of the multinational corporation. Specific policies should therefore exist that would motivate subsidiary managers to avoid making decisions that would be in conflict with overall corporate goals. If transfer pricing policies lead to an inaccurate financial measure of the subsidiary's performance, this should be taken into account when a performance evaluation is made.

Use of Transfer Prices to Achieve Corporate Objectives

Three philosophies of transfer pricing have emerged over time: (1) cost based (direct cost or cost-plus), (2) market based (discounted "dealer" price derived from end market prices), and (3) **arm's-length price,** or the price that unrelated parties would have reached on the same transaction. The rationale for transferring at cost is that it increases the profits of affiliates, and their profitability will eventually benefit the entire corporation. In most cases cost-plus is used, requiring every affiliate to be a profit center. Deriving transfer prices from the market is the most marketing-oriented method, because it takes local conditions into account. Arm's-length pricing is favored by many constituents, such as governments, to ensure proper intracompany pricing. However, the method becomes difficult when sales to outside parties do not occur in a product category. Additionally, it is often difficult to convince external authorities that true negotiation occurs between two entities controlled by the same parent. In a study of 32 U.S.-based multinational corporations operating in Latin America, a total of 57 percent stated that they use a strategy of arm's-length pricing for their shipments, while the others used negotiated prices, cost-plus, or some other method.[8]

The effect of environmental influences in overseas markets can be alleviated by manipulating transfer prices.[9] High transfer prices on goods shipped to a subsidiary and low ones on goods imported from it will result in minimizing the tax liability of a subsidiary operating in a country with a high income tax. For example, with the lowering in 1986 of the cor-

[7] "How to Free Blocked Funds via Supplier Surcharges," *Business International,* December 7, 1984, 387.

[8] Robert Grosse, "Financial Transfers in the MNE: The Latin American Case," *Management International Review* 26 (1986): 33–44.

[9] James Shulman, "When the Price Is Wrong—By Design," *Columbia Journal of World Business* 4 (May–June 1967): 69–76.

porate tax rate in the United States to 34 percent, which is one of the lowest rates among industrialized nations, many multinational corporations now have an incentive to report higher profits in the United States and lower profits in other countries. On the other hand, a higher transfer price may have an effect on the import duty, especially if it is assessed on an ad-valorem basis. Exceeding a certain threshold may boost the duty substantially when the product is considered a luxury, and will have a negative impact on the subsidiary's competitive posture. Adjusting transfer prices for the opposite effects of taxes and duties is, therefore, a delicate balancing act.

Transfer prices may be adjusted to balance the effects of fluctuating currencies when one partner is operating in a low-inflation environment and the other in one of rampant inflation. Economic restrictions such as controls on dividend remittances and allowable deductions for expenses incurred can also be blunted. For example, if certain services performed by corporate headquarters (such as product development or strategic planning assistance) cannot be charged to the subsidiaries, costs for these services can be recouped by increases in the transfer prices of other product components. A subsidiary's financial and competitive position can be manipulated by the use of lower transfer prices. Start-up costs can be lowered, a market niche carved more quickly, and long-term survival guaranteed.

With the increase of government regulation on foreign participation, transfer pricing becomes an important tool for recouping of expanses from joint ventures, especially if there are restrictions on profit repatriation. A study of transfer price setting in Canada found that the impetus toward a high or low transfer price depends on the level of ownership in the subsidiary, the dividend payout ratios, the effective marginal tax rates in both parent and subsidiary countries, and the tariff on goods transferred.[10] A study of national differences in the use of transfer prices found that British companies set transfer prices at their best estimate of market prices, while the dominant feature of French companies is the use of transfer prices that are roughly equivalent to marginal cost.[11] Of two U.S. companies studied, one used a system of market prices, while the second used a system of marginal cost prices. Top management in the U.S. companies, however, was found to be more conscious than the British or the French of the importance and the difficulty of establishing transfer prices, and corporate headquarters played a far more active role in price setting.

Transfer pricing problems grow geometrically as all of the subsidiaries with differing environmental concerns are added to the planning exercise, calling for more detailed intracompany data for decision making. Further, fluctuating exchange rates make the planning even more challenging.

[10] D. J. Fowler, "Transfer Prices and Profit Maximization in Multinational Enterprise Operations," *Journal of International Business Studies* (Winter 1975): 9–26.

[11] David Granick, "National Differences in the Use of Internal Transfer Prices," *California Management Review* 17 (Summer 1975): 28–40.

However, to prevent double taxation and meet arm's-length requirements, it is essential that the corporation's pricing practices are uniform. Many have adopted a philosophy that calls for an obligation to maintain a good-citizen fiscal approach (that is, recognizing the liability to pay taxes and duties in every country of operation and to avoid artificial tax-avoidance schemes), and a belief that the primary goal of transfer pricing is to support and develop commercial activities.[12]

Transfer Pricing Challenges

Two general type of challenges exist to transfer pricing policies. The first is internal to the multinational corporation and concerns the motivation of those affected by the pricing policies of the corporation. The second, an external one, deals with relations between the corporation and tax authorities in both the home country and the host countries.

Performance Measurement Manipulating intracorporate prices complicates internal control measures and, without proper documentation, will cause major problems. If the firm operates on a profit-center basis, some consideration must be given to the effect of transfer pricing on the subsidiary's apparent profit performance and its actual performance. To judge a subsidiary's profit performance as not satisfactory when it was targeted to be a net source of funds can easily create morale problems. The situation may be further complicated by cultural differences in the subsidiary's management, especially if the need to subsidize less efficient members of the corporate family is not made clear. An adjustment in the control mechanism is called for to give appropriate credit to divisions for their actual contributions. The method may range from dual bookkeeping to compensation in budgets and profit plans. Regardless of the method, proper organizational communication is necessary to avoid conflict between subsidiaries and headquarters.

Taxation Transfer prices will by definition involve the tax and regulatory jurisdictions of the countries in which the company does business, as is pointed out in The International Marketplace 17.1. Sales and transfers of tangible properties and transfers of intangibles such as patent rights and manufacturing know-how are subject to close review and to determinations about the adequacy of compensation received. This quite often puts the multinational corporation in a difficult position. U.S. authorities may think the transfer price is too low, whereas it may be perceived as too high by the foreign entity, especially if a less-developed country is involved. **Section 482** of the Internal Revenue Code gives the Commissioner of the IRS vast authority to reallocate income between controlled foreign operations and U.S. parents, and between U.S. operations of foreign corporations.

---

[12] Michael P. Casey, "International Transfer Pricing," *Management Accounting* 66 (October 1985): 31–35.

Prior to the early 1960s, the enforcement efforts under 482 were mostly domestic. However, since 1962, the U.S. government has attempted to stop U.S. companies from shifting U.S. income to their foreign subsidiaries in low- or no-tax jurisdictions and has affirmed the arm's-length standard as the principal basis for transfer pricing. Because unrelated parties normally sell products and services at a profit, an arm's-length price normally involves a profit to the seller.

A significant portion of Section 482 adjustments, including those resulting from the 1986 Tax Reform Act, have focused on licensing and other transfer of intangibles such as patents and trademarks. Historically, transfer pricing from a U.S. company's point of view has meant the shifting of income out of the United States. But with the lower corporate tax rate, the question now is how to use transfer pricing to shift profits into the United States.

According to Section 482, there are four methods of determining an arm's-length price and they are to be used in the following order:

1. The comparable uncontrolled price method
2. The resale price method
3. The cost-plus method
4. Any other reasonable method

Guidelines of the Organization for Economic Cooperation and Development (OECD) to transfer pricing are similar to those used by U.S. authorities.[13]

The starting point for testing the appropriateness of transfer prices is a comparison with *comparable uncontrolled* transactions, involving unrelated parties. Uncontrolled prices exist when (1) sales are made by members of the multinational corporation to unrelated parties, (2) purchases are made by members of the multinational corporation from unrelated parties, and (3) sales are made between two unrelated parties, neither of which is a member of the multinational corporation. In some cases, marketers have created third-party trading where none existed before. Instead of selling 100 percent of the product in a market to a related party, the seller can arrange a small number of direct transactions with unrelated parties to create a benchmark against which to measure related-party transactions.

If this method does not apply, the *resale* method can be used. This usually applies best to transfers to sales subsidiaries for ultimate distribution. The arm's-length approximation is arrived at by subtracting the subsidiary's profit from an uncontrolled selling price. The appropriateness of the amount is determined by comparison with a similar product being marketed by the multinational corporation.

The *cost-plus* approach is most applicable for transfers of components or unfinished goods to overseas subsidiaries. The arm's-length approxima-

[13] *1979 Report on Transfer Pricing* (Paris: Organization for Economic Cooperation and Development, 1979), para. 45.

tion is achieved by adding an appropriate markup for profit to the seller's total cost of the product.[14] The key is to apply such markups consistently over time and across markets.

Such comparisons, however, are not always possible even under the most favorable circumstances, and may remain burdened with arbitrariness. Comparisons are impossible for products that are unique or when goods are traded only with related parties. Adjusting price comparisons for differences in the product mix, or for the inherently different facts and circumstances surrounding specific transactions between unrelated parties, undermines the reliance that can be placed on any such comparisons. The most accepted of the other *reasonable* methods is the functional analysis approach.[15] The functional analysis measures the profits of each of the related companies and compares it to the proportionate contribution to total income of the corporate group. It addresses the question of what profit would have been reported if the intercorporate transactions had involved unrelated parties. Understanding the functional interrelationships of the various parties (that is, which entity does what) is basic to determining each entity's economic contribution vis-à-vis total income of the corporate group.

The most difficult of cases are those involving intangibles, because comparables are absent in most cases. The IRS requires that the price or royalty rate for any cross-border transfer be commensurate with income; that is, it must result in a fair distribution of income between the units. This requires marketers to analyze and attach a value to each business function (R&D, manufacturing, assembly, marketing services, and distribution). Comparable transactions when available—or, if absent, industry norms—should be used to calculate the rates of return for each function. Take, for example, a subsidiary that makes a $100 profit on the sale of a product manufactured with technology developed and licensed by the U.S. parent. If the firm identifies rates of return for manufacturing and distribution of 30 percent and 10 percent, then $40 of the profit must be allocated to the subsidiary. The remaining $60 would be taxable income to the parent.[16] Needless to say, many of the analyses have to be quite subjective, especially in cases such as the one described in The International Marketplace 17.2, and may lead to controversies and disputes with tax authorities.

In the host environments, the concern of multinational corporations is to maintain the status of good corporate citizenship. Many corporations, in drafting multinational codes of conduct, have specified that their intracorporate pricing will follow arm's length.

---

[14] David P. Donnelly, "Eliminating Uncertainty in Dealing with Section 482," *The International Tax Journal* 12 (Summer 1986): 213–227.

[15] Gunther Schindler, "Income Allocation under Revenue Code Section 482," *Trade Trends* 2 (September 1984): 3.

[16] "MNCs Face Tighter Net over Transfer Pricing Rules," *Business International*, October 31, 1988, 337–338.

17.2   **THE INTERNATIONAL MARKETPLACE**

> ***Taxing Mr. Smith's Brain***   *The U.S. Internal Revenue Service plans to extend its "commensurate with income" standard to include services provided by key employees. For example, a U.S. executive travels to the company's Argentine subsidiary to assist in the construction of a plant. The U.S. parent and the subsidiary agree to a $100 per diem fee as Mr. Smith's compensation. The subsidiary ultimately generates substantial income for many years from products manufactured at this plant. The IRS has suggested that the U.S. company may be required to quantify the value and contribution of Mr. Smith's knowledge and skills to reflect his actual benefit to the plant.*

> Source: "MNCs Face Tighter Net over Transfer Pricing Rules," *Business International*, October 31, 1988, 337–338.

PRICING WITHIN INDIVIDUAL MARKETS

Pricing within the individual markets in which the company operates is determined by (1) corporate objectives, (2) costs, (3) customer behavior and market conditions, (4) market structure, and (5) environmental constraints.[17] Because all of these factors vary among the countries in which the multinational corporation might have a presence, the pricing policy must vary as well. Despite the controversy over the desirability of uniform pricing in multinational markets, price discrimination is an essential characteristic of the pricing policies of firms conducting business in differing markets.[18] In a study of the price decision making for nondomestic markets of 42 U.S.-based multinational corporations, the major problem areas in international pricing were meeting competition, cost, lack of competitive information, distribution and channel factors, and government barriers.[19]

Although many multinational marketers, both U.S. based[20] and foreign based,[21] emphasize nonprice methods of competition, they rank pricing

---

[17] Helmut Becker, "Pricing: An International Marketing Challenge" in *International Marketing Strategy*, eds. Hans Thorelli and Helmut Becker (New York: Pergamon Press, 1980), 206–217.

[18] Peter R. Kressler, "Is Uniform Pricing Desirable in Multinational Markets?" *Akron Business and Economic Review* 2 (Winter 1971): 3–8.

[19] James C. Baker and John K. Ryans, "Some Aspects of International Pricing: A Neglected Area of Management Policy," *Management Decisions* (Summer 1973): 177–182.

[20] J. J. Boddewyn, Robin Soehl, and Jacques Picard, "Standardization in International Marketing: Is Ted Levitt in Fact Right?" *Business Horizons* 29 (November–December 1986): 69–75.

[21] Saeed Samiee, "Pricing in Marketing Strategies of U.S.- and Foreign-Based Companies," *Journal of Business Research* 15 (March 1987): 17–30.

high as a marketing tool overseas, even though the nondomestic pricing decisions are made at middle management level in a majority of firms. Pricing decisions also tend to be made more at the local level with coordination from headquarters in more strategic decision situations.[22]

Corporate Objectives

Multinational marketers must set and adjust their objectives based on the prevailing conditions in each of their markets. Pricing may well influence the overall strategic moves of the company as a whole. This is well illustrated by the decision of many foreign-based companies, automakers for example, to begin production in the United States rather than to continue exporting. To remain competitive in the market, many have had to increase the dollar component of their output. Apart from trade barriers, many have had their market shares erode because of higher wages in their home markets, increasing shipping costs, and unfavorable exchange rates. Market share very often plays a major role in pricing decisions, in that marketers may be willing to sacrifice immediate earnings for market share gain or maintenance. This is especially true in highly competitive situations; for example, Fujitsu's 1983 net income was only 5 percent of sales compared to IBM's 12.7 percent worldwide and 7.6 percent in Japan.

Pricing decisions will also vary depending on the pricing situation. The basics of first-time pricing, price adjustment, and product-line pricing were discussed in Chapter 10 and apply to pricing within nondomestic situations as well. For example, companies such as Kodak and Xerox, which introduce all of their new products worldwide within a very short time period, have an option of either **skimming** or **penetration pricing.** If the product is an innovation, the marketer may decide to charge a premium for the product. If, however, competition is keen or expected to increase in the near future, lower prices may be used to make the product more attractive to buyers and the market less attractive to competition. The Korean general trading companies (such as Goldstar, Hyundai, and Samsung) were able to penetrate and capture the low end of many consumer goods markets both in the United States and Europe based on price competitiveness (as shown in Table 17.2).

For the most part, the Korean general trading companies have competed in the world marketplace, especially against the Japanese, on price rather than product traits with the major objective of capturing a foothold in various markets. For example, Samsung was able to gain access to U.S. markets when J.C. Penney was looking for lower priced microwave ovens in

---

[22] For an example of pricing processes by multinational marketers, see John U. Farley, James M. Hulbert, and David Weinstein, "Price Setting and Volume Planning by Two European Industrial Companies: A Study and Comparison of Decision Processes," *Journal of Marketing* 44 (Winter 1980): 46–54.

TABLE 17.2 ▪ **South Korea's Price Edge over Japan**

	Korean Brand		Japanese Brand	
	1985	1989	1985	1989
SUBCOMPACT AUTOS	Excel (Hyundai)		Sentra (Nissan)	
	$5,500–6,000	$5,999	$7,600	$7,299
PERSONAL COMPUTERS	Leading Edge (Daewoo)		Advanced-3 (NEC)	
	$1,495	$898	$1,695	$998
VIDEOCASSETTE RECORDERS	Samsung		Toshiba	
	$270	$189	$350	$299
COMPACT REFRIGERATORS	Goldstar		Sanyo	
	$149	$88	$265	$99
13-IN. COLOR TELEVISIONS	Samsung		Hitachi	
	$148	$159	$189	$199
MICROWAVE OVENS	Goldstar		Toshiba	
	$149	$79	$180	$99
VIDEOCASSETTES	SKC (Sunkyong)		TDK	
	$6	$6	$7	$7.50

Source: L. Helm, "The Koreans Are Coming," *Business Week*, December 23, 1985, 46–52; direct manufacturer/retailer inquiries.

the early 1980s. Samsung's ovens retailed for $299 whereas most models averaged between $350 and $400 at the time.[23]

Price changes may be frequent if the company's objective is to undersell a major competitor. A marketer may, for example, decide to maintain a price level 10 to 20 percent below that of a major competitor; price changes would be necessary whenever the competitor made significant changes in its prices. Price changes may also be required because of changes in foreign-exchange rates. Many multinational marketers were forced to increase prices in the United States on goods of non-U.S. origin when the dollar weakened during the 1980s.

Product-line pricing occurs typically in conjunction with positioning decisions. The international marketer may have a premium line as well as a standard line and, in some cases, sell directly to retailers for their private label sales. Products facing mass markets have keener competition and smaller profit margins than premium products, which may well be priced more liberally because there is less competition. For example, for decades

[23] Ira C. Magaziner and Mark Patinkin, "Fast Heat: How Korea Won the Microwave War," *Harvard Business Review* 67 (January–February 1989): 83–92.

Caterpillar's big-ticket items virtually sold themselves. But environmental factors, such as the U.S. budget deficit, the Gulf States oil crunch, and the Latin American debt crisis, resulted in fewer large-scale highway and construction projects. The company then focused on smaller equipment to remain competitive globally.[24]

Costs

Costs are frequently used as a basis for price determination, largely because they are easily measured and provide a floor under which prices cannot go in the long term. These costs include procurement, manufacturing, logistics, and marketing costs as well as overhead. Quality at an affordable price drives most procurement systems. The decision to turn to offshore suppliers may often be influenced by their lower prices, which enable the marketer to remain competitive.[25] Locating manufacturing facilities in different parts of the world may lower various costs, such as labor or distribution costs, although this may create new challenges. For example, during the 1980s many multinational corporations established plants in the Far East in search of cheaper labor. Toward the end of the decade, however, labor costs rose dramatically (for example, the average industrial wage in South Korea rose 110 percent between 1984 and 1988), labor strife increased, and labor shortages developed. These challenges were compounded by strengthened local currencies, adding to the upward pressure on prices.[26]

Varying inflation rates will have a major impact on the administration of prices, especially because they are usually accompanied by government controls. The task of the parent company is to aid subsidiaries in their planning to ensure reaching margin targets despite unfavorable market conditions, as illustrated in The International Marketplace 17.3. Inflationary environments call for constant price adjustments; in markets with hyperinflation, pricing may be in a stable currency with daily translation into the local currency.

Internally, controversy may arise in determining which manufacturing and marketing costs to include. For example, controversy may arise over the amounts of research and development to charge to subsidiaries or over how to divide the costs of a pan-regional advertising campaign when costs are incurred primarily on satellite channels and viewership varies dramatically from one market to the next.

[24] Ronald Henkoff, "This Cat Is Acting like a Tiger," *Fortune*, December 19, 1988, 69–76.

[25] "The Why, How, and What of Overseas Purchasing," *Purchasing*, June 25, 1987, 54–55.

[26] "Is the Era of Cheap Asian Labor Over?" *Business Week*, May 15, 1989, 45–46.

| 17.3 | THE INTERNATIONAL MARKETPLACE |

Coping with Inflation, Avon Style   Avon Products Inc., the multinational marketer of cosmetics and accessories, has developed a pricing tool to help local subsidiaries cope with extremely high inflation rates as well as major devaluations. The objective of the approach is to respond quickly to changes in the price level and thus preserve local-currency margins. This is crucial for the international marketers, who usually need longer lead times for creative marketing planning.

The first step of the approach requires local managers from the various functional areas to predict future replacement costs and adjust prices quickly in relation to both market conditions and inflation rate. Local vendors are instrumental in helping make these projections. After the projections are completed, the marketing department uses these costs to prepare sales campaigns as far as one year into the future—a long time in a country suffering hyperinflation. Regular meetings are scheduled to approve, or revise, prices before sales campaigns go into effect. Contingency plans must be ready to handle dramatic changes in the inflation rate. For example, in Argentina, inflation ranged from as high as 1,000 percent to close to zero under price and wage controls.

Source: "Close-In Pricing System Protects Avon's Margins in Hyperinflationary Nations," *Business International*, February 3, 1986, 33–34; and "Avon's Close-In Pricing: Four Steps toward Implementing the Strategy," *Business International*, February 10, 1986, 42–46.

Demand and Market Factors

Demand will set a price ceiling in a given market. Despite the difficulties in obtaining data on foreign markets and forecasting potential demand, the international marketer must make judgments concerning the quantities that can be sold at different prices in each foreign market. The prices will have to be set not only with ultimate consumers in mind but also the intermediaries involved. For example, if a company wants to undercut its competition, it has to make sure retailers' margins remain adequate and competitive.

Care has to be taken that the price–quality perception of consumers will not turn against the international marketer. However, competitively priced goods have made inroads against even well-entrenched competitors. One of the fastest selling personal computers in the United States is the Leading Edge Model D, made by the Korean Daewoo Corporation, which sells for half of the price of the comparable IBM model.[27] Another example is

[27] L. Helm, "The Koreans Are Coming," *Business Week*, December 23, 1985, 46–52.

the Soviet-made Belarus tractor, which fared quite well both in Western Europe and the United States mainly because of its highly attractive price. On the other hand, the marketer who wants to charge a premium price must make sure that customers are willing to pay the price; that is, positioning of the product and marketing communication become crucial.

Market Structure and Competition

Competition often helps set the price for a market within the parameters of costs and demand. To hold onto its eroding worldwide market share, Caterpillar shrank costs and moved away from its old practice of competing mainly by building advanced, enduring machines and selling them at premium prices. Instead, the company cut prices and called on joint venture partners overseas to produce competitive equipment.

IBM's operation in Japan lost market share in mainframes largely because competitors undersold it. A Japanese mainframe was typically listed at 10 percent less than its IBM counterpart, and it frequently carried an addition 10 to 20 percent discount beyond that. This created an extremely competitive market. IBM's reaction was to respond in kind with aggressive programs of its own, with the result that it began regaining its lost share.

The international marketer's freedom in pricing may be restricted if a channel member holds the power in distribution. For example, in the United Kingdom, large retail multiples control access to the consuming public in daily staples and will therefore demand price concessions from the producers. Profit margins will naturally be squeezed if the marketer is not able to generate alternative distribution modes.

Environmental Constraints

Governmental interference in multinational corporation pricing causes hardship on many organizations. Once under **price controls,** the subsidiary is operating in a regulated industry. The setting of maximum prices has been defended primarily on political grounds: it stops inflation and an accelerating wage–price spiral and consumers want it. Supporters also maintain that price controls raise the income of the poor. Operating in such circumstances is difficult. Achieving change in prices can be frustrating; for example, a company may wait 30 to 45 days for an acknowledgment of a price increase petition.

To fight price controls multinational corporations can demonstrate that they are getting an unacceptable return on investment and that, without an acceptable profit opportunity, future investments will not be made and production perhaps will be stopped.[28] Cadbury Schweppes sold its plant

[28] Victor H. Frank, "Living with Price Control Abroad," *Harvard Business Review* 63 (March–April 1984): 137–142.

in Kenya in April 1982 because price control made its operation unprofitable. In 1983, Coca-Cola and PepsiCo withdrew their products from the shelves in Mexico until they received a price increase. Pakistani milk producers terminated their business when they could not raise prices, and Glaxo, a pharmaceutical manufacturer, canceled its expansion plans in Pakistan because of price controls.

In general, company representatives can cite these consequences in arguing against price controls: (1) the maximum price often becomes the minimum price if a sector is allowed a price increase, because all businesses in the sector will take it regardless of cost justification; (2) the wage–price spiral advances vigorously in anticipation of controls; (3) labor often turns against restrictions because they are usually accompanied by an income policy or wage restrictions; (4) noninflationary wage increases are forestalled; (5) government control not only creates a costly regulatory body but control is also difficult to enforce; (6) authorities raise less in taxes because less money is made; and (7) a government may have to bail out many companies with cheap loans or make grants to prevent bankruptcies and unemployment.[29] Once price controls are invoked, management will have to devote much time to resolving the many difficulties that controls present. The best interest of multinational corporations is therefore served by working with governments, especially in the developing countries, to establish an economic policy centered around a relatively free market in order to ameliorate the problem of rapidly escalating prices without price controls.

PRICING COORDINATION

The issue of standard worldwide pricing is mostly a theoretical one because of the influence of the factors already discussed. However, coordination of the pricing function is necessary especially in larger, regional markets such as the European Community. Standardization efforts usually involve price levels and the use of pricing as a positioning tool. For example, a particular product may be priced as a premium product in every market, regardless of the absolute price.

Of greatest importance to multinational corporations is the control and coordination of pricing to intermediaries. When currency exchange rate discrepancies widen, gray markets emerge. In this respect, many multinational marketers view 1992 with trepidation. The concern is that when Europe is without trade barriers, goods sold in a country at a lower price can easily find their way into another country where the pricing structure for the same product is higher. Badedas shower gel, for example, is priced

---

[29] Helm, "The Koreans Are Coming," 46–52.

in the middle of the market in West Germany by its marketer, Ligner & Fischer. In the United Kingdom, Beecham positions Badedas as a high-price product.[30] This discrepancy causes parallel imports to U.K. retailers from West Germany. Though not illegal, such transshipments have been held at bay in Europe to some extent by complicated customs and shipping procedures. When the trade barriers fall, parallel imports by strong retail chains will start to flourish. Multinational marketers' only response in addition to stricter distribution control is a careful scrutiny of pricing policies.

The need for pricing coordination is not limited to regions such as the European Community. With more global and regional brands in the multinational marketer's offering, control in pricing is increasingly important. Of course, this has to be balanced against the need for allowing subsidiaries latitude in pricing so they may quickly react to specific market conditions.

Studies have shown that foreign-based multinational corporations allow their U.S. subsidiaries considerable freedom in pricing. This has been explained by the size and unique features of the market. Further, it has been argued that these subsidiaries often control the North American market (that is, a Canadian customer cannot get a better deal in the United States, and vice versa) and that distances create a natural barrier against arbitrage practices that would be more likely to emerge in Europe.[31] However, recent experience (as discussed in Chapter 12) has shown that pricing coordination has to be worldwide because parallel imports will surface in any markets in which price discrepancies exist regardless of distances.

SUMMARY

In a world of increasing competition, government regulation, accelerating inflation, and widely fluctuating exchange rates, international marketers must spend increasing amounts of time planning pricing strategy. Because pricing is the only revenue-generating element of the marketing mix, its role in meeting corporate objectives is enhanced. However, it comes under increasing governmental scrutiny as well, as evidenced by intracompany transfer pricing.

The three philosophies of transfer pricing that have emerged over time are cost based, market based, and arm's-length. Transfer pricing concerns are both internal and external to the company. Internally, manipulating transfer prices may complicate control procedures and documentation.

---

[30] Kevin Cote, "1992: Europe Becomes One," *Advertising Age*, July 11, 1988, 46.

[31] Samiee, "Pricing in Marketing Strategies of U.S.- and Foreign-Based Companies," 17–30.

Externally, problems arise from the tax and regulatory entities of the countries involved.

Pricing decisions are typically left to the local managers; however, planning assistance is provided by the parent company. Pricing in individual markets comes under the influence of environmental variables, each market with its own unique set. This set consists of corporate objectives, costs, customer behavior and market conditions, market structure, and environmental constraints. Their individual impact and the result of their interaction must be thoroughly understood by the international marketer, especially if regional, or even worldwide, coordination is attempted.

Questions for Discussion

1. Comment on the pricing philosophy, "Sometimes price should be wrong by design."

2. The standard worldwide base price is most likely looked upon by management as full-cost pricing, including an allowance for manufacturing overhead, general overhead, and selling expenses. What factors are overlooked?

3. In combating price controls, multinational corporations will deal with agency administrators rather than policymakers. How can they convince administrators that price relief is fair to the company and also in the best interest of the host country?

4. Should there be governmental action against gray markets? Are gray markets not an expression of free trade?

5. Which elements of pricing can be standardized?

6. The approach of Avon Products, reported in The International Marketplace 17.3, is an example of headquarter's guidance in pricing. What are benefits of this approach?

7. If a price edge is based on cost advantages, such as those between Korea and most industrialized countries, what can the international marketer do to compete with a Korean marketer?

8. Describe the circumstances under which an international marketer can utilize a skimming strategy and charge what the market will bear.

Recommended Readings

"Setting Intercorporate Pricing Policies." *Business International.*

Fuller, James P. *International Tax Aspects of the Transfer or Use of Intangibles.* Palo Alto, Calif.: Fenwick, Davis & West, 1985.

Harper, Donald V., and Jack L. Caldwell. "Pricing." In *Marketing Manager's Handbook*, edited by Steuart Henderson Britt and Norman F. Guess. Chicago: Dartnell Press, 1983.

Robinson, Richard D. *International Business Management*. Hinsdale, Ill.: Dryden, 1985.

Schuettinger, Robert, and Eamonn Butler. *Forty Centuries of Wage and Price Controls*. Washington: The Heritage Foundation, 1980.

CHAPTER 18

International Logistics

THE INTERNATIONAL MARKETPLACE

> ***Airfreight: The New Marketing Tool*** It is axiomatic that freight
> moves by air only when it is so time sensitive that a shipper will
> bear the higher cost of air shipment. It is also axiomatic that ship-
> pers are concerned only with moving their goods by the least
> expensive method available.
>
> That may once have been true. Today, however, increasing global
> competitiveness is driving a change in the axiom. Because manu-
> facturers perceive the need to be more customer-service oriented
> and to cast a wider net in search of customers, commodities now
> move regularly by air that in the not-too-distant past were not
> considered "air eligible."
>
> And, perhaps of greater significance, the modal transportation
> decision is being made by new players. Where once the traffic man-
> ager made the transportation decision, today the decision is being
> made in consultation with marketing and financial executives.
> Marketing executives get into the act because they deal with cus-
> tomers and are involved in determining the conditions of sale.
> Finance personnel look at the cost of working capital tied up in
> inventory as well as the speed of payment. They are looking at
> the total cost impact on the corporation.
>
> Source: Lawrence H. Kaufman, "Shipping: The New Marketing Tool," *Air Com-
> merce,* March 27, 1989, 3T.

For the international firm, customer locations and sourcing opportunities
are widely dispersed. The physical distribution and logistics aspects of
international marketing therefore have great importance. To obtain and
maintain favorable results from the complex international environment,
the international manager must coordinate activities and gain the cooperation of all departments. The firm can attain a strategically advantageous
position only if system synergism exists. Neglect of distribution and logistics issues brings not only higher costs but eventual noncompetitiveness,
which will result in diminished market share, more expensive supplies,
or lower profits.

This chapter will focus on international logistics activities. Primary areas of concern are transportation, inventory, packaging, storage, and logistics management. The logistics problems and opportunities that are peculiar to international marketing will also be highlighted.

THE FIELD OF INTERNATIONAL LOGISTICS

The concept of business logistics is relatively new. Although some aspects were discussed as early as 1951, John F. Magee is generally credited with publishing the first article on logistics theory in 1960.[1] The theoretical development of international logistics is even more recent, probably originating in a 1966 article by Robert E. McGarrah on "Logistics for the International Manufacturer."[2] The importance of international logistics has quickly been recognized by practitioners of international business.

Logistics costs currently comprise between 10 and 25 percent of the total landed cost of an international order, and they continue to increase.[3] International firms have already achieved many of the cost reductions that are possible in financing, communication, and production, and they are now beginning to look at international logistics as a competitive tool. Managers realize that "competition is the name of the game" in international business and that logistics "is key to making—and keeping—customers."[4] They also believe that future sales growth in the international market will come mainly from the development of wider and better logistics systems.[5]

A Definition of International Logistics

International logistics is defined as the designing and managing of a system that controls the flow of materials into, through, and out of the international corporation. It encompasses the total movement concept by covering the entire range of operations concerned with product movement. An overview of the logistics function is provided in Figure 18.1.

Two major phases in the movement of materials are of logistical importance. The first phase comprises materials management, or the timely movement of raw materials, parts, and supplies into and through the firm. The second phase is physical distribution, which involves the movement of the firm's finished product to its customers. In both phases, movement

[1] John F. Magee, "The Logistics of Distribution," *Harvard Business Review* 38 (July–August 1960).

[2] Robert E. McGarrah, "Logistics for the International Manufacturer," *Harvard Business Review* 44 (March–April 1966).

[3] "Distribution's Vital Role," *Distribution* 79 (October 1980).

[4] Dennis Davis, "New Involvement in the Orient," *Distribution* 78 (October 1979).

[5] U.S. Department of Commerce, *Survey of Export Management Companies on the Export Trading Company Concept* (Washington, D.C.: Government Printing Office, 1977).

FIGURE 18.1 ▪ **The Logistics Function**

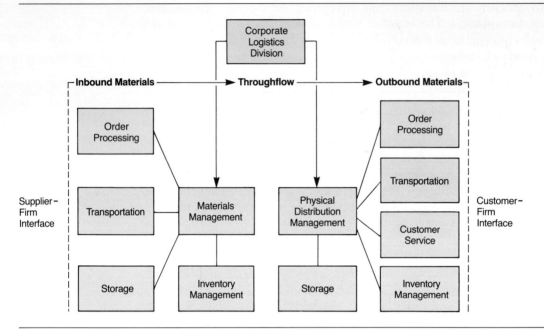

is seen within the context of the entire process. Stationary periods (storage and inventory) are therefore included. The basic goal of logistics management is the effective coordination of both phases and their various components to result in maximum cost effectiveness while maintaining service goals and requirements. In the words of the director of international logistics operations of General Motors Corporation, the purpose of international logistics is "to plan cost-effective systems for future use, attempt to eliminate duplication of effort, and determine where distribution policy is lacking or inappropriate. Emphasis is placed on consolidating existing movements, planning new systems, identifying useful ideas, techniques, or experiences, and working with various divisions toward implementation of beneficial changes."[6]

The growth of logistics as a field has brought to the forefront three major new concepts: the systems concept, the total cost concept, and the trade-off concept. The systems concept is based on the notion that materials-flow activities within a firm are so extensive and complex that they can be considered only in the context of their interaction. Instead of each corporate function and division operating with the goal of individual optimization, the systems concept stipulates that some function or division may have to work suboptimally in order to maximize the benefits of the system as a

[6]Rex R. Williams, "International Physical Distribution Management," in *Contemporary Physical Distribution and Logistics*, 4th ed., eds. James C. Johnson and Donald F. Wood (Tulsa, Okla.: Penwell Books, 1981), 150.

whole. Clearly, the systems concept intends to provide the firm with the synergism expected from size.

A logical outgrowth of the systems concept is the development of the total cost concept. In order to evaluate and optimize logistical activities, cost is used as a basis for measurement. The purpose of the total cost concept is to minimize the firm's overall logistics cost by implementing the systems concept appropriately. Increasingly, however, the total cost concept is being partially supplanted by a total after-tax profit concept. This takes into account the impact of national tax policies on the logistics function and has the objective of maximizing after-tax profits rather than minimizing total cost. Because tax variation in the international arena can often have major consequences, this new focus appears quite appropriate.[7]

The trade-off concept, finally, recognizes the linkages within the logistics systems that result in an interaction among the logistics components. For example, locating a warehouse near the customer may reduce the cost of transportation. However, additional costs are associated with new warehouses. Similarly, a reduction of inventories will save money but may increase the need for costly emergency shipments. Managers can maximize performance of logistic systems only by formulating decisions based on the recognition and analysis of these trade-offs.

Differences between Domestic and International Logistics

In the domestic environment, logistics decisions are guided by the experience of the manager, possible industry comparison, an intimate knowledge of trends, and discovered heuristics—or rules of thumb. The logistics manager in the international firm, on the other hand, frequently has to depend on educated guesses to determine the steps required to obtain a desired service level. Variations in locale mean variations in environment. Lack of familiarity with these variations leads to uncertainty in the decision-making process. By applying decision rules based on a decision variable developed at home, the firm will be unable to adapt well to the new environment, and the result will be inadequate profit performance. The long-term survival of international activities depends on an understanding of the differences inherent in the international logistics field. These variations can be classified as basic differences and country-specific differences.[8]

Basic Differences   Basic differences in international logistics emerge because the corporation is active in more than one country. One example of a basic difference is distance. International marketing activities frequently require goods to be shipped farther to reach final customers. These distances in turn result in longer lead times, more opportunities for things to

---

[7] Paul T. Nelson and Gadi Toledano, "Challenges for International Logistics Management," *Journal of Business Logistics* 1 (No. 2, 1979): 7.

[8] Ibid., 2.

go wrong, more inventories—in short, greater complexity. Currency variation is a second basic difference in international logistics. The corporation must adjust its planning to incorporate the existence of different currencies and changes in exchange rates. The border-crossing process brings with it the need for conformance with national regulations, an inspection at customs, and proper documentation. As a result, additional intermediaries participate in the international logistics process. They include freight forwarders, customs agents, customs brokers, banks, and other financial intermediaries. Finally, the **transportation modes** may also be different. Most transportation domestically is either by truck or by rail whereas the multinational corporation quite frequently ships its products by air or by sea. Airfreight and ocean freight have their own stipulations and rules that require new knowledge and skills.

Country-Specific Differences   Within each country, the firm faces specific logistical attributes that may be quite different from those experienced at home. Transportation systems and intermediaries may vary. The reliability of carriers may be different. The computation of freight rates may be unfamiliar. Packaging and labeling requirements differ from country to country. Management must consider all of these factors in order to develop an efficient international logistics operation.

INTERNATIONAL TRANSPORTATION ISSUES

International transportation is of major concern to the international firm, because transportation determines how and when goods will be received. Further, transportation costs represent 7 to 15 percent of the total landed cost of an international order,[9] and therefore deserve special attention. The transportation issue can be divided into three components: infrastructure, the availability of modes, and the choice of modes among the given alternatives.

Transportation Infrastructure

In the United States, firms can count on an established transportation network. Internationally, however, major infrastructural variations may be encountered. Some countries may have excellent inbound and outbound transportation systems but weak transportation links within the country. This is particularly true in former colonies, where the original transportation systems were designed to maximize the extractive potential of the countries. In such instances, shipping to the market may be easy, but distribution within the market may represent a very difficult and time-consuming task.

[9]Robert L. Vidrick, "Transportation Cost Control—The Key to Successful Exporting," *Distribution* 79 (March 1980).

The international marketer must therefore learn about existing and planned infrastructures abroad. In some countries, for example, railroads may be an excellent transportation mode, far surpassing the performance of trucking, while in others the use of railroads for freight distribution may be a gamble at best. The future routing of pipelines must be determined before any major commitments are made to a particular location if the product is amenable to pipeline transportation. The transportation methods used to carry cargo to seaports or airports must be investigated.

Extreme variations also exist in the frequency of transportation services. For example, a particular port may not be visited by a ship for weeks or even months. Sometimes only carriers with particular characteristics, such as small size, will serve a given location. All of these infrastructural concerns must be taken into account in the initial planning of the firm's transportation service.

Availability of Modes

Even though some goods are shipped abroad by rail or truck, international transportation frequently requires ocean or airfreight modes, which many corporations only rarely use domestically. In addition, combinations such as land bridges or sea bridges frequently permit the transfer of freight among various modes of transportation, resulting in intermodal movements. The international marketer must understand the specific properties of the different modes in order to use them intelligently.

Ocean Shipping   Three types of vessels operating in ocean shipping can be distinguished by their service: liner service, bulk service, and tramp or charter service. Liner service offers regularly scheduled passage on established routes. Bulk service mainly provides contractual services for individual voyages or for prolonged periods of time. Tramp service is available for irregular routes and is scheduled only on demand.

In addition to the services offered by ocean carriers, the type of cargo a vessel can carry is also important. Most common are conventional (break bulk) cargo vessels, container ships, and roll-on-roll-off vessels. Conventional cargo vessels are useful for oversized and unusual cargoes but may be less efficient in their port operations. Container ships carry standardized containers that greatly facilitate the loading and unloading of cargo and intermodal transfers. As a result, the time the ship has to spend in port is reduced. Roll-on-roll-off (RORO) vessels are essentially ocean-going ferries. Trucks can drive onto built-in ramps and roll off at the destination. Another vessel similar to the RORO vessel is the LASH (lighter aboard ship) vessel. LASH vessels consist of barges stored on the ship and lowered at the point of destination. These individual barges can then operate on inland waterways, a feature that is particularly useful in shallow water.

The availability of a certain type of vessel, however, does not automatically mean that it can be used. The greatest constraint in international

TABLE 18.1 ▪ **International Air Freight, 1960–1988**[a]

Year	Tonne-kilometers (billions)
1960	1.0
1965	2.6
1970	6.4
1975	11.7
1980	20.3
1983	24.9
1985	39.8
1988 [b]	52.9

[a]Based on data supplied by member states of the International Civil Aviation Organization (ICAO). As the number of member states increased from 116 in 1970 to 150 in 1983, there is some upward bias in the data, particularly from 1970 on when data for the U.S.S.R. were included for the first time.

[b]Preliminary figure.

Source: *Civil Aviation Statistics of the World* (Montreal: ICAO, 1989).

ocean shipping is the lack of ports and port services. For example, modern container ships cannot serve some ports because the local equipment is unable to handle the resulting traffic. This problem is often found in developing countries, where local authorities lack the funds to develop facilities. In some instances, nations purposely limit the development of ports to impede the inflow of imports. Increasingly, however, nations have begun to recognize the importance of an appropriate port facility structure and are developing such facilities in spite of the heavy investments necessary. If such investments are accompanied by concurrent changes in the overall infrastructure, transportation efficiency should, in the long run, more than recoup the original investment.

Large investments in infrastructure are always necessary to produce results. Selective allocation of funds to transportation usually achieves only the shifting of bottlenecks to some other point in the infrastructure. If these bottlenecks are not removed, the consequences may be felt in the overall economic performance of the nation. A good example is provided by the Caribbean Basin Initiative. This initiative, designed to increase the exports of the Caribbean region to the United States, has still not taken full effect, mainly because of inadequate transportation links and an inadequate infrastructure. The Caribbean nations continue to be poorly served by ocean carriers, and products that could be exported from the region to the United States are at a disadvantage because they take a long time to reach the U.S. market. For many products quick delivery is essential because of required high levels of industry responsiveness to orders. From a regional perspective, maintaining adequate facilities is therefore imperative in order to remain on the list of areas and ports served by international carriers.

FIGURE 18.2 ▮ **Advertisement of an International Airfreight Specialist**

At Northern we give you more than a good price. We become your partners in transportation. Here are some intelligent reasons for making Northern your partner.

1. Air freight doesn't have to cost more. (Time and density save you money.)

Northern introduced density based pricing almost 15 years ago. It simply means the more an item weighs per cubic foot, the lower the rate per pound. Compare our FREIGHT MISER* two- to four-day time definite delivery to LTL, and you may be getting more of your shipments off the ground.

3. Overseas doesn't mean out of sight. (Having connections makes a world of difference.)

International shipping is a whole new frontier for a lot of companies. At Northern we know the territory. Supported by a strong network of international partners, we take care of all the details. From the paperwork to clearing customs, nothing gets lost in translation.

Other air freight companies show you how much. Northern shows you how.

2. "Just-in-time" means just what it says. (Not sooner, or later.)

A day early can be as bad as a day late if you have a production schedule built around a shipment. Northern's domestic overnight and second day service guarantees your delivery, or we pay your shipping costs up to $200 per shipment. You'll have no surprises, because our computer tracking system lets you know exactly where it is every step of the way—domestically and internationally.

4. Smart distribution can improve your bottom line. (Moving it can cost almost as much as making it.)

Distribution costs come in with the price of raw materials, and go out with the price of finished goods. Northern can streamline your shipping setup to cut those costs down to size.

If all you're getting from your air freight company is a price, call Northern for more intelligent ways to save money and time with air freight shipping.

Call Toll-Free: 1-800-624-4099
Telex: 4979607 (ITT)
FAX: (206) 646-7188

NORTHERN Air Freight

FREIGHT MISER* is a registered trademark of Northern Air Freight.

Source: Courtesy Danzas–Northern Air Freight, Inc.

Air Shipping **Airfreight** is available to and from most countries. This includes the developing world, where it is often a matter of national prestige to operate a national airline. The tremendous growth in international airfreight over past decades is shown in Table 18.1. However, the total volume of airfreight in relation to total shipping volume in international business remains quite small. It accounts for less than one percent of the total volume of international shipments, although it often represents more than 20 percent of the value shipped by industrialized countries.[10] Clearly,

[10] Gunnar K. Sletmo and Jacques Picard, "International Distribution Policies and the Role of Air Freight," *Journal of Business Logistics* 6 (No. 1, 1984): 35–52.

FIGURE 18.3 ▪ **Automobiles Being Loaded into a Jumbo Jet**

Source: *Lufthansa Bordbuch*, 4, 1987, 66.

high-value items are more likely to be shipped by air, particularly if they have a high density, that is, a high weight to volume ratio.

Over the years airlines have made major efforts to increase the volume of airfreight. Many of these activities have concentrated on developing better, more efficient ground facilities, introducing airfreight containers, and providing and marketing a wide variety of special services to shippers. In addition, some airfreight companies have specialized and become partners in the international logistics effort, as Figure 18.2 shows.

Changes have also taken place within the aircraft. As an example, 30 years ago the holds of large propeller aircraft could take only about 10 tons of cargo. Today's jumbo jets can hold more than 30 tons and can therefore, as Figure 18.3 shows, transport bulky products. In addition, aircraft manufacturers have responded to industry demands by developing both jumbo cargo planes and combination passenger and cargo aircraft. The latter carry passengers in one section of the main deck and freight in another. These hybrids can be used by carriers on routes that would be uneconomical for passengers or freight alone.[11]

From the shipper's perspective, the products involved must be amenable to air shipment in terms of their size. In addition, the market situation for any given product must be evaluated. For example, airfreight may be needed if a product is perishable or if, for other reasons, it requires a short transit time. The level of customer service needs and expectations can also play a decisive role. For example, the shipment of an industrial product that is vital to the ongoing operations of a customer is usually much more

[11] Klaus Wittkamp, "Rickshaws for Taiwan or Cattle for China, It's All Air Freight," *The German Tribune* (Hamburg), June 26, 1983, 10.

urgent than the shipment of most consumer products. The joint decision by traffic, marketing, and financial managers about which products are "air eligible" is discussed in The International Marketplace 18.1 at the beginning of the chapter.

Choice of Modes

The international marketer must make the appropriate selection from the available modes of transportation. This decision of course will be heavily influenced by the needs of the firm and its customers. The manager must consider the performance of each mode on four dimensions: transit time, predictability, cost, and noneconomic factors.

Transit time   The period between departure and arrival of the carrier varies significantly between ocean freight and airfreight. For example, the 45-day transit time of an ocean shipment can be reduced to 24 hours if the firm chooses airfreight. The length of transit time will have a major impact on the overall logistical operations of the firm. As an example, a short transit time may reduce or even eliminate the need for an overseas depot. Also, inventories can be significantly reduced if they are replenished frequently. As a result, capital can be freed up and used to finance other corporate opportunities. Transit time can also play a major role in emergency situations. For example, if the shipper is about to miss an important delivery date because of production delays, a shipment normally made by ocean freight can be made by air.

Perishable products require shorter transit times. Transporting them rapidly prolongs the shelf life in the foreign market. As was seen in The International Marketplace 18.2, for products with a short lifespan, air delivery may be the only way to successfully enter foreign markets. For example, international sales of cut flowers have reached their current volume only as a result of airfreight.

This interaction between selling price, market distance, and form of transportation is not new. Centuries ago, Johann von Thünen, a noted German economist, developed models for the market reach of agricultural products that incorporated these factors. Yet, given the forms of transportation available today, these factors no longer pose the rigid constraints postulated by von Thünen, but rather offer new opportunities in international business.

Predictability   Providers of both ocean and airfreight service wrestle with the issue of reliability. Both modes are subject to the vagaries of nature, which may impose delays. Yet, because **reliability** is a relative measure, the delay of one day for airfreight tends to be seen as much more severe and "unreliable" than the same delay for ocean freight. However, delays tend to be shorter in absolute time for air shipments. As a result, arrival time via air is more predictable. This attribute has a major influence on corporate strategy. For example, because of the higher predictability of air freight, inventory safety stock can be kept at lower levels.

18.2 ## THE INTERNATIONAL MARKETPLACE

Maine Lobster: A Christmas Dinner Tradition—in Europe
Eighty tons of fresh lobsters were shipped at Christmastime in 1987 from Maine to Europe, where the delicacy has become something of a Christmas dinner tradition. The 160,000 pounds of crustaceans were about 35,000 pounds more than the amount of Maine lobster delivered to Europe for Christmas a year earlier.

The lobsters, harvested from the frigid Atlantic waters off Maine and Nova Scotia, were distributed to markets throughout France, Luxembourg, and Belgium. Bruce Saunders, who acted as an independent agent for nine lobster suppliers, attributed the success of the sizable sale to the shipping crew, which quickly loaded the freshly caught cargo aboard a 747 charter plane at the Bangor airport. Saunders arranged to have the lobsters carted and packed so they were out of water for less than 24 hours before they went to market.

Source: "Christmas Gift to Europeans: Maine Lobsters," *The Journal of Commerce,* December 28, 1987, 4A.

Greater predictability can also serve as a useful sales tool for foreign distributors, who are able to make more precise delivery promises to their customers. If inadequate port facilities exist, airfreight may again be the better alternative. Unloading operations from ocean-going vessels are more cumbersome and time-consuming than for planes. Finally, merchandise shipped via air is likely to suffer less loss and damage from exposure of the cargo to movement. Therefore, once the merchandise arrives, it is more likely to be ready for immediate delivery—a facet that also enhances predictability.

Cost of Transportation   A major consideration in choosing international transportation modes is the cost factor. International transportation services are usually priced on the basis of both cost of the service provided and the value of the service to the shipper. Because of the high value of the products shipped by air, airfreight is often priced according to the value of the service. In this instance, of course, price becomes a function of market demand and the monopolistic power of the carrier.

The international marketer must decide whether the clearly higher cost of airfreight can be justified. In part, this will depend on the cargo's properties. For example, the physical density and the value of the cargo will affect the decision. Bulky products may be too expensive to ship by air, whereas very compact products may be more amenable to airfreight transportation. High-priced items can absorb transportation cost more easily than low-priced goods, because the cost of transportation as a percentage of total product cost will be lower. As a result, sending diamonds by airfreight is easier to justify than sending coal by air.

Most important, however, are the overall logistical considerations of the firm. The manager must determine how important it is for merchandise to arrive on time. The need to reduce or increase international inventory must be carefully measured. Related to these considerations are the effect of transportation cost on price and the need for product availability abroad. For example, some firms may wish to use airfreight as a new tool for aggressive market expansion. Airfreight may also be considered a good way to begin operations in new markets without making sizable investments for warehouses and distribution centers.

Although costs are the major consideration in modal choice, the overall cost perspective must be explored. Simply comparing transportation modes on the basis of price alone is insufficient. The manager must factor in all corporate activities that are affected by the modal choice and explore the total cost effects of each alternative.

Noneconomic Factors Often noneconomic dimensions will enter into the selection process for a proper form of transportation. The transportation sector, nationally and internationally, both benefits and suffers from heavy government involvement. Carriers may be owned or heavily subsidized by governments. As a result, governmental pressure is exerted on shippers to use national carriers, even if more economical alternatives exist. Such preferential policies are most often enforced when government cargo is being transported. Restrictions are not limited to developing countries. For example, in the United States, all government cargo and all official government travelers must use national flag carriers when available.

For balance of payments reasons, international quota systems of transportation have been proposed. The United Nations Commission on International Trade and Development (UNCTAD), for example, has recommended a treaty whereby 40 percent of the traffic between two nations is allocated to vessels of the exporting country, 40 percent to vessels of the importing country, and 20 percent to third country vessels. However, stiff international competition among carriers and the price sensitivity of customers frequently render such proposals ineffective, particularly for trade between industrialized countries.

Although many justifications are possible for such national policies, ranging from prestige to national security, they may distort the economic choices of the international corporation. These policies are a reflection of the international environment within which the firm must operate. Proper adaptation is necessary.

INTERNATIONAL INVENTORY ISSUES

Inventories tie up a major portion of corporate funds. As a result, capital used for inventory is not available for other corporate opportunities. Because annual **inventory carrying costs** (the expense of maintaining inventories) can easily comprise up to 25 percent or more of the value of the inventories themselves,[12] proper inventory policies should be of major concern to the international marketing manager. In addition, new just-in-time inventory policies are increasingly adopted by multinational manufacturers. These policies minimize the volume of inventory by making it available only when it is needed for the production process. Firms using such a policy will choose suppliers on the basis of their delivery and inventory performance. Proper inventory management may therefore become a determinant variable in obtaining a sale.

Although inventories are closely monitored domestically, this is often not the case internationally. One observer wrote, "As the risk of foreign operations increases, companies are less likely to follow prescribed procedures for optimizing models related to inventory management."[13] This lack of preoccupation, however, does not reduce the importance of the issue. In its international inventory management, the multinational corporation is faced not only with new situations that affect inventories negatively but also with new opportunities and alternatives.

The purpose of establishing inventory—to maintain product movement in the delivery pipeline in order to satisfy demand—is the same for domestic and international inventory systems. The international environment, however, includes unique factors such as currency exchange rates, greater distances, and duties. At the same time, international operations provide the corporation with an opportunity to explore alternatives not available in a domestic setting, such as new sourcing or location alternatives. In international operations the firm can make use of currency fluctuations by placing varying degrees of emphasis on inventory operations, depending on the stability of the currency of a specific country. Entire operations can be shifted to different nations to take advantage of newly emerging opportunities. International inventory management can therefore be much more flexible in its response to environmental changes.

In deciding the level of inventory to be maintained, the international marketer must consider three factors: the order cycle time, desired customer service levels, and use of inventories as a strategic tool.

Order Cycle Time   The total time that passes between the placement of an order and the receipt of the merchandise is referred to as order cycle time. Two dimensions are of major importance to inventory management: the length of the total order cycle and its consistency. In international marketing, the order cycle is frequently longer than in domestic business. It comprises the time involved in order transmission, order filling, packing and preparation for shipment, and transportation. Order transmission time varies greatly internationally depending on whether telex, telephone, fax, or mail is used in communicating. The order filling time may also be increased because lack of familiarity with a foreign market makes the antic-

---

[12] Bernard J. LaLonde and Paul H. Zinszer, *Customer Service: Meaning and Measurement* (Chicago: National Council of Physical Distribution Management, 1976).

[13] David A. Ricks, *International Dimensions of Corporate Finance* (Englewood Cliffs, N.J.: Prentice-Hall, 1978).

ipation of new orders more difficult. Packing and shipment preparation require more detailed attention. Finally, of course, transportation time increases with the distances involved. As a result, total order cycle time can frequently approach 100 days or more.[14] Larger inventories may have to be maintained both domestically and internationally in order to bridge these time gaps.

Consistency, the second dimension of order cycle time, is also more difficult to maintain in international marketing. Depending on the choice of transportation mode, delivery times may vary considerably from shipment to shipment. This variation requires the maintenance of larger safety stocks in order to be able to fill demand in periods when delays occur.

The international marketer should attempt to reduce order cycle time and increase its consistency without an increase in total costs. This objective can be accomplished by altering methods of transportation, changing inventory locations, or by improving any of the other components of the order cycle time, such as the way orders are transmitted. By shifting order placement from mail to telephone or to direct computer order entry, for example, the order cycle time can easily be reduced by three to eight days. Yet, because such a shift is likely to increase the cost of order transmittal, offsetting savings in other inventory areas must be achieved.

Customer Service Levels The level of customer service denotes the responsiveness that inventory policies permit for any given situation. Customer service is therefore a management determined constraint within the logistics system. A customer service level of 100 percent could be defined as the ability to fill all orders within a set time—for example, three days. If within these three days only 70 percent of the orders can be filled, the customer service level is 70 percent. The choice of customer service level for the firm has a major impact on the inventories needed. In their domestic operations, U.S. companies frequently aim to achieve customer service levels of 90 to 95 percent. Often such "homegrown" rules of thumb are then used in international inventory operations as well.

Many managers do not realize that standards determined heuristically and based on competitive activity in the home market are often inappropriate abroad. Different locales have country-specific customer service needs and requirements. Service levels should not be oriented primarily around cost or customary domestic standards. Rather, the level chosen for use internationally should be based on customer expectations encountered in each market. These expectations are dependent on past performance, product desirability, customer sophistication, the competitive status of the firm, and whether a buyers' or sellers' market exists.

Because high customer service levels are costly, the goal should not be the highest customer service level possible, but rather an acceptable level. If, for example, foreign customers expect to receive their merchandise

---

[14]Michael R. Czinkota, Harvey J. Iglarsh, Richard L. Seeley, and James Sood, "The Role of Order Cycle Time for the Latin American Exporting Firm," presented at the annual meeting of the Academy of International Business, New Orleans, La., October 21, 1980, 9.

within 30 days, for the international corporation to promise delivery within 10 or 15 days does not make sense. Customers may not demand or expect such quick delivery. Indeed, such delivery may result in storage problems. In addition, the higher prices associated with higher customer service levels may reduce the competitiveness of a firm's product.

Inventory as a Strategic Tool   International inventories can be used by the international corporation as a strategic tool in dealing with currency valuation changes or hedging against inflation. By increasing inventories before an imminent devaluation of a currency, instead of holding cash, the corporation may reduce its exposure to devaluation losses. Similarly, in the case of high inflation, large inventories can provide an important inflation hedge. In such circumstances, the international inventory manager must balance the cost of maintaining high levels of inventories with the benefits accruing to the firm from hedging against inflation or devaluation. Many countries, for example, charge a property tax on stored goods. If the increase in tax payments outweighs the hedging benefits to the corporation, it would be unwise to increase inventories before a devaluation.

Despite the benefits of reducing the firm's financial risk, inventory management must still fall in line with the overall corporate market strategy. Only by recognizing the trade-offs, which may result in less than optimal inventory policies, can the overall benefit to the corporation be maximized.

INTERNATIONAL PACKAGING ISSUES

Packaging is of particular importance in international logistics because it is instrumental in getting the merchandise to the ultimate destination in a safe, maintainable, and presentable condition. Packaging that is adequate for domestic shipping may be inadequate for international transportation because the shipment will be subject to the motions of the vessel on which it is carried. Added stress in international shipping also arises from the transfer of goods among different modes of transportation. Figure 18.4 provides examples of some sources of stress in intermodal movement that are most frequently found in international transportation.

The responsibility for appropriate packaging rests with the shipper of goods. The U.S. Carriage of Goods by Sea Act of 1936 states: "Neither the carrier nor the ship shall be responsible for loss or damage arising or resulting from insufficiency of packing." The shipper must therefore ensure that the goods are prepared appropriately for international shipping. This is important because it has been found that "the losses that occur as a result of breakage, pilferage, and theft exceed the losses caused by major maritime casualties, which include fires, sinkings, and collision of vessels. Thus the largest of these losses is a preventable loss." [15]

[15] Charles A. Taft, *Management of Physical Distribution and Transportation*, 7th ed. (Homewood, Ill.: Irwin, 1984), 324.

FIGURE 18.4 ▪ **Stresses in Intermodal Movement**

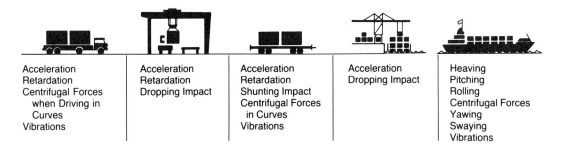

Acceleration	Acceleration	Acceleration	Acceleration	Heaving
Retardation	Retardation	Retardation	Dropping Impact	Pitching
Centrifugal Forces	Dropping Impact	Shunting Impact		Rolling
when Driving in		Centrifugal Forces		Centrifugal Forces
Curves		in Curves		Yawing
Vibrations		Vibrations		Swaying
				Vibrations

Note: Each transportation mode exerts a different set of stresses and strains on containerized cargoes. The most commonly overlooked are those associated with ocean transport.

Source: Reprinted with permission from *Handling and Shipping Management*, September 1980 issue, p. 47; David Greenfield, "Perfect Packing for Export." Copyright © 1980, Penton Publishing, Cleveland, Ohio.

Packaging decisions must also take into account differences in environmental conditions—for example, climate. When the ultimate destination is very humid or particularly cold, special provisions must be made in order to prevent damage to the product. The task becomes even more challenging when one considers that, in the course of long-distance transportation, dramatic changes in climate can take place.

Packaging issues also need to be closely linked to overall strategic plans. The individual responsible for international packaging should utilize transportation modes as efficiently as possible. This requires appropriate package design. The International Marketplace 18.3 provides an example of packaging efficiencies.

The weight of packaging must also be considered, particularly when airfreight is used, as the cost of shipping is often based on weight. At the same time, packaging material must be sufficiently strong to permit stacking in international transportation. Another consideration is that, in some countries, duties are assessed according to the gross weight of shipments, which includes the weight of packaging. Obviously, the heavier the packaging, the higher the duties will be.

The shipper must pay sufficient attention to instructions provided by the customer for packaging. For example, requests by the customer that the weight of any one package should not exceed a certain limit, or that specific package dimensions should be adhered to, usually are made for a reason. Often they reflect limitations in transportation or handling facilities at the point of destination.

Although the packaging of a product is often used as a form of display abroad, international packaging can rarely serve the dual purpose of protection and display. Therefore double packaging may be necessary. The

18.3 THE INTERNATIONAL MARKETPLACE

London Brewery Taps United States with New Keg   A small South London brewery that still makes local deliveries by horse-drawn dray is set to revolutionize the way in which beer is shipped to overseas markets. Determined to break into the U.S. market and exploit the growing demand for draught beer but hampered by the cost of transporting beer in metal kegs, Young & Co.'s brewery— better known to real ale aficionados on both sides of the Atlantic as the Ram Brewery—is experimenting with a nonreturnable plastic container.

Young's is the first brewery to employ lightweight 30-liter kegs that were developed by Johnson Enterprises of the United States and are manufactured in Britain by Metal Box PLC. The first exports to the United States using the new-style kegs, which are more elongated in shape than traditional 10- and 20-liter metal ball-shaped kegs, began in March 1987 and initial response was very favorable. In the first four months shipments across the Atlantic doubled from two to four containers a month, and in 1988 the firm expected to sell 5,000 U.K. barrels (210,000 U.S. gallons) of beer in the United States.

Young's export manager, Dan Kopman, estimated that the company will enjoy a savings of some 25 percent through lower freight charges because of the weight differential and the elimination of costs associated with the returnable keg system. "Plastic kegs could completely change the way in which beer is shipped around the world," he predicted.

Beer is one of the most important commodities transported across the North Atlantic. For example, the United States accounts for more than one-third of all U.K. beer exports, with shipments in 1986 reaching 213,000 U.K. barrels, or more than $40 million.

Source: Janet Porter, "Small London Brewery Hopes to Tap the U.S. with New Keg," *The Journal of Commerce,* July 29, 1987, 1A–2A.

---

display package is for future use at the point of destination; another package surrounds it for protective purposes.

One solution to the packaging problem in international logistics has been the development of intermodal containers—large metal boxes that fit on trucks, ships, railroad cars, and airplanes and ease the frequent transfer of goods in international shipments. In addition, containers offer greater safety from pilferage and damage. Of course, if merchandise from a containerized shipment is lost, frequently the entire container has been removed. Developed in different forms for both sea and air transportation, containers also offer better utilization of carrier space because of standardization of size. The shipper therefore may benefit from lower transportation rates.

Container traffic is heavily dependent on the existence of appropriate handling facilities, both domestically and internationally. In addition, the quality of inland transportation must be considered. If transportation for containers is not available and the merchandise must be removed and reloaded, the expected cost reductions may not materialize.

In some countries, rules for the handling of containers may be designed to maintain employment. For example, U.S. union rules obligate shippers to withhold containers from firms that do not employ members of the International Longshoreman Association for loading or unloading of containers within a 50-mile radius of Atlantic or Gulf ports. Such restrictions can result in an onerous cost burden.

Overall, close attention must be paid to international packaging. The customer who ordered and paid for the merchandise expects it to arrive on time and in good condition. Even with replacements and insurance, the customer will not be satisfied if there are delays. This dissatisfaction will usually translate directly into lost sales.

INTERNATIONAL STORAGE ISSUES

Although international logistics is discussed as a movement or flow of goods, a stationary period is involved when merchandise becomes inventory stored in warehouses. Heated arguments can arise within a firm over the need for and utility of warehousing internationally. On the one hand, customers may expect quick responses to orders and rapid delivery. Accommodating the customer's expectation may require locating many distribution centers around the world. On the other hand, warehousing space is expensive. In addition, the larger volume of inventory increases the inventory carrying cost. The international marketer must consider the trade-offs between service and cost to determine the appropriate levels of warehousing. Other trade-offs also exist within the logistics function. As an example, fewer warehouses will allow for consolidation of transportation and therefore lower transportation rates to the warehouse. However, if the warehouses are located far from customers, the cost of outgoing transportation from the warehouse will increase.

Storage Facilities

The international marketer is faced with the location decision of how many distribution centers to have and where to locate them. The availability of facilities abroad will differ from the domestic situation. For example, while public storage is widely available in the United States, such facilities may be scarce or entirely lacking abroad. Also, the standards and quality of facilities abroad are often not comparable to those offered in the United States. As a result, the storage decision of the firm is often accom-

18.4 THE INTERNATIONAL MARKETPLACE

The Cost of Warehousing in Japan *One of the major shortcomings of the Japanese distribution system is its lack of warehousing facilities. Even though the Japanese government has begun to introduce change by making warehousing facilities more widely available and by legislating the building of distribution centers, the cost of storage space is quite high. In order to obtain space in an existing distribution center, tenants often must pay a number of charges. Some of these charges (based on an exchange rate of $1 = 125 yen) are:*

- *Construction contribution fund: Participation in this fund consists of a one-time payment, which is refundable only after ten years, with no interest payment. Usually this one-time payment amounts to approximately $400 per square meter.*
- *Security deposit: This deposit amounts to $1,000 per square meter and is refundable only at the end of the lease, with no interest payment.*
- *Monthly rent: $25 per square meter.*
- *Administrative charges: These charges are paid for administrative support that is rendered by the management of the distribution center. They amount to approximately $8 per square meter per month.*

Leases typically must be signed for a minimum of ten years. Despite these quite substantial costs, vacancy rates at existing distribution centers are extremely low, with outside turnover often being less than 2 percent.

Source: Michael R. Czinkota and Jon Woronoff, *Japan's Market: The Distribution System* (New York: Praeger, 1986), 86.

---

panied by the need for large-scale, long-term investments. An example of the possible costs encountered by a firm seeking warehouse space internationally is given in The International Marketplace 18.4. Despite the high cost, international storage facilities should be established if they support the overall marketing effort. In many markets, adequate storage facilities are imperative in order to satisfy customer demands and to compete successfully.

Once the decision is made to utilize storage facilities abroad, the warehouses must be carefully analyzed. As an example, in some countries warehouses have low ceilings. Packaging developed for the high stacking of products is therefore unnecessary. In other countries, automated warehousing is available. Proper bar coding of products and the use of package dimensions acceptable to the warehousing system are basic requirements.

In contrast, in warehouses still stocked manually, weight limitations will be of major concern.

To optimize the logistics system, the marketer should analyze international product sales and then rank order products according to warehousing needs. Products that are most sensitive to delivery time may be classified as "A" products. "A" products would be stocked in all distribution centers, and safety stock levels would be kept high. Products for which immediate delivery is not urgent may be classified as "B" products. They would be stored only at selected distribution centers around the world. Finally, products for which short delivery time is not important, or for which there is little demand, would be stocked only at headquarters. Should an urgent need for delivery arise, airfreight could be considered for rapid shipment. Classifying products enables the international marketer to substantially reduce total international warehousing requirements and still maintain acceptable service levels.

Foreign Trade Zones

Special areas where foreign goods may be held or processed and then reexported without incurring duties are called trade zones.[16] Trade zones can be found at major ports of entry and also at inland locations near major production facilities. For example, Kansas City, Missouri, has one of the largest foreign trade zones in the United States.

The existence of trade zones can be quite useful to the international firm. For example, in a particular country the benefits derived from lower factor costs, such as labor, may be offset by high duties and tariffs. As a result, location of manufacturing and storage facilities in that country may prove uneconomical. Foreign trade zones are designed to exclude the impact of duties from the location decision. This is done by exempting merchandise in the foreign trade zone from duty payment. The international firm can therefore import merchandise; store it in the foreign trade zone; and process, alter, test, or demonstrate it—all without paying duties. If the merchandise is subsequently shipped abroad (that is, reexported), no duty payments are ever due. Duty payments become due only if and when the merchandise is shipped into the country from the foreign trade zone.

Firms can also make use of sharp differentials in factor endowments, such as, for example, labor costs, between adjoining countries, by locating close to their border. For instance, the maquiladora program between the United States and Mexico permits firms to carry out their labor-intensive operations in Mexico, while sourcing raw materials or component parts from the United States, free of Mexican tariffs. Subsequently, the semi-

---

[16] Ronald H. Ballou, *Basic Business Logistics: Transportation, Materials Management, Physical Distribution* (Englewood Cliffs, N.J.: Prentice-Hall, 1987).

FIGURE 18.5   ▪   **Major Locations of Japanese Plants along the U.S. Border
with Mexico**

Source: "Japan's Launching Pad." Copyright 1987, *U.S. News & World Report.* Reprinted
with permission from the August 3, 1987 issue, p. 40.

finished or assembled products are shipped to the U.S. market and are assessed duties only for the foreign labor component. By 1988 over 1,000
firms were participating in this program, employing close to 300,000
Mexican citizens and accounting for close to $2 billion in revenue.[17] The
benefits of the maquiladora program are available for any firm that chooses
to locate close to the border and are therefore not restricted to U.S. companies alone. Figure 18.5 shows how Japanese firms have made use of this
program.

Both parties to the arrangement benefit from foreign trade zones. The
government maintaining the trade zone achieves increased employment.
The firm using the trade zone obtains a spearhead in or close to the foreign
market without incurring all of the costs customarily associated with such
an activity. As a result, goods can be reassembled and large shipments can
be broken down into smaller units. Also, goods can be repackaged when
packaging weight becomes part of the duty assessment. Finally, goods can
be given domestic "made-in" status if assembled in the foreign trade zone.
Thus, duties may be payable only on the imported materials and component parts rather than on the labor that is used to finish the product.
Whenever use of a trade zone is examined, however, the marketer must
keep the additional cost of storage in mind before making a decision.

[17]Charles R. Patton, William W. Thompson, and Donald R. Moak, "Understanding the
Present Controversy about the Maquiladora Program: A Primer for Marketing Executives and
Professors," *Developments in Marketing Science,* vol. 11, ed. K. Bahn (Miami: Academy of
Marketing Science, 1988), 492.

MANAGEMENT OF INTERNATIONAL LOGISTICS

Because the very purpose of a multinational firm is to benefit from system synergism, a persuasive argument can be made for the coordination of international logistics at corporate headquarters. Without coordination, subsidiaries will tend to optimize their individual efficiency but jeopardize the overall performance of the firm.

Centralized Logistics Management

A significant characteristic of the centralized approach to international logistics is the existence of headquarters staff that retains decision-making power over logistics activities affecting international subsidiaries. If headquarters exerts control, it must also take the primary responsibility for its decisions. Clearly, ill will may arise if local managers are appraised and rewarded on the basis of performance they do not control. This may be particularly problematic if headquarters staff suffers from a lack of information or expertise.

To avoid internal problems, both headquarters staff and local logistics management should report to one person. This person, whether the vice president for international logistics or the president of the firm, can then become the final arbiter to decide the firm's priorities. Of course, this individual should also be in charge of determining appropriate rewards for managers, both at headquarters and abroad, so that corporate decisions that alter a manager's performance level will not affect the manager's appraisal and evaluation. Further, this individual can contribute an objective view when inevitable conflicts arise in international logistics coordination. The internationally centralized decision-making process leads to an overall logistics management perspective that can dramatically improve profitability.

Decentralized Logistics Management

An alternative to the centralized international logistics system is the "decentralized full profit center model." [18] The main rationale for such decentralization is the fact that "when an organization attempts to deal with markets on a global scale, there are problems of coordination." [19] Particularly when the firm serves many international markets that are diverse in nature, total centralization would leave the firm unresponsive to local adaptation needs.

If each subsidiary is made a profit center in itself, each one carries the full responsibility for its performance, which can lead to greater local

[18] Jacques Picard, "Physical Distribution Organization in Multinationals: The Position of Authority," *International Journal of Physical Distribution and Materials Management* 13 (No. 2, 1983): 24.

[19] Philip B. Schary, *Logistics Decisions* (Hinsdale, Ill.: Dryden, 1984), 407.

management satisfaction and to better adaptation to local market conditions. Yet often such decentralization deprives the logistics function of the benefits of coordination. For example, while headquarters, referring to its large volume of overall international shipments, may be able to extract bottom rates from transportation firms, individual subsidiaries by themselves may not have similar bargaining power.

Overall, given the desire for system synergism, a firm's international logistics operations would appear to be best served if major control is exercised from headquarters, particularly in the international movement of products. Once products are within a specific market, however, increased input from local logistics operations should be expected and encouraged. At the very least, local managers should be able to provide input into the logistics decisions generated by headquarters. Ideally, within a frequent planning cycle, local managers can identify the logistics benefits and constraints existing in their particular market and communicate them to headquarters. Headquarters can then either adjust its international logistics strategy accordingly or can explain to the manager why system optimization requires actions different from the ones recommended. Such a justification process will help greatly in reducing the potential for animosity between local and headquarters operations.

SUMMARY

The relevance of international logistics was not widely recognized in the past. As competitiveness is becoming increasingly dependent on cost efficiency, however, the field is emerging as one of major importance, because international distribution comprises between 10 and 25 percent of the total landed cost of an international order.

International logistics is concerned with the flow of materials into, through, and out of the international corporation and therefore includes materials management as well as physical distribution. The logistician must recognize the total systems demands of the firm in order to develop trade-offs between various logistics components.

International logistics differs from domestic activities in that it deals with greater distances, new variables, and greater complexity because of country-specific differences. One major factor to consider is transportation. The international marketer needs to understand transportation infrastructures in other countries and modes of transportation such as ocean shipping and airfreight. The choice among these modes will depend on the customer's demands and the firm's transit time, predictability, and cost requirements. In addition, noneconomic factors such as government regulations weigh heavily in this decision.

Inventory management is another major consideration. Inventories abroad are expensive to maintain yet often crucial for international success. The marketer must evaluate requirements for order cycle times and customer service levels in order to develop an international inventory policy that can also serve as a strategic management tool.

International packaging is important because it ensures arrival of the merchandise at the ultimate destination in safe condition. In developing packaging requirements, consideration must be given to environmental conditions such as climate and freight and handling conditions.

The marketer must also deal with international storage issues and determine where to locate inventories. International warehouse space will have to be leased or purchased and decisions made about utilizing foreign trade zones.

International logistics management is increasing in importance. Centralized operations seem to be the most effective way to improve logistics operations.

Questions for Discussion

1. Why do international firms pay so little attention to international logistics issues?

2. Contrast the use of ocean shipping to airfreight.

3. Explain the meaning and impact of transit time in international logistics.

4. How and why do governments interfere in "rational" freight carrier selection?

5. What is your view of the 40/40/20 freight allocation rule of the United Nations Commission on International Trade and Development?

6. How can an international firm reduce its order cycle time?

7. Why should customer service levels differ internationally? Is it, for example, ethical to offer a lower customer service level in developing countries than in industrialized countries?

8. Given all the uncertainties in the international environment, is it worthwhile to attempt to model international logistics?

Recommended Readings

Ballou, Ronald H. *Basic Business Logistics.* Englewood Cliffs, N.J.: Prentice-Hall, 1987.

Blanding, Warren. *Practical Handbook of Distribution/Customer Service.* Washington, D.C.: Traffic Service Corporation, 1985.

LaLonde, Bernard, Martha Cooper, and Thomas Noordewier. *Customer Service, A Management Perspective.* Oakbrook, Ill.: Council of Logistics Management, 1988.

LaLonde, Bernard, and Martha Cooper. *Partnerships in Providing Customer Service: A Third Party Perspective.* Oakbrook, Ill.: Council of Logistics Management, 1989.

Owen, Wilfried. *Transportation and World Development.* Baltimore, Md.: Johns Hopkins University Press, 1987.

Schary, Philip B. *Logistics Decisions.* Hinsdale, Ill.: Dryden Press, 1984.

Shapiro, Roy D., and James L. Heskett. *Logistics Strategy: Cases and Concepts.* St. Paul, Mn.: West, 1985.

Stephenson, Frederick J., Jr. *Transportation USA.* Reading, Mass.: Addison-Wesley, 1987.

CHAPTER 19

International Promotion

THE INTERNATIONAL MARKETPLACE

Compaq Prepares for European Boom Compaq Computer Corp. is fine-tuning its international advertising strategy to take advantage of Europe's fast-growing $15 billion personal-computer market. Its sales rose 151 percent to $734 million in 1988, and in the pre-Christmas rush the company had to charter three cargo jets to bring goods from Texas because it could not book enough space on commercial flights.

The company is ready to launch its first pan-European campaign to position Compaq as the high-performance PC leader. The ads provide an "umbrella overlay" to develop Compaq's brand across borders, largely in anticipation of 1992. Although the company believes it has done an excellent job in country penetration and brand development, more must be done to tie things together.

Despite the plan for a regional campaign, Compaq will continue to rely heavily on its successful approach to central marketing strategy planning at headquarters in Houston. Instead of a single European campaign translated by country, media and creative strategies are tailored to the particular nation. "Individual executions allow you to take advantage of a country's culture, mores, history, and points of view whereas a single worldwide approach can become meaningful for no one," stated James D'Arezzo, Compaq Vice President–International Marketing. Relying on one marketing strategy for product and brand efforts, however, is essential to achieve consistency, accuracy, and direction for all executions.

When the company planned ads around its fast growth, the U.K. ad was a reprint of a news account headlined "Compaq Beats Apple Record for Fastest Entry to Fortune 500." The humor showed up at the bottom of the ad with the line, "Sorry, old fruit." The Germans dismissed the idea as arrogant and perhaps as an indication that the company grew so fast because its products were too high-priced. Their theme: "Compaq's 386. Full acceleration at any level." The Swiss chose "We're being followed." In this approach, ideas cross borders, but not necessarily executions. In addition, the company strives for a worldwide look through, for example, graphics consistency.

"We are not putting handcuffs on anyone, but we want to make sure that when it comes to execution, it is done with certain guidelines. The most important thing is that we get the message across and differentiate it from the competition in a tone that the individual country understands," said D'Arezzo.

Ogilvy & Mather, led by its Houston office, handles Compaq through 16 offices worldwide. The Australian account is the only one handled by a local agency.

Source: Richard I. Kirkland, Jr., "Europe Goes Wild for Yankee PCs," *Fortune*, June 5, 1989, 257–260; and Jennifer Lawrence, "Compaq Prepares for European Push," *Advertising Age*, June 12, 1989, 38.

The general requirements of effective marketing communications discussed in Chapter 11 apply to the multinational corporation as well; however, the environments and the situations usually are more varied and call for coordination of the promotional effort. Market conditions increasingly call for pan-regional approach or even the use of one global campaign, as can be seen in The International Marketplace 19.1.

The technology is in place for global communication efforts, but difficult challenges still remain in the form of cultural, economic, ethnic, regulatory, and demographic differences in the various countries and regions. Standardization of any magnitude requires sound management systems and excellent communication to ensure uniform strategic and tactical thinking of all the professionals in the overseas marketing chain. One marketer has suggested the development of a worldwide visual language that will be understandable and that would not offend cultural sensitivities.[1] Innovations in promotional approaches will be needed. One possibility is to increase the use of **infomercials** that offer educational advice using the sponsor's product as an example.

This chapter will analyze the elements to be managed in promotional efforts in terms of environmental opportunities and constraints. A framework is provided for the planning of promotional campaigns. Although the discussion focuses mostly on advertising, other elements of the promotion mix, especially sales promotion and publicity, fit integrally into the planning model. Naturally, all of the mass selling methods have to be planned in conjunction with personal selling efforts. For example, personal selling often relies on updated direct mailing lists and promotional materials sent to prospects before the first sales call.

PLANNING INTERNATIONAL PROMOTIONAL CAMPAIGNS

The planning for promotional campaigns consists of the following seven stages, which usually overlap or take place concurrently, especially after

[1]John Eger, "Globalancing Act Is Real," *Advertising Age*, January 30, 1984, 20, 24.

the basics of the campaign have been agreed upon. The stages are as follows:

1. Determine the target audience.
2. Determine specific campaign objectives.
3. Determine the budget.
4. Determine media strategy.
5. Determine the message.
6. Determine the campaign approach.
7. Determine campaign effectiveness.[2]

The actual content of these stages will change by type of campaign situation; compare, for example, a local campaign for which headquarters provides support versus a global corporate-image campaign.

The Target Audience

Multinational marketers face multiple audiences beyond customers. The expectations of these audiences have to be researched to assure the appropriateness of the campaign decision making. Consider the following publics with whom communication is necessary: suppliers, intermediaries, government, the local community, bankers and creditors, media organizations, shareholders, and employees. Each can be reached with an appropriate mix of tools. A multinational corporation that wants to boost its image with the government and the local community may sponsor events. Exxon, for example, sponsored an exhibition of Colombian art in the United States. The acclaim this received created a better understanding of South American culture and led to the Colombian government's awarding Exxon its highest decoration. This initiative helped Exxon to secure its market position as well as to create a favorable public image throughout South America.[3]

Some campaigns may be targeted at multiple audiences. For example, British Airways' "Manhattan Landing" campaign (in which Manhattan Island takes to the air and lands in London) was directed not only at international business travelers but at employees, the travel industry, and potential stockholders (the campaign coincided with the privatization of the airline in 1983).[4]

An important aspect of research is to determine multimarket target audience similarities. If such exist, pan-regional or global campaigns can be attempted. Grey Advertising checks for commonalities in variables such as economic expectations, demographics, income, and education. Consumer needs and wants are assessed for common features. An example of such commonalities is provided in The International Marketplace 19.2.

[2] Dean M. Peebles and John K. Ryans, *Management of International Advertising: A Marketing Approach* (Boston, Mass.: Allyn & Bacon, 1984), 72–73.

[3] Edgar P. Hibbert, *Marketing Strategy in International Business* (London: McGraw-Hill, 1989), 76–77.

[4] "Berkeley Square Takes on Madison Avenue," *The Economist*, September 17, 1988, 25–28.

THE INTERNATIONAL MARKETPLACE **19.2**

Gillette Uses Sports to Cross Culture Barriers   Toiletries are geared to cultures and lifestyles, and Gillette International, in taking the Trac II razor to Europe in 1972, faced some knotty problems in preparing a marketing plan to fit European lifestyles. The plan involved everything from the product's name to advertising strategy.

The name Trac II was changed to GII after market ·studies revealed that "trac" in some of the Romance languages meant "fragile." Gillette wanted the target audience to see the product as strong and not as one that might easily break. Gillette sends all copy to its London office, where all words are checked for accuracy, when taking products overseas.

Another problem in the introduction was how to deliver the concept, "the closest shave." In 1970, when Gillette introduced the Trac II, it used the principle of hysteresis. Animation was used to show how the second blade strategically placed alongside the first cuts the whisker again. To introduce the product to a European market meant finding a universal appeal to all types of Europeans. The answer: sports. The sports analogy suggested that a synchronization of two moves resulted in the scoring of a goal, in the product's case, the closest shave. The approach fit the intended target of young active men.

Similarly, when Eraser-Mate pens were introduced in Europe, the concept "to erase" was understood only in the English-speaking countries. The problem was to get the concept across the cultural barrier. In the search for a new name, Gillette found that everyone understood the word "replay." The reason: whenever a goal is scored in soccer games televised throughout Europe the word Replay blinks on the screen, signaling a repeat of what had just been seen. It fit Gillette's concept exactly: you erase it and do it again.

Gillette has since expanded this approach to new markets. As an official sponsor of the 1986 World Cup of soccer, it paid $10 million to put its corporate logo on stadium walls where it could be picked up by television cameras seen by approximately a billion people, nearly 25 percent of the world's population. The company believes that the United States and some of the European markets are mature for its products and is hoping that a World Cup connection will help persuade Third World customers. Gillette is a major sponsor of European satellite television shows such as Eurosport.

Sources: Jamie Talan, "Yankee Goods—and Know-How—Go Abroad," *Advertising Age*, May 17, 1982, M-14, M-16; and "The Selling of the Biggest Game on Earth," *Business Week*, June 9, 1986, 102–103.

Often, however, problems may emerge. For example, Tang was marketed in the United States as an orange juice substitute, which did not succeed in testing abroad. In France, for example, Tang was repositioned as a refreshment because the French rarely drink orange juice at breakfast. In countries like the Philippines, Tang could be marketed as a premium drink, whereas in Brazil, it was a low-priced item.[5] Audience similarities are more easily found in business markets.[6]

Campaign Objectives

Nothing is more essential to the planning of international promotional campaigns than the establishment of clearly defined, measurable objectives. These objectives can be divided into overall global and regional objectives as well as local objectives. Compaq, for example, has set as its worldwide objective to consistently rank number two for business PCs. For Compaq to reach this goal, international sales will represent 50 percent of total sales by 1992.[7] Such objectives offer the general guidelines and control needed for broad-based campaigns.

The objectives that are set at the local level are more specific and set measurable targets for individual markets. These objectives may be product- or service-related, or related to the corporation itself. Typical goals are to increase awareness, enhance image, or improve market share in a particular market. Whatever the objective, it has to be measurable for control purposes.

Local objectives are typically developed as a combination of headquarters–country organization involvement. Basic guidelines are initiated by headquarters, whereas local organizations set the actual country-specific goals. These goals are subject to headquarters approval, mainly to ensure consistency. Although some campaigns, especially global ones, may have more headquarters involvement than usual, local input is still quite important, especially to ensure appropriate implementation of the subsequent programs at the local level.

The Budget

The promotional budget links established objectives with media, message, and control decisions. Ideally, the budget would be set as a response to the objectives to be met, but resource constraints often preclude this approach. Many multinational marketers use an objective–task method, as a recent survey of 484 advertising managers for consumer goods in 15 countries indicates (see Table 19.1); however, realities may force compromises

---

[5] "Global Marketing Campaigns with a Local Touch," *Business International*, July 4, 1988, 205–210.

[6] Robert E. Hite and Cynthia Fraser, "International Advertising Strategies of Multinational Corporations," *Journal of Advertising Research* 28 (August–September 1988): 9–17.

[7] Jennifer Lawrence, "Compaq Prepares for European Push," *Advertising Age*, June 12, 1989, 38.

TABLE 19.1 ▪ **Budgeting Methods for Promotional Programs**

Budgeting Method	Percentage of Respondents Using This Method[a]	Major Differences	
		Lowest Percentages	Highest Percentages
Objective and Task	64	Sweden (36%) Argentina (44%)	Canada (87%) Singapore (86%)
Percentage of Sales	48	Yugoslavia (22%) Germany (31%)	Brazil (73%) Hong Kong (70%)
Executive Judgment	33	Finland (8%) Germany (8%) Yugoslavia (13%)	USA (64%) Denmark (51%) Brazil (46%) Great Britain (46%)
All-You-Can-Afford	12	Argentina (0%) Israel (0%)	Sweden (30%) Germany (25%) Great Britain (24%)
Matched Competitors	12	Denmark (0%) Israel (0%)	Germany 33% Sweden (33%) Great Britain (22%)
Same as Last Year Plus a Little More	9	Israel (0%)	
Same as Last Year	3		
Other	10	Finland (0%) Germany (0%) Israel (0%)	Canada (24%) Mexico (21%)

[a] Total exceeds 100 percent because respondents checked all budgeting methods that they used.

Source: Nicolaos E. Synodinos, Charles F. Keown, and Laurence W. Jacobs, "Transnational Advertising Practices," *Journal of Advertising Research* 29 (April–May 1989): 43–50.

between ideal choices and resources available.[8] As a matter of fact, available funds may dictate the basis from which the objective–task method can start.

Budgets can also be used as a control mechanism if headquarters retains final budget approval. In these cases, headquarters decision makers must have a clear understanding of cost and market differences to be able to make rational decisions.

Media Strategy

Target audience characteristics, campaign objectives, and the budget form the basis for the choice between media vehicles and the development of a media schedule. The major factors determining the choice of the media

[8] Nicolaos E. Synodinos, Charles F. Keown, and Laurence W. Jacobs, "Transnational Advertising Practices: A Survey of Leading Brand Advertisers in Fifteen Countries," *Journal of Advertising Research* 29 (April–May 1989): 43–50.

FIGURE 19.1 ■ **Worldwide Advertising Spending (average per person, $52)**

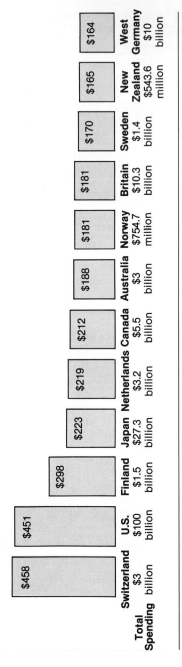

Note: Figures reflect advertising expenditures for 68 countries in 1987.

Source: "Where the Pitch Is Loudest." Copyright 1989, *U.S. News & World Report.* Reprinted with permission from the March 20, 1989 issue, p. 90.

vehicles to be used are (1) the availability of the media in a given market, (2) the product or service itself, and (3) media habits of the intended audience.

Media Availability   Media spending varies dramatically around the world, as seen in Figure 19.1. In absolute terms, the United States spends more money on advertising than 68 of the other major advertising nations combined. Other major spenders are Japan, the United Kingdom, West Germany, Canada, and France. The mature U.S. market anticipates slower growth in the future, but the opening of the European market in 1992 and the development of the Pacific Rim's consumer markets are likely to fuel major growth.[9] An estimate of growth in overall foreign spending for 1989 was set at $136 billion, whereas spending in the United States is expected to rise to only $126 billion.

Naturally, this spending varies by market. Countries devoting the highest percentage to television were Peru (88 percent), Costa Rica (78 percent), and Venezuela (64 percent). In countries where commercial television and radio are not available or are in limited use, the percentage devoted to print is high: Oman (100 percent), Norway (97 percent), and Sweden (96 percent). Radio accounts for more than 20 percent of total measured media in only a few countries such as Trinidad and Tobago, Nepal, and Mexico. Outdoor/transit advertising accounted for 48 percent of Bolivia's media spending but only 1.6 percent in the United States.[10] Cinema advertising is important in countries such as India and Nigeria. The prevailing advertising technique used by the Chinese consists of 7,000 outdoor boards and posters found outside factories.

The media available to the international marketer in major Latin American countries are summarized in Table 19.2. The breakdown by media points to the enormous diversity in how media are used in a given market. These figures do not tell the whole story, however, which emphasizes the need for careful homework on the part of the international manager charged with media strategy. As an example, Brazil has five television networks but one of them—TV Globo—corners 70 percent of all television advertising spending. Throughout Latin America, the tendency is to allocate half or more of total advertising budgets into television, with the most coveted spots on prime-time soap operas that attract viewers from Mexico to Brazil. In general, advertising in Latin America requires flexibility and creativity. Inflation rates have caused advertising rates to increase dramatically in countries like Argentina. In Mexico, advertisers can use the "French Plan," which protects participating advertisers from price increases during the year and additionally gives the advertiser two spots for the price of one. For these concessions the advertiser must pay for the year's entire advertising schedule by October of the year before.

---

[9]Julie S. Hill, "Euro, Pacific Spending Spree," *Advertising Age*, April 10, 1989, 4, 55.

[10]Lena Vanier, "U.S. Ad Spending Double All Other Nations Combined," *Advertising Age*, May 16, 1988, 36.

TABLE 19.2 ▪ **Latin American Media Breakdown**

	Argentina	Brazil	Chile
Total advertising expenditure, 1983[a]	N.A.	$2.1 billion	$105 million
Breakdown by Media			
Television	29.6%	61%	45.1%
Newspapers	23.5	14.7	35.1
Radio	8.4	8	10.8
Magazines	5.7	12.9	6.1
Outdoor	7.6	2.3	2.8
Cinema	2.4	0.4	0.1
Media Ownership			
Television	Government (Buenos Aires); private outside Buenos Aires	TV Globo and other private	Chilean universities in Santiago
Newspapers	Private, mostly family owned	Private, largely family owned	Edwards chain and other private
Radio	Private, government	Private	Private and government
Commission Structure	17.5% on gross, plus volume discounts; media wholesalers	20% on gross media, 15% on gross production, plus volume discounts and price cutting	17.65% of net, plus volume discounts

[a]These figures are based on average exchange rates for 1983; high rates of inflation and extreme currency devaluations should be taken into account.

The major problems affecting international promotional efforts involve conflicting national regulations. J. Walter Thompson, one of the ten largest advertising agencies in the world, has estimated that advertising expenditures on Western European television would be $2.4 to $3.3 billion more should these regulations be eased.[11] Some of the regulations include limits on the amount of time available for advertisements, ranging from complete prohibition (Sweden) to 15 to 20 minutes per day in blocks of 3 to 5 minutes (West Germany). France and Italy limit the percentage of revenues that the state monopoly systems can derive from advertising. In France, where U.S. computer manufacturers are especially desperate for

[11]D. Pridgen, "Satellite Television Advertising and the Regulatory Conflict in Western Europe," *Journal of Advertising* 14 (Winter 1985): 23–29.

Colombia	Mexico	Peru	Venezuela
$337.8 million	$200 million	$74 million	$186 million
52%	50.6%	53.9%	50.5%
18	12.3	25.7	25.9
25	16.9	12.2	17.1
5	9.2	3.8	2.0
—	3.0	{ 4.4	2.3
—	1.5		0.9
Government controls, but hires out to private companies	Televisa	One government, five private channels	Private and government
Private	Private	Private	Private
Government controls, but hires out to private companies	Televisa and other private, government	Private	Private
17.65% on net billings; discounts prevalent	17.65%; French plan prevalent	17.65% on net billings and 15% on gross; discounts common	15.2% on gross media and production plus volume discounts

Source: "Latin American Media Breakdown," *Advertising Age*, July 5, 1984, 22. Reprinted with permission from *Advertising Age*. Copyright Crain Communications, Inc. All rights reserved.

more television advertising time in a fast-growing market, they have had to wait up to 18 months for allocation of airtime. This means that marketers cannot use TV as a tactical medium for new-product introductions. Strict separation between programs and commercials is almost a universal requirement, preventing U.S.-style sponsored programs. Restrictions on items such as comparative claims and gender stereotypes are prevalent; for example, Germany prohibits the use of superlatives such as "best." Many of these regulations may be standardized by coordination efforts of such bodies as the Council of Europe and the EC.

Until now, with few exceptions, most nations have been very successful in controlling advertising that enters their borders. When commercials were not allowed on the state-run stations, advertisers in Belgium had been accustomed to placing their ads on the Luxembourg station. Radio

Luxembourg has traditionally been used to beam messages to the United Kingdom. By the end of the 1990s, however, approximately half of the homes in Europe will have access to additional television broadcasts through either cable or direct satellite, and television will no longer be restricted by national boundaries. The implications of this to international marketers are significant. The viewer's choice will be expanded, leading to competition between government-run public channels, competing state channels from neighboring countries, private channels, and pan-European channels.

This development will add to available advertising time on television but it will also create a complex market in which to buy effectively. With the advent of cross-boundary television competition and satellite channels, marketers need to make sure that advertising works not only within markets but across countries as well.[12] This has major implications for other areas of marketing, such as branding and positioning.

Product Influences Marketers and advertising agencies are currently frustrated by wildly differing restrictions on how products can be advertised. Agencies often have to produce several separate versions to comply with various national regulations. Consumer protection in general has dominated the regulatory scene in the 1980s.[13] Changing and standardizing these regulations, even in an area like the EC, is a "long and difficult road."[14]

A summary of product-related regulations found in Western Europe is provided in Table 19.3. Tobacco products and alcoholic beverages are the most heavily regulated products in terms of promotion; however, the manufacturers of these products have not abandoned their promotional efforts. Philip Morris engages in corporate image advertising using its cowboy-spokesperson. John Player sponsors sports events, especially Formula One car racing. Some European cigarette manufacturers have diversified into the entertainment business (restaurants, lounges, movie theaters) and named them after their cigarette brands. Tobacco and alcohol advertisers have also welcomed an innovation in advertising: in-flight ads. Brown & Williamson Tobacco Corporation, marketer of Kool cigarettes, sponsors the Kool Jazz Network, a music channel on American Airlines.

Certain products are subject to special rules. In the United Kingdom, for example, advertisers cannot show a real person applying an underarm deodorant; the way around this problem is to show an animated person applying the product. What is and is not allowable is very much a reflection of the country imposing the rules. Explicit advertisements of contra-

---

[12] John Clemens, "Television Advertising in Europe," *Columbia Journal of World Business* 22 (Fall 1987): 35–41.

[13] Jean J. Boddewyn, "Advertising Regulation in the 1980s," *Journal of Marketing* 46 (Winter 1982): 22–28.

[14] Kevin Cote, "The New Shape of Europe," *Advertising Age*, November 9, 1988, 98–100, 148.

TABLE 19.3 ▪ **Restrictions on Advertisements for Specific Products in Selected Western European Countries**

	Cigarettes and Tobacco Products	Alcoholic Beverages	Pharmaceutical Products
France	Banned	Banned	Prior authorization from appropriate government health authority required
Republic of Ireland	Cigarettes—banned Cigars and pipe tobacco—permitted but regulated	Liquor—banned Beer and wine—permitted but regulated	Advertisements for certain products or treatments prohibited, others regulated
Luxembourg (pursuant to voluntary code)	Banned	Permitted but regulated	Permitted but regulated
Netherlands	Banned	Permitted but regulated	Prior opinion sought from self-regulatory bodies
Switzerland	Banned	Banned	Banned
United Kingdom (Independent Broadcasting Authority)	Cigarettes—banned Pipe tobacco and cigars—permitted but regulated	Permitted but regulated	Prior opinion sought from Medical-Advisory Board; advertisements for certain products or treatments prohibited

Source: D. Pridgen, "Satellite Television Advertising and the Regulatory Conflict in Western Europe," *Journal of Advertising* 14 (Winter 1985): 23–29.

ceptives are commonplace in Sweden, for example, whereas they can be found almost nowhere else in the world.

Audience Characteristics A major objective of media strategy is to reach the intended target audience with a minimum of waste. As an example, Amoco Oil Company wanted to launch a corporate image campaign in the People's Republic of China in the hope of receiving drilling contracts. Identifying the appropriate decision makers was not difficult, because they all work for the government. The selection of appropriate media proved to be equally simple, because most of the decision makers overseeing petroleum exploration were found to read the vertical trade publications: *International Industrial Review, Petroleum Production,* and *Offshore Petroleum.*

If conditions are ideal, and they seldom are in international markets, the media strategist would need data on (1) media distribution, that is, the number of copies of the print medium or the number of sets for broadcast; (2) media audiences; and (3) advertising exposure. For instance, an advertiser interested in using television in Brazil would like to know that the music show "Cassino do Chacrinha" averages a 25 rating and a 50 percent share of audience for the 4:00 p.m. to 6:00 p.m. time slot. In markets where more sophisticated market research services are available, data on advertising perception and consumer response may be available.[15] In many cases, advertisers have found circulation figures to be unreliable or even fabricated.

Global Media Media vehicles that have target audiences on at least three continents and for which the media buying takes place through a centralized office are considered to be **global media.** Global media have traditionally been publications that, in addition to the worldwide edition, have provided advertisers the option of using regional editions. For example, *Time* provides 133 editions, enabling advertisers to reach a particular country, continent, or the world. Other global publications include *International Herald Tribune, The Wall Street Journal,* and *National Geographic.*

Advertising in global media is dominated by major consumer ad categories, particularly airlines, financial services, communications, automobiles, and tobacco. The aircraft industry represents business-market advertisers.[16] Companies spending in global media include AT&T, IBM, and General Motors. In choosing global media, the three most important media characteristics for media buyers are targetability, client-compatible editorial, and editorial quality.[17] Some global publications have found that some parts of the globe are more appealing to advertisers than others; *International Management,* for example, had to eliminate its editions in Latin America, Africa, and Asia-Pacific because of lack of advertising.[18]

In broadcast media, pan-regional radio stations have been joined in Europe by television as a result of satellite technology. The pan-European satellite channels, such as Sky Channel and Super Channel, were conceived from the very beginning as advertising media. Many are skeptical about the potential of these channels, especially in the short term, because of the challenges of developing a cross-cultural following in Europe's still highly nationalistic markets.[19] Pan-European channels have had to cut back, while native-language satellite channels like French-language Tele 5

[15] Terence A. Shimp and M. Wayne DeLozier, *Promotion Management and Marketing Communications* (Hinsdale, Ill.: Dryden, 1986), 399–420.

[16] R. Craig Endicott, "International Print Builds Rates, Reach," *Advertising Age,* December 19, 1988, 21–22.

[17] David W. Stewart and Kevin J. McAuliffe, "Determinants of International Media Buying," *Journal of Advertising* 17 (Fall 1988): 22–26.

[18] Lawrence Wentz, "Why 'IM' Heads Away from Global," *Advertising Age,* December 2, 1985, 45, 58.

[19] Laurel Wentz, "Murdoch's Sky Takes a Fall," *Advertising Age,* October 3, 1988, 68.

and RTL Plus in Germany have increased their viewership. British Satellite Broadcasting, which will compete directly with U.K. networks ITV and the BBC, estimates that it alone will have 10 million viewers and ad revenues of $1.7 billion by the turn of the century.[20]

The Promotional Message

The creative people must have a clear idea of the characteristics of the audience expected to be exposed to the message. In this sense the principles of creating effective advertising are the same as in the domestic marketplace. The marketer must determine what the consumer is really buying—that is, the customer's motivations. They will vary, depending on:

1. The diffusion of the product or service into the market. For example, to penetrate Third World markets with business computers is difficult when few potential customers know how to type.
2. The criteria on which the customer will evaluate the product. For example, in traditional societies, advertising the time-saving qualities of a product may not be the best approach, as Campbell Soup Company learned in Italy and Brazil, where housewives felt inadequate as homemakers if they did not make soups from scratch.
3. The product's positioning. For example, Parker Pen's upmarket image around the world may not be profitable enough in a market that is more or less a commodity business. The solution is to create an image for a commodity product and make the public pay for it—for example, the positioning of Perrier in the United States as a premium mineral water.

The ideal situation in developing message strategy is to have a world brand—a product that is manufactured, packaged, and positioned the same around the world. A good example of this type of situation is provided in The International Marketplace 19.3, which describes the promotional program developed by Xerox Corporation for the introduction of its new worldwide copier line. Companies that have been successful with the global approach have shown flexibility in the execution of the campaigns. The idea may be global, but overseas subsidiaries then tailor the message to suit local market conditions and regulations.

Executing an advertising campaign in multiple markets requires a balance between conveying the message and allowing for local nuances. The localization of global ideas can be achieved by various tactics, such as adopting a modular approach, localizing international symbols, and using international advertising agencies.[21]

[20]"European Satellite TV: Just So Much Pie in the Sky?" *Business Week*, October 24, 1988, 39–42.

[21]"Global Marketing Campaigns with a Local Touch," *Business International*, July 4, 1988, 205–210.

19.3	THE INTERNATIONAL MARKETPLACE

Xerox Combats Worldwide Competition　When Xerox Corporation's leading position in photocopying started to decline in the mid-1970s, the company wanted to develop one comprehensive plan to combat competition, to stop the sales decline, and to restore its international leadership position.

A new line of products was developed by the various entities of the corporation. Fuji Xerox developed two copiers, the 1020 and the 1035, for the low-volume segment. Rank Xerox came up with an internationally developed entry, the 1045, for the middle-volume segment; and Xerox U.S. designed the Xerox 1075 for the high-volume market. With the product ready for global introduction, Xerox needed a comprehensive communications program. It wanted to promote the products with a single, powerful message instantly understood anywhere to convey the endurance of its products. The symbol chosen: the marathon.

The media program combined international with local media. An umbrella campaign in English-language print media (such as

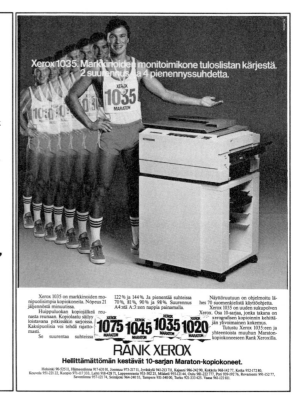

the international editions of Time, Newsweek, Business Week, *and* Fortune, *and the European and Far Eastern editions of* The Wall Street Journal *and* Herald Tribune *) was supported by appropriate advertising in local languages. The ad on the left is part of the global campaign, while the ad on the right is an example of a local (Finnish) execution. Xerox also used two media aimed at business travelers: a high-visibility poster program in major airports and a two-minute, editorial-style commercial shown before movies on international flights.*

To reinforce the advertising program, Xerox sponsored marathon races around the world. World-class runners (such as Grete Waitz and Rob de Castella) agreed to appear in six races a year in Team Xerox uniforms.

The effort paid off in sales results. Although many factors contributed to the increase, the marathon campaign played a key role in generating speedy awareness of the new line of products.

Source: William Wells, John Burnett, and Sandra Moriarty, *Advertising: Principles and Practice* (Englewood Cliffs, N.J.: Prentice-Hall, 1989), 580–583.

Marketers may develop multiple broadcast and print ads from which country organizations can choose the most appropriate for their operations. This can provide local operations with cost savings and allow them to use their budgets on tactical campaigns (which may also be developed around the global idea). For example, the "Membership Has Its Privileges" campaign of American Express, which has run in 24 countries on TV and three more in print, was adjusted in some markets to make sure that "privileges" did not have a snob or elitist appeal, especially in countries with a strong caste or class system. Product-related regulations will affect advertising messages as well. When General Mills Toy Group's European subsidiary launched a product line related to G.I. Joe-type war toys and soldiers, it had to develop two television commercials, a general version for most European countries and another for countries that bar advertisements for products with military or violent themes. As a result, in the version running in West Germany, Holland, and Belgium, jeeps replaced the toy tanks, and guns were removed from the hands of the toy soldiers. Other countries, such as the United Kingdom, do not allow children to appear in advertisements.

Marketers may also want to localize their international symbols. Some of the most effective global advertising campaigns have capitalized on the popularity of pop music worldwide and used well-known artists in the commercials, such as Pepsi's use of Tina Turner. In some versions, local stars have been included in the ads with the international stars to localize the campaign. Aesthetics play a role in localizing campaigns. The international marketer does not want to chance the censoring of the company's ads or risk offending customers. For example, even though importers of

FIGURE 19.2 ▪ **Adjustment of a Standardized Campaign**

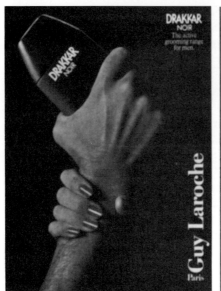

Source: Michael Field, "Fragrance Marketers Sniff Out Rich Aroma," *Advertising Age,* January 30, 1986, 10.

perfumes into Saudi Arabia want to use the same campaigns as are used in Europe, they occasionally have to make adjustments dictated by moral standards, as illustrated in Figure 19.2. The European version shows a man's hand clutching a perfume bottle and a woman's hand seizing his bare forearm. In the Saudi Arabian version, the man's arm is clothed in a dark suit sleeve, and the woman's hand is merely brushing his hand.

The use of one agency—or only a few agencies—ensures consistency. The use of one agency allows for coordination, especially when the multinational marketer's operations are decentralized. It also makes the exchange of ideas easier and may therefore lead, for example, to wider application of a modification or a new idea.

The environmental influences that call for these modifications, or in some cases totally unique approaches, are culture, economic development, and lifestyles. Of the cultural variables, language is most apparent in its influence on promotional campaigns. The European community alone has nine languages: English, French, German, Dutch, Danish, Italian, Greek, Spanish, and Portuguese. Advertisers in the Arab world have sometimes found that the voices in a TV commercial speak in the wrong Arabic dialect. The challenge of language is often most pronounced in translating themes. For example, Coca-Cola's worldwide theme, "Can't Beat the Feeling" is the equivalent of "I Feel Coke" in Japan, "Unique Sensation" in Italy, and "The Feeling of Life" in Chile. In Germany, where no translation really worked, the original English-language theme was used. One way of getting around this is to have no copy or very little copy and to use innovative approaches, such as pantomime. Using any type of symbolism will naturally require adequate copy testing to determine how the target market perceives the message.

The stage of economic development—and therefore the potential demand for and degree of awareness of the product—may vary and differentiate the message from one market to another. Whereas developed markets may require persuasive messages (to combat other alternatives), a developing market may require a purely informative campaign. Campaigns may also have to be dramatically adjusted to cater to lifestyle differences in regions that are demographically quite similar. For example, N.W. Ayer's Bahamas tourism campaign for the European market emphasizes clean water, beaches, and air. The exceptions are in West Germany, where it focuses on sports activities, and in the United Kingdom, where it features humor.

Unique market conditions may require localized approaches. Although IBM has utilized global campaigns (the Little Tramp campaign, for example), it has also used major local campaigns in Japan and Europe for specific purposes. In Japan, it used a popular television star in poster and door-board ads to tell viewers, "Friends, the time is ripe" (for buying an IBM 5550 personal computer). The campaign was designed to bolster the idea that the machine represents a class act from America. At the same time, IBM was trying to overcome a problem in Europe of being perceived as "too American." Stressing that IBM is actually a "European company," an advertising campaign told of IBM's large factories, research facilities, and tax-paying subsidiaries within the EC.

The Campaign Approach

Many multinational corporations are staffed and equipped to perform the full range of promotional activities. In most cases, however, they will rely on the outside expertise of advertising agencies and other promotions-related companies such as media buying companies and specialty marketing firms. In the organization of promotional efforts, a company has two basic decisions to make: (1) what type of outside services to use and (2) how to establish decision-making authority for promotional efforts.

Outside Services   Of all the outside promotion-related services, advertising agencies are by far the most significant. A list of the world's 50 top agencies and agency groups is given in Table 19.4. Of the top 50 agencies, 27 are based in the United States, 13 in Japan, and the rest in the United Kingdom, France, Australia, and South Korea. While the Japanese agencies tend to have few operations outside their home country, U.S. and European agencies are engaged in worldwide expansion. Size is measured in terms of gross income and billings. Billings are the cost of advertising time and space placed by the agency plus fees for certain extra services, which

TABLE 19.4 ▪ Top 50 Agencies Worldwide, 1989

Rank	Agency	Worldwide Gross Income	Worldwide Billings
1	Dentsu Inc.	$1,229	$9,450
2	Young & Rubicam	758	5,390
3	Saatchi & Saatchi Advertising Worldwide	740	5,035
4	Backer Spielvogel Bates Worldwide	690	4,678
5	McCann-Erickson Worldwide	657	4,381
6	FCB-Publicis	653	4,358
7	Ogilvy & Mather Worldwide	635	4,110
8	BBDO Worldwide	586	4,051
9	J. Walter Thompson Co.	559	3,858
10	Lintas: Worldwide	538	3,586
11	Hakuhodo International	522	3,939
12	Grey Advertising	433	2,886
13	D'Arcy Masius Benton & Bowles	429	3,361
14	Leo Burnett Co.	428	2,865
15	DDB Needham Worldwide	400	3,020
16	WCRS Worldwide	290	2,029
17	HDM	279	1,938
18	Roux, Seguela, Cayzac & Goudard	210	1,527
19	Lowe, Howard-Spink & Bell	197	1,316
20	N W Ayer	185	1,348
21	Bozell, Jacobs, Kenyon & Eckhardt	179	1,283
22	Dai-Ichi Kikaku	142	978
23	Daiko Advertising	140	1,127
24	Tokyu Advertising Agency	135	1,115
25	Wells, Rich, Greene	117	836
26	Scali, McCabe, Sloves	107	771
27	Ketchum Communications	106	776
28	Asatsu Advertising	105	755
29	I&S Corp.	97	691
30	Ogilvy & Mather Direct Response	97	647
31	TBWA	97	672
32	Yomiko Advertising	90	660
33	Ross Roy Group	85	568
34	Mojo MDA	72	455
35	Asahi Advertising	71	440
36	BDDP Group	69	462
37	Chiat/Day	65	520
38	FCA! Group	58	387
39	Hill, Holliday, Connors, Cosmopulos	50	335
40	Chuo Senko Advertising	47	346
41	Nihon Keizaisha	47	283
42	Lowe Marschalk	46	304
43	Korea First Advertising	45	194
44	AC&R Advertising	44	356
45	BMP Davison Pearce	43	300
46	W. B. Doner	42	303
47	Orikomi Advertising	41	420
48	Admarketing Inc.	40	225
49	Jordan, McGrath, Case & Taylor	39	300
50	Man-Nen-Sha	36	493

Note: Figures are in millions.

Source: Julie S. Hill, "No. 1 Dentsu Hits Lofty $1.2 Billion in Gross Income," *Advertising Age*, March 29, 1989, 71. Reprinted with permission from *Advertising Age*. Copyright 1989 Crain Communications, Inc. All rights reserved.

TABLE 19.5 ▪ **Megagroups in Advertising, 1989**

Rank	Group	Worldwide Gross Income	Billings Worldwide	Billings U.S.
1	Saatchi & Saatchi PLC	$1,990	$13,529	$6,316
2	Interpublic Group of Cos.	1,260	8,402	3,095
3	WPP Group PLC	1,173	7,825	4,256
4	Omnicom Group	986	7,072	4,344
5	Ogilvy Group	865	5,703	2,702
6	Eurocom	500	3,343	212
7	WCRS Group	335	2,914	764
8	Lowe, Howard-Spink & Bell	197	1,316	397
9	Bozell Inc.	194	1,347	1,185
10	GGK Holding AG	85	578	174
11	Lopex PLC	68	452	64

Note: Billing figures are in millions.

Source: "Saatchi Leads Top 11 Mega-Groups," *Advertising Age*, March 29, 1989, 80.

are converted by formula to correspond to media billings in terms of value of services performed. Agencies do not receive billings as income; in general, agency income is approximately 15 percent of billing.

Agencies form world groups for better coverage. The largest world "super" group, Saatchi & Saatchi Co., includes such entities as Saatchi & Saatchi Advertising Worldwide, McCaffrey & McCall, Backer Spielvogel Bates Worldwide, Dorland Worldwide, and AC&R. Billings of this group were $13.5 billion in 1988 (see Table 19.5). Smaller advertising agencies have affiliated local agencies in foreign markets.

The choice of an agency will largely depend on the quality of coverage the agency will be able to give the multinational company. Global marketing requires global advertising, according to proponents of the globalization trend. The reason is not that significant cost savings can be realized through a single worldwide ad campaign but because such a global campaign is inseparable from the idea of global marketing. Saatchi & Saatchi Advertising Worldwide, which promotes itself as the leading world-brand agency, predicts that the whole industry will be concentrated into a few huge multinational agencies by the end of the decade.[22] Agencies with networks too small to compete have become prime takeover targets in the creation of worldwide mega-agencies. Many believe that local, midsized agencies can compete in the face of globalization in developing local solutions.[23]

Although the forecast that six large agencies will eventually place most international advertising may be exaggerated, global marketing is the new

[22] Myron Magnet, "What Makes Saatchi & Saatchi Grow," *Fortune*, March 11, 1984, 46–56.

[23] "Ad Exec: Going Global Is Not Always the Best Choice an Agency Can Make," *Marketing News*, August 1, 1988, 15.

19.4 THE INTERNATIONAL MARKETPLACE

Getting Ready for 1992   *Since 1988, there has been a rush of activity among multinational marketers and advertising agencies in Western Europe. Although marketers readily admit that they do not know precisely how 1992 will affect the competitiveness of their brands, developments reflect rapid restructuring by clients and related responses by their advertising agencies.*

- *Johnson & Johnson's $35 million rollout of its Silhouette feminine hygiene products in 1988 approached Europe as a single market, rather than as a collection of distinct countries. Saatchi & Saatchi coordinated the effort.*
- *Agencies are gearing up as multinational clients increasingly assign budgets for specific brands on a pan-European basis; for example, 3M Europe is breaking ties with some 50 agencies and would like to appoint only two to four in all of Europe.*
- *When Backer Spielvogel Bates Worldwide announced the merger of its Ted Bates Ltd. and Dorland offices in London, the reason was to strengthen Bates' European network through the presence of a heavyweight London office.*
- *United Pictures International—the export marketing organization for Paramount, Universal, and MGM/UA studios in the United States—fired a grab bag of ad agencies in national European markets and appointed Young & Rubicam to manage the $30 million of film promotion.*
- *The alliance of Foote, Cone & Belding and France's Publicis was FCB's bid to position itself with a strong European partner.*

Source: Kevin Cote, "1992: Europe Becomes One," *Advertising Age*, July 11, 1988, 46.

---

wave and is having a strong impact on advertising. In the 1980s, the major multinational agencies increased their share of the advertising market from 14 percent to over 20 percent.[24] Major realignments of client-agency relationships have occurred due to mergers and to clients' reassessment of their own strategies. In Europe, anticipation of 1992 has provided the major impetus, as can be seen from The International Marketplace 19.4.

New markets are also emerging, and agencies are establishing their presence in them. For example, DDB Needham, which has been servicing its clients in the Chinese market from Hong Kong, was forming a joint venture with the Chinese government in 1989.[25] In September 1988, Young &

[24] Myron Magnet, "Saatchi & Saatchi Will Keep Gobbling," *Fortune*, June 23, 1986, 36–40.
[25] Nancy Giges, "DDB Needham to Enter China for Asian Growth," *Advertising Age*, May 1, 1989, 57–58.

Rubicam signed a letter of intent to form a joint venture with the largest ad agency in the Soviet Union, Vneshtorgreklama.[26]

Agency–client relations for the major multinational corporations and their international advertising agencies are shown in Table 19.6. According to a Grey Advertising survey of 50 multinational marketers, 76 percent believe the ideal situation is to use the same agency worldwide, with some local deviation as necessary. The same percentage believes an advertising agency should be centrally run, and 72 percent believe in using the same advertising strategy worldwide.[27] Most large companies typically use more than one agency, with the division of labor usually along product lines. For example, Matsushita Electric Industrial Company, an innovator in the consumer electronics industry, uses two major agencies. Backer Spielvogel Bates Worldwide handles everything involving portables, audio, VHS, and television. Grey Advertising handles the hi-fi area, the Technics label, and telephone products. Panasonic, one of Matsushita's U.S. brands, has a small agency for primarily nonconsumer items.

The main concern arising from the use of mega-agencies is conflict. With only a few giant agencies to choose from, the international marketer may end up with the same agency as the main competitor. The mega-agencies believe they can meet any objections by structuring their companies as rigidly separate, watertight agency networks (such as the Interpublic Group) under the umbrella of a holding group. Following that logic, Procter & Gamble, a client of Saatchi & Saatchi Advertising Worldwide, and Colgate-Palmolive, a client of Ted Bates, should not worry about falling into the same network's client base. However, when the Saatchi & Saatchi network purchased Ted Bates, Colgate-Palmolive left the agency.

Despite the globalization trend, local agencies will survive as a result of governmental regulations. In Peru, for example, a law mandates that any commercial aired on Peruvian television must be 100 percent nationally produced. Local agencies also tend to forge ties with foreign agencies for better coverage and customer service and thus become part of the general globalization effort. A basic fear in the advertising industry is that accounts will be taken away from agencies that cannot handle world brands. An additional factor is contributing to the fear of losing accounts. In the past, many multinational corporations allowed local subsidiaries to make advertising decisions entirely on their own. Others gave subsidiaries an approved list of agencies and some guidance. Still others allowed local decisions subject only to headquarters' approval. Now the trend is toward centralization of all advertising decisions, including those concerning the creative product.

Decision-Making Authority The alternatives for allocating decision-making authority range from complete centralization to decentralization.

---

[26] Charles Joseph, "Soviet Union," *Advertising Age*, November 9, 1988, 114.

[27] Dennis Chase, "Global Marketing: The New Wave," *Advertising Age,* June 25, 1984, 49, 74.

TABLE 19.6 ▪ Major Advertiser–Agency Relationships

	N W Ayer	BBDO	BDDP	Backer Spielvogel Bates Worldwide	Bozell, Jacobs, Kenyon & Eckhardt	Leo Burnett Co.	DDB Needham Worldwide	DMB&B	Foote, Cone & Belding	GGK	Grey Advertising	Hakuhodo Inc.	HDM	Ketchum Communications	LintasWorldwide	Lowe International	McCann-Erickson Worldwide	Mojo	Ogilvy & Mather Worldwide	Publicis International	Roux, Seguela, Cayzac & Goudard	Saatchi & Saatchi Advertising	Scali, McCabe, Sloves	TBWA Advertising	J. Walter Thompson Co.	Univas	WCRS/Belier	Young & Rubicam
American Airlines					•		•																					
American Cynamid				•				•	•													•						
American Express																	•		•									
American Home Products								•											•									•
Anheuser-Busch							•	•																				
BAT				•							•				•				•								•	
Bayer	•										•						•		•			•					•	
Beecham											•									•	•	•						
Beiersdorf									•	•															•			
BMW				•															•								•	
Bristol-Myers							•	•			•								•								•	
BSN Gervais Danone		•										•							•					•			•	•
Cadbury-Schweppes								•											•			•						
Campbell Soup	•							•															•					
Cheesebrough-Pond's																	•								•			
Ciba Geigy				•													•		•									
Citicorp							•	•	•						•										•			
Coca-Cola Co.															•		•		•									
Colgate-Palmolive Co.								•				•																•
CPC International								•				•					•						•					
Dow Chemical Co.								•				•					•										•	
Du Pont	•	•										•											•					•
Duracell								•											•									
Eastman Kodak Co.																			•				•		•			•
Electrolux				•							•																	
General Foods								•			•								•									•
General Motors	•							•									•	•										
Gillette Co.	•	•							•										•									
Guinness								•														•						
H.J. Heinz						•	•	•																				•
Henkel	•							•				•					•	•							•			
Hewlett Packard						•					•																	
Heublein																	•	•										
IBM						•	•																•		•			

	N W Ayer	BBDO	BDDP	Backer Spielvogel Bates Worldwide	Bozell, Jacobs, Kenyon & Eckhardt	Leo Burnett Co.	DDB Needham Worldwide	DMB&B	Foote, Cone & Belding	GGK	Grey Advertising	Hakuhodo Inc.	HDM	Ketchum Communications	Lintas: Worldwide	Lowe International	McCann-Erickson Worldwide	Mojo	Ogilvy & Mather Worldwide	Publicis International	Roux, Seguela, Cayzac & Goudard	Saatchi & Saatchi Advertising	Scali, McCabe, Sloves	TBWA Advertising	J. Walter Thompson Co.	Univas	WCRS/Belier	Young & Rubicam
Jacobs Suchard													•								•				•			•
Johnson & Johnson		•					•				•				•		•		•									•
S.C. Johnson				•					•										•									
Kimberly-Clark								•	•										•									
Kraft						•			•									•							•			
Mars				•				•																				
Mars Petfood				•				•																				
Philip Morris						•																		•				
Nestlé		•							•						•				•								•	
L'Oreal													•				•			•						•		
Parker Pen											•								•									
PepsiCo		•				•	•												•						•			•
N.V. Philips		•						•			•				•				•			•			•			
Polaroid		•																	•									
Procter & Gamble						•		•			•											•						
Qantas																	•											•
Quaker Oats Co.								•							•		•								•			
Reckitt & Colman											•				•		•	•				•			•			
Remy Martin															•													•
Richardson-Vicks				•				•									•											
RJR Nabisco						•			•						•							•			•			
Rothmans	•	•									•																	
Rowntree-Macintosh		•													•				•									
Seagram					•														•							•		
Shell				•															•									
3M				•							•			•					•									
Unilever		•													•				•						•			
Volkswagen					•					•																		
Wm. Wrigley Jr. Co.		•							•										•									
Warner-Lambert Co.				•																					•			•
Xerox		•																	•								•	

With complete centralization, the headquarters level is perceived to have all the right answers and has adequate power to impose its suggestions on all of its operating units. Decentralization involves relaxing most of the controls over foreign affiliates and allowing them to pursue their own promotional approaches.

The Grey Advertising survey found that only 21 percent of multinational corporations surveyed were run centrally, but 41 percent were moving in that direction. However, multinational corporations are at various stages in their quest for centralization. Procter & Gamble and Gillette generally have an approved list of agencies, whereas Quaker Oats and Johnson & Johnson give autonomy to their local subsidiaries, but will veto those decisions occasionally.

The important question is not who should make decisions but how advertising quality can be improved at the local level. Gaining approval among multinational corporations is an approach somewhere between centralization and decentralization, called **coordinated decentralization.**[28] This six-step program, which is summarized in Figure 19.3, strives for development of common strategy but flexible execution. The approach maintains strong central control but at the same time capitalizes on the greatest asset of the individual markets—market knowledge. Interaction between the central authority and the local levels takes place at every single stage of the planning process. The central authority is charged with finding the commonalities in the data provided by the individual market areas. This procedure will avoid one of the most common problems associated with acceptance of plans: the NIH syndrome (not invented here) by allowing for local participation by the eventual implementors.

A good example of this approach was Eastman Kodak's launch of its Ektaprint copier–duplicator line in 11 separate markets in Europe. For economic and organizational reasons, Kodak did not want to deal with different campaigns or parameters. It wanted the same ad graphics in each country, accompanied by the theme "first name in photography, last word in copying." Translations varied slightly from country to country, but the campaign was identifiable from one country to another. A single agency directed the campaign, which was more economical than campaigns in each country would have been and was more unified and identifiable through Europe. The psychological benefit of association of the Kodak name with photography was not lost in the campaign.

Agencies are adjusting their operations to centrally run client operations. Many accounts are now handled by a lead agency, usually in the country where the client is based. More and more agencies are moving to a strong international supervisor for global accounts. This supervisor can overrule local agencies and make personnel changes. Specialty units have emerged as well. For example, McCann-Erickson has a global advertising

[28] Dean M. Peebles, John K. Ryans, and Ivan R. Vernon, "Coordinating International Advertising," *Journal of Marketing* 42 (January 1978): 28–34.

FIGURE 19.3 ▪ **Coordinated Approach to International Advertising**

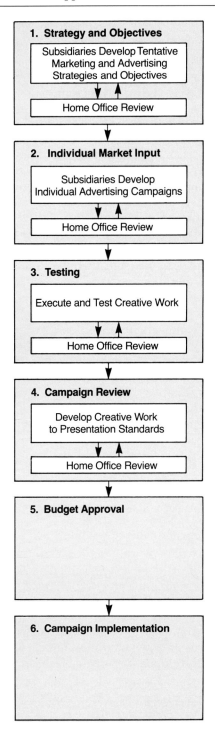

Source: Dean M. Peebles, John K. Ryans, and Ivan R. Vernon, "Coordinating International Advertising," *Journal of Marketing* 42 (January 1978): 30, published by the American Marketing Association.

625

unit of 25 professionals at headquarters in New York that specializes in developing global campaigns for its clients.[29]

Measurement of Advertising Effectiveness

John Wanamaker reportedly said, "I know half the money I spend on advertising is wasted. Now, if I only knew which half." Whether or not advertising effectiveness can be measured, most companies engage in the attempt. Measures of advertising effectiveness should range from pretesting of copy appeal and recognition to posttesting of recognition all the way to sales effects. The measures most used are sales, awareness, recall, executive judgment, intention to buy, profitability, and coupon return.[30]

The technical side of these measurement efforts does not differ from that in the domestic market, but the conditions are different. Very often syndicated services, such as A. C. Nielsen, are not available to the international marketer. If available, their quality may not be at an acceptable level. Testing is also quite expensive and may not be undertaken for the smaller markets. Compared to the U.S. market, the costs of research are higher in relation to the overall expenditure on advertising.[31] The biggest challenge to advertising research will come from the increase of global and regional campaigns. Comprehensive and reliable measures of campaigns for a mass European market, for example, are difficult because audience measurement techniques and analysis differ for each country. Advertisers are pushing for universally accepted parameters to compare audiences in one country to those in another.

OTHER PROMOTIONAL ELEMENTS

Personal Selling

Advertising is often equated with the promotional effort; however, a number of other efforts are used to support advertising. The marketing of industrial goods, especially of high-priced items, requires strong personal selling efforts. In some cases, personal selling may be truly international; for example, Boeing and Northrop salespeople engage in sales efforts around the world. However, in most cases, personal selling takes place at the local level. The best interests of any firm in the industrial area lie in establishing a solid base of dealerships staffed by local people. Personal selling efforts can be developed in the same fashion as advertising. For the

---

[29] "International Approach of McCann," *The New York Times*, February 27, 1989, 34.

[30] Nicolaos E. Synodinos, Charles F. Keown, and Laurence W. Jacobs, "Transnational Advertising Practices: A Survey of Leading Brand Advertisers in Fifteen Countries," *Journal of Advertising Research* 29 (April–May 1989): 43–50.

[31] Joseph T. Plummer, "The Role of Copy Research in Multinational Advertising," *Journal of Advertising Research* 26 (October–November 1986): 11–15.

multinational company, the main question again involves the enhancement and standardization of personal selling efforts, especially if the product offering is standardized.

Eastman Kodak has developed a line-of-business approach to allow for standardized strategy throughout a region.[32] In Europe, one person is placed in charge of the entire copier–duplicator program in each country. That person is responsible for all sales and service teams within the country. Typically, each customer is served by three representatives, each with a different responsibility. Sales representatives maintain ultimate responsibility for the account; they conduct demonstrations, analyze customer requirements, determine the right type of equipment for each installation, and obtain the orders. Service representatives install and maintain the equipment and retrofit new-product improvements to existing equipment. Customer service representatives are the liaison between sales and service. They provide operator training on a continuing basis and handle routine questions and complaints. Each team is positioned to respond to any European customer within four hours.

The training of the salesforce usually takes place in the national markets, but multinational corporations' headquarters will have a say in the techniques used. For instance, when Kodak introduced the Ektaprint line, sales team members were selected carefully. U.S. copier personnel could be recruited from other Kodak divisions, but most European marketing personnel had to be recruited from outside the company and given intensive training. Sales managers and a select group of sales trainers were sent to the Rochester, New York, headquarters for six weeks of training. They then returned to Europe to set up programs for individual countries so that future teams could be trained there. To assure continuity, all the U.S. training materials were translated into languages of the individual countries. To maintain a unified program and overcome language barriers, Kodak created a service language consisting of 1,200 words commonly found in technical information.

Foreign companies entering the Japanese market face challenges in establishing a salesforce. Recruitment poses the first major problem in that well-established, and usually local, entities have an advantage in attracting personnel. Many have, therefore, entered into joint ventures or distribution agreements to obtain a salesforce. Companies can also expect to invest more in training and organizational culture building activities than in the United States. These may bring long-term advantages in building loyalty to the company.[33]

Personal selling also has a major role in establishing and maintaining reseller relationships. These issues are discussed in Chapter 12.

---

[32] Joseph A. Lawton, "Kodak Penetrates the European Copier Market with Customized Marketing Strategy and Product Changes," *Marketing News*, August 3, 1984, 1, 6.

[33] John L. Graham, Shigeru Ichikawa, and Yao Apasu, "Managing Your Sales Force in Japan," *Euro-Asia Business Review* 6 (January 1987): 37–40.

Sales Promotion

Sales promotion has been used as the catchall term for promotion that does not fall under advertising, personal selling, or publicity. Sales promotion directed at consumers involves such activities as couponing, sampling, premiums, consumer education and demonstration activities, cents-off packs, point-of-purchase materials, and direct mail. The use of sales promotions as alternatives and to support advertising is increasing worldwide.[34] The appeal is related to several factors: cost and clutter of media advertising, simpler targeting of customers compared to advertising, and easier tracking of promotional effectiveness (for example, coupon returns provide a clear measure of effectiveness).

The success in Latin America of Tang, General Foods' presweetened powder juice substitute, is for the most part traceable to successful sales promotion efforts. One promotion involved trading Tang pouches for free popsicles from Kibon, General Foods' Brazilian subsidiary. Kibon also placed coupons for free groceries in Tang pouches. In Puerto Rico, General Foods ran Tang sweepstakes. In Argentina, in-store sampling featured Tang pitchers and girls in orange Tang dresses. Decorative Tang pitchers were a hit throughout Latin America. Sales promotion directed at intermediaries, also known as trade promotion, includes activities such as trade shows and exhibits, trade discounts, and cooperative advertising.

For sales promotion to be effective, the campaigns planned by manufacturers, or their agencies, must gain the support of the local retailer population. Coupons from consumers, for example, have to be redeemed and sent to the manufacturer or to the company handling the promotion. A. C. Nielsen tried to introduce cents-off coupons in Chile and ran into trouble with the nation's supermarket union, which notified its members that it opposed the project and recommended that coupons not be accepted. The main complaint was that an intermediary, like Nielsen, would unnecessarily raise costs and thus the prices to be charged to consumers. Also, some critics felt that coupons would limit individual negotiations, because Chileans often bargain for their purchases.

Tools of sales promotion fall under varying regulations, as can be seen from Table 19.7. A particular level of incentive may be permissible in one market but illegal in another. The Scandinavian countries present the greatest difficulties in this respect, because every promotion has to be approved by a government body. In France a gift cannot be worth more than 4 percent of the retail value of the product being promoted (subject to a maximum of 10 francs), while the maximum prize value in the Netherlands is 250 guilders, making certain promotions virtually impossible. Although competitions are allowed in most of Western Europe, to insist on receiving proofs of purchase as a condition of entry is not permitted in West Germany.

---

[34] Jean J. Boddewyn, *Premiums, Gifts and Competitions* (New York: International Advertising Association, 1986), Chap. 1.

TABLE 19.7   ▪   **Regulations Regarding Premiums, Gifts, and Competitions in Selected Countries**

Country	Category	No Restrictions or Minor Ones	Authorized with Major Restrictions	General Ban with Important Exceptions	Almost Total Prohibition
Australia	Premiums	x			
	Gifts	x			
	Competitions		x		
Austria	Premiums				x
	Gifts		x		
	Competitions		x		
Canada	Premiums	x			
	Gifts	x			
	Competitions		x		
Denmark	Premiums			x	
	Gifts		x		
	Competitions			x	
France	Premiums	x			
	Gifts	x			
	Competitions	x			
Germany	Premiums				x
	Gifts		x		
	Competitions		x		
Hong Kong	Premiums	x			
	Gifts	x			
	Competitions	x			
Japan	Premiums		x		
	Gifts		x		
	Competitions		x		
Korea	Premiums		x		
	Gifts		x		
	Competitions		x		
United Kingdom	Premiums	x			
	Gifts	x			
	Competitions		x		
United States	Premiums	x			
	Gifts	x			
	Competitions	x			
Venezuela	Premiums		x		
	Gifts		x		
	Competitions		x		

Source: J. J. Boddewyn, *Premiums, Gifts and Competition*, 1988, published by International Advertising Association, 342 Madison Avenue, Suite 2000, NYC, NY 10017. Reprinted with permission. Copies are available prepaid at the above address, U.S. $60 plus $5 postage and handling.

19.5 THE INTERNATIONAL MARKETPLACE

The "Pepsi Challenge" Worldwide   Cola wars are raging wherever the two giants, Coca-Cola Company and Pepsi International, meet. The best known of the warfare tactics have been various comparison campaigns, but other approaches have been utilized as well.

Local bottlers started using the "Pepsi challenge" campaign at a time when Coca-Cola outsold Pepsi in 108 of 148 markets, including most of the major ones. The challenge has been modified in most countries to fit laws and local customs. Usually this has meant softening the comparison claims by not naming Coke. In Malaysia, Pepsi was required to include a third cola so as not to imply that Coke and Pepsi were the only drinks available in the market. In Mexico, the Coca-Cola bottler installed its own tasting booths in front of Pepsi's and doubled its advertising budget. Further, Coke officials complained to the Mexican National Consumer Institute that the campaign was unethical.

In South Korea, where Coke outsells Pepsi by more than 5 to 1, Coca-Cola received a major boost from its status as an official worldwide Olympic sponsor. To counter this, Pepsi used "ambush tactics," such as offering free Pepsis to patrons of selected restaurants, including Pepsi's Pizza Huts, on days when the South Korean team won gold medals. Pepsi also gave away 50,000 sun visors with its logo to spectators of events such as the marathon. On a 45-inch TV screen outside Seoul's largest shopping center, Pepsi showed videotaped highlights of the Games and U.S. Pepsi shots, including commercials featuring Michael Jackson.

The hottest battle rages in the world's third-largest cola market: Brazil. Coke outsells Pepsi 4 to 1 but Pepsi is trying to catch up. Some novel tactics have been employed. In an operation called "The Mission," employees in São Paulo were dressed in battle fatigues, told they represented the "Blue Liberation Army," and then sent out to persuade distributors to drop Coke and try Pepsi. When Pepsi launched a Tina Turner publicity campaign, Coke responded with Sting, before signing up Xuxa, a local idol. Pepsi's announced goal is to be number one by the year 2000, which Coca-Cola bottlers will challenge with an investment of $150 million a year over a five-year period.

Sources: Dennis Chase, "Pepsi Uses 'Challenge' to Fight Coke Abroad," *Advertising Age*, March 25, 1985, 60–62; Oles Gadacz, "Diet Soft-Drink War Invades South Korea," *Advertising Age*, September 12, 1988, 85; and "Pepsi Aims to Liberate Big Market in Brazil from Coke's Domination," *The Wall Street Journal*, November 30, 1988, B6.

Regulations such as these make truly international sales promotions rare and difficult to launch.[35] Although only a few multinational brands have been promoted on a multiterritory basis, the approach can work. The International Marketplace 19.5 describes a program executed on a multiterritory basis: PepsiCo's Pepsi Challenge. In general, such multicountry promotions may be suitable for products such as soft drinks, liquor, airlines, credit cards, and jeans, which span cultural divides. Naturally, local laws and cultural differences have to be taken into account at the planning stage. Although many of the promotions may be funded centrally, they will be implemented differently in each market so that they can be tied with the local company's other promotional activities. For example, 7Up's multiterritory Music Machine promotion carries a common theme—youth-oriented rock music. The promotion involves sponsored radio shows, featuring specially recorded concerts by leading contemporary artists, and promotional gifts such as music videos and audiotapes.

In the province of Quebec in Canada, advertisers must pay a tax on the value of the prizes they offer in a contest, whether the prize is a trip, money, or a car. The amount of the tax depends on the geographical extent of the contest. If it is open only to residents of Quebec, the tax is 10 percent; if open to all of Canada, 3 percent; if worldwide, 1 percent. Subtle distinctions are drawn in the regulations between a premium and a prize. As an example, the Manic soccer team was involved with both McDonald's and Provigo Food stores. The team offered a dollar off the price of four tickets, and the stubs could be cashed for a special at McDonald's. Provigo was involved in a contest offering a year's supply of groceries. The Manic–McDonald's offer was a premium that involved no special tax; Provigo, however, was taxed, because it was involved with a contest. According to the regulation, a premium is available to everyone, whereas a prize is available to a certain number of people among those who participate. In some cases, industries may self-regulate the use of promotional items.

Public Relations

Image—how a multinational corporation relates to and is perceived by its key constituents—is a bottom-line issue for management. Public relations is the marketing communications function charged with executing programs to earn public understanding and acceptance, which means both internal and external communication.

Especially in multinational corporations, internal communication is important to create an appropriate corporate culture. The Japanese have perfected this in achieving a **wa** (we) spirit. Everyone in an organization is, in one way or another, in marketing and will require additional targeted information on issues not necessarily related to their day-to-day functions. A basic part of most internal programs is the employee publication pro-

[35] "An English Plan Abroad," *Sales Promotion*, April 25, 1985, 2–6.

FIGURE 19.4   ▪   **Internal Media: Deere & Company**

Source: Deere & Company.

duced and edited typically by the company's public relations or advertising department. Some, such as the example in Figure 19.4 from Deere & Company, have foreign-language versions. More often, as in the Mobil Corporation, each affiliate publishes its own employee publication. The better this vehicle can satisfy the information needs of employees, the less

TABLE 19.8 ▪ **Image-Enhancing Activities of Multinational Corporations**

- Gulf & Western Industries, Inc., through its Dominican Foundation, has awarded more than $11.8 million to various community development projects such as scholarship funds and education, health, and recreation programs.
- McDonald's Corporation sponsors Ronald McDonald tennis schools for youngsters in all of the markets where it operates.
- Since 1949, Caltex has provided road networks, bridges, low-cost housing, schools, and scholarships for the people of Indonesia.
- Colgate-Palmolive attracts up to 800,000 young participants each year to the Colgate Olympics in Brazil.
- In Pakistan, Exxon's affiliate operates a medical center specializing in snakebite treatment. It is credited with saving 1,000 lives in an area 60 miles from a hospital.
- A new freshwater supply system and a canal for the 2,000 residents of a Nigerian community were donated by Gulf Oil in cooperation with the Nigerian National Petroleum Company.

Sources: Oliver Williams, "Who Cast the First Stone?" *Harvard Business Review*, 62 (September–October 1984): 151–160; and S. Watson Dunn, *Public Relations* (Homewood, Ill.: Irwin, 1986), 585–586.

tion.[39] He proposes that the marketer's role is one of enlightened self-interest; reasonable critics understand that the marketer cannot compromise the bottom line. Complicating the situation often is the fact that groups in one market criticize what the marketer is doing in another market. For example, the Interfaith Center on Corporate Responsibility urged Colgate-Palmolive to stop marketing Darkie toothpaste under that brand name in Asia because of the term's offensiveness elsewhere in the world. Darkie toothpaste was sold in Thailand, Hong Kong, Singapore, Malaysia, and Taiwan, and packaged in a box that featured a likeness of Al Jolson in blackface.[40] Colgate-Palmolive changed the package and the brand name to Darlie.

The public relations function can be handled in-house or with the assistance of an agency. Some multinational corporations maintain public relations staffs in their main offices around the world, while others use the services of firms such as Burson-Marsteller, Hill and Knowlton, and Grey & Company on specific projects.

SUMMARY

As multinational corporations manage the various elements of the promotions mix in differing environmental conditions, decisions must be made about channels to be used in the communication, the message, who is to

[39] Oliver Williams, "Who Cast the First Stone?" *Harvard Business Review* 62 (September–October 1984): 151–160.

[40] "Church Group Gnashes Colgate-Palmolive," *Advertising Age*, March 24, 1986, 46.

execute or help execute the program, and how the success of the endeavor is to be measured. The trend is toward more harmonization of strategy, at the same time allowing for flexibility at the local level and incorporating local needs early into the promotional plans.

The effective implementation of the promotional program is a key ingredient in the marketing success of the firm. The promotional tools must be used within the opportunities and constraints posed by the communications channels as well as laws and regulations governing marketing communications.

Advertising agencies are key facilitators in communicating with the firm's constituent groups. Many multinational corporations are realigning their accounts worldwide in an attempt to streamline their promotional efforts and achieve a global approach.

The use of other promotional tools, especially personal selling, tends to be more localized to fit the conditions of the individual markets. Decisions concerning recruitment, training, motivation, and evaluation must be made at the affiliate level, with general guidance from headquarters.

An area of increasing challenge to multinational corporations is public relations. Multinationals, by their very design, draw attention to their activities. The best interest of the marketer lies in anticipating problems with both internal and external constituencies and managing them, through communications, to the satisfaction of the parties.

Questions for Discussion

1. Comment on the opinion that, "practically speaking, neither an entirely standardized nor an entirely localized advertising approach is necessarily best."

2. Discuss problems associated with measuring advertising effectiveness in foreign markets.

3. Should a company ever attempt perfect standardization of an advertising message? Is recognizability (by the consumer) enough for the general benefits of standardization to be achieved?

4. What type of adjustments must advertising agencies make as more companies want "one sight, one sound, one sell" campaigns?

5. What problems are created when an advertising message is extended to other markets through direct translation?

6. Assess the programmed management approach for coordinating international advertising efforts.

7. Is international personal selling a reality? Or is all personal selling national, regardless of who performs it?

8. How can the multinational corporation exert influence and strive for standardization in personal selling?

9. In June 1986, a campaign sponsored by 80 U.S. businesses in South African newspapers asserted that "apartheid laws are totally contrary

to the idea of free enterprise." The ad listed demands such as the release of political prisoners and acknowledged that U.S. companies faced increasing pressure to divest. Argue for and against this type of involvement by the international marketer.

Recommended Readings

Copeland, Lennie, and Lewis Griggs. *Going International: How to Make Friends and Deal Effectively in the Global Marketplace.* New York: Random House, 1985.

Dunn, S. Watson, Arnold M. Barban, Dean M. Krugman, and Leonard N. Reid. *Advertising: Its Role in Modern Marketing.* Hinsdale, Ill.: Dryden, 1990.

Kaynak, Erdener, ed. *The Management of International Advertising: A Handbook and Guide for Professionals.* Westport, Conn.: Quorum Books, 1989.

Kleinman, Philip. *Saatchi & Saatchi: The Inside Story.* Lincolnwood, Ill.: NTC Business Books, 1988.

Niefeld, Jaye S. *The Making of an Advertising Campaign: The Silk of China.* Englewood Cliffs, N.J.: Prentice-Hall, 1989.

Peebles, Dean, and John K. Ryans. *Management of International Advertising.* Boston: Allyn & Bacon, 1984.

Roth, Robert F. *International Marketing Communications.* Chicago: Crain Books, 1982.

Starch INRA Hooper. *Twenty-third Survey of World Advertising Expenditures: A Survey of World Advertising Expenditures in 1987.* Mamaroneck, N.Y.: Starch INRA Hooper, 1989.

CHAPTER 20

International Marketing Organization and Control

THE INTERNATIONAL MARKETPLACE

Doing More with Less at Headquarters *As the operations of multinational marketers have grown into large corporate entities, their organizational structures have become equally complex. As a result, many multiproduct, multicountry companies have abandoned their international divisions in favor of worldwide product groups, matrices, and hybrid organizations. For some, however, the international division structure still makes sense. An example is the Loctite Corporation, a worldwide leader in the development and marketing of high-performance adhesives and sealants for industrial and consumer applications. In 1987, the company derived 50 percent of its $337 million in sales from foreign markets.*

The international division structure at Loctite, in which authority and responsibility rest primarily with strong country managers, complements the company's decentralized management style, integrated product lines, and its emphasis on marketing and service.

The company's philosophy is "not to have a huge headquarters staff—but to provide all the support and expertise possible on the local scene." The major role of headquarters is to provide strong strategic direction for international operations. An international group resident, supported by a staff of two, oversees international operations consisting of 28 wholly owned subsidiaries, four joint ventures, and distributors in 50 countries.

Loctite has divided the world outside the United States into three regions—Europe, Latin America, and the Pacific—each of which is managed by a regional vice president. Managers responsible for country operations report to their respective regional heads. The primary responsibilities of each country manager are to satisfy local customer needs, manage the growth of country-specific businesses, help cross-fertilize ideas, and execute global strategies.

Source: "How Loctite Prospers with 3-Man Global HQ, Strong Country Managers," *Business International*, May 2, 1988, 129–130.

As companies evolve from purely domestic entities to multinationals, their organizational structure and control systems must change to reflect new strategies. With growth comes diversity in terms of products and services, geographic markets, and personnel, leading to a set of challenges for the company. Two critical issues are basic to addressing them: (1) the type of organization that provides the best framework for developing worldwide strategies and maintaining flexibility with respect to individual markets and operations and (2) the type and degree of control to be exercised from headquarters to maximize total effort.

This chapter will focus on the advantages and disadvantages of the organizational structures available as well as their appropriateness at various stages of internationalization. A determining factor is where decision-making authority within the organizational structures will be placed. Also, the roles of the different entities of the organization must be defined. The chapter will also outline the need for devising a control system to oversee the international operations of the company, emphasizing the control instruments needed in addition to those used in domestic business, as well as the control strategies of multinational corporations. The appropriateness and eventual cost of the various control approaches will vary as the firm expands its international operations. Overall, the objective of the chapter is to study intraorganizational relationships in the firm's attempt to optimize competitive response in areas most critical to its business.

ORGANIZATIONAL STRUCTURE

The basic functions of an organization are to provide (1) a route and locus of decision making and coordination and (2) a system for reporting and communications. Authority and communication networks are typically depicted in the organizational chart.

Organizational Designs

The basic configurations of international organization correspond to those of purely domestic ones; the greater the degree of internationalization, the more complex the structures can become. The types of structures that companies use to manage foreign activities can be divided into three categories based on the degree of internationalization:

1. Little or no formal organizational recognition of international activities of the firm. This category ranges from domestic operations handling an occasional international transaction on an ad hoc basis to separate export departments.
2. International division. Firms in this category recognize the ever-growing importance of international involvement.
3. Global organizations. These can be structured by product, area, function, process, or customer.

Hybrid structures may exist as well, in which one market may be structured by product, another by areas. Matrix organizations have emerged in large multinational corporations to combine product, regional, and functional expertise. As worldwide competition has increased dramatically in many industries, the latest organizational response is networked global organizations in which heavy flows of technology, personnel, and communication take place between strategically interdependent units to establish greater global integration.

Little or No Formal Organization   In the very early stages of international involvement, domestic operations assume responsibility for international marketing activities. The share of international operations in the sales and profits of the corporation is initially so minor that no organizational adjustment takes place. No consolidation of information or authority over international sales is undertaken or is necessary. Transactions are conducted on a case-by-case basis either by the resident expert or quite often with the help of facilitating agents, such as freight forwarders.

As demand from the international marketplace grows and interest within the firm expands, the organizational structure will reflect it. An export department appears as a separate entity. This may be an outside export management company—that is, an independent company that becomes the de facto export department of the firm. This is an indirect approach to international involvement in that very little experience is accumulated within the firm itself. Alternatively, a firm may establish its own export department, hiring a few seasoned individuals to take full responsibility for international activities. Organizationally, the department may be a subdepartment of marketing (alternative b in Figure 20.1) or may have equal ranking with the various functional departments (alternative a). This choice will depend on the importance assigned to overseas activities by the firm. Because the export department is the first real step for internationalizing the organizational structure, it should be a full-fledged marketing organization and not merely a sales organization.

Licensing is the international entry mode for some firms. Responsibility for licensing may be assigned to the R&D function despite its importance to the overall international strategy of the firm. A formal liaison among the export, marketing, production, and R&D functions should be formed for the maximum utilization of licensing.[1] A separate manager should be appointed if licensing becomes a major activity for the firm.

As the firm becomes more involved in foreign markets, the export-department structure will become obsolete. The firm may then undertake joint ventures or direct foreign investment, which require those involved to have functional experience. The firm therefore typically establishes an international division.

---

[1]Michael Z. Brooke, *International Management: A Review of Strategies and Operations* (London: Hutchinson, 1986), 173–174; and "Running a Licensing Department," *Business International*, June 13, 1988, 177–178.

FIGURE 20.1 ▪ **The Export Department Structure**

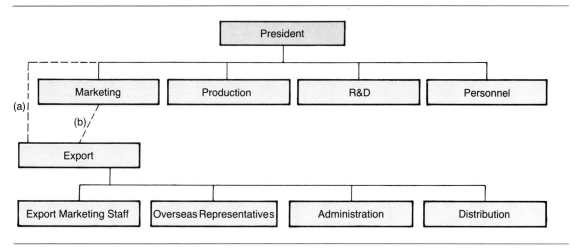

FIGURE 20.2 ▪ **The International Division Structure**

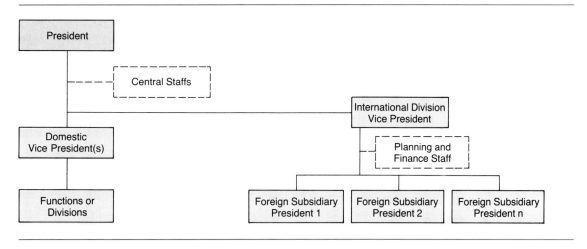

Some firms that acquire foreign production facilities pass through an additional stage in which foreign subsidiaries report directly to the president or to a manager specifically assigned this duty.[2] However, the amount of coordination and control that is required quickly establishes the need for a more formal international organization in the firm.

The International Division The international division centralizes in one entity, with or without separate incorporation, all of the responsibility for international activities, as illustrated in Figure 20.2. The approach aims to

---

[2] Stefan Robock and Kenneth Simmonds, *International Business and Multinational Enterprises* (Homewood, Ill.: Irwin, 1983), 414.

eliminate a possible bias against international operations that may exist if domestic divisions are allowed to independently serve international customers. In some cases, international markets have been found to be treated as secondary to domestic markets. The international division concentrates international expertise, information flows concerning foreign market opportunities, and authority over international activities. However, manufacturing and other related functions remain with the domestic divisions in order to take advantage of economies of scale.

To avoid situations in which the international division is at a disadvantage in competing for production, personnel, and corporate services, coordination is necessary between domestic and international operations. Coordination can be achieved through a joint staff or by requiring domestic and international divisions to interact in strategic planning and to submit the plans to headquarters. At Loctite Corporation, for example, international division headquarters is bolstered by two corporate staff functions specially created to promote a global flow of product information. One of the staff functions is the New Business Development group responsible for all research and new-product development.[3] Loctite's philosophy of "doing more with less" is described in The International Marketplace 20.1. Coordination is also important because domestic operations are typically organized along product or functional lines whereas international divisions are geographically oriented.

International divisions best serve firms with few products that do not vary significantly in terms of their environmental sensitivity, and when international sales and profits are still quite insignificant compared to those of the domestic divisions.[4] Companies may outgrow their international divisions as their international sales grow in significance, diversity, and complexity. This is especially true of European multinationals, which have typically outgrown the structure because of the relatively small size of their domestic markets. A number of U.S.-based companies in the 1970s shifted from a traditional organizational structure with an independent international division to entities built around worldwide or global structures with no differentiation between "domestic" and "international" operations.[5]

Size in itself is not a limitation to the use of the international division structure. Some of the world's largest corporations rely on international divisions.[6] The management of these companies believe that specialization is needed primarily in terms of the environment.

---

[3] "How Loctite Prospers with 3-Man Global HQ, Strong Country Managers," *Business International*, May 2, 1988, 129–130.

[4] Richard D. Robinson, *Internationalization of Business: An Introduction* (Hinsdale, Ill.: Dryden, 1984), 84.

[5] William H. Davidson, "Shaping a Global Product Organization," *Harvard Business Review* 59 (March–April 1982): 69–76.

[6] L. S. Walsh, *International Marketing* (Plymouth, England: MacDonald and Evans, 1981), 161.

Global Organizational Structures   Global structures have grown out of competitive necessity. In many industries competition is on a global basis, with the result that companies must have a high degree of reactive capability. European firms have traditionally had a global structure because of the relatively small size of their domestic markets. N. V. Philips, for example, could have never grown to its current prominence by relying on the Dutch market.

Five basic types of global structures are available:

1. Global product structure, in which product divisions are responsible for all manufacture and marketing worldwide
2. Global area structure, in which geographic divisions are responsible for all manufacture and marketing in their respective areas
3. Global functional structure, in which the functional areas (such as production, marketing, finance, and personnel) are responsible for the worldwide operations of their own functional areas
4. Global customer structure, in which operations are structured based on distinct worldwide customer groups
5. Mixed—or hybrid—structure, which may combine the other alternatives

Product Structure   The **product structure** is the one that is most used by multinational corporations.[7] This approach gives worldwide responsibility to strategic business units for the marketing of their product lines, as shown in Figure 20.3. Most consumer-product firms utilize some form of this approach, mainly because of the diversity of their products. One of the major benefits of the approach is improved cost efficiency through centralization of manufacturing facilities. This is crucial in industries in which competitive position is determined by world market share, which in turn is often determined by the degree to which manufacturing is rationalized.[8] Adaptation to this approach may cause problems because it is usually accompanied by consolidation of operations and plant closings. A good example is Black & Decker, which in the mid-1980s rationalized many of its operations in its worldwide competitive effort against Makita, the Japanese power-tool manufacturer. Similarly, Goodyear reorganized itself in 1988 into a single global organization with a complete business team approach for tires and general products. The move was largely prompted by tightening worldwide competition.[9]

---

[7] See Joan P. Curhan, William H. Davidson, and Suri Rajan, *Tracing the Multinationals* (Cambridge, Mass.: Ballinger, 1977), 15; M. E. Wicks, *A Comparative Analysis of the Foreign Investment Evaluation Practices of U.S.-Based Multinational Corporations* (New York: McKinsey & Co., 1980), 3; and Lawrence G. Franko, "Organizational Structures and Multinational Strategies of Continental European Enterprises," in *European Research in International Business*, eds. Michel Ghertman and James Leontiades (Amsterdam, Holland: North Holland, 1977), 111–137.

[8] William H. Davidson and Philippe Haspeslagh, "Shaping a Global Product Organization," *Harvard Business Review* 59 (March–April 1982): 69–76.

[9] "How Goodyear Sharpened Organization and Production for a Tough World Market," *Business International*, January 16, 1989, 11–14.

FIGURE 20.3 ▪ **The Global Product Structure**

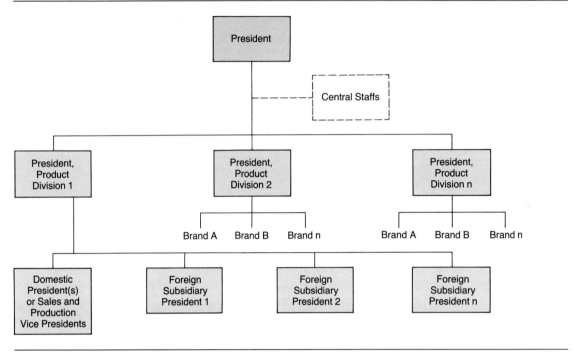

Another benefit is the ability to balance the functional inputs needed by a product and the ability to react quickly to product-specific problems in the marketplace. Even smaller brands receive individual attention. Product-specific attention is important because products vary in terms of the adaptation they need for different foreign markets. All in all, the product approach ideally brings about the development of a global strategic focus in response to global competition.

At the same time, this structure fragments international expertise within the firm, because a central pool of international experience no longer exists. The structure assumes that managers will have adequate regional experience or advice to allow them to make balanced decisions. Coordination of activities among the various product groups operating in the same markets is crucial in order to avoid unnecessary duplication of basic tasks. For some of these tasks, such as market research, special staff functions may be created and then hired by the product divisions when needed. If product managers lack an appreciation for the international dimension, they may focus their attention on only the larger markets, often with emphasis on the domestic markets, and fail to take the long-term view.

Area Structure The approach adopted second most frequently is the **area structure,** illustrated in Figure 20.4. The firm is organized on the basis of geographical areas; for example, operations may be divided into

FIGURE 20.4 ▪ **The Global Area Structure**

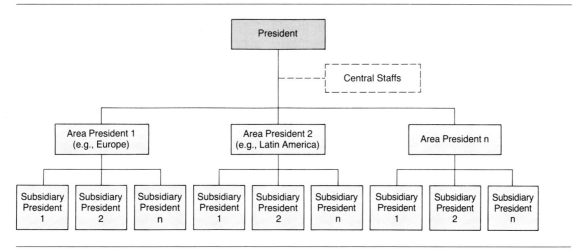

those dealing with North America, the Far East, Latin America, and Europe. Regional aggregation may play a major role in this structuring; for example, many multinational corporations have located their European headquarters in Brussels, where the EC has its headquarters. Similarly, many U.S. companies have their headquarters for Latin American operations in Miami. Ideally, no special preference is given to the region in which the headquarters is located—for example, North America or Europe. Central staffs are responsible for providing coordination support for worldwide planning and control activities performed at headquarters.

The area approach follows the marketing concept most closely because individual areas and markets are given concentrated attention. If market conditions with respect to product acceptance and operating conditions vary dramatically, the area approach is the one to choose. Companies opting for this alternative typically have relatively narrow product lines with similar end uses and end-users. However, expertise is most needed in adapting the product and its marketing to local market conditions. Once again, to avoid duplication of effort in product management and in functional areas, staff specialists—for product categories, for example—may be used.

Without appropriate coordination from the staff, essential information and experience may not be transferred from one regional entity to another. Also, if the company expands in terms of product lines and if end markets begin to diversify, the area structure may become inappropriate.

Functional Structure Of all of the approaches, the **functional structure** is the most simple from the administrative viewpoint because it emphasizes the basic tasks of the firm—for example, manufacturing, sales, and research and development. This approach, illustrated in Figure 20.5, works best when both products and customers are relatively few and similar in nature. Because coordination is typically the key problem, staff

FIGURE 20.5　▪　**The Global Functional Structure**

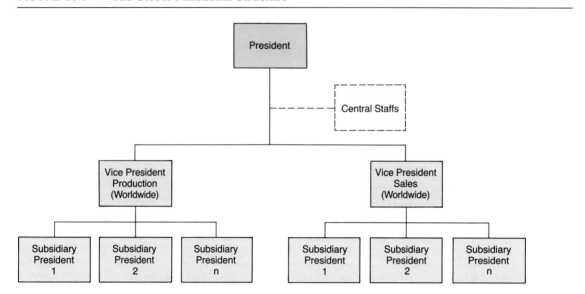

functions have been created to interact between the functional areas. Otherwise, the company's marketing and regional expertise may not be exploited to the fullest extent.

A variation of this approach is one that uses processes as a basis for structure. The **process structure** is common in the energy and mining industries, where one corporate entity may be in charge of exploration worldwide and another may be responsible for the actual mining operation.

Customer Structure　Firms may also organize their operations using the **customer structure,** especially if the customer groups they serve are dramatically different—for example, consumers versus businesses versus governments. Catering to these diverse groups may require the concentrating of specialists in particular divisions. The product may be the same but the buying processes of the various customer groups may differ. Governmental buying is characterized by bidding, in which price plays a larger role than when businesses are the buyers.

Mixed Structure　Mixed, or hybrid, organizations also exist. A **mixed structure,** such as the one in Figure 20.6, combines two or more organizational dimensions simultaneously. It permits attention to be focused on products, areas, or functions as needed. This approach may occur in a transitionary period after a merger or an acquisition or it may come about because of a unique customer group or product line (such as military hardware). It may also provide a useful structure before the implementation of the matrix structure.[10]

[10]Daniel Robey, *Designing Organizations: A Macro Perspective* (Homewood, Ill.: Irwin, 1982), 327.

FIGURE 20.6   ▪   **The Global Mixed Structure**

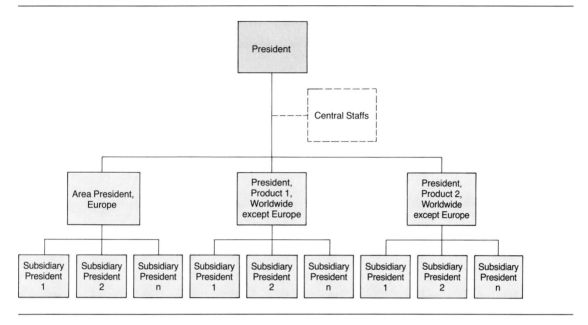

Organization structures are of course never as clear-cut and simple as they have been presented here. Whatever the basic format, inputs are needed for product, area, and function. One alternative, for example, might be an initial product structure that would eventually have regional groupings. Another alternative might be an initial area structure with eventual product groupings. However, in the long term, coordination and control across such structures become tedious.

Matrix Structure   Many multinational corporations—in an attempt to facilitate planning, organizing, and controlling interdependent businesses, critical resources, strategies, and geographic regions—have adopted the **matrix structure.**[11] Eastman Kodak shifted from a functional organization to a matrix system based on business units. Business is driven by a worldwide business unit (for example, photographic products or commercial and information systems) and implemented by a geographic unit (for example, Europe or Latin America). The geographical units, as well as their country subsidiaries, serve as the "glue" between autonomous product operations.[12]

Organizational matrices integrate the various approaches already discussed, as the N. V. Philips example in Figure 20.7 illustrates. The matrix structure manager has functional, product, and resource managers report-

[11] Thomas H. Naylor, "International Strategy Matrix," *Columbia Journal of World Business* 20 (Summer 1985): 11–19.

[12] "Kodak's Matrix System Focuses on Product Business Units," *Business International*, July 18, 1988, 221–223.

FIGURE 20.7 ■ The Global Matrix Structure at N. V. Philips

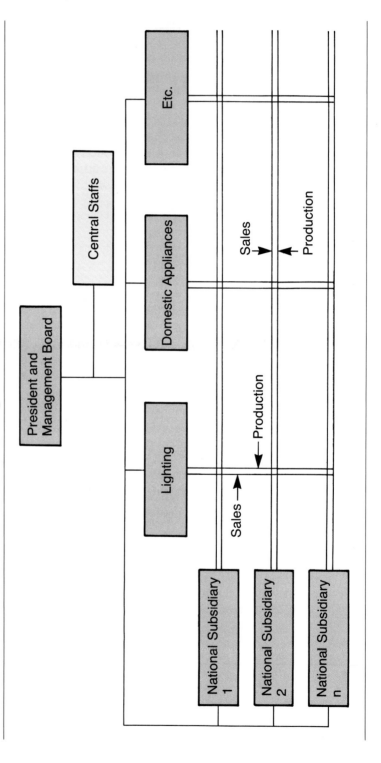

ing to him or her. The approach is based on team building and multiple command, each team specializing in its own area of expertise. It provides a mechanism for cooperation between country managers, business managers, and functional managers on a worldwide basis through increased communication, control, and attention to balance in the organization.

The matrices used vary according to the number of dimensions needed. For example, Dow Chemical's matrix is three-dimensional, consisting of six geographic areas, three major functions (marketing, manufacturing, and research), and more than 70 products. The matrix approach helps cut through enormous organizational complexities by building in a provision for cooperation among business managers, functional managers, and strategy managers. However, the matrix requires sensitive, well-trained middle managers who can cope with problems that arise from reporting to two bosses—for example, a product-line manager and an area manager. At 3M, for example, every management unit has some sort of multidimensional reporting relationship, which may cross functional, regional, or operational lines. On a regional basis, group managers in Europe, for example, report administratively to a vice president of operations for Europe. But functionally, they report to group vice presidents at headquarters in Minneapolis–St. Paul.[13]

Many companies have found the matrix structure problematic.[14] The dual reporting channel easily causes conflict, complex issues are forced into a two-dimensional decision framework, and even minor issues may have to be resolved through committee discussion. Ideally, managers should solve problems themselves through formal and informal communication; however, physical and psychic distance often make that impossible. Especially when competitive conditions require quick reaction, the matrix with its inherent complexity may actually lower the reaction speed of the company.

Evolution of Organizational Structures Companies develop new structures in stages as their product diversity develops and the share of foreign sales increases.[15] At the first stage are autonomous subsidiaries reporting directly to top management, followed by the establishment of an international division. With increases in product diversity and in the importance of the foreign marketplace, companies develop global structures to coordinate subsidiary operations and rationalize worldwide production. As multinational corporations have faced pressures to adapt to local market conditions while trying to rationalize production and globalize com-

[13] "How 3M Develops Managers to Meet Global Strategic Objectives," *Business International*, March 21, 1988, 81–82.

[14] Thomas J. Peters, "Beyond the Matrix Organization," *Business Horizons* 22 (October 1979): 15–27.

[15] See John M. Stopford and Louis T. Wells, *Managing the Multinational Enterprise* (New York: Basic Books, 1972), 25; also A. D. Chandler, *Strategy and Structure* (Cambridge, Mass.: MIT Press, 1962), 3; and B. R. Scott, *Stages of Corporate Development* (Boston, Mass.: ICCH, 1971), 2.

FIGURE 20.8 ▪ **Evolution of International Structures**

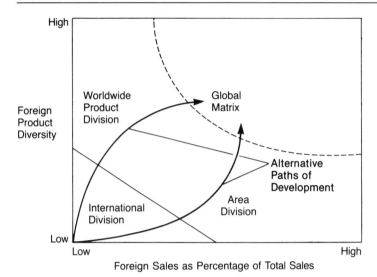

Source: From Christopher A. Bartlett, "Building and Managing the Transnational: The New Organizational Challenge," in Michael E. Porter, ed., *Competition in Global Industries.* Boston: Harvard Business School Press, 1986, p. 368. Reprinted by permission.

petitive reaction, many have opted for the matrix structure.[16] The evolutionary process is summarized in Figure 20.8.

Locus of Decision Making

Organizational structures themselves do not indicate where the authority for decision making and control rests within the organization. If subsidiaries are granted a high degree of autonomy, the result is termed **decentralization.** In decentralized systems controls are relatively loose and simple, and the flows between headquarters and subsidiaries are mainly financial; that is, each subsidiary operates as a profit center. On the other hand, if controls are tight and strategic decision making is concentrated at headquarters, the result is termed **centralization.** Firms are typically neither totally centralized nor totally decentralized. Some functions, such as finance, lend themselves to more centralized decision making, whereas other functions, such as promotional decisions, lend themselves to far less. Research and development is typically centralized in terms of both decision making and location, especially when basic research work is involved. Partly because of governmental pressures, some companies have added R&D functions on a regional or local basis. In many cases, however,

[16] Stanley M. Davis, "Trends in the Organization of Multinational Corporations," *Columbia Journal of World Business* 11 (Summer 1976): 59–71.

variations in decision making are product and market based; for example, Corning Glass Works' television tube marketing strategy requires global decision making for pricing and local decisions for service and delivery.

Allowing maximum flexibility at the subsidiary level takes advantage of the fact that subsidiary management knows its market and can react to changes quickly. Problems of motivation and acceptance are avoided when decision makers are also the implementers of the strategy. On the other hand, many multinational companies faced with global competitive threats and opportunities have adopted global strategy formulation, which by definition requires some degree of centralization. What has emerged as a result can be called coordinated decentralization. This means that overall corporate strategy is provided from headquarters, while subsidiaries are free to implement it within the range established in consultation between headquarters and the subsidiaries.

Factors Affecting Structure and Decision Making

The organizational structure and locus of decision making in multinational corporations are determined by a number of factors. They include (1) the degree of involvement in international operations, (2) the business(es) in which the firm is engaged (in terms, for example, of products marketed), (3) the size and importance of the markets, and (4) the human resource capability of the firm.[17]

The effect of the degree of involvement on structure and decision making was discussed earlier in the chapter. With low degrees of involvement by the parent company, subsidiaries can enjoy high degrees of autonomy as long as they meet their profit targets. The same situation can occur in even the most globally involved companies, but within a different framework. As an example, consider North American Philips Corporation, a separate entity of the Dutch N. V. Philips. It enjoys an independent status in terms of local policy setting and managerial practices but is nevertheless within the parent company's planning and control system.

The firm's country of origin and the political history of the area can also affect organizational structure and decision making. For example, Swiss-based Nestlé, with only 3 to 4 percent of its sales in the small domestic market, has traditionally had a highly decentralized organization. Moreover, European history for the past 75 years, particularly the two World Wars, has often forced subsidiaries of European-based companies to act independently in order to survive.

The type and variety of products marketed will have an effect on organizational decisions. Companies that market consumer products typically have product organizations with high degrees of decentralization, allowing for maximum local flexibility. On the other hand, companies that market technologically sophisticated products, such as General Electric's

[17] Rodman Drake and Lee M. Caudill, "Management of the Large Multinational: Trends and Future Challenges," *Business Horizons* 24 (May–June 1981): 83–91.

turbines, display centralized organizations with worldwide product responsibilities. Even in matrix organizations, one of the dimensions may be granted more say-so in decisions; for example, at Dow Chemical geographical managers have the strongest voice.

Apart from situations that require the development of an area structure, the characteristics of certain markets or regions may require separate arrangements for the firm. For many Japanese and European companies, the North American market has been granted such attention with, for example, direct organizational links to top management at headquarters.

The human factor in any organization is critical. Managers both at headquarters and in the subsidiaries must bridge the physical and psychic distances separating them. If subsidiaries have competent managers who rarely need to consult headquarters about their problems, they may be granted high degrees of autonomy. In the case of global organizations, subsidiary management must understand the corporate culture, because decisions must sometimes be made that meet the long-term objectives of the firm as a whole but are not optimum for the local market.

The Networked Global Organization

No international structure is ideal, and some have challenged the wisdom of even looking for an ideal one. They have called attention to new processes that would, in a given structure, develop new perspectives and attitudes to reflect and respond to complex demands of the opposite forces of global integration and local responsiveness.[18] Rather than a question of which structural alternative is best, the question is thus one of how best to take into account the different perspectives of various corporate entities when making decisions. In structural terms, nothing may change. As a matter of fact, N. V. Philips still has its basic matrix structure, yet major changes have occurred in internal relations.[19] The basic change was from a decentralized federation model to a networked global organization; the effects are depicted in Figure 20.9. The term **glocal** has been coined to describe the approach.[20]

The network avoids the problems of duplication of effort, inefficiency, and resistance to ideas developed elsewhere by giving subsidiaries the latitude, encouragement, and tools to pursue local business development within the framework of the global strategy. Headquarters considers each unit as a source of ideas, skills, capabilities, and knowledge that can be utilized for the benefit of the entire organization. This means that the subsidiaries must be upgraded from the role of implementation and adap-

[18]Christopher Bartlett, "MNCs: Get Off the Reorganization Merry-Go-Round," *Harvard Business Review* 60 (March–April 1983): 138–146.

[19]Cheryll Barron, "Format Fears at Philips," *Management Today*, August 1978, 35–41, 101–102.

[20]Thomas Gross, Ernie Turner, and Lars Cederholm, "Building Teams for Global Operations," *Management Review*, June 1987, 32–36.

FIGURE 20.9   ▪   **The Networked Global Organization**

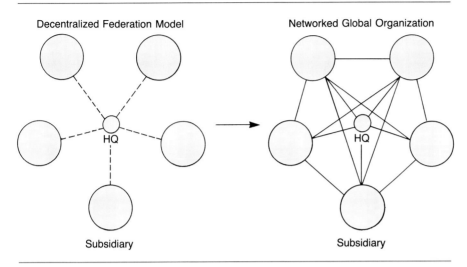

Source: Thomas Gross, Ernie Turner, and Lars Cederholm, "Building Teams for Global Operations," *Management Review*, June 1987, 34.

tation to that of contribution and partnership in the development and execution of worldwide strategies. Efficient plants may be converted into international production centers, innovative R&D units may become centers of excellence (and thus role models), and leading subsidiary groups may be given a leadership role in developing new strategy for the entire corporation. At Ford Motor Company, development of a specific car or component will be centralized in whichever Ford technical center worldwide has the greatest expertise in that product (see The International Marketplace 20.2).[21]

The main tool for implementing this approach is international teams of managers who meet regularly to develop strategy. Although final direction may come from headquarters, the input has included information on local conditions, and implementation of the strategy is enhanced because local managers were involved from the beginning. This approach has worked even in cases that, offhand, would seem impossible because of market differences. Both Procter & Gamble and Henkel have successfully introduced pan-European brands for which strategy was developed by European strategy teams. These teams consisted of local managers and staff personnel to smooth eventual implementation and to avoid unnecessarily long and disruptive discussions about the fit of a new product to individual markets.

As the discussion indicates, the networked approach is not a structural adaptation but a procedural one that requires a change in management mentality. Adjustment is primarily in the coordination and control functions of the firm.

[21] "Can Ford Stay on Top?" *Business Week*, September 28, 1987, 78–86.

Ford's Centers of Excellence To carry its momentum in the 1990s, Ford is organizing design and engineering teams into centers of excellence. The approach has two goals: to avoid duplicating efforts and to capitalize on the expertise of Ford's specialists. Savings are estimated in "hundreds of millions of dollars."

Located in several countries, the centers will work on key components for cars. One will, for example, work on certain kinds of engines. Another will engineer and develop common platforms—the suspension and other undercarriage components—for similar-sized cars.

Designers in each market will then syle exteriors and passenger compartments to appeal to local tastes. Each car will usually be built on the continent where it is to be sold.

NORTH AMERICA
Dearborn, Mich.

- *Platform for cars to replace midsize Taurus, Sable, and Europe's Scorpio*
- *Six- and eight-cylinder engines*
- *Air-conditioning systems*
- *Automatic transmissions*
- *Scheduled for introduction in 1994*

FORD OF EUROPE
Brentwood, England

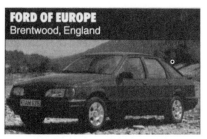

- *Platform for replacement of North American compacts Tempo and Topaz and Europe's Sierra*
- *Four-cylinder engines*
- *Manual transmissions*
- *Schedule for introduction in 1993*

MAZDA (25% owned by Ford)
Hiroshima, Japan

- *Platform for replacement of Escort subcompact, the best-selling car in the world*
- *Cars smaller than Escort*

ASIA–PACIFIC
Melbourne, Australia

- *Specialty sports cars, beginning with two-seater Capri*
- *First introduced in the fall of 1988*

Source: "Can Ford Stay on Top?", reprinted from September 28, 1987 issue of *Business Week*, pp. 78–86 by special permission, copyright © 1987 by McGraw-Hill, Inc.

FIGURE 20.10 ▪ **Roles for Country Organizations**

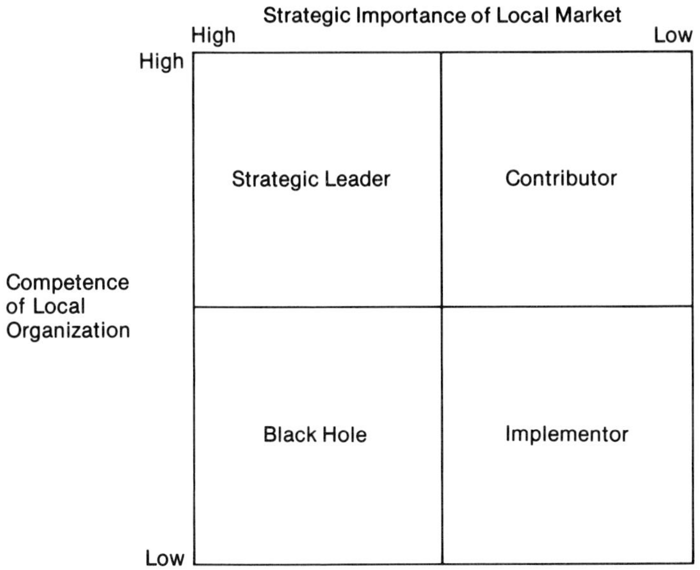

Source: Reprinted by permission of *Harvard Business Review*. An exhibit from "Tap Your Subsidiaries for Global Reach," by Christopher A. Bartlett and Sumantra Ghoshal, 64 (November/December 1986), p. 90. Copyright © 1986 by the President and Fellows of Harvard College; all rights reserved.

The Role of Country Organizations

Country organizations should be treated as a source of supply as much as they are considered a source of demand. Quite often, however, heaquarters managers see their role as the coordinators of key decisions and controllers of resources and perceive subsidiaries as implementors and adapters of global strategy in their respective local markets. Furthermore, all country organizations may be seen as the same. This view severely limits the utilization of the firm's resources by not using country organizations as resources and by depriving country managers of possibilities of exercising their creativity.[22]

The role that a particular country organization can play depends naturally on that market's overall strategic importance as well as the competences of its organization. Using these criteria, four different roles emerge (see Figure 20.10).

The role of **strategic leader** can be played by a highly competent national subsidiary located in a strategically critical market. The country organization serves as a partner of headquarters in developing and implementing strategy. Procter & Gamble's Eurobrand teams, which analyze opportunities for greater product and marketing program standardization,

[22]Christopher A. Bartlett and Sumantra Ghoshal, "Tap Your Subsidiaries for Global Reach," *Harvard Business Review* 64 (November–December 1986): 87–94.

20.3   THE INTERNATIONAL MARKETPLACE

Finding a Headquarters–Country Organization Balance   In 1983, Campbell Soup CEO Gordon McGovern decided to take action to correct long-standing problems at Campbell Canada. The subsidiary had changed its top executive nine times in 11 years, profitability had been in decline for seven years, and leading Campbell brands were steadily losing Canadian market share.

According to McGovern, the subsidiary's problems stemmed primarily from the "classic branch plant management approach Campbell used, which meant taking what was done in the U.S. and introducing it in other markets with no adaptation to local conditions. This was further complicated by the fact that Campbell Canada was run mainly by Americans: overall strategy and operational and functional activities were directed by headquarters." Decisions were often made in Camden, N.J., by senior management and staff without full knowledge and acceptance of the differences between the U.S. and Canadian companies and markets. A massive policy manual dictated every operating decision that was made by a Campbell operation anywhere.

What Campbell did to remedy the situation was to cut the Canadian subsidiary lose in several critical respects. It recruited a Canadian CEO, who built a strong local management team. It delegated a great deal of operational authority to the subsidiary, even allowing it to adapt Campbell's product lines to suit its markets better—something unthinkable earlier. The critical element of success for this new approach is consistent maintenance of constructive dialogue and exchange of ideas, and removal of the parent's voice in key local operating decisions.

The relationship balances on the U.S. headquarters' continued financial control. Campbell Soup maintains sufficient reporting controls so that "if things go off the rails badly they know about it in time to begin to challenge local managers." Headquarters retains final approval over capital spending above certain set limits, all compensation matters, and strategic plans developed in Canada. But once headquarters has signed off on the strategic plan, the subsidiary is held completely accountable for its implementation. Today most decisions that once required endless meetings and many layers of approvals across the border are made by seven Canadian executives.

Source: "How Decentralization Sparked a Revival for Campbell Canada," *Business International*, January 25, 1988, 20–21.

are chaired by a brand manager from a "lead country."[23] The experience of Campbell Soup in delegating authority to its Canadian subsidiary is described in The International Marketplace 20.3.

A **contributor** is a country organization with a distinctive competence, such as product development. Increasingly, country organizations are the source of new products. These range from IBM's recent breakthrough in superconductivity research, generated in its Zurich lab, to low-end innovations like Procter & Gamble's liquid Tide, made with a fabric-softening compound developed in Europe.[24]

The critical mass for the international marketing effort is provided by **implementors.** These country organizations may exist in smaller, less-developed countries in which corporate commitment for market development is less. Although most entities are given this role, it should not be slighted, because the implementors provide the opportunity to capture economies of scale and scope that are the basis of a global strategy.

The **black hole** is a situation that the international marketer has to work out of. As an example, in strategically important markets, such as the European Community, local presence is considered necessary for maintaining the company's overall global competitiveness and, in some cases, to anticipate competitive moves in other markets. One of the major ways of exiting this position is to enter into strategic alliances. AT&T, which had long restricted itself to its domestic market, needed to go global fast. Some of the alliances it formed were with Philips in telecommunications and Olivetti in computers and office automation.[25] In some cases, firms may use their presence in a major market as an observation post to keep up with developments before a major thrust for entry is executed.

Depending on the role, the relationship between headquarters and the country organization will vary from loose control based mostly on support to tighter control in making sure strategies are implemented appropriately. Yet, in each of these cases it is imperative that country organizations have enough operating independence to cater to local needs and to provide motivation to the country managers. For example, an implementor should be heard for input in the development of a regional or a global strategy or program. Strategy formulation should make sure that appropriate implementation can be achieved at the country level.

CONTROL

The function of the organizational structure is to provide a framework in which objectives can be met. A set of instruments and processes is needed, however, to influence the behavior and performance of organiza-

[23] John A. Quelch and Edward J. Hoff, "Customizing Global Marketing," *Harvard Business Review* 64 (May–June 1986): 59–68.

[24] Richard I. Kirkland, Jr., "Entering a New Age of Boundless Competition," *Fortune*, March 14, 1988, 18–22.

[25] Louis Kraar, "Your Rivals Can Be Your Allies," *Fortune*, March 27, 1989, 66–76.

tion members to meet the goals. Controls focus on actions to verify and correct actions that differ from established plans. Compliance needs to be secured from subordinates through various means of coordinating specialized and interdependent parts of the organization.[26] Within an organization, control serves as an integrating mechanism. Controls are designed to reduce uncertainty, increase predictability, and ensure that behaviors originating in separate parts of the organization are compatible and in support of common organizational goals despite physical, psychic, and temporal distances.[27] The critical issue is the same as with organizational structure: what is the ideal amount of control? On the one hand, headquarters needs information to ensure that international activities contribute maximum benefit to the overall organization. On the other hand, controls should not be construed as a code of law and allowed eventually to stifle local initiative.

Types of Controls

Most organizations display some administrative flexibility, as demonstrated by variations in the application of management directives, corporate objectives, or measurement systems. A distinction should be made, however, between variations that have emerged by design and those that are the result of autonomy. The one is the result of management decision, whereas the other has typically grown without central direction and is based on emerging practices. In both instances some type of control will be exercised. Here we are concerned only with controls that are the result of headquarters initiative rather than consequences of tolerated practices. Firms that wait for self-emerging controls often find that such an orientation may lead to rapid international growth, but may eventually result in problems in areas of product-line performance, program coordination, and strategic planning.[28]

Not all control systems evolve in the way they were originally envisioned. For example, shifts may be triggered by changes over time in the relative importance of international activity. Hoover Corporation provides an example. Initially, Hoover's U.S. headquarters had strong control capability. As the European operations grew in importance, however, they assumed an increasing role in overall corporate planning and control.

In the design of the control system, a major decision concerns the object of control. Two major objects are typically identified: output and behavior.[29] Output controls consist of balance sheets, sales data, production

---

[26] Amitai Etzioni, *A Comparative Analysis of Complex Organizations* (Glencoe, England: Free Press, 1961), 8.

[27] William G. Egelhoff, "Patterns of Control in U.S., U.K., and European Multinational Corporations," *Journal of International Business Studies* 15 (Fall 1984): 73–83.

[28] William H. Davidson, "Administrative Orientation and International Performance," *Journal of International Business Studies* 15 (Fall 1984): 11–23.

[29] William G. Ouchi, "The Relationship between Organizational Structure and Organizational Control," *Administrative Science Quarterly* 22 (March 1977): 95–112.

TABLE 20.1 ▪ **Comparison of Bureaucratic and Cultural Control Mechanisms**

	Type of Control	
Object of Control	Pure Bureaucratic/ Formalized Control	Pure Cultural Control
Output	Formal performance reports	Shared norms of performance
Behavior	Company policies, manuals	Shared philosophy of management

Source: B. R. Baliga and Alfred M. Jaeger, "Multinational Corporations: Control Systems and Delegation Issues," *Journal of International Business Studies* 15 (Fall 1984): 28.

data, product-line growth, or a performance review of personnel. Measures of output are accumulated at regular intervals and forwarded from the foreign operation to headquarters, where they are evaluated and critiqued based on comparisons to the plan or budget. Behavioral controls require the exertion of influence over behavior after, or ideally before, it leads to action. This influence can be achieved, for example, by providing sales manuals to subsidiary personnel or by fitting new employees into the corporate culture.

In order to institute either of these measures, corporate officials must decide on instruments of control. The general alternatives are bureaucratic/formalized or cultural.[30] **Bureaucratic controls** consist of a limited and explicit set of regulations and rules that outline desired levels of performance. **Cultural controls,** on the other hand, are much less formal and are the result of shared beliefs and expectations among the members of an organization. A comparison of the two types of controls and their objectives is provided in Table 20.1.

Bureaucratic/Formalized Control   The elements of bureaucratic/formalized control are (1) an international budget and planning system, (2) the functional reporting system, and (3) policy manuals used to direct functional performance. **Budgets** are short-term guidelines in such areas as investment, cash, and personnel, whereas **plans** refer to formalized long-range programs with more than a one-year horizon. The budget and planning process is the major control instrument in headquarters–subsidiary relationships. Although systems and their execution vary, the objective is to achieve the best fit possible with the objectives and characteristics of the firm and its environment.

[30] B. R. Baliga and Alfred M. Jaeger, "Multinational Corporations: Control Systems and Delegation Issues," *Journal of International Business Studies* 15 (Fall 1984): 25–40.

The budgetary period is typically one year because budgets are tied to the accounting systems of the company. The budget system is used for four main purposes: (1) allocation of funds among subsidiaries; (2) planning and coordination of global production capacity and supplies; (3) evaluation of subsidiary performance; and (4) communication and information exchange between subsidiaries, product organizations, and corporate headquarters.[31] Long-range plans, on the other hand, extend over periods of two years up to ten years, and their content is more qualitative and judgmental in nature than that of budgets. Shorter periods, such as two years, are the norm because of the uncertainty of diverse foreign environments.

Although firms strive for uniformity, this may be comparable to trying to design a suit to fit the average person. The budget and planning processes themselves are formalized in terms of the schedules to be followed.

Functional reports comprise another control instrument used by multinational corporations. The reports required by headquarters from subsidiaries vary in number, amount of detail, and frequency. Table 20.2 summarizes the various types of functional reports in a total of 117 multinational corporations in three countries—the United States, Germany, and Japan. The structure and elements of these reports are typically highly standardized to allow for consolidation at the headquarters level.

The frequency and types of reports to be furnished by subsidiaries are likely to increase because of the globalization trend. Managers in subsidiaries must therefore see the rationale for this often time-consuming task. When explaining the need for additional reports, two approaches used in tandem facilitate the process: participation and feedback. Involving the preparers of reports in their ultimate use serves to avoid the perception at subsidiary levels that reports are "art for art's sake." When this is not possible, feedback about results and consequences is an alternative. Through this process, communication is also enhanced.

Headquarters may want to guide the way in which subsidiaries make decisions and implement agreed-upon strategies. U.S.-based multinational companies, relying heavily on manuals for all major functions, tend to be far more formalized than their Japanese and European counterparts.[32] The manuals are for functions such as personnel policies for recruitment, training, motivation, and dismissal. The use of policy manuals as a control instrument correlates with the level of reports required from subsidiaries.

Cultural Control In countries other than the United States, less emphasis is placed on formal controls, which are viewed as rigid and too quantitatively oriented. Rather, the emphasis is on corporate values and culture, and evaluations are based on the extent to which an individual or entity fits in. Cultural controls require an extensive socialization process

---

[31] Laurent Leksell, *Headquarters–Subsidiary Relationships in Multinational Corporations* (Stockholm, Sweden: Stockholm School of Economics, 1981), chap. 5.

[32] Anant R. Negandhi and Martin Welge, *Beyond Theory Z* (Greenwich, Conn.: JAI, 1984), 16.

TABLE 20.2 ■ **Types of Functional Reports in Multinational Corporations**

Type of Report	U.S. MNCs (33)	German MNCs (44)	Japanese MNCs (40)
Balance Sheet	97	49	42
Profit and Loss Statements	91	49	42
Production Output	94	50	47
Market Share	70	48	31
Cash and Credit Statement	100	41	39
Inventory Levels	88	46	38
Sales per Product	88	37	44
Performance Review of Personnel	9	15	2
Report on Local Economic and Political Conditions	33	32	12

Source: Anant R. Negandhi and Martin Welge, *Beyond Theory Z* (Greenwich, Conn.: JAI, 1984), 18.

and informal, personal interaction is central to the process. Substantial resources must be spent to train the individual to share the corporate culture, that is, "the way things are done at the company."[33]

The instruments of cultural control focus on the careful selection and training of corporate personnel and the institution of self-control. The choice of cultural controls rather than bureaucratic controls can be justified if the company enjoys a low turnover rate. Cultural controls are thus applied, for example, when companies offer lifetime or long-term employment, as many Japanese firms do.

In selecting home-country nationals and, to some extent, third-country nationals, multinational companies are exercising cultural control. They assume that these managers have already internalized the norms and values of the company. For example, only four of 3M's 53 managing directors of overseas subsidiaries are local nationals. The company's experience is that nonnationals tend to run a country operation with a more global view.[34] In some cases the use of headquarters personnel to ensure uniformity in decision making may be advisable; for example, for the position of financial officer Volvo uses a home-country national. Expatriates are used in subsidiaries not only for control purposes but also to initiate change, which has caused concern especially in Third World countries. Companies control the efforts of management specifically through compensation, promotion, and replacement policies.

[33] Richard Pascale, "Fitting New Employees into the Company Culture," *Fortune*, May 28, 1984, 28–40.

[34] "How 3M Develops Managers to Meet Global Strategic Objectives," 81–82.

When the expatriate corps is small, headquarters can exercise control through other means. Management training programs for overseas managers as well as visits to headquarters will indoctrinate individuals to the company's way of doing things. For instance, a Chinese executive selected to run Loctite's new operation in China spent two years at the company's headquarters before taking over in Beijing.[35] Similarly, visits to subsidiaries by headquarters teams will promote a sense of belonging. These may be on a formal basis, as for a strategy audit, or less formal—for example, to launch a new product.

Corporations rarely use one pure control mechanism. Rather, emphasis is placed on both quantitative and qualitative measures. Corporations are likely, however, to place different levels of emphasis on the types of performance measures and on the way the measures are taken.

Exercising Control

Within most corporations, different functional areas are subject to different guidelines. The reason is that each function is subject to different constraints and varying degrees of those constraints. For example, marketing as a function has traditionally been seen as incorporating many more behavioral dimensions than does manufacturing or finance. As a result, many multinational corporations employ control systems that are responsive to the needs of the function. Yet such differentiation is sometimes based less on appropriateness than on personality. One researcher hypothesized that manufacturing subsidiaries are controlled more intensively than sales subsidiaries because production more readily lends itself to centralized direction, and technicians and engineers adhere more firmly to standards and regulations than do sales people.[36]

In their international operations, U.S.-based multinational corporations place major emphasis on obtaining quantitative data. Although this allows for good centralized comparisons against standards and benchmarks, or cross-comparisons between different corporate units, several drawbacks are associated with the undertaking. In the international environment, new dimensions—such as inflation, differing rates of taxation, and exchange rate fluctuations—may distort the performance evaluation of any given individual or organizational unit. For the global corporation, measurement of whether a business unit in a particular country is earning a superior return on investment relative to risk may be irrelevant to the contribution an investment may make worldwide or to the long-term results

---

[35] Nathaniel Gilbert, "How Middle-Sized Corporations Manage Global Operations," *Management Review*, October 1988, 46–50.

[36] R. J. Alsegg, *Control Relationships between American Corporations and Their European Subsidiaries*, AMA Research Study No. 107 (New York: American Management Association, 1971), 7.

of the firm. In the short-term, the return may even be negative.[37] Therefore, the control mechanism may quite inappropriately indicate reward or punishment. Standardizing the information received may be difficult if the environment fluctuates and requires frequent and major adaptations. Further complicating the issue is the fact that, although quantitative information may be collected monthly, or at least quarterly, environmental data may be acquired annually or "now and then," especially when crisis seems to loom in the horizon.

In order to design a control system that is acceptable not only to headquarters but also to the organization and individuals abroad, great care must be taken to use only relevant data. Major concerns, therefore, are the data collection process and the analysis and utilization of data. Evaluators need management information systems that provide for maximum comparability and equity in administering controls. The more behaviorally based and culture-oriented controls are, the more care that needs to be taken.[38]

In designing a control system, management must consider the costs of establishing and maintaining it and trade them off with benefits to be gained. Any control system will require investment in a management structure and in systems design. As an example, consider the costs associated with cultural controls: personal interaction, use of expatriates, and training programs are all quite expensive. Yet these expenses may be justified in savings through lower employee turnover, an extensive worldwide information system, and a potentially improved control system.[39] Moreover, the impact goes beyond the administrative component. If controls are erroneous or too time-consuming, they can slow or misguide the strategy implementation process and thus the overall capability of the firm. The result will be lost opportunity or, worse, increased threats. In addition, time spent on reporting takes time away from other tasks. If reports are seen as marginally useful, the motivation to prepare them will be low. A parsimonious design is therefore imperative. The control system should collect all the information required and trigger all the intervention necessary, but should not create a situation that resembles the pulling of strings by a puppeteer.

The impact of the environment must also be taken into account when designing controls. First, the control system should measure only dimensions over which the organization has control. Rewards or sanctions make

[37] John J. Dyment, "Strategies and Management Controls for Global Corporations," *Journal of Business Strategy* 7 (Spring 1987): 20–26.

[38] Hans Schoellhammer, "Decision-Making and Intra-Organizational Conflicts in Multinational Companies," presented at the Symposium on Management of Headquarter-Subsidiary Relationships in Transnational Corporations, Stockholm School of Economics, June 2–4, 1980.

[39] Alfred M. Jaeger, "The Transfer of Organizational Culture Overseas: An Approach to Control in the Multinational Corporation," *Journal of International Business Studies* 14 (Fall 1983): 91–106.

little sense if they are based on dimensions that may be relevant for overall corporate performance but over which no influence can be exerted; for example, price controls. Neglecting the factor of individual performance capability would send wrong signals and severely impede the motivation of personnel. Second, control systems should harmonize with local regulations and customs. In some cases, however, corporate behavioral controls have to be exercised against local customs even though overall operations may be affected negatively. This type of situation occurs, for example, when a subsidiary operates in markets where unauthorized facilitating payments are a common business practice.

Corporations are faced with major challenges to appropriate and adequate control systems in today's business environment. With an increase in local (government) demands for a share in the control of companies established, controls can become tedious, especially if the multinational company is a minority partner. Even in a merger, such as the one between ASEA and Brown Boveri—or a new entity formed by two companies as when Toyota and GM formed NUMMI—the backgrounds of the partners may be sufficiently different to cause problems in terms of the controls.

SUMMARY

The structures and control mechanisms needed to operate internationally define relationships between the firm's headquarters and subsidiaries and provide the channels through which these relationships develop.

International firms can choose from a variety of organizational structures, ranging from a domestic operation that handles ad hoc export orders to a full-fledged global organization. The choice will depend primarily on the degree of internationalization of the firm, the diversity of international activities, and the relative importance of product, area, function, and customer variables in the process. Another determining factor is the degree to

TABLE 20.3 ▪ **Organizational and Control Characteristics of Nine Multinational Corporations**

	Parent Company Characteristics	
Company	*Dominant Organizational Concept*	*Planning and Control*
American Cyanamid Company (U.S.)	Product divisions with global responsibility	Heavy reliance on strategic planning: under guidance of Corporate Planning and Development Department; plans prepared by designated business units; accompanied by annual profit plan; investment priority matrix to facilitate allocation of funds

which headquarters wants to decide important issues concerning the corporation as a whole or the subsidiaries individually. Organizations that function effectively still need to be reviewed periodically to ensure that they will remain responsive to changing environments. Some of the responses may not take the form of structural changes but rather are changes in internal relations. Of these, the primary one is the use of subsidiaries as resources, not merely as implementors of headquarters' strategy.

The control function is of increasing importance, because of the high variability in performance that results from divergent local environments and the need to reconcile local objectives with the corporate goal of synergism. It is important to grant autonomy to country organizations so that they can be responsive to local market needs, but it is equally important to ensure close cooperation between units.

Control can be exercised through bureaucratic means, emphasizing formal reporting and evaluation of benchmark data. It can also be exercised through a cultural control process in which norms and values are understood by individuals and entities that comprise the corporation. U.S. firms typically rely more on bureaucratic controls, whereas multinational corporations headquartered in other countries frequently control operations abroad through informal means and rely less on stringent measures.

The implementation of controls requires great sensitivity to behavioral dimensions and to the environment. The measurements used must be appropriate and must reflect actual performance rather than marketplace vagaries. Entities should be measured only on factors over which they have some degree of control.

A summary of organizational and control characteristics of nine of the world's most successful multinational corporations is provided in Table 20.3. As can be seen, they display wide variation in their approaches, yet they all achieve an overall balance between control and attention to local conditions.

Parent Company Characteristics		
Research and/or Product Development	*U.S. Companies: Handling of International Business*	*European Companies: Handling of U.S. Business*
Research and product development activities carried out by product divisions at five separate centers, each concentrating on a particular technology and/or market	Separate international operating divisions organized into two geographic areas; limited authority, serving primarily in staff capacity	(not applicable)

(Continued)

TABLE 20.3 ▪ **Continued**

| | Parent Company Characteristics | |
Company	Dominant Organizational Concept	Planning and Control
Ciba-Geigy Limited (Switzerland)	Product divisions with global responsibility, but gradual strengthening of key regional organizations	Moderate reliance on strategic planning by global product divisions: gradual buildup of the role of key regional companies in the planning process; operational plans and capital budgets by country organizations and their product divisions, with the latter playing the more active role
The Dow Chemical Company (U.S.)	Decentralized geographically into six regional companies: central coordination through World Headquarters Group	Coordination of geographic regions through World Headquarters Group, particularly the Corporate Product Department; strategic planning at the corporate level on a product basis, and in the operating units on a regional basis; operational plans and capital budgets by geographic region; control function at the corporate level
General Electric Company (U.S.)	Product-oriented strategic business units on a worldwide basis	Heavy reliance on strategic planning: under guidance of Corporate Planning and Development Department; plans prepared by designated strategic business units; investment priority matrix to facilitate allocation of funds
Imperial Chemical Industries Limited (U.K.)	Product divisions with global responsibility, but gradual strengthening of regional organizations	Coordination of planning through Central Planning Department; strategic planning and operational planning at the divisional and regional levels; tight financial reporting and control by headquarters
Nestlé S.A. (Switzerland)	Decentralized regional and country organizations	Increasing emphasis on strategic planning, with recent formation of Central Planning and Information Services Department; annual plans (budgets) by each major company; tight financial reporting and control by headquarters
N. V. Philips (The Netherlands)	Product divisions with global responsibility, but gradual strengthening of geographic organizations; U.S. company financially and legally separate from parent	Moderate to heavy reliance on strategic planning by planning units in product divisions, selected national organizations, and Central Planning Department; operational plans by division and national organizations, with initiative from the former; monthly review of performance

	Parent Company Characteristics	
Research and/or Product Development	*U.S. Companies: Handling of International Business*	*European Companies: Handling of U.S. Business*
Research and product development activities carried out by domestic product divisions and certain product divisions in key geographic areas	(not applicable)	Dual reporting relationship, with U.S. company reporting directly to headquarters and its local divisions also reporting to their counterpart domestic divisions
Research and development activities heavily process-oriented and usually associated with manufacturing facilities reporting to geographic regions; central coordination by World Headquarters Group	Highly decentralized organization of six geographic areas, each with almost complete authority over planning and operations	(not applicable)
Centralized research, with supportive product development activities at the operating level	International business sector, together with overseas activities in other sectors; nine country strategic business units, which prepare an international integration plan to coordinate activities with product SBUs	(not applicable)
Research and product development activities carried out by headquarters and selected regional organizations	(not applicable)	U.S. organization oversees ICI activities in the Americas, and reports directly to headquarters; U.S. board has considerable authority regarding local decisions and activities
Highly centralized research, but local product development by regional and country organizations	(not applicable)	U.S. activities divided among three main companies, each with special reporting relationship to headquarters
Highly centralized research, but with product development by product divisions and large national organizations; other research centers located in four key countries	(not applicable)	No formal chain of command between headquarters and U.S. organization; latter operating under direction of U.S. Philips Trust

(Continued)

TABLE 20.3 ▪ **Continued**

	Parent Company Characteristics	
Company	Dominant Organizational Concept	Planning and Control
Rhône-Poulenc S.A. (France)	Product divisions with global responsibility, but major country organizations retain special status	Moderate reliance on strategic planning by Central Strategy and Planning Department; in addition, strategic planning at the operational level, primarily by product divisions; operational plans and capital budgets by divisions and country organizations; monthly review of performance
Solvay & Cie S.A. (Belgium)	Product divisions with global responsibility, but national and subsidiary organizations allowed to exercise a reasonable degree of autonomy	Increasing emphasis on strategic planning with the recent formation of Central Planning Department; operational plans and capital budgets by country organizations

Source: Reprinted from "Management of the Large Multinational: Trends and Future Challenges," by Rodman Drake and Lee M. Caudill, *Business Horizons* 24 (May–June 1981): 88–90. Copyright 1981 by the Foundation for the School of Business at Indiana University. Used with permission.

Questions for Discussion

1. Firms differ, often substantially, in their organizational structures even within the same industry. What accounts for these differences in their approaches?

2. Discuss the benefits gained in adopting a matrix approach in terms of organizational structure.

3. What changes in the firm and/or in the environment might cause a firm to abandon the functional approach?

4. Is there more to the "not invented here" syndrome than simply hurt feelings on the part of those who believe they are being dictated to by headquarters?

5. If the purposes of the budget are in conflict, as is sometimes argued, what can be done about it?

6. Performance reviews of subsidiary managers and personnel are required rarely, if at all, by headquarters. Why?

7. Why do European-based multinational corporations differ from U.S.-based corporations in the instruments they choose for exerting control?

8. One of the most efficient means of control is self-control. What type of program would you prepare for an incoming employee?

	Parent Company Characteristics	
Research and/or Product Development	U.S. Companies: Handling of International Business	European Companies: Handling of U.S. Business
Research and product development activities carried out by product divisions; several large centers, each focusing on different specializations	(not applicable)	Special reporting relationship directly to headquarters; U.S. company coordinates activities with product divisions at headquarters
Centralized research and product development activities; major national organizations also carry out product development	(not applicable)	U.S. organization functions as legal entity, overseeing Solvay's activities in the United States; however, several of the U.S. businesses report independently to headquarters

Recommended Readings

Davidson, William H., and José de la Torre. *Managing the Global Corporation.* New York: McGraw-Hill, 1989.

Deal, Terrence E., and Allen A. Kennedy. *Corporate Cultures: The Rites and Rituals of Corporate Life.* Boston: Addison-Wesley, 1982.

Goehle, Donna D. *Decision-Making in Multinational Corporations.* Ann Arbor, Mich.: UMI Research Press, 1980.

Hedlund, Gunnar, and Per Åman. *Managing Relationships with Foreign Subsidiaries.* Stockholm, Sweden: Mekan, 1984.

Hulbert, John M., and William K. Brandt. *Managing the Multinational Subsidiary.* New York: Holt, Rinehart, and Winston, 1980.

Negandhi, Anant, and Martin Welge. *Beyond Theory Z.* Greenwich, Conn.: JAI, 1984.

Otterbeck, Lars, ed. *The Management of Headquarters-Subsidiary Relationships in Multinational Corporations.* Aldershot, England: Gower, 1981.

Porter, Michael E., ed. *Competition in Global Industries.* Boston, Mass.: Harvard Business School Press, 1986.

Stopford, John N., and Louis T. Wells. *Managing the Multinational Enterprise: Organization of the Firm and Ownership of the Subsidiary.* New York: Basic Books, 1972.

CHAPTER 21

The International Marketing of Services

THE INTERNATIONAL MARKETPLACE

> *International Services are Important* According to the conventional wisdom, we don't export services. Services are consumed locally by the goods makers, who do export. But the facts are just the opposite. Since about 1975, we have done well sending our services abroad despite a comparative lack of success moving our goods.
>
> Asked what you think are the largest exports of New Haven, New York City, Seattle, or the United States, it would surprise no one if your guess were textiles, computers, garments, airplanes, or food. But these guesses, of course, would be wrong. Three of the largest exporters out of New Haven are Yale University, Yale New Haven Medical Center Inc., and The Knights of Columbus (The Knights is one of the largest private life insurance providers in the world, insuring its own members). New York City's largest export is legal services. Seattle now exports more services than goods, despite Boeing's presence there. And the United States as a whole is now a large net services exporter, while importing far more goods than it sells abroad.
>
> Source: David L. Birch, "No Respect," *INC* Magazine, May 1987.

The international marketing of services is becoming a major component of world business. As a reflection of this development, this chapter will highlight marketing dimensions that are specific to services, with particular attention given to their international aspects. A definition of services will be provided, followed by a discussion of the differences between the marketing of services and of products. The roles of services in the U.S. economy and in the world economy will then be discussed. The chapter will explore the opportunities and new problems that have arisen from the increase in international service marketing, focusing particularly on the worldwide transformations of industries as a result of profound changes in the environment and in technology. The strategic responses to these transformations by both governments and firms will be described. Finally, the chapter will outline the initial steps that firms need to undertake in order to offer services internationally—and will look at the future of international service marketing.

DIFFERENCES BETWEEN SERVICES AND PRODUCTS

We rarely contemplate or analyze the precise role of services in our lives. Services often accompany products but they are also, by themselves, increasingly an important part of our economy, domestically and internationally as The International Marketplace 21.1 indicates. One writer has contrasted services and products by stating that "a good is an object, a device, a thing; a service is a deed, a performance, an effort."[1] This definition, although quite general, captures the essence of the difference between products and services. Services tend to be more intangible, personalized, and custom-made than products. In addition, services are the fastest growing sector in world business. These major differences bring with them the need for a major differentiation, because they add dimensions to services that are not present in products.

Linkage between Services and Products

Services may complement products; at other times products may complement services. The offering of products that are in need of substantial technological support and maintenance may be useless if no proper assurance for service can be provided. For this reason, the initial contract of sale often includes the service dimension. This practice is frequent in aircraft sales. When an aircraft is purchased, the buyer contracts not only for the physical product—namely, the plane—but often for training of personnel, maintenance service, and the promise of continuous technological updates. Similarly, the sale of computer hardware is critically linked to the availability of proper servicing and software.

This linkage between products and services often makes international marketing efforts quite difficult. A foreign buyer, for example, may wish to purchase helicopters and contract for service support over a period of ten years. If the sale involves a U.S. firm, both the product and the service sale will require an export license. Such licenses are issued only for an immediate sale. Therefore, over the ten years, the seller will have to apply for an export license each time service is to be provided. Because the issuance of a license is often dependent on the political climate, the buyer and the seller are haunted by uncertainty. As a result, sales may be lost to firms in countries that can unconditionally guarantee the long-term supply of product-supporting services.

Services can be just as dependent on products. For example, an airline that prides itself on providing an efficient reservation system and excel-

[1]Leonard L. Berry, "Services Marketing Is Different," in *Services Marketing*, ed. Christopher H. Lovelock (Englewood Cliffs, N.J.: Prentice-Hall, 1984), 30.

FIGURE 21.1   ▪   **Tangible and Intangible Offerings of Airlines**

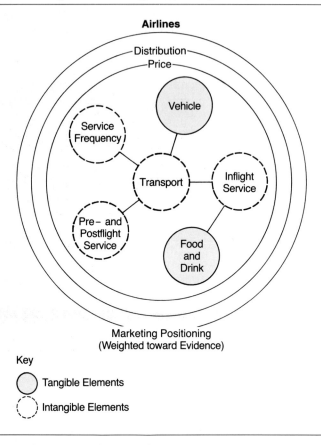

Source: G. Lynn Shostack, "Breaking Free from Product Marketing," in *Services Marketing*, ed. Christopher H. Lovelock (Englewood Cliffs, N.J.: Prentice-Hall, 1984), 40.

lent linkups with rental cars and hotel reservations could not survive if it were not for its airplanes. As a result, many offerings in the marketplace consist of a combination of products and services. A graphic illustration of the tangible and intangible elements in the market offering of an airline is provided in Figure 21.1.

The simple knowledge that services and products interact, however, is not enough. Successful managers must recognize that different customer groups will frequently view the service/product combination differently. The type of use and usage conditions will also affect evaluations of the market offering. For example, the intangible dimension of "on-time arrival" by airlines may be valued differently by college students than by business executives. Similarly, a 20-minute delay will be judged differently by a passenger arriving at his or her final destination than by one who has just missed an overseas connection. As a result, adjustment possibilities in both the service and the product area emerge that can be used

FIGURE 21.2 ∎ **Scale of Elemental Dominance**

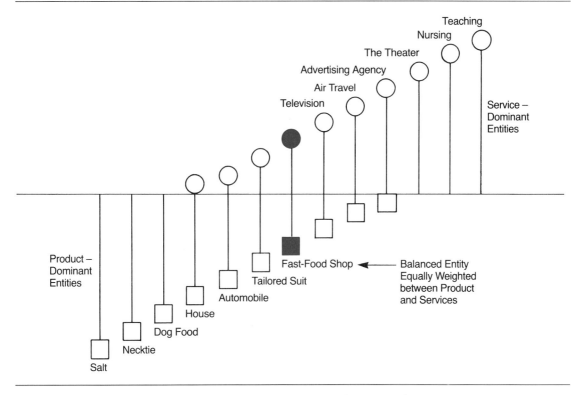

Source: G. Lynn Shostack, "How to Design a Service," in *Marketing of Services*, eds. J. Don-nelly and W. George, 1981, p. 222, published by the American Marketing Association.

as a strategic tool to stimulate demand and increase profitability. As Figure 21.2 shows, service and product elements may vary substantially. The marketer must identify the role of each and adjust all of them to meet the desires of the target customer group. By rating the offerings on a scale ranging from dominant tangibility to dominant intangibility, the marketer can obtain a mechanism for comparison between offerings and also information for subsequent market positioning strategies.

Stand-Alone Services

Services do not always come in unison with products. Increasingly, they compete against products and become an alternative offering. For example, rather than buy an in-house computer, the business executive can contract computing work to a local or foreign service firm. Similarly, the purchase of a car (a product) can be converted into the purchase of a service by leasing the car from an agency.

Services may also compete against each other. As an example, a store may have the option of offering full service to consumers who purchase there or of converting to the self-service format. Only checkout services may be provided by the store, with consumers engaging in other activities such as selection, transportation, and sometimes even packaging and pricing.

Services differ from products most strongly in their **intangibility:** they are frequently consumed rather than possessed. Even though the intangibility of services is a primary differentiating criterion, it is not always present. For example, publishing services ultimately result in a tangible product, namely, a book or an article. Similarly, construction services eventually result in a building, a subway, or a bridge. Even in those instances, however, the intangible component that leads to the final product is of major concern to both the producer of the service and the recipient of the ultimate output, because it brings with it major considerations that are nontraditional to products.

One major difference concerns the storing of services. Because of their nature, services are difficult to inventory. If they are not used, the "brown around the edges" syndrome tends to result in high services **perishability.** Unused capacity in the form of an empty seat on an airplane, for example, becomes nonsaleable quickly. Once the plane has taken off, selling an empty seat is virtually impossible—except for an in-flight upgrade from coach to first class—and the capacity cannot be stored for future usage. Similarly, the difficulty of inventorying services makes it troublesome to provide service backup for peak demand. To maintain **service capacity** constantly at levels necessary to satisfy peak demand would be very expensive. The marketer must therefore attempt to smooth out demand levels in order to optimize overall benefits.

For many service offerings, the time of production is very close to or even simultaneous with the time of consumption. This fact points toward close **customer involvement** in the production of services. Customers frequently either service themselves or cooperate in the delivery of services. As a result, the service provider often needs to be physically present when the service is delivered. This physical presence creates both problems and opportunities, and it introduces a new constraint that is seldom present in the marketing of products. For example, close interaction with the customer requires a much greater understanding of and emphasis on the cultural dimension. A good service delivered in a culturally unacceptable fashion is doomed to failure. A common pattern of internationalization for service businesses is therefore to develop stand-alone business systems in each country.[2] At the same time, however, some services have become "delocalized," as advances in modern technology have made it possible for firms to delink production and service processes and switch labor intensive service performance to countries where qualified, low-cost labor is plentiful. The International Marketplace 21.2 provides some examples.

[2] *Winning in the World Market* (Washington, D.C.: American Business Conference, November 1987), 17.

THE INTERNATIONAL MARKETPLACE   `21.2`

International Services Help U.S. Firms   The ticket stub you turn in at an American Airlines boarding gate may be heading off on a trip of its own—to Barbados. And your benefits claim from New York Life Insurance might land in Ireland. In both cases, the paperwork is caught up in one of the office world's latest trends: exporting back-office jobs. The reason lies not only in the low wages of Third World countries but also in the fact that, thanks to a very low unemployment rate, U.S. firms have trouble finding and keeping workers in back-office jobs. Examples of firms using international services to stay on top of paperwork including the following:

■ *Mead Data Center International uses typists in Asia to enter court opinions into its Lexis computer service.*

■ *American Airlines flies ticket stubs to Barbados and to the Dominican Republic, where 600 workers punch in flight data for American's main computer in Tulsa, Oklahoma.*

■ *New York Life is training 22 claim processors in Castleisland, Ireland, where they begin work on claims five hours before workers in the United States reach their desks.*

Source: Mark Memmott, "Big Firms Export Their Paper Work," *USA TODAY,* June 6, 1988, p. 1.

The close interaction with customers also points toward the fact that services often are custom-made. This contradicts the desire of a firm to standardize its offering; yet at the same time it offers the service provider an opportunity to differentiate the service from the competition. The concommitant problem is that in order to fulfill customer expectations, **service consistency** is required. As with anything offered on-line, however, consistency is difficult to maintain over the long run. The human element in the service offering therefore takes on a much greater role than in the product offering. Errors can enter the system and nonpredictable individual influences can affect the outcome of the service delivery. The issue of quality control affects the provider as well as the recipient of services. In fact, efforts to increase such control through uniform service may sometimes be perceived by customers as a limiting of options. It may therefore have a negative market effect.[3]

Buyers have more problems in observing and evaluating services than products. This is particularly true when a shopper tries to choose intelligently among service providers. Even when sellers of services are willing and able to provide more **market transparency,** the buyer's problem is

[3]G. Lynn Shostack, "Service Positioning through Structural Change," *Journal of Marketing* 51 (January 1987): 38.

TABLE 21.1 ▪ **Restriction on Foreign Motion Pictures in Brazil**

The most significant trade barrier for motion pictures has been the CONCINE Resolution 98 requirement for foreign home videocassette distributors. They must maintain an inventory including at least 25 percent Brazilian titles and 25 percent copies each month. Because the supply of Brazilian home videocassettes is limited, this requirement restricts the number of foreign videos that may be distributed and therefore imported.

Resolution 98 also significantly increases distributors' operating expenses since they must: (a) purchase video rights from national producers; (b) buy blank cassettes for duplicating national films; (c) pay for duplicating national films (a high cost since there is only one Brazilian printing company); (d) pay for national film packaging and publicity; and (e) pay all relevant taxes on national films.

It also artificially increases demand for the limited Brazilian home videocassettes that are available, thus driving up their prices considerably. Finally, limited availability of legitimately imported cassettes creates an environment that perpetuates widespread piracy of home video programming.

Other barriers include:

- A discriminatory requirement to exhibit a Brazilian short subject film along with any foreign feature film.
- Dividing 3.4 percent of the gross box office receipts among Brazilian short subject producers and the national distributor of Brazilian films, Embrafilme.
- Subjecting each foreign film title imported for theatrical or television distribution to government censorship review before distribution. A fee is required for each foreign title but not imposed on Brazilian films.
- A requirement on all Brazilian movie theaters to exhibit Brazilian feature films at least 140 days every year.
- A requirement to print all color feature films distributed for television broadcast and theatrical exhibition in Brazilian laboratories. Brazil has only one such laboratory.
- A five-year waiting period for theatrical television distribution.

Source: *1987 National Trade Estimate Report on Foreign Trade Barriers* (Washington, D.C.: Office of the United States Trade Representative, 1987), 42–43.

complicated: customers receiving the same service may use it differently, service quality may vary for each delivery, and service offerings are not directly comparable. Services therefore often defy quality measurement and transparency efforts. As a result, the reputation of the service provider plays an overwhelming role in the customer choice process.

Services often require entirely new forms of distribution. Traditional channels are often multitiered and long and therefore slow. They often cannot be used because of the perishability of services. A weather news service, for example, either reaches its audience quickly, or it rapidly loses its value. As a result, direct delivery and short distribution channels are often required. When they do not exist—which is often the case domestically and even more so internationally—service providers need to be distribution innovators in order to reach their market.

All these aspects of services exist in both international and domestic settings. However, their impact takes on greater importance for the international marketer. For example, because of the longer distances involved, service perishability that may be an obstacle in domestic business becomes a barrier internationally. Similarly, the issue of quality control for international services may be much more difficult to deal with due to different service uses, changing expectations, and varying national regulations.

Because services are delivered directly to the user, they are frequently much more sensitive to cultural factors than are products. Sometimes their influence on the individual may even be considered with hostility abroad. For example, the use of U.S. films for cinemas or television abroad is often attacked as an imposition of U.S. culture. National leaders who place strong emphasis on national cultural identity frequently denounce foreign services and attempt to hinder their market penetration. Table 21.1 gives an example of how the distribution of motion picture services is inhibited in Brazil.

THE ROLE OF SERVICES IN THE U.S. ECONOMY

Since the industrial revolution, the United States has seen itself as a primary international competitor in the area of production of goods. In the past few decades, however, the U.S. economy has increasingly become a service economy, as Figure 21.3 shows. The service sector produces 68 percent of the GNP[4] and employs 83 percent of the full-time and part-time work force.[5] The service sector accounts for most of the growth in total nonfarm employment. During the period from 1982 to 1987, for example, the service sector added about 11 million new jobs, compared to 650,000 new jobs in manufacturing.[6] In excess of 45 percent of the average U.S. family's budget is spent on services.[7]

Of course, only a limited segment of the total range of services is sold internationally. Federal, state, and local government employees, for example, sell few of their services to foreigners. U.S. laundries and restaurants only occasionally service foreign tourists. However, many service industries that do market abroad often have at their disposal large organizations, specialized technology, or advanced professional expertise. Strength in these characteristics has enabled the United States to become the world's largest exporter of services. Total U.S. services exported grew from $6 billion in 1958 to over $188 billion in 1988.[8] For a long time, this growth of services trade enabled the United States to maintain a favorable balance of payments, even though the U.S. merchandise trade account was in deficit. The contribution of services to the balance of payments is high-

---

[4]U.S. Department of Commerce, *Survey of Current Business,* July 1988.

[5]David R. Barton and William B. Sullivan, "Highlights of the 1988 U.S. Industrial Outlook," *1988 U.S. Industrial Outlook* (Washington, D.C.: Government Printing Office, 1988), 8.

[6]Allen Sinai and Michael Drury, "Services and the Job Quality Debate," *The Service Economy* (October 1988): 20.

[7]Berry, "Services Marketing Is Different," 29.

[8]U.S. Department of Commerce, *Survey of Current Business,* March 1989.

FIGURE 21.3 ▪ **Employment in Industrial Sectors as a Percentage of the Total Labor Force**

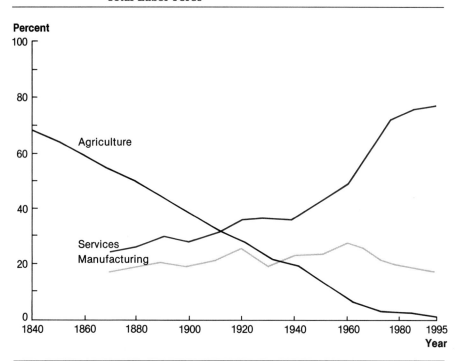

Source: J. B. Quinn, "The Impacts of Technology on the Services Sector," *Technology and Global Industry: Companies and Nations in the World Economy,* © 1987 by the National Academy of Sciences, Washington, D.C. Reprinted with permission.

lighted in Table 21.2. It shows that even though the U.S. services trade balance is still producing a substantial surplus, it can no longer make up for the huge deficits in merchandise trade.

Because of statistical convention, foreign investment income and payments are included in the services balance. Until 1984 the United States was a major international creditor, in terms of both direct and indirect foreign investments, and a good portion of U.S. services trade exports therefore actually reflected investment and interest income. Since 1985, however, the United States has become a net foreign debtor. As this debt grows, investment income flows are counterbalanced by payments that the United States has to make to compensate for the increased foreign investment that has taken place in the United States in recent years. The overall service account surplus is therefore expected to gradually decline, even though business service activities are likely to maintain substantial international growth.

International service trade has had very beneficial results for many U.S. firms. Citibank, for example, receives 65 percent of its total revenues from foreign operations; the top ten U.S. advertising agencies make 51 percent of their total billings abroad. All of the ten largest U.S. management con-

TABLE 21.2 ■ **Balances of Trade in Goods and Services, 1988 (in billions)**

Exports of Goods and Services:	$508
Goods	320
Services	188
Services as a percentage of goods: 59%	
Imports of Goods and Services:	630
Goods	447
Services	183
Services as a percentage of goods: 41%	
Balance on Goods Trade	−127
Balance on Services	+5
Balance on Goods and Services	−122

Source: U.S. Department of Commerce, *Survey of Current Business*, March 1989.

TABLE 21.3 ■ **The 10 Largest U.S. Management Consulting Firms**

Firm	1987 Worldwide Consulting Revenues (in millions)	Percentage Earned Overseas
1. Arthur Andersen	$838	38%
2. Marsh & McLennan	530	26
3. McKinsey[1]	510	50
4. Towers Perrin	465	18
5. Peat Marwick Main	438	42
6. Booz-Allen & Hamilton	412	16
7. Coopers & Lybrand	381	48
8. Ernst & Whinney	374	38
9. Price Waterhouse	345	54
10. Saatchi & Saatchi	267	34

[1]Estimated by *Consultant News*.

Source: Kennedy & Kennedy (Fitzwilliams, N.H.), *Consultant News*, June 1988, 2–3.

sulting firms derive a substantial volume of their revenue from overseas, as Table 21.3 shows. Some of the service firms have become truly international and formidable in size. For example, the merger of Peat Marwick with Klynveld Maine Goerdeler in 1987 created the world's largest professional service organization, with a worldwide network of 58,000 partners and staff. KPMG, the resulting organization, is headquartered in Amsterdam and operates in 101 countries.[9] Services form the major export component of 19 industries as shown in Table 21.4.

[9]Harry L. Freeman and Beth Bogie, *Statistics, Company Achievements and Statements on Diverse Aspects of the Service Sector* (New York: American Express Company, 1988), 8.

TABLE 21.4   ▪   **Major U.S. Exporters of Services, by Industry**

Accounting	Franchising
Advertising	Health Service Consulting
Banking and Other Financial Services	Hospital Management
	Insurance
Communications	Leasing
Computers	Legal
Construction, Engineering, and Architecture	Lodging and Catering
	Management and Catering
Equipment Maintenance and Repair	Management Consulting
	Technical Consulting
	Education and Training

Large international growth, however, is not confined to U.S. firms. The import of services into the United States is also increasing dramatically. In 1988, the United States imported $183 billion of services.[10] A study conducted for the Distribution, Research, and Education Foundation predicted that, by 1990, ten percent of the wholesale distribution industry in the United States will consist of foreign-owned companies and 15 percent of sales will be supplied by foreign firms. Even though this percentage may seem small, this market share will represent more than $450 billion of the industry's sales and will therefore represent a significant presence in the U.S. marketplace.[11]

Competition in international services is also increasing rapidly at all levels. Years ago, for example, U.S. construction firms could count on a virtual monopoly in large-scale construction projects. Today firms from South Korea, Italy, Yugoslavia, and other countries are taking a major share of the international construction business. Similarly, in other service industries such as banking, insurance, and advertising, Hong Kong and Singapore and Western European countries are increasingly active. The overall result of these developments is that the American share of international service trade was estimated to have declined in relative terms—from 25 to 20 percent of the world market—within a decade.

THE ROLE OF INTERNATIONAL SERVICES IN THE WORLD ECONOMY

The United States is not unique in its conversion to a service economy. Similar changes have taken place internationally. The world market for services grew over a ten-year period at an annual rate of about 16 percent,

[10] U.S. Department of Commerce, *Survey of Current Business,* March 1989.

[11] Arthur Andersen & Company, *Future Trends in Wholesale Distribution* (Washington, D.C.: The Distribution Education and Research Foundation, 1983), 21.

compared to a rate of about 7 percent for merchandise trade.[12] As a result, trade in services constitutes roughly 20 to 25 percent of overall world trade and, in some regions, accounts for well above 40 percent of merchandise trade.[13] At the current time, services trade is taking place mainly between the developed countries, with the 12 member nations of the Organization for Economic Cooperation and Development (OECD) alone accounting for approximately 70 percent of total trade.[14] Within these countries, the names of such firms as American Express, McDonald's, Club Med, Thomas Cook, Mitsubishi, and Hilton have become widely familiar. The meteoric rise of these firms internationally, together with the increased service orientation of the global developed world economy, has led to predictions that by the year 2000 more than half of all multinational enterprises will be service corporations.[15]

GLOBAL TRANSFORMATION IN THE SERVICES SECTOR

One question that can be asked is, what changes accounted for the dramatic rise in service marketing? The two major factors seem to result from environmental and technological developments.

One primary environmental change that has taken place in the past decade is the reduction of governmental regulation of services. This deregulatory development is most clearly seen within the United States. In the mid-1970s a philosophical decision was made to reduce government interference in the marketplace, in the hope that this would enhance competitive activity. As a consequence some service sectors have benefited, and others have suffered, from the withdrawal of government intervention. The primary deregulated industries in the United States have been transportation, banking, and telecommunications. As a result, new competitors participate in the marketplace. Regulatory changes were initially thought to have primarily domestic effects, but they have rapidly spread internationally. For example, the 1984 **deregulation** of AT&T has not only given rise to competition in the United States. Japan's telecommunication monopoly, NT&T, was deregulated in 1985. In the United States, other firms such as MCI and Sprint now offer their services internationally to, for example, the United Kingdom and Australia.

Similarly, deregulatory efforts in the transportation sector have had international repercussions. New air carriers have entered the market to compete against established trunk carriers and have done so successfully by pricing their services differently both nationally and internationally.

[12]"The U.S. Lead in Service Exports Is Under Siege," *Business Week*, September 15, 1980, 70.

[13]Andre Sapir and Ernst Lutz, *Trade in Non-Factor Services: Past Trends and Current Issues*, discussion draft, World Development Report, 1980, 2.

[14]*World Invisible Trade* (London: British Invisible Export Council, 1985).

[15]J. J. Boddewyn, Marsha Baldwin Halbric, and A. C. Perry, "Service Multinationals: Conceptualization, Measurement, and Theory," paper presented at the Annual Meeting of the Academy of International Business, Cleveland, Ohio, October 1984, 1.

Deregulatory efforts therefore have also affected international regulations, such as **conference pricing,** and have caused deregulation in foreign countries. Obviously, a British airline can count only to a limited extent on government support in order to remain competitive with new low-priced fares offered by other carriers also serving the British market. The deregulatory movement that originated in the United States has spread internationally, particularly to Europe, and fostered the emergence of new competition and new competitive practices. Because many of these changes resulted in lower prices, demand stimulation has taken place and has led to a rise in the volume of international services trade.

Another major environmental change in the United States has been the decreased regulation of service industries by their industry groups. For example, business practices in fields such as health care, law, and accounting are increasingly becoming more competitive and aggressive. New economic realities require firms in these industries to search for new ways to attract market share and expand their markets, as The International Marketplace 21.3 shows. International markets are one frequently untapped possibility for market expansion and have therefore become a prime target for such service firms.

Technological advancement is the second major change that has taken place. Increasingly, progress in technology is offering new ways of doing business and is permitting businesses to expand their horizons internationally. Through computerization, for instance, service exchanges that previously would have been prohibitively expensive are now feasible. For example, Ford Motor Company uses one major computer system to carry out its new car designs in both the United States and Europe. This practice not only lowers expenditures on hardware but also permits better utilization of existing equipment and international design collaboration by allowing design groups in different time zones to use the equipment around the clock. However, this development could take place only after advances in data transmission procedures.

In a similar fashion, more rapid data transmission has permitted financial institutions to expand their service delivery through a worldwide network. Again, were it not for advances in technology, such expansion would rarely have been possible or cost efficient.

Another result of these developments is that service industry expansion has not been confined to the traditional services that are labor intensive and could therefore have been performed better in areas of the world where labor possesses a comparative advantage because of lower prices. Rather, increasingly technology-intensive services are becoming the sunrise industries of the 1990s.

INTERNATIONAL TRADE PROBLEMS IN SERVICES

Together with the increase in the importance of service marketing, new problems have emerged that beset the service sector. Even though many of these problems have been characterized as affecting mainly the negotia-

THE INTERNATIONAL MARKETPLACE 21.3

Legal Services Span the Globe Edwards and Angell, a medium-sized law firm based in New York, was the first American law firm to formally establish a joint working arrangement with a Chinese law firm, the Beijing Foreign Economic Law Office. The agreement was signed in June 1988, after more than a year of negotiations. Such aggressive international expansion is a good example of niche marketing by law firms looking for growth areas in the increasingly competitive American legal community. With U.S. business more and more attuned to international opportunities and with international firms increasingly active in the United States—buying properties, staking major financial positions, and operating businesses—there is a growing market for law firms with an international orientation.

Also spurring interest in overseas operations is the realization that the weakness of the U.S. dollar is making American firms more competitive. The value of the dollar affects services as much as manufactured goods. "When I was practicing for an American law firm in France in the early 1980s, we were very expensive," said Robert Horner, head of the International Division of Goldstein and Manello. "Now American legal services are very competitive."

China was particularly attractive to Edwards and Angell because, from the standpoint of Western corporate law, it is relatively virgin territory. "We felt that China was a good place for us to go because it was young, and there was less competition," said Louis B. Goldman, the Edward and Angell partner in charge of its international practice. More importantly, Edwards and Angell had clients who were in business in China. By establishing its own representation in China, the law firm could capitalize on this existing business base.

In the past, companies that needed international legal representation either relied on their U.S. attorney's old-boy network to connect them with someone who had the proper experience, or they turned to one of a few giant law firms with international divisions. In China the situation was especially difficult, because only a handful of U.S. international law firms maintained even a token presence there. To actually practice law, the U.S. firms in China had to work through local law firms.

The agreement will not only provide Edwards and Angell clients with full representation in China, but may direct some of China's U.S. business interests to Edwards and Angell. "This is a two-way street," explained Goldman. "We expect a lot of business from U.S. companies that want to do business there, but we also expect a lot of business from there to come this way."

Source: Allen Radding, "Law Firm Sets Agreement with Beijing," *Northeast International Business* (September 1988): 9.

tions between nations, they are of sufficient importance to the firm in its international activities to merit a brief review.

Data Collection Problems

The data collected on service trade are quite poor. Service transactions are often "invisible" statistically as well as physically. The fact that the U.S. Department of Commerce has precise data on the number of trucks exported down to the last bolt, but has little information on reinsurance flows, reflects past governmental inattention to services. Only recently has it been recognized that the income generated and the jobs created through the sale of services abroad are just as important as income and jobs resulting from the production and exportation of goods. In spite of increased attention paid to the issue, official government sources have stated that "we don't really know how much is being earned from service exports, but we do know that service exports are growing substantially."[16] As a result, estimates of services trade value vary widely. Total actual U.S. trade in services is believed to be almost double the amount shown by official statistics.[17]

When considering the dimension of the problem of data collection on services in the United States, with its sophisticated data gathering and information system, it is easy to imagine how many more problems are encountered in countries lacking such elaborate systems and unwilling to allocate funds for such efforts. The gathering of information is of course made substantially more difficult because services are intangible and therefore more difficult to measure and to trace than products. Insufficient knowledge and information has led to a lack of transparency, making it difficult for nations either to gauge or to influence services trade. As a result, regulations are often put into place without precise information as to their repercussions on actual trade performance.

U.S. Disincentives to International Services

In spite of its commitment to free trade, the United States has erected and maintained major barriers to international services. These disincentives affect both inbound and outbound services. Barriers to services destined for the U.S. market result mainly from regulatory practices. The fields of banking, insurance, and accounting provide some examples. These industries are regulated at both federal and state levels, and the regulations often pose a formidable barrier to potential entrants from abroad.

The chief complaint of foreign countries is not that the United States discriminates against foreign service providers, but rather that the United

[16] U.S. Department of Commerce, *Current Developments in the U.S. International Service Industries* (Washington, D.C.: Government Printing Office, 1980).

[17] "The Problem of Data on Services," *International Services Newsletter*, January–June 1981, 11.

States places more severe restrictions on them than do other countries. In addition, the entire U.S. regulatory process gives little weight to international policy issues and often operates in isolation from executive branch direction.[18] These barriers are of course a reflection of the decision-making process within the U.S. domestic economy and are unlikely to change in the near future. A coherent approach toward international commerce in services is hardly likely to emerge from the disparate decisions of agencies such as the Interstate Commerce Commission (ICC), the Federal Communications Commission (FCC), the Securities and Exchange Commission (SEC), and the many licensing agencies at the state level.

Various domestic laws and regulations also often impede the export of U.S. services. One disincentive frequently mentioned is the Foreign Corrupt Practices Act, which arguably discourages U.S. businesses and particularly services industries from competing overseas. Similarly, export control legislation increasingly is extended to the services sector and may restrict the potential of services exporters.

National Regulations of Services Abroad

Obstacles to service trade abroad can be categorized into two major types: barriers to entry and problems in performing services abroad.

Barriers to entry are often justified by reference to **national security** and **economic security.** For example, the impact of banking on domestic economic activity is given as a reason why banking should be carried out only by nationals or indeed be operated entirely under government control. Sometimes the protection of service users is cited, particularly of bank depositors and insurance policyholders. Some U.S. trading partners have economic systems that are based on the premise that competition is wasteful and should be avoided. Another justification for barriers is the frequently used **infant industry** argument: "With sufficient time to develop on our own, we can compete in world markets." Often, however, this argument is used simply to prolong the ample licensing profits generated by restricted entry. Yet, defining a barrier to service marketing is not always easy. For example, Taiwan gives an extensive written examination to prospective accountants (as do most countries) in order to ensure that licensed accountants are qualified to practice. Naturally, the examination is given in Chinese. The fact that few U.S. accountants read and write Chinese, and hence are unable to pass the examination, does not necessarily constitute a barrier to trade in accountancy services.[19]

Even if barriers to entry are nonexistent or can be overcome, service companies have difficulty performing abroad effectively once they have achieved access to the local market. One reason is that rules and regula-

---

[18]Gary C. Hufbauer, remarks, Seminar on Services in the World Economy, organized by the United States Council of the International Chamber of Commerce, New York, May 5, 1980, 3.

[19]Dorothy I. Riddle, *Key LDC's: Trade in Services*, American Graduate School of International Studies, Glendale, Arizona, March 1987, 346–347.

tions based on tradition may inhibit innovation. A more important reason is that governments aim to pursue social objectives through national regulations. Of primary importance here is the distinction between **discriminatory** and **nondiscriminatory regulations.** Regulations that impose larger operating costs on foreign service providers than on the local competitors, that provide subsidies to local firms only, or that deny competitive opportunities to foreign suppliers are a proper cause for international concern. The discrimination problem becomes even more acute when foreign firms face competition from government-owned or government-controlled enterprises, which are discussed in more detail in Chapter 23. On the other hand, nondiscriminatory regulations may be inconvenient and may hamper business operations, but they offer less opportunity for international criticism.

All of these regulations make it difficult for the international service marketer to penetrate world markets. At the governmental level services frequently are not recognized as a major facet of world trade or are viewed with suspicion because of a lack of understanding, and barriers to entry often result. To make progress in tearing them down, much educational work needs to be done.

MACRO RESPONSES TO PROBLEMS IN INTERNATIONAL SERVICES MARKETING

U.S. Developments

Greater experience and know-how give the United States a major comparative advantage in the international marketing of services. As a result, the United States has been the country most concerned with international problems in the providing of services. This concern originated in the private sector in the 1960s. International insurance companies began to organize into advisory committees, shortly to be joined by companies in the banking and transportation sectors.

A major boost to this effort occurred when the **Trade Act of 1974** pointedly expanded the definition of international trade to include trade in services, gave the president a mandate to negotiate reduced services barriers, and made provision for presidential retaliation against countries that discriminate against U.S. service companies. In 1976, a White House study made a series of recommendations on services issues, including suggestions for international negotiations and government reorganization.[20] In 1978, the U.S. Chamber of Commerce founded its International Services Industry Committee to influence the formulation of policy.

The recommendation to reorganize resulted in 1978 in the creation of an international services division within the U.S. Department of Commerce.

---

[20] "U.S. Service Industries in World Markets," *Current Problems in Future Policy Development*, White House Interagency Study, December 1976.

However, responsibility for services issues remained far-flung and dispersed across departments such as State, Treasury, and Transportation. The Trade Act of 1979 and trade reorganization plan assigned policy leadership in the area of services trade to the Office of the **United States Trade Representative,** (USTR), and created a Services Policy Advisory Committee.

In its international efforts aimed at improving the climate for service trade, the United States has had some success with bilateral negotiations. For many decades, selected services had general coverage in bilateral treaties of Friendship, Commerce, and Navigation. Since 1980, however, specific services negotiations and agreements have been concluded with major trading partners. For example, bilateral negotiations resulted in Japan's lifting of restrictions on U.S. computer service sales. In 1983, the Korean insurance market began to open to foreign firms. In 1984, the banking sector in Japan was opened to foreign participation in offering financial services and syndicated loans. In 1987, U.S. lawyers were permitted to begin operations in Japan.

In addition, the United States has initiated various steps to strengthen its hand in future international negotiations. Most of these actions consist of threatening retaliation in the event other nations refuse to liberalize services trade. The **International Banking Act of 1978,** for example, which established a comprehensive federal government role in the regulation of foreign bank participation, directed the government to submit a report to Congress on "the extent to which U.S. banks are denied, whether by law or practice, national treatment in conducting bank operations in foreign countries."[21] Congress has also added **reciprocity provisions** for services in various fields, with the general thrust that reciprocity should be a significant factor in determining whether and to what extent foreign firms would be able to participate in regulated industries in the United States. Usually this approach demands that, in order for foreign firms to participate in the U.S. market, U.S. firms must have access to the foreign market.

International Developments

Less progress has been made on the global level. The **GATT** provides a framework for disciplining national restraint of trade in goods, but no similar framework exists for trade in services. Even though the original ITO incorporated thoughts on services, the considerations were not part and parcel of the subsequently implemented GATT framework.

One of the early postwar multilateral efforts to liberalize international trade in services was the OECD code on invisible transactions, which in the 1950s removed some barriers to service trade. Within the GATT, the U.S. attempted in the late 1970s, near the end of the **Tokyo Round,** to add

---

[21]Geza Feketekuty, "International Trade in Banking Services: The Negotiation Agenda," draft, prepared for the International Law Institute conference on the International Framework for Money and Banking in the 1980s, Washington, D.C., April 30–May 1, 1981, 8.

service issues to the agenda. However, this move was greeted with international suspicion. Because the United States has the largest service economy and the most service exports, other nations suspected that any liberalization would principally benefit the United States. Moreover, some of the negotiating partners had the same lack of knowledge about services trade that U.S. negotiators had had a few years before.

As a result, services were addressed only to a very limited extent in the Tokyo Round. Services are therefore covered in the international trade framework only by the **Government Procurement Code** and the **Subsidies and Countervailing Measures Code.** The former covers services only to the extent that they are ancillary to purchases of goods and do not exceed the goods in value. The latter is restricted to services that are ancillary to trade in goods.

Currently, the United States is pushing hard to have services included in international trade negotiations. As part of this effort, the United States has obtained agreement on the establishment of a study group on services trade barriers within the **OECD.** The information produced may eventually improve the climate for a services trade agreement.

In a major breakthrough in Punta del Este in 1986, the United States also obtained agreement from the major GATT participants to conduct services trade negotiations parallel with product negotiations in the Uruguay Round. However, many developing nations, particularly Brazil and India, continue to be opposed to such negotiation because they believe that product issues should be resolved first and that any agreement on services trade would restrict their future international competitiveness. In addition, given the slow progress of international negotiations, the service field can be expected to be embattled for years to come.

CORPORATE INVOLVEMENT IN INTERNATIONAL SERVICES MARKETING

Typical International Services

Although many firms are already active in the international service arena, others often do not perceive their existing competitive advantage. Numerous services that are efficiently performed in the United States have great potential for internationalization.

U.S. financial institutions can offer some functions very competitively internationally in the field of banking services. In particular, U.S. banks possess advantages in fields such as credit card operations, customer service, and collection management as Figure 21.4 shows. In the general area of international finance, however, U.S. banks need to expend major efforts in order to remain competitive. Increasingly, leadership is taken by banks in Japan and Europe, which are boosted by large assets and solid income performance, as seen in Table 21.5 on pages 690–691.

FIGURE 21.4 ▪ **Advertisement Showing How a Financial Services Firm Positioned Itself in the International Marketplace**

EN ESPAÑA SOMOS ESPAÑOLES.

IN DEUTSCHLAND SIND WIR DEUTSCHE.

IN AUSTRALIA, WE ARE AUSTRALIAN.

日本では、日本人。

IN CANADA, WE ARE CANADIAN.

IN NEDERLAND ZIJN WE NEDERLANDS.

IN ENGLAND, WE ARE ENGLISH.

IN DER SCHWEIZ SIND WIR SCHWEIZER.

在香港我們是中國人。

IN AMERICA, WE ARE AMERICAN.

DI SINGAPURA KAMI IALAH ORANG SINGAPURA.

EN FRANCE, NOUS SOMMES FRANÇAIS.

AROUND THE WORLD WE ARE THE
CS FIRST BOSTON GROUP.

Announcing a worldwide investment banking firm that draws its strength from established investment banks in the world's financial capitals.

Operating as First Boston in the Americas, Credit Suisse First Boston in Europe and the Middle East, and CS First Boston Pacific in the Far East and Asia, the CS First Boston Group – together with Credit Suisse – offers unparalleled expertise in capital raising, mergers and acquisitions, securities sales, trading and research, asset management, and merchant banking.

So regardless of what language you speak, the words for powerful investment banking are the same all over the world – CS First Boston Group.

| **CS First Boston Group** | First Boston | Credit Suisse First Boston | CS First Boston Pacific |

Source: Courtesy First Boston Corporation.

Another area with great international potential is construction, design, and engineering services. Because of vast U.S. experience, economies of scale can be effected not only for machinery and material but also in areas such as personnel management and the overall management of projects. Particularly for international projects that are large scale and long term, the experience advantage could weigh heavily in favor of U.S. firms. The economic significance of these services far exceeds their direct turnover, because they encourage subsequent demand for capital goods. For ex-

TABLE 21.5 ▪ **The Leading International Banks**

		Assets		Performance			Market Value
		$ Million	Change from 1987	Net Income $ Million	Change from 1987	Real Profitability	5/31/89 $ Million
1. Dai-Ichi Kangyo Bank[a]	Japan	$383,767.8	10.40%	$1,360.1	28.00%	1.095	$68,859
2. Sumitomo Bank[a]	Japan	368,981.8	13.57	1,500.0	69.20	1.110	71,341
3. Fuji Bank[a]	Japan	354,026.5	12.22	1,301.1	27.50	1.097	66,604
4. Mitsubishi Bank[a]	Japan	346,169.4	11.10	1,266.3	31.20	1.097	61,313
5. Sanwa Bank[a]	Japan	338,399.4	12.82	1,176.2	28.80	1.094	50,823
6. Industrial Bank of Japan[a]	Japan	259,509.1	8.01	707.3	18.70	1.069	73,903
7. Norinchukin Bank[a]	Japan	243,761.7	5.21	308.6	12.50	1.043	NT
8. Tokai Bank[a]	Japan	222,879.7	6.21	455.4	14.00	1.054	31,463
9. Credit Agricole	France	210,595.8	−2.85	643.7	39.80	1.047	NT
10. Citicorp	U.S.	207,666.0	1.99	1,858.0	NM	1.150	9,602
11. Mitsui Bank[a]	Japan	205,053.7	5.90	600.6	23.70	1.077	30,424
12. Bank of Tokyo[a]	Japan	199,735.2	22.86	472.0	22.30	1.055	23,732
13. Banque Nationale de Paris	France	196,954.8	7.82	534.6	−5.10	1.059	NT
14. Barclays	Britain	189,368.4	15.86	1,616.0	313.60	1.144	8,485
15. Credit Lyonnais	France	178,877.5	6.26	356.2	−19.30	1.043	NT
16. National Westminster Bank	Britain	178,505.2	10.25	1,708.3	111.10	1.157	7,895
17. Taiyo Kobe Bank[a]	Japan	174,972.8	5.02	404.7	22.90	1.062	17,689
18. Long-Term Credit Bank of Japan[a]	Japan	173,630.9	4.05	535.6	31.90	1.079	33,687
19. Mitsubishi Trust & Banking[a]	Japan	172,906.2	9.38	587.0	12.70	1.079	25,728
20. Deutsche Bank	West Germany	167,133.3	0.81	675.6	59.70	1.089	9,892
21. Sumitomo Trust & Banking[a]	Japan	161,171.7	15.14	556.7	10.80	1.082	23,616
22. Societe Generale	France	155,482.9	1.61	590.5	17.70	1.085	4,496
23. Mitsui Trust & Banking[a]	Japan	143,624.1	6.64	458.4	12.50	1.075	18,016
24. Dresdner Bank	West Germany	127,312.1	−1.30	291.6	−1.10	1.049	4,607
25. Daiwa Bank[a]	Japan	123,272.3	10.30	295.8	5.70	1.054	16,688
26. Paribas Group	France	121,617.4	−0.54	732.5	18.90	1.114	4,455
27. Nippon Credit Bank[a]	Japan	119,675.5	8.84	287.4	17.00	1.065	17,743
28. Yasuda Trust & Banking[a]	Japan	117,854.8	8.33	396.4	17.20	1.079	12,672
29. Hongkong & Shanghai Banking	Hong Kong	113,151.2	6.60	634.7	7.80	1.056	4,618
30. Union Bank of Switzerland	Switzerland	109,396.8	−12.18	517.5	−12.40	1.087	8,219

ample, the fact of having an engineering consultant of a certain nationality increases the chances that contracts for the supply of equipment, technology, and know-how will be won by an enterprise of the same nationality, given the advantages enjoyed in terms of information, language, and technical specification.[22]

Because of long-standing insurance practices in the United States, insurance services marketed internationally can offer the benefit of substantial knowledge about insurance, underwriting, risk evaluation, and insurance operations. Firms in the fields of legal and accounting services can aid U.S. firms abroad through support activities; they can also aid foreign firms and countries in improving business and governmental operations.

[22] *Engineering, Technical and other Services to Industry*, Synthesis Report, Organization for Economic Cooperation and Development, Paris, 1988.

		Assets		Performance			Market Value
		$ Million	Change from 1987	Net Income $ Million	Change from 1987	Real Profit- ability	5/31/89 $ Million
31. Kyowa Bank[a]	Japan	104,999.2	1.83	273.1	1.60	1.067	11,912
32. Swiss Bank	Switzerland	101,487.6	−10.48	448.9	−12.30	1.081	6,122
33. Midland Bank	Britain	100,848.7	11.88	760.0	NM	1.111	4,355
34. Cqmmerzbank	West Germany	99,633.6	−0.94	275.0	2.80	1.064	2,528
35. Bank of China	China	97,827.5	20.13	1,135.0	9.00	1.064	NT
36. Chase Manhattan	U.S.	97,455.1	−1.76	1,058.9	NM	1.159	3,206
37. Saitama Bank[a]	Japan	96,851.0	11.29	219.4	14.60	1.060	10,986
38. Bankamerica	U.S.	94,647.0	1.95	726.0	NM	1.098	4,754
39. Lloyds Bank	Britain	93,800.2	12.26	1,118.3	NM	1.220	4,919
40. Toyo Trust & Banking[a]	Japan	91,924.4	9.25	310.1	3.20	1.080	11,373
41. Shoko Chukin Bank[a]	Japan	91,754.9	−0.09	71.1	43.93	1.019	NT
42. Bayerische Vereinsbank	West Germany	91,319.4	−2.35	152.8	2.80	1.039	2,337
43. Westdeutsche Landesbank Girozentrale	West Germany	90,726.7	−3.84	90.4	43.90	1.020	NT
44. Banca Nazionale del Lavoro	Italy	87,782.4	−5.02	−46.7	NM	0.942	1,371
45. Zenshinren Bank[b]	Japan	85,925.8	32.16	209.7	32.40	1.067	NT
46. Algemene Bank Nederland	Netherlands	85,176.3	0.36	313.6	5.80	1.086	2,402
47. Amsterdam-Rotterdam Bank	Netherlands	84,072.0	3.83	295.1	8.10	1.085	2,220
48. J. P. Morgan	U.S.	83,923.0	11.28	1,001.8	NM	1.221	6,754
49. Bank of Yokohama[a]	Japan	82,389.6	7.34	153.6	6.40	1.047	10,937
50. Royal Bank of Canada[c]	Canada	82,389.6	14.19	591.0	NM	1.126	4,694

[a] Fiscal year ended Mar. 31, 1989.

[b] Fiscal year ended Mar. 31, 1988.

[c] Fiscal year ended Oct. 31, 1988.

NM = not meaningful. NT = not traded.

Source: Reprinted from June 26, 1989 issue of *Business Week*, p. 115, by special permission, copyright © 1989 by McGraw-Hill, Inc.

In the field of computer and data services, the United States has a longer experience horizon than most other countries. Knowledge of computer operations, data manipulations, data transmission, and data analysis are insufficiently exploited internationally by many small and medium-sized firms.

Similarly, U.S. communication services may encounter substantial future international market opportunities. For example, U.S. activities in the areas of videotext, home banking, and home shopping may be valuable abroad, particularly where geographic obstacles make the establishment of retail outlets cumbersome and expensive.

Many U.S. organizations have vast experience in the field of teaching services. Both the educational and the corporate sector, which largely have concentrated their work in the domestic market, have expertise in management motivation as well as the teaching of operational, manage-

TABLE 21.6 ▪ **Demand for Consulting Services in Selected Countries, 1987**

Practice Areas	Percent of Consulting Revenues						
	Canada	West Germany	Italy	Japan	Spain	United Kingdom	United States
Administration/Information Management	5	15	17	6	10	15	5
Information Systems	30	35	7	4	17	15	11
Financial Consulting	16	3	4	7	8	15	3
General Management	9	12	18	26	6	7	18
Government Administration	9	7	1	5	5	15	6
Executive Search	6	5	8	2	15	4	3
Human Resources	5	4	12	17	10	4	14
Manufacturing	4	5	19	2	13	12	17
Marketing	7	3	11	16	8	7	13
Procurement	—	1	1	—	2	1	—
Research/Development	—	3	1	2	1	2	—
Specialized Services	9	7	1	13	5	3	10

Source: *U.S. Industrial Outlook 1989* (Washington, D.C., U.S. Government Printing Office, 1989), 59–2.

rial, and theoretical issues. In the same vein, management consulting services can be provided by U.S. firms to the many foreign institutions and corporations in need of them. Of particular value could be management expertise in areas where U.S. firms maintain global leadership such as the transportation and logistics sector. Such U.S.-based expertise can be provided by management consulting firms and also by U.S. corporations willing to sell their management experience abroad. Yet consulting services are particularly sensitive to the cultural environment. As Table 21.6 shows, the use of consulting services varies significantly by country and field of consulting, which delineates the fact that while many companies seek outside consulting assistance, the areas in which they require such help differ markedly across national borders.

All service expenditures funded from abroad by foreign citizens in a country also represent a service export. This makes tourism an increasingly important area of U.S. services trade, as suggested in The International Marketplace 21.4. Every foreign visitor who spends foreign currency in the United States contributes to an improvement in the current account. With the value of the dollar declining, and given the vast natural resources and beauty offered by the United States, tourism services may well be destined to become a key national export factor. On a regional basis in the United States, tourism already is the largest employer in 13 states, with Nevada and Hawaii taking the lead, where 33 percent and 21 percent of all jobs are attributable to tourism.[23] The same also holds

[23] Ilkka A. Ronkainen and Richard J. Farano, "United States' Travel and Tourism Policy," *Journal of Travel Research* 25 (Spring 1987): 2–8.

THE INTERNATIONAL MARKETPLACE 21.4

Tourism Dollars Are Exports Too! German tourists just love the United States—especially when the dollar weakens against the deutsche mark. As one German tourist said, "America still has the image to Germans of being full of adventure and miracles. I think that for most Germans, America is a dream country." Another tourist compared America's vastness with Germany's dense population: "Here you can ride in a car for ten hours and not see any houses almost." Germans have a general fascination with America and Americans. They are attracted by America's vastness, sights, monuments, and friendliness. One tourist explained, "We hunger for traveling and seeing new things, unknown things."

The U.S. Travel and Tourism Administration (USTTA), a branch of the Commerce Department, reported that 1,153,000 Germans visited America in 1988. In 1985, when the exchange rate was about three deutsche marks to the dollar, 509,000 visited the United States. With the exchange rate at 1.8 deutsche marks to the dollar, USTTA predicted 1,200,000 would visit in 1989.

Ron Erdman, a USTTA market research analyst, has described the German tourist influx as "a continuous rise, but it's based mainly on the dollar. The devaluation of the dollar makes the United States a travel bargain. Many of the German travelers are repeat visitors." Returnees in 1988 were 72 percent of total travelers.

The United States is the preferred overseas destination for Germans, Erdman said. It far outdistances East Asia and South Asia, which are in second place. Most Germans come in spring and summer; more females than males visit. Favorite activities are shopping and sightseeing, followed by water sports and art galleries and museums. Germans are pretty much independent travelers and so packages will entice few. Only 14 percent come on package tours; more than 60 percent travel alone. They are quite adventuresome too. "Outdoors is a big thing for them. You will see them at the Grand Canyon in Arizona," Erdman said.

Washington ranks fifth as a destination choice, behind top-rated California, New York, Florida, and Arizona, according to USTTA. The usual visit includes two or three states. The average stay is 25.4 nights and 70 percent stay in hotels for part of their trip. While in the United States, Germans spend 43 dollars per day on the average. "That adds up to a substantial sum if they are here for 25 days," Erdman pointed out, "and this does not include airline tickets and package tours."

Source: Sarah Wersan, "Declining Dollar Brings More Germans to U.S.," *The Washington Times*, September 2, 1988, D4.

true for U.S. health services offered to citizens from abroad and U.S. education provided to foreign students. Yet, in order to be even more effective exporters, firms in these service industries need to properly prepare and promote their offerings to such new clients.

International services should not be viewed from the U.S. perspective only, however. Many other countries possess factor advantages that make some of their services very competitive. In Japan, for example, because of the lack of privacy legislation, retailers can obtain a substantial amount of information about their customer groups and their usage habits that can be useful to foreign firms. Similarly, India is increasingly participating in the provision of international data services. Although some aspects of the data field are high-technology intensive, many operations still require skilled human service input. The coding and inputting of data often has to be performed manually, because appropriate machine-readable forms may be unavailable or not useable. Because of lower wages, Indian companies can offer data inputting service at a rate much lower than in more industrialized countries. As a result, data are transmitted in raw form to India, encoded on a proper medium there, and returned to the ultimate user. To some extent, this transformation can be equated to the value-added steps that take place in the transformation of a raw commodity into a finished product. Obviously, using its comparative advantage for this labor-intensive task, India can compete in the field of international services.

A proper mix in international services might also be achieved by pairing the strengths of different partners. For example, U.S. information technology could be combined with the financial resources of individuals and countries abroad. The strengths of both partners can then be used to obtain maximum benefits.

Combining international advantages in services may ultimately result in the development of an even newer and more drastic comparative lead. For example, the United States has an international head start in such areas as high technology, information gathering, information processing, and information analysis and teaching. Ultimately, the major thrust of U.S. international services might not rely on providing these service components individually but rather in ensuring that, based on all U.S. resources, better decisions are made. If better decision making is transferable to a wide variety of international situations, that in itself might become the overriding future comparative advantage of the United States in the international market.

Starting to Market Services Internationally

For services that are delivered mainly in the support of or in conjunction with products, the most sensible approach for the international novice is to follow the path of the product. For years, many large accounting and banking firms have done so by determining where their major multinational clients have set up new operations and then following them. Smaller service marketers who cooperate closely with manufacturing firms can determine where the manufacturing firms are operating internationally. Ideally, of course, it would be possible to follow clusters of manufacturers in order to obtain economies of scale internationally, while, at the same time, looking for entirely new client groups abroad.

For service providers whose activities are independent from products, a different strategy is needed. These individuals and firms must search for market situations abroad that are similar to the domestic market. Such a search should concentrate in their area of expertise. For example, a design firm learning about construction projects abroad can investigate the possibility of rendering its design services. Similarly, a management consultant learning about the plans of a foreign country or firm to computerize can explore the possibility of overseeing a smooth transition from manual to computerized activities. What is required is the understanding that similar problems are likely to occur in similar situations.

Another opportunity consists of identifying and understanding points of transition abroad. Just as U.S. society has undergone change, foreign societies are subject to a changing domestic environment. If, for example, new transportation services are introduced, an expert in containerization may wish to consider whether to offer his or her service to improve the efficiency of the new system.

Leads for international service opportunities can also be gained by keeping informed about international projects sponsored by domestic organizations such as the U.S. Agency for International Development as well as international organizations such as the United Nations, the International Finance Corporation, or the World Bank. Very frequently such projects are in need of support through services. Overall, the international service marketer needs to search for similar situations, similar problems, or scenarios requiring similar solutions in order to formulate an effective international expansion strategy.

Strategic Implications of International Service Marketing

To be successful in the international service offering, the marketer must first determine the nature and the aim of the services offering core—that is, whether the service will be aimed at people or at things and whether the service act in itself will result in tangible or intangible actions. Table 21.7 provides examples of such a classification that will help the marketer to better determine the position of the services effort.

During this determination, the marketer must consider other tactical variables that have an impact on the preparation of the service offering. For example, in the field of research, the measurement of capacity and delivery efficiency often remains highly qualitative rather than quantitative. In the field of communications, the intangibility of the service reduces the

TABLE 21.7 ▪ **Understanding the Nature of the Service Act**

Nature of the Service Act	Direct Recipient of the Service	
	People	*Things*
Tangible Actions	Services directed at people's bodies:	Services directed at goods and other physical possessions:
	Health care	Freight transportation
	Passenger transportation	Industrial equipment repair and maintenance
	Beauty salons	
	Exercise clinics	Janitorial services
	Restaurants	Laundry and dry cleaning
	Haircutting	Landscaping/lawncare
		Veterinary care
Intangible Actions	Services directed at people's minds:	Services directed at intangible assets:
	Education	Banking
	Broadcasting	Legal services
	Information services	Accounting
	Theaters	Securities
	Museums	Insurance

Source: Christopher H. Lovelock, *Managing Services: Marketing, Operations, and Human Resources*, 1988, p. 47. Reprinted by permission of Prentice-Hall, Inc., Englewood Cliffs, New Jersey.

marketer's ability to provide samples. This makes communicating the service offered much more difficult than communicating a product offer. Brochures or catalogs explaining services often must show a "proxy" for the service in order to provide the prospective customer with tangible clues. A cleaning service, for instance, can show a picture of an individual removing trash or cleaning a window. However, the picture will not fully communicate the performance of the service. Because of the different needs and requirements of individual consumers, the marketer must pay very close attention to the two-way flow of communication. Mass communication must often be supported by intimate one-on-one follow-up.

The role of personnel deserves special consideration in the international marketing of services. Because the customer interface is intense, proper provisions need to be made for training of personnel both domestically and internationally. Major emphasis must be placed on appearance. Most of the time the person delivering the service—rather than the service itself—will communicate the spirit, value, and attitudes of the service corporation.

This close interaction with the consumer will also have organizational implications. For example, while tight control may be desired over personnel, the individual interaction that is required points toward the need for an international decentralization of service delivery. This, in turn, requires delegation of large amounts of responsibility to individuals and service "subsidiaries" and requires a great deal of trust in all organizational units. This trust, of course, can be greatly enhanced through proper methods of training and supervision.

The areas of pricing and financing require special attention. Because services cannot be stored, much greater responsiveness to demand fluctuation must exist, and therefore much greater pricing flexibility must be maintained. At the same time, flexibility is countered by the desire to provide transparency for both the seller and the buyer of services in order to foster an ongoing relationship. The intangibility of services also makes financing more difficult. Frequently, even financial institutions with large amounts of international experience are less willing to provide financial support for international services than for products. The reasons are that the value of services is more difficult to assess, service performance is more difficult to monitor, and services are difficult to repossess. Therefore, customer complaints and difficulties in receiving payments are much more troublesome to evaluate for a lender in the area of services than for products.

Finally, the distribution implications of international services must be considered. Usually, short and direct channels are required. Within these channels, closeness to the customer is of overriding importance in order to understand what the customer really wants, to trace the use of the service, and to aid the consumer in obtaining a truly tailor-made service.

SUMMARY

Services are taking on an increasing importance in international marketing. They need to be considered separately from the marketing of goods because they no longer simply complement products. Often, products complement services or are in competition with them. Because of service attributes such as their intangibility, their perishability, their custom-madeness, and cultural sensitivity, the international marketing of services is frequently more complex than that of goods.

Services play an increasing role in the economy of the United States and other industrialized nations. As a result, international growth and competition in this sector has begun to outstrip that of merchandise trade and is likely to intensify in the future. Even though services are unlikely to replace production, the sector will account for the shaping of new comparative advantages internationally.

The many service firms now operating domestically need to investigate the possibility of going global. Historical patterns that had service providers following manufacturers abroad have become obsolete as stand-alone services become more important to world trade. Management must therefore assess its vulnerability to service competition from abroad and explore opportunities to provide its services internationally.

Questions for Discussion

1. Discuss the major reasons for the growth of international services.

2. Why has the U.S. world market share in trade in services declined?

3. Why does the United States have a comparative advantage in many services sectors?

4. How does the international sale of services differ from the sale of goods?

5. What are some of the international marketing implications of service intangibility?

6. What are some ways for a firm to expand its services internationally?

7. Some predict that "the main future U.S. international service will be to offer better decisions." Do you agree? Why or why not?

8. How can a firm in a developing country participate in the international services boom?

9. Which services would be expected to migrate abroad in the next decade? Why?

Recommended Readings

Bateson, John E. G. *Managing Services Marketing*. Hinsdale, Ill.: Dryden Press, 1989.

Berry, Leonard L., David R. Bennett, and Carter W. Brown. *Service Quality*. Homewood, Ill.: Dow Jones-Irwin, 1989.

Blum, Julius M. "World Trade in Services: Opportunities and Obstacles." In *1985 Proceedings of the Southwestern Marketing Association*. Denton, Tex.: Southwestern Marketing Association, 1985.

Czepiel, John, Michael R. Solomon, and Carol F. Surprenant, eds. *The Service Encounter*. Lexington, Mass.: Lexington Books, 1985.

Feketekuty, Geza. *International Trade in Services*. Cambridge, Mass.: Ballinger, 1988.

Heskett, James L. *Managing in the Service Economy*. Boston, Mass.: Harvard Business School Press, 1986.

Lovelock, Christopher H. *Services Marketing*. Englewood Cliffs, N.J.: Prentice-Hall, 1990.

Shames, Germaine W. and W. Gerald Glover. *World-Class Service*. Yarmouth, Maine: Intercultural Press, 1989.

Shelp, Ronald. *Beyond Industrialization: Ascendancy of the Global Service Economy*. New York: Praeger, 1981.

U.S. Chamber of Commerce and the Bretton Woods Committee. *How U.S. Firms Can Boost Exports through Overseas Development Projects*. Washington, D.C.: Government Printing Office, 1986.

CHAPTER 22

Countertrade

THE INTERNATIONAL MARKETPLACE

How PepsiCo Sells to Cashless Buyers   *Many American companies marketing to Third World countries rely on countertrade. Economists argue that such deals make little sense. Countertrade adds unnecessarily to the cost of doing business, critics say, and countries would be better off developing export industries themselves. Marketing executives agree that countertrade is no panacea, but they see little choice, especially because the problem of Third World debt shows no signs of easing. They see the additional cost as an investment in future market share.*

PepsiCo does a lot of countertrade. PepsiCo World Trade Corporation, a subsidiary, helps generate foreign exchange that enables soft drink bottlers to buy concentrate. In Mexico, Pepsi's largest foreign soft drink market, the company rehabilitated a locally owned pineapple canning factory and found U.S. buyers for its product. It has also bought a frozen broccoli operation. The Sudan pays for its concentrate with sesame seeds, while Tanzania provides sisal, which is used for making rope.

In breaking into the Indian market, PepsiCo cut a deal that makes India look like Tom Sawyer getting paid to let PepsiCo whitewash a fence. India will earn five times as much hard currency as it shells out for PepsiCo ingredients. PepsiCo will export fruit juices and tomato paste and do research and develop high-yield and disease-resistant export crops. Robert H. Bebey, president of PepsiCo International, has said: "It mesmerizes us when there is a market we are not in. We want to be in Albania. We want to be in Burma. We wouldn't make much, if anything, but we want to be there when windows of opportunity open. Countertrade is instrumental. We are selling something that is nonessential, so we have to give them more than we are getting."

Source: Louis Kraar, "How to Sell to Cashless Buyers," Fortune, November 7, 1988: 147–154.

General Motors exchanged automobiles for a trainload of strawberries. Control Data swapped a computer for a package of Polish furniture, Hungarian carpet backing, and Soviet greeting cards. Ford traded cars for sheepskins from Uruguay, potatoes from Spain, toilet seats from Finland, cranes from Norway, and coffee from Columbia.[1] Pepsi has accepted, in exchange for soft-drink concentrate, products ranging from sesame seeds to sisal for making rope, as described in The International Marketplace 22.1.

All of these are examples of countertrade activities carried out around the world. This chapter will focus on the ancient, yet new, form of barter and countertrade that is emerging again in world trade. It will first explain the types of countertrade that currently exist and discuss why these types of transactions are reemerging. Policy issues associated with countertrade will be explored by examining the attitudes held toward countertrade by both national governments and international bodies such as the GATT, the OECD, and the UN. The countertrade situation of corporations will then be reviewed with an examination of what firms do, and why they do it. Finally, information will be provided on how to organize for countertrade, what problems to look out for, and how countertrade can be used as an effective international marketing tool.

COUNTERTRADE DEFINED

Countertrade is a sale that encompasses more than an exchange of goods, services, or ideas for money. In the international market, countertrade transactions "are those transactions which have as a basic characteristic a linkage, legal or otherwise, between exports and imports of goods or services in addition to, or in place of, financial settlements."[2] Historically, countertrade was mainly conducted in the form of barter, which is a direct exchange between parties of goods of approximately equal value, with no money involved. These transactions were the very essence of business at times during which no money—that is, a common medium of exchange—existed or was available. Over time, money emerged as a convenient medium that unlinked transactions from individual parties and permitted greater flexibility in trading activities. Repeatedly, however, we can see returns to the barter system as a result of environmental circumstances. For example, because of tight financial constraints, Georgetown University during its initial years of operation after 1789 charged its students part of the tuition in foodstuffs and required students to participate in the construction of university buildings. During periods of high inflation in Europe in the 1920s, goods such as bread, meat, and gold were seen as much more useful and secure than paper money, which decreased in real value

[1] Raj Aggarwal, "International Business through Barter and Countertrade," *Long Range Planning*, June 1989, 75–81.

[2] "Current Activities of International Organizations in the Field of Barter and Barter-like Transactions," *Report of the Secretary General*, United Nations, General Assembly, 1984, 4.

by the minute. Even more recently, in the late 1940s, American cigarettes were an acceptable medium of exchange in most European countries, much more so than any currency except the dollar.

Countertrade transactions have therefore always arisen when economic circumstances made it more efficient to exchange goods directly than to use money as an intermediary. Conditions that encourage such business activities are lack of money, lack of value of money, lack of acceptability of money as an exchange medium, or greater ease of transaction by using goods.

These same reasons prevail in today's resurgence of countertrade activities. Beginning in the 1950s, countertrade and barter transactions were mainly carried out with countries from the Socialist bloc. The currencies of these countries are not acceptable elsewhere because they are not freely convertible. At the same time, the countries do not want their currency distributed outside their economic bloc, and they do not possess sufficient foreign "hard" currency to make purchases of Western goods that are not available within COMECON but are crucial for further economic development. To some extent, these countries solved their currency problem by depleting their gold reserves—which indirectly, because of the world market price for gold, was a financial transaction. Even so, these measures did not permit sufficient importation. Many of these countries therefore insisted in their dealings with Western nations that goods they produced be taken in exchange so as to reduce their need for foreign currencies.

In the 1980's, the use of countertrade steadily increased and eventually stabilized. In 1972, countertrade was used by only 15 countries. By 1979, the countries conducting countertrade transactions numbered 27, and by 1989 the number was 94. Figure 22.1 lists countries that are currently requesting countertrade transactions from their trading partners. Estimates as to the total volume of global countertrade vary widely. A consensus of expert opinions has put the percentage of world trade financed through countertrade transactions at between 20 and 25 percent.[3] Such an estimate conflicts with IMF figures, which attribute only a very small percentage of world trade to countertrade. Yet, if all business transactions in which countertrade plays some kind of role are considered, the estimate of 20 to 25 percent could be reasonable.

Increasingly, countries are deciding that countertrade transactions are more beneficial to them than transactions based on financial exchange alone. A primary reason is that the world debt crisis has made ordinary trade financing very risky. Many countries, particularly in the developing world, simply cannot obtain the trade credit or financial assistance necessary to afford desired imports. Heavily indebted countries, faced with the possibility of not being able to afford imports at all, resort to countertrade in order to maintain at least some trickle of product inflow.

---

[3] Sam Okoroafo, "Determinants of LDC Mandated Countertrade," *International Marketing Review*, Winter 1989, 16–24.

FIGURE 22.1 ▪ **Countries Requesting Countertrade**

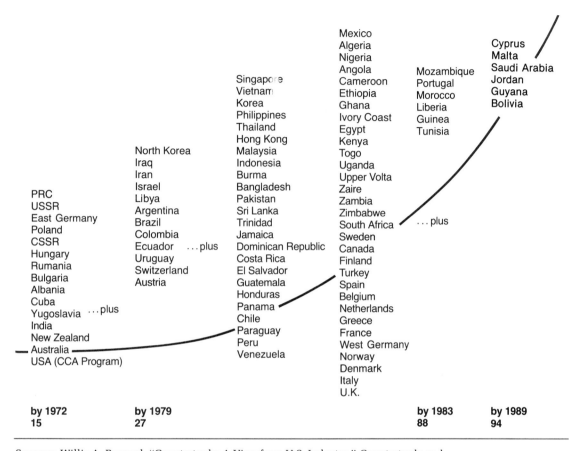

by 1972	by 1979		by 1983	by 1989
15	27		88	94

Sources: Willis A. Bussard, "Countertrade: A View from U.S. Industry," *Countertrade and Barter Quarterly*, May 1984, 54; and Pompiliu Verzariu, Office of Barter and Countertrade, U.S. Department of Commerce, May 1989.

A second reason is that many countries are again enamored by the notion of bilateralism. Thinking along the lines of "you scratch my back, and I'll scratch yours," they prefer to exchange goods with countries that are their major business partners.

Countertrade is also often viewed by firms and nations alike as an excellent mechanism to gain entry into new markets. When a producer feels that marketing is not its strong suit, particularly in product areas that face strong international competition, countertrade is seen as useful. The producer often hopes that the party receiving the goods will serve as a new distributor, opening up new international marketing channels and ultimately expanding the original market.

Conversely, because countertrade is highly sought after in many enormous, but semiclosed, markets such as China, the Eastern Bloc, South

America, and the Third World, engaging in such transactions can provide major growth opportunities for Western firms.[4] In increasingly competitive world markets, countertrade can be a good way to attract new buyers. By providing marketing services, the seller is in effect differentiating his product from those of his competitors.[5]

Finally, countertrade can provide stability for long-term sales. For example, if a firm is tied to a countertrade agreement, it will need to source the product from a particular supplier, whether it wishes to do so or not. This stability is often valued highly because it eliminates, or at least reduces, vast swings in demand and thus allows for better planning.

TYPES OF COUNTERTRADE

Under the traditional types of barter arrangements, goods are exchanged directly for other goods of approximately equal value. As Table 22.1 shows, such transactions can encompass the exchange of a wide variety of goods—for example, bananas for cars, or sugar for toys—and are carried out not only in the Socialist bloc but also in the developing and the developed countries. However, such straightforward barter transactions, which were quite frequent in the 1950s, are less often used today, "because it is difficult to find two parties prepared to make a simultaneous or near-simultaneous exchange of goods of equivalent value."[6]

Increasingly, participants in countertrade have resorted to more sophisticated versions of exchanging goods that often also include some use of money. One refinement of simple barter is the **counterpurchase,** or **parallel barter,** agreement. The participating parties sign two separate contracts that specify the goods and services to be exchanged. Frequently, the exchange is not of precisely equal value; therefore some amount of cash will be involved. However, because an exchange of goods for goods does take place, the transaction can rightfully be called barter. A special case of parallel barter is that of reverse reciprocity, "whereby parallel contracts are signed, granting each party access to needed resources (for example, oil in exchange for nuclear power plants)."[7]

Another common form of countertrade is the **buy-back** or compensation arrangement. One party agrees to supply technology or equipment that enables the other party to produce goods with which the price of the supplied products or technology is repaid. These arrangements often "include larger amounts of time, money, and products than straight barter

---

[4]Bill Neale, "Countertrade: Reactive or Proactive?" *Journal of Business Research* 16 (December 1988): 327–335.

[5]Jong H. Park, "Is Countertrade Merely a Passing Phenomenon? Some Public Policy Implications," *Proceedings of the 1988 Conference,* ed. R. King (Charleston, S.C.: Academy of International Business, Southeast Region, 1988), 67–71.

[6]"Current Activities of International Organizations," 4.

[7]Christopher M. Korth, "The Promotion of Exports with Barter," in *Export Promotion,* ed. M. Czinkota (New York: Praeger, 1983), 42.

TABLE 22.1 ■ **A Sample of Barter Agreements**

Country		Exported Commodity	
A	B	A	B

Brazil	Mexico	Foodstuff:
		  Soybeans (160,000 MT)
		  Sunflower seeds
		Petrochemicals
		Oil products
		Oil-drilling equipment
		Total, $3 billion
			Oil at 80,000 barrels a day

Ecuador	U.S.S.R.	Bananas	LADA cars NIVA cars SKM pickup trucks

Jamaica	U.S.—
	  General
	  Motors
		Bauxite	Cars

U.S.S.R.	Japan	Raw cotton, 10,000 T	Synthetic fiber:
			  synthetic cotton
			  polyester

China	East
	  Germany
		Rice
		Canned fruit
		Vegetables
		Textiles
		Chemicals
		Machine tools
			Scientific
			  instruments
			Printing machines
			Trucks
			Chemical fertilizers

Sweden	Iran	Paper and pulp,
		  U.S. $29 million
		Glass products,
		  U.S. $22 million
		Vicose,
		  U.S. $6 million
		General machinery,
		  U.S. $7.8 million
			Crude oil (to be
			  delivered before
			  manufactured
			  goods are
			  exported)

Pakistan	Iran	Sugar, 50,000 T Wheat, 130,000 T Rice Chemical fertilizer	Crude oil
New Zealand	Iran	Frozen lamb	Crude oil

Note: MT—metric tons; T—tons.

Source: Donna Vogt, *U.S. Government International Barter*, Congressional Research Service, Report No. 83-211 ENR (Washington, D.C.: Congressional Research Service, 1983), 74–77.

arrangements."[8] They originally evolved "in response to the reluctance of communist countries to permit ownership of productive resources by the private sector—especially by foreign private sectors."[9] One example of

[8] Donna U. Vogt, *U.S. Government International Barter*, Report No. 83- 211 ENR (Washington, D.C.: Congressional Research Service, 1983), 65.

[9] Korth, "The Promotion of Exports with Barter," 42.

such a buy-back arrangement is an agreement entered into by Levi Strauss and Hungary. The company transferred the know-how and the Levi's trademark to Hungary. A Hungarian firm began producing Levi's products. Some of the output is sold domestically and the rest is marketed in Western Europe by Levi Strauss, in compensation for the know-how. In the past decade, buy-back arrangements have extended far beyond the Communist bloc and now encompass many developing and newly industrialized nations.

Another form of more refined barter, aimed at reducing the effect of the immediacy of the transaction, is called **clearing account barter.** Here, clearing accounts are established to hold deposits and effect withdrawals for trades. These currencies merely represent purchasing power, however, and are not directly withdrawable in cash. As a result, each party can agree in a single contract to purchase goods or services of a specified value. Although the account may be out of balance on a transaction by transaction basis, the agreement stipulates that over the long term a balance in the account will be restored. Frequently, the goods available for purchase with clearing account funds are tightly stipulated. In fact, funds have on occasion been labeled "apple clearing dollars" or "horseradish clearing funds." Sometimes, additional flexibility is given to the clearing account by permitting **switch-trading,** in which credits in the account can be sold or transferred to a third party. Doing so can provide creative intermediaries with opportunities for deal making by identifying clearing account relationships with major imbalances and structuring business transactions to reduce them.

Another major form of barter arrangement is called **offset.** These arrangements are most frequently found in the defense-related sector and in sales of large-scale, high-priced items such as aircraft. For example, a country purchasing aircraft from the United States might require that certain portions of the aircraft be produced and assembled in the purchasing country. Such a requirement is often a condition for the award of the contract, and is frequently used as the determining attribute for contract decisions. Offset arrangements can take on many forms, such as coproduction, licensing, subcontracting, or joint ventures.

A final, newly emerging form of countertrade consists of **debt swaps.** These swaps are carried out particularly with lesser developed countries in which both government and the private sector face large debt burdens. Because the debtors are unable to repay the debt any time soon, debt holders have increasingly grown amenable to exchange of the debt for something else. Four types of swaps are most prevalent. One of them consists of a **debt-for-debt swap.** Here the loan held by one creditor is simply exchanged for a loan held by another one. For example, a U.S. bank may swap Argentine debt with a European bank for Chilean debt. Through this mechanism, debt holders are able to consolidate their outstanding loans and concentrate on particular countries or regions. A second form of debt swap consists of debt-for-equity swaps. Here, debt is converted into foreign equity in a domestic firm. The swap therefore serves as the vehicle for foreign direct investment. Although the equity itself is denominated into local currency, the terms of conversion may allow the investor future access to foreign exchange for dividend remittances and capital repatriation.[10]

In some countries these **debt-for-equity swaps** have been very successful. For example, investments in Chile have so far retired about $2.9 billion of external debt, representing over 10 percent of the country's foreign debt.[11]

A third method of debt swaps consists of **debt-for-product swaps.** Here, debt is exchanged for products received. Usually, these transactions require that additional cash payment be made for the product. For example, First Interstate Bank of California concluded an arrangement with Peruvian authorities whereby a commitment was made to purchase $3 worth of Peruvian products for every $1 of products paid by Peru against debt.[12]

The newest emerging form of debt swaps is that of swapping debt for social purposes. For example, environmental concerns can be addressed by applying debt to the preservation of nature. The International Marketplace 22.2 gives an example of such activity. As repayment of debt becomes more and more difficult for an increasing number of nations, the swap of debt for social causes is likely to increase. In addition to the environmental fields, these increases can occur in many other areas of need. For example, it has already been suggested by the U.S. government that portions of the debt burden be used for a **debt-for-education swap** where more U.S. students could study abroad, which could greatly contribute to the international orientation, language training, and cultural sensitivity of the U.S. education system.[13]

With the increasing sophistication of countertrade, the original form of straight barter is the least-used form today. Most frequently used is the counterpurchase agreement. Because of the rapid increase in military expenditures, offsets are the second most frequently used. Figure 22.2 presents the results of a survey showing that, for U.S. firms at least, straight barter transactions are the least common of all, a finding that has also been confirmed by other research.[14]

---

[10]Richard A. Debts, David L. Roberts, and Eli M. Remolona, *Finance for Developing Countries* (New York: Group of 30, 1987), 18.

[11]Pompiliu Verzariu, "An Overview of Nontraditional Finance Techniques in International Commerce," in *Trade Finance: Current Issues and Developments* (Washington, D.C.: Government Printing Office, 1988), 48.

[12]Ibid., 50.

[13]Michael R. Czinkota and Martin J. Kohn, *A Report to the Secretary of Commerce: Improving U.S. Competitiveness–Swapping Debt for Education* (Washington, D.C.: Government Printing Office, 1988).

[14]Donald J. Lecraw, "The Management of Countertrade: Factors Influencing Success," *Journal of International Business Studies* 20 (Spring 1989): 41–59.

22.2   THE INTERNATIONAL MARKETPLACE

Swapping Debt for Nature   Environmentalists have seldom had much time for financiers. This makes welcome a new understanding between the brown-sandal nature lovers and the black-Gucci bankers. Conservation agencies want banks to sell them Third World debts at a hefty discount. The agencies can then give the debt back to an indebted country, so long as it agrees to spend some of it on conservation. Banks like it; they get at least some money for their nonperformance loans, while developing countries gain from retiring the debt at a discount.

Some transactions have already taken place. Conservation International, an American environmental group, paid Citicorp $100,000 for $650,000 of Bolivian debt. The Americans then returned the debt to Bolivia, which agreed to make a wildlife sanctuary from a 4-million-acre stretch of the Amazon basin and pay for its upkeep.

Other Third World governments are lining up to participate in such swaps. The Costa Rican government agreed to pay 75 percent of the face value of any debt donated for conservation projects. The Philippines will swap up to $2 million for the peso equivalent of $2 million of cash targeted for conservation. The Malagasy Republic, keen to preserve its many endangered species of lemur, has talked to the World Wild Life Fund about debt for nature swaps.

Source: "Greensback-Debt," *The Economist*, August 6, 1988, 62–63.

FIGURE 22.2   ▪   **Countertrade Usage—By Types**

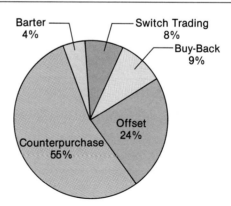

Source: Willis A. Bussard, "An Overview of Countertrade Practices of Corporations and Individual Nations," in *International Countertrade*, C. Korth, ed. (Quorum Books, a division of Greenwood Press, Inc., Westport, CT, 1987), p. 18. Copyright © 1987 by Christopher M. Korth. Reprinted with permission.

OFFICIAL ATTITUDES TOWARD COUNTERTRADE

Official U.S. Policy

When trying to ascertain official U.S. government attitudes, the investigator must look at the different departments within the executive, the legislative, and judicial branches. On occasion, a coherent policy view can be identified. More often than not, discrepancies among the different groups will become visible because they have different outlooks and serve different constituencies. Such discrepancies are particularly obvious when looking at the issue of countertrade.

A report of President Carter's on U.S. competitiveness makes a strong statement against countertrade. The report briefly examines the incidence of countertrade, its growth, and the incentives behind its practice. It concludes that "the transactions are purely bilateral in nature and are not competitive since they squeeze out competition from a third market or specify the export market. Trade is formulated on the basis of the willingness to countertrade and not on economic considerations."[15]

The Department of the Treasury tends to take a similarly dim view of countertrade. Treasury officials stated with regard to offsets and coproduction that they "suspect that offset and coproduction agreements mandated by governments (do not) promote . . . economic . . . efficiency. They may constitute implicit subsidies to the industry of the purchasing countries. They may result in diversion of business away from efficient U.S. producers . . . thus causing economic inefficiency and dislocations. . . . Since these practices appear to involve spillover effects on nondefense production and trade, they may have adverse effects on future U.S. production, trade, employment, and tax revenue."[16]

The Office of the U.S. Trade Representative, which is the chief U.S. trade negotiator, is somewhat more flexible. At a House of Representatives hearing a negotiator testified that "our position is that countertrade is a second-best option for international trade transactions. It represents a distortion of international trade and is contrary to an open, free trading system. It is not in the long-run interest of the United States or the U.S. business community. Nevertheless, as a matter of policy the U.S. government does not oppose U.S. companies participating in countertrade arrangements unless such actions could have a negative impact on national security. If a company believes a countertrade transaction is in its interest, the company is in a better position than we are to make that business decision."[17]

[15] *Report of the President on U.S. Competitiveness*, transmitted to Congress on September 1980, V-45.

[16] John D. Lange, Jr., Director, Office of Trade Finance, U.S. Department of the Treasury, testimony before the House of Representatives, Economic Stabilization Subcommittee, Committee on Banking, Finance, and Urban Affairs, 97th Cong., 1st sess., September 24, 1981.

[17] Donald W. Eiss, Statement before the Subcommittee on Arms Control, International Security and Science and the Subcommittee on International Economic Policy and Trade, Committee on Foreign Affairs, U.S. House of Representatives, July 1, 1987, 4–5.

The Department of Defense is concerned with enhancing its principles of RSI, or rationalization, standardization, and interoperability. This means that the Department strongly encourages other nations allied with the United States to use similar equipment, which can be interchanged in case of an armed conflict. For this reason, the Department of Defense tries to encourage foreign acquisitions of U.S. military hardware. Because such acquisition is likely to come about only through promises of offsets and coproduction, the department tends to display a policy of "positive neutrality" toward countertrade methods.

This attitude makes a lot of sense from the perspective of production cost. Given the economies of scale and the learning curve effects inherent in the manufacture of arms, more international sales result in longer production runs, which in turn permit weapons manufacturers to offer their products at a lower price. If the Department of Defense can encourage more international sales, it either can buy a given number of products for less money or can purchase more products with a given budget. From that perspective one could argue that countertrade transactions contribute to the U.S. national security.

The Department of Commerce displays the most supportive view of countertrade in the policy community. Given its mandate to help U.S. firms compete internationally, the department has its own Office of Barter and Countertrade, which provides advice to firms interested in such transactions. However, the establishment of this office came about only after significant congressional pressure.

While all these different views exist within the departments of the administration, on the legislative side Congress repeatedly has passed bills that permit or even encourage countertrade transactions. This legislation has primarily focused on barter possibilities for U.S. agricultural commodities or for stockpiling purposes. As a result, the **Commodities Credit Corporation** (CCC) and the **General Services Administration** (GSA) have been carrying out countertrade transactions for years. An example was the swap of U.S. agricultural commodities for Jamaican bauxite. This large-scale transaction was designed to reduce the U.S. surplus of agricultural products in exchange for increasing national stockpiles of a strategic material.

On the judicial side, countertrade involvement stems mostly from the enforcement activities of the Internal Revenue Service. The IRS is of course primarily concerned with the valuation of countertrade transactions and with ensuring that proper tax payments are made. A proper assessment of taxes, however, usually requires a painstaking determination of all facets of the transaction. Difficulties are often encountered in ascertaining the exact value of the countertraded goods, the time when the income has been received, and the profitability of the entire transaction. As a result of these problems, tax authorities are not in favor of countertrade. Other judicial activities are mainly concerned with valuation issues for import purposes. One major issue is the threat of dumping, whereby goods obtained through countertrade transactions may be disposed of cheaply in the domestic market and therefore harm domestic competitors, who do not benefit from the sales end of a countertrade transaction.

One can conclude that as a nation the United States is ambivalent toward countertrade. There are differing views within the administration and on the legislative and the judicial side. Countertrade is partially encouraged as long as no major negative effects within the domestic economy on nonparticipants are visible.

Foreign Government Views

Most industrialized countries, including Western Europe, Japan, New Zealand, and Australia, have participated actively in the growing countertrade phenomenon. Frequently, they are catalysts for countertrade transactions. Countries in the Eastern bloc have continued to maintain a procountertrade stance because of their continued need to preserve hard currencies. Countries in the developing world have taken different positions. Indonesia, for example, cited two choices it faced as its export revenues declined dramatically: one was to drastically limit its imports, the other was to liberalize its trade with alternative measures such as countertrade. As a result, the government officially instituted a mandatory countertrade requirement for any transaction exceeding a value of $500,000.

In a similar vein, Mexico has created a countertrade office in the Ministry of Foreign Trade. Several U.S. companies have been told that they can increase their exports to Mexico only if new sales are linked to imports from Mexico. Other developing countries have more subtle policies but are implementing and supporting countertrade nonetheless. Brazil, for example, keeps a low profile. Although the country "has issued no countertrade regulations and does not officially sanction its practice, CACEX, the foreign trade arm of the central bank, has made it quite clear that awards of import licenses and export performance are linked at the level of the firm."[18] This is a position taken more and more frequently by lesser developed countries. Although officially abhorring the use of countertrade, unofficially they have made it clear that, in order to do business, countertrade transactions are mandatory.

Attitudes of International Organizations

International organizations almost uniformly condemn countertrade. Public statements by both the IMF and GATT indicate that their opposition "is based on broad considerations of macroeconomic efficiency." These authorities complain that instead of a rational system of exchange, based on product quality and price, countertrade introduces extraneous elements into the sales equation. Arthur Dunkel, Director General of the GATT, went so far as to warn that the very viability of GATT is threatened by

---

[18] Steven M. Rubin, "Countertrade Controversies Stirring Global Economy," *The Journal of Commerce*, September 24, 1984, 14.

the proliferation of countertrade. He cautioned that if the trend continued, world trade practices would become inconsistent with the GATT principle of nondiscriminatory, most-favored-nation treatment in international trade. In addition, he warned that government-mandated bilateral arrangements could politicize international trade and diminish the purely commercial considerations that are now the cornerstone of multilateral, liberalized trade and its related institutions.[19]

Officials from the OECD (Organization for Economic Cooperation and Development) also deplore countertrade arrangements. They feel that such arrangements would lead to an increase in trade conflicts as competitive suppliers, unwilling to undertake countertrade arrangements, are displaced by less competitive suppliers willing to undertake countertrade arrangements.[20]

The international organization most neutral toward countertrade is the United Nations. A report of the Secretary General stated only that there appeared to be some economic and financial problems with countertrade transactions, and that any global, uniform regulation of countertrade may be difficult to implement because of the complexity and variety of transactions. The report lacks any kind of general conclusion, because such conclusions "may be somewhat hazardous in the absence of a sufficient volume of contracts that are easily available."[21]

This statement highlights one of the major problems faced by policymakers interested in countertrade. Corporation executives consider the subject of countertrade to be sensitive, because public discussion of such practices could imply that a product line is difficult to sell or indicate that the corporation is willing to conduct countertrade. Because such knowledge would result in a weakening of the corporation's international negotiation position, executives are usually tight-lipped about countertrade transactions.[22] At the same time, rumors about countertrade deals are often rampant, even though many of the transactions gossiped about may never materialize. To some extent, the public view of countertrade may resemble an inverted iceberg: there is much more on the surface than below. Policymakers are therefore uncertain about the precise volume and impact of countertrade, a fact that makes it all the more difficult to take proper policy actions.

Countertrade does appear to be on the increase. The main reason for that conclusion is the fact that countertrade may perhaps be the only practical solution to the fundamental difficulties in the world economy of which the proliferation of countertrade is a symptom. Access to devel-

[19]"GATT Director Dunkel Criticizes Trend toward Unilateral Trade Law Interpretations," *U.S. Export Weekly,* July 20, 1982, 557.

[20]Jacques de Miramon, "Countertrade: A Modern Form of Barter," *OECD Observer,* January 1982, 12.

[21]"Current Activities of International Organizations," 4.

[22]Michael R. Czinkota, "New Challenges in U.S.-Soviet Trade," *Journal of the Academy of Marketing Science* 5 (Special Issue, Summer 1977): 17–20.

oped markets for the lesser developed countries has become increasingly limited. Balance of payment crises, debt problems, and other financial difficulties have hurt their ability to import needed products. In the face of limited trade opportunities, both lesser developed countries and developed countries appear to regard countertrade as an alternative solution to no trade at all.[23]

THE CORPORATE SITUATION

A few years ago, most executives claimed both in public and in private that countertrade is a hindrance to international marketing and is avoided by their firms. More recently however, changes in corporate thought have taken place. Even though companies may not like countertrade transactions, if they refuse to engage in them business will be lost to foreign rivals who are willing to participate in countertrade. Increasingly, companies that are forced to take countertraded goods are altering their perspective from a reactive to a proactive one. In the past, corporations frequently resorted to countertrade only because they were compelled by circumstances to do so. However, times have changed, as The International Marketplace 22.3 shows, and companies have now begun to use countertrade as a tool to improve their market position. Rockwell International Corporation, for example, uses its own internal barter capabilities through its trading subsidiary, which Rockwell created several years ago. As a result, Rockwell's products have a special appeal abroad, because of the company's willingness to engage in countertrade.

Increasingly, companies are formulating market penetration strategies and are planning to acquire market share from their competition by instructing their staff to seek out countertrade opportunities if they lead to an expansion of their own product sales. These companies go beyond the traditional view that some sales, even those subject to countertrade, are better than no sales. They are using countertrade systematically as a marketing tool that brings with it favorable government consideration and a larger extent of pricing flexibility.

For longer range countertrade transactions, executives may not be as risk averse as for shorter range transactions. By the time the countertrade requirements fall due, which may be five to ten years in the future, they may not be around to take the blame if problems arise, because they may have been promoted, have changed positions, or have retired. On the other hand, for these long-term risks, many companies make it clear that the preferred compensation is cash, preferably dollars, and that any kind of countertrade transaction is not acceptable. However, the number of stalwart defenders of strictly noncountertrade deals is decreasing.

Companies and countries imposing countertrade believe that there are more merits to these transactions than purely conserving foreign cur-

---

[23] Michael R. Czinkota and Anne Talbot, "Countertrade and GATT: Prospects for Regulation," *International Trade Journal* (Winter 1986): 155–174.

22.3 THE INTERNATIONAL MARKETPLACE

Countertrade as Marketing Strategy at Daimler-Benz   German automaker Daimler-Benz is entering world countertrade arrangements in its effort to export commercial vehicles. There seems to be no immediate risk of a decline in demand for Daimler-Benz trucks, but world markets are becoming tougher. So in the long term the company's Stuttgart strategists are banking on barter, offset, and countertrade.

No likelihood exists of trading trucks in return for apples, as some critics over-hastily imagine. But, according to Gerhard Liener, head of finance and supplies at Daimler-Benz headquarters, "In many countries we no longer have any choice except some degree of countertrade."

Daimler-Benz established in the early 1970s a subsidiary that has dealt with barter and offset facilities. Such arrangements have been on a small scale. For example, warning triangles that are part of the equipment with which Mercedes cars are supplied were countertraded with the Eastern Bloc. Screwdrivers and jacks were similarly accepted for exchange, except that a single Daimler-Benz truck is worth the equivalent of an entire year's production of screwdrivers of a small factory.

For many developing or threshold countries, commodities are the only means of payment that they can call their own. Daimler-Benz management, lacking any idea of how to sell freighter loads of ore, has joined forces with Metallgesellschaft, which has this know-how. In February 1988, a joint countertrade subsidiary was formed between the two firms. Metallgesellschaft is rated number two worldwide in countertrade and deals mainly in raw materials.

At Daimler-Benz, Gerhard Liener has said: "We are now in a position to talk countertrade terms with the government of countries without money. Now we are going on to the offensive."

Source: Klaus Dieter Oehler, "Daimler-Benz Sees Countertrade as Key to Marketing Strategy," *The German Tribune*, June 12, 1988, 7.

---

rency. For example, the countertrade partner can be used as a marketing arm to explore new markets. Long-term countertrade requirements can ensure markets for future output, which are particularly important to producers in industries highly sensitive to capacity utilization. Security and stability of purchasing and sales arrangements can also play a major role. Some countries also see counterpurchases as a major way of insuring that technology transfer is carried out as promised, because the transferor will have to take back the product produced and will therefore ensure that the repayment will be of high quality.

Other reasons for engaging in countertrade by sellers of countertraded products can be more effective introduction of new products, the desire to more effectively enter new markets, and the goal of expanding a company's market share. Countertrade has been found to provide "outlets for integrative growth in addition to market penetration and development."[24] Finally, countertrade can provide markets and open up new trade channels for surplus products that could not be marketed otherwise.[25] Particularly when a world market glut exists for commodities that are in ample supply in some countries yet scarce in others, countertrade transactions may be an appealing trade mechanism.

THE EMERGENCE OF NEW INTERMEDIARIES

The rise in countertrade transactions has resulted in the emergence of new specialists to handle such transactions. These intermediaries can be either in-house or outside the corporation. Some companies have been founded to facilitate countertrade transactions for other firms. By purchasing unwanted inventories from companies at a steep discount, sometimes very high profit margins can be obtained. For example, Fred Tarter of Deerfield Communications founded his company on this principle and made $17,000,000 when he sold it in 1984 to Integrated Barter International of New York. He took on inventory from companies and paid for it in cash or advertising time or both. When he paid in advertising, of course, he exchanged bartered goods for other bartered commodities that were more desirable.

Other intermediaries that have benefited from the rise of countertrade are trading companies or trading houses that act frequently as third party intermediaries. Figure 22.3 shows an advertisement by such a firm. Because of their widespread connections, they can dispose of unwanted countertraded goods more easily than individual corporations. They are also more capable of evaluating the risks of such transactions and can benefit from both the discount and the markup portion of the exchange. Firms that deal with trading houses in order to receive assistance in their countertrade transactions need to be aware that the fees charged are often quite steep and may be cumulatively increasing. For example, there may be an initial consulting fee when the transaction is contemplated, a fee for the consummation of the acquisition, and a subsequent steep discount for the disposal of the acquired products. Also, these trading houses frequently refuse to take countertraded goods on a nonrecourse basis, which means that the company that has obtained countertraded goods still shares some of the risks.

[24] Sandra M. Huszagh and Hiram C. Barksdale, "International Barter and Countertrade: An Exploratory Study," *Journal of the Academy of Marketing Science* 14 (Spring 1986): 21–28.

[25] Lynn G. Reiling, "Countertrade Revives 'Dead Goods,'" *Marketing News*, August 29, 1986, pp. 1, 22.

FIGURE 22.3 ▪ **Advertisement Offering Countertrade Services**

International banks have also begun to increase their countertrade capabilities in order to serve their clients better and to increase their own profitability. One pertinent development for the U.S. banking industry is the Export Trading Company Act of 1982. This law stipulates that banks can participate in international trading activities, including countertrade transactions. U.S. banks can therefore be expected to become more active in this field in the future. Banks may be able to use their experience in international trade finance and apply it to the financial aspects of countertrade transactions. Banks may also have a comparative advantage over trading

FIGURE 22.4 ▪ **Countertrade Services Employed**

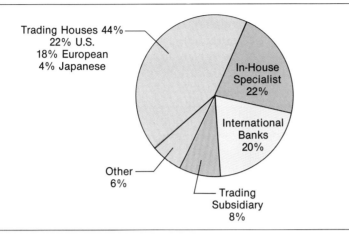

Trading Houses 44%
22% U.S.
18% European
4% Japanese

In-House Specialist 22%

International Banks 20%

Other 6%

Trading Subsidiary 8%

Source: Willis A. Bussard, "An Overview of Countertrade Practices of Corporations and Individual Nations," in *International Countertrade*, C. Korth, ed. (Quorum Books, a division of Greenwood Press, Inc., Westport, CT, 1987), p. 21. Copyright © 1987 by Christopher M. Korth. Reprinted with permission.

firms by having more knowledge and expertise in financial risk management, and more information about and contacts with the global market.

Countertrade intermediaries need not be large in size. Smaller firms can successfully compete by pursuing a niche strategy. An entrepreneur who exploits specialized geographic or product knowledge and develops countertrade transactions that may be too small for a multinational firm can conduct trades with little capital, yet receive sound profit margins.

Another new type of intermediary is represented by countertrade information service providers. These firms are exemplified by Batis Ltd. in London and ACECO in France. They provide databases on countertrade products and regulations in various countries, which subscribers may tap into. They are beginning also to provide computerized matchmaking services between companies in debt to some country's counterpurchase system and those in credit, or those willing to buy counterpurchase items.[26]

As Figure 22.4 shows, the vast majority of countertrade transactions in the United States are currently consummated by countertrade specialists outside the corporation.

PREPARING FOR COUNTERTRADE

Companies may wish to consider carrying out countertrade transactions in-house. If this can be done, the need for steep discounts may decrease, and the profitability of countertrade may improve. Developing an in-house capability for handling countertrade should be done with great caution.

[26] Kate Mortimer, "Countertrade in Western Europe," in *International Countertrade*, ed. C. Korth (Westport, Conn.: Quorum Books, 1987), 41.

First, from a strategic corporate perspective, the company should determine the import priorities of its products to the country or firm to which it is trying to sell. Goods that are highly desirable and/or necessary for a country mandating countertrade are less likely to be subject to countertrade requirements or are subject to less stringent requirements than imports of goods considered luxurious and unnecessary. As a next step, the company needs to identify which countertrade arrangements and regulations exist in the country to which it exports. An awareness of the alternatives available, and of the countertrade percentages demanded, will strengthen the company's bargaining position at the precontract stage. Obtaining this information is also important in order to incorporate possible countertrade cost into the pricing scheme. It is quite difficult to increase the price of goods once a "cash-deal" price has been quoted, and a subsequent countertrade demand is presented.

At this stage, the most favored countertrade arrangement from the buyer's perspective should be identified. The company should find out why this particular arrangement is the most favored one and explore whether other forms of transactions would similarly meet the objectives of the countertrading partner. In order to do this, the goals and objectives of the countertrading parties need to be determined. As already discussed, these can consist of import substitution, a preservation of hard currency, export promotion, and so on.

The next step is to match the strengths of the firm with current and potential countertrade situations. This requires an assessment of corporate capabilities and resources. It should be explored whether any internal sourcing needs exist that can be used to fulfill a countertrade contract. This may mean that raw materials or intermediate products currently sourced from other suppliers could now be obtained from the countertrade partner. However, this assessment should not be restricted to the internal corporate use of a countertraded product. The company should also determine whether it can use, for example, its distribution capabilities or its contacts with other customers and suppliers to help in its countertrade transactions. Moreover, an increase in the use of mandated countertrade by governments, combined with a more proactive approach toward such transactions by firms, may well result in companies expecting their suppliers to share in the burdensome effects of countertrade. Based on the notion that the supplier benefits from the export taking place due to the countertrade, it could very well be that main contractors will demand that major suppliers participate in disposing of the countertraded goods. As a result, companies that do not see themselves as international marketers may suddenly be confronted with countertrade demands.

At this point, the company can decide whether it should engage in countertrade transactions. The accounting and taxation aspects of the countertrade transactions should be considered, because they can often be quite different from current procedures. The use of an accounting or tax professional is essential in order to comply with difficult and obscure IRS regulations in this area.

Next, all of the risks involved in countertrade must be assessed. This means that the goods to be obtained need to be specified, that the delivery time for these goods needs to be determined, and that the reliability of the supplier and the quality and consistency of the goods need to be assessed. It is also useful to explore the impact of countertrade on the future prices, both for the price of the specific goods obtained and for the world market price of the category of goods. For example, a countertrade transaction may appear to be quite profitable at the time of agreement. Because several months or even years may pass before the transaction is actually consummated, however, a change in world market prices may severely affect the profitability. The effect of a countertrade transaction on the world market price should also be considered. In cases of large-volume transactions the established price may be affected due to a glut of supply. Such a situation may not only affect the profitability of a transaction but can also result in possible legal actions by other suppliers of similar products.

In conjunction with the evaluation of the countertraded products, which should be specified in as much detail as possible rather than left open as a general requirement, the company must explore the market for these products. This includes a forecasting of future market developments, paying particular attention to competitive reaction and price fluctuations. It is also useful at this stage to determine the impact of the countertraded products on the sales and profits of other complementary product lines currently marketed by the firm. What, if any, repercussions will come about from outside groups should also be investigated. Such repercussions may consist of antidumping actions brought about by competitors or reactions from totally unsuspected quarters. For example, McDonnell Douglas ran into strong opposition when it used bartered Yugoslavian ham in its employees' cafeteria and as Christmas gifts. The local meat-packers' union complained vociferously that McDonnell Douglas was threatening the jobs of its members.

Using all of the information obtained, the company can finally evaluate the length of the intended relationship with the countertrading partner, and the importance of this relationship for its future plans and goals. These parameters will be decisive for the final action, because they may form constraints overriding short-term economic effects. Overall, management needs to remember that, in most instances, a countertrade transaction should remain a means for successful international marketing and not become an end in itself.

SUMMARY

Countertrades are business transactions in which the sale of goods is linked to other goods rather than to money only. Such transactions are emerging with increasing frequency, due to hard-currency shortfalls in many nations around the world.

Concurrent with their increased use, countertrade transactions have also become more sophisticated. Rather than exchange goods for goods in a straight barter deal, companies and countries now structure counter-purchase, compensation, and offset agreements to aid in their industrial policies.

Governments worldwide and international organizations are concerned about the trend toward countertrade, yet in light of existing competition and the need to find creative ways of financing trade, very little interference with countertrade is exercised.

Corporations are increasingly using countertrade as a competitive tool in order to maintain or increase market share. The complexity of these transactions requires careful planning in order to avoid major corporate losses. Management must consider how the acquired merchandise will be disposed of, what the potential for market disruptions is, and to what extent countertraded goods fit with the corporate mission.

New intermediaries have emerged to facilitate countertrade transactions. Their services can be very expensive. However, they can enable firms without countertrade experience to participate in this growing business practice.

Questions for Discussion

1. What are some of the major causes for the resurgence of countertrade?

2. What forms of countertrade exist and how do they differ?

3. Discuss the advantages and drawbacks of countertrade.

4. How would you characterize the U.S. government's position toward countertrade?

5. How consistent is countertrade with the international trade framework?

6. Why would a firm take goods rather than cash?

7. Why would a buyer insist on countertrade transactions?

8. What particular benefits can an outside countertrade intermediary offer to a firm engaged in such transactions?

9. How would you prepare your firm for countertrade?

10. Discuss some of the possible accounting and taxation ramifications of countertrade.

11. Develop a corporate goals statement that uses countertrade as a proactive tool for international expansion.

12. Explain why countertrade may be encouraged by the increasing technology transfer taking place.

13. What are some of the dangers of using countertraded goods in-house?

14. What is your view of the future of countertrade?

Recommended Readings

Alexandrides, C. G., and B. L. Bowers. *Countertrade: Practices, Strategies and Tactics.* New York: Wiley, 1987.

Elderkin, Kenton W., and Warren E. Norquist. *Creative Countertrade.* Cambridge, Mass.: Ballinger, 1987.

Kopinski, Thaddeus C. *Negotiating Countertrade and Offsets: Avoiding Legal and Contractual Pitfalls.* Arlington, Va.: Asian Press, 1987.

Korth, Christopher M. (ed.). *International Countertrade.* Westport, Conn.: Quorum Books, 1987.

Schaffer, Matt. *Winning the Countertrade War.* New York: Wiley, 1989.

Countertrade and Barter. A magazine published by Metal Bulletin Inc., New York, N.Y.

CHAPTER 23

Marketing with Governments

23.1 THE INTERNATIONAL MARKETPLACE

Major Trade Changes in the Soviet Union *The U.S.S.R. Council of Ministers' foreign trade decree of December 10, 1988, will fundamentally change the way companies do business in the Soviet Union. New foreign trade organizations, new currency exchange rules, new foreign trade incentives, and a new tariff system will be introduced.*

Perhaps the most radical innovation is one that could bring hundreds of new Soviet foreign trade organizations onto the scene. As of April 1, 1989, all Soviet enterprises, associations, production cooperatives, and other organizations with goods or services able to compete on foreign markets will gain the legal right to set up their own foreign trade firms—although the State Foreign Trade Commission/GVK retains the right of veto.

This does not mean that all the enterprises interested in foreign trade will rush out to form their own FTOs right away. Presumably most will choose to work through existing FTOs for at least several years. Even so, given the sheer size of the Soviet economy, the results could still be dramatic. If only 1 percent of the U.S.S.R.'s 45,000 largest state enterprises decided to set up foreign trade units, for example, the number of FTOs would reach 450.

The decree encourages local republic councils of ministers and other territorial bodies (in Moscow and Leningrad, the city executive committees) to set up small departments to support local enterprises that want to conduct foreign trade. These units will employ only two to three people, but could be a useful stop for Western businessmen trying to research local markets.

Another innovation is the decree's provision for foreign currency auctions, to be supervised by Vneshekonombank. This goes further than prior legislation, which allowed enterprises to transfer their hard currency to one another at mutually agreed exchange rates but did not set up any specific institutional framework or procedure for such transactions.

Countertrade linkage could gradually begin to be eased by a provision of the new decree allowing Soviet enterprises and other units to set up consortia, associations, trading houses, or even joint stock companies for marketing and other foreign trade coordination. The long-term possibilities here are vast.

Although some of the decree's provisions may take many years to implement fully, the direction of change is clear: Soviet enterprises themselves are to conduct foreign trade. The traditional foreign trade straightjacket is to be dismantled.

Source: "New Soviet Trade Decree Promises Major Changes," *Business Eastern Europe*, January 2, 1989, 1–2. Reprinted with permission from Business International, London/New York.

This chapter addresses the international marketing activities of firms dealing with Communist or Socialist countries and state-owned enterprises. Marketing to **Communist nations** is singled out because these countries, which have also been labeled "second world countries," have **centrally planned economies.** International marketing success does not therefore depend on market forces, but rather on the government and its plans.

The fact that most of the countries with centrally planned economies are currently undergoing major economic and political changes provides for environmental shifts and potential business opportunities that international marketers need to be aware of. State-owned enterprises are included because, even though many of them exist in free market economies, they reflect to a significant extent the wishes and desires of their governments. The international marketer must focus on the nature of the government and the policies and politics surrounding the business transaction when dealing with these institutions.

The chapter will begin with a brief description of the emerging international trade structures in Communist countries. Market entry possibilities, negotiation approaches, and the challenges and opportunities facing the international marketer when dealing with governments and their enterprises are then discussed. Joint venture activities between Western firms and centrally planned economies are proliferating and are therefore an important part of the future trade relationship between Socialist and Western countries; this subject was dealt with in Chapter 14.

MARKETING WITH CENTRALLY PLANNED ECONOMIES

The major centrally planned economies are the Soviet Union, Eastern Europe, and the People's Republic of China (PRC). In modern times the design of central planning originated within the Soviet Union and has subsequently been adopted by other countries. However, gradual changes and "deviations" have come about in Eastern Europe and China, resulting in differences in strategies and tactics.

It is often believed that business ties between the Western world and Communist nations are a new phenomenon. However, that is not the case. For example in the 1920s General Electric and RCA helped to develop the

Soviet electrical and communications industries. Ford constructed a huge facility in Gorky to build Model A cars and buses. Du Pont introduced its technology to Russia's chemical industry. By the mid-1930s, however, most American companies had withdrawn from the scene or were forced to leave. Since then, centrally planned economies and Western corporations engaged in international marketing have had rather limited contact.[1]

To a large extent, this limitation has been the result of an ideological wariness on both sides. Socialist countries have often perceived international marketers as "aggressive business organizations developed to further the imperialistic aims of Western, especially American, capitalists the world over."[2] Furthermore, many aspects of capitalism, such as the private ownership of the means of production, were seen as exploitative and antithetical to Communist ideology.[3] Western managers, in turn, often saw Socialism as a threat to the Western world and the capitalistic system in general.

Over time, however, these rigid stances have been modified on both sides. Decision makers in centrally planned economies have recognized the need to purchase products and technology that are unavailable domestically or that can be produced only at a substantial comparative disadvantage.

They have decided that in order to achieve economic growth and improve the very much neglected standard of living in their society, the potential benefits of Socialist–Capitalist cooperation in many instances outweigh the risks of decentralized economic power and reduced reliance on plans. As a result, government planners in Socialist economies have begun to include some market considerations in their activities and have opened up their markets significantly to Western businesses.

At the same time, the greater openness on the part of Socialist governments has resulted in more flexibility in Western government controls of East-West trade. A drive toward modernization of production and growing consumer demand, combined with the new legislation and attitudes toward international business discussed in The International Marketplace 23.1, have greatly raised the attractiveness of doing business with Socialist economies. Furthermore, many firms have a great need to diversify their international business activities away from traditional markets because of current major trade imbalances in the West, and they are constantly searching for new opportunities. The large populations of Socialist countries may well offer them, as Table 23.1 shows. Therefore, corporations and managers in the West have come to understand that centrally planned economies can represent substantial new markets with vast sales potential

[1] Richard M. Hammer, "Dramatic Winds of Change," *Price Waterhouse Review* 33, no. 1 (1989): 23–27.

[2] Peter G. Lauter and Paul M. Dickie, "Multinational Corporation in Eastern European Socialist Economies," *Journal of Marketing* 35 (Fall 1975): 40–46.

[3] Alan B. Sherr, "Joint Ventures in the USSR: Soviet and Western Interests with Considerations for Negotiations," *Columbia Journal of World Business* 23 (Summer 1988): 25–37.

TABLE 23.1 ▪ **Population and GNP of Communist Nations**

	Population[a] (millions)	GNP[b] (billions)	GNP per Capita[b]
Bulgaria	8,966	$ 61.2	$ 6,800
China	1,088,169	286.0	280
Cuba	10,354	18.7	1,800
Czechoslovakia	15,620	143.9	9,280
German Democratic Republic	16,597	187.5	11,300
Hungary	10,588	84.0	7,910
Mongolia	2,067	1.7	880
Poland	37,958	259.8	6,930
Romania	23,041	138.0	6,030
Soviet Union	286,435	2,356.7	8,375
Vietnam	65,185	12.4	200
Total	1,564,980	3,549.9	

[a] As of July 1988.

[b] As of 1986.

Source: *The World Fact Book, 1988* (Washington, D.C.: Central Intelligence Agency, 1988).

that is far from realized. This is apparent from the relatively small but growing trade volumes shown in Tables 23.2 and 23.3.

This gradual enlightenment on both sides, coupled with political developments that at times have encouraged trade, has led to increased business interaction between Western international marketers and Socialist countries.

The Socialist Trade Apparatus

The Soviet system of foreign trade dates back to a decree signed by Lenin on April 22, 1918. It established that the state would have a monopoly on foreign trade and that all foreign trade operations were to be concentrated in the hands of organizations specifically authorized by the state. These organizations served as the basis for all trade, as well as economic, scientific, and technical operations with foreign countries.[4] This system of monopoly direction issued by the state was also adopted by the East European allies of the Soviet Union and by the Peoples' Republic of China.

This trade apparatus in effect isolated the firms and consumers in Socialist economies from the West. Any international transaction was cumbersomely reviewed by foreign trade organizations, ministries, and a multitude of state committees. In addition, rigid state bureaucracies regulated the entire economy. Over time, domestic economic problems emerged. In spite of some top–down and bottom–up planning interaction, the lack of market forces resulted in misallocated resources; the lack of competition

[4] Raymond J. Waldmann, *Managed Trade: The New Competition among Nations* (Cambridge, Mass.: Ballinger Press, 1986), 136.

TABLE 23.2 ▪ **Leading U.S. Exports to Centrally Planned Economies**
(C.I.F. value in thousands of dollars)

Schedule E

Number	Description	1984	1985	1986	1987	1988
041	Wheat, Unmilled	1,756,288	265,957	13,548	595,555	1,556,496
044	Corn or Maize, Unmilled	1,500,957	1,599,361	370,269	529,296	1,000,374
562	Fertilizers and Fertilizer Material	291,242	349,744	404,668	539,764	621,524
588	Synthetic Resins, Rubber, and Plastic Materials	238,607	233,373	199,289	261,336	608,385
247	Wood, in the Rough	271,835	323,456	178,515	164,640	438,065
792	Aircraft, Spacecraft, and Associated Equipment	114,484	657,457	296,261	486,428	338,266
517	Organic Chemicals and Products	111,491	103,942	104,732	170,493	302,792
081	Animal Feeding	77,781	46,118	51,314	89,380	260,038
875	Measuring, Checking Instruments	192,895	293,531	271,286	229,256	244,539
222	Oilseed and Oleaginous Fruit for Soft Oils	176,510	54,472	395,786	219,598	230,576
728	Specialized Industrial Machinery	41,161	131,663	175,913	164,482	228,985
752	Automatic Data Processing Machines	79,385	159,284	197,113	156,225	161,683
251	Pulp and Waste Paper	25,136	20,973	36,983	82,901	122,233
723	Civil Engineering and Contractors' Equipment	169,533	343,722	193,174	76,409	107,857
764	Telecommunication Equipment, TV, Radio Equipment	26,715	47,650	69,296	87,796	106,773
525	Inorganic Chemicals and Products	215,798	125,277	48,943	88,641	84,336
714	Internal Combustion Engines	17,593	65,284	59,794	48,543	79,071
641	Paper and Paperboard	32,274	26,959	60,630	104,927	76,739
971	Nonmonetary Gold, except Ores	2	31	3	4	76,259
322	Coal and Lignite	41,280	78,883	53,328	50,463	73,062
263	Cotton	173,550	67,826	1,436	11,644	68,874
266	Noncellulosic Fibers Suitable for Spinning	86,789	103,259	14,704	25,351	65,577
931	Special Transactions Not Classified	54,548	67,085	59,852	63,231	65,176
743	Pumps, Compressors, Filter Equipment	22,838	46,558	33,899	59,354	62,335
674	Iron or Steel Plates and Sheets	1,603	5,242	5,654	4,678	61,476
211	Hides, Skins, except Fur Skins	126,145	105,468	70,530	41,840	61,270
891	Articles of Rubber or Plastics	58,790	65,494	69,120	67,802	60,212
267	Cellulosic Fiber Suitable for Spinning	22,660	20,857	40,810	43,412	59,433
741	Heating and Cooling Equipment and Parts	21,891	51,219	61,315	62,226	58,637
334	Petroleum Products, Refined	22,760	48,255	58,626	54,831	55,729
736	Metalworking Machinery, Tools	24,416	44,931	68,888	70,268	55,606
759	Parts for Office Machines	27,427	37,527	55,418	42,391	50,993
057	Fruits and Nuts, except Oil Nuts	24,852	67,420	38,847	28,809	47,385
778	Electrical Machinery and Apparatus	20,083	36,150	48,334	35,146	46,772
774	Electromedical and Radiological Apparatus	32,229	42,354	50,260	32,162	46,592

TABLE 23.2 ▪ **Continued**

784	Parts of Road Vehicles and Tractors	53,978	54,036	45,428	44,716	46,047
724	Textile and Leather Working Machinery	10,358	22,666	17,509	29,447	42,728
598	Miscellaneous Chemical Products	27,647	28,697	28,892	24,938	37,715
651	Textile Yarn and Thread	42,386	130,223	41,691	5,210	37,015
712	Steam and Other Vapor Power Units	13,006	30,187	51,843	54,305	36,578
Total of Items Shown		6,248,920	6,002,593	4,043,899	4,947,896	7,784,203
Total Other		967,419	1,085,764	1,082,642	766,077	918,623
Total of All Commodities		7,216,339	7,088,357	5,126,541	5,713,973	8,702,826

Source: U.S. Department of Commerce, *1988 U.S. Foreign Trade Highlights* (Washington, D.C.: Government Printing Office, 1989), 364.

TABLE 23.3 ▪ **Leading U.S. Imports from Centrally Planned Economies (C.I.F. value in thousands of dollars)**

Schedule A Number	Description	1984	1985	1986	1987	1988
894	Baby Carriages, Toys, etc.	136,647	292,066	420,394	790,280	1,177,967
843	Outwear Apparel, Cotton, Wool	423,970	394,140	751,551	812,523	805,034
334	Petroleum Products	1,140,340	854,938	703,696	645,489	656,565
845	Sweaters and Other Outwear Apparel	155,426	225,472	526,661	625,895	561,595
658	Made-Up Articles of Textile Materials	141,676	203,217	250,816	392,056	485,317
831	Luggage, Handbags, and Similar Articles	110,860	163,519	213,681	329,129	476,962
333	Crude Petroleum	249,017	758,086	540,452	391,421	452,067
851	Footwear, New, except Military or Orthopedic	99,241	112,778	123,867	211,755	443,100
842	Outer Garments except Shirts	232,844	215,978	265,526	355,822	324,093
775	Household Type Equipment	3,129	11,708	33,559	102,803	319,128
848	Fur	79,062	82,322	98,696	148,572	299,779
036	Shellfish, Fresh, Frozen, Salted	28,871	33,973	66,760	119,869	299,118
899	Manufactured Articles not Further Specified	150,739	148,694	142,302	200,414	278,736
762	Radio Receivers (am and am/fm)	20,165	27,357	32,463	119,782	236,011
014	Meat, in Airtight Containers	129,690	153,254	178,576	202,076	174,173
846	Undergarments, Knit	115,682	92,059	194,108	197,998	169,189
764	Telecommunications Equipment	8,256	9,519	24,412	80,607	154,924
821	Furniture and Parts Thereof	72,404	71,961	84,293	121,159	139,552
891	Articles of Rubber or Plastics	12,320	19,296	29,622	59,296	137,235
844	Shirts	97,382	117,761	135,938	172,261	128,425
778	Electrical Machinery and Apparatus	24,140	39,438	40,555	68,664	128,202

(Continued)

TABLE 23.3 ▪ Continued

763	Phonographs, TV, Image, and Sound Reproduction Equipment	1,456	934	3,732	36,386	125,108
522	Inorganic Chemicals, Elements, Oxides	159,532	136,812	96,959	78,988	119,029
659	Floor Coverings, Tapestries	103,845	103,972	108,620	108,569	118,879
666	Pottery	51,038	46,178	54,244	84,050	118,254
652	Fabric, Cotton, Woven	127,542	109,220	168,873	144,208	116,296
681	Silver, Plated	86,433	49,488	85,952	103,632	114,639
931	Special Transactions	20,014	32,545	75,272	68,211	112,277
896	Artworks, Collectors' Pieces, and Antiques	60,159	57,219	108,224	134,760	110,783
517	Organic Chemicals and Related Products	81,440	94,227	103,714	95,172	99,319
056	Vegetables, Roots and Tubers	62,547	63,517	57,950	77,814	91,844
674	Plates and Sheets, Iron and Steel	147,830	133,027	47,200	64,303	87,090
694	Nails, Screws, and Other Fasteners	56,179	52,170	35,625	66,223	74,663
699	Manufactures and Semimanufactures, Base Metal	14,714	19,441	25,119	42,256	74,364
743	Pumps, Compressors, Fans, etc.	8,213	5,191	4,941	25,534	70,302
562	Fertilizers and Fertilizer Materials	151,361	121,448	143,055	38,594	69,531
695	Tools, for Hand or Machine Use	23,671	23,529	26,942	41,114	67,686
665	Glassware	52,953	43,091	46,345	57,226	66,049
291	Animal Materials, Crude	32,580	32,971	42,306	58,329	60,075
278	Crude Minerals	57,473	52,870	29,426	40,639	59,866
Total of Items Shown		4,730,840	5,205,387	6,122,426	7,513,880	9,603,222
Total Other		1,007,109	1,136,973	1,325,830	1,517,836	2,057,046
Total All Commodities		5,737,949	6,342,360	7,448,255	9,031,716	11,660,268

Source: U.S. Department of Commerce, *1988 U.S. Foreign Trade Highlights* (Washington, D.C.: Government Printing Office, 1989), 473.

promoted inefficiency. Centralized allocation prevented the emergence of effective channels of distribution. Managers of plants were more concerned with producing the quantities stipulated by a rigid **central plan** (often five-year plans, one following another) than with producing the products and the quality desired. Overfulfillment of the plan was discouraged because it would result in a quota increase for the following year. Entrepreneurship was disdained, innovation risky. In consequence, Socialist economies produced very lackluster growth, and their citizens fell far behind the West in their standard of living.

In the early 1980s the economic orientation of centrally planned economies began to change. Hungary and Poland started to cautiously encourage their firms to develop an export-oriented strategy. Exporting itself was nothing new, because much trade took place between the countries belonging to the **Council for Mutual Economic Assistance (CMEA).** What was new was the fact that government policy emphasized trade with the West and increasingly exposed domestic enterprises to the pressure of international competition.[5] In addition, Socialist countries began to import more equipment from the West and started to encourage direct investment by foreign firms.

In the mid-1980s the Soviet Union developed two bold new programs: **perestroika** and **glasnost.** Perestroika was to fundamentally reform the Soviet economy by improving the overall technological and industrial base as well as improving the quality of life for Soviet citizens through improved availability of food, housing, and consumer goods. Glasnost was to complement these efforts by encouraging the free exchange of ideas and discussion of problems, pluralistic participation in decision making, and increased availability of information.[6]

These major domestic steps were followed shortly by legislative measures that thoroughly reformed the Soviet foreign trade apparatus. In 1986 the Soviet Union officially requested membership in the **General Agreement on Tariffs and Trade (GATT).** In a major move away from previous trade centralization through the channels of the Ministry of Foreign Trade, national agencies, large enterprises, and research institutes were authorized to handle their own foreign transactions directly. A 1987 decree asserted that it was essential to develop economic ties with the capitalist world in order to consistently move along the strategic course of using the advantages of the world division of labor, strengthen the positions of the U.S.S.R. in international trade, and introduce the achievements of world science and technology into the national economy.[7] By 1989, all Soviet enterprises that could compete in foreign markets were permitted to apply for independent trading rights. By July 1989, over 5,000 such entities were registered.[8]

Concurrent with the steps taken in the Soviet Union, other Socialist countries also initiated major reforms affecting international marketers. China began to launch major programs of modernization and developed multinational corporations of its own, as The International Marketplace 23.2 shows. Virtually all Socialist countries began to invite foreign investors to form joint ventures and to produce in their countries to satisfy both domestic and international demand. Some advertisements of firms in these countries became almost undistinguishable from those in the West, as can be seen in Figure 23.1. By the late 1980s the macroeconomic systems of the Soviet Union, China, and Eastern Europe had begun to move

---

[5]Mihaly Simai, "Problems, Conditions, and Possibilities for an Export-Oriented Economic Policy in Hungary," in *Export Policy: A Global Assessment,* eds. M. Czinkota and G. Tesar (New York: Praeger, 1982), 20–30.

[6]Eugene Theroux and Arthur L. George, *Joint Ventures in the Soviet Union: Law and Practice,* rev. ed. (Washington, D.C.: Baker & McKenzie, 1989), 1.

[7]Sherr, "Joint Ventures in the USSR," 27.

[8]"Bolshoi Bang," *The Economist,* July 15, 1989, 69.

CITIC: Communist China's Thriving Capitalist Enterprise

Nationalize a massive banking holding company like Citicorp, merge it with an investment house like Goldman Sachs, put a Rockefeller in charge of the resulting organization, and you'd have the American equivalent of the China International Trust and Investment Corporation.

Although it can't compare financially to those American institutions, CITIC—a large financial company that functions like a national investment banker for China and owns Delaware's CitiSteel steel plant—has that kind of clout.

Founded less than a decade ago, CITIC has developed a reputation for aggressive investing that rivals any western firm.

Inside China, it is the major investor in joint venture projects with American companies such as Otis Elevator and Occidental Petroleum. Outside China, it owns interests in an Australian aluminum smelter, a bank and a habor tunnel in Hong Kong, and the Hong Kong-based airline Cathay Pacific. It also has interests in real estate and timber, paper, logging, and gold mining operations in the United States and Canada.

Rong Yiren, a former industrialist from Shanghai who remained in China after 1949, is CITIC's chairman and driving force. Beaten by the Red Guards during the Cultural Revolution, Rong returned to favor in the 1970s as Deng Xiaoping's economic reform philosophies gained ascendency. In 1979 Deng asked Rong to found CITIC, reportedly on the premise that it "be boldly creative."

CITIC staffers are well educated and knowledgeable about international banking practices. Study abroad and fluency in a foreign language are said to be prerequisites to a CITIC job. Many senior staff members have advanced degrees from prestigious universities throughout the world.

Since its founding, CITIC has grown at a remarkable rate—it quadrupled both its assets and its earnings between 1984 and 1986—but it also has generated controversy. A subsidiary called Poly Technologies, which imports radar systems, aircraft, and ambulances to China, is believed to have been deeply involved in the sale of Silkworm missiles to Iran. The subsidiary also has been competing with other major Chinese government agencies for the U.S. gun market, principally in the sale of AK47 assault rifles, until an indefinite import ban was imposed on those weapons.

CITIC has invested $50 million in Citifor, a timber company in Washington State, and an undisclosed amount in real estate in Phoenix. It recently bought an interest in a gold mine in Colorado, and is said to be considering buying a group of companies on the West Coast that includes another lumber operation.

FIGURE 23.1 ▪ **Chinese Ad Resembling Western Ads**

Source: *China Daily*, April 9, 1988, 8.

clearly in the direction of increased market involvement. Figure 23.2 provides a graphic display of this beginning market orientation.

All of these changes do not occur without problems. One major difficulty encountered is the lack of an appropriate infrastructure of information about markets. For example, very little knowledge exists about pricing, advertising, research, and trading, and few institutions are able to accurately assess and channel supply to the points of demand. As a result, major educational missionary work needs to be carried out in order to provide such information. The International Marketplace 23.3 gives an example of such efforts.

A second set of problems is encountered in the bureaucratic implementation of change. Managers still are worried about the qualitative demands of export production and have little incentive to master the technicalities

FIGURE 23.2 ▪ **Macroeconomic Systems of the U.S.S.R. and Eastern Europe**

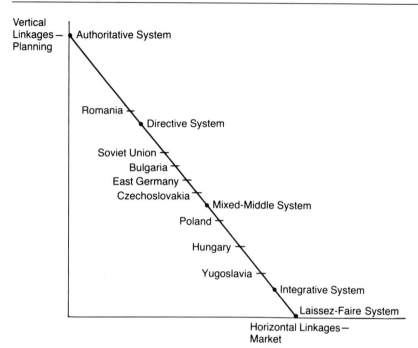

Source: A. Coskun Samli, "Changing Marketing Systems in Eastern Europe: What Western Marketers Should Know," *International Marketing Review* 3 (Winter 1986): 8.

of international trade and finance.[9] Because of the total lack of prior market orientation, even easy reforms require an almost unimaginable array of decisions about business licenses, the setting of optimal tax rates, rules of business operation, definitions of business expenses for taxation purposes, safety standards and nondiscrimination rules, consumer protection measures, and the establishment of a reliable supply system.[10]

Of greatest concern, however, is the continuing struggle between conflicting **ideologies.** By no means is it settled that centrally planned economies will leave all past orientations permanently behind and base themselves on market forces. Resistance against such change comes from various quarters and for differing reasons. For example, the availability of greater financial latitude for firms also requires that inefficient firms be permitted to go into bankruptcy—a concept not cherished by many. Wage reforms threaten to relegate blue-collar workers, who were traditionally favored by the Socialist system, to second-class status, while permitting the emergence of a new entrepreneurial class of the rich, which has not

[9]H. Stephen Gardner, "Restructuring the Soviet Foreign Trade System," *Columbia Journal of World Business* 23 (Summer 1988): 7–12.

[10]Jerry F. Hough, *Opening Up the Soviet Economy* (Washington D.C.: The Brookings Institution, 1988), 46.

THE INTERNATIONAL MARKETPLACE 23.3

New Education in Hungary   *At Karl Marx University in Budapest,*
Das Kapital no longer is required reading. These days, Hungary's
managerial hopefuls seem more keen to learn about American
businessman Dale Morris.

The Oklahoman's effort to market a new seasoning product is
just one of several case studies that form the core curriculum at the
International Management Center (IMC), a joint-venture business
school set up by Hungarian Credit Bank president Sandor Demjan
to train Western-style managers. Operating since April 1989 from a
restored 19th century manor on the outskirts of Budapest, the cen-
ter sees itself as an incubator for East-bloc entrepreneurs. By creat-
ing a "manager's identity," the IMC hopes to rebuild expertise
eroded by four decades of Communist central planning. "We have
to make up for our 'lost decades,'" explained Tamas Toth, a former
IBM executive and the center's deputy managing director.

Hungary's search for excellence appears to be paying off. Within
the first three months after IMC's opening, some 200 students had
completed eight semester-length courses taught by a faculty of four
foreign and four Hungarian instructors. "They came up with some
very good ideas," reported Robert Hisrich, one of the professors. "It
just shows how deep the entrepreneurial spirit is in this country."
The school next began to offer a 10-month class costing $10,000
that gives young managers business-degree credits at the Univer-
sity of Pittsburgh.

Source: Mihaly Batki, "East Bloc Meets Mysterious West." Copyright 1989, *U.S.
News & World Report.* Reprinted with permission from the July 31, 1989 issue, p. 42.

been seen in many decades. Retail price reforms may endanger the safety
net of large population segments, while wholesale price changes introduce inflation and cyclical fluctuations into the economy. Furthermore,
many decision makers in Socialist countries may not be prepared to provide the legal transparency and institutional security that are the basic
conditions for the stability of economic change.[11]

As a result, it is probably appropriate to speak of the development of a
Socialist market orientation that retains much of the social fabric of central planning and in its implementation differs substantially from a free
market society, particularly when conflicts with ideological postulates
occur.

In spite of the apparent international thawing of the rigid lines drawn by
ideology, the international marketer must remember that government dic-

[11]Mihaly Simai, *East-West Co-Operation at the End of the 1980s: Global Issues, Foreign Direct Investments and Debts* (Budapest: Hungarian Scientific Council for World Economy,
1989), 62.

23.4 THE INTERNATIONAL MARKETPLACE

China Business after Tiananmen Square   *"When are you coming back?" implore the telexes, faxes, and phone calls from China to foreign partners. In raising the question—and in their hurried, nervous efforts to reassure Western investors that their country is still a good place to do business—Chinese managers are taking their cue from Deng Xiaoping. Despite his bloody swerve to the right, the 84-year-old strongman insists China's door is still open to foreign capital and technology.*

But business will not go on as usual—not anytime soon. Deng may genuinely want to keep the door open, and he may be able to do so despite the reemergence of more conservative leaders who want less contact with the West. The question is whether Westerners will want to walk through such an uncertain opening.

The immediate foreign reaction to the Tiananmen massacre was dramatic. Western buyers of such Chinese goods as toys and garments canceled orders, unwilling to risk the possibility that future turmoil would disrupt production. Japanese steelmakers, for whom China is a major export market, announced a production cut because of uncertainties about future demand. China's $230 million purchase of New Zealand steel fell through, apparently scuttled by edgy foreign lenders. Scores of companies active in China rushed to shift some operations to Thailand and other low-cost countries.

As a semblance of order returns, U.S., European, and Japanese companies with operations in China will likely crank up again. But many executives say they will postpone—or cancel—future investments. Some plan to shift orders for Chinese goods to Asian neighbors—Thailand and the Philippines among them. Tourists, who regard automatic-weapons fire as worse than losing traveler's checks, will certainly stay away. And many Chinese students and scholars studying and working abroad will not return.

China is the biggest loser. "The Chinese economy will slow down significantly," predicts Kenji Dobashi, managing director of Nomura Research International in Hong Kong. The tortuous, ten-year experiment with capitalist incentives, which produced stunning growth and held such promise for the future, is stalled. Not for a long time will liberal-minded economists press hard for more reform.

In such a fluid situation, the best advice is to make no big decisions about China until you absolutely must. When the time comes to place your bet, it's wise to remember that even your best assumptions are just that—your assumptions, not necessarily those of the aging cadres in Zhongnanhai, the placid compound near Tiananmen Square where China's senior leaders live and jockey for power.

Source: Ford S. Worthy, "What's Next for Business in China," FORTUNE, July 17, 1989, 110–112. © 1989 The Time Inc. Magazine Company. All rights reserved.

tates and postulates are still the overriding determinant in Socialist countries. Regardless of the public liberalization measures taken, doing business with nonmarket economies continues to involve state trading, and therefore continues to be subject not only to market but also to political imperatives. Shifts can come about rather quickly and harshly, making carefully laid plans rapidly obsolete. The occurrences in China during the spring of 1989 are one example of such rapid turns of events. The International Marketplace 23.4 provides a realistic portrayal of the subsequent business uncertainty. The international marketer must remember the fragility of change and evaluate risks carefully when appraising the new opportunities presented by Socialist economies.

Given the current flux within the trade apparatus of Socialist economies, establishing the initial contact can be quite difficult. Even though many organizations may be registered to carry out international transactions, shortcomings in capabilities may make some of them inappropriate trading partners. Frequently, the **foreign trade organizations (FTO)** continue to be a good initial vehicle for contact because of their expertise and widespread contacts.

Awareness of products can sometimes be established through the embassies of nonmarket economies or organizations that represent them, such as Amtorg, which represents Soviet FTOs in the United States. In addition, introductory letters can be written to the FTO. The drawback to this approach is that, without end-user contact, precise needs are difficult to determine. If the identity and special problems of the ultimate user are not known, presenting a viable product proposition is difficult.

A better approach is to participate in a **trade fair.** If handled properly, fairs offer a major opportunity for market entry.[12] However, thorough preparation and proper follow-up are crucial in successful trade fair participation. Although the international marketer cannot be expected to be fully versed in all details of trade fair participation, assistance by both governmental and nongovernmental organizations is becoming increasingly available, as The International Marketplace 23.5 demonstrates.

Trade fairs are held frequently in nonmarket economies. Some of them have become the main point of contact for foreign buyers and sellers. For example, twice a year, China holds the Guangzhou (formerly Canton) Fair, which is considered an excellent place to initiate business. However, because participation is by invitation only, advance preparation is essential; this would include contact initiation and translation of major materials into the host-country language. The major advertised fairs are not the only ones that can be of use to the international marketer. Increasingly, smaller minifairs are held on a regional basis and may be of equal value if the region where the fair is offered is where most end-users are located. When participating in such an event, the international marketer should keep in mind that contracts are rarely signed on the first visit. Rather, the purpose

[12]Cecil G. Howard, "Follow These Tips When Entering East European Markets," *Marketing News,* August 17, 1984, 17, 20.

THE INTERNATIONAL MARKETPLACE

Participating in an East European Trade Fair Technik and Trade, a company based in Cleveland, Ohio, has displayed substantial initiative in exhibiting at the Leipzig trade fair. The firm's president, Dr. Bernd Brunner, was granted a stand as a main exhibitor and he sublets space to other Ohio firms, among them the International Trade Development Office of the State of Ohio, Accu-Ray of Columbus, Agri-Tec of Spencerville, and TRW of Cleveland. However, Brunner does not simply offer exhibit space. He has developed a package concept that includes background training on the history and politics of East Germany and on the city of Leipzig for the personnel at the exhibit on East-West trade. He is also planning to make arrangements for fair exhibits that will include distributing company literature to the right officials before the fair, setting up appointments during the fair, and helping with post-fair follow-up, including visits to plants and farms when possible. Brunner has persuaded a German trade official to address company representatives at his exhibit before the fair, thus making certain that the attention focused on firms that sublet space from him is well out of proportion to the size of their trade levels with the German Democratic Republic.

Source: "U.S. Trading Firm Takes Initiative, Tackles GDR," *Business Eastern Europe,* June 14, 1985, 188–189.

of fair participation is to stimulate demand-pull from end-users vis-à-vis their foreign trade apparatus.

Another major form of market entry is the seminar route. Here, representatives of firms offer to present their technology, product information, and expertise through **technical seminars.** In this way, initial product familiarity and awareness are achieved, and subsequent negotiations can be initiated. Again, detailed technical preparation is necessary, because invitations are required in order to present seminars in most nonmarket economies.

Gradually, however, the rigid isolation of end-users is fading. Western executives report that more recently direct interaction is facilitated and that unscheduled visits to end-user plants are increasingly permitted. To assist in the task of identifying potential end-users and facilitating contact with them, research organizations formed either by the government or by the private sector are increasingly available,[13] not just in the capitals of countries, but also on a state or province level.[14]

[13] Wolfgang J. Koschnick, "Russian Bear Bullish on Marketing," *Marketing News,* November 21, 1988, 1, 18.

[14] For example, in 1988, the Ukrainian state government formed a Centre for Business Analysis and Marketing Research in Kiev.

The Negotiation Process

Virtually every international marketing transaction carried out with centrally planned economies requires negotiations. Very rarely are purchase orders simply forwarded.[15]

The **negotiations process** typically is divided into technical negotiations and commercial negotiations. The process is customarily initiated with **technical negotiations,** which can be quite lengthy, sometimes taking up to three years to complete. The rationale is that the product–service offering of the seller needs to be fully understood before commercial terms can be discussed. The reason for frequent delays at this stage of the negotiations can again be found in the structure of the trade apparatus.

First of all, in spite of the liberalization measures taken, many layers of review still exist for each proposal. More important, there still seems to be little incentive to hasten negotiations. For example, Chinese negotiators do not appear to earn plaudits for a job well done, but they are vulnerable to censure should the contract not adequately protect China's and their unit's interests. There is no encouragement to bring their discussions to an end, either in order to return to their job or to earn a bonus for completing a job. Once the current set of contracts is signed, they simply move on to a new round of negotiations.[16]

At this stage of the negotiations, the foreign firm is expected to share vast amounts of its technical information. At the same time, socialist negotiators will often be unwilling to share their data. This of course makes it very difficult for Western negotiators to be fully responsive to their potential client's needs.

An additional problem results from export control provisions. In order to disclose technical information, Western firms often need export licenses from their governments. Delays in obtaining the license often protract the initial negotiation process. Yet the licensing requirement for the disclosure of technical data can also be seen as helpful, because it provides an advance indication of whether the product under negotiation can be sold to the negotiation partner.

Continuing the negotiation process, **commercial negotiations** serve to define delivery terms, financing, countertrade requirements, and other contractual terms and conditions. These negotiations also can be quite time-consuming. Very often, the time involved is used as a negotiation tactic in itself, with negotiators in centrally planned economies aware that Western industrial firms and their managers are frequently subject to stringent time demands and under pressure to produce results quickly. Protracted negotiations may, therefore, produce results more favorable to the party that can more afford to wait things out, namely, the negotiator from the centrally planned economy.

[15] Mikhail Nite, "Getting to Da," *Export Today,* Summer 1985, 37–40.

[16] Kenneth Lieberthal and Michel Oksenberg, "Understanding China's Bureaucracy," *The China Business Review,* November–December, 1986, 24–31.

The major issues covered in commercial negotiations are financing, pricing, and performance. Centrally planned economies place major emphasis on reducing their hard currency outflow. This goal frequently results in demands for buy-backs, compensation deals, or barter arrangements. In price negotiations, representatives of nonmarket economies are unwilling to discuss factors such as inflation and price-escalation clauses. They prefer to insist on fixed-price contracts. Because many projects involve lengthy time spans for their completion, however, Western negotiators insist on some price adjustment possibility. Nonmarket economies often characterize transactions as a "foot in the door." Negotiators encourage international marketers to offer a low price in order to gain a foothold in the market. However, because of the uncertainty of follow-up orders, most marketers experienced in trading with nonmarket economies suggest that any particular transaction should be required to stand financially on its own, or should not be consummated at all.

Major attention is also paid to specifying details of contract performance. Here, factors such as "acts of God" are rarely accepted by Communist countries. However, using a slightly different phrasing, **force majeure,** often enables the Western negotiator to include clauses that describe specific circumstances in which the contracting parties are released from fulfilling the contractual obligations.

In contracts that call for cooperative efforts, a detailed clarification of the responsibilities of each trading partner is very important. Otherwise, obligations that were anticipated to be the duty of one contracting party may result in costs to the other. As an example, Rosenlew Oy, a major Finnish industrial corporation, had to pay a $600,000 fine to Hungary's Chemokomplex for delays in the completion of a furfural plant. Parts to be provided by the Hungarian side seldom appeared on time, but Rosenlew, as the major contractor, was held responsible.[17]

Overall, contracts negotiated with centrally planned economies are usually more specific and detailed than contracts customarily encountered in the Western world. Although arriving at contract terms may be a lengthy and time-consuming process, the international marketer can fully expect that the terms, once agreed upon, will be stringently adhered to.[18] By the same token, compliance requirements for the Western trading partner are also quite stringent. This practice may be burdensome, but it does provide benefits to the international marketer in that expectations are known and the outcome of contracts is therefore more predictable.

Negotiators in nonmarket economies frequently view the negotiation process as a test for potential trading partners. They reason that a company that can survive a complex and lengthy negotiation process is much

---

[17] "Negotiating in Eastern Europe," *Business Eastern Europe,* October 17, 1980, 320–330.

[18] Simon Chilewich, "Why Trade with the Russians?" in *Common Sense in U.S.–Soviet Trade,* eds. M. Chapman and C. Marcy (Washington, D.C.: American Committee on East-West Accord, 1983), 51.

more likely to be a good trading partner than one who balks at delays.[19] Also, the participation by top management in negotiations is seen as an indication of a firm's commitment to the particular international marketing transaction. Although negotiations are unlikely to result in personal friendships between the parties, the development of a close official relationship is definitely sought. In the People's Republic of China, for example, for the international marketer to earn the title "old friend" is very valuable. It is used only for people who can be counted on personally and, in turn, can be relied on to recommend other trustworthy parties.[20]

Marketing Challenges and Opportunities

The pressure for change in many centrally planned economies represents vast opportunities for the future expansion of international marketing activities.[21] Large populations offer potential consumer demand and production supply that is unmatched by any other region in the world. Furthermore, the knowledge of the international marketer may be particularly useful to centrally planned economies where marketing skills are only rudimentarily developed. These countries need assistance and contacts to reshape their domestic economies and penetrate foreign markets. For example, the Soviet Union is already asking for help in areas such as business and personnel training, marketing, banking, auditing and compilation of statistics.[22]

Doing business with Socialist governments also presents multiple challenges. Centrally planned economies inherently have substantially less flexibility than free market economies in adjusting to market demands. This lack of adjustment capability is often not a problem, because market demand is frequently not of primary concern to the decision makers. Nevertheless, the lack of capability to react to changes quickly, coupled with the difficulty of developing comprehensive plans, results in inefficiency and great difficulties for the international marketer.

A second major concern is the limitation placed on goods that can be sold to centrally planned economies. The international marketer needs to consider the current and future political environments when planning long-term business commitment. A third major challenge is the lack of contact with end-users. The entire marketing discipline is founded on the basic objective of satisfying the needs and wants of individuals and organizations. Unable to ascertain their desires, the international marketer

---

[19] Nite, "Getting to Da," 37.

[20] John W. De Pauw, *U.S.–Chinese Trade Negotiations* (New York: Praeger, 1981), 64.

[21] Jonathan Sanders, "A New Era in Soviet–American Trade," *Columbia Journal of World Business* 23 (Summer 1988): 5–6.

[22] Janet Porter, "Western Consultants Benefit as Soviets Restructure Business," *The Journal of Commerce*, July 12, 1988, 1A, 3A.

must use secondary information, such as hearsay, educated guesses, and elaborations of intermediaries.

Finally, the major difficulty encountered in marketing to governments is the frequent unavailability of hard currency. Products, however necessary, often cannot be purchased by centrally planned economies because no funds are available to pay for them. As a result, many of these countries resort to barter and countertrade mechanisms. This places an additional burden on the international marketer, who not only must market products to the government but must take products back that in turn have to be marketed to other consumers and institutions.

Similar problems are encountered when the international marketer attempts to source products from centrally planned economies. Many firms have found that "selling" is not part of the economic culture of most centrally planned economies. The descriptive materials that are made available are often poorly written and devoid of useful information. To obtain additional information on a product may be difficult and time-consuming. This situation is a result of a system that does not encourage risk taking and often punishes mistakes severely.[23]

The quality of the products obtained can also represent a major problem. Centrally planned economies tend to place primary emphasis on product performance and, to a large extent, neglect any concern with style or product presentation. The result is "a willingness to leave equipment rough and unfinished when lack of finishing does not significantly affect function."[24] Before sourcing products from centrally planned economies, therefore, the international marketer needs to forge agreements that require the manufacturer to improve quality, provide for technical control, and ensure prompt delivery. Such demands for improvement frequently produce problems and tensions that hamper further cooperation.[25]

Even when satisfactory products are obtained from centrally planned economies, the marketing of these products in other markets can be a major problem. One study has shown that negative **attitudes** exist toward products sourced from centrally planned economies. This appears to be particularly true for consumer products. International marketers "will find a portion of the population [in the United States] hesitant to purchase [such] goods."[26]

Nevertheless, sufficient opportunity exists to make consideration of these international marketing activities worthwhile. Centrally planned

[23] John W. Kiser, "Tapping Soviet Technology," in *Common Sense in U.S.–Soviet Trade*, eds. M. Chapman and C. Marcy (Washington, D.C.: American Committee on East-West Accord, 1983), 108.

[24] Ibid, 104.

[25] Leon Zurawicki, "The Cooperation of the Socialist State with the MNC's," *Columbia Journal of World Business* 10 (Spring 1975): 112.

[26] Robert D. Hisrich, Michael P. Peters, and Arnold K. Weinstein, "East-West Trade: The View from the United States," *Journal of International Business Studies* 12 (Winter 1981): 109–121.

TABLE 23.4 ▪ **Active Soviet Licenses in the United States**

Technology	_Sold To_	_Approximate Date_
Surgical Stapling Instruments	U.S. Surgical Corp.	1964
	3M	1979
Hydraulic Rock Crusher	Joy Manufacturing	1969
Pneumatic Underground Punch "Hole Hog"	Allied Steel & Tractor	1971
Evaporative Stave Cooling of Blast Furnaces	Andco Engineering	1972
Aluminum Silicon Alloy	Ethyl Corporation	1973
Production of Hollow Ingots by Electroslag Remelting	Cabot	1973
Flux Cored Electrodes	Chemetron	1974
Magnetic Impact Bonding	Maxwell Laboratories	1974
Drug Pyrroxan for Treating Central Nervous System Disorders	American Home Products	1974
Ethnozin for Treating Cardiac Arrest	Dupont	1974
Electromagnetic Casting of Aluminum	Kaiser Aluminum	1975
	Reynolds Aluminum	
	Alcoa	
Carboxide Insect Repellant	American Home Products	1975
In-Situ Underground Coal Gasification	Texas Utilities Services, Inc.	1975
Carminomycin and Ftorafur Anti-Cancer Agents	Bristol Myers	1976
Bulat Process for Titanium Nitriding	Multiarc Vacuum Systems	1979
Flash Butt Welding of Large Diameter Pipes	J. R. McDermott	1980
Electromagnetic Casting of Copper Alloys	Olin Brass	1980
Cone Crusher	Rexnord	1981
Air Column Separator	Air Products	1981
Medical Preparation Riocidin	Ciba-Geigy USA	1982
Biodegradable Polymer Pin for Orthopedics	Medco	1982

Source: John W. Kiser, III, "Tapping Soviet Technology," in _Common Sense in U.S.—Soviet Trade,_ eds. M. Chapman and C. Marcy (Washington, D.C.: American Committee on East-West Accord, 1983), 107–108.

economies do have products that can be of use in free market economies and are often unique in their product performance. For example, Table 23.4 lists Soviet licenses that are used in the United States. Most of these licenses are for industrial rather than consumer products, which is a reflection of the Soviet orientation in terms of research and development.

FIGURE 23.3   ▪   **Advertisement for Soviet Launch Services**

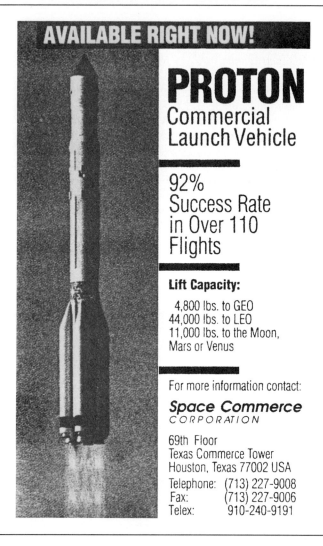

Similarly, industrial services are provided very competitively, as Figure 23.3 shows.

Consumer products may in time play a larger role. Lower labor costs and, in some instances, the greater availability of labor may enable centrally planned economies to offer consumers in free market economies a variety of product choice at a lower cost. This is particularly likely for consumer products with a high value-added component, an example of which is shown in Figure 23.4.

FIGURE 23.4   ▪   **New Soviet Consumer Products for the Decadent West**

Source: *The Wall Street Journal*, August 24, 1987, 17.

Centrally planned economies do not have to follow the **product life cycle** of the industrialized nations, which consists of domestic product introduction, gradual market penetration, and subsequent exports. Because the satisfaction of domestic demand is dependent on government directives, new products can immediately be exported. The People's Republic of China might therefore, for example, produce vast quantities of low-cost cars and designate virtually all of the production for export. This capability to quickly develop important export sectors is reason for the international marketer to maintain relations with centrally planned economies in order not to lose a potentially valuable source of supply.

MARKETING WITH STATE-OWNED ENTERPRISES

One phenomenon that has increasingly emerged in non-Communist countries over the past two decades is the **state-owned enterprise.** Figure 23.5 provides an overview of the extent to which this form of corporation exists in various industrial sectors of major economies. Many of these enterprises are active on an international level. In 1979, state enterprises were responsible for more than 20 percent of world sales by the 500 largest international business corporations headquartered outside the United States.[27] State-owned enterprises represent a formidable pool of international suppliers, customers, and competitors to the international marketer.

Reason for the Emergence of State-Owned Enterprises

Various economic and noneconomic factors have contributed to the dramatic increase of state-owned enterprises. Two primary ones are **national security** and economic security. Many countries believe that, for national security purposes, certain industrial sectors need to be under state control. Typically, these sectors include the telecommunications, airline, banking, and energy industries.

The citing of **economic security** reasons occurs primarily in countries that are heavily dependent on specific industries for their economic performance. This may be the case when countries are heavily commodity-dependent. For example, in 18 African countries, one commodity contributes more than half of export revenues.[28] Governments frequently believe that, given such heavy national dependence on a particular industrial sector, government control is necessary to ensure national economic health.

Other reasons have also contributed to the development of state-owned enterprises. On occasion, the sizable investment required for the develop-

---

[27] Douglas F. Lamont, *Foreign State Enterprises* (New York: Basic Books, 1979).

[28] Martin C. Schnitzer, Marilyn L. Liebrenz, and Connard W. Kubin, *International Business* (Cincinnati, Ohio: South-Western Publishing Company, 1985), 421.

FIGURE 23.5 ▪ Frontiers of the State: The International Extent of Public Enterprise at the Start of the 1980s

Private Sector:
○ More Than 75%

Public Sector:
◕ 25%   ◑ 50%
◕ 75%
● More Than 75%

	Posts	Telecommunications	Electricity	Gas	Oil Production	Coal	Railways	Airlines	Motor Industry	Steel	Shipbuilding	
Australia	●	●	●	●	○	○	●	◕	○	○	na	Australia
Austria	●	●	●	●	●	●	●	●	●	●	na	Austria
Belgium	●	●	◔	◔	na	○	●	●	○	◑	○	Belgium
Brazil	●	●	●	●	●	●	◕	○	◕	○		Brazil
Britain	●	●	●	●	◔	●	●	◕	◑	◕	●	Britain
Canada	●	◕	●	○	○	○	◕	◕	○	○	○	Canada
France	●	●	●	●	na	●	●	◕	◑	◕	○	France
West Germany	●	●	◕	◑	◕	◑	●	●	◕	○	◕	West Germany
Holland	●	●	◕	◕	na	na	●	◕	◑	◕	○	Holland
India	●	●	●	●	●	●	●	●	○	◕	●	India
Italy	●	●	◕	●	na	na	●	●	◕	◕	◕	Italy
Japan	●	●	○	○	na	○	◕	◕	○	○	○	Japan
Mexico	●	●	●	●	●	●	●	◑	◕	◕	●	Mexico
South Korea	●	●	◕	○	na	◕	●	○	○	◕	○	South Korea
Spain	●	◑	○	◕	na	◑	●	●	○	◑	◕	Spain
Sweden	●	●	◑	●	na	na	●	◑	○	◕	◕	Sweden
Switzerland	●	●	●	●	na	na	●	◕	○	○	na	Switzerland
United States	●	○	◕	○	○	○	◕	○	○	○	○	United States

Source: *The Economist*, December 21, 1985, p. 72. © 1985 *The Economist*, distributed by Special Features. Reprinted by permission.

ment of an industry is not available from the private sector. Governments, therefore, close the gap between national needs and private sector resources by developing industries themselves. In addition, governments often decide to rescue failing private enterprises by placing them in government ownership. In so doing, they fulfill important policy objectives such as the maintenance of jobs, the development of depressed areas, or the increase of exports.

Finally, some governments have held that state-owned firms may be better for the country than privately held companies, because they may be more societally oriented and therefore contribute more to the greater good. This is particularly the case in areas such as telecommunications and transportation, where **profit maximization,** at least from a governmental perspective, may not always be the appropriate primary objective.

Relevance of State-Owned Enterprises to the International Marketer

Three types of activities in which the international marketer is likely to encounter state-owned enterprises are market entry, the sourcing or marketing process, and international competition.

On occasion, the very existence of a state-owned enterprise may inhibit or prohibit foreign market entry by the international marketer. For reasons of development and growth, governments frequently make market entry from the outside quite difficult so that the state-owned enterprise can perform according to plan. Even if market entry is permitted, often the conditions under which the international marketer can conduct business are substantially less favorable than the conditions under which the state-owned enterprises operate. Therefore, the international marketer may be placed at a competitive disadvantage and may not be able to perform successfully, even though economic factors would indicate success.

The international marketer also faces a unique situation when sourcing from or marketing to state-owned enterprises. Even though the state-owned firm may appear to be simply another partner in the marketing process, ultimately it is an extension of the government and its activities. This may mean that, quite often, a state-owned enterprise conducts its transactions according to the policy of the country rather than according to economic rationale because political forces have a much greater impact on public sector organizations than on private sector organizations.[29] For example, political considerations can play a decisive role in the determination of purchasing decisions. Contracts may be concluded for non-economic reasons rather than based on product offering and performance. Contract conditions may depend on foreign policy outlook, prices may be altered to reflect government displeasure, and delivery performance may change to "send a signal." Exports and imports may be delayed or encouraged depending on the needs of government. Even though an economic rationale appears to exist within a state-owned enterprise, the interests and concerns of the owners—the state—may lead it to be driven by policy issues.[30]

This also holds true when the international marketer encounters international competition from state-owned enterprises. Very often, the con-

[29]Charles W. Lamb, Jr., "Public Sector Marketing Is Different," *Business Horizons*, July–August 1987, 56–60.

[30]Renato Mazzolini, "European Government-Controlled Enterprises: An Organizational Politics View," *Journal of International Business Studies* 11 (Spring–Summer 1980): 48–58.

TABLE 23.5 ▪ **Corporate Responses to Government Policies Protecting Home Industries**

Country	Industry	Details of Policy Implementation	Competitive Response
Brazil	Aerospace/ Commuter Aircraft	—controlled technology transfer —home market protection —defense procurement —export credit subsidies —state-owned enterprise	—sell components to Embraer: 55 percent import content —enter into joint ventures with Embraer —request U.S. government (U.S.I.T.C.) retaliation
Brazil	Computers	—market reserve for domestic corporation for eight years —ban on foreign ownership —government supervised licensing of technology —tax subsidies	—license older technology —establish indirect market presence in anticipation of removal of controls —obtain market share in related industry—software—in antic- ipation of similar controls
France	Computers/Tele- communications	—government funds for R&D and capital investment in five-year electronics plan —dependence on government- owned companies —domestic firms favored in government procurement	—enter into joint venture with French firms —obtain access to nonreserved share of market, for example AT&T —obtain indirect market share through other EC firms
France	Aerospace/ Airbus Industry	—state-owned enterprise —government funding of R&D losses over 17 years —export credit subsidies —countertrade	—obtain U.S. government— Exim Bank credit subsidies —concentrate on new product development —match Airbus's sales terms

Source: Ravi Sarathy and Samuel Rabino, "Corporate Responses to Industrial Policy," *International Marketing Review* 4 (Summer 1987):40.

centration of these firms is not in areas of comparative advantage, but rather in areas that at the time are most beneficial for the government owning the firm. Factor input costs often pale in their importance compared to policy objectives. Sometimes, state-owned enterprises may not even know the value of the products they buy and sell, because prices themselves have such a low priority. As a result, the international marketer may be confronted with competition that is very tough to beat.

The Strategic Response to the State-Owned Enterprise

Given the problems that state-owned enterprises can represent for the international marketer, various strategic alternatives for dealing with this challenge should be considered. Table 23.5 provides some examples of corporate responses to government policies that protect home industries.

One major alternative is that of demonstrating the benefits of working through private sector and free market activities rather than government control. If results can show that the benefits gained from government control are far outweighed by its cost, foreign policymakers may reconsider the value of creating state-owned enterprises. The United States, for example, has taken an international lead by deregulating some industries that were tightly controlled or regulated. As a result of U.S. activity, a philosophical realignment has taken place in other countries, reversing the trend toward state ownership. The International Marketplace 23.6 explains the rationale and process of such **privatization** in the United Kingdom.

A second type of response to the state-owned enterprise is that of international negotiations and government intervention to "level the playing field." Whenever discriminatory market conditions are encountered by the international marketer, complaints can be launched to the home government. These complaints in turn can be accumulated and aired at meetings of international trade negotiators, with the goal of changing the discrimination. Alternatively, particularly in the United States, lawsuits can be brought in court against unfair competition from abroad. If the findings are favorable, penalties for subsidization or dumping are frequently imposed against foreign firms.

A third response lies in the antitrust area, particularly for firms or industries in which economies of scale play a major role. In order to provide relief for firms that are subject to pressures by large-scale state-owned enterprises, governments can consider reducing the application of antitrust provisions. In the United States, for example, antitrust laws were originally written with strictly domestic competition rather than global competitiveness in mind. Their relaxation permits domestic firms to cooperate in domestic and international activities through such measures as joint research and development efforts.

The strategic responses described may be valuable in the medium and long term. For the short term, the international marketer needs to persevere in the international marketplace in spite of the existence of state-owned enterprises, and this often means dealing with such enterprises. In doing so, the international marketer must be wary of current policy objectives and policy changes. Marketing proposals for either sourcing or selling must be structured with the **economic rationale** in mind, but also consider the policy imperative under which the state-owned enterprise operates. In addition, the marketer must develop alternative sources of supply and contingency plans for cases of rapid shifts in demand in order to remain at least partially insulated from sudden policy actions by state-owned enterprises.

The international marketer can also seek opportunities that are created by the very existence of state-owned enterprises. For example, there may be room for joint ventures or cooperation agreements. Alternatively, the international marketer may be able to provide services such as management training or distribution agreements. Moreover, the current trend to-

THE INTERNATIONAL MARKETPLACE   **23.6**

Privatization in the United Kingdom   In 1979, the government of
the United Kingdom embarked on an ambitious program of returning state-owned corporations to the private sector. The intention
behind the government's privatization and competition policies
was to replace the surrogate market with the real market.

Privatization is intended to benefit customers, employees, and
the economy as a whole. Customers benefit when the greater efficiency that can be achieved through privatization is passed on to
them, for example, in the form of prices that are lower than they
would otherwise have been, wider choice, and better service. Privatized businesses are likely to be more responsive to changing
customer demands and more innovative in introducing new
products to the market.

For employees, privatization means working in a company with
clear objectives, the resources to achieve them, and rewards for
success. This, in turn, reinforces the concern for the customer that
is at the heart of any successful business.

The economy benefits through higher returns on capital in the
privatized industries, which can no longer preempt resources from
elsewhere in the economy but must compete for funds in the open
capital markets. And as the products and services of privatized industries underpin much activity elsewhere in the economy, there
are substantial benefits for other businesses.

These advantages are borne out in the success for privatized
companies. Among companies that have been in the private sector
for a number of years, the profits for Cable and Wireless, British
Aerospace, Amersham International, and the National Freight Consortium have increased significantly. Among more recent entrants
to the private sector, British Telecom has eliminated waiting lists
for telephone installations; Jaguar has made major advances in
product quality, sales, and profits; and British Gas has increased
profits and the number of its customers.

Seventeen major companies had been privatized as of May 1988.
Receipts were some 17 billion pounds, with future sales projected
at a rate of about 5 billion per year. About 650,000 jobs had been
transferred to the private sector.

Source: *Current Major Themes in Industrial Policy: Privatization,* submission by the
Delegation of the United Kingdom, Organization for Economic Cooperation and Development, DSTI/IND/88.22/17, Paris, October 12, 1988.

ward privatization in many countries may also offer new opportunities to the international marketer.

State-owned enterprises often originate very large projects. Because domestic supply is frequently insufficient for the needs of such projects, there may be room for the participation of foreign firms, particularly when new technology or sophisticated project management techniques are required. Yet proper caution must be exercised so that the marketer can be assured of participating in a successful venture.

In many instances, large-scale projects are cofinanced by international institutions such as the World Bank or regional institutions like the Interamerican Development Bank. Even though these organizations make allowances for the policy aims of the borrower, they also impose stringent requirements regarding the efficiency of the project. They may therefore provide for a domestic sourcing preference but insist on limits to the extent of such a preference. Cofinanced projects therefore offer interesting opportunities to the international marketer, particularly because their contracting requirements are reasonably tightly defined and easily available internationally through the financing institutions.

SUMMARY

Special concerns must be considered by the international marketer when dealing with governments or with state-owned enterprises. The centrally planned economies of the Soviet Union, Eastern Europe, and China work with a foreign trade apparatus that is significantly different from the accustomed market forces.

In these countries the state has a major impact on trade. Purchasing and selling decisions are often made based on plans that have been developed by the government. Even though the trading systems in these countries have begun to open up to the West in recent years, the international marketer must always remember that trade has not only an economic but also a political price tag and that political winds may shift.

The centrally planned system also makes it very difficult to establish contact with the end-user. The initial contact is most often made through an intermediary. Participation in trade fairs or in international seminars are also possibilities.

Negotiations are usually lengthy, difficult, and quite detailed. Their format is a function of the trade apparatus, the system-inherent risks and rewards, the continued distrust in Western trading partners, and the need for negotiators to assess their trading partner's commitment to the relationship. Once negotiations are completed, however, scrupulous adherence to the terms agreed upon can be expected.

Often, the international marketer is also faced with state-owned enterprises, which have been formed in non-Communist nations for reasons of national or economic security. These firms may inhibit or prohibit foreign market entry, and frequently reflect in their transactions the overall domestic and foreign policy of a country rather than economic rationale.

The marketer must recognize these effects, encourage his or her government to negotiate relief from them, and consider them in any negotiations.

Questions for Discussion

1. Where do you see the greatest potential in future trade between Socialist countries and the West?

2. Planning is necessary, yet central planning is inefficient. Why?

3. What sales materials should a U.S. firm prepare for distribution at a Chinese trade fair?

4. Compare U.S. and Soviet negotation and contract philosophies.

5. Discuss the observation that "Soviet products do what they are supposed to do—but only that."

6. How can U.S. consumer acceptance of Soviet products be altered?

7. Do you see potential for a Chinese yang-tse car to successfully enter the U.S. market in 1995?

8. What lessons can one learn from the Chinese crackdown on Tiananmen Square?

9. Under what circumstances would you be in favor of state-owned enterprises?

10. What are some of the dangers of dealing with a state-owned enterprise?

11. Structure a service package that a state-owned enterprise could use in its international marketing efforts.

12. What are the benefits of privatization?

Recommended Readings

Bubnov, Boris. *Foreign Trade with the USSR: A Manager's Guide to Recent Reforms*. New York: Pergamon Press, 1987.

Carvounis, Chris, and Brinda Z. Carvounis. *U.S. Commercial Opportunities in the Soviet Union*. Westport, Conn.: Quorum Books, 1989.

Hough, Jerry F. *Opening up the Soviet Economy*. Washington, D.C.: The Brookings Institution, 1988.

Knight, Misha G. *How to Do Business with Russians: A Handbook and Guide for Western World Business People*. Westport, Conn.: Greenwood Press, 1987.

Simai, Mihaly. *East–West Cooperation at the End of the 1980s: Global Issues, Foreign Direct Investments and Debts*. Budapest: Hungarian Scientific Council for World Economy, 1989.

Theroux, Eugene, and Arthur L. George. *Joint Ventures in the Soviet Union: Law and Practice*. Washington, D.C.: Baker & McKenzie, 1989.

Trade between the United States and the Nonmarket Economy Countries. Quarterly publication of the United States International Trade Commission, Washington, D.C.

U.S. Department of Commerce. *Doing Business with China*. Washington, D.C.: Government Printing Office, 1983.

U.S.–Soviet Trade. Columbia Journal of World Business (Summer 1988).

CHAPTER 24

The Future

THE INTERNATIONAL MARKETPLACE

The Future   *Grand forecasts often become too embarrassing to invite reexamination. Those who saw the Futurama at the 1964–1965 New York World's Fair surely remember the displays of underwater resorts, lunar outposts, and other visions that remind us how naive we were. Such fairground futurism may be fun, but it's not much help in deciding where to bet with real money. Forgetting underwater resorts and all that, what kind of world can managers expect in the Nineties?*

A few things seem certain, and one is that "globalization" will continue to be an inescapable buzzword. Businesses will operate in an ever more interconnected world. With continuing advances in computers and communications, world financial markets will meld. Manufacturing prowess will appear almost suddenly in new Taiwans and South Koreas.

A shrinking world will mean an expanding clock. Managers will have to shape organizations that can respond quickly to developments abroad. As speed and agility become paramount virtues, we will see even more decentralization, with responsibility closer to the operating level.

American consumers will be within buying distance of an ever larger number of producers, so competition for the customer's money will intensify. Companies will have to tailor products to hot market segments, to fast-growing regions, to preferences of ethnic groups. With increasing globalization, companies will be unavoidably enmeshed with foreign customers, competitors, and suppliers. Futurist Marvin Cetron, president of Forecasting International, predicts that by the year 2000 industrial countries, on average, will be importing nearly 40 percent of the parts used in domestic manufacturing.

Companies will be forced to develop products and make decisions faster. They will adopt fluid structures that can be altered as business conditions change. More than being helped by computers, companies will live by them, shaping strategy and structure to fit new information technology. They will engage in even more joint ventures, gaining access to techniques and markets they might not have developed on their own. And they will have to cope with a work force made more demanding by a scarcity of labor.

The Nineties will be tougher than the Eighties, which seemed pretty tough. American companies did much to raise productivity and quality; they will have to do even more in the next decade. Says Ray Stata, chairman of Analog Devices: "What the electronics industry has to do to stay competitive in the next five years is incredible. It almost seems impossible." GE Chairman Jack Welch told his stockholders recently that "the Nineties will be a white-knuckle decade for global business . . . fast . . . exhilarating."

International marketers are constantly faced with a changing global environment, as The International Marketplace 24.1 shows. This is not a new situation nor one to be feared because change provides the opportunity for the emergence of new market positions. Recognizing the importance of change and adapting creatively to new situations is the daily bread of marketing professionals.

Recently, however, changes are occurring more frequently, more rapidly, and have a more severe impact. The past has lost much of its value as a predictor of the future. What occurs today may be not only altered in the future, but may be completely overturned or reversed. For example, some countries find that their major exports, which have increased steadily over decades, can drop off to zero in a matter of weeks. A nation's political stability can be completely disrupted over the course of a few months. Countries that have been considered enemies, and to which no business executive would dream of selling, suddenly become close allies and offer a wealth of business opportunities. Just a short time later, these opportunities may shrink dramatically because of new government policies. In all, international marketers today face complex and rapidly changing economic and political conditions.

This chapter will discuss possible future developments in the international marketing environment, highlight the implications of these changes for international marketing management, and offer suggestions for a creative response. The chapter will also explore the meaning of both environmental and strategic changes to the reader, with particular emphasis on career choice and career path alternatives in international marketing.

THE INTERNATIONAL MARKETING ENVIRONMENT

This section analyzes the international marketing environment by looking at political, financial, societal, and technological conditions of change and providing a glimpse of possible future developments as envisioned by a panel of experts.*

* This section draws heavily on research carried out at the Center for International Business and Trade at Georgetown University.

The Political Environment

The international political environment will continue to be shaped by the direction of trade among political blocs. Currently, this environment consists of the East-West blocs and the North-South blocs, but new formations are beginning to emerge.

The East-West Relationship Economic arguments are not expected to be the dominant force in the East-West relationship. Rather, strategic considerations will form the basis of business activity. Because of the impact of political shifts on business relationships, long-term planning will be difficult for the international manager. In spite of a desire for stability and consistency, businesses must be ready to adjust rapidly to new realities. U.S. goods and technology will continue to be stamped with a political price tag as well as an economic one.[1] In the East-West context, international marketers must remember that many policymakers view their activities as a privilege and not a right.[2] Nevertheless, policymakers will have to recognize that other nations' concerns must be taken into account, particularly because trade is increasingly important to the survival of their firms. Therefore, a reduction is needed in the number of short-term policy shifts, giving firms a broader planning horizon for their international marketing activities.

Interesting changes may also occur in the nature of economic competition within and from centrally planned economies. With increasing attention paid to market forces, production in Socialist countries may well achieve some gains in international competitiveness, leading not only to increased international market participation but also to decreased demand for traditional imports. At the same time, however, market forces may demand a vast increase in the import of consumer products that were heretofore considered inappropriate.

The North-South Relationship The distinction between developed and less developed countries is likely to continue. Some theoreticians argue that the economic gap among these two groups will diminish, whereas others hold that the gap will increase. Both arguments lead to the conclusion that a gap will endure for some time. Because of the relative poverty of the less developed countries, they will intensify the pressure on developed countries to quicken the pace of development. The international marketer will have a number of alternatives for effectively conducting business within this North-South context.

One clear alternative is that of continued international cooperation. The developed countries could relinquish part of their economic power to less developed ones, thus contributing actively to their development through a sharing of resources and technology. While **cross-subsidization** will be

---

[1] Richard M. Nixon, quoted by Lawrence J. Brady in "Trade Policy," *Business Week*, November 21, 1983, 23.

[2] Office of Technology Assessment, *Technology and East-West Trade* (Washington: Government Printing Office, 1979).

useful and necessary for the development of less developed countries, it will result in a declining rate of increase in the standard of living in the more developed ones.

A second alternative is that of confrontation. Because of an unwillingness to share resources and technology sufficiently (or excessively, depending on the point of view), the developing and the developed areas of the world may become increasingly hostile toward one another. As a result, the volume of international trade, both by mandate of governments and by choice of the private sector, could be severely reduced.

A third alternative is that of isolation. While there may be some cooperation between the two major blocs, both groups, in order to achieve their domestic and international goals, may choose to remain economically isolated. This alternative may be particularly attractive if the countries in each bloc believe that they face unique problems and must therefore seek their own solutions.

New Orientations   The people of some nations will quite possibly decide to reprioritize their values. The aim for financial progress and improved standards of living may well give way to priorities based on religion, the environment, social relations, or other factors. Such reorientation may result in complete reversals of currently held business values and consumption orientation and may require a major readjustment of the activities of the international corporation in these countries. A continuous scanning of newly emerging national values thus becomes even more important to the international marketer.

The International Financial Environment

Even though the international debt situation appears temporarily subdued, it will remain a major international trade and business issue throughout this century. Debt constraints and low commodity prices will continue to offer slower growth prospects for many developing countries. They will be forced to reduce their levels of imports and to exert more pressure on industrialized nations to open up their markets. Even if these markets are opened, however, demand for most primary products will be far lower than their supply. Ensuing competition for market share will therefore continue to depress prices.

A key issue in resolving the debt crisis will be how the indebted less developed and newly industrialized countries can pursue necessary or imposed austerity policies and achieve reasonable development goals without seriously damaging the growth requirements and exports of other countries. Developed nations in turn will have a strong incentive to help the debtor nations. This incentive consists of the market opportunities that economically healthy developing countries can offer and of national security concerns. As a result, industrialized nations may very well be in a situation in which a funds transfer to debtor nations, accompanied by major debt relief measures, is necessary to achieve economic stimulation back home.

The dollar will remain the major international currency, with little probability that gold will return to its former status in the near future. The system of floating currencies will likely continue, with occasional attempts by nations to manage exchange rate relationships. However, given the vast flows of financial resources across borders, it would appear that market forces, rather than government action, will be the key determinant of a currency's value. Factors such as investor trust, economic conditions, earnings perceptions, and political stability are therefore likely to have a much greater effect on the international value of currencies than domestic monetary and fiscal experimentation.

Given the close linkages between financial markets, financial shocks in one market can quickly translate into rapid shifts in others and easily overpower the financial resources of individual governments. Even if governments decide to pursue coordinated fiscal and monetary policies, they will not be able to negate in the long term market effects that are a response to economic fundamentals.

A looming concern in the international financial environment will be the **international debt load** of the United States. Both domestically and internationally, we are encountering debt figures that would have been inconceivable only a decade ago. For example, in the 1970s the accumulation of financial resources by the Arab nations was of major policy concern in the United States. Congressional hearings focused on whether or not Arab money was "buying out America." At that time, however, Arab holdings in the United States were only $10 to $20 billion. We are seeing now a rapid accumulation of foreign funds in the United States that is leading to much more significant shifts in foreign holdings.

In 1985, the United States became a debtor internationally. The United States enters the 1990's with an international debt of more than $800 billion, making it the largest debtor nation in the world, owing more to other nations than all the developing countries combined. The only saving grace is that all of these debts are denominated in dollars and that, even at such a large volume, the U.S. international debt will be a small proportion of its GNP. The accumulation of foreign funds may very well introduce entirely new dimensions in international business relationships among individuals and nations. Once the debt has reached a certain level, the creditor as well as the debtor is hostage to the loans.

Because foreign creditors expect interest payments on the loans, much of U.S. international trade activity will have to be devoted to generating sufficient funds for such repayment. At the current rate of growth of the U.S. international debt, export earnings will need to grow geometrically if foreign interest and debt repayments are to be made concurrent with payments for necessary imports. This would indicate that international business and marketing will become a greater priority both domestically and internationally than it is today. Such a development will also mean that, rather than being a drag on the economy, international marketing will become a major source of economic growth in the United States.

To some degree, foreign holders of dollars may also choose to convert their financial holdings into real property and investment in the United States. This will result in an entirely new pluralism in U.S. society. It will become increasingly difficult to distinguish between domestic and foreign products—as is already the case with Hondas made in Ohio. Senators and congressmen, governors, municipalities, and unions will gradually be faced with conflicting concerns in trying to develop a national consensus on international trade and marketing. National security concerns may also be raised as major industries become majority-owned by foreign firms.

The Societal Environment

The population discrepancy between less developed nations and the industrialized countries will continue to increase. In the industrialized world, **population growth** will become a national priority, given the fact that in many countries, particularly in Western Europe, the population is shrinking rather than increasing. This shrinkage may lead to labor shortages and to major societal difficulties in providing for a growing elderly population.

In the developing world, the management of population growth will continue to be one of the major challenges of governmental policy. In spite of well-intentioned economic planning, continued rapid increases in population will make it more difficult to ensure that the pace of economic development exceeds population growth. If we determine the standard of living of a nation by dividing the GNP by its population, any increase in the denominator will require equal increases in the numerator to maintain the standard of living. Therefore, if the population's rate of growth continues at its current pace, even greater efforts must be made to increase the economic activity within these nations.

Another problem found by many less developed countries is an **expectation–reality gap** felt by their population. Because the persistence of unfulfilled expectations fosters discontent, these countries must close the gap. This can be accomplished either by improving economic reality—that is, offering more goods at lower prices and increasing the general standard of living—or by reducing the expectations. Although nations will attempt to improve the living standards of their people, substantial efforts to reduce expectations also appear quite likely. The efforts to reduce expectations may increasingly require the use of de-marketing techniques on a national level. The goal would be the reduction of communication that fosters expectations—a quite difficult task as explained below—and a conscientious restriction of the products and services offered or permitted.

The Technological Environment

The concept of the global village is commonly accepted today and indicates the importance of communication in the technological environment. It is already feasible to build satellite dishes out of easily obtainable components. The rapid growth of telefax machines, portable telephones, and computer communication devices all point in the direction of unrestricted communication flows. Concurrently, the availability of information to be communicated is increasing dramatically. For example, the *Directory of Online Databases* lists 3,699 databases available worldwide.[3] Because of all this information includes details about lifestyles, opportunities, and aspirations, international communication will be a great "equalizer" in the future.

Changes in other technologies will be equally rapid and will have a major effect on business in general. For example, the appearance of superconductive materials, high polymers, and composite materials has made possible the development of new systems in fields such as transportation and electric power, pushing the frontiers of human activity into as-yet unexplored areas such as outer space and the oceans. The development of biotechnology is already leading to revolutionary progress not only in medicine and chemistry but also in manufacturing systems within industry.[4]

High technology is expected to become one of the most volatile areas of economic activity. For example, order of magnitude changes in any technology can totally wipe out private and public national investment in a high-technology sector. In the hard-hitting race toward technological primacy, some nations inevitably will fall behind and others will be able to catch up only with extreme difficulty. Even those firms and countries that are at the leading edge of technology will find it increasingly difficult to marshal the funds necessary for further advancements. For example, investments in semiconductor technology are increasingly measured in billions rather than millions of dollars and do not bring any assurance of success. To spread the size of these commitments and to reduce the risk of permanent losses by participants in the race, technology will increasingly be shared among nations provided payment is made for such shared information. In addition, on the level of the firm developments such as cooperative agreements, joint ventures and strategic partnerings will grow vastly in their prevalence.

CHANGES IN TRADE RELATIONS

The international trade framework, consisting primarily of the General Agreement on Tariffs and Trade (GATT), will remain under siege in the years to come. The GATT is greatly strained already in attempting to cope with the complexities of international trade. The framework will need to incorporate newly industrialized countries into its structure, requiring these countries to play by the established rules and to remove preferential tariffs and offer equal access to their markets. Obviously, such require-

[3] "Information Services," *U.S. Industrial Outlook 1989* (Washington, D.C.: Government Printing Office, 1989), 45–46.

[4] Shinji Fukukawa, *The Future of the U.S.–Japan Relationship and Its Contribution to New Globalism* (Tokyo: Ministry of International Trade and Industry, 1989): 10–11.

ments will be resisted by the new participants in international trade, because many of them will believe that the rules inhibit their economic development. The GATT will therefore also need to shoulder greater responsibilities for the poor participants in world trade and offer trade development alternatives in exchange for market access.

In addition, the GATT will need to pay more attention to new forms of international trade that are currently not under its regulatory supervision. These include trade in services, trade in high technology, new forms of subsidization, and countertrade. The GATT must also consider abolishing or regulating trade arrangements that now occur outside of the GATT forum and substantially distort trade flows such as orderly or voluntary market restraint agreements.

A key question will be whether the GATT can be restructured to accommodate its current challenges or a new organization will be the requisite and feasible alternative. The success of **multilateral trade negotiations** is essential to the survival of the multilateral trade system. The diverging interests of the participants in such trade negotiations, however, make it difficult to achieve major success quickly. If trade relations cannot be continued on a multilateral basis, **bilateral agreements** and treaties would become more prevalent. As a result, protectionism would increase on a global scale as individual industrial policies are followed, and the volume of international trade would decline.

International trade relations will also be shaped by new participants bringing with them the potential to restructure the composition of trade. For example, new entrants with exceptionally large productive potential, such as the People's Republic of China, may substantially alter world trade flows. As trading nations like China, Korea, and Taiwan step up their international trade efforts, governments of nations that are highly successful in international trade, such as Japan, are very concerned about the future of their international competitiveness.

Finally, the efforts of governments to achieve self-sufficiency in economic sectors, particularly in agriculture and heavy industries, have ensured the creation of long-term worldwide oversupply of some commodities and products, many of which had historically been traded widely. As a result, after some period of intense market share competition aided by subsidies and governmental support, a gradual and painful restructuring of these industries will have to take place.

GOVERNMENTAL POLICY

A clear worldwide trend exists toward increased management of trade by governments.[5] International trade activity now affects domestic policy more than in the past. Governments, in their desire to structure their domestic economic activity, will be forced to intervene more and more in

[5]Raymond J. Waldmann, *Managed Trade: The New Competition between Nations* (Cambridge, Mass.: Ballinger Press, 1986), 5.

international markets. For example, trade flows can cause major structural shifts in employment. As a result of these shifts, other industries subsequently begin to experience similar structural readjustment needs. Most recently, the United States footwear manufacturing industry has experienced an import penetration level of over 70 percent. Similarly, the textile industry in the United States is increasingly under pressure from foreign imports. These industries may be faced with a need to substantially restructure their employment outlook because of productivity gains and competitive pressures. Yet such restructuring is not necessarily negative. Since the turn of the century, farm sector employment in the United States dropped from more than 40 percent of the population to less than 3 percent. At the same time, the farm industry feeds 250 million people in the United States and produces large surpluses. A restructuring of industries can therefore greatly increase productivity and competitiveness and can provide the opportunity for resource allocation to newly emerging sectors of an economy.

Governments cannot be expected, for the sake of the theoretical ideal of "free trade," to sit back and watch the effects of de-industrialization on their countries. The most that can be expected is that they will permit an open-market orientation subject to the needs of domestic policy. Even an open market orientation is maintainable only if governments can provide reasonable assurances to their own firms and citizens that this openness applies not only to their own markets but to foreign markets as well. Therefore, unfair trade practices such as governmental subsidization, dumping, and industrial targeting will be examined more closely, and retaliation for such activities will be increasingly swift and harsh.

Increasingly, governments will attempt to coordinate policies that affect the international marketing environment. The development of international indexes and trigger mechanisms will be a useful step in that direction. Yet, in order for them to be effective, governments will need to muster the political fortitude to implement the policies necessary for successful cooperation. For example, international monetary cooperation will work, in the long term, only if domestic fiscal policies are responsive to the achievement of the coordinated goals.

Governmental policymakers must understand the international repercussions of domestic legislation. For example, the imposition of a special surcharge tax on the chemical industry designed to provide for the cleanup of toxic waste products will need to be carefully considered in light of its repercussions on the international competitiveness of the chemical industry. Similarly, antitrust laws should be revised if these laws hinder the international competitiveness of domestic firms.

Policymakers also need a better understanding of the nature of the international trade issues confronting them. Most countries today face both short-term and long-term trade problems. Trade balance issues, for example, are short term in nature, whereas competitiveness issues are much more long term. All too often, however, short-term issues are attacked with long-term trade policy mechanisms, and vice versa. In the United States, for example, the desire to "level the international playing field" with mechanisms such as a strikeforce, vigorous implementation of import restrictions, or voluntary restraint agreements may serve long-term competitiveness well, but does little to alleviate the publicly perceived problem of the trade deficit. Similarly, a further opening of Japan's market to foreign corporations will have only a minor immediate effect on that country's trade surplus. Yet, it is the expectation and hope of many in both the public and the private sectors that such immediate changes will occur. For the sake of the credibility of policymakers, it becomes therefore increasingly imperative to precisely identify the nature of the problem, to design and use policy measures that are appropriate for its resolution, and to communicate the hoped-for end results.

Any kind of official **industrial policy** in the United States is unlikely in the immediate future. However, the accuracy of this statement lies only in the context of an official posture. The United States is opposed to any industrial policy because of the historical rationale that bureaucrats will be less successful than the free market in choosing winners. Historically, we can see that industrial policies were in fact implemented, although indirectly. For example, when transportation across the country was vital, railroads were built, later followed by highways. When education became a national priority, substantial government funding was provided to create and upgrade universities in the scientific fields. In a similar way, it can be expected that firms that provide employment will gather more and more political clout and will in all likelihood benefit from governmental action in the areas of taxation and governmental spending.

Governments are also likely to jawbone interindustry cooperation. For example, industries that benefit from the free trade stance of their government currently reap those benefits without any quid pro quo. At the same time, firms that lose out in the free trade environment are left to fend for themselves. Increasingly, it can be expected that governments will aim at a cross-fertilization between the industries benefiting and losing from free trade. This may mean that firms that are successful internationally will be asked to consider locating new plants or capacity expansion in those areas that suffer from high unemployment as a result of foreign competition. If quiet admonitions are not helpful in obtaining such objectives, governments may be substantially less enthusiastic in fighting for market access for their own industries abroad.

The concept of **administrative guidance** will likely enter increasingly into the policy of governments that have heretofore pledged to believe only in the invisible hand of the free market. This may mean that even the best product offered at the lowest price may be at the mercy of vagaries of the nonmarketing environment. The international marketer will then have to spend an increased amount of time and effort on dealing with governments and on avoiding being held hostage to politics, pressure, and protectionism.

THE FUTURE OF INTERNATIONAL MARKETING MANAGEMENT

Environmental changes result in an increase in international risk. One shortsighted alternative for risk-averse managers would be the termination of international activities altogether. However, businesses will not achieve long-run success by engaging only in risk-free actions. Furthermore, other factors make the continuance of international marketing highly probable.

International markets continue to be a source of high profits, as a quick look at the list of Fortune 500 firms will show. International markets help cushion slack in domestic sales resulting from recessionary or adverse domestic market conditions and are crucial to the very survival of the firm. International markets also provide firms with foreign experience that helps them compete more successfully with foreign firms in the domestic market. Finally, international activities are necessary to compensate for foreign product and service inflows into the economy and to at least contribute to an equilibration of the balance of trade. As long as supply potential exceeds demand on an international level, an inherent economic motivation will exist for international marketing.

International Planning and Research

The focus on the customer will remain a major factor in marketing. The international marketer must continue to serve customers well. At the same time, government will increasingly emerge as a coequal partner in the international marketing arena. This means that the international marketing manager will have to take general governmental concerns into account when planning a marketing strategy.

The diverging needs of foreign consumers will result in more available niches in which firms can create a distinct international competence. This points toward increased specialization and segmentation. Firms will attempt to fill very narrow and specific demands or to resolve very specific problems for their international customers. Identifying and filling these niches will be easier in the future because of the greater availability of international research tools.

The international marketer will also increasingly face problems of social responsibility. Governmental forces will demand that private marketing practices not increase public costs. Governments will expect marketers to serve their customers equally and nondiscriminately.[6] This concept runs directly counter to marketers' desire to serve first the markets that are most profitable and least costly. International marketers will therefore be torn in two directions and, in order to provide results that are acceptable both to customers and to the societies they serve, they must walk a fine line, balancing the public and the private good.

[6] Robert Bartels, *Global Development and Marketing* (Columbus, Ohio: Grid Publishing, 1981), 111.

International Product Policy

Two major trends are emerging in the product policies of multinational corporations. On one hand, automation and the search for increasing economies of scale demand that they serve more markets. Even large domestic markets such as the United States or Japan may be "too small to absorb the output of the world class automated plants needed for economies of scale in many product areas."[7] Europe, Japan, and the United States harbor the greatest buying power and demand concentration in the world for many products. For example, these three regions account for nearly 85 percent of the world's demand for consumer electronic goods; they consumed 85 percent of the computers and 70 percent of the machine tools produced in the world in 1985.[8] According to these facts, production should be concentrated in one of these regions and output widely distributed.

Although this trend would argue for greater exports and greater standardization of products, a counterargument holds that, because of increasing protectionist policies and the desire of nations to obtain and develop their own technology, exports will be replaced by foreign direct investment.[9] If this is the case, marketing across international borders would be replaced by marketing abroad within foreign borders. As long as firms have the flexibility of choice of location, managers will have substantial leverage over domestic legislation and regulations that would affect their international marketing effort. Governments will run the risk of unemployment growth if domestic firms, because of an unsatisfactory **competitive platform,** move their operations abroad.

Regardless of which avenue firms take for marketing their products internationally, it appears certain that worldwide introduction of products will occur much more rapidly in the future. Already, **international product life cycles** have accelerated substantially. Whereas product introduction could previously be spread out over several years, firms now must prepare for product life cycles that can be measured in months or even weeks.[10,11] As a result, firms must design products and plan even their domestic marketing strategies with the length of the international product cycle in mind. Product introduction will grow more complex, more expensive, and more risky, yet the rewards to be reaped from a successful product will have to be accumulated more quickly.

Factor endowment advantages have a significant impact on the decisions of international marketers. Given the acceleration of product life

---

[7] Kenichi Ohmae, "Only Triad Insiders Will Succeed," *The New York Times*, November 2, 1984, 2f.

[8] Ibid.

[9] Bartels, *Global Development and Marketing*, 111.

[10] Michael R. Czinkota, "Conclusions on Export Policy" in *Export Policy: A Global Assessment*, eds. M. Czinkota and G. Tesar (New York: Praeger, 1982), 162.

[11] Michael R. Czinkota, "Distribution of Consumer Products in Japan," *International Marketing Review* 2 (Fall 1985): 39–51.

TABLE 24.1   ▪   **Foreign Patents Granted in the United States in 1988**

Country	Patents	Country	Patents
Japan	16,984	Poland	8
West Germany	7,501	Singapore	8
France	2,792	Chile	7
United Kingdom	2,757	Colombia	6
Canada	1,642	Portugal	5
Switzerland	1,300	Monaco	4
Italy	1,172	Philippines	4
Netherlands	898	Trinidad/Tobago	4
Sweden	891	Bahamas	3
Taiwan	536	Costa Rica	3
Australia	486	Iceland	3
Austria	351	Zimbabwe	3
Belgium	328	El Salvador	2
Israel	249	Indonesia	2
Finland	239	Iraq	2
Denmark	208	Malaysia	2
Norway	137	Morocco	2
Spain	132	Saudi Arabia	2
South Korea	124	Thailand	2
South Africa	107	Turkey	2
Hong Kong	104	Barbados	1
Soviet Union	97	Cayman Islands	1
Hungary	94	Cyprus	1
New Zealand	70	Guadeloupe	1
China	48	Iran	1
Ireland	47	Kuwait	1
East Germany	46	Malta	1
Mexico	45	Mauritius	1
Luxembourg	38	North Korea	1
Brazil	37	Panama	1
Czechoslovakia	33	Peru	1
Bulgaria	23	Romania	1
Venezuela	20	Sri Lanka	1
Yugoslavia	20	Uruguay	1
Argentina	18		
Greece	15	Total Foreign Patents	39,702
India	14	Total Patents	84,272
Liechtenstein	11		

Source: Technology Assessment and Forecast Database, U.S. Patent and Trademark Office, Washington, D.C., 1989.

cycles, nations with low production costs will be able to replicate products more cheaply. Countries such as India, Israel, and the Philippines offer large pools of skilled people at labor rates much lower than in Europe, Japan, or the United States. For example, India has the third largest number of engineers after the United States and the Soviet Union.[12] All

[12]Vern Terpstra, "The Evolution of International Marketing," *International Marketing Review* 4 (Summer 1987): 60.

this talent also results in a much wider dissemination of technological creativity, a factor that will affect the innovative capability of firms. For example, in 1988, nearly half of all the patents in the United States were granted to foreign entities. Table 24.1 provides an overview of the foreign patents granted.

This indicates that firms need to make such foreign advantages part of their production strategies, or they need to develop consistent comparative advantages in production technology in order to stay ahead of the game. Similarly, workers engaged in the productive process must attempt, through training and skill enhancement, to stay ahead of foreign workers who are willing to charge less for their time. However, this will be very difficult for a firm producing only in an industrialized country.

As a result, an increase will occur in the trend toward **strategic alliances,** or partnerings, permitting the formation of collaborative arrangements between firms. These alliances will enable firms to take risks that they could not afford to take alone, facilitate technological advancement, and ensure continued international market access.

International Communications

The advances made in international communications will have a profound impact on the international marketer. Entire industries are becoming more footloose in their operations; that is, they are less tied to their current location in their interaction with markets. For example, Best Western Hotels in the United States has channeled its entire reservation system through a toll-free number that is being serviced out of the prison system in Utah. Companies could as easily concentrate their communications activities in other countries. Communications for worldwide operations, for example, could be located in Africa or Asia and not impair international corporate activities.

Advances in computer technology will enable firms to reach a wider audience as well as to reach consumers directly. As a result, precise targeting and fine-tuning to meet the specific needs and requirements of the consumer will be possible.

Distribution Strategies

Worldwide distribution systems are beginning to emerge. Currently, only a few integrated systems, labeled sea bridges and land bridges, are operational. However, major trading routes that offer substantial distribution economies of scale are being developed. International marketers will experience relative ease in distribution as long as they stay within the established routes, but will encounter difficulties when attempting to deviate from them. Customers who are on the routes will benefit in turn from the low cost of distribution and will see their choice of products widened. More distant customers will probably have their product choices reduced and pay increased prices for foreign products. Because of a lack of international competition, they will also have to live with high prices for domestic products. The distribution systems will often become the deciding factor in whether markets can be served. Because communications advances will ensure that the customers in different markets are informed about product availability, distribution limitations will become even more painful.

International Pricing

Price competition will become increasingly heated for the international marketer. Many products, as they become distributed more widely throughout the world, will take on commodity characteristics, as semiconducters have in the 1980s. Therefore, price differentials of one cent per unit may become crucial in making international sales. However, because many new products and technologies will address completely new needs, firms will be forced to engage in forward pricing by distributing development cost over the anticipated volume of sales. This task will become increasingly difficult and controversial because demand levels for totally new products are impossible to predict accurately, with the result that firms will be open to charges of dumping.

Even for consumer products, price competition will be substantial. Because of the increased dissemination of technology, the country of origin of the manufacture will no longer be able to justify higher prices; domestically produced products of similar or equal quality will be quickly introduced. As a result, exchange rate movements may play more significant roles in maintaining the competitiveness of the international firm. Firms can be expected to prevail on their governments to manage the country's currency in order to produce a favorable exchange rate or to compensate them for the effects of adverse currency fluctuations.

Government management of trade will continue to influence international pricing in other ways. Through subsidization, targeting, and government contracts, nations will attempt to stimulate their international competitiveness. Because of the price sensitivity of many products, the international marketer will be forced to identify such unfair practices quickly, communicate them to his or her government, and insist on either similar benefits or government negotiation of an internationally level playing field.

CAREERS IN INTERNATIONAL MARKETING

The student reader of this book will, it is hoped, have learned about the intricacies, complexities, and thrills of international marketing. Of course, a career in international marketing does not consist only of jet travel between Rome, London, and Paris. It is hard work and requires knowledge and expertise. As The International Marketplace 24.2 shows, students need to be well versed in the specific business functions and may wish to

THE INTERNATIONAL MARKETPLACE **24.2**

Education for Global Awareness *Reflecting the growing role of internationalism, the American Society for Training and Development published an article in its journal deploring American managerial unpreparedness in this period of increasing globalization of markets.*

One of the coauthors, Denise S. Wallace, a marketing research consultant for the Wilson Learning Corporation of Eden Prairie, Minnesota, said that generally United States managers, "because of their educational background, lack experience and diversity that many of their offshore counterparts have." They need, she added, "organizational expatriate experiences along with knowledge of languages, cultures, and foreign business systems."

"Continuous change and chaos will be the dominant influences. The global leader needs a cosmopolitan perspective that comes from traveling and working abroad. He or she needs a knowledge of international relations and must be sensitive to diversity of beliefs and social forces. Yet such leaders must be grounded in their own skills."

An earlier survey of 100 top managers of major companies by Egon Zehnder, a large worldwide management recruiting firm, found that 96 percent of the respondents agreed that over the next five years their companies' ability to compete against foreign firms is essential to long-term success. Yet the survey showed that few companies had managers abroad who could fluently speak the languages of the countries in which they were stationed.

"We wonder how a manager can assess business opportunities in a foreign country if he does not speak the language and has little knowledge of the culture," said Kai Linholst, managing partner of Egon Zehnder. Management by walking around, visiting foreign operations, and keeping in touch by telephone is not enough.

Source: Elizabeth M. Fowler, "Education for Global Awareness," *The New York Times,* April 25, 1989, D27; and Elizabeth M. Fowler, "Promoting Overseas Markets," *The New York Times,* December 16, 1986, D27.

---

take summer internships abroad, take language courses, and travel not simply for pleasure but to observe business operations abroad and gain a greater understanding of different peoples and cultures.

Further Training

One option for the student is to obtain further in-depth training by enrolling in graduate business school programs that specialize in international business education. Even though the international orientation of U.S. uni-

TABLE 24.2 ▪ A Listing of Master's Degree Programs in International Business

Master's Degree Programs in IB

School	Average GMAT	Percentage Foreign Students	Average Age	Number of 1985 Grads (MBA)	Number of 1985 MBA Grads with IB Majors	Other
AGSIM (Thunderbird)	510	26%	25	—	—	MIM—893
Alabama	550	9%	25	40	2	None
American University	525	18%	27	219	18	7 grads MS in IB
Baylor	532	5%	25	107	?	6 grads MIM
Brigham Young	563	7%	27	295	7	None
Columbia	620	16%	25	639	57	None
CUNY (Baruch)	510	9%	28	378	11	3 grads MBA in IM
Georgetown	579	22%	26	62	58	None
George Washington	531	17%	26	670	84	18 grads MA in IB
Georgia State	538	40%	28	?	31	None
Hawaii	546	13%	29	104	?	None
Houston	556	12%	27	550	40	None
Indiana University	576	12%	25	271	30	None
MIT	640	20%	26	?	?	MS in IB
Monterey	528	20%	25	48	48	None
New Mexico	540	15%	30	112	9	4 grads IB in Lat. Amer.
NYU	591	25%	26	998	120	None
Northwestern	619	11%	28	300	50	None
Notre Dame	533	25%	23	142	27	None
Ohio State	584	21%	25	150	5	6 grads MA in IB
Pennsylvania State	?	14%	25	140	5	1 grad MS in IB
St. Louis	494	12%	25	200	12	None
Southern California	583	14%	26	400	7	None
South Carolina (MIBS)	556	19%	25	305	None	138 grads MIBS
Temple	550	10%	28	241	12	2 grads MS in IB—7 courses
Texas-Austin	599	10%	25	376	40	None
Texas-Dallas	521	35%	25	380	8	31 grads MA in IB
Toledo	500	11%	29	136	5	None
Washington	586	16%	28	225	15	None
Wisconsin	567	11%	25	400	14	None

Source: Lee C. Nerth, "The Ranking of Masters Programs in International Business," *Journal of International Business Studies* 18 (Fall 1987): 91–99. Reprinted with permission.

| | IB Courses Offered | | | | | | | | | | | | | | | |
Intro. to IB	Intl. Mgmt.	Intl. Mktg.	Intl. Corp. Fin.	Intl. Acctg.	Intl. Banking	Comp. Mgmt.	Comp. Labor	Comp. Bus. Sys.	Area Studies	IB Law	IB Negotiations	IB Seminar	Intl. Transportation	IB Strategy	IB Courses Required for Major	Required Nonbusiness Courses?
	x	x	x	x	x	x	x		8	x		x		x	5	Cross-cultural courses + 3 area courses in pol. sci., history, econ. dev., etc.
x	x	x	x	x											5	None
x		x	x	x	x					x		x			4	None
	x	x	x												3	4 courses in pol. sci.
		x	x	x					x					x	3	None
x		x	x						2			x		x	4	None
x		x	x							x		x	x	x	5	None
x	x	x	x								x	x			3	None
x		x	x	x	x	x			4	x	x				5	None
x	x	x	x	x				x		x		x			5	None
x		x	x	x		x	x								4	None
x		x	x											x	3	None
x	x	x	x				x	x							4	None
x	x		x			x	x			x					4	None
x		x	x	x						x					5	One regional course
x	x	x	x	x					3			x			5	For IB in Lat. Amer. needs 2 Lat. Am. courses
x	x	x	x	x	x	x			5	x	x	x			4	None
x		x	x				x								3	None
x		x	x	x					x					x	6	None
x		x	x			x	x							x	3	None
x		x						x				x		x	3	None
	x	x	x		x				x	x					5	None
	x	x	x	x											3	None
x	x	x	x	x	x		x		3		x	x		x	8	2 courses
x	x	x	x	x		x	x								4	None
x		x	x	x					3	x		x			3	None
x	x	2	x	x	x	x	x		6	3		x	x		5	None
x		x	x					x				x	x		3	None
x	x		x	x	x	x			3			x			3	None
	x	x	x					x		x			x		3	None

TABLE 24.3 ▪ **Some Information Sources for Study and Travel Abroad**

WHERE TO WRITE

For information on year-off programs, contact youth groups, trade associations, embassies, travel and scientific groups, and educational foundations. Here are a few sources:

American Institute for
  Foreign Study
102 Greenwich Avenue
Greenwich, Conn. 06830
(203) 869-9090

British American Educational
  Foundation
351 East 74th Street
New York, N.Y. 10021
(212) 772-3890

Center for Interim Programs
233 Mount Lucas Road
Princeton, N.J. 08540
(609) 924-0441

Dynamy
57 Cedar Street
Worcester, Mass. 01609
(617) 755-2571

Earthwatch Expeditions Inc.
680 Mount Auburn Street,
  Box 403N
Watertown, Mass. 02272
(617) 926-8200

Foundation for Field Research
787 South Grade Road
Alpine, Calif. 92001
(619) 445-9264

International Christian
  Youth Exchange
134 West 26th Street
New York, N.Y. 10001
(212) 206-7307

Institute of International Education
809 United Nations Plaza
New York, N.Y. 10017
(212) 883-8200

Kibbutz Aliya Desk
27 West 20th Street, Ninth Floor
New York, N.Y. 10011
(212) 255-1338

Open Door Student Exchange
250 Fulton Avenue, P.O. Box 71
Hempstead, N.Y. 11551
(516) 486-7330

Up With People
3103 North Campbell Avenue
Tucson, Ariz. 85719
(602) 327-7351

Volunteers in Service to America
VISTA
Washington, D.C. 20525
(202) 634-9108
or contact your state ACTION office

Source: "Boning Up on the Best Programs." Copyright © 1988, *U.S. News & World Report.* Reprinted with permission from the February 29, 1988 issue, p. 68.

versities is relatively recent, a substantial number of schools has developed specific international programs. Table 24.2 provides a nonexhaustive listing of such institutions together with some of the international courses offered by them. In addition, universities abroad specialize in developing international managers. INSEAD in France, the London Business School in England, the University of Western Ontario in Canada, IMEDE in Switzerland, and the Stockholm School of Economics are only a few examples of such universities.[13]

Many organizations are able to assist students interested in studying abroad or in gathering foreign work experience. Apart from individual

[13]Donald A. Ball and Wendell H. McCulloch, Jr., "International Business Education Programs in American and Non-American Schools: How They Are Ranked by the Academy of International Business," *Journal of International Business Studies* 19 (Summer 1988): 295–299.

WHAT TO READ

Academic Year Abroad, Institute of International Education, New York, N.Y., $16.95: Lists more than 1,100 study programs from eight weeks to a full year. IIE also publishes *Vacation Study Abroad*, $19.95, which lists more than 1,000 summer and short-term programs at all postsecondary-eucation levels.

Advisory List of International Educational Travel and Exchange Programs, Council on Standards for International Educational Travel, 1906 Association Drive, Reston, Va. 22091, $5: Describes and evaluates 36 international organizations that run travel and study programs for high-school students and graduates.

Archaeological Fieldwork Opportunities Bulletin, Archaeological Institute of America, 675 Commonwealth Avenue, Boston, Mass. 02215: $6, published annually. Forty pages describing worldwide digs and their sponsors, sites, and costs.

The Young American's Scholarship Guide to Travel and Learning Abroad, Intravco Press, 211 East 43rd Street, Suite 1303, New York, N.Y. 10017, by mail only, $14.95:

Lists about 70 organizations with wide variety of interim programs and information about fees, scholarships, and locations.

The Teenager's Guide to Study, Travel and Adventure Abroad, Council on International Educational Exchange, St. Martin's Press, New York, N.Y., $8.95: A how-to book that describes more than 150 programs, their sponsors and costs, and housing; interviews with participants and their parents.

Transitions Abroad, P.O. Box 344, Amherst, Mass. 01004, published five times a year, $15: Articles and listings cover overseas programs, seminars, publications, tips on travel, relocating, finding work, housing.

International Workcamp Directory, VFP International Workcamps, Belmont, Vt. 05730, $10 (includes membership): Booklet that lists Volunteer for Peace member work camps worldwide.

Volunteer Vacations, Chicago Review Press, $11.95: Lists volunteer organizations that offer science and community-service projects.

universities and their programs for study abroad, various nonprofit institutions stand ready to help and to provide informative materials. Table 24.3 lists some of the programs and institutions that can be contacted.

For those ready to enter or rejoin the "real world," different employment opportunities need to be evaluated.

Employment with a Large Firm

One career alternative in international marketing is to work for a large multinational corporation. These firms constantly search for personnel to help them in their international operations. For example, a Western Union recruiting advertisement is reproduced in Figure 24.1.

Many multinational corporations, while seeking specialized knowledge like languages, expect employees to be firmly grounded in the practice

FIGURE 24.1 ▪ **Advertisement Recruiting International Marketers**

Source: Courtesy Western Union Corporation.

and management of business. Rarely, if ever, will a firm hire a new employee at the starting level and immediately place him or her in a position of international responsibility. Usually, a new employee is expected to become thoroughly familiar with the company's domestic internal operations before being considered for an international position. It is very expensive to send an employee overseas. To transfer a manager to an overseas post has been estimated to cost up to $100,000. The annual cost of maintaining that manager overseas is about two to three times the cost of hiring a local manager.[14] Companies want to be sure that the benefit they will receive is worth the expenditure.

Although many firms depend on their international operations for a substantial amount of sales volume and profits, less than 2 percent of U.S. companies have an overseas placement plan for rising young executives. Some claim that only a few major U.S. companies have effective international management development programs.[15] Given the fact that management development programs are scarce, it is not surprising that reentry

[14]Frederica Hoge Dunn, "Preparing for the Overseas Job," *Clipper Magazine*, September 1978, 58, 63.

[15]"Overseas Executives: The Cost of Cutting Costs," *World Business Weekly*, February 25, 1980, 13.

programs are even more difficult to find. Quite often, employees who have taken the international route come back to headquarters only to find that few positions are open for them. Apart from such organizational difficulties, which may result in a career that is placed in a holding pattern, financial pressures and family problems may lead to significant executive stress during reentry.[16]

There is some truth to the saying that the best place to be in international marketing is on the same floor as the chairman at headquarters. It is therefore a tough decision for the internationalist to decide to go abroad, make his or her mark, and hope to return to an equivalent or even better position. However, as corporations begin to recognize the importance of international operations, they are likely to give more consideration to proper management of overseas personnel.

The reason an employee is sent abroad, more often than not, is that the company expects him or her to reflect the corporate spirit, to be tightly wed to the corporate culture, and to communicate well with both local and corporate management personnel. In this liaison position, the employee will have to be exceptionally sensitive to both headquarters and local operations. As an intermediary, the expatriate must be empathetic, understanding, and yet fully prepared to implement the goals set by headquarters.

Employment with a Small or Medium-Sized Firm

A second alternative is to begin work in a small or medium-sized firm. Very often, these firms have only recently developed an international outlook and the new employee will arrive on the "ground floor." Initial involvement will normally be in the export field—evaluating potential foreign customers, preparing quotes, and dealing with mundane activities such as shipping and transportation. With a very limited budget, the export manager will only occasionally visit foreign markets to discuss marketing strategy with foreign distributors. Most of the work will be done by mail, via telex, or by telephone. The hours are often long, because of the need to reach a contact overseas, for example, during business hours in Hong Kong. Yet the possibilities for implementing creative business methods are virtually limitless, and the contribution made by the successful export manager will be visible in the firm's growing export volume.

Alternatively, international work in a small firm may involve importing—finding new, low-cost sources for domestically sourced products. Decisions often must be based on limited information, and the import manager is faced with many uncertainties. Often things do not work out as planned. Shipments are delayed, letters of credit are canceled, and products almost never arrive in exactly the form and shape anticipated. Yet the problems are always new and offer an ongoing challenge.

---

[16] Michael G. Harvey, "Repatriation of Corporate Executives: An Empirical Study," *Journal of International Business Studies* 20 (Spring 1989): 131–144.

TABLE 24.4 ▪ **Approximate Budget Requirements for an International Market Consulting Service**

	Monthly	Annual
Rent (750 sq. ft. @ $25/sq. ft.)	$ 1,562.50	$ 18,750.00
Secretary/Receptionist	1,500.00	18,000.00
Administrative/Office Manager	1,750.00	21,000.00
Withholding/Employer Contributions	975.00	11,700.00
Employee Health Insurance	270.00	3,240.00
IBM Word Processor (purchase)	—	4,500.00
Telex*	—	250.00
IBM Selectric II	—	850.00
Telephone (4 lines)		
Installation (one time)		250.00
Hardware (3 phones)		900.00
Computer Box (lease)	70.00	840.00
C&P Basic Service	200.00	2,400.00
Copier		
Lease*	250.00	3,000.00
Supplies/Paper	100.00	1,180.00
Long Distance Phone	600.00	7,200.00
Telex Usage	800.00	9,600.00
Brochure, Design and Print (2,000)	—	10,000.00
Newsletter *Copywriting (12 issues, 4 pages)	334.00	4,000.00
Printing Charges*	200.00	2,400.00
Business Stationery		
Layout/Design		300.00
Printing/Supply		1,000.00
Postage*		
Leasing of Meter (quarterly)	65.00	260.00
Postage (estimate)	400.00	5,000.00
Business Development		
Domestic T&E*	4,000.00	48,000.00
Total	$13,076.50	$174,620.00

*Denotes expenses that are partially recoverable from clients.

Source: President, Robert D. Keezer & Associates, Washington, D.C. Reprinted with permission.

As a training ground for international marketing activities, there is probably no better place than a smaller firm. Ideally, the person with some experience may find work with an export trading or export management company, resolving other people's problems and concentrating virtually exclusively on the international arena.

Self-Employment

A third alternative is to hang up a consultant's shingle or to establish a trading firm. Many companies are in dire need of help for their international marketing effort and are quite prepared to part with a portion of their profits to receive it. Yet it requires in-depth knowledge and broad experience to make a major contribution to a company's international mar-

FIGURE 24.2 ▪ A Price Comparison for Business Travelers

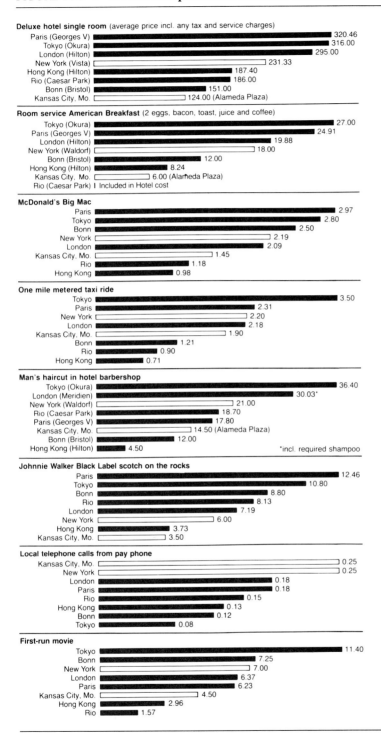

Deluxe hotel single room (average price incl. any tax and service charges)
- Paris (Georges V) — 320.46
- Tokyo (Okura) — 316.00
- London (Hilton) — 295.00
- New York (Vista) — 231.33
- Hong Kong (Hilton) — 187.40
- Rio (Caesar Park) — 186.00
- Bonn (Bristol) — 151.00
- Kansas City, Mo. — 124.00 (Alameda Plaza)

Room service American Breakfast (2 eggs, bacon, toast, juice and coffee)
- Tokyo (Okura) — 27.00
- Paris (Georges V) — 24.91
- London (Hilton) — 19.88
- New York (Waldorf) — 18.00
- Bonn (Bristol) — 12.00
- Hong Kong (Hilton) — 8.24
- Kansas City, Mo. — 6.00 (Alameda Plaza)
- Rio (Caesar Park) — Included in Hotel cost

McDonald's Big Mac
- Paris — 2.97
- Tokyo — 2.80
- Bonn — 2.50
- New York — 2.19
- London — 2.09
- Kansas City, Mo. — 1.45
- Rio — 1.18
- Hong Kong — 0.98

One mile metered taxi ride
- Tokyo — 3.50
- Paris — 2.31
- New York — 2.20
- London — 2.18
- Kansas City, Mo. — 1.90
- Bonn — 1.21
- Rio — 0.90
- Hong Kong — 0.71

Man's haircut in hotel barbershop
- Tokyo (Okura) — 36.40
- London (Meridien) — 30.03*
- New York (Waldorf) — 21.00
- Rio (Caesar Park) — 18.70
- Paris (Georges V) — 17.80
- Kansas City, Mo. — 14.50 (Alameda Plaza)
- Bonn (Bristol) — 12.00
- Hong Kong (Hilton) — 4.50

*incl. required shampoo

Johnnie Walker Black Label scotch on the rocks
- Paris — 12.46
- Tokyo — 10.80
- Bonn — 8.80
- Rio — 8.13
- London — 7.19
- New York — 6.00
- Hong Kong — 3.73
- Kansas City, Mo. — 3.50

Local telephone calls from pay phone
- Kansas City, Mo. — 0.25
- New York — 0.25
- London — 0.18
- Paris — 0.18
- Rio — 0.15
- Hong Kong — 0.13
- Bonn — 0.12
- Tokyo — 0.08

First-run movie
- Tokyo — 11.40
- Bonn — 7.25
- New York — 7.00
- London — 6.37
- Paris — 6.23
- Kansas City, Mo. — 4.50
- Hong Kong — 2.96
- Rio — 1.57

Source: "Sticker Shock: U.S. Travelers Face Trauma of Sharply Devalued Dollar," *The Wall Street Journal*, December 4, 1987, p. 41. Reprinted by permission of *The Wall Street Journal*, © Dow Jones & Company, Inc. 1987. All Rights Reserved Worldwide.

keting effort from the outside or to successfully run a trading firm. Specialized services that might be offered by a consultant include international market research, international strategic planning, or, particularly desirable, beginning-to-end assistance in international market entry or international marketing negotiations.

Table 24.4 gives an idea of some of the initial expenses incurred in setting up an international market consulting service. The up-front costs are substantial and are not covered by turnover but rather have to be covered by profits. For an international marketing expert, the hourly billable rate typically is as high as $200 for experienced principals and $100 for staff. Whenever international travel is required, overseas activities are often billed at the daily rate of $1,600 plus expenses, which can add up quickly to a substantial amount, as Figure 24.2 shows. When trading on one's own, income and risk can be limitless. Even at these relatively high rates, solid groundwork must be completed before all the overhead is paid. The advantage is the opportunity to become a true international entrepreneur. Consultants and owners of trading firms will work at a higher degree of risk than employees, but with the opportunity for higher rewards.

SUMMARY

This final chapter has provided an overview of the environmental changes facing international marketers and alternative managerial responses to these changes. International marketing is a complex and difficult activity, yet it affords many challenges and opportunities. "May you live in interesting times" is an ancient Chinese curse. For the international marketer, this curse is a call to action. Observing changes and analyzing how best to incorporate them in the international marketing mission is the bread and butter of the international marketer. If the international environment were constant, there would be no challenge. The frequent changes are precisely what make international marketing so fascinating to those who are active in the field. It must have been international marketers who were targeted by the old Indian proverb, "When storms come about little birds seek shelter, while eagles soar."

Questions for Discussion

1. For many developing countries debt repayment and trade are closely interlinked. What does protectionism mean to them?

2. Should we worry about the fact that the United States is a debtor nation?

3. What are some alternatives for governments in closing the expectation–reality gap of the populace?

4. With low wages prevalent abroad, how can U.S. workers expect to compete?

5. How can you advocate free trade when 200,000 workers in the U.S. textile industry are losing their jobs to foreign competition?

6. Is international marketing segmentation ethical if it deprives the poor of products?

7. How would our lives and our society change if imports were completely banned?

Recommended Readings

Behrman, Jack N. *The Rise of the Phoenix.* Boulder, Colo.: Westview Press, 1987.

Boddewyn, Jean J. "Comparative Marketing: The First Twenty-five Years." *Journal of International Business Studies* 12 (Spring–Summer 1981): 61–79.

Cohen, Marjorie A. *Work Study Travel Abroad 1988–1989.* 9th ed. New York: St. Martin's Press, 1987.

Czinkota, Michael R. "International Trade and Business in the Late 1980s: An Integrated U.S. Policy Perspective." *Journal of International Business Studies* 17 (Spring 1986): 127–134.

Drucker, Peter F. "The Changed World Economy." *Foreign Affairs* 64 (Spring 1986): 768–791.

Graham, John L., and Kjell Gronhaug. "Ned Hall Didn't Have to Get a Haircut; Or, Why We Haven't Learned Much about International Marketing in the Last Twenty-Five Years." *The Journal of Higher Education* 60 (March–April 1989): 152–187.

Judkins, David. *Study Abroad: The Astute Student's Guide.* Hawthorne, N.J.: The Career Press, 1989.

Schwartz, Peter, and Jerry Saville. "Multinational Business in the 1990's—A Scenario." *Long Range Planning* 19 (December 1986): 31–37.

Sethi, Prakash S. "Opportunities and Pitfalls for Multinational Corporations in a Changed Political Environment." *Long Range Planning* 20 (December 1987): 45–53.

Smith, Allen E., James M. MacLachlan, William Lazer, and Priscilla LaBarbera. *Marketing 2000: Future Perspectives on Marketing.* Chicago: American Marketing Association, 1989.

Terpstra, Vern. "The Evolution of International Marketing." *International Marketing Review* 4 (Summer 1987): 47–59.

The Total Guide to Careers in International Affairs. Poolesville, Md.: Jeffries and Associates, 1987.

Thurow, Lester C. "A Weakness in Process Technology." *Science* 238 (December 1987): 1659–1663.

Win, David. *International Careers: An Insider's Guide.* Hawthorne, N.J.: Career Press, 1987.

Parker Pen Company

Parker Pen Company, the manufacturer of writing instruments based in Janesville, Wisconsin, is one of the world's best known companies in its field. It sold its products in 154 countries and considered itself number one in "quality writing instruments," a market that consists of pens selling for $3 or more.

In early 1984, the company launched a global marketing campaign in which everything was to have "one look, one voice," and with all planning to take place at headquarters. Everything connected with the selling effort was to be standardized. This was a grand experiment of a widely debated concept. A number of international companies were eager to learn from Parker's experiences.

Results became evident quickly. In February 1985, the globalization experiment was ended, and most of the masterminds of the strategy either left the company or were fired. In January 1986, the writing division of Parker Pen was sold for $100 million to a group of Parker's international managers and a London venture-capital company. The U.S. division was given a year to fix its operation or close.

GLOBALIZATION

Globalization is a business initiative based on the conviction that the world is becoming more homogeneous and that distinctions between national markets are not only fading but, for some products, they will eventually disappear. Some products, such as Coca-Cola and Levi's, have already proven the existence of universal appeal. Coke's "one sight, one sound, one sell" approach is a legend in the world of global marketers. Other companies have some products that can be "world products," and some that cannot and should not be. For example, if cultural and competitive differences are less important than their similarities, a single advertising approach can exploit these similarities to stimulate sales everywhere, and at far lower cost than if campaigns were developed for each individual market.

Compared to the multidomestic approach, globalization differs in these three basic ways:

1. The global approach looks for similarities between markets. The multidomestic approach ignores similarities.
2. The global approach actively seeks homogeneity in products, image,

Source: This case was prepared by Ilkka A. Ronkainen for discussion purposes and not to exemplify correct or incorrect decision making. The case draws facts from Joseph M. Winski and Laurel Wentz, "Parker Pen: What Went Wrong?" *Advertising Age*, June 2, 1986, 1, 60–61, 71; and Lori Kesler, "Parker Rebuilds a Quality Image," *Advertising Age*, March 21, 1988, 49.

marketing, and advertising message. The multidomestic approach produces unnecessary differences from market to market.

3. The global approach asks, "Should this product or process be for world consumption?" The multidomestic approach, relying solely on local autonomy, never asks the question.

Globalization requires many internal modifications as well. Changes in philosophy concerning local autonomy, concern for local operating results rather than corporate performance, local strategies designed for local—rather than global—competitors, are all delicate issues to be solved. By design, globalization calls for centralized decision making; therefore, the "not invented here" syndrome becomes a problem. This can be solved by involving those having to implement the globalization strategy at every possible stage as well as keeping lines of communication open.[1]

GLOBALIZATION AT PARKER PEN COMPANY

In January 1982, James R. Peterson became the president and CEO of Parker Pen. At that time, the company was struggling, and global marketing was one of the key measures to be used to revive the company. While at R. J. Reynolds, Peterson had been impressed with the industry's success with globalization. He wanted for Parker Pen nothing less than the writing-instrument equivalent of the Marlboro man.

For most of the 1960s and 1970s, a weak dollar had lulled Parker Pen into a false sense of security. About 80 percent of the company's sales were abroad, which meant that when local-currency profits were translated into dollars, big profits were recorded.

The market was changing, however. The Japanese had started marketing inexpensive disposable pens with considerable success through mass marketers. Brands such as Paper Mate, Bic, Pilot, and Pentel each had greater sales, causing Parker's overall market share to plummet to 6 percent. Parker Pen, meanwhile, stayed with its previous strategy and continued marketing its top-of-the-line pens through department stores and stationery stores. Even in this segment Parker Pen's market share was eroding because of the efforts of A. T. Cross Company and Montblanc of West Germany.

Subsidiaries enjoyed a high degree of autonomy in marketing operations, which resulted in broad and diverse product lines and 40 different advertising agencies handling the Parker Pen account worldwide.

When the dollar's value skyrocketed in the 1980s, Parker's profits plunged and the loss of market share became painfully evident.

Peterson moved quickly upon his arrival. He trimmed the payroll, chopped the product line to 100 (from 500), consolidated manufacturing

---

[1] Laurence Farley, "Going Global: Choices and Challenges," presented at the American Management Association Conference, June 10, 1985, Chicago, Illinois.

operations, and ordered an overhaul of the main plant to make it a state-of-the-art facility. Ogilvy & Mather was hired to take sole control of Parker Pen advertising worldwide. (Among the many agencies terminated was Lowe Howard-Spink in London, which had produced some of the best advertising for Parker Pen's most profitable subsidiary.)

A decision was also made to go aggressively after the low end of the market. The company would sell an upscale line called Premier, mainly as a positioning device. The biggest profits were to come from a roller-ball pen called Vector, selling for $2.98. Plans were drawn to sell an even cheaper pen called Itala—a disposable pen never thought possible at Parker.

Three new managers, to be known as Group Marketing, were brought in. All three had extensive marketing experience, most of it in international markets. Richard Swart, who became marketing vice president for writing instruments, had handled 3M's image advertising worldwide and taught company managers the ins and outs of marketing planning. Jack Marks became head of writing instruments advertising. At Gillette he had orchestrated the worldwide marketing of Silkience hair-care products. Carlos Del Nero, brought in to be Parker's manager of global-marketing planning, had broad international experience at Fisher-Price. The concept of marketing by *centralized* direction was approved.

The idea of selling pens the same way everywhere did not sit well with many Parker subsidiaries and distributors. Pens were indeed the same, but markets, they believed, were different: France and Italy fancied expensive fountain pens; Scandinavia was a ballpoint market. In some markets, Parker could assume an above-the-fray stance; in others it had to get into the trenches and compete on price. Nonetheless, headquarters communicated to them all:

> Advertising for Parker Pens (no matter model or mode) will be based on a common creative strategy and positioning. The worldwide advertising theme, "Make Your Mark With Parker," has been adopted. It will utilize similar graphic layout and photography. It will utilize an agreed-upon typeface. It will utilize the approved Parker logo/design. It will be adapted from centrally supplied materials.

Swart insisted that the directives were to be used only as "starting points," and that they allowed for ample local flexibility. The subsidiaries perceived them differently. The U.K. subsidiary, especially, fought the scheme all the way. Ogilvy & Mather London strongly opposed the "one world, one brand, one advertisement" dictum. Conflict arose, with Swart allegedly shouting at one of the meetings: "Yours is not to reason why; yours is to implement." Local flexibility in advertising was out of the question (see Figure 1).

The London-created "Make Your Mark" campaign was launched in October 1984. Except for language, it was essentially the same: long copy, horizontal layout, illustrations in precisely the same place, the Parker logo at the bottom, and the tag line or local equivalent in the lower right-

FIGURE 1 ▪ **Ads for Parker's Global Campaign**

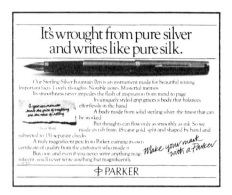

hand corner. Swart once went to the extreme of suggesting that Parker ads avoid long copy and use just one big picture.

Problems arose on the manufacturing side. The new $15 million plant broke down repeatedly. Costs soared and the factory turned out defective products in unacceptable numbers. In addition, the new marketing approach started causing problems as well. Although Parker never aban-

doned its high-end position in foreign markets, its concentration on low-price, mass-distribution products in the United States caused dilution of its image and ultimately losses of $22 million in 1985. Conflict was evident internally and the board of directors began to turn against the concept of globlization.

In January 1985, Peterson resigned. Del Nero left the company in April, Swart was fired in May, Marks in June.

Questions for Discussion

1. Should the merits of global marketing be judged by what happened at Parker Pen Company?

2. Was the globalization strategy sound for writing instruments? If yes, what was wrong in the implementation? If not, why not?

3. What marketing miscalculations were made by the advocates of the globalization effort at Parker Pen?

4. The task is to "fix it or close it." What should be done?

Nova Scotia

THE U.S. MARKET FOR CANADIAN TRAVEL SERVICES

The more than 12 million Americans who travel to Canada annually constitute 42 percent of all departures from the United States. The U.S. market is of crucial importance to the Canadian tourism industry because 95 percent of all tourists are Americans, who spend approximately $2.7 billion a year on these trips.

The 1980s have witnessed a major escalation in campaigns that try to lure tourists to a particular state or foreign country. Tourism areas spent over $100 million in U.S. media in 1985, and the level is expected to grow considerably. Tourism Canada, the government tourist organization, in 1986 launched a campaign with the theme "Come to the world next door" as an umbrella campaign for Canada as a whole. The provinces will conduct their own independent campaigns to segments they deem most attractive and profitable. For example, ads for Manitoba are mostly written for the outdoor vacationer.

The Canadian Government Office of Tourism (CGOT) sponsored a large-scale benefit-segmentation study of the American market for pleasure travel to Canada, the results of which are summarized in Table 1. Segmenting the market by benefits provides many advantages over other methods. Segmenting by attitude toward Canada or by geographic area would be feasible if substantial variation occurred. This is not the case, however. Segmenting by benefits reveals what consumers were and are seeking in their vacations. Knowing this is central to planning effective marketing programs.

A BENEFIT-MATCHING MODEL

Figure 1 summarizes a strategic view for understanding tourism behavior and developing a marketing campaign. The model emphasizes the dominant need to define markets by benefits sought and the fact that separate markets seek unique benefits or activity packages. Membership in the segments will fluctuate from year to year; the same individuals may seek rest and relaxation one year and foreign adventure the next.

Identifying benefits is not enough, however. Competitors (that is, other countries or areas) may present the same type of benefits to the consumers. Because travelers seriously consider only a few destinations, a sharp focus is needed for promoting a destination. This also means that a destination should avoid trying to be "everything to everybody" by promoting

Source: This case was written by Arch G. Woodside and Ilkka A. Ronkainen for discussion purposes and not to exemplify correct or incorrect decision making. The case is largely based on Arch G. Woodside, "Positioning a Province Using Travel Research," *Journal of Travel Research* 20 (Winter 1982): 2–6.

TABLE 1 ∎ **Benefit Segments of U.S. Travelers to Canada**

Segment I: Friends and relatives—nonactive visitor (29 percent). These vacationers seek familiar surroundings where they can visit friends and relatives. They are not very inclined to participate in any activity.

Segment II: Friends and relatives—active city visitor (12 percent). These vacationers also seek familiar surroundings where they can visit friends and relatives, but they are more inclined to participate in activities—especially sightseeing, shopping, and cultural and other entertainment.

Segment III: Family sightseers (6 percent). These vacationers are looking for a new vacation place that would be a treat for the children and an enriching experience.

Segment IV: Outdoor vacationer (19 percent). These vacationers seek clean air, rest and quiet, and beautiful scenery. Many are campers and availability of recreation facilities is important. Children are also an important factor.

Segment V: Resort vacationer (19 percent). These vacationers are most interested in water sports (for example, swimming) and good weather. They prefer a popular place with a big-city atmosphere.

Segment VI: Foreign vacationer (26 percent). These vacationers look for a place they have never been before with a foreign atmosphere and beautiful scenery. Money is not of major concern but good accommodation and service are. They want an exciting, enriching experience.

Source: Shirley Young, Leland Ott, and Barbara Feigin, "Some Practical Considerations in Market Segmentation," *Journal of Marketing Research* 15 (August 1978): 405–412.

FIGURE 1 ∎ **Benefit Matching Model**

Markets	Benefits Sought	Benefit Match	Benefits Provided	Destinations
A ⟶	A_s, B_s ⟶	S ⟵	A_p, B_p ⟵	X
B ⟶	B_s, C_s ⟶	M ⟵	C_p, D_p ⟵	Y
C ⟶	C_s, D_s ⟶	N ⟵	E_p, F_p ⟵	Z

S = Supermatch, M = Match, N = Mismatch.

Source: Arch G. Woodside, "Positioning a Province Using Travel Research," *Journal of Travel Research* 20 (Winter 1982): 3.

too many benefits. Combining all of these concerns calls for positioning; that is, generating a unique, differentiated image in the mind of the consumer.

Three destinations are shown in Figure 1. Each destination provides unique as well as similar benefits for travelers. Marketers have the opportunity to select one or two specific benefits from a set of benefits when developing a marketing program to attract visitors. The benefits selected for promotion can match or mismatch the benefits sought by specific market segments. The letters S, M, and N in the figure express the degree of fit between the benefits provided and those sought. For example, a mismatch is promoting the wrong benefit to the wrong market; e.g., promoting the scenic mountain beauty of North Carolina to Tennessee residents.

THE CASE OF NOVA SCOTIA

Canada has a rather vague and diffuse image among Americans. This is particularly true of the Atlantic provinces (see Figure 2). The majority of Nova Scotia's nonresident travelers reside in New England and the mid-Atlantic states of New York, Pennsylvania, and New Jersey. Most of these travelers include households with married couples having incomes substantially above the U.S. national average; that is, $50,000 and above. Such households represent a huge, accessible market—10 million house-

FIGURE 2 ▪ **Nova Scotia and Its Main Markets**

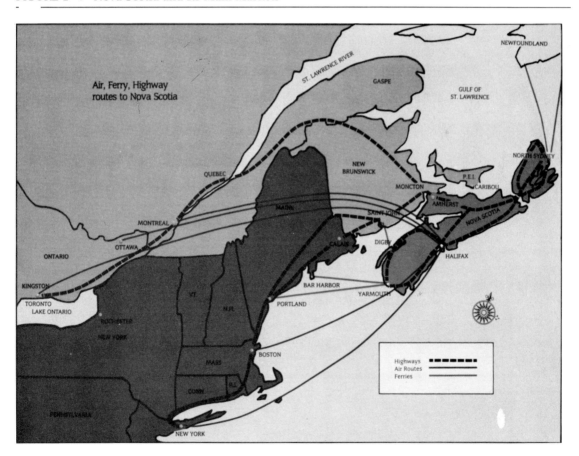

Source: "Nova Scotia," *The Travel Agent,* February 27, 1986, 14.

FIGURE 3   ■   **Example of "There's So Much to Sea" Campaign**

Source: "Nova Scotia Insert," *Travel Weekly,* April 15, 1986.

holds that are 1 to 2½ days' drive from Halifax, the capital. Most house-holds in this market have not visited the Atlantic provinces and have no plans to do so. Thus, the market exhibits three of the four requirements necessary to be a very profitable customer base for the province: size, accessibility, and purchasing power. The market lacks the intention to visit for most of the households described. Nova Scotia is not one of the destinations considered when the next vacation or pleasure trip is being planned. Worse still, Nova Scotia does not exist in the minds of its largest potential market.

In the past, Nova Scotia had a number of diverse marketing themes, such as "Good times are here," "International gathering of the clans," "The 375th anniversary of Acadia," "Seaside spectacular," and the most recent, "There's so much to sea" (see Figure 3). These almost annual changes in marketing strategy contributed to the present situation both by confusing the consumer as to what Nova Scotia is all about and by failing to create a focused image based on the relative strengths of the province. Some critics argue that Novia Scotia is not being promoted on its unique features but benefits that other locations can provide as well or better.

EXAMPLES OF SUCCESSFUL POSITIONING

Most North Atlantic passengers flying to Europe used to have a vague impression of Belgium. This presented a problem to the tourism authori-ties, who wanted travelers to stay for longer periods. Part of the problem was a former "Gateway to Europe" campaign that had positioned Belgium as a country to pass through on the way to somewhere else.

The idea for new positioning was found in the *Michelin Guides,* which rate cities as they do restaurants. The Benelux countries have six three-star cities (the highest ranking), of which five are in Belgium and only one (Amsterdam) is in Holland. The theme generated was, "In Belgium, there are five Amsterdams." This strategy was correct in three different ways: (1) it related Belgium to a destination that was known to the traveler, Amsterdam; (2) the *Michelin Guides,* another entity already known to the traveler, gave the concept credibility; and (3) the "five cities to visit" made Belgium a *bona fide* destination.[1]

The state of Florida attracts far more eastern North American beach seekers than does South Carolina. Tourism officials in South Carolina had to find a way in which the state could be positioned against Florida.

The positioning theme generated was, "You get two more days in the sun by coming to Myrtle Beach, South Carolina, instead of Florida." Florida's major beaches are a one-day drive beyond the Grand Strand of South Carolina—and one additional day back. Most travelers to Florida go in the May-to-October season when the weather is similar to that in

---

[1] Al Ries and Jack Trout, *Positioning: The Battle for Your Mind* (New York: McGraw-Hill, 1980), 171–178.

South Carolina. Thus, more beach time and less driving time became the central benefit provided by the state.

POSITIONING NOVA SCOTIA

The benefits of Nova Scotia as a Canadian travel destination cover segments III to VI of U.S. travelers (see Table 1). Those providing input to the planning process point out water activities, seaside activities, camping, or scenic activities. The segment interested in foreign adventure could be lured by festivals and other related activities.

The argument among planners centers not so much on which benefits to promote, but which should be emphasized if differentiation is desired. The decision is important because of (1) the importance of the industry to the province and (2) the overall rise in competition for the travelers in Nova Scotia's market, especially by U.S. states.

Questions for Discussion

1. How would you position Nova Scotia to potential American travelers? Use the benefit-matching model to achieve your supermatch.

2. Constructively criticize past positioning attempts, such as "There's so much to sea."

3. What other variables, apart from positioning, will determine whether Americans will choose Nova Scotia as a destination?

Union Carbide at Bhopal

On Sunday, December 3, 1984, the peaceful life of a U.S. corporate giant was joltingly disrupted. The Union Carbide plant at Bhopal, a city less than 400 miles from New Delhi, India, had leaked poisonous gas into the air. Within one week over 2,000 people died and more remained critically ill. Over 100,000 people were treated for nausea, blindness, and bronchial problems. It was one of history's worst industrial accidents.

Union Carbide is America's 37th largest industrial corporation, with more than 100,000 employees, and an annual sales volume of over $9 billion. The firm is active in petrochemicals, industrial gases, metals and carbon products, consumer products, and technology transfers.

Union Carbide operated 14 plants in India. Total Indian operations accounted for less than 2 percent of corporate sales. In spite of a policy by the Indian government to restrict foreign majority ownership of plants, Union Carbide owned 50.9 percent of the Bhopal plant. This special arrangement was granted by the government because the plant served as a major technology transfer project. In order to achieve the goal of technology transfer, management of the plant was mostly carried out by Indian nationals. General corporate safety guidelines applied to the plant, but local regulatory agencies were charged with enforcing Indian environmental laws. Only three weeks before the accident, the plant had received an "environmental clearance certificate" from the Indian State Pollution Board.

The accident resulted in wide public awareness in the United States. A poll showed that 47 percent of those questioned linked Union Carbide's name to the Bhopal disaster. The direct impact of this awareness on Union Carbide's business remains uncertain. Most U.S. consumers do not connect the Union Carbide name to its line of consumer products, which consists of brands such as Energizer, Glad, and Presto. Industrial users, on the other hand, are highly aware of Union Carbide's products. One area that could be particularly affected is that of technology transfer, which in 1983 accounted for 24 percent of Union Carbide's revenues. The firm has concentrated increasingly on that sector, selling mainly its know-how in the fields of engineering, manufacturing, and personnel training.

THE PUBLIC REACTION

Internationally, the reaction was one of widespread consumer hostility. Environmentalists demonstrated at Union Carbide plants in West Ger-

Source: This case study was written by Michael R. Czinkota by adapting secondary source materials from: Alan Hall, "The Bhopal Tragedy Has Union Carbide Reeling," *Business Week*, December 17, 1984, 32; Clemens P. Work, "Inside Story of Union Carbide's India Nightmare," *U.S. News & World Report*, January 21, 1985, 51–52; Armin Rosencranz, "Bhopal, Transnational Corporations, and Hazardous Technologies," *Ambio* 17, no. 5 (1988): 336–341; and other public information sources.

many and Australia. Some facilities were firebombed, most were spray painted. Plans for plants in Scotland had to be frozen. The operation of a plant in France was called into question by the French government.

Major financial repercussions occurred as well. Within a week of the accident, Union Carbide stock dropped by $10, a loss in market value of nearly $900 million. A $1.2 billion line of credit was frozen.

In the ensuing debate of the Bhopal disaster, three basic issues were highlighted—responsible industrial planning, adequate industrial safety measures, and corporate accountability. In terms of industrial planning, both Union Carbide and the Indian government were said to have failed. The Indian subsidiary of Union Carbide did little to inform workers about the highly toxic methyl isocyante (MIC) the plant was producing and the potential health threat to neighboring regions. When the accident occurred, the subsidiary's management team reportedly resisted the parent company's instructions to apply first aid to victims for fear of generating widespread panic within the corporation and the region. The Indian government, on the other hand, seemed to regard technology transfer to be a higher priority than public safety. The local government readily approved construction of the plant with little medical and scientific investigation into its biological effects on the environment and on people.

The second issue was the absence of a "culture of safety" among Indian technicians, engineers, and management. From the very beginning, the project lacked a team of experienced maintenance personnel who would have recognized the need for higher safety measures and, more important, a different choice of technology. When the entire Indian government wholeheartedly approved the import of the most advanced chemical production facility in any developing country without qualified personnel to handle the material and without insight into appropriate precautionary measures in case of an accident, the seeds were sown for potential disaster.

The third area of interest in the Bhopal incident is that of corporate accountability. There are three general norms of international law concerning the jurisprudence of the home government over the foreign subsidiary:

1. Both state and nonstate entities are liable to pay compensation to the victims of environmental pollution and accidents.
2. The corporation is responsible for notifying and consulting the involved officials of actual and potential harm involved in the production and transport of hazardous technologies and materials.
3. The causer or originator of environmental damage is liable to pay compensation to the victims.

These and other developing norms of international law serve to make transnational corporations more responsible to the region of their operation.

COMPENSATION TO VICTIMS

Five days after the incident the first damage suit, asking for $15 billion, was filed in U.S. Federal District Court. Since then more than 130 suits have been filed in the United States and more than 2,700 in India. Union Carbide offered to pay $300 million over a period of 30 years to settle the cases before the courts in the United States and India. The Indian government rejected the offer, claiming that the amount was far below its original request of $615 million. By 1986 most U.S. lawsuits had been consolidated in the New York Federal Court. In May 1986, however, the judge presiding over the collective Bhopal cases ruled that all suits arising out of the accident should be heard in the Indian judicial system, claiming that "India is where the accident occurred, and where the victims, witnesses and documents are located." While this decision appeared to benefit Union Carbide because of lower damage awards in India, the judge explicitly stated that (1) Union Carbide (USA) and its Indian affiliate will have to submit to the jurisdiction of the Indian court system, (2) Union Carbide must turn over all relevant documents to the plaintiffs' lawyers in India as they would if in the United States, and (3) Union Carbide must agree to whatever judgment is rendered in India. This decision had a major effect on Union Carbide (USA) because (1) both Union Carbide (USA) and its Indian subsidiary now had to answer to the Indian court and (2) the entire company's assets had become involved.

In India, the class suit traveled from the Bhopal district court to the Madhya Pradesh High Court and finally to the Indian Supreme Court, where it stood as of July 1989. Although a settlement agreement was reached between Union Carbide and the Indian government, the descendents of the 2,000 victims were not satisfied. Several victims' consumer groups and public-interest lawyers filed petitions contesting the authority of the government to handle the lawsuit on behalf of the victims' descendents. The petitions claim that the government has no right to represent the victims because governmental negligence caused the accident in the first place and the government should be as much a target as Union Carbide in the suit itself. If the Indian Supreme Court were to uphold this rationale, then the government would be unable to settle on the victims' behalf, thereby nullifying the agreed amount. Until further action can be taken, the Supreme Court of India has ordered the government to issue monthly compensation checks of $50 to the descendents of victims.

The lessons learned? Several chemical companies have reduced the size of their storage tanks of toxic materials while others have cut their inventories by as much as 50 percent. Many have provided information to the communities in which they manufacture. Some have even invested in risk assessment studies of their operations of hazardous materials.

Questions for Discussion

1. How could Union Carbide have planned for an event such as Bhopal?

2. How would such planning have improved corporate response to the disaster?

3. Does it make sense to base corporate strategy on worst-case scenarios?

4. Which other firms are exposed to similar risks?

5. What are the future implications for the management of Union Carbide?

6. What are the future implications for the government of India?

7. In general, should joint venture partners absorb part of the blame and cost when accidents occur?

Puig Doria

In August 1985, one week before the arrival of representatives of Daimatsu and C. Itoh–Japan,[1] Miguel Villar[2] and Josep Maria Puig Doria sat down to discuss how negotiations with the Japanese had gone to date. It had been almost two years since Puig Doria was first approached by the Japanese, who were interested in selling his designs in Japan, yet both Villar and Puig Doria were somewhat uneasy about the way things had developed. The worry stemmed from Puig Doria's deep personal feelings about his jewelry. He was reluctant to put his designs in hands that had not proven their ability to recreate the aura he demanded for their display and sale. At the same time, the Japanese represented a great opportunity if handled correctly.

Puig Doria had commented: "I don't want to relinquish too much control over the marketing of my jewelry. It's just too important, a rather integral part of the Puig Doria image. Yet, I approve of what they have done so far, and I don't want to give in to my feelings prematurely."

A tremendous amount of prestige was attached to successfully exporting to Japan, not to mention the sales that would result from having access to a market of 120 million affluent people. Considering Puig Doria's feelings, however, it was worth asking if anything more could be done to protect his interests while at the same time solidifying the fragile bond that existed with the Japanese.

BACKGROUND

Puig Doria is a prestigious jewelry establishment located on Avenida Diagonal in Barcelona, Spain, the Fifth Avenue of the city, where it is surrounded by other retail outlets featuring the products of several internationally known designers, such as Cartier and Yves St. Laurent. Its proprietor, Josep Maria Puig Doria, started designing jewelry in the 1950s. By 1968, his international reputation was firmly established and his designs were being featured in some of the world's most famous showrooms, including Saks Fifth Avenue, Bloomingdale's, and Van Cleef & Arpels. The proprietor's growing renown had prompted him to open the large and elegant showroom on Avenida Diagonal, which was the ex-

Source: Copyright 1986 by Instituto de Estudios Superiores de la Empresa, Universidad de Navarra, Barcelona, Spain. Prepared by Melissa Martincich, MED Alumni, under the supervision of Francesco Parés, Lecturer, and Professor Lluís G. Renart, February 1986. This case was prepared as a basis for class discussion rather than to illustrate either effective or ineffective handling of an administrative situation.

[1]C. Itoh is one of Japan's largest general trading companies. See Appendix A.

[2]Puig Doria is actually the name of the store and showroom where its owner and designer displays his jewelry. In this case, the name Puig Doria is used to describe all administrative functions, including sales and production.

clusive showroom for his designs, and the location of all of Puig Doria's administrative and commercial activities.

Although Puig Doria took exclusive responsibility for the design of his jewelry, he relied on independent craftsmen to realize the jewel itself, as this eliminated much of the administrative burden associated with maintaining inhouse production facilities, and provided Puig Doria with a great degree of flexibility relative to production capacity. Although production went on all year long, Puig Doria formally presented his new collection for the coming year in November, in time for the Christmas holiday season, when the demand for jewelry was at its peak. While some of the designs were reproduced many times for sale, one-of-a-kind pieces were designed and sold at a premium. These were often created with a particular woman in mind. In that case Puig Doria insisted on seeing or meeting her; he hoped to capture her essence in his work.

For Puig Doria, jewelry was a very personal form of expression: "When someone wants to buy one of my jewels I often get emotional. It is a very special moment when I must part with something that I value. Sometimes I feel tempted to embrace my client. I am awfully sentimental. After all, each one of my jewels is a part of my soul."

Puig Doria extended the care he put into the design of his jewels to the environment in which they were displayed and sold. He felt this was just one of many important details surrounding the creation and sale of a high-quality jewel. As a result, the Puig Doria store was color coordinated in grey and chestnut, and each jewel elegantly displayed in individual, carefully lit exhibits set into the walls throughout the establishment. The store staff was also elegantly dressed in grey and chestnut, wearing shirts especially designed to show off jewels they might be asked to model by a potential client. In addition, a section of the store had been recently devoted to a line of accessories, which included ties, briefcases, umbrellas, and scarves in Puig Doria colors, each discreetly displaying the Puig Doria insignia.

EXPORT ACTIVITIES

In 1971 Puig Doria designed a line of economical silver jewelry to be produced in quantity for export to the United States and West Germany under the Puig Doria name which, by 1977, was selling overseas in sufficient volume to justify a continuing effort. Puig Doria was compelled, however, to seriously curtail export activities when, in a serious breech of company loyalty, a former employee began producing and selling copies of the designs without any licensing agreement. Puig Doria was strongly affected by this incident and began to feel that this particular type of export activity made his designs particularly vulnerable to piracy.

As a result, he began to believe that it might be more appropriate to export not just his designs, but the Puig Doria concept as a whole, which was defined by its prestige, its elegance, and its unique style, all well represented in the showroom in Barcelona. The idea then developed to license the name "Puig Doria" to suitable retail establishments in major cities throughout the world. They would, in turn, adopt the commercial focus characteristic of Puig Doria Barcelona. These establishments would be provided with Puig Doria wrapping paper, ribbon, and a variety of other sales amenities that would provide consistency to the image. Ideally, these franchised showrooms would sell only Puig Doria designs, produced in and exported from Barcelona. In this way, the proprietor hoped to control not only where but how his designs were sold.

In 1978, Puig Doria authorized the opening of a Puig Doria store in Geneva. The store was forced to close in 1982, however, after an unsuccessful search for suitable management. Although the firm had not engaged in any export activities since then, Puig felt that international activity was an important element of prestige in his field. He stated in an interview with "Aurum": "I'm still trying to develop my business on an international level. Actually, I would like to find someone who could market my jewelry in the United States and Japan."

CONTACT WITH C. ITOH

C. Itoh, the fourth largest general trading company, or *Sogoshosha*, in Japan, maintained a branch office in Madrid that was primarily involved in trading commodities in Spain, principally aluminum. Because the margins earned in commodity trading were extremely low, it was decided in 1981 to investigate the possibility of diversifying into higher margin businesses in Spain. One result of this investigation was the decision to search for a jewelry supplier who could provide high-quality, branded jewelry with exclusive designs at a price of between $500 and $1,000 per piece, and who also offered a full range of complementary accessories.

Toward the end of 1981, after being identified as a suitable supplier, Puig Doria was contacted by Yuichi Oka, C. Itoh's Metals Department director in Madrid, to discuss the possibility of importing Puig Doria jewelry to Japan. When the person in charge of the discussions with Oka subsequently left Puig Doria, however, the relationship was abruptly broken, and it was not until the end of 1983 that Oka once again attempted to make contact. He was then put in touch with Miguel Villar,[3] who had had some previous experience exporting and knew of Puig Doria's desire to commercialize his product in Japan. Oka proposed the following: While C. Itoh would actually purchase jewelry from Puig

---

[3]Miguel Villar had been working for Puig Doria for nearly 17 years. Starting out in 1968 as administrative director, in 1982 he also became responsible for the production of the jewels, with special responsibility for those jewels with precious stones. In 1985, he defined his position as "administrative staff." He estimated that he had devoted less than five percent of his time to export-related business.

Doria, Daimatsu, a manufacturer of high-quality silk kimonos, would choose the jewels, and would be responsible for selling them to the public through retail outlets that handled, among other products, their silk kimonos and jewelry. This jewelry by Spanish standards would be considered medium quality relative to design. Daimatsu's intention was to, over time, open departments dedicated to Puig Doria in retail outlets located in ten of Japan's most important cities. C. Itoh would obtain a letter of credit to pay Puig Doria for the jewels and would earn a commission from Puig Doria over the F.O.B. price of jewelry purchased. Essentially, C. Itoh acted as buyer and importer, reselling Puig Doria jewels to Daimatsu in Japan. It was not known what, if anything, Daimatsu paid C. Itoh for this service.

At the same time, Daimatsu extended an invitation to Puig Doria to visit Japan, and insisted it would be best if he became personally acquainted with Daimatsu, its management, its clients, and Japan in general. Daimatsu hoped that Puig Doria would take an interest in promoting his products in Japan by making personal appearances at showings and becoming a live force behind his creations. Puig Doria, however, was reluctant to work with Daimatsu under the terms that they were suggesting. He made it clear to C. Itoh that while he was interested in selling his jewelry in Japan, he would work with Daimatsu only if they were willing to open retail outlets dedicated exclusively to Puig Doria products. He described plans to grant concessions featuring the Puig Doria concept as a whole. While Daimatsu was not immediately receptive to this idea, the negotiations were kept alive by C. Itoh of Japan, who patiently persisted in trying to mediate an agreement.

Eventually, three purchases were made of Puig Doria jewels, chosen personally by representatives of Daimatsu who traveled to Barcelona for the first time in January 1984. The Daimatsu representatives had said they intended to use their purchases to test the Japanese market, but after the third purchase, in December 1984, Puig Doria decided to discontinue the relationship for two reasons. First, each of the three purchases had consisted of only one unit of a particular piece of jewelry, and Puig Doria was concerned that the Japanese might simply intend to copy his designs. Since his first experience with piracy, he had had other serious incidents of his designs being reproduced without consent, and he was not unfamiliar with the stereotype of the Japanese as skillful copiers. Second, Puig Doria still wanted to export the Puig Doria concept as a whole through exclusive showrooms fashioned after his store in Barcelona, and he felt that the negotiations with Daimatsu were not leading to this end.

Between December 1984 and March 1985 communication between Puig Doria and C. Itoh was minimal, and it appeared the negotiations for the commercialization of Puig Doria jewelry in Japan had reached their end. In April 1985, however, C. Itoh forwarded two market studies to Puig Doria in an effort to convince him to continue negotiating the sale of his jewelry through Daimatsu. The first of these studies was intended

TABLE 1 ∎ **Summary of Significant Points of Japanese Market Study**

A. Buying Habits of the Japanese
    1. Unmarried young females purchase the greatest amount of gold jewelry.
    2. Seventy-five percent of gold jewelry purchased is without gemstones. Of jewelry with gemstones, 40% contains diamonds.
    3. Over 90% of females buy gold jewelry for themselves.
    4. The most popular price range of gold jewelry is ¥20,000 to ¥40,000 (Pts 15,000 to Pts 30,000).
    5. Over 60% of females purchase at a special discount or sale.
    6. Japanese jewelry consumers tend to look for quality, placing great importance on the design. They are not concerned with the "name value of the famous brands."

B. Characteristics of Gold Jewelry Markets in Spain and Japan
    1. Source of purchase
        Spain: 82% of all gold jewelry is purchased in jewelry stores, 2% in department stores, and the balance in "other."
        Japan: 39% of all gold jewelry is purchased in jewelry stores, 28% in department stores, and the balance in "other."
    2. Purchaser profile as a percentage of all gold jewelry bought
        Spain: 56% of purchases are made by women, 44% by men.
        Japan: 76% of purchases are made by women, 24% by men.
    3. Categories of purchase as a percentage of all items bought
        Spain: Rings 38%, necklaces 26%, wristwear 11%, earrings 19%, watches 2%, and brooches 4%.
        Japan: Rings 37%, necklaces 36%, wristwear 18%, earrings 6%, watches 2%, and brooches 1%.
    4. Gifts and self-purchase as a percentage of all gold jewelry bought
        Spain: 64% purchased as a gift, 36% self-bought.
        Japan: 18% purchased as a gift, 82% self-bought.
    5. Occasion of purchase as a percentage of all gold jewelry bought
        Spain: 71% purchased for a special occasion such as Christmas or birthday, 29% for no special occasion.
        Japan: 35% purchased for a special occasion, 65% for no special occasion.

Note: To allow for direct comparison, the figures are from the Intergold publication "Gold Jewelry Market, International Review," published in 1985.

to demonstrate the difficulty in establishing new retail outlets in Japan. Among other problems, Japan suffered from a shortage of suitable rental locations, extremely high rents, and exorbitant overhead, which could be attributed mostly to high wages. The second document was a market study on the Japanese gold jewelry market conducted by Intergold,[4] which seemed to indicate that the buying habits of the Japanese were significantly different from those of Spanish jewelry purchasers (Table 1). These two studies convinced Puig Doria that perhaps in Japan selling

[4]Intergold is an associate company of the Chamber Mines of South Africa, a private organization acting on behalf of South Africa's gold mines, which produce more than 50 percent of the world's gold. Intergold has spent $200 million in the past decade for the promotion of gold sales, the major portion of which has been expended to assist manufacturers and sellers of jewelry to market their products.

his jewels through exclusive showrooms was not a realistic expectation. As a result, he decided to continue working with C. Itoh and Daimatsu, reluctantly reaching the conclusion that he must become more flexible in his demands if he wished to reach any agreement at all with the Japanese.

THE FUTURE

In August 1985, Puig Doria had called Villar to his office to once again try to analyze his reluctance to commit himself to a commercial venture with C. Itoh and Daimatsu. Villar went over the document that had been the basis for the decision to continue working with the Japanese, pondering the prominent differences between the Japanese and the Spanish jewelry buyer. Because of limited knowledge of the Japanese market, Puig Doria had taken no part in choosing the jewelry that was being sent to Japan. He wondered, however, if they should somehow be more involved in creating a Japanese collection of Puig Doria jewels. Puig Doria himself was studying the large color catalog that featured the collection of Puig Doria jewelry chosen by Daimatsu during its trips to Barcelona. The catalog had been published in the fall of 1984 as the first step in launching Puig Doria in Japan, and the first 11 pages and the cover elegantly and professionally displayed the Puig Doria collection. Daimatsu had presented Puig Doria as the personality and the creative force behind the jewels by including a photo and some quotes about his work. Puig Doria had been satisfied with the presentation of his jewels, which was both creative and in good taste. While the remaining 41 pages of the catalog were devoted to Daimatsu's own collection of jewels, Puig Doria's high quality and exclusive design were clearly evident in contrast. It was obvious that Puig Doria was Daimatsu's most sophisticated line, intended to relay a sense of prestige to all the other products offered by Daimatsu.

Villar thought the catalog did justice to Puig Doria's work. But he wondered who would read it. Was it offered for sale or free to customers of Daimatsu stores, or was it intended for the management of these retail outlets? Villar was in fact unclear about many things concerning Daimatsu. He did not know what Daimatsu's exact relationship with its retail outlets was or even how many of them there were, nor could he say for sure how Puig Doria's jewels were being handled in Japan, aside from what he had seen in the catalog. While Puig Doria and Daimatsu had signed a statement outlining their intentions with one another, it was in no way specific. As a result of C. Itoh's persistence, the interests of all three parties had come closer to being met, yet Mr. Villar worried that Puig Doria was risking too much.

At the next meeting Daimatsu's representatives, among other things, intended to choose several examples of a variety of jewels to take back to Japan. They had opened the first department dedicated to Puig Doria in a retail outlet in Nagoya, and were beginning to get a feel for which designs would be successful in Japan and which would not. Villar knew they would also again extend an invitation to Puig Doria to visit Japan. As far as they were concerned things were progressing just fine, but, like Puig Doria, Villar had the uneasy sense that the Puig Doria firm was not exploiting the situation as well as it might. He continued to ponder what, if anything, they should do about it.

Questions for Discussion

1. What has made Puig Doria successful in Barcelona? What do you see as the firm's key success factors? Are they exportable?

2. Evaluate Puig Doria's previous attempts at exporting (silver jewelry and the Geneva retail outlet).

3. What has been C. Itoh's contribution in the attempt by Puig Doria to export to Japan? What is the cost of C. Itoh's services? Should Puig Doria continue using C. Itoh? Why or why not?

4. Who controls the whole export-import process in this relationship? What does control mean in this context? What objectives does each partner or stakeholder have?

5. Examine, from Puig Doria's point of view, what has been done so far with C. Itoh and Daimatsu. Has any real progress been made? How do you evaluate the situation reviewed by Puig Doria and Villar in August 1985?

   a. Should your evaluation be Positive—that is, if you feel that Puig Doria is on the right track—prepare a list of specific recommendations for consolidating the relationship with Daimatsu and to progressively increase the sales volume to the Japanese market.

   b. Should your evaluation be Negative—that is, if you feel that Puig Doria is on the wrong track—be ready to articulate the reasons why you think so; describe what you see as specifically wrong (the export strategy, the implementation, or both); explain how Puig Doria should have acted in a different way to start exporting to Japan; outline the alternative courses of action that are open; and recommend one of the alternatives.

Appendix A: General Trading Companies of Japan (Sogoshosha)

The general trading company is a uniquely Japanese commercial institution that has played an integral role in Japan's impressive economic development. Originating during the Meiji period (1868–1912), when it became the priority of the Japanese government to industrialize and modernize Japan, most modern trading companies began as independent import-export agents that acted as international representatives for Japan's budding manufacturing sector.

By 1939 and the advent of World War II, trading companies had become the common element of Japan's foreign transactions, and played an important role in mobilizing the resources necessary for Japan's war effort. With the support of the Japanese government, several large trading companies participated in a virtual monopoly over Japan's international business sector, thereby consolidating a tremendous amount of power.

POST–WORLD WAR II DEVELOPMENT

After World War II the Allied occupation considered trading companies counter to the ideal of a democratic free market economy, and an attempt was made to diminish their power by breaking them down into smaller, unrelated enterprises. In 1951, upon gaining political autonomy, the Japanese government allowed general trading companies to reconsolidate, although in a somewhat modified form. Today's trading companies are also Japan's largest multinationals, with interests in overseas trading, manufacturing, resource extraction, and a variety of other nontrading activities.

The principal areas of activity of the modern trading company can be broken down into three categories:

1. Information gathering: Each major trading company has developed a vast network with the capacity to collect information on economic, social, and political activity in almost every country in the world.
2. Quasi-banking: Trading companies maintain a reservoir of money that is used to provide short- and medium-term credit in connection with their trade intermediating activities.
3. Organizing/coordinating: Trading companies apply the skills and expertise they have gained working in international markets to coordinating and organizing large development projects outside of Japan, especially in Third World countries.

C. ITOH AND COMPANY LTD.

Founded in 1858 as a textile wholesaler, C. Itoh was one of the small trading companies that flourished at the end of World War II and is now the fourth largest trading company in Japan, with 10,000 employees, 36 branches in Japan, and 144 representative offices in 87 countries overseas. C. Itoh is active in textiles, machinery, metals, foodstuffs, commodities, energy, chemicals, construction, and a variety of other industries. Its trade volume in 1983 was $54 billion.

C. Itoh's branch office in Spain's capital of Madrid was established in 1970 and has 14 employees. Its primary activity has been in the area of metals, chemicals, and machinery.

The Audi 5000: The Case of Sudden Acceleration

In July 1989, Audi of America published multiple advertisements in business publications, newspapers, and journals across the United States declaring the "case closed" on the issue of sudden acceleration that had severely hampered its sales, stock values, and public relations during the preceding three years.

COMPANY BACKGROUND

Audi AG traces its history to 1909 when August Horch left his own company, A. Horch & Cie, to form a new firm called August Horch Automobilwerke GmbH. By 1914 the plant, in Ingolstadt, Germany, was manufacturing a range of models. In 1925 total production climbed to 1,116 vehicles. From 1912 through 1928, Audi was also involved in the production of military vehicles for the German army.

In 1932, because of the depression, Audi merged with Horch, Zschopauer Maschinenfabrik J. S. Rasmussen (DKW) and the car division of Wanderer Werke to form the Auto Union AG, with Daimler-Benz holding the majority of shares. Total production of the new company quickly rose to approximately 62,100 cars and 63,500 motorcycles.

Another year of transition was 1969, when Volkswagenwerk AG purchased Auto Union's stock from Daimler-Benz and merged the firm with the Neckarsulmer Strickmaschinenfabrik (NSU). This action brought together a conglomeration of expertise in the manufacturing of bicycles, motorcycles, typewriters, automobiles, aircraft, and submarine parts. The newly formed Audi NSU Auto Union AG experienced an explosive rate of expansion throughout the 1970s.

Throughout the history of the company, Audi cars were known for their performance, durability, and quality. Recent awards won by Audi cars include the 1986 U.S. Sports Car Club of America PRO Rally Manufacturers' Championship and the 1986 and 1987 championships in the Pikes Peak Hill Climb.

ENTRY IN THE UNITED STATES

Auto Union GmbH had exported to the United States as early as 1940. From 1949 through 1960, Auto Union exported to the United States a total of 5,801 vehicles. Exports climbed slowly, and by the end of 1970 the newly formed Audi sold just under 7,700 cars through 138 dealers in

Source: This case was written by Michael R. Czinkota and Bao-Nga Tran based on public sources such as *Automotive News* and *Automotive Litigation Reporter*; the videotape "Unintended Acceleration: The Myth and the Reality," Audi of America, Troy, Michigan, 1989; *History of Progress 1988*, Audi AG, Ingolstadt, West Germany, 1988; and interviews with executives of Audi of America and Volkswagen of America.

the United States. A wholly owned subsidiary, Audi of America Inc., was established on September 1, 1985, and assumed from the American subsidiary of Volkswagen AG the functions of sales, service, advertising, merchandising, and public relations for Audi operations. By 1985, Audi of America's sales reached 74,061, capturing over 35 percent of Volkswagen of America's total sales in the United States. Vice President Peter Fischer of Audi of America estimated in 1985 that Audi's "5000 series will be the 'backbone' of Audi's lineup and will represent 64 percent of Audi's U.S. sales in 1986."

ADVERSE MEDIA COVERAGE

In March 1986, the Center for Auto Safety submitted a petition to Audi of America, requesting the recall of all 1978 through 1986 Audi 5000 models because of repeated cases of dangerous malfunction. At the beginning of November 1986, New York's attorney general Robert Abrams publicly asked Audi of America to stop selling Audi 5000 automobiles with automatic transmissions. Both parties claimed that hundreds of accidents had been caused by the improper acceleration of Audi 5000s. Then, on the evening of November 23, 1986, CBS broadcast a "60 Minutes" episode with the Audi 5000 featured as one of its segments.

During this single broadcast Audi was accused before 65 million viewers of manufacturing and distributing the Audi 5000 series without warning the public of the possible danger of a phenomenon known as "sudden acceleration." Sudden acceleration was hypothesized to occur when "the driver starts the engine and moves the shift lever from 'park' into reverse or drive. The car [at times suddenly] hurtles forward or backward at great speed, with the driver unable to stop."

During the segment, CBS interviewed several drivers who claimed to have experienced the problem of unintended sudden acceleration. One man claimed he suffered shin splints because he pressed his foot too hard on the brake pedal. Another witness broke the car seat while fighting to brake her uncontrollable Audi. The most dramatic account of all came from Mrs. Brodosky, whose car killed her own son when it suddenly accelerated and pinned his body against the wall. These interviews quickly placed Audi on the defensive because the drivers were seen as helpless victims while operating a luxury automobile promised by Audi to be reliable and safe.

The "60 Minutes" broadcast included professional input from an automotive engineer and a representative of the American Standards Testing Bureau, who speculated on the cause of sudden acceleration. These professional opinions were both the same: "The idle stabilizer which keeps gas flowing to the engine may be fooled into sending too much. This transient malfunction would totally bypass the accelerator system, leaving the driver helpless, and would not leave any internal engine damage." To test this hypothesis, CBS had an engineer demonstrate how

sudden acceleration could occur. The demonstrating driver shifted into drive with no foot on the brake or the accelerator pedals, and the car lurched forward.

AUDI'S RESPONSE

Following the CBS broadcast, Audi AG and Volkswagen of America denied the allegations, stating that sudden acceleration results from the negligence of the drivers. Through letters to Audi dealers and owners, both Audi and Volkswagen attempted "not only to counteract the ("60 Minutes") report, but really more to educate (consumers) as to the issue and assure them [they] are building safe cars." Audi, in addition, spent over $1 million in December 1986 placing ads in *The Wall Street Journal*, *USA Today*, and over 100 newspapers in 33 major cities, highlighting the fact that other manufacturers such as Nissan, Mercedez-Benz, and Volvo had received similar complaints.

By January 1987, Audi was forced to take more decisive action and recalled 25,000 of the 5000 series to install an idle stabilizer that required the driver to place a foot on the brake pedal before shifting gears. Further, Audi publicly denounced the CBS "60 Minutes" news team for news manipulation. In their opinion, CBS was unethical in not revealing to the public that the engineer interviewed on the program had to "dismantle three internal pressure relief valves, drill a hole into the transmission housing, and introduce artificial pressure from outside, pressure far greater than could ever occur in normal operation of the vehicle" in order to accelerate without pressing on the gas pedal. Audi executives believed that, had this been revealed, the impact of the CBS theory would have been lessened.

THE MARKET RESPONSE

Within a year and a half following the CBS broadcast, Audi was beset with huge financial losses and faced hundreds of court cases from its customers and dealers.

In the four year period from 1985 to 1988, the company's sales dropped from 74,061 to 22,943, as shown in Table 1. According to Audi AG Chairman Ferdinand Piech, the impact of falling sales resulted in a loss of $120 million in 1987 alone. In addition, Volkswagen's stocks, which closed on July 30, 1986, at 454.0, plummeted to a low of 248.5 by the close of July 29, 1988. A loss of public faith and interest is reflected in decreasing resale values of Audi 5000s in comparison to the Volvo 740 GLE and the BMW 325i 6, as highlighted in Table 2.

Along with the financial losses, Audi of America and Volkswagen of America faced court suits for injuries suffered due to sudden acceleration and the loss of resale car value. For example, in the class action suit

TABLE 1 ▪ **Audi Sales in the United States, 1985–1988**

Year	Number of Sales	Percent of Total Import Sales	Loss in Sales Since 1985
1985	74,061	2.61	—
1986	59,797	1.84	19.3%
1987	41,322	1.31	44.2
1988	22,943	0.75	69.0

TABLE 2 ▪ **New versus Used Car Prices, 1985–1988**

	1985	1986	1987	1988
NEW PRICES				
Audi 5000	$18,160	$19,575	$20,460	$22,850
BMW 325i 6	21,105	20,455	22,850	25,150
Volvo 740 GLE	18,585	18,980	20,610	21,850
USED CAR WHOLESALE PRICES				
Audi 5000	$ 5,400	$ 7,650	$11,175	$14,550
BMW 325i 6	11,300	10,300	16,600	24,500
Volvo 740 GLE	10,325	11,000	13,100	15,850

Note: Figures effective for four-door sedans with automatic transmission.

Source: *Official Used Car Guide* (McLean, Virginia: National Auto Dealers Association, 1989).

of Paul Perona et al. v. Audi AG et al., the plaintiffs list the following points of redress:[1]

- Breach of implied warranty of merchantability under the Uniform Commercial Code
- Violation of Consumer Fraud and Deceptive Trade Business Practice Act
- Breach of express warranties under the Uniform Commercial Code
- Breach of implied covenant of good faith and fair dealing
- Willful and wanton violation of Consumer Fraud and Deceptive Trade Business Practice Act
- Breach of contract

In addition, many owners have filed independent suits against Audi and Volkswagen. By 1988 court fees alone were estimated to have cost Audi over $10 million. Over $4.6 million in payments have been awarded to injured parties throughout the United States, but Audi and Volkswagen

[1] *American Litigation Reporter*, April 7, 1987, 8, 449–457.

continue to face a multitude of unsettled individual lawsuits involving sudden acceleration.

AUDI'S REPOSITIONING

With increasingly declining sales and bulging inventories, Audi once again was forced to take drastic action. In the spring of 1988, the firm began to offer $4,000 rebates to previous Audi owners toward the purchase of a new Audi 5000 model. In addition, to control costs, Audi of America reduced its work force by several hundred in response to the shutdown of an Audi assembly plant in Westmoreland, Pennsylvania. Concurrently, Audi's parent company, Volkswagen of America, executed four major shake-ups in Audi's top management.

Audi continued to run full one- and two-page advertisements directly addressing the issue of sudden acceleration. According to *Automotive News*, "ads captioned 'It's Time We Talked' . . . suggest that Audi erred at first when it decided to let the facts speak for themselves."[2] In February 1989, Audi kicked off the advertising year with the theme, "The Alternate Route." Promotions during the year highlighted Audi's longer warranties and four-wheel-drive system as standard features of its newest lines. The new marketing approach was budgeted by Audi of America at approximately $60 million, almost twice the amount of previous years' promotional budgets.

In 1989 Audi discontinued the 5000 models and introduced a new 100/200 line to divorce itself from the issues that plagued the 5000 series. The new line represents "a major step in Audi's recovery program, as it refines, upgrades, and improves on the original 5000 series." With a better-built car and longer servicing warranties, Audi hopes its faithful clientele—as well as its own management—will encounter fewer complications and amend their relationship. To entice previous 5000 owners to accept their new offer, Audi has provided a resale guarantee, limited to the first through fourth years of ownership, that would pay the customer the entire difference in retail trade-in values between the Audi 5000 and the comparable 260 E Mercedez-Benz, Volvo 740, and BMW 525.

CASE CLOSED

A March 1989 National Highway Traffic Safety Administration study concluded that sudden acceleration may occur on a number of automobiles for a variety of reasons: "close lateral pedal placements, similarity of pedal force displacement, pedal travel and vertical offset, and

---

[2]David Versical, "Audi Reports U.S. Loss, Beefs Up Ad Campaign," *Automotive News*, April 4, 1988: 3.

FIGURE 1 ▪ **Audi Advertisement Announcing Final Decision of the National Highway Traffic Safety Administration**

Case Closed.

Is there anyone who has not heard the rumors of "sudden acceleration" and Audi? We doubt it.

What you may not know, however, is that the final chapter has just been written.

Because on July 11, 1989, the National Highway Traffic Safety Administration officially completed its investigation and closed the file.

An investigation involving over 20 manufacturers, thousands of pages of test data and various other materials.

Their conclusion? No mechanical or electrical defect which would cause "sudden acceleration".

Their explanation? Pedal misapplication.

These findings coincide with similar investigations by the governments of Canada and Japan. As well as Audi's own analysis of the "sudden acceleration" incidents.

While there can be no happy ending to such a sad episode, the faith of our loyal owners and dealers has been justified.

Audi has been vindicated. Case closed.

© 1989 Audi of America

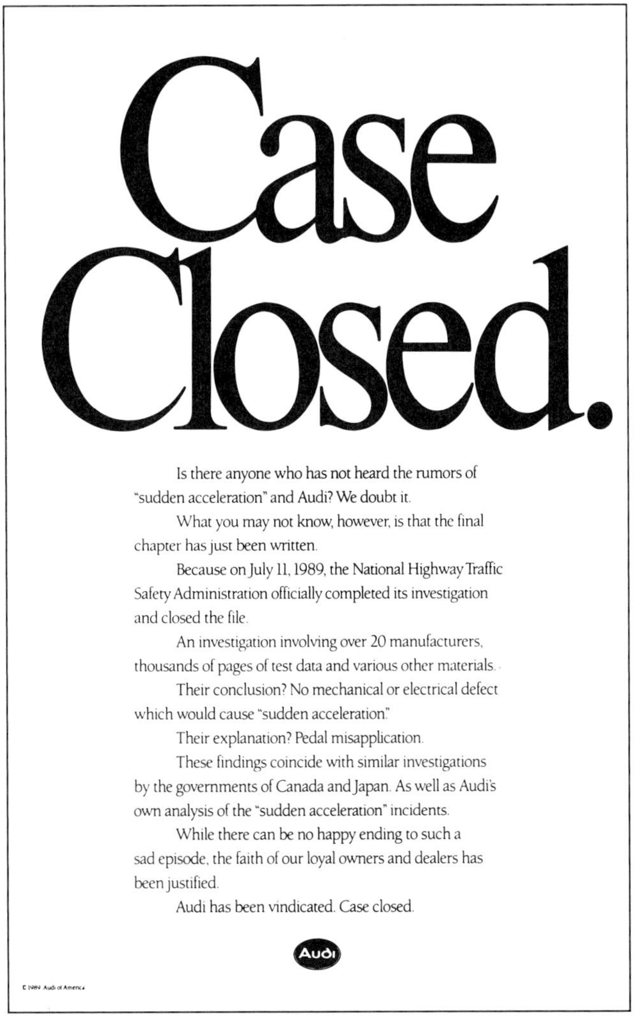

Source: *Washington Post*, July 1989.

vehicle acceleration capability that allows an error to occur before a driver has time to take corrective action." The study also explicitly stated that changes to the pedal design and placement in future models would only reduce the number of occurrences and not eliminate them altogether.

In July 1989, Audi of America took advantage of this conclusion and ran the "Case Closed" advertisement shown in Figure 1.

Questions for Discussion

1. Would a U.S. carmaker have responded differently to the CBS "60 Minutes" broadcast?

2. Evaluate the "re-marketing" efforts of Audi of America for 1986–1988 and 1989.

3. Design an alternative response to maintain customer satisfaction.

4. Do you believe the case is closed on the Audi 5000?

Agencia de Publicidad Aramburu S.A. (APA)

Mr. Aramburu was worried about the growing complexity of the operations of his advertising agency, from the point of view of both creativity and implementation of the advertising campaigns.

The agency not only created and implemented advertising campaigns for various Spanish products for the Spanish market but also had been creating and implementing since 1975—at least in part—the advertising campaigns for Semo semolina, manufactured by Invesa, in various East African countries, in Morocco, and in the Middle East; subsequently, since 1983, it had agreed to create advertising campaigns for African or Arab customers to be aired in their respective countries.

On the one hand, it seemed worthwhile to put to use the body of knowledge acquired over the last ten years on how to advertise in Africa and the Middle East. On the other hand, he wondered if these markets really offered any opportunities in the medium term or if the good results obtained so far owed more to having ridden on the crest of a wave of favorable circumstances.

PREVIOUS INTERNATIONAL EXPERIENCE

Agencia de Publicidad Aramburu S.A. (APA), had its origin in 1940 as the advertising department of a food comglomerate (Vascalisa) and gradually developed into Publicom S.A., a wholly owned subsidiary of Vascalisa. In 1985, APA was founded as the result of a management buy-out. The buy-out came about because Vascalisa was an industrial group with only limited interest in advertising activities. Even as a separate entity APA continued to work with Vascalisa during a transitional period, on the basis of fees and other conditions stated in the purchasing contract.

EXPORTING ADVERTISING SERVICES

In 1975 Vascalisa set up an export department to sell semolina to countries in Africa and the Middle East. For this purpose, "Semo" was developed in 1977, a semolina which could be defined as a tropicalized durum formula Semolín. In the same year, the Vascalisa subsidiary Internacional Vasca Export S.A. (Invesa) was created as the company within the group that would manufacture and market Semo. Invesa soon began to open markets in Central and East Africa, especially in the countries that made up the Horn of Africa.

Source: This case was prepared by Pere Gil, student 2° MED, under the supervision of Francesco Parés, Lecturer, and Professor Lluís G. Renart. It is intended to be used as a basis for class discussion rather than to illustrate either effective or ineffective handling of an administrative situation. Copyright © 1987, IESE, Barcelona, Spain. Reprinted with permission. No part of this publication may be reproduced without the permission of IESE.

Vascalisa decided to rename its export semolina, calling it Semo—which locally sounds something like "semu"—which sounded better and was easier to pronounce than Semolín. The product itself was tropicalized too to make it more resistant in the environment of extreme climatic conditions, especially considering the length of time that passed between manufacture in Spain and consumption in countries such as Somalia, Tanzania, or Sudan. The product would be retailed in small individual bags, following local usage and to increase rotation, instead of boxes containing several bags, which was the format used to sell Semolín in Spain.

Right from the start, Vascalisa turned to Publicom S.A. for help in designing its marketing strategy in Africa. The product's name, the adaptation of the product's quality to the markets it would enter, its presentation (without box) were all minutely analyzed. From the business point of view, Publicom S.A. treated Vascalisa just like any other company, providing full service within the legal restrictions imposed by each African country. Vascalisa paid Publicom S.A. in Spain, using pesetas for the services provided.

In 1979, both Vascalisa and Publicom S.A. began to feel the need to evolve toward a more aggressive sales strategy; by 1980, this feeling had become a determination to gradually progress from push marketing to pull marketing.

As Mr. Aramburu explained: "At first, we had to feel our way; it did not seem reasonable to us to invest in expensive advertising campaigns in markets whose possibilities we did not exactly know. Later on, we saw that the sales of Semo were growing, that we had a large potential market, and that it could be profitable to invest money in 'pulling' the product from the point of sale. We also understood that any campaign we made had to be aimed at promoting a specific demand, and not just a purely generic demand, as some Italian brands had already been around over there for much longer than us."

The first task was to decide *how to advertise*. It was obvious that the methods and ideas used in Spain could not be easily exported to the markets in East Africa. There was also the language problem: in Tanzania, for example, the only official language was Swahili,[1] a widely used native language that was written using the Latin alphabet, although English was fairly common at certain levels; there were also several major dialects that were spoken but not written. In view of the reduced level or even nonexistence of television and the low readership levels, especially among women, the media that seemed to be the most suitable was radio; in any case, there were no audience surveys and it also had to

---

[1] Swahili is a Bantu language spoken in Tanzania (including Zanzibar) and Kenya, where it is the official language; in Uganda, where it is the official language with English, and in some areas of the Congo River basin. It is the most widely spoken Black African language and has been considerably influenced by Arab and Persian. Although originally written in Arab characters, in the 19th century Latin characters were introduced. Swahili is widely used as a written language in magazines and newspapers.

be borne in mind that the radio stations were usually run by the respective governments, with very little room for maneuver, and centered on news. The same could be said about television in those countries where it existed, to the extent that there were no censuses of the number of television sets.

"Advertising," commented Mr. Aramburu, "is just one more cultural phenomenon. Each advertisement must stimulate the consumer's preference toward the brand, and the advertisement's message cannot be dissociated either from the product that sponsors it or from the idiosyncrasies of the potential consumer it is directed toward. We avoided 'advertising colonization' as much as possible because of our lack of knowledge concerning the region and because it seemed advisable to us from the point of view of working relationships with the government authorities. Thus, only an observant and open-minded person would realize that in those countries the housewife appearing in TV commercials would have to be a plump and well-fed woman; or that a dish must be tasted almost unavoidably with the fingers.

"In those countries where they existed, we reached agreements with local agencies. This was the case in Tanzania, Somalia, Ethiopia, and Kenya. In other countries where there were no established advertising agencies, we had to work directly with the advertising departments of the broadcasting stations."

Publicom S.A. tried to generate ideas in the meetings held with the staff of the local agencies. Normally, these were young people who had studied in Europe or occasionally an English expatriate who had started up on his own. All their ideas, collected in the field and processed in Bilbao, were expressed in a video, in a radio spot, in a jingle, in an image, that Publicom S.A. then showed in Madrid to a group of contacts from the country concerned—mostly students—to ensure that the message was appropriate.

"In Kenya, in 1983, we ran a campaign consisting of a truck with a film projector that toured through the jungle and when it arrived at a village, showed a promotional film; the driver–operator then handed out free samples of Semo to the audience. In 1984, we launched the multimedia campaign 'The Four Pleasures' in Tanzania, a country which has color television. It referred to the four pleasures of cooking: the purchase of the ingredients, the preparation of the dish by the housewife, the offering of the food to the head of the family (the father), without whose approval the meal cannot be served, and the tasting of the dish by him. The commercial was announced by a 'kotch-barma,' a mythical character, a king's witch doctor, a kind of oracle who—unlike other counselors who may indulge in intriguing—always tells the truth. This character combs his hair with two perpendicular partings so that it is divided into four parts, like a harlequin. In the commercial, the witch doctor shows his head with his hair dyed in the four colors of the Semo bags while he recommends its use for cooking to be able to enjoy the four pleasures it provides to the consumer. Before launching the message on the market,

we wanted to be sure that the video would not be sacrilegious or scandalous and so we showed it to about a dozen Tanzanians we had contacted in Madrid who could read and write Swahili. This campaign was shown on television in two countries and broadcast on radio in a further five; produced in 14 different dialects, as well as Swahili, French, and English. At the time, it was the basic advertising communication in those markets.

"In 1984, we also launched a jingle on the radio in Uganda with such intensity that many thought that it was the national anthem and stook up every time they heard it. In each case, we tried to get maximum advertising benefit from the media available to us and for this we had to know the particular features of each region and the coverage of the various media. Thus, we discovered that in some villages it was the custom for families to get together in large groups to watch television. On other occasions, it was impossible for us to get around the pressure we were subjected to by associated agencies or the media themselves to advertise through certain media, such as newspapers, which seemed ineffective to us.

"We also launched two blind-test commercials; in these, people tasted two different soups, one of which was made with Semo. Everybody delightedly guessed which was Semo after successively dipping their fingers in each and licking them."

THE TRIPS TO AFRICA

In line with his philosophy of adapting the advertising and marketing to the particular idiosyncrasies of each national market, Mr. Aramburu went to Africa for the first time in 1982. The purpose of the trip was to "smell out" the market on the spot, to find out for himself what it was like. In Dar-es-Salaam, Carlos Aramburu had the opportunity to deal directly with the distributor of Semo, with some of his salesmen, and with retailers.

"One thing that stands out straight away is the vital importance of the point of sale for effectively marketing the product. In the markets of the large capitals, the stalls measure barely one meter square. They may be open-air or lightly covered and are usually attended by a mammy. [*Mammy* or, perhaps less frequently, *mummy* is used generically in Africa to refer to women who sell in the market.] These mammies are usually extraordinarily fat women who sit on a box and arrange the consumer products they sell on the ground in front of them. In the countryside, the retail outlets are shacks where no more than a dozen different brands are stacked.

"I have visited a large number of these bazaars and street markets, sticking stickers or offering posters showing the Semo squares, colors, and logo; this aspect of loyalty to an image is vital in those countries where the written transmission of slogans or even of the product's name is virtually useless. This direct contact with the mammies, with the salesmen, with the agents, even with the personnel of the media advertising departments, with the market, and with the country in general has been very useful. We have found out what the market is really like, it's given us ideas, it's enabled us to gain the channel's trust. In fact, I don't think that any other manufacturer has made so much effort to get close to the market. The fact is that we are gaining market share and I suppose the other manufacturers are getting pretty worried."

DIVERSIFICATION OF APA'S EXPORT BUSINESS AND ITS OPENING UP TO LOCAL ADVERTISERS

Little by little, on the basis of the reputation gained from the marketing of Semo, Publicom S.A. began to make a name for itself in some of the countries in which it operated. The distributors were pleasantly surprised by the success of Publicom S.A.'s campaigns; the personal contacts made during the visits helped to create an atmosphere of rapprochement and trust; the dinners held in the Carvajal family's house, to which the small but warm-hearted Spanish colony in Dar-es-Salaam was invited, were the scene of interminable conversations which gave Carlos Aramburu a clearer idea of life in those countries.

The importers and/or distributors of Semo were usually influential men of Indopakistani or Lebanese origin who had businesses in several industrial and commercial sectors. Mr. Aramburu spoke of them with a certain air of indecision. "In my opinion, it is vital to deal directly with people. I think that everyone likes being treated on an equal footing in a natural and respectful manner; I have always tried to establish a climate of polite deference and I think that it has opened a lot of doors for me. In any case, not all Europeans agree with me and there are some who have had undoubted success in the area in spite of—or perhaps thanks to—their rather arrogant and scornful attitude."

In the spring of 1983, the importer of Semo in Tanzania requested Publicom S.A. to design the advertising campaign for the umbrellas it manufactured and sold, bypassing Counterpoint, which was the local agency that Vascalisa, Publicom S.A., and the importer itself had worked with right from the first day Semo was marketed there. In another two countries, Publicom S.A. was also given direct assignments from the respective importers. The importer of Semo in Zanzibar also sold a line of Italian detergents and it placed Publicom S.A. in charge of the advertising campaign for these detergents.

The main problems facing Publicom S.A. at that time were basically two-fold. First, the importers did not have or were simply not used to providing the type of information on the market, the channel, and the markups that was essential to organize a meaningful campaign. "Over there," said Mr. Aramburu, whose voice had recovered its forceful tone, "you've got to be prepared to listen. If you hand the potential client your

BID,[2] the chances are he won't be able to fill it in because to do so, certain basic knowledge is required not of marketing but of the market, of what you really want to achieve. Also, in addition to the problem of the lack of a qualified sales manager, you've also got the lack of statistics on media audiences and, worse still, the lack of awareness of advertising techniques."

There was also the problem of payment because until then Publicom S.A. had always been paid by Vascalisa in Spain, using pesetas. When it started to work directly for local companies, as the product that Publicom S.A. sold to its new companies was an intangible consisting of advertising ideas and action techniques, sometimes it was difficult to justify the origin of the dollars received in fees to the customs authorities at the airport when leaving the country.

BASIC FEATURES OF EXPORTING ADVERTISING SERVICES TO AFRICA

"In all these countries," said Mr. Aramburu, "the normal procedure is to start talking about money. When they decide to invest, it is because they feel it is advisable to do so but normally they don't know how much. It can even occur that they say to you, 'I've got so many million shillings. What can I do with them? Maybe I could put posters on buses, or print ads in the newspapers?' They are at that point where a country or company is starting to feel interested in advertising. It happened in Spain 30 years ago and it's happening to them now.

"The advertiser has no information on the market in his own country and neither do we. So somehow we have to complement the 'empirical' information available. Mr. Abdullah Bequer, for example, does not know for sure who is buying his products; he knows his customers are natives because he knows the points of sale. But he doesn't know their social class, their age, their background. Neither does he know to what extent his customers are loyal, that is, repeat buyers, or whether his sales are usually only occasional first purchases. You have to work a bit on trial and error to get an idea of the situation.

"Also, and as a result of the above, major changes may occur in the course of the campaign. For example, if it is seen that the campaign is successful, its budget may be considerably increased."

In Spain, on the other hand, the process was usually started on the advertiser's initiative, who nearly always had a certain idea of the market situation. The advertiser selected an agency, who proposed his fees and method. Advertiser–agency "marriages" were frequent, i.e., an advertiser

---

[2]The BID—or Basic Information Document—was, in APA's terminology, what is usually known as a briefing or questionnaire often used by advertising agencies to gain information on the basic features of its client and the product to be marketed. This questionnaire is filled in by the potential client or by the agency itself after initial contact and will be used to draw the general lines of the advertising campaign.

may consistently use the same agency to advertise some or all its products. After preparing the briefing, the agency was in a position to be able to define the campaign's total cost. After that, it started to develop the creativity, the idea, or concept to communicate and the way to communicate it most effectively. The next steps were media definition, budget distribution, contracting the media chosen, and putting the campaign into action and monitoring it.

In other cases, it was the agency that took the initiative, seeking out a client with whom to reach an initial agreement for the presentation of a tentative campaign based on an overall budget. From that mutual loose commitment, the agency developed the creativity to present it to the advertiser. If the advertiser was satisfied with the agency's ideas, it implemented the ensuing steps of defining the media, distributing the budget, contracting the media, and executing the campaign. On the other hand, if the ideas created by the agency were not to the budding client's liking, it could cancel the contract on the spot.

Carlos Aramburu commented on the differences between the situation in Africa and the normal working methods used in Spain: "You cannot place all the local agencies under the same heading. For example, in Mogadishu, Vascalisa has its local agency, Oggi, which is very dependable. Oggi contracts the media and bills Vascalisa locally for them. Also, Oggi creates the idea, designs the storyboard, and films the commercial or records the spot or prepares the original graphics. Our function in this case is to closely supervise the operations and ensure that the standards desired by Vascalisa are met.

"In other cases, for example, the United Arab Emirates, APA does the complete creativity and the local agency buys the media, supervises the copy, determines the amount of posters to be printed, and gives information on local culture.

"Finally, in those countries where there are no local agencies, APA resorts to the managers of the advertising media for advice on local culture, review of the copy in the local language, hire actors and speakers."

CARLOS ARAMBURU'S CONCERNS IN SEPTEMBER 1986

Carlos Aramburu was aware of the prudence required to manage a company recently starting out on its own and with rather limited financial resources. He also liked to define himself as a businessman "like they used to be," concerned to get the most out of every peseta spent and unwilling to take on additional expenditure items if it was not clear that they were absolutely necessary.

As part of this line of thought, APA's prime goal was to consolidate a market in Spain. The image its team of professionals had created for themselves over the last 30 years, the successes achieved, and the enormous amount of creativity shown by campaigns as varied as those for a major Japanese photocopier manufacturer ("Japanese through a Tube"), a

well-established Bilbao newspaper ("In Writing, Please"), a chain of supermarkets covering the entire Basque Country, Navarre, and Rioja ("We
Sell Quality"), or a cookie manufacturer ("Heaps Better"), among many
others, provided a major business asset which had to be capitalized upon.

Furthermore, the team of professionals in APA had been working in
the sector for many years, knew everybody in Spain, and were in a position to present themselves as a group experienced in working together,
that had been enriched after the purchase of Publicom S.A. with new
human and technical resources and was able to offer each advertiser a
dual response of creativity and service adapted to each client's particular
situation.

However, the general manager of APA did not want to give up the idea
of strengthening his markets abroad and he was well aware that a significant part of the agency's billing for creativity—excluding therefore the
buying of media—came from Vascalisa and the overseas clients.

Carlos Aramburu realized the enormous prospects that were opening
up to him in the East African and Arab countries. The multinational
agencies had yet to establish any significant presence in these quasi-
virgin territories and Mr. Aramburu was afraid that, if he let time slip by,
he would end up losing his lead to them. He had noticed that the sales
office of an Italian agency in Mogadishu had been recently relaunched
after years of inactivity. In this area, he considered that he had several
possible alternatives: establish branches (wholly owned subsidiaries),
continue as until now cooperating with the agencies existing in each
country on the basis of agreed "contractual" collaborations, or form associations with the local agencies, buying some of their shares and providing basically technical assistance, such as training personnel in Spain or
dealing with certain aspects of the creativity. In any case, it seemed clear
that each country would require individual treatment.

APA, both in Spain and in the other nine countries it had worked in,
had developed a know-how and an image that it should not let go to waste.
They had been four years of work well done by Publicom S.A. and APA
in Tanzania, Somalia, Kenya, Uganda, or Morocco; four years of traveling, learning, contacting markets, agencies, and media, of winning the
company's first clients. To wait two years, which was the least time required to ensure continuity in Spain, for pushing strongly abroad, was
not without risk.

Mr. Aramburu did not forget Vascalisa, the temporarily captive customer he had gained with the agency buy-out, which for the time being
guaranteed a certain minimum billing for the agency. In any case, the
terms were not particularly generous and Mr. Aramburu was considering
renegotiating—updating—some of the clauses because, in his opinion,
the quality of the service given by APA was improving day by day and in
some cases was significantly higher than that given when the contract for
the management buy-out of Publicom S.A. was written.

In Mr. Aramburu's opinion, the policy of exporting advertising services could be focused along two approaches: the European companies

that exported to Africa and the Middle East and the local companies. APA had already made contacts with some Spanish companies that were looking for markets in those regions.

In addition to these general issues, Mr. Aramburu also pondered on a number of other more specific but no less important problems.

Among these was the question of the profitability of the foreign clients. Most of these were medium-sized companies and—especially in the case of the foreign clients—required traveling. This inevitably meant an increase in the cost of the service, should traveling expenses be charged direct to the clients, or a significant decrease in profitability should APA include such costs as one more item in its income statement. Mr. Aramburu wondered to what extent, in the medium term, these charges could be borne by him or by his customers and, looking at the problem from another viewpoint, what should APA's fees be for it to be worthwhile for him and for his clients.

Mr. Aramburu was also aware that, in September 1986, APA had no export manager; there was the feeling in the agency that such a position would unnecessarily burden the overhead and the time for such a person was not yet ripe. As Mr. Aramburu explained: "There's no doubt that an export manager—or foreign accounts manager as we would call him— would significantly lighten my workload and enable me to give greater attention to the Spanish market. In November, for instance, I should be going to three countries and the way things are, it looks that I won't be able to go. A trip abroad, in addition to totally absorbing your attention for a few days, always leaves a few loose ends to be tied up because when you get back you have to send a leaflet or agenda to the inquisitive government officer who asked for them, send an answer to this or that client, review the conclusions of this or that matter, write a letter of intent, report to the board. But I think that it's best to wait a while because to fill this position would cost money and it's got to be done properly. We would need someone who would fit in with the company's corporate philosophy, who was familiar with the bureaucratic problems existing over there, who knew the methods of payment and the systems of credit, and who could feel at ease in those countries.

"Then there's what I call advertising 'colonization' and which we have consistently avoided: we sell creativity not preconceived ideas tailored to the European markets; also, you've got to bear in mind our own limitations, our lack of in-depth knowledge of the reality and idiosyncrasies of each country, of the need to know how to work with people over there."

THE CONCEPTION OF A BUSINESS STRATEGY: STRENGTHS AND POSSIBILITIES

Deep down, what worried Mr. Aramburu most was the doubt he constantly had as to the suitability of the present business strategy. Sometimes, he caught himself muttering, "The idea of a medium-sized Basque

agency going out and running campaigns in Africa is ridiculous! A thousand things could happen to convert it into instant disaster."

In any case, Carlos Aramburu tried to look at the situation from another viewpoint. He was aware that the agency he owned and managed had not yet had time to attain large volumes but he knew that he had a wide range of possibilities before him and the decision he took—which under no circumstances should endanger the company's continuity—could differentiate the advertising product he offered and speed up the company's growth path. In short, APA seemed to be facing the following strategic options:

1. Stop all exporting of advertising services—giving up also Vascalisa with a billing volume of 23 million pesetas and a margin of 12 million pesetas a year—in view of the risk that in the medium-term, as local agencies appeared in the various countries, the local advertisers would leave APA, preferring to work with these native agencies. Mr. Aramburu could not quite get out of his mind the niggling sensation that all that had been achieved through Vascalisa was only a fly-by-night affair without any real substance.

2. Continue to let itself be carried along by Vascalisa without actively trying to gain new clients for campaigns outside Spain. This meant continuing to sell "without pushing," to carry on "waiting for them to come"; in any case, even if this option was chosen, it seemed advisable to define the time when such a strategy would no longer be sufficient and the company should launch itself with more determination in the conquest of new markets.

3. Continue to think how to make best use of the know-how acquired but to preferably direct efforts toward Spanish companies with sales activities in those countries. Mr. Aramburu could not wait to find out who was exporting to the countries that APA knew so well; Mr. Aramburu would initiate contacts—first by letter/pamphlet and then by personal visit to each of those exporters—to offer them APA's services, backed by the successes achieved with Vascalisa. This offer could be made in at least two ways:

   ▪ Directly approach the exporting companies.
   ▪ Approach these companies' advertising agencies. APA could act as a specialist consultant in those countries.

   Or, looking at things from another point of view:

   ▪ Only approach those companies that were already exporting.
   ▪ Try to find out (how? where?) which companies were potential exporters to the countries in the area and approach them.

4. Preferably direct efforts at the native companies in each African country, which to a certain extent was the path followed so far under Vascalisa's wing. In any case, it seemed clear that the BID to be used for these local clients would have to be refocused.

In addition to these four options related to client segments, at a more general level of the organization there existed the possibility of seeking associations with another larger advertising agency or even with some group that wished to create, develop, or cultivate markets in East Africa. This idea did not particularly appeal to Mr. Aramburu from a "personal fulfilment" viewpoint but he was sure that any company who bought APA would be buying valuable know-how that would enable it to gain rapid penetration in certain countries. This know-how was an asset that increased the company's value and, in a services company—which is what an advertising agency is par excellence—this meant a great deal. After all, Mr. Aramburu said to himself with a slight smile of self-satisfaction, "I don't know any other agency apart from APA that has in its files, for instance, the prices of market media in Kenya."

Questions for Discussion

1. Which course of action do you recommend?
2. Who should implement the course of action?
3. Does APA supply the same services in Africa as it does in Spain?

Megabox Inc.

Megabox Inc. is a major manufacturer of color television sets and video cassette recorders (VCRs), with its major production facility and final assembly plant in Western Pennsylvania. Competition from Far Eastern manufacturers has compelled the company to trim its product line and to concentrate on a limited number of quality products while attending to the needs of specialized market segments.

The leap of the oil-producing Middle Eastern countries into contemporary consumer society has made them important markets for Megabox products. Television broadcasts have been introduced during the past two decades, but VCRs are newcomers to these markets, and their sales have been growing fast during the past couple of years.

As Megabox distribution manager Joe Perez reviewed sales forecasts for the coming year, he was concerned about transportation of the products to Zumburu, one of the larger Middle Eastern markets. The government of Zumburu never seemed to have an economic policy, and with the drying up of oil revenues, Perez was concerned that the government might suddenly impose higher import duties, or limit imports in some other manner, in order to control the outflow of foreign currency. Because he had insufficient space available in cargo airlines serving Zumburu, he was considering entering into a 12-month contract with a carrier that would provide him with more space, but he had to commit himself to ship at least 4,000 cubic feet per week during the contract period. He was concerned about erratic changes in demand because of possible government action. (The freight rates for this carrier were 10 percent below scheduled carriers.)

For distribution planning purposes, the product lines of Megabox were divided into four characteristic products, three television sets and a VCR, as shown in Table 1.

The sales forecast (Table 2) was prepared by the marketing department and Perez normally discounted it by 10 percent, because he knew from his past experience that these forecasts were actually marketing tools that were seldom met. Sales were expected to peak in the second quarter (the camel-racing season), and to be somewhat below the quarterly average in the third quarter.

Shipping services to Zumburu were available by air or by sea. Scheduled air cargo flights left John F. Kennedy airport three times a week, and Perez could secure at least 3,000 cubic feet per week on these flights. (More space could be used on a space-available basis.) If need be, Perez could use charter cargo flights at a cost 20 percent higher than the scheduled service. (On a full-load basis, at least 4,000 cubic feet per shipment, these flights did not have return cargo.)

Source: This case was prepared by David Ronen, Naval Postgraduate School, Monterey, California.

TABLE 1 ▪ **Distribution Characteristics of Products (per unit basis)**

Product	Shipping Volume (cubic feet)	Shipping Weight (kilo-grams)	Selling Price (F.O.B. plant)
TV1	16	18	$360
TV2	10	15	230
TV3	2	4	120
VCR	3	7	300

TABLE 2 ▪ **Zumburu Sales Forecast (units)**

Product	Quarter				Total
	1	2	3	4	
TV1	3,000	5,200	2,200	2,800	13,200
TV2	2,200	3,200	1,800	2,000	9,200
TV3	1,200	2,400	1,400	1,200	6,200
VCR	6,300	11,100	6,500	7,200	31,100

Sea service was provided by a weekly sailing of a conference container vessel, on which Perez could get as much space as he needed, but was limited to shipping in 40-foot container loads (CL) or in less than container load (LCL). Because of the high sensitivity of the products to pilferage, loss, and damage, Perez did not consider using general cargo vessels (which were also 40 percent to 50 percent slower than container vessels). He had also been approached by outsiders (ship operators who are not members of the conference) who offered him use of their semimonthly container service to Zumburu, using 20-foot containers at 15 percent discount over the conference freight rates.

At Perez's request, his assistant compiled several tables of pertinent data, in consultation with their freight forwarder. Transit time estimates for the various modes are given in Table 3. (Perez suspected that some of these estimates, especially those for the labor-intensive operations, were somewhat optimistic.)

Information concerning sizes of sea containers is provided in Table 4.

Air shipments were trucked from the assembly plant to the carrier's terminal, where they were stuffed by the carrier into air containers. The carrier unstuffed the containers at the other end of the trip, and the products were stored at an air cargo terminal until they were cleared through customs and shipped to the local distributor.

Sea shipments required containerization (CL shipments) or crating (LCL shipments), and these operations took place at a packer's facility

TABLE 3 ▪ **Transit Time Estimates (days)**

	Air (scheduled)	Sea (conference)	
		CL	LCL
Plant	1	1	1
↓	—	1	1
Export Packer/Container Stuffing	—	4	7
↓	1	1	1
Loading Port/Airport	1	4	4
↓			
Vessel/Airplane	1	18	18
↓			
Discharge Port	1	3	2
↓	—	—	1
Unpacking/Unstuffing	1	—	5
↓	1	1	1
Consignee	2	3	2
Total	9	36	43

TABLE 4 ▪ **Sizes of Sea Containers**

Nominal Length (feet)	Outside Measures (feet)	Inner Volume[a] (cubic feet)
20	8 by 8 by 20	1100
40	8 by 8 by 40	2000

[a]Because of incompatibility of package sizes, only about 90 percent of the inner volume can be utilized for cargo.

close to the loading port. Perez wondered if he should not move these operations into the assembly plant, thus saving on handling and transportation. Equipment incompatibility (truck box trailers are 40 feet to 50 feet long, sea containers are 20 feet or 40 feet long) made such analysis complicated, but possible use of rail service to move full sea containers to the loading port might make such an alternative attractive.

After containerization/crating the shipment would be trucked to the loading port, where it would wait for the next ship. Although the average interval between sailings of conference ships was one week, there were frequent delays, so that interval ranged from three to ten days. At the other end, after the shipment was unloaded, full container shipments were trucked to the distributor (after clearing customs). LCL shipments were unstuffed in the port and then, after customs clearance, moved to the distributor.

TABLE 5 ∎ **Breakdown of Distribution Costs (per cubic foot)**

| | Air (scheduled) | Sea (conference) | |
		CL[a]	LCL
Transportation to Packer	—	$0.50	$0.50
Packing/Container Stuffing	—	1.80	2.40
Transportation to Port	$0.50	0.20	0.20
Freight[b]	9.60	2.00	2.80
Unpacking/Unstuffing	—	—	0.70
Transportation to Consignee	0.40	0.40	0.40

[a] In 40-foot containers.

[b] Freight rates are on "liner terms" and include handling in ports on both ends.

Although CL shipments are cheaper, not all the shipments were large enough to fill a container. In the past year 70 percent of the volume of sea shipments went in CL and the rest in LCL. Perez estimated that this ratio would shift to 90 percent CL by using 20-foot containers.

Megabox was selling its product to its local distributor in Zumburu on C.I.F. (cost, insurance, freight) terms. Perez was therefore concerned about the reduction of all transportation-related costs and the cost of in-transit inventory. (Megabox used 28 percent for inventory-carrying cost, 15 percent of which was the cost of capital.) Megabox paid all the expenses up to the storage point at the destination port, where title on the goods was transferred, and the local distributor paid for the shipment within 30 days after receiving the shipment's documents.

Some of the shipping costs might be allocated on the basis of the volume shipped. These are presented in Table 5 (in dollars per shipped cubic foot).

Other associated costs are:

1. Consular fee—1 percent of F.O.B. plant price, paid for Zumburu import license, used to finance the operations of the Zumburu embassy in the United States.
2. Cargo insurance—1 percent of C.I.F. value plus 10 percent for air shipments, 1.4 percent for CL, and 1.6 percent for LCL (larger losses and damages).
3. Documentation—$220 per shipment, paid to the forwarder for the preparation of the U.S. export documentation and the import documents of Zumburu.
4. Wharfage—charged by the unloading seaport at 2 percent of the shipment's landed value (C.I.F. value).
5. Customs duties—40 percent of value at the exit gate of the port (excluding port storage charges, but including wharfage).

6. Storage fees at destination ports—0.24 $/kg per day for air cargo and 0.02 $/kg per day for sea cargo.

The distributor receiving the goods is interested in receiving frequent small shipments to reduce average inventory and thus prefers air shipments. Moreover, on air shipments the distributor pays lower customs duties, because no wharfage is included in the value for customs duties calculation. Megabox therefore grants the distributor a 2 percent discount on sea shipments off C.I.F. prices, which are $496 for TV1, $317 for TV2, $165 for TV3, and $432 for VCR.

Questions for Discussion

1. Evaluate the cost of inventory in transit.
2. Prepare a comparative cost analysis of the different shipping alternatives.
3. Should Perez enter into the 12-month contract with the air carrier?

American Trade Consortium

On March 30, 1989, a trade agreement was signed between the American Trade Consortium (ATC) comprised of six U.S. multinational corporations and more than 30 Soviet trade and economic organizations. The agreement ranks as the biggest and most complex in Western–Soviet trade. It established a legal and business framework for at least 25 American joint ventures in the Soviet Union involving investments of between $5 and $10 billion during a 15-year period. By comparison, bilateral trade between the United States and the Soviet Union in 1987 amounted to only $1.6 billion.

The six U.S. companies—Chevron, Eastman Kodak, Johnson & Johnson, RJR Nabisco, Archer-Daniels-Midland, and Mercator—see the agreement as offering important access to largely untapped Soviet markets. For the Soviets the agreement was equally as attractive. They generally favor big projects with prestigious companies. "What made this go," said James H. Giffen, president of Mercator and one of the key negotiators, "was the support of the top leadership of the U.S.S.R."

REFORMS IN THE SOVIET ECONOMY

In 1986, General Secretary Mikhail Gorbachev opened the 27th Party Congress of the Soviet Union with this statement: "The acceleration of the country's social and economic development is the key to all our problems; . . . bold measures are needed to switch the economy to the intensive path." The terms "radical reform" and "revolutionary change" are characteristic of Gorbachev's plan to invigorate the performance of the Soviet economy. He is moving at an unprecedented pace to achieve the fundamental objectives of his economic strategy.

The changes have been on two fronts. On the one hand, the focus has been on the improvement of labor productivity through concentration on the human factor: raising the level of labor morale and discipline through a combination of incentives and penalties. On the other, the aim is to increase productivity through the introduction of advanced technology to modernize the industrial base. Reform is sought by streamlining the

Source: This case was prepared by Ilkka A. Ronkainen. It is based largely on "The Twain Are Meeting—and Cutting Deals," *Business Week*, December 7, 1987, 88; "Reforming the Soviet Economy," *Business Week*, December 7, 1987, 76–88; "Vain Kapitalisti Menestyy Moskovassa," *Talouselama*, March 18, 1988, 64–66; Bruce Steinberg, "Reforming the Soviet Economy," *Fortune*, November 25, 1985, 90–96; George Ginsburgs, "Joint Ventures in the Soviet Union," *PlanEcon Report*, September 18, 1986, 1–12; Yuri D. Shcherbina, "A Soviet View on U.S.–U.S.S.R. Trade," special publication, National Center for Export-Import Studies #19, January 1987; "The Deal of the Decade May Get Done in Moscow," *Business Week*, February 27, 1989, 54–55; "Soviets, 6 U.S. Firms Reach Trade Accord," *The Wall Street Journal*, March 30, 1989, A10; "Pact with U.S. Firms Is Pet Soviet Project," *The Wall Street Journal*, March 31, 1989, A12; and "Soviets Open to Deals with West," *The Christian Science Monitor*, April 4, 1989, 9.

planning apparatus, including the control of foreign trade. In addition to allowing production ministries and some enterprises to deal directly with the West, direct investment is actively being sought.

In the 1970s, Soviet leader Leonid Brezhnev had tried to give a similar boost to Soviet industry, without compromising the Soviet system of ownership, by buying technology from the West. The results fell short of expectations because Soviet managers were not provided with incentives to spread the know-how throughout Soviet industry and thus spur home-grown technological advances.

Gorbachev's push to get the Soviet Union to participate to the fullest degree in the world trading system permits foreign investment flows to the country for the first time since the demise of Lenin's New Economic Policy, which allowed foreigners to run mines and plants. A pragmatic reason for this dramatic change is the steadily worsening trade deficit caused by the sharp drop in the price of Soviet oil exports. The only long-term solution to the problem of paying for technology imports to modernize Soviet industry is to export more manufactured goods. A significant role in this are joint ventures with Western companies that would produce export-quality goods for sale in world markets as well as the Soviet Union. The intent, however, is to bring more than technology into the Soviet Union. Western management methods may be one way to introduce internal cost effectiveness into Soviet industry.

Soviet regulations governing equity joint ventures were approved in January 1987. Among the provisions are (1) a maximum foreign share of 49 percent, (2) special low taxation rates and the right to freely repatriate profits and other assets, (3) management decisions on a joint basis with each partner having a veto, (4) Western quality control measures, and (5) the exclusion of joint ventures from central planning targets. Typically, the biggest hurdles in negotiations have been determining the Western partner's management role and deciding how to repatriate profits. For example, the Soviets initially stipulated that the Western partner could repatriate profits only if the venture earned hard currency.

Many Westerners believe that the eventual winners will be those who get an early foothold, and hundreds have indicated an interest in joint ventures. Interest is growing: In the first six weeks of 1989, 67 joint ventures were registered with the Soviet government, compared with 168 in all of 1988. Among the industries represented is oil, with Occidental Petroleum Corporation and Italy's Montedison agreeing to build a $6 billion petrochemical complex with the Soviets. A service-industry venture is Finnair's renovation in Moscow of the Berlin Hotel, renamed The Savoy.

THE ATC AGREEMENT

The concept of a consortium of companies to engage in business with and in the Soviet Union originated in December 1984 when Dwayne Andreas, chairman of Archer-Daniels-Midland, and James Giffen held a two-hour meeting with Gorbachev in the Kremlin. Gorbachev was interested in boosting trade, and the three men discussed various approaches. "It was clear that he was not just interested in projects, but an overview," James Giffen has said. After several similar meetings, the initial proposal of setting up a consortium was submitted to the Soviets in August 1987 and was approved by the Council of Ministers within 30 days. By April 1988, the creation of the consortium was announced and negotiations with the Soviets on a trade agreement followed soon after. The signed General Trade Agreement is envisioned as a "model joint-venture contract that could be a blueprint for other enterprises."

The ATC, which was incorporated in New York State in March 1988 as a nonprofit organization, acts more as a negotiator and facilitator than a trading company. Mercator is both a member of the consortium and its merchant banker; in effect, its manager. A participant pays Mercator a general fee at the beginning of its participation and a "success fee" upon establishment of an actual venture. The ATC negotiates the umbrella agreements, while the individual members work on their own deals.

The ATC's counterpart is the Soviet Foreign Economic Consortium (SFEC). It represents numerous organizations in foreign trade, including the Ministry for Foreign Economic Relations, the Bank for Foreign Economic Affairs, the Finance Ministry, and the State Planning Committee, as well as 23 enterprises and production associations under nine different industrial ministries.

HOW THE ATC IS TO WORK

The ATC is designed to cut through red tape and quicken the process of setting up joint ventures. At the core of the agreement, however, is an arrangement whereby the U.S. companies can repatriate their profits in dollars. Export-oriented ventures that earn hard currency, such as dollars, will be able to sell their cash to ventures aimed solely at the Soviet domestic market. Chevron will, at least initially, serve as the cash cow by operating petrochemical facilities in either the Archangelsk or Ural region and exporting oil for hard currency. The other participants—such as Kodak, with its plans for ventures in blood analyzers, floppy disks, and photographic products and services—will sell to the Soviet market for rubles. Chevron's earnings would be used to meet the Soviet requirement that joint ventures must earn enough hard currency to cover any profits they want to repatriate. As other export-oriented participants get started, their hard-currency earnings would be added to the pool. The plan is long-term, allowing the ATC 15 years to balance its hard-currency accounts.

Initially, at least, things have progressed smoothly. Archer-Daniels-Midland is negotiating four agro-industrial projects, including oilseed processing, edible-oil refining, and the production of starch and sweeteners. Johnson & Johnson is conducting studies for health product ventures, while RJR Nabisco has looked into making Ritz crackers, biscuits,

cereals, and cigarettes. Kodak has seven joint-venture programs at various stages of development.

Beyond the difficult negotiations, the only setback thus far has been the withdrawal of Ford Motor Company. Ford, probably the biggest player with Chevron in the consortium, was to have helped the Soviets revitalize their auto industry. The plan called for Ford to start by exporting its executive Scorpio model and gradually shift production to the Soviet Union over a five-year period. An assembly line would have been built near the Gorkovsky Automobilnyi Zavod (GAZ), which Ford helped build in the 1930s. The last-minute withdrawal was "disappointing" to Ford executives. "The project that Ford was discussing included a substantial initial investment. To succeed it would have required the Soviets to adopt new and innovative financial arrangements. Unfortunately, although there was progress, the framework of understandings between ATC and SFEC was not sufficient to make a project of Ford's scope and complexity feasible."

The progress of the ATC is being closely monitored by other Western nations and business entities interested in increasing their trade with the Soviet Union. Young & Ernst, one of the Big Five accounting firms, is working with British firms to develop a similar consortium, and firms in countries such as Italy and West Germany are expected to follow suit.

Questions for Discussion

1. What are the concerns of the various constituents in establishing such joint ventures as the one by ATC or in general with Soviet partners? Consider the businesses and the governments involved, as well as the world trading environment as a whole.

2. Should Ford's withdrawal be construed as a warning to ATC participants? According to a Coopers & Lybrand report, seven out of ten joint ventures fail even when the partners come from a similar background. What odds do you give for arrangements such as the one described?

Kaline

Kaline is a joint venture undertaken by a Swedish firm and a large U.S. company, each owning 50 percent. Both parent firms are known for their high technological standards, although they specialize in somewhat different product lines.

Kaline was formed in 1970. The president of the U.S. firm wanted to start a company with a new product line and sought out the Swedish partner because of its reputation. When the joint venture was formed, a detailed contract was signed by the partners. Products to be produced and marketed were specified, as were the conditions for technical support and other services, dividend policy, and profit distribution. Both parties clearly stated how they saw the new venture as a major part of their mission. Half of the board of directors was to be elected by each party, the chairman was to be elected from the U.S. board members, and the chairman of the shareholders meeting was to be elected by the Swedish partner. All major decisions specified in the agreement required a qualified majority (two-thirds) of the board members.

The agreement also contained a divorce clause, which specified that "either party can take the initiative to sell its shares at a price named in the notice. Such offer may be accepted by the noninitiating party or the noninitiating party may treat the offer as binding the initiating party to buy the noninitiating party's shares at the same price. Conversely, the initiating party may offer to buy the other party's shares at a price named in a notice. Such offer may be accepted by the noninitiating party or the noninitiating party may treat the offer as binding the initiating party to sell its shares at the same price. In any event, offers and acceptances must be for all the shares of the party."

In the initial year of formation, the Swedish partners were enthusiastic about the formation of Kaline. Prior to the joint venture, sales of Kaline's product line were flat. Because of new production technology brought to the table by the U.S. partner, however, Kaline was able to produce in the United States about 30 percent cheaper than in Sweden, including shipping costs and duties. The U.S. partner also had a ready and functioning sales organization. The joint venture therefore pursued a policy of entering the market and gaining market share and volume through price cutting.

Two years after the signing of the joint venture contract, Kaline had several hundred employees. Sales were high but financial results were disastrous. Both parents were unwilling to invest new equity. The president of the U.S. firm took over also as president of Kaline. The initiator of the joint venture, he also had an excellent personal relationship with

Source: Lars Otterbeck, "Management of Joint Ventures," presented at the seminar on the Management of Headquarters/Subsidiary Relationships in Transnational Corporations, Stockholm School of Economics, June 2–4, 1980, 27–32.

the president of the Swedish partner. He made several visits to Sweden to clear the air and succeeded in obtaining more updated technological knowledge and production rights.

Kaline's lack of profits during these years had severe effects on the quality of its personnel. Kaline as well as the U.S. partner had bonus pay plans that were based on the profitability of the firm. Because no bonuses were paid at Kaline, an exodus of managers from Kaline back to the profitable parent firm resulted. Kaline became known as the dump ground for managers.

In the fourth year of the joint venture, a young engineer in the U.S. parent company who had taken evening classes in marketing met with the president of Kaline. He had found that in some segments Kaline's product was one of the three market leaders. He suggested that the only possible cure for Kaline was to segment the market, emphasize the unique features of the product, differentiate it slightly, and raise prices. This suggestion was quite contrary to the previous high-volume philosophy. Only through personal intervention by the president of the U.S. partner directly with the president of the Swedish firm was the necessary technology transferred and the new policy cleared.

This process was by no means easy. Because of their culture, the Swedish engineers were totally against the idea. Sharing know-how and sharing it with a company that did not understand that volume was the oxygen of business was an alien thought.

One year later, the young engineer was president of Kaline, the company was a price-leader, its volume had gone up in the midst of a recession, and the company was making money. This success gave independence. The following exchange of communications regarding reporting routines illustrates the point.

The headquarters of the Swedish parent had sent a memo on corporate reporting to Kaline. Kaline's president responded by letter. "Your memo strikes us wrong. In essence it dictates a rigid policy of outside and inside auditing. Perhaps you do not recognize that Kaline is somewhat unique in your organization. The shares are not owned in a majority by you. We do realize that as a separate matter you do own 2 percent shares of our U.S. parent. This, however, does not give you control of us. The above is a statement of the relationship as we see it. I do propose that Kaline continue to be cooperative."

On the day the letter was received, the controller of the Swedish parent sent the following telex to Kaline: "The memo was sent to you by mistake. We are well aware of the uniqueness of Kaline. It is my intention to visit your company to discuss these questions. I think such a discussion will further improve our already good cooperation."

Two weeks later Kaline's president wrote the Swedish parent: "Thank you for your telex, which clears the air completely. We would very much welcome your visit to Kaline in the near future."

This letter was filed at the Swedish headquarters together with a memo from the controller: "We should not demand more information from Kaline than they are prepared to give us. If we want the same information that is required from other subsidiaries, the matter must probably be dealt with by the presidents of the two parents. I have talked to the president of Kaline. He has nothing against giving information on Kaline to us. But he does not want to change his reporting routines."

Questions for Discussion

1. How would you have changed the initial joint venture agreement?
2. Would you characterize the relationship between Kaline and its parent companies as formal or informal?
3. How can a firm retain the profit incentive while making allowance for start-up costs?
4. Is it a sensible policy to structure controls as a function of profitability?
5. Discuss the current interaction between Kaline and its parent companies. How can the goal of corporate synergy accommodate the need for individualism?

Goodyear and South Africa

Many U.S. corporations doing business in South Africa are feeling the heat from many and diverse groups and entities. Of the 326 U.S. companies operating in South Africa in 1982, only 131 remained in 1989 (see Table 1). The companies staying are convinced that their presence can be an effective force for peaceful change in a country torn by racial tensions manifested by violent protests against the system of apartheid. For example, Texaco Chief Executive James Kinnear says "walking away is not the right way to fight apartheid" in helping Caltex's 476 black employees. However, the Interfaith Center on Corporate Responsibility, a group that advocates disinvestment, believes that Caltex is very vulnerable as the last U.S. oil company in South Africa.

Antiapartheid activists are organizing boycotts of products and arranging demonstrations outside corporate headquarters demanding an end to all operations in South Africa. The pension funds of cities, states, and universities are selling off stock of companies with investments in South Africa. The University of California regents, for example, voted in 1986 to divest $3.1 billion from companies operating in South Africa. U.S. Congress has agreed to impose economic sanctions, and the pressure on the South African government is likely to continue and strengthen. Mobil chairman Allen Murray concedes that his company was pressured into leaving by the Rangel Amendment, a law that prevents U.S. companies from deducting taxes paid to South Africa.

SOUTH AFRICA AND THE SYSTEM OF APARTHEID

South Africa occupies the southern tip of the African continent. The country is known as a leading producer of gold and diamonds as well as a trove of strategic metals essential to industry.

South Africa has a long history of segregation. The area was populated by Europeans during the 17th and 18th centuries and controlled as a colony by the Dutch East India Company. The British took over in 1795 and conflicts broke out between the earlier settlers—the Afrikaners—and the British, who excluded the Afrikaners from the governing of the country. The conflict culminated in the Boer War of 1899 to 1902, which the British won, but the Afrikaners steadfastly maintained their lifestyle. The Afrikaners took over in 1948 and expanded on a policy of racial apartness put into effect by the British. In the 40 years since, extensive legislation has been passed ranging from bans on interracial marriage to controlling movements of blacks through so-called "pass" laws and forcing them to live in all-black townships.

Source: This case was prepared by Ilkka A. Ronkainen for discussion purposes and not to exemplify correct or incorrect decision making. The case draws facts from Felix Kessler, "Goodyear Toughs It Out," *Fortune*, September 30, 1985, 24–26.

TABLE 1 ▪ **South Africa: Who's Quit, Who's Staying**

Those Gone	*Those Leaving*	*Those Staying*
Exxon	Mobil	Goodyear
General Motors	RJR Nabisco	International Paper
General Electric	Control Data	Caltex Petroleum
Coca-Cola	NCR	Johnson & Johnson
Chase Manhattan	Hewlett-Packard	United Technologies

Source: Frederick H. Katayama, "Did Mobil Help or Hurt Apartheid?" *Fortune*, June 5, 1989, 16–17.

Racial tensions have increased since the mid-1970s, with increasing outbreaks of violence in the mid-1980s. Some groups opposing apartheid, such as the African National Congress, advocate violence to overthrow the white minority government.

U.S. COMPANIES IN SOUTH AFRICA

At best, U.S. companies had approximately $2.5 billion of direct investment in South Africa and employed some 100,000 people. As a shield against increasing criticism, especially from groups in the United States, nearly two-thirds of these companies were signatories to the so-called Sullivan Principles.

The Sullivan Principles, which were drafted in 1977, were a voluntary code of conduct for U.S. companies doing business in South Africa. These principles are summarized in Table 2. The signatories also agreed to additional demands beyond the principles. For example, they agreed to observe minimum-wage rules that do not apply to nonsignatory competitors, and acknowledged the right of black trade unions to organize. Charitable efforts were called for as well. During the 1980s, companies have spent nearly $80 million on social programs. The participating companies were graded on their compliance and are urged to do more every year. Spokesmen for American companies feel that the principles generated effective moral and economic pressures.

The investment of most U.S. companies in South Africa represents less than 1 percent of their total assets. Within the South African economy, however, U.S. subsidiaries play a significant role. Before IBM left in 1987, U.S. companies controlled 70 percent of the South African computer market. An estimated 40 percent of oil-refining capacity was in the hands of two U.S. companies. General Motors held 9 percent of the automobile market.

Combined with political pressure, the souring of economic conditions in South Africa has caused some U.S. companies to leave. Many companies are tired of being caught in the middle, attacked in the United States by liberals and in South Africa for being too liberal. Sanctions by

TABLE 2 ▪ **The Sullivan Principles**

I. Nonsegregation of the races in all eating, comfort, and work facilities
II. Equal and fair employment practices for all employees
III. Equal pay for all employees doing equal or comparable work for the same period of time
IV. Initiation of and development of training programs that will prepare, in substantial numbers, blacks and other nonwhites for supervisory, administrative, clerical, and technical jobs
V. Increase in the number of blacks and other nonwhites in management and supervisory positions
VI. Improvement in the quality of employees' lives outside the work environment in such areas as housing, transportation, schooling, recreation, and health facilities

Source: Stratford P. Sherman, "Scoring Corporate Conduct in South Africa," *Fortune*, July 9, 1984, 168.

Congress are providing another incentive to leave. Furthermore, Reverend Leon Sullivan, after whom the Sullivan Principles were named, set a deadline of May 31, 1987, for the abolishment of apartheid. Since then he has actively called for the withdrawal of all companies from the country.

Many companies state their intention to stay, both because of the millions of dollars of assets invested and because of a moral commitment to continue to work for a positive change. Many are confident that divestiture would harden white segregationist attitudes and harm the black workers it is supposed to help. Some companies say they will leave South Africa only when profitability falls below acceptable levels. Most of the companies that have left have kept indirect ties that permit their products to continue to be manufactured and sold in South Africa through licensing and distribution agreements.

GOODYEAR AND SOUTH AFRICA

Goodyear is a $10 billion company with operations in 29 countries, one of them South Africa. Overseas operations contribute one-third of all sales. Goodyear began selling tires in South Africa in 1916 and started its manufacturing operations in 1947, a year before the Afrikaner government imposed apartheid on the already segregated nation. Today, Goodyear has a $100 million investment that accounts for 2,500 jobs, making it the biggest American employer in the country. The subsidiary contributes 1 percent of the company's $411 million annual profits.

In a recent international policy meeting held at the company's Akron headquarters, the problems of operating in South Africa amid the rising protests calling for disinvestment were discussed. The following is a summary of some of the issues discussed:

Despite South Africa's three-year recession and months of civil unrest, sales by Goodyear's subsidiary at Uitenhage in South Africa's East Cape have rebounded, reports assistant controller H. Jay Elliott. The plant managers and black workers appear to be coping with the turmoil and a government curfew that overlaps the factory's night shift; absenteeism at the plant has declined from 30 percent to 6 percent. Joseph C. Garden, vice president in charge of international manufacturing, says that a $20-million expansion enabling the South African plant to produce radial truck tires will go into full operation ahead of schedule. Emmett H. Sellars, international vice president for tire sales, comments in passing that Goodyear's profit margins in South Africa have been among the best it achieves in any country.

Yet Goodyear's subsidiary is not free of serious problems. The plunge of the South African currency, the rand, to record lows has depressed the division's earnings. Many workers are withdrawing contributions they had made to the company's pension fund, jeopardizing the retirement plan's viability. Those at the meeting speculate that a black boycott of white shopkeepers has boosted living costs for black employees, making it necessary for them to dip into savings.

One subject not raised: the notion that Goodyear should consider withdrawing from South Africa. Since Goodyear's managers are in unanimous agreement, there is no need to debate the topic. "Who isn't against apartheid?" asks Robert E. Mercer, Goodyear's chairman. But he argues that a sudden pullout would only hurt blacks and stiffen the government's determination not to amend the racist laws. "If the government would emulate the kind of integrated microenvironment we have in that plant," says William R. Miller, "it would resolve most of the country's problems."

Goodyear has other compelling reasons for staying, such as profits and its high global visibility. "Because South Africa has always been profitable," says Jacques Sardas, Goodyear International President, "we have not considered leaving. Our presence there is good for our shareholders as well as South Africans—all of them." Furthermore, Goodyear does not want to set a negative precedent by giving in to pressure. "Things would really have to deteriorate a lot more for us even to consider the possibility of selling out," says Sardas.

If Goodyear were to leave the market, the protective trade barriers that have helped make South Africa a profitable proposition would then effectively shut Goodyear out of the market it helped to develop. Leaving would also mean being stuck with whatever take-it-or-leave-it price a South African or European competitor like Dunlop might offer.

Although Goodyear always received top marks on its compliance with the Sullivan Principles (for example, it spent $6 million on nonwhite education and housing programs), shareholder pressure has been rising. About 3 percent of the company's outstanding shares are held by universities, pension funds, and financial institutions.

The biggest concern at Goodyear is U.S. sanctions aginst technology transfers and new investments. These would have a negative effect on the quality of the products manufactured, an issue on which Goodyear is not willing to compromise.

So far the profit margin still outweighs the South African hassle factor. "But if it gets to be 20 percent of our troubles," says chairman Mercer, "we have to reassess what we are doing."

Questions for Discussion

1. Is staying in South Africa a vote for apartheid? Consider that
   according to the U.S. Investor Responsibility Research Center, six
   different polls by U.S., British, German, and South African
   researchers show most black South Africans oppose divestment,
   while Archbishop Desmond Tutu has said that "foreign investors
   fatten on black misery, cheap labor and the destruction of black
   family life."

2. Goodyear cites its high global visibility as a reason for staying in
   South Africa. Could this visibility not be an equal reason for getting
   out and using indirect modes of operating there?

3. How does one handle the rising criticism of groups that may
   eventually affect Goodyear's corporate image and marketing efforts?

Name Index

837

Subject Index